The Complete A+ Guide to PC Repair

Cheryl A. Schmidt
Florida Community College
at Jacksonville

Illustrations by LeeAnne Dollison, KC Frick, and Donna McAfee Tucker

Scott/Jones Inc., *Publishers*

P.O. Box 696, El Granada, CA 94018
Voice: (650) 726-2436
Fax: (650) 726-4693
E-mail: marketing@scottjonespub.com
Web: www.scottjonespub.com

The Complete A+ Guide to Computer Repair

Cheryl A. Schmidt

432 XYZ

ISBN: 1-57676-057-X

Composition: Martie Bateson Sautter
Book Manufacturing: Von Hoffman Graphics
Art Production: LeeAnne Dollison,
    Donna McAfee Tucker, and KC Frick

Cover Design: Martie Bateson Sautter
Copy Editing: Cathy Baehler, Jule Marne, and
    Heather Bennett
Clipart: Nova Development Corporation (now
    Microsoft Corporation)

Scott/Jones Publishing Company
Sponsoring Editorial Group: Richard Jones, Leata Holloway, Patricia Myacki
Marketing & Sales: Hazel Dunlap, Donna Cross, Victoria Chamberlain, and Page Mead
Business Operations: Michelle Robelet, Cathy Glenn, and Natascha Hoffmeyer
Production: Heather Bennett, Audrey Anderson

The Publisher wishes to acknowledge the memory of James F. Leisy. Thanks Jim. We miss you.

A Word About Trademarks

PREFACE

The Complete A+ Guide to PC Repair is intended for one or more courses geared toward A+ Certification, computer repair, and operating systems. The book is written so that it is easy to read and understand because concepts are presented in building-block fashion. The book focuses on hardware, software, and basic networking. Appendix A contains information on how to subnet.

Some of the best features of the book include the coverage of difficult subjects in a step-by-step manner, good graphics to illustrate concepts, reinforcement questions, hands-on exercises at the end of each chapter, practice certification review questions, and is written by a teacher (someone who understands the value of a textbook in this field). I have written another book, *A+ Certification Self-Study,* to further prepare students for the A+ Certification exam. Contact the publisher for a copy.

Organization of the Text

The text is organized to allow thorough coverage of all topics, but also to be a flexible teaching tool; it is not necessary to cover all the chapters, nor do the chapters have to be covered in order.

- Chapter 1 covers beginning terminology and computer part and port identification.
- Chapter 2 details components, features, and concepts related to motherboards including microprocessors, cache, expansion slots, and chipsets.
- Chapter 3 deals with configuration basics for the system and the different types of adapters installed in a system. System resources are also explained.
- Chapter 4 steps the student through how to disassemble and reassemble a computer. Tools, ESD, EMI, and preventive maintenance are discussed for the first time. Subsequent chapters also include preventive maintenance topics.
- Chapter 5 deals with basic electronics and computer power.
- Chapter 6 is a basic section covering troubleshooting skills and error codes.
- Chapter 7 covers memory concepts, installation, configuration, and troubleshooting.
- Chapter 8 involves floppy drive concepts, installation, configuration, and troubleshooting.
- Chapter 9 deals with hard drive installation, preparation, and troubleshooting.
- Chapter 10 covers multimedia devices including CD and DVD technologies as well as sound cards.
- Chapter 11 deals with serial devices theory and configuration. An in-depth modem section includes information on digital modems, 56K modems, and troubleshooting. The chapter also looks at mice, and keyboards.
- Chapter 12 handles video including video memory issues.
- Chapter 13 covers dot matrix, ink jet, and laser printers including troubleshooting and preventive maintenance techniques.
- Chapter 14 covers DOS skills essential for technicians. Topics covered include basic DOS commands, DOS file structure, the AUTOEXEC.BAT file, and the CONFIG.SYS file. The exercises include steps for executing DOS commands from a Windows environment.
- Chapter 15 covers Windows 98 basics such as formatting a disk, copying a file, starting applications, using Explorer, using the Find utility, using Help, and backing up the registry. An excellent section in this appendix involves the Windows 98 boot process including troubleshooting startup problems.

- Chapter 16 covers NT Workstation and includes how to install NT, troubleshoot the installation process, troubleshoot boot problems, and install hardware and software.
- Chapter 17 covers 2000 Professional and has the same types of material as the NT Chapter, but also includes the plethora of tools that comes with this operating system.
- Chapter 18 is a chapter that introduces the students to networking. Basic concepts, terminology, and exercises make this chapter a favorite.
- Appendix A contains an introduction to subnetting. Even though this subject is not covered on the A+ exam, students need it for (1) other exams and (2) the work environment. The chapter also contains practice problems at the end.
- Appendix B has practice certification review questions.
- Appendix C is the glossary.
- Appendix D is the index.

Features

Easy-to-Understand Text

Each section is written in building-block fashion beginning at the most basic level and continuing on to the more advanced. Students taught using this method understand new technologies better because of a good foundation.

End-of-Chapter Review Questions

Each chapter contains numerous review questions in various formats including true/false, multiple choice, matching, fill-in-the-blank, and open-ended.

Tech Tips

Each chapter contains technical tips that are highlighted and preceded by a Sherlock Holmes picture.

Hands-on Exercises

Computer repair cannot be learned by theory and lecture alone, but is reinforced through practice and experience. Exercises at the end of each chapter help with this task.

Certification Questions

Appendix B contains certification review questions that are designed to help students practice for the A+ Certification exam.

Objectives and Terminology

At the beginning of each chapter is a list of objectives. Following the objectives are the key terms defined and used throughout the chapter.

Instructor Support

All the pedagogical features outlined here are unique to this book. They should make the instructor's job easier. In addition, an instructor's CD containing answers to the review and exercise questions can be obtained from the publisher. By mid 2002 a test generator and test items will be available from the publisher. By mid 2002 PowerPoint slides will be available from the publisher.

A Note to Students

All the way through the book, I had to refrain from telling my stories, stay on track, and avoid using my mnemonics. Writing a textbook is really different from teaching class. My personality lies buried in this book. Only in a few places can you see or feel my teaching style, but I hope it comes through in subtle ways. My students are like my children except that I do not have to feed them and send them to college, so I am happy to claim any of you. I wish that I could be in each classroom as you start your computer career. How exciting!

Another thing that I tell my students is that I am not an expert and to watch out for those who say or think they are. Computer repair is an ever-changing field. I have been at it a long time, but there are always products and standards being developed that I do not know very much about. Humility is a wonderful trait to keep in computer repair because if you are not humble, the industry will prove you wrong sooner or later.

To my future technicians, I offer one important piece of advice:

Consistent, high quality service boils down to two equally important things: caring and competence.
— Chip R. Bell and Ron Zemke

I can help you with the competence, but you are going to have to work on the caring part. Do not ever forget that there are people behind those machines that you love to repair. Taking care of people is as important as taking care of the computers. To my future technicians, I offer one important piece of advice:

A Note to Teachers

Whenever people ask me what I do, my first response is "I fix computers." In my heart, I will always be a technician. Everything else is just a facet of that skill set, whether it is managing a computer and network support department, building a new lab and networking it, or teaching microprocessors. All of these boil down to knowing technical things. Sharing what I know is as natural as walking to me, but sitting still to write down what I know is unnatural, so composing this text has been one of my greatest challenges. I managed to do it only because I needed a better textbook.

I taught computer repair classes long before I became a full-time faculty member. I was very frustrated with not having an appropriate book. During the first two terms, I taught without a textbook and my students nicknamed me "The Handout Queen." The book I have used most often is one of the best books on the subject of computer repair, but it is not a textbook. I hope this book can offer better support to teachers.

Acknowledgments

Many people have helped me along my career and life paths. Thanks to my fellow faculty members John Debo and Kevin Hampton. You two keep me sane. Ernie Friend, my new boss, has been a great strength for me, as have David Brown and Lance Wallace who help with my labs! LeeAnne Dollison and Martie Bateson Sautter, my new graphic artist and typesetter are a joy and true professionals. Richard Jones of Scott/Jones Publishing, I could not imagine working for another publisher. You are the best!

No acknowledgements can be complete without speaking of my family—Karl is the love of my life and completes me. I could never ask for better daughters, Raina and Karalina. They are such blessings!

Many parts of the manuscript have also been class-tested at Florida Community College at Jacksonville. My colleagues and students have offered numerous valuable suggestions for improvement. Finally, the faculty members who reviewed individual chapters have my undying gratitude for their input.

Reviewers

Don Casper
Eastern Idaho Technical College, ID

Martin Kanu
Canada College, CA

Richard Gohman
Yavapai Community College, AZ

Alan Block
Black Hawk Technical College, WI

Roger Peterson
Northland Community Technical College, MN

Phillip Regalbuto
Trident Technical College, SC

Russell Foszcz
McHenry County College, IL

Richard Kalman
Atlantic Cape Community College, NJ

Mike Beaver
University of Rio Grande, OH

Donald Hoffmann
Grayson County College, TX

Steve Cain
Tidewater Community College, VA

Terry Dummar
Midland Community College, TX

Jee Laird
Nashville State Technical Community College, TN

Nancy Smith
Kirkwood Community College, IA

John Gazak
Herkimer County Community College, NY

Greg Steffanelli
Carroll Community College, MD

John Haney
Snead State Community College, AL

Ron Carswell
San Antonio College, TX

These people made a huge impact on the book's final form, but I am responsible for any remaining errors. Please contact me with any corrections or suggestions at either of the following e-mail addresses:

CSchmidt@fccj.org or let the publisher know at ScotJones2@aol.com

Other Titles of Interest from Scott/Jones Publishing

The Complete A+ Guide to Computer Repair
A+ Certification Self-Study, 2nd edition
Quick Start to IP Subnetting
What CCNAs Should Really Know
   Cheryl A. Schmidt

The Windows 2000 Server Lab Manual
   Gerard Morris

Windows XP Step-by-Step
Windows 2000 Professional, Step-by-step
   Leslie Hardin and Debby Tice

Student Lab Manual for the Complete Computer Repair Textbook, 3rd ed
   Don Casper

Starting out with C++, 3rd edition
Starting out with C++, 3rd alternate edition
Starting out with Visual Basic
Starting out with Java
   Tony Gaddis

The Windows XP Textbook
The Windows 2000 Professional Textbook
   Stewart Venit

Operating Systems for Technicians
   Todd Meadors

TABLE OF CONTENTS

Chapter 14: Introduction to DOS 14-1

Chapter 15: Windows 98 15-1

Chapter 17: Windows 2000 Professional 17-1

INDEX OF FIGURES & TABLES

Chapter 3: System Configuration

Chapter 4: Disassembly/Reassembly

Chapter 5: Basic Electronics and Power

Chapter 6: Logical Troubleshooting

Chapter 7: Memory

Chapter 8: Floppy Drives

Chapter 9: Hard Drives

Chapter 10: Multimedia Devices

Chapter 11: Serial Devices, Mice, and Keyboards

Chapter 12: Video

Chapter 13: Printers

Chapter 14: Introduction to DOS

Chapter 15: Windows 98

Chapter 16: Windows NT Workstation

Chapter 17: Windows 2000 Professional

Chapter 18: Introduction to Networking

Appendix A: Subnetting

1

Chapter 1:

Introduction to Computer Repair

OBJECTIVES

After completing this chapter you will
- Understand basic computer terms.
- Identify computer parts.
- Recognize and identify external computer connectors.

KEY TERMS

adapter	memory
ARCnet	microcomputer
bus mouse	modem
capacitive keyboard	monitor
CD-ROM drive	motherboard
cold boot	mouse
D-shell connector	mouse port
DIN connector	operating system
Ethernet	parallel port
expansion slot	port
female port	POST
firmware	power supply
floppy disk	RAM
floppy drive	riser board
game port	ROM
hard drive	ROM BIOS
hardware	serial port
integrated motherboard	software
keyboard	sound card
keyboard port	Token Ring
keyed	USB port
male port	video port
mechanical keyboard	warm boot

OVERVIEW

A computer technician must be a jack-of-all-trades: a software expert in various operating systems and applications; a hardware expert on everything ranging from microprocessors to the latest laser printer; a communicator extraordinaire to handle the occasional irate, irrational, or computer-illiterate customer; a good listener to elicit computer symptoms from customers (and from the computer); an empathetic counselor to make the customers feel good about their computers and confident in the technician's skills; and finally, a master juggler of time and priorities. These traits do not come overnight and not all of them can be taught, but a technician can constantly develop and fine-tune each.

This book covers computer repair basics, knowledge to get you started in the computer repair industry. Standards relating to computer repair are important and technicians must recognize both old and current standards and stay abreast of emerging ones. Some computer standards allow a great deal of leeway for manufacturers and therefore more heartburn for computer technicians. However, if a technician understands the basics of computer repair, the problems from manufacturer design or hardware not covered in this book can still be resolved.

There is no substitute for experience, and no substitute for knowing the basics of how individual computer parts work. The basics help you understand other emerging technologies as well as proprietary devices. Once a technician has a job in the industry, hands-on time will increase his or her depth of knowledge and experience. Use the hands-on time in the classroom wisely. The classroom is the place to learn the ropes, the basics.

Having a teacher to guide you through the basics, classmates to share information with, and a book to supplement your instruction are all important to getting you started. This book is a textbook. Other books are excellent reference books. Most technicians have *Upgrading and Repairing PCs* by Scott Mueller and *The Complete PC Upgrade & Maintenance Guide* by Mark Minasi on their bookshelves or in their vehicles. This book is not a reference book, but instead, it supplements your instructor as a textbook on computer repair.

The best quality a technician can possess is a logical mind. A good technician narrows a problem to a general area, subdivides the problem into possible culprits, and eliminates the possibilities one-by-one in a timely and logical manner. A technician is like a detective, constantly looking for clues, using common sense and deductive reasoning, gathering information from the computer and the computer user, and finally solving the mystery. As one computer teacher puts it, "a computer technician works smart, not hard." Because detective work is so important to a technician's job, a computer detective precedes every important technical tip in the book:

An industry standard certification called A+ Certification is important for new technicians. It does not guarantee you a job, but it helps you get an interview. The A+ certification consists of two exams: Core and Operating System. My book, *The Complete A+ Guide to PC Repair*, covers all aspects of the A+ exam. *The Complete Computer Repair Textbook* focuses on the hardware exam, but does have material on operating systems as well as chapters on Windows 98 and networking, which are included on the Operating

System Exam. Located throughout both books are practice review questions. I also have another book called *A+ Certification Self-Study* that contains over 1,000 practice questions to help you if certification is your goal.

Repairing computers is very rewarding, but can be frustrating if you do not understand the basics. With good reasoning ability and a good foundation in computer repair, no problem will remain unsolved. Never forget that if every repair is simple, no one would need technicians. Enjoy the class!

SAFETY NOTE

Even though safety is covered in the power chapter, no book on computer repair can begin without stating the fact that both the technician and the computer can be harmed by poor safety habits. To protect both yourself and the computer, make sure the computer power is off when disassembling, installing or removing hardware, or doing preventive maintenance (cleaning). Never take the monitor or power supply apart unless you have been specifically trained on these components. The power supply and monitor have capacitors (electronic parts which hold an electrical charge) that can hurt you even if the power has been removed. The type of equipment you need and things that you can do to prevent harm to the computer are covered more explicitly in the power and disassembly chapter.

BEGINNING TERMINOLOGY

A technician must be familiar with and thoroughly understand computer terminology to (1) speak intelligently to other technical support staff, (2) explain to the user what the problem is, and (3) be proficient in a chosen field. Unfortunately, some computer technicians use the technical language of the trade around people who are not attuned to this type of lingo. Using too many technical terms around end-users serves only to confuse and irritate them. (Even calling them "users" can irritate them.)

In addition to knowing and using the correct terminology, a technician must use it appropriately, and explain computer terms with simple, everyday language and examples. This book illustrates the terminology in easy-to-understand terms and analogies that can be used with customers.

BASIC COMPUTER PARTS

Computer systems are composed of hardware, software, and firmware. **Hardware** is something you can touch and feel; the physical computer itself is an example of hardware. The monitor and keyboard are hardware components. The parts inside the computer are hardware. **Software** is the operating system and applications that make the hardware work. NT Workstation, Windows 98, Windows 95, DOS, Microsoft Word, Lotus 1-2-3, Netscape Communicator, Adobe Acrobat Reader, Office XP, and WordPerfect are all examples of software. A computer is nothing more than a doorstop unless there is software that allows the hardware to accomplish something. An important piece of software that every computer needs is an operating system. An **operating system** coordinates the interaction between hardware and software applications. The operating system also handles the interaction between a user and the computer. Examples of operating systems include DOS, Windows 95, Windows 98, NT Workstation, Windows 2000, Windows XP, and Unix. **Firmware** combines hardware and software into important chips inside the microcomputer that you can touch and feel like hardware, but with software written into them. The reason it is called firmware is because it is a chip, which is hardware, and it also has software built into the chip. An example of firmware is the ROM chip. ROM chips are electronic chips that have software inside them all of the time.

The simplest place to start learning about microcomputer repair is with the hardware components and their common names. A **microcomputer**, sometimes called a computer or a PC, is a unit that performs tasks using software applications. Microcomputers come in three basic models: (1) a desktop model that normally sits on top of a desk, (2) a tower model that sits under a desk, and (3) a laptop model, which is portable. A fourth type of computer is a handheld computer or PDA (Personal Digital Assistant). Handheld computers are normally used to manage schedules, contact names, phone numbers, and addresses, for exchanging e-mail, and for simple note taking. PDAs are gaining in popularity, but are beyond the scope of this book.

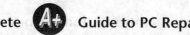

The microcomputer consists of a case (chassis), a **keyboard** that allows users to communicate with the computer, a **monitor** that displays information, and a **mouse** that allows data input or is used to select menus and options. Two types of keyboards are mechanical and capacitive. The **mechanical keyboard** is the cheapest and most common. It has mechanical switches that close when a key is depressed. The **capacitive keyboard** uses a change in capacitance to detect a key being depressed. The capacitive keyboard is more expensive, but also more reliable. Introduction Figure #1 shows a desktop computer's case, monitor, keyboard, and mouse.

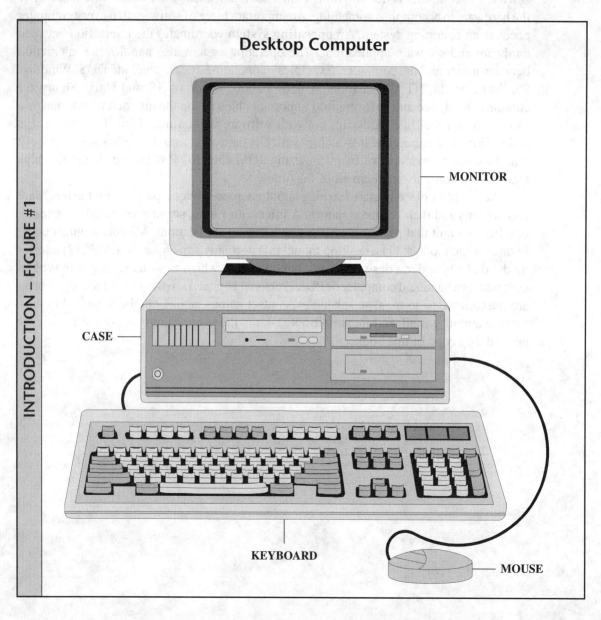

INTRODUCTION – FIGURE #1

Desktop Computer

MONITOR

CASE

KEYBOARD

MOUSE

Introduction Figure #2 shows an illustration of a tower computer's case, monitor, keyboard, and mouse. Tower computers are very popular for home and business.

Tower Computer

INTRODUCTION – FIGURE #2

Monitor

Case

Mouse

Keyboard

Once the case is removed from the computer, the parts inside can be identified. The easiest part to identify is the power supply. The **power supply** is the metal box normally located in a back corner of the case. A power cord goes from the power supply to a wall outlet or surge strip. One purpose of the power supply is to convert the AC voltage that comes out of the wall to DC voltage the computer can use. The power supply also supplies DC voltage to the internal parts of the computer. A fan located inside the power supply keeps the computer cool to avoid damage to the components.

A computer usually has a device to store software applications and files. Two common storage devices are the floppy drive and the hard drive. A slot in the front of the computer easily identifies the floppy drive. The **floppy drive** allows data storage to **floppy disks** (sometimes called diskettes or disks) that can be used in other computers. Floppy disks store less information than hard drives. The **hard drive**, sometimes called hard disk, is a rectangular box normally inside the computer's case that is sealed to keep out dust and dirt. In a desktop computer, the hard drive is normally mounted below or beside the floppy drive. A **CD-ROM drive** holds disks (CDs) that have data, music, or software applications on them. A popular alternative to a CD-ROM drive is a DVD. A **DVD (Digital Versatile Disk)** drive supports CDs as well as music and video DVDs. See Introduction Figure #3 for an illustration of a desktop power supply, a floppy drive, hard drive, and a CD-ROM drive.

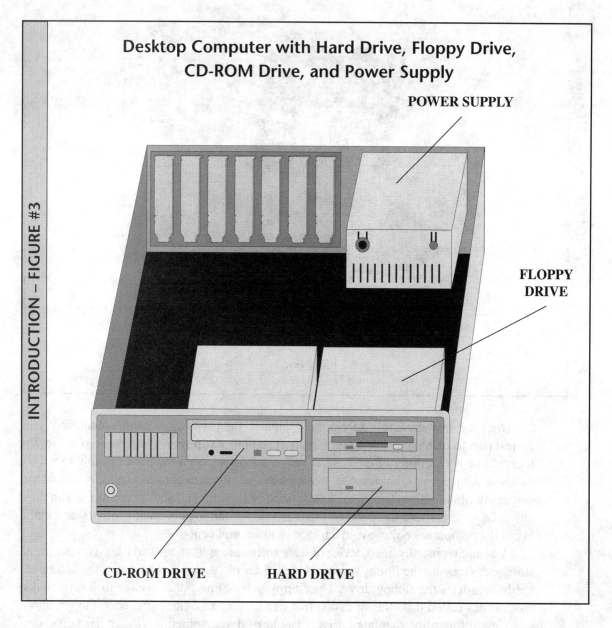

Desktop Computer with Hard Drive, Floppy Drive, CD-ROM Drive, and Power Supply

INTRODUCTION – FIGURE #3

POWER SUPPLY

FLOPPY DRIVE

CD-ROM DRIVE   HARD DRIVE

Introduction Figure #4 shows a tower computer with a hard drive, floppy drive, power supply, and DVD drive.

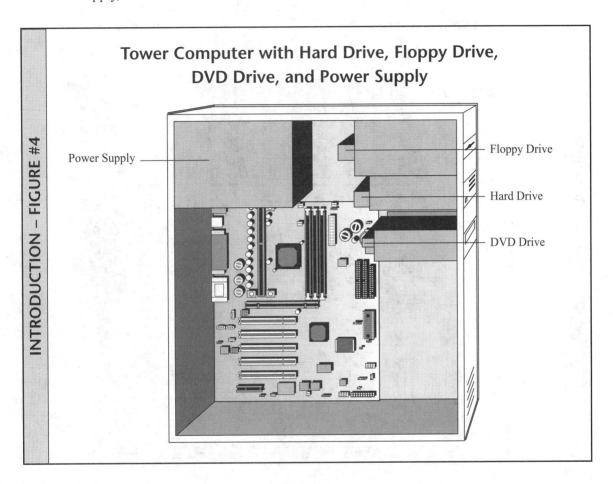

Tower Computer with Hard Drive, Floppy Drive, DVD Drive, and Power Supply

Power Supply

Floppy Drive

Hard Drive

DVD Drive

The **motherboard** is the main circuit board and contains the most electronics. It is normally located on the bottom of a desktop or laptop computer and mounted on the side of a tower computer. Other names for the motherboard include mainboard, planar, or systemboard. The motherboard is the largest electronic circuit board in the computer. The keyboard frequently connects directly to the back of the motherboard, although some computers have a keyboard connection in the front of the case.

Some devices have a cable that connects the device to the motherboard. Other devices require an adapter. **Adapters** are smaller electronic circuit cards that normally plug into an **expansion slot** on the motherboard. Other names for an adapter are controller, card, controller card, circuit card, circuit board, and adapter board. The number of available expansion slots on the motherboard depends on the manufacturer. See Introduction Figure #5 for an illustration of a motherboard, various expansion slots, and an adapter in an expansion slot.

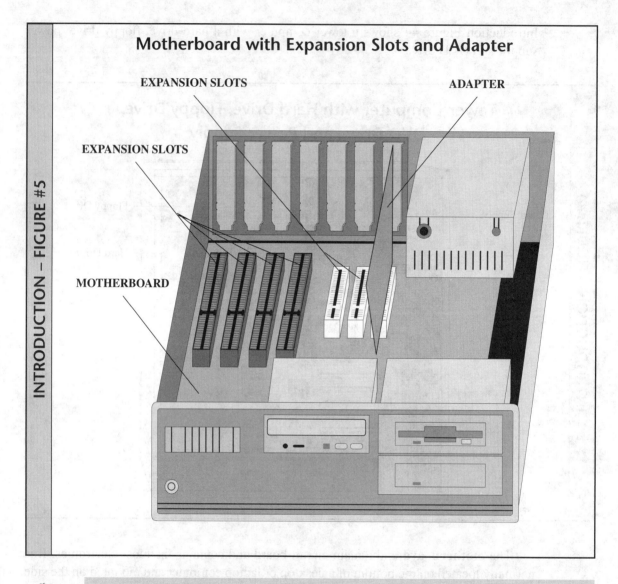

INTRODUCTION – FIGURE #5

Motherboard with Expansion Slots and Adapter

EXPANSION SLOTS   ADAPTER

EXPANSION SLOTS

MOTHERBOARD

Tracing the cable(s) attached to the adapter or looking at the device connected to the adapter can usually help with identifying an adapter's function. For example, typically a monitor has a cable going between it and a video adapter or motherboard connector.

An adapter may control multiple devices such as the CD-ROM and speakers. All these devices have a cable connecting to the adapter inside the computer or to the adapter's connector on the back of the computer.

An alternative to an adapter plugging directly into the motherboard is the use of a riser board. A **riser board** has its own expansion slots and the riser board plugs into the motherboard. Adapters can plug into the riser board's expansion slots instead of directly into the motherboard. Introduction Figure #6 shows an illustration of a riser board.

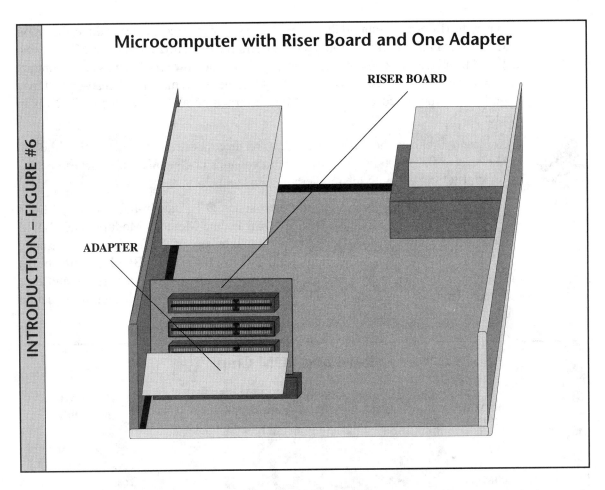

INTRODUCTION – FIGURE #6

Microcomputer with Riser Board and One Adapter

RISER BOARD

ADAPTER

Memory is an important part of any computer. Memory chips hold applications, part of the operating system, and user documents. Two basic types of memory are RAM and ROM. **RAM (Random Access Memory)** is volatile memory meaning the data inside the chips is lost when power to the computer is shut off. When a user types a document in a word processing program, both the word processing application *and* the document are in RAM. If the user turns the computer off without saving the document to a disk or the hard drive, the document is lost because the information *does not* stay in RAM when power is removed.

Software inside ROM chips will remain even when the power is removed. **ROM (Read-Only Memory)** is non-volatile memory because data stays inside the chip even when the computer is turned off. An important chip on the motherboard that can be ROM is the BIOS (Basic Input/Output System) chip, frequently called the ROM BIOS. The **ROM BIOS** has start-up software that must be present for a computer to operate. The ROM BIOS also contains software instructions for communication with input/output devices, as well as important hardware parameters that determine, to some extent, what hardware can be installed. For example, if you intend to install a large capacity hard drive in an older computer, the BIOS must support that drive, if the system is to recognize the drive. Common ROM BIOS manufacturers for today's computers include AMI (American Megatrends, Inc.) and Phoenix. Many computer companies produce their own BIOS chips or subcontract with AMI or Phoenix to customize the BIOS. Also, the BIOS may not be read-only. It may be a different type called Flash BIOS. More information about this type of BIOS is in Chapter 3.

 You cannot replace the ROM BIOS with one from a different vendor unless the motherboard supports it. Check the motherboard's documentation to determine which BIOS works with the motherboard.

RAM and ROM chips come in four different styles: DIP (Dual In-line Package), SIMM (Single In-line Memory Module), DIMM (Dual In-line Memory Module), and RIMM (Rambus Inline Memory Module). RAM chips can be any of the four types, but usually are SIMM or DIMM. Some ROM chips are DIP chips. If the ROM BIOS is a DIP chip, it is usually distinguishable by a sticker that shows the manufacturer, version, and date produced. Memory chips are covered in great detail in the Memory chapter. Introduction Figure #7 shows RAM and ROM chips.

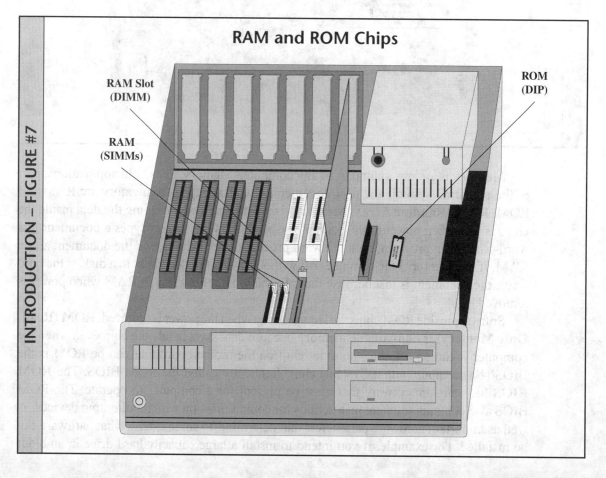

INTRODUCTION – FIGURE #7

RAM and ROM Chips

RAM Slot
(DIMM)

RAM
(SIMMs)

ROM
(DIP)

Part of the startup software the motherboard BIOS contains is the POST. The **POST (Power On Self Test)** performs a basic test of the individual hardware components such as the motherboard, RAM memory chips, keyboard, floppy drive, and the hard drive. When a computer is turned on with the power switch, BIOS executes POST. Numbers appearing in the upper left corner of the monitor indicate that POST is checking RAM. Turning the computer on with the power switch is known as a **cold boot**. Users perform a cold boot every time they come to work and power on their computers. A technician performs a cold boot when he is troubleshooting a computer and needs POST to execute.

A computer can be restarted with a **warm boot** by holding down the CTRL key, the ALT key, and the DEL key all at the same time. Pushing the reset button on the front of the computer can also perform a warm boot. A warm boot does not put as much strain on a computer. Frequently, a technician makes changes to the files that execute when the computer powers on. These files control some of the computer components. Warm booting the computer causes the changes to take effect.

Other devices such as Zip drives, sound cards, and tape backup units can be installed in a computer, but the most basic components are the monitor, keyboard, mouse, power supply, floppy drive, hard drive, CD-ROM drive, motherboard, and adapters.

EXTERNAL CONNECTORS

A motherboard sometimes has the keyboard, mouse, parallel, serial, network, or video ports built in. A **port** is a connector on the motherboard or on a separate adapter that allows a device to connect to the computer. Motherboards that have ports built into them are called **integrated motherboards**. A technician needs to be able to readily identify these common ports to be sure that (1) the correct cable plugs into the port, and (2) the technician can troubleshoot problems in the right area.

Most port connections are called male or female ports. **Male ports** have metal pins that protrude out from the connector. A male port requires a cable with a female connector. **Female ports** have holes in the connector. The male cable's pins insert into these holes.

Most connectors on integrated motherboards are either D-shell connectors or DIN connectors. A **D-shell connector** has more pins or holes on top than on the bottom so a cable connected to the D-shell connector can only be inserted in one direction and not accidentally flipped upside down. Parallel, serial, and video ports are examples of D-shell connectors. A **DIN connector (*Das Ist Norm*—that is the norm)** is round with small holes and is normally keyed. When a connector is **keyed**, it has an extra metal piece or notch that matches with an extra metal piece or notch on the cable and the cable can only be inserted into the DIN connector one way. Keyboard and mouse connectors are examples of DIN connectors. Introduction Figure #8 shows the back of a computer with an integrated motherboard. On the motherboard are various D-shell and DIN connectors.

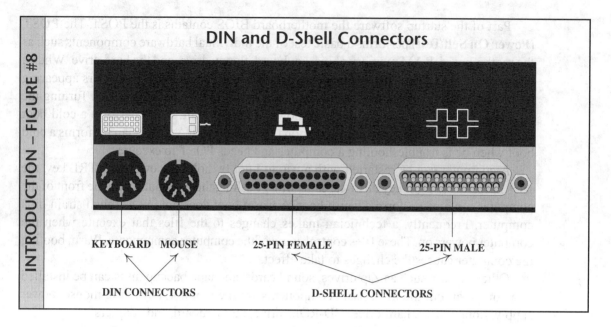

DIN and D-Shell Connectors

KEYBOARD   MOUSE   25-PIN FEMALE   25-PIN MALE

DIN CONNECTORS   D-SHELL CONNECTORS

INTRODUCTION – FIGURE #8

VIDEO PORTS

Two different connectors are available for **video port** connections: a 9-pin female D-shell and a three row, 15-pin female D-shell. The 9-pin connector is used with older monitors such as monochrome, CGA, and EGA monitors. The 15-pin female connector is used with today's monitors and connects to VGA, SVGA, or XGA monitors. Introduction Figure #9 shows examples of video ports.

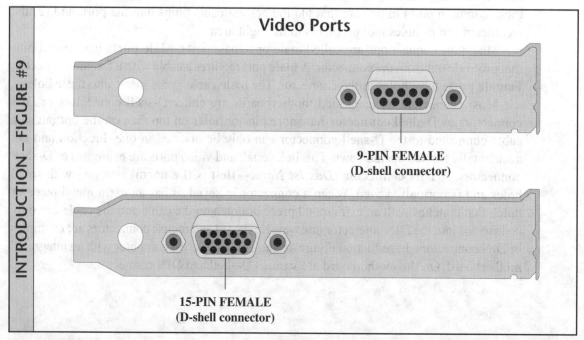

Video Ports

9-PIN FEMALE
(D-shell connector)

15-PIN FEMALE
(D-shell connector)

INTRODUCTION – FIGURE #9

PARALLEL PORT

The **parallel port** is a 25-pin female D-shell connector used to connect a printer to the computer. Some motherboards have a small picture of a printer etched over the connector. Parallel ports transfer eight bits of data at a time to the printer or any other parallel device connected to the parallel port. Other parallel devices include tape drives, Iomega's Zip drive, scanners, and external hard drives. Look at Introduction Figure #10 for an illustration of a parallel port.

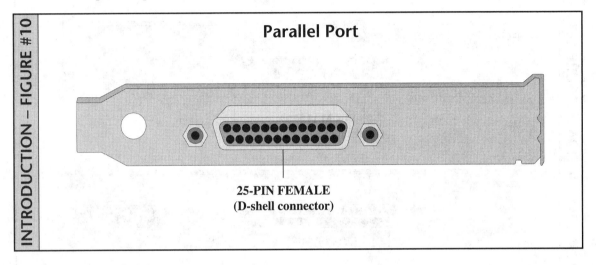

Parallel Port

INTRODUCTION – FIGURE #10

25-PIN FEMALE
(D-shell connector)

SERIAL PORTS

A **serial port** (also known as a COM port) connector can be a 9-pin male D-shell connector or a 25-pin male D-shell connector. Introduction Figure #11 shows the two different serial ports.

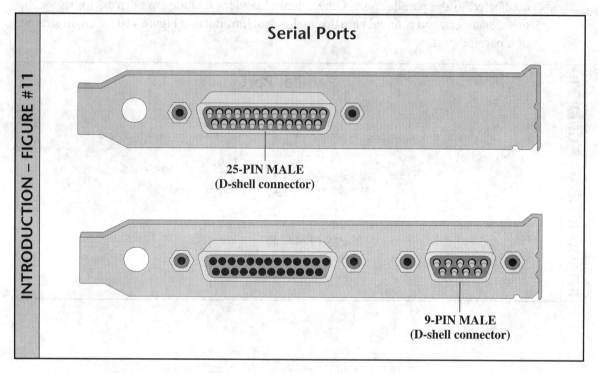

INTRODUCTION – FIGURE #11

Serial Ports

25-PIN MALE
(D-shell connector)

9-PIN MALE
(D-shell connector)

The most common type of serial port is the 9-pin connector.

Serial ports are used for a variety of input devices including mice, external modems, digitizers, and trackballs. The serial port transmits one bit at a time and is much slower than the parallel port that transmits eight bits at a time. Special connectors are available to convert a 9-pin serial port to a 25-pin port or to convert a 25-pin port to a 9-pin one. This converter is needed if someone has a 25-pin serial cable and the computer has a 9-pin serial port connector on the back or if the reverse situation was true. Serial ports sometimes have a small picture of two rows of square blocks (two digital square waves) tied together etched over the connector. The other type of picture sometimes shown above a serial port is a series of 1s and 0s. Look back at Introduction Figure #8 for an example of the picture over the 25-pin male serial connector.

Serial and parallel ports are typically bi-directional, which means that data transfers to/from the port to the motherboard/adapter in both directions. Video, keyboard, and mouse ports are typically unidirectional. The mouse and keyboard are normally input-only devices, so data flows from the device to the computer. The monitor is normally an output device and data flows from the computer to the monitor.

MOUSE AND KEYBOARD PORTS

The **mouse** and **keyboard ports** are DIN connectors. Three types of DIN connectors are the 5-pin, 6-pin, and 9-pin. The 5-pin connector is actually bigger than the 6-pin connector and is only used for a keyboard. The 6-pin keyboard or mouse connector is commonly known as a mini-DIN or a PS/2 mouse connection. The 9-pin DIN is normally on a bus mouse adapter. A **bus mouse** is used in a computer without a mouse port built in. The 9-pin DIN is not as common as the 5 or 6-pin DIN connectors. Most manufacturers put a small diagram of a keyboard and of a mouse over the connectors. Look back to Introduction Figure #8 to see the diagrams over the connectors.

On most motherboards, the mouse and keyboard ports are not interchangeable even though they are of the same pin configuration. The keyboard cable must plug into the keyboard port connector. The mouse cable must plug into the mouse port connector.

A common converter for technicians to have in their toolkit is a 5 to 6-pin DIN converter or a 6 to 5-pin DIN converter.

Introduction Figure #12 shows a 5-pin DIN and the 6-pin mini-DIN connectors used with a keyboard or a mouse.

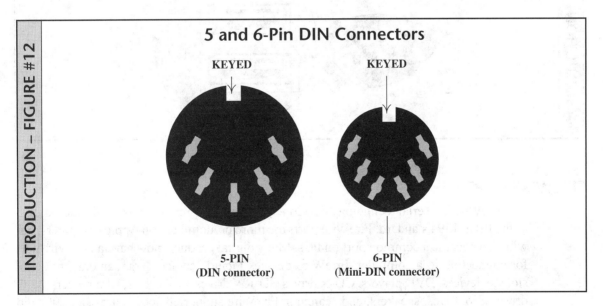

INTRODUCTION – FIGURE #12

5 and 6-Pin DIN Connectors

KEYED

KEYED

5-PIN
(DIN connector)

6-PIN
(Mini-DIN connector)

USB PORTS

USB stands for Universal Serial Bus. A **USB port** is a four-wire connector that allows up to 127 devices to transmit at either 12Mbps (12 million bits per second) or 1.5Mbps. USB 2.0 allows speeds up to 240Mbps. Compare these speeds to parallel port transfers of 150Kbps (150 thousand bits per second). Devices that can connect to the USB port include printers, scanners, mice, joysticks, CD-ROMs, tape drives, floppy drives, flight yokes, digital cameras, Web cams, modems, speakers, telephones, video phones, data gloves, and digitizers. In order for the computer to use the USB port, the computer must have a Pentium or higher microprocessor, an operation system that supports USB such as Windows 95/98, Windows 2000, or NT, and a chipset that acts as a host controller. Many motherboards have two integrated USB ports. Introduction Figure #13 shows a close up view of two USB ports.

USB Ports

INTRODUCTION –FIGURE #13

FIREWIRE PORTS

FireWire is a serial technology developed by Apple Computer. It is sometimes known as the IEEE 1394 standard. FireWire ports are more predominant on Apple computers, but will also become a common port on PCs. Many digital products now have a FireWire port for connecting to a computer. FireWire devices include camcorders, cameras, printers, storage devices, DVD players, CD-R drives CD-RW drives, tape drives, film readers, M-O drives, Zip drives, speakers, and scanners. FireWire supported speeds are 100, 200, and 400Mbps. As many as 63 devices, (using cable lengths up to 14 feet), can be connected together with FireWire. Windows 98, Windows 2000, Windows Millennium, and Windows XP support FireWire. FireWire supports hot swapping (plugging and unplugging devices with the power on), plug and play, and power for low power devices. The FireWire cable has six wires, four for data and two for power. Introduction Figure #14 shows a FireWire port.

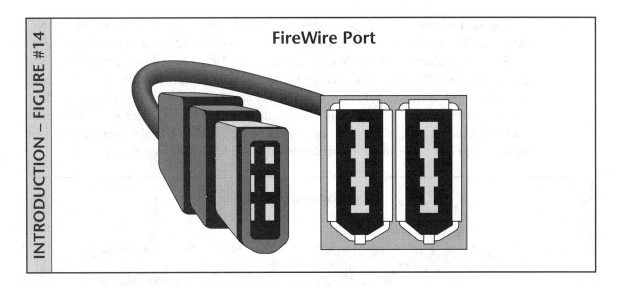

INTRODUCTION – FIGURE #14

FireWire Port

NETWORK PORTS

Three different network adapters, ARCnet, Ethernet, and Token Ring, are available. The ports on these adapters can be quite confusing because the connectors are sometimes the same. **ARCnet** ports can have a BNC connector, a RJ-45 connector, or both, on the adapter. ARCnet adapters sometimes have DIP switches that are used to select a network address. A network address is a unique hexadecimal number assigned to each ARCnet adapter. ARCnet adapters are not very common in today's networks. Introduction Figure #15 is an example of an ARCnet adapter.

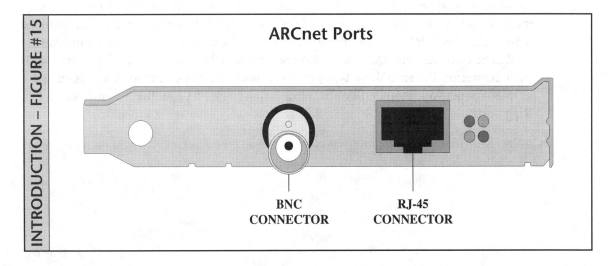

ARCnet Ports

BNC
CONNECTOR

RJ-45
CONNECTOR

Ethernet adapters are the most common types of network card. They can have a BNC, a RJ-45, a 15-pin female D-shell connector, or a combination of these on the same adapter. The BNC connector attaches to thin coax cable. The 15-pin D-shell connector connects to thick coax cable. The RJ-45 connector connects to UTP (Unshielded Twisted Pair) cable and is the most common Ethernet port used. The 15-pin female D-shell connector is confusing because this connector is also used with **game ports.** The RJ-45 connector looks like a phone jack, but it uses eight wires instead of four like the phone cable does. Introduction Figure #16 shows examples of different Ethernet adapter ports.

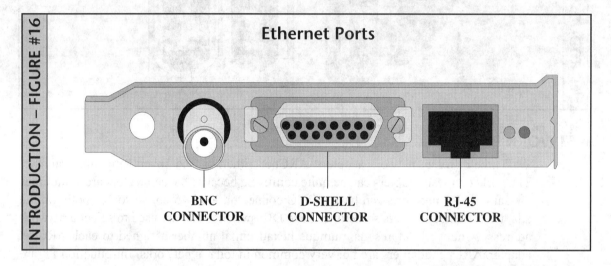

INTRODUCTION – FIGURE #16

Ethernet Ports

BNC CONNECTOR   D-SHELL CONNECTOR   RJ-45 CONNECTOR

Token Ring adapters have two different connectors: RJ-45 or 9-pin female D-shell connectors. Some adapters have a little green sticker with the numbers 4/16 on it. The 4/16 indicates the two speeds, 4Mbps and 16Mbps, at which Token Ring adapters can run. The 4/16 sticker is a helpful indicator that the port is a Token Ring port. Token Ring adapters used to be confused with the older video ports because both ports have a 9-pin female D-shell connector. Because these types of video ports are not common today, assume the adapter is a network adapter. Look at Introduction Figure #17 for the two different Token Ring ports.

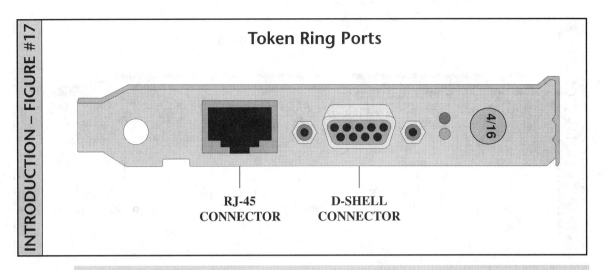

Token Ring Ports

INTRODUCTION – FIGURE #17

RJ-45
CONNECTOR

D-SHELL
CONNECTOR

Network ports are often confusing because there are so many similar ports on the three different network adapters. Sometimes the only way to identify the port is to look on the adapter for the name.

SOUND CARD PORTS

A **sound card** is an adapter that has several ports on it. Sound cards are also called audio cards. A sound card's main purpose is to convert digital computer signals and convert them to sound as well as the reverse. Sound cards can have a variety of ports, but the most common ones include a port for a microphone, one or more ports for speakers, and an input port for a joystick or MIDI (Musical Instrument Digital Interface) device. Examples of MIDI devices include an electronic keyboard or external sound module. The joystick port is sometimes known as a game port. Game ports are 15-pin female D-shell connectors. Game ports are sometimes confused with older Ethernet connectors. See Introduction Figure #18 for an illustration of a game port.

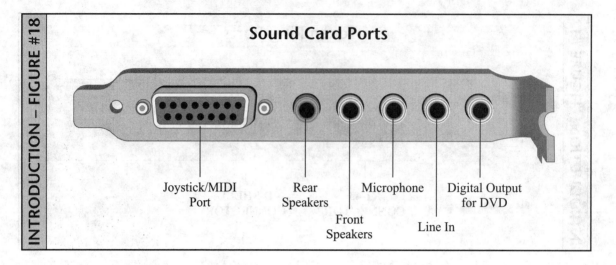

MODEM PORTS

A **modem** connects a microcomputer to a phone line. A modem can be an internal modem or an external modem. An internal modem is an adapter that has one or two RJ-11 connectors on the outside. An external modem is a separate device that sits outside the computer and connects to a 9-pin or 25-pin serial port. The external modem can also have one or two RJ-11 connectors. The RJ-11 connectors look like phone jacks in a home. With two RJ-11 connectors, one connector can be used for a telephone and the other connector has a cable that connects to the wall jack. The RJ-11 connector labeled *Line* is for the connection to the phone wall jack. The RJ-11 connector labeled *Phone* is to connect a telephone. An internal modem with only one RJ-11 connector connects to the phone wall jack. Look at Introduction Figure #19 that shows an internal modem with two ports.

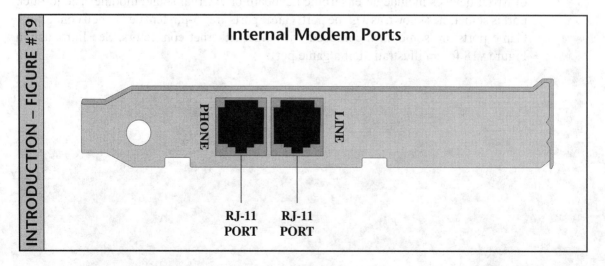

Being able to identify ports quickly and accurately is a critical skill in computer repair.

PROS AND CONS OF INTEGRATED MOTHERBOARDS

An integrated motherboard provides expandability because ports are built in and do not require separate adapters. Serial and parallel ports can be on the same adapter. If the motherboard includes the serial, parallel, and video ports, there is more space available for other adapters such as network or sound cards. The number of available expansion slots in a system depends on the motherboard manufacturer.

Ports built into the motherboard are faster than those on an expansion board. All adapters in expansion slots run slower than the motherboard components. Computers with integrated motherboards are easier to set up because the manufacturer configures the ports. Systems with integrated motherboards are normally easier to troubleshoot because the components are on one board. The drawback is that the motherboard must be replaced when one port goes bad, unless the motherboard supports disabling the faulty port. This is a lot more expensive than replacing an adapter.

One important feature to look for on an integrated motherboard is the ability to disable a port. If a port is faulty, disable the port and add an adapter.

If a motherboard has an integrated parallel port and the port is faulty, disabling the port and adding a $15 parallel port adapter is an inexpensive repair. However, not all integrated motherboards allow this. An integrated motherboard with ports that cannot be disabled can be very costly or cause some configuration problems with other expansion cards. Beware of integrated motherboards that do not allow the flexibility of disabling the ports!

A closely related feature to look for is the ability to change the configuration of the port. Ports have different parameters set to keep one port from interfering with another. The ability to alter the configuration is important to a technician. Of course, having good documentation on the features and abilities of an integrated motherboard is crucial for you. Without documentation, you cannot disable a port or change a port's settings. In addition, you cannot know the features of the individual ports or of the other motherboard components. The Internet is a great resource for documentation.

Name _____

INTRODUCTION REVIEW QUESTIONS

1. List three qualities of a good computer technician.

2. Describe how a computer technician must be like a detective.

3. [T / F]   A monitor can cause harm to an improperly trained technician.

4. List an example of an operating system.

5. What is firmware?

6. List one purpose of a power supply.

7. List three common components found inside a computer.

8. Which holds more data, a hard drive or a floppy disk?

9. What is an alternative to a CD-ROM drive?

10. Where is the motherboard located on a tower computer?

11. List three names for an adapter.

12. How can you determine an adapter's function?

13. What is the difference between RAM and ROM?

14. List one function of the ROM BIOS.

15. [T / F]   One cannot randomly change the ROM BIOS to a different manufacturer.

16. List two types of RAM chips.

17. What is the difference between a cold and a warm boot?

18. What is another name for a connector on the motherboard or an adapter?

19. Why must technicians be able to identify common ports?

20. What is the difference between male and female ports?

21. What type of connector do keyboards and mice use?

22. What is the difference in data transmission between the serial and parallel ports?

23. What are some common parallel devices?

24. List two common serial devices that connect to the serial port.

25. [T / F] Serial and parallel ports normally transmit in both directions.

26. How can you distinguish between a serial and a parallel port?

27. [T / F] The keyboard and mouse cables can always plug into either DIN port on the back of a computer.

28. How can one distinguish between a keyboard port and a mouse port?

29. What speeds are supported by USB?

30. [T / F] 2000 Professional supports USB devices.

31. What is another name for FireWire?

32. What speeds are supported by FireWire?

33. Which ports are often confused with Ethernet ports?

34. What is an easy way to identify a Token Ring port?

35. List at least two identification tips for distinguishing between network adapters.

36. What is the most common type of network adapter?

37. What normally connects to a game port?

38. What device converts analog signals to digital and vice versa as well as connects a computer to a phone line?

39. What type of connectors are found on an internal modem?

40. [T / F]   An internal modem with one RJ-11 jack has a phone connected to the port.

41. What are at least two advantages of an integrated motherboard?

42. Why is documentation an important issue with ports on an integrated motherboard?

Name _____

INTRODUCTION FILL-IN-THE-BLANK

1. An operating system is an example of _____. The floppy drive, hard drive, and monitor are examples of _____.

2. A small input device connected to the motherboard or an adapter is a _____.

3. The _____ provides DC voltage to various parts of a computer.

4. Disks used to store data insert into the _____.

5. The largest electronic circuit board in the microcomputer is the _____.

6. Adapters plug into a/an _____ on the motherboard.

7. A _____ plugs into the motherboard and holds adapters in some computer models.

8. Two basic types of memory found inside the microcomputer are _____ and _____.

9. The chip that contains software to start the computer is the _____.

10. _____ performs a hardware check during a cold boot.

11. An _____ is a motherboard that has multiple ports built into it.

12. Most integrated motherboard connectors are either _____ or _____ connectors.

13. A connector with a notch or an extra metal piece that allows a cable to be inserted only one way is said to be _____.

14. A three row, 15-pin female D-shell connector is a _____ port.

15. The 25-pin female D-shell connector is used for the _____ port.

16. The 9-pin or 25-pin male D-shell connector is a _____ port.

17. The keyboard or mouse connector can be a _____ or a _____.

18. A _____ port allows connection of up to 127 devices.

19. The most common connector used on the Ethernet port is _____.

20. A _____ converts digital signals to audio.

 Name _____

IDENTIFICATION OF DESKTOP COMPUTER PARTS PAPER EXERCISE

Objective: To identify various computer parts correctly

Identify each computer part shown in Introduction Exercise Figure #1.

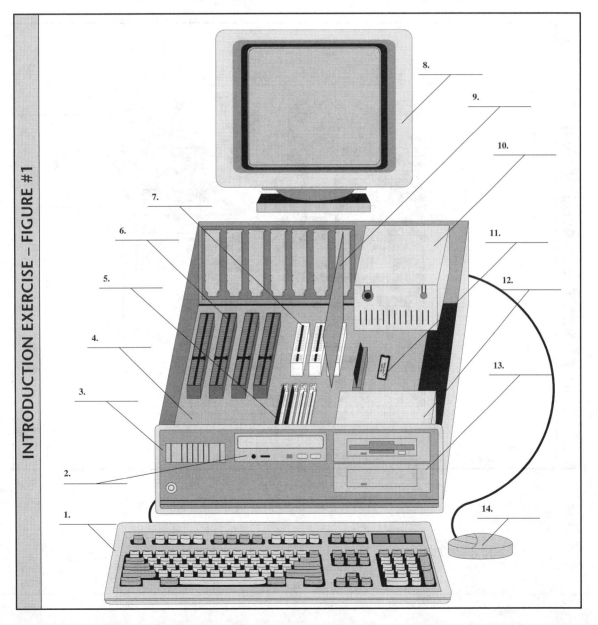

INTRODUCTION EXERCISE – FIGURE #1

Name _____

IDENTIFICATION OF TOWER COMPUTER PARTS PAPER EXERCISE

Objective: To identify various computer parts correctly

Using Introduction Exercise Figure #2, identify each computer part.

INTRODUCTION EXERCISE – FIGURE #2

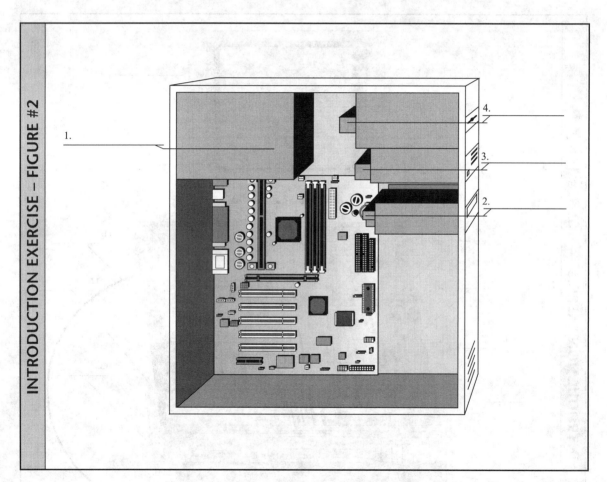

 Name _____

IDENTIFICATION OF COMPUTER PORTS PAPER EXERCISE

Objective: To identify various computer ports correctly

Identify the specific ports shown in Exercise Figure #3.

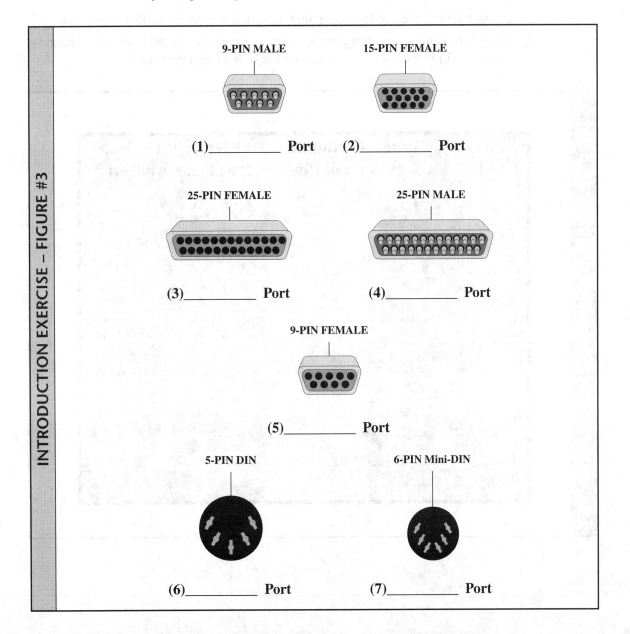

INTRODUCTION EXERCISE – FIGURE #3

9-PIN MALE

15-PIN FEMALE

(1)_____ **Port**   (2)_____ **Port**

25-PIN FEMALE

25-PIN MALE

(3)_____ **Port**   (4)_____ **Port**

9-PIN FEMALE

(5)_____ **Port**

5-PIN DIN

6-PIN Mini-DIN

(6)_____ **Port**   (7)_____ **Port**

Name _____

PORT IDENTIFICATION EXERCISE

Objective: To identify various computer ports correctly

Parts: Computer ports, either built into a specific computer or as separate adapters

1. Contact your instructor for a computer on which to work or to obtain adapters.

2. Identify the computer port(s) given to you by the instructor. Using Introduction Exercise Table #1, fill in the connector type, number of pins, and port type.

INTRODUCTION EXERCISE – TABLE #1

Connector Type (D-Shell, DIN, etc.)	Number of Pins	Port Type (Video, Parallel, Serial, etc.)
1.		
2.		
3.		
4.		
5.		
6.		
7.		
8.		
9.		
10.		

 Name _____

INTERNET DISCOVERY

Objective: To obtain specific information on the Internet regarding a computer or its
associated parts

Parts: Access to the Internet

The following scenario relates to questions 1–7:
You have a customer who has an ASUS P2L97-S motherboard.

Question 1:   Determine from documentation whether the mouse port is built into the motherboard.

Question 2:   If the mouse port is built into the motherboard, determine how many pins the mouse
port has.

Question 3:   Determine from documentation how many serial ports are built into the motherboard.

Question 4:   Determine how many pins the serial port(s) have.

Question 5:   Determine from documentation if the motherboard has USB ports.

Question 6:   Determine how many expansion slots are available for adapters.

Question 7:   Determine how many pins the keyboard port has.

The following information relates to questions 8–14:
You have a customer who has a Dell V400C Dimension computer.

Question 8:   Determine if the computer has a network adapter built into the motherboard.

Question 9:   If the motherboard has an integrated network adapter, what type of port is it?
[BNC / RJ-45 / 15-pin female]

Question 10:   Discover what operating system the computer ships with.

Question 11:   Determine if the computer ships with a modem.

Question 12:   If the computer ships with a modem, what type of modem is installed?

Question 13:   What is the warranty period on the computer?

Question 14:   Does the computer include a CD-ROM or a DVD?

The following information relates to questions 15–20:
A customer owns an Acer 6000-C333A computer.

Question 15:   Discover what operating system(s) the computer ships with.

Question 16:   Determine if the computer includes a network adapter.

Question 17:   If the computer contains a network adapter, what type of port is it?
[BNC / RJ-45 / 15-pin female]

Question 18:   Discover how many storage bays for hard drives, floppy drives, etc. are included?

Question 19:   Find out how many serial ports are integrated into the motherboard.

Question 20:   List three software packages that ship with the computer.

NOTES

2

Chapter 2:

On the Motherboard

OBJECTIVES

After completing this chapter you will

- Understand the major components on a motherboard including the microprocessor, chipset, math coprocessor, and expansion slots.
- Understand the basic operation of a microprocessor and what must be considered when upgrading it.
- Recognize and identify the microprocessor.
- Understand the differences among the various architectures and buses.
- Recognize different expansion slots.
- Recognize an adapter's architecture or bus.

KEY TERMS

3DNow!	HyperTransport	PC
AGP	IEEE 1394 (FireWire)	PC Card
bit	InfiniBand	PCI
bus	internal data bus	petabyte
bus-mastering	ISA	pipeline
byte	jumper	RapidIO
cache memory	kilobyte	SEC cartridge
CardBay	L1 cache	SEPP cartridge
CardBus	L2 cache	Slot A
chipset	L3 cache	SmartMedia
clone	local bus	Socket A
COAST	math coprocessor	SSE
CPU	MCA	Super 7 socket
DIB	megabyte	terabyte
EISA	megahertz	USB
exabyte	microprocessor	VL-bus
expansion slot	MMX	VRM
external data bus	multiplier	word size
form factor	on-die cache	write-back cache
FSB	overclocking	write-through cache
gigabyte	overdrive	ZV port
gigahertz		

MICROPROCESSOR OVERVIEW

At the heart of every microcomputer is a special motherboard chip called the **microprocessor** (or processor) that determines, to a great extent, how powerful a computer can be. The microprocessor is also called the **CPU (Central Processing Unit)**. The CPU executes instructions, performs math calculations, and coordinates input/output operations. Each motherboard has electronic chips that work with the CPU and are designed to certain specifications. Whether or not these other components can keep up with the microprocessor depends on the individual component's specifications. The major microprocessor manufacturers today are Intel, Motorola, Cyrix (now Via), and AMD (Advanced Micro Devices, Inc.). The microprocessors designed by Motorola have been used in Apple computers for years. Intel designed the microprocessors IBM used in their first computers.

IBM put microcomputers in the workplace and the home. Those early computers influenced a lot of what happened in the computer industry. The machines sold by companies who copied IBM's first computers were known as **clones** or IBM-compatibles. These two terms are still used in the computer industry today even though companies are not copying IBM at this point. Another name for the computer is **PC** or Personal Computer. This book focuses on compatibles (non-Apple computers) because they are the majority used in businesses today. Intel and AMD microprocessors are covered extensively because they are the most common in the computer industry.

MICROPROCESSOR BASICS

All microprocessors use 1s and 0s. One *1* or one *0* is a **bit**. Eight bits grouped together are a **byte**. The letter *A* looks like 01000001 to the microprocessor. Each character on a keyboard appears as one byte or eight bits to the microprocessor. Approximately 1,000 bytes are a **kilobyte**. (1,024 bytes to be exact, but the computer industry rounds the number off to the nearest thousand for ease of calculation.) Ten kilobytes are shown as 10K or 10KB. Approximately one million bytes are a **megabyte**. 540 megabytes are shown as 540MB or 540M. A true megabyte is 1,048,576 bytes. Approximately one billion bytes (1,073,741,824 bytes) are a **gigabyte** and are shown as 1GB or 1G. Beyond the gigabyte is a **terabyte** that is approximately one trillion bytes. A **petabyte** is one thousand terabytes (or 2 to the fiftieth power) and finally, an **exabyte** is approximately one billion times one billion bytes or 2 to the sixtieth power.

The number of bits processed at one time is the microprocessor's **word size**. Each word contains eight bytes or eight characters. Another term some industry books and magazines use is *register size*. Intel's 8086 microprocessor's word size was 16 bits or two bytes. Today's microprocessors have word sizes of 32 bits. Future microprocessors will have 64-bit word sizes. The result of this will be the development of 64-bit operating systems and 64-bit applications.

The 1s and 0s must travel from one place to another inside the microprocessor as well as outside to other electronic chips. To move the 1s and 0s around, electronic lines called a **bus** are used. The electronic lines inside the microprocessor are known as the **internal**

data bus. In the 8086, the internal data bus is comprised of 16 separate lines with each line carrying one *1* or one *0*. The word size and the number of lines for the internal data bus are equal. The 8086, for example, had a 16-bit word size and 16 lines carried 16 bits on the internal data bus. In today's microprocessors, several groups of 32 internal data bus lines operate concurrently.

For the microprocessor to communicate with devices in the outside world, the 1s and 0s travel on the **external data bus**. The external data bus connects the microprocessor to adapters, the keyboard, the mouse, the floppy drive, the hard drive, and other devices. The external data bus is also known as the external data path. One can see the external data lines by looking between the expansion slots on the motherboard. Some solder lines between the expansion slots are used to send data out along the external data bus to the expansion slots. The Intel 8088 had an 8-bit external data bus. Today's microprocessors have 64-bit external data paths.

To make sense of all of this, take a look at a letter typed on a computer that starts out: "DEAR MOM." To the microcomputer, the letters of the alphabet are different combinations of eight 1s and 0s. For example, the letter *D* is 01000100; the letter *E* is 01000101. The 8086 microprocessor has a word size of 16-bits and an external data path of 16-bits. Therefore, the letters *D* and *E* travel together down the bus; the letters *A* and *R*, then the letters (*space*) and *M*, and finally the letters *O* and *M* travel as 1s and 0s. Each 1 or 0 travels along a data path line. Intel's 80386DX microprocessor has 32-bit internal and external data buses. In the same "DEAR MOM" letter, the letters *D*, *E*, *A*, and *R* are processed at the same time, followed by (*space*), *M*, *O*, and *M*. You can see that the size of the bus greatly increases performance on a microcomputer. Motherboard Table #1 shows the different models of Intel microprocessors and their internal and external data paths. Many Intel microprocessors are known as the x86 family because of the numbering scheme Intel used in naming the microprocessors.

Intel Microprocessors

MOTHERBOARD – TABLE #1

Microprocessor	Word Size (in bits)	External Data Bus Size (in bits)
8088	16	8
8086	16	16
80286	16	16
80386DX (386)	32	32
80386SX (386SX)	32	16
80486DX (486)	32	32
80486SX (486SX)	32	32
Pentium	32*	64
Pentium Overdrive	32*	32
Pentium Pro	32*	64
Pentium II	32*	64
Celeron	32*	64
Pentium III	32*	64
Pentium 4	32*	64

*Multiple 32-bit paths

Notice in Motherboard Table #1 that the 8088 microprocessor has a 16-bit internal data path and an 8-bit external data path. This is bad news. Imagine the "DEAR MOM" letter as it is processed in the computer. The microprocessor handles the letters *D* and *E* simultaneously, but when the letters go outside the microprocessor—to the monitor, for example—the letter *D* goes out the external data bus, followed by the letter *E*. Having an external data path one-half the size of the internal data path slows down a microcomputer considerably. Why would a manufacturer make such a product? The answer is simple— lower costs. In many issues relating to microcomputers, the bottom line is profit.

Motherboard Table #1 shows Intel's Pentium, Pentium Overdrive, Pentium Pro, Pentium II, Pentium III, and Pentium 4 microprocessors as having 32* bits for the internal data buses. These microprocessors have multiple **pipelines** (separate internal buses) that operate simultaneously. The microprocessor handles 32 bits at a time and has separate paths, each of which handle 32 bits. For example, the Pentium microprocessor has two pipelines. In the "DEAR MOM" scenario, the letters *D, E, A,* and *R* can be in one pipeline, while (*space*), *M, O, M* can be in the other pipeline. Motherboard Figure #1 shows some of Intel's microprocessors.

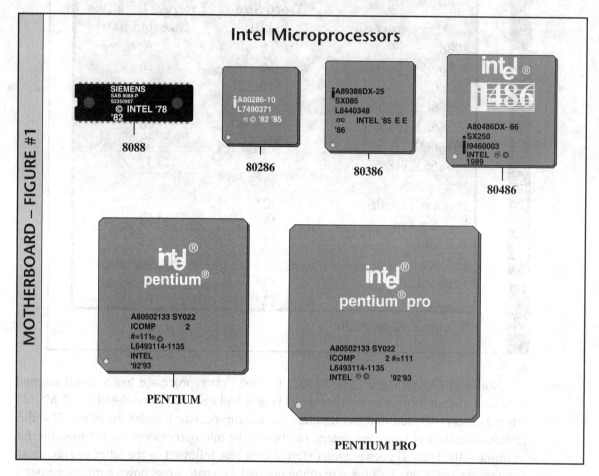

MOTHERBOARD – FIGURE #1

Intel Microprocessors

8088

80286

80386

80486

PENTIUM

PENTIUM PRO

The Pentium II has five execution pipelines, although they only output 64 bits at a time to the external data bus. AMD's K-6 microprocessor has six execution pipelines; the Athlon has nine execution pipelines. Intel has changed the microprocessor pipeline to include more stages. The Pentium III has a 10-stage pipeline and a Pentium 4 has a 20-stage pipeline. Debate continues about whether a longer pipeline improves performance.

The Pentium II microprocessor looks different than the other rectangular and square microprocessors. To achieve speeds up to 300MHz, Intel redesigned the microprocessor casing for the Pentium II. It uses an **SEC (Single Edge Contact) cartridge** to mount onto the motherboard into an Intel Slot 1 connector. Motherboard Figure #2 shows the Pentium II SEC cartridge.

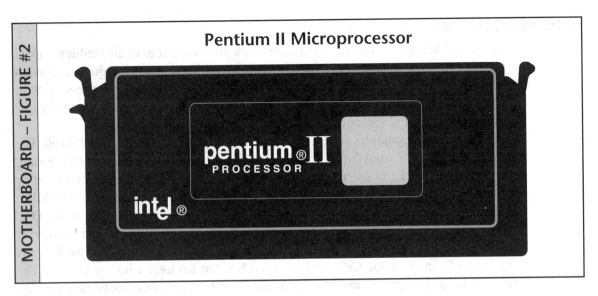

Pentium II Microprocessor

Intel's Celeron microprocessor was released for low-cost workstations. The CPU uses the P6 architecture similar to the Pentium II, but it is not expandable and does not include as much cache (explained later in the chapter) as the Pentium II. The Celeron uses a **SEPP (Single Edge Processor Package) cartridge**. This cartridge is similar to the Pentium II's SEC cartridge and it maintains compatibility with the 242-pin slot connector (known as a Slot 1 connector) the Pentium II uses. The Celeron processor is also available in a 370-pin PGA and FCPGA (Flip-Chip Pin Grid Array). The Pentium II Xeon and Pentium III Xeon CPUs insert into a 330-pin Intel Slot 2 connector. This Slot 2 connector allows communication between the CPU and L2 cache at the CPU's full speed, whereas the Slot 1 connector allows communication with the L2 cache at only one-half CPU speed. Pentium 4 processors use a 423-pin PGA socket and Xeons use a 603-pin PGA socket.

Distinguishing a 486 from a Pentium or Pentium Pro is accomplished by looking at the microprocessor's size. The 486 uses a 169-pin socket; the Pentium uses a 273 or 296-pin socket; the Pentium Pro uses a 387-pin socket. The 486 socket frequently has extra holes for a Pentium upgrade. The Pentium II and Pentium III CPUs are in an SEC cartridge. Pentium 4s and Xeons use large PGAs.

The microprocessor to watch for is a joint venture between Intel and Hewlett-Packard with the code name Merced. The Merced is a 64-bit microprocessor with a new architecture called IA-64. It will still be able to run applications designed for the older X86, Pentium, and Pentium II line. The clock speed of the Merced is expected to be 2GHz and higher. Other Intel processors in the works have the codenames Madison and Deerfield; both of these will use the IA-64 architecture.

AMD PROCESSORS

Advanced Micro Devices, Inc (AMD) makes a product similar to the Pentium known as the K5. The K5 processor fits in the same 296-pin socket as the Pentium. Even though a motherboard might physically accommodate the K5, the BIOS may not recognize it. (The BIOS may have to be upgraded.) Located on the AMD web site is a list of motherboards that accept the K5 CPU without an upgrade.

The different K5 modules are PR75, PR90, PR100, PR120, PR133, and PR166. The numbers after the *PR* are not the CPU speed. Instead, they are what is known as a P-rating, which is the clocked CPU speed when running a specific application as agreed upon by Cyrix, IBM, SGS-Thomson Microelectronics, and AMD. The speeds are actually 75MHz, 90MHz, 100MHz, 90MHz, 100MHz, and 116.7MHz respectively, according to AMD.

The AMD K6 is a sixth-generation processor to rival Intel's Pentium and Pentium II line. The K6 comes in three flavors—K6, K6-2, and K6-III. Even though the K6 was designed to fit in the same CPU socket as the K5, the K6 uses a higher voltage. The bottom line is that not all motherboards work with K6 processors because of the motherboard voltage and BIOS. Always check AMD's web site at www.amd.com for compatibility.

The K6-2 and K6-III models added speed to the CPU and system bus as well as more support for multimedia applications. Both CPUs fit into something known as a **Super 7 socket**, which is a redesigned Socket 7 that allows for higher bus speeds (from 66MHz to 95 or 100MHz). The Super 7 motherboards allow higher CPU speeds, support for AGP, support for ultra DMA hard drives, and have advanced power management features.

AMD's sixth-generation CPUs are the Athlon and Duron. The Duron is a scaled down version of the Athlon and has more cache memory than Intel's Celeron. The AMD Duron can access the cache through a 200MHz bus not shared by the chipset, RAM, AGP, PCI, and so forth. This CPU targets the home and business user or anyone who executes everyday applications like word processing and spreadsheet applications, e-mail, or Internet access. The Duron is available in 600-950+MHz versions.

The Duron and Athlon both use a new socket called **Socket A**. Socket A is a 462-pin PGA socket. Motherboard Figure #3 shows AMD's Socket A.

MOTHERBOARD – FIGURE #3

AMD's Socket A

The Athlon is AMD's powerhouse CPU available in 1 to 1.8+GHz versions. The Athlon can communicate with its L2 cache via a 200 or 266MHz bus. The Athlon is best suited for those who use desktop publishing, CAD, CAE, digital imaging, voice recognition, and scientific applications, or 3D gaming. The Athlon is also used in network servers; it rivals Intel's Pentium 4. The Athlon can execute up to nine instructions simultaneously as well as rearrange up to 72 instructions simultaneously. The Athlon uses either the 462-pin Socket A or the Slot A. The **Slot A** Athlon cartridge is similar to Intel's Pentium III, but they are not interchangeable! The same holds true for the AMD Socket A and Intel's Socket 370—only Intel CPUs function in the Socket 370.

Both the Athlon and Duron use the E6 design from DEC (Digital Equipment Corp.) compared to Intel's GTL+. The E6 design uses a 100MHz or 133MHz bus and double clocks data yielding a 200MHz or 266MHz bus to the CPU. The E6 design was originally developed for the 21264 Alpha CPU, but was redesigned for AMD. The AMD Athlon is shown in Motherboard Figure #4.

MOTHERBOARD – FIGURE #4

AMD Athlon

The Thunderbird is one of the best of Athlon's CPUs. It uses the 462-pin Socket A and is available in speeds of 750GHz to 1.4+GHz. The AMD Athlon Pro, code named Mustang, has a 12-stage pipeline. The successor to the Athlon is called SledgeHammer and it will have 64-bit instruction registers, but still contain 32-bit instructions for backward compatibility with today's operating systems and applications. The SledgeHammer will also include 64-bit memory addressing, which allows up to 18EB (Exabytes) addressing space. Future AMD processors include SledgeHammer, ClawHammer, and Barton. AMD has announced that the Hammer chip family will use a new type of bus called NUMA (Non-Uniform Memory Access) Lightning Data Transport bus. This will probably mean a new CPU socket or slot.

MMX, SSE, AND 3DNOW!

MMX is a microprocessor technology from Intel designed for the X86 microprocessors. Intel placed 57 new commands in the MMX microprocessors that help with multimedia and communications software. Keep in mind almost all software applications now include some pictures, sounds, or movies. If a particular application is not specifically written using the 57 new instructions, the software application's performance can still show a 10 to 20 percent increase in performance. On the flip side, with a particular application written to take advantage of the MMX technology, the software can still operate on non-MMX microprocessors, but the application speed will be slower. All Pentium II and higher microprocessors include the 57 MMX instructions.

MMX technology is not exclusive to Intel microprocessors. AMD and Cyrix processors also use MMX instructions in their command set. For future applications and faster multimedia applications, the MMX technology is necessary.

MMX2 technology places 70 new instructions beyond MMX. The instructions speed up applications including 2-D games, image editors, speech recognition software, and video encoding. The MMX2 technology is available in Intel's Pentium III microprocessor and is sometimes called KNI (Katmai New Instructions).

Today's applications require intense mathematical calculations because of the emphasis on video and audio integration. Inside the microprocessor is a part called the FPU (Floating Point Unit), which is responsible for handling floating-point numbers. Floating-point numbers are those that use decimals such as 1024.7685 and –581.3724985 compared to integers, which are numbers like 10, 561, and –86. The FPU has registers that hold bits. The more bits the register has, the more accurate a calculation the FPU can perform. Both video and audio applications use floating-point numbers.

Today's applications and games use 3-D graphics. A 3-D graphic is made up of small polygons. One 3-D figure could be 500 to 1500 polygons or more. Each time the figure changes, the polygons have to be redrawn and each polygon corner has to be recalculated using floating-point numbers. Four things help speed up calculations: (1) a faster CPU, which also means faster FPU, (2) more CPU pipelines, (3) built-in 3-D instructions that software applications can use, and (4) a good video adapter with a built-in processor and memory installed on the board.

Intel's response to 3-D needs comes through **SSE (Streaming SIMD Extensions).** SIMD stands for Single Instruction Multiple Data, which means that one instruction can be executed by multiple data items. To put this in English, imagine an instructor with 20 students in a classroom. The instructor could go to each student individually and tell him or her the daily assignment. On the other hand, the instructor *could* stand at the front of the room, stating the assignment to the entire class. The "telling once" scenario is similar to SIMD.

SSE is 50 new instructions that allow floating-point calculations to occur simultaneously. SSE uses 64-bit registers. An upgrade to SSE is known as SSE2 and it uses 128-bit registers. SSE2 contains 144 new instructions and is available in Pentium III and 4 processors. AMD's eighth generation CPUs (the 64-bit processors) may support SSE2, but AMD has its own method of dealing with 3-D.

AMD developed the **3DNow!** Technology, which became available with the K6-2 CPU. 3DNow! has 21 specific instructions and support for SIMD. Two 3DNow instructions can be handled simultaneously along with four floating-point calculations. The upgrade to 3DNow! is known as Enhanced 3DNow! and is available in the Athlon microprocessor. AMD will continue to include 3DNow! in future CPUs.

MATH COPROCESSORS

The difference between the 80486SX and the 80486DX microprocessors is in their ability to perform math calculations. The 80486DX microprocessor has the math coprocessor built right into the microprocessor; the 80486SX does not. In prior microprocessors, a separate computer chip called a **math coprocessor,** or a numeric processor, was added to the motherboard to perform some of the number-crunching functions. All microprocessors since Intel's 486DX and AMD's AM486 include the math coprocessor. On older computers, adding a math coprocessor sped up performance, especially with programs such as AutoCAD, spreadsheet applications, and graphics-intensive applications. To install a math coprocessor on a machine with an 80486SX microprocessor, add an 80487SX chip to the motherboard. The 80487SX is a microprocessor and math coprocessor combined, similar to the 80486DX. The 80487SX microprocessor takes over for the 80486SX processor. Each microprocessor without math coprocessing abilities has a specific math coprocessor designed to work with it. Motherboard Table #2 shows Intel's microprocessors with their associated math coprocessors, as well as the ones with built-in math coprocessing abilities.

Intel Math Coprocessors

Microprocessor	Math Coprocessor
8088	8087
8086	8087
80286	80287
80386DX	80387DX
80386SX	80387SX
80486DX	N/A
80486SX	80487SX
Pentium	N/A
Pentium Overdrive	N/A
Pentium Pro	N/A
Pentium II	N/A
Celeron	N/A
Pentium III	N/A
Pentium 4	N/A

MOTHERBOARD – TABLE #2

Notice in Motherboard Table #2 how the 80486DX, Pentium, Pentium Overdrive, Pentium Pro, Pentium II, Celeron, Pentium III, and Pentium 4 microprocessors do not have math coprocessors. This is because the math coprocessing ability is built into these microprocessors.

PROCESSOR SPEEDS

Math coprocessors and microprocessors come in a variety of speeds. The speed of a microprocessor and math coprocessor is measured in **megahertz** or **gigahertz**. Hertz is a measurement of cycles per second. One hertz equals one cycle per second. One megahertz is one million cycles per second or 1MHz. One gigahertz is one billion cycles per second or 1GHz. The 8088 microprocessor ran at 4.77MHz. Today's microprocessors run at speeds over 1GHz.

The numbers on top of the chip indicate the speed of a microprocessor and math coprocessor. Look for the number after the hyphen. Examples of chip speeds are in Motherboard Figure #5. The Pentium microprocessor runs at 133MHz. The 80486 microprocessor runs at 66MHz.

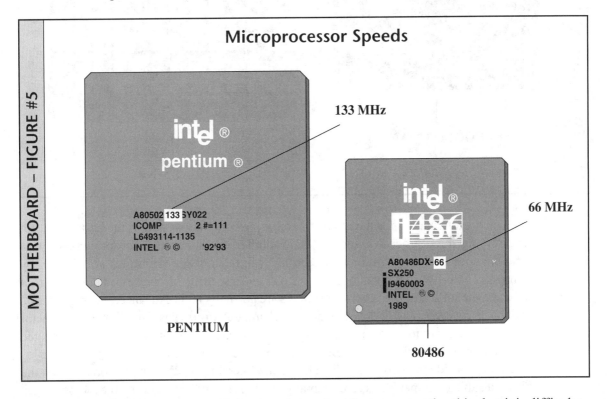

PENTIUM

80486

The processor speed is easy to determine if you can see the chip, but it is difficult to determine the speed of the 80486 and higher CPUs. These processors frequently have fans or heat sinks attached to them for cooling. A heat sink looks like metal bars protruding from the microprocessor. The largest chip or cartridge on or inserted into the motherboard with a fan or a heat sink attached is easily recognized as the microprocessor. The fans and heat sinks are very large in today's systems. Some systems have multiple fans to keep the CPU cool. Motherboard Figure #6 shows a microprocessor with a fan and another one with a heat sink.

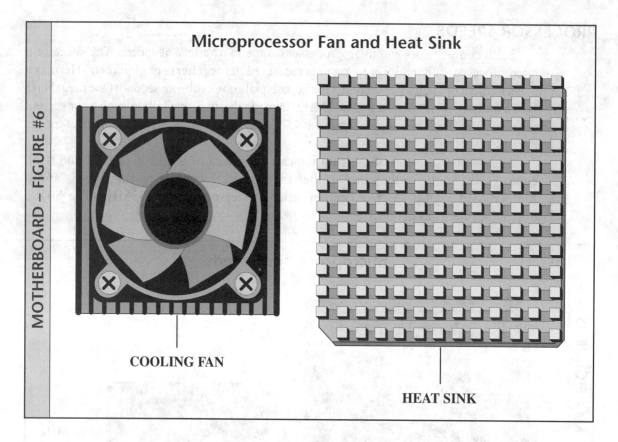

Microprocessor Fan and Heat Sink

COOLING FAN

HEAT SINK

The documentation for the motherboard or the computer system is the best source for determining microprocessor speed. Many motherboards accept microprocessors with different speeds. The microprocessor settings can be configured through software or by jumpers. The software is contained in the BIOS and a specific key is pressed during startup to access the software. The processor settings are normally in the Advanced Settings section and this is covered in more detail in the next chapter. A **jumper** is a small metal connector with a plastic cover used to connect two metal pins together. A jumper is normally located on a jumper block. Pins protrude upward from the jumper block. A jumper is enabled when it is placed over two pins. When the jumper is removed, the connection between the pins is disabled. Jumper blocks are normally labeled JP1, JP2, JP3, etc. on the motherboard.

A motherboard manufacturer determines the motherboard configuration, the number of jumpers on the motherboard, the jumper labels, and the use for each jumper. Each jumper can have more than one setting. For example, consider a motherboard with a jumper block and three pins labeled 1, 2, and 3. The jumper can be placed over pins 1 and 2 for one setting or pins 2 and 3 for a different setting. For example, jumper pins 1 and 2 may need to be jumpered together to configure the motherboard for a 166MHz microprocessor. In that case, the jumper is placed over pins 1 and 2; pin 3 is left uncovered. Refer to Motherboard Figure #7 for an illustration of JP1 pins 1 and 2 jumpered together.

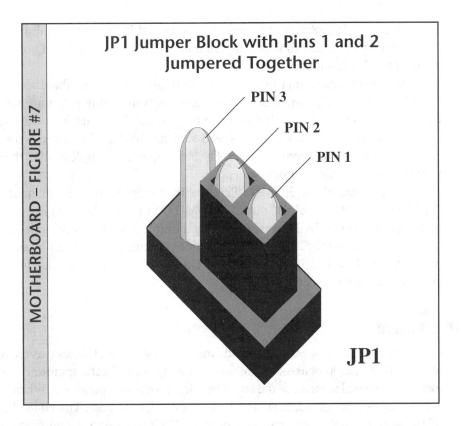

JP1 Jumper Block with Pins 1 and 2 Jumpered Together

PIN 3

PIN 2

PIN 1

JP1

MOTHERBOARD – FIGURE #7

Motherboard Figure #7 shows an enlarged jumper; the jumper blocks and jumpers on a motherboard are much smaller. When a jumper is not in use, instead of putting it in a desk drawer, a baggie, or in a drawer somewhere, place the jumper over a single pin in the jumper block. Although connecting the jumper over a single pin does not enable anything, it keeps the jumper safe and convenient for when needed later.

When working on a motherboard, look at it to see what jumpers are set. Then refer to the motherboard documentation for the microprocessor speed. Because microprocessors now have math coprocessing functions built in, knowing the CPU's speed is no longer an issue unless you are upgrading the computer to a faster microprocessor or configuring the motherboard.

Many people think that the higher the CPU speed, the faster the computer. This is very seldom true. Several factors contribute to computer speed. One factor is bus speed. Bus speed describes how fast the CPU can communicate with motherboard components, such as memory, chipset, or PCI bus. The first Pentium CPUs ran at a bus speed of 60MHz, however the CPUs got faster and the buses stayed the same. Advances in technology had not reached the rest of the motherboard components.

A **multiplier** is a number that, when multiplied by the bus speed, gives the CPU speed. For example, a 90MHz Pentium is determined by the 60MHz bus speed multiplied by 1.5 (the multiplier) yielding 90MHz. Common multipliers used are 1.5, 2, 2.5, 3, 3.5, 4, 4.5, 5,

5.5, 6, 6.5, 7, 7.5, 8, 8.5, 9, 9.5, and 10. The available multiplier and the bus speed are determined by the motherboard manufacturer. Common motherboard bus speeds include 60, 66, 68, 75, 83, 100, and 133MHz.

When upgrading a microprocessor or installing a new one, there are frequently two sets of motherboard jumpers or motherboard software settings that are very important: CPU bus frequency and bus frequency multiple. The CPU bus frequency setting allows the motherboard to run at a specific speed, such as 66MHz. This speed is the external rate data travels *outside* the microprocessor. The bus frequency multiple enables the motherboard to recognize the *internal* processor speed.

Take for example, a 333MHz Pentium II microprocessor. Its internal clock rate is 333MHz and external clock rate is 66.6MHz. The CPU bus frequency is set on the motherboard to 66MHz. The bus frequency multiple is set to 5. Five times 66MHz equals the internal clock rate of 333MHz. Both settings are configured, either by enabling jumpers on the motherboard or by accessing the BIOS software. An exercise at the end of the chapter helps with this concept.

CACHE MEMORY

The first microprocessor to include math coprocessing abilities was the 80486. It was also the first microprocessor to include cache memory. **Cache memory** is a fast type of memory designed to increase the speed of microprocessor operations. When located inside the microprocessor, it is known as **L1 cache** or as L1 memory. The 80486 has 8K or 16K of L1 write-through cache memory built in. **Write-through cache** uses a technique in which the microprocessor writes 1s and 0s into the cache memory at the same time it writes data to regular memory.

The type of L1 cache used in a Pentium or Pentium Pro microprocessor is different from the type used in the 80486. Instead of using a write-through cache, the Pentium and higher processors use a write-back cache. **Write-back cache** is more efficient than write-through cache. The 1s and 0s are stored and then later written to regular memory when the microprocessor is not busy.

The Pentium and Pentium Pro microprocessors come with 16K of L1 cache divided into two 8K segments. One 8K segment of cache handles microprocessor instructions (commands that tell the microprocessor what to do). The other 8K of cache handles data—1s and 0s as in the "DEAR MOM" letter. Two separate caches and two 32-bit internal data paths speed up the microprocessor tremendously. The Pentium II microprocessor has 32K of L1 cache.

L2 cache memory is a special type of memory similar to L1 cache memory. **L2 cache** holds a small amount of data that is "guesstimated" to be the next data the microprocessor will need. It is on the motherboard for Pentium and lower microprocessors, but starting with the Pentium Pro, the L2 cache is inside the microprocessor packaging. Whenever the L2 cache is housed in the microprocessor packaging, it is known as the **on-die cache**. When L2 cache is integrated into the same processor cartridge as the CPU, speed is increased. The cache speed stays the same, but the speed in which the processor accesses the data increases. The microprocessor is not limited by the motherboard routing speed constraints. The Pentium III and 4 have 256KB of L2 cache built into the microprocessor packaging. AMD's Duron has 64KB and the Athlon has 256KB of L2 cache.

When the L1 and L2 cache are included with the processor packaging, any cache installed on the motherboard is called **L3 cache**. Currently, little advantage is gained by more cache on the motherboard when the L1 and L2 cache are included in the microprocessor.

Cache chips on the motherboard can be a DIP (Dual In-line Package) chip, or a **COAST (Cache On A STick)** module. COAST memory modules resemble a small SIMM (Single In-line Memory Module). A DIP chip has a row of legs down each side. A COAST memory module is easier to install and holds more information than a DIP chip. Older motherboards use DIP chips. Newer motherboards, such as those used with 80486 and higher microprocessors, use COASTs for the cache. Motherboard Figure #8 shows the two different types of cache memory chips.

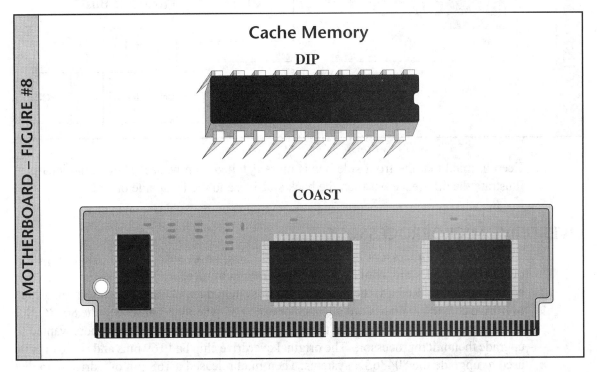

Accessing L2 cache and motherboard components has always been a bottleneck in systems up to the Pentium and K5 processors. This is because with older systems, the CPU must use the same bus to communicate with RAM, L2 cache, the chipset, PCI bus, and other motherboard components. Intel's Pentium Pro and AMD's Athlon/Duron CPUs take a different approach called DIB. With **DIB (Dual Independent Bus)**, two buses are used: a back side bus and a front side bus. The back side bus connects the CPU to the L2 cache. The **FSB (front side bus)** connects the CPU to the motherboard components. The Celeron uses a 66MHz FSB; Pentium II, K6-2, and K6-III use a 100MHz FSB; the Pentium III and the K6-3 use a 133MHz FSB; the Duron and some Athlon models use a 200MHz FSB; some Athlon models have a 266MHz FSB; and the Pentium 4 uses a 400MHz FSB. Because the Athlon uses the E6 architecture, each CPU installed in a multiprocessor system has its own 200MHz FSB. Motherboard Figure #9 illustrates the concept of a front side bus.

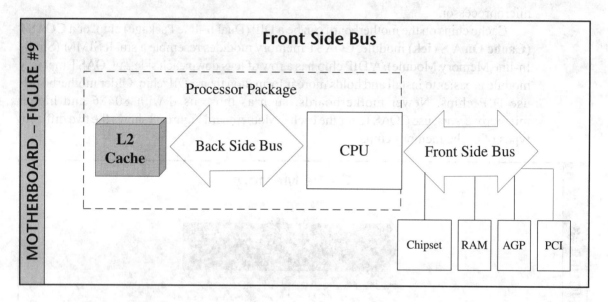

MOTHERBOARD – FIGURE #9

Keep in mind that the front side bus is more detailed than what is shown; the idea is to illustrate the difference between the back side bus and the front side bus.

OVERDRIVE MICROPROCESSORS

Older microprocessors can be upgraded using an **overdrive** chip. Many types of overdrive upgrades are available. When upgrading a microprocessor, be sure to get the correct overdrive. Refer to the motherboard or system documentation to determine which overdrive chip the motherboard allows. For example, when Intel produced the 80486DX2 microprocessor that runs at twice the motherboard speed, many 80486 owners wanted to upgrade their microprocessors. The original overdrive chip had 169 pins and could only be used to upgrade the 80486SX systems. Then Intel released a 168-pin overdrive chip that could be used in 80486DX or 80486SX systems.

Another upgrade chip is the Pentium Overdrive with 32K (16K more than the original Pentium) of L1 cache. However, the Pentium Overdrive chip only has one 32-bit external data path, not two as the Pentium has. The original Pentium Overdrive fit in a 238-pin socket on the motherboard, but the newer 80486 motherboards have an improved 235- or 237-pin socket.

Most 80486 motherboards can be upgraded with an overdrive chip depending on (1) the processor currently installed and (2) the socket(s) available on the motherboard. Documentation for the motherboard or computer system *might* give upgrade details, if not, go to Intel's web site.

MICROPROCESSOR STUDY GUIDES

Motherboard Table #3 shows a consolidated list of Intel microprocessors, word size, external data path, memory address lines (covered in Chapter 7), and common pin configurations.

Intel Microprocessor Study Table

CPU	Internal Data Path	External Data Path	Memory Address Lines	Common Pins/Slot
8088	16	8	20 (1MB)	40 (DIP)
80286	16	16	24 (16MB)	68 (PGA)
80386DX	32	32	32 (4GB)	132 (PGA)
80386SX	32	16	32 (4GB)	100 (PGA)
80486DX	32	32	32 (4GB)	168 (PGA)
80486SX	32	32	32 (4GB)	168 (PGA)
Pentium	32*	64	32 (4GB)	296 (PGA) & 320 (PGA)
Pentium Pro	32*	64	36 (64GB)	387 (PGA)
Pentium II	32*	64	36 (64GB)	242 (Slot 1 cartridge)
Celeron	32*	64	36 (64GB)	242 (Slot 1 cartridge) & 370 (PGA)
Pentium III	32*	64	36 (64GB)	370 (PGA) & Slot 1 cartridge
Pentium II/III Xeon	32*	64	36 (64GB)	330 (Slot 2 SEC cartridge)
Pentium 4	32*	64	36 (64GB)	423 (PGA)

*Multiple 32-bit paths

MOTHERBOARD – TABLE #3

The 320-pin Socket 7 the Pentium uses actually contains 321 pins, but the Pentium only uses 320 of them. AMD's processors, starting with the K5, are listed with their associated pin or slot configurations in Motherboard Table #4.

AMD Processors

Processor	Pin/Slot Configuration
K5	320 (PGA—Socket 7)
K6	320 (PGA—Socket 7)
K6-2	320 (PGA—Socket 7 & Super 7)
K6-III	320 (PGA—Super 7)
Duron	462 (PGA—Socket A)
Athlon	462 (PGA—Socket A) & Slot A

MICROPROCESSOR UPGRADE OVERVIEW

Two common questions asked of technicians are "*Can* a computer be upgraded to a higher or faster microprocessor?" and "*Should* a computer be upgraded to a higher or faster microprocessor?" Whether or not a computer *can* be upgraded to a higher or faster microprocessor depends on the capability of the motherboard. When a customer asks if a microprocessor *should* be upgraded, the technician should ask, "What operating system and applications are you using?" If the response is DOS or Windows 95 running mostly DOS and Windows 3.x applications, then the original Pentium is the optimum microprocessor. Even though Windows 95 is a 32-bit operating system, most of the code designed for the operating system is 16-bit and users are still using 16-bit applications designed for Windows 3.1. If the user wants to run Windows 98, Me, NT, or 2000 Professional, then a Pentium II/K6 or higher microprocessor is best.

A quick glance at the motherboard for extra holes around the microprocessor or an extra processor socket/slot is a good place to start in determining if the motherboard can accept a new microprocessor. Also look for the new SEC socket for a Pentium II upgrade. Read the documentation for the motherboard to determine if it can accept a faster microprocessor.

> Do not upgrade the microprocessor unless the documentation or manufacturer states the motherboard supports a newer or faster microprocessor.

Another issue to consider with microprocessor speeds is the voltage level of the microprocessor. All Intel microprocessors used in desktop or tower models up to the 80486DX use 5 volts supplied from the motherboard. The 80486SX, 80487SX, and 80486DX2 microprocessors also run on 5 volts. The 80486DX4 microprocessor runs on 3.3 volts. Members of the Pentium microprocessor family use varying voltages. The lower voltage microprocessors run cooler than the higher voltage ones. Newer microprocessors operate at 2 volts or lower.

Some motherboards can be changed from 5 volts to 3.3 volts needed by the processor, as required by some microprocessor upgrades. If you accidentally insert a 3.3-volt microprocessor into the socket without changing the setting on the motherboard from 5 volts to 3.3 volts, the 5 volts going in the new microprocessor will likely destroy it. Getting the correct microprocessor upgrade and setting configuration jumpers on the motherboard for the correct speed and voltage are critical to a successful microprocessor upgrade. Because the 150MHz and higher Pentiums require a lower voltage, Intel has socket designs (Socket 7 and Socket 8) specifically for these Pentiums. The Socket 7 or Socket 8 can have a **VRM (Voltage Regulator Module)** mounted beside the socket, thus providing the appropriate voltage to the new microprocessor.

Upgrading things other than the microprocessor can also increase speed in a microcomputer. Installing more memory, a faster hard drive, or a motherboard with a faster front side bus sometimes improves a computer's performance more than installing a new microprocessor. All devices and electronic components must work together transferring the 1s and 0s efficiently. The microprocessor is only one piece of the puzzle. Many people do not realize upgrading one computer component does not always make a computer faster or better.

INSTALLING AND OVERCLOCKING MICROPROCESSORS

Whenever a microprocessor is purchased, it includes installation instructions. Also, motherboard manuals (documentation) include the steps to upgrade or install the CPU. Outlined below are general steps for processor installation.

Parts: Proper microprocessor for the motherboard (refer to motherboard documentation)

Microprocessor extractor tool if necessary (normally comes with an upgrade kit)

Anti-static materials

1. Be sure power to the computer is *off*.
2. Place the anti-static wrist strap around your wrist and attach the other end to a ground on the computer.
3. Remove the old processor. During upgrading, some older processors require the use of an extractor tool included with the microprocessor upgrade. If necessary, insert the microprocessor extractor tool under one side of the microprocessor. Pry the chip up slightly. Remove the microprocessor extractor tool. Insert the microprocessor extractor tool under a side of the microprocessor adjacent to the side just lifted. Pry the side up slightly. Repeat for the remaining two sides of the microprocessor until the microprocessor lifts from its socket. If the microprocessor is in a ZIF (Zero Insertion Force) socket, lift the retaining lever outward and upward. The microprocessor will lift gently out of the socket. Gently pull the microprocessor straight upward. Put the old microprocessor into an anti-static bag. To remove a cartridge CPU, push down on the retaining

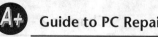
locks that release the cartridge. Some locks have to be pushed inward before the processor can be removed. Lift the cartridge out of the slot.

4. Before installing the new CPU, you must configure the motherboard by jumpers or through software configuration. Refer to the motherboard manual for exact steps. If necessary, set any jumpers or switches on the motherboard necessary for proper operation or press the correct key to enter the Setup program that allows you to set the CPU speed and proper multiplier. Some manuals refer to the multiplier as the stepping value. Refer to the motherboard's documentation. Check yourself. A saying that definitely applies to computers and networks is "Think twice, replace once."

5. Insert the new microprocessor into the socket ensuring that pin 1 on the microprocessor (indicated by a dot or a notched corner) aligns with pin 1 of the motherboard socket (indicated by a dot or a notched corner). Newer processors insert only one way into the socket or slot. If the microprocessor is a SEC cartridge, the cartridge has a lock on both sides near the top (away from the connectors). Hold the cartridge over the CPU expansion slot ensuring that the CPU connector aligns in the correct direction with the notch in the expansion slot. Push the locks inward and slide the cartridge into the expansion slot. Some motherboards have a retention mechanism used with microprocessors equipped with mounted heat sinks.

Overclocking is changing the front side bus speed and/or multiplier to boost CPU and system speed. Before describing the steps, we must discuss the overclocking issues.

- Because the CPU is normally covered with a heat sink and/or fan, you cannot easily tell the CPU speed. Some vendors sell a system advertised with a higher rated CPU speed than what is installed.
- CPU speed ratings are conservative.
- The CPU, motherboard, memory, and other components can be damaged by overclocking, especially if it is not performed in a logical, cautious manner.
- Applications may crash, the operating system may not boot, and/or the system may hang when overclocking. If these issues are frustrating to you, do not overclock.
- The warranty is void on the CPU if you overclock.
- When you increase the speed of the CPU, the processor's heat increases. Extra cooling by fans and larger heat sinks are essential.
- PCI and SCSI devices may not react well to the overclocking.
- The hard drive PIO mode may need to be changed because of overclocking.
- The memory chips may need to be upgraded to be able to keep up with the faster CPU.
- You may consider overclocking dishonest. If this is the case, do not do it.

In order to overclock, you must have the motherboard documentation to determine whether the system board supports different CPU speeds and different multipliers. The changes to the motherboard will be made through jumpers or through BIOS Setup. Determine which method is used with your motherboard. A few motherboards do not support speed or multiplier changes. Keep in mind that overclocking is a trial and error situation. There are web sites geared toward documenting specific motherboards and overclocked CPUs.

The first change to make is to increase the bus speed. In the motherboard manual, locate the settings for External Bus Speed, External Frequency, CPU Bus Frequency, External Bus Frequency or something along those lines. The common speeds seen are 50, 55, 60, 66, 75, and 83. Make a note about the current setting (and put it to the side for future reference in case you need to return the setting to the original configuration). Always make changes one step at a time; increase the external bus speed by one setting.

The next change that can be made is to change the multiplier. This setting is frequently marked or documented as Multiplier, Bus Frequency Multiple, CPU to Bus Frequency Ratio, Clock Ratio, or something along those lines. The bus speed times the multiplier equals the CPU speed. Again, only make one change at a time and only increase the multiplier by a .5 increment. For example, if the current setting is 2.0, the next increment would be 2.5. Do not change the setting to 3.0 or 3.5. Do not rush the procedure.

The CPU voltage may need to be increased. Many motherboards allow the CPU voltage to be adjusted. As you can tell, overclocking cannot be accomplished without the motherboard manual. Increase the CPU voltage only in small increments.

The number one problem with overclocking is insufficient cooling. Make sure you purchase the larger heat sink and/or extra fans before starting the overclocking process. When you make a change and start the computer, enter the BIOS Setup program (see Chapter 3). If the Setup program will not load, power off the computer and return the CPU and multiplier settings to the original setting or the setting that previously worked. After each change, enter the Setup program. If that works, load the operating system. If that works, stay with the setting, or continue making incremental changes.

DUAL PROCESSORS

You may ask: "What must I do to install two or more CPUs into a motherboard?" To install more than one processor into a motherboard, both the operating system and the applications must support SMP (Symmetric Multiprocessing), and the motherboard must support multiple CPUs. Most home and business users do not need multiple processors. Give them a power CPU, a good front side bus, lots of memory and hard drive space and they should be fine. Network servers *do* need multiple processors, and network operating systems, such as Novell, NT, 2000 Server, Linux, Microsoft XP, and Unix, support SMP. 2000 Server supports up to four CPUs on a motherboard. Windows 95, 98, and Me do not support multiple CPUs. Motherboard manufacturers have developed system boards that support the Celeron, Pentium II, Pentium III, Pentium Xeon, Pentium 4 Xeon (sometimes called Xeon DP), Athlon MP, and Duron processors.

When installing multiple processors, place the same processor model in each slot and install as much RAM as the customer can afford. If a second processor is added without adding more RAM, both processors have to make do with the same amount of RAM. The general rule of thumb is to double (at least) the amount of RAM when upgrading to two or more CPUs. Because a system has two CPUs installed does not mean that performance will double. A gain of 50 to 70 percent in performance is considered to be excellent. Most applications that support SMP show only a 10 to 15 percent performance gain. Applications that support multiprocessors include Adobe's Photoshop, Discreet's 3D StudioMax, GameSpy Industries, and Quake III.

When installing multiple processors ensure the computer is powered off. Install the processor according to the directions that came with the processor or according to the motherboard documentation. Ensure the system has adequate cooling including a heat sink and/or fan for the new processor. Some motherboards do not come with the second VRM (voltage regulator module) for the second processor slot. The customer may need to purchase one before installing the CPU onto the motherboard. Go into the Advanced Settings portion of BIOS Setup or set the motherboard jumpers according to the documentation. Ensure that the processor speed and multiplier settings are correct. The operating system and/or any applications that support multiple processors may have to be reinstalled before they will recognize new processor(s). The best advice is to install as many processors as needed before loading any applications or operating systems, or to buy the system with multiple processors already installed.

ARCHITECTURES AND BUSES

If the computer is to be useful, the microprocessor must communicate with the outside world including other components on the motherboard and adapters plugged into the motherboard. An architecture or bus is a set of rules that control how many bits can be transferred at one time to an adapter, what signals are sent over the adapter's gold connectors, how the adapter is set up or configured, etc. Three architectures used in PCs are ISA (Industry Standard Architecture), EISA (Extended Industry Standard Architecture), and MCA (MicroChannel Architecture). Note that EISA and MCA are not common in today's computers. ISA is also becoming rare and is only available to handle old adapters. The buses most common today are PCI (Peripheral Component Interconnect), AGP (Accelerated Graphics Port), USB (Universal Serial Bus), IEEE 1394 (FireWire), and PC Card. A technician must be able to distinguish among adapters and ports designed for each bus type and configure the adapters/devices for each bus. The technician must also realize the abilities and limitations of each bus when installing upgrades, replacing parts, or making recommendations to customers.

ISA (INDUSTRY STANDARD ARCHITECTURE)

The **Industry Standard Architecture**, better known as **ISA**, is the oldest architecture used with X86 microprocessors and it still has limited use in today's computers. ISA allows 16-bit transfers to adapters installed in ISA slots. A slot or **expansion slot** is the place to plug in an adapter. The number of expansion slots available depends on the manufacturer of the motherboard. ISA is also referred to as the AT bus. Because computer manufacturers want customers to be able to use their old adapters in an upgraded motherboard or a new computer, ISA is still on the market.

ISA operates at 8MHz although some vendors reliably achieve 10MHz throughput. Some vendors have achieved 12MHz, but the industry pronounced 10MHz the maximum speed for ISA. With today's microprocessor speeds, it's easy to see how the ISA architecture can be a detriment. Adapters, such as network memory and video, which require high-speed transfers, are hampered by the slowness of the ISA standard. Many people still do not realize how much an ISA adapter handicaps the devices it controls.

A memory expansion card should *never* be placed in a 386 or higher's ISA expansion slot. All the computer's memory runs at the speed of the ISA expansion slot—10MHz.

ISA was designed to be backward compatible with IBM's first two computer models, the PC and the XT. The PC and XT had an 8-bit external data bus. The only adapters that worked in the PC and the XT computers were 8-bit adapters. The ISA architecture allows an 8-bit adapter to fit and operate in the 16-bit ISA slot. Reference Motherboard Figure #10 for an example of the difference between an 8-bit ISA adapter and a 16-bit ISA slot.

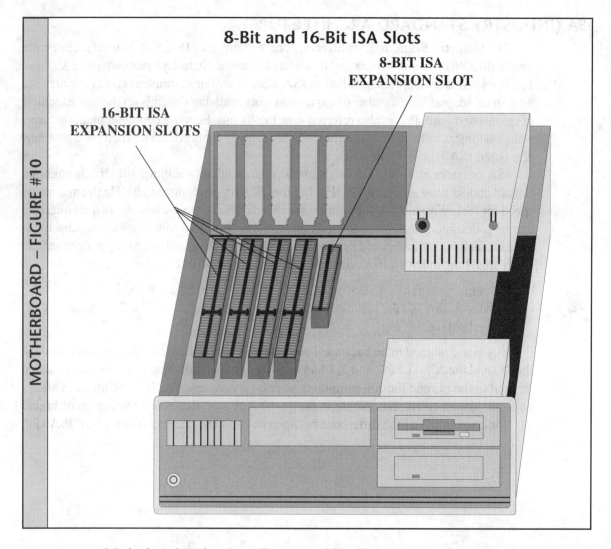

8-Bit and 16-Bit ISA Slots

8-BIT ISA EXPANSION SLOT

16-BIT ISA EXPANSION SLOTS

Motherboards today normally come with only 16-bit ISA slots because an 8-bit ISA adapter fits perfectly in a 16-bit slot. The extension connector on the 16-bit slot remains empty. Many books, advertisements, and vendors call 8-bit adapters ISA cards, but a true ISA adapter is a 16-bit card. The original architecture for computers that used the 8088 microprocessor was the PC bus. Nevertheless, because some rules from the PC bus were incorporated into the ISA standard, most people call 8-bit adapters ISA adapters.

ISA adapters are frequently configured through switches and jumpers. This is time-consuming for a technician because most computer owners do not have the documentation for the ISA adapters installed in their systems. This documentation is frequently lost or destroyed. Most companies have adapter documentation on their web sites. However, some adapters do not have identifiers on them so a technician cannot tell which manufacturer produced them. Newer ISA adapters can also be configured through software, which is much easier than setting jumpers or switches.

MCA (MICROCHANNEL ARCHITECTURE)

When IBM computers were cloned and IBM started losing its share of the microcomputer market, IBM decided to develop its own architecture called **MicroChannel Architecture** or **MCA** for short. The MicroChannel Architecture is *incompatible* with ISA. MCA adapters will *not* fit in ISA expansion slots, nor will ISA adapters fit in MCA expansion slots.

The MicroChannel Architecture includes a 32-bit bus, although most MCA adapters are 16-bit adapters. Some MCA cards are able to do 64-bit transfers using a technique called streaming. MicroChannel is a proprietary architecture and any vendor who designs an MCA adapter pays IBM a fee. IBM has maintained strict controls on this architecture, so it has not been cloned.

MCA adapters are much easier to configure than ISA adapters because the adapters are set up through software. When an MCA adapter is sold, a disk ships with the adapter that allows the MCA computer to recognize the adapter and any changes in the adapter's configuration. The drawback to this method is computer users frequently lose the adapter software disk. IBM no longer manufactures computers with only MCA expansion slots.

The MicroChannel Architecture introduced a feature called **bus-mastering**. This allows an adapter to take over the external data bus from the microprocessor and execute operations with another bus-mastering adapter without going through the microprocessor. The ISA standard only allowed one bus-master adapter in an ISA machine. However, ISA bus-master adapters are rare. The PCI bus (covered later in the chapter) now supports bus-mastering too. Bus-mastering is important for network and video adapters especially because of their need for speed.

EISA (EXTENDED INDUSTRY STANDARD ARCHITECTURE)

The computer industry was upset by IBM's move to a proprietary architecture. A group of nine vendors: Compaq, Hewlett-Packard, Zenith, Epson, NEC, Wyse, AST, Tandy, and Olivetti got together to develop a new non-proprietary architecture to rival IBM's MicroChannel Architecture. The result was the development of **EISA (Enhanced Industry Standard Architecture).** EISA is a 32-bit 10MHz standard that allows ISA adapters to operate in the EISA expansion slots. The ISA adapters do not have access to all the upgraded features the EISA expansion slot offers. Only an EISA adapter is able to take advantage of the upgraded features of the EISA expansion slot. An EISA expansion slot is the same physical length as an ISA expansion slot. The difference between the two is the depth of each expansion slot. The EISA expansion slot is twice as deep as the ISA expansion slot. An EISA adapter has two rows of gold connectors. Reference Motherboard Figure #11 for an example of a motherboard with EISA and ISA expansion slots.

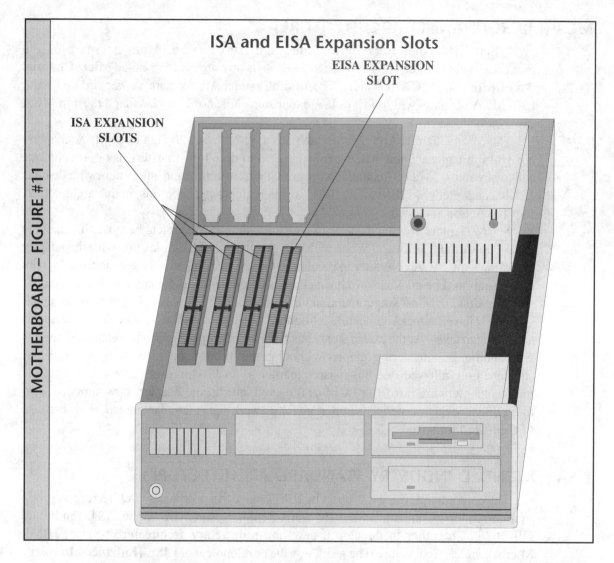

ISA and EISA Expansion Slots

EISA EXPANSION
SLOT

ISA EXPANSION
SLOTS

EISA adapters, like MCA adapters, are configured through software, which is simple for technicians. Also, EISA adapters can do bus-mastering like the MCA adapters. However, EISA never really caught on as well as the designers hoped.

All three architectures, ISA, MCA, and EISA, are limited by speed. EISA expansion slots are useful because ISA and EISA adapters fit and work in the expansion slots. MCA is very consistent in how all adapters are configured. MCA and EISA both support software configuration and bus-mastering which are a great improvement over ISA. Motherboard Figure #12 compares ISA, MCA, and EISA adapter connectors.

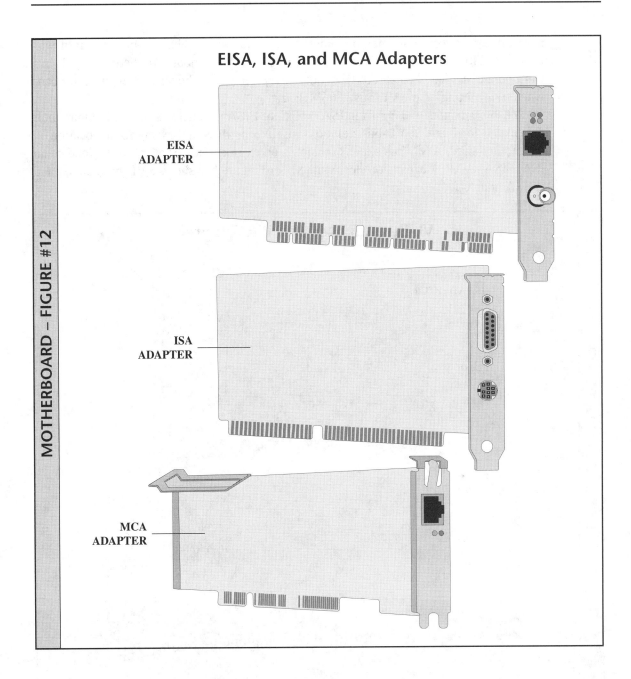

MOTHERBOARD – FIGURE #12

EISA, ISA, and MCA Adapters

EISA
ADAPTER

ISA
ADAPTER

MCA
ADAPTER

VL-BUS

One of the biggest industries affected by the slowness of ISA, EISA, and MCA is the video industry. Video needs a wide, fast path to transmit all the 1s and 0s to generate millions of colors, create detailed pictures, and provide video motion. So, the video industry developed their own local bus standard called the **VL-bus** or VESA (Video Electronics Standards Association) bus. Other industries have taken advantage of the VL-bus, including hard drive, network, and memory adapter manufacturers. The VL-bus standard was formulated for the 80486 microprocessor and is a 32-bit standard. In theory, the VL-bus can operate at speeds up to 66MHz (but some testing has shown that errors can occur when transmitting on the VL-bus at 66MHz).

VL-bus adapters will *not* fit in ISA, MCA, or EISA expansion slots, and require their own expansion bus. The VL-bus slot looks just like an MCA slot except for its location on the motherboard. A VL-bus expansion slot is an extra connector added to the end of an ISA, EISA, or MCA expansion slot. Motherboard Figure #13 shows a VL-bus adapter and an ISA adapter.

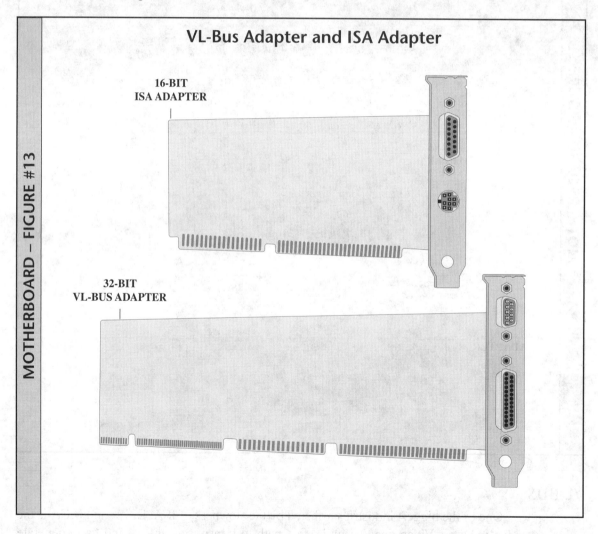

VL-Bus Adapter and ISA Adapter

**16-BIT
ISA ADAPTER**

**32-BIT
VL-BUS ADAPTER**

MOTHERBOARD – FIGURE #13

Notice in Motherboard Figure #13 how the VL-bus adapter has three different connectors on it. Two of the VL-bus connectors are just like an ISA adapter's connectors, but the third connector to the far left is what makes the adapter a VL-bus.

VL-bus expansion cards configure through jumpers and switches. However, some VL-bus adapter manufacturers provide the capability of software configuration. More configuration issues are covered in Chapter 3.

PCI (PERIPHERAL COMPONENT INTERCONNECT)

The most popular local bus is **PCI (Peripheral Component Interconnect)** bus. PCI comes in four varieties: (1) 32-bit 33MHz, (2) 64-bit 33MHz, (3) 64-bit 66MHz, and (4) the new proposed standard called PCI-X 64-bit 133MHz. The PCI bus has almost reached its limit in terms of speed. The PCI-X bus is backward compatible with the previous versions of the bus, but allows faster speeds. A chip called the PCI bridge controls the PCI devices and PCI bus. With the PCI-X bus, a separate bridge controller chip is added. Motherboard Figure #14 shows how the PCI-X bus integrates into the system board.

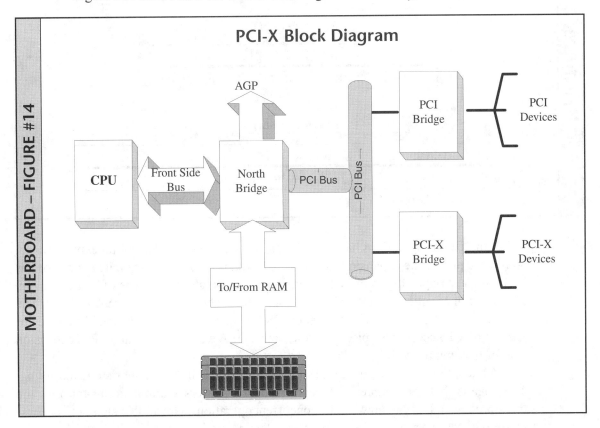

PCI expansion slots are not extensions of another architecture's expansion slots, as is the case with VL-bus connectors. Instead, PCI expansion slots are separate connectors. The expansion slots come in four configurations based on voltage level and number of bits that transfer in or out of the slot. Motherboard Figure #15 shows the different types of individual PCI expansion slots.

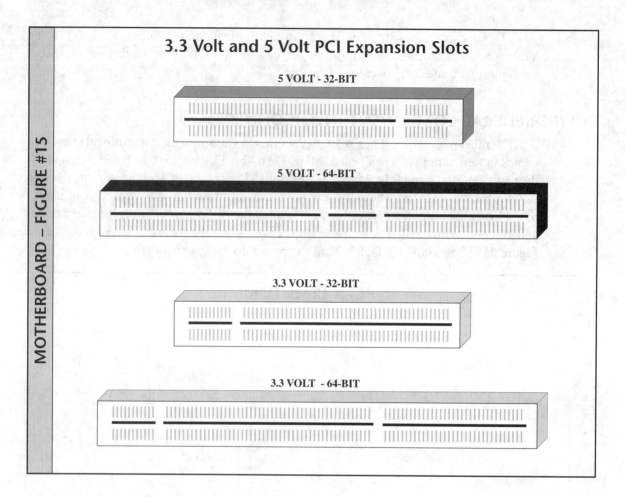

3.3 Volt and 5 Volt PCI Expansion Slots

Both PCI configurations have a 32-bit and a 64-bit version. The 64-bit expansion slot adds more pins to the expansion slot. The PCI expansion slot as a separate connector has been the most popular type of PCI expansion slot until lately. One type of PCI expansion slot, sometimes called a combo slot, is a connector that combines both ISA and PCI. The expansion slot allows insertion of either one ISA adapter *or* one PCI adapter. The connector is one molded piece, but the piece contains both an ISA expansion slot and a PCI expansion slot for maximum flexibility.

PCI adapters are configured with software and the standard supports bus-mastering. This means that the adapter can perform data transfers without going through the microprocessor. PCI can now handle concurrent operations. Not all PCI slots support bus-mastering. Always refer to the motherboard documentation.

Many adapters are now available for PCI expansion slots. Unlike VL-bus, the PCI standard can be used with both PCs and Apple computers. PCI expansion cards can take advantage of the speed and throughput of today's microprocessors such as Intel's Pentium III and Pentium 4 as well as AMD's Athlon processors. PCI expansion slots are farther from the back of the computer than ISA, EISA, or MCA slots. The VL-bus slot is also the same dimension. Most motherboards today come with ISA and PCI slots. Reference Motherboard Figure #16 for an example of a motherboard with PCI and ISA expansion slots.

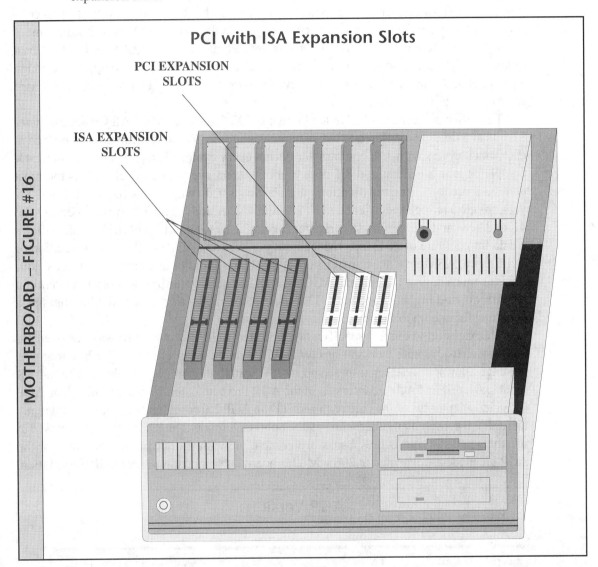

AGP (ACCELERATED GRAPHICS PORT)

AGP (Accelerated Graphics Port) is a bus interface for graphics adapters developed from the PCI bus. Intel does the majority of the development for AGP and the specification was originally designed around the Pentium II processor. AGP speeds up 3-D graphics, 3-D acceleration, and full-motion playback.

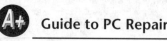

With AGP, the processor on the video adapter can directly access RAM on the motherboard when needed. This helps with video-intensive applications. 3-D graphics, for example, are resource-intensive and use a lot of memory. Software developers can produce better and faster 3-D graphics using AGP technology. The best performance is achieved when applications use the RAM on the AGP adapter. However, because more memory than the amount on the adapter is needed, motherboard RAM is the next best option. Previous video adapters have been limited by the bottleneck caused by going through an adapter and a bus shared with other devices. With AGP, the video subsystem is isolated from the rest of the computer.

The different versions of AGP are known as 1X, 2X, 4X, and 8X. All versions transfer 32-bits at a time. The difference between the versions is how many transfers take place in each clock cycle. With 1X, one transfer occurs every cycle; 2X makes two transfers; 4X completes four transfers; and 8X does eight transfers every clock cycle. 2X is the most common version. The specifications are shown as 1.0 (which was for the 1X and 2X versions), 2.0 (which specified the 1X, 2X, and 4X versions), and 3.0 (which specifies the 4X and 8X standards). AGP data transfers occur 32-bits at a time at 66MHz, which allows a data transfer rate of 264Mbps (Megabytes per second). AGP2X, the next generation of AGP, has a 528Mbps data transfer rate. AGP4X has a data transfer rate of 1Gbps, four times as much data as the original AGP. AGP4X has been optimized to work with Pentium III, Athlon, and higher processors. The latest recommendation is for AGP8X that has a data transfer rate up to 2Gbps.

An extension to the 2.0 specification is called AGP Pro. AGP Pro was designed for more powerful graphics workstations. With AGP Pro, the connector is longer, has improved cooling, allows an adapter to draw up to 110 watts, and supports both the 2X and 4X modes. All original AGP adapters fit in the AGP Pro connector. In order to install an AGP 4X video adapter two things are required: (1) an AGP 2.0 compliant 4X video adapter and an AGP 2.0 compliant motherboard that supports 4X mode. The 8X version is supposed to use the same slot, but is only backward compatible with the 4X mode. Products for the AGP 8X mode are expected in 2003. Motherboard Table #5 summarizes AGP information.

AGP Versions

AGP Version	1X	2X	4X	8X
Bus Speed	66MHz	133MHz	266MHz	533MHz
Transfer Rate	256Mbps	512Mbps	1Gbps	2Gbps
Data Path	32 bits	32 bits	32 bits	32 bits
Connector Voltage	3.3V	3.3V	1.5V	1.5V

MOTHERBOARD – TABLE #5

In order to implement AGP, the motherboard must have an AGP expansion slot, the chipset (covered later in the chapter) must support AGP, and an appropriate operating system, such as Windows 95 OSR2.1, Windows 98, Windows Me, or Windows 2000, must be installed.

Some motherboards allow you to set the amount of memory the AGP can use. The most common default setting is 64MB. This setting is known as the AGP Aperture and is configured through the BIOS Setup program (covered in the next chapter). If the computer has an ample amount of RAM, increasing this setting can increase performance especially in applications (such as games) that use 3D graphics. AGP slots are normally brown (compared with PCI slots, which are usually white). Motherboard Figure #17 shows an illustration of an AGP slot compared with PCI and ISA expansion slots.

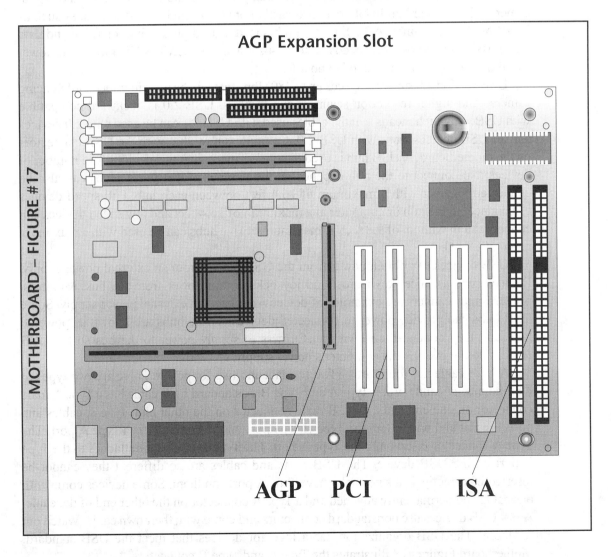

AGP Expansion Slot

MOTHERBOARD – FIGURE #17

AGP   PCI   ISA

USB (UNIVERSAL SERIAL BUS)

The **USB (Universal Serial Bus)** was developed cooperatively by Compaq, DEC, IBM, Intel, Microsoft, NEC, and Northern Telecom. USB allows connection of up to 127 external devices without degradation of speed. Devices that can use USB include keyboards, mice, joysticks, modems, speakers, phones, video phones, storage devices, printers, scanners, digital cameras, webcams, and CD-ROMs. Operating systems that support USB include Windows 95 Service Release 2, Windows 98, Windows Me, Windows NT, and Windows 2000. USB devices are hot-swappable, that is they can be plugged into the computer or hub while the computer is powered. USB devices support plug and play.

The original release of USB includes two speeds, 12Mbps and 1.5Mbps. The 12Mbps rate is for devices such as modems, CD-ROMs, printers, scanners, monitors, and digital cameras. The higher bandwidth can also easily connect to high-speed interfaces such as ISDN or T1 phone lines. A T1 line is a high-speed, leased phone line for voice and data transmission that allows for speeds up to 1.544Mbps. The 1.5Mbps USB rate is for lower speed devices such as mice and keyboards.

USB version 2.0 supports speeds up to 480Mbps that will be used for videoconferencing cameras and higher resolution scanners and printers. USB 2.0 is backward compatible with USB1.1, which means that the cables used with USB 1.1 can be used with 2.0 devices and all USB devices work with USB 2.0. Computers now ship with the USB connectors on the motherboard. A USB hub is used to connect more than two devices. The number of devices that connect to the hub depends on the number of hub ports. Hubs can also be connected together with a maximum of 16.4 feet between each hub. Full speed devices can connect to the hub or computer at a maximum of 16.4 feet and low speed devices can connect at a maximum of 9.8 feet. A maximum of five hubs can be used with a maximum range of 88.5 feet.

USB devices can obtain power from the USB bus or from an external power supply. Devices such as mice, keyboards, and joysticks obtain power from the bus. Monitors, printers, and scanners are examples of devices that have an external power supply. Some USB hubs can provide power to connected devices. These hubs are known as powered hubs and they contain their own transformers to supply power to the bus so the USB devices do not overtax the computer's power supply.

A USB cable has four wires—two for data and two for power. There are two types of USB connectors and ports—Type A and Type B. A standard USB cable has a Type A male connector on one end and a Type B male connector on the other end. Type A cables and ports are flat and wider than the Type B. The port on the computer is a Type A port. The Type A connector inserts into the Type A port. The Type B connector attaches to the Type B port on the USB device. The USB ports and cables are so different they cannot be inserted incorrectly. Hubs normally have Type A ports on them. Some devices come with one cable end permanently attached and a Type A connector on the other end of the cable. A few USB devices use nonstandard connectors and come with their own cable. Watch out for these! The USB organization has a logo for devices that meet the USB standard. Motherboard Figure #18 illustrates the Type A and Type B connectors.

MOTHERBOARD – FIGURE #18

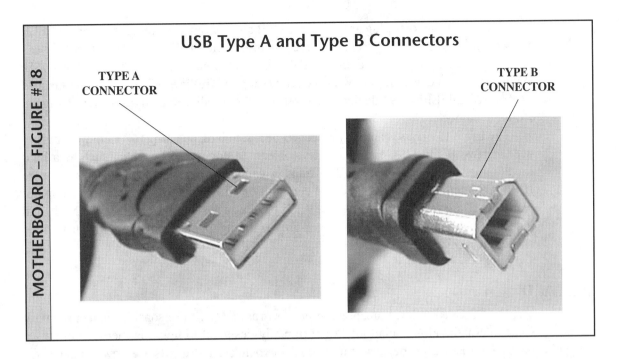

USB Type A and Type B Connectors

TYPE A CONNECTOR

TYPE B CONNECTOR

The Universal Serial Bus devices are plug and play devices. A motherboard-based USB host controller and the system software manage the bus. An older system without a USB host controller can be upgraded with a PCI adapter with two USB connectors.

IEEE 1394 (FIREWIRE)

Texas Instruments and Apple Computer, Inc developed the **IEEE 1394** serial bus. IEEE 1394 is commonly known as FireWire and it supports speeds higher than traditional serial buses. The IEEE 1394 bus allows automatic installation and configuration of up to 63 devices such as a modem, keyboard, mouse, monitor, scanner, hard drive, CD-ROM, printer, and an audio/video device. Each device can connect to up to 14.7 feet away and up to 16 devices can be on a single chain. The maximum distance for all devices combined is approximately 236 feet. IEEE 1394 supports speeds of 100Mbps, 200Mbps, or 400Mbps. A proposed addition to the existing standard, IEEE 1394b or FireWire2, expands the bandwidth to 800Mbps and increases cable lengths to 100 meters.

The big excitement over the standard stems from its ability to handle digital audio and video devices such as VCRs, camcorders, and televisions. Audio and video equipment have traditionally been proprietary devices and connecting them to computers was nearly impossible. The existing computer buses could not accommodate the throughput necessary for quality audio and video transfer. A 30-frames-per-second, high quality video at a 640x480 resolution, using 16.7 million colors transfers at 221Mbps, is too fast for the standard computer serial bus. FireWire has the potential to affect video for microcomputers dramatically.

IEEE 1394 supports plug and play like USB and the devices are hot swappable. IEEE 1394 devices (like USB devices) can receive power from the IEEE 1394 bus, or they can have an external power source, but FireWire is more expensive to implement than USB. Windows 98, Windows Me, and Windows 2000 support FireWire. When a device is attached or removed, all IEEE 1394 devices are reset. They reinitialize and all devices are assigned a unique number.

The IEEE 1394 bus is actually a peer-to-peer standard, meaning that a computer is not needed. Two IEEE 1394-compliant devices can be connected together (such as a hard drive and a digital camera) and data transfer can occur across the bus. Many compare IEEE 1394 with USB or place them in competition with one another; but in the computer world, there are applications for each. IEEE 1394 was designed for high-speed audio and video devices and the standard has much greater throughput for applications such as video conferencing.

PC CARD

The **PC Card** architecture, previously known as PCMCIA (Personal Computer Memory Card International Association), was originally designed to upgrade memory in laptop computers. However, because the standard expanded, PC Cards are now available for modems, hard drives, network adapters, and so forth. The PC Card's local bus can also be installed in a desktop computer, but that is not common.

The original standard was a 16-bit local bus standard with 64MB of memory addressing. The new standard called **CardBus** allows 32-bit transfers at speeds up to 33MHz (133Mbps). CardBus was designed as a combination of the old PC Card architecture and PCI. The PC Card's CardBus also supports bus-mastering, direct memory accessing (DMA) covered in Chapter 3, and up to 4GB of memory addressing. PC Cards are about the size of a credit card, though thicker. Motherboard Figure #19 shows a PC Card.

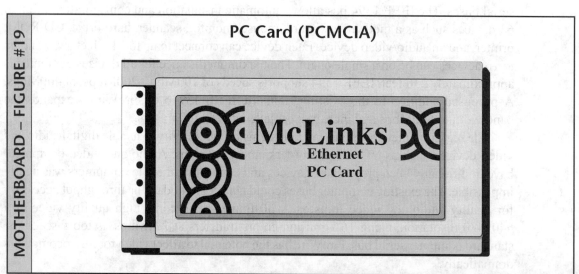

PC Card (PCMCIA)

MOTHERBOARD – FIGURE #19

McLinks
Ethernet
PC Card

The number of PC Card slots available on a computer varies among manufacturers and computer models. A PC Card inserts into the PC Card slot. However, each PC Card can control more than one PC Card slot. In theory, any PC Card can be used for any type of device. However, their use is normally denoted by the PC Card's thickness. There are three major PC Card types of different sizes known as Type I, Type II, and Type III. The Type I PC Cards are 3.3mm thick and are normally memory cards. These memory cards can be RAM, FLASH memory, OTP (One-Time-Programmable) memory, and SRAM.

Upgrading memory in a 486 or higher laptop with a 16-bit PC Card is not the best solution. Because of the 16-bit transfers, a PC Card memory upgrade should be done only as a last resort. However, for some laptops, this is the only option.

Type II PC Cards are 5mm thick and used for modem and network functions. A laptop computer with a Type II PC Card slot accepts Type II and Type I PC Cards in the slot, but only one at a time! The easiest way to think of this is that the thinner cards fit in the thicker slots, but a thick card cannot fit in the thinner slots.

Type III PC Cards are 10.5mm thick and are for rotating devices such as hard drives, CD-ROMs, floppy drives, etc. Type III PC Card slots also accept Type I and II PC Cards. Motherboard Table #6 recaps the PC Card types, sizes, and uses. This table is important to those studying for the A+ Certification.

MOTHERBOARD – TABLE #6

PC Cards

PC Card Type	Size	Usage
I	3.3mm	Memory and applications
II	5mm	Modems and network adapters
III	10.5mm	Storage devices such as floppy drive, hard drives, and CD-ROMs

PC Cards now support power management in the following ways: as security tokens, GPS (Global Positioning System), wireless network adapters, sound cards, video capture/frame grabber cards, TV tuners, and video conferencing cards.

A **SmartMedia** card is used with digital cameras, voice or sound recorders, PDA, electronic musical instruments, faxes, printers, scanners, and game machines. The SmartMedia card is smaller than a credit card and is used to hold pictures and audio files similar to a floppy disk. In order to connect a SmartMedia card to a PC Card slot, an adapter must be inserted into the PC Card slot.

The **ZV port (zoomed video port)** allows direct data transfer from a PC Card to a video controller. The data is transferred over the ZV bus instead of the system bus. With this new bus a notebook computer can connect to a video device such as a camera.

The **CardBay** standard allows laptop computers to be compatible with the USB and IEEE 1394 serial interfaces. CardBay supports all versions of USB and all USB operating modes. With CardBay, a controller switches the CardBay card to the appropriate bus (USB or IEEE 1394). If the CardBay card is USB, the USB bus configures it and treats it just like any other USB device. CardBay does not require a driver, nor does it have to be supported by an operating system. CardBay is backward compatible with previous PC Cards.

PC Cards ship with software called device drivers to allow the adapters to operate. The device drivers are frequently operating system dependent. Be sure the PC Card is supported by the operating system installed on the laptop. After configuration, some PC Cards can be hot swapped, that is, they can be inserted into the expansion slot after the computer has been powered on.

FUTURE BUSES

Great progress has been made in CPU and memory enhancement. However, the I/O (input/output) bus is the number one bottleneck for a computer. The I/O bus is what connects the motherboard components and devices to the CPU and memory. The I/O architectures of the past use what is known as a shared bus technology. Devices must compete and share the same path to the microprocessor. PCI and AGP have alleviated the bottleneck to some degree, but the congestion still exists.

PCI is on its last legs. PCI-X is probably the last version of PCI to be seen in a computer. The future lies in new I/O architectures. The ones to watch are HyperTransport, InfiniBand, 3GIO, and RapidIO. The trend is toward simultaneous point-to-point connections, allowing two devices to communicate without interfering with any other communication session.

AMD is the force behind the **HyperTransport** architecture, which is a serial-link design scalable to 128Gbps and beyond. HyperTransport has a great deal of industry support and input into the design and is compatible with PCI-based products. Being compatible with existing devices and adapters is important to an industry where billions of dollars are invested in hardware each year. With HyperTransport, devices can be daisy chained, connecting one device to another like Christmas light sets. Each communication consists of two unidirectional point-to-point links. Transmission can occur in 4, 8, 16, and 32 bits in each direction. The HyperTransport architecture can be applied to computers, network workstations, network servers, network routers, network switches, handheld devices, and game consoles. The architecture is not limited to the motherboard. Some articles have described HyperTransport as the "universal link."

A similar technology is the InfiniBand architecture. Compaq, Dell, Hewlett-Packard, IBM, Intel, Microsoft, and Sun Microsystems are behind this I/O architecture and form a group known as IBTA (InfiniBand Trade Association). **InfiniBand** uses a point-to-point connection between devices, CPUs, servers, networks, server clusters, etc. The connections are made through a switching fabric. Switching fabric is a combination of hardware and software that allows data to move between two devices without interfering with communications occurring between other devices. InfiniBand is a high-speed bi-directional serial link between an HCA and a TCA. An HCA (Host Channel Adapter) connects memory to the switch fabric. A TCA (Target Channel Adapter) connects end devices to the switch fabric.

InfiniBand can use 2, 8, or 24 channels. Half the channels are used for sending and the other half are used for receiving with theoretical bandwidths of 5Gbps, 20Gbps, and 60Gbps. The link that is created is only there for the duration of the communication session. When the devices finish communicating, the link is torn down. The InfiniBand architecture is compatible with PCI, PCI-X, and Fibre Channel, making it a viable choice for the future.

Intel recently announced its idea for the future called 3GIO (Third Generation I/O). 3GIO is a point-to-point serial interface that supports copper and optical interfaces. 3GIO is supposed to support speeds in excess of 10GHz.

RapidIO is the result of work done by Motorola and Mercury Computers, who have joined with numerous other technology companies to form the RapidIO Trade Association. **RapidIO** is an architecture designed for network and embedded applications (signal processing, data storage, and multimedia), but which can be applied to I/O interconnection for chip-to-chip, board-to-board, and device-to-device communication. RapidIO technology permits PCI and PCI-X devices to coexist in the same computer because the PCI bridges can be connected together using RapidIO switches.

The current specification has 8- and 16-bit versions. The 8-bit version allows for bandwidths up to 20Gbps and the 16-bit version up to 40Gbps. The RapidIO Trade Association states "RapidIO can be thought of as the mechanism to connect devices together to form the computer system." Motorola originally designed RapidIO as an interface used with their microprocessors, but the technology can be applied to compatibles and networks.

Technicians must stay current with emerging technologies such as these. Once one or two architectures are integrated into the motherboard, the technician must support them. The Internet has opened up immense resources for technicians to stay current. A technician should subscribe to at least one magazine (on-line or traditional) to stay abreast of these issues.

PROPRIETARY LOCAL BUS SLOTS

Some older computers have an expansion slot built into the motherboard that is neither a VL-bus slot nor a PCI slot. These expansion slots are proprietary: the adapters that fit in them are expensive and must be purchased from the slot manufacturer (if it is still in business). Motherboard Figure #20 shows a proprietary 32-bit expansion slot on a motherboard.

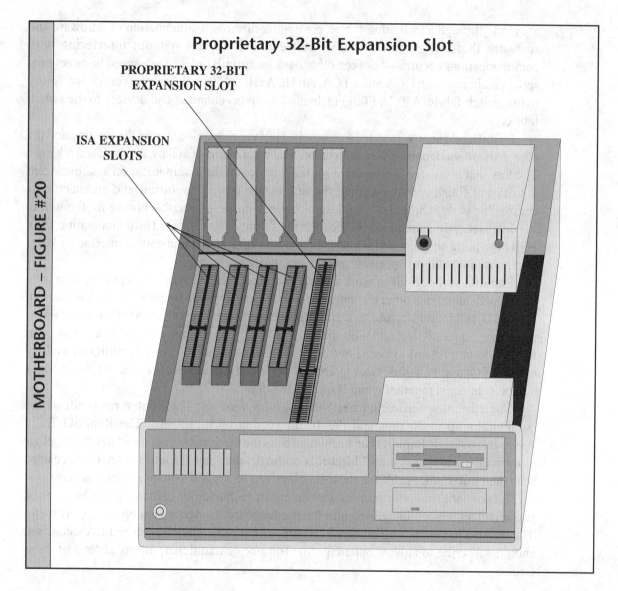

MOTHERBOARD – FIGURE #20

Proprietary 32-Bit Expansion Slot

PROPRIETARY 32-BIT
EXPANSION SLOT

ISA EXPANSION
SLOTS

Beware of proprietary slots! Expansion cards are usually hard to obtain and the documentation for adapters is even scarcer.

The different architectures and local buses can be overwhelming. Motherboard Table #7 allows viewing the differences at a glance.

MOTHERBOARD – TABLE #7

Architecture and Bus Overview

Architecture or Local Bus	Bits	Speed	Bus-Mastering
ISA	8/16	8/10MHz	Y (only 1 adapter)
MCA	16/32	10MHz	Y
EISA	32	10MHz	Y
VL-bus	32	25/33MHz	Y
PCI	32/64	33/66/133MHz	Y
AGP	32	66/133/266/533MHz	N/A
USB	1 (serial bus)	1.5Mbps/12Mbps/ 480Mbps	Y
IEEE 1394	1 (serial bus)	100Mbps/200Mbps/ 400Mbps/800Mbps	Y
PC Card	16/32	33MHz	Y

CHIPSETS

The principle chips on the motherboard that work in conjunction with the microprocessor are known as a **chipset**. These allow certain features on the computer. For example, chipsets control the maximum amount of motherboard memory, the type of RAM chips, the motherboard's capacity for two or more microprocessors, and whether the motherboard supports the latest version of PCI. Common chipset manufacturers include Intel, Via Technologies, Acer Labs (ALI), Silicon Integrated Systems (SiS), AMD, and OPTi.

Usually a chipset goes with a particular microprocessor and determines which memory chips a motherboard can have. Chipsets determine a lot about what a motherboard *can* allow or *can* support. When buying a motherboard, pick both a proper microprocessor and a good chipset.

Let's take a look at some different Intel chipsets. Intel's 440AX chipset supports a 100MHz external bus, PC100 SDRAM, AGP X1 and X2 modes, Ultra DMA/33 and 66, USB, and two memory banks. Intel's 440EX and 810 chipsets are used with the Celeron microprocessor. The 450NX chipset supports up to four Pentium III Xeon microprocessors, 100MHz external bus, 16MB and 64MB EDO DRAM, a maximum of 8GB of RAM and bus-master IDE. Intel's 850 chipset supports Pentium 4, 400MHz bus, 4 RIMMs, up to 4GB PC 600/800 RDRAM, AGP4X, four USB ports, and the USMA100 ATA standard. The AMD-760 Athlon chipset supports AGP4x, 266MHz front side bus, 4GB RAM, PC1600 and PC2100 DDR SDRAM, and the USMA100 ATA standard.

A technician must keep well informed of the chipsets on the market; customers will always ask for recommendations about motherboard upgrades and new computer purchases.

TYPES OF MOTHERBOARDS

Motherboards come in different sizes known as **form factors**. The most common motherboards are the AT, baby AT, ATX, NLX, μATX (MicroATX), FlexATX, and ITX. AT motherboards were named after IBM's original AT computer motherboard. Clones that used a smaller motherboard were referenced as baby AT motherboards. The ATX motherboard is similar in size to the baby AT except it is rotated 90 degrees. The microprocessor no longer sits near the expansion slots on an ATX motherboard. The ATX provides easier installation of full-length cards, easier cabling, and more cost-effective cooling. Look back to Motherboard Figure #17 for an example of an ATX motherboard.

The NLX motherboard is designed around the Pentium II and higher microprocessors and provides more space for expansion. The NLX design has a riser board that contains the expansion slots. Motherboard Figure #21 shows an NLX motherboard layout.

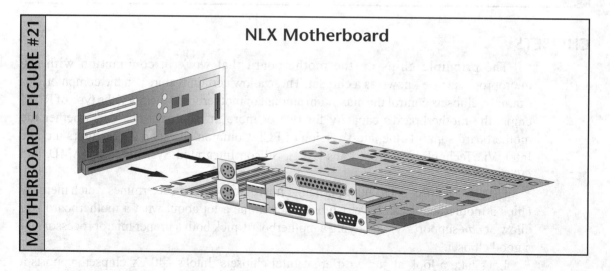

MOTHERBOARD – FIGURE #21

NLX Motherboard

The μATX (MicroATX) motherboard has a maximum size of 9.6 inches by 9.6 inches and fits in a standard ATX case or other smaller tower models. FlexATX is smaller than the MicroATX form factor, is 9 inches by 7.5 inches, and is backward compatible with ATX and μATX cases. An even smaller motherboard (8.5 inches by 7.5 inches) is the ITX form factor, which is made for a smaller power supply.

Manufacturers can also design their case so that it requires a proprietary motherboard. With these designs, a replacement motherboard must be purchased from the original manufacturer and is usually more expensive.

When building a computer or replacing a motherboard, it is important to obtain the correct form factor so the board fits in the computer case.

UPGRADING AND REPLACING MOTHERBOARDS

Whenever upgrading a motherboard, several issues must be taken into account. The following list helps guide a technician through making the decision (or helping a customer make a decision) of whether or not to upgrade a motherboard.

1. Why is the computer being upgraded? For example, does the computer need more memory? Are more expansion slots needed? Does the computer need a bigger and faster microprocessor to run certain operating systems or applications? Sometimes, upgrading the motherboard does not help unless the other computer components are upgraded. The most expensive and fastest motherboard in the world will not run applications well unless it has the proper amount of memory. Hard drives are another issue. If software access is slow, the solution might not be a new motherboard, but a faster and larger hard drive, more cache memory, or more RAM.

2. Which type (ISA, EISA, MCA, PCI, or VL-bus) and how many adapters are needed from the old motherboard? Does the new motherboard have the required expansion slots?

3. Could any devices such as the hard drive or CD-ROM that currently require an adapter, plug directly into the upgraded motherboard? This would free up expansion slots as well as speed up the devices.

4. What type of chipsets does the new motherboard support? What features, if any, would this bring to the new motherboard? What expense is incurred if the new chipset is purchased? Will the chipset from the old motherboard operate in the new motherboard?

5. Will the new motherboard fit in the case of the computer to be upgraded?

6. Does the motherboard allow for future microprocessor upgrades?

7. How much memory (RAM) does the motherboard allow? What memory chips are required on the new motherboard?

Before replacing a motherboard, the adapters must be removed from the expansion slots. Also, the power connectors must be disconnected from the motherboard, any external connectors, such as keyboard, mouse, and printer, must be disconnected, and the CPU and RAM must be removed. Replacement motherboards do not normally come with RAM or a microprocessor, so the old ones are removed from the bad motherboard. Make note of the CPU orientation before removing it from the motherboard. When installing the CPU into the replacement motherboard, refer to these notes. Most motherboards support a variety of microprocessors.

Make note of any jumper settings on the old motherboard. Set the new motherboard's settings to match the old settings if the two boards are identical.

Motherboards contain most of the circuitry for a microcomputer and are very important to its operation. Technicians must keep current with the options, features, microprocessors, and chipsets. Most technicians subscribe to computer magazines to help them fulfill this responsibility.

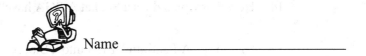 Name _____

MOTHERBOARD REVIEW QUESTIONS

1. What is a microprocessor?

2. List two CPU manufacturers.

3. What is a PC?

4. What is a bus?

5. What is the difference between the internal data bus and external data bus?

6. [T / F]   A computer's word size and external data path are always the same number of bits.

7. [T / F]   The Pentium II has a 64-bit external data path.

8. What is a microprocessor's pipeline?

9. Why did Intel use the Single Edge Connector (SEC) cartridge on the new Pentium II and Pentium III microprocessors?

10. What is the easiest way to distinguish the 80486, Pentium, and Pentium Pro microprocessors?

11. You insert an AMD K5 CPU into a motherboard and the chip inserts easily. However, the system will not boot. What is one possible problem?

12. What are the three versions of K6 AMD processors?

13. What is the most powerful AMD processor?
    [K8 / Pentium 4 / Greece / Athlon]

14. How many pins does a Socket A PGA have?

15. [T / F]   A Pentium III fits into a Slot A.

16. What is the difference between MMX and MMX2?

17. List one advantage an Intel MMX microprocessor has over a microprocessor without MMX.

18. What is the name of AMD's popular technology for 3-D graphics rendering?

19. What is the difference between an 80486SX microprocessor and an 80486DX microprocessor?

20. [T / F]   A Celeron processor needs an external math coprocessor for maximum performance.

21. Which microprocessor speed is the fastest 10MHz, 25MHz, 100MHz, or 266MHz?

22. List two methods for determining microprocessor speed.

23. Is the microprocessor speed the same speed as the chips on the motherboard?

24. A 1.2GHz processor is installed onto a motherboard that has a 100MHz bus. What multiplier is used?

25. What is the CPU speed for a 66MHz motherboard with a multiplier of 2?

26. List two advantages of a Pentium microprocessor over an 80486 microprocessor.

27. What is L3 cache?

28. What is the difference between a front side bus and a back side bus?

29. [T / F]   With DIB, the path to L2 cache is shared with the PCI controller.

30. How does DIB speed up computer operations?

31. How would you know what overdrive chip a system could handle?

32. What type of socket or slot is used for Intel's Pentium 4?

33. A customer wants to upgrade her microprocessor. What questions are you going to ask her before making a recommendation?

34. How can you tell if a motherboard accepts a faster or more powerful microprocessor?

35. [T / F]   A 3.3 volt microprocessor automatically converts the incoming 5 volts to a lower voltage.

36. Describe how to remove a CPU that is packaged in a cartridge.

37. A motherboard has no visible jumpers or switches. How would the multiplier be set on this type of system board?

38. When overclocking, what setting should be changed first?

39. What is the most common problem with overclocking?

40. List two operating systems that support multiple CPUs.

41. [T / F]   The Celeron processor can be used in multiple CPU systems.

42. [T / F]   A 800MHz and a 1.2GHz Athlon can be installed on the same motherboard.

43. What is a computer architecture?

44. Name three microcomputer architectures.

45. List three common buses.

46. Why must a technician be familiar with the different architectures?

47. What is ISA's biggest drawback?

48. Why should a memory expansion adapter never be placed in an expansion slot?

49. [T / F] Computers today still use ISA.

50. List two drawbacks to the MicroChannel Architecture.

51. What is bus-mastering?

52. [T / F] An EISA adapter can operate in an ISA slot.

53. List one limitation common to microcomputer architectures.

54. List the four PCI versions.

55. [T / F] PCI-X is backward compatible with 32-bit 33MHz PCI.

56. [T / F] PCI is a better bus standard than VL-bus.

57. [T / F] PCI is set up via jumpers and switches on the PCI adapter.

58. Match the following definitions with the most correct term.
    _____ VL-bus   A.   A local bus primarily used in laptop computers
    _____ PC Card   B.   A local bus standard developed by the video industry
    _____ PCI   C.   A 64-bit local bus standard

59. What is a bus interface for graphic adapters developed to speed up 3-D applications?

60. What is different about AGP Pro compared to AGP?

61. A customer wants to install a 4X AGP video adapter into her system. What would you have the customer check?

62. At what speeds can USB operate under the original specification?

63. What is the maximum number of USB hubs that can be connected together?

64. [T / F]   USB scanners normally receive power from an external power supply.

65. What type of USB port is found on motherboards?

66. How many devices can connect on a single IEEE 1394 chain?

67. What speeds are currently supported by FireWire?

68. What types of devices are best suited for the IEEE 1394 bus?

69. How many bits at a time does the CardBus transfer?

70. What are the three types of PC Cards and for what are they used?

71. What new laptop standard allows portable computers to use USB devices and IEEE 1394 serial devices?

72. What is AMD's I/O serial architecture called?

73. What I/O architecture uses the terms HCA and TCA?

74. What are some features a computer chipset provides?

75. What form factor is 9.6-inch x 9.6-inch?

76. List at least three recommendations to keep in mind when upgrading or replacing a motherboard.

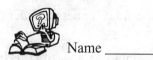
Name _____

MOTHERBOARD FILL-IN-THE-BLANK

1. The main chip found on the motherboard that executes software instructions is the _____.

2. In computer technology, a 1 or a 0 is a _____.

3. A combination of eight 1s and 0s is a _____.

4. Approximately 1,000 (one thousand) bytes are a _____.

5. Approximately 1,000,000 (one million) bytes are a _____.

6. Approximately 1,000,000,000 (one billion) bytes are a _____.

7. Approximately 1,000,000,000,000 (one trillion) bytes are a _____.

8. The number of bits that the microprocessor processes at one time is the microprocessor's _____.

9. The AMD _____ CPU is similar to Intel's Pentium.

10. The AMD K6-2 and K6-III processors fit into a _____ socket.

11. The AMD _____ CPU is a scaled-down version of the Athlon.

12. _____ microprocessors have 57 multimedia instructions built into them.

13. _____ is the acronym used to describe the technology that allows multiple data items to use one instruction.

14. A microprocessor speed is measured in _____ or _____.

15. To keep today's microprocessors cool _____ or _____ are used.

16. A _____ converts 5VDC down to a voltage appropriate for the microprocessor.

17. A plastic cover over two pins that enables a computer option is a _____.

18. The _____ setting is the speed at which the CPU's external bus operates.

19. The type of memory that has always been found inside the microprocessor is _____.

20. The type of memory previously outside the microprocessor on the motherboard, but now inside the microprocessor packaging is _____.

21. The type of cache memory written immediately to regular memory is known as _____.

22. The type of cache memory written to regular memory whenever the microprocessor is not busy is known as _____.

23. Cache chips can be _____ chips or a _____ memory module.

24. _____ provides a front side bus and a back side bus.

25. The AMD Athlon inserts into a _____-pin socket commonly known as Socket _____ or into a Slot _____ connector.

26. A _____ socket has a lever beside it to facilitate CPU insertion and removal.

27. Pin 1 on a processor is indicated by a _____ or a _____ corner.

28. Increasing CPU speed is commonly known as _____.

29. In order to install two or more processors, the operating system must support _____ and the operating system and applications must support it as well.

30. AMD's _____ and _____ processors can be installed as dual processors.

31. The oldest architecture is _____.

32. An _____ allows an adapter to be added to a motherboard or a riser board.

33. An adapter that communicates directly with another adapter without going through the microprocessor uses _____.

34. The _____ was a standard created by VESA.

35. The 64-bit 66MHz PCI version is commonly called _____.

36. The _____ allocates how much RAM the AGP adapter can use from motherboard RAM.

37. _____ allows connectivity for up to 127 devices.

38. A customer has four USB devices and zonly two ports on his system. A USB _____ can be used to connect all USB devices and provide for future devices.

39. USB cable connectors are either Type _____ or Type _____.

40. USB devices normally have a _____ port.

41. Another name for the IEEE 1394 standard is _____.

42. The _____ architecture is mainly for laptop computers.

43. The _____ port allows a camera to be connected to a laptop computer.

 Name _____

EXPANSION SLOT IDENTIFICATION EXERCISE

Using Motherboard Exercise Figure #1, label the expansion slots.

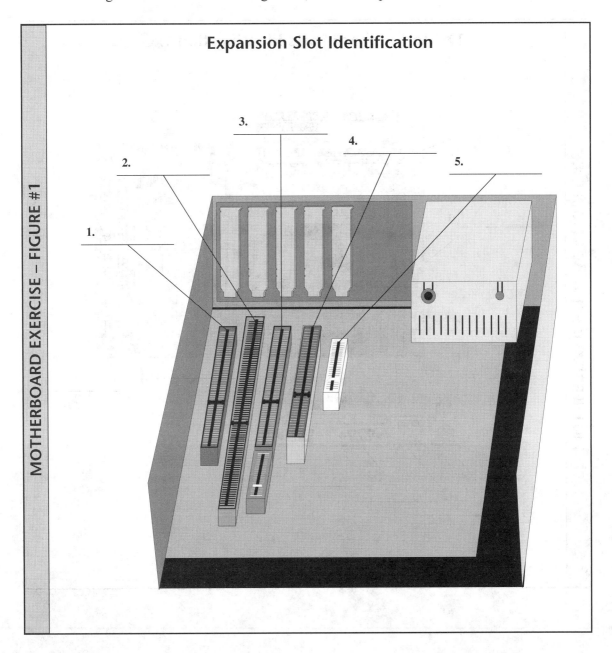

Name _____

ATX MOTHERBOARD PARTS IDENTIFICATION EXERCISE

Using Motherboard Exercise Figure #2, label each of the ATX motherboard parts.

ATX Motherboard Parts Identification Exercise

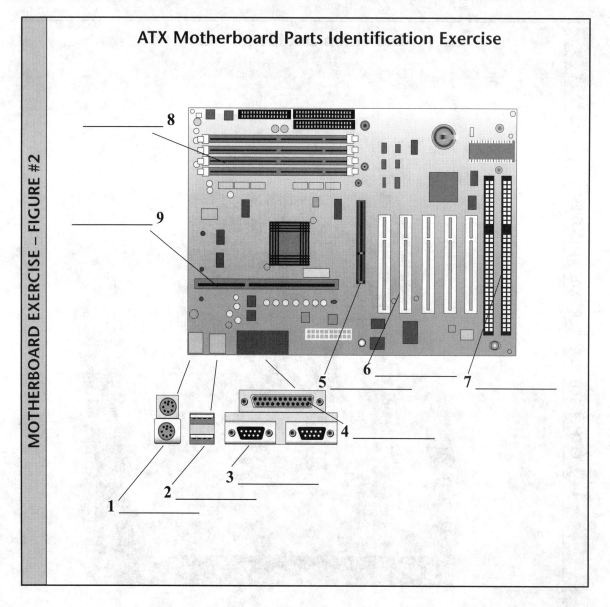

MOTHERBOARD EXERCISE – FIGURE #2

Name _____

ADAPTER AND EXPANSION SLOT IDENTIFICATION EXERCISE

Objective: To identify the adapter type and the architecture or local bus expansion slot type by looking inside a computer

Parts: Computer with adapters installed

Step 1. Remove the cover from a computer shown to you by your instructor.

Step 2. Identify all adapters installed in the microcomputer as ISA, EISA, MCA, VL-bus, PCI, AGP, or PCMCIA/PC Card. Use Motherboard Exercise Table #1 to list the adapter type (video, hard drive controller, network adapter, etc.) and the architecture or local bus expansion slot used for the adapter.

Note: You can sometimes identify the adapter type by observing the cables attached to the adapter. For example, the hard drive controller has one or two cables that attach to the hard drive. Many computers have multi-function adapters able to control more than one device such as the floppy and hard drive.

	Adapter Type (video, network, sound, floppy, hard, etc.)	Expansion Slot Type (ISA, EISA, MCA, VL-bus, PCI, AGP, or PC Card)
MOTHERBOARD EXERCISE – TABLE #1	1.	
	2.	
	3.	
	4.	
	5.	
	6.	
	7.	
	8.	
	9.	
	10.	

Name _____

ADAPTER'S EXPANSION SLOT IDENTIFICATION EXERCISE

Objective: To identify the adapter type and the architecture or local bus expansion slot type by looking at an adapter

Parts: Various adapters

Step 1.   Obtain an adapter from your instructor.

Step 2.   By looking at the adapter, (1) determine the type of adapter—video, hard drive controller, or network adapter— and (2) determine the expansion slot architecture the adapter uses. Record your results in Motherboard Exercise Table #2.

Adapter Type (video, network, sound, floppy, hard, etc.)	Expansion Slot Type (ISA, EISA, MCA, VL-bus, PCI, AGP, or PC Card)
1.	
2.	
3.	
4.	
5.	
6.	
7.	
8.	
9.	
10.	

MOTHERBOARD EXERCISE – TABLE #2

Name _____

MICROPROCESSOR UPGRADE
PAPER CONFIGURATION EXERCISE

Look at the drawing shown in Motherboard Exercise Figure #3. Using the documentation included with the figure, draw a jumper (a rectangular box) around the pins to be jumpered if installing a Pentium II 300MHz microprocessor.

MOTHERBOARD EXERCISE – FIGURE #3

Pentium II Microprocessor Upgrade Configuration Exercise

J1 J2 J3 J4 J5 J6

BUS FREQUENCY

Frequency	J1	J2	J3
66MHz	1-2	1-2	1-2
66MHz	1-2	1-2	1-2
66MHz	1-2	1-2	1-2
66MHz	1-2	1-2	1-2

PENTIUM II CPU FREQUENCY

Frequency	J4	J5	J6
233MHz	2-3	1-2	1-2
266MHz	2-3	1-2	2-3
300MHz	1-2	2-3	1-2
333MHz	1-2	2-3	2-3

Name _____

DETERMINING CPU FREQUENCY

The multiplier and bus speed are used to determine CPU frequency. Determine the CPU frequency, bus speed, or multiplier used when given two of the three parameters. Fill in the missing parameter using Motherboard Exercise Table #3.

MOTHERBOARD EXERCISE – TABLE #3

CPU Frequency	Bus Speed	Multiplier
_____	66MHz	3
250MHz	83MHz	_____
850MHz	_____	8.5
_____	133MHz	7.5
166MHz	66MHz	_____
300MHz	_____	3.5
_____	60MHz	1.5
1.13GHz	133MHz	_____
150MHz	_____	2

Name _____

PROCESSOR SPEED, PROCESSOR SOCKET, USB PORTS, AND IEEE 1394 (FIREWIRE) PORTS

Objective: To identify various computer features such as the type of processor being used, processor socket, and additional expansion ports.

Parts: Access to the Internet
Computer

Step 1.   Boot a computer and determine the microprocessor speed by watching the computer boot. Write the speed in the space below.

Step 2.   Power off the computer. Remove the cover. What type of processor socket or slot is on the motherboard. If unsure, use the Internet as a resource. Write the processor socket or slot type in the space below.

Step 3.   Look at the back of the computer where the ports are located. Does the computer have USB ports? If so, how many USB ports does the computer have? If the computer has at least one USB port, what type of connector is it? Write all of the answers in the space below.

Step 4.   Locate a picture of an IEEE 1394 port or connector on the Internet. Write the URL for where you found this information in the space below.

Step 5.   Using the Internet, locate one vendor that makes a motherboard that supports IEEE 1394 or has an integrated IEEE 1394 port. Write the vendor's name and the URL where you found the information in the space below.

_____ *Instructor's Initials*

Name _____

INTERNET DISCOVERY

Objective: To obtain specific information on the Internet regarding a computer or its associated parts.

Parts: Access to the Internet

The following scenario relates to questions 1–10:

Your customer has a Super Micro SUPER P4DC6 motherboard. Using documentation found on the Internet, answer the following questions.

Question 1:   Does the motherboard support multiple CPUs?

Question 2:   What chipset is installed?

Question 3:   How many 64-bit 66MHz PCI slots are on the motherboard?

Question 4:   What form factor does this motherboard use?

Question 5:   What processor is used on this motherboard?

Question 6:   What processor speeds are supported?

Question 7:   Does the motherboard have a ZIF socket or a processor slot?

Question 8:   What is the CNR motherboard slot used for?

Question 9:   What type of memory does this motherboard accept?

Question 10: The Super P4DC6 motherboard uses the term *Clock Ratio* for the clock multiplier. What settings are supported by this motherboard?

Question 11: Locate a web site that lists information about various Intel chipsets and write the URL in the space below.

Question 12: Find a vendor for a motherboard that accepts an AMD Athlon 1.4GHz processor with a 266MHz front side bus. Write the vendor's name in the space below.

Question 13: Find an Internet site that describes the difference between the North Bridge and the South Bridge and write a brief description of each term.

NOTES

3

Chapter 3:

System Configuration

OBJECTIVES

After completing this chapter you will

- Understand the different ways to configure a microcomputer.
- Understand how to replace a battery.
- Understand and be able to identify system resources such as interrupts, DMA channels, memory addresses, and I/O addresses.
- Understand how different architectures and local bus adapters are configured.
- Understand the effects of plug and play, Windows 95, 98, NT, and 2000 on configuring adapters.

KEY TERMS

card services

cascaded interrupt

CMOS

device driver

Device Manager

DIP switch

DMA channel

Flash BIOS

generic enabler

I/O address

IML

interrupt

IRQ steering

memory address

MSD

non-cascaded interrupt

NT diagnostics

plug and play

point enabler

reference disk

registry

Setup

socket services

switch bank

system partition

system resources

vendor-specific enabler

CONFIGURATION OVERVIEW

When assembling a computer for the first time, a technician must go into a Setup program to configure the system. The **Setup** program indicates how much RAM is in the computer, the type and number of hard and floppy drives installed, where the computer should find its boot disk, the current date and time, and so forth. An error message is displayed if the information in the Setup program fails to match the hardware or if a specific device does not work properly.

SETUP SOFTWARE

Most computers require Setup software to access the Setup program. Often this software is built into the BIOS chip on the motherboard and accessed by specific keystrokes determined by the manufacturer of the BIOS chip. At the initial Startup, most computers will display a message stating which keystrokes will launch the Setup program. Configuration Table #1 shows keystroke(s) commonly used by BIOS manufacturers.

CONFIGURATION – TABLE #1

Setup Keystrokes

BIOS Manufacturer	Keystroke(s)
AMI	DEL
Award	CTRL+ALT+ESC or DEL
Compaq	F1 or F10
Dell	CTRL+ALT+ENTER or DEL
Gateway	F1
IBM	CTRL+ALT+INS (When the cursor is in the right corner), F1, or Reference Disk
MR (Microid Research)	ESC
NEC	F1 or F10
Phoenix	CTRL+ALT+S, CTRL+ALT+ESC, or F2
Zenith	CTRL+ALT+INS

The BIOS sometimes needs updating. This can mean replacing one or more chips on the motherboard or downloading a file from the Internet and executing that file. There are various reasons a computer needs a BIOS upgrade: to provide support for more floppy drives or different floppy drive capacities, support for higher capacity hard drives, virus protection, password protection, or to solve problems with the current BIOS.

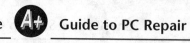

Some older computers have a software disk that contains the Setup program. Older Compaqs, Zeniths, IBM ATs, and some IBM PS/2 MicroChannel computers come with a Setup program on a disk. The older IBM PS/2 Setup disk is called a **reference disk**. Besides containing the Setup software, the reference disk contains advanced diagnostics and special utilities for the hard drive.

Advanced diagnostics and low-level format software for the hard drive are accessible on the older IBM PS/2 MicroChannel reference disk by pressing the *CTRL+A* keys when the main menu appears. After accessing the Setup program, notice the different options that appear on the menu. The directions for changing the menu options usually appear on the bottom of the screen.

FLASH BIOS

Flash BIOS is a type of memory computer manufacturers use as an alternative to the ROM BIOS chip(s). It is the most common type of BIOS today. A Flash BIOS allows changing the BIOS without installing a new chip or chips. A flash update contains system fixes and upgrades. Systems that contain Flash BIOS allow updates via files downloaded from the Internet. Always read the instructions for installing the update. The following is one example of how to flash the BIOS:

1. Once the BIOS upgrade is downloaded, create a boot disk and copy the downloaded file onto the boot disk.
2. Let the system boot from the floppy drive through the Setup program.
3. Insert the boot disk that contains the BIOS update and boot the computer.
4. Follow the directions on the screen or from the manufacturer.
5. Remove the disk and reboot the computer.

Because the Flash BIOS is frequently write-protected, a motherboard jumper or switch may need to be changed to allow the update. Refer to the computer or motherboard documentation to find the exact procedure for removing the write protection and updating the Flash BIOS.

Viruses can infect the Flash BIOS. Keep the BIOS write-protected until you need to update it.

CMOS MEMORY

Once the configuration is set, information is saved into a special type of static memory on the motherboard that technicians call the **CMOS** "chip." CMOS stands for **Complementary Metal Oxide Semiconductor**. *CMOS chip* is actually a misnomer because many chips use this technology. Part of the BIOS software routine that runs after the computer is turned on checks CMOS for information about what components are supposed to be installed. These components are then tested.

The CMOS chip can run on low power for a long time. The information inside CMOS memory can be kept there for several years using a small battery. All batteries are going to die one day. When the battery dies, all configuration information in CMOS is lost and must be entered again. The Setup information inside CMOS is the computer's *current* configuration—what the computer currently has installed.

Recall from Chapter 1 that POST (Power On Self Test) runs whenever the computer cold boots. POST knows what hardware is *supposed* to be in the computer by obtaining the settings from CMOS. POST performs a hardware check on the installed computer components.

> The wrong configuration information causes POST error codes or error messages that would normally indicate a hardware problem.

When working on a computer with a POST error code, be certain that the user or another technician (1) has not changed the configuration through the Setup program or (2) removed or installed any hardware without changing the Setup program or updating the operating system.

> Technicians should keep a record of the current settings for all the computers they service. If the wrong information is entered into the Setup program and saved into CMOS, a computer can operate improperly and may not boot. Correct Setup information is crucial.

BATTERIES

Computer batteries come in various shapes and sizes. The most common battery used today is a lithium battery about the size of a nickel. Look at Configuration Figure #1 for a motherboard containing a lithium battery.

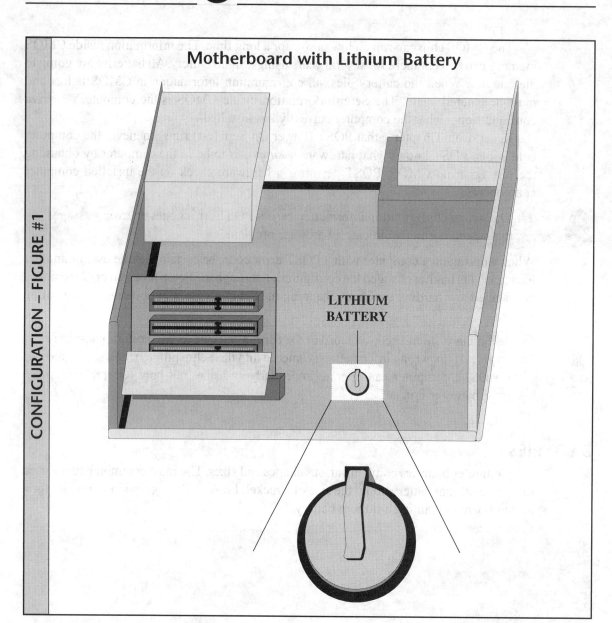

CONFIGURATION – FIGURE #1

Motherboard with Lithium Battery

LITHIUM
BATTERY

Also used in older computer systems is a 1.5-inch cylindrical battery. The battery, usually blue in color, solders onto the motherboard. Configuration Figure #2 shows this particular type of battery.

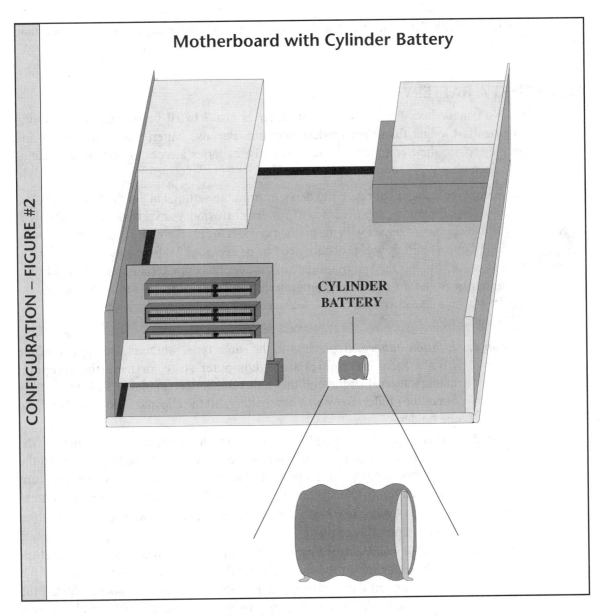

Motherboard with Cylinder Battery

CYLINDER BATTERY

Cylinder batteries fail after only a few years. Some people have had the experience of purchasing a motherboard and finding the cylinder battery already dead.

Other computer systems use a 3.6-volt cylinder of lithium batteries or alkaline 4.5-volt batteries. AA batteries found in common electronic equipment are sometimes used inside computers. They are mounted in a container secured by velcro to the inside of the computer case. Still, other computer manufacturers use a battery pack.

The battery is usually visible on the motherboard. If you cannot find the battery, look for a riser board. This board extends up from the motherboard to hold expansion cards and may contain the battery. Some computer and motherboard manufacturers use a real-time clock chip with the battery inside the chip. These are more expensive to replace than regular batteries.

REPLACING A BATTERY

No battery lasts forever. Computer batteries last 7 to 10 years. The newer lithium batteries last longer than their predecessors did. Because batteries now last longer and people replace their computers more frequently, batteries are not as serious an issue as they once were.

Before replacing a battery, write down or print the settings in Setup. Also, check the motherboard for any evidence of battery corrosion and verify that no battery acid has come in contact with the motherboard. If the motherboard is contaminated with battery acid, it will probably need to be replaced. A first indication that a battery is failing is the loss of the date or time on the computer. The battery should be replaced before more configuration information is lost. When batteries die, several options are available to the technician, depending on which type of battery is installed.

Option 1: *Lithium battery:* Replace with the same type, which is usually obtainable from a local electronics store, computer store, or from the computer manufacturer. Lift the clip that holds the battery in place. Slide the battery out of the holder. To insert a new battery, lift the clip and slide the battery into the holder.

Option 2: *Battery pack:* Locate the battery and note which way the wires connect to the motherboard. The leads that attach a battery pack or battery holder to the motherboard must connect properly. Remove the wires from the motherboard first, then remove the battery pack. Reinstall by reversing these procedures.

Option 3: *AA or AAA batteries:* Replace these batteries the same way you would replace them in a portable radio.

Option 4: *Real-time clock chip:* Obtain a replacement chip. Locate the real-time clock chip by referring to the motherboard documentation. Note which way the chip orients on the motherboard. Pull the chip out of its socket. Install the replacement chip by orienting its pins over the socket. Push the chip firmly in.

Option 5: *Soldered battery:* If the battery solders onto the motherboard, your choices include the following: (1) use an external battery pack, (2) purchase a battery holder, or (3) solder a new battery into place. For option 1, look on the motherboard or in the documentation for an external battery connector usually located near the existing battery. An external battery pack can be purchased at a local computer or electronics store. Many motherboards require a jumper to be set or enabled to allow the external connector to operate. Refer to the documentation for the motherboard to find this setting. In option 2, the battery holder snaps onto the leads of the battery soldered to the motherboard. This holder permits the installation and removal of a battery while bypassing the dead battery on the motherboard. Battery holders are also sold in electronics stores. Option 3 is not for the average person; it requires special skills, tools, and ESD considerations. But if you decide to do it, obtain a replacement battery. Disconnect the battery from the motherboard by cutting the leads to the battery and solder the new battery into place.

Always refer to the motherboard documentation for the exact battery replacement specifications. Replace the battery with one of the proper voltage and check on any recharging procedures.

Some technicians change the battery with the power on so that the configuration is not lost. The best procedure is always to have the configuration written down in any case.

INITIAL MICROCODE LOAD (IML)

IBM uses a method called **Initial Microcode Load (IML)**, which keeps the BIOS information in a hidden place on the hard drive. Machines that use IML do not have a reference disk. Instead, the BIOS information is already pre-loaded in this special section on the hard drive. Once the information is accessed, make a backup of the configuration and the reference disk. The IML method eliminates the need for a reference disk. However, if anything ever happens to the hard drive, the only way to get back into the system is to boot from a backup reference disk. Always make a backup reference disk for an IBM computer containing the Setup software on the hard drive.

The drawback to Setup software on a floppy disk is that if the configuration ever disappears or changes, a Setup disk is needed to reboot. Many users lose these disks. For a technician, this is bad news, though all is not lost. Setup disks are frequently available across the Internet.

PLUG AND PLAY

A specification called **plug and play (PnP)** allows automatic configuration of an adapter. A plug and play adapter plugs into an expansion slot without the technician having to configure the board or worry about the adapter conflicting with other adapters already installed in the system. Most computers today support plug and play. The motherboard BIOS must be the type that supports plug and play. PCI and AGP support plug and play and the latest revision to the VL-bus is supposed to support plug and play. ISA, EISA, and MCA architectures can also be used in a plug and play environment. More information on configuring adapters that support plug and play is available later in the chapter and in the various hardware and operating system chapters.

CONFIGURATION THROUGH SWITCHES

Some old computers such as IBM's PC and XT models do not have batteries installed; nor do they have CMOS memory or any type of Setup program. Instead, they use **DIP switches** to set the computer's configuration. The DIP switches are normally located on the motherboard. DIP switches can also be found on today's motherboards and ISA adapters. The switches allow different configurations for the motherboard or adapter. Learning how to properly set a DIP switch is important to a technician. There are two basic models of DIP switches: slide and rocker.

SLIDE DIP SWITCH

With the slide DIP switch, a sliding tab sticks up from each switch in the **switch bank**. A switch bank is a group of switches. Each switch is normally numbered from 1 to the number of switches in the bank. Each side of the switch bank is normally labeled with either On/Off, 1/0, or Closed/Open. On, 1, and Closed all mean the same thing; Off, 0, and Open all mean the same thing. How the switch bank is labeled is up to the manufacturer of that switch bank.

To change a switch in the slide DIP switch bank, move the tab on one switch with an ink pen or small tweaker (flat-tipped) screwdriver to one of the two positions. For example, say that a switch needs positions 5 and 8 turned ON. A technician turns the computer off, removes the computer cover, and moves the tabs in switch positions 5 and 8 to ON. Configuration Figure #3 shows an example of a slide type DIP switch with the sliding tabs in positions 5 and 8 in the ON position. Notice in Configuration Figure #3 that the switch bank actually has eight individual switches.

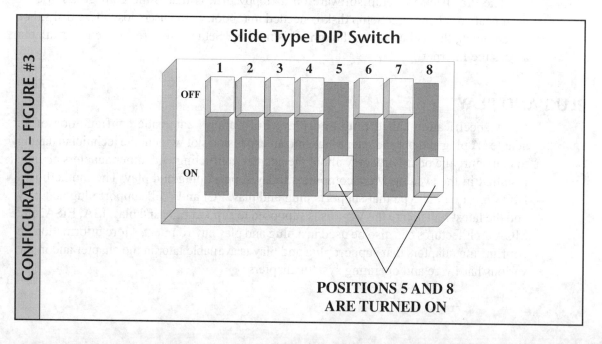

CONFIGURATION – FIGURE #3

Slide Type DIP Switch

POSITIONS 5 AND 8
ARE TURNED ON

ROCKER DIP SWITCH

A rocker DIP switch does not have a sliding tab on each switch position. Instead, each switch position has a rocker switch that presses down to either the On position or the Off position. To change a rocker DIP switch position, use an ink pen or small tweaker screwdriver to push *down* on one side of the rocker switch. One end of the switch will be pushed down into the switch bank and the other end will extend up from the switch bank. The side of the rocker switch that is pushed down determines whether the switch is On or Off, 1 or 0, or Open or Closed. For example, Configuration Figure #4 illustrates a rocker type DIP switch with switch positions 1, 4, and 5 Closed (which also means On or 1). Positions 2, 3, and 6 are Open (which also means Off or 0).

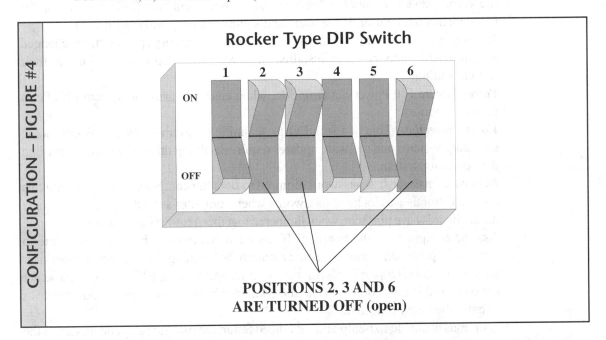

Rocker Type DIP Switch

**POSITIONS 2, 3 AND 6
ARE TURNED OFF (open)**

CONFIGURATION – FIGURE #4

NEVER use a *pencil* to change a DIP switch because the pencil lead may break off into the switch. The lead is conductive. If it breaks off into the switch, the switch may be ruined.

ADVANCED CONFIGURATION INFORMATION

Many computers have an Advanced Setup with options such as Memory Test, Boot Sequence, Shadow RAM, Memory Speeds, NUMLOCK, and Power Saver. Some of the possible options are listed below.

Memory Test Enable/Disable: If this option is disabled, POST runs faster, but the RAM above 1MB is not tested. It is recommended to keep this option enabled.

Boot Sequence: This option determines if the computer looks first to the floppy drive, the hard drive, CD-ROM, or DVD for the operating system.

System BIOS Shadow or System BIOS Cacheable: This setting puts a copy of the software contained in the BIOS into RAM. Running the BIOS software in RAM speeds up a system because accessing the information in RAM is faster than accessing it from the ROM chip.

Video ROM Shadow or Video BIOS Cacheable: This option copies the contents of the Video ROM into RAM for faster access.

AGP Aperture Size: Sets the amount of RAM (in Megabytes) dedicated for the AGP adapter's use.

NUMLOCK ON/OFF: Use the NUMLOCK setting to determine if the system sees the keypad keys as numbers (On) or as cursor movement keys (Off). The setting for this depends on the user. If the user inputs numbers frequently, set it to On.

Memory Speeds: Some computer systems allow the memory speed settings changed for the RAM memory chips installed. It is recommended to leave them at their current setting.

Power Saver: The Power Saver option, when enabled, turns the system off after a period of non-use.

Virus Protection: This is a small virus scanning program located in BIOS. Some operating systems and software updates require disabling this option when installing the operating system.

Power-on Password: A password required to boot the computer can be set with this option. Computer users need passwords when computer security is an issue. Some motherboards have pins that, when jumpered together, remove the power-on password. Ask the computer, motherboard, or BIOS manufacturer for the exact procedure to remove the power-on password. Some motherboards distinguish between a Supervisor password and a User password. Another security option some BIOSes have is whether the password is needed every time the computer boots or only when someone tries to enter the Setup program.

The options available in Setup and Advanced Setup are machine-dependent due to the different BIOS chips and the different chipsets installed on the motherboard. Refer to the computer or motherboard documentation for the meaning of each option!

> When a power-on password is set and forgotten, some motherboards have pins that, when jumpered together, remove the power-on password. With other motherboards, the only way to remove the password is by jumpering pins together to clear all the CMOS settings.

You must save your changes to the configuration. Many technicians make errors on this step. Options available depend on the BIOS being used. Examples from one type of BIOS include the options Save & Exit Setup, Exit Without Saving, Load Fail-Safe Defaults, and Load Optimized Defaults. The Save & Exit Setup option is the one most commonly used by technicians when changes are made. The Exit Without Saving option is used when changes have been made that are in error and the technician wants to do more research, or try the adapter/device in another machine. The Load Fail-Safe Defaults sets the defaults programmed by the motherboard manufacturer. These generally provide the most stable computer operation. Load Fail-Safe Defaults would seldom be required except when overclocking and when the technician fears a motherboard component has been damaged. The last option, Load Optimized Defaults, is also programmed by the manufacturer, but has more aggressive settings than the Load Fail-Safe Defaults. This setting would seldom be used except when overclocking or when adjusting memory timing.

OTHER CONFIGURATION PARAMETERS

Other possible parameters contained and set via the Setup program are IRQs (Interrupt Requests), I/O (Input/Output) addresses, DMA (Direct Memory Access) channels, and memory addresses. These parameters are assigned to individual adapters and ports, such as disk controllers, and the serial, parallel, and mouse ports. Sometimes these ports must be disabled through Setup in order for other devices or adapter ports to work. No matter how the parameters are assigned, collectively they are known as **system resources**. These are not the same system resources used when discussing Windows 3.x, Windows 9x, NT, or Windows 2000. Let's take a look at four important system resources: (1) IRQs, (2) I/O addresses, (3) DMA channels, and (4) memory addresses.

IRQ (INTERRUPT REQUEST)

Imagine being in a room of twenty students when four students want the teacher's attention. If all four students talk at once, the teacher is overloaded and not able to respond to the four individuals' needs. Instead, a teacher needs an orderly process of acknowledging each request, prioritizing the request (which student gets to go first), and then answering each question. The same thing happens inside a microcomputer when multiple devices want the attention of the microprocessor. For example, which device gets to go first if a key on the keyboard is pressed and the mouse moved simultaneously? The answer lies in what interrupt request numbers are assigned to the keyboard and the mouse. Every device requests permission to do something by interrupting the microprocessor (similar to the device raising its hand). The microprocessor must have a priority system to handle such situations.

The microprocessor prioritizes device requests through the use of interrupts. An **interrupt** or **IRQ (Interrupt ReQuest)** is a number assigned to expansion adapters or ports so orderly communication can occur between the device or port and the microprocessor. The IRQ number is a priority system for the microprocessor. For example, if you press a key on a keyboard and move the mouse simultaneously, which device first gets the attention of the microprocessor? The answer lies in the IRQ number assigned to each device. The keyboard, by the way, has the highest priority.

IBM's PC and XT computers had only eight interrupts available, IRQs 0 through 7. Today's computers have 16 interrupts numbered 0 through 15. The chip that controls the interrupts is known as the interrupt controller chip. In a system with 16 interrupts, two interrupt controller chips are on the motherboard. Two methods of operation exist with the interrupt controller chips: cascaded and non-cascaded interrupts.

In a system that uses **cascaded interrupts**, the interrupt controller chip handling IRQs 0–7 uses IRQ2 to cascade, or bridge over, to the other interrupt controller chip. All interrupts handled by the second interrupt controller chip go to the microprocessor through IRQ2 on the first interrupt controller chip. For example, if an adapter or device has the interrupt IRQ12, the interrupt request goes to IRQ2 on the first interrupt controller chip, and then on to the microprocessor. Configuration Figure #5 shows the concept of two interrupt controller chips using cascaded interrupts.

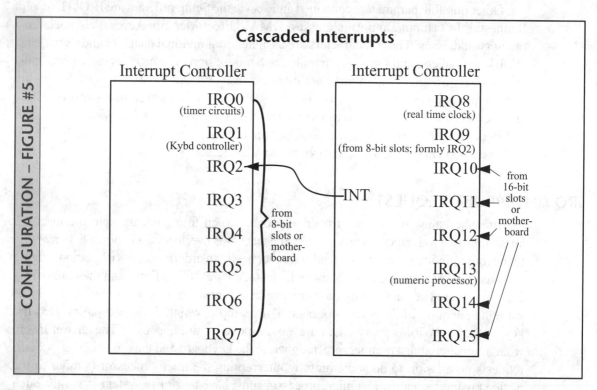

CONFIGURATION – FIGURE #5

Cascaded Interrupts

Interrupt Controller

Interrupt Controller

IRQ0
(timer circuits)

IRQ1
(Kybd controller)

IRQ2

IRQ3

IRQ4

IRQ5

IRQ6

IRQ7

from
8-bit
slots or
mother-
board

INT

IRQ8
(real time clock)

IRQ9
(from 8-bit slots; formly IRQ2)

IRQ10

IRQ11

IRQ12

IRQ13
(numeric processor)

IRQ14

IRQ15

from
16-bit
slots
or
mother-
board

Notice in Configuration Figure #5 how the INT signal from the second interrupt controller chip connects to the first interrupt controller chip's IRQ2. Motherboards using cascaded interrupts reroute any signals from IRQ2 over to IRQ9 on the second controller chip.

The computer's timing circuitry that keeps all operations running always uses IRQ0. The keyboard controller uses IRQ1. IRQ8 is used by the computer's real-time clock. The math coprocessor uses IRQ13. IRQs 0, 1, 2, 8 and 13 are not available to adapters. IRQ0 has the highest priority of all interrupts. IRQ1 has the next highest priority, then IRQ2. The next highest priority depends on whether the system uses cascaded interrupts. Any interrupt handled by the second interrupt controller chip gets the same priority level as if it were IRQ2. So, if an adapter has an interrupt level of 15, that adapter has priority over an adapter with an interrupt level of IRQ5 to the system using cascaded interrupts. Still, on the second interrupt controller chip, a priority system exists. For example, IRQ12 has a higher priority than IRQ15.

Non-cascaded interrupts occur when two interrupt controller chips are not bridged together. Each chip handles eight interrupts that connect directly to the microprocessor. Keep in mind that the interrupt controller chips are integrated with the motherboard's chipset. With non-cascaded interrupts, the lower a device's IRQ number, the higher its priority is to the microprocessor. Configuration Table #2 lists commonly assigned interrupts or IRQs in computers. Interrupt assignments are important to know for the A+ exam as well as when working with computers. Configuration Table #2 shows common assignments. Each adapter and computer can be assigned differently.

CONFIGURATION – TABLE #2

Common Interrupt Assignments

IRQ	Function
0	System timer
1	Keyboard controller
2	Used to bridge to IRQs 8-15 when using cascaded interrupts
3	COM2 and COM4
4	COM1 and COM3
5	Sound cards or LPT2
6	Floppy disk controller
7	LPT1
8	Real-time clock
9	Former IRQ2 from 8-bit slots
10	
11	
12	PS/2 mouse
13	Math coprocessor
14	Primary IDE controller
15	Secondary IDE controller

USB (Universal Serial Bus) and IEEE 1394 (FireWire) require at least one IRQ for their bus controller.

Different interrupts are assigned to adapters and devices. No two ISA devices should have the same interrupt. However, two serial devices can share the same interrupt *if* they have different I/O addresses. More detail is given in the Serial Devices chapter.

Interrupts for some ports and devices can be set through the system's Setup program. Other adapters and device interrupts are set by enabling or disabling switches or jumpers, running a Setup program included with the adapter or device, using **Device Manager** in Windows 95/98/2000, using **NT Diagnostics** with NT Workstation, or using various control panels in Windows 95, 98, NT, or 2000.

To access Device Manager in Windows 9x, click on the *Start* button, point to *Settings*, and click on the *Control Panel* option. Double-click on the *System* control panel icon. Click on the *Device Manager* tab. Double-click on the *Computer* item and the Computer Properties window appears. Select the appropriate radio button (Interrupt request [IRQ] for interrupt information). When using 2000 Professional, click on the *Start* button, point to *Settings*, and click on the *Control Panel* menu option. When the Control Panel window opens, scroll down to the *System* icon and double-click on it. Click on the *Hardware* tab and click on the *Device Manager* button. Click on the *View* menu option and select *Resources by Type*.

CONFIGURATION – FIGURE #6

IRQs in Device Manager

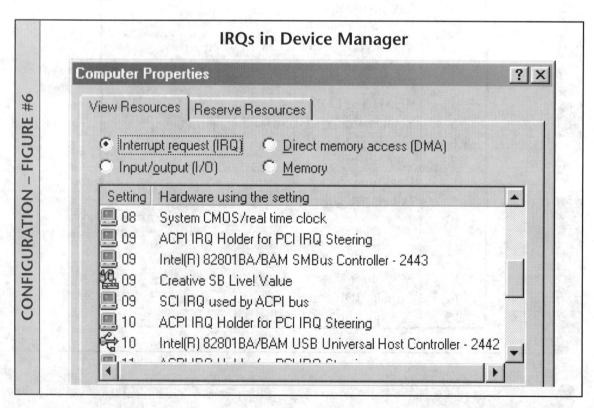

Computer Properties

View Resources | Reserve Resources

- ⊙ Interrupt request (IRQ)   ○ Direct memory access (DMA)
- ○ Input/output (I/O)   ○ Memory

Setting	Hardware using the setting
08	System CMOS/real time clock
09	ACPI IRQ Holder for PCI IRQ Steering
09	Intel(R) 82801BA/BAM SMBus Controller - 2443
09	Creative SB Live! Value
09	SCI IRQ used by ACPI bus
10	ACPI IRQ Holder for PCI IRQ Steering
10	Intel(R) 82801BA/BAM USB Universal Host Controller - 2442
11	ACPI IRQ Holder for PCI IRQ Steering

When adapters or devices have resource conflicts or are disabled, Device Manager marks them with a yellow circle with an exclamation point inside it or with a red X over the device icon. You may have to click on the plus sign beside each category type to see the indication. To avoid conflicts, select adapters that have the several interrupts to choose from when installing in a system.

Windows 98 and Windows 2000 have a great utility called MSINFO (System Information) that shows conflicts without having to expand each Device Manager category. To access MSINFO in Windows 98, click on the *Start* button, point to *Programs*, *Accessories*, and *System Tools*. Click on the *System Information* item. Double-click on the *Hardware Resources* option. Click on the *Conflicts/Sharing* selection and after a couple of seconds, the right side will show the IRQ number, along with the name of the device, and often the manufacturer.

To access System Information in 2000 Professional or 2000 Server, click on the *Start* button and point to the *Settings* selection. Point to the *Control Panel* option and double-click on the *Administrative Tools* control panel icon. Double-click on the *System Information* icon. Click on the + *(plus sign)* next to the *Components* folder. Click on the *Problem Devices* folder. Any devices with hardware conflicts are listed in the right window.

Once you have identified a conflict, use Device Manager or the specific device control panel to correct any problems with resource allocation. Within Device Manager, double-click on the **device/adapter** with the problem. Click on the *Properties* button and then click on the *Resources* tab. The Resources tab sometimes allows you to change a device/adapter's resources.

Indications of a resource conflict (including IRQ, DMA, I/O address, and memory address conflicts) are as follows:

- The new device is installed and the new device or a device already installed does not work.
- The computer locks up or restarts when performing a specific function. An example could be playing or recording audio.
- The computer hangs during startup or shutdown.
- A device does not work properly or fails to work at all.

Notice that in Configuration Figure #6, some interrupts have multiple entries. Multiple entries do not always indicate a resource conflict. They are allowed because PCI devices may share IRQs. The next section goes into more detail on this issue.

PCI INTERRUPTS

PCI devices use interrupts called INTA, INTB, INTC, and INTD. Some documentation uses the numbers 1, 2, 3, and 4 to replace the letters A, B, C, and D. PCI devices are allowed to share interrupts. Most PCI adapters are set to INTA and share this interrupt with other PCI adapters. PCI interrupts must still be mapped to one of the traditional interrupts. With so few interrupts available and so many devices installed in today's computers, this presents a problem solved with a technique called IRQ steering.

IRQ steering allows multiple PCI adapters to be mapped to the same traditional IRQ. In order to use IRQ steering, both the operating system and the BIOS must support it. Starting with Windows 95B (OSR2), Microsoft's operating systems support IRQ steering. Note that with Windows 95, IRQ steering is disabled by default. With the other operating systems, IRQ steering is enabled by default. When IRQ steering is enabled and when a PCI/AGP adapter needs an interrupt, the operating system finds an available interrupt (which may be currently used by an ISA device that does not need it) and allows the PCI device to use it. By default, on ACPI (Advanced Configuration and Power Interface) systems, PCI devices share IRQ9. Look back at Configuration Figure #9 to see how IRQ 9 is used.

The PCI Special Interest Group (PCI-SIG) has a diagnostic program that tests if the BIOS supports IRQ steering and is available from their web site at www.pcisig.com. The name of the diagnostic is PCI DIAG.

To access the IRQ steering settings in Windows 9x, click on the *Start* button, point to *Settings*, and click on *Control Panel*. Double-click on the *System* control panel. Click on the *Device Manager* tab. Locate the *System Devices* and double-click on this option. Locate and double-click on the *PCI Bus* selection. Click on the *IRQ Steering* tab. If the Use IRQ Steering checkbox has a check inside it, IRQ steering is enabled. If the checkbox is empty, IRQ steering is disabled.

To access IRQ steering settings in 2000 Professional, click on the *Start* button, point to *Settings*, and click on the *Control Panel* menu option. When the Control Panel window opens, scroll down to the *System* icon and double-click on it. Click on the *Hardware* tab and click on the *Device Manager* button. Configuration Figure #7 shows the PCI bus Properties window where IRQ steering is configured.

IRQ Steering Window

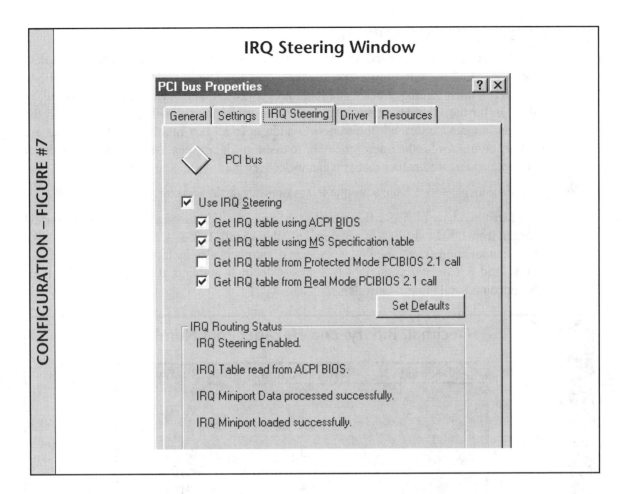

PCI bus Properties

General | Settings | IRQ Steering | Driver | Resources

◇   PCI bus

☑ Use IRQ Steering
  ☑ Get IRQ table using ACPI BIOS
  ☑ Get IRQ table using MS Specification table
  ☐ Get IRQ table from Protected Mode PCIBIOS 2.1 call
  ☑ Get IRQ table from Real Mode PCIBIOS 2.1 call

Set Defaults

IRQ Routing Status
  IRQ Steering Enabled.
  IRQ Table read from ACPI BIOS.
  IRQ Miniport Data processed successfully.
  IRQ Miniport loaded successfully.

Notice that Configuration Figure #7 lists four IRQ routing table checkboxes. A routing table controls IRQ steering. The table Windows uses can be selected through the checkboxes. The order in which Windows searches for a table is the same order shown in Configuration Figure #7, ACPI BIOS, MS Specification, Protected Mode PCIBIOS 2.1, and finally Real Mode PCIBIOS 2.1. In Windows 95, there is only one checkbox for the PCIBIOS 2.1 tables. By default, Windows 98 does not enable the third checkbox, Get IRQ table from Protected Mode PCIBIOS 2.1 call.

Under Windows 95, if a PCI device is having an interrupt problem, select the *PCIBIOS 2.1 table* option and restart Windows 95. Under Windows 98, uncheck the *ACPI BIOS* checkbox and restart the operating system. If that does not work, enable the *Protected Mode PCIBIOS 2.1 call* checkbox and restart Windows 98.

I/O (INPUT/OUTPUT) ADDRESSES

I/O addresses, otherwise known as input/output addresses, or port addresses allow the device and the microprocessor to exchange data. The I/O address is like a mailbox number: it must be unique or the mailman gets confused. The device places data (mail) in the box for the microprocessor to pick up. The microprocessor delivers the data to the appropriate device through the same I/O address (mail box number). I/O addresses are simply addresses for the microprocessor to distinguish between the devices with which it communicates. Remember that you cannot deliver mail without an address.

Each device *must* have a unique I/O address; there are no exceptions!

Most PCs have 65,535 different I/O addresses. I/O addresses are shown in hexadecimal format from 0000 to FFFF. Hexadecimal numbers are 0, 1, 2, 3, 4, 5, 6, 7, 8, and 9 just like the decimal numbers we use, but hexadecimal numbers also include the numbers A, B, C, D, E, and F. Configuration Table #3 shows decimal numbers 0 through 15 with their hexadecimal and binary equivalents.

CONFIGURATION – TABLE #3

Decimal, Binary, and Hexadecimal Numbers

Decimal	Hexadecimal	Binary
0	0	0000
1	1	0001
2	2	0010
3	3	0011
4	4	0100
5	5	0101
6	6	0110
7	7	0111
8	8	1000
9	9	1001
10	A	1010
11	B	1011
12	C	1100
13	D	1101
14	E	1110
15	F	1111

An example of an I/O address is 390h where the small "h" denotes hexadecimal. Configuration Table #4 uses this method and shows common I/O addresses used in computers. Pay particular attention to I/O addresses 2E8, 2F8, 378, 3E8, and 3F8 for the A+ certification exam.

Common I/O Addresses

I/O Address	Device or Port
000-00Fh	DMA controller (channels 0-3)
020-021h	Interrupt controller 1
040-043h	System timers—clocks
060h	Keyboard
070h or 071h	Real-time clock/CMOS/NMI mask
081-083h and 087h	DMA page register (0-3)
089-08Bh and 08Fh	DMA page register (4-7)
0A0-0A1h	Interrupt controller 2
0C0-0DEh	DMA controller (channels 4-7)
0F0-0FFh	Math coprocessor
108-12Fh	May be reserved on some systems
150-1EFh	May be reserved on some systems
170-177h	Secondary IDE controller
1F0-1F7h	Primary IDE controller
200-207h	Game port
20C-20Dh	Reserved
21Fh	Reserved
220-233h	Sound card
278-27Fh	LPT2
2E8-2EFh	COM4
2F8-2FFh	COM2
330-331h	Midi port
378-37Fh	LPT1
388-38Bh	FM synthesizer
3E8-3EFh	COM3
3F0-3F7h	Floppy controller
3F8-3FFh	COM1
FF80-FF9F	USB

CONFIGURATION – TABLE #4

The addresses in Configuration Table #4 are common assignments. Each adapter and computer can be assigned differently.

Notice that Configuration Table #4's left column lists a range of I/O addresses. Devices normally need more than one hexadecimal address location. The number of extra addresses depends on the individual device and what business it does with the microprocessor. In manuals or documentation for a device or adapter, a technician might see the adapter has an I/O address range instead of just one I/O address. Configuration Table #4 lists what I/O addresses *can* be used in computers. The manufacturer of the computer or an adapter can set the I/O address specifically or allow different I/O addresses to be set. I/O addresses are set for some devices and ports through the computer's Setup program, Device Manager in Windows 9x and 2000, NT Diagnostics in NT Workstation, or various control panels in Windows 95, 98, or NT Workstation. Other devices are configured by setting jumpers, switches, or through installation software included with the device or adapter.

The important thing to remember is that every device must have a separate I/O address or the microprocessor cannot distinguish between installed devices. Technicians need to document the I/O addresses used in a system before adding a new device or troubleshooting a newly installed device. I/O address conflicts are a frequent source of problems.

One problem for technicians is that some documentation and some Setup programs only give the starting hexadecimal I/O address and not the ending I/O address. The range of addresses the adapter uses can conflict with another adapter or device. The only resolution is for the technician to change the I/O address on one of the two conflicting devices or adapters and try the devices again. Given poor documentation, this is a hit or miss process.

Configuration Figure #8 illustrates a partial view of I/O addresses from the System Information window.

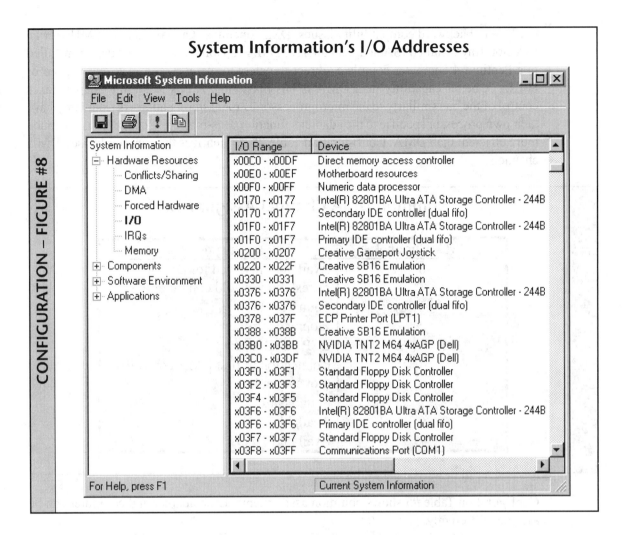

DMA (DIRECT MEMORY ACCESS) CHANNELS

A **DMA channel** is a number assigned to an adapter. The DMA assignment allows the adapter to bypass the microprocessor and communicate directly with the RAM chips. Transferring the data directly to memory speeds up transfers. Devices that frequently take advantage of DMA are drives, tape backup units, and multimedia adapters such as sound cards. A drawback to DMA transfers is the microprocessor may be put on hold until the DMA data transfer is complete. Well-written software allows the microprocessor to function periodically during the DMA operation.

Older computers have four DMA channels labeled 0, 1, 2, and 3. DMA channel 0 was normally reserved for refreshing the RAM chips. A single DMA controller chip controls four DMA channels. Today's computers normally have two DMA controller chips, giving a total of eight DMA channels. DMA channel 4 is normally reserved for connecting the two DMA controller chips. Keep in mind the DMA controller chips are integrated with the motherboard's chipset in computers today.

Due to backward compatibility issues, DMA operates at a maximum of 8MHz for an ISA slot. Any installed ISA adapter can have DMA capabilities. Even an adapter installed in a Pentium 4 computer completes direct transfers to memory at a maximum speed of 8MHz. A better capability than DMA is bus-mastering. A bus-mastering adapter takes control of the bus similarly to the microprocessor. Bus-mastering adapters frequently have their own processor specific to the adapter's function. Bus-mastering capabilities are much more efficient than DMA. Configuration Table #5 summarizes the commonly used DMA channels.

CONFIGURATION – TABLE #5

Common DMA Channel Assignments

DMA Channel	Purpose
0	Available (reserved for DRAM refresh on very old computers)
1	Sound card
2	Floppy controller
3	ECP parallel port
4	Connection to first DMA controller (not available)
5	Sound card
6	Available
7	Available

Configuration Table #5 shows common assignments. Each adapter and computer can be assigned differently.

Assign DMA channels through the Setup program; Windows 9x or 2000 Professional's Device Manager; NT Workstation's NT Diagnostics; various control panels in Windows 9x, NT Workstation, 2000 Professional; or through the adapter or the device installation process by setting jumpers, switches, or running the configuration software.

No two devices or adapters should have the same DMA channel number!

MEMORY ADDRESSES

The last important system resource is the memory address. A **memory address** is a unique address assigned to the ROM BIOS (or Flash BIOS), any other ROM chips installed in the system, and RAM chips installed in the system. The memory address is used by the microprocessor when it accesses information inside the chip. Configuration problems are normally associated with the ROM memory addresses.

Memory addresses are shown in hexadecimal. Refer back to the I/O address section for a discussion of hexadecimal. The memory address ranges used for all of the different ROM chips installed in the system are usually from A00000h to FFFFFh. This is the notation shown in books. However, some documentation drops the last digit and doesn't include the full memory range that the ROM chip takes. For example, a ROM chip on an adapter might be listed as C800h. In reality, this is C8000-C8FFFh. When you look at the memory address on the computer, the address may be shown with more hexadecimal places such as 000A0000-000AFFFFh. This is due to the number of address lines supported by the motherboard. Even though a microprocessor might be able to support 36 address lines, the motherboard may not support that many. Remember that each hexadecimal number represents four binary numbers. If a motherboard supported all 36 address lines, the maximum memory address would be FFFFFFFFF (nine Fs with each F representing four bits). These different notations are very confusing to new technicians. Configuration Table #6 lists common ROM addresses.

CONFIGURATION – TABLE #6

Common Memory Address Assignments

Memory Address	Purpose
A0000-BFFFFh	Video RAM
C0000-C7FFFh	Video ROM
C8000-CFFFFh	SCSI disk adapters
F0000-FFFFFh	Motherboard ROM

Some ROM addresses are preset and cannot be changed. Others can be changed through jumpers, switches, Device Manager on Windows 9x and 2000 Professional, NT Diagnostics in NT Workstation; or various control panels in Windows 95, Windows 98, and NT Workstation. Windows 98 and 2000 Professional's System Information is another place to view memory addresses. Configuration Figure #9 shows memory addresses viewed through System Information.

CONFIGURATION – FIGURE #9

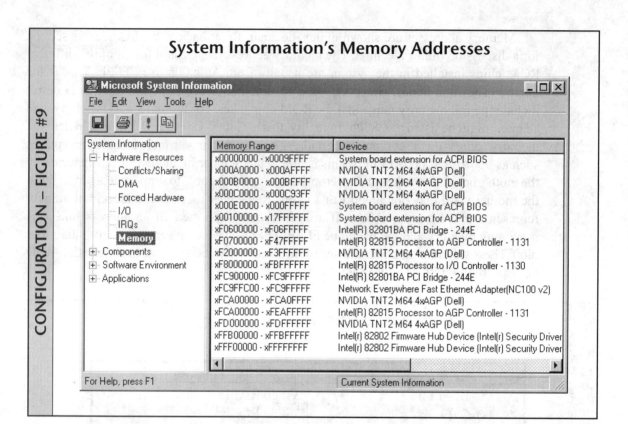

System Information's Memory Addresses

Notice in Configuration Figure #9 how the video card (NVIDIA TNT2 M64 4xAGP) is using the memory address ranges 00A0000-000AFFFFh, 00B0000-00BFFFFh, and 000C000-000C93FF. The first two ranges are for video RAM and the last address range is for the video ROM chip. The first two ranges are very standard in industry. The last address range normally starts at C000, but the ending range depends on the video ROM size.

Every ROM chip must have a unique memory address or the microprocessor will not be able to access the information inside it. Memory address conflicts can prevent a device or adapter from functioning properly.

IRQs, I/O addresses, DMA channels, and memory addresses cause headaches for technicians. Documentation and utility programs are the best source of relief. Documentation for adapters is rare. Even when it is available, such documentation is often hard to read, has mislabeled settings, contains incomplete information, and is simply inadequate. Utility programs are frequently the only source of information to help with DMA, IRQ, and I/O address conflicts. However, be advised, no utility program detects all adapter and device configuration information. Always consult several utility programs, the documentation, and vendor technical support. *Assume nothing!* Exercises at the end of the chapter help with identifying IRQs, I/O addresses, DMA channels, and memory addresses for various devices and operating systems.

UTILITIES

Some computers have their own utility programs that show the interrupt, DMA, and I/O address information. Refer to the computer's documentation for directions on accessing such programs. Microsoft DOS and Windows 3.x have a utility called MSD (Microsoft Diagnostics). MSD allows the viewing of IRQs and some port I/O addresses. Be careful using MSD though. MSD usually does okay detecting what is installed on the motherboard, but it is frequently wrong on adapters.

Windows 9x and 2000 Professional have a tool called Device Manager that shows IRQs, I/O addresses, DMA channels, and memory addresses. Windows 98 and 2000 Professional also have the System Information utility. Exercises at the end of the chapter help you use these utilities. NT Workstation comes with a program called NT Diagnostics that performs a similar function to Device Manager.

DiagSoft's QA Info is another program available with some computers, devices, and adapters sold today. The QA Info software shows hardware configuration, IRQ, DMA, and I/O address information. Other utilities used by technicians in resolving DMA, IRQ, and I/O address conflicts include Symantec's Norton Utilities' SYSINFO, Helix Software Corporation's Nuts & Bolts, and Touchstone Software Corporation's CheckIt. Public domain software such as Steve Grant's SYSID and Snooper are also available for technicians. Because operating systems come with so many utilities today and because they support plug and play, technicians do not buy external utilities as much as they did in years past.

CONFIGURATION ACCORDING TO ARCHITECTURE OR BUS

ISA, EISA, and MCA adapters must be configured for the proper IRQ, I/O address, memory address, and DMA channel. The method of configuration normally depends on the system architecture. The same is true for VL-bus, PCI, and AGP adapters. However, even though there are standards, the manufacturer of any adapter has the final word on configuration issues. Always refer to the adapter's documentation to find the correct configuration method.

CONFIGURATION OF ISA ADAPTERS

Some ISA adapters' interrupt, I/O address, or DMA channel are configured with jumpers, switches, and/or software. Not all adapters are able to use DMA, nor do the manufacturers of the adapters allow choosing the interrupt and I/O addresses for a particular adapter. However, this is not normally the case for today's ISA adapters due to the number of potential conflicts this can cause. The manufacturer of an adapter for today's computers wants to have as many combinations of interrupts and I/O addresses as possible so the adapter is useable in any system.

Other ISA adapters come with configuration software on a disk. The configuration software allows different settings and saves the configuration to the adapter. This method of configuration is much easier for a technician. The only drawback is that sometimes the disk has been misplaced or thrown away. However, most manufacturers have the configuration software available on their web sites.

Some manufacturers stencil the possible jumper or switch settings right on the adapter. Other manufacturers rely on paper documentation shipped with the adapter. Adapter documentation is frequently available through the Internet. Technicians must become familiar with using the Internet to download documentation, support files, and software drivers needed to configure ISA adapters.

Steps for installing ISA adapters:

1. Use an anti-static wrist strap when handling adapters. Electrostatic Discharge, ESD, can damage electronic parts. (See the Disassembly/Reassembly chapter for more details on ESD.)
2. Gather information about the computer in which the adapter is being installed such as interrupts, I/O addresses, and any DMA channel used by the adapters previously installed.
3. If necessary, set the appropriate (non-conflicting) interrupt, I/O address, or DMA channel on the adapter by referring to its documentation.
4. Be sure the computer is powered off.
5. Attach any internal device cables that connect to the adapter, if necessary.
6. Install the ISA adapter in a free expansion slot. Remove any brackets from the case or plastic covers from the rear of the computer that may prevent adapter installation.
7. Attach any cables that go to an external port on the adapter, if necessary.
8. Attach any external or internal devices to the opposite ends of the cable, if necessary.
9. Power on any external devices connected to the ISA adapter, if applicable.
10. Power on the computer.
11. If the adapter requires configuration software, refer to the adapter's documentation and load the software. Configure the adapter so it does not conflict with other installed devices.
12. Load any application software or device drivers needed for the devices attached to the ISA adapter.
13. Test the devices connected to the ISA adapter.

Configuring adapters by setting jumpers or switches is very time consuming. Reduce the time required to configure the adapter by investigating the system's interrupts, I/O address, DMA channels, and memory addresses *before* installing the adapter!

CONFIGURATION OF MCA ADAPTERS

IBM's MicroChannel computers are configured through software. Three times you might access the configuration software are (1) when an adapter or device is added or removed, (2) during a reconfiguration, such as when changing the interrupt or I/O address for a port, and (3) so that you can document the current configuration. MicroChannel configuration software ships on a disk with the adapter. The configuration files end in a .ADF extension. These files are text files and may be viewed with any text editor, such as the MS-DOS EDIT program. The configuration file included with an MCA adapter adds to the MicroChannel computer's current configuration using configuration software. The MicroChannel computer has two methods to access this software: (1) through a reference disk and (2) using a special partition on the hard drive called the IML (Initial Microcode Loader). Older MicroChannel computers include a reference disk that is unique for each IBM computer model. A reference disk for an IBM PS/2 Model 60 will *not* work in an IBM PS/2 Model 55. To access the configuration software, insert a backup copy of the reference disk into the A: drive. Then, power on the computer or perform a warm boot. Once the computer boots from the reference disk, the adapter's configuration file must be added to the existing configuration software.

Always make a backup of the reference disk in case of damage or loss of the original disk. Also, any adapters are added to the MicroChannel computer, the software that configures the adapter must be added to the reference disk. The IBM reference disk does not allow writing to the original disk. This write-protect feature is permanently enabled. Put a piece of tape over the write-protect hole or make a backup of the disk.

Newer MicroChannel computers use the IML (Initial Microcode Loader) process. The IML process loads software normally in the ROM BIOS from a special partition (section) on the hard drive or from a disk. A ROM BIOS chip is still used, but not as much information is stored there. The special section or partition on the hard drive is called the **system partition**. In addition to the IML boot record (formerly kept in the ROM BIOS), the system partition contains the system programs. The system programs include the diagnostic software, Setup software, and software to back up the system partition. The systems programs that IBM previously shipped on the reference disk are now in the system partition.

Access the system partition by warm booting (*CTRL+ALT+DEL*) or cold booting the computer. A cursor appears in the upper left corner of the screen. When the cursor moves to the right corner, press the *CTRL+ALT+INS* keys to access the system programs software. Use this same procedure when installing MicroChannel adapters.

Steps for installing MicroChannel adapters:

1. Use an anti-static wrist strap when handling adapters.
2. Gather information about the computer in which the adapter will be installed such as interrupts, I/O addresses, and DMA channel currently used by adapters in the system. Even though the MicroChannel architecture allows the sharing of interrupts, set each adapter to a different interrupt for the best results.
3. Verify the computer is powered off.

4. Install any necessary internal cables that connect to the adapter.
5. Install the MCA adapter in an available expansion slot. Remove any brackets from the case or possible plastic covers from the rear of the computer.
6. Attach any cable that connects to the adapter's external port, if necessary.
7. Attach any external or internal devices to the other ends of the cable as necessary.
8. Power on any external devices connected to the MCA adapter, if applicable.
9. Power on the computer. A POST error code will appear. If the MCA computer is an older one that requires a reference disk, insert the disk into the floppy drive. If the MCA computer uses the IML, the computer automatically goes into the Setup software.
10. Once the Setup software loads, a prompt appears stating that a configuration change has occurred and asking if the system should be automatically configured. Choose *N* for No.
11. From the main menu, choose *Copy an Option Disk* and follow the directions given on the screen. This option copies the adapter software to the reference disk or the system partition. If you are using a reference disk, it may need to be inserted into the floppy drive, alternating with the adapter's option disk, until the .ADF file finally copies onto the reference disk. If you are using a computer with the IML, only the option disk is necessary.
12. At the main menu, choose the *Set Configuration* option.
13. From the Set Configuration menu, choose the *Run Automatic Configuration* option.
14. Press *Y* for Yes so the system will configure itself for the new adapter.

On an MCA computer with an IML, after the option disk copies, make another backup of the system partition that contains the reference disk software!

When configuring a MicroChannel computer and prompted from the Setup software to *Automatically configure the computer (Y/N)?*, most users press *Y* for Yes. Beware of this apparently easy option. In a networked environment, it can configure a Token Ring adapter to the wrong speed. Also, conflicts between certain adapters such as external 5.25-inch and 3270 emulation adapters are not automatically detected. Sometimes it is better to choose *N* for No, go into the *Change Configuration* menu, and set the configuration settings manually. Verify that the settings are saved before exiting the configuration software.

Steps for backing up the System Partition on a MicroChannel computer:

1. Enter the system partition programs by pressing *CTRL+ALT+DEL* on the keyboard.
2. The cursor will move from the upper left to the upper right corner of the screen. While the cursor is on the right side, press *CTRL+ALT+INS*. The main menu appears.
3. From the main menu, choose the *Backup/Restore System Programs* option.
4. From the Backup/Restore System Programs menu, choose the *Backup the System Partition* option.

5. Follow the instructions on the screen for inserting a blank disk, etc.
6. After the backup of the system partition is made, press *Enter*.
7. Press *F3* to return to the main menu.
8. Press *F3* again to exit the software and reboot the computer.

CONFIGURATION OF EISA ADAPTERS

Some EISA adapters are configured with software, like the MicroChannel adapters. However, instead of a filename extension .ADF like the MCA adapters, EISA configuration files have the filename extension .CFG. Most EISA adapters are set up through software. However, some EISA adapters still require setting jumpers or switches to configure them. A technician must refer to the documentation included with the EISA adapter for configuration information.

Some EISA systems come with a configuration disk. The software used to configure the EISA computer may also be pre-loaded on the hard drive. Either way, make a backup of the configuration software. When executed, it shows the current configuration held in CMOS, searches for any EISA adapters, allows new EISA adapter configuration files to be added, and writes the new configuration information to CMOS. An EISA adapter can be installed into a system in an EISA expansion slot using the same procedures as with any adapter. Start the EISA configuration utility software. The .CFG configuration file that ships with the adapter is added to the configuration software. The new adapter is configured. Finally, the settings are saved to CMOS and the computer reboots. Always refer to the EISA computer documentation as well as the adapter's documentation to find complete installation instructions.

> When you configure an EISA system, the computer manufacturer sometimes recommends removing the ISA adapters from the system for initial configuration. However, this is obviously not feasible if the ISA adapter is the video adapter!

CONFIGURATION OF VL-BUS ADAPTERS

VL-bus adapters are usually configured through jumpers and switches or through software. VL-bus adapters have connectors for (1) the traditional buses: ISA, EISA, or MCA and (2) the VL-bus connector. The traditional connector part of the VL connector establishes connection for the ISA, EISA, or MCA resources, such as interrupts and DMA channels. This is *not* provided by the VL-bus. Most VL-bus cards are an extension of ISA and therefore configured through jumpers and switches, just the way traditional ISA adapters are configured. Some manufacturers have developed their own software Setup utilities. Always refer to the VL-bus adapter's documentation for installation instructions and watch out for the same old interrupt and I/O address conflicts.

MORE ABOUT PLUG AND PLAY

Plug and play (PnP) is one of the latest configuration techniques. Plug and play is a software and hardware standard designed to make hardware installation easier. The system board and BIOS chip must support plug and play to use it. Plug and play works with many existing ISA, EISA, MCA, PC Card, or PCI adapters and devices. Windows 95, 98, and 2000 Professional fully support plug and play whereas Windows NT only minimally supports it. There may be extra steps in a Windows NT environment. Even if a system has plug and play capabilities, older adapters must still be configured manually.

A plug and play device or adapter has built-in registers reached through a set of three I/O port addresses so the system BIOS or operating system can control the configuration. In a fully compatible plug and play computer, both the BIOS and the operating system support plug and play. The BIOS has the ability to control the plug and play adapters, determine what resources the adapter requires, and resolve conflicts among devices. Some plug and play computers allow choices through the Setup program: either (1) all plug and play adapters and devices are BIOS-configured and activated or (2) the plug and play adapters are checked by the BIOS, but only the adapters needed to boot the machine are activated. If Setup does not allow a choice of these two options, assume the BIOS does not configure the plug and play adapter unless the adapter is necessary for booting the computer. If the BIOS does not configure the plug and play adapters, the operating system will do so.

If a plug and play adapter is needed to boot the computer (for example, a video or drive adapter), that adapter starts up in an active mode. The adapter comes online similar to conventional boards using resources assigned as power-on defaults. Because the video and hard drive adapters start the system, traditional conflicts with interrupts, I/O addresses, and the like can still be a problem, even if the adapters are plug and play. Other plug and play adapters that do not activate during the boot-up process stay inactive until the operating system activates them.

Plug and play helps with some installation problems, but vendors implement the plug and play features in different ways. Most manufacturers offer plug and play cards that can operate in a computer with a plug and play BIOS as well as in the old (non-plug and play BIOS) computers. This is usually accomplished through a software utility provided by the manufacturer.

All devices and adapters, whether ISA, EISA, MCA, VL-bus, PCI, or plug and play, require configuration of some sort. Plug and play cannot always resolve all the system resource conflicts. Even if a BIOS and an operating system support plug and play, not all adapters within a given computer system will support plug and play. The plug and play software may not determine the traditional (non-plug and play) adapter's resources. Ensuring that all devices and adapters inside the computer are at a DMA channel, an I/O address, and an interrupt that no other device possesses has always been a challenge to technicians. Nothing beats good adapter, device, and computer documentation. However, never forget that documentation is not always accurate. Question everything and always ask the manufacturer of the device or adapter for clarification or better documentation.

CONFIGURATION OF PCI ADAPTERS

PCI adapters are the easiest adapters to configure. They do not have problems with interrupt conflicts because the PCI standard allows interrupt sharing. A PCI device is configured through the BIOS and system Setup software as well as through software provided with the PCI adapter. PCI adapters have special registers that store the configuration information. Furthermore, the PCI standard lends itself to plug and play. When installing a PCI adapter, always refer to the documentation for installation instructions.

When you install a PCI adapter in a DOS/Windows environment, you normally use the configuration software for the adapter. When you install a PCI adapter in a Windows 9x and 2000 Professional environment, the operating system detects installation and adds the adapter's configuration information to the registry. The **registry** is a central database that holds hardware information and other data. All software applications access the registry for configuration information instead of going to the adapter. In a plug and play operating system, the system prompts for either the operating system disks or CD, or for a software disk from the PCI adapter manufacturer. Windows NT does not fully support plug and play, but PCI adapters still work well. Windows NT does not always automatically detect an adapter's installation. However, after the configuration information is added to Windows NT's registry, applications know the adapter's resources. As in Windows 95/98, applications running under Windows NT access the registry instead of going to the adapter or the BIOS. No matter which method of configuration is used, it is always simpler than traditional ISA adapter configuration.

CONFIGURATION OF ADAPTERS USING WINDOWS 9X AND 2000 PROFESSIONAL

Windows 9x and 2000 Professional support plug and play and work in conjunction with a plug and play BIOS to configure adapters automatically. Windows attempts to make hardware installation easier and it keeps track of the computer's configuration. When Windows boots, it compares the saved configuration with what is detected during initialization. When adding or removing any hardware, use Windows' Add New Hardware/ Add Remove Hardware wizard. (The Add New Hardware is in Windows 95/98 and the Add Remove Hardware wizard is used in 2000.) This wizard lets the operating system search for the new piece of hardware or allows you to specifically select the type of device or adapter.

One way to access the Add New Hardware/Add Remove Hardware wizard is through the *Control Panel* option (accessed through Start menu's *Settings* option). The icon is in the Control Panel window. Double-clicking on the icon starts the wizard. Once the *Next* button is clicked, the wizard asks if Windows should search for the new hardware. If the Yes option is chosen, then the operating system searches for new hardware. Directions for installation appear in the windows throughout the process. If the No option is chosen, a list of hardware types appears in a window. Click on the specific hardware category, click on the *Next* button, and follow the directions on the screen. Letting the operating system search for new hardware can be a time-consuming process. If you are familiar with installing hardware, select the *No* option and pick the hardware category to save time. Selecting the No option may also save time because Windows may automatically select system resources that conflict with other devices already installed.

> Whether or not Windows searches for the new hardware, use the specific operating system driver provided with the adapter for optimum performance. If the driver is missing, check the adapter manufacturer's web site to see if a driver exists and if a new version is available.

CONFIGURATION OF ADAPTERS IN NT WORKSTATION

All hardware devices must have NT drivers in order to operate with NT Workstation. An important thing to remember is that the only type of user who can install hardware components by default is the Administrator. The Administrator uses various control panels to add hardware components in NT Workstation. To access the control panels, click on the *Start* button. Point to the *Settings* option and then click on the *Control Panel* menu option. The number of control panels is determined by what hardware is installed in the computer. Knowing which control panel to use and which specific tab will allow installation of a hardware device driver is sometimes confusing in NT. The following procedures help with the most common NT hardware installations.

- To load a monitor device driver, use the *Display* control panel, click on the *Settings* tab, and click on the *Change* button.
- To load a keyboard driver, use the *Keyboard* control panel, click on the *General* tab, and click on the *Change* button. To load a modem driver, use the *Modem* control panel, click on the *Add* button.
- To load a multimedia device driver such as a CD-ROM, joystick, or MIDI driver, use the *Multimedia* control panel, click on the *Devices* tab, and click on the *Add* button.
- To install a NIC driver, use the *Network* control panel, click on the *Adapters* tab, and click on the *Add* button.
- To install a SCSI adapter device driver, use the *SCSI Adapter* control panel, click on the *Drivers* tab, and click on the *Add* button.
- To install a tape drive device driver, use the *Tape Devices* control panel, click on the *Detect* button.

> Two important things to remember about NT Workstation: (1) you must have administrator rights to install a hardware driver and (2) the driver you install needs to be compatible with NT.

CONFIGURATION OF PC CARDS

PC Cards also support plug and play and can be used for a variety of purposes: network interface adapters, memory expansion, hard drive, floppy drive, CD-ROM drive access, applications, video, etc. PC Cards require different layers of software to allow them to operate. The most basic PC Card software is **socket services**. Socket services software can include drivers or device drivers. A **device driver** is a small piece of software that allows an operating system to access a piece of hardware. In the DOS environment, a device driver loads through the CONFIG.SYS file. In the Windows 9x, NT, or 2000 environment, a device driver loads through the CONFIG.SYS file or through the VMM32.VxD file that loads any virtual device drivers referenced in the registry.

Socket services allow each PC Card type to co-exist in the same system. Socket services software is similar to the software contained in the BIOS. In fact, some computer manufacturers place the socket services software in the BIOS. Socket services software isolates the PC Card software from the system hardware and allows detection of PC Card insertion and removal. Check the computer's documentation on the procedures for loading or enabling socket services.

A socket services driver must match your computer system. A driver from one laptop computer may not work in another one.

The second layer of software for PC Cards is **card services** software. It is included with operating systems such as PC DOS, MS DOS, OS/2, Windows 9x, NT, and 2000 Professional. Card services software can load through the CONFIG.SYS file (although it can also be an executable file run through a batch file). Newer software now loads as part of the registry. Some card services' software files are quite large in size. For this reason, many laptop computers require multiple boot options. For example, the computer can have one boot option if the computer is used with a network and another one if it is used as a stand-alone computer. Pieces of software needed for each scenario will load, while the others will not.

Socket services software loads before card services software. In fact, card services software needs socket services software to operate. Some computers and some PC Cards support hot swapping. Hot swapping allows the PC Card to be inserted into the slot when the computer is powered on. Both the computer and the PC Card must support hot swapping if automatic configuration is to occur. Whether or not hot swapping is possible, each PC Card takes up system resources, such as memory addresses and interrupts, just as other adapters do. Card services software manages the allocation of system resources and keeps PC Cards from interfering with one another. However, the system resources allocated to PC Cards may interfere with adapters other than PC Cards. For this reason, a third piece of software may be necessary: an enabler (sometimes called a super driver). A **generic enabler** can operate with different PC Cards and allows assignment of interrupts and I/O addresses. PC Card manufacturers can provide a vendor-specific enabler with their own PC Cards. **Vendor-specific enablers** operate with one specific PC Card and require socket services and card services software.

Problems can occur if both a generic enabler and a vendor-specific enabler are loaded in the same computer. If the PC Card you want to use can be configured by the generic enabler, do not load the vendor-specific enabler. The exception to this rule is if the PC Card is the only PC Card in the system. Contact the manufacturer of the vendor-specific enabler first if problems occur. The Internet is a wonderful source of information for situations like this.

The last type of PC Card software is a point enabler. A **point enabler** is similar to the vendor-specific enabler in that it works with a specific PC Card. A point enabler is different from the vendor-specific enabler in that this software *does not* require socket services or card services software. This is good if memory management is a problem. The point enabler software ignores any loaded socket services or card services software. However, it may also cause other adapters that use socket services and card services software to malfunction.

Point enablers should be used only if the PC Card it supports is the only one installed in the computer.

Configuration Figure #10 illustrates how all the software pieces fit together to communicate with the PC Card. Keep in mind that this illustration is an overview and not the final authority on configuring a PC Card. Always refer to the computer and PC Card documentation for instructions on configuring and installing the adapter.

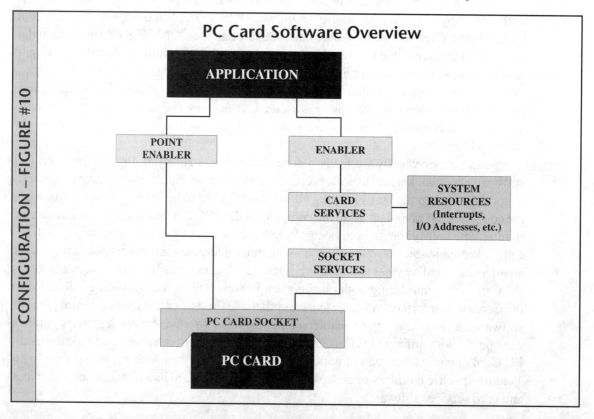

When installing PC Cards, some manufacturers recommend that you insert the installation CD or floppy, start the installation software, and then insert the PC Card. Other manufacturers have you install the PC Card with the power off and then boot the computer. You may need the operating system CD to install any new devices.

PC Cards, especially modems and network cards, can be frustrating in their conflicts with other installed devices. When using Windows 9x or 2000 Professional, you should confirm the PC Card installation using Device Manager. When using NT Workstation, use NT Diagnostics to ensure that no resource conflicts exist. For example, if the PC Card is a LAN+Modem card, you should check in both the network card's control panel and the modem control panel. In both places, you should double-click on the Device Manager icon where you will bring up a message such as, "This device is working properly." For faster confirmation, use the System Information tool in Windows 98 and 2000 Professional to ensure no conflicts exist. If a yellow exclamation mark shows in Device Manager, troubleshoot the resource conflict. If a red X appears over the device's icon, click on the appropriate checkbox under Properties to enable the PC Card device.

Some versions of NT do not support power management and this causes the PC Card to fail after a suspend/resume session. Disable power management in the system BIOS, upgrade NT, or upgrade the BIOS to solve this problem. Common problems that can occur with PC Cards are listed below:

- The card is not fully inserted into the slot.
- The computer's BIOS is not up to date.
- Use Device Manager or NT Diagnostics to troubleshoot resource conflicts.
- The system shows multiple installations of the same PC Card.
- The appropriate cable is not connected properly or in the right PC Card connector.
- An old driver was used.
- If two devices will not work when installed simultaneously, but will work when only one or the other is installed, then reverse the order of installation. Install one device and test it, then install the second device. If this does not work, uninstall both devices and reverse the order.

INSTALLING A USB DEVICE

A USB device can be installed if the operating system is Windows 95 OSR2, Windows 98, or Windows 2000. You also need a USB port on the computer. If the computer does not have one or more USB ports, you can add an adapter that contains USB ports. Once the adapter is installed (according to the adapter manufacturer's instructions), you plug your USB device into the USB port with the computer powered on, and a Found New Hardware dialog box appears. Follow the directions on the screen. If necessary, have the USB device's driver disk handy and insert it when prompted. With Windows 98, you must often reboot the computer to get the USB device to finish installing. A few USB devices require you to load the driver before connecting the device to the computer. Always follow the USB device manufacturer's instructions.

Name _____

CONFIGURATION REVIEW QUESTIONS

1. What is the purpose of the Setup program?

2. What is the best source of information for finding out how to enter the Setup program?

3. What is the difference between ROM BIOS and CMOS?

4. What is the purpose of a Flash update?

5. A computer has a write-protected BIOS. What can you do to update the Flash BIOS?

6. [T / F]   A virus can infect a Flash BIOS.

7. How does the POST program know which hardware components to test?

8. [T / F]   Entering the wrong Setup information can cause a POST error.

9. What component keeps the information in CMOS memory even when the computer is powered off?

10. List two things to remember when replacing a battery inside a microcomputer.

11. What is one indication a battery is beginning to fail?

12. A failing battery is soldered to the motherboard. How will you handle the problem?

13. Can you replace a computer battery with one that has a higher voltage?

14. Can you replace a computer battery with one that has a lower voltage?

15. Using Configuration Exercise Figure #1, determine how the switches would be changed if positions 1, 2, and 6 are the only positions to be *enabled*.

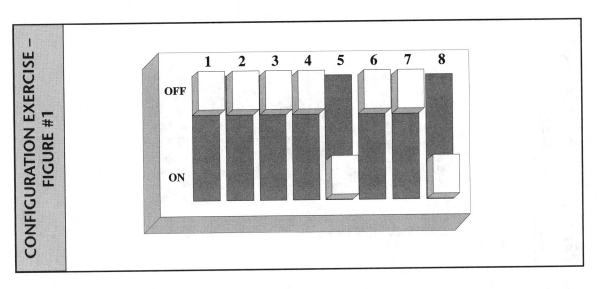

16. A switch block has the top labeled 1 and the bottom labeled 0 as shown in Exercise Figure #2. Which switches are off?

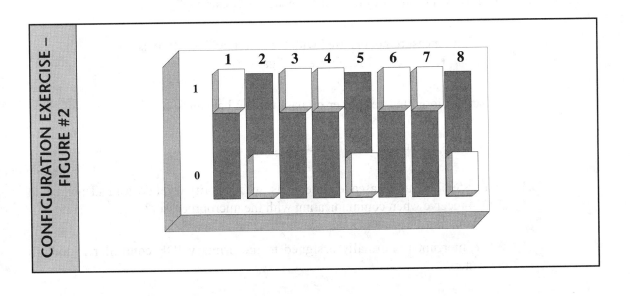

17. Using Configuration Exercise Figure #3, determine which side of each switch position is pressed if positions 1, 3, 4, & 6 are the only ones to be *disabled*?

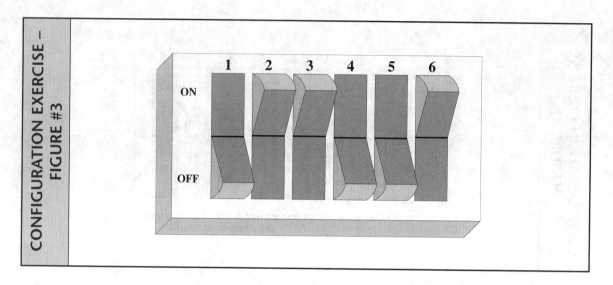

CONFIGURATION EXERCISE – FIGURE #3

18. [T / F] A pencil should be used to change a DIP switch because the tip is thinner than an ink pen's tip.

19. What is the purpose of the Boot Sequence BIOS setting?

20. What base measurement is used with the Aperture Size BIOS setting?
[Bytes / Kilobytes / Megabytes / Gigabytes]

21. A user has forgotten her power-on password. What can you do?

22. What IRQs are unavailable for adapters?

23. In a system that uses cascaded interrupts, what priority level does an adapter set to IRQ14 receive when communicating with the microprocessor?

24. What interrupt is normally assigned to the primary IDE controller in today's computers?

25. A system has a network card on IRQ3, a PS/2 mouse on IRQ12, and a printer on IRQ7. The computer uses cascaded interrupts. Which device has the highest priority when communicating with the CPU?
    [Network card / Printer / Mouse]

26. A system has an EIDE hard drive controller on IRQ14, a floppy controller on IRQ6, and a serial port on IRQ4. The computer uses cascaded interrupts. Which device has the lowest priority when communicating with the CPU?
    [Floppy / Hard drive / Serial port]

27. List two Windows 98 tools used to view IRQs.

28. Describe two visual signs of a resource conflict detected by Device Manager.

29. What Windows 98 Device Manager item is checked to see if PCI steering is enabled?

30. [T / F] Every device must have a separate I/O address to communicate with the microprocessor.

31. What is the decimal number 14 in hexadecimal?

32. What is the common I/O address for the COM1 serial port?

33. What is the common I/O address for the LPT1 parallel port?

34. What NT program is used to view I/O addresses?

35. What DMA channel is frequently used to connect to the first DMA controller?

36. How many DMA channels do today's computers have?

37. List one disadvantage to using a DMA channel.

38. What type of address is unique for every ROM installed in the computer?

39. Why are utilities important when assigning system resources?

40. [T / F] ISA adapters can be installed with power applied to the computer.

41. What configuration method do MicroChannel adapters use?
    [Jumpers / Switches / Plug and play / Software]

42. What makes a computer plug and play compatible?

43. Which adapters [ISA / EISA / MCA / VL-bus / PCI] are the easiest to configure?

44. [T / F] Using plug and play always ensures that no interrupt or I/O address conflicts exist within a system.

45. [T / F] If a BIOS supports plug and play, during boot up the BIOS searches the system for plug and play adapters and assigns each unique system resources for those adapters detected.

46. [T / F] ISA adapters do not support plug and play.

47. What control panel is used with Windows 98 when installing a new adapter?

48. What NT control panel is used to add a network adapter?

49. Describe the difference between PC Card socket services and card services software.

50. [T / F] A PC Card generic enabler can be used with a variety of PC Cards rather than one particular PC Card.

51. What tool do you use to verify the PC card installed properly with Windows 98 and 2000 Professional?

52. List two common PC Card installation problems.

53. [T / F] All versions of Windows support USB devices.

54. A friend of yours bought a USB printer and asks you to install it. You look on the computer and there are no USB ports on the motherboard. What will you recommend?

 Name _____

CONFIGURATION FILL-IN-THE-BLANK

1. To set the configuration for today's computers, go into the _____ program.

2. The _____ holds the Setup program.

3. A computer has an Award BIOS. To enter Setup, press either the _____ or _____ keys.

4. The configuration software for older IBM MicroChannel computers comes on a _____.

5. An alternative to the ROM BIOS chip is _____.

6. A special type of memory where configuration information is saved is _____.

7. The _____ keeps information in CMOS.

8. A special place on a MicroChannel hard drive that contains system programs is the _____.

9. PCI supports _____, which allows PCI adapters to be configured automatically.

10. On a rocker DIP switch, other settings for "on" are _____ or _____.

11. The _____ setting copies the motherboard ROM chip contents into RAM.

12. _____ is the name given when collectively referring to IRQs, I/O addresses, DMA channels, and memory addresses.

13. An _____ is a number assigned to an adapter so the microprocessor can recognize higher priority devices first.

14. An adapter that uses IRQ2 has the interrupt re-routed to _____.

15. The normal IRQ for COM1 is _____.

16. The reason IRQ8 cannot be used for an adapter is because it is used for the _____.

17. Windows 2000's System Information Tool is available through the _____ control panel.

18. _____ allows an external PCI modem and a PCI network card to share the same interrupt.

19. An _____ allows communication between a microprocessor and an adapter.

20. An I/O address is normally shown using the _____ numbering system.

21. A _____ is a number assigned to an adapter that allows bypassing the microprocessor.

22. Memory addresses are shown as _____ numbers.

23. Video RAM normally uses the address space _____ to _____.

24. EISA configuration files end in a _____ extension.

25. _____ allocate system resources to PC Cards.

26. The lowest level of software for a PC card is _____.

Name _____

CONFIGURATION METHOD EXERCISE AND REVIEW

Objective: To determine which configuration method a computer uses

Parts: A computer

    Step 1.   Open the computer and look at the motherboard. Determine whether the computer uses (1) switches, (2) a battery to maintain CMOS information, or (3) Flash BIOS.

Question 1:   What is an advantage of having a battery that keeps CMOS information instead of switches?

Question 2:   What is an advantage of Flash BIOS over a normal BIOS chip?

Question 3:   What is one of the first indications of a failing battery?

Question 4:   What determines the keystroke required to access the Setup program?

_____ *Instructor's Initials*

Name _____

BACKING UP CMOS CONFIGURATION DATA

Objective: To use a CMOS backup utility to back up and restore CMOS configuration data

Parts: Windows 2000 Professional, Windows NT, Windows 95/98, or DOS workstation
Several third-party and shareware utilities allow backing up and restoring CMOS configuration data. This is especially useful in the event the CMOS configuration is changed or becomes corrupted. In this lab, you will use a shareware utility called CMOS.EXE to back up and restore the CMOS configuration data.

Step 1.   From a computer having Internet access, connect to the following URL: http://www.demesne.freeserve.co.uk/dos/

Question 1:   What does the acronym URL stand for? (*Hint:* If you do not know, use the Internet to find out.)

Step 2.   When the above web page opens, scroll down to the **Miscellaneous** section.

Step 3.   Select the **CMOS V1.2** utility, and download it to your local harddrive. The CMOS V1.2 utility is downloaded in a compressed or zipped format. The zipped file's name is CMOS.ZIP. In order to use the utility it must first be decompressed or unzipped.

Step 4.   Using an unzip utility such as WINZIP or PKZIP, unzip the **CMOS.ZIP** file to a floppy disk. Two files, CMOS.DOC and CMOS.EXE will be written to the disk.

To use the CMOS.EXE backup utility, follow these steps:

Step 5.   From your workstation, open a **command prompt**.

Step 6.   Insert the floppy disk containing CMOS.EXE into the appropriate drive.

Step 7.   Change the command prompt to the appropriate drive (normally A:\), type **CMOS / W CMOS.BIN** and press **Enter**. The current CMOS data in memory will be written to a file called CMOS.BIN on the floppy disk.

Question 2:   What does the /W switch do? (*Hint:* Read the CMOS.DOC file.)

Step 8.   Browse the floppy disk to verify the **CMOS.BIN** file was created.

To restore the CMOS configuration from the backup, follow these steps:

Step 9. From your workstation, open a **command prompt.**

Step 10. Insert the floppy disk containing the CMOS.EXE and the CMOS.BIN backup file into the appropriate drive.

Step 11. Change the command prompt to the appropriate drive (normally A:\) and type **CMOS /C CMOS.BIN** and press **Enter.**

Question 3: What does the /C switch do?

Step 12. The current CMOS configuration data will be compared with the backup file and, if necessary, the backup file will overwrite the new data.

_____ *Instructor's Initials*

Name _____

USING MICROSOFT DIAGNOSTICS (MSD)

Objective: To evaluate a computer's resources using Microsoft Diagnostics

Parts: A computer that has Microsoft Diagnostics (MSD) loaded

Step 1.   Power on the computer and be sure the computer is at a DOS prompt such as C:\>. For DOS skills, refer to Appendix A.

Step 2.   Type **CD\WINDOWS** and press **Enter**. The prompt changes to C:\WINDOWS>. If this does not happen, retype the command.

Step 3.   Type **MSD** and press **Enter**. The Microsoft Diagnostics program appears.

Step 4.   Press the letter **C** on the keyboard for COM PORTS. The COM PORTS screen appears.

Question 1:   What I/O address (port address) does COM1: use?

Step 5.   Press **Enter** to return to the main MSD menu.

Step 6.   Press the letter **Q** on the keyboard for IRQ STATUS. The IRQ STATUS screen appears.

Question 2:   For what device or port is IRQ7 used?

Question 3:   For what device or port is IRQ3 used?

Step 7.   Press **Enter** to return to the main MSD menu.

Step 8.   Press **F3** on the keyboard to exit MSD.

_____ *Instructor's Initials*

Name _____

INTERRUPT, I/O ADDRESS, & DMA CHANNEL CONFIGURATION (ON 286 OR HIGHER COMPUTERS USING KEYSTROKES TO ENTER SETUP PROGRAM)

Objective: To access a computer's resources through the Setup program

Parts: A 286 or higher computer that uses keystrokes to enter the Setup program

Step 1.   Power on the computer.

Step 2.   Press the appropriate key(s) to enter the Setup program.

Step 3.   Go through the various menus or icons until you find an interrupt (IRQ) setting for a particular device or port. Write the device or port and the associated IRQ in the space below:

IRQ	Device or Port

Question 1:   Why do different devices generally not have the same interrupt?

Step 4.   Go through the various menus or icons until you find an I/O address setting for a particular device or port. Write the device or port in the space below along with the associated I/O address.

I/O Address	Device or Port

Question 2:   Why must all devices and ports have a separate and unique I/O address?

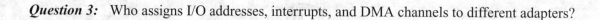

Question 3: Who assigns I/O addresses, interrupts, and DMA channels to different adapters?

Question 4: What is the best source of information on how to set interrupts, I/O addresses, and DMA channels for technicians installing a new adapter into a system?

Step 5. Exit the **Setup** program.

Step 6. Go into the MSD program (DOS/Windows 3.x computer), Device Manager (Windows 95/98 computer), or NT Diagnostics (NT Workstation computer) and determine if the information collected in steps 3 and 4 is the same.

_____ ***Instructor's Initials***

Name _____

VIEWING I/O ADDRESSES AND IRQS
IN WINDOWS 2000 PROFESSIONAL

Objective: To view memory area assignments in Windows 2000 Professional using the System Information utility

Parts: Computer with Windows 2000 Professional installed

At times, it may become necessary to view memory area assignments in order to troubleshoot and/or configure your system.

Step 1.   Turn the computer on and verify that Windows 2000 Professional loads.

Step 2.   Logon to Windows 2000 Professional using the userid and password provided by the instructor or lab assistant.

Step 3.   From the **Start** menu, choose **Programs, Accessories, System Tools,** and then select **System Information**. If the System Tools option is not available, click on the Start button, point to the Settings option, and click on the Control Panels option. Double-click on the Administrative Tools control panel and then double-click on the System Information icon. The System Information utility opens.

Question 1:   What system information is available through the System Information utility?

Step 4.   Expand the **Hardware Resources** folder.

Step 5.   Expand **I/O**. The system I/O address assignments will appear.

Question 2:   Which I/O address range is the video adapter using?

Step 6.   Expand **IRQ**s. The system IRQ assignments appear.

Question 3:   Which IRQ(s) is the video adapter using?

Step 7.   Close the **System Information** utility.

_____ *Instructor's Initials*

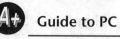

 Name _____

EXAMINING SYSTEM RESOURCES USING WINDOWS 95/98

Objective: To understand how to access a computer's resources using Windows 95/98

Parts: A computer that has Windows 95 or Windows 98 loaded

Step 1.   Power on the computer and verify that the desktop appears.

Step 2.   Click once on the **Start** button. (Press **CTRL+ESC** if the Start button is not visible.)

Step 3.   Place the mouse pointer over the **Settings** option.

Step 4.   Click once on the **Control Panel** option.

Step 5.   Double-click on the **System** icon.

Step 6.   Click once on the **Device Manager** tab. The window shows a list of hardware devices sorted by hardware types. All the system resources seen throughout the rest of the exercise can be printed from the current window. Take note of the Print button located near the bottom of the window.

Step 7.   Double-click on the **Computer** icon.

Step 8.   The View Resources tab lists the IRQs. Use Exercise Table #1 to document the IRQs currently used.

CONFIGURATION EXERCISE – TABLE #1

IRQ	Device	IRQ	Device
0	System timer	8	
1	Keyboard	9	
2		10	
3		11	
4		12	
5		13	
6		14	
7		15	

Step 9.   Click on the **Input/Output I/O** radio button located on the top portion of the window.

Step 10.   The I/O addresses used by the system are displayed.

Always write down the possible I/O addresses for a new adapter and then check the I/O addresses shown on the screen to see which I/O address is available for the adapter to use.

Step 11.   Click on the **Direct memory access (DMA)** radio button located on the top portion of the window.

Step 12.   Using Exercise Table #2, write down the DMA channels used in the system.

CONFIGURATION EXERCISE – TABLE #2

DMA	Device	DMA	Device
0	System timer	4	
1	Keyboard	5	
2		6	
3		7	

Step 13.   Click on the **Memory** radio button located on the top portion of the window. Memory addresses that appear are used by ROM chips on the adapters and the ROM chips on the motherboard.

Question 1:   List two memory addresses that are used by ROMs.

Question 2:   List one memory range used by the ROM BIOS.

Step 14.   Click once in the window's **Close** box (the X in the upper right corner).

Step 15.   Click once in the **System Properties Close** box.

Step 16.   Click once in the **Control Panel Close** box.

_____ *Instructor's Initials*

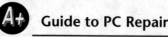

 Name _____

EXAMINING SYSTEM RESOURCES USING NT WORKSTATION

Objective: To understand how to access a computer's resources using NT Workstation

Parts: A computer that has NT Workstation loaded

Step 1. Power on the computer and verify that NT Workstation loads.

Step 2. Click on the **Start** button. (Press **CTRL+ESC** if the Start button is not visible.)

Step 3. Place the mouse pointer over the **Programs** option.

Step 4. Place the mouse pointer over the **Administrative Tools (Common)** option.

Step 5. Click on the **Windows NT Diagnostics** option.

Step 6. Click on the **Resources** tab.

Step 7. Click on the **IRQ** button at the bottom of the window.

Question 1: What IRQs are used?

Step 8. Click on the **I/O Port** button at the bottom of the window.

Question 2: List two I/O addresses for common ports such as the serial and parallel port.

Step 9. Click on the **DMA** button at the bottom of the window.

Question 3: List two DMA channels used.

Step 10. Click on the **Memory** button at the bottom of the window.

Question 4: List two memory address ranges used by ROM chips.

Step 11. Click on the **OK** button to close Windows NT Diagnostics.

_____ *Instructor's Initials*

 Name _____

EXAMINING SYSTEM RESOURCES
USING WINDOWS 2000 PROFESSIONAL

Objective: To understand how to examine system resource information for use in troubleshooting

Parts: Windows 2000 Professional Workstation

In order to configure and troubleshoot a Windows 2000 Professional workstation effectively, you must be able to examine the system resource information to identify conflicts, resources used, and resources available.

Step 1.   Turn the computer on and verify that Windows 2000 Professional loads.

Step 2.   Logon to Windows 2000 Professional using the userid and password provided by the instructor or lab assistant.

Step 3.   From the Start menu, choose **Programs, Accessories, System Tools,** and then select **System Information**. If System Tools is not a choice, click on the **Start** button, point to **Settings,** click on **Control Panels,** double-click on the **Administrative Tools** control panel, and double-click on the **System Information** icon. The System Information utility opens.

Step 4.   Open the **System Summary** folder. A summary of your system information will be displayed.

Question 1:   How much Total Physical Memory is installed in your system?

Step 5.   Expand **Hardware Resources**. From this folder you can view memory usage information, IRQ usage information, I/O address range information, Forced Hardware information (if any), DMA usage information, and Hardware Conflicts/Sharing information (if any).

Question 2:   The video adapter is using which I/O address ranges?

Step 6.   Expand **Components**. From this folder you can view system information related to Multimedia, Display, Modems, Network Storage, and so forth. Explore the available system information under Components.

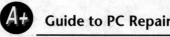

Question 3: How many storage drives are listed under the Storage/Drives option?

Step 7. Expand **Software Environment**. From this folder you can view system information related to Software Applications and the Operating System. Explore the system information available under Software Environment.

Question 4: How many services are listed?

Step 8. Expand **Internet Explorer 5**. From this folder you can view system information related to the Internet Explorer 5 application.

Step 9. Close the System Information utility and return to the Windows 2000 Professional desktop.

_____ *Instructor's Initials*

Name _____

386 AND HIGHER CONFIGURATION

Objectives: To understand how to configure a 386 or higher computer

                To understand the effects of changing a computer's configuration

Parts: A computer with a 386 or higher microprocessor

Note: Different BIOS manufacturers specify different keystroke(s) to access the Setup program. Refer to the computer manual or Configuration Table #1 for the appropriate keystroke(s).

Step 1.   Power on the computer.

Step 2.   Press the appropriate key(s) on the keyboard to access the Setup program.

Question 1:   What key(s) did you press to access the Setup program?

Step 3.   Using the keys shown on the menu, go to the menu screen that allows changes to the installed floppy drives.

Question 2:   What type of floppy drive is installed as drive A: according to the current Setup information?

Step 4.   Using the appropriate keys, change the drive type for the A: drive to a type other than the one installed.

Step 5.   Save the configuration information by pressing the appropriate key and exit the Setup program. Follow the directions shown on the screen to restart the computer.

Question 3:   Did any error codes or messages appear during POST? If so, write the code or message in the space below.

Step 6. Go back into the Setup program and change the type of floppy drive back to the original configuration. Refer to Question 2 for the original floppy drive type.

Step 7. Save the configuration and exit the Setup program by pressing the appropriate keys as displayed on the screen.

Step 8. Reboot the computer.

Question 4: Did the computer boot without any errors? If not, be sure that the correct floppy drive type was entered into the Setup program.

_____ *Instructor's Initials*

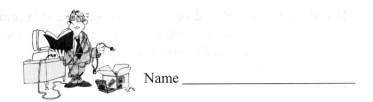

Name _____

ISA ADAPTER INSTALLATION EXERCISE

Objective: To install an ISA adapter properly, by setting the configuration so the adapter does not conflict with other adapters

Parts: ISA adapter and documentation (if possible)
Software for the adapter (if applicable)
Tools
Anti-static materials

CAUTION: Observe proper grounding procedures when installing an adapter.

Step 1.   Using any appropriate method or available software, determine what IRQs are available in the system. Use Exercise Table #3 to document the IRQs currently in use.

CONFIGURATION EXERCISE – TABLE #3

IRQ	Device	IRQ	Device
0	System timer	8	
1	Keyboard	9	
2		10	
3		11	
4		12	
5		13	
6		14	
7		15	

Question 1:   Using the adapter's documentation and information in Configuration Exercise Table #3, determine what IRQs are available for the ISA adapter being installed. What are the adapter's possible IRQ settings?

Step 2.   Using any appropriate method or software available, determine what I/O addresses other adapters and devices in the computer currently use.

Question 2:   According to the information found in Step 2 and the adapter's documentation, what I/O addresses can the adapter use that are *not* used by any other adapter or device?

Step 3.   If necessary, use appropriate methods or available software to determine which DMA channels are currently used and to which DMA channels the adapter can be set. Make notes if necessary.

Step 4.   If the adapter is configured by setting jumpers and switches, go ahead and configure the adapter for the proper interrupt, I/O address, and any other system resources needed.

Step 5.   Verify that the computer is powered off.

Step 6.   Remove the computer's cover.

Step 7.   Find an available ISA expansion slot.

Step 8.   If necessary, attach any internal device cables that connect to the adapter.

Step 9.   Remove any brackets from the case or plastic covers from the rear of the computer that prevent adapter installation.

Step 10.   Install the adapter in the expansion slot.

Step 11.   If necessary, attach any cables that go to an external port on the adapter.

Step 12.   If necessary, attach any external or internal devices to the other end of the cables.

Step 13.   If applicable, power on any external devices that connect to the ISA adapter.

Step 14.   Power on the computer.

Step 15. If the adapter is configured through software, load the configuration software, following the directions included with the adapter or the README file on the software disks. Configure the adapter using the software verifying the settings chosen do not conflict with other devices. Refer to Exercise Table #3, Questions 2 and 3, and Step 3's notes when configuring the adapter.

Step 16. Load any application software or device driver needed for the ISA adapter. Always refer to the documentation for exact loading procedures.

Step 17. Test any devices that connect to the ISA adapter.

Question 3: Does the adapter (and any devices that connect to it) work properly? If not, refer to the adapter's documentation and review all installation steps.

_____ *Instructor's Initials*

Step 18. If applicable, power off any external devices.

Step 19. Power off the computer.

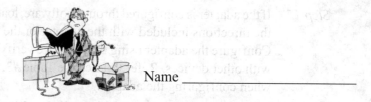

Name _____

PCI ADAPTER INSTALLATION EXERCISE

Objective: To install a PCI adapter

Parts: PCI adapter and documentation (if possible)
Software for the adapter (if applicable)
Tools
Anti-static materials

Note: Observe proper grounding procedures when installing an adapter.

Step 1.   Using any appropriate method or available software, determine what IRQs are available in the system. Use Exercise Table #4 to document the IRQs currently in use.

CONFIGURATION EXERCISE – TABLE #4

IRQ	Device	IRQ	Device
0	System timer	8	
1	Keyboard	9	
2		10	
3		11	
4		12	
5		13	
6		14	
7		15	

Question 1:   What type of PCI adapter is being installed?

    Step 2.   Using the adapter manufacturer's instructions, install the adapter and software into the system. If necessary, attach any cables that go to an external port on the adapter. If necessary, attach any external or internal devices to the ends of the cables.

    Step 3.   Power on the computer.

    Step 4.   Test any devices that connect to the adapter.

Question 2:   Using any utility or tool available with the operating system, determine which I/O address the adapter is using and write that address in the space below.

Question 3:   Determine if the adapter uses any ROM space. Refer to documentation and use any utility or tool available with the operating system. Write the memory address in the space below.

Question 4:   Does the adapter (and any devices that connect to it) work properly? If not, refer to the adapter's documentation and review all installation steps. Troubleshoot as necessary.

_____ *Instructor's Initials*

    Step 5.   If applicable, power off any external devices.

    Step 6.   Power off the computer.

Name _____

INTERNET DISCOVERY

Objective: To obtain specific information on the Internet regarding a computer or its associated parts

Parts: Access to the Internet

Your customer owns a Dell 4100 Dimension computer. Answer questions 1 and 2 based on this information.

Question 1:   Determine the procedure for accessing the computer's Setup program. Write the key(s) to press and the URL where you found this information.

Question 2:   Determine how to remove a power-on password that has been set and forgotten. Write the solution and the URL where you found this information.

Question 3:   A customer has an ABIT KT7A motherboard. What is the name of the file for the latest Flash BIOS version for this motherboard and at which URL did you find this information?

Question 4:   A customer has a Tyan Tomcat i815T motherboard. What chipset does this motherboard use?

Question 5:   A customer has a Tyan Tomcat i815T motherboard. What type of battery does this motherboard use? Describe its location on the motherboard. Write the URL you found and the answers in the space below.

Question 6: A customer has an MSI (Micro-Star International) MS-6341 motherboard. What is the Swap Floppy Drive Setup configuration setting used for?

Question 7: A customer has an MSI (Micro-Star International) MS-6341 motherboard. What is the default option for the AGP Data Transfer Mode BIOS setting?

Question 8: You have just purchased a 3Com 3C905C-TX-M Ethernet PCI adapter. What is the minimum processor this computer must have? Into what type of PCI slot does the adapter install? At which URL did you find this information?

NOTES

4

Chapter 4:

Disassembly/ Reassembly

OBJECTIVES

After completing this chapter you will
- Understand how static electricity can damage a computer.
- Understand what type of equipment causes RFI and EMI.
- Know which tools a technician needs.
- Understand the importance of diagramming when disassembling a computer.
- Be able to disassemble and reassemble a computer.

KEY TERMS

anti-static wrist strap	pin 1
EMI	preventive maintenance
ESD	return
grounding	RFI
head parking utility	self-parking heads
hot	solder joints
keyed	standoffs
MSDS	

DISASSEMBLY OVERVIEW

It is seldom necessary to completely disassemble a computer. However, when a technician is first learning about microcomputers, disassembly can be both informative and fun. Some technicians disassemble a computer to perform a preventive cleaning on it. It may also be appropriate to disassemble a computer when it has a problem of undetermined cause. Sometimes, the only way to diagnose a problem is to disassemble the computer outside the case or remove components one by one. Sometimes disassembling the computer outside the case helps with grounding problems. A **grounding** problem occurs when the motherboard or adapter is not properly installed and a trace (metal line on the motherboard or adapter) touches the computer frame, causing the adapter and possibly other components to cease working.

ELECTROSTATIC DISCHARGE (ESD)

Many precautions must be taken when disassembling a microcomputer. The electronic circuits located on the motherboard and adapters are subject to **electrostatic discharge** or **ESD**. Static electricity can be very damaging to electronic equipment without the technician feeling the static electricity. An average person requires a static discharge of 3,000 volts before he or she feels it. An electronic component can be damaged with only 30 volts of static electricity. Some electronic components may not be damaged the first time static electricity hits them. However, the effects of static electricity can be cumulative, weakening or eventually destroying the component. An ESD event is not recoverable. Nothing can be done about the damage it induces. CMOS and RAM chips are most susceptible to ESD strikes.

Atmospheric conditions affect static electricity. When humidity is low, the potential for ESD is greater than at any other time. Keep humidity above 50 percent to reduce the threat of ESD.

A technician can prevent ESD using a variety of methods. The most common tactic is to use an **anti-static wrist strap.** One end encircles the technician's wrist. At the other end is an alligator clip that attaches to the computer. The clip attaches to a grounding post or a metal part such as the power supply. The electronic symbol for ground follows:

This method allows the technician and the computer to be at the same voltage potential. As long as the technician and the computer or electronic part are at the same potential, static electricity does not occur. An exercise at the end of the chapter demonstrates how to attach an anti-static wrist strap and how to perform maintenance on it.

Technicians should use an ESD wrist strap whenever possible. The one time a technician *should not* wear an ESD wrist strap is when working inside a monitor because of the high voltages there. A resistor inside the wrist strap protects the technician in case something accidentally touches the ground to which the strap attaches while she is working inside a computer. This resistor could not protect the technician against the voltages possible inside

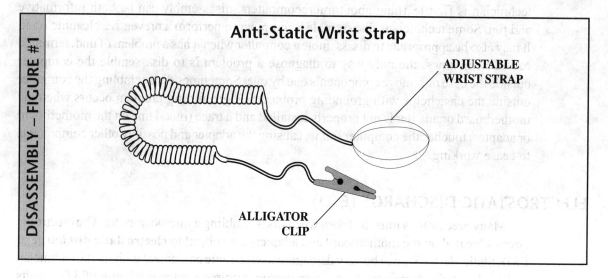

DISASSEMBLY – FIGURE #1

Anti-Static Wrist Strap

ADJUSTABLE WRIST STRAP

ALLIGATOR CLIP

a monitor. Refer to Disassembly Figure #1 for an illustration of an anti-static wrist strap.

Anti-static bags are good for storing spare adapters and motherboards when the parts are not in use. Anti-static mats are available to place underneath a computer being repaired; many of the mats have a snap for connecting the anti-static wrist strap.

If an anti-static wrist strap is not available, you can still reduce the chance of ESD damage by using an alternate method. After removing the computer case, if you are right-handed, place your bare left arm on the power supply. Remove the computer parts one-by-one, always keeping the left elbow (or some bare part of the arm) connected to the power supply. If you are left-handed, place your right arm on the power supply. By using an elbow on the power supply, both hands are free to remove computer parts. This method is *not* as safe as using an anti-static wrist strap. It is an effective way of keeping the technician and the computer at the same voltage potential, thus reducing the chance of ESD damage. Also, removing the power cable from the back of the computer is a good idea for new technicians. In the past, leaving the power cable plugged into the wall socket and the computer's power supply was the best method for ensuring a good ground; however, today's power supplies provides a small amount of power to the motherboard, even when the computer is powered off. Always unplug the computer and use an anti-static wrist strap!

EMI (ELECTROMAGNETIC INTERFERENCE)

EMI (ElectroMagnetic Interference, sometimes called EMR for ElectroMagnetic Radiation), is noise caused by electrical devices. Many devices can cause EMI, such as the computer, a pencil sharpener, a motor, a vacuum cleaner, an air conditioner, and fluorescent lighting. The FCC (Federal Communications Commission) has two classes of computer specifications, Class A and Class B. The Class A specification is for computers in the design stage or devices for commercial and business use. The Class B specification covers consumer computing devices. A Class B certification is not difficult to obtain because computers do not emit much noise anyway. The electrical devices around the computer, including the computer monitor and speakers, cause more problems than the computer. EMI can significantly affect a monitor. If a monitor's output is distorted, try moving the computer to a different location to see if EMI is the problem source.

A specific type of electromagnetic interference that affects computers is **RFI (Radio Frequency Interference)**. RFI is simply those noises that occur in the radio frequency range. Anytime a computer has an intermittent problem, check the surrounding devices for the source of that problem. For example, if the computer only goes down when the pencil sharpener operates or when a CD plays in the CD player, then EMI could be to blame. EMI problems are very hard to track to the source. EMI can also come through the power lines. Move the computer to a different wall outlet or to a totally different circuit to determine if the power outlet is the problem source. EMI can also affect files on a disk or hard drive.

DISASSEMBLY

Before a technician disassembles a computer, several steps should be performed or considered. The list below helps with these steps:

1. Back up, write down, or print out the CMOS Setup configuration.
2. If disassembling an IBM MicroChannel computer, locate the reference or adapter disks and set aside. If they are unavailable, do not disconnect the battery from the motherboard.
3. Do not disconnect the battery from the motherboard if at all possible or the CMOS configuration information will be lost.
4. Use proper grounding procedures to prevent ESD damage.
5. Keep paper and pen nearby for note taking and diagramming. Even if you have taken computers apart for years, you might find something unique or different inside this one. Good technicians continue to diagram throughout their careers.
6. Have ample workspace.
7. When removing adapters, do not stack the adapters on one another.
8. If possible, place removed adapters inside a special ESD protective bag.
9. Take note of any jumper or switch settings on the motherboard or adapters before removing them from the computer. Notes are helpful if the switches or jumpers are accidentally changed.
10. Handle each adapter or motherboard on the side edges. Avoid touching the gold contacts on the bottom of adapters. Sweat, oil, and dirt cause problems.
11. Hard disk drives require careful handling. A very small jolt can cause damage to stored data.

TOOLS

No chapter on disassembly and reassembly is complete without the mention of tools. Many technicians do not go on a repair call loaded down with a full tool case. Most repairs are accomplished with a few tools. Tools can be divided into two categories: (1) do not leave the office without these tools and (2) nice to have in the office, home, or car tools.

Ninety-five percent of all computer repair calls are completed with a couple of basic tools:

- Medium flat-tipped screwdriver
- Small, flat-tipped tweaker screwdriver
- #1 Phillips screwdriver
- #2 Phillips screwdriver
- 1/4-inch nut driver
- 3/16-inch nut driver
- Pair of small diagonal cutters
- Pair of needlenose pliers

The screwdrivers and nut drivers take care of most disassemblies and reassemblies. Sometimes, manufacturers place tie wraps on new parts, new cables, or the cables inside the computer case. The diagonal cutters are great for removing the tie wraps without cutting cables or damaging parts. The needlenose pliers are good for getting disks or disk parts out of disk drives, straightening DIP chip legs bent from using a DIP chip inserter tool, straightening bent pins on cables or connectors, and about a million other uses. The small tweaker screwdriver and the needlenose pliers are irreplaceable.

Many technicians start with a basic $15 microcomputer repair kit and build from there. A specialized Swiss army knife with screwdrivers is the favorite of some technicians. Other technicians prefer the all-in-one tool carried in a pouch that connects to the belt. Individual taste and convenience sets each person's standard. However, you should be aware that some tools included with the basic microcomputer repair toolkits are not useful. For example, both a DIP chip insertion tool and DIP chip removal tool are worthless. If you are asked however, for A+ certification about what tool to use with DIP chips, answer "DIP chip insertion" or "DIP removal" tools. More DIP chip legs are bent when using the insertion tool than when inserting chips by hand. DIP chip legs are bent when the chip is removed because applying equal pressure while lifting straight up on the DIP chip is nearly impossible.

One tool to avoid is a magnetic screwdriver. A magnetic screwdriver can cause permanent loss of data on hard or floppy disks. Magnetism can also induce currents into components and damage them. Technicians who have a magnetic screwdriver use it when they drop a small part such as a screw into a hard-to-reach place or when something rolls under the motherboard. Alternatives to the magnetic screwdriver include a screw pick-up tool and common sense. The screw pick-up tool is used in the hard-to-reach places and sometimes under the motherboard. If a screw rolls under the motherboard and cannot be reached, tilt the computer so the screw rolls out. Sometimes the case must be tilted in different directions until the screw becomes dislodged.

Tools no one thinks of as tools, but which need to go on the service call every time include: a pen or pencil to take notes and fill out the repair slip, and a bootable disk containing the technician's favorite repair utilities. Usually a technician has several bootable disks for different operating systems and utilities as well as a few blank disks for saving files or testing a floppy drive. Another item is a small reference book by Sequoia Publishing, *Pocket PCRef*. It contains many useful error codes, commands, and common repair recommendations. A flashlight comes in handy when least expected. Some rooms and offices are dimly lit. Last, do not forget to bring a smile and a sense of humor.

Tools that are nice to have, but not used on a day-to-day or hour-to-hour basis, include:

- Multimeter for checking voltages and cable continuity
- Screw pick-up tool
- Screwdriver extension tool for making a Phillips or flat-tipped screwdriver longer for printers that require longer screwdrivers
- Soldering iron, solder, and flux
- Screw-starter tool
- Medium-size set of diagonal cutters
- Metric nut drivers
- Cable-making tools, such as wire strippers and crimpers
- AC circuit tester
- Right-angled, flat-tipped and Phillips screwdrivers for hard-to-reach areas
- Hemostats
- Pliers
- Floppy disk read/write head cleaning kit
- Chip removal tools for PGA (Pin Grid Array), PLCC (Plastic Leaded Chip Carrier), and PQFP (Plastic Quad Flat Pack) chips are handy to have around, but not needed every day.

You could get some nice muscle tone from carrying each of these nice to have, but normally unnecessary tools. Sometimes, T-10 and T-15 Torx screwdrivers are needed for some manufacturer's screws as well as a tamper-proof Torx driver. Loopback plugs help when testing some standard connectors. Not often do the ports need testing, but when they do, some utilities require such a tool for a loop-back test.

When first starting in computer repair, get the basics. As your career path and skill level grow, so will the toolkit. Nothing is worse than getting to a job site and not having the right tool. However, because there are no standards or limitations on what manufacturers can use in their product line, *always* having the tool on hand is impossible. Always remember that no toolkit is complete with an anti-static wrist strap.

REASSEMBLY

Reassembling a microcomputer is easy if the technician is careful and diagrams properly during the disassembly. Simple tasks such as inserting the floppy drive in the correct drive bay become confusing after many parts have been removed. Writing down reminders takes less time than troubleshooting the computer because of poor reassembly. Reinsert all components into their proper place; be careful to replace all screws and parts.

Three major reassembly components are motherboards, cables, and connectors. Motherboards frequently have plastic connectors called **standoffs** on the bottom. The standoffs slide into slots on the computer case. Do not remove the standoffs from the motherboard. Take the motherboard out of the case with the standoffs attached. The first step in removing a motherboard involves removing the screws that attach the motherboard to the case. Then, the motherboard, (including the standoffs), slides to one side and lifts up. Follow the reverse procedure when reinstalling the motherboard.

When reinstalling the motherboard, insert the plastic standoffs evenly into the edge of the case slots. The motherboard will gently slide toward the power supply until it clamps firmly into the slots. This procedure requires practice but eventually a technician will be able to tell when a motherboard's standoffs seat properly into the slots. Visual inspection can also help.

CABLES AND CONNECTORS

Cables that connect a device to an adapter or motherboard can be tricky when reassembling a microcomputer. Inserting a cable backward into a device or adapter can damage the device, motherboard, or adapter. Some cables are **keyed** so the cable only inserts into the connector one way. However, some cables or connectors are *not* keyed.

Each cable has a certain number of pins and all cables have a **pin 1**. Pin 1 on the cable connects to pin 1 on the connector.

Pin 1 on a cable is easily identified by the colored stripe that runs down the edge of the cable.

In the unlikely event the cable is *not* easily identified, both ends of the cable should be labeled with either a number 1 or 2 on one side or a higher number, such as 24, 25, 49, 50, etc., on the other end. Pins 1 and 2 are always on the same end of a cable. If you find a higher number, pin 1 is on the opposite end. Also, the cable connector usually has an arrow etched into its molding showing the pin 1 connection. Disassembly Figure #2 shows pin 1 on a ribbon cable.

Ribbon Cable's Pin 1

**ARROW
SHOWS PIN 1
ON THE CABLE**

**STRIPE
SHOWS PIN 1
ON THE CABLE**

**ARROW
SHOWS PIN 1
ON THE CABLE**

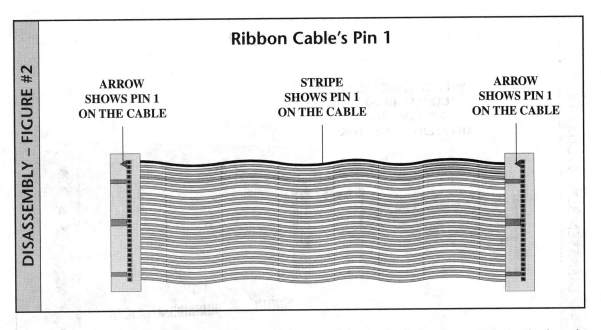

Just as all cables have a pin 1, all connectors on devices, adapters, or motherboards have a pin 1. Pin 1 on the cable inserts into pin 1 on the connector. Some manufacturers stencil a number 1 or a number 2 by the connector on the motherboard or adapter. However, on a black connector, seeing the small number is difficult. Adapter numbers are easier to distinguish. Even if the number 2 is etched beside the adapter's connector, connect the cable's pin 1 to this side. Remember that pins 1 and 2 are always on the same side whether it is on a connector or on a cable. Disassembly Figure #3 shows an example of a stenciled marking beside the adapter's connector.

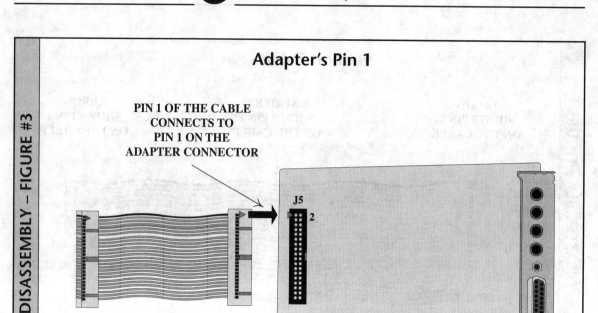

DISASSEMBLY – FIGURE #3

Adapter's Pin 1

PIN 1 OF THE CABLE
CONNECTS TO
PIN 1 ON THE
ADAPTER CONNECTOR

J5

2

Even though Disassembly Figure #3 illustrates the number 2 etched onto the adapter, other manufacturers do just the opposite; they stencil a higher number, such as 33, 34, 39, or 40, beside the opposite end of the connector.

> If a higher number is stenciled beside the connector, connect pin 1 of the cable **to the opposite end of that connector**.

Some manufacturers make connections really tough and do not put any markings on the cable connector; even so, there is a way to determine which way to connect the cable. Remove the adapter, motherboard, or device from the computer. Look where the connector solders or connects to the motherboard or adapter. Turn the adapter over. Notice the silver blobs, known as **solder joints**, on the back of the motherboard or adapter. Solder connects electronic components to the motherboard or adapter. All chips and connectors mount onto a motherboard in the same direction—all pin 1s normally orient in the same direction. The connector's solder joints are normally all round, *except for the solder joint for pin 1*! Pin 1's solder joint is square. Look for the square solder joint on the back of the connector. If the square solder joint is not apparent on the connector needle, look for other connectors or solder joints that are square. Keep in mind if one pin 1 is found, the other connectors orient in the same direction. Insert the cable so pin 1 matches the square solder joint of the connector. Disassembly Figure #4 shows a square solder joint for a connector on the back of an adapter.

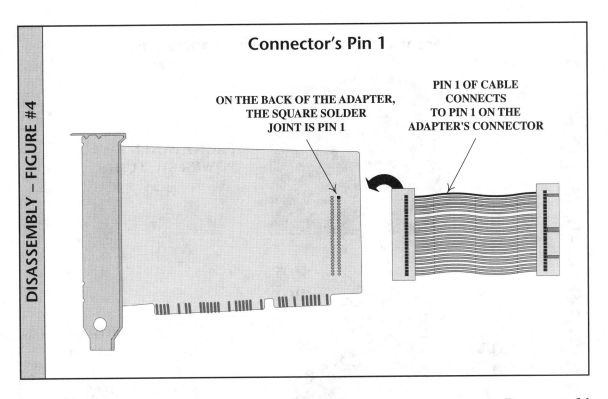

Connector's Pin 1

ON THE BACK OF THE ADAPTER, THE SQUARE SOLDER JOINT IS PIN 1

PIN 1 OF CABLE CONNECTS TO PIN 1 ON THE ADAPTER'S CONNECTOR

DISASSEMBLY – FIGURE #4

The power supply provides power to the different computer components. Be very careful when disconnecting power supply connections. Watch out for the set of cables connecting the power supply to the motherboard. Also, be very careful with any power connections from the power supply to the PC's front panel. The four wires (black, blue, white, and brown) bring AC voltage to the front panel. AC wiring has both a **hot** and a **return**. The hot and return go out to the front panel from the power supply and back into the power supply. One wire connects the hot from the power supply to the front panel. Another wire is the return side for the black. A third wire connects the hot from the power supply to the front panel and a fourth wire is the return side for it. Pushing the front panel power switch causes the wires to make a connection to the power supply. The power supply chapter covers more of this in detail.

Diagramming how the wiring attaches to the front panel is very important when reassembling. Most power supplies of this type have a wiring diagram stenciled on the top. If a technician reverses the cables, the computer can catch on fire. Disassembly Figure #5 shows an example of front panel switch wiring. Always check the power supply's documentation and color schemes before reassembling.

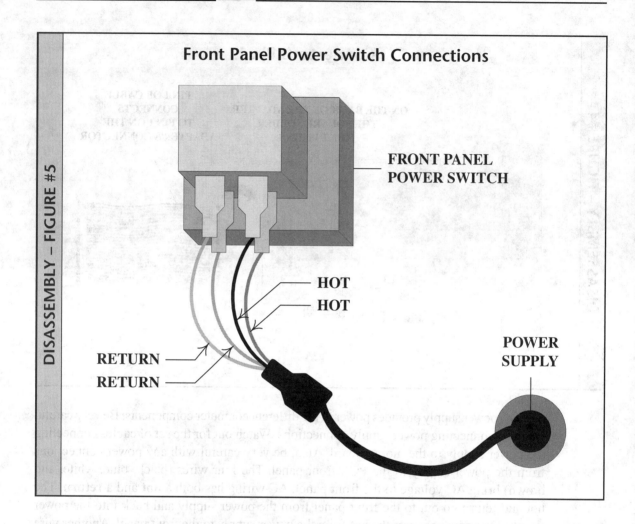

DISASSEMBLY – FIGURE #5

Front Panel Power Switch Connections

FRONT PANEL
POWER SWITCH

HOT
HOT

RETURN
RETURN

POWER
SUPPLY

HARD DRIVES

Hard drives must be handled with care when disassembling a microcomputer. Inside the hard drives are hard platters with tiny read/write heads located just millimeters above the platters. A small jolt can make the read/write heads drop down and touch the platter, causing damage to the platter and/or the read/write heads. The platter is used to store data and applications. With older hard drives, a **head parking utility** locks the heads in place away from the area where data is stored on the platter. Today's hard drives have **self-parking heads** that do not require software to make them pull away to a safe area. Instead, when the computer powers off, the heads pull away automatically. Always be careful neither to jolt nor to jar the hard drive when removing it from the computer. Even with self-parking heads, improper handling can cause damage to the hard drive. An exercise at the end of the chapter contains step-by-step directions for disassembling and reassembling a microcomputer.

PREVENTIVE MAINTENANCE

A computer should be cleaned at least once a year in a normal working environment. A computer runs longer and more efficiently if preventive maintenance is periodically undertaken. **Preventive maintenance** includes certain procedures performed to prolong the life of the computer. Some computer companies sell maintenance contracts that include a preventive maintenance program. Typical preventive measures include vacuuming the computer and cleaning floppy drive heads, keyboard keys, printers, and the monitor screen. Preventive exercises for many individual devices are described in their respective chapters. For example, the exercise that explains how to clean floppy drive heads is included as part of the floppy chapter. This section gives an overview of a preventive maintenance program and some general tips about cleaning solvents.

Repair companies frequently provide a preventive maintenance kit for service calls. The kit normally includes a portable vacuum cleaner, special vacuum cleaner bags for laser printers, a can of compressed air, a floppy head cleaning kit, urethane swabs, monitor wipes, lint-free cloths, general purpose cloths, general purpose cleanser, denatured alcohol, an anti-static brush, gold contact cleaner, and a CD cleaning kit.

The vacuum is used to suck dirt out of the inside of the computer. Some vacuum cleaners have the ability to blow air out. Vacuum first and then set the vacuum cleaner to blow. The blowing action is used to get dust out of hard to reach places. Compressed air can also be used in these situations. The floppy head cleaning kit is used to clean the read/write heads on the floppy drive. Monitor wipes are used on the front of the monitor screen. The monitor wipes with anti-static solution are best.

Do not use monitor wipes on laptop displays. A dry cloth is the best option.

Urethane swabs are used to clean between the keys on a keyboard. The general-purpose cleanser is used to clean the outside of the case (after removing the case from the computer), and to clean the desktop areas under and around the computer. Denatured alcohol is used on rubber rollers, such as those found inside printers. An anti-static brush can be used to brush dirt away from hard-to-reach places. The gold contact cleaner is used to clean adapter's contacts. If the gold contact cleaner is unavailable, some technicians use an artist or drafting eraser. This type of eraser does not leave as much residue as a pencil eraser. The gold contact cleaner is the best solution. A CD cleaning kit can include a lens cleaner that removes dust and debris from an optical lens, a disk cleaner that removes dust, dirt, fingerprints, and oils from the CD, and a scratch repair kit used to resurface, clean, and polish CDs.

When using cleaning solutions, many companies have **MSDS (Material Safety Data Sheets)** that contain information about a product, its toxicity, storage, and disposal. Your state may also have specific disposal procedures for chemical solvents.

When performing preventive maintenance, power on the computer to be certain it operates. It is a terrible feeling to perform preventive maintenance on a computer, only to power it on and find it does not work. You always wonder if the cleaning you performed caused the problem or if the computer had a problem before the preventive maintenance.

Once the computer powers up, go into Setup and copy the current settings in case the battery dies. Keep this documentation with the computer. Some technicians tape it to the inside of the case.

Power off the computer and vacuum the computer with a non-metallic attachment. Do *not* start with compressed air or by blowing dust out of the computer because the dirt and dust simply go into the air and eventually fall back into the computer and surrounding equipment. After vacuuming as much as possible, use compressed air to blow the dust out of hard-to-reach places, such as inside the power supply and under the motherboard. Inform anyone in the immediate area that they might want to leave the area if they have allergies.

If you remove an adapter from an expansion slot, replace it into the same slot. If the computer battery is on a riser board, it is best to leave the riser board connected to the motherboard so the system does not lose its configuration information. The same steps covered in the chapter's disassembly portion hold true for performing preventive maintenance.

While you perform preventive maintenance, take inventory of what is installed in the computer, such as the hard drive size, amount of RAM, available hard drive space, etc. During the maintenance procedure, communicate with the users. Ask if the computer has been giving them any trouble lately or if it has been performing adequately. Computer users like to know that you care about their computing needs. Also, users frequently ask common sense questions, such as whether sunlight or cold weather harms the computer. Always respond with answers the user can understand. For example, computers are designed to work within a range of temperatures. Any sudden change is not good for them. If a laptop computer is in a car all night and the temperature drops, then the laptop should be returned to room temperature before you power it on. It is bad for a computer to sit in direct sunlight, just as it is bad for a person to sit in the sun too long. Inside the computer case it is usually 40° hotter than outside. Direct sunlight will make a computer run hotter, which may cause a particular component to exceed its temperature rating. Users appreciate it when you explain things in terms they understand and that make sense.

The preventive maintenance call is the perfect opportunity to check the computer for viruses. Normally you would clean the computer first. Then, while the virus checker is running, you might clean external peripherals, such as printers. Preventive maintenance measures help limit computer problems as well as provide a chance to interact with customers and help with difficulty that may seem minuscule, but could worsen. In a preventive maintenance call, entry level technicians can see the different computer types and begin learning the computer components.

Name _____

DISASSEMBLY/REASSEMBLY REVIEW QUESTIONS

1. How often does a technician normally disassemble a computer?

2. If someone says that a motherboard might be *grounding out*, what does that mean?

3. If you are out on a service call without an anti-static wrist strap, how can you nevertheless reduce ESD?

4. How do you solve an RFI problem?

5. Why is it important to write down the CMOS settings before disassembling a computer?

6. Why should you *not* touch an adapter's gold contacts?

7. Which tools are usually necessary to disassemble a microcomputer?

8. Which tool is used to straighten chip leads and for removing floppy disks from drives?

9. Which tool(s) should be avoided if a screw inadvertently rolls under the motherboard?

10. What can be done if a screw drops and rolls under the motherboard?

11. What does a cable being *keyed* mean?

12. How can you easily identify a ribbon cable's pin 1?

13. [T / F]   On a cable, pin 2 is on the same end as pin 1.

14. [T / F]   A square solder joint is on the opposite end from pin 1.

15. Is orienting cables a difficult task? Why or why not?

16. Why is it important to connect the hot and return wires correctly on a power supply that connects AC to the front panel power switch?

17. [T / F] Even with self-parking heads, improper handling can damage a hard drive.

18. List three common tasks performed during preventive maintenance. What is the name of the test the computer performs to check hardware each time the computer powers on?

19. List three common things found in a preventive maintenance kit.

20. [T / F] The first step in preventive maintenance is cleaning the computer with compressed air.

21. [T / F] Leaving the computer plugged in during disassembly is the best method for ensuring a good ground.

22. What is the most frustrating component of a microcomputer to remove?

23. What is the most frustrating component to install when reassembling the microcomputer?

24. How can the frustration referred to in Question 23 be avoided?

Name _____

DISASSEMBLY/REASSEMBLY FILL-IN-THE-BLANK

1. _____ is static electricity that enters an electronic component causing damage to it.

2. _____ volts need to be present before an average person can feel static electricity.

3. As little as _____ volts of static electricity can damage an electronic component.

4. _____ and _____ chips are most susceptible to ESD strikes.

5. An _____ connects a technician to the computer and places both at the same potential.

6. An anti-static wrist strap should not be used when working inside a _____.

7. Random noise caused by a pencil sharpener that interferes with a computer speaker is an example of _____.

8. All home computers should adhere to the FCC _____ specification.

9. Before you disassemble a computer, make note of the _____ settings.

10. A _____ tool is used for screws or small parts dropped during disassembly/reassembly.

11. No toolkit is complete without an _____.

12. The plastic connectors on the bottom of the motherboard are _____.

13. Cable pin numbers _____ and _____ are always toward the cable's stripe.

14. The power supply connections to the front panel are called the _____ and the
    _____.

15. Most power supplies have a _____ stenciled on top.

16. Hard drives that do not need to execute special software before moving a computer
    are said to have _____.

17. Measures taken to prolong the life of computer components are collectively known
    as _____.

18. The _____ contains information about how to dispose of a particular chemical
    solvent.

19. A _____ can include a lens cleaner, scratch repair kit, and disk cleaner.

Name _____

PERFORMING MAINTENANCE ON AN ANTI-STATIC WRIST STRAP

Objective: To understand how to care for and properly use an anti-static wrist strap

Parts: Anti-static wrist strap
Computer chassis

Electrostatic discharge (ESD) has great potential to harm the electronic components inside a computer. Given this fact, it is vitally important that you practice proper ESD precautions when working inside a computer case. One tool you can use to prevent ESD is an anti-static wrist strap. This tool channels any static electricity from your body to the computer's chassis, where it is dissipated safely.

To use and maintain an anti-static wrist strap, follow these steps:

Step 1.   Examine the wrist strap for any obvious defects such as worn or broken straps, loose grounding lead attachments, dirt or grease buildup, etc.

Step 2.   If necessary, remove any dirt or grease buildup from the wrist strap, paying close attention to the electrical contact points such as the wrist contact point, the ground lead attachment point, and the computer chassis attachment clip. Use denatured alcohol to clean these contact points.

Step 3.   If possible, use a multimeter to check continuity between the wrist contact point and the computer chassis attachment clip. A reading of zero ohms of resistance indicates a good electrical pathway.

Question 1:   How many volts of static electricity does it take to harm a computer's electrical components?

Step 4.   Adjust the wrist strap so it fits snugly yet comfortably around your wrist. Ensure that the wrist contact is in direct contact with your skin, with no clothing, hair, etc. being in the way.

Step 5.   Attach the ground lead to the wrist strap, and ensure it snaps securely into place.

Step 6.   Attach the computer chassis attachment clip to a clean metal attachment point on the computer chassis.

Step 7.   Any static electricity generated or attracted by your body will now be channeled through the anti-static wrist strap to the computer chassis, where it will be safely dissipated.

Question 2:   How many volts will an ESD be before you will feel it?

_____

Question 3:   Should you use an anti-static wrist strap when working inside a monitor?

_____

_____ *Instructor's Initials*

Name _____

COMPUTER DISASSEMBLY/REASSEMBLY EXERCISE

Objective: To disassemble and reassemble a microcomputer correctly

Parts: A computer to disassemble
             A toolkit
             An anti-static wrist strap (if possible)

Note: Observe proper ESD handling procedures when disassembling and reassembling a microcomputer.

Step 1.   Gather the proper tools needed to disassemble the computer.

Step 2.   Clear as much workspace as possible around the computer.

Step 3.   Power on the computer, go into Setup, and write down or print all configuration information. Use the space below to write down the configuration. Pay particular attention to the hard drive type information.

Question 1:   Why is it important to write down the configuration information of any computer that is disassembled?

Step 4.   Turn the computer and all peripherals *off*. Remove the power cable.

Step 5.   Note where the monitor cable plugs into the back of the computer. Disconnect the monitor including the power cord, and move it to a safe place. Write any notes in the space below.

External Cables

Step 6.   Remove all external cables from the back of the computer. Take notes on the location of each cable. Move the peripheral devices to a safe place. Use the space below for any notes regarding external cables.

Question 2:   Did the mouse cable connect to the motherboard or to an adapter?

Computer Case Removal

Step 7. Remove the computer case. Use the space below to diagram the screw locations. Keep the cover screws separate from other screws. An egg carton or a container with small compartments makes an excellent screwholder. Label each compartment and reuse the container.

Adapter Placement

Step 8. Use Disassembly Exercise Figure #1 to indicate the placement of each adapter in the slots. Make any additions, deletions, or modifications to the drawing as they apply to the system being disassembled. If necessary, make a new drawing.

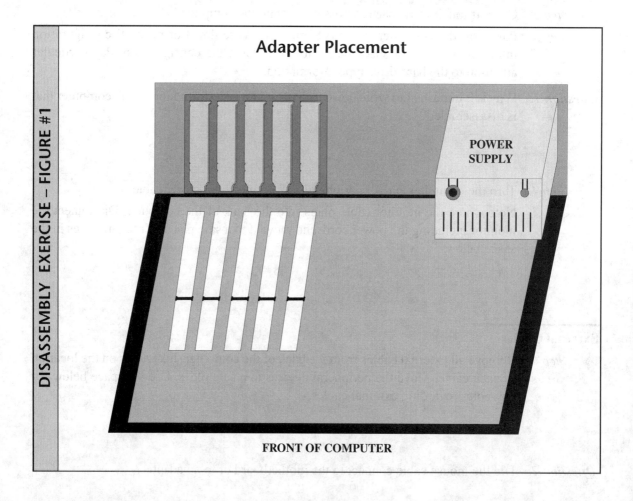

DISASSEMBLY EXERCISE – FIGURE #1

Adapter Placement

POWER SUPPLY

FRONT OF COMPUTER

Step 9. Use Disassembly Exercise Figure #2 to draw the internal cable connections *before* removing any adapters or cables from the computer. Make notes regarding how and where the cable connects to the adapter. Do not forget to include cables that connect to the motherboard or to the computer case. Modify the drawing as necessary or create a new one.

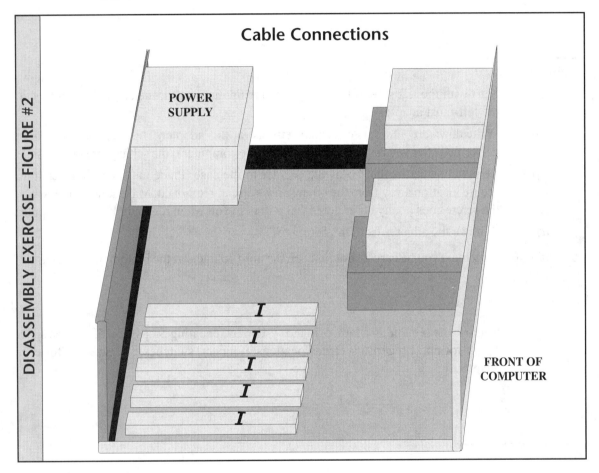

Question 3: List some ways to determine the location of pin 1 on an adapter or cable.

Internal Cable Removal

Step 10. Remove all internal cables. Make appropriate notes below for the cable connections. Some students find that labeling the cables and their associated connectors makes reassembly much easier. However, a few notes usually suffice.

Adapter Removal

Step 11. Start with the left side of the computer (facing the front of the computer) and locate the left-most adapter.

Step 12. Write down any jumpers or switch settings for this adapter. This step may need to be performed after you remove the board from the computer if the settings are inaccessible.

Step 13. Remove the screw that holds the adapter to the case. Place the screw in a separate, secure location away from the other screws already removed. Make notes about where the screw goes or any other notes that will help you when reassembling the computer.

Step 14. Remove the adapter from the computer.

Question 4: Why must you be careful not to touch the gold contacts at the bottom of each adapter?

Step 15. Remove the remaining adapters in the system by repeating Steps 12–15. Use the space below for notes regarding screw locations, jumpers, switches, and so forth for each adapter.

Drives

Step 16. Remove all power connections to drives, such as hard drives, floppy drives, CD-ROM drives, etc. Use Disassembly Exercise Figure #3 and the space below to note the placement of each drive and each cable, and any reminders needed for reassembly.

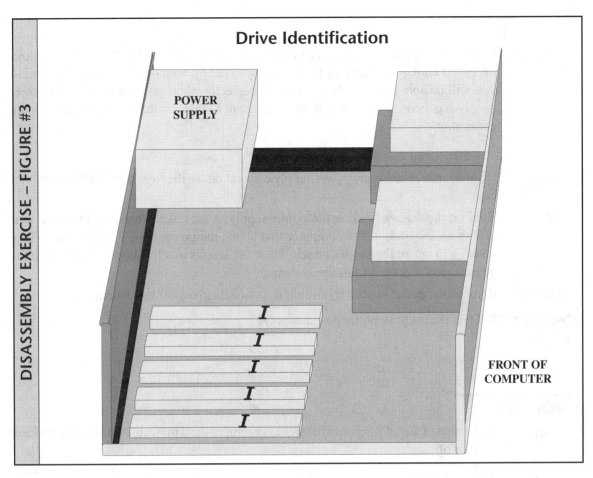

Step 17. Remove any screws holding the disk drives in place. In the space below, make notes as to where these screws go. Keep the disk drive screws separate from earlier removed screws.

Step 18. Remove all disk drives.

Question 5: Why must you be careful handling a hard drive?

Power Supply

Step 19. Remove the connectors that connect the power supply to the motherboard. Also remove the power cord going from the power supply to the AC wall outlet. Make notes here so you will be able to insert the connectors correctly when reassembling. If the power supply has connections to a front panel switch, make notes regarding the switch connections.

Step 20. If applicable, remove any power supply connections to the front panel of the computer case.

Step 21. Remove the screws holding the power supply to the case. Normally, there are four screws on the back of the computer that attach the power supply to the case. Make notes as to where the screws attach. Place the screws in a location separate from the other screws removed from the system.

Step 22. Remove the power supply by sliding it toward the front of the computer.

Question 6: What is the purpose of the power supply?

Motherboard

Step 23. Make note of any motherboard switches or jumpers and indicate if the switch position is on or off.

Question 7: What is the importance of documenting switches and jumpers on the motherboard?

Step 24. Remove any remaining connectors *except* those that connect a battery to the motherboard. Use the space below to write notes.

Step 25. Remove any screws that hold the motherboard to the case. Place these screws in a different location from the other screws removed from the system. Write any notes below pertaining to the motherboard screws.

Step 26.   Remove the motherboard. Write any notes pertaining to the motherboard removal in the space below. The computer case should be empty after you complete this step.

_____*Instructor's Initials*

Reassembly

Step 27.   Reassemble the computer by reversing the steps for disassembly. Pay particular attention to cable orientation when reinstalling cables. Refer to your notes. The first step is to install the motherboard in the computer case and reconnect all motherboard connections and screws.

Step 28.   Install the power supply by attaching all screws that hold the power supply in the case. Attach the power connectors to the motherboard. Attach any power connectors to the front panel. Refer to your notes for Steps 20, 21, and 22.

Step 29.   Install all drives by attaching screws, cables, and power connectors. Refer to your notes for Steps 17 and 18. Attach any cables that connect the drive to the motherboard. Refer to your notes from Step 10 and in Disassembly Exercise Figure #2.

Step 30.   Install all adapters beginning with the one closest to the power supply and working toward the outside of the case. Attach all screws and cables from the adapter to the connecting device. Refer to your previous notes and diagrams.

Step 31.   Connect any external connectors to the computer. Refer to previously made notes when necessary.

Step 32.   Replace the computer cover.

Step 33.   Reinstall the computer's power cable.

Step 34.   Once the computer is reassembled, power on all external peripherals and the computer.

Question 8:   Did the computer power on with POST error codes? If so, recheck all diagrams, switches, and cabling. Also, check a similar computer model that still works to see if you made a diagramming error. A chapter on logical troubleshooting comes later in the book. However, at this point in the course, the most likely problem is with a cable connection or with an adapter not seated properly into its socket.

_____ *Instructor's Initials*

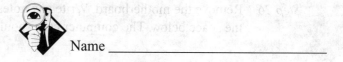

Name _____

INTERNET DISCOVERY

Objective: To obtain specific information on the Internet regarding a computer or its associated parts

Parts: Access to the Internet

You have a customer who owns a Dell OptiPlex GX1p. Please answer Questions 1 through 12.

Question 1:   Does the computer come with a NIC adapter or is it built into the motherboard?

Question 2:   How many externally accessible drive bays does a minitower have?

Question 3:   How many internally accessible drive bays does a minitower have?

Question 4:   Does the computer use gold, tin (or both) contact DIMM memory modules?

Question 5:   How many PCI motherboard connectors share an expansion slot with ISA connectors in a minitower?

Question 6:   What type of battery is installed on the motherboard?

Question 7:   What is the recommended room temperature for operating the computer?

Question 8:   Which microprocessors are supported on the GX1p?

Question 9:   Which type of microprocessor slot is on the motherboard?

Question 10:   Which chipset does the motherboard use?

Question 11:   How many DMA channels does the motherboard provide?

Question 12:   How many interrupt levels are provided?

NOTES

5

Chapter 5:

Basic Electronics and Power

OBJECTIVES

After completing this chapter you will

- Understand basic electronic terms that relate to computer support.
- Be able to perform basic checks, such as voltage and continuity.
- Understand the purpose of a power supply.
- Be able to connect a power supply to the front panel (if necessary), motherboard, and devices.
- Know the power supply output voltages.
- Recognize different power connectors.
- Know the reasons to upgrade or replace a power supply.
- Be able to solve power problems.
- Know the purpose of different power protection devices.
- Know what to do in case of an electrical fire.

KEY TERMS

AC	hot	spike
AC circuit tester	joule dissipation capacity	SPS
ACPI	line conditioner	square wave
amp	modem isolator	surge
APM	Molex connector	surge protector
ATX12V	MOV	TVS rating
Berg connector	ohm	Type A-B-C fire extinguisher
blackout	overvoltage	Type C fire extinguisher
brownout	phone line isolator	undervoltage
capacitor	power	UPS
clamping speed	power good signal	volt
clamping voltage	resistance	voltage
continuity	return	Wake on LAN
current	sag	Wake on Ring
DC	sine wave	watt

BASIC ELECTRONICS OVERVIEW

A technician needs to know a few basic electronic terms and concepts when testing components. The best place to start is with electricity. There are two types of electricity: AC and DC. The electricity provided by a wall outlet is **AC (Alternating Current)** and the type of electricity used by computer components is **DC (Direct Current)**. Devices such as radios, TVs, and toasters use AC power. Low voltage DC power is used for the computer's internal components or anything powered by batteries. The computer's power supply converts AC electricity from the wall outlet to DC for the internal components. Electricity is nothing more than electrons flowing through a conductor, just as water runs through a pipe. With AC, the electrons flow alternately in both directions. With DC, the electrons flow in only one direction.

ELECTRONIC TERMS

Voltage, current, power, and resistance are common electronic terms used in the computer industry. **Voltage** is measured in **volts** and is a measure of the pressure pushing electrons through a circuit. A power supply's output is measured in volts. Power supplies typically put out +5 volts, –5 volts, +12 volts, and –12 volts. Newer power supplies output +3.3 volts. The term *volts* is also used to describe voltage from a wall outlet. The wall outlet voltage is normally 120VAC (120 volts AC). Exercises at the end of the chapter teach you how to take voltage readings.

Polarity is the condition of being positive or negative with respect to some reference point.

Polarity is only important when measuring DC voltage. For example, when a technician measures the voltage coming out of a power supply, the black meter lead (which is negative) connects to the black wire from the power supply (which is ground). The red meter lead connects to either the +5 or +12 volt wires from the power supply.

The reading on the meter could be the opposite of what it should be if the meter's leads are reversed. Since electrons flow from one area where there are many of them (negative polarity) to an area where there are few electrons (positive polarity), polarity shows which way an electric current will flow. Polarity is not important when measuring AC.

Monitors and power supplies have voltage levels that can be dangerous. Monitors can have up to 35,000 volts going to the back of the CRT. 120 volts AC is present inside the power supply. Power supplies and monitors have capacitors inside them. A **capacitor** is a component that holds a charge even after the computer is turned off. Capacitors inside monitors can hold a charge for several hours after the monitor has been powered off. Capacitance is measured in *farads*.

Monitors require high voltage meters and special precautions. Do not work inside a monitor unless you have special training.

Another important consideration when taking voltage readings is to set the meter for the correct type of current. The AC voltage setting is for alternating current and the DC voltage setting is for direct current. Meters may have different symbols for AC and DC voltage, but the common symbol found on a meter for AC voltage is as follows:

$\sim$ or $\sim_V$

The common meter symbol for DC voltage is as follows:

$-$ or $\cdots$ or $\overline{V}$

Always refer to the meter's documentation if you are unsure of the symbols. Know whether you are measuring AC or DC voltage and set the meter to the appropriate setting. Also note that some meters have voltage ranges (such as 0-10V, 0-100V, etc.) that must be set *before* taking a measurement.

> When measuring an unknown voltage, set the meter to the highest setting before taking any readings. The meter may be damaged if it is set to a low range and the measured voltage is a much higher level.

Current is measured in **amps (amperes)**, which is the number of electrons going through a circuit every second. In the water pipe analogy, voltage would be how much pressure is applied to force the water through the pipe and current would be the amount of water flowing. Every device needs a certain amount of current to operate. The power supply is rated for the amount of total current (in amps) it can supply at each voltage level. For example, a power supply could be rated at 20 amps for the 5-volt level and 8 amps for the 12-volt level.

Power is measured in **watts**, which is how much electrical work is being done. Power is found by multiplying volts by amps. Power supplies are described as providing a maximum number of watts. This is the sum of all outputs: for example, 5 volts x 20 amps (100 watts) plus 12V x 8 amps (96 watts) equals 196 watts.

> A technician needs to replace a power supply with one that provides an equal or greater amount of power. Not all power supplies are the same. Search the Internet for power supply reviews. A general rule of thumb is that if two power supplies are equal in wattage, the heavier one is better because it uses a bigger transformer, bigger heat sinks, and more quality components.

> Always unplug an ATX power supply before working inside the computer. The ATX power supply provides power to the motherboard, even if the computer is powered off.

An exercise at the end of the chapter helps you understand how current and power relate to a technician's job.

Resistance is measured in **ohms**, the amount of opposition to current in an electronic circuit. The resistance range on a meter can be used to check continuity or whether a fuse is good. A conductor in a cable or a good fuse will have very low resistance to electricity (close to zero ohms). A broken wire or a bad fuse will have very high resistance (millions of ohms, sometimes shown as infinite ohms). A **continuity** check is used to determine if a wire has a break in it. For example, a cable is normally made up of several wires that go from one connector to another. If you were to measure the continuity from one end of a wire to the other, it should show no resistance. If the wire has a break in it, the meter shows infinite resistance. Power Figure #1 show an example of a good wire reading and a broken wire reading.

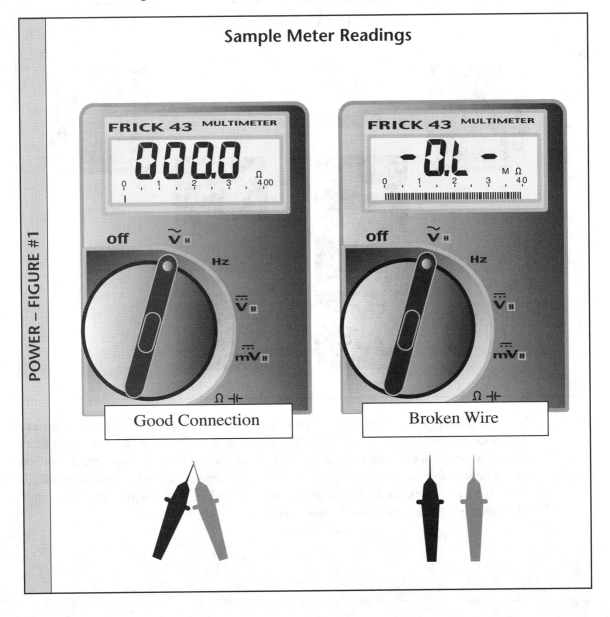

POWER – FIGURE #1

Sample Meter Readings

Good Connection

Broken Wire

When checking continuity, the meter is placed on the ohms setting as shown in Power Figure #1. The ohms setting is usually illustrated by an omega symbol (W).

Polarity is not important when performing a continuity check. Either meter lead (red or black) can be placed at either end of the wire. However, you do need a pin-out (wiring list) for the cable before you can check continuity. Pin 3 at one end of the cable does not always connect to pin 3 at the other end. Power Figure #2 shows a 25-pin to 25-pin serial cable.

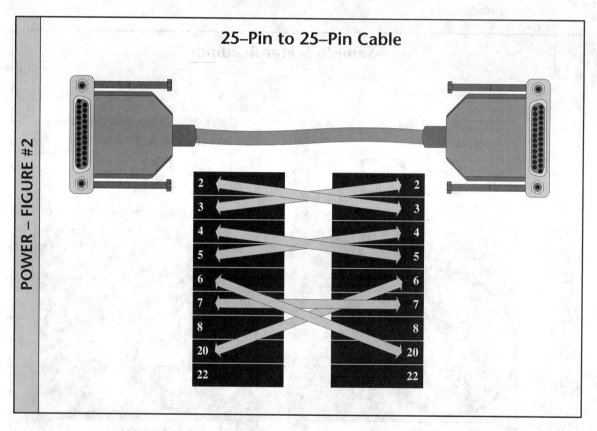

POWER – FIGURE #2

25–Pin to 25–Pin Cable

2	2
3	3
4	4
5	5
6	6
7	7
8	8
20	20
22	22

Notice in Power Figure #2 that all 25 pins are not used. Also notice how pin 2 on the left connector connects to pin 3 on the right connector. If you were to measure continuity using pin 2 on both ends, you would see infinite resistance. This *would not* mean that you have a faulty cable or a broken wire. To measure continuity, touch one of the meter's leads to the left connector's pin 2; then touch the other meter lead to the right connector's pin 3. The same technique is used for the other wires.

Sometimes a pin on one connector is wired to two or more pins on the other end. To perform a continuity check in this situation, touch one meter lead to the pin number on the first connector. Touch the other meter lead to one of the second connector's pins. Check the continuity. Move the meter lead to the other pins that connect to the first connector's pins. Do continuity checks on each pin that connects to the first connector's pin.

If you know a cable works, but you do not know how it is wired, you can create your own pin diagram. For example, a cable has a 25-pin connector at both ends, one labeled Connector A and the other labeled Connector B. On a piece of paper, write a vertical column of numbers from 1 to 25. Label the column "Connector A." Write a corresponding column of numbers directly across from the first column. Label the new column "Connector B." Touch a meter lead to Connector A's pin 1. Touch the other meter lead to every one of Connector B's pins. Each pin that shows zero resistance is a connection. Document your findings on your diagram. An exercise at the end of the chapter steps you through this method.

Some connectors have small pin connections. Use a thin meter probe or insert a thin wire, such as a paper clip, into the hole and touch the meter to the wire to take your reading.

The same concept of continuity applies to fuses. A fuse has a tiny wire inside it that extends from end to end. The fuse is designed so that the wire melts (breaks) if too much current flows through it. The fuse keeps excessive current from damaging electronic circuits or starting a fire.

A fuse is rated for a particular amount of current. For example, a 5-amp fuse protects a circuit if the amount of current exceeds 5 amps.

Never replace a fuse with one that has a higher amperage rating. You could destroy electronic circuits or cause a fire by allowing too much current to be passed by the fuse, defeating the fuse's purpose.

Take the fuse out of the circuit before testing it. A fuse that is good has a meter reading of 0 ohms. A fuse that is blown shows a meter reading of infinite ohms. A technician must sometimes check a fuse and an exercise at the end of this chapter shows how.

A technician needs to be familiar with basic electronic terms and checks. Power Table #1 consolidates this information.

Basic Electronics

Term	Value	Usage
Voltage	Volts	Checking AC voltage on a wall outlet (typically 120VAC). Checking the DC output voltage from a power supply (typically +/- 12 and +/-5VDC)
Current	Amps (Amperes)	Each device needs a certain amount of current to operate. The power supply is rated for total current in amps for each voltage level (such as 20 amps for 5 volt power and 8 amps for 12 volt power).
Resistance	Ohms	Resistance is the amount of opposition there is to electric current. Resistance is used to check continuity on cables and fuses. A cable that shows little or no resistance has no breaks in it. A fuse that shows no resistance is a good fuse. If a cable has a break in it or if a fuse is bad, the resistance is infinite.
Wattage	Watts	Watts is a measure of power and is derived by multiplying amps by volts. Power supply output is measured in watts. Also, UPSs are rated in Volt-Amps. The size of UPS purchased depends on how many devices plug in to it.

POWER – TABLE #1

POWER SUPPLY OVERVIEW

The power supply is an essential component within the computer; no other internal computer devices work without it. The power supply converts AC to DC, distributes lower voltage DC power to components throughout the computer, and provides cooling through the use of a fan located inside the power supply. The power supply is sometimes a source of unusual problems. The effects of the problems can range from those not noticed by the user to those that shut down the system.

There are two basic types of power supplies: switching and linear (constant voltage). The type a computer uses is a switching power supply. It provides efficient power to all the computer's internal components (and possibly to some external ones like USB devices). It also generates minimum heat and comes in relatively small sizes. A switching power supply requires a load (something attached to it) in order to operate properly. With today's power supplies, a motherboard is usually a sufficient load, but always check the power supply's specifications to be sure.

> Do not power on a power supply without connecting to the motherboard and possibly a device such as a floppy or hard drive. An ATX power supply usually requires only a motherboard connection. Powering on a power supply without anything attached could damage that power supply.

Frequently, technicians overlook the power supply when troubleshooting. For example, suppose a new computer will not boot. The POST error code indicates a hard drive problem. The problem does not go away after the technician puts in a new hard drive. The technician replaces the hard drive cable connected to the motherboard; the problem does not go away. The motherboard is replaced and the computer finally boots. Two days later the same problem returns. Finally, after trying everything else, the technician swaps the power supply and the problem is fixed. Connecting the power supply to the various components, identifying the different types of power connectors, knowing what to look for when upgrading a power supply, and troubleshooting power supply problems are all important skills for a technician.

POWER SUPPLY FORM FACTORS

Just as motherboards come in different shapes and sizes, so do power supplies. The older power supplies were known as PC/XT, AT, AT/Tower, and Baby AT. Today's most common power supply form factors are LPX, SFX, and ATX. The LPX power supply is used with LPX motherboards. The SFX (Small Form Factor) power supply is used with MicroATX motherboards. The ATX power supply is the most common and is used with ATX, MicroATX, and NLX motherboards. Power Table #2 summarizes power supply form factors.

Power Supply Form Factors

Power Supply Form Factor	Motherboards
PC/XT	PC and XT
AT	AT Desktop
AT/Tower	AT Tower
Baby AT	Baby AT and AT Desktop
LPX	LPX
SFX	MicroATX
ATX	ATX, MicroATX, and NLX

POWER – TABLE #2

Because of higher power requirements for newer processors, AMD now certifies specific power supplies that can handle their Athlon products. Intel's Pentium 4 requires a minimum of at least 250 watts from the power supply and also requires a specific type of ATX power supply known as an **ATX12V.** This power supply has a new 4-pin connection to the motherboard and provides extra +12 volts. Some ATX power supply manufacturers make a two-row, six-pin connector that provides additional +5 and +3.3 volts to the motherboard. These voltages are used to monitor and control the CPU's cooling fan, monitor the 3.3V signal to the motherboard, provide power and grounding to IEEE1394 (FireWire) devices, and allow the operating system and motherboard to monitor and control the fan. The connector looks very similar to one of the old motherboard power connectors. A web site containing information in this area is www.formfactors.org.

PURPOSES OF A POWER SUPPLY

The power from a wall outlet is high voltage AC. The type of power computers need is low voltage DC. All computer parts (the electronic chips on the motherboard and adapters, the electronics on the drives, and the motors in the floppy drive, hard drive, and CD-ROM drive) need DC power to operate. One purpose of the power supply is to convert AC to DC so the computer has proper power to run its components.

Power supplies with a switch on the front panel have a cable that connects AC directly to the front panel switch with four color-coded wires. Be very careful with these connectors. AC wiring has both a hot and a return. The blue and brown wires connect the 110VAC to the switch. These wires are dangerous if the power supply is plugged into the wall outlet.

Disconnect the 120V AC cable from the wall outlet to the power supply when connecting the power supply's wires to the front panel.

The black and white wires bring the AC back to the power supply. The black and white wires should be dangerous only when the power supply is connected to the wall outlet *and* the front panel switch is turned on (pushed in). Some power supplies have a fifth wire, usually green or green striped. This wire is a safety ground and attaches to the computer case or designated ground.

When connecting the power supply wires to the front panel, the brown and blue wires are normally across from one another and the black and white wires are normally across from one another. Keep in mind that power supply manufacturers can wire the connections differently, so look at the documentation, which is frequently located on the top of the power supply. If you reverse the AC connections, the computer can catch on fire. 120V AC power can kill you if you do something that allows it to pass through your body from arm to arm or arm to leg. Some pointers for you to keep in mind: keep one hand in your pocket when working around AC power; wear rubber soled shoes; be sure the floor around your workspace is dry. Power Figure #3 shows a sample front panel switch connection.

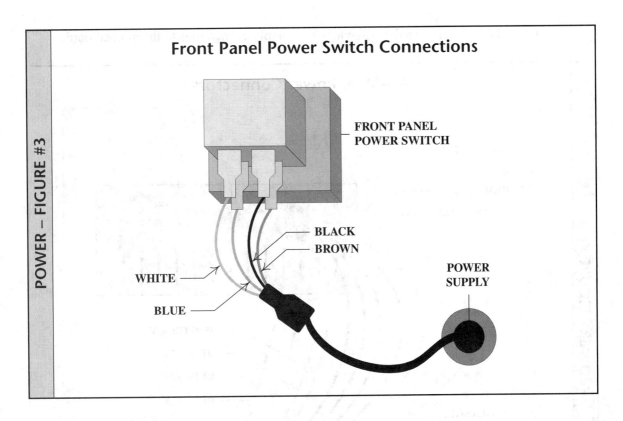

POWER – FIGURE #3

Front Panel Power Switch Connections

FRONT PANEL POWER SWITCH

BLACK
BROWN
WHITE
BLUE
POWER SUPPLY

The ATX power supply does not connect to the front panel switch as the AT-style power supplies do in tower computers. With the ATX power supply, a connection from the front panel switch to the motherboard simply provides a 5-volt signal that allows the motherboard to tell the power supply to turn on. This 5-volt signal allows ATX power supplies to support APM (Advanced Power Management), which is covered later in the chapter, and also lets the motherboard and operating system control the power supply. Some ATX power supplies do not have external on/off switches. Instead, the operating system powers down the computer.

If an ATX power switch is present and in the *off* position, the motherboard and operating system cannot turn the power supply on.

Another purpose of the power supply is to distribute proper DC voltage to each component. Coming out of the power supply are several cables with connectors. In older computers, two power supply connectors plug directly to the AT-style motherboard to provide DC power to the motherboard's components. Other connectors supply power to the hard drive, CD-ROM, floppy drive, and so forth.

With AT-style motherboards, the power supply's black wires must be placed next to each other in the center of the P8 and P9 connectors when plugged into the motherboard.

Power Figure #4 shows the AT-style power supply connections to the motherboard.

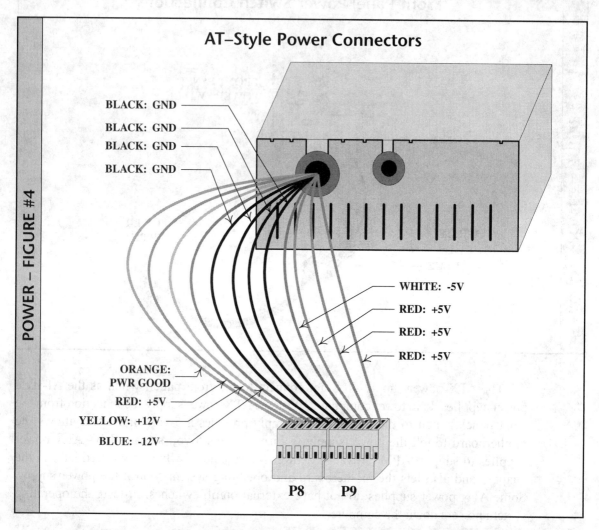

AT–Style Power Connectors

POWER – FIGURE #4

BLACK: GND
BLACK: GND
BLACK: GND
BLACK: GND

WHITE: -5V
RED: +5V
RED: +5V
RED: +5V

ORANGE:
PWR GOOD
RED: +5V
YELLOW: +12V
BLUE: -12V

P8   P9

When connecting the power supply to the motherboard, insert the connectors properly or the motherboard may be damaged when the computer is powered on. Look at the power connectors that attach to the motherboard, and notice that each connector has differently colored wires. Also, notice that both connectors have black wires.

Notice in Power Figure #4 how +5, -5, +12, and -12 volts are supplied to the motherboard. The motherboard itself normally uses +5 volts. If the motherboard has integrated serial ports, they sometimes use +12- and -12-volt power. The ISA bus specified that -5 volts be supplied to the ISA connectors, but ISA adapters rarely use -5-volt power anymore.

With ATX motherboards, there is only one 20-pin connector. The power connector inserts only one way into the motherboard connector. With the ATX-style power supply,

+3.3 volt power can be delivered to the motherboard for AGP, PCI adapters, DIMMs, some serial ports, some laptop cooling fans, and motherboard components. The other voltages, +5V, –5V, +12V, and –12V, are also supplied. Power Figure #5 shows the ATX power supply connections.

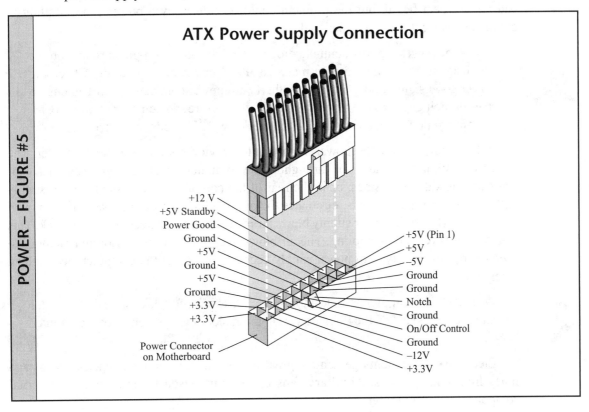

POWER – FIGURE #5

ATX Power Supply Connection

+12 V
+5V Standby
Power Good
Ground
+5V
Ground
+5V
Ground
+3.3V
+3.3V

Power Connector
on Motherboard

+5V (Pin 1)
+5V
–5V
Ground
Ground
Notch
Ground
On/Off Control
Ground
–12V
+3.3V

Notice in Power Figure #5 how the power cable is only one connector, notched so the cable inserts only one way into it. This is a much better design than older power supplies when two connectors were used and they could be reversed. Also, notice in both Power Figure #4 and Power Figure #5 that a **power good signal** goes to the motherboard. When the computer is turned on, part of POST is to allow the power supply to run a test on each of the voltage levels. The voltage levels must be correct before any other devices are tested and allowed to initialize. If the power is OK, a power good signal is sent to the motherboard. If the power good signal is not sent from the power supply, a timer chip on the motherboard resets the microprocessor. Once a power good signal is sent, the microprocessor begins executing software from the BIOS.

A high-quality power supply delays sending the power good signal until all of the power supply's voltages have a chance to stabilize. Some cheap power supplies do not delay the power good signal. Other cheap power supplies do not provide the power good circuitry at all, but instead, tie five volts to the signal, sending a "power good" even when it is not there.

If a computer does not boot properly, but when you press *CTRL+ALT+DEL* the computer *does* boot, the power good signal is the likely problem. Some motherboards are more sensitive to the power good signal than others. An example is when a motherboard has been replaced and the system does not boot. At first glance, this may appear to be a bad replacement board, but the problem could be caused by a power supply failing to output a consistent power good signal.

Check the power supply documentation to see if the power supply outputs a power good signal (rather than the normal +5 volts). Turn the computer on. Check the power good signal going into the motherboard power connector's pin 1 to ensure that it is being sent to the motherboard. Do this before replacing the motherboard. A power supply with a power good signal below +3V needs to be replaced.

A third purpose for the power supply is to provide cooling for the computer. The power supply's fan circulates air throughout the computer. Most computer cases have air vents on one side, both sides, or in the rear of the computer. The AT-style power supply pulls air through the air vents, circulates the air, and blows it out the back of the power supply. The ATX-style power supply blows air inside the case instead of out the back. This is known as reverse flow cooling. The air blows over the microprocessor and memory to keep them cool. This type of power supply keeps the inside of the computer cleaner than older styles.

Whether the computer is a desktop model, a tower model, or a desktop model mounted in a stand on the floor, be sure nothing blocks the air vents in the computer case!

Electronic components generate a great deal of heat, but are designed to withstand fairly high temperatures. Auxiliary fans can be purchased to help cool the internal components of a computer.

Be careful when installing an auxiliary fan. Place the fan so the outflow of air moves the same direction as the flow of air generated by the power supply. If an auxiliary fan is installed inside the case in the wrong location, the auxiliary airflow could work against the power supply airflow, reducing the cooling effect.

TYPES OF POWER SUPPLY CONNECTORS

Two different connectors that extend from the power supply to devices are a **Molex connector** and a **Berg connector**. Power Figure #6 shows an illustration of each.

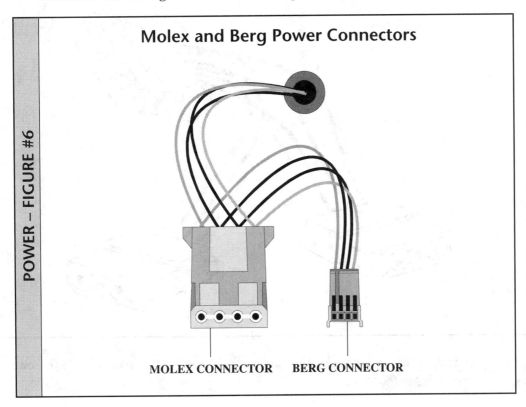

POWER – FIGURE #6

Molex and Berg Power Connectors

MOLEX CONNECTOR   BERG CONNECTOR

Most power supplies have the Molex and Berg connectors, but if a device requires a Berg connector and the only one available is a Molex, a Molex-to-Berg connector converter can be purchased. The Molex and Berg connectors coming from the power supply can connect to any device; there is *not* a specific connector for the hard drive, the floppy drive, and so forth. Also, the number of available connectors from the power supply varies among manufacturers. If there are not enough connectors from the power supply for the number of devices installed in the computer, a Y power connector can be purchased at a computer or electronics store. The Y connector adapts a single Molex connector to two Molex connectors for two devices. Verify that the power supply can output enough power to handle the extra device being installed! Power Figure #7 shows a Y power connector.

POWER – FIGURE #7

Y Power Connector

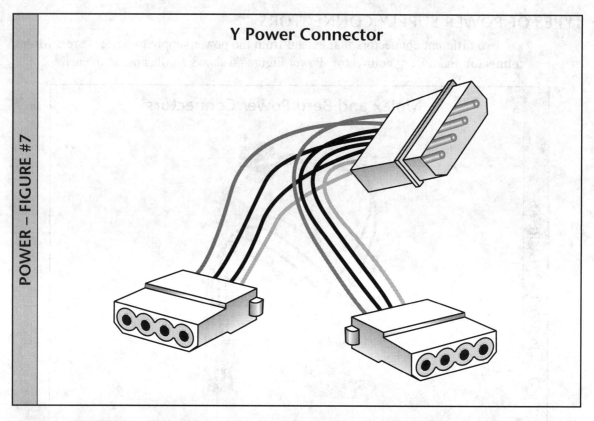

 A technician is well advised to carry a Molex-to-Berg converter and a Y power connector in the toolkit.

POWER SUPPLY VOLTAGES

The wires from the power supply carry the following levels of DC voltage: +5 volts, −5 volts, +12 volts, −12 volts, and +3.3 volts. The motherboard, as well as most adapters, uses only +5 volts. Newer motherboards have some chips that run on 3.3 volts or less. A voltage regulator on the motherboard takes the 5 volts from the power supply and reduces it, unless it is an ATX power supply and motherboard. The ATX power supply provides +3.3 volts directly to the motherboard. Devices such as the floppy drive and the hard drive use +5 volts and +12 volts. The +12 voltage is used to operate the device motors found in drives. Drives are now being made that use +5 volt motors. Chips use +5 volts and +3.3 volts. The +3.3 volts are also used for memory, PCI adapters, and some laptop fans. The negative voltages are seldom used.

A technician must occasionally check voltages in a system. There are four basic checks for power supply situations: (1) wall outlet AC voltage, (2) DC voltages going to the motherboard, (3) DC voltages going to a device via a Molex or Berg connector, and (4) ground with an outlet tester.

When checking voltages, the power supply should always have a load. Be sure the power supply connects to the motherboard and to at least one device, such as the hard drive. A motherboard is normally load enough for an ATX power supply.

A good power supply has internal circuitry that shuts it down if it is not connected to something, meaning the power supply is without a load. However, some cheap power supplies can burn up if powered on without a device or the motherboard connected. Exercises at the end of the chapter familiarize the technician with voltage checks on a microcomputer. Exercise extreme caution when taking AC voltage checks; AC voltage is high enough to harm the technician! Also, be careful when checking DC voltages. Touching the meter to two different voltages simultaneously or to a DC voltage and another circuit can damage the computer!

APM (ADVANCED POWER MANAGEMENT)

Today's computer user needs to leave the computer on for extended periods of time in order to receive faxes, run computer maintenance tasks, automatically answer the phone, download software upgrades and patches, such as for anti-virus programs. Network managers want control of their computers so they can push software upgrades out, perform backups, download software upgrades and patches, and perform tests. Laptop users have always been plagued by power management problems, such as short battery life, inconsistent handling of screen blanking, and screen blanking in the middle of presentations. This was because the BIOS controlled power. Power management has changed. APM, ACPI, and OnNow are common terms used when describing how a computer manages power.

APM (Advanced Power Management) was originally developed by Microsoft, Toshiba, and Intel. It was geared toward the portable computer market but has evolved to include all computers and operating systems. APM allows the operating system to control devices such as the hard drive and monitor when the computer is not in use. APM could not originally manage external devices' power.

APM further developed into a standard known as **ACPI (Advanced Configuration and Power Interface)**, which combines the features of APM and plug and play to give the motherboard and operating system control over various devices' power and modes of operation. Windows 98, 2000, and XP support ACPI. In order for a computer to support ACPI, the motherboard, BIOS, operating system, applications, and attached devices need to be ACPI-compliant. Microsoft maintains a list of hardware compatible with ACPI. You can also check the device manufacturer's web site. Common components that can be controlled through ACPI include the CPU, hard drive, CD-ROM, DVD, monitor, network adapter, and printer; and devices controlled through the computer, such as VCR, TV, phone, fax machine, and stereo. All ACPI user preferences are set through the operating system, although the computer must first have ACPI turned on through the system's Setup program. Microsoft calls the operating system's ability to support ACPI OnNow.

With ACPI, the user can control how the power switch operates and when power to specific devices, such as the hard drive and monitor, is lowered. For example, the Instant on/off BIOS setting can control how long the power switch is held in before the power supply turns on or off. Case temperatures, CPU temperatures, and CPU fans can be monitored. The power supply can be adjusted for power requirements. Allowing the BIOS and operating system to work together to control power and allowing the computer user to set the parameters has changed the computer environment.

ACPI has six operating states: S0 Working, S1 Sleep, S2 Sleep, S3 Sleep, S4 Hibernate, and S5 Off. There are also device ACPI states. In the S0 Working state, the computer is fully functional with no power management active. Both the Sleep and Hibernate modes are frequently called Standby mode. When in the S1 Sleep mode, the CPU is slowed or stopped and unused devices are powered down. RAM is still being refreshed. The S2 Sleep mode requires less power than the S1 Sleep mode because the CPU is not being powered. Information in RAM is still there and being refreshed and the system is restored instantly upon user intervention. In the S3 Sleep mode, the power supply is in a reduced state. S4 is known as the Hibernate mode. Information in RAM is saved to the hard disk. When a user interacts with the computer, the information is retrieved from the hard drive and the system resumes in the same state it was in at the time of the last user interaction. In the S5 Off mode, a computer is shut down through the operating system; the user must reboot the computer to use it again.

Two common BIOS and adapter features that take advantage of ACPI are Wake on LAN and Wake on Ring. The **Wake on LAN** feature allows a network administrator to control the power to a workstation remotely and directs the computer to come out of sleep mode. Software applications can also use the Wake on LAN feature to perform updates, upgrades, and maintenance tasks. The feature can also be used to bring up computers right before the business day starts. Wake on LAN can be used with web or network cameras to start recording when motion is detected or to bring a network printer up so that it can be used when needed. The **Wake on Ring** allows a computer to come out of sleep mode when the telephone rings. This lets the computer receive phone calls, faxes, and e-mails when the user is not present.

The Wake on LAN feature is enabled on adapters as well as through the motherboard for built-in network adapters. Wake on Ring is usually a pin connector on the motherboard that allows a cable connection between the motherboard and the device that uses Wake on Ring. Common BIOS settings related to ACPI are listed below.

- *Delay Prior to Thermal* defines the number of minutes the system waits to shut the system down once an overheating situation occurs.
- *CPU Warning Temperatures* specifies the CPU temperature at which a warning message is displayed on the screen.
- *ACPI Function* enables or disables ACPI. This is the preferred method for disabling ACPI in the event of a problem.

When not all devices or applications support ACPI and generate system errors, when the computer randomly goes to standby mode, or when the computer freezes coming out of standby mode, you may need to disable ACPI. The best way to do this is through the computer's Setup program. Look for the key words APM, ACPI, or Power Management. If the system still has ACPI-related problems, disable ACPI through the operating system's Power Options or Power Management control panel.

- *Soft-off* specifies the length of time a user must press the power button to turn the computer off.
- *Wake Up by PCI Card* allows the computer to wake when a PCI adapter contains the Wake on LAN feature.
- *Power on by Ring* or *Wakeup from Serial* allows the computer to wake when an adapter or external device supports Wake on Ring.
- *Wake Up on LAN* allows the computer to wake when a Wake on LAN signal is received across the network.
- *CPU THRM Throttling* allows a reduction in CPU speed when the system reaches a specific temperature.
- *Power on Function* specifies which key (or key combination) will activate the system's power.
- *Hot Key Power On* defines the keystrokes that will reactivate system power.

Sometimes when a computer comes out of Sleep mode, not all devices respond and the computer's power or reset button has to be pressed to reboot the computer. Various things can cause this to happen:

- Screen saver conflicts with ACPI.
- All adapters/devices are not ACPI-compliant.
- An adapter/device has an outdated driver.

To see if the screen saver causes the problem, use the Display control panel and set the screen saver option to None. Identifying a problem adapter, device or driver will take Internet research. Check each adapter, device, and driver one by one.

To configure power management in Windows 98, access the Power Management control panel. Under 2000 Professional, use the Power Options control panel. The Power Schemes tab allows you to configure generic settings for the computer. Power Figure #8 shows this window.

POWER – FIGURE #8

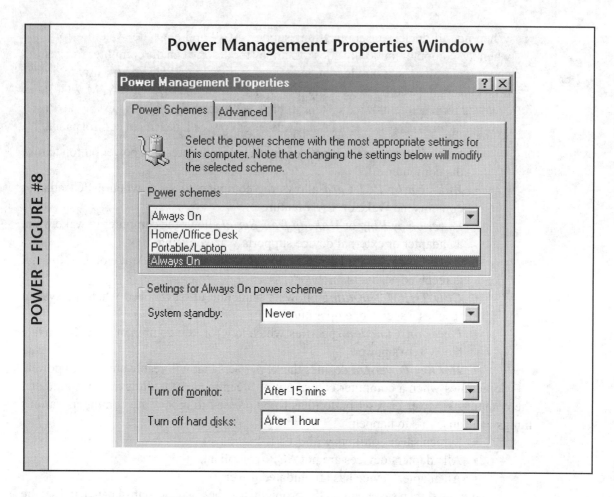

The Advanced tab in this window allows you to specify whether the power control icon appears in the taskbar, whether a password is required to bring the computer out of Standby mode, and how the computer's power and sleep buttons behave. Power Figure #9 shows the Advanced tab settings.

POWER – FIGURE #9

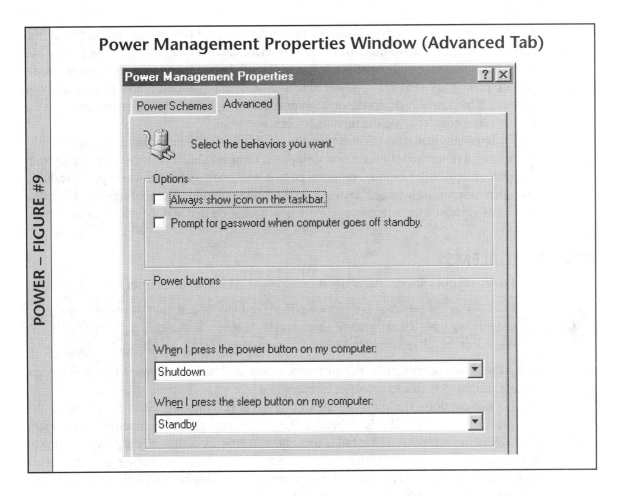

Power Management Properties Window (Advanced Tab)

If the computer does not go into the Sleep mode, check the following.

- Is ACPI enabled in BIOS?
- Disable third party TSRs. Problems often arise with anti-virus programs.
- Set the screen saver to None to see if it is causing the problem.
- Are all device drivers ACPI-compliant?
- Is power management enabled through the operating system? In Windows 98, use the Power Management control panel and in 2000 use the Power Options control panel.
- Some USB devices can cause problems. Disconnect them to see if this is the case.

REPLACING OR UPGRADING A POWER SUPPLY

Power supplies are rated in watts. Computers in use today have power supplies with ratings ranging from 250 to 300 watts, although powerful computers, such as network servers, can have power supplies rated 600 watts or higher. Each device inside the computer

uses a certain amount of power and the power supply must provide enough to run all the devices together. One example of a "not powerful enough" supply is that in a very old computer, such as an 8088 or 8086. Another potential power supply problem would be an old computer converted into a power machine with multiple hard drives and a variety of adapters. The power each device or adapter requires is defined in the documentation for the device or adapter or on the manufacturer's web site.

Different physical sizes of power supplies are available. When replacing a power supply, purchasing a power supply for a new computer, or upgrading a power supply, verify that the power supply will fit in the computer case. Also, verify that the power supply produces enough power for the installed devices and for future upgrades. Do not forget to check that the on/off switch on the new power supply is in a location that matches the computer case.

POWER PROBLEMS

Power supplies are not normally disassembled. Manufacturers often rivet them shut.

Even when the power supply can be disassembled, you should not take it apart unless you have a background in electronics. Replace the entire power supply when it is faulty; power supplies are inexpensive.

Swap the power supply, make the customer happy, and be on your way! Power problems are not usually difficult to detect or troubleshoot.

Do not overlook the most obvious power supply symptom. Start by checking the computer's power light. If it is off, check the power supply's fan by placing your palm at the back of the computer. If the fan is turning, it means the wall outlet is providing power to the computer and the technician can assume the wall outlet is functioning. An **AC circuit tester** can verify that a wall outlet is wired properly. The following troubleshooting questions help you determine the location of a power problem:

1. Has the power supply ever worked before? If not, check the 115/230 switch on the power supply and verify it is on the 115 setting.
2. Is the power supply's fan turning? If yes, go to Question 5. If not, check the wall outlet for proper AC voltages. If the wall outlet is okay, go on to Question 3.
3. Is a surge strip used? If so, check to see if the surge strip is powered on, then try a different outlet in the surge strip, or replace the surge strip.
4. Is the computer's power cord okay? Verify that the power cord plugs snugly into the outlet and into the back of the computer. Swap the power cord to verify it is functioning.
5. Are the voltages going to the motherboard at the proper level? Check the voltages to the motherboard. If they are low, something may be overloading the power supply. Disconnect the power cable to one device and check the voltages again. Replace the power cable to the device. Remove the power cable from another device and check the motherboard voltages again. Continue

doing this until the power cord for each device has been disconnected and the motherboard voltages have been checked. A single device can short out the power supply and cause the system to malfunction. Replace any device that draws down the power supply's output voltage and draws too much current. If none of the devices cause the problem, replace the power supply. If replacing the power supply does not solve the problem, replace the motherboard.

Build the computer outside the computer case, on an anti-static mat if possible. Start with only a power supply, motherboard, and speaker connected. Even though it will normally produce a POST audio error, just verify that the power supply fan will turn. Most power supplies issue a click before the audio POST beeps. Next, verify the voltages from the power supply. If the fan turns and the voltages are correct, power down the machine and add a video adapter and monitor to the system. If the machine does not work, put the video adapter in a different expansion slot and try again. If placing the video adapter in a different expansion slot does not work, swap out the video adapter.

If the video adapter works, continue adding devices one by one and checking the voltages. Just as any one device can cause the system not to operate properly, so can any one adapter. If one particular adapter causes the system to malfunction, try a different expansion slot before trying a different adapter.

If the expansion slot proves to be a problem, check the slot for foreign objects. If none are found, but the problem still occurs, place a note on the expansion slot so that no one will use it.

SYMPTOMS OF POWER SUPPLY PROBLEMS

The following list offers symptoms of a power supply problem:

- The computer's power light is off.
- The power supply fan does not turn when the computer is powered on.
- The computer sounds a continuous beep (this could also be a bad motherboard or stuck key on keyboard).
- When the computer powers on, it does not beep at all (could also be bad motherboard).
- When the computer powers on, it sounds repeating short beeps (could also be bad motherboard).
- During POST, a 02X or parity POST error code appears (where X is any number). One of the POST checks is a "power good" signal from the power supply. A 021, 022, ... error message indicates that the power supply did not pass the POST test.

LAPTOP BATTERIES

Portable computers (laptops) sometimes use a battery as their power source so this chapter is a good place to discuss battery issues. Laptop users always complain about how long their batteries last. Battery technologies have improved in the past five years, probably due to the development of more devices that need battery power, such as digital cameras, portable CDs and DVDs, and PDAs (Personal Digital Assistants).

Up until 1996, the NiCad (Nickel Cadium) battery was the most popular type of portable computer battery. NiCad batteries were said to cause a memory effect, which means that the battery could not be fully recharged if it was not fully drained before recharging. In reality, the NiCad battery memory effect is rare.

NiCad batteries have been replaced with NiMH (Nickel-Metal Hydride) batteries that are lighter because they are made with lighter metals. NiMH batteries can store up to 50 percent more power than their predecessors. These batteries are being replaced with Li-Ion (Lithium Ion) batteries, which are very light and can hold a charge longer than any other type. They are also more expensive. Many other devices, such as mobile phones and digital cameras, use Li-Ion batteries.

Li-Ion Polymer batteries are similar to Li-Ion batteries, except they are packed in pouched cells. This design allows for smaller batteries and a more efficient use of space, which is important in the portable computer and mobile device industries. For environmentalists, the zinc-air battery is the one to watch. AER Energy Resources, Inc. has several patents on a battery that uses oxygen to generate electricity. Air is allowed to flow during battery discharge and is blocked when the battery is not in use. This battery holds a charge for extended periods of time. In a mobile phone test, the battery lasted 12 hours.

ADVERSE POWER CONDITIONS

There are two adverse AC power conditions that can damage or adversely affect a computer: overvoltage and undervoltage. **Overvoltage** occurs when the output voltage from the wall outlet (the AC voltage) is over the rated amount. Normally the output of a wall outlet is 110 to 130 volts AC. When the voltage rises above 130 volts, an overvoltage condition exists. The power supply takes the AC voltage and converts it to DC. An overvoltage condition is harmful to the components because too much DC voltage destroys electronic circuits. An overvoltage condition can be a **surge** or a **spike**. A surge has a longer duration than a spike. (A surge is three or more nanoseconds whereas a spike lasts one to two nanoseconds. A nanosecond is a billionth of a second). Another name for a surge is transient voltage. Causes of surges include lightning, poorly regulated electricity, faulty wiring, and devices that turn on periodically, such as elevators, air conditioners, and refrigerators. A spike is harder to guard against than a surge because it has such short duration and high intensity.

Electric companies are offering surge protection for homes. Frequently, there are two choices. The basic package protects larger appliances, such as refrigerators, air conditioners, washers, and dryers. It allows no more than 800 volts to enter the electrical system. The premium package protects against more sensitive devices (TVs, VCRs, stereos, and computers) and reduces the amount of voltage allowed in to 323 volts or less. Some suppressors handle surges up to 20,000 volts. The exterior surge arrestor does not protect against voltage increases that originate inside the building, such as those caused by faulty wiring.

When the voltage falls below 110 volts AC, an **undervoltage** condition exists. If the voltage is too low, a computer power supply cannot provide enough power to all the components. Under these conditions, the power supply draws too much current, causing it to overheat. If the power supply overheats, its components can be weakened or damaged. An undervoltage condition is known as a brownout or sag. A **brownout** is when power circuits become overloaded. On occasion, an electric company intentionally causes a brownout to reduce the power drawn by consumers during peak periods. A **sag** occurs when the voltage from the wall outlet drops momentarily. A **blackout** is a total loss of power.

ADVERSE POWER PROTECTION

Power supplies have built-in protection against adverse power conditions. However, the best protection for a computer is to unplug it during a power outage or thunderstorm. Three devices are commonly used to protect against adverse power conditions: a surge protector, a line conditioner, or an Uninterruptable Power Supply (UPS). Each device has a specific purpose and guards against certain conditions. A technician needs to be familiar with each device to make recommendations for customers.

SURGE PROTECTORS

A **surge protector**, also known as a surge strip or surge suppressor, is commonly a six-outlet strip with built-in protection against overvoltage. Power Figure #10 shows a picture of a surge protector.

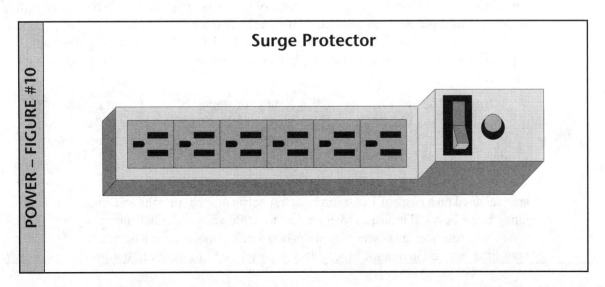

POWER – FIGURE #10

Surge Protector

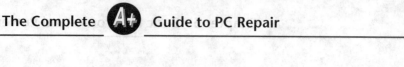
Surge protectors do not protect for the undervoltage condition; they protect against voltage increases. Most surge protectors have an electronic component called a **MOV** (**Metal Oxide Varistor**), which protects the computer or device that plugs into one of the outlets on the surge strip. The MOV is positioned between the AC coming in and the outlet into which you plug devices. When a surge occurs, the MOV takes the extra voltage and prevents it from passing to the outlets. The MOV, however, has some drawbacks. If a large surge occurs, the MOV will take the hit and be destroyed, which is better than damaging the computer. However, with smaller overvoltages, each small surge weakens the MOV. A weakened MOV might not give the proper protection to the computer if there is a bigger surge. Also, there is no simple check for the MOV's condition. Some MOVs have indicator lamps attached, but these only indicate when the MOV has been destroyed, not when it is weakened. Still, having an indicator lamp is better than nothing at all. Some surge protectors also have replaceable fuses and/or indicator lamps for the fuse. A fuse only works once and is destroyed in order to protect devices plugged into surge protector outlets.

Several surge protector features deserve consideration. **Clamping voltage** is the level at which the surge protector starts protecting the computer. **Clamping speed** is how much time elapses before that protection begins. Surge protectors cannot normally protect against power spikes (overvoltages of short duration) because of their rated clamping speed. Another feature to look at is the **joule dissipation capacity** (sometimes called energy absorption). The greater the number of joules that can be dissipated, the more effective and durable a surge protector is. A surge protector rated at 630 joules is more effective than one rated at 210 joules.

Another feature to look for in a surge protector is how fast the surge protector responds to an adverse condition. Surge protectors that respond within picoseconds (trillionths of seconds) are preferable to surge protectors that respond in nanoseconds (billionths of seconds). Also, for greater surge protection, choose a lower **Transient Voltage Suppressing (TVS) rating** (sometimes known as response time). A 330 TVS-rated surge protector is better than a 400 TVS-rated surge protector. Look for modem protection in the power strip features. This topic is covered in detail later in the chapter.

Underwriter's Laboratories developed the UL1449 standard to regulate surge suppressors—the 497A standard is for phone line protection, and the 1283 standard is for EMI/RFI.

When purchasing or recommending a surge protector, be sure it conforms to the UL1449 standard and has a MOV status lamp. Also, check to see if the vendor offers to repair or replace the surge protected equipment in the event of damage during a surge.

The federal government designates surge suppressor grades—A, B, and C. Suppressors are evaluated on a basis of 1,000 surges at a specific number of volts and amps. A Class A rating is the best and indicates tolerance up to 6,000 volts and 3,000 amps.

Surge protectors are not the best protection for a computer system because most provide very little protection against other adverse power conditions. Even the good ones only protect against overvoltage conditions. Those with the UL 1449 rating and a MOV status lamp are usually more expensive. Unfortunately, people tend to put their money into their computer parts, not the protection of those parts.

LINE CONDITIONERS

An alternative for computer protection is the line conditioner. **Line conditioners**, sometimes known as power conditioners, are more expensive than surge protectors, but do protect the computer from overvoltages, undervoltages, and adverse noise conditions over electrical lines. The line conditioner monitors AC electricity. If the voltage is too low, a line conditioner boosts voltage to the proper range. If the voltage level is too high, a line conditioner clamps the voltage down and sends the proper amount to the computer.

Be careful not to plug too many devices into a line conditioner. A line conditioner is rated for a certain amount of current. Laser printers, for example, can draw a great deal of current (up to 15 amps). Some line conditioners are not rated to handle these devices. Because laser printers draw so much current, if a computer and a laser printer are on the same electrical circuit, that circuit should be wired to a 20-amp circuit breaker. Most outlets are on 20-amp breakers in today's buildings.

UNINTERRUPTABLE POWER SUPPLY (UPS)

A **UPS** (**Uninterruptable Power Supply**), sometimes called online UPS or true UPS, provides power to a computer or device for a limited amount of time when there is a power outage. The UPS provides enough time to save work and bring the computer down safely. Some operating systems do not operate properly if power abruptly cuts off and the computer is not brought to a logical stopping place. A network server, the main computer for a network, is a great candidate for a UPS. Network operating systems are particularly susceptible to problems in a power outage. Some UPSs have a connection for a serial cable and special software that automatically maintains voltages to the computer, quits all applications, and powers the computer off. The UPS provides the necessary power and time to do this. Some newer UPSs will protect network cables.

A UPS also provides power conditioning for the devices attached to it. The AC power is used to charge a battery inside the UPS. The battery inside the UPS supplies power to an inverter. The inverter makes AC for the computer. When AC power from the outlet fails, the battery inside the UPS continues to supply power to the computer. The battery inside the UPS outputs DC power and the computer accepts (and expects) AC power. Therefore, the DC power from the battery must be converted back to AC voltage. AC voltage looks like a **sine wave** when it is in its correct form, but cheaper UPSs produce a **square wave** that is not as effective. Some computer systems and peripherals do not work well on a 120V AC square wave. Power Figure #11 illustrates a sine wave and a square wave.

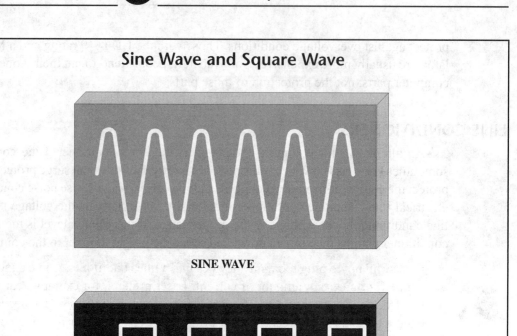

Sine Wave and Square Wave

SINE WAVE

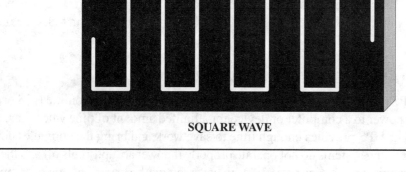

SQUARE WAVE

POWER – FIGURE #11

Be sure the UPS produces a proper waveform for optimum operation. The UPS documentation should specify the waveform type. The amount of time the UPS provides power to a computer or device and the number of devices that can attach to the UPS varies from model to model. Generally, the more time and the more devices a UPS can handle, the more expensive it is.

UPSs are the best protection against adverse power conditions because they protect against both over- and undervoltage conditions and they provide power so a system can be brought down and turned off properly. When purchasing a UPS, be sure that (1) the amount of battery time is sufficient to protect all devices, (2) the amount of current the UPS produces is sufficient to protect all devices, and (3) the output waveform is a sine wave.

 Do not plug a laser printer into a UPS unless it has a rating less than 1400 VA. Most UPSs cannot handle the very high current requirements of a laser printer when it powers up.

When a UPS is first plugged in, the battery is not charged. Read the UPS manufacturer's directions before plugging any devices into the UPS. Do not drop a UPS. A UPS has a battery inside similar to a car battery (except that the UPS battery is sealed). The battery contains acid. Never throw a UPS in the trash. Research your state's requirements for recycling batteries. All batteries fail after some time and most UPSs have replaceable batteries. Again, do not throw the UPS battery in the trash. Recycle it!

STANDBY POWER SUPPLY (SPS)

A device similar to the UPS is the **Standby Power Supply** or **SPS**. An SPS contains a battery like the UPS, but the battery only provides power to the computer when it loses AC power. It does not provide constant power like the UPS. An SPS is not as effective as the UPS because an SPS provides no protection against noise or under/over voltages. The SPS must detect a power-out condition first, then switch over to the battery to supply power to the computer. As a result, SPS switching time is important. Any time under five milliseconds is fine for most systems.

PHONE LINE ISOLATOR

Just like AC power outlets, the phone outlet can experience power fluctuations. These enter the computer through a modem, a device used to connect a computer to a phone line. Not only can a modem be damaged by a power surge on the phone line, but other electronics inside the computer, such as the motherboard, can also be damaged. A **phone line isolator**, sometimes called a **modem isolator**, can be purchased at an electronics store and provides protection against phone line surges. No computer connected to a phone line through a modem should be without one. Many surge protectors now come with a modem isolator built into the strip. Power Figure #12 shows a phone/modem isolator that is an individual unit.

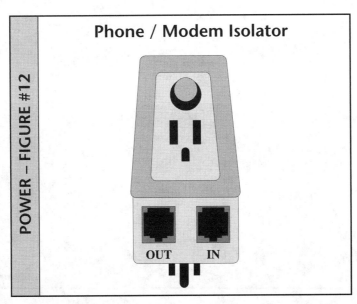

POWER – FIGURE #12

Phone / Modem Isolator

OUT   IN

Power supplies and associated protection equipment are not very exciting to a technician, but they are very important. Power problems can catch you unaware. Always keep power as a potential suspect in your mind when troubleshooting a computer.

ELECTRICAL FIRES

No discussion of power is complete without a brief warning about fire. Electrical fires are uncommon in computers, but if one ever occurs, a technician needs to be aware of what to do. If a fire occurs inside a computer or peripheral, unplug the equipment if possible. Do not put yourself in harm's way attempting to do this. Use a **Type C** or a **Type A-B-C fire extinguisher** to put out the fire. Type C fire extinguishers are made specifically for Type C (electrical) fires. Type A-B-C fire extinguishers can be used for Class A, Class B, and Class C fires. Class A fires involve paper, wood, cloth, or other normal combustibles. Class B fires involve flammable liquids and gases.

When a fire occurs, pull out the fire extinguisher pin. Aim the fire extinguisher nozzle at the base (bottom) of the fire. Squeeze the fire extinguisher's handle and move the nozzle back and forth in a slow sweeping motion.

 Name _____

BASIC ELECTRONICS AND POWER REVIEW QUESTIONS

1. Describe the difference between AC and DC power.

2. What device provides DC power to the computer's internal components?

3. Describe how polarity is important when measuring DC voltage.

4. Name two devices with potentially dangerous voltage levels?

5. Of the two devices mentioned in Question 4, which one is the most dangerous?

6. Draw an AC voltage symbol found on a meter.

7. Draw a DC voltage symbol found on a meter.

8. If you do not know what the symbols on a meter mean, what are you going to do?

9. What meter setting is used when measuring an unknown voltage?
   [Infinite / Highest / Amps / Lowest]

10. What is current?

11. How is current related to computer repair?

12. How do watts relate to power?

13. What computer component's output is described in watts?

14. When replacing a power supply, how is wattage applicable?
    A. It must be lower than the total requirement of all components installed.
    B. It is not applicable.
    C. It relates to the amount of capacitance the power supply provides.
    D. It must be equal to or greater than the total requirement of all components installed.

15. When working inside an ATX computer, why should the computer be unplugged even if it is powered down?

16. What term describes the amount of opposition to current in a circuit?
    [Resistance / Wattage / Capacitance / Voltage]

17. What type of check is performed on a cable to determine if each wire is good?

18. What type of check is performed on a fuse to determine if it has blown?

19. [T / F] When checking continuity, polarity does not matter.

20. [T / F] When checking continuity on pin 2 on both ends of the cable, the meter will always show no resistance if the wire is good.

21. Describe how you can make your own pin-out diagram with a good cable.

22. Why is it not recommended to replace a fuse with one that has a higher amp rating?

23. What is the most common power supply form factor?

24. What is different about an ATX12V power supply?

25. List three purposes of a power supply.

26. For computers that have power supply connections to the front panel, what is the purpose of the fifth (green or green-striped) wire?

27. What could be the result of improper power supply connection wiring?

28. [T / F] An ATX power supply has 120VAC going to the front panel switch.

29. How do you power off a computer that has an ATX power supply?

30. How many power connectors are used to connect to the AT-style motherboard?

31. Describe the correct power supply connections to the AT-style motherboard.

32. What style of power supply outputs 3.3 volts to the motherboard?

33. What could be the result of a faulty "power good" signal?

34. List one precaution to take when installing an additional cooling fan inside a computer.

35. What can be done if a power supply does not have an available Berg connector for a device that requires one?

36. What can be done if a power supply does not have enough power connectors?

37. What are the five output voltages of a power supply?

38. Of the five output voltages of a power supply, which are used for electronic chips?

39. Of the five output voltages of a power supply, which is used for most drive motors?

40. Why should a power supply be tested with "a load"?

41. What is the difference between the Sleep and Hibernate ACPI modes?

42. What is the difference between Wake on LAN and Wake on Ring?

43. How can you determine if the screen saver is causing ACPI problems?

44. Which Windows 98 Power Management tab allows you to control the hard drive motor?

45. What should you take into account when replacing a power supply?

46. [T / F] Power supplies are frequently disassembled for repair.

47. Describe how you can go about troubleshooting a power supply problem.

48. [T / F] Most power supplies issue a single click during the boot process.

49. List three power supply problem symptoms.

50. What is the difference between a surge and a spike?

51. [T / F] Power supplies have their own internal protection against power problems.

52. What features should you look for in a surge protector?

53. Why is having a MOV status lamp in a surge protector important?

54. What is the optimum power protection for a computer during a storm?

55. [T / F] Powerful computers that are the main component in a network should always have a UPS attached for power protection.

56. What features are important in a UPS?

57. What is the difference between a UPS and an SPS?

58. [T / F] Power surges can occur over phone lines and damage internal components of a microcomputer.

59. What is the difference between a Class A and a Class C fire?

60. Describe how to use a fire extinguisher.

Name _____

BASIC ELECTRONICS AND POWER FILL-IN-THE-BLANK

1. The type of power provided through a wall outlet is known as _____.

2. The type of power the computer uses is known as _____.

3. The measurement used to describe the power supply's output is _____, which is also the term that describes how much pressure pushes electrons through a circuit.

4. Typical power supply output voltages are _____.

5. A wall outlet is typically _____ AC volts.

6. A _____ is an electronic component found in power supplies and monitors that stores a charge even after power is removed.

7. Capacitance is measured in _____.

8. Amps are a measurement of _____.

9. Power is measured in _____.

10. Ohms are a measure of _____.

11. When measuring a broken wire, the meter shows _____.

12. A good fuse shows _____ ohms on a meter.

13. There are two basic types of power supplies. Computers use a _____ type power supply.

14. Do not power on a power supply without a _____ because the power supply can be damaged.

15. An SFX power supply is used with _____ motherboards.

16. When working with a power supply that connects to a front panel power switch, disconnect the _____ when attaching the cables from the power supply to the switch.

17. _____ motherboards have only one 20-pin power supply connector.

18. The _____ signal is sent to the motherboard when the power supply's voltages are at their proper levels.

19. When installing an auxiliary fan, the airflow must be in the _____ direction as the airflow generated by the power supply.

20. Two power supply connectors that attach to devices are the _____ and the _____.

21. All power supplies have the _____ connectors.

22. If a Molex power connector is the only connector available and the device needs a Berg connector, use a _____.

23. Intel, Microsoft, and Toshiba developed the _____ standard that was geared primarily toward controlling laptop power.

24. _____ combines APM and plug and play technologies to allow an operating system and BIOS to control various devices' power.

25. The _____ BIOS setting is used to enable/disable ACPI.

26. The best way to disable ACPI is through the _____.

27. An _____ is used to test wall outlet connections.

28. _____ laptop batteries replaced NiMH batteries in industry because they were lighter weight.

29. An _____ condition is when the AC electrical force exceeds the rated amount.

30. Two overvoltage conditions are a _____ and a _____.

31. Two undervoltage conditions are a _____ and a _____.

32. A total loss of power is also known as a _____.

33. A _____ only protects against the overvoltage condition.

34. A common component in a surge protector is the _____.

35. A surge protector's _____ is the voltage level at which protection begins.

36. A surge protector's _____ is the time it takes for the surge protector to react to an adverse overvoltage condition.

37. The _____ guards against overvoltages and undervoltages, but not against a blackout.

38. The _____ provides power from a battery to the computer during a power outage and during normal power conditions.

39. A _____ provides power to the computer from a battery only during a power outage.

40. _____ provides protection for modems.

41. To extinguish a computer fire, use a Class _____ or _____ fire extinguisher.

42. An electrical fire is classified as a Class _____.

Name _____

AMPS AND WATTAGE EXERCISE

Objective: To determine the correct capacity and wattage of a power supply

Parts: Power supply
                Internet access (as needed)

Step 1.   Locate the documentation stenciled on the power supply, if possible.

Question 1:   Can you determine from the documentation how many amps of current the power supply is rated for at 5 volts? If not, proceed to optional Step 1a.

Optional Step 1a.   Use the Internet to find the power supply's documentation. Go to the power supply manufacturer's web site to find this information. Use the information you find to answer the remaining questions.

Question 2:   How many amps is the power supply rated for at 5 volts?

Question 3:   How many amps is the power supply rated for at 12 volts?

Question 4:   What is the maximum rated output power of the power supply in watts?

_____ *Instructor's Initials*

Name _____

CONTINUITY CHECK EXERCISE

Objective: To perform a continuity check on a cable and find any broken wires

Parts: Multimeter
Cable and pin-out diagram

Step 1.   Obtain a meter, cable, and pin-out diagram from your instructor.

Step 2.   Set the meter to ohms.

_____ *Instructor's Initials*

Step 3.   Power on the meter.

Step 4.   Lay the cable horizontally in front of you. The connector on the left is referred to as Connector A. The connector on the right is referred to as Connector B.

Step 5.   Using the table on the next page and the pin-out diagram from your instructor, check the continuity of each wire. Document your findings by placing a checkmark beside each pin number with a good continuity check. Use only as many pin numbers as you need. Add more pin numbers to the table or use a separate piece of paper if you run out of space.

Connector A	Connector A
1	1
2	2
3	3
4	4
5	5
6	6
7	7
8	8
9	9
10	10
11	11
12	12
13	13
14	14
15	15
16	16
17	17
18	18
19	19
20	20

Question 1: What meter setting did you use to check continuity and what meter symbol is used for this setting?

Step 6. Power off the meter and return all supplies to the instructor.

_____ *Instructor's Initials*

Name _____

PIN-OUT DIAGRAMMING EXERCISE

Objective: To draw a pin-out diagram using a working cable

Parts: Multimeter
Good cable

Step 1.   Obtain a meter and a good cable from your instructor.

Step 2.   Set the meter to ohms.

_____ ***Instructor's Initials***

Step 3.   Power on the meter.

Step 4.   Lay the cable horizontally in front of you. The connector on the left is referred to as Connector A. The connector on the right is referred to as Connector B.

Step 5.   Touch one meter lead to Connector A's pin 1. Touch the other meter lead to every Connector B pin. Notice when the meter shows zero resistance, indicating a connection. Using the table below, draw a line from Connector A's pin 1 to any Connector B pins that show zero resistance. Add more pin numbers as needed to the table or use a separate piece of paper. Remember that all pins do not have to be used in the connector.

Connector A	Connector A
1	1
2	2
3	3
4	4
5	5
6	6
7	7
8	8
9	9
10	10
11	11
12	12
13	13
14	14
15	15
16	16
17	17
18	18
19	19
20	20

Step 6.   Power off the meter.

_____ *Instructor's Initials*

Step 7.   Return all supplies to the instructor.

Name _____

FUSE CHECK EXERCISE

Objective: To determine if a fuse is good

Parts: Multimeter
    Fuse

Step 1. Obtain a meter and a fuse from your instructor.

Step 2. Look at the fuse and determine its amp rating.

Question 1: What is the amperage rating of the fuse?

Step 3. Set the meter to ohms.

_____ *Instructor's Initials*

Step 4. Power on the meter.

Step 5. Connect one meter lead to one end of the fuse. Connect the other meter lead to the opposite end.

Step 6. Look at the resistance reading on the meter.

Question 2: What is the resistance reading?

Question 3: Is the fuse good?

Step 7. Power off the meter.

_____ *Instructor's Initials*

Step 8. Return all materials to the instructor

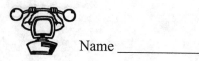

Name _____

WALL OUTLET AND POWER CORD AC VOLTAGE CHECK

Objective: To check the voltage from a wall outlet and through a power cord

Parts: Multimeter
Computer power cord

CAUTION: Exercise extreme caution when working with AC voltages!

Step 1.   Set the multimeter to **AC VOLTAGE** (refer to the meter's manual if you are unsure about this setting). **Important:** Using a current or resistance setting could destroy the meter.

Step 2.   Power on the multimeter.

Step 3.   Insert the meter's **black** lead into the **round** (Ground) AC outlet plug.

Step 4.   Insert the meter's **red** lead into the **smaller flat** (Hot) AC outlet plug. The meter reading should be around 120 volts. Use the table below to record the reading.

Step 5.   Move the meter's **red** lead into the **larger flat** (Neutral) AC outlet plug. The meter reading should be 0 volts. Use the table below to record the reading.

Step 6.   Remove both leads from the wall outlet.

Step 7.   Insert the meter's **black** lead into the **smaller flat** (Hot) AC outlet plug.

Step 8.   Insert the meter's **red** lead into the **larger flat** (Neutral) AC outlet plug. The meter reading should be around 120 volts. Use Power Exercise Table #1 to record the reading.

POWER EXERCISE – TABLE #1

Wall Outlet AC Checks

Connections	Expected Voltage	Actual Voltage
GND to Hot	120VAC	
GND to Neutral	0VAC	
Hot to Neutral	120VAC	

Step 9. Plug the computer power cord into the AC wall outlet that was checked using Steps 3 through 8.

Step 10. Verify the other end of the power cord is *not* plugged into the computer.

Step 11. Perform the same checks you performed in Steps 3 through 8, except this time check the power cord end that plugs into the computer. Use Power Exercise Table #2 to record the reading.

POWER EXERCISE – TABLE #2

Power Cord AC Checks

Connections	Expected Voltage	Actual Voltage
GND to Hot	120VAC	
GND to Neutral	0VAC	
Hot to Neutral	120VAC	

Step 12. If the voltage through the power cord is correct, power off the meter. Notify the instructor of any incorrect voltages.

_____ *Instructor's Initials*

Name _____

AT-STYLE MOTHERBOARD DC VOLTAGE CHECK

Objective: To check the power supply voltages sent to the motherboard.

Parts: Multimeter

AT-style computer

Step 1. Set the multimeter to **DC VOLTAGE**.

Step 2. Power on the multimeter.

Step 3. Power off the computer.

Step 4. Remove the computer case.

Step 5. Locate the power connectors that go *from* the power supply *to* the motherboard. They are normally located close to the power supply. Do *not* remove the connectors; just locate them.

Step 6. Power on the computer.

Step 7. Check the +5 volt DC output from the power supply by placing the meter's **black** lead or common on one of the ground wires* (a black wire) and the meter's **red** lead on one of the +5 volt wires (usually a red wire) on the connector to the motherboard. Consult Power Exercise Figure #1, the power supply documentation, or the motherboard documentation for the layout of the power supply connections. Power Exercise Figure #1 contains the table of acceptable voltage levels.

*Use and check all four ground connections (black wires going into the motherboard). Do not perform all the voltage checks using the same ground connection.

Write the voltage level found for each +5 volt wire in the Power Exercise Table #3.

POWER EXERCISE – TABLE #3

Voltage Being Checked:	Voltage Found:
+5 volts	
+5 volts	
+5 volts	
+5 volts	

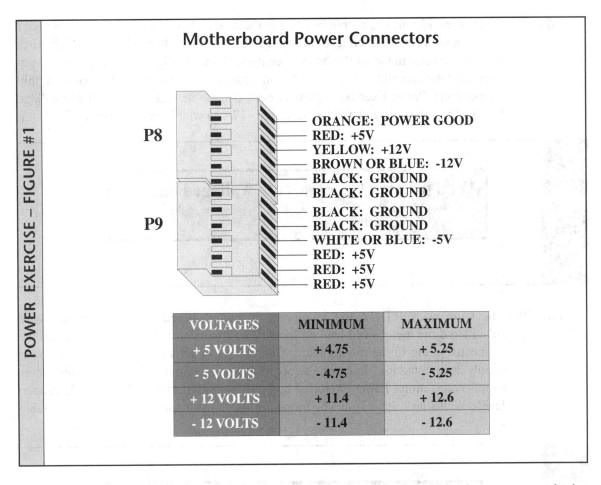

Motherboard Power Connectors

VOLTAGES	MINIMUM	MAXIMUM
+ 5 VOLTS	+ 4.75	+ 5.25
- 5 VOLTS	- 4.75	- 5.25
+ 12 VOLTS	+ 11.4	+ 12.6
- 12 VOLTS	- 11.4	- 12.6

Step 8. Check the –5 volt DC output by placing the meter's **black** lead on one ground wire (black) and the meter's **red** lead on the –5 volt wire (normally a blue or white wire) on the connector to the motherboard (usually a white or blue wire). Consult Power Exercise Figure #1, the power supply documentation, or the motherboard documentation for the layout of the power supply connections. Power Exercise Figure #1 contains a table of acceptable voltage levels. Write the voltage level found for the –5 volt wire in Power Exercise Table #4:

Voltage Being Checked:	Voltage Found:
-5 volts	

Step 9. Check the –12 volt DC output by placing the meter's **black** lead on one ground wire (black) and the meter's **red** lead on the –12 volt wire (normally a brown or blue wire) on the connector to the motherboard. See Power Exercise Figure #1, the power supply documentation, or the motherboard documentation for the layout of the power supply connections. Power Exercise Figure #1 contains a table that lists acceptable voltage levels. Write the voltage level found for the –12 volt wire in Power Exercise Table #5:

POWER EXERCISE – TABLE #5

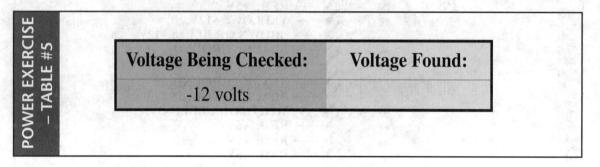

Voltage Being Checked:	Voltage Found:
-12 volts	

Step 10. Check the +12 volt DC output by placing the meter's **black** lead on one ground wire (black) and the meter's **red** lead on the +12 volt wire (usually a yellow wire) on the connector going to the motherboard. Consult Power Exercise Figure #1, the power supply documentation, or the motherboard documentation for the layout of the power supply connections. Power Exercise Figure #1 contains the table of acceptable voltage levels. Write the voltage level you found for the +12 volt wire in Power Exercise Table #6.

POWER EXERCISE – TABLE #6

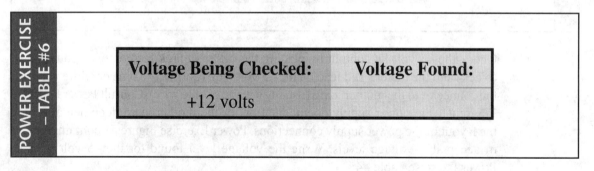

Voltage Being Checked:	Voltage Found:
+12 volts	

Step 11. Notify the instructor of any voltages out of range.

Step 12. Power off the meter.

_____ *Instructor's Initials*

Step 13. Power off the computer.

Name _____

ATX-STYLE MOTHERBOARD DC VOLTAGE CHECK

Objective: To check the power supply voltages sent to the motherboard

Parts: Multimeter
                 ATX-style computer

Step 1.   Set the multimeter to **DC VOLTAGE**.

Step 2.   Power on the multimeter.

Step 3.   Power off the computer.

Step 4.   Remove the computer case.

Step 5.   Locate the power connectors that go *from* the power supply *to* the motherboard. They are normally located close to the power supply. Do *not* remove the connectors; just locate them.

Step 6.   Power on the computer.

Step 7.   Check the +5 volt DC output from the power supply by placing the meter's **black** lead or common on one of the ground wires* and the meter's **red** lead on one of the +5 volt wires on the connector to the motherboard. Refer to Power Exercise Figure #1, the power supply's documentation, or the motherboard documentation for the layout of the power supply connections. Power Exercise Figure #2 contains the table of acceptable voltage levels.

   *Use and check all seven ground connections. Do not perform all the voltage checks using the same ground connection.

   Write the voltage level found for each +5 volt wire in the Power Exercise Table #7.

POWER EXERCISE – TABLE #7

Voltage Being Checked	Voltage Found
+5 Volts	
+5 Volts	
+5 Volts	
+5 Volts	
+5 Volts	
+5 Volts	
+5 Volts	

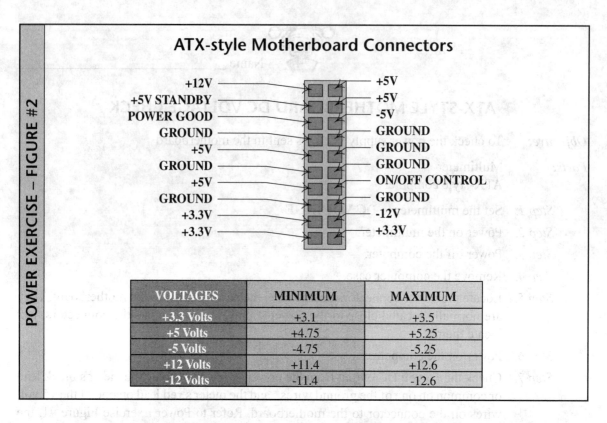

ATX-style Motherboard Connectors

+12V — +5V
+5V STANDBY — +5V
POWER GOOD — -5V
GROUND — GROUND
+5V — GROUND
GROUND — GROUND
+5V — ON/OFF CONTROL
GROUND — GROUND
+3.3V — -12V
+3.3V — +3.3V

VOLTAGES	MINIMUM	MAXIMUM
+3.3 Volts	+3.1	+3.5
+5 Volts	+4.75	+5.25
-5 Volts	-4.75	-5.25
+12 Volts	+11.4	+12.6
-12 Volts	-11.4	-12.6

Step 8. Check the –5 volt DC output by placing the meter's **black** lead on one ground wire and the meter's **red** lead on the –5 volt wire on the connector to the motherboard. See Power Exercise Figure #2, the power supply's documentation, or the motherboard documentation for the layout of the power supply connections. Power Exercise Figure #2 contains a table of acceptable voltage levels. Write the voltage level found for the –5 volt wire in Power Exercise Table #8:

Voltage Being Checked	Voltage Found
-5 Volts	

Step 9. Check the –12 volt DC output by placing the meter's **black** lead on one ground wire and the meter's **red** lead on the –12 volt wire on the connector to the motherboard. Consult Power Exercise Figure #2, the power supply's documentation, or the motherboard documentation for the layout of the power supply connections. Power Exercise Figure #2 contains a table that lists the acceptable voltage levels. Write the voltage level found for the –12 volt wire in Power Exercise Table #9:

POWER EXERCISE – TABLE #9

Voltage Being Checked	Voltage Found
-12 Volts	

Step 10. Check the +12 volt DC output by placing the meter's **black** lead on one ground wire and the meter's **red** lead on the +12 volt wire on the connector going to the motherboard. Refer to Power Exercise Figure #2, the power supply's documentation, or the motherboard documentation for the layout of the power supply connections. Power Exercise Figure #2 contains the table of acceptable voltage levels. Write the voltage level found for the +12 volt wire in Power Exercise Table #10.

POWER EXERCISE – TABLE #10

Voltage Being Checked	Voltage Found
+12 Volts	

Step 11. Check the +3.3 volt DC output by placing the meter's **black** lead on one ground wire and the meter's **red** lead on the +12 volt wire on the connector going to the motherboard. See Power Exercise Figure #2, the power supply's documentation, or the motherboard documentation for the layout of the power supply connections. Power Exercise Figure #2 contains the table of acceptable voltage levels. Write the voltage level found for the +3.3 volt wire in Power Exercise Table #11.

POWER EXERCISE – TABLE #11

Voltage Being Checked	Voltage Found
+3.3 Volts	

Step 12. Notify the instructor of any voltages out of range.

Step 13. Power off the meter.

_____ *Instructor's Initials*

Step 14. Power off the computer.

Name _____

DEVICE DC VOLTAGE CHECK

Objective: To check the power supply voltages sent to various devices

Parts: Multimeter
                Computer

Step 1.   Set the multimeter to **DC VOLTAGE** (refer to the meter's manual if unsure about the setting).

Step 2.   Power on the multimeter.

Step 3.   Power off the computer.

Step 4.   Remove the computer case.

Step 5.   Locate a Molex or Berg power connector. If one is not available, disconnect a power connector from a device.

Step 6.   Power on the computer.

Step 7.   Check the +5 volt DC output from the power supply by placing the meter's **black** lead in (if the connector is a Molex) or on (if the connector is a Berg) one of the grounds* (a black wire). Place the meter's **red** lead on the +5 volt wire (normally a red wire) in or on the connector. Consult Power Exercise Figure #3 for the layout of the Molex and Berg power supply connections. Power Exercise Figure #3 also contains a table with the acceptable voltage levels.

*Use and check both ground connections (black wires going into the connector); do not check all the voltages using only one ground connection.

Write the voltage level found for the +5 volt wire in Power Exercise Table #12:

POWER EXERCISE – TABLE #12

Voltage Being Checked	Voltage Found
+5 Volts	

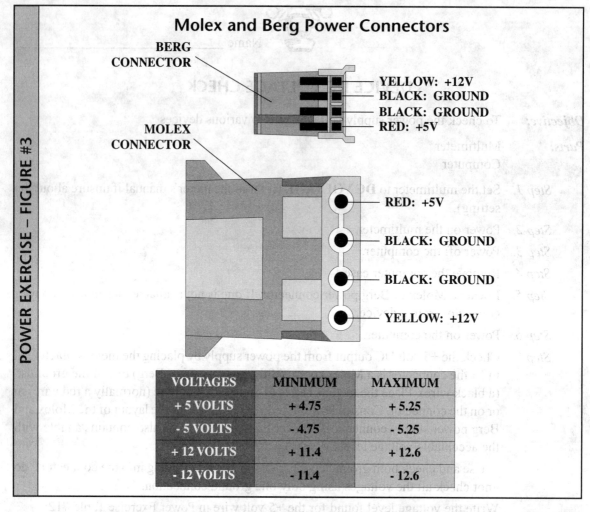

Molex and Berg Power Connectors

POWER EXERCISE – FIGURE #3

BERG CONNECTOR

YELLOW: +12V
BLACK: GROUND
BLACK: GROUND
RED: +5V

MOLEX CONNECTOR

RED: +5V

BLACK: GROUND

BLACK: GROUND

YELLOW: +12V

VOLTAGES	MINIMUM	MAXIMUM
+ 5 VOLTS	+ 4.75	+ 5.25
- 5 VOLTS	- 4.75	- 5.25
+ 12 VOLTS	+ 11.4	+ 12.6
- 12 VOLTS	- 11.4	- 12.6

Step 8. Check the +12 volt DC output by placing the meter's **black** lead in (if the connector is a Molex) or on (if the connector is a Berg) one of the grounds. Place the meter's **red** lead on the +12 volt wire in or on the connector. See Power Exercise Figure #3 for the layout of the Molex and Berg power supply connections. Power Exercise Figure #3 also contains a table with acceptable voltage levels. Write the voltage level found for the +12 volt wire in Power Exercise Table #13:

POWER EXERCISE – TABLE #13

Voltage Being Checked	Voltage Found
+12 Volts	

Step 9.   Notify the instructor of any voltages out of range.

Step 10.   Power off the meter.

_____ *Instructor's Initials*

Step 11.   Power off the computer.

Name _____

INTERNET DISCOVERY

Objective: To obtain specific information on the Internet regarding a computer or its associated parts

Parts: Access to the Internet

Question 1:   Locate a power company that provides surge protection service for homes. Write the cost(s) of the service and the URL where you found the information in the space below.

Question 2:   A customer owns a Belkin 8-outlet Surge Master II Gold. What is the warranty amount for this surge protector?

Question 3:   A customer has a Sparkle Power Inc. (SPI) FSP300-60BN power supply. What is the power supply's maximum power output (in watts)?

Question 4:   A customer has an Enermax EG265P-VB power supply. Does this power supply support Pentium 4 motherboards? At what Internet site did you find this information?

Question 5:   A customer has an Enermax EG265P-VB power supply. How many device power cables does this power supply have and what type of connector does it use?

Question 6:   What type of battery does the HP Omnibook 6000 laptop use and where did you find this information?

Question 7:   Your company has an APC SU1000X127 UPS. What is the part number and cost for a replacement battery? At what Internet site did you find this information?

Question 8:   Locate a Class C fire extinguisher. Give the model, cost, and URL where you found this information.

NOTES

6

Chapter 6:

Logical Troubleshooting

OBJECTIVES

After completing this chapter you will

- Understand the basic procedures for troubleshooting a microcomputer.
- Understand how the POST error codes help troubleshoot a computer.
- Understand the importance of good communication with the computer user.

KEY TERMS

patch
service release

TROUBLESHOOTING OVERVIEW

When a computer does not work properly, technicians must exhibit one essential trait—the will to succeed. A technician must have a good attitude and a large amount of perseverance and drive. Solving a computer problem can be easier if a troubleshooter uses logical reasoning and takes logical steps. Logical troubleshooting can be broken down into six simple steps:

1. Re-create the problem.
2. Divide the problem into hardware or software.
3. Divide and conquer: divide the problem into logical areas to isolate it.
4. Repair the problem or go back to test another theory.
5. Test the solution.
6. Provide feedback to the user.

RE-CREATE THE PROBLEM

Computer problems come in all shapes and sizes. Many problems relate to the people who operate computers—the users. They frequently perceive the computer as the problem. The problem may end up being the user's behavior, such as failing to choose the correct printer, pushing the wrong key for a specific function, or issuing an incorrect command.

Have the user demonstrate or re-create the problem. Because the user himself is often the problem, you can save a great deal of time with this step. Do not assume anything! A user may complain that "my hard drive does not work" when in fact, there is no power to the computer. Users often repeat computer terms they have heard or read, but cannot use them correctly or in the right syntax. By asking a user to re-create a problem, a technician creates the chance to see it as the client sees it. Even in a phone consultation, the same rule applies: never assume and have the user re-create the problem step-by-step.

HARDWARE OR SOFTWARE

A technician determines if the computer problem is hardware or software related (or both) by using his or her senses: sight, hearing, and smell can tell you a great deal. Watch the computer boot up, look for lights, listen for beeps, and take notes. Frequently a hardware problem is detected during POST (Power On Self-Test) executed by the BIOS during a cold boot. POST checks out the hardware in a sequential order and if it finds an error, the BIOS issues a beep and/or displays a numerical error code. Make note of any error codes or beeps. The number or duration of beeps and the numerical error codes that appear are different for different computers. The secret is knowing the manufacturer of the BIOS chip. Major manufacturers of motherboard BIOS chips include Award (now merged with Phoenix Technologies), AMI, IBM, and Phoenix. Logical Table #1 lists the audio beeps heard on a computer with an AMI ROM BIOS chip installed.

LOGICAL – TABLE #1

AMI BIOS Audio Beeps

Beeps	Description of Problem
1	OK if screen appears. If not, DRAM refresh (memory)
2	Parity circuit (memory)
3	1st 64KB of RAM or CMOS
4	System timer/memory
5	Microprocessor (memory/motherboard)
6	Keyboard controller or A20 line
7	Virtual mode exception error (CPU)
8	Video memory (read/write test)
9	BIOS
10	CMOS shutdown (read/write test)
11	Cache memory
1 long, 3 short	RAM (conventional or extended)
1 long, 8 short	Video

Logical Table #2 lists the audio beeps heard on a computer with an IBM BIOS chip installed.

LOGICAL – TABLE #2

IBM POST Audio Beeps

Beeps	Description
No beeps	Power supply or motherboard failure
Continuous beep	Power supply or motherboard failure
Repeating beeps	Power supply, motherboard or keyboard failure
1 short beep	Successful POST
2 short beeps	Initialization error on video
1 long, 1 short beep	System board failure
1 long, 2 short beeps	Video adapter failure
1 long, 3 short beeps	EGA video adapter failure

Logical Table #3 lists the audio beeps heard on a computer with a PHOENIX BIOS chip installed.

LOGICAL – TABLE #3

Phoenix Audio Beeps

Beeps	Description	Beeps	Description (cont.)
None/1-1-2	CPU register test	3-1-1	DMA register failure (motherboard)
1-1-3	CMOS failure	3-1-2	DMA register failure (motherboard)
1-1-4	BIOS failure (checksum test)	3-1-3	Interrupt mask register failure (motherboard)
1-2-1	Programmable Interval Timer failure (motherboard)	3-1-4	Interrupt mask register failure (motherboard)
1-2-2	DMA failure (motherboard)	None/3-2-2	Interrupt vector loading
1-2-3	DMA page register failure (motherboard)	3-2-4	Keyboard controller failed
1-3-1	RAM refresh (motherboard)	None/3-3-1	CMOS RAM power bad
None/1-3-2	1st 64K of RAM test	None/3-3-2	CMOS config valid. in progress
1-3-3	1st 64K RAM chip failure/ motherboard	3-3-4	Video failure
1-3-4	1st 64K RAM failure/ motherboard	3-4-1	Video initialization failure
1-4-1	1st 64K RAM failure/ motherboard	3-4-2	Video retrace test failure
1-4-2	1st 64K RAM failure (parity)	None/3-4-3	Video ROM search in progress
1-4-3	EISA timer test in progress	None	Video scan failure
1-4-4	EISA NMI port test in progress	None	Screen is running with Video ROM
2-1-1	1st 64K RAM failure (bit 0)	None	Screen (mono) is operable
2-1-2	1st 64K RAM failure (bit 1)	None	Screen (color 40) is operable
2-1-3	1st 64K RAM failure (bit 2)	None	Screen (color 80) is operable
2-1-4	1st 64K RAM failure (bit 3)	4-2-1	Timer tick interrupt (motherboard)
2-2-1	1st 64K RAM failure (bit 4)	4-2-2	Shutdown test (keyboard/ motherboard)
2-2-2	1st 64K RAM failure (bit 5)	4-2-3	Gate A20 (keyboard/motherboard)
2-2-3	1st 64K RAM failure (bit 6)	4-2-4	Unexpected interrupt (adapter/motherboard)
2-2-4	1st 64K RAM failure (bit 7)	4-3-1	RAM test (motherboard/memory)
2-3-1	1st 64K RAM failure (bit 8)	4-3-3	Interval timer (motherboard)
2-3-2	1st 64K RAM failure (bit 9)	4-3-4	Time of day clock (battery/power supply/motherboard)
2-3-3	1st 64K RAM failure (bit 10)	4-4-1	Serial port
2-3-4	1st 64K RAM failure (bit 11)	4-4-2	Parallel port
2-4-1	1st 64K RAM failure (bit 12)	4-4-3	Math coprocessor
2-4-2	1st 64K RAM failure (bit 13)	4-4-4	Cache test failed
2-4-3	1st 64K RAM failure (bit 14)	*1-1-2	System board select failed
2-4-4	1st 64K RAM failure (bit 15)	*1-1-3	Extended CMOS RAM failed

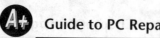

In addition to hearing audio tones, a technician might see numerical error codes. Like audio clues, the numerical error codes are BIOS dependent. Logical Table #4 lists IBM POST codes. These codes are somewhat generic and similar to those found on other systems as well.

LOGICAL – TABLE #4

IBM POST Error Codes

Error	Description	Error	Description
01X	Undetermined problem	115	Cache parity, ROM cksum, or DMA error
02X	Power supply	116	Port read/write error
1XX	**Motherboard Errors**	118	Parity or L2 cache error
101	Processor interrupt failed	120	Microprocessor failure
102	Timer or PS/2 real time clock failed	121	Unexpected interrupt error
103	Timer int. failed;PS/2 CMOS fail.	131-4	PS/2 DMA error
104	Protected mode failed	151	Battery or CMOS failure
105	8042 keybd cont. failed	152	PS/2 real time clock/CMOS error
106	Converting logic test failed	160	PS/2 sys bd ID not recognized
107	NMI failure	161-2	Battery; CMOS SETUP error
108	Bus test failure	163	CMOS date & time error
109	DMA failure	164	CMOS memory size error
110	PS/2 parity check failure	165	PS/2 SETUP error
111	PS/2 parity check failure	166	PS/2 adapter timeout
112	PS/2 MCA arbitration failed	167	PS/2 clock not updating
113	PS/2 MCA arbitration failed	168	CMOS math coprocessor error
114	PS/2 external ROM failed	199	User indicated configuration error

IBM POST Error Codes (cont.)

Error	Description	Error	Description
2XX	**Memory Errors (RAM)**	626	Disk data compare error
201	Memory failure	648	Format test failed
202	Memory address failure (0-15)	649	Incorrect media type
203	Memory address failure (ISA 16-23) (MCA 16-31)	650	Drive speed error
210	Parity error	651	Format failed
211	PS/2 1st 64K failure	652	Verify failed
3XX	**Keyboard Errors**	653	Read failed
301	Kybd reset failure/stuck key	654	Write failed
302	Keylock is enabled error	655	Adapter failed
303	Keyboard controller failure	**7XX**	**Math Coprocessor Errors**
304	Keyboard or sys board failure	**9XX**	**Parallel Adapter Errors**
305	+5v error; PS/2 kybd fuse (on system board) error	**10XX**	**Alternate Parallel Port Adapter Errors**
306	Unsupported keyboard	**11XX**	**Primary Async (Serial COM1) Errors**
342	Keyboard cable error	1101	Adapter failure
366	Keyboard cable error	1107	Cable error
4XX	**Monochrome Display Errors**	1113	Transmit error
401	Mono mem., horiz. synch, or video test failure; PS/2 parallel port failure	1114	Receive error
432	Parallel port failure	1142	No IRQ4
5XX	**CGA Display Errors**	1143	No IRQ3
501	Mem., horiz. synch, vert. synch., or video test failure; CRT failure	1148	Time-out error
503	Adapter failure	1152	No DSR
6XX	**Floppy Errors**	1156	No CTS
601	Drive or controller error	**12XX**	**Alternate Async (Serial COM2, 3, 4) Errors**
602	Disk boot record error	1201	Adapter failure
603	Disk size error	1202	Internal modem failed
607	Write-protect error	1207	Cable error
610	Disk initialization error	1213	Transmit error
611	Drive time-out error	1214	Receive error
613	Adapter DMA test failure	1242	No IRQ4
621	Drive seek error	1243	No IRQ3
622	Drive CRC error	1248	Time-out error
623	Record not found error	1252	No DSR
624	Bad address mark error	1256	No CTS

LOGICAL – TABLE #4

IBM POST Error Codes (cont.)

Error	Description	Error	Description
104XX	ESDI or MicroChannel IDE Errors	166XX	Primary TokenRing Adapter Errors
10450	Read/write test failure	208XX	SCSI Device Errors
10451	Read verify test failure	209XX	SCSI Removable Disk Errors
10452	Seek test failed	210XXXX	SCSI Hard Drive Errors
10453	Wrong drive type in CMOS	1st X after 210	SCSI ID number
10454	Controller buffer test failed	2nd X after 210	Logical Unit Number
10455	Controller failure	3rd X after 210	Host adapter slot number
10456	Controller diagnostic failure	4th X after 210	Drive capacity
10461	Drive format error	215XX	SCSI CD ROM Errors
10462	Controller head select problem	I99900XX	IML Errors
10463	Drive read/write error	I999001X	Invalid disk IML record
10464	Drive defect map problem	I999002X	Disk IML record load error
10465	Controller ECC error	I999003X	Disk IML incompatible with motherboard
10466	Controller ECC error	I999004X	Disk IML incompatible with processor
10467	Drive seek problem	I999005X	Disk IML not attempted
10468	Drive seek problem	I999006X	IML not supported on drive
10473	Read verify problem	I99900X2	Disk IML load error
10480	Drive 0 seek error	I99900X3	IML incompatible w/sys.board
10481	Drive 1 seek error	I99900X4	Disk IML incompatible with processor
10482	Controller transfer error	I99903XX	No Bootable Device Errors
10483	Controller reset error	I9990302	Invalid disk boot record
10484	Controller: hd select 3 error	I9990303	System partition boot failed
10485	Controller: hd select 2 error	I9990304	No bootable device found
10486	Controller: hd select 1 error	I9990305	No bootable media found
10487	Controller: hd select 0 error	I9990306	Invalid SCSI device boot record
112XX	SCSI Adapter Errors	I99904XX	IML/System Mismatch Errors
113XX	SCSI (on sys bd) Errors	I99906XX	IML Errors

The Award (now Phoenix Technologies) BIOS is sold to various computer manufacturers, who are allowed to create their own error codes and messages. Look in the motherboard/ computer manual or on the manufacturer's web site for a listing of exact error messages.

Logical Table #5 lists some of the more generic Award error codes.

Award (Now Phoenix Technologies) BIOS Codes

Error Message	Description of Problem
BIOS ROM checksum error — System halted	BIOS is corrupted
CMOS battery failed	Replace battery
CMOS checksum error — defaults loaded	Check and/or replace battery
Floppy disk(s) fail	Check Setup for correct floppy drive type/floppy cable/floppy drive
Keyboard error or no keyboard present	Check keyboard, cable, and/or keys
Keyboard is locked out —Unlock the key	Check for pressed or stuck keys
Memory test fail	RAM
Override enabled—Defaults loaded	If the system cannot read current CMOS configuration, the system can boot with a set of system defaults. Check battery and CMOS settings
Primary master hard disk fail	Check primary master IDE/EIDE
Primary slave hard disk fail	Check primary slave IDE/EIDE device
Secondary master hard disk fail	Check secondary master IDE/EIDE device
Secondary slave hard disk fail	Check secondary slave IDE/EIDE device

LOGICAL – TABLE #5

POST error codes only direct a technician to the right general area. Sometimes multiple POST errors occur. If this is the case, start the troubleshooting process with the first error code detected.

Because manufacturers constantly produce BIOS upgrades, you must contact the chip manufacturer for a current list of error codes or use the Internet to download the latest copy of error codes.

Hardware errors might also occur. For example, the monitor might suddenly go black, the floppy drive's access light might not go on when it attempts to access the floppy disk, or the printer might repeatedly flash an error code. Hardware errors are usually obvious because of POST error codes or errors that occur when accessing a particular device.

Software errors, on the other hand, occur when the computer user accesses a particular application or when the system boots. Files that affect the booting process are operating system-dependent. Examples include CONFIG.SYS, AUTOEXEC.BAT, BOOT.INI, and files in the Startup folder. If in doubt as to whether a problem is hardware or software, run diagnostics on the hardware to eliminate that possibility. Some computers come with a diagnostic disk or diagnostics built into the Setup program. There are also third party diagnostics. Every software program has problems (bugs) when first released. Software manufacturers offer a software **patch** or a **service release** that fixes known problems. Patches or service releases are usually available on the Internet from the software manufacturer.

DIVIDE AND CONQUER

Divide the problem into logical areas and continue sub-dividing the problem until it is isolated. For example, if an error appears each time the computer user saves to a floppy disk, then the logical place to look is the floppy drive system. The floppy drive system includes the user's disk, the floppy drive, electronics that tell the floppy drive what to do, a cable that connects the floppy drive to the electronics, and the software program currently being used. Any of these may be the problem.

Ernie Friend, a technician of many years, advises students to divide a problem in half; then divide it in half again; then continue to divide until the problem is manageable. This way of thinking carries a technician a long way. Always keep in mind too, that you will beat the problem at hand! You are smarter than any problem!

Use Ernie's philosophy with the floppy problem: divide the problem in half and determine if the problem is hardware or software. To determine if the software application is causing the floppy problem, try saving a document to the floppy disk from another application. If the second application saves properly, then the problem is in the first application. If both applications have problems saving data to the disk, the problem is most likely in the disk or in the floppy hardware system. The next easiest thing to eliminate as a suspect is the floppy disk. Try a different floppy. If a different disk works, then the first disk was the problem. If neither disk accepts data, the problem is the floppy drive, cable, or electronics. Swap parts one at a time until you locate the problem.

If a hardware problem is evident once a POST error or peripheral access/usage error occurs, consider the problem a subunit of the entire computer. For example, if a 601 floppy drive error occurs, the subunit is the floppy drive subsystem. The floppy drive subsystem consists of the floppy drive, the cable, and the controlling circuits that may be on an adapter or the motherboard.

If the problem is software, narrow it to a specific area. For example, determine if the problem is related to the CONFIG.SYS or AUTOEXEC.BAT files. Determine if the problem occurs only when a specific application executes.

When isolating the problem to a specific area, be practical; change or check the easy stuff first. Time is money, both to the company or person whose computer is down and to the company paying the technician's salary. If a monitor is down, swap the monitor with another before opening up the computer and swapping the video adapter. Also, check with the computer user to see if anything about the computer has changed recently. For example, ask if anyone installed or removed something from the computer or if new software was loaded before or since the problem started. If the problem is hardware, diagnostics can narrow it down to a subunit, but isolating a problem frequently requires part swapping. Try not to replace good parts. If a replacement part does not solve the problem, put the old part back in.

Ethics are an important part of any job, including the job of being a technician. Do not fall into the trap of charging customers for parts that do not fix the problem. When a replacement part does not fix the job, do not leave it in the machine and charge the customer anyway. Good technicians, like good automobile mechanics, take pride in doing an honest day's work. Start practicing these good habits in the classroom.

If you do not hear any unusual audio beeps or see any POST error codes, and you suspect a software error, reboot the computer. Depending on the operating system, you may need to step through the boot process and files. Usually this is done through a Startup menu, but with Windows 98, press and hold the CTRL key down while the computer boots. Select a menu option, such as Step-by-Step Confirmation. For Windows 95 and 2000 Professional, use the F8 key to bring up the menu.

REPAIR THE PROBLEM OR GO BACK TO TEST ANOTHER THEORY

Swapping a part, checking hardware settings, referring to documentation — all are necessary steps in troubleshooting. Noting error or beep codes is just one element in the diagnostic routine. Determining what the problem is usually takes longer than fixing it. Software problems frequently involve reloading software applications, software drivers, or getting software updates and patches from the appropriate vendor. The Internet is an excellent resource for these files.

Hardware problem resolution simply involves swapping the damaged part. If swapping a part or reloading the software does not solve the problem, go back to logical troubleshooting. Step 2 reminds you to divide the problem into hardware and software. Go back to this step if necessary. Step 3 advises you to divide and conquer. This step is the most likely place to resume your troubleshooting. Eliminating what could be the problem is important. Take notes during these steps so that you know what you have tried.

People who troubleshoot randomly—repairing parts or replacing files without a plan are known as "gunslingers." Gunslingers are the most dangerous technicians to have on staff. Sometimes gunslingers get lucky and fix a problem faster than a logical technician would, but gunslingers frequently cause more problems than they solve. Consistent, logical troubleshooting is a better path. Be methodical and there is no problem you cannot solve.

TEST THE SOLUTION

Never assume the hardware component or the replaced software repairs the computer. The computer can have multiple problems, or the repair may not offer a complete solution. Test the computer yourself *and* have the user test the computer in normal conditions to prove that the problem is indeed solved.

PROVIDE FEEDBACK TO THE USER

Unfortunately, one of the biggest problems with technicians is their inability to communicate effectively with users. The best computer technicians are the ones the users trust, and those who explain problems in a way the customers understand. A computer repair is never finished until the user is updated. Do not use technical terms with users who are not technically competent. Treat computer users as if they are intelligent, even if they are not proficient in technical terminology.

Each computer repair is a different scenario because of the plethora of vendors, products, and standards in the marketplace. But that is what makes the job so interesting and challenging. Break each problem down into a manageable task, isolate the problem, and use all available resources, including other technicians, documentation, and the Internet, to solve it. Never forget to give feedback.

The remaining chapters are dedicated to specific devices or areas of the computer. Each device or area has troubleshooting techniques that can be used once a problem is narrowed. For example, if you find you have a memory problem, go to the memory chapter for details of operation and troubleshooting techniques.

Name _____

LOGICAL TROUBLESHOOTING REVIEW QUESTIONS

1. Explain how users can be a computer problem.

2. How can a technician determine if a problem is hardware or software?

3. [T / F] The manufacturer of the RAM chip determines what error codes are shown during POST.

4. If a computer beeps once during POST and the computer has an AMI BIOS, what is the problem?
    A. Keyboard
    B. CPU register test
    C. DRAM refresh
    D. Video initialization error

5. If an IBM computer beeps once during POST, what is the problem?
    A. There is no problem
    B. CPU register test
    C. DRAM refresh
    D. Video initialization error

6. What BIOS manufacturer uses multiple beeps with pauses in between such as two beeps, pause, four beeps, pause, and then three beeps?
   [AMI / Award / IBM / Phoenix]

7. Where can you find the latest information on POST error codes?

8. [T / F] ROM BIOS can be upgraded.

9. [T / F] After swapping a part and powering on, you can assume a computer problem is solved.

10. What is the last and most important step in resolving a computer problem?

Name _____

LOGICAL TROUBLESHOOTING FILL-IN-THE-BLANK

1. _____ checks out hardware sequentially.

2. The _____ chip executes POST.

3. An IBM POST error code _____ indicates a date and time error.

4. To help determine if a problem is in the startup files, press the _____ key when the message, "Starting MS-DOS" or "Starting Windows 95" appears.

5. If a problem is hardware, _____ can be useful in getting the problem narrowed to a subunit.

6. The _____ error code appears if the keyboard is not plugged in correctly.

 Name _____

LOGICAL TROUBLESHOOTING EXERCISE

Objective: To solve a computer problem with logic

Parts: Computer with a problem

Step 1.   Power on a computer with a problem and perform the steps shown in the flow chart of Logical Exercise Figure #1. Answer the questions that follow.

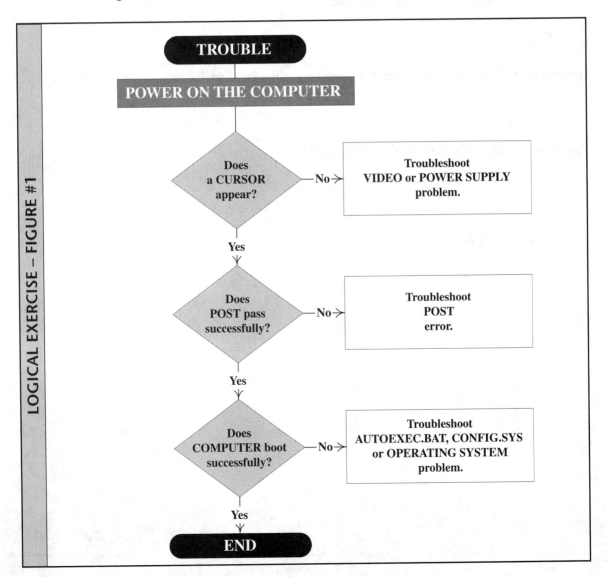

Question 1:   Do you hear any audio clues? If yes, list the symptoms below.

Question 2:   Are any POST error codes seen? If so, list the errors below in the order in which they occur.

Question 3:   Are there any CONFIG.SYS or AUTOEXEC.BAT errors? If so, list them below in the order in which they occur.

Question 4:   Are there any application-specific problems? If so, list the symptoms below.

Question 5:   Describe your solution to the problem.

_____ *Instructor's Initials*

Name _____

LOGICAL TROUBLESHOOTING FOR WINDOWS 95

Objective: To understand a logical troubleshooting approach using a Windows 95 computer

Parts: Windows 95 computer

Note: The student should leave the room while the instructor or lab assistant creates a problem with the Windows 95 computer. When the student returns to the room, the instructor/lab assistant will play the part of the user and the student will isolate and repair the problem.

By following a logical troubleshooting procedure, you, as a technician, will be able to isolate and repair PC problems more efficiently. To accomplish the exercise, use the six logical troubleshooting steps:

1. Re-create the problem.
2. Divide the problem into hardware or software.
3. Divide and conquer: divide the problem into logical areas.
4. Repair the problem or test another theory.
5. Test the solution.
6. Provide feedback to the user.

Step 1.   Re-create the problem.

    A. Have the user demonstrate the problem for you.

    B. Ask questions to isolate the general problem.

Question 1:   What does the general problem seem to be?

Question 2:   Does the problem stem from user error?

Step 2.   Divide the problem into hardware or software.

    A. Will the computer start?

      • *No:*   Check power cables, etc.

      • *Yes:*   Watch for POST error messages or beep codes.

Question 3: Are there any POST error messages or beep codes? If so, list them below.

B. Confirm computer startup step-by-step.
- Boot the Windows 95 computer.
- Press the **F8** function key when the words "Starting Windows 95" appear. The Startup menu opens.
- From the Startup menu, select **Step-by-step confirmation**.
- You will now confirm each startup command by pressing the **Y** key. Any error messages display on the screen and can easily be associated with the command that caused the error.

Question 4: Were any error messages displayed during step-by-step confirmation? List them below.

C. Use the System control panel to view resource conflicts.
- From the Start menu, choose **Settings** and then **Control Panel.**
- From Control Panel, double-click on the **System** icon, and then select **Device Manager**.
- Browse the devices in Device Manager and note any disabled devices and/or resource conflicts.

Question 5: Are any disabled devices or resource conflicts visible from within Control Panel? List them below.

Step 3. Divide and conquer.

A. Divide the problem into logical areas

Question 6: Using the information gathered in the previous steps, can you isolate the probable cause of the problem to one or more logical areas? List these logical areas below.

Question 7:   For each of the possible areas listed in Question 6, formulate possible solutions. List these solutions below.

Note: Try fixing the easy things first. For example, if you believe the problem is with the video subsystem, try a different monitor before replacing the video adapter.

Step 4.   Repair the problem, or go back and test another theory.

   A.   Implement possible solutions one at a time.
   - If you implement more than one solution at a time, you will not know which solution worked.

   B.   Try a fix and see if it works.
   - If the solution does not work, return the computer to its previous condition and try another solution.

Step 5.   Test the solution.

   A.   Try to re-create the problem after you think it has been repaired.
   B.   If the problem does not recur, it has probably been solved.

Step 6.   Provide feedback to the user.

   A.   Demonstrate to the user that the problem has been solved.
   B.   Have the user try to re-create the problem.
   C.   Document the results of your troubleshooting for future reference.

_____ *Instructor's Initials*

Name _____

LOGICAL TROUBLESHOOTING FOR WINDOWS 98

Objective: To understand a logical troubleshooting approach using a Windows 98 computer

Parts: Windows 98 computer

Note: The student should leave the room while the instructor or lab assistant creates a problem with the Windows 98 computer. When the student returns to the room, the instructor/ lab assistant will play the part of the user, and the student will isolate and repair the problem.

By following a logical troubleshooting procedure, you, as a technician, will be able to isolate and repair PC problems more efficiently. To accomplish the exercise, use the six logical troubleshooting steps:

1. Re-create the problem.
2. Divide the problem into hardware or software.
3. Divide and conquer: divide the problem into logical areas.
4. Repair the problem or test another theory.
5. Test the solution.
6. Provide feedback to the user.

Step 1.   Re-create the problem.

A. Have the user demonstrate the problem for you.
B. Ask questions to isolate the general problem.

Question 1:   What does the general problem seem to be?

Question 2:   Does the problem stem from user error?

Step 2.   Divide the problem into hardware or software.

A. Will the computer start?
- *No:* Check power cables, etc.
- *Yes:* Watch for POST error messages or beep codes.

Question 3:   Are there any POST error messages or beep codes? If so, list them below.

        B. Confirm computer startup step-by-step.
- Boot the Windows 98 computer.
- Press and hold the **CTRL** key during the boot process to open the Startup menu.
- From the Startup menu, select **Step-by-step confirmation**.
- Confirm each startup command by pressing the **Y** key. Any error with the command that caused the error.

Question 4:   Were any error messages displayed during step-by-step confirmation? If so, list them below.

        C. Use the System control panel to view resource conflicts.
- From the Start menu, choose **Settings** and then **Control Panel**.
- From the Control Panel window, double-click on the **System** icon, and then select **Device Manager**.
- Browse the devices in Device Manager and note any disabled devices and/or resource conflicts.

Question 5:   Are any disabled devices or resource conflicts visible from within Control Panel? If so, list them below.

    Step 3. Divide and conquer.
        A. Divide the problem into logical areas

Question 6:   Using the information gathered in the previous steps, can you isolate the probable cause of the problem to one or more logical areas? List these logical areas below.

Question 7:   For each of the possible areas listed in Question 6, formulate possible solutions. List these solutions below.

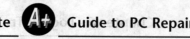

Note: Try fixing the easy things first. For example, if you believe the problem is with the video subsystem, try a different monitor before replacing the video adapter.

Step 4. Repair the problem, or go back and test another theory.

    A. Implement possible solutions one at a time.
- If you implement more than one solution at a time, you will not know which solution worked.

    B. Try a fix and see if it works.
- If the solution does not work, return the computer to its previous condition and try another solution.

Step 5. Test the solution.

    A. Try to re-create the problem after you think it has been repaired.

    B. If the problem does not recur, it has probably been solved.

Step 6. Provide feedback to the user.

    A. Demonstrate to the user that the problem has been solved.

    B. Have the user try to re-create the problem.

    C. Document the results of your troubleshooting for future reference.

_____ *Instructor's Initials*

Name _____

LOGICAL TROUBLESHOOTING FOR NT WORKSTATION

Objective: To understand a logical troubleshooting approach using Windows NT Workstation

Parts: Windows NT Workstation

Note: The student should leave the room while the instructor or lab assistant creates a problem on the Windows NT Workstation. When the student returns to the room, the instructor/lab assistant will play the part of the user, and the student will isolate and repair the problem.

By following a logical troubleshooting procedure, you, as a technician, will be able to isolate and repair PC problems more efficiently. To accomplish the exercise, use the six logical troubleshooting steps:

1. Re-create the problem.
2. Divide the problem into hardware or software.
3. Divide and conquer: divide the problem into logical areas.
4. Repair the problem or test another theory.
5. Test the solution.
6. Provide feedback to the user.

Step 1.   Re-create the problem.

   A. Have the user demonstrate the problem for you.
   B. Ask questions to isolate the general problem.

Question 1:   What does the general problem seem to be?

Question 2:   Does the problem stem from user error?

Step 2.   Divide the problem into hardware or software.

   A. Will the computer start?
   - *No:*   Check power cables, etc.
   - *Yes:*   Watch for POST error messages or beep codes.

Question 3:   Are there any POST error messages or beep codes? If so, list them below.

      B. Use Event Viewer to view System and Application events.
- From the Start menu, choose **Programs**, **Administrative Tools**, and then **Event Viewer**.
- From Event Viewer, open and view the System and Application logs.

Question 4:   Are there any error messages in the System or Application logs that relate to the problem? If so, list them below.

      C. Use various control panels to view resource conflicts.
- From the Start menu, choose **Settings** and then **Control Panel**.
- From the Control Panel, open and view the properties and resource settings of devices, such as Network adapters, Ports, Sound cards, and Mice.

Question 5:   Are any resource conflicts visible from within any of the control panels? If so, list them below.

Step 3.   Divide and conquer.

      A. Divide the problem into logical areas

Question 6:   Using the information gathered in the previous steps, can you isolate the probable cause of the problem to one or more logical areas? List these logical areas below.

Question 7:   For each of the possible areas listed in Question 6, formulate possible solutions. List these solutions below.

Note: Try fixing the easy things first. For example, if you believe the problem is with the video subsystem, try a different monitor before replacing the video adapter.

Step 4.   Repair the problem, or go back and test another theory.

     A.   Implement possible solutions one at a time.
- If you implement more than one solution at a time, you will not know which solution worked.

     B.   Try a fix and see if it works.
- If the solution does not work, return the computer to its previous condition and try another solution.

Step 5.   Test the solution.

     A.   Try to re-create the problem after you think it has been repaired.

     B.   If the problem does not recur, it has probably been solved.

Step 6.   Provide feedback to the user.

     A.   Demonstrate to the user that the problem has been solved.

     B.   Have the user try to re-create the problem.

     C.   Document the results of your troubleshooting for future reference.

_____ ***Instructor's Initials***

Name _____

LOGICAL TROUBLESHOOTING FOR 2000 PROFESSIONAL

Objective: To understand a logical troubleshooting approach using Windows 2000 Professional

Parts: Windows 2000 Professional computer

Note: The student should leave the room while the instructor or lab assistant creates a problem on the Windows 2000 Professional computer. When the student returns to the room, the instructor/lab assistant will play the part of the user and the student will isolate and repair the problem.

By following a logical troubleshooting procedure, you, as a technician, will be able to isolate and repair PC problems more efficiently. To accomplish the exercise, use the six logical troubleshooting steps:

1. Re-create the problem.
2. Divide the problem into hardware or software.
3. Divide and conquer: divide the problem into logical areas.
4. Repair the problem or test another theory.
5. Test the solution.
6. Provide feedback to the user.

Step 1.   Re-create the problem.

A. Have the user demonstrate the problem for you.
B. Ask questions to isolate the general problem.

Question 1:   What does the general problem seem to be?

Question 2:   Does the problem stem from user error?

Step 2.   Divide the problem into hardware or software.

A. Will the computer start?
   *   *No:*   Check power cables, etc.
   *   *Yes:*   Watch for POST error messages or beep codes.

Question 3:   Are there any POST error messages or beep codes? If so, list them below.

B. Enable Boot Logging during system startup.
   • From the Windows Boot Menu, press **F8**.
   • From the Windows 2000 Advanced Options menu, choose **Enable Boot Logging** and press **Enter**.
   • The Enable Boot Logging option creates a boot log text file called NTBTLOG.TXT in the WINNT directory. After booting, browse to and open the NTBTLOG.TXT file. Examine the file for any error messages.

Question 4:   Are there any error messages in the NTBTLOG.TXT file? If so, list them below.

C. Use Event Viewer to view System and Application events.
   • From the Start menu, choose **Settings**, **Control Panel**, and then double-click **Administrative Tools**.
   • Double-click **Event Viewer**.
   • From Event Viewer, open and view the System and Application logs.

Question 5:   Are there any error messages in the System or Application logs that relate to the problem? If so, list them below.

D. Use the System Information tool to view resource conflicts.
   • From the Start menu, choose **Programs, Accessories, System Tools**, and then select **System Information**.
   • Expand the **Hardware Resources** folder and then open the **Conflicts/Sharing** folder.

Question 6:   Are any resource conflicts listed in the Conflicts/Sharing folder? If so, list them below.

Step 3. Divide and conquer.

    A. Divide the problem into logical areas.

Question 6: Using the information gathered in the previous steps, can you isolate the probable cause of the problem to one or more logical areas? List these logical areas below.

Question 7: For each of the possible areas listed in Question 6, formulate possible solutions. List these solutions below.

Note: Try fixing the easy things first. For example, if you believe the problem is with the video subsystem, try a different monitor before replacing the video adapter.

Step 4. Repair the problem, or go back and test another theory.

    A. Implement possible solutions one at a time.

       • If you implement more than one solution at a time, you will not know which solution worked.

    B. Try a fix and see if it works.

       • If the solution does not work, return the computer to its previous condition and try another solution.

Step 5. Test the solution.

    A. Try to re-create the problem after you believe it has been repaired.

    B. If the problem does not recur, it has probably been solved.

Step 6. Provide feedback to the user.

    A. Demonstrate to the user that the problem has been solved.

    B. Have the user try to re-create the problem.

    C. Document the results of your troubleshooting for future reference.

_____ ***Instructor's Initials***

Name _____

INTERNET DISCOVERY

Objective: To obtain specific information on the Internet regarding a computer or associated parts

Parts: Access to the Internet

Question 1:   Locate a web site that has a troubleshooting flow chart and write the web address in the space below.

Question 2:   Locate one web site that lists the Phoenix BIOS beep codes.

Question 3:   What does the A08 Flash BIOS upgrade do for a Dell Dimension 4100 computer? Write the answer and URL where you found the answer in the space below.

Question 4:   Go to the http://www.spu.edu/~time/say/comphelp.html URL. In "Tim's 7-Step Guide to Computer Troubleshooting," what does Tim recommend to do before starting any of the seven steps?

Question 5:   On a Compaq computer, you hear two long and two short beeps. What is the problem (and the solution) and on what Internet site was the answer found?

NOTES

Chapter 7:
Memory

OBJECTIVES

After completing this chapter you will
- Understand memory-related terminology.
- Be able to install and remove memory chips.
- Understand how memory works with different operating systems.
- Be able to optimize memory under different operating systems.
- Be able to troubleshoot memory problems.

KEY TERMS

access time	LIM	RIMM
bank	memory map	ROM
burst EDO	nanosecond	SDRAM
C-RIMM	non-parity	SGRAM
CAS	non-volatile memory	SIMM
cache memory	page	SIPP
chipset	parity	SO-DIMM
conventional memory	parity chip	SO-RIMM
DDR DIMM	PC100	SPD
DDR RAM	PC133	SRAM
DIMM	Performance Monitor	swap file
DIP	Performance utility	System Monitor
DRAM	pipeline burst cache	thread
ECC	pipelining	UMA
EDO	protected mode	UMB
EMS	RAM	VCM
expanded memory	RAM drive	virtual memory
extended memory	RDRAM	volatile memory
external data lines	real mode	VRAM
flash memory	refresh	WRAM
FPM	registered SDRAM	XMS
HMA	reserved memory area	

MEMORY OVERVIEW

Computer systems need software to operate; the computer is an expensive doorstop without software. For the computer to operate, the software must reside in the computer's memory. Memory is simple to upgrade, but a technician must understand memory terminology, determine the optimum amount of memory for a system, install the memory, fine-tune it for the best performance, and finally, troubleshoot and solve any memory problems.

The two main types of memory are **RAM (Random Access Memory)** and **ROM (Read Only Memory)**. RAM is found on the motherboard and stores the operating system (DOS, Windows 95, Windows 98, or NT Workstation), the software applications (word processing, spreadsheet, database, etc.), and the data being used by all of this software. RAM is also found on adapters such as video cards. RAM is **volatile memory**; the information in RAM is lost when you power off the computer. ROM is **non-volatile memory**; the information is in ROM even when the computer is powered off.

RAM is divided into two major types: **DRAM (Dynamic RAM)** and **SRAM (Static RAM)**. DRAM is less expensive, but slower than SRAM. With DRAM, the 1s and 0s inside the chip must be refreshed. Over time, the *charge*, which represents information inside a DRAM chip, leaks out. The information, stored in 1s and 0s, is periodically rewritten to the memory chip through the **refreshing** process. The refreshing is accomplished inside the DRAM while other processing occurs. Refreshing is one reason DRAM chips are slower than SRAM.

Most memory on the motherboard is DRAM, but a small amount of SRAM can be found on a motherboard or, as is the norm for today's computers, inside the microprocessor. SRAM is also known as **cache memory**. The cache memory holds the most frequently used data so the microprocessor does not return to the slower DRAM chips to obtain the data. For example, on a motherboard with a bus speed of 100MHz, accessing DRAM could take as long as 180 nanoseconds. (A **nanosecond** is a billionth of a second.) Accessing the same information in cache could take as little as 45 nanoseconds.

Some cache memory (L2 cache) is known as **pipeline burst cache**. When computers use this memory technology, it is known as pipelining. **Pipelining** is the process by which microprocessors and memory obtain computer software instructions in a timely fashion.

To understand pipelining, take the example of a fast food restaurant. In the restaurant, say there are five steps (and one employee per step) to making a burger and giving it to the customer: (1) take the order and input it into the computer system, (2) brown the buns and cook the burgers, (3) take the bun and burger and add condiments, (4) wrap the burger, add fries, and insert them into a sack, (5) take the customer's money and give the sack to the customer. Keep in mind that the person taking the customer's order cannot serve another customer until the first customer receives their order. To make this burger process go faster, you could (1) allow the person taking the order to serve other customers until the first order is ready to be given to the first customer or (2) allow more registers to be opened so more customers can be served simultaneously.

To relate this to processors, the CPU fetches a software instruction from memory and then the processor sits idle. This is the same as not allowing waiting customers to be served until the first customer has his/her food. With pipelining, the processor is allowed to obtain more software instructions without waiting for the first instruction to be executed. Having more registers is the same as having more pipelines that have the task of fetching instructions. Both techniques are used in today's processors. The bottom line is that the CPU should never have to wait to receive an instruction. Using pipelined burst cache speeds up processing for software applications.

The data or instruction that the microprocessor needs is usually in one of three places: cache, DRAM, or the hard drive. Cache gives the fastest access. If the information is not in cache, the microprocessor looks for it in DRAM. If the information is not in DRAM, it is retrieved from the hard drive and placed into DRAM or the cache. Hard drive access is the slowest of the three. An analogy is the best way to explain this. Consider a glass of cold lemonade, a pitcher of lemonade in the refrigerator, and a can of frozen concentrated lemonade in the freezer. If you are thirsty, you would drink from the glass because it is the fastest and easily accessible. If the glass is empty, you would pour lemonade from the pitcher to refill the glass. If the pitcher is empty, you would go to the freezer to get the frozen concentrate to make some more. The glass of lemonade is like cache memory. It is easily accessible. The pitcher of lemonade is like DRAM. If the glass is empty, you have to get more lemonade from the pitcher. If the 1s and 0s are not in cache, they are retrieved from DRAM. The pitcher holds more lemonade than the glass just like DRAM holds more information than cache memory. The concentrated lemonade is like the hard drive. Concentrated lemonade takes longer to make and get to than the glass or the pitcher. In a computer, it takes roughly a million times longer to access information from the hard drive than it does from DRAM or cache.

Usually the more cache memory a system has, the better that system performs, but this is not always true. System performance also depends on the efficiency of the cache controller (the chip that manages the cache memory), the system design, the amount of available hard drive space, and the speed of the microprocessor. When determining a computer's memory requirements, you must take into consideration what operating system is used, what types of applications are used, and what hardware is installed. DOS computers take a lot less memory than 2000 Professional computers. High-end games and desktop publishing take more RAM than word processing. Free hard drive space and video memory are often as important as RAM in improving a computer's performance. RAM is only one piece of the puzzle. All of the computer's parts must work together to provide good system performance.

MEMORY PHYSICAL PACKAGING

A **DIP (Dual In-line Package)** chip has a row of legs running down each side. The oldest motherboards used DIP chips for the DRAM. **SIMMs (Single In-line Memory Modules)** came along next. Two types of SIMMs are available: 30-pin and 72-pin. The most popular memory chip, a **DIMM (Dual In-line Memory Module)**, has 168 pins. It works in Pentium, Pentium Pro, Pentium II, or Pentium III motherboards.

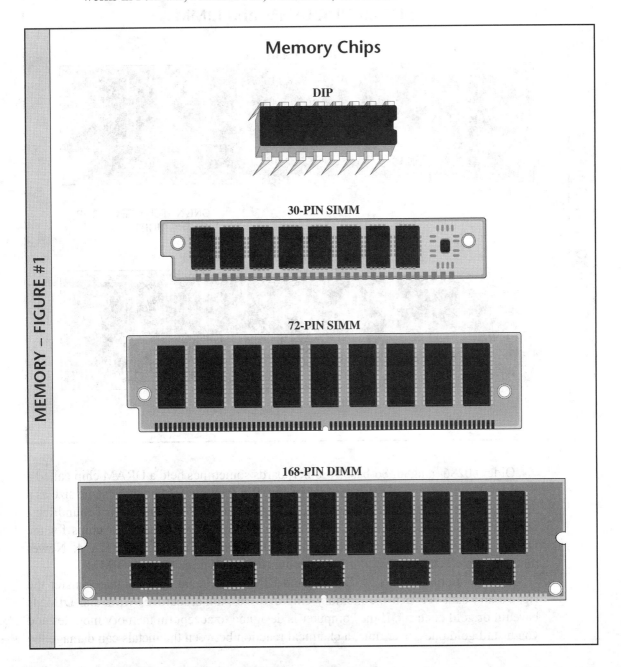

Memory Chips

DIP

30-PIN SIMM

72-PIN SIMM

168-PIN DIMM

MEMORY – FIGURE #1

Other memory packages available today include the 184-pin DIMM and the 168-pin RIMM. **DDR DIMMs** are used in AMD Athlon computers and higher-end servers. **RIMMs** are used in Intel Pentium 4 computers. Memory Figure #2 illustrates these types. Notice the single notch at the bottom of the 184-pin DDR DIMM. This distinguishes it from the other dual-notched DIMMs. The RIMM has two notches in the center.

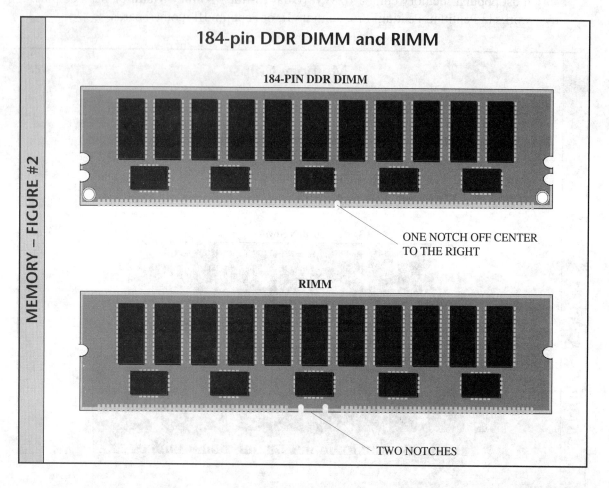

184-pin DDR DIMM and RIMM

184-PIN DDR DIMM

ONE NOTCH OFF CENTER
TO THE RIGHT

RIMM

TWO NOTCHES

MEMORY – FIGURE #2

Older 80286- and 80386-based motherboards sometimes held a DRAM chip called a SIPP, but these are rare. A **SIPP (Single In-line Pin Package)** is about the same size as a 30-pin SIMM. Instead of a card-edged connector, the SIPP has one row of round legs. Older 8088, 8086, 80286, and even a few 80386 motherboards had DIP chips for the DRAM, but 386, 486, and Pentium computers use SIMMs for the RAM. Newer motherboards (Pentium, Pentium Pro, Pentium II, and Pentium III) use DIMMs.

At the bottom of a SIMM, DIMM, and RIMM are metal contacts that transfer the signals and data between the memory chip and the motherboard. SIMMs and DIMMs have tin or gold contacts. If the computer is designed to accept tin memory modules and you install gold ones, over time, a chemical reaction between the metals can damage the connector. The bottom line is this: purchase the appropriate memory module for the computer. This can be determined by referring to the documentation or by examining other chips already installed.

SIMMs, DIMMs, and RIMMs come in parity and non-parity versions. **Parity** is a method for checking the accuracy of data going in or out of the memory chips. For every eight bits of data, one parity bit is used. Parity chips can detect memory errors, but cannot correct them. **Non-parity** memory chips are simply chips that do not use any error checking.

> A computer system that uses parity *must* have parity memory chips installed. Some computers that are non-parity systems can use either parity or non-parity SIMMs. It is best to use the manufacturer-specified memory chips.

If the SIMM is a parity chip, the parity bit is ignored by the non-parity system. However, non-parity memory chips are usually less expensive than parity memory chips. Some motherboards allow a choice of parity and non-parity memory by setting a motherboard jumper or using the Setup program. Still other motherboards, when checking memory during POST, automatically disable the parity checking if all memory banks do not contain parity bits. Pentium-based microcomputers with Intel's Triton-series chipset do *not* support parity.

How parity functions depends on whether the system uses even parity or odd parity. For example, if the system uses even parity and the data bits 10000001 go into memory, the ninth bit or parity bit is a 0 because an even number of bits (2) are 1s. The parity changes to a 1 only when the number of bits in the data is an odd number of 1s. If the system uses even parity and the data bits 10000011 go into memory, the parity bit is a 1. There are only three 1s in the data bits. The parity bit adjusts the 1s to an even number. When checking data for accuracy, the parity method detects if one bit is incorrect. However, if two bits are in error, parity does not catch the error.

An alternative to parity checking is the ECC method. **ECC (Error Correcting Code)** uses a mathematical algorithm to verify data accuracy. ECC can detect up to four-bit memory errors and correct one-bit memory errors. ECC memory checking is more expensive to implement than parity. The motherboard or memory controller must have additional circuitry to process ECC bits generated and compared during each data transfer. ECC is used in computers such as network servers, database servers, or workstations running database applications. These systems need very high quality data for proper operation.

MEMORY CHIP CAPACITY

DIP chips normally have 64Kb, 256Kb, or 1Mb capacities. Notice the lowercase *b* indicates the size measured in *bits*, not bytes. A 64-kilobit chip holds approximately 64,000 bits. Eight 64Kb DIP chips work together to provide 64KB (the uppercase *B* indicates bytes) of memory. Thirty-pin SIMM sizes are 256KB, 512KB, 1MB, 2MB, and 4MB, with 1MB and 4MB the most common sizes. Seventy-two-pin SIMM sizes are 4MB, 8MB, 16MB, 32MB, 64MB, and 128MB capacities. DIMM sizes are 8MB, 16MB, 32MB,

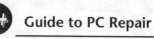
64MB, 128MB, 256MB, 512MB, and 1024MB. RIMMs come in 64MB, 128MB, and 256MB capacities.

IDENTIFYING CHIP CAPACITY AND SPEED

Sometimes, you can tell the capacity of a memory chip by examining the numbers printed on it. For example, on a DIP chip, the numbers M41256A indicate a 256Kb chip and the numbers M51004 indicate a 1Mb chip. On a SIMM chip, the numbers K264096P0 indicate a 4MB SIMM and the numbers K268192P0 indicate an 8MB SIMM.

Memory chip numbers can be misleading. The only way to be certain of the capacity is to install the SIMM in a computer or research the manufacturer's number on the Internet. Memory Figure #3 shows a DIP chip and a SIMM.

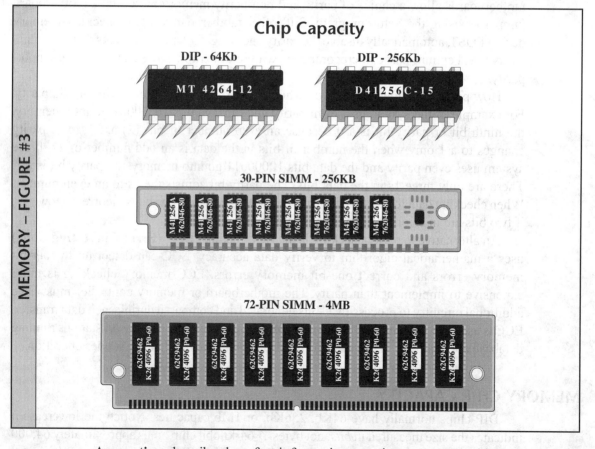

Access time describes how fast information goes into a memory chip or is removed from the chip. DRAM chip access time is measured in nanoseconds, abbreviated ns. A nanosecond is a billionth of a second. DIMMs have access times of 15, 12, 10, 7, and lower nanoseconds. SIMMs have access times of 50, 60, 70, or 80 nanoseconds. Older computers that used DIP DRAM chips have access times of 100, 120, or 150 nanoseconds.

The lower the number of nanoseconds, the faster the access time of the memory chips. If possible, identify the access time by looking at the numbers on the memory chip or on an attached sticker. On the chip the number(s) following the dash indicate the access time.

Memory Figure #4 shows the access time indicated on different memory chips.

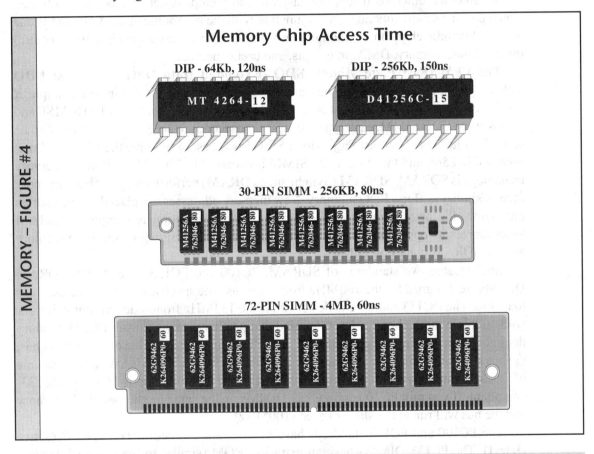

MEMORY – FIGURE #4

Memory Chip Access Time

DIP - 64Kb, 120ns

MT 4264-**12**

DIP - 256Kb, 150ns

D41256C-**15**

30-PIN SIMM - 256KB, 80ns

72-PIN SIMM - 4MB, 60ns

Installing memory chips with a faster access time *does not* speed up a computer. The motherboard is designed to operate with memory chips that have a specific access time. Adding faster memory chips does not speed up the motherboard because faster memory chips do not change the motherboard design. Faster memory chips can be added, but the memory will operate at the original access time.

MEMORY CHIP TECHNOLOGIES

Technology has provided faster DRAM speeds without increasing the cost too greatly. These DRAM technologies include FPM (Fast Page Mode) RAM, EDO (Extended Data Out) RAM, BEDO (Burst EDO) RAM, SDRAM (Synchronous DRAM), DDR RAM, and RDRAM (Rambus DRAM). The motherboard must be designed to use one of these technologies or the faster memory *will not* speed up the computer.

Whether a motherboard supports faster memory chips is determined by the chipset, which performs most functions in conjunction with the microprocessor. A **chipset** is one to five electronic chips on the motherboard. The chipset contains the circuitry to control the local bus, memory, DMA, interrupts, and cache memory.

The **FPM (Fast Page Mode)**, **EDO (Extended Data Out)**, and **Burst EDO** technologies speed up DRAM on sequential accesses to the memory chip. For example, if you have a 50ns DRAM SIMM, a 50ns Fast Page Mode SIMM, a 50ns EDO SIMM, and a 50ns Burst EDO SIMM, each type takes 50 nanoseconds to access the first time. On the second try however, the Fast Page Mode SIMM is accessed in 40ns, the EDO SIMM is accessed in 25ns, and the Burst EDO SIMM is accessed in 15ns. The follow-on memory technology is SDRAM. **SDRAM (Synchronous DRAM)** performs very fast burst memory access, similar to Burst EDO memory. New memory addresses are placed on the address bus before the prior memory address retrieval and execution is complete. SDRAM synchronizes its operation with the microprocessor's clock signal to speed up memory access. SDRAM comes on DIMMs.

Intel created two standards of SDRAM, PC100 and PC133. The **PC100** SDRAM DIMMs are designed for the 100MHz front-side bus. The specification calls for the chips to be 8ns. The **PC133** standard is designed for the 133MHz front-side bus, but will work with 100MHz motherboards. Keep in mind that just because you install PC133 memory does not mean the bus will go 133MHz. If PC133 memory is installed on a 100MHz bus, the bus still communicates with memory at 100MHz. PC133 DIMMs have an access time of 7.5ns. Manufacturers affix a label that certifies the memory chip is PC100 or PC133-compliant. If you mix PC100 and PC133 DIMMs on the same motherboard, all memory and the bus will run at the slower speed (100MHz).

The PC100 and PC133 standards have a new feature called **SPD (Serial Presence Detect)**. The PC133 DIMMs have an extra EEPROM (similar to the Flash BIOS) that holds information about the DIMM, such as capacity size, voltage, error detection/correction, refresh rates, data width, etc. The BIOS can read and use this information to adjust motherboard timings for the best CPU-to-RAM performance.

Another distinction between SDRAM types is that some are registered and some unbuffered. **Registered SDRAM** is sometimes called buffered SDRAM and is used in network servers and higher end computers. This type of memory delays all data transfers by one clock to ensure accuracy. It also allows for larger capacity DIMMs. Some computers only accept Registered SDRAM. The opposite of Registered SDRAM is unbuffered SDRAM and this is the memory type most often used in home computers and in low- to medium-powered computers.

An alternative to SDRAM is **VCM (Virtual Memory Channel)**, which was created by NEC Electronics, Inc.). VCM fits in DIMM slots, but the chipset must support it. Intel chipsets do not support VCM, but VIA chipsets do. The VC133 memory module is designed for the 133MHz front-side bus.

SDRAM is a good memory technology for Pentium and higher systems. However, as microprocessors and motherboard components got larger than 200MHz, memory technologies evolved to include RDRAM and DDR RAM. **RDRAM (Rambus DRAM)** is technology developed by Rambus, Inc. Intel uses RDRAM in Pentium 4 computers. RDRAM is also used on some video adapters. RDRAM is packaged in RIMMs. (RIMM is not an acronym, but a trademark of Rambus, Inc.) In order for a computer to use a RIMM, the BIOS and the chipset must both support the technology. RIMMs come in 600, 700, and 800MHz versions.

When RIMMs are used, all memory slots must be filled even if the slot is not needed because the memory banks are tied together. Put a **C-RIMM (Continuity RIMM)**, which is a blank module, in any empty (unfilled) slot.

RDRAM is proprietary; it is licensed by Rambus, Inc. and has not caught on as previously predicted. Intel now has a chipset (the i845) that allows Pentium 4 motherboards to support DDR RAM. RDRAM is more expensive than DDR RAM.

DDR RAM (Double Data Rate RAM) was developed from SDRAM technology. With SDRAM, data is only sent on the rising clock signal. With DDR RAM, data can be transmitted on both sides of the clock signal (rising and falling edges). If this does not make sense, just think of it this way: DDR RAM can send twice as much data as SDRAM. DDR RAM uses 184-pin DIMMs that are different from SDRAM DIMMs. They will not fit in the same socket. The two most popular versions of DDR RAM are PC1600 and PC2100. PC1600 is for the 200MHz front-side bus (it doubles 100MHz) and PC2100 is for the 266MHz front-side bus (it doubles 133MHz). You can mix PC1600 and PC2100 DIMMs on the same motherboard, but the bus will run at the PC1600 speed (200MHz). Some AMD processor-based motherboards (such as for the Thunderbird) use DDR RAM.

Memory technology is moving quite quickly today. Chipsets also change constantly. Technicians are continually challenged to keep up with the features and abilities of the technology so that they can make recommendations to their customers! Trade magazines and the Internet are excellent resources for updates. Never forget to check the motherboard's documentation when dealing with memory. Information is a technician's best friend. Take a look at HSDRAM (High Speed Synchronous DRAM), ESDARM (Enhanced SDRAM), and SLDRAM (Synchronous-Link DRAM) for some interesting memory developments.

Even though video memory is covered in the video chapter, when studying memory and for the A+ Certification, it never hurts to see something twice. **VRAM (Video RAM)** is a memory type found on a video card. A closely related type of memory is **WRAM (Windows RAM)**. Both of these memory technologies are dual-ported, which means that they can read from memory and output to the monitor simultaneously. WRAM is faster and cheaper than VRAM and was developed by Samsung Electronics. Another video memory technology that can deliver data at speeds up to 100MHz is **SGRAM (Synchronous Graphic Random Access Memory)**. SGRAM memory chips are frequently used on video adapters and graphics accelerators, and have special memory techniques that speed up graphics-intensive functions.

MEMORY BANKS

The process of installing memory in a system is called "populating the memory." A few basic concepts are important in understanding how to add or remove memory in a system. The best way to explain memory is to begin with how the 8088 microprocessor used on the original IBM PCs addressed memory, and continue to the microprocessors of today.

Memory chips work together in a group called a **bank**. The number of chips in a memory bank depends on how many **external data lines** extend from the microprocessor to the memory chips. Data lines are different from address lines. The address lines pick which memory location on a chip (mailbox) to access. The data lines carry binary 1s and 0s of data (the mail) into the memory location (mailbox). The 8088 microprocessor has an eight-bit external data path. Memory Figure #5 illustrates how the 8088's external data path connects to the banks of memory.

MEMORY – FIGURE #5

8088 Memory Banks

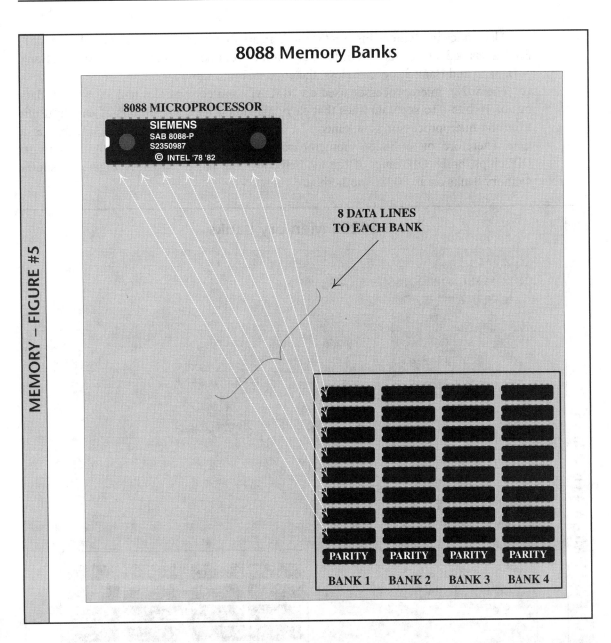

Notice in Memory Figure #5 that the microprocessor outputs or accepts input of eight 1s or 0s at a time. Each data line from the microprocessor connects to one chip in the memory bank. The chips in the bank work together to transfer data to or from the microprocessor. Therefore, a bank of memory chips for an 8088 accepts eight bits of data at a time. On most 8088-based computers, a bank of memory contains *nine* DIP chips. The ninth chip is a **parity chip**. The parity chip checks the accuracy of the eight bits transferred into the bank of memory together. Look at Memory Figure #5 and notice the last chip in the bank is labeled *parity*.

Also notice in Memory Figure #5 that there are four banks of memory labeled Bank 1, Bank 2, Bank 3, and Bank 4. A different manufacturer might label the banks Bank 0, Bank 1, Bank 2, and Bank 3; nevertheless, the concept is the same.

The 80286 microprocessor used on IBM ATs and compatibles had an external data bus of 16 bits—16 separate lines that carry a 1 or a 0. Because 16 bits of data transmit from the microprocessor simultaneously, each bank of memory processes 16 bits at a time. Therefore, on an 80286 motherboard, one bank of memory normally contains 16 DIP chips, or 18 DIP chips if the motherboard uses parity. Memory Figure #6 shows memory banks on an 80286 motherboard.

MEMORY – FIGURE #6

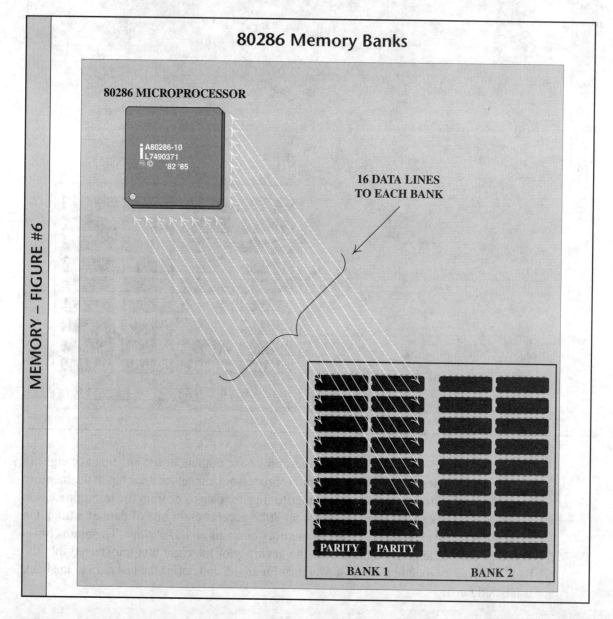

80286 Memory Banks

80286 MICROPROCESSOR

A80286-10
L7490371
'82 '85

16 DATA LINES
TO EACH BANK

PARITY   PARITY

BANK 1   BANK 2

Notice in Memory Figure #6 how each bank of memory contains two rows of chips instead of just one row of chips as on the 8088 motherboard. Each bank contains two rows of chips because the 80286 microprocessors have 16 external data lines. Each chip connects to one data line. The 80286 microprocessor could handle more RAM on the motherboard, so memory chip manufacturers started making 1 megabit (1Mb) DIP chips. 1Mb memory chips are two pins longer than the 64Kb and the 256Kb DIP chips. Many motherboards accepted both physical sizes of DIP chips.

When the 80386 came out with 32 address lines and 32 external data lines, manufacturers started using 30-pin SIMMs on the motherboard. These accept eight bits of data from the microprocessor at one time. Therefore, one 30-pin SIMM is like one entire bank of memory in a XT. Memory Figure #7 shows this concept.

MEMORY – FIGURE #7

How a 30-Pin SIMM Compares with a Bank of DIP Chips

8088 MICROPROCESSOR

8 DATA LINES
TO EACH BANK

BANK 1   BANK 2   BANK 3   BANK 4

8088 MICROPROCESSOR

8 DATA LINES
TO EACH BANK

BANK 1 BANK 2 BANK 3 BANK 4

Notice that even though Memory Figure #7 shows a comparison of how the data lines connect to each SIMM, the 8088-based motherboards did not use SIMMs. Memory Figure #7 simply illustrates how the SIMM replaced eight or nine chips by placing them on a small circuit board, making memory easier to install, easier to manage, and easier to troubleshoot.

Because the 80386 microprocessor has a 32-bit external data path, four 30-pin SIMMs are normally found in each bank of memory. Refer to Memory Figure #8 for an illustration of an 80386 motherboard with SIMM sockets instead of DIP chips.

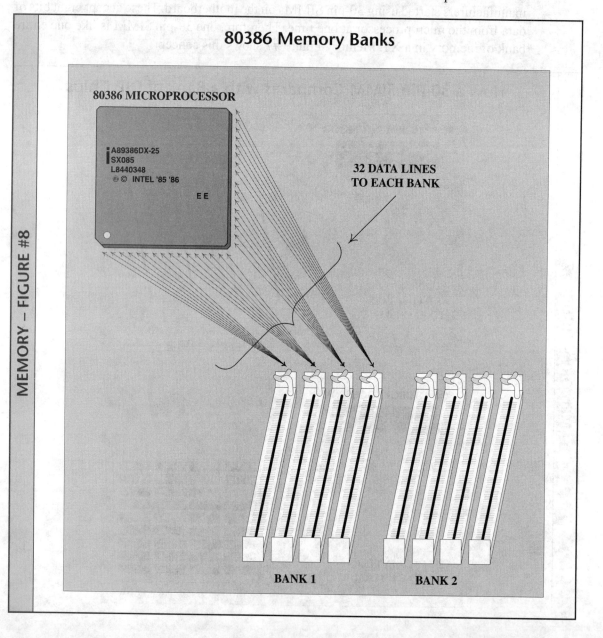

MEMORY – FIGURE #8

80386 Memory Banks

80386 MICROPROCESSOR

A89386DX-25
SX085
L8440348
Ⓜ © INTEL '85 '86

E E

32 DATA LINES
TO EACH BANK

BANK 1   BANK 2

30-pin SIMM sizes are 256KB, 512KB, 1MB, 2MB, and 4MB, although the 1MB and the 4MB are most common. Exactly which SIMM can be used on a motherboard depends on the manufacturer of the motherboard. Memory Figure #9 illustrates an 80386 motherboard populated with 10MB of memory using 2MB and 512KB SIMM chips.

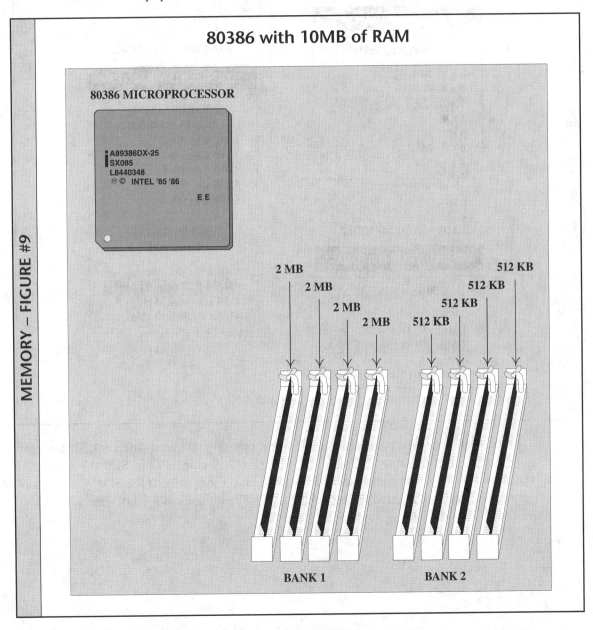

Memory sales advertisements and technical manuals list 30-pin SIMMs in different ways. Understanding the different lists can be difficult. Memory Figure #10 shows three different memory advertisements.

MEMORY – FIGURE #10

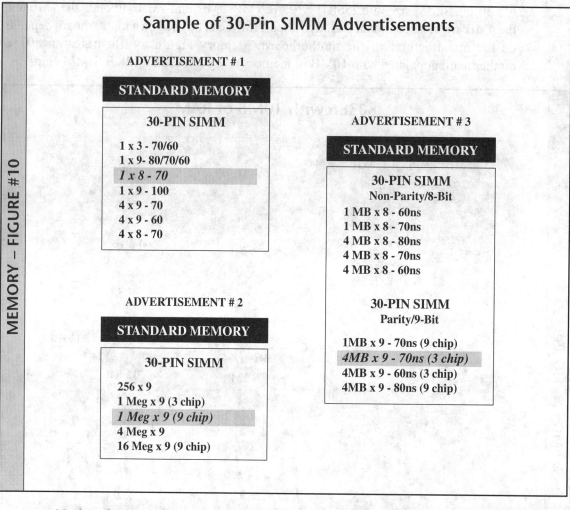

Sample of 30-Pin SIMM Advertisements

ADVERTISEMENT # 1

STANDARD MEMORY

30-PIN SIMM

1 x 3 - 70/60
1 x 9- 80/70/60
1 x 8 - 70
1 x 9 - 100
4 x 9 - 70
4 x 9 - 60
4 x 8 - 70

ADVERTISEMENT # 2

STANDARD MEMORY

30-PIN SIMM

256 x 9
1 Meg x 9 (3 chip)
1 Meg x 9 (9 chip)
4 Meg x 9
16 Meg x 9 (9 chip)

ADVERTISEMENT # 3

STANDARD MEMORY

30-PIN SIMM
Non-Parity/8-Bit

1 MB x 8 - 60ns
1 MB x 8 - 70ns
4 MB x 8 - 80ns
4 MB x 8 - 70ns
4 MB x 8 - 60ns

30-PIN SIMM
Parity/9-Bit

1MB x 9 - 70ns (9 chip)
4MB x 9 - 70ns (3 chip)
4MB x 9 - 60ns (3 chip)
4MB x 9 - 80ns (9 chip)

Notice that each advertisement in Memory Figure #10 has a different SIMM chip highlighted. Advertisement #2 shows a "1Meg x 9 (9 chip) 30-pin SIMM." The "x 9" portion of the advertisement means the SIMM chip uses parity. If the SIMM was a non-parity chip, the highlighted listing would say "x 8" as it does in Advertisement #1.

When purchasing SIMMs for a microcomputer, be sure if the computer uses parity that you buy parity SIMMs. The documentation included with the motherboard should state whether or not the system uses parity. If a computer system does *not* use parity, SIMMs with the extra parity chip can be installed. The parity chip will simply be ignored.

In Advertisement #3, a "4MB x 9 70ns (3 chip)" line is highlighted. Some 9-bit SIMM chips have nine individual memory chips mounted on the SIMM while other 9-bit SIMM chips have only three individual memory chips mounted on the SIMM. Each of the three memory chips on the SIMM handles three bits at a time.

Some motherboards are very particular about the type of SIMM installed (how many chips are mounted on the SIMM). Systems that already have nine chips on a 30-pin SIMM have been known to lock up when upgraded to SIMMs with only three chips on the SIMM. Not all memory retailers specify in their advertisements if the SIMM is a three-chip or a nine-chip SIMM.

When upgrading a system that uses 30-pin SIMMs, open the system and look inside at the existing memory SIMMs. Order the appropriate type of SIMM, three-chip or nine-chip, to match what is already in the system. If you are installing 30-pin SIMMs on a motherboard without SIMMs, refer to the documentation included with the motherboard.

Manufacturers started using 72-pin SIMMs on the 80386-based motherboards. A 72-pin SIMM accepts 32 bits of data at a time from the microprocessor. Therefore, one 72-pin SIMM takes the place of four 30-pin SIMMs. See Memory Figure #11 for a comparison of banks of memory for 30-pin SIMMs and 72-pin SIMMs.

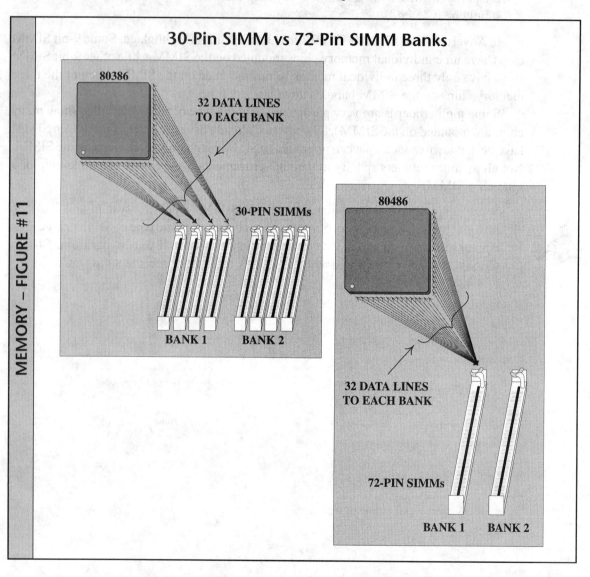

MEMORY – FIGURE #11

30-Pin SIMM vs 72-Pin SIMM Banks

80386

32 DATA LINES
TO EACH BANK

30-PIN SIMMs

BANK 1   BANK 2

80486

32 DATA LINES
TO EACH BANK

72-PIN SIMMs

BANK 1   BANK 2

Notice in Memory Figure #11 that a bank of four 30-pin SIMMs on an 80386-based motherboard equates to a bank of one 72-pin SIMM on an 80486-based motherboard. Some 80386-based motherboards use 72-pin SIMMs or a combination of 30-pin and 72-pin SIMMs to give consumers the choice of which to buy and the ability to use older SIMMs from another machine.

BUYING THE RIGHT 72-PIN SIMM

72-pin SIMMs are available in 1MB, 2MB, 4MB, 8MB, 16MB, 32MB, and 64MB capacities. As with 30-pin SIMMs, advertisements of 72-pin SIMMs can be very confusing. Refer to Memory Figure #12 for samples.

MEMORY – FIGURE #12

Sample of 72-Pin SIMM Advertisements

ADVERTISEMENT # 1

STANDARD MEMORY

72-PIN SIMM

1 x 32 Pin
2 x 32 Pin
2 x 32 Pin - EDO
4 x 32 Pin
8 x 32 Pin

ADVERTISEMENT # 2

STANDARD MEMORY

72-PIN SIMM

1MB x 32 - 60ns
1MB x 32 - 70ns
1MB x 32 - 60ns - EDO
1MB x 32 - 70ns - EDO
2MB x 32 - 60ns
2MB x 32 - 60ns - EDO
4MB x 32 - 60ns
4MB x 32 - 60ns - EDO
8MB x 32 - 60ns
8MB x 32 - 60ns - EDO

1MB x 36 - 60ns
1MB x 36 - 70ns
2MB x 36 - 60ns
2MB x 36 - 70ns
4MB x 36 - 60ns
4MB x 36 - 70ns
8MB x 36 - 60ns
8MB x 36 - 70ns

ADVERTISEMENT # 3

STANDARD MEMORY

72-PIN SIMM
256 x 36 - 70 (1MB)
512 x 36 - 70 (2MB)
1 x 36 - 70/60 (4MB)
2 x 36 - 70/60 (8MB)
4 x 36 - 70/60 (16MB)
8 x 36 - 70/60 (32MB)
16 x 36 - 70/60 (64MB)

72-PIN SIMM
Non-Parity

1 x 32 - 70/60 (4MB)
2 x 32 - 70/60 (8MB)
4 x 32 - 70/60 (16MB)
8 x 32 - 70/60 (32MB)
16 x 32 - 70/60 (64MB)

Notice in Memory Figure #12 that Advertisement #1 highlights the 1 x 32 pin. This particular advertisement does not list the memory chip's access time, which a technician needs to know when installing memory. The "1" in 1 x 32 stands for 1 megabit. The "32" in 1 x 32 stands for 32 bits. The chip accepts 32 bits at one time. The total capacity for this chip is found by multiplying 1 megabit by 32 bits, which is the same as 4 megabytes. (Approximately 1,000,000 bits times 32 bits equals 32,000,000 bits. 32,000,000 bits divided by 8 equals the number of bytes.) So, an advertisement that lists 1 x 32 for a 72-pin SIMM reveals a capacity of 4MB.

A "x 32" is a non-parity SIMM chip. If the SIMM is a parity 72-pin SIMM, some advertisements list "x 36" instead of "x 32." Remember, there is one parity bit for every eight bits. With 32-bits, four additional bits are needed for parity, one for every eight bits, totaling 36 bits. Every chip shown in Advertisement #1 is a non-parity 72-pin SIMM.

Notice in Advertisement #2 that the memory chips are divided into non-parity SIMMs at the top and parity SIMMs at the bottom. Also, this particular company sells EDO memory. Another good feature of Advertisement #2 is the list of access speeds. However, as in Advertisement #1, Advertisement #2 does not list the total capacity of the SIMM. Also, the "MB" listed in the highlighted "2MB x 36-60ns SIMMs" line of Advertisement #2 is a misnomer. The correct listing should be "2M*b* x 36-60ns SIMMs." Most manufacturers and retailers do not list the SIMMs in the correct format. A 2MB x 36-60ns SIMM has a total capacity of 8MB with four bits used for parity.

Memory Figure #12's Advertisement #3 is the best of these three. The retailer lists the total capacity of the chip in parentheses beside each SIMM. The access time is given to the right of each chip in the advertisement. Notice the highlighted "1 x 36-70/60 (4MB) chip." The 70/60 is the access times available for this particular model of SIMM. Finally, this particular advertisement separates parity and non-parity SIMMs.

POPULATING PENTIUM AND HIGHER MOTHERBOARDS

Intel's Pentium, Pentium Pro, Pentium II, Pentium III, and Pentium 4 microprocessors have an external data path of 64 bits. So do the AMD processors. If the system uses 72-pin SIMMs, each bank of memory has two 72-pin SIMM sockets. See Memory Figure #13 for a layout of the 72-pin memory sockets on a Pentium-based motherboard.

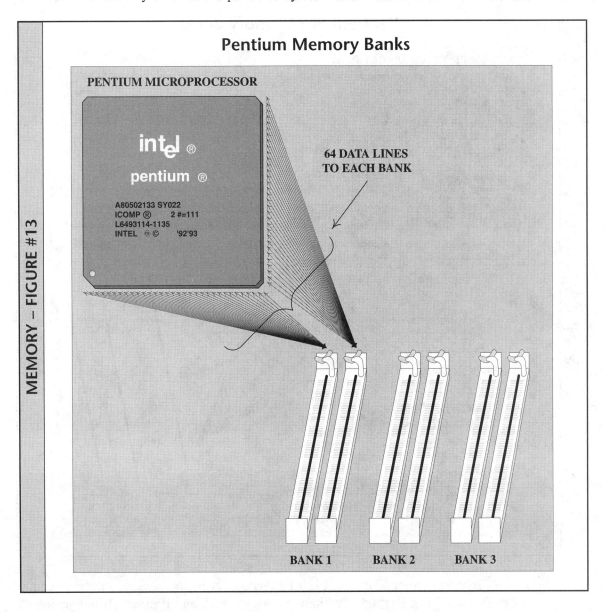

On a machine that uses a Pentium microprocessor and SIMM sockets, two SIMMs must be inserted into at least one bank for the computer to operate. Pentium and higher motherboards also use DIMMs (Dual In-line Memory Modules).

Some manufacturers produce motherboards that contain 72-pin SIMM sockets and 168-pin DIMM sockets. Memory Figure #14 shows a Pentium Pro-based motherboard that has both a DIMM socket and SIMM sockets. Bank 1 contains one DIMM socket and Bank 2 contains two 72-pin SIMM sockets.

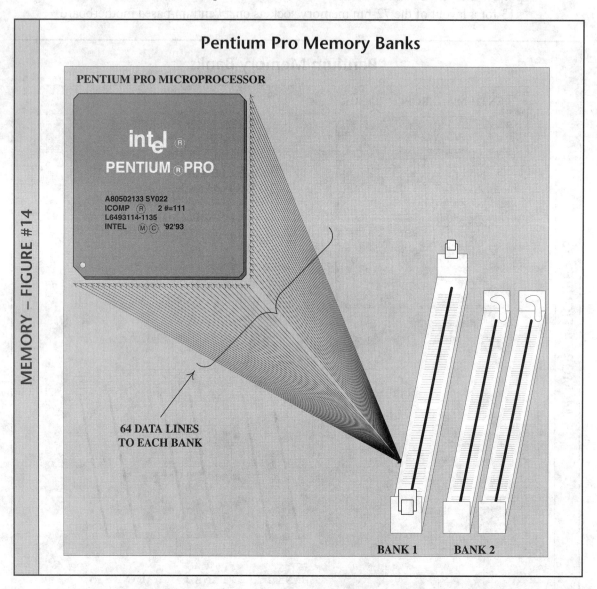

MEMORY – FIGURE #14

Pentium Pro Memory Banks

PENTIUM PRO MICROPROCESSOR

intel ®
PENTIUM ® PRO

A80502133 SY022
ICOMP ® 2 #=111
L6493114-1135
INTEL Ⓜ Ⓒ '92'93

**64 DATA LINES
TO EACH BANK**

BANK 1   BANK 2

As seen in Memory Figure #14, a DIMM socket is one bank of memory for the motherboards. Most Pentium, Pentium Pro, Pentium II, and Pentium III motherboards ship with only DIMM sockets. Pentium 4s ship with DIMM or RIMM sockets (but not both).

BUYING THE RIGHT DIMM OR RIMM

DIMMs have capacities of 8MB, 16MB, 32MB, 64MB, 128MB, 256MB, 512MB, and 1024MB (although larger capacities are sure to come). DIMMs have parity and non-parity versions. The 8MB parity DIMM lists as 1MB x 72 and the non-parity 8MB DIMM lists as 1MB x 64. The 72 on the parity DIMM is calculated by adding one parity bit for every eight bits. There are 64 bits on the DIMM, so it needs eight extra bits to handle parity checking. 64 + 8 = 72 total bits. Be careful when dealing with DIMMs. ECC DIMMs are also shown with 72 bits. Memory Figure #15 shows sample ads for DIMMs.

MEMORY – FIGURE #15

Sample 168-Pin DIMM Advertisements

ADVERTISEMENT # 1

STANDARD MEMORY

168-PIN SDRAM

32MB 4x64-10
64MB 8x64-10
128MB 16x64-10
64MB 8x64-7 PC100
128MB 16x64-7 PC100
256MB 32x64-7 PC100

ADVERTISEMENT # 2

STANDARD MEMORY

DIMMs

128MB EDO Buffered
32MB EDO 3.3 Unbuffered
64MB EDO 3.3 Unbuffered
32MB SDRAM PC 100MHz BX
64MB SDRAM PC 100MHz BX
128MB SDRAM PC 100MHz BX

ADVERTISEMENT # 3

STANDARD MEMORY

SDRAM 66MHz
4 x 64   32MB
8 x 64   64MB
16 x 64   128MB
SDRAM ECC 66MHz
4 x 72 ECC   32MB
8 x 72 ECC   64MB
16 x 72 ECC   128MB
PC100 SDRAM 100MHz
8 x 64-100   64MB
16 x 64-100   128MB
32 x 64-100   256MB
PC100 ECC SDRAM 100MHz
8 x 72-100 ECC   64MB
16 x 72-100 ECC   128MB
PC100 CAS2 SDRAM 100MHz
8 x 64-100 CAS2   64MB
16 x 64-100 CAS2 128MB
PC133 SDRAM 133MHz
8 x 64-133   64MB
16 x 64-133   128MB

Memory Figure #15 Advertisement #1's highlighted portion shows the total capacity of the chip, "64MB"; the amount of bits transferred at a time, which is 64 bits, "8 x 64"; followed by the speed of the chip, 10ns, "-10." Many DIMM advertisements omit the speed of SDRAM chips, as shown in Advertisement #2. The advertiser in this ad is more specific about the type of chip offered, but no speed is listed. The highlighted DIMM in Advertisement #2 is a 128MB SDRAM DIMM that runs on a 100MHz system bus speed motherboard. The BX denotes that the DIMM is compatible with an Intel chipset. In

Advertisement #3, a SDRAM ECC DIMM that runs on a 100MHz-system board is shown. The "8 x 72" in the advertisement shows that it uses ECC memory checking. An ECC chip might also be listed as a "x 80." If the advertisement shows "x 72" and it does not say ECC, it could mean that it is a parity chip. In the advertisement, the total capacity for the chips is shown at the end of each line. The highlighted DIMM is a 64MB PC100 SDRAM chip.

Memory Figure #16 lists advertisements for DDR RAM DIMMs and RIMMs.

MEMORY – FIGURE #16

Sample DDR RAM DIMM and RIMM Advertisements

ADVERTISEMENT #1

DDR DIMM
PC1600 (200MHz Bus) 128MB 16x64 (184-pin)
PC2100 (266MHz Bus) 128MB DDR 16x64 (184-pin)
PC2100 (266MHz Bus) 128MB ECC DDR 16x72 (184-pin)
PC1600 (200MHz Bus) 128MB ECC DDR 16x72 (184-pin)
PC2100 (266MHz Bus) 128MB DDR 16x64 (184-pin) unbuffered CAS 2.5
PC2100 (266MHz Bus) 256MB DDR 32x64 (184-pin)
PC2100 (266MHz Bus) 512MB ECC Registerd DDR 64x72 (184-pin)

ADVERTISEMENT #2

RDRAM RIMMs
600MHz Non-ECC 4-Device
600MHz ECC 4-Device
700MHz Non-ECC 4-Device
700MHz ECC 4-Device
800MHz Non-ECC 4-Device
800MHz ECC 4-Device

Notice in Memory Figure #16 that the highlighted item in Advertisement #1 has the letters CAS. **CAS (Column Address Strobe)** actually is CAS latency, which is the amount of time (clock cycles) that pass before the processor moves on to the next memory address. RAM is made up of cells where data is held. A cell is the intersection of a row and a column. Think of it as a spreadsheet application. The CAS signal picks which memory column to select and a signal called RAS (Row Address Strobe) picks which row to select. The intersection of the two is where the data is stored. A CAS latency of 2 is better than a CAS latency of 3 (fewer clock cycles to wait). PC133 SDRAM modules normally have a

CAS latency (sometimes called simply CAS or CL) of 2. PC1600 and PC2100 DDR DIMMs normally have a CAS latency of 2.5.

Advertisement #1 shows a 128MB DDR module as "16 x 64." 16 bits times 64 million bits equals 1,024,000,000 bits. 1,024,000,000 bits divided by eight equals 128MB (the memory capacity of the chip). Also, notice how the advertiser lists that it is a 184-pin module. All DDR RAM modules are 184-pin DIMMs.

Advertisement #2 shows the different RIMM modules—600, 700, and 800MHz. All three come as either ECC or non-ECC. The highlighted line in Advertisement #2 has the words "4-Device." According to the RIMM specifications, a RIMM can be designed for 1 to 16 RDAM devices (chips). A RIMM advertised as a "4-Device," has four RDRAM devices (chips) on that module.

The exercises at the end of the chapter help you understand how to populate memory banks for different microprocessors. Before memory chips are installed into a system, you must make a plan of action and refer to the documentation.

MEMORY INSTALLATION RULES

When installing memory in banks, a few rules must be observed. They are listed below with their explanations.

- When you start a bank, fill a bank.
- Use memory chips of the same capacity in a memory bank.
- All the chips in a bank should have the same access speed, if possible.
- All the chips in a bank should be of the same type , if possible.
- Some manufacturers require that higher capacity chips be placed in the first bank.

START A BANK, FILL A BANK

When installing memory chips into a bank, whether DIPs, SIMMs, or DIMMs, do not leave any slot or socket of the bank empty. This does not mean that all banks have to be filled. Rather, if you start putting memory chips into a bank, fill that bank. The number of bits of memory must equal the number of bits the data bus will support. Do not forget that with RIMMs, empty banks must be filled with C-RIMMs.

Memory chips in the bank work together to transfer data to and from the microprocessor and the entire bank must be completely filled with memory chips if it is to operate correctly. For example, if a motherboard has banks of memory with two memory chips per bank, then you must install two memory chips at a time. You cannot put one memory chip into a bank and expect it to work. Remember, the memory bank works as a single unit transferring information to and from the microprocessor.

SAME CAPACITY CHIPS IN A BANK

Because memory chips in a bank work together, each chip in the bank must be able to hold the same number of bits as other chips. In 8088-based computer systems, 64Kb and 256Kb chips were the most common. Bank 1, for example, might contain nine 256Kb chips, totaling 256KB of memory. The ninth chip, the parity chip, must be the same capacity as the memory chips so it can check the accuracy of data transferred into the eight memory chips. With later microprocessors, a bank with two SIMM sockets requires two equal capacity SIMMs. On today's motherboards, there is only one DIMM per memory bank because each DIMM transfers 64 bits at a time. Matching DIMM size will not be an issue until 128-bit data path microprocessors are released.

SAME ACCESS SPEED

Memory chips *should* have the same access speed as other chips in the bank. Mixing in chips with faster access times may work, but this simply depends on the motherboard. If you are working on a system that requires an 80ns DRAM memory chip, a faster chip may work as a replacement for a failed DIP or SIMM chip.

Never use a slower access speed chip as a replacement chip!

SAME CHIP TYPE

Some motherboards allow mixing different chip technologies, such as FPM and EDO SIMMs. The Triton FX chipset allows FPM and EDO chips to be installed in the same bank. However, when you mix technologies, the bank will run at the slower speed. For example, if you install FPM and EDO chips in the same bank, the bank will run at the speed of the slower FPM chip(s).

For best performance, use the same chip technology with all of the memory chips installed.

Another thing to watch out for is motherboards that accept SIMMs and DIMMs. Some motherboards require that if DIMMs are to be installed, all SIMM banks must be empty. Others require that all SIMM banks be fully populated before any DIMMs can be added. Always refer to the motherboard documentation before purchasing memory chips.

HIGHER CAPACITY CHIPS

Some manufacturers require that higher capacity memory chips be placed in the lower banks such as Bank 0 or Bank 1. The only way to know if this is a requirement is to check the documentation included with the motherboard or computer system.

If no documentation exists, experiment! Try the higher capacity chips in the lower banks. If that does not work, swap the memory chips and try the lower capacity chips in the lower bank numbers.

Installing memory chips into a system can be broken down into three steps:

Step 1.   Obtain the proper type, size, and capacity of chip(s) needed for the system.

Step 2.   Remove and/or install the memory chips.

Step 4.   Configure the computer for the new memory.

MEMORY TYPE, SIZE, AND CAPACITY

Step 1 involves research and planning using the documentation included with the motherboard or the computer system. Determine for the memory chip: the proper type (gold lead or tin lead; DIP, SIPP, SIMM, or DIMM); the proper size (30-pin, 72-pin, or 168-pin); the proper capacity (4MB, 8MB, 16MB, 32MB, etc.); and the proper access speed (50ns, 60ns, 70ns, etc.). Many frustrations, headaches, and problems can be avoided when this first step is taken.

If you are upgrading a computer's memory and no documentation exists, look at the memory chips already installed for clues to access speeds, type, and size. Trial and error can also be helpful. Many vendors will allow the return or swap of memory chips if you ordered the wrong type or size. The Internet is a great source for motherboard documentation.

LAPTOP MEMORY

Portable computers are a major part of today's business environment. The memory chips used with laptops are different than the ones used in desktop or tower computers. Portables that use DIMMs use a special type called **SO-DIMM (Small Outline DIMM)** and those that use RIMMs use **SO-RIMM (Small Outline RIMM)**. Some laptop manufacturers require proprietary memory modules, but that is not as common as it once was. Many laptops only have one memory slot, so when you upgrade, you must replace the module that is installed. Always refer to the manufacturer's documentation when doing this. Laptops can also be upgraded with PC Cards, but this type of memory is not as fast as the memory installed on the motherboard.

FLASH MEMORY

Flash memory is a type of non-volatile memory that holds data even when the computer power is off. Flash memory is popular with laptops because it is small, fast, and consumes little power. This is especially important when running a computer off a battery. PCs also use flash memory as a replacement for the BIOS chip. Network devices use flash memory to store the operating system and instructions. Digital cameras use flash memory to store pictures; scanners use flash memory to store images; printers use flash memory to store fonts. Flash memory does not have to be refreshed like DRAM and it does not need constant power like SRAM. A drawback to flash memory is that it is erased in blocks rather than by bytes like RAM.

INSTALLING MEMORY CHIPS

The best method to determine which memory chips to install in each bank is described in the following steps:

1. Determine which chip capacities can be used for the system. Look in the documentation included with the motherboard or the computer for this information.
2. Determine how much memory is needed. Ask the user which operating system is installed and which applications they are using. Refer to documentation for each application to determine the amount of RAM recommended. Plan for growth!
3. Determine what capacity chips go in each bank by drawing a diagram of the system, planning the memory population on paper, and referring to the documentation of the system or motherboard.

REMOVING/INSTALLING MEMORY CHIPS

Depending on the type of motherboard, the number of banks available on the motherboard, whether the computer memory is being upgraded, or whether the memory is a new installation, some memory chips may need to be removed to put higher capacity chips into the bank. Look at what is already installed in the system, refer to the documentation, and remove any banks of memory necessary to upgrade the memory. Use an anti-static wrist strap when removing or installing memory chips.

REMOVING A DIP CHIP

For A+ certification, the recommended DIP chip removal tool is a DIP chip extractor. However, when using this tool, students frequently bend the DIP chip legs. A small flat-tipped screwdriver is the most practical tool to use when removing a DIP chip. Carefully insert the small screwdriver under one end of the DIP chip. Rotate the screwdriver back and forth *gently* until the end of the chip rises slightly above the socket. Carefully, insert the screwdriver under the *opposite* end of the DIP chip. Rotate the screwdriver back and forth a few times until this end of the chip starts to rise above the socket. Keep inserting the screwdriver into alternate ends of the DIP chip until it gently lifts from the socket. Refer to Memory Figure #17 for an illustration of how to remove a DIP chip.

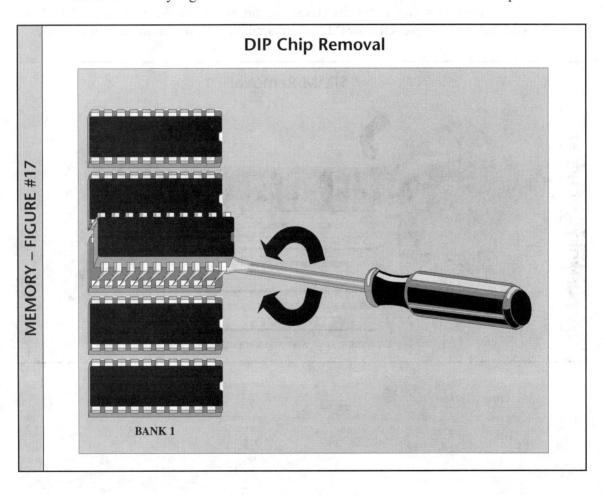

MEMORY – FIGURE #17

DIP Chip Removal

BANK 1

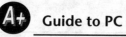
REMOVING A SIMM

Removing a SIMM or a DIMM is much easier than removing a DIP chip. A SIMM socket has two clasps, one on either side of the socket. These hold the memory chip into the socket. A metal or plastic clasp is normally used with SIMM sockets.

 Be extremely careful when working with plastic clasps. If they break, they are expensive to replace and sometimes you have to purchase a new motherboard. Memory Figure #18 shows how the clasps are *gently* pulled away from the SIMM to remove the memory module from the socket.

Grasp the two clasps on either side of the socket with your thumbs resting on the inner side of the clasps. Gently pry the clasps out and away from the memory module. With your index finger, press the SIMM forward until it pulls away from the clasps.

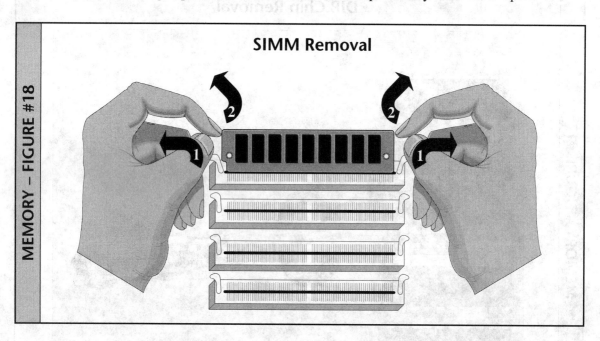

MEMORY – FIGURE #18

SIMM Removal

REMOVING A DIMM/RIMM

Removing a DIMM or a RIMM is very similar to removing a SIMM except that you push *down* on the outside edges of the DIMM's retaining tabs. The DIMM/RIMM lifts slightly out of the socket. Lift the module out of the socket once it is released. Memory Figure #19 shows how to remove a DIMM/RIMM.

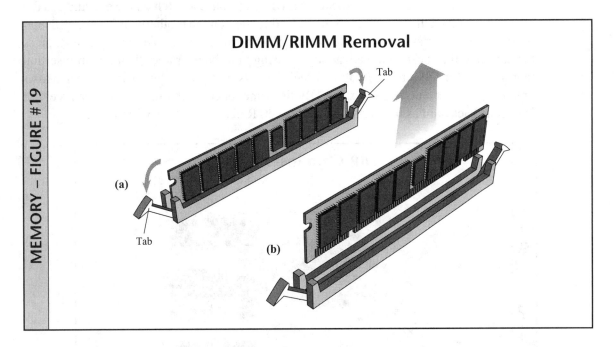

MEMORY – FIGURE #19

DIMM/RIMM Removal

(a)

Tab

Tab

(b)

INSTALLING A DIP CHIP

To insert a DIP chip, verify that all legs on the DIP chip are straight and even before installing. If the legs are bent, use a pair of small needlenose pliers to straighten and align the legs before inserting the chip into the socket. Place the DIP chip over one side of the chip socket, *barely* placing each leg into the holes on one side of the socket. Be sure the DIP chip orients properly in the socket. All DIP chips have a notch on the end and usually all notches of the DIP chips face in the same direction on the motherboard (or any adapter for that matter). Press gently on the DIP chip's opposite side legs. At the same time, press the chip into the socket. One advantage to using your hands rather than a chip insertion tool to install a DIP chip, is you can feel the legs going into the socket properly after practicing this technique a few times. By the same token, with practice, you can feel if a leg bends backward as it inserts into the socket. Reference Memory Figure #20.

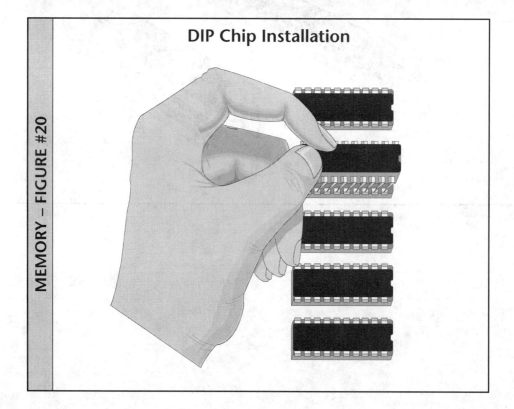

DIP Chip Installation

MEMORY – FIGURE #20

INSTALLING A SIMM

A SIMM inserts only one way into the socket, so it cannot be inserted improperly (oriented the wrong way) as the DIP chip can. The SIMM has a notch on one side. If you look carefully at the socket, you can see a plastic tab on one side. The notch on the memory module lines up with the side of the socket with the plastic tab. See Memory Figure #21 for a picture of a SIMM notch and the SIMM socket.

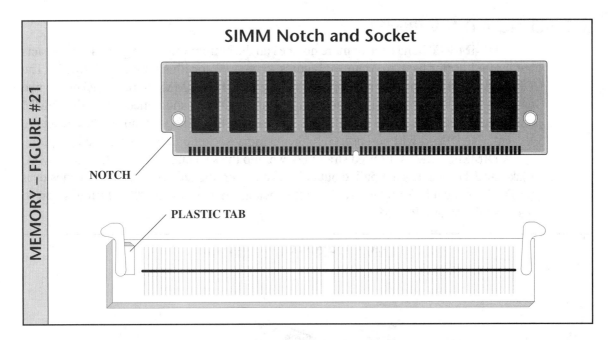

SIMM Notch and Socket

NOTCH

PLASTIC TAB

MEMORY – FIGURE #21

Insert the SIMM memory module at a tilt into the socket. Insert the chip's metal contacts *firmly* into the socket. Press the memory module backward into the socket until the two clasps clamp against the memory module. Memory Figure #22 shows this procedure. Notice in Memory Figure #22 there is a hole on either side of the memory module. A plastic pin on each side of the memory socket inserts into the memory module's holes when the module inserts properly into the socket.

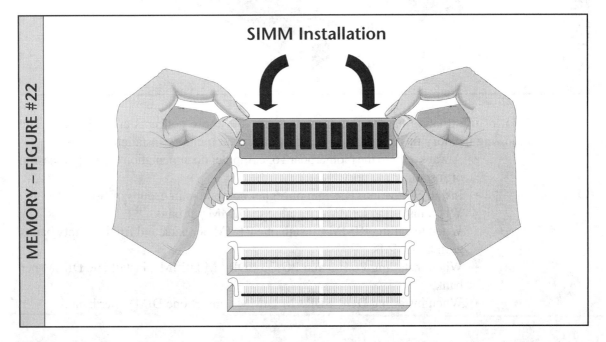

SIMM Installation

MEMORY – FIGURE #22

INSTALLING A DIMM/RIMM

A DIMM/RIMM has one or more notches on the bottom where the gold or tin contacts are located. Refer back to Memory Figures #1 and #2 for illustrations of DIMMs. The DIMM only inserts into the memory socket one way. The DIMM memory socket has two tabs that align with the DIMM notches. Look at the DIMM and notice where the DIMM notches are located. Look at the DIMM socket and notice where the tabs in the socket are located. The DIMM will not insert into the memory socket unless it is oriented properly.

A DIMM/RIMM is inserted straight down into the socket, not at a tilt like the SIMM. Make sure the side tabs are pulled out before you insert the DIMM and close the tabs over the DIMM once it is firmly inserted into the socket. Memory Figure #23 illustrates how to insert a DIMM or a RIMM.

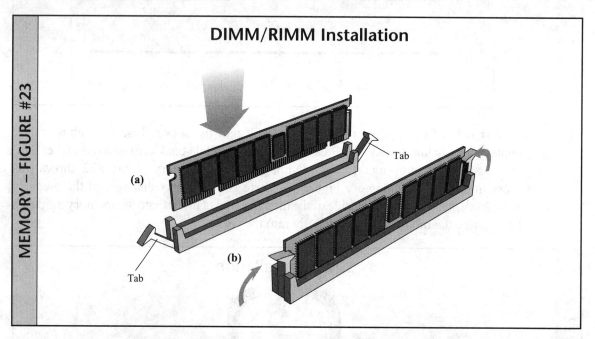

DIMM/RIMM Installation

MEMORY – FIGURE #23

(a) Tab

(b) Tab

A lot of information has been presented so far, but these concepts are important. The following memory tips summarize the most important memory installation steps.

- Always refer to the motherboard or computer documentation before purchasing or installing memory.
- Install SIMM into Pentium or higher computers in groups of two.
- When installing DIMMs, install one DIMM per bank.
- When installing RIMMs, install one RIMM per bank and fill the empty banks with C-RIMMs.
- When installing PC100 and PC133 SDRAM DIMMs, install one DIMM per bank.
- When installing DDR SDRAM DIMMs, insert one DIMM per bank.

CONFIGURING THE COMPUTER

Older motherboards require setting of jumpers or switches to denote how much memory installs on the motherboard, but newer ones automatically recognize new memory. Still other computers require no setting except through CMOS Setup. Always refer to the motherboard or the computer system's documentation for this information.

After you install the memory, power the computer on. Some computers show a POST error message or automatically go into the Setup program. This is normal. The important thing to notice during POST is that the memory count should equal the amount of memory installed. Refer to Memory Figure #24 for an example of the memory configuration screen, keeping in mind every BIOS chip is different and different messages appear depending on which one is installed. This is only a sample.

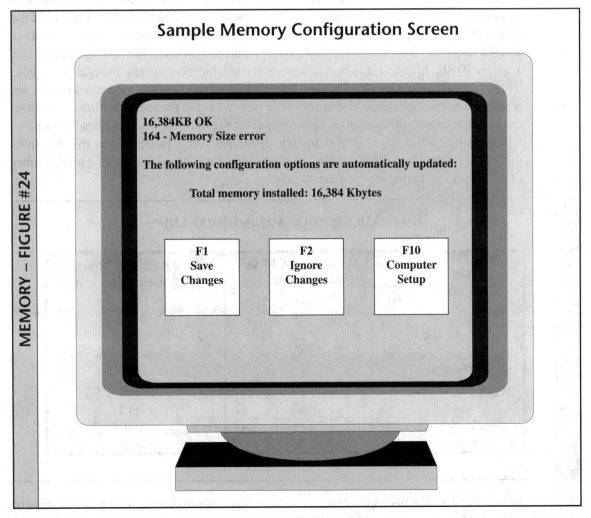

MEMORY – FIGURE #24

Sample Memory Configuration Screen

16,384KB OK
164 - Memory Size error

The following configuration options are automatically updated:

Total memory installed: 16,384 Kbytes

F1	F2	F10
Save	Ignore	Computer
Changes	Changes	Setup

With the system illustrated in Memory Figure #24, the F1 key is pressed to configure CMOS and save the memory installation changes.

HOW MUCH MEMORY?

The amount of memory that can be installed on the motherboard depends on two things: (1) the motherboard manufacturer and (2) the microprocessor.

RAM system memory should *always* be installed on the motherboard and not on a memory expansion adapter because *the memory on the motherboard will slow down to the adapter memory's speed*. The adapter memory's speed is at the speed of the adapter bus (ISA, MicroChannel, EISA, VL-bus, or PCI), which is always slower than the motherboard.

Microprocessors have a specific number of address lines connecting each memory chip with the CPU. Each memory location is like a mailbox for data to be placed into it or retrieved from it. The processor can connect to only a limited number of mailboxes or addresses. A mathematical relationship exists between the number of address lines and the total number of addresses the CPU recognizes. A simple (but non-realistic) example is that if a microprocessor had three address lines (and each address line can be a binary 1 or a binary 0), the different mailbox addresses the microprocessor can have are 000, 001, 010, 011, 100, 101, 110, or 111. With three address lines, eight different addresses are possible. The mathematical relationship is $2x$ where x is the number of address lines from the microprocessor. (The number "2" comes from the fact that address lines have one of two possible states, a 1 or a 0 binary digit. Memory Table #1 recaps the Intel microprocessors, giving the number of address lines for each, along with the total number of addresses the microprocessor can access.

Intel Microprocessor Address Lines

Processor	Number of Address Lines	Max. Amount of Memory Addresses
8088	20	1MB
80286	24	16MB
80386DX	32	4GB
80486DX	32	4GB
Pentium	32	4GB
Pentium Pro	36	64GB
Pentium II	36	64GB
Pentium III	36	64GB
Pentium 4	36	64GB

MEMORY – TABLE #1

Notice that the 8088 microprocessor can address up to approximately one million different addresses because 2^{20} = 1MB (1,048,576 addresses to be exact). The 80286 was the first Intel microprocessor allowing access to memory above 1MB. It was the first CPU to support protected mode. **Protected mode** allows applications to access memory above 1MB. Applications must be specifically written for protected mode in order to use it. **Real mode** describes early computers that could not access memory above 1MB. Most DOS applications were written for real-mode microprocessors. The Pentium Pro, Pentium II, Pentium III, and Pentium 4 processors can address up to 68,719,476,736 (64GB) different addresses. However, not all memory address locations are for RAM chips. The microprocessor uses the address lines for all memory chips including ROM chips on the motherboard and on various installed adapters.

To look at the whole picture of the address lines' usage, a **memory map** is used. It makes things easier to see. Memory Figure #25 illustrates the memory map for the 8088 microprocessor's address space, as designated by IBM on the first PC.

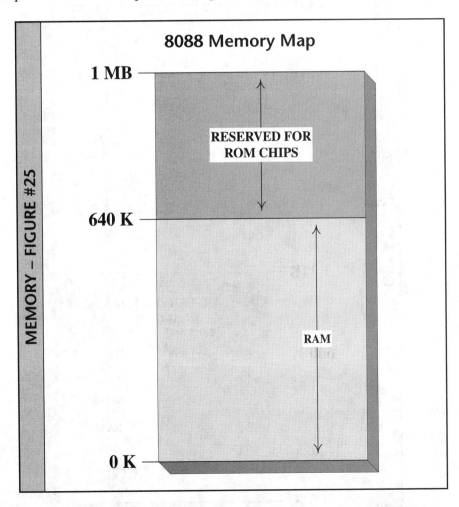

MEMORY – FIGURE #25

8088 Memory Map

1 MB

RESERVED FOR ROM CHIPS

640 K

RAM

0 K

Notice that the 0KB to 640KB space is for RAM chips. The upper addresses are for various ROM chips in the system. This address space is frequently defined as the **reserved area** or the **UMA (Upper Memory Area)**. On an Intel 8088 microprocessor-based IBM compatible computer, the maximum amount of memory on the motherboard is 640KB.

Today's applications and operating systems need much more than 640KB of RAM. Later microprocessors allow for this increase. Memory Figure #26 shows the memory map for an 80386, an 80486, and a Pentium.

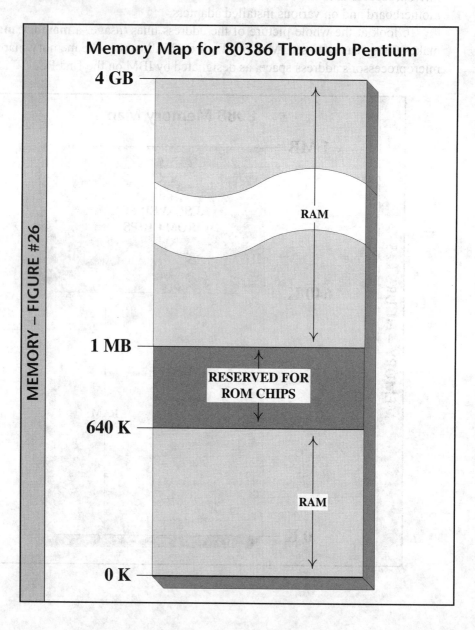

MEMORY – FIGURE #26

Memory Map for 80386 Through Pentium

4 GB

RAM

1 MB

RESERVED FOR ROM CHIPS

640 K

RAM

0 K

Notice that the area above 1MB in Memory Figure #26 allows for more RAM to be installed in a system. Just because the microprocessor supports the additional address lines does not mean a computer system has 4GB of RAM (less the 360KB reserved for ROM chips). This is where the manufacturer of the motherboard comes into the picture. The amount of RAM placed on the motherboard depends on the manufacturer. Most manufacturers of Pentium-based motherboards do not allow the full amount of RAM because few computers need 4GB of memory. This information is usually in the documentation that comes with the computer or motherboard. The Intel Pentium Pro through Pentium 4 processors have a similar memory map; however, the map extends further, to 64GB at the top.

MEMORY AND SOFTWARE CONSIDERATIONS

Physically installing memory in the computer is fine, but not all applications can use the available memory. Whether or not an application can use all the RAM in a system depends on the operating system/environment installed on the computer and the operating system for which the application is written. Three examples include:

- An application specifically written for the DOS/Windows environment running on a system with Windows 9x, NT, or 2000 behaves as if it was installed on a system with DOS.
- An application specifically written for Windows NT will not operate in a Windows 9x or DOS/Windows 3x environment.
- An application specifically written for Windows 9x will not run in the DOS/Windows environment.

DOS/WINDOWS 3.X AND MEMORY

To understand the memory limitations of DOS, start with the 8088 microprocessor of the original IBM PC. From there we can move forward because all computers, even today's computers, are backward compatible with older microprocessors. Microprocessor designers want consumers to be able to run the software that ran on their old computers.

The 8088 microprocessor has 20 address lines for a total of 1,048,576 possible addresses. Keep in mind that all memory chips, RAM and ROM alike, have different memory addresses that fit into a memory map for a specific microprocessor. Memory Figure #27 illustrates the 8088 memory map.

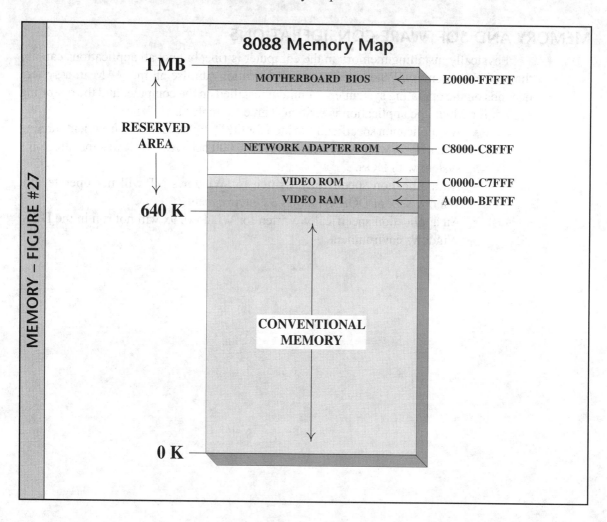

MEMORY – FIGURE #27

CONVENTIONAL MEMORY

The area from 0 to 640KB is for the RAM chips installed in the 8088-based computer and is normally called **conventional memory**. DOS and all DOS applications written for the 8088 computers ran in conventional memory. The application, such as a word processor, would load into the RAM chips. Any document created within the application, such as a letter, was also kept in the RAM chips and mapped into the 0 to 640KB area of the memory map. Windows 9x also uses conventional memory.

UPPER MEMORY AREA (RESERVED MEMORY)

The area of the memory map designated Reserved is for the ROM chips in the computer. The Reserved area is also known as the Upper Memory Area or UMA. Refer back to Memory Figures #25, #26, and #27 to see this memory area. The Reserved area is subdivided into blocks of memory that are illustrated with hexadecimal memory addresses. Hexadecimal is easier to process than the computer's binary 1s and 0s. The area from E0000 to FFFFF is used by the BIOS chip(s) on the motherboard. The hard drive controller in 8088-based computers has ROM chips on the adapter that normally use the memory address range of C8000 to CBFFF. If the computer has an EGA monitor installed, the ROM chip on the EGA adapter fits into the memory map at C0000-C3FFF. All ROM chips in the system must fit in a space on the memory map not occupied by any other ROM chip.

Computer users, especially the ones who created large spreadsheets in spreadsheet software such as Lotus, frequently ran out of conventional memory due to the 0 to 640KB limitation. Lotus, Intel, and Microsoft worked together to develop a new memory standard called **LIM (Lotus, Intel, Microsoft)** which solves the limitation of conventional memory. The LIM memory standard is also known as **expanded memory** or **EMS (Expanded Memory Specification)**.

EXPANDED MEMORY

To break the 640KB memory limitation with 8088-based microprocessors, users had to buy an expanded memory adapter with more RAM chips. For the microprocessor to communicate with this RAM, the memory chips had to fit in the memory map, but the 8088 had only 20 address lines. The EMS standard occupies a 64KB portion of the Reserved area in the memory map not used by any ROM chips, such as the 832KB to 896KB range. The 64KB block of memory map space is divided into four 16KB blocks used to address the memory chips on the expanded memory adapter. The EMS standard allows up to 32MB of EMS memory. Refer to Memory Figure #28 for an illustration of how EMS memory fits into the 8088's memory map.

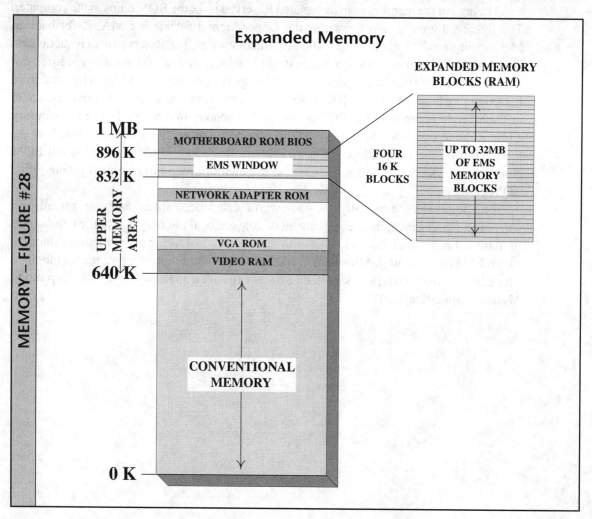

MEMORY – FIGURE #28

The spreadsheet data or any other data using expanded memory loads into the RAM chips on the expanded memory adapter. The microprocessor accesses this data by swapping it into the four 16KB blocks of memory in the Reserved area. If more data is needed, the original data is taken out of one of the four 16KB blocks and placed into the expanded memory block. The new data is then swapped or paged into the old data's slot in the Reserved area. Expanded Memory is also known as paged memory because it pages (swaps) the data in and out of the reserved area in four 16KB chunks. Expanded memory is *very* slow because it pages in and out of the memory map.

Not all applications can use expanded memory. The application must be specifically written for it. Years ago, a disk containing software, sometimes called a driver, was included with the purchase of an expanded memory adapter. When the software driver was loaded into the CONFIG.SYS file, a 64KB window was made available in the memory map for use as expanded memory.

Expanded memory no longer requires a separate adapter. Instead, if an older application requires expanded memory, a specified amount (up to 32MB) of the RAM on the motherboard can be specified as expanded memory. The rest is for extended memory covered in the next section. In this scheme, even though the memory is on the motherboard, data is still paged in and out of the memory map through the 64KB window to access the RAM chips. A driver is still needed in the CONFIG.SYS file. DOS and Windows both have an expanded memory manager, called EMM386.EXE, for 80386 and higher microprocessors.

EXTENDED MEMORY

A better alternative to expanded memory is extended memory and it became available with the 80286 microprocessor. **Extended memory**, also known as **XMS (Extended Memory Specification)**, is the area of the memory map above the 1MB mark. The 80286 microprocessor has 24 address lines with 2^{24} (16,777,216) different addresses available to the microprocessor. Refer to Memory Figure #29 for an illustration of the memory map for an 80286 microprocessor.

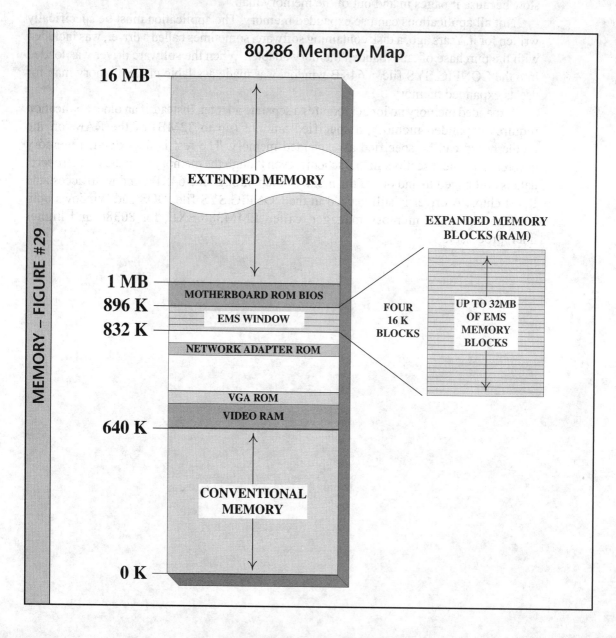

MEMORY – FIGURE #29

80286 Memory Map

16 MB

EXTENDED MEMORY

EXPANDED MEMORY BLOCKS (RAM)

1 MB
896 K — MOTHERBOARD ROM BIOS
832 K — EMS WINDOW

FOUR 16 K BLOCKS

UP TO 32MB OF EMS MEMORY BLOCKS

NETWORK ADAPTER ROM

VGA ROM
VIDEO RAM
640 K

CONVENTIONAL MEMORY

0 K

Extended memory is much faster than expanded memory. With the 80386, 80486, and Pentium-based systems the same memory map exists, except that the extended memory range is from 1MB to 4GB (4,294,963,296 different addresses). Refer to Memory Figure #30 for the memory map of the 80386, 80486, and Pentium microprocessors.

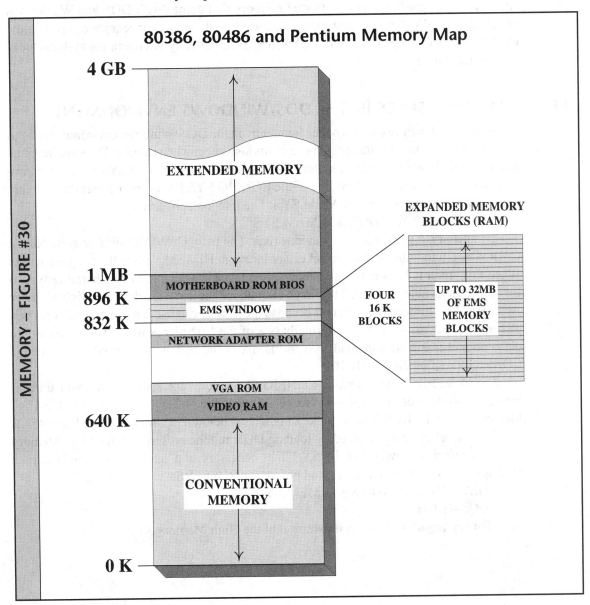

MEMORY – FIGURE #30

80386, 80486 and Pentium Memory Map

- 4 GB
- EXTENDED MEMORY
- 1 MB
- 896 K — MOTHERBOARD ROM BIOS
- EMS WINDOW
- 832 K
- NETWORK ADAPTER ROM
- VGA ROM
- VIDEO RAM
- 640 K
- CONVENTIONAL MEMORY
- 0 K

EXPANDED MEMORY BLOCKS (RAM)

FOUR 16 K BLOCKS

UP TO 32MB OF EMS MEMORY BLOCKS

The Pentium Pro through Pentium 4 processors have 36 address lines. The memory maps for the Pentium Pro and Pentium II look exactly like the illustration in Memory Figure #30 except the highest memory address extends beyond 4GB to 64GB.

For a system to use extended memory, a driver must be installed in the CONFIG.SYS file. The driver used to access extended memory that comes with DOS and Windows is HIMEM.SYS. Windows 95 and higher operating systems do not require a driver in the CONFIG.SYS file because HIMEM.SYS loads automatically. All operating systems today use extended memory.

FREEING MEMORY SPACE IN THE DOS/WINDOWS ENVIRONMENT

Insufficient memory errors occur frequently in the DOS/Windows environment due to conventional memory limitations. These errors also occur when running DOS applications under the Windows 9x operating system. A close look at the CONFIG.SYS file is necessary to understand memory. The first line of the CONFIG.SYS file normally lists the software driver for extended memory, HIMEM.SYS. The line looks like this:

DEVICE=C:\WINDOWS\HIMEM.SYS

The command DEVICE= loads a device driver. The path, C:\WINDOWS, may be named C:\DOS or C:\ to indicate the correct driver location. HIMEM.SYS is the program name. When this driver is loaded, the area above 1MB is made available to the operating system for applications able to use it. The first 64KB above the 1MB mark is the High Memory Area (HMA). This area is important because the system can use it as an extended portion of conventional memory. DOS, normally one of the first pieces of software loaded into conventional memory, can load into the HMA if the following special line is in the CONFIG.SYS file: DOS=HIGH.

The BUFFERS= statement in CONFIG.SYS allows for speeding up data transfer between two devices. The memory space reserved for buffers also goes into the High Memory Area with DOS if the number of buffers is below 42 (with DOS 6x). Up to 47KB of conventional memory is saved by loading DOS and the buffers into the High Memory Area. Therefore, the two CONFIG.SYS lines necessary to place DOS and the buffers in the High Memory Area that must load before the BUFFERS= command are these:

DEVICE=C:\WINDOWS\HIMEM.SYS
DOS=HIGH

See Memory Figure #31 for an illustration of the High Memory Area.

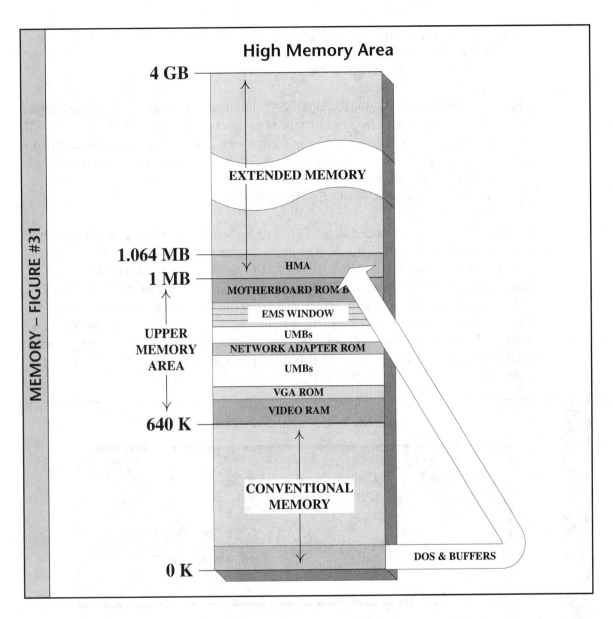

High Memory Area

MEMORY – FIGURE #31

4 GB

EXTENDED MEMORY

1.064 MB — HMA
1 MB — MOTHERBOARD ROM B
EMS WINDOW

UPPER
MEMORY
AREA

UMBs
NETWORK ADAPTER ROM

UMBs

VGA ROM
VIDEO RAM

640 K

CONVENTIONAL
MEMORY

DOS & BUFFERS

0 K

Another conventional memory saver occurs when the unused blocks of memory in the Reserved area are available for use with files normally loaded in conventional memory. The blocks of memory in the Reserved area that can be used for software other than ROM chips are also known as the **Upper Memory Blocks** or the **(UMBs)**. The UMBs are part of the Upper Memory Area. To make the UMBs available to the system, two lines are needed in the CONFIG.SYS file:

```
DEVICE=C:\WINDOWS\EMM386.EXE
DOS=UMB
```

These two lines must follow the extended memory manager CONFIG.SYS line:

    DEVICE=C:\WINDOWS\HIMEM.SYS
    DEVICE=C:\WINDOWS\EMM386.EXE
    DOS=UMB

The DEVICE=C:\WINDOWS\EMM386.EXE line loads the expanded memory driver, which allows the system to *see* the upper memory blocks as part of DOS. The DOS=UMB line allows the system to *use* the upper memory blocks. A more common use of the DOS=UMB line is to combine it with the DOS=HIGH line, as illustrated in this example:

    DEVICE=C:\WINDOWS\HIMEM.SYS
    DEVICE=C:\WINDOWS\EMM386.EXE
    DOS=HIGH,UMB

After these lines are placed in the CONFIG.SYS file, any other device drivers (lines that begin DEVICE=) can load into the upper memory blocks, if space is available, by changing the statement to DEVICEHIGH=. Also, any lines in the AUTOEXEC.BAT file that load TSR (Terminate and Stay Resident) programs can be preceded by the LOADHIGH or LH command to load the software into the upper memory blocks, not into conventional memory. The switches (numbers or letters following the program name) available for use with the EMM386 command change the way the system accesses and/or uses the upper memory blocks. Memory Table #2 lists the proper switch to use with the EMM386 command.

MEMORY – TABLE #2

EMM386.EXE Switches

Do You Need Expanded Memory?	Do You Need UMB Access?	EMM386 Switch
NO	NO	N/A
YES	NO	N/A
YES	YES	*XX* where *XX*=amt of mem in KB (64 to 32,768)
NO	YES	NOEMS

Most applications do *not* require expanded memory. The most frequently used EMM386 switch is NOEMS. If this switch is needed, the line in CONFIG.SYS is:

    DEVICE=<path>EMM386.EXE NOEMS

The NOEMS switch is popular because expanded memory is *not* needed by most applications. 64KB of UMB space is needed to load software normally found in conventional memory, therefore freeing precious space in the conventional memory range. The MSD and the MEM programs can be used to view the Upper Memory Blocks. Exercises at the end of the chapter show how.

All this memory management has now been automated with the latest DOS versions. Microsoft's memory management utility is MEMMAKER and IBM's memory management utility is RAMBOOST. A technician always needs to know the basics of memory management. The memory exercises at the end of the chapter help you understand the techniques.

ADDING MORE CACHE/RAM

Most computers today have cache built into the processor. The motherboard manufacturer determines if any L3 cache can be installed. Check the documentation included with the motherboard or computer to determine the correct amount of cache (SRAM).

Adding more RAM can make a noticeable difference in computer performance (up to a point, of course). When a computer user is sitting in front of a computer waiting for a document to appear, or waiting to go to a different location within a document, it might be time to install more RAM. Do not purchase a computer today if it has less than 128MB of RAM.

DISK CACHE

With older computers, a technician could increase computer speed by installing a disk cache program. A disk cache will set aside a portion of memory (RAM to be used when applications or data are read from the disk drive (which is inherently slow). Under these circumstances more data than requested is read and placed in RAM, where the disk cache is located. Some hard drives have their own caching controllers. Caching hard drive controllers have memory installed that speeds up the system by using memory chips on the adapter rather than the motherboard RAM for the disk cache.

DOS, Windows 3x, and Windows 9x have a disk caching program called SmartDrive (SMARTDRV.EXE). This program caches data from floppy disks, CD-ROMs, hard drives, and InterLink drives. Windows 98 includes the SmartDrive program to be backward compatible with some older devices. Normally, this program is not used with Windows 98 and higher operating systems. Windows 9x, NT, and 2000 have an integrated caching program for CD-ROMs that works better than SmartDrive. Refer to the hard drive and CD-ROM chapters for more information on caching programs.

The Windows 95 Setup program sometimes hangs if SmartDrive double buffering is not enabled. Some hard drives require double buffering. Use the Setup /C command to prevent SmartDrive from loading during the Windows 95 installation process. If the installation process hangs after running Setup from Windows 3x, try disabling 32-bit disk access from the 386 enhanced control panel before starting the Setup program again. If that does not work, run the Setup program from the DOS prompt.

WINDOWS 9X/NT/2000 DISK CACHING

Windows 95 has disk caching built in to the operating system through the use of the VCACHE program. Even though SmartDrive is used to load Windows 95, VCACHE is used during normal Windows 95 operations.

Windows 98/NT/2000 have a more efficient memory management through VMM (Virtual Memory Manager). **Virtual memory** is a method of using hard disk space as if it were RAM. The disk cache is dynamic—it increases or decreases the cache size as needed. If the system begins to page frequently and is constantly swapping data from RAM to the hard drive, the cache size automatically shrinks.

Windows 9x uses a temporary swap file, WIN386.SWP, that increases or decreases in size as necessary based on the amount of RAM installed in the computer and the amount of memory needed to run the application(s). A **swap file** is a block of hard drive space used like RAM by applications. Other names for the swap file include page file or paging file. For optimum performance in any Windows operating system, set aside as much free hard disk space as possible to allow ample room for virtual memory and caching. As a default, the swap file is on the same hard drive as the Windows 95/Windows 98 directory.

If multiple hard drives are available, a technician might want to move the swap file to a different drive. Always put the swap file on the fastest hard drive unless that hard drive lacks space. NT and 2000 Professional allow you to have the swap file on multiple hard drives. It is best to keep the swap file on a hard drive that does not contain the operating system.

In Windows 9x, to adjust the virtual memory swap file size
1. Open *Control Panel*
2. Double-click on the *System* control panel icon
3. Click the *Performance* tab
4. Click the *Virtual Memory* button
5. Click the *Let me specify my own virtual memory settings* option
6. Click the *down arrow* in the area to the right of the *Hard disk* option
7. Choose a different hard drive from the list
8. Click *OK*. The settings for the minimum and maximum size of the swap file can also be changed.

In NT, to adjust the virtual memory size
1. Open *Control Panel*
2. Double-click on the *System* control panel icon
3. Click on the *Performance* tab
4. Click on the *Change* button
5. In the area designated as *Paging File Size for Selected Drive*, change the size parameters
6. Click on the *OK* button.

In 2000 Professional, to adjust the virtual memory size

1. Open *Control Panel*
2. Double-click on the *System* control panel icon
3. Click on the *Advanced* tab
4. Click on the *Performance Options* button
5. Click on the *Change* button
6. Change the size parameters and click on the *OK* button.

Windows 98, NT, and 2000 Professional use virtual memory differently than Windows 3x. With Windows 3x, memory is divided into different sized segments each up to 64KB. Windows 98/NT/2000 use 32-bit demand-paged virtual memory and each process gets 4GB of address space divided into two 2GB sections. One 2GB section is shared with the rest of the system while the other 2GB section is reserved for the one application. All the memory space is divided into 4KB blocks of memory called **pages**. The operating system allocates as much available RAM as possible to an application. Then the operating system swaps or pages the application to and from the temporary swap file as needed. The operating system determines the optimum setting for this swap file; however, the swap file size can be changed. Memory Figure #32 illustrates how Windows 98, NT, and 2000 Professional uses virtual memory.

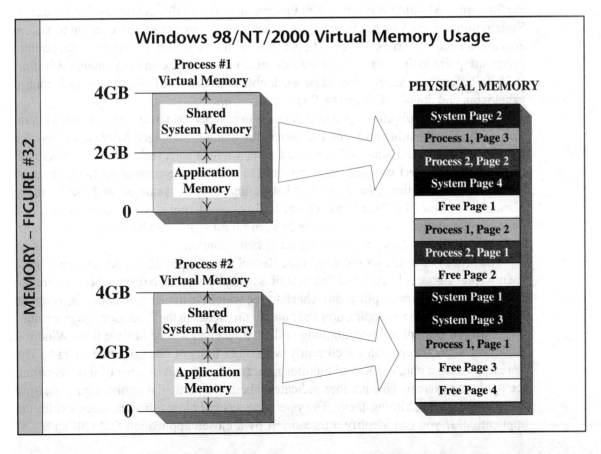

In Memory Figure #32, notice how each application has its own memory space. The Memory Pager maps the virtual memory addresses from the individual processes' address space to physical pages in the computer's memory chips.

A great freeware utility to use for virtual memory (as well as other computer components) is Sisoftware's Sandra at www.sisoftware.demon.co.uk/Sandra. Download the *Sandra Standard*. Install the software according to the instructions. Load a lot of games and applications into memory, then access the Sandra program by clicking on *Programs*, pointing to *SiSoft Utilities*, and clicking on the *SiSoft Sandra 2001te Standard* option. Click on the *OK* button to clear the utility tip. Double-click on the *Windows Memory Information* icon. Write down the number listed to the right of the Current Page File; this is how much of your hard drive space has been reserved for virtual memory. Locate the Free Page File setting; it shows how much of the set aside hard drive space is being used at this point. The Free Physical Memory setting is how much (if any) of your RAM chips are still available for use.

MONITORING MEMORY USAGE UNDER WINDOWS 95/98/NT

System Monitor is a utility that comes with Windows 9x; NT's utility is called **Performance Monitor** and with 2000 Professional, the **Performance utility**. To access System Monitor, click on the *Start* button, point to the *Programs* selection, point to *System Tools*, and click on *System Monitor*. In NT Workstation, click on the *Start* button, point to *Programs*, point to the *Administrative Tools* selection, and click on *Performance Monitor*. In 2000 Professional, access *Control Panel*, double-click on the *Administrative Tools* control panel icon, and double-click on the *Performance Utility*.

Each of these tools allows you to evaluate different performance areas: the file system, the IPX/SPX compatible protocol, the kernel, the memory manager, Microsoft Client for NetWare Networks and Microsoft Network Client, Microsoft Network Server, and Microsoft Network Monitor Performance Data. In regard to memory, the areas of particular interest are the Kernel Monitor (the Processor Usage and Threads settings) and the Memory Manager Monitor (the Page-Outs, Discards, Locked Memory, Allocated Memory, and Page Faults settings). You can access the System Monitor program by selecting *Programs, Accessories, System Tools,* and clicking on *System Monitor.*

The processor usage setting within the Kernel monitor provides a percentage of time the microprocessor is busy. If the Processor Usage values are high (even when you are not doing anything with an application), check to see which particular application is using the microprocessor. Close an application and note the difference in the Processor Usage settings.

A **thread** is a unit of programming code that receives a slice of time from Windows 95, 98, or NT so it can run concurrently with other units of code or other threads. The Threads setting within the Kernel monitor indicates the current number of threads within the operating system. This number indicates whether a particular application is starting threads and not reclaiming them. The operating system closes threads when exiting an application. If you can identify a thread left by a closed application that still shows as being open in the task list, that application may need to be restarted then exited again so the thread closes.

The Memory Manager's Discards setting is the number of pages of memory discarded per second. The pages of memory are not swapped to the hard disk because the information is already stored there. The Page-outs setting is the number of pages of memory swapped out of memory and written to the disk per second. If these two values are high and indicate a lot of activity, more RAM may be needed.

The Memory Manager's Locked Memory setting shows the amount of memory, including the disk cache, that cannot be paged out. To determine the exact amount of locked RAM, subtract the disk cache size amount from the locked memory amount. The Allocated Memory setting in the Memory Manager indicates the total amount of allocated memory not stored in the swap file (Other Memory) and the number of bytes in use from the swap file (Swapable Memory). If the Locked Memory values are a large portion of the Allocated Memory value, then the system does not have enough free memory and this affects performance. Also, an application might be locking memory unnecessarily and not allowing the memory to be paged out. This comes from poorly written software or software that needs to be reloaded.

The Memory Manager's Page Faults setting shows the number of page faults occurring each second. If this value is high, the application currently in use has memory requirements higher than what is installed in the computer. In this case, recommend that the customer purchase more RAM for the computer.

USING A RAM DRIVE

A **RAM drive** is a virtual (not real) hard disk drive created from RAM. It's the opposite of virtual memory. The RAM set aside for a RAM drive is not available to the system as normal memory. A RAM drive can be created out of conventional, expanded, or extended memory, but extended memory is preferred. A RAM drive is located in memory and operates much faster than retrieving data from a hard drive. The drawback to a RAM drive is that anything written to this area of memory will be lost when the computer restarts or shuts down. Therefore, permanent data should not be stored in a RAM drive. Also, because the memory allocated to the RAM drive is no longer available to the system, a RAM drive should only be created if there is RAM to spare in a system.

In older DOS versions, the RAM disk device driver was VDISK.SYS. In today's operating system, the RAM disk driver is RAMDRIVE.SYS. To create a RAMDRIVE from extended memory, insert the following line into the CONFIG.SYS file:

DEVICE=[path]RAMDRIVE.SYS /e [size]

[path] is the directory where you find the RAMDRIVE.SYS file. [size] is the size of the RAM drive in kilobytes. The default is 64KB and the possible range is 16KB to 4,096KB.

DOS APPLICATIONS UNDER WINDOWS 9X

Most DOS applications run fine under Windows 9x, but those with problems can be run in the Windows 9x's MS-DOS mode. In MS-DOS mode, the operating system removes almost all of itself from memory, finishes all tasks currently running, loads a real-mode copy of MS-DOS into memory, uses a customized CONFIG.SYS file and a customized AUTOEXEC.BAT file, then turns over the computer resources to the DOS application. When the DOS application finishes running, Windows 9x restarts and loads itself back into memory. DOS applications require ample available conventional memory, just as a non-Windows 9x computer does. Therefore, a DOS application that executes using the Windows 9x MS-DOS mode should have a customized CONFIG.SYS containing the HIMEM.SYS; DOS=HIGH,UMB; and EMM386.EXE statements. Load all possible device drivers and TSRs into the UMBs.

When a DOS application is started with Windows 9x's Run utility (from the Start button), the DOS application appears in a window as any application does. Windows 9x's memory management and task management features are still in effect when DOS applications are started this way.

Another alternative is to run the DOS application after starting Windows 9x in the Command Prompt Only mode. To start Windows 95 in a different mode, press the *F8* key when the "Starting Windows 95" message appears on the screen as the system first boots. Then, choose the *Command Prompt Only* option from the menu that appears. For Windows 98, hold the *CTRL* key down while Windows 98 boots. When the Startup menu appears, select the number for the *Command Prompt Only* option.

DOS APPLICATIONS UNDER NT WORKSTATION/2000

Each DOS application runs in an NT/2000 process called NT Virtual DOS Machine (NTVDM). The NTVDM process simulates a 486 computer running DOS. Each DOS application runs in its own address space. However, 16-bit applications share address space in the NT environment. Many DOS applications do not operate in the NT/2000 environment. DOS applications frequently make direct calls to hardware, which neither NT nor 2000 allows. If DOS applications are still being used, you might want to recommend a different operating system to the user until all applications are 32-bit.

TROUBLESHOOTING OTHER MEMORY PROBLEMS

You can get out of memory errors with any operating system. System resource errors were more common in Windows 3x than they are with current operating systems because these systems use hard drive space more efficiently. No matter which operating system or environment is being used, check the amount of free space on the hard drive. Delete files that are no longer needed. Empty the Recycle Bin to free up more hard drive space. Change the virtual memory settings so that the hard drive has more space. Finally, closing applications that are not being used can help with memory problems. Sometimes you must close all applications, reboot the computer, and open only the application that was running when the out of memory error occurred because some applications do not release the memory space they held. Windows 9x, NT, and 2000 have memory troubleshooting wizards that can help with this task. Click on the *Start* button, click on the *Help* option, click on the *Index* tab, and type in *Memory*. Select the option under this heading for troubleshooting. Keep in mind that sometimes there is nothing to do but buy more RAM— but try the aforementioned tips first. The following tips help with memory management.

- Add more RAM. Nothing helps memory performance as much as adding physical memory to the computer. To see the amount of physical memory (RAM) installed, right-click on the *My Computer* desktop icon and click on the *Properties* item.
- Adjust virtual memory size. Refer to the previous steps for adjusting this setting for various operating systems.
- Turn off the screen saver or use the Blank option. Screen savers do not protect monitors from burn-in anymore; instead, they take up memory.
- Remove the desktop wallpaper scheme or use a very plain one. Wallpaper schemes take up memory.
- Put the swap file on the fastest hard drive.
- Do not put the swap file on multiple partitions that reside on the same hard drive. Use multiple hard drives if possible.
- Put the swap file on a hard disk partition that does not contain the operating system.
- Adjust your Temporary Internet Files setting. From Internet Explorer, click on either the *View* or the *Tools* menu option (depending on your operating system). Click on *Internet Options* and click on the *Settings* button. A slide bar allows you to adjust how much disk space is set aside for caching web files. To increase the amount of disk space (faster access), move the sliding bar to the right. For those who do not have a lot of free hard disk space, move the sliding bar to the left. Adjust this setting as necessary.
- Defragment the hard drive. See the hard drive chapter for steps.
- Remove (uninstall) unnecessary files and applications from the hard drive to free up hard drive space.
- Empty the Recycle Bin to permanently remove deleted files and free up hard drive space.

POST usually detects a problem with a memory chip and most BIOS chips show a "2XX POST" error code. Some computers have the CMOS option to disable extended memory checking. This is not a good idea. Endure the few seconds it takes to check the memory chips to get an early warning of a memory failure. When POST issues a memory error, turn off the computer, remove the cover and press down on any DIP memory chips. If SIMMs or DIMMs are installed, clean out the sockets with compressed air and reseat the chips in the memory sockets. Also, gold contact swabs can be used to clean the SIMM/ DIMM sockets. Reseating memory chips often corrects memory errors.

If this does not work, turn the computer on again and watch the memory count in the upper left corner of the screen. The memory count is an excellent clue for where to start troubleshooting a memory problem. For example, on a computer with 16MB of RAM installed, if the memory in the upper left corner gets to 8,378KB and a POST memory error appears, then the memory problem is on a chip somewhere after the first 8MB of RAM. If the system is a Pentium with two 8MB, 72-pin SIMMs installed, the problem is probably in the second SIMM socket. Swap the SIMM in the first socket with the SIMM in the second socket. If the POST error code appears more quickly as the first 8MB of memory counts on the screen, the problem is the SIMM that was in the second socket, but later moved to the first socket.

The key to good memory chip troubleshooting is to divide and conquer. Narrow the problem to a suspected bank of memory, then start swapping memory chips (SIMM/DIMMS). Keep in mind most memory problems are not in the hardware, but in the software, especially if operating in the DOS/Windows environment.

Most DOS memory problems are attributed to the lack of conventional memory. Use the MEM command to view and verify as many programs as possible load into the Upper Memory Blocks. TSRs and device drivers in the AUTOEXEC.BAT and CONFIG.SYS files can be reordered. Sometimes more programs can be loaded into the Upper Memory Blocks just by reordering the programs. You can still run MEMMAKER under Window 9x to load real-mode drivers into the Upper Memory Blocks. For Windows 98, the program is located on the CD under the TOOLS\OLDMSDOS directory.

ROM address conflicts are a frequent source of problems for the technician. The ROM chips on some adapters have addresses that are selectable while others are pre-set and cannot be changed. All ROM chips throughout the computer system must have a separate, unique ROM address to operate within the memory map. See the System Configuration chapter for more information on memory addresses.

One of the first symptoms of a ROM address conflict is if a particular adapter will not function. Or, when a new adapter is installed in a system and the computer will not boot off the hard drive, a ROM conflict is the likely culprit. Do not forget to consider interrupt and I/O address conflicts also.

For DOS or Windows 3x computers, MSD (Microsoft Diagnostics) is a good place to begin checking the currently used ROM locations *before* installing any new adapters. There are other programs and utilities that perform the same function, but MSD ships with Microsoft DOS and Windows. For Windows 9x and 2000 computers, the Device Manager is used to see the various ROM addresses. For NT computers, use NT Diagnostics located under Programs, Administrative Tools option.

Name _____

MEMORY REVIEW QUESTIONS

1. Describe the difference between RAM and ROM.

2. What is meant by "memory chip refreshing"?

3. Which types of memory chips require constant refreshing? (Pick all that apply.)
   [ROM / DRAM / SRAM / SDRAM / EDO / FPM / Burst EDO]

4. [T / F]   Most memory on the motherboard is SRAM.

5. Describe how cache increases computer speed.

6. What motherboards commonly use DIMMs? (Pick all that apply.)
   [386 / 486 / Pentium / Pentium Pro / PentiumII / Pentium III]

7. [T / F]   A non-parity system can use parity memory chips.

8. Describe how to determine a memory chip's access time.

9. [T / F]   An 8ns memory chip is faster than a 10ns memory chip.

10. [T / F]   Installing faster memory chips always increases computer speed.

11. At what speed do PC100 DIMMs operate?

12. How can you tell if a DIMM is PC100 or PC133-compliant?

13. What is SPD and how is memory different with SPD?

14. What is the difference between buffered and unbuffered SDRAM?

15. What speeds do RDRAM RIMMs come in?

16. What are the two versions of DDR RAM modules?

17. Describe the difference between address lines and external data lines.

18. [T / F]   Pentium-based motherboards commonly use DIMMs.

19. [T / F]   A 2MB x 32 72-pin SIMM has a total capacity of 8MB.

20. [T / F]   A 2MB x 36 72-pin SIMM does not use parity.

21. Explain how the 168-pin DIMM replaces two 72-pin SIMMs.

22. A DDR DIMM memory chip is advertised as 256MB CAS 2.5. What does the CAS 2.5 mean?

23. Which is better CAS 2 or CAS 2.5?

24. A RIMM is listed as 700 MHz ECC 4-Device. What does the 4-Device mean?

25. Which of the following are rules for populating memory? (Pick all that apply.)
    A. If a bank of memory is to be used, it must be filled entirely with memory chips.
    B. All memory chips in a bank must be the same capacity.
    C. Every bank on a motherboard must be filled with memory chips to operate properly.
    D. Memory chips in the same bank should have the same access speed.
    E. The memory chips in every memory bank on the motherboard must be the same capacity.

26. Describe how you can determine how much memory to install in a system.

27. [T / F]   Laptop memory is best upgraded with a PC Card.

28. [T / F]   Flash memory contents are lost when power is removed.

29. What is the best tool for removing a DIP memory chip?

30. Which is easier to install a SIMM or a DIP and why?

31. How is a DIMM installation different from a SIMM?

32. [T / F]   There is normally one DIMM per bank.

33. [T / F]   A POST error message is normal after upgrading memory on some computers.

34. Which area of the 80286 memory map is the area from 0 to 640KB?
[Conventional / Expanded / Upper Memory Blocks / High Memory Area / Extended]

35. Which area of the 8088 memory map is a maximum of 32MB divided into 16KB blocks and pages in and out of a 64KB space?
[Conventional / Expanded / Upper Memory Blocks / High Memory Area / Extended]

36. Which area of the 80386 memory map is the area from 640KB to 1MB?
[Conventional / Expanded / Upper Memory Area / High Memory Area / Extended]

37. Which area of the 80486 memory map is the area from 1MB to 4GB?
[Conventional / Expanded / Upper Memory Area / High Memory Area / Extended]

38. Which area of the memory map operates the slowest because it pages in and out of the memory map?
[Conventional / Expanded / Upper Memory Area / High Memory Area / Extended]

39. Which area of the Pentium memory map is the first 64KB of memory above the 1MB mark?
[Conventional / Expanded / Upper Memory Area / High Memory Area / Extended]

40. Which type of memory is faster, conventional or expanded?

41. What DOS command provides access to extended memory?
    [EMM386.EXE / HIMEM.SYS / DOS=HIGH / DOS=UMB]

42. Which of the following CONFIG.SYS lines will load most of DOS into the HMA?
    [EMM386.EXE / HIMEM.SYS / DOS=HIGH / DOS=UMB]

43. Which of the following CONFIG.SYS lines allows the use of the UMBs for loading device drivers and TSRs?
    [EMM386.EXE / HIMEM.SYS / DOS=HIGH / DOS=UMB]

44. [T / F] Processors today have cache built into them.

45. Explain how virtual memory works.

46. Which control panel is used in 2000 Professional to set personalized virtual memory settings?

47. [T / F] Each 32-bit application running within 2000 Professional is allowed 4GB of address space.

48. Which of the following is Windows 95/98's performance monitoring tool, useful in troubleshooting memory problems?
    [VCACHE / VIRTUAL / My Computer / System Monitor]

49. What is a RAMDrive?

50. What is the difference between running a DOS application using the RUN utility and running the application under Windows 95's MS-DOS mode?

51. [T / F] All DOS applications operate in the NT environment.

52. List four things to help with memory performance.

53. Which screen saver takes the least amount of memory?

54. Describe how to allocate memory for Internet Explorer.

55. What is a common POST error code for memory?

56. What is a symptom of a ROM address conflict?

Name _____

MEMORY FILL-IN-THE-BLANK

1. The two main types of memory are _____ and _____.

2. An example of non-volatile memory is _____.

3. The major types of RAM are _____ and _____.

4. The SRAM chips on the motherboard are also known as the _____.

5. _____ is the process of performing more than one instruction at the same time.

6. The *type* of memory chip used for RAM in today's systems is _____, with either tin or gold contact edges.

7. The RAM memory chips used on older motherboards and for cache memory are known as _____. These have one row of legs down each side of the chip.

8. Athlon motherboards can use _____ DIMMs, which have 184-pins.

9. Pentium 4 motherboards use _____, which hold RDRAM.

10. _____ is a method of memory error checking in which an extra bit is used to check a group of 8 bits going into the bank of memory.

11. Most SIMMs have capacities measured in _____.

12. DIMMs have capacities measured in _____.

13. Memory access time is measured in _____.

14. Whether a system can use Fast Page Mode, EDO, or Burst EDO RAM chips depends on the _____ and the chipset used on the motherboard.

15. _____ was developed by Rambus, Inc. and is used on Pentium 4 motherboards.

16. All unused RIMM slots must contain a _____.

17. _____ transmits data on both sides of the clock signal and uses 184-pin DIMMs.

18. Two dual-ported video memory types are _____ and _____.

19. All the memory chips that must transmit simultaneously to the microprocessor are called a _____.

20. The number of sockets in a bank of memory is determined by the number of bits in a microprocessor's _____.

21. A SIMM advertised as 4x36 has a total capacity of _____.

22. A DIMM advertised as a PC100 chip runs on a motherboard that has a bus speed of _____.

23. The absolute maximum amount of RAM that can be connected to a microprocessor is determined by the number of _____ from the microprocessor.

24. The maximum number of address lines in a computer with a Pentium microprocessor is _____.

25. A laptop DIMM is called _____ because its form factor is smaller.

26. The maximum amount of addressable RAM and ROM in a Pentium II computer is _____.

27. _____ mode applications can access memory above 1MB.

28. DOS applications traditionally use _____ mode.

29. A graphical representation of how a system uses memory is known as a _____.

30. The area from 640K to 1MB on an 8088 memory map is known as the _____ or the _____.

31. In the memory map between 640K and 1MB are ROM chips and _____ RAM.

32. The area between 0 and 640K is known as _____.

33. _____ is also known as LIM or EMS memory.

34. _____ is located above the 1MB mark in the memory map.

35. The first 64K above the 1MB line on a memory map is known as _____.

36. The _____ file loads memory management drivers for the DOS environment.

37. A _____ file is the use of some hard drive space by applications because there is not enough RAM.

38. Windows 98, NT, and 2000 Professional have memory space divided into _____.

39. NT's utility for monitoring memory performance is called _____.

Name _____

PAPER MEMORY POPULATION EXERCISE FOR 8088-BASED MOTHERBOARDS

Use the drawing shown in Memory Exercise Figure #1 to populate the motherboard with 640KB of memory. The DIP memory chips to use with this motherboard are 64Kb and 256Kb.

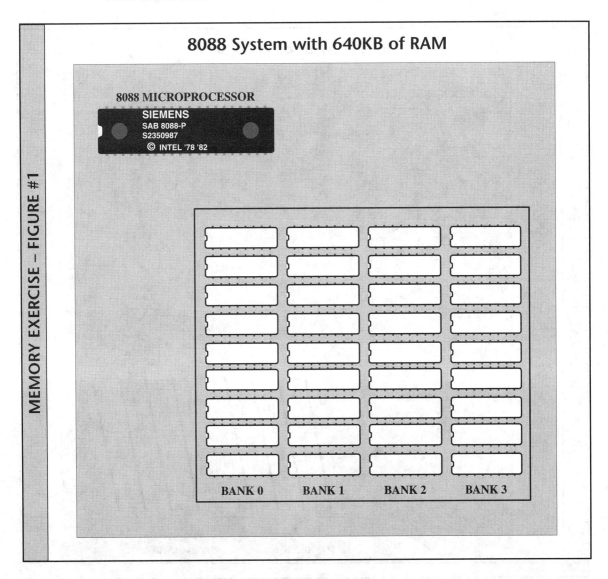

Name _____

PAPER MEMORY POPULATION EXERCISE FOR 80386-BASED MOTHERBOARDS

Use the drawing shown in Memory Exercise Figure #2 to populate the motherboard with 8MB of memory. The 30-pin SIMMs available to use with this motherboard are 256KB, 512KB, 1MB, and 4MB.

MEMORY EXERCISE – FIGURE #2

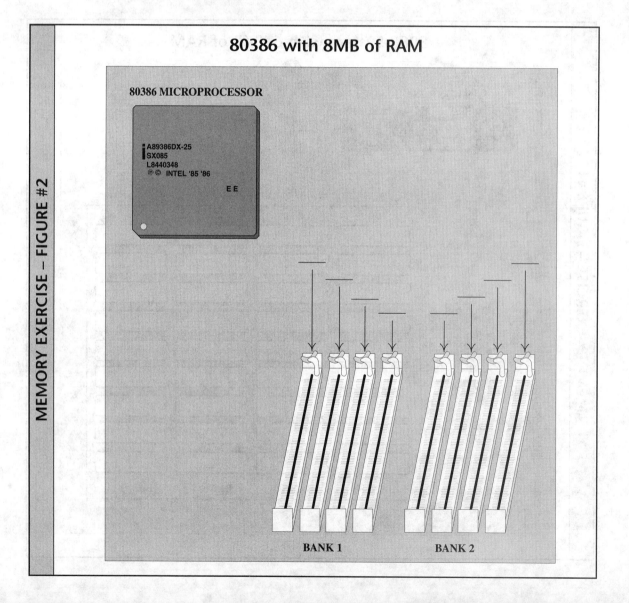

80386 with 8MB of RAM

80386 MICROPROCESSOR

A89386DX-25
SX085
L8440348
® © INTEL '85 '86

E E

BANK 1   BANK 2

Name _____

SECOND PAPER MEMORY POPULATION EXERCISE FOR 80386-BASED MOTHERBOARDS

Use the drawing shown in Memory Exercise Figure #3 to populate the motherboard with 5MB of memory. The 30-pin SIMMs available to use with this motherboard are 256KB, 512KB, 1MB, and 4MB.

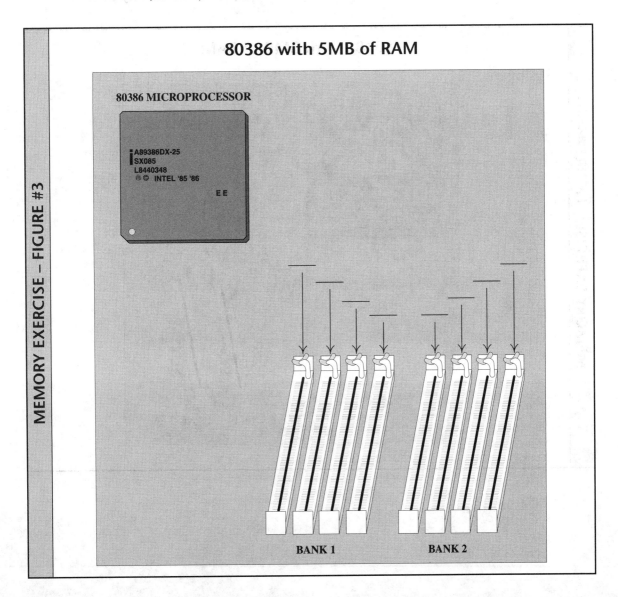

MEMORY EXERCISE – FIGURE #3

80386 with 5MB of RAM

80386 MICROPROCESSOR

A89386DX-25
SX085
L8440348
® © INTEL '85 '86

E E

BANK 1   BANK 2

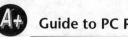

 Name _____

PAPER MEMORY POPULATION EXERCISE FOR
80486-BASED MOTHERBOARDS

Use the drawing shown in Memory Exercise Figure #4 to populate the motherboard with 8MB of memory. The 72-pin SIMMs available to use with this motherboard are 2MB, 4MB, and 8MB (these are the total capacities of the memory chips).

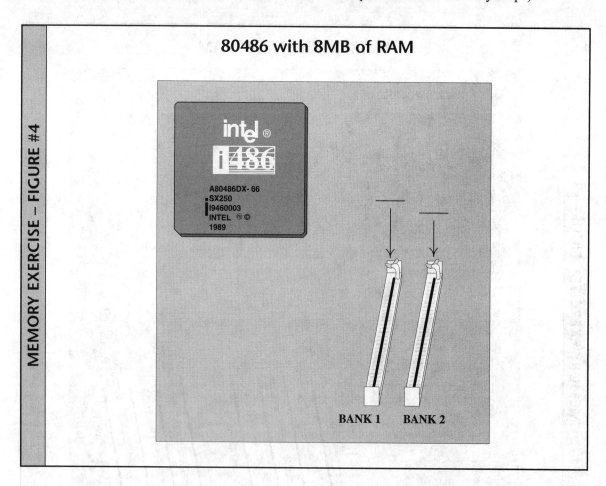

MEMORY EXERCISE – FIGURE #4

80486 with 8MB of RAM

 Name _____

SECOND PAPER MEMORY POPULATION EXERCISE FOR 80486-BASED MOTHERBOARDS

Use the drawing shown in Memory Exercise Figure #5 to populate the motherboard with 16MB of memory. The 72-pin SIMMs available to use with this motherboard are 1MB x 36, 2MB x 36, 4MB x 36, 8MB x 36, and 16MB x 36.

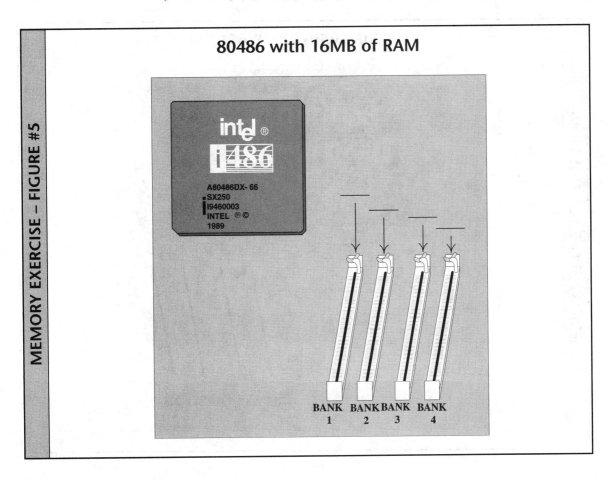

MEMORY EXERCISE – FIGURE #5

80486 with 16MB of RAM

Name _____

THIRD PAPER MEMORY POPULATION EXERCISE FOR
80486-BASED MOTHERBOARDS

Use the drawing shown in Memory Exercise Figure #6 to populate the motherboard with 20MB of memory. The 72-pin SIMMs available to use with this motherboard are 1MB x 36, 2MB x 36, 4MB x 36, 8MB x 36, and 16MB x 36.

MEMORY EXERCISE – FIGURE #6

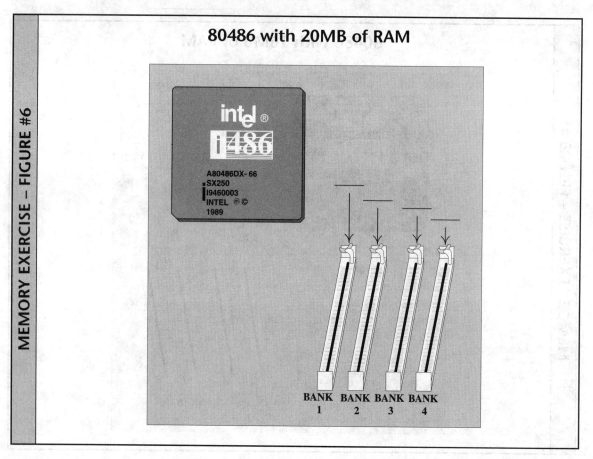

80486 with 20MB of RAM

Name _____

PAPER MEMORY POPULATION EXERCISE FOR
PENTIUM-BASED MOTHERBOARDS

Use the drawing shown in Memory Exercise Figure #7 to populate the motherboard with 16MB of memory. The 72-pin SIMMs available to use with this motherboard are 1MB x 36, 2MB x 36, 4MB x 36, 8MB x 36, and 16MB x 36.

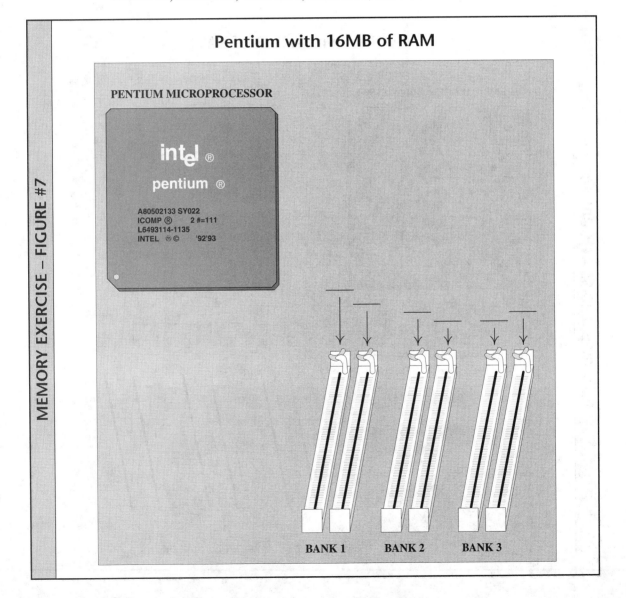

Name _____

SECOND PAPER MEMORY POPULATION EXERCISE FOR PENTIUM-BASED MOTHERBOARDS

Use the drawing shown in Memory Exercise Figure #8 to populate the motherboard with 40MB of memory. The 72-pin SIMMs available to use with this motherboard are 1MB x 36, 2MB x 36, 4MB x 36, 8MB x 36, and 16MB x 36.

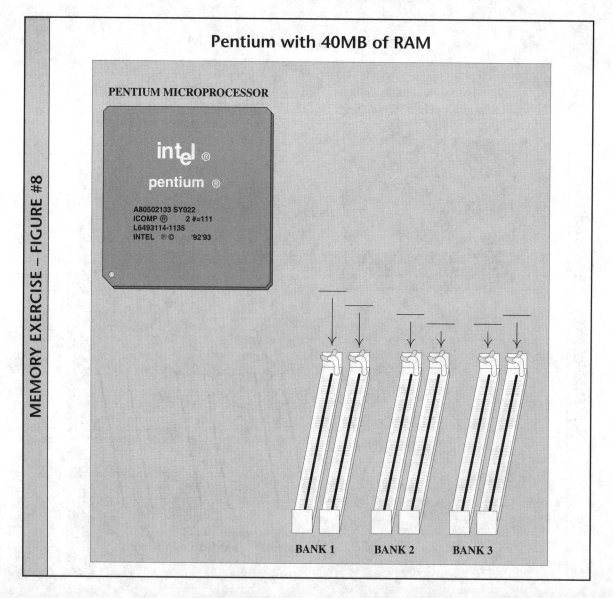

MEMORY EXERCISE – FIGURE #8

Pentium with 40MB of RAM

PENTIUM MICROPROCESSOR

intel ®
pentium ®

A80502133 SY022
ICOMP ®   2 #=111
L6493114-1135
INTEL ® ©   '92'93

BANK 1   BANK 2   BANK 3

Name _____

PAPER MEMORY POPULATION EXERCISE FOR PENTIUM II AND HIGHER MOTHERBOARDS

Use the drawing shown in Memory Exercise Figure #9 to populate the motherboard with 176MB of memory. The 168-pin DIMMs available to use with this motherboard are 1MB x 64, 2MB x 64, 4MB x 64, 8MB x 64, and 16MB x 64.

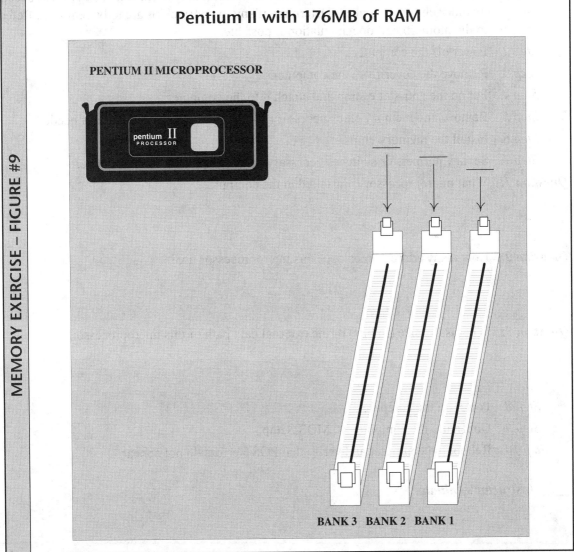

Pentium II with 176MB of RAM

PENTIUM II MICROPROCESSOR

pentium II PROCESSOR

BANK 3   BANK 2   BANK 1

Name _____

MEMORY INSTALLATION EXERCISE

Objective: To correctly install memory into a computer

Parts: Memory chips
Anti-static strap
Documentation for the motherboard

Step 1.   Plan the memory installation. Determine what size, type, capacity, and access speed memory chip(s) you need. Determine if any memory chips are to be removed. Refer to the motherboard documentation if possible.

Step 2.   Power off the computer.

Step 3.   Remove the cover from the computer.

Step 4.   Put on the anti-static strap and attach it to the computer.

Step 5.   Remove any memory chips necessary for the upgrade or installation if needed.

Step 6.   Install the memory chips.

Step 7.   Set any jumpers or switches necessary for a computer memory change.

Question 1:   What microprocessor is installed in the computer?

Question 2:   How many address lines does this microprocessor use?

Question 3:   What is the size (in bits) of the external data path of this microprocessor?

Step 8.   Power on the computer.

Step 9.   Configure the computer's CMOS Setup.

Step 10.   Reboot the computer and verify that POST errors do not appear.

_____ *Instructor's Initials*

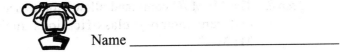

Name _____

SEEING THE RESULTS OF MEMORY MANAGEMENT

Objective: To see how software affects conventional memory and how to load software into the Upper Memory Blocks

Parts: One blank disk
A computer with DOS 6x loaded
Optional software from the instructor

Step 1.   Make a bootable disk with the version of DOS currently on the computer. For DOS skills, refer to the DOS chapter.

Step 2.   Create a CONFIG.SYS file that contains the following lines:

FILES=20

BUFFERS=20

Step 3.   Reboot the computer from the bootable disk.

The system is at the A:\> prompt after rebooting.

Step 4.   Go to the C: drive by typing

C:

The prompt changes to C:\>.

Step 5.   Type

Prompt PG

Step 6.   Go to the DOS directory by typing

CD\DOS

The prompt changes to C:\DOS>

Step 7.   The MEM command allows you to view memory information on the computer. Type

MEM

Question 1:   How many bytes of total conventional memory are available?

Question 2:   What size is the largest executable program?

Step 8. The MEM /C command allows you to see a memory summary with details of the different memory classifications such as conventional and UMBs. Type **MEM /C**

Question 3: What is the first program to load into conventional memory?

Question 4: How much space (in bytes) does this program occupy?

Question 5: How much conventional memory is available?

Question 6: How much contiguous extended memory is available? (Contiguous memory is not broken up; it is adjacent to other memory locations.)

Step 9. No matter how much contiguous extended memory is available, none is usable without a memory manager, such as the HIMEM.SYS program, shipped with DOS, Windows 3x, and Windows 95. Modify the CONFIG.SYS file and insert the HIMEM.SYS file in the first line. Verify that the correct path statement directs the system to the HIMEM.SYS file.

Question 7: Write your CONFIG.SYS file in the space below:

Step 10. Create an AUTOEXEC.BAT file that contains the following files:
PROMPT PG
PATH=C:\DOS

Step 11. Reboot the computer with the bootable disk inserted in the A: drive.

Step 12. At the prompt, type
MEM /C

Question 8: How much conventional memory does the HIMEM.SYS file take?

Step 13.   Modify the CONFIG.SYS file on the boot disk to add the line **DOS=HIGH** after the DEVICE=C:\WINDOWS\HIMEM.SYS statement.

Step 14.   Reboot the computer with the bootable disk inserted into the A: drive.

Step 15.   At the prompt, type

MEM

Question 9:   How many bytes of free conventional memory are available?

Step 16.   Modify the CONFIG.SYS file on the boot disk to include the **EMM386.EXE** expanded memory manager after the HIMEM.SYS statement.

Step 17.   Reboot the computer with the bootable disk inserted in the A: drive.

Question 10:   Using the MEM command, how much conventional memory does the EMM386.EXE file require?

Question 11:   Using the MEM command, how much extended memory is available for use?

Step 18.   Modify the CONFIG.SYS file to add **,UMB** to the DOS=HIGH line so that the line reads: DOS=HIGH,UMB.

Step 19.   Reboot the computer with the bootable disk inserted into the A: drive.

Question 12:   Using the MEM command, how much UMB space is now available?

Question 13:   How much extended memory is now available?

Question 14:   Why did the total amount of free extended memory reduce in size by adding ,UMB to the DOS=HIGH statement?

Step 20.   Modify the CONFIG.SYS statement on the bootable disk to include the NOEMS switch on the EMM386.EXE line.

Step 21.   Reboot the computer with the bootable disk inserted in the A: drive.

Question 15:   Using the MEM command, how much Upper Memory Block space is now available (in bytes)?

Question 16:   How much extended memory is now available?

Note: Steps 22 through 30 are optional. Check with the instructor to see if these steps are to be completed.

Step 22.   Using a device driver supplied by the instructor, load the device driver by modifying the CONFIG.SYS file on the bootable disk.

Question 17:   Write the CONFIG.SYS statements now contained on the bootable disk in the space below:

Step 23.   Reboot the computer with the bootable disk inserted in the A: drive.

Step 24.   Type
MEM /C/P

Question 18:   Using the MEM command, how much space in conventional memory does the driver loaded in Step 22 require?

Step 25.   Modify the CONFIG.SYS file on the bootable disk to load the driver installed in Step 22 to the Upper Memory Blocks.

Step 26.   Reboot the computer with the bootable disk inserted in the A: drive.

Question 19:   Did the driver loaded in Step 25 go into the Upper Memory Blocks? How can you tell? If the driver did not load correctly, redo Steps 25 and 26.

Step 27.   Obtain a TSR (Terminate and Stay Resident) program from the instructor.

Step 28. Modify the AUTOEXEC.BAT file on the bootable disk to load the TSR into the Upper Memory Blocks using the LOADHIGH (LH) command.

Step 29. Reboot the computer with the bootable disk inserted in the A: drive.

Step 30. Verify that the TSR loaded in Step 27 loads in the UMBs.

Question 20: Did the TSR load high? Explain how you determined if it loaded high.

_____ *Instructor's Initials*

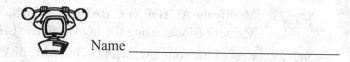

Name _____

USING MICROSOFT'S MEMMAKER (EXPRESS) EXERCISE

Objective: To see how software affects conventional memory and how to load software into the Upper Memory Blocks

Parts: A computer with MS-DOS 6x loaded

Question 1:   Using the MEM command, determine the amount of free conventional memory. Type **MEM** from the command prompt. For DOS skills, refer to the DOS chapter. Write the amount of free conventional memory in the space below:

Step 1.   From the C:\> command prompt, type
MEMMAKER
For DOS skills, refer to the DOS chapter. The screen displays a choice of Express or Custom Setup.

Step 2.   Express Setup is the default option. Press **Enter** to accept the default. A screen appears asking you to specify if any programs require expanded memory.

Step 3.   Because most applications today do *not* require expanded memory, the default option of **No** is the most common answer. Press **Enter** to accept the default.

Optional Step 4. If MemMaker cannot find your Windows 3x, MemMaker might prompt for the location of these files. If so, type in the directory where Windows 3x is located. Contact the instructor if you are unsure.

Step 5.   Later, MemMaker displays a screen stating the computer must be restarted. As the screen instructs, press **Enter** to restart the computer. After restarting, MemMaker determines the optimum memory configuration. MemMaker determines the order for loading the device drivers and TSRs into the Upper Memory Blocks to free up the most conventional memory. This process may take a few moments depending on the complexity of the AUTOEXEC.BAT and CONFIG.SYS files.

Step 6.   After determining the optimum configuration, MemMaker changes the CONFIG.SYS and AUTOEXEC.BAT files. If the computer does not respond after a long period of time, press **CTRL+ALT+DEL** to restart MemMaker, then choose the **Try again with conservative settings** option. Follow the directions on the screen. If the computer performs correctly, it still must be restarted for the changes to take effect. When prompted to do so, press **Enter** to load MemMaker to optimize the CONFIG.SYS and AUTOEXEC.BAT files.

Step 7. Watch carefully for any errors that appear during the restart process. MemMaker displays a question as to whether or not any errors appear. If no error messages appear, press **Enter** to accept the default of YES. If errors appear or you suspect problems, press the **spacebar** once to change the default to NO, then press **Enter**.

Step 8. If everything boots successfully, MemMaker displays the amount of memory available before and after running MemMaker.

Question 2: How much free conventional memory is now available?

Step 9. Press **Enter** to quit MemMaker.

_____ *Instructor's Initials*

Optional Step 10. Contact the instructor to see if the configuration changes made by MemMaker are to be undone. If so, type **MEMMAKER /UNDO** at the command prompt. Press **Enter** to restore the original AUTOEXEC.BAT and CONFIG.SYS files.

Name _____

CONFIGURING WINDOWS 3X FOR 32-BIT DISK ACCESS AND VIRTUAL MEMORY

Objective: To correctly configure Windows 3x 32-bit disk access and set the virtual memory type

Parts: A computer with Windows 3x loaded in the 386 Enhanced mode

Step 1. Power on the computer.

Step 2. Run a disk compacting utility such as DEFRAG.

Step 3. Start Microsoft Windows 3x.

Step 4. Open the **Main** window.

Step 5. Open the **Control Panel** window.

Step 6. Double-click on the **386 Enhanced** icon.

Step 7. Click in the **Virtual memory** box.

Step 8. Click once in the **Change** box.

Step 9. At the bottom of the window is a checkbox for 32-bit disk access *if* Windows determines the hard disk controller is WD1003-compatible. If the 32-bit disk access checkbox is available, click once inside the checkbox. If the checkbox is not available, skip to Step 12.

Step 10. Save the settings by clicking in the **OK** box.

Step 11. A prompt appears stating Windows must be restarted for the changes to take effect. Click in the box that says **Restart Windows**.

Question 1: What is an advantage of using 32-bit disk access?

Step 12. After Windows restarts, open the **Main** window.

Step 13. Open the **Control Panel** window.

Step 14. Double-click on the **386 Enhanced** icon.

Step 15. Click in the **Virtual memory** box.

Step 16. Click once in the **Change** box.

Step 17. Click in the **Type** box **down arrow** (which either says permanent or temporary).

Step 18. Ignore the Recommended size and set the Permanent Swap file New Size to the settings given in Memory Exercise Table #1 according to the amount of RAM installed on the motherboard.

Step 19.   Click on **OK**.

Permanent Swap File Settings

Installed RAM	Permanent Swap File Setting
8MB	1024K
16MB	2048K
32MB	4096K

Step 20.   A dialog box appears asking, "Are you sure you want to make changes to the Virtual memory settings?" Click in the **Yes** box.

Step 21.   A dialog box appears stating, "You need to quit and restart Windows so that the changes you made will take effect. Do not press CTRL+ALT+DEL to restart Windows—this will result in loss of information. Restart Windows now?" Click in the **Restart Windows** box.

Step 22.   Verify that Windows 95 starts properly after changing the virtual memory settings.

_____ *Instructor's Initials*

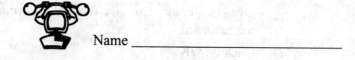

Name _____

WINDOWS 3X MODE AND SYSTEM RESOURCES

Objective: To determine Windows 3x operation mode and what percentage of system resources is available

Parts: A computer with Windows 3x loaded

Step 1.   Power on the computer and start Microsoft Windows.

Step 2.   From the Program Manager, click on **Help**.

Step 3.   Click on **About Program Manager**.

Question 1:   What percentage of system resources is available?

Question 2:   In what Windows mode is the machine running?

Question 3:   How much memory does the machine have available?

Step 4.   Click on **OK**.

Step 5.   Open up the **Accessories Program Group** window.

Step 6.   Open the Microsoft **Write** application.

Step 7.   Click in the **Program Manager** window, leaving the Write application running.

Step 8.   Click on **Help** within the Program Manager window.

Step 9.   Click on **About Program Manager**.

Question 4:   What percentage of system resources is now available?

Step 10.   Click on **OK**.

Step 11.   Return to the Microsoft **Write** application and **Exit** the program.

Question 5: Which memory heap, USER.EXE or GDI.EXE, handles the size of the Microsoft Write application document?

Question 6: Which memory heap, USER.EXE or GDI.EXE, handles the printing of a Microsoft Write document?

_____ *Instructor's Initials*

Name _____

USING MSD FOR ROM ADDRESS CONFLICTS

Objective: To use MSD to view ROM addresses

Parts: A computer with MS-DOS or Windows 3x loaded

Step 1.   Power on the computer.

Step 2.   Change to the directory where the MSD.EXE program is located. For DOS skills, refer to the DOS chapter.

Step 3.   At the command prompt, execute the Microsoft Diagnostics by typing **MSD**.

Step 4.   From the Main Menu, press **M** for Memory.

Step 5.   Using the scroll bars on the right side of the screen, examine the memory areas from A000 to FFFF. Look for areas that contain Fs in the blocks of memory. They are the areas of memory that are available. Any new adapter with a ROM chip must have the ROM address set to one of the available areas shown in MSD.

Question 1:   List at least two memory address ranges available for use by a new adapter.

Question 2:   If a new adapter does not have an option available for one of the ROM addresses listed in Microsoft Diagnostics, what could you as the technician do?

Step 6.   Exit the MSD program by pressing **ALT**, then **F**, then **X**.

_____ *Instructor's Initials*

Name _____

INSTALLING AND RUNNING WINDOWS 95 SYSTEM MONITOR

Objective: To install and properly use System Monitor

Parts: A computer with Windows 95 loaded, or a Windows 95 CD or installation disk

Step 1. Power on the computer and start Microsoft Windows 95.

Step 2. Click on the **Start** button.

Step 3. Click on the **Settings** button.

Step 4. Double-click on the **Control Panel** option to open the Control Panel window.

Step 5. Double-click on the **Add/Remove Programs** icon.

Step 6. Click on the **Windows Setup** tab.

Step 7. In the **Components** list, be sure **Accessories** is enabled or checked. If Accessories is not checked, click on it to enable it.

Step 8. Click on **Accessories**.

Step 9. Click on **Details**.

Step 10. In the **Components** list, verify **System Monitor** is enabled or checked. If System Monitor is not checked, click on it to enable it.

Step 11. Click **OK**. The screen returns to the Windows Setup window.

Step 12. Click **OK**. A prompt may appear asking you to insert the Windows 95 CD-ROM disk or a Windows 95 installation disk.

Step 13. Click **OK** after inserting the proper CD or disk into the appropriate drive.

Step 14. Close the **Control Panel** window.

Step 15. Click the **Start** button.

Step 16. Click on the **Run** option.

Step 17. Type **SYSMON** and press **Enter.**

Objective: To use the System Monitor utility to track performance problems:

Step 1.   Click the **Edit** menu.

Step 2.   Click on **Add Item**.

Step 3.   In the Item List, click on the resource(s), such as **Kernel** or **Memory Manager**, to be monitored. To select more than one resource, press and hold **CTRL** while clicking on the resource.

Step 4.   Click **OK**. The System Monitor window appears with the various options checked in Step 4. Open and close various applications to see the effects on memory usage.

_____ ***Instructor's Initials***

 Name _____

ADJUSTING MEMORY FOR A MS-DOS APPLICATION RUNNING IN THE WINDOWS 9X MS-DOS MODE

Objective: To adjust the memory configuration for a DOS application in the Windows 9x MS-DOS mode

Parts: A computer with Windows 9x loaded
DOS application

Step 1. Power on the computer and start Microsoft Windows 9x.

Step 2. Double-click on the **My Computer** icon.

Step 3. Right-click on the **drive** icon that contains the DOS application.

Step 4. Click once on the **Explore** option.

Step 5. Find the appropriate DOS application .EXE or .COM file which starts the application.

Step 6. Right-click the DOS application's **.EXE** file.

Step 7. Click on the **Properties** option.

Step 8. Click on the **Memory** tab. If the DOS application is configured in the Advanced settings for MS-DOS mode, not the Suggest MS-DOS Mode as Necessary option, memory cannot be configured for the application.

Step 9. Adjust the conventional, extended, or MS-DOS Protected Mode (DPMI) memory as needed. MS-DOS Protected Mode memory is automatically provided by Windows 95 as expanded memory if the EMM386 statement is included in the CONFIG.SYS file. Do not use the NOEMS switch if you want to use MS-DOS Protected Mode memory.

Question 1: Because DPMI (DOS Protected Mode) memory access is provided by the EMM386 statement, where on the memory map is DPMI memory located?

Step 10. Click **OK** when all properties are set.

Step 11. Close the **Exploring** window.

Step 12. Close the **My Computer** window.

_____ *Instructor's Initials*

Name _____

USING WINDOWS 9X'S DEVICE MANAGER
FOR VIEWING VARIOUS MEMORY AREAS

Objective: To use Device Manager to help avoid memory conflicts

Parts: A computer with Windows 9x loaded

Step 1. Power on the computer and start Microsoft Windows 9x.

Step 2. Right-click on the **My Computer** icon. A sub-menu appears.

Step 3. Click on the **Properties** menu option. The System Properties window appears.

Step 4. Click on the **Device Manager** tab.

Step 5. Verify that the Computer option is highlighted. If not, click once on the **Computer** option.

Step 6. Click on the **Properties** button. The Computer Properties window appears. Currently listed are the system's interrupts or IRQ in use.

Step 7. Click on the **Memory** radio button. The system's ROM addresses used by motherboard ROM chips or ROM chips on various adapters are listed on the screen. Keep in mind that no two ROM chips can share the same memory map space.

Step 8. Click on the **Performance** tab.

Question 1: What is the amount of RAM installed?

Question 2: What percentage of system resources is available?

Question 3: What, if any, recommendations can you make for this machine in regard to memory management?

_____ *Instructor's Initials*

Step 9. Click on the **Close** box in the upper right corner.

Name _____

USING WINDOWS 98'S SYSTEM INFORMATION TOOL

Objective: To use Microsoft's System Information to see how memory is being used by the system

Parts: A computer with Windows 98 loaded

Step 1. Power on the computer and start Microsoft Windows 98.

Step 2. Click on the **Start** button.

Step 3. Select the **Programs** option.

Step 4. Select the **Accessories** option.

Step 5. Select the **System Tools** option.

Step 6. Click on the **System Information** option.

Step 7. Three components are listed in the left window: Hardware Resources, Components, and Software Environment. Notice how the words "System Information" are highlighted in the left window and general information is available in the right window. If this is not shown, click on **System Information** in the left window.

Question 1: What percentage of system resources is available for other programs to use?

Step 8. Click on the **Start** button.

Step 9. Select the **Programs** option.

Step 10. Select the **Accessories** option.

Step 11. Click on the **WordPad** option. If WordPad is not available, select **any accessory** that ships with the system.

Step 12. Click on the **Microsoft System Information** button on the toolbar at the bottom of the screen. The System Information application reappears on the screen.

Step 13. Click on the **View** menu option.

Step 14. Click on the **Refresh** option.

Question 2: What percentage of system resources is available now that WordPad or another application has started?

Step 15.   Click on the **plus sign (+)** by Hardware Resources.

Step 16.   Click on the **Memory** option available under Hardware Resources in the left panel.

Question 3:   List one memory address range and its purpose.

_____ *Instructor's Initials*

Step 17.   Click on the **plus sign (+)** by Software Environment.

Step 18.   Click on the **plus sign (+)** by Drivers. Kernel Drivers, MS-DOS Drivers, and User-Mode Drivers appear under the Drivers section.

Step 19.   Click on the **Kernel Drivers** option in the left window.

Step 20.   Locate the **PAGESWAP** driver in the right window.

Question 4:   Using the horizontal scroll bar at the bottom of the window, determine from where the PAGESWAP driver is loaded. Write your answer in the space below.

Step 21.   Click on the **MS-DOS Drivers** option in the left window.

Question 5:   How many DOS drivers are currently loaded?

Step 22.   Click on the **Running Tasks** option in the left window.

Step 23.   Locate the **EXPLORER.EXE** program in the right window.

Question 6:   Using the horizontal scroll bar at the bottom of the window, determine from which directory the EXPLORER.EXE program loads.

Question 7:   How do you think the System Information program could help you solve a memory problem?

Step 24.   Close the **Microsoft System Information** program.

Step 25.   Click the **WordPad** program or whatever program loaded in Step 11.

Name _____

VIEWING MEMORY AREAS IN WINDOWS 2000 PROFESSIONAL

Objective: To use the System Information utility to view memory area assignments in
Windows 2000 Professional

Parts: Computer with Windows 2000 Professional installed.
At times, it may become necessary to view memory area assignments in order to
troubleshoot and/or configure your system

Step 1.   Turn the computer on and verify that Windows 2000 Professional loads.

Step 2.   Logon to Windows 2000 Professional using the userid and password provided by the
instructor or lab assistant.

Step 3.   From the Start menu, choose **Programs, Accessories, System Tools,** and then select
System Information. The System Information utility opens.

Question 1:   What system information is available through the System Information utility?

Step 4.   Expand the **Hardware Resources** folder, and then expand **Memory**. The System's
memory assignment information will be displayed.

Question 2:   Which memory area is assigned to your video adapter?

_____ *Instructor's Initials*

Step 5.   Close the **System Information** utility.

Name _____

MEMORY TROUBLESHOOTING EXERCISE

Objective: To correctly identify and solve a memory problem

Parts: A computer with a memory problem

   Step 1.   Power on a computer that has a memory problem inserted.

Question 1:   What is the first indication that there is a memory problem?

Question 2:   List all troubleshooting steps taken to solve this problem.

Question 3:   Were there any CONFIG.SYS or AUTOEXEC.BAT errors? If so, list the errors in the space below in the order the errors occurred:

Question 4:   Describe the solution to the problem.

_____ *Instructor's Initials*

Name _____

INTERNET DISCOVERY

Objective: To become familiar with researching memory chips using the Internet

Parts: A computer with Internet access

Step 1. Power on the computer and start the Internet browser.

Step 2. Using any search engine, locate three different vendors that sell memory chips.

Step 3. Fill in the table below based on your findings at each of the memory sites.

Internet Site	Smallest Capacity 72-pin SIMM	Largest Capacity DIMM	Pros of Web site	Cons of Web site

Question 1: Of the three Internet sites you found, which one was your favorite and why?

NOTES

Chapter 8:

Floppy Drives

OBJECTIVES

After completing this chapter you will
- Understand the basic terms associated with floppy drives.
- Understand the different parts of the floppy drive system.
- Be able to recognize the different floppy disk capacities.
- Be able to clean floppy drive read/write heads.
- Be able to install and configure a floppy drive system.
- Be able to perform basic floppy drive troubleshooting techniques.

KEY TERMS

1.2MB disk	jumper
1.44MB disk	LS-120 drive
2.88MB disk	read/write head
360KB disk	sector
720KB disk	straight-through cable
a:drive	terminator
cluster	track
disk	twisted cable
drive select setting	write-protect notch
floptical drive	write-protect window
formatted (disk)	Zip drive
hub ring	

FLOPPY DRIVE OVERVIEW

The floppy drive subsystem consists of three main parts: (1) the electronic circuits or the controller, (2) the 34-pin ribbon cable, and (3) the floppy drive. The electronic circuits give the floppy drive instructions: "Floppy drive go to this location and read some data! Floppy drive go to this other location and write some data!" The electronic circuits can be on an adapter or built into the motherboard. For today's computers, the electronic circuits are normally built into the motherboard. A technician needs to know that the control circuits can go bad. The floppy cable connects the floppy drive to the electronic circuits. The floppy drive is the device that allows saving data to disk media.

Troubleshooting and installing floppy drives involves these three main areas and the media. Media refers to the disks inserted in the floppy drive. Floppy drives are classified in two ways: by the physical size of disk used (3.5" or 5.25") and the storage capacity of disk used (360KB, 1.2MB, 720KB, 1.44MB, and 2.88MB). Note that today's floppy drives are 3.5" 1.44MB.

FLOPPY MEDIA

The media inserted in a floppy drive is a **disk** or floppy disk. (These words are used interchangeably.) Though 5.25" floppy disks are not prevalent today, it is possible to find them. They have two capacities: 360KB and 1.2MB. The disks have a different coating of material on their surface that is significant in determining the amount of data a disk can hold. Manufacturers label 360KB disks in various ways to identify them. The **360KB disks** are commonly known as double-sided, double-density and are labeled 2S2D, DS2D, or DSDD to indicate this. Some disks have no identifying labels and a technician should be able to tell the disk capacity by just looking at it. A 360KB disk normally has a reinforced center—a darker, thicker material that is sometimes a different color. This is frequently called the **hub ring**. Floppy Figure #1 shows the two 5.25" disk capacities and the hub ring.

1.2MB disks *do not* have a hub ring. The common name for the 1.2MB disk is double-sided, high-density, or simply a high-density disk. However, a 1.2MB floppy is labeled differently than a 360KB floppy disk. The labels you commonly see on a 1.2MB disk are DSHD, 2SHD, or HD located on the outside jacket of the disk.

5.25" disks are protected against accidental erasure by a **write-protect notch** found on the right side of the disk. Look at Floppy Figure #1 for an illustration of the write-protect notch. Cover this notch to prevent data from being written to the disk.

Using the proper disk in the floppy drive is very important. A 360KB floppy disk works best when used in a 360KB floppy drive. *A 1.2MB disk only works in a 1.2MB floppy drive.*

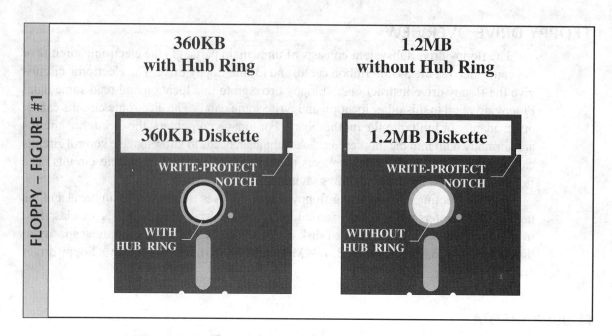

FLOPPY – FIGURE #1

360KB
with Hub Ring

1.2MB
without Hub Ring

360KB Diskette

WRITE-PROTECT
NOTCH

WITH
HUB RING

1.2MB Diskette

WRITE-PROTECT
NOTCH

WITHOUT
HUB RING

3.5" floppy disks have two major capacities: 720KB and 1.44MB. For a while IBM sold computers that used 2.88MB disks. **720KB disks** are double-sided, double-density and are labeled DSDD, DD, 2S2D similar to 360KB disks. You can identify a 720KB disk by visual inspection. Look at the top of the disk and there is one small window in the lower left corner called the write-protect window. The **write-protect window** normally has a sliding tab that closes or opens the window. If you close the window, data can be written to the disk. If the window is open, the disk is write-protected and data cannot be written on the disk. This is true for all 3.5" disks. 720KB disks work best in 720KB drives. Floppy Figure #2 shows a 720KB disk with its write-protect window.

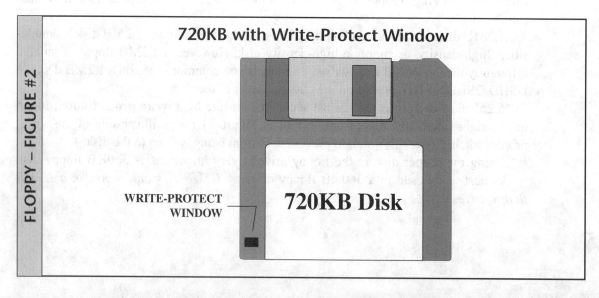

FLOPPY – FIGURE #2

720KB with Write-Protect Window

WRITE-PROTECT
WINDOW

720KB Disk

1.44MB disks are high-density disks and are labeled by manufacturers as HD or 2HD. They are easily identified by the presence of two windows on the disk, almost directly across from each other. Floppy Figure #3 shows the two-windowed high-density disk.

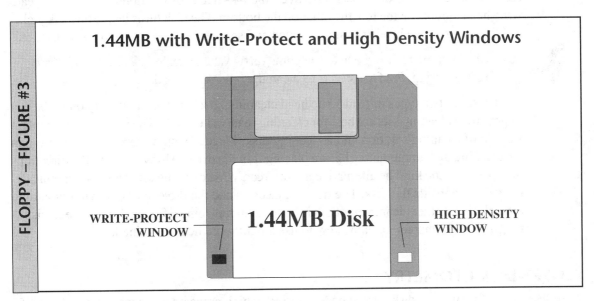

FLOPPY – FIGURE #3

1.44MB with Write-Protect and High Density Windows

WRITE-PROTECT WINDOW   **1.44MB Disk**   **HIGH DENSITY WINDOW**

The extra window on the right side is used by some floppy drives to detect the disk is high density. 1.44MB disks work best in 1.44MB drives and *cannot be read by 720KB drives*. Floppy Table #1 is a summary table to help you understand the different types of disks and floppy drives.

FLOPPY – TABLE #1

Types of Disks

Physical Size	Capacity	Markings	Identification Clues	Drives Used In
5.25"	360KB	DSDD, DD, 2S2D	Reinforced hub ring	360KB, 1.2MB
5.25"	1.2MB	2SHD, HD, DSHD	No hub ring	1.2MB
3.5"	720KB	DSDD, DD, 2S2D	1 left window	720KB, 1.44MB, 2.88MB
3.5"	1.44MB	2HD, HD, DSHD	2 windows across from one another	1.44MB, 2.88MB
3.5"	2.88MB	EHD, ED	2 windows; the right one is higher than the left	2.88MB

FLOPPY DRIVE CONSTRUCTION

Floppy drives have two **read/write heads** responsible for placing the data, the 1s and 0s, onto the disk. The disk inserts between the two heads of the floppy drive. One read/write head mounts on the top, the other on the bottom. The disk turns inside the disk jacket and the floppy drive heads physically touch and scan the disk to read and write data.

Over time, the read/write heads become dirty. When a technician sees read/write errors occuring, the first step is to clean the read/write heads.

There are two types of read/write head cleaning kits: a wet one and a dry one. The wet floppy drive cleaning kits are best for cleaning read/write heads. The cleaning kits contain a bottle of cleaning solution and a cleaning disk. Place a couple drops of the solution on the cleaning disk immediately before placing it in the drive. Always refer to the directions included with the kit. The alternative is a dry read/write cleaning kit that uses a chemically treated cloth inside the disk. The disk is placed inside the drive and used without adding any solution. Either cleaning method is better than replacing a floppy drive. An exercise at the end of this chapter explains how to use a read/write head cleaning kit.

FLOPPY DISK GEOMETRY

Before using a disk it must be **formatted,** which prepares it to accept data. Many 3.5" disks are formatted by the manufacturer. If not, the disk *must* be formatted before it can be used in a computer. To format a disk and make it bootable in a DOS/Windows-based computer, go to the command prompt and type FORMAT A: /S. A prompt appears on the screen to insert a disk. Insert the disk and press *Enter.* To format a disk and make it bootable in a Windows 9x-based computer, double-click on the *My Computer* desktop icon. Right-click on the *3-1/2" (A:) icon.* Select *Format* from the drop-down menu. Click to enable the *Copy system files* option. Click the *Start* button to begin the format process.

A handy tool for any technician is a bootable system disk. There are many versions of operating systems and a bootable disk may be your only hope in repairing certain problems.

When a disk is formatted, whether by the manufacturer, the user, or the technician, concentric circles called **tracks** are drawn on that disk. The 360KB disk has 40 tracks. The 1.2MB, 720KB, 1.44MB, and 2.88MB disks all have 80 tracks. Floppy Figure #4 shows a disk with tracks.

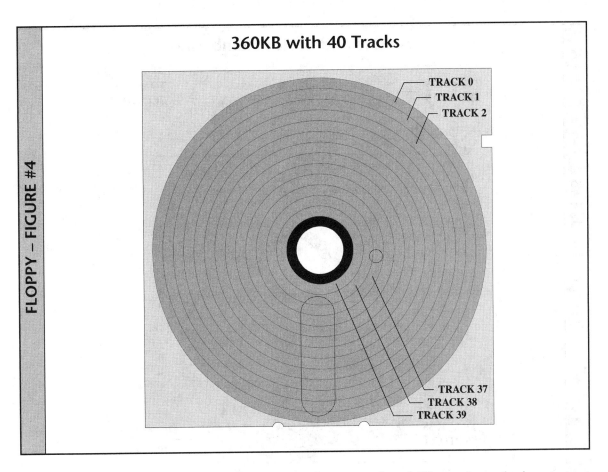

360KB with 40 Tracks

TRACK 0
TRACK 1
TRACK 2

TRACK 37
TRACK 38
TRACK 39

FLOPPY – FIGURE #4

Floppy Figure #4 illustrates how the tracks are numbered. The track numbering starts at the outermost ring beginning with the number 0. The eighty tracks on a 1.44MB high-density disk number from 0 to 79.

The tracks are further subdivided into pie-shaped wedges. The section defined between a track and an intersecting line is a **sector** that holds 512 bytes of information. Each sector is identified by a track number and a sector number. Floppy Figure #5 shows various numbered sectors on a disk.

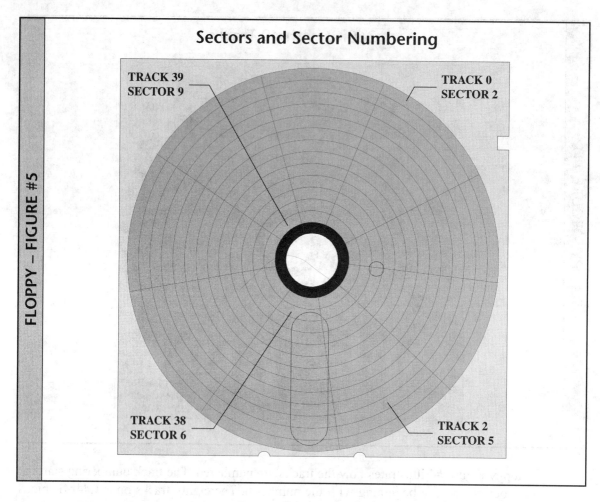

Sectors and Sector Numbering

TRACK 39
SECTOR 9

TRACK 0
SECTOR 2

TRACK 38
SECTOR 6

TRACK 2
SECTOR 5

When you save a file, the data is stored in two sectors on the floppy disk. If the file is larger than two sectors, two additional sectors are allocated for the file. The *minimum* amount of space one file occupies is defined as a **cluster**. On a floppy disk, a cluster is 1,024 bytes or two sectors. As a file grows in size, it uses more clusters.

FLOPPY MEDIA PROBLEMS

The 360KB disk has only 40 tracks with nine sectors per track divided across the surface of the disk. The 360KB tracks are the widest of any disk mentioned in this chapter. The 360KB floppy drive heads rest in the middle of the tracks to read and write the 1s and 0s. On the other hand, the 1.2MB floppy drives have much smaller read/write heads. The 1.2MB disk has 80 tracks and 15 sectors per track, allowing it to store more data. The 1.2MB disk also has a coating of a different magnetic material. The smaller 1.2MB read/write heads can read the big 1s and 0s the 360KB disk has written to it. However, when you write information to a high-density disk with a 1.2MB drive, it has two tracks of data for every one track on a 360KB disk.

That is why you should *never* try to read information written by a 1.2MB drive in a 360KB floppy drive. If you write information on a 360KB disk with a 360KB drive, the 1.2MB drive is able to read the information. But, if you write to that same disk using a 1.2MB drive, the information may or may not be read by the 360KB drive.

Floppy Table #2 summarizes this information.

FLOPPY – TABLE #2

What Disks Work in What Drives

	360KB Floppy Drive		1.2MB Floppy Drive	
	Read	**Write**	**Read**	**Write**
360KB Disk	Yes	Yes	Yes	Yes, but might not be read by a 360KB drive
1.2MB Disk	No	No	Yes	Yes

3.5" drives are a different animal. All the read/write heads are the same size. The disks have a different coating and each capacity type has a different number of sectors per track: 720KB disks have 9 sectors per track, 1.44MB disks have 18 sectors per track, and 2.88MB disks have 36 sectors per track. Each time you format a disk, the operating system tries to format it to the highest capacity, unless (1) you tell DOS otherwise through the FORMAT command switches or through the Windows format window, or (2) you have a floppy drive with a sensor that detects what type of disk has been inserted. This is why 3.5" disks have the windows on the right side of the higher capacity disks. Some floppy drive manufacturers make floppy drives without the sensor. The disk does not get the 1s and 0s written properly causing data errors. The easiest way to determine the floppy drive capacity is to go into the computer's Setup program and look at the configuration.

The two biggest causes of read/write errors on floppy drives are dirty read/write heads or the wrong type of disk used in a floppy drive.

FLOPPY DEVELOPMENTS

IBM tried to create a new floppy standard with their 2.88MB floppy drive, but the rest of the computer industry did not follow. Three other markets have come close to influencing the floppy drive market: (1) the CD-ROM market, (2) the floptical or laser servo technology market, and (3) the zip disk market. CD-ROM drives have made floppy drives almost obsolete because software applications are now so large, the applications require 20 or more floppy disks. CDs are preferable for the installation and running of applications, but are not suitable for storing small amounts of data. The price for a CD drive that can write and read data has dropped drastically, but it is still not comparable to the price of a floppy drive. Computer buyers usually include a floppy drive with their systems.

Floptical drives are floppy drives that use optical technology to move the read/write heads over the disk surface. They were the topic of many trade articles during the last several years, but floptical drives never made a big impact until now. Some people in the computer industry predicted the demise of the floppy drive by the year 2000. The product is called the **a:drive**. It holds 120MB of data, can read from and write to traditional 720KB and 1.44MB disks, fits in existing drive bays, and accesses data up to five times faster than the traditional drive. The a:drive (also called a **LS-120 drive** for laser servo 120MB) uses a patented laser servo technology developed by O.R. Technology, Compaq Computer Corp., Imation, and Matsushita-Kotobuki Electronics Industries Ltd. (MKE). The a:drive connects to an IDE cable on the system. (See the hard drive chapter for configuring and cabling IDE (ATAPI) devices.) The a:drive sells for around $120 and the 120MB disks sell for about $20. Windows 95 Service Release 2, Windows 98, and Windows NT have built-in support for the a:drive. If ever a device has the possibility of tapping into a market stagnant for years, the a:drive is a perfect example of such a device.

The last product that has challenged the floppy drive market is Iomega's **Zip drive**. The Zip drive is not backward compatible with a floppy drive. A Zip disk holds 100MB of data and the external model runs off the parallel or USB port. A 250MB model, SCSI model, and a 1GB model are also available.

FLOPPY DRIVE CONFIGURATION

Some floppy drives require configuration before they are installed. Configuring a floppy drive requires two steps at most: (1) setting the correct drive select number and (2) terminating the floppy drive system. The **drive select setting** is a number assigned to a drive that enables the controlling circuits to distinguish between two floppy drives. Some drives have the drive select setting already configured and it cannot be changed. But if a drive has a drive select setting, a technician assigns a drive select number to the drive by placing a plastic **jumper** over two pins. Having documentation for the drive is best at this point (but not very common). Drive select jumpers are normally found at the bottom rear or at the very back of the floppy drive. Floppy drives can have up to four drive select numbers. They are normally labeled Drive Select numbers 0, 1, 2, or 3 or Drive Select numbers 1, 2, 3, or 4. The floppy drive manufacturer determines how to label the drive select numbers. Floppy Figure #6 shows two different floppy drives and the different drive select number labels.

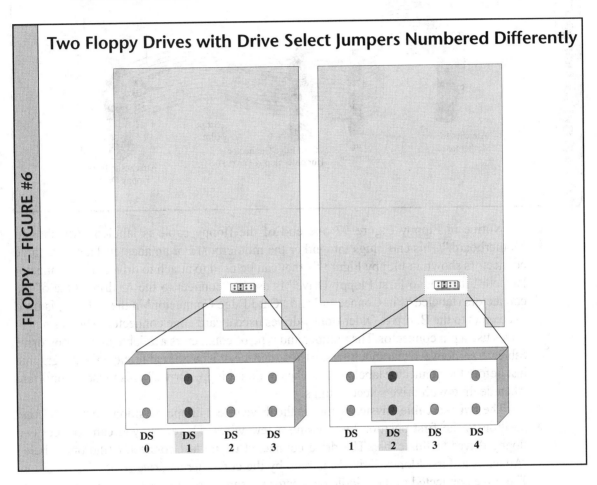

Each floppy drive that connects to one floppy cable must have a separate drive select number. Notice how both drives shown in Floppy Figure #6 have the jumpers over the second drive select. It does not matter how the drive select numbers are labeled. The second drive select may be numbered 1 or 2, but it is still the second drive select position. Floppy drives come from most manufacturers pre-set to the second drive select. The original cabling for floppy drives had a lot to do with why the drive select jumper is set to the second position. Floppy Figure #7 shows a common floppy drive cable.

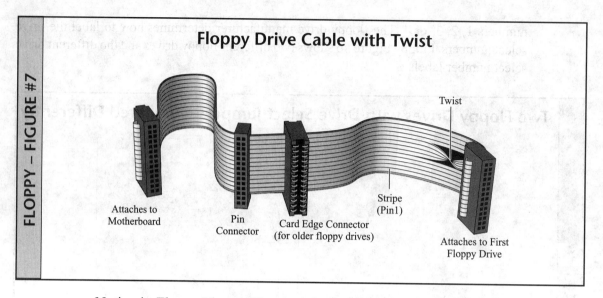

Floppy Drive Cable with Twist

Twist

Attaches to
Motherboard

Pin
Connector

Card Edge Connector
(for older floppy drives)

Stripe
(Pin1)

Attaches to First
Floppy Drive

Notice in Floppy Figure #7 one end of the floppy cable is labeled "Attaches to Motherboard." This end plugs into either the motherboard or an adapter. There are three connectors shown in Floppy Figure #7 that can be used to attach to drives. The connector labeled "Attaches to First Floppy Drive" is used to connect to the A: drive. One of the connectors (labeled "Pin Connector" and "Card Edge Connector" in the graphic) is used to connect to the B: drive. Older floppy drives used a card edge connector, whereas newer drives use a pin connector. The number and type of connectors available on a floppy drive cable varies between manufacturers. Also notice the twist in the cable shown in the graphic just before the connector labeled "Attaches to First Floppy Drive." This twist is important when dealing with drive select settings.

The **twisted cable** physically moves the drive select jumper position from the second position to the first position by crossing a few wires. Therefore, you can connect two floppy drives to this cable. The drive connected to the last connector (the one labeled "Attaches to First Floppy Drive"), is seen by the computer as drive select first position. The drive connected to the middle connector is seen as drive select second position. The controller can now distinguish between the drives even though they are both set to the second position drive select.

The operating system assigns drive letters to each drive detected. The drive at the end of the cable is the A: drive and is set to the second drive select number, but is seen as drive select first position due to the twist in the cable. Drive A: always connects to the last connector on the cable. The drive connected to the middle connector, which is also set to the second drive select number, is assigned B: by the operating system. Floppy Figure #8 shows two sample drives and their drive select jumpers set to the second drive select number.

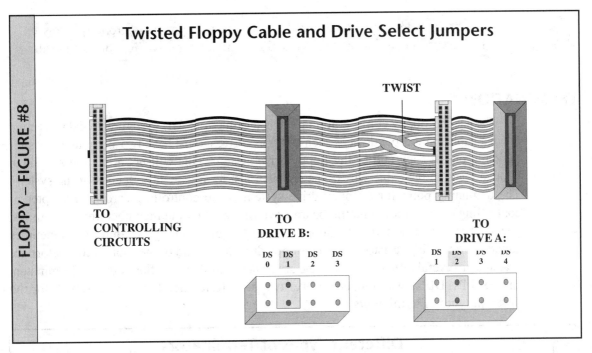

FLOPPY – FIGURE #8

Twisted Floppy Cable and Drive Select Jumpers

TWIST

TO
CONTROLLING
CIRCUITS

TO
DRIVE B:

TO
DRIVE A:

Not all manufacturers use floppy cables with a twist before the last connector. Cables without the twist are **straight-through cables**. If a system has a straight-through cable, set the A: drive to the first drive select number and the B: drive to the second drive select number and the controller can tell the difference between the drives. Floppy Figure #9 shows the drive select jumpers using a cable without a twist.

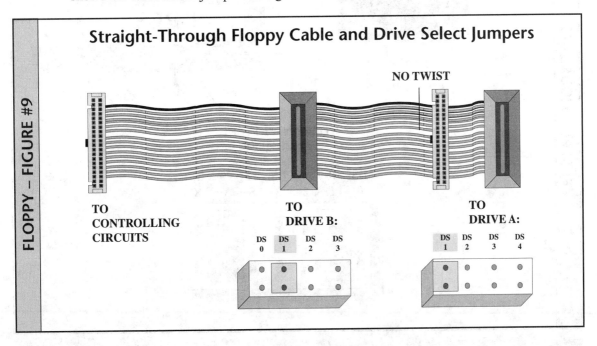

FLOPPY – FIGURE #9

Straight-Through Floppy Cable and Drive Select Jumpers

NO TWIST

TO
CONTROLLING
CIRCUITS

TO
DRIVE B:

TO
DRIVE A:

A good way to tell if you configured the drive select jumpers improperly is to see if both drive lights turn on at the same time or if neither drive light turns on at all.

TERMINATION

The second floppy configuration issue is termination. Any system with data traveling down a cable to multiple devices such as floppy drives, must have two stopping places for the data; one at each end of the floppy drive system. This will not allow the signals to bounce back up the cable wires. The signals must terminate at both ends of the system. The beginning point for a floppy drive system is the controlling card. The adapter or controlling circuits on the motherboard are terminated by the manufacturer. Sometimes, you must designate the end of the floppy drive system by installing a **terminator**, sometimes called a terminating resistor, onto the floppy drive at the end of the cable. Terminators are available in several forms and colors and are on devices other than floppy drives. Terminators can be SIPs, DIPs, or a jumper set over two pins. Reference Floppy Figure #10 for the different types of terminators.

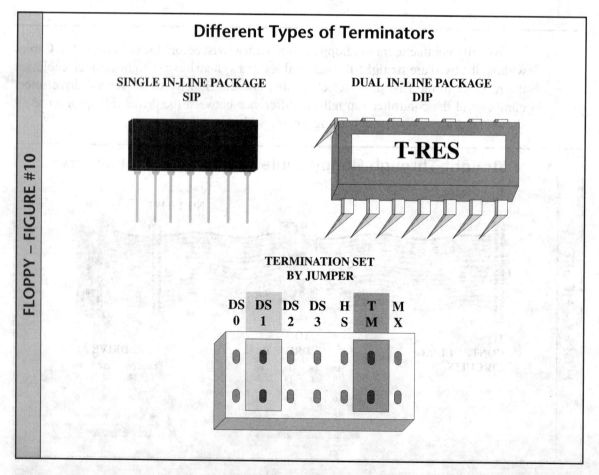

FLOPPY – FIGURE #10

Different Types of Terminators

SINGLE IN-LINE PACKAGE
SIP

DUAL IN-LINE PACKAGE
DIP

T-RES

TERMINATION SET
BY JUMPER

DS 0   DS 1   DS 2   DS 3   H S   T M   M X

The terminator installs on the last drive at the end of the cable, the A: drive. Remove the terminator on the B: drive.

Another function of the terminator is to provide the correct amount of electrical resistance for the system. With terminators installed on both drives in a two drive system, too much current can flow through the floppy system. You might not detect an incorrectly terminated system by an error code or an immediate failure. Over time, this can possibly cause both drives and the controlling circuits to fail.

RELATED FLOPPY DRIVE ISSUES

Some floppy drives do not have drive select jumpers. Assume that the drive select jumper is set to the second position. Also, some drives do not have terminators they are self-terminating. The drives terminate themselves if necessary and un-terminate if they are installed as the B: drive.

In summary, no matter what type of cable is used, if installing only one floppy drive, connect it to the last connector on the cable and terminate. If you are installing two drives, connect the A: drive to the connector at the end of the cable and terminate. Connect the B: drive to the middle connector on the cable and *remove* the terminator. Floppy Figure #11 shows two different floppy drive scenarios.

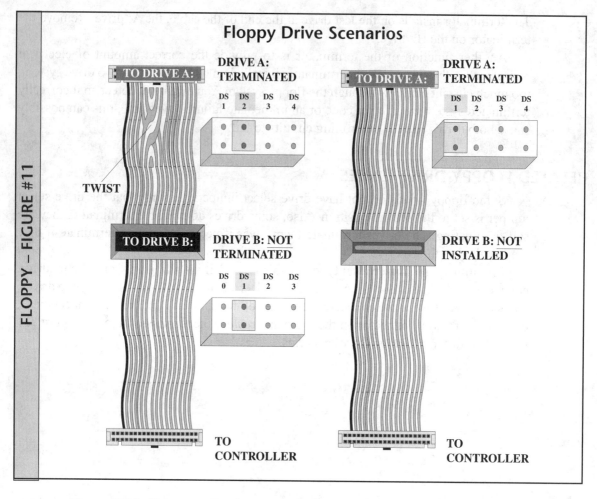

FLOPPY – FIGURE #11

Floppy Table #3 summarizes how to configure a floppy drive based on what cable is in the system.

Floppy Drive Configuration Summary

FLOPPY – TABLE #3

| | Drive Select Jumper | | | |
	Cable With a Twist	Cable Without a Twist	Terminator	Cable Connector
A: Drive	2nd position	1st position	Yes	Farthest from controller
B: Drive	2nd position	2nd position	No	Middle connector

The best way to tackle any hardware device installation and configuration is to (1) have the proper documentation, (2) install or remove any jumpers and switches before the device is installed, and (3) think through the installation and configuration thoroughly.

The exercises at the end of the chapter help you understand floppy drive configurations.

FLOPPY DRIVE INSTALLATION

Installation of floppy drives is simple after doing some preliminary homework:
* Be sure that the computer's BIOS supports the drive being installed by referring to the documentation or going into the computer's Setup program and changing the parameters for the floppy drive to see the possible types.
* Be sure there is a drive bay available.
* Be sure there is a power connection available.
* Be sure there is a floppy cable connector available, if installing a second floppy drive.
* Be sure the floppy cable has the proper connector for the drive being installed (card-edged or pin).
* Purchase any necessary mounting hardware for installing the drive into the case. The floppy drive attaches to the computer chassis. Normally, side brackets and screws attach to the floppy so the drive slides into the drive bay. Floppy drive brackets and screws normally are included with a computer case, but are also available cheap at local computer stores.

After resolving these issues, installation is nothing more than mounting the floppy drive to the computer case and connecting the cable between the drive and motherboard or adapter. Make sure you configure the floppy's drive select setting and termination properly before you mount the drive into the case.

When connecting any cable to an adapter or a device, match pin 1 of the cable to pin 1 of the adapter or device! Devices, adapters, controlling circuits, etc., can be damaged if a cable plugs into the connector the wrong way. Some cables are keyed so they insert only one way into the connector. Most cables that connect to the floppy drive are keyed, but the other end of the cable that connects to the controlling circuits is frequently not keyed.

Pin 1 of a cable is easy to identify. There is a colored stripe down one side of the cable. This stripe connects to pin 1. If by chance, the stripe has faded or is hard to detect, look on the cable's connector end. There is normally an arrow that points to pin 1.

Pin 1 on an adapter or motherboard is not as easy to find. Some manufacturers put a small 1 or 2 by the end where the cable's pin 1 inserts. Other manufacturers put larger numbers at the opposite end. For example, if you saw the number 33 or the number 34 on the motherboard where the floppy cable inserts, pin 1 and pin 2 are on the *opposite* end of the connector.

If there are no pin number markings, look at other connections on the adapter. If you find a number 1 or 2 on a different connector, the floppy connector's pin 1 or 2 orients in the same direction. If you find a higher number (such as 39, 40, 33, 34), then pin 1 is on the opposite end. The floppy cable's pin 1 will be in the same direction as the other connector's pin 1. Also, if there are other cables plugged into the adapter, look for their colored stripe to see which way they orient; the floppy cable will orient in the same direction. If all else fails, remove the adapter from the computer and look on the back of the adapter. Most manufacturers use a square solder joint on the back of the board for the pin 1 connection and round solder joints for the other connections. If you can find one square pin 1 solder joint, then all other pin 1s orient in the same direction.

TROUBLESHOOTING FLOPPY DRIVES

Problems with the floppy drive can be narrowed down to four areas:
- Disk
- The floppy drive
- The cable that connects the drive to the controlling circuits
- The floppy controlling circuits

The most common problem for read or write errors is the disk. Disk problems can include the user using the wrong capacity disk, a bad area of a disk, and a damaged disk. Disks are affected by magnetic fields. Having a disk near a monitor, speaker, or even a kitchen magnet can damage the data contained on it. The easiest way to determine if the problem is the disk is to try a different disk in the drive or test the original disk in another floppy drive.

An easy problem to fix is dirty read/write heads on the floppy drive. These cause errors frequently because the heads physically touch the disk surface. Drive read/write head cleaning kits are available at computer and retail stores. The exercise at the end of this chapter explains how to clean the heads.

After eliminating the disk as the problem, the next most likely culprit is the floppy drive. Mechanical devices fail more frequently than electronic parts. If the read/write heads are clean and the drive still shows errors, the floppy drive is the next suspect. Anytime a device has moving parts such as read/write heads or motors, these devices are more likely to fail than an electronic part, such as a controller.

The least common problem with floppy drives is the cable. Cables do not normally malfunction unless they have been cut, which is not very likely. Cables are sometimes torn when replacing and removing computer cases, so be very careful during disassembly and reassembly.

POST is always a good indicator there is a problem with the floppy drive system. Floppy drive problems give a 6xx series error code for many systems. Refer to the Logical Troubleshooting chapter for a list of different POST error codes. Also, there are diagnostic programs that test a floppy drive, but after a technician works on computers for some time very few continue to use these programs. A good method for troubleshooting an intermittent floppy system problem is to execute a simple batch file that copies information from the hard drive to the floppy drive, deletes the data, and then starts over again. Use a new floppy disk when using this method. An example of such a batch file follows:

```
Echo Floptest.bat
A:
PATH=C:\DOS
MD\TEST
CD\TEST
COPY C:\DOS\F*.*
COPY C:\DOS\A*.*
DEL F*.*
DEL A*.*
FLOPTEST
```

After running the batch file or testing the drive with diagnostics, replace the suspect component. If the batch file runs fine for a while then starts showing floppy errors, the problem may be the floppy drive's electronics or the controlling circuits. Replacing a floppy drive is usually cheaper in today's computers because the floppy controller is built into the motherboard or built into an adapter that controls other devices as well.

Name _____

FLOPPY REVIEW QUESTIONS

1. List the three parts of a floppy drive system.

2. List the two types of 5.25" floppy drives.

3. List two types of 3.5" floppy drives.

4. Why is it not a good idea to write information on a 1.2MB disk and then try to read the information on a 360KB floppy drive?

5. Why is it important to know about drive select jumpers?

6. What drive letter is assigned the first floppy drive detected in a system?

7. List one purpose of a terminator.

8. What determines whether or not you terminate a floppy drive?

9. What harm could you do if you installed both terminators on a multi-drive system?

10. If a floppy cable has two connectors and only one drive is to be connected, to which connector do you attach the drive?

11. How do you know the proper orientation to connect the cable onto the floppy controller?

12. List three considerations when adding or installing a floppy drive.

13. What is the most common part to fail in a floppy drive system?

14. What should a technician do when a computer system shows the message, "Error Reading Drive A:"?

15. What is the common POST error code series for the floppy drive system?

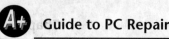

Name _____

FLOPPY FILL-IN-THE-BLANK

1. The circuitry that gives the floppy drive instructions can be on the _____ or on a separate adapter.

2. A _____ is a device that allows data saving to disk media.

3. The markings on the label of a 360KB disk can be _____, _____, or _____.

4. The markings on the label of an 1.2MB disk can be _____, _____, or _____.

5. The _____ is a part of a 5.25" disk that has been cut away to protect the disk from accidental erasure.

6. A _____ floppy drive is the smallest capacity of 3.5" floppy drives.

7. The markings on the label of a 720KB disk can be _____, _____, or _____.

8. The markings on the label of a 1.44MB disk can be _____, _____, or _____.

9. The _____ is a window on the left side of a 3.5" disk that, when closed, allows data to be written to the disk.

10. One purpose of the _____ is to write 1s and 0s to the disk surface.

11. A disk must be _____ before it is used for the first time.

12. Concentric circles on the surface of the disk are commonly called _____.

13. 512 bytes of information are stored in a _____.

14. The smallest amount of space DOS allocates for one file is called a _____.

15. The _____ floppy drive has the largest read/write heads.

16. The _____ floppy drive has read/write heads half the size of the 360KB floppy drive.

17. A _____ floppy disk drive accepts only 5.25" double-sided, double-density disks.

18. A _____ floppy drive can accept 3.5" high-density or double-density disks.

19. The _____ allows the floppy controller to distinguish between two installed floppy drives.

20. A cable with a _____ is installed if both floppy drives connected to the cable have their drive select jumpers set to the second position.

21. A _____ cable is installed if the A: floppy drive has its drive select jumper set to the first position and the B: floppy drive has its drive select jumper set to the second position.

22. The _____ is used to prevent signals from bouncing back up the cable and to provide the correct resistive load for the floppy drive system.

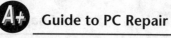
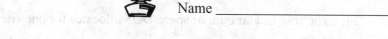

Name _____

PAPER CONFIGURATION OF FLOPPY DRIVES EXERCISE

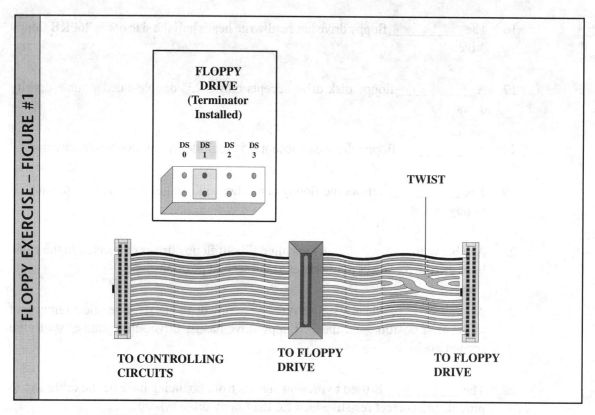

Reference Floppy Exercise Figure #1 for Questions 1–3:

Question 1: Assume you are installing one floppy drive into a system and it is the only floppy drive in the system. The drive select jumper is set to the second position (DS1) as shown in Floppy Exercise Figure #1. Also, notice the cable has a twist at one end. To install the drive, do you move the drive select jumper to a new position or leave it set to the second position? If the drive select jumper must be moved, to which drive select number (DS0, DS1, DS2, or DS3) would you move the jumper?

Question 2:   If using the cable shown in Floppy Exercise Figure #1, to which connector on the cable will you connect the floppy drive you are installing?

Question 3:   The floppy drive has a terminator installed by the manufacturer. Will you leave it installed or remove it?

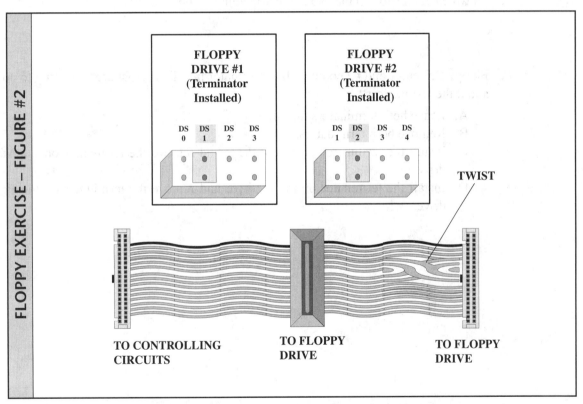

Reference Floppy Exercise Figure #2 for Questions 4–8:

Question 4:   Assume you are going to install the floppy drives shown in Floppy Exercise Figure #2 into the same system and you will be using the cable shown. Notice the cable has a twist at one end. Set up Floppy Drive #1 as the A: drive. Both drives have the drive select jumper already set to the second position. Which drive select (DS0, DS1, DS2, or DS3) will you choose for Drive #1?

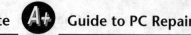

Question 5: Set up Floppy Drive #2 as the B: drive. Which drive select (DS1, DS2, DS3, or DS4) will you choose for the B: drive?

Question 6: To which connector on the cable will you connect the A: drive?

Question 7: To which connector on the cable will you connect the B: drive?

Question 8: Floppy Drives #1 and #2 come with a terminator installed. What are you going to do about the terminators?

    A. Leave both terminators installed.

    B. Remove both terminators.

    C. Install the terminator on the B: drive and remove the terminator on the A: drive.

    D. Install the terminator on the A: drive and remove the terminator on the B: drive.

Name _____

CLEANING FLOPPY DRIVE HEADS EXERCISE

Objective: To clean a floppy drive's read/write heads to prevent errors

Parts: Wet floppy drive cleaning kit for 5.25" or 3.5" drive

Step 1. Power on the computer.

Step 2. Verify the DOS prompt is on the screen.

Step 3. Follow the directions on the floppy cleaning kit for applying the proper number of cleaning fluid drops on the special cleaning disk.

Step 4. Insert the moistened disk into the floppy drive.

Step 5. Type the appropriate drive letter (A or B) followed by a colon. For example, **A:** and press **Enter.**

Step 6. Type **DIR** and press **Enter**. A *normal* error message appears such as "Error reading Drive A: Abort (A), Retry (R), or Ignore (I)?

Step 7. Press **R** for Retry. Do this three or four times.

Step 8. Press **A** for Abort.

Step 9. Remove the special cleaning disk.

Question 1: What is an indication that the read/write heads need cleaning?

_____ *Instructor's Initials*

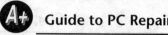

 Name _____

SINGLE FLOPPY DRIVE INSTALLATION EXERCISE

Objective: To install a single floppy drive in a computer correctly

Parts: Floppy drive
Floppy cable
Anti-static materials
Data disk

CAUTION: Observe proper grounding procedures when installing floppy drives.

Step 1.   Remove the cover from the computer. Use proper anti-static procedures.

Step 2.   Attach the 34-pin cable to the adapter or motherboard. Check to be sure the cable's pin 1 attaches to the adapter or motherboard connector's pin 1.

Question 1:   How can you determine which is pin 1 on the adapter or motherboard connector?

Step 3.   Set the drive select jumper on the floppy drive. Refer to the documentation that came with the floppy drive, if possible. If the drive's 34-pin cable has a twist in the cable immediately before the last connector on the cable, then set the drive select jumper to the second drive select position. If the drive's 34-pin cable *does not* have a twist in the cable immediately before the last connector on the cable, then set the drive select jumper to the first drive select position.

Question 2:   How are the drive select jumpers numbered on the drive being installed?

Question 3:   What drive select did you choose for the floppy drive?

Step 4.   If necessary, terminate the floppy drive. Refer to the documentation included with the floppy drive. Most floppy drives are terminated by the manufacturer.

Question 4:   Why do you have to place a terminator on the floppy drive?

Step 5.   Install any mounting hardware required on the sides of the floppy drive.

Step 6.   Install the floppy drive into the computer and secure with screws.

Step 7.   Connect the power cable to the drive.

Step 8.   Connect the floppy cable that connects to the floppy drive. Check and be sure the cable's pin 1 connects to the floppy drive connector's pin 1. Most floppy cables are keyed to insert only one way onto the drive. **If you have a cable with two connectors on the end and the floppy is to be the A: drive, attach the cable connector that is the FARTHEST from the adapter to the floppy drive.**

Question 5:   How do you determine where pin 1 is on the cable?

Step 9.   If this is a PC or XT-type computer, go to Step 16.

Step 10.   Power up the system. Go into the computer's Setup program to configure the CMOS. (Frequently, the power-on screen displays the keystrokes required to enter Setup. If this is not the case, refer to the computer's documentation.) Choose the floppy drive type that matches the floppy drive you are installing (360KB, 720KB, 1.2MB, or 1.44MB). Contact your instructor if you have any questions. Entering the wrong parameters into CMOS will prohibit your drive from working properly or to it's fullest capacity and possibly cause POST errors.

Question 6:   How did you get into CMOS Setup?

Step 11.   Save the Setup information by following the directions on the screen.

Step 12.   Perform a warm boot by pressing **CTRL+ALT+DEL**.

Question 7:   Did the computer boot without a POST error? If not, refer to the chapter section on troubleshooting. Check all previously performed steps. Do not proceed until you solve all POST errors.

Step 13.   Insert a data disk into the floppy drive you just installed.

Step 14.   Verify you are at the DOS prompt. Type the following:

DIR A:

Question 8:   Did the drive perform the read operation successfully? If not, check all previously performed steps as well as the chapter section on troubleshooting.

Step 15.   Reinstall the computer cover.

_____ *Instructor's Initials for 286 or higher microcomputer*

The following steps are for a PC or a XT model computer:

Step 16.   Set the switches on the motherboard for the number of floppy drives installed. For one floppy drive, SW1 position 1 should be OFF, position 7 and 8 should be ON. Use an ink pen or small screwdriver to set the switches.

Question 9:   Why should you *not* use a pencil when setting switches on the motherboard?

Step 17.   Power on the computer.

Question 10:   Did the computer boot without a POST error? If not, refer to the section on troubleshooting. Check all previously performed steps. Do not proceed until all POST errors are solved.

Step 18.   Insert a data disk into the floppy drive you just installed.

Step 19.   Verify you are at the DOS prompt. Type the following:

DIR A:

Question 11:   Did the drive perform the read operation successfully?

Step 20.   Reinstall the computer cover.

_____ *Instructor's Initials for PC or XT microcomputer*

Name _____

INTERNET DISCOVERY

Objective: To obtain specific information on the Internet regarding a computer or associated parts

Parts: Access to the Internet

Question 1:   Locate a motherboard that supports LS-120 drives. Write the name of the motherboard manufacturer and the URL of the Internet site where you found the information.

Question 2:   On the Microsoft web site, locate troubleshooting tips for floppy drives installed into Windows 98 computers. What mode of operation does Microsoft recommend that you go into to test the drive? Do these Microsoft guidelines apply to Windows 95 too? Write the answers and URL in the space below.

Question 3:   Find a web site that has floppy troubleshooting guidelines. Write the URL in the space below.

Question 4:   Describe the steps to change the drive letter for an Iomega Zip drive when using 2000 Professional. Also write the URL of the Internet location where you found this information in the space below.

Question 5:   What is the CMOS setting for an internal Iomega ATAPI Zip 100 drive installed in an NT Workstation computer? Write the answer and the URL in the space below.

NOTES

9

Chapter 9:
Hard Drives

OBJECTIVES

After completing this chapter you will
- Understand hard drive terminology.
- Understand the different hard drive types.
- Be able to set up and configure different types of hard drives.
- Be able to troubleshoot hard drive problems.
- Understand and be able to perform hard drive preventive maintenance.

KEY TERMS

active terminator	FAT16	Raid 5 volume
actuator arm	FAT32	read/write head
ATA standard	FDISK	SCAM
ATAPI	file system	SCANDISK
basic disk	FPT	SCSI
basic storage	fragmentation	SCSI bus
boot partition	head crash	SCSI channel
boot sector virus	high-level format	SCSI ID
boot volume	host adapter	SCSI segment
busmaster DMA	HVD	SE
cable select	IDE	sector
CHS addressing	INT13 interface	sector translation
cluster	interface	serial ATA
CRC	interleaving	service
crosstalk	LBA	simple volume
cylinder	Logical Disk Management	single
daisy chaining	logical drive	slave
DBR	lost clusters	S.M.A.R.T.
defragmentation	low-level format	spanned volume
differential terminator	LVD	ST506
disk cache	master	striped volume
Disk Cleanup	MBR	system partition
drive type	NTFS	system volume
dynamic disk	NTFS5	track
dynamic storage	partition table	translating BIOS
ECHS	partitioning	UDMA
encoding	pass through terminator	VCACHE
ERD	passive terminator	VFAT
ESDI	petabyte	virus
exabyte	platter	volume
extended partition	primary partition	zone bit recording
FAT		

HARD DRIVE OVERVIEW

Hard drives are the most popular device for storing data. They store more data than floppy drives and move data faster than tape drives. Today's hard drive capacities range from 10 to 40GB. Hard drives are frequently upgraded in a computer, so it is important for you to understand all the technical issues. These issues include knowing the parts of the hard drive subsystem, how the operating system and the BIOS work with a hard drive, how to configure a hard drive, and how to troubleshoot it.

The hard drive subsystem consists of four parts: (1) the hard drive; (2) possibly an adapter that connects the hard drive subsystem to the motherboard; (3) the chips that control the hard drive; and (4) one or two cables that connect the drive to the motherboard or adapter. Some hard drives connect directly to the motherboard.

HARD DRIVE GEOMETRY

Hard drives have multiple hard metal surfaces called **platters**. Each platter normally holds data on both sides and normally has two read/write heads, one for the top and one for the bottom. The **read/write heads** write and read 1s and 0s to and from the hard drive surface. The read/write arms hold the read/write heads and operate as one unit on an **actuator arm**. The heads move over the hard drive surface as the platters rotate. The read/write heads float on a cushion of air without touching the platter surface. If a read/write head touches the platter, a **head crash** occurs. This can damage the platters or the read/write head causing corrupt data. See Hard Figure #1 for an illustration of a hard drive's arms, heads, and platters.

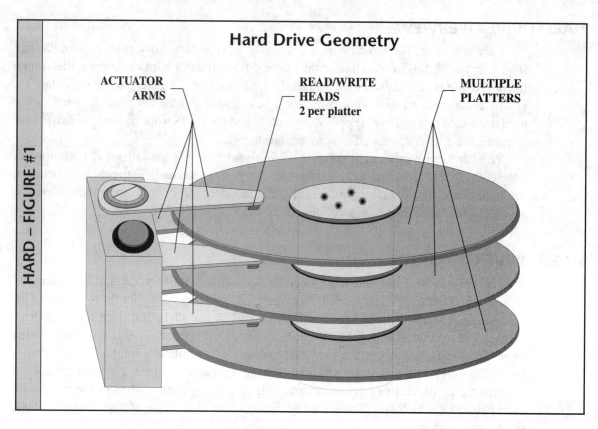

Hard Drive Geometry

ACTUATOR ARMS

READ/WRITE HEADS
2 per platter

MULTIPLE PLATTERS

HARD – FIGURE #1

Each hard drive surface is metallic and has concentric circles, each of which is called a **track**. Tracks are numbered starting with the outermost track, which is called track 0. One corresponding track on all surfaces of a hard drive is a **cylinder**. For example, cylinder 0 consists of all the track 0s; all of the track 1s make cylinder 1, and so on. The number of tracks and cylinders are the same, but they are *not* the same thing. A track is a single circle on one platter. A cylinder is the same track on all platters. Hard Figure #2 shows the difference between tracks and cylinders.

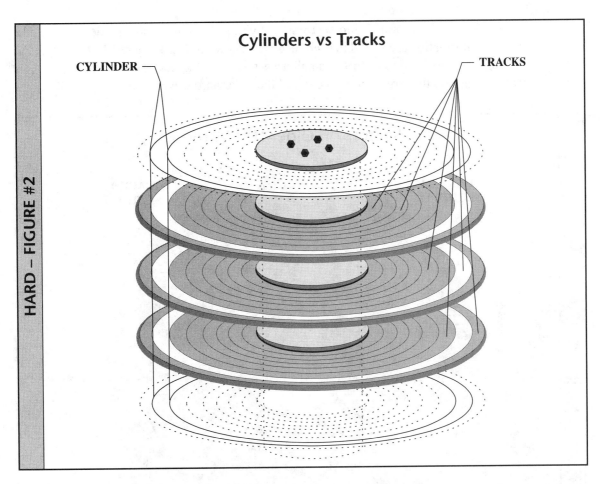

Notice in Hard Figure #2 how a concentric circle makes an individual track. A single track on all the surfaces makes an individual cylinder.

Each track is separated into **sectors** by dividing the circle into smaller pieces. 512 bytes of information are stored in each sector. As shown in Hard Figure #3, if 512 bytes of information can be stored on the smaller sectors near the center of the drive, there is wasted space on the larger, outer sectors of the older hard drives.

HARD – FIGURE #3

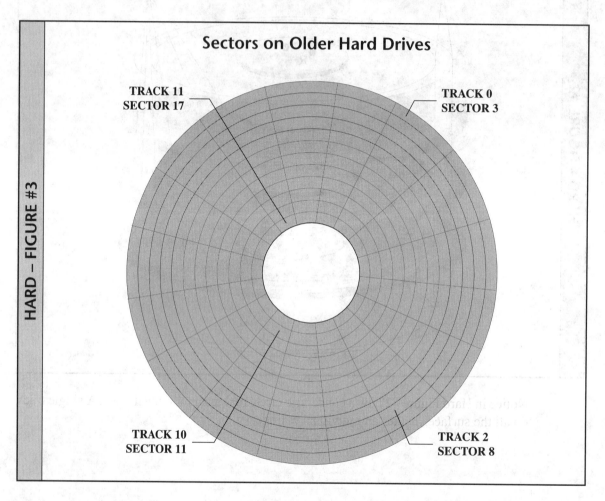

Sectors on Older Hard Drives

TRACK 11
SECTOR 17

TRACK 0
SECTOR 3

TRACK 10
SECTOR 11

TRACK 2
SECTOR 8

Keep in mind that Hard Figure #3 does not show as many tracks or sectors as an older hard drive actually has, but the concept is the same.

Hard drive manufacturers developed a way to use the wasted space on the outer tracks. **Zone bit recording** efficiently uses the hard drive surface by placing more sectors on the outer tracks than on the inner tracks. Other names for this include zone recording or multiple zone recording (MZR). Instead of using pie-shaped wedges, the drives can have a different number of sectors on each track. The outer tracks of the hard drive contain more sectors than the inner tracks because each sector is the same physical size. Reference Hard Figure #4 for an illustration of newer hard drive sectors.

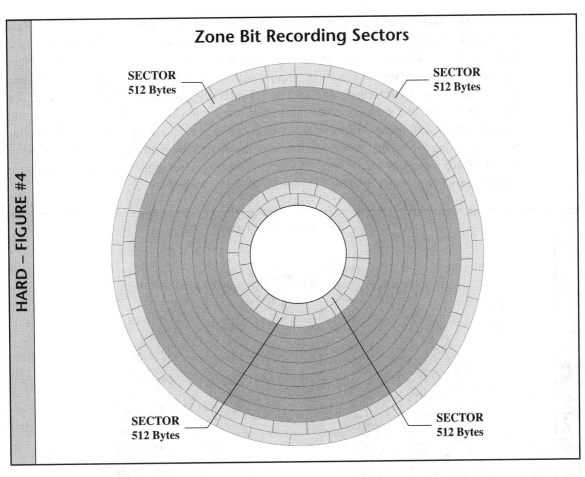

The basic operation of the hard drive is that the read/write heads pick up data and transfer it to the controller, which passes the data to the motherboard. Then, the controller asks for more data. As this occurs and the platter continues to spin, the read/write heads may not be positioned over the next sector. Therefore, the read/write heads must wait for data as the disk spins and the next sector is positioned under the read/write heads. A more efficient method for data transfer comes from numbering the sectors differently.

Interleaving is a method of numbering sectors for the most efficient transfer of data between the hard drive and the controller. The numbering sequence for the sectors is the interleave factor. If a hard drive has a 1:1 (pronounced "one to one") interleave, the sectors on each track number consecutively beginning with the number 1. Older hard drives require a 2:1, 3:1, 5:1, or 6:1 interleave factor. The 1:1 interleave factor is not efficient for older drives because of the slow speed of their electronics. On older hard drives, interleaving provides the fastest means of transferring data between the hard drive and the controller without waiting for the disk to rotate all the way around to the required sector. Some books list interleave factors as 1:2, 1:3, or 1:5. The concept is the same though — the sectors are not numbered consecutively. Hard Figure #5 shows 3:1 interleaving.

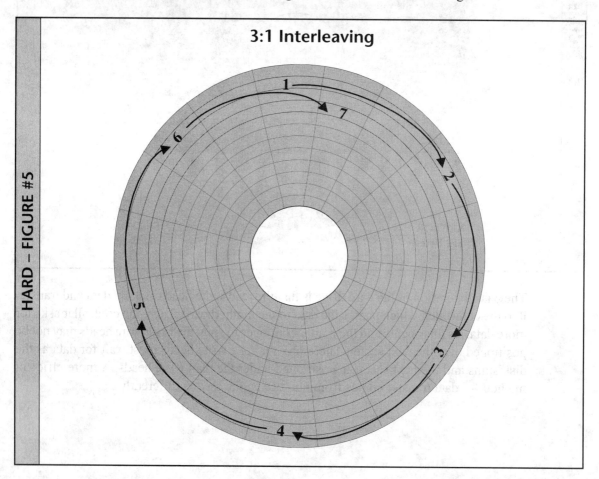

HARD – FIGURE #5

3:1 Interleaving

In Hard Figure #5, sector 1 is not adjacent to sector 2; it is two sectors away from sector 1. Numbering the sectors on every third sector determines the 3:1 interleave factor. Software programs such as Gibson Research's SpinRite allows the interleave factor to be changed, but it is normally set when the hard drive is first prepared for use. The procedure to set the interleave factor is covered in the Configuration and Setup portion of this chapter.

Today's hard drives normally use a 1:1 interleave. Setting the interleave factor is not an issue in today's hard drive configurations due to (1) faster hard drive electronics, (2) caching hard drive controllers (hard drive controllers that contain memory on the adapter), and (3) faster system board buses.

The time required for the disk to rotate from sector 1 to sector 2 now matches the time required by the electronics to get ready for the next burst of data.

HARD DRIVE INTERFACES

A hard drive system must have a set of rules to operate. These rules specify the number of heads on the drive, what commands the drive responds to, the cables used with the drive, the number of devices supported, the number of data bits transferred at one time, and so forth. These rules make up a standard called an **interface** that governs communication with the hard drive. There are four hard drive interfaces:

- ST506
- ESDI
- IDE (ATA)
- SCSI

ST506 INTERFACE

The **ST506** interface is the oldest standard and it evolved from the floppy drive interface. It requires two cables: one 34-pin cable for control signals, and one 20-pin cable for data. This interface is very susceptible to electrical noise and outside interference can easily affect the hard drive signals causing a loss of data. ST506 hard drives transmit data serially (one bit at a time), at a mere 5Mbps (Megabits per second) or 7.5Mbps, depending on the encoding method.

Encoding is the way the 1s and 0s are placed on the drive. ST506 has two encoding schemes, MFM and RLL. MFM (Modified Frequency Modulation) is the oldest encoding scheme used with hard drives and limits the sectors per track to 17. RLL (Run Length Limited) is an enhanced version of encoding that requires fewer electronic pulses than MFM to write the same data; RLL allows more sectors per track because fewer pulses require less space.

Any ST506 hard drive using MFM to write the 1s and 0s onto the surface must have a MFM controller card. Any ST506 hard drive using RLL encoding must have a RLL controller. Today's more advanced hard drive interfaces, use encoding methods known as ARLL (Advanced RLL) or ERLL (Enhanced RLL).

The controlling electronics for the ST506 are placed on a separate adapter and connect to the hard drive(s) via two cable connections per drive. The electronic circuits instruct the drive to read or write information, what cylinder to go to, and what head to use. One problem with ST506 hard drives is the controlling circuitry can only tell the drive to move one cylinder at a time, another reason for the ST506 slowness. As with all interfaces, a ST506 hard drive requires a ST506 adapter.

One can see there are many limitations to the ST506 interface. Hard drive interfaces were bound to get better, faster, smarter, and more advanced. The first step in this growth was the evolution of a hard drive interface known as ESDI (Enhanced Small Devices Interface).

ESDI (ENHANCED SMALL DEVICES INTERFACE)

The **ESDI (Enhanced Small Devices Interface)** hard drive uses the same 34-pin and 20-pin cables as the ST506. ESDI drives corrected two problems with ST506 by allowing increased hard drive capacities and by supporting drives of up to 256 heads, whereas ST506 drives had a maximum of 16 heads.

An ESDI drive holds geometry information such as number of heads, tracks, and sectors on the drive itself. This information is then sent to the controller. A ST506 drive requires extensive setup during configuration to ensure the controller knows the ST506 hard drive's geometry information.

ESDI hard drives have transfer speeds up to 24Mbps. ST506 and ESDI drives are found mostly in 8088, 8086, and 80286 computers. ESDI hard drives were never popular, and the only time you should purchase an ESDI or a ST506 hard drive is if there is already an adapter for the hard drive in the system. If the customer wants the same drive type, try to talk them out of it. Today's computer manufacturers use one of two other interfaces for hard drives: IDE (Integrated Drive Electronics) or SCSI (Small Computer System Interface).

IDE (INTEGRATED DRIVE ELECTRONICS)

IDE (Integrated Drive Electronics) is the most current type of hard drive and is used for other internal devices such as tape drives, Zip drives, CD-ROMs, and DVDs. The original IDE standard was developed for hard drives. A 40-pin cable connects the IDE hard drive to an adapter or the motherboard, which makes it easy to identify. Most motherboards have two IDE connectors. Each IDE connector can support two IDE devices. An example of an adapter that has an IDE connector is a sound card that handles other devices as well as a possible IDE hard drive.

The original IDE interface supported up to two drives and is also known as the **ATA Standard (AT Attachment Standard)**. ATA is the set of rules, or the standard, to which an IDE drive should conform. ATA-2 is an enhanced version of ATA. The ATA-2 standard has faster transfer rates (8.3MBps, then later 16.6MBps) than the original ATA standard of 3.3MBps. The ATA-2 standard also improves drive compatibility through an Identify Drive command that allows the BIOS to better determine the drive's properties. This is essential for plug and play computers. DMA (Direct Memory Access) transfers are supported by the ATA-2 standard. The DMA mode allows data transfer between the hard drive and RAM without having to go through the CPU.

There are two ways to transfer data between and IDE hard drive and the rest of the computer: PIO and DMA. The PIO (Programmed Input/Output) mode is a speed standard for data transfers to and from the hard drive and data passes through the CPU. The DMA mode allows data transfer between the hard drive and memory without passing through the CPU. PIO is a slower mode than DMA.

PIO is defined in different modes according to the transfer speed and will probably be removed in future ATA standards. Hard Table #1 shows the PIO modes available with IDE hard drives.

HARD – TABLE #1

PIO Modes for IDE Hard Drives

PIO Mode	Transfer Rate (MBps)
0	3.3
1	5.2
2	8.3
3	11.1
4	16.6

Some manufacturers list a PIO Mode 5, which has transfers of 22.2MBps, but this is not in the ATA standards.

The slowest DMA mode, DMA0, transferred data at 2.1MBps. DMA1, the mode used with Fast ATA, transfers data at a maximum of 13.3MBps using multiple words. Hard Table #2 shows the DMA modes. Multi-word DMA is not a popular option with industry.

HARD – TABLE #2

DMA Modes for IDE Hard Drives

DMA Mode	Transfer Rate (MBps)
DMA0 (Single word)	2.1
DMA0 (Multi-word)	4.2
DMA1 (Single word)	4.2
DMA1 (Multi-word)	13.3
DMA2 (Single word)	8.3
DMA2 (Multi-word)	16.6

You cannot use PIO mode to control one device and DMA to control another device when both are connected to the same IDE channel (on the same cable). Do not put a DMA-capable device on the same cable with a device that can only do a PIO mode.

The latest type of DMA transfers is called **UDMA (Ultra-DMA)** or **busmaster DMA**. With regular DMA, a DMA controller located on the motherboard is used. With UDMA, the interface gains control of the bus. IDE hard drives use the PCI bus. UDMA comes in different modes, which represent different transfer speeds. Hard Table #3 shows the Ultra-DMA modes for ATA hard drives.

Ultra-DMA Modes for IDE Hard Drives

Ultra-DMA Mode	Transfer Rate (MBps)
UDMA0	16.7
UDMA1	25
UDMA2	33
UDMA3	44
UDMA4	66
UDMA5	100

HARD – TABLE #3

To install an Ultra DMA device in a computer, the system must include three elements:

1. The motherboard or adapter must support Ultra DMA.
2. The BIOS on the motherboard must be compatible with Ultra DMA.
3. The operating system must support and be enabled for DMA transfers. (All Microsoft operating systems starting with Windows 98 support DMA transfers.)

Hard drive manufacturers frequently ship software that allows you to configure the hard drive transfer mode. Most hard drives supporting DMA transfers ship with the Ultra DMA transfer function enabled. If your computer or operating system does not support DMA transfers, you may need to configure the hard drive for a slower transfer rate until the system is upgraded with a new motherboard or with a driver for the operating system. Windows 98 and higher Microsoft operating systems include bus master drivers.

ATA-3 does not provide a faster transfer rate but does include power management features and a new technology called **S.M.A.R.T (Self-Monitoring Analysis & Report Technology)**. S.M.A.R.T. lets the drive send messages to the user about possible failures or data loss. The ATA-4 standard includes faster transfer modes and is called Ultra-ATA or

Ultra DMA/33 that allows transfers up to 33MBps. It implements bus mastering and uses CRC for data integrity and verification.

CRC (cyclic redundancy checking) is an advanced method of checking the data for errors. The drive and controller (host) calculate a value based on a mathematical algorithm. This value is compared to ensure it is the same in both places. If the value is different, the controller (host) drops to a slower transfer mode and requests a retransmission. CRC is only used when the drive is operating in Ultra DMA transfer mode.

The ATA-5 standard is also known as Ultra ATA/66 or simply ATA/66. This standard allows transfers up to 66MBps. A 40-pin cable is used with this standard as with the other standards, but the cable is different. The ATA-5 40-pin cable has 80 conductors. The 40 extra conductors are ground lines and are physically located between the existing 40 wires. These ground lines reduce crosstalk. **Crosstalk** is when signals from one wire interfere with the signals on an adjacent wire. Extra grounding also improves the accuracy of data transfers and allows faster speed. The 80-conductor cable is backward compatible with older IDE devices.

UDMA modes 3 and higher require the newer 80-conductor (40-pin) cable.

To determine whether or not an IDE adapter supports Ultra DMA, refer to the adapter's documentation or contact the adapter manufacturer. If the system has the proper chipset and is running Windows 95, some Windows 95 files must be modified for an Ultra DMA device to work. Older versions of Windows 95 do not support DMA transfers. However, a DMA driver can be obtained and installed to enable DMA transfers. Intel has a utility available through their web site that will update the Windows 95 files.

Sometimes when you enable DMA transfers through the operating system, you could experience problems—Windows 95 or 98 could boot into Safe Mode or produce a fatal exception error. This could be caused by the BIOS not supporting Ultra DMA transfers. If a BIOS upgrade is unavailable for your system, then an adapter can be purchased that supports Ultra DMA transfers.

To verify if the operating system supports DMA transfers, use Device Manager. Click on the *Disk Drives* option to expand the selections. Click on the specific hard drive you want to check. Click on the *Properties* button and select the *Settings* tab. Look for a DMA check box. If the checkbox has a check inside it, the DMA transfer mode is enabled. If unchecked, click inside the box, click on the *OK* button and restart the computer. Go into Device Manager again. If the box is unchecked, your BIOS does not support DMA transfers. If the computer locks because you enabled DMA transfers through the operating system and then does not allow you to disable it, disable DMA in CMOS Setup. Once disabled, start the operating system and disable DMA in the operating system.

If the hard drive is connected to an adapter and the hard drive does not show a DMA checkbox, it is because the adapter is automatically designed for DMA transfers. Hard Table #4 shows a concise listing of the ATA standards.

IDE ATA Standards

ATA Std.	Speed	Cable	Notes
ATA-1	3.3Mbps	40-pin	IDE hard drives
ATA-2	8.3 & 16.6Mbps	40-pin	Sometimes called EIDE
ATA-3	8.3 & 16.6Mbps	40-pin	Includes SMART (Self-Monitoring Analysis & Report Technology)
ATA-4	33Mbps	40-pin	Also Called Ultra DMA/33 or Ultra ATA/33
ATA-5	66Mbps	40-pin (80-conductor)	Also called Ultra DMA/66 or Ultra ATA/66

The ATA-6 standard is currently being defined. A recommendation is to change the number of bits for LBA (Logical Block Addressing—see BIOS Limitations section later in the chapter) from 28-bits to 48-bits. The bottom line is more bits would allow hard drive sizes to be as large as 144PB. PB stands for **petabytes**; 144PB is about 144,000,000 gigabytes. The current standard does not allow hard drives larger than 137GB. Another suggested change is to add new commands that help with multimedia applications.

In July 2001, Maxtor recommended a new industry standard called Ultra ATA/133 that allows data transfers of 133MBps. This standard will be backward compatible with all other Ultra ATA standards, use the same 80-conductor, 40-pin cable as other standards, and support CRC for data accuracy. A new standard called **Serial ATA** will probably follow ATA/133. Maxtor, APT, IBM, Dell, Intel, and Seagate are part of the working group to develop this standard.

EIDE and Fast ATA are two terms frequently associated with IDE devices. EIDE (Enhanced Integrated Drive Electronics) is a Western Digital term. Many think EIDE is an IDE standard, but EIDE is a marketing program from Western Digital (and a very good one at that). EIDE has two parts: software and hardware. On the software side, the *enhanced* is the enhanced BIOS requirement—a BIOS that supports drives larger than 504MB. On the hardware side of EIDE, Western Digital specifies that the drive must conform to the ATA-2 standard and the ATAPI standard. **ATAPI** stands for AT Attachment Packet Interface and is designed for devices such as CD-ROMs and tape drives.

Many mistakenly think EIDE provides the ability to connect four IDE devices (two devices on one cable and two devices on a second cable). A second IDE port was included in a computer's input/output map for years but at that time, most ROM BIOS chips did not support the second connector. With the huge growth in hard drive capacities, CD-ROM purchases, and the decline in hard drive prices, the second IDE connector became a necessity. BIOS manufacturers began to include support for the secondary IDE port in their chips. This occurred at the same time that Western Digital was pushing EIDE. Computer users wanted to connect more IDE devices and Western Digital set a specification (EIDE) that stated BIOS supports two IDE connectors (four devices) and the devices must support the ATAPI standard. The term *EIDE* and the concept of four devices then became synonymous.

Fast ATA is a term Seagate Technology started using and was later endorsed by the Quantum Corporation. Fast ATA defines devices that support the ANSI (American National Standards Institute) PIO Mode 3 standard and the multi-word DMA1 protocol. PIO Mode 3, used with Fast ATA, transfers data at a maximum of 11.1MBps. Fast ATA-2 is also a Seagate term for devices that support PIO Mode 4 and Multi-word DMA Mode 2 protocols. Fast ATA-2 has a maximum transfer rate of 16.6MBps.

Another misconception with IDE hard drives concerns 32-bit transfers. Some people believe Fast ATA-2 can transfer 32 bits at a time. Currently, the IDE interface allows for a maximum of 16-bit data transfer. An adapter manufacturer who claims a 32-bit IDE data transfer is actually saying one of two things: either the adapter is a local bus adapter or the PCI motherboard bus can combine two 16-bit data transfers into a 32-bit stream to send these bits to the microprocessor.

IDE devices are quite common in today's computers. Two IDE connectors are contained on many motherboards and BIOS support for IDE devices is the standard, not the exception. IDE is a popular choice for computer users because of its ease of installation and low cost. IDE devices are a common upgrade request for technicians. The IDE interface's biggest competitor is the fourth hard drive interface type, SCSI.

SCSI (SMALL COMPUTER SYSTEM INTERFACE)

SCSI (Small Computer System Interface) defines many different devices such as scanners, tape drives, hard drives, optical drives, disk array subsystems (RAID), and CD-ROMs. The SCSI standard allows connection of multiple devices to the same adapter. All devices that connect to the same SCSI controller share a common data bus called the **SCSI bus** (or SCSI chain). With features such as increased speed and multiple device support comes added cost. SCSI is more expensive than any other interface used with hard drives.

SCSI hard drives have the "intelligence" built into the drive similar to IDE and EIDE hard drives. The SCSI host adapter (it's usually a separate card) connects the SCSI device to the motherboard and coordinates the activities of the other devices connected. Three basic standards of SCSI are called SCSI-1, SCSI-2, and SCSI-3.

The original SCSI standard, SCSI-1, left a lot of room for vendor specifications on the wide range of devices that SCSI supports. Technicians had to cope with the fact that not all SCSI adapters handled all SCSI devices. SCSI-1 was primarily for hard drives because the standard included a set of software commands defined for hard drives. However, other device manufacturers, such as those making tape drives, made do with SCSI-1 and adapted their devices as they saw fit. SCSI-1 supports up to eight devices on one SCSI 8-bit bus at a transfer rate of up to 5MBps. SCSI-2 improves on SCSI-1 by supporting 16 devices and speeds up to 20MBps. SCSI-2 hardware is compatible with SCSI-1 devices. SCSI-3 improves on data transfer rates and includes fiber optical cable standards.

Fast SCSI is a term associated with the SCSI-2 interface. It transfers data at 10MBps, eight bits at a time. 32-bit SCSI was defined in SCSI-2, but never adopted by industry, so the 32-bit standard was dropped in SCSI-3. An improvement on the SCSI-2 interface is SCSI-3. The various SCSI-3 standards all start with the word "Ultra." Ultra-Wide SCSI transfers 16 bits of data at 40MBps, Ultra2 SCSI transfers eight bits of data at 40MBps, and Ultra2-Wide SCSI transfers 16 bits of data at 80MBps.

SCSI-3 is made up of different SPI (SCSI Parallel Interface) standards that include SPI, SPI-2, SPI-3, and SPI-4. SPI is commonly called Ultra SCSI; SPI-2 is called Ultra2 or Fast-40 SCSI; SPI-3 is called Ultra3 or Ultra 160 SCSI; SPI-4 is known as Ultra4 or Fast-80DT SCSI. SPI-3 has five main features: (1) increase in speed to 160MBps, (2) CRC error checking added, (3) performs optimum speed test before data transfers occur, (4) a device that wants to transmit can have access to the SCSI bus faster, and (5) data, commands, and status messages that used to be transmitted separately can now transmit as a packet. Devices that support the first three features are sometimes called Ultra 160 SCSI, and devices that support all five features are known as Ultra 160+ SCSI. Hard Table #5 shows a breakdown of the common SCSI standards.

HARD – TABLE #5

SCSI Standards

SCSI Standard	SCSI Term	Speed (MBps)
SCSI-1	N/A	5
SCSI-2	N/A	5
	Fast	10
	Wide	20
	Fast-Wide	20
SCSI-3	Ultra	20
	Ultra2	40
	Ultra-Wide	40
	Ultra2-Wide	80
	Ultra3	160
	Ultra 160	160
	Ultra 160+	160
	Ultra 320	320

SCSI SOFTWARE STANDARDS

All SCSI devices require software to operate. Most SCSI hard drives have software built into the hard drive's BIOS chip. But, if the SCSI device needs software drivers, one of three types of SCSI software standards is used:

1. ASPI (Advanced SCSI Programming Interface)
2. CAM (Common Access Method)
3. LADDR (Layered Device Driver Architecture)

A SCSI device may have all three types of software drivers written for it. The important thing to remember is if the host adapter has an ASPI driver, then any device that connects to the adapter also needs an ASPI driver. All devices along the SCSI bus (including the host adapter) should speak the same language. CAM software comes with OS/2 2.X and SCO UNIX and LADDR ships with OS/2 1.X to work with Microsoft's LAN Manager.

HARD DRIVE CONFIGURATION OVERVIEW

The configuration of a hard drive usually includes setting jumpers on the drive and sometimes on the hard drive adapter, terminating properly, and performing a few software commands. Remember from Chapter 8 that termination is the installation of a resistor to avoid signal reflection on the cable. Each hard drive type has a normal configuration method. However, individual drive manufacturers may develop their own configuration steps. *Always* refer to the documentation included with the hard drive and the adapter or motherboard for configuration and installation information.

ST506 & ESDI HARD DRIVE CONFIGURATION

To configure a ST506 or an ESDI hard drive, three steps must be performed:

1. Set the proper drive select jumper or switch.
2. Set or remove termination.
3. Connect the drive to the proper cable connector.

ST506 and ESDI drives have drive select jumpers similar to the drive select jumpers found on floppy drives. ESDI drive systems can handle more drives, so they frequently have more drive select options than ST506 drives. Setting the drive select jumper and the terminator is the same process for ST506 and ESDI hard drives. Hard Figure #6 shows two types of drive select jumpers and two different physical placements of the terminator.

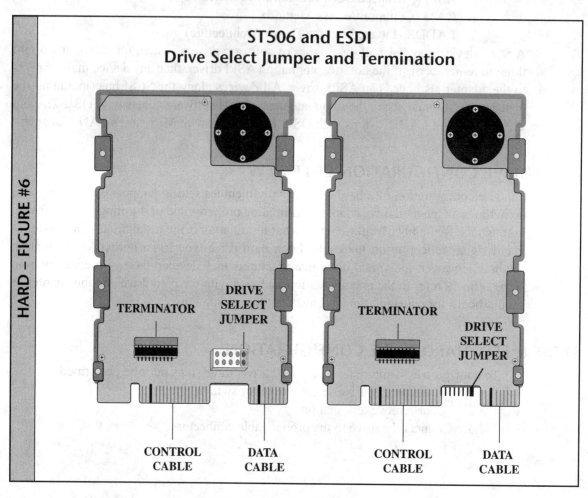

**ST506 and ESDI
Drive Select Jumper and Termination**

HARD – FIGURE #6

TERMINATOR

DRIVE
SELECT
JUMPER

TERMINATOR

DRIVE
SELECT
JUMPER

CONTROL
CABLE

DATA
CABLE

CONTROL
CABLE

DATA
CABLE

Just as with floppy drives, some hard drive manufacturers label the drive select jumpers as 0, 1, 2, and 3; and some manufacturers label the jumpers as 1, 2, 3, and 4. The correct setting for the drive select jumper or switch depends on (1) whether multiple drives are connected and (2) which cable is used.

The 34-pin hard drive cable is *not* the same 34-pin cable used with floppy drives. Hard Figure #7 shows the difference between a 34-pin floppy cable and a 34-pin hard drive cable used with ST506 and ESDI hard drives.

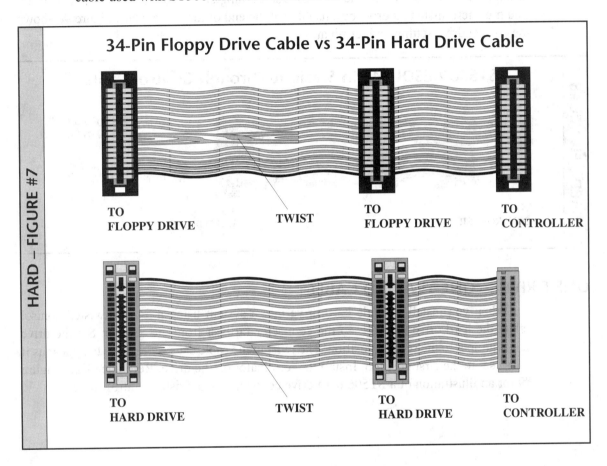

Notice in Hard Figure #7 how the twist on the hard drive cable is farther from pin 1 than the floppy drive cable.

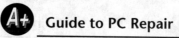
ONE DRIVE — ONE CABLE

If the ST506 or ESDI drive is the only drive in the system and it connects to a straight-through 34-pin control cable, then the drive select jumper is always set to the first position. You must terminate this drive because it is at the end of the cable. Hard Figure #8 shows the correct drive setting and termination.

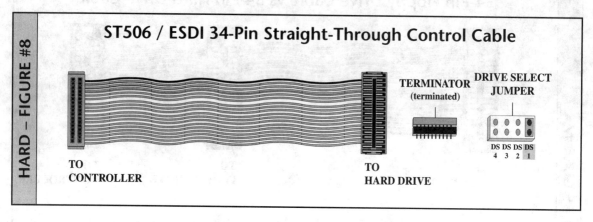

HARD – FIGURE #8

ST506 / ESDI 34-Pin Straight-Through Control Cable

TO
CONTROLLER

TO
HARD DRIVE

TERMINATOR
(terminated)

**DRIVE SELECT
JUMPER**

DS DS DS DS
4 3 2 1

ONE DRIVE — ONE TWISTED CABLE

When you install a single hard drive into a system using a 34-pin twisted control cable, the hard drive connects to the connector farthest from the adapter. Set the drive select jumper to the second position. The twist in the cable causes the drive to appear as if it was set to the first position. Install the terminator on the drive. Reference Hard Figure #9 for an illustration of a ST506 hard drive connected to a twisted control cable.

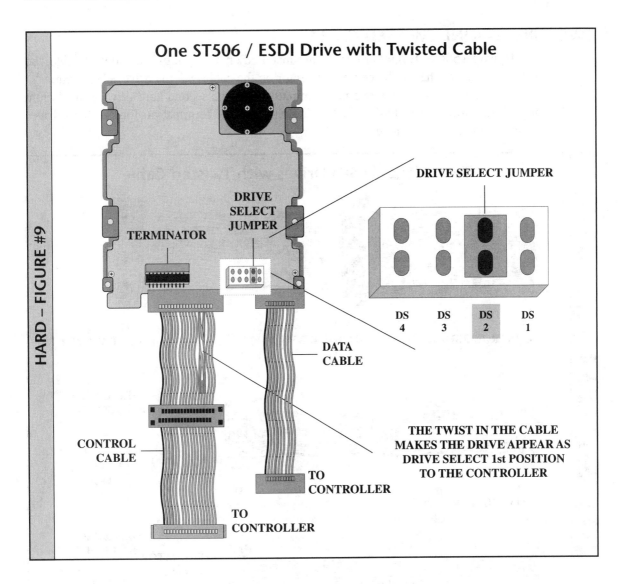

One ST506 / ESDI Drive with Twisted Cable

HARD – FIGURE #9

DRIVE SELECT JUMPER

TERMINATOR

DRIVE SELECT JUMPER

DS 4   DS 3   DS 2   DS 1

DATA CABLE

THE TWIST IN THE CABLE MAKES THE DRIVE APPEAR AS DRIVE SELECT 1st POSITION TO THE CONTROLLER

CONTROL CABLE

TO CONTROLLER

TO CONTROLLER

TWO DRIVES — ONE CABLE

If two ST506 or ESDI hard drives connect to the same adapter, use a single 34-pin cable with two drive connectors. A separate 20-pin data cable then connects to each drive. If one hard drive is connected to a 34-pin cable with two connectors, use one connector and save the other connector for future expansion. Just as in a floppy drive configuration, only the last drive connected at the end of the cable is terminated.

TWO DRIVES—ONE TWISTED CABLE

If two ST506 or ESDI hard drives are installed on a 34-pin twisted control cable, the second drive attaches to the center connector on the cable. Set the drive select jumper to the second position and remove the terminator from the second hard drive. Hard Figure #10 shows how to set the drive select jumpers and the termination for two hard drives connected to a twisted cable.

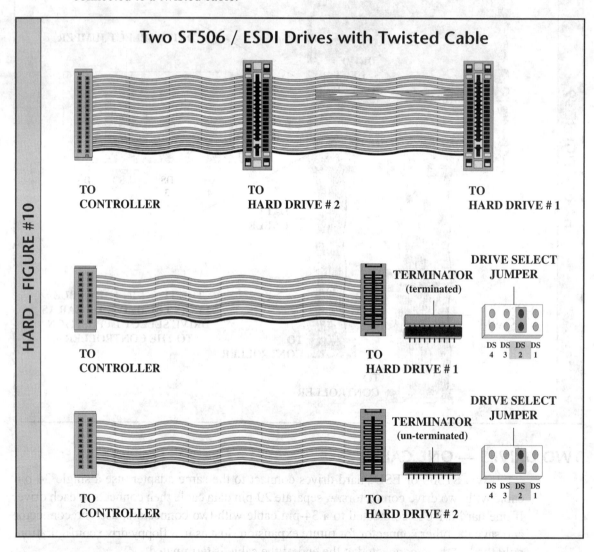

HARD – FIGURE #10

Two ST506 / ESDI Drives with Twisted Cable

Notice in Hard Figure #10 that a separate 20-pin data cable is used for the second hard drive. Again, the twist in the control cable causes the drive to appear to the controller card as if it is set to the first position. The hard drive at the end of the cable is seen as the first hard drive in the system. The cables from the hard drive to the controller must connect to the proper adapter connectors to operate properly. Hard Figure #11 shows two different ST506 or ESDI hard drive controllers and their cable connections.

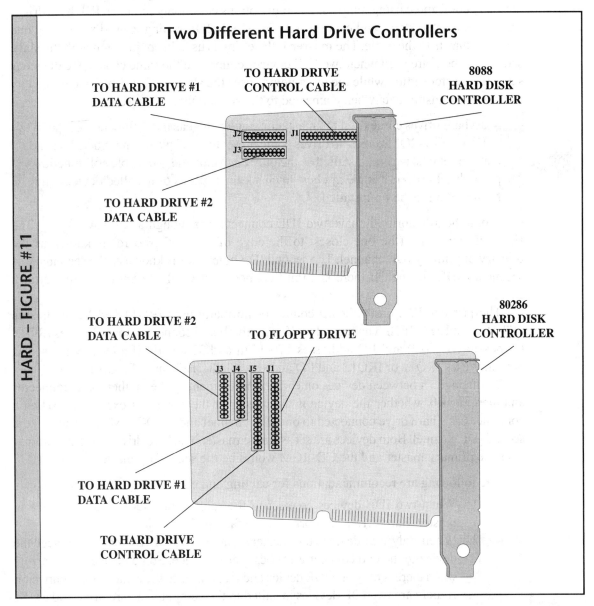

Two Different Hard Drive Controllers

HARD – FIGURE #11

TO HARD DRIVE #1 DATA CABLE

TO HARD DRIVE CONTROL CABLE

8088 HARD DISK CONTROLLER

TO HARD DRIVE #2 DATA CABLE

80286 HARD DISK CONTROLLER

TO HARD DRIVE #2 DATA CABLE

TO FLOPPY DRIVE

TO HARD DRIVE #1 DATA CABLE

TO HARD DRIVE CONTROL CABLE

Hard drives are assigned drive letters by the operating system just like floppy drives. The first hard drive seen by the system is assigned the drive letter C:. The only time the first hard drive will not receive the drive letter C: is if a system supports more than two floppy drives installed in the system. However, most computers have the drive letter C: for the first hard drive installed into the system.

IDE HARD DRIVE CONFIGURATION

IDE devices (including hard drives) are the simplest to configure. IDE hard drives are normally configured using jumpers. The four options commonly found on IDE hard drives are single, master, slave, and cable select. The **single** IDE setting is used when only one device connects to the cable. The **master** IDE setting is used in conjunction with the **slave** setting and both are used when two IDE devices connect to the same cable. One device is set to the master setting while the other uses the slave setting. Only one of the two devices can transmit data when connected to the same IDE channel (cable).

Most hard drives come preset to master or single whereas most other devices such as DVDs, CD-ROMs, and Zip drives come preset to the slave setting. Such devices that are set to slave and installed as the only device on the IDE cable still function properly. However, it is always best to check the settings of installed devices and for new devices being installed.

Motherboards normally have two IDE connectors (although a few have three). The first IDE connector (the one closest to the edge of the motherboard) is known as the primary or primary IDE channel. The second IDE connector is known as the secondary or secondary IDE channel. If there is a third connector, it would be known as the tertiary channel.

The primary IDE motherboard connector normally uses IRQ14 and I/O addresses 1F0-1F7h and 3F6-3F7h. The secondary IDE motherboard connector normally uses IRQ15 (or possibly IRQ10) and I/O addresses 170-177h and 376-377h. If a tertiary is used, it normally uses IRQ11 or IRQ12 and I/O addresses 1E8-1EFh and 3EE-3Efh.

To distinguish between devices on each channel, identify the motherboard connector and then identify whether the device is the master or the slave. For example, say that a computer has a hard drive connected to one IDE channel and a CD-ROM connected to the second IDE channel. Both devices are set as single/master. The hard drive would be referred to as the primary master and the CD-ROM would be the secondary master.

The following are recommendations for cabling and configuring IDE devices.

1. When two IDE devices connect to the same cable, set the faster device to master. Hard drives are normally the fastest IDE devices.
2. When only one device (the master) connects to an IDE cable, connect the device to the end connector for best performance. Some devices show errors when there is only one IDE device and it connects to the center cable connector.
3. If there are two IDE devices installed in the computer, a hard drive and a CD-ROM/DVD, install the hard drive on one IDE channel (primary) and the CD-ROM/DVD on the second IDE channel.
4. If only one device connects to an IDE cable, put it on the very last connector (the farthest from the motherboard or adapter).
5. Avoid putting a hard drive and an ATAPI device such as an optical drive (CD-ROM or DVD) on the same channel. The ATAPI device uses a more

complicated command set than the hard drive and it can slow the hard drive down.

6. If a hard drive can do DMA bus mastering, never put an ATAPI device that cannot do DMA transfers on the same channel. The channel will use PIO and the hard drive will have to use that mode too.

7. If you have a CD-RW drive and a CD-ROM drive and you transfer data frequently between the two, it is best to put them on a separate channel. However, putting one of these devices with a hard drive is not a good idea either. So, the best solution would be to purchase a PCI IDE adapter that supports bus mastering.

8. For optimum performance, connect the hard drive that you boot from to the primary IDE motherboard connector and configure it as master.

9. The maximum IDE cable length is 18 inches and this presents a problem with tower computers. Some companies sell 24 or 36-inch IDE cables. These do not meet specifications. If IDE problems or intermittent problems occur, replace the cable with one that meets specifications.

The **cable select** IDE option replaces the master/slave setting. To use the cable select option, a special cable is needed. The cable has pin 28 disabled. The device is automatically set to either the master setting or the slave setting depending on which cable connector the device is attached.

With the older cable select option, the device connected to the middle connector is the master. The device connected to the last connector is the slave. When the cable select became a standard with ATA-5, the master connector (the black connector) is at the end of the cable. The slave connector (the gray one) is in the middle of the connector and the blue connector attaches to the motherboard. All 80-conductor (40-pin) cables that meet the ATA specifications automatically support cable select and the connectors are color-coded according to the specifications. The 80-conductor (40-pin) cable must be used in Ultra DMA Mode 3 and higher, but can be used in lower modes as well.

Three criteria must be met to use the cable select option:

1. A special IDE cable select cable or the 80-conductor (40-pin) cable must be used.

2. The host interface (controlling circuits) must support the cable select option.

3. Any attached device must be set to the cable select option.

Do not set an IDE device to the cable select option unless the special cable is installed and the host interface supports this option. If two devices are set to the cable select option and a regular IDE cable is used, both devices will be configured as master and not work properly.

Almost all IDE devices ship with the master/slave setting configured instead of the cable select option. IDE drives connect to a 40-pin ribbon cable. Termination is not an issue when configuring IDE devices because there are no terminators on IDE devices. Hard Figure # 12 shows an illustration of an IDE hard drive configured as the master. In Hard Figure #12, the table shows several possible configurations. A similar table is found either on top of the hard drive or in the documentation included with the hard drive. The third alternative is to use the manufacturer's Internet site. If only one IDE hard drive is to be installed the drive is normally set as the master. For the drive shown in Hard Figure #12, a jumper is installed over J1 to make the drive the master. When documentation shows an option as closed, this means to put a jumper over the two pins.

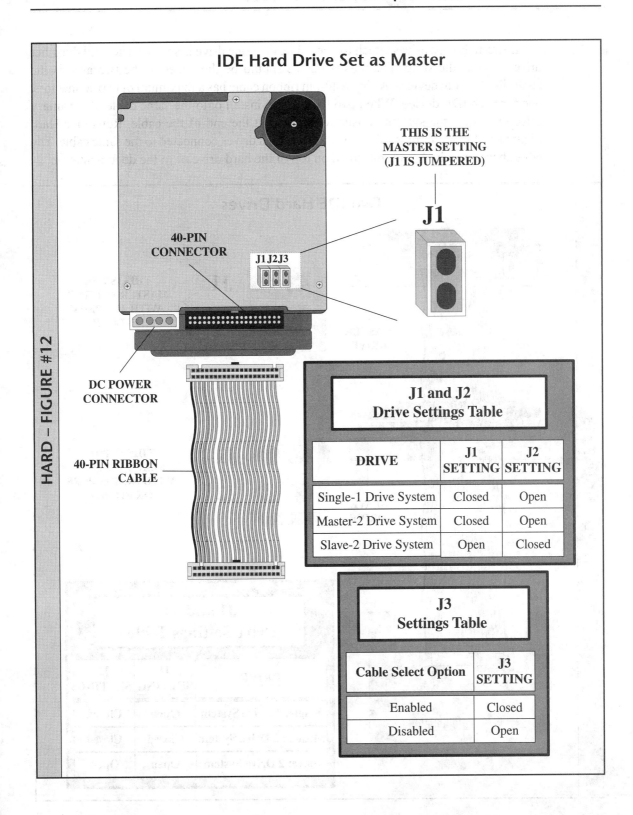

IDE Hard Drive Set as Master

THIS IS THE
MASTER SETTING
(J1 IS JUMPERED)

J1

40-PIN
CONNECTOR

J1 J2 J3

DC POWER
CONNECTOR

40-PIN RIBBON
CABLE

HARD – FIGURE #12

J1 and J2 Drive Settings Table

DRIVE	J1 SETTING	J2 SETTING
Single-1 Drive System	Closed	Open
Master-2 Drive System	Closed	Open
Slave-2 Drive System	Open	Closed

J3 Settings Table

Cable Select Option	J3 SETTING
Enabled	Closed
Disabled	Open

If two IDE hard drives attach to one cable, then one drive is set as master and the other drive is set as the slave. The master device should be the faster of the two as it is the controller for both devices. A single 40-pin ribbon cable has a maximum of two connectors, one for each IDE device. When two hard drives install onto the same cable, the primary drive that boots the system is usually installed at the end of the cable. Reference Hard Figure #13 for an example of settings for two hard drives connected to the same cable. The table shown may be found imprinted on top of the hard drive or in the documentation.

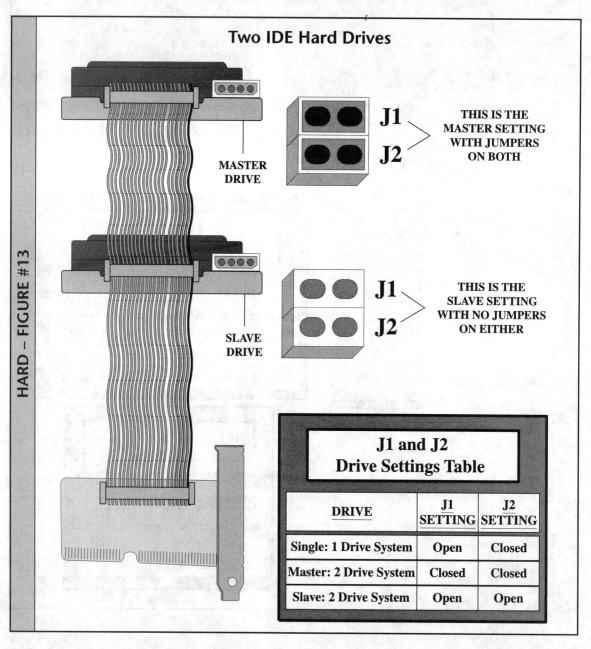

Two IDE Hard Drives

MASTER DRIVE

J1
J2
> THIS IS THE MASTER SETTING WITH JUMPERS ON BOTH

SLAVE DRIVE

J1
J2
> THIS IS THE SLAVE SETTING WITH NO JUMPERS ON EITHER

HARD – FIGURE #13

J1 and J2 Drive Settings Table

DRIVE	J1 SETTING	J2 SETTING
Single: 1 Drive System	Open	Closed
Master: 2 Drive System	Closed	Closed
Slave: 2 Drive System	Open	Open

Documentation is important when setting up a hard drive. In Hard Figure #13 the documentation table is different from the documentation shown in Hard Figure #12. This particular drive manufacturer lists three possible drive configurations. Single: 1 Drive System is a single drive attached to one cable. There is no slave in a single IDE drive configuration because there is only one device. Master: 2 Drive System is two IDE devices connected to one cable. If the IDE drive is to be the master of the two devices, then this setting is correct. Slave: 2 Drive System is two IDE devices connected to the same cable with the IDE device set to slave, not master. The other device on the cable is set as master for the two devices to operate. How a manufacturer uses the terms and configures the drive is up to the manufacturer. The technician must learn to adjust to poorly written and sometimes confusing documentation. Jumpers other than the master/slave jumpers may be present, but you must refer to the hard drive's documentation for the proper settings. If documentation is unavailable, use the Internet; most manufacturers place their jumper setting documentation online.

DASP (Drive Active/Slave Present) is a signal in the ATA interface on pin 39 of the IDE connector some manufacturers use to indicate the presence of a slave IDE device. Some older IDE devices do not support the DASP signal so they must connect to a master IDE device that recognizes them. Some manufacturers put a SP (Slave Present) jumper on the IDE device so it recognizes another device connected as a slave.

If an IDE device has a Slave Present setting, the setting is only used when installing two IDE devices on one cable where one device does not support the DASP signal. The Slave Present setting, when set on the master device, tells the slave device it is controlled by the master. The master IDE is the controller for both devices.

On some older IDE drives, the Master/Slave or Slave Present jumpers are not available. If you install a drive like this in a two-drive IDE system, one drive must be considered the master and the other drive is designated as the slave. The drive without the jumpers still may not work in a two-drive system. The only way to know is to try it.

NOTEBOOK IDE HARD DRIVES

Two methods are used with IDE hard drives installed in portable computers: proprietary or removable. With the proprietary installation, the hard drive is installed in a location where it cannot be changed, configured, or moved very easily. Proprietary cables and connectors are used. With removable IDE hard drives, the laptop has a hard drive bay that allows installation/removal through a 44-pin connector. This connector provides power as well as data signaling. The drive is usually mounted in a carrier that attaches to the 44-pin connector and is the primary master device. If an ATAPI CD-ROM is installed, it is normally configured as the secondary master. Laptops do not normally allow a second IDE hard drive. Instead, add an additional hard drive to the USB or parallel port or install a PC Card.

SCSI CONFIGURATION

A SCSI device is configured by
1. Setting the proper SCSI ID
2. Terminating both ends of the SCSI chain
3. Connecting the proper cable(s)

The SCSI chain consists of several SCSI devices cabled together. The SCSI chain includes SCSI devices and a single controller, sometimes called a **host adapter**. The SCSI controller is usually a separate adapter, but it may be built into the motherboard. The SCSI chain includes internal SCSI devices that connect to the SCSI host adapter and any external SCSI devices that connect to an adapter's external port. Multiple SCSI chains can exist in a system and a computer can contain up to four SCSI host adapters. A SCSI-1 host adapter supports up to seven internal or external devices. SCSI-2 or higher adapters support up to 15 internal or external devices. These types of adapters are known as Wide SCSI adapters because they support 16-bit transfers.

Each device on a SCSI chain, including the SCSI host adapter, is assigned a **SCSI ID**. (Some SCSI hard drive manufacturers refer to this setting as the drive select ID.) The SCSI ID allows each device to share the same SCSI bus and it assigns a priority for each device. The SCSI interface allows a SCSI device to communicate directly with another SCSI device connected on the same SCSI chain. The higher the SCSI number, the higher the priority of the device on the SCSI chain. SCSI IDs are normally set using switches, jumpers, SCSI BIOS software, or manufacturer-provided software.

SCSI ID CONFIGURATION

When a computer is first powered on, the system BIOS searches the system for other adapter ROM chips that must initialize the devices they control. When the system BIOS allows the ROM chip on the SCSI host adapter to initialize, the SCSI host adapter scans the SCSI bus for any attached SCSI devices. The host adapter then determines the priority of these devices on the SCSI bus based on their SCSI IDs.

Power on all external SCSI devices before powering on the computer. The host adapter detects all SCSI devices along the SCSI chain during the bootup sequence. However, if a SCSI device is not used frequently the device can be powered off. The rest of the SCSI devices operate even if a SCSI device is powered off. If two devices have the same SCSI ID, a SCSI ID conflict occurs and the devices will not work properly. Setting an improper SCSI ID (priority) setting results in slower SCSI device performance.

Standard SCSI devices (8-bit devices) recognize SCSI IDs 0 through 7. Wide SCSI devices (16-bit devices) recognize SCSI IDs 0 through 15. The SCSI ID priority values are as follows from highest priority value to lowest.

Highest														Lowest
7	6	5	4	3	2	1	0	5	14	13	12	11	10	9	8

   The SCSI host adapter is normally preset to SCSI ID 7, the highest priority and should not be changed. The host adapter is always a high priority because the adapter is the link to the rest of the computer system. Slow devices such as scanners or CD-ROMs should be assigned a higher SCSI ID number such as SCSI ID 6 or 5 for a standard SCSI device and 15 or 14 for a Wide SCSI device. By assigning the slow devices a higher priority SCSI ID number, the slower devices receive ample time to move data on the SCSI bus. Make sure that a device such as a CD-RW or video encoder that cannot tolerate delays is given a high priority SCSI ID. If a hard drive is to boot the system, its setting should be SCSI ID 0. This is the only time you would set a slow device to a high priority.

   The SCSI priority system is logical. SCSI hard drives normally move data quickly. If a SCSI hard drive has a higher priority than a scanner, the scanner will not access the SCSI bus often because it must wait as the hard drive is continually accessing software. An exception to this is that some IBM PS/2 computers have the hard drive preset to SCSI ID 6. The PS/2 computer will boot only if the first hard drive is set to SCSI ID 6. If you add a second hard drive, set the drive to SCSI ID 5. SCSI ID 0 is the default for most SCSI hard drives.

As long as each SCSI device has a unique SCSI ID number, the sequence of the devices cabled to the adapter is insignificant. SCSI devices do not have to be cabled in SCSI ID order. SCSI IDs are normally set using jumpers, a switch block, or software. Technicians should always refer to the documentation included with the SCSI device or adapter for setting the SCSI ID. Many SCSI manufacturers use three jumpers or three switches and standard binary counting to set the SCSI IDs. For example, a setting of 000 is SCSI ID 0 and a setting of 010 is SCSI ID 2. Table #6 illustrates the sixteen possible SCSI settings with the most significant bit on the left. If a device only has three positions, ignore the first "Settings" column on the left. Be aware that a manufacturer may reverse the SCSI setting and place the most significant bit on the right.

HARD – TABLE #6

SCSI ID Settings
(Most Significant Bit to the Left)

SCSI ID	Setting*	Setting*	Setting*	Setting*
0	0	0	0	0
1	0	0	0	1
2	0	0	1	0
3	0	0	1	1
4	0	1	0	0
5	0	1	0	1
6	0	1	1	0
7	0	1	1	1
8	1	0	0	0
9	1	0	0	1
10	1	0	1	0
11	1	0	1	1
12	1	1	0	0
13	1	1	0	1
14	1	1	1	0
15	1	1	1	1

*0=OFF 1=ON

To combine this information, Hard Figure #14 shows two internal SCSI devices cabled to a SCSI host adapter. It shows the SCSI ID setting for each SCSI device and the SCSI adapter. The SCSI host adapter has a switch block for setting its SCSI ID. Switch block 1 (S1) positions 1, 2, and 3 control the SCSI ID number. (This information is in the documentation for the adapter). The first device in the chain is the SCSI hard drive that boots the system and is set to SCSI ID 0. The hard drive uses jumpers to set its SCSI ID. Then, the last device on the chain is a SCSI CD-ROM that is set to SCSI ID 5. The CD-ROM also has jumpers that set its SCSI ID. The documentation for both the hard drive and the CD-ROM shows how to set each SCSI ID. If the documentation is not available, the Internet is the next best place to obtain the documentation.

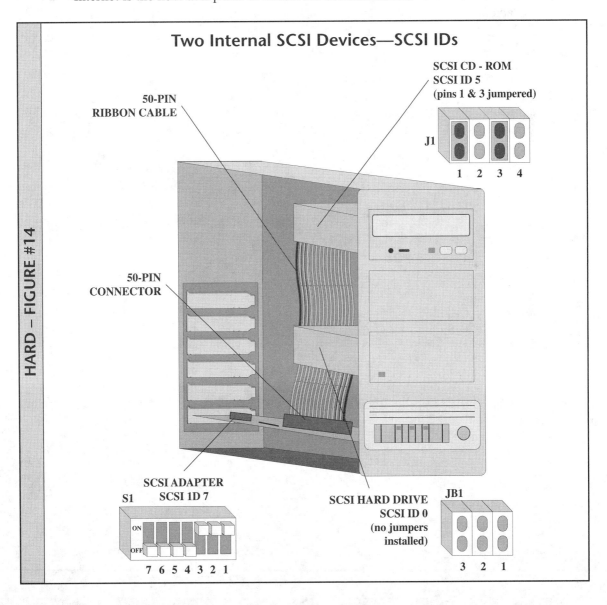

HARD – FIGURE #14

Two Internal SCSI Devices—SCSI IDs

SCSI CD - ROM
SCSI ID 5
(pins 1 & 3 jumpered)

J1

1 2 3 4

50-PIN
RIBBON CABLE

50-PIN
CONNECTOR

SCSI ADAPTER
SCSI 1D 7

S1

ON

OFF

7 6 5 4 3 2 1

SCSI HARD DRIVE
SCSI ID 0
(no jumpers
installed)

JB1

3 2 1

All devices connected to the same SCSI host adapter make up a SCSI chain. If multiple external devices connect to the same SCSI controller, a SCSI cable daisy chains each external device to another external SCSI device. The SCSI ID on the external device is normally set by a thumbwheel switch, jumpers, or switches located on the back of the SCSI device where the cables connect. External SCSI devices usually have two connectors on the back of the device. If the external device is in the center of the SCSI chain, the two connectors have cables that connect to other SCSI devices in the SCSI chain. For example, if a SCSI bus has two external devices such as a CD-ROM and a scanner attached, the CD-ROM has a cable that connects it to the SCSI adapter. A separate cable connects the CD-ROM drive to the scanner. Hard Figure #15 shows two SCSI devices cabled to a SCSI adapter.

HARD – FIGURE #15

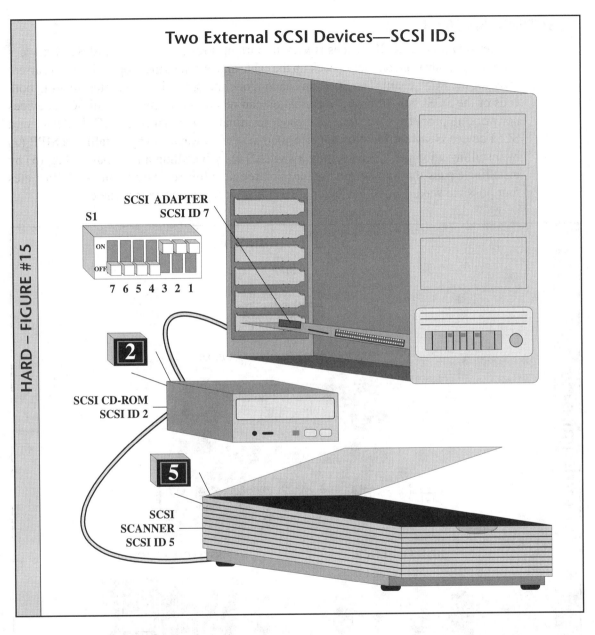

Two External SCSI Devices—SCSI IDs

SCSI ADAPTER
SCSI ID 7

S1

ON
OFF

7 6 5 4 3 2 1

2

SCSI CD-ROM
SCSI ID 2

5

SCSI
SCANNER
SCSI ID 5

A development that is supposed to be helpful in setting SCSI IDs is **SCAM (SCSI Configured AutoMatically)**. Devices and adapters that support SCAM allow automatic SCSI ID assignment. To enable the SCAM feature, check the host adapter's documentation. Using SCAM, each device connected to the SCSI adapter is assigned a unique SCSI ID during boot-up. When purchasing a SCSI adapter or device, be sure it supports SCAM for easy installation and to avoid SCSI ID conflicts. Many have found this to cause more problems that help.

SCSI TERMINATION

Termination of SCSI devices is very important. Proper termination of SCSI devices keeps the signals from bouncing back up the cable and provides the proper electrical current level for the SCSI chain. The SCSI bus cannot operate properly without terminating both ends of the SCSI bus. Improper termination can result in one, many, or all SCSI devices not working properly. Over time, improper termination can damage a SCSI adapter or a SCSI device. SCSI termination is performed in several ways: (1) by installing a SIPP, (2) by installing a jumper, (3) by setting a switch, (4) by installing a terminator plug, (5) by installing a pass-through terminator, or (6) through software. Hard Figure #16 illustrates four possible ways a SCSI device or a SCSI host adapter may be terminated.

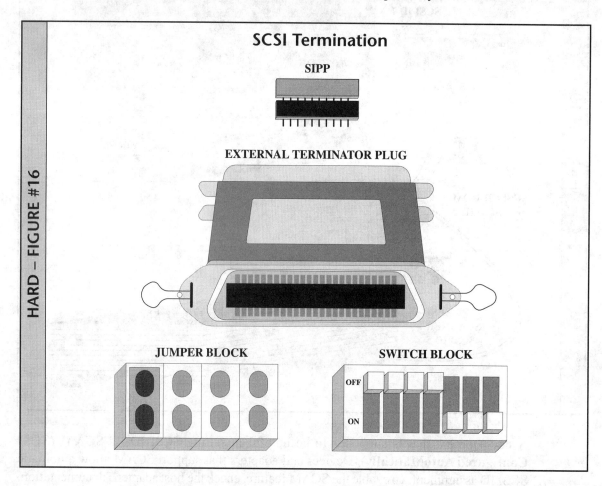

SCSI Termination

SIPP

EXTERNAL TERMINATOR PLUG

JUMPER BLOCK

SWITCH BLOCK

OFF

ON

HARD – FIGURE #16

When setting or removing termination, refer to the documentation included with the adapter or device. If the terminator to an external SCSI device is not provided with the device, it must be purchased separately. Some internal SCSI cables do not have a terminator built into the SCSI cable.

There are several types of SCSI electrical signals and terminators. The three major categories of electrical signals and terminators are SE, HVD, and LVD. **SE (Single Ended)** is used the most in SCSI devices. It can use passive and active terminators and it has a limited bus length of 9 feet (less when more devices are installed). **Passive terminators** are used on SCSI-1 devices and they are not good for long cable distances because they are susceptible to noise interference. **Active terminators** were introduced with SCSI-2, but can be used on SCSI-1, SCSI-2, and SCSI-3 devices. They allow for longer cable distances and provide the correct voltage for SCSI signals. Active terminators must be used with Fast, Wide, or Fast-Wide SCSI devices. The SCSI-2 standard recommends active termination be used at both ends of the SCSI chain, but passive termination can be used if a Fast, Wide, or Fast-Wide SCSI device is not installed. A passive terminator and an active terminator can be used on the same SCSI chain. SCSI-3 requires active termination. A special type of active terminator is called **FPT (Forced Perfect Termination)** and it can be used with SE devices.

HVD (High Voltage Differential) was used in a few SCSI-2 devices and it allows a longer SCSI bus length of 82 feet. HVD has been removed from the SCSI-3 standards. HVD cannot be mixed with other signal types. HVD devices must use HVD terminators and HVD SCSI host adapters. An HVD bus (SCSI bus with all HVD devices) uses what is known as a **differential terminator**. The HVD signaling method uses two wires for each signal.

LVD (Low Voltage Differential) is backward compatible with SE and required on all devices that adhere to the Ultra SCSI standards. LVD uses two wires per signal like HVD, but uses a lower voltage than HVD. LVD allows longer cable lengths than SE. LVD bus length can be up to 39 feet (depending on the number of devices). LVD was first defined in SCSI-3 (SPI-2) and LVD devices use either LVD terminators or LVD/SE terminators. LVD/SE terminators and devices can determine whether the bus needs to run in LVD mode or SE mode and adjusts itself appropriately. If SE devices are installed on the same bus with LVD devices, the SE signaling method is used. If all devices on the SCSI bus are LVD devices, the LVD signaling method is used.

Most internal hard drives use pass through terminators. A **pass through terminator** has an extra connector and allows a device that does not have terminators to be terminated through the connector that attaches to the cable. The majority of terminators in use are either active or the FPT active terminator. Hard Figure #17 shows an internal pass through terminator and an external active terminator.

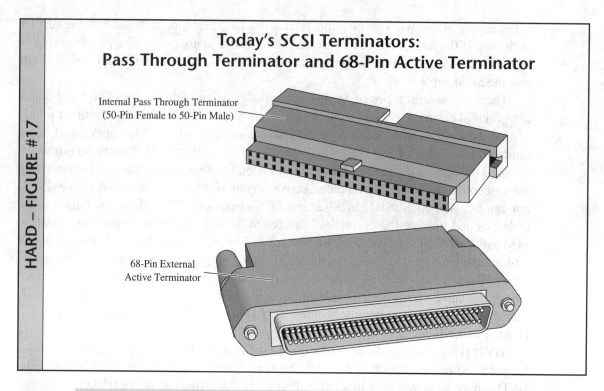

Today's SCSI Terminators:
Pass Through Terminator and 68-Pin Active Terminator

Internal Pass Through Terminator
(50-Pin Female to 50-Pin Male)

68-Pin External
Active Terminator

 Never connect an HVD device/terminator to a SCSI bus/adapter that uses a SE, LVD, or LVD/SE bus. Equipment can be damaged!

Some SCSI host adapters can support multiple SCSI segments and channels. A **SCSI segment** takes the SCSI bus and divides it into two electrical sections, but it is still logically one bus. A good example of a SCSI segment is when using both SE and LVD devices. Put the SE devices on one segment and the LVD devices on a second segment. All of the devices must have a unique SCSI ID because they are still on one bus and they share the SCSI bandwidth, though they operate on separate electrical requirements. This prevents the SE devices from making the LVD devices work in SE mode and allows them to have longer cable lengths. In order for a SCSI host adapter that supports SCSI segments to function, a driver for the specific operating system is installed.

A host adapter that supports **SCSI channels** has the ability to have more than one SCSI bus. In this scenario, the devices connected to one channel have to have unique SCSI IDs and the other channel's devices must have unique IDs.

Being able to distinguish among various SCSI devices is very difficult because there are so many SCSI flavors. Special icons are placed on SCSI devices to differentiate them. Hard Figure #18 shows these icons.

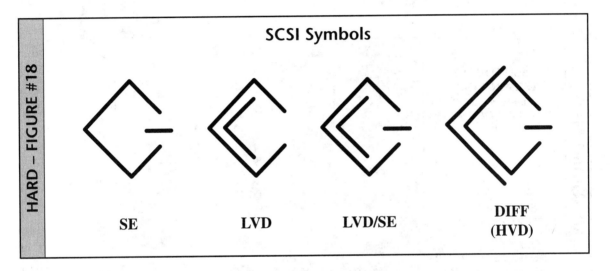

SCSI Symbols

SE   LVD   LVD/SE   DIFF (HVD)

HARD – FIGURE #18

If only internal devices connect to the SCSI host adapter, terminate the adapter and the last internal device connected to the cable. Remove the termination from all other devices. Look at Hard Figure #19 to see how the SCSI chain is terminated if two internal SCSI devices connect to the same host adapter. The SCSI chain has a SCSI host adapter, an internal hard drive, and an internal CD-ROM. The two ends of the SCSI chain are the host adapter and the CD-ROM drive. Both of these devices must be terminated. The internal hard drive, which connects in the center of the SCSI chain, is not terminated.

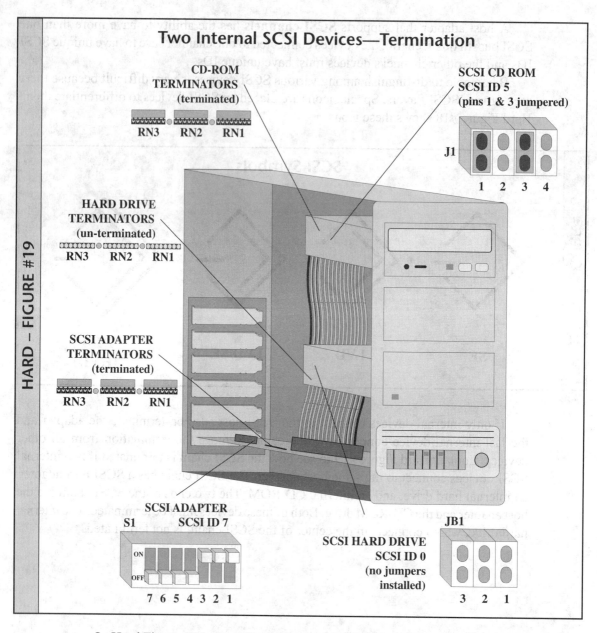

Two Internal SCSI Devices—Termination

CD-ROM
TERMINATORS
(terminated)
RN3   RN2   RN1

SCSI CD ROM
SCSI ID 5
(pins 1 & 3 jumpered)

J1

1   2   3   4

HARD DRIVE
TERMINATORS
(un-terminated)
RN3   RN2   RN1

SCSI ADAPTER
TERMINATORS
(terminated)
RN3   RN2   RN1

SCSI ADAPTER
S1   SCSI ID 7

ON
OFF

7 6 5 4 3 2 1

SCSI HARD DRIVE
SCSI ID 0
(no jumpers
installed)

JB1

3   2   1

HARD – FIGURE #19

In Hard Figure #19, the SIP terminator sockets are labeled RN1, RN2, and RN3. The RN stands for resistor network. The three SIP terminators work together to provide the proper mount of voltage and resistance for the SCSI bus.

When connecting only external devices to the SCSI host adapter, terminate the adapter and the last external device. Remove the termination from all other external devices. See Hard Figure #20 for an illustration of termination when connecting two external SCSI devices.

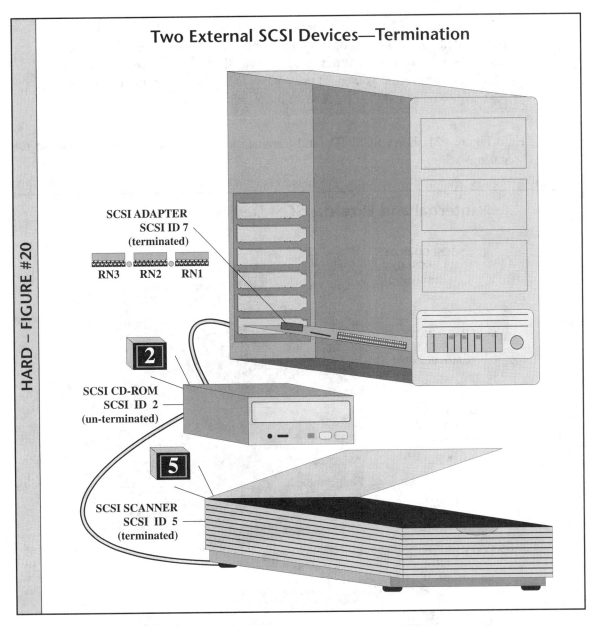

Two External SCSI Devices—Termination

HARD – FIGURE #20

SCSI ADAPTER
SCSI ID 7
(terminated)

RN3   RN2   RN1

2

SCSI CD-ROM
SCSI ID 2
(un-terminated)

5

SCSI SCANNER
SCSI ID 5
(terminated)

In Hard Figure #20, the SCSI chain consists of the host adapter, an external CD-ROM, and an external scanner. The two devices on each end of the SCSI chain are the adapter and the scanner; therefore, these devices are terminated. The external CD-ROM is not terminated.

Notice how two cables connect to the back of the CD-ROM. One cable connects the CD-ROM to the host adapter. A separate SCSI cable connects the CD-ROM to the scanner. The scanner also has two connectors on the back. One connector, of course, contains the cable connecting the scanner to the CD-ROM. The scanner's other connector contains a terminator because the scanner is the last device on the SCSI chain.

Not all external SCSI devices have two connectors on the back and are permanently terminated. This is not a problem if only one device is designed this way because the device can be placed at the end of the SCSI chain. However, with two SCSI devices on the chain, you could use a pass-through terminator, which allows the cable to connect and the device to be the termination point.

Hard Figure #21 shows SCSI IDs and termination for an internal and external device scenario.

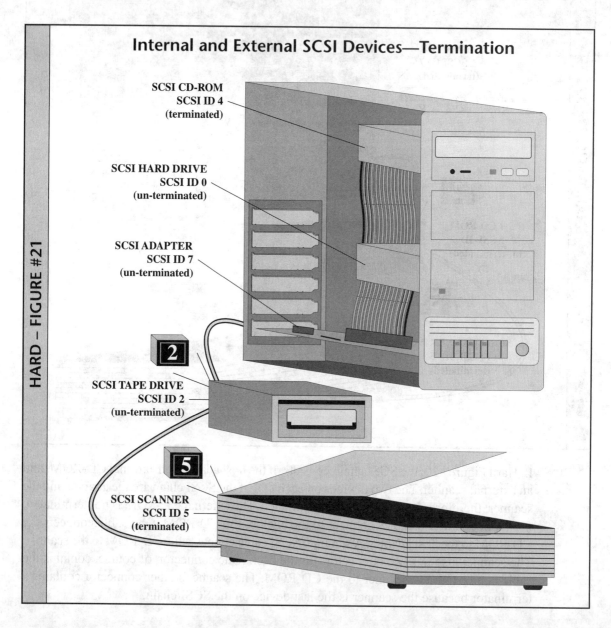

HARD – FIGURE #21

Internal and External SCSI Devices—Termination

SCSI CD-ROM
SCSI ID 4
(terminated)

SCSI HARD DRIVE
SCSI ID 0
(un-terminated)

SCSI ADAPTER
SCSI ID 7
(un-terminated)

2

SCSI TAPE DRIVE
SCSI ID 2
(un-terminated)

5

SCSI SCANNER
SCSI ID 5
(terminated)

If both internal and external devices attach to the SCSI host adapter, the last internal device connected to the SCSI cable is terminated as well as the last external device. All other devices and the SCSI host adapter must have their terminators removed. The SCSI chain in Hard Figure #21 consists of two internal SCSI devices, (a CD-ROM and a hard drive), and two external SCSI devices, (a tape drive and a scanner). The two ends of the SCSI chain that must be terminated are the CD-ROM and the scanner. All other devices are not terminated.

A smart technician plans the configuration of the drive before installing the drive in the system. A good plan of attack is the best strategy to avoid problems during installation. Draw the configuration on a piece of paper to help get the installation straight in your mind. To help new technicians with different configurations, the exercises at the end of the chapter contain sample practice configurations.

SCSI CABLES

SCSI cabling allows multiple devices to be connected to one SCSI host adapter and share the same SCSI bus; this is called **daisy chaining**. Daisy chaining is like connecting multiple Christmas light sets together. If *multiple* internal SCSI devices attach to the SCSI adapter, then use an internal SCSI cable with multiple connectors. Most internal SCSI-1 cables are 50-pin ribbon cables. To connect external devices, a 50-pin Centronics to 50-pin Centronics cable is used. The SCSI-1 cable is also known as an A-Cable. The SCSI-2 standard has a different cable for connecting to the first external SCSI device. This cable has a 50-pin D-shell connector that connects to the SCSI host adapter, and a Centronics connector that connects to the external device. For 16-bit SCSI devices, a second 68-pin cable, called the B-Cable, must be used in addition to the A-Cable. This B-Cable is not in the SCSI-3 specifications because industry did not fully support it. SCSI-3 has a new 68-pin cable called the P-Cable for Fast Wide SCSI or Ultra SCSI devices. A cable, known as the Q-Cable, was to be used in conjunction with the P-Cable, but it did not catch on.

The most common internal SCSI cables found are the A cable and the P cable. They can be internal or external. Hard Figure #22 illustrates some SCSI cables. Also, look back to Hard Figure #17 to see the HD (High Density) 68-pin external connector.

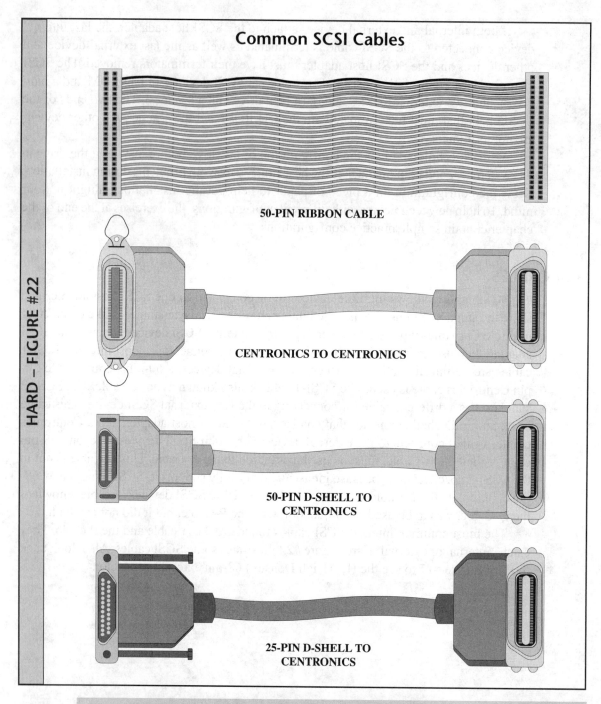

HARD – FIGURE #22

Common SCSI Cables

50-PIN RIBBON CABLE

CENTRONICS TO CENTRONICS

50-PIN D-SHELL TO CENTRONICS

25-PIN D-SHELL TO CENTRONICS

Not all SCSI cables are created equal. Do not recommend or buy the cheaper, thinner SCSI cables available for external devices. These cheaper cables are susceptible to outside noise. The section on Configuration and Setup Procedures covers more cabling issues.

SYSTEM CONFIGURATION FOR HARD DRIVES

On a 286 or higher system, the hard drive is configured through the Setup program. As mentioned previously, Setup is accessed through keystrokes, a Setup disk from the manufacturer (IBM AT is one example), or a Reference disk (IBM's older MicroChannel computers). Once in Setup, you must enter a Drive Type number. The **Drive Type** is a number that corresponds to a drive's geometry (the number of cylinders, heads, and sectors). In times past, a number was entered and the drive geometry information appeared to the right of the Drive Type number. In today's computers, the setting is Auto and the BIOS automatically detects the hard drive type. The drive type information is saved in CMOS. If the computer's battery fails, the drive type information is lost and the computer cannot boot from the hard drive.

For most ESDI hard drive installations, the documentation recommends setting the Drive Type to 1. The ESDI controller and drive take over from there even though that is not the correct parameters for the drive. The drive's geometry information is sent to the controller by the ESDI hard drive.

For SCSI hard drive installations, the most common CMOS setting for the hard drive type is type 0 or None. Once the system boots, the SCSI controller ROM BIOS initializes and the SCSI hard drive takes over and boots the system. Even though the Drive Type number is set to 0 or None, if this step is omitted, the hard drive will not operate.

IDE hard drives are normally configured using the Auto-Detect feature included with BIOS. The Auto-Detect feature automatically determines the Drive Type for the system. Older IDE hard drive manufacturers recommend setting the CMOS drive type to 1 and using a special software package such as Ontrack's Disk Manager or Western Digital's EZ-Drive to allow the system to see the hard drive.

If an IDE and a SCSI hard drive are in the same system, set the system to boot from the SCSI drive. If this is not an option, boot from the IDE drive, upgrade the BIOS, replace the motherboard, or configure the IDE hard drive as an extended partition with logical drives (see next section) and configure the SCSI drive as the primary partition. The last option is not guaranteed to work.

Drive manufacturers normally include documentation describing how to configure the drive in CMOS Setup. Also, they provide software for any system that does not recognize the drive.

With an older ROM BIOS chip that does not support the hard drive, no configuration software is available, and one of the drive types available through Setup must be chosen, certain precautions should be followed:
- Do *not* pick a drive type with more cylinders than the hard drive.
- Do *not* pick a drive type with a different write precompensation cylinder.
- Do *not* pick a drive type with more heads than the hard drive.

Pick the largest total capacity drive type that remains after considering these precautions.

BIOS CONFIGURATIONS FOR HARD DRIVES

The motherboard BIOS must detect and recognize the installed hardware components, including the hard drive. The BIOS chip is the liaison between the operating system and the hard drive. BIOS chips were designed to work with ST506, ESDI, or IDE hard drives. A SCSI hard drive normally connects to an adapter containing a ROM chip. The adapter's ROM chip takes control from the BIOS chip on the motherboard and becomes the liaison between the SCSI hard drive and the operating system. Some motherboards have commands added to the BIOS for built-in SCSI support, but these are more expensive than most motherboards and are not the norm.

Most system BIOS chips manufactured before 1994 do not recognize hard drives larger than 504MB. The reason for this is due to a standard that many drive manufacturers use called the INT13 interface. INT13 (Interrupt 13) is the BIOS interrupt that handles reading and writing to the hard disk. BIOS sees the location of data on the hard drive at the specific cylinder, head, and sector number. The **INT13 interface** is the standard that governs how the BIOS locates data on the hard drive.

A hard drive has a specific number of cylinders, heads, and sectors. The BIOS talks to the hard drive based on the number of cylinders, heads, and sectors using **CHS** (cylinders, heads, sectors) **addressing**. The cylinders, heads, and sectors information is translated inside the hard drive so the BIOS recognizes the information. INT13 can only process a CHS of 1024 cylinders, 63 sectors, and 16 heads. Each sector holds 512 bytes of information; therefore, with 1024 cylinders there are 528,482,304 bytes of data (cylinders x bytes per sector x sectors x heads). The maximum amount of hard drive space the INT13 can handle is 528,482,304 bytes or 504MB. Many books and magazine articles call the maximum 528MB, but 504MB is more accurate because 504MB equals 528,482,304 bytes.

Another way for the BIOS to handle the hard drive is **Extended CHS** or **ECHS**. A BIOS that supports Extended CHS frequently has a Large option in the hard drive section of Setup. Select the *Large* setting to activate Extended CHS. Normally, the hard drive translates the real number of cylinders, heads, and sectors for the BIOS. Then, the BIOS processes the interaction between the operating system and the hard drive. With Extended CHS, in addition to the hard drive translating the cylinders, heads, and sectors, the BIOS performs a second translation. However, having the cylinders, heads, and sectors translated by both the drive and the BIOS chip causes slower response than straight CHS.

A third option for the BIOS to communicate with the hard drive is **LBA** or **Logical Block Addressing**. This is a method of **sector translation**. Today's hard drive manufacturers put intelligence into the drive to track data in a linear fashion. Each sector is assigned a number beginning with the first cylinder, first head, and first sector of user data. The drive continues numbering the sectors until the last track, last head, and last sector are numbered. The drive must translate the cylinder, sector, and head information from the BIOS into a single number that the drive understands. This allows larger drives to be installed under the BIOS INT13 limitation. LBA supports hard drives up to 8GB in capacity. The 8GB limitation is inherent to the INT13 interface. IBM and Microsoft developed an extension to the INT13 interface known as the Extended INT13 interface to support hard drives larger than 8GB.

The last BIOS option is Auto (sometimes seen as IDE HDD Auto Detection), which allows the BIOS to automatically detect and configure itself for the IDE hard drive. This is the most popular and frequently used setting in today's computers. A system BIOS that supports hard drives larger than 504MB is known as a **translating BIOS**. The IDE hard drive SETUP options for the translating BIOS chips are Normal for CHS (Cylinder, Head, Sector), Large for ECHS (Extended CHS), LBA for Logical Block Addressing, and Auto for Automatic Detection. Refer to the installation manual included with the hard drive and the motherboard/computer documentation to choose the correct option. Hard Table #7 shows the most commonly used hard drive settings.

Common Hard Drive Setup Settings

HARD – TABLE #7

Hard Drive Type	Common Setting
IDE/EIDE	AUTO
SCSI	TYPE 0
ST506/ESDI	Specific Number in the TYPE field

If the BIOS chip installed on the motherboard is not a translating BIOS chip, then two options are available:

- Upgrade the BIOS chip(s) on the motherboard to a translating BIOS chip.
- Use a software program such as Ontrack's Disk Manager or Western Digital's EZ-Drive to allow the system to see the larger hard drive.

On-Track's Disk Manager & Western Digital's EZ-Drive programs cannot be used simultaneously on two different drives installed in the same computer system. One software program must be used on both hard drives.

Two other BIOS settings related to hard drives are Block mode and 32-Bit transfers. The block mode allows multiple commands to be sent over the IDE interface and only uses one interrupt to the microprocessor. Every time a device wants to use the bus, it must request permission from the CPU by setting an interrupt. With Block mode enabled in the BIOS, 16 to 32 sectors can be sent and only one interrupt request made to the processor. The 32-bit transfer BIOS setting is sometimes listed as 32-bit access. The IDE/ATA standard transfers data 16-bits at a time normally using the PCI bus (when the IDE connectors are built into the motherboard). The PCI bus allows 32-bit transfers. When the 32-bit transfer BIOS option is enabled, two 16-bit transfers can occur simultaneously increasing IDE performance.

HARD DRIVE PREPARATION OVERVIEW

Once a hard drive is installed and configured properly, and the hard drive type is entered into the CMOS Setup program (on a 286 or higher), the drive must be prepared to accept data. The three steps of hard drive preparation are as follows:

1. Low-level format*
2. Partition
3. High-level format

*The low-level format is not performed on today's hard drives.

The low-level format is performed on very old drives such as the ST506 drives. It is sometimes available for SCSI drives, but is performed at the hard drive manufacturing site. Low-level formatting creates the tracks and sectors on the hard drive platters. Partitioning the hard drive allows a drive letter to be assigned to one or more parts of the hard drive. High-level formatting prepares the drive for use for a particular operating system. This allows the drive to accept data from the operating system. For today's computers, a drive cannot be used until it has been partitioned and high-level formatted. Technicians should be very familiar with the partitioning and high-level formatting installation steps.

LOW-LEVEL FORMAT

The **low-level format** creates and numbers the sectors on the hard drive surface and erases all data from the hard drive. On ST506 drives, the interleave factor is chosen during the low-level format process. The drive and controller are matched in a way that the controller knows the number of tracks, sectors per track, heads, and both the write precompensation and reduced write current cylinders. Write precompensation is the starting inner cylinder number where data is compressed because of the smaller amount of space available. Reduced write current is the starting inner cylinder number where magnetic levels are weaker so more data can be written to a smaller amount of space. For ST506 hard drives, this step is critical. The controller must recognize and properly identify the hard drive to be able to instruct it.

ESDI hard drives have their geometry information built into the drive, so less information is input during the low-level format process. However, ESDI drives still require the installer to perform a low-level format. IDE and SCSI drives are low-level formatted at the factory.

The DOS DEBUG program or the use of special low-level format software such as Ontrack's Disk Manager can be used to low-level format ST506 or ESDI hard drives. If you use DOS DEBUG, the hard drive controller must have a ROM chip that contains the formatting software. DEBUG is just a program to access this software. The most common ROM addresses are in Hard Table #8.

HARD – TABLE #8

Common Hard Drive ROM Addresses for ST506 Drives

C800:5	C800:CCC
D800:5	D800:CCC
C000:5	C000:CCC
D000:5	D000:CCC

To use DEBUG in low-level formatting the hard drive, type *DEBUG* at the DOS prompt. A dash (–) appears on the screen. Type *G=* followed by the starting address of the low-level format software contained on the ROM chip. The starting address is a hexadecimal address where the low-level software begins. The software routine should appear on the screen. If nothing appears on the screen after approximately 30 seconds, reboot the computer and type *DEBUG* again. After the dash, type *G=* followed by a different address. Continue this routine until either the software routine appears or all addresses do not work. If no address works, two options remain: contact the adapter manufacturer to obtain the starting address or use special low-level format software.

Once the software appears on the screen, (whether it is from the ROM chip or from a disk), the software asks for certain information. The required information depends on the software and/or the adapter's ROM chip. Some information that might be needed is listed below:

- How many cylinders does the drive have?
- How many heads does the drive have?
- How many sectors per track does the drive have?
- What is the reduced write current cylinder?
- What is the write precompensation cylinder?
- What is the landing zone cylinder?
- What is the model of the drive being formatted?

The number of questions and the format for the typed answer depends on the software. The information is in the documentation included with the hard drive or on the manufacturer's Internet site.

Low-level formatting must be performed on a newly installed ST506 or ESDI hard drive. Low-level formatting is also a good idea when a ST506 or ESDI hard drive begins to have read and/or write errors. All possible data should be backed up before beginning the low-level formatting. If you install a replacement ST506 hard drive controller, the hard drive usually must be low-level formatted. Good backups are critical for all hard drives.

 Never low-level format an IDE hard drive unless there is no alternative. An example of this is if an older IDE hard drive is getting numerous read errors. The data has been backed up and reloaded, but the drive still gets read errors.

The only alternative at this point is to try the special utilities or buy a new hard drive. Some manufacturers supply formatting software with the computer. IBM provides low-level format software with their MicroChannel machines. From the main menu of the Reference Disk software, press *CTRL+A* for the Advanced Diagnostics to find the low-level format option.

PARTITIONING

The second step in preparing a hard drive for use is partitioning. **Partitioning** a hard drive divides the drive so the computer system sees the hard drive as more than one drive. DOS, Windows 95, and Windows 98 have a software program called **FDISK** that partitions hard drives. Windows NT and 2000 partitions can be set up using FDISK or by using the Disk Administrator program that is available after the operating system is installed. Partitioning provides advantages that include:

- Dividing a hard drive into separate subunits which are then assigned drive letters such as C: or D: by the operating system.
- Organizing the hard drive to separate multiple operating systems, applications, and data.
- Providing data security by placing data in a different partition to allow ease of backup as well as protection.
- Using the hard drive to its fullest capacity.

The original purpose of partitioning was to allow for loading multiple operating systems. This is still a good reason today because placing each operating system in its own partition eliminates the crashes and headaches caused by multiple operating systems and multiple applications co-existing in the same partition. The type of partition and how big the partition can be depends on the file system being used. A **file system** defines how data is stored on a drive. The most common file systems are FAT16, VFAT, FAT32, and NTFS. The file system that can be used depends on what operating system is installed. DOS versions before release 3 used **FAT (File Allocation Table).** This file system was used for floppy disks and hard drives smaller than 16MB. Starting with DOS 3, a file system called **FAT16** (or 16-bit FAT) was used. FAT16, when used with DOS, Windows 95, or Windows 98, supports partitions up to 2GB. Windows NT and 2000 supports FAT16 partitions up to 4GB.

Windows 95 shipped with a file system called **VFAT (Virtual File Allocation Table)** that has the same partition limitations as FAT16, but VFAT supports long file names instead of the traditional 8.3 filenames supported by FAT and FAT16. When using Windows 95's VFAT, drive partitions are still limited to 2GB.

Windows 9x supports a file system called **FAT32**. FAT32 only comes with Windows 95's service release 2. Windows 9x's FAT32 (32-bit FAT) supports hard drive sizes up to 2TB; Windows 2000 only allows FAT32 volumes up to 32GB because Microsoft wants users to go to NTFS. Volumes created on Windows 9x that are greater than 32GB are recognized by Windows 2000 but the operating system cannot create volumes that large.

FAT32 does not support drives smaller than 512MB, nor does it support disk compression. If a computer is to be dual-booted with Windows NT, it cannot use the FAT32 file system, but Windows 2000 can.

To determine whether the operating system uses FAT32, go to the desktop and right-click on the *My Computer* desktop icon. Select the *Properties* option. In the window under the *General* tab, the third line down shows the type of file system being used.

When FDISK is used to partition the hard drive and you select the option to create a partition, a message appears that asks if you wish to enable large disk support. This option is what allows FAT32 to be installed. If you select N (for No) when this question is asked, FAT32 will not be installed.

> Windows 98 comes with a utility called Drive Converter that converts a FAT16 partition to FAT32. To access this utility, click on the Start button. Point to the Programs, Accessories, System Tools selections, and then click on the Drive Converter menu option. Follow the prompts and continue to click on the Next button to convert the partition. Windows 2000 does not ship with a FAT16 to FAT 32 partition converter program, but you can use the CVT program that ships with Windows 98 to convert it.

Windows NT ships with a new file system called **NTFS (NT File System)**. Windows 2000 also uses this file system, but it is called **NTFS5**. To distinguish between the two some people use the terms NTFS4 and NTFS5, but they do have some things in common. NTFS is not compatible with FAT, FAT16, VFAT, and FAT32. It can only be used when loaded as an operating system in Windows NT or 2000. The NTFS file system supports partitions as large as 16EB (Exabytes), but in practice, it currently has a 2TB limit. An **exabyte** is equal to one billion gigabytes. A terabyte is approximately a thousand gigabytes. NTFS allows faster file access and uses hard drive space more efficiently. NTFS supports individual file compression and better file security than the other file systems.

NTFS5 supports disk quotas, which means that individual users can be limited on the amount of hard drive space. It can also automatically repair disk problems. For example, when a hard drive sector is going bad, the entire cluster is moved to another cluster.

> In NT, to convert a FAT16 partition to NTFS, or in Windows 2000, to convert a FAT16/FAT32 partition to NTFS, use the CONVERT.EXE program. Access a command prompt window. Type the following command:
>
> **CONVERT *x:* /FS:NTFS** (where *x:* is the drive letter of the partition being converted to NTFS)
>
> Press *Enter* and then press the *Y* key (for Yes) and press *Enter.* Close the command prompt window and restart the computer. You can add a /V switch to the end of the command for a more verbose operation mode.

When installing 2000 on a hard drive that already has a partition created, you are prompted to convert the partition to NTFS. If you agree to the conversion, no other prompts appear to confirm this decision. The partition is converted to NTFS. Any NTFS partitions are automatically upgraded to NTFS5. NTFS5 can only read NTFS partitions if they are NTFS5. Any type of partition conversions requires free hard drive space. The amount depends on the size of the partition.

> Windows 2000 automatically converts any NTFS partition to NTFS5. In order for an NT computer to read or write to NTFS5 partitions, service pack 4 or higher must be installed. Even when the service pack is installed, the additional features in NTFS5 are not installed, nor do they function in the NT Workstation environment. To take advantage of the NTFS5 features, Windows 2000 must be installed.

Hard Table #9 recaps the different file systems.

HARD – TABLE #9

File Systems

Name	Operating System	Characteristics
FAT (FAT12)	Pre-DOS 3.x	Floppy disks and hard drives <16MB
FAT16	DOS 3.x and higher Windows 95 Windows 98 Windows NT	2GB partition limitation with DOS, Windows 95, and 98. 4GB partition limitation with NT. Filenames are limited to 8.3 in length.
VFAT	Windows 95	2GB partition limitation. Smaller clusters than FAT16. Supports long filenames.
FAT32	Windows 95 Windows 98	Supports drives up to 2TB. Does not support drives smaller than 512MB.
NTFS	NT Server NT Workstation 2000 Professional 2000 Server	Drives up to 16EB (but in practice, it is 2TB). Supports file compression and file security. NTFS4 is available on NT Workstation and Server. NTFS5 ships with Windows 2000 and NT service pack 4 and higher.

An even better reason for partitioning than loading multiple operating systems is to partition the hard drive for more efficient use of space.

The operating system sets aside one cluster as a minimum for every file. A **cluster** is the smallest amount of space reserved for one file. A cluster is made up of a specific number of sectors. Memory Figure #23 illustrates the concept of a cluster. Keep in mind that the number of hard drive sectors per track varies. The outer tracks hold more information (have more sectors) than the inner tracks.

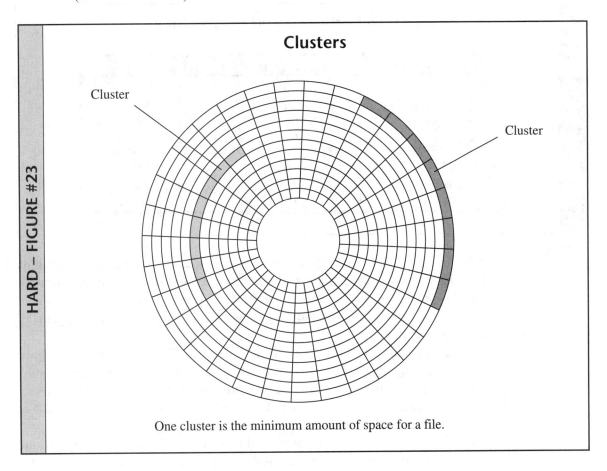

Clusters

Cluster

Cluster

One cluster is the minimum amount of space for a file.

HARD – FIGURE #23

The size and type of a hard drive's partition determines the cluster size! Remember that a cluster is the smallest amount of space reserved for one file. The size of the cluster is determined by the partition size.

For example, if a letter is being typed
     DEAR MOM,
and the phone rings, you quickly save the file to the hard disk. If the hard disk has a 20MB FAT16 partition, then the file saves in a cluster of four sectors or 2,048 bytes (2KB) even though the file is only nine bytes long.

If the file is on a 128MB partition, then a cluster of eight sectors, or 4KB of space, is reserved for the file. A 1GB partition sets aside 16KB of space for the same nine characters in the file. If the file grows larger than one cluster in size, additional clusters are used in sizes relational to the size of the hard drive partition. Inefficient partitioning wastes space on the hard drive. Hard Table #10 illustrates how the hard drive's FAT partition size affects cluster size.

HARD – TABLE #10

FAT 16 Partitions and Cluster Size

Partition Size	No. of Sectors	Cluster Size
0-15MB	8	4K
16MB-127MB	4	2K
128MB-255MB	8	4K
256MB-511MB	16	8K
512MB-1GB	32	16K
1GB-2GB	64	32K
2GB-4GB	128	64K

One can see in Hard Table #10 that partitioning today's large drives into one partition wastes hard drive space. Most end users do not have big files. An efficiently partitioned hard drive allows more files to be saved because less of the hard drive is wasted. Computer users with CAD (Computer Aided Drafting) software would naturally have bigger files and need larger partitions.

Applications should be in a separate partition than data files. There are several good reasons for partitioning the hard drive and separating data files from application files:

- Multiple partitions on the same hard drive divide the drive into smaller sub-units which makes it easier and faster to back up the data (which should be backed up more often than applications).
- The data is protected from operating system failures, unstable software applications, and any unusual software problems that occur between the application and the operating system.
- The data is in one location, which makes the files easier and faster to back up, organize, and locate.

Windows 9x and Windows 2000 systems use FAT32 partitions. The FAT32 file system makes more efficient use of the hard drive. Hard Table #11 shows the cluster size for FAT32 partitions.

FAT32 Partitions and Cluster Size

HARD – TABLE #11

Partition Size	No. of Sectors	Cluster Size
0-511MB	N/A	N/A
512MB-8GB	8	4K
8GB-16GB	16	8K
16GB-32GB	32	16K
>32GB	64	32K

The NTFS file system is a very efficient one. NTFS can use cluster sizes as small as 512 bytes per cluster. Hard Table #12 lists the default cluster sizes for Windows NT and 2000.

NTFS Partitions and Cluster Size

HARD – TABLE #12

Partition Size	No. of Sectors	Cluster Size
0-511MB	1	512 bytes
512MB-1GB	2	1KB
1GB-2GB	4	2KB
2GB-4GB	8	4KB
4GB-8GB	16	8KB
8GB-16GB	32	16K
16GB-32GB	64	32K
>32GB	128	64K

The FDISK program is used with DOS and Windows 9x to partition a hard drive. With NT and 2000, the FDISK program can be used before the operating system is loaded, the NT/2000 Setup installation program can be used to create a partition, and the Disk Administrator utility can be used once the operating system is installed. Hard Figure #24 shows a screen capture from NT's Disk Administrator. The one in Windows 2000 has a similar look.

HARD – FIGURE #24

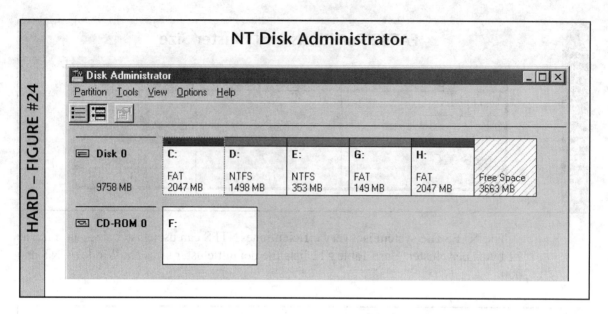

NT Disk Administrator

Partitions are defined as primary and extended. If there is only one hard drive installed in a system and the entire hard drive is one partition, it is the **primary partition**. The primary partition on the first detected hard drive is assigned the drive letter C:. DOS requires that the first hard drive in a system be a primary partition and must be marked as active if the drive boots the system.

If the drive is divided so only part of the drive is the primary partition, the rest of the cylinders can be designated as the **extended partition**. An extended partition allows a drive to be further divided. A second operating system can reside in an extended partition. A single hard drive can be divided into a maximum of four primary partitions, but some operating systems such as DOS, allow only one primary partition to be visible at one time. Look at Hard Figure #25 for an illustration of how one hard drive can be divided into partitions. The sectors are in pie-shaped wedges for easy explanation and illustration. Today's hard drives do not use sectors drawn in pie-shaped wedges; they use zone bit recording which has a different number of sectors for every track. Reference Hard Figure #4 earlier in the chapter for a refresher.

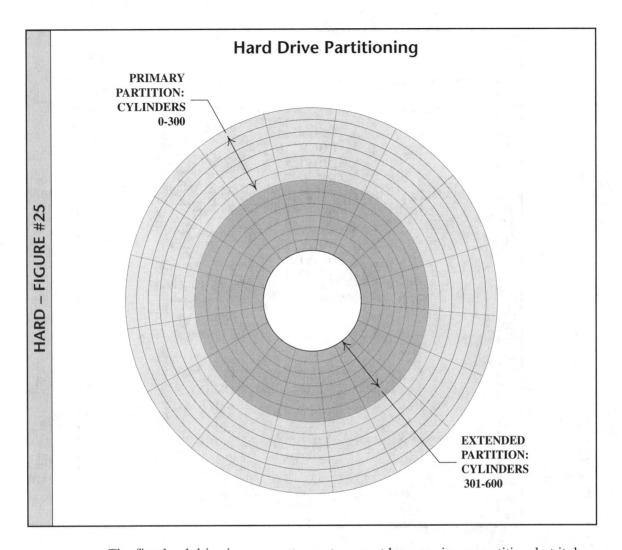

HARD – FIGURE #25

Hard Drive Partitioning

PRIMARY PARTITION: CYLINDERS 0-300

EXTENDED PARTITION: CYLINDERS 301-600

The first hard drive in a computer system must have a primary partition, but it does not require an extended partition. If the drive has an extended partition, it can be further subdivided into **logical drives** that appear as separate hard drives to the computer system. Logical drives created in the extended partition are assigned drive letters such as D:, E:, or others. The only limit for logical drives is the number of drive letters. An extended partition can have a maximum of 23 logical drives with the drive letters D: through Z:. Hard Figure #26 shows an illustration of a hard drive divided into a primary partition and an extended partition further subdivided into two logical drives.

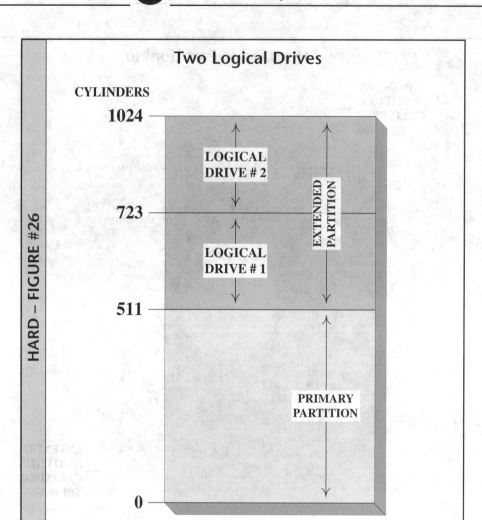

If two hard drives are installed in one computer system, the first hard drive *must* have a primary partition. The second hard drive is not required to have a primary partition and may simply have a single extended partition. If the second hard drive does have a primary partition, it can have an extended partition too.

When a partition is deleted, all information in the partition is lost. A partition can be resized by deleting the partition and re-creating it, but the FDISK or Disk Administrator program removes all information in the deleted partition. When logical drives in an extended partition are deleted, all data is lost. The other logical drives within the extended partition retain their information.

When a hard drive is first installed and partitioned, the outermost track on the platter (cylinder 0, head 0, physical sector 1) is reserved for the partition table. The **partition table** holds information about the types of partitions created and in what cylinders these partitions reside. The partition table is part of the **MBR (Master Boot Record)** that contains a program that reads the partition table, looks for the primary partition marked as active, and goes to that partition to boot the system.

NTFS has two additional terms that you need to be aware of as a technician: system partition and boot partition. An NT/2000 **system partition** is the partition on the hard drive that holds the hardware-specific files needed to load the operating system. An NT/2000 **boot partition** is the partition on the hard drive that contains the operating system. The boot partition and the system partition can be on the same partition with NT or 2000.

HOW DRIVE LETTERS ARE ASSIGNED

DOS, or any operating system, assigns drive letters during the partitioning step. The order in which the partitions are assigned drive letters depends on three factors: (1) the number of hard drives, (2) the type of partitions on the hard drives (primary or extended), and (3) the operating system. Microsoft's MS-DOS assigns drive letters in a hierarchical fashion based on what drives (floppy, hard, or other drives) are detected, how many drives are detected, and the order in which the system detects the drives. The following outline shows the order in which DOS, Windows 9x, and NT assigns drive letters; other operating systems may assign the drive letters in a different order.

1. The first floppy drive detected is assigned drive letter A:.
2. If a second floppy drive is detected, it is assigned drive letter B:. If a second floppy drive is not found, a logical drive B: is created and assigned to the first floppy drive (in addition to the drive letter A:).
3. The first hard drive primary partition detected receives drive letter C:. DOS supports up to eight different hard drives. DOS and older Windows 95 support a maximum partition size of 2.1GB. Windows 95 (Service Release 2) and Windows 98 support a maximum partition size of 2TB. NT and 2000 have a maximum partition size of 16EB.
4. Any other primary partitions found, beginning with the second hard drive, receive the next drive letters.
5. Logical drives within any extended partitions, beginning with the first physical hard drive, are assigned the next drive letters.
6. After all logical drives are assigned drive letters, drive letters are assigned to drives such as RAM drives or CD-ROM drives that use software drivers loaded through the CONFIG.SYS file. The order in which the drive letters are assigned depends on the order in which the drivers load in the CONFIG.SYS file. One exception is RAM drives are assigned drive letters before CD-ROMs no matter what order the drivers load.

Windows 2000 has changed how drive letters are assigned. The Mount Manger program assigns the drive letters in the following order:

1. The first floppy drive detected is assigned drive letter A:.
2. If a second floppy drive is detected, it is assigned drive letter B:. If a second floppy drive is not found, a logical drive B: is created and assigned to the first floppy drive (in addition to the drive letter A:).
3. The first primary partition marked at active receives the drive letter C:.
4. Logical drives on hard drives and removable drives (MO and Jazz) are assigned drive letters.
5. Remaining primary partitions are assigned drive letters.
6. CD-ROMs and DVDs receive drive letters.

The following examples are based on the DOS, Windows 9x, and NT drive assignment scheme.

Example 1: A single hard drive is partitioned into one primary partition. With this scenario, DOS assigns the drive letter C: to the primary partition and this partition must be marked as active if the drive boots the system.

Example 2: A single hard drive is partitioned into one primary and one extended partition. Two logical drives are allocated in the extended partition. DOS assigns the drive letter C: to the primary partition, drive letter D: to the first logical drive in the extended partition, and drive E: to the second logical drive in the extended partition.

Example 3: Two hard drives are in the same system. Drive 1 is partitioned into one primary and one extended partition. The extended partition has one logical drive that occupies the entire partition. Physical Drive 2 also has one primary partition and one extended partition with one logical drive. The operating system assigns drive C: to the primary partition of Hard Drive 1, drive D: to Hard Drive 2's primary partition, drive E: to Hard Drive 1's logical drive in the extended partition. Drive F: is assigned to Hard Drive 2's logical drive in the extended partition. Hard Figure #27 displays the drive letter assignments for the two hard drives in this scenario.

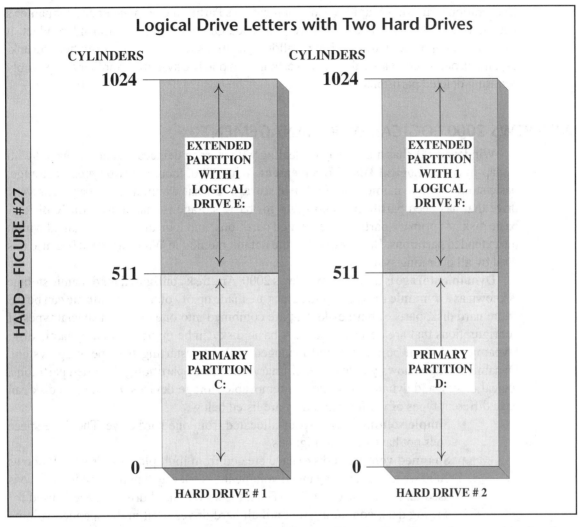

Logical Drive Letters with Two Hard Drives

HARD – FIGURE #27

CYLINDERS

1024

EXTENDED
PARTITION
WITH 1
LOGICAL
DRIVE E:

511

PRIMARY
PARTITION
C:

0

HARD DRIVE # 1

CYLINDERS

1024

EXTENDED
PARTITION
WITH 1
LOGICAL
DRIVE F:

511

PRIMARY
PARTITION
D:

0

HARD DRIVE # 2

Partitioning can be a little confusing, but the best way to learn about partitioning is to perform the procedure. The partitioning exercises later in the chapter provide practice to reinforce the partitioning concepts and steps.

To determine the type of partition installed on a DOS or Windows 3.x computer, use the FDISK program. Select Option 4—Display Partition Information.

To determine the type of partition on a Windows 9x, Windows NT, or 2000 computer, double-click on the My Computer icon. Right-click on a drive letter. Click on the Properties menu option. Click on the General tab. The type of file system used in the partition is shown in the window.

Special products can be used that partition the hard drive and allow repartitioning *without any data loss*. Examples include Paragon Software's Partition Manager, PowerQuest

Corporation's Partition Magic, V Communication's Partition Commander and Symantec's Partition-IT. Note that since Symantec purchased Quarterdeck's Partition-IT product, it has not been updated. Partition Magic allows partitions to be created, formatted, shrunk, expanded, or moved. It also allows converting from one file system to another and possibly restoring deleted partitions.

WINDOWS 2000 LOGICAL DISK MANAGEMENT

Windows 2000 has a new way of dealing with storage devices that are managed with a snap-in called **Logical Disk Management**. With 2000, there are two types of storage, basic storage and dynamic storage. **Basic storage** is what we think of as partitions. Any drive that has been partitioned and setup for basic storage is known as a **basic disk**. A basic disk has primary partitions, extended partitions, and logical drives contained within the extended partitions. Basic storage is the default method in Windows 2000 because it is used by all operating systems.

Dynamic storage is unique to Windows 2000. Any disk configured for dynamic storage is known as a **dynamic disk**. Dynamic disks are made up of volumes. A **volume** can be the entire hard disk, parts of hard disks that are combined into one unit, and special types of configurations that are described later. A basic disk can be upgraded to a dynamic disk. Dynamic disks can be resized and managed without restarting the operating system. Dynamic storage allows you to create primary (the norm) partitions, extended partitions, logical drives, and dynamic volumes on removable storage devices. A dynamic disk can have different types of volumes and they are listed below:

- **Simple volume** is disk space allocated from one hard drive. The drive space does not have to be contiguous.
- **Spanned volume** is disk space created from multiple hard drives. Windows 2000 writes data to a spanned volume in such a way that the first hard drive is used until the space is filled. Then, the second hard drive's space is used for writing data, continuing on until all hard drives used in the spanned volume are utilized.
- **Striped volume** is when data is written across two to thirty-two hard drives. This appears to be like a spanned volume, but it is different in that each drive is use alternately. Another name for this is striping or Raid 0.
- **Raid 5 volume** puts data on three or more hard drives and one of the hard drive spaces is used for parity. Data that is written using this method is recoverable if one hard drive crashes.
- **System volume** holds the files needed to load 2000.
- **Boot volume** holds the 2000 operating system. The system volume and the boot volume can be one and the same.

Use the Disk Management snap-in tool (found in the Computer Management console) to work with dynamic disks or to convert a basic disk to a dynamic one. Once accomplished, the conversion process cannot be reversed. Only 2000 computers recognize dynamic disks.

The 2000 Setup program does not recognize dynamic disk volumes, but it can recognize a dynamic disk that was converted from a basic disk. When there are problems with 2000, the dynamic volumes are not displayed accurately in the text mode portion of Setup or with the Recovery Console. Hopefully, Microsoft will provide a service pack that addresses this issue.

HIGH-LEVEL FORMAT

The last step in preparing a hard drive for use is high-level formatting. A **high-level format** must be performed on all primary partitions and logical drives located within extended partitions before data can be written to the hard drive. The high-level format sets up the file system so it can accept data.

> Included with Windows 95's Service Release 2 and Windows 98 are new FDISK, FORMAT, SCANDISK, and DEFRAG commands that can handle the FAT32 32-bit addressing. FAT32 is incompatible with some existing DOS drivers, DOS games, and DOS disk compression and defragmentation utilities. Neither Windows 3.x nor Windows NT can read the Windows 95/98 FAT32 hard disk volumes. Windows 2000 can read FAT32 partitions.

Windows NT and 2000's file system, NTFS, allows support for multiple data streams and support for every character in the world. NTFS also automatically remaps bad clusters to other sections of the hard drive without any additional time or utility. Hard Figure #28 shows the difference between how a FAT16 partition and an NTFS partition is set up when the high-level format step is completed.

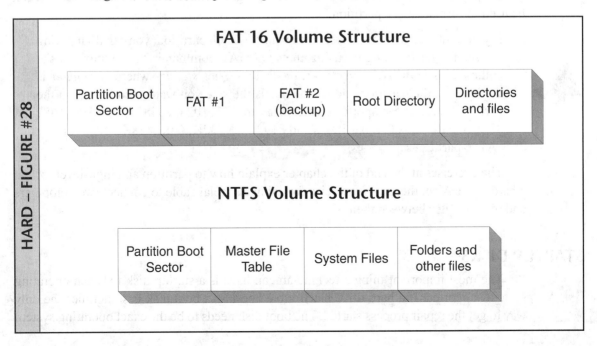

HARD – FIGURE #28

FAT 16 Volume Structure

| Partition Boot Sector | FAT #1 | FAT #2 (backup) | Root Directory | Directories and files |

NTFS Volume Structure

| Partition Boot Sector | Master File Table | System Files | Folders and other files |

With FAT16 and FAT32, the high-level format creates two file allocation tables (FATs), one primary and one secondary. It also creates the root directory that renumbers the sectors. The FAT keeps track of the hard disk's file locations. It is similar to a table of contents in a book as it lists where the files are located in the partition. FAT partitions are recognized by DOS, Windows 95, Windows 98, and OS/2 operating systems and are limited to 2.1GB. NT/2000's FAT partitions are limited to 4GB, but are unrecognizable by other operating systems when made this large.

No matter what operating system is being used, high-level formatting can be performed using the FORMAT command. The /S FORMAT command switch makes the partition bootable. In DOS, three files are required to make the hard disk bootable: two hidden files and COMMAND.COM. The FORMAT C: /S command copies these three files to the hard disk. This command should always be used to make the primary partition bootable.

The area of the disk that contains information about the system files is the **DOS Boot Record** or the **DBR** and is located on the hard drive's cylinder 0 head 1 sector 1. The more common term for this today (since DOS is no longer a major operating system) is **boot sector** or volume boot record. With DOS, the boot sector points to where the two hidden files, IO.SYS and MSDOS.SYS, are stored and attempts to load them. The FORMAT command does NOT erase all data from the hard drive, it only removes the FAT. If a backup of the original FAT can be restored to the hard drive or an "unformat" utility is used on a logical drive that has accidentally been high-level formatted, no data is lost.

FAT32 partitions are less susceptible to boot failures than FAT16 partitions. The FAT32 boot record has been expanded to include a backup of critical data. Unlike FAT16, FAT32 can relocate the root directory and use the backup file allocation table if the default table has a problem. Windows NT and 2000 have a program called Disk Administrator that can be used to format an NT partition.

If you want to adjust the cluster size on an NT/2000 partition, you can do it during the high-level format step using the FORMAT command. The syntax for the command is FORMAT *driveletter*: /FS:NTFS /A:*clustersize* where *driveletter* is the letter of the partition and *clustersize* is the size you want each cluster in the partition to be. The supported cluster sizes are 512, 1024, 2048, 4096, 8192, 16K, 32K, or 64K for NTFS partitions and 8192, 16K, 32K, 64K, 128K, and 256K for FAT16 partitions.

The exercises at the end of the chapter explain how to partition and high-level format a hard drive. Also, there is an exercise for using a special cable to connect two computers and transfer files between them.

STARTUP DISKS

The most important thing a technician can have is a startup disk for each operating system supported. If a hard drive has trouble booting, a boot disk is sometimes the only way to get the repair process started. The boot disk needs to be the exact operating system version that is installed on the computer. The problem with this is that the computer users do not always know what operating system, much less what version is installed on their computer.

A web site called BOOTDISK.COM (www.bootdisk.com) allows you to create a boot disk for most operating systems. To create a boot disk on a DOS or Windows 3.x computer, at the DOS prompt, type *FORMAT A: /S*. Insert a disk and follow the prompts on the screen. Even though this creates a bootable disk, it does not transfer the commands commonly needed for troubleshooting such as ATTRIB or FDISK, SYS. The boot disk also will not contain the drivers needed for devices such as a CD-ROM or mouse. If the hard drive requires special drivers in order to operate, these drivers must be copied over to the boot disk or the hard drive will never be accessible.

To create a boot disk on a Windows 9x computer, click on the *Start* button. Point to the *Settings* option and click on the *Control Panel* menu option. Double-click on the *Add/ Remove Programs* icon. Click on the *Startup* disk tab. Click on the *Create Disk* button and follow the prompts on the window.

To create a Windows 98 startup disk that can create or read FAT32 partitions, use a special program called FAT32EBD. This program is located on the Windows 98 CD in the MTSUTIL folder (which is located under the TOOLS folder). Use Windows Explorer to locate the folder. Double-click on the *FAT32EBD* file and follow the instructions on the screen.

You can also make an NT/2000 startup disk, but it is quite complex.

1. Click on the *Start* button and then click on the *RUN* utility.
2. Type *Format A: /S*, insert a blank floppy into the drive, and press Enter.
3. Start the Windows NT Explorer program. Click on *View* and then click the *Options* menu option.
4. On the View tab, click on the *Show all files* option and then click on the *OK* button.
5. Click on the needed files (a list follows later in the chapter).
6. On the File menu option, click on the *Properties* option.
7. Click on the *General* tab. In the Attributes box at the bottom, make sure the Read Only, System, and Hidden check boxes are unchecked (clear). Click on the *OK* button.
8. Select the files from Explorer and copy them over to the floppy disk.

An easier method for creating Windows NT startup disks is to use the NT/2000 startup disk or the installation CD. An exercise at the end of the chapter details the required steps. Another important disk that can be used in conjunction with the NT/2000 boot disk is an **ERD (Emergency Repair Disk)**. An ERD can help when the operating system has problems booting, problems with a person's working environment, damaged system files, or if new hardware has been installed and the system will not boot. An option to create this disk is presented during the NT/2000 installation, but one can also be created later. To create an ERD, click on the *Start* button and click on *Help*. Click on the *Index* tab and type in the word *repair*. In the search results, click on the *Repair Disk utility* option and click on the

Display button. In the window, click on the *arrow* to start the utility. Click on the *Create Repair Disk* button and follow the instructions on the screen.

In NT, the same can be achieved using the RDISK command from the RUN utility. The RDISK command backs up the system and software registry hives. RDISK /S backs the system, software, and security registry hives as well as the SAM (Security Accounts Manager)—the database that NT uses to track things.

Windows 2000 does not ship with the RDISK command. To create an ERD in Windows 2000, click on the *Start* program, point to *Programs, Accessories, and System Tools*. Click on the *Backup* option. Once the window appears, click on the *Tools* menu option and select the *Create an Emergency Repair Disk* selection. Follow the prompts on the screen.

Hard Table #13 lists the startup files commonly found on a floppy disk for MS-DOS, Windows 9x, Windows NT, and 2000. Keep in mind that the files may be different depending on what hardware is installed.

Boot Files

HARD – TABLE #13

MS-DOS	Windows 9x	NT/2000
COMMAND.COM	COMMAND.COM	NTLDR
IO.SYS	IO.SYS	BOOT.INI
MSDOS.SYS	MSDOS.SYS	NTDETECT
	ATTRIB.EXE	BOOTSECT.DOS
	CHKDSK.EXE	NTBOOTDD.SYS
	CONFIG.SYS	
	DEBUG.EXE	
	DRVSPACE.BIN	
	EBD.SYS	
	EDIT.COM	
	FDISK.EXE	
	FORMAT.EXE	
	HIMEM.SYS	
	EXTRACT.EXE	

When loading NT or 2000 and planning to use NTFS, a good suggestion is to make a small FAT16 partition as the first partition, then create a NTFS partition and install NT into the NTFS partition. NT is a very stable environment, but when it crashes, it is difficult to troubleshoot if the only partition on the drive is a NTFS partition. By having a small FAT16 partition, you can create a DOS or Windows 9x boot disk just to access the FAT16 partition and NT files if needed. An emergency rescue disk can be created to help with corrupt system files, Registry, or partition boot sector.

VIRUSES

A **virus** is a program written to cause a device not to operate in its normal fashion. Common types of viruses include the BIOS virus, the MBR or boot sector virus, the file-infecting virus, the macro virus, the Trojan horse virus, and the worm virus. Hard Table #14 lists the most common types of viruses and a description of them.

Types of Viruses

Program	Description
BIOS virus	Designed to attack computers with Flash BIOS. Rewrites the BIOS code so the computer does not boot.
Boot sector (MBR) virus	Replaces or alters information in boot sectors or in the Master Boot Record. These viruses spread whenever you boot off a disk. Examples include Michaelangelo, Junkie, and Ohio.
File-infecting virus	Most common type of virus. Attaches to EXE, COM, SYS, DLL, & OVL files. Can also be triggered for a particular event such as a date. Examples include Friday the 13th, Enigma, Loki, and Nemesis.
Macro virus	A program written in the macro language that is built into some applications. Most often attacks in Microsoft Office products and Ami Pro.
Trojan horse programs	Does not replicate as a virus does, but does destroy data. Frequently hides a virus program because it appears as a legitimate program to virus checkers. Examples include Aids Information, Twelve Tricks A and B, and Darth Vader
Worm virus	A self-contained program that spreads to other computers usually through a network.

Common errors that display when a MBR or boot sector virus has infected the computer are Invalid partition table, Error loading operating system, and Missing operating system. See the specific operating system chapters for more details on viruses.

LOGICALLY TROUBLESHOOTING NEWLY INSTALLED DRIVES

Most problems with new drive installation stem from improper configuration of the drive select jumpers, SCSI ID jumpers, termination, problems with cabling, or drive type configuration. The following steps assist with checking possible problems.

1. Check the drive select or SCSI ID jumper setting(s).
2. Check termination (if needed).
3. Check cabling. Pin 1 of the cable should be attached to pin 1 of the adapter connector.
4. Check the drive type setting in CMOS. Refer to the documentation, contact the manufacturer of the drive for the correct setting, or use the Internet to obtain the setting.
5. If after you have configured the drive, installed it, and powered it on, the CMOS shows the drive type as "None, Not installed," or displays all 0's in the drive parameters even though you set it to automatically detect the drive, then the BIOS is not able to detect it. Check all your jumper settings, check cable connections, and check the power connection. If there are two drives connected to the same cable, disconnect the slave drive. If the drives can be detected individually, but not together, they are incompatible on the same cable. In Setup, reduce any advanced features such as Block mode, multi-sector transfer, PIO mode, 32-bit transfers, etc. to their lowest values or disable them. Increase the amount of time the computer takes to initialize the hard drive by going into Setup and enabling such features as above 1MB memory testing and floppy drive seek at boot. You many also increase the initialization time, increase the hard drive boot delay, or set the boot speed to the lowest value. This gives the hard drive more time to spin up and reach its appropriate RPM before data is read from it. Make sure the controller port on the motherboard is enabled either by a jumper or through Setup.
6. If the drive is a new ST506 or ESDI drive, has the drive been low-level formatted?
7. Has the drive been partitioned?
8. Has the drive been high-level formatted?
9. Were the boot files copied over?
10. Verify the mounting screw to hold the drive in the case is not too tight. Loosen the screw and power up the computer.
11. If during partitioning, the "No fixed disks present" error appears, check the hard drive cabling, power connection, configuration jumpers (drive select, master/slave, SCSI ID), termination, and CMOS configuration.

12. If the hard drive does not format to full capacity: (a) the drive parameters may be set incorrectly in Setup, (b) the BIOS does not support large hard drives, or (c) translation is not set up for the hard drive in the Setup program. See the section on BIOS limitations. Confirm the drive's parameters reported by FDISK with the drive's actual parameters and capacity.

13. If the error messages "No ROM Basic—System Halted" or "Disk Boot failure" appear, check to see that the primary partition is marked active.

14. If the error message "Non-System disk" appears, the system files are missing from the primary partition. Boot from a bootable disk and type *SYS C:*.

15. If on initial boot, the computer locks up or shows a much smaller drive capacity. Let the system try to boot for at least two minutes. Then, turn the system off, check the cable to the hard drive and to the adapter or motherboard for correct pin 1 orientation and check the configuration jumpers. Try to enter *CMOS Setup* and set the drive type to auto configuration. If the system still does not respond, the computer's BIOS may not support the large hard drive.

16. If on initial boot after setting up a hard drive in CMOS Setup, you see the message "HDD Controller Failure, Press F1 to continue." This error message occurs if the system is not partitioned or high-level formatted. Press the *F1* key and boot from a floppy disk, then partition and high-level format the hard drive. If the message still continues, check the cabling and jumper configuration(s) on the hard drive.

17. During power-on, the hard drive does not spin up or the hard drive spins down after a few seconds. Check the power connector. Check the pin 1 orientation on the cable. Check the drive type in CMOS Setup. Check Master/Slave settings. Check for energy management jumpers or settings in Setup. Check for any software that came with the drive that enables power management. Disable power management in CMOS. Try installing the drive in another system.

18. Some SETUP programs try to be helpful by using drive letters to identify multiple hard drives, but inadvertently assign the drive letters to the wrong hard drives. Do not trust the Setup program to identify hard drives. Instead, use the FDISK program for accurate drive lettering.

19. If the drive uses an adapter, check that the adapter seats properly in the expansion slot.

20. Run a virus checker on the system from a bootable floppy.

21. Try a warm boot (CTRL+ALT+DEL). If the drive is recognized after the warm boot, the Setup program may be running too fast for the drive to initialize. One solution is to slow down the computer. If the computer has a turbo switch, press it to slow the computer's processor. Some computers require keystrokes to change the turbo setting. Refer to the computer or motherboard documentation for the exact procedure. Once the computer powers up properly, the system can be returned to the faster speed.

22. If the hard drive attaches to an adapter, check the IRQ, I/O address, and ROM address for conflicts with other installed adapters.

If the new hard drive is a new SCSI drive, the following are some things to check:

1. If the "Drive Not Ready" error message appears on the screen, verify that the hard drive has the spin-up on power-up option enabled (usually through a jumper setting).

2. If you are installing a new SCSI adapter and a SCSI (non-hard drive) peripheral and an error message appears such as "No boot drives found," the BIOS on the SCSI adapter should be disabled (usually through a jumper setting).

3. An IDE hard drive and a SCSI hard drive are in the same system, but the computer does not boot off the SCSI hard drive. This is because a bootable IDE or ESDI hard drive always takes precedence over the SCSI drive; however, with some computers today, the BIOS allows a SCSI device to be the boot device. Look for either the Boot Device or Boot Order (or something similar) section in the Setup program.

4. If the SCSI ASPIDISK.SYS driver loads and the error message "Too many block devices" appears, change the LAST DRIVE= statement in the CONFIG.SYS file to a higher drive letter.

5. If the system hangs on boot-up after a SCSI adapter and hard drive are installed, check for an interrupt, ROM address, I/O address, or DMA conflict. If all appears okay with each setting, disconnect the SCSI hard drive (and any other SCSI devices connected to the adapter) from the SCSI adapter. Power on the system. If the system boots properly, check for a termination problem, SCSI ID conflict, or improper cabling.

6. Verify with the drive or the SCSI host adapter manufacturer that the two devices are compatible. Not all SCSI devices work with the various SCSI adapters.

Hard drive troubleshooting can best be handled if the technician understands the boot process. With DOS, the boot sequence only works if all elements in the hard drive hardware (controller, cables, and drive) are functional and configured properly. The steps are as follows:

1. BIOS performs POST. If the computer has a plug and play BIOS, the plug and play devices are located, tested, and configured.

2. The partition table is read.

3. The boot record is read.

4. The hidden files load.

5. Depending on the operating system, IBMBIO.COM or IO.SYS executes. The message "Starting MS-DOS" or "Starting PC DOS" appears. IBMBIO.COM or IO.SYS reads the CONFIG.SYS file (if IBMBIO.COM or IO.SYS finds this file).

6. IBMDOS.COM or MSDOS.SYS executes.

7. COMMAND.COM loads.

8. COMMAND.COM executes the AUTOEXEC.BAT file (if COMMAND.COM finds this file).

For Windows 9x, the boot procedure is a little different. The steps for Windows 95 booting are as follows:

1. BIOS performs POST. If the computer has a plug and play BIOS, the plug and play devices are located, tested, and configured.
2. The partition table is read.
3. The boot record is read.
4. IO.SYS executes.
5. Windows 9x checks the MSDOS.SYS file for boot configuration parameters.
6. The message "Starting Windows 9x," appears.
7. The SYSTEM.DAT file loads.
8. If a CONFIG.SYS file exists, the CONFIG.SYS file processes the commands.
9. If an AUTOEXEC.BAT file exists, its commands execute.
10. The WIN.COM file executes.
11. The VMM32.VxD and any other virtual device drivers referenced in the registry or the SYSTEM.INI files load.
12. The core files (Kernel, USER, and GDI) files load. If any network support is installed, it loads.
13. Any applications located in the part of the registry labeled Hkey_Local_Machine\Software\Microsoft\Windows\CurrentVersion\RunOnce will load.

The Windows NT/2000 boot process is different from either DOS or Windows 9x. The NT boot process is listed below:

1. BIOS performs POST.
2. The Master Boot Record is located.
3. The Master Boot Record scans the partition table for a system partition.
4. NTLDR file loads from the root directory. A message appears stating "OS Loader V4.0."
5. NTLDR switches the processor to a 32-bit flat memory mode.
6. The BOOT.INI file is read and a menu appears with the available operating systems.
7. When NT is selected, NTLDR executes NTDETECT.COM.
8. NTDETECT.COM gathers hardware information. A message appears to "Press spacebar now to invoke Hardware Profile/Last Known Good menu."
9. If the spacebar is *not* pressed, NTLDR loads the NTOSKRNL.EXE file.
10. NTOSKRNL.EXE starts and a message similar to "Microsoft Windows NT Version 4.0 1 System Processor (128MB Memory) appears.
11. NTOSKRNL.EXE loads device drivers and services. An NT **service** is software loaded into memory that controls a process. Also, other applications and processes can use this service. Examples of services include printing, file sharing, and printer sharing. Specific services are selected and installed when

NT is installed for the first time. They also can be added after installation.

12. WINLOG.EXE executes and the Logon dialog window appears prompting to press *CTRL+ALT+DEL* to logon.

By knowing the boot process, a technician has a much better shot at locating the source of trouble. Troubleshooting begins in the section of the boot process where problems or error messages start occurring.

LOGICALLY TROUBLESHOOTING PREVIOUSLY INSTALLED DRIVES

The following are generic guidelines for hard drives that did work, but are now having problems.

1. Run a virus-checking program after booting from a virus-free boot disk. Many viruses are specifically designed to attack the hard drive.

2. Has someone recently added any new software or hardware? If so, be sure a device driver was not inserted into the CONFIG.SYS file that might conflict with the hard drive. Verify that there are no interrupt, I/O address, or ROM address conflicts if a new adapter was recently installed.

3. Has there been a recent cleaning of the computer or has someone recently removed the top from the computer? If so, check all cables and verify they correctly connect pin 1 to pin 1 of the adapter or motherboard. Push down firmly on all DIP chips on the hard drive adapter. Check the power connection to the hard drive.

4. Can you boot from a bootable floppy disk and see the hard drive when you type *C:* and press *Enter*? If so, type *A:* (press *Enter*). Make sure the floppy drive has FDISK on it. Type *FDISK* (press *Enter*). Press *4* for Display Partition Information. Does the partition look correct for this drive? Is there a partition marked as active? If not, return to the main partition menu and make the primary partition active. If the partition information looks unusual (not the way the drive was originally set up), escape from the FDISK program back to the A: prompt. Run a virus-checking program or a partition table repair utility. If you have DOS 6 or higher, type *FDISK /MBR* to fix the partition table. If you do not have DOS 6, use a hard drive utility such as Norton Disk Doctor or PC Tools to repair the partition information. Before running FDISK /MBR, back up the partition table using a special utility or the MIRROR /PARTN. This command places the partition table in a file called PARTNSAV.FIL. Copy the backup copy to a floppy. Use the UNFORMAT /PARTN command to restore the partition to the hard drive. Windows 95 users do not have UNFORMAT or MIRROR commands, so the partition table can only be backed up with third party utilities.

5. If the partition table is not the problem, but you can still boot from a floppy disk and see the hard drive, then the system files are the most likely suspects. Boot from a bootable floppy of the same DOS version as the version on the

hard drive. Make sure the floppy disk has SYS.COM on the disk. At the A: prompt, type *SYS C:* (press *Enter*). You will receive a message that the system files transferred. Another solution is to run a utility that repairs the DOS Boot Record. If the DOS version is lower than DOS 5, copy the COMMAND.COM file to the hard drive. Some lower DOS versions require COMMAND.COM be the first viewable file in the root directory. Sometimes on the older DOS versions, it is necessary to copy all of the files from the root directory into a temporary directory. Delete all files from the root directory, copy COMMAND.COM from the bootable floppy, and then copy the files in the temporary directory back into the root directory.

6. Place a hand on top of the drive as you turn on the computer. Does the drive spin at all? If not, the problem is probably a "sticky" drive or a bad drive. A hard drive must spin at a certain rpm before the heads move over the surface of the hard drive. To check if the drive is sticking, remove the drive and try spinning the spindle motor by hand. Otherwise, remove the drive, hold the drive in your hand, and give a quick jerk with your wrist. Another trick that works is to remove the hard drive from the case, place the drive in a plastic bag, and put in the freezer for a couple of hours. Then, remove the drive and allow the drive to warm up to room temperature. Reinstall the drive into the system and try it. As a *last resort*, try bopping the top of the hard drive with a heavy reference book such as a dictionary as the system powers on.

7. If the hard drive flashes quickly on boot up, the controller is trying to read the partition table in the Master Boot Record. If this information is not found, various symptoms can be shown, such as the error messages "Invalid Drive Specification, 0 drives found" or "0 drives ready." Sometimes, there are no error messages if there is a problem with the partition table. To solve this problem, run FDISK /MBR or use a hard drive utility to repair the partition table. Before running FDISK /MBR, make a backup of the partition table using a special utility or type *MIRROR /PARTN*. This command places the partition table in a file called PARTNSAV.FIL. Copy the backup copy to a floppy. Use the UNFORMAT /PARTN command to restore the partition to the hard drive. Windows 95 users do not have UNFORMAT or MIRROR commands, so the partition table can only be backed up with third party utilities.

8. Beware of hard drive software that creates a small partition for its use. These partitions require a special software driver that may be missing from the CONFIG.SYS file or is a corrupt file on the hard disk and needs to be reloaded.

9. Do you receive a message such as "Disk Boot Failure," "Non-System Disk," or "Disk Error"? These errors may indicate a boot record problem. The solution is to boot from a bootable floppy and transfer the hidden files with the SYS command (SYS C:). You may also use a hard disk utility such as Mace Utilities, Norton Utilities, or PC Tools to repair the boot record. With NT and 2000, use

the ERD to replace the system files. Also, verify the primary partition is marked as active.

10. Do you receive the message "Bad or Missing Command Interpreter"? If so, boot from a bootable floppy disk that is the *same* DOS version as the version on the hard drive. Copy COMMAND.COM to the hard drive.

11. Do you receive a message such as "File Allocation Table bad, drive C:"? If so, the FAT is most likely damaged. Type *R* for Retry when the "Abort or Retry?" message appears on the screen. Use a FAT repairer such as PC Tools or Norton Utilities.

12. If the error message "Error Reading Drive C:" appears, boot the computer from a virus-free bootable disk. Run a virus-scanning program on the hard drive. Also, run the DOS SCANDISK and DEFRAG programs. Another thing to try is re-creating the Master Boot Record. Boot off a bootable floppy that contains the FDISK command. Type *FDISK /MBR* to repair the boot record. Before running FDISK /MBR, make a backup of the partition table using a special utility or type *MIRROR /PARTN*. This command places the partition table in a file called PARTNSAV.FIL. Copy the backup copy to a floppy. Use the UNFORMAT /PARTN command to restore the partition to the hard drive. Windows 95 users do not have UNFORMAT or MIRROR commands, so the partition table can only be backed up with third party utilities.

13. Does Windows 95 show more hard drives than it should? If so, the drive configurations or partitions have been changed more than once. One solution is to disable any changes, create a new Hardware Profile, shut the computer down, restore the changes and reboot under the new hardware profile. Another solution, which is permanent, but riskier, is to use REGEDIT and edit the Registry. Be sure to make a backup of the Registry before trying this. Go to the section HKEY_LOCAL_MACHINE\SystemCurrentControlSet\Services\Class\hdc. Delete all the keys beneath it, but do not delete the hdc key.

14. Does the message "No Operating System Found" appear? If so, boot from a boot disk and type *C:*. If the system allows you to access the hard drive, type *DIR*. Do any files appear? If yes, the system files are missing and you must reinstall them. If no files appear, a virus is present or someone has accidentally formatted the drive. Use an unformat program or reinstall the operating system. If the system does not allow you to access the C: drive, boot from a bootable floppy that contains the FDISK program. Type *FDISK /MBR* to repair the partition table. If this does not fix it, type *FDISK* to see if the drive is visible to the system. If it is, use an unformat program or reinstall Windows. If the system does not see the hard drive, check the hard drive cables and power connectors. Check to see if the BIOS is configured properly for the drive. If all looks good, there is a hardware problem (hard drive, cables, or controller).

15. Does either error message "Write fault error writing drive C" or "A serious disk error has occurred while writing to drive C" appear? If so, check to see if

there is a BIOS setting which write protects the boot sector.

16. Sometimes when creating a dual-boot or when running a disk management utility, the NT boot sector is overwritten. If NT or 2000 fails to boot, use the ERD to restore the system files or re-create the BOOT.INI file.

17. If an error message appears stating that a drive/folder is inaccessible, a file/folder/directory is corrupt, or a file/directory/folder is unreadable, the FAT could be damaged. Use the CHKDSK program or a third party utility.

18. If Windows 2000 does not allow you to convert a FAT32 partition to NTFS and the drive is larger that 20GB, obtain a Windows 2000 service pack from Microsoft.

19. If you get an error message stating that the operating system is missing, the problem is most likely the MBR or partition table. Check the hard drive for a virus. Check and see if the BIOS settings have been changed or are lost because of a dead or weak battery. Boot to a command prompt and run the FDISK / MBR program to repair that Master Boot Record. Use a third party utility to check the MBR and partition table.

20. If you receive the message "Invalid Drive Specification," the partition table has been damaged or the drive has not been partitioned yet.

21. If you receive the message "Invalid Media Type," the FAT is corrupt, a volume boot record is corrupt, or the drive has not been formatted yet. Use a disk utility to check the drive or format the drive (if unformatted).

22. If you receive the error message "Hard Disk Controller Failure," do not assume that the motherboard/adapter is faulty. Check BIOS settings. A weak or dead battery can cause the information in CMOS to be wrong or missing. Check hard drive cabling and power. Use another power cable. This error can also be caused by a faulty hard drive, faulty cable(s), a bad adapter, or a faulty motherboard.

23. When Windows 2000 has startup problems, the ERD, Recovery Console, and the Advanced Options menu are used. Many times startup problems are due to a virus. The AVBoot disk can be used to check the computer for a virus. Other utilities that help with MBR, boot sector, and system files are FIXBOOT, FIXMBR, System File Checker, and the Advanced Options menu. To use FIXBOOT, type *FIXBOOT x:* command where *x:* is the drive letter of the volume that has the problem. To use FIXMBR, type *FIXMBR* from a command prompt. Both the FIXBOOT and FIXMBR commands are covered in the Recovery Console section later in the chapter. The System File Checker program can be run from the Run dialog box by typing *x:\WINNT\SYSTEM32\SFC.EXE /scannow* where *x:* is the drive letter of the drive on which 2000 is installed. Indications that there is a problem with the Master Boot Record or the system files are as follows: "Invalid partition table," "Error loading operating system," "Missing operating system," "A disk read error has occurred," "NTLDR is missing," or "NTLDR is corrupt."

When Windows 2000 has startup problems due to incompatible hardware or software, or a corrupted installation process, the Windows 2000 Advanced Options menu can help. This option can be selected by pressing the *F8* key when the *For troubleshooting and advanced startup options for Windows 2000, press F8* message appears on the screen during the boot process.

ST506 SPECIFIC ERRORS

1. If an error Code 80 appears during the low-level format routine, the drive select jumpers are set wrong.
2. If an error Code 20 or 40 appears during the low-level format routine, check the cable connections. Verify that the 34-pin hard drive cable is not a floppy control cable.
3. If on an 8088 (PC or XT) computer, the hard drive light is always on, check the cables.
4. A 1790 POST error generally indicates an unformatted hard drive.

ST506 hard drives normally give 17XX POST error codes. Refer to the Logical Troubleshooting chapter for the specifics on these error codes.

ESDI SPECIFIC ERRORS

ESDI hard drives normally give 104XX POST error codes. Refer to the Logical Troubleshooting chapter for the specifics on these error codes.

IDE/EIDE SPECIFIC ERRORS

1. Has an IDE hard drive recently been installed and now the floppy drive does not work so the hard drive cannot be configured? Verify that the IDE drive is not connected to the floppy connector on the adapter or motherboard. Make sure that the IDE cable pin 1 connects to the drive pin 1 and the adapter or motherboard pin 1.
2. If the second slave IDE hard drive does not work, check if the first IDE hard drive is older. If so, check the documentation of the first IDE hard drive and be sure it can operate with a slave drive present. Some older IDE hard drives will not work in a two-drive system.
3. If you have to keep running a utility to repair the partition table on an IDE/EIDE hard drive, the CMOS Setup is most likely set to a drive type with greater values than the drive or values the drive does not support. Back up the data and try another drive type in CMOS Setup. The data must be reinstalled after the change.

SCSI SPECIFIC ERRORS

SCSI POST error codes are quite extensive and sometimes difficult to read. Refer to the Logical Troubleshooting chapter for error code specifics, including the 210XX SCSI error codes.

1. If the BIOS on the SCSI adapter initializes, but the drive does not boot, check for an interrupt, I/O address, DMA channel conflict, or a termination problem.
2. If the SCSI adapter sees seven hard drives when only one drive is attached, check the SCSI ID on the hard drive.
3. If the computer boots up and the SCSI ROM message does not appear on a system where the SCSI adapter has the BIOS enabled, check the adapter for a memory address conflict between the adapter's ROM chip and other ROM chips in the system.
4. If the system is booting and the "No SCSI Device Found" error message appears, check the SCSI adapter for a ROM address conflict. Set the hard drive type to None, 0, or Not Installed in the CMOS Setup. Check the SCSI cables, SCSI IDs, and termination. Check the power connection to the SCSI device. Check the SCSI hard drive documentation to see if the parity jumper on the hard drive needs to be enabled or disabled.

AUTOEXEC.BAT AND CONFIG.SYS ERRORS

People are frequently baffled by errors that occur during the boot process and often call technicians with the complaint that their hard drive is bad. The best way to be sure that the problem is not an AUTOEXEC.BAT or CONFIG.SYS problem is to step through the AUTOEXEC.BAT and CONFIG.SYS files one command or one driver at a time. DOS 6 allows this by pressing the *F8* key when the message "Starting PC DOS" or "Starting MS DOS" appears on the screen. On older versions of DOS, one must "REM out" problem lines individually to find conflicts. (A REMed out line will be treated as a remark and not executed.) For Windows 95-based computers, press the *F8* key when the message "Starting Windows 95" appears on the screen. From the menu that appears, select the option for *step-by-step confirmation.* For Windows 98 computers, hold the *CTRL* key down during the boot process. If this does not work, press the *F8* key while booting.

NT's command prompt is accessed in any of the following ways:

-   Click on the *Start* button, point to *Programs,* and click on the *Command Prompt* option.
-   Click on the *Start* button, click on the *Run* option, type in *cmd* in the dialog box, and click on the *OK* button.
-   Click on the *Start* button, click on the *Run* option, type in *command* in the dialog box, and click on the *OK* button.

For Windows 2000, the options you can use are as follows:

- Click on *Start* button, click on the *Run* option, and type *command* in the dialog box.
- Click on *Start* button, point to the *Programs* option, point to the *Accessories* option, and click on the *Command* prompt option.
- Click on the *Start* button, click on the *Run* option, and type *cmd* in the dialog box.

PREVENTIVE MAINTENANCE FOR HARD DRIVES

Keeping the computer system in a clean and cool operating environment extends the life of a hard drive. Performing preventive maintenance on the entire computer is good for all components found inside the computer, including the hard drive subsystem.

A program called CHKDSK locates clusters disassociated from data files. These disk clusters occupy disk space. When CHKDSK executes and reports there are **lost clusters**, this means the FAT cannot determine to which file or directory these clusters belong. Typing *CHKDSK /F,* saves lost clusters and gives them filenames in the root directory, beginning with FILE0000.CHK. These .CHK files can sometimes, but not very often, be recovered.

A better program for detecting and repairing lost clusters is the **SCANDISK** program included with DOS 6 and Windows 9x. NT and 2000 do not include the SCANDISK program, but to check the hard drive's integrity follow the procedures outlined below:

1. Double-click on the *My Computer* desktop icon and right-click on the appropriate hard drive icon.
2. Click on the *Properties* option and select *Tools*.
3. In the Error-checking section, click on the *Check Now* option.

Exercises at the end of this chapter demonstrate the procedures for running both the CHKDSK and the SCANDISK programs.

Windows 2000 has a new program called **Disk Cleanup** that removes temporary files, removes offline Internet files, empties the Recycle Bin, compresses unused files, removes unused programs, and prompts you before doing any of this. To access Disk Cleanup use the following procedures:

1. Access a command prompt and type *CLEANMGR* and press *Enter* or click on the *Start* button, point to *Programs*, *Accessories*, *System Tools*, and click on the *Disk Cleanup* option.
2. Select the drive letter and click on the *OK* button.
3. On the Disk Cleanup tab, click in the checkboxes for the options desired and click on the *OK* button.

HARD DRIVE FRAGMENTATION

Over time, as files are added to a hard drive, the files will be come fragmented. **Fragmentation** means the clusters that make up the file are not adjacent to one another. Fragmentation slows down the hard drive in two ways: (1) the FAT has to keep track of scattered clusters and (2) the hard drive read/write head assembly must move to different locations on the drive's surface to access a single file. Hard Figure #29 illustrates fragmentation.

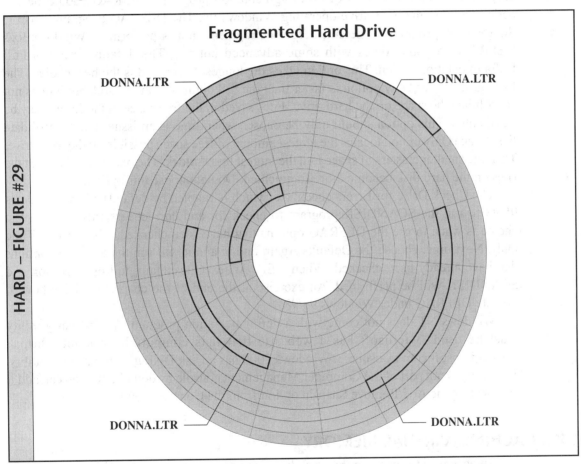

HARD – FIGURE #29

Defragmentation is the process of placing files in contiguous sectors. Some operating systems include a program that defragments the hard drive. This program places the file clusters in adjacent sectors. Defragmenting the hard drive makes for faster hard disk access. These measures also extend the life of the hard drive because the drive's mechanical movements are reduced.

Defragment and re-order the files periodically on a hard drive. Users who delete files often and have large files that are constantly revised should run these utilities more often. A hard drive running DOS should be defragmented frequently depending on how often files are deleted and how much hard drive space is available. At a minimum, a hard drive should be defragmented once a month.

Even though fragmentation under Windows 9x is less a problem than under DOS, Windows 9x comes with its own defragmentation program. DEFRAG should be run periodically on the hard drive operating Windows 9x. The DEFRAG program runs the SCANDISK program by default before defragmentation is performed. Windows 9x's DEFRAG program comes with some advanced options. The default option is Full Defragmentation option. This option takes the longest to run and is the best choice. The Defragment Files Only option is faster than the full optimization method, but it does not consolidate the space on the hard drive. Files saved in the free space in the future may be fragmented. This option should only be chosen when time is an issue. The Consolidate Free Space Only option locates the largest amount of free space possible on the hard drive. Then the smaller clusters of space join the largest found block. The result could be that the files on the hard disk become more fragmented. Do not choose this option.

The Check Drive for Errors checkbox (which is enabled by default) allows Windows 95/98 to run the SCANDISK program to check for and correct lost clusters. The last choice is when to use the DEFRAG options that have been checked. Choose This Time Only. Next time, choose the Defaults Again option and it will run the advanced options that have already been checked. When DEFRAG executes again, full optimization and SCANDISK will be performed. An exercise at the end of the chapter explains how to execute DEFRAG under Windows 95/98.

Windows NT does not come with a defragmentation program. A third-party utility must be used. Microsoft has a web site that lists compatible products: http://www.microsoft.com/infosource. Windows 2000 has a Disk Defragmenter snap-in utility. The utility is not part of the Computer Management console by default, but you can add it by selecting the Add/Remove Snap-in option from the Console menu.

DISK CACHING/VIRTUAL MEMORY

An easy way to speed up the hard drive is to create a **disk cache**. This puts data into RAM where it can be retrieved much faster than if the data is still on the hard drive. When data is read from the hard drive, the next requested data is frequently located in the adjacent clusters. Disk caching reads more data from the hard drive than requested. The data is placed in a reserved portion of RAM called the cache. Cache on a hard drive controller, sometimes called a data buffer, allows the read/write heads to read more than just one sector at a time. A hard drive can read up to an entire track of information and hold this data until needed without returning to the hard drive for each sector.

The BUFFERS statement in the CONFIG.SYS (now in the IO.SYS) file is a very rudimentary caching program used in prior years to cache file transfers. The BUFFERS command provides a small amount of RAM for transferring files from one device to another, such as from the floppy drive to the hard drive or from memory to the floppy drive.

With Windows 9x, SmartDrive is used, but once Windows 9x loads, it uses a disk caching program called VCACHE that also uses read-ahead and write-behind caching by default for hard drives. The Windows 9x **VCACHE** program caches the hard drive and uses a separate cache for CD-ROMs. Instead of being a set size as in DOS and Windows, Windows 9x's disk cache is dynamic. The cache grows or shrinks according to the needs of the system. The VCACHE program works with fragmented sectors on the hard drive as well as with continuous sectors. As with any hard drive or any operating system, defragmented hard drives work faster and more efficiently.

Any settings for the SHARE or SmartDrive programs must be removed from the AUTOEXEC.BAT file. Any entries for SmartDrive that are in the CONFIG.SYS file also must be removed. Windows 95/98 no longer uses these programs to handle the caching for the disk drive. If a lot of disk activity is going on, the cache will shrink automatically for optimum performance. However, if the amount of disk activity is constant to the point where the system's performance is extremely slow, check if the hard disk is using a driver made for the DOS/Windows environment. If so, contact the hard drive manufacturer to obtain a Windows 95/98 driver.

Windows 98/NT/2000 have a more efficient memory management through VMM (Virtual Memory Manager). Virtual memory is a method of using hard disk space as if it were RAM. The disk cache is dynamic—it increases or decreases the cache size as needed. If the system begins to page (constantly swapping data from RAM to the hard drive), the cache size automatically shrinks.

If multiple hard drives are available, a technician might want to move the swap file to a different drive. Always put the swap file size on the fastest hard drive unless that hard drive lacks space. NT and 2000 Professional allow you to have the swap file on multiple hard drives. It is best to keep the swap file on a hard drive that does not contain the operating system.

In Windows 9x, to adjust the virtual memory swap file size, perform the following steps:

1. Open *Control Panel*.
2. Double-click on the *System* control panel icon.
3. Click the *Performance* tab.
4. Click the *Virtual Memory* button.
5. Click the *Let me specify my own virtual memory settings* option.
6. Click the *down arrow* in the area to the right of the *Hard disk* option.
7. Choose a different hard drive from the list.
8. Click *OK*. The settings for the minimum and maximum size of the swap file can also be changed.

In NT, to adjust the virtual memory size:

1. Open *Control Panel*.
2. Double-click on the *System* control panel icon.
3. Click on the *Performance* tab.
4. Click on the *Change* button.
5. In the area designated as *Paging File Size for Selected Drive*, change the size parameters.
6. Click on the *OK* button.

In 2000 Professional, to adjust the virtual memory size:

1. Open *Control Panel*.
2. Double-click on the *System* control panel icon.
3. Click on the *Advanced* tab.
4. Click on the *Performance Options* button.
5. Click on the *Change* button.
6. Change the size parameters and click on the *OK* button.

Windows 98, NT, and 2000 Professional use virtual memory differently than Windows 3.x. With Windows 3.x, memory is divided into different sized segments each up to 64KB. Windows 98/NT/2000 use 32-bit demand-paged virtual memory and each process gets 4GB of address space divided into two 2GB sections. One 2GB section is shared with the rest of the system while the other 2GB section is reserved for the one application. All the memory space is divided into 4KB blocks of memory called "pages." The operating system allocates as much available RAM as possible to an application. Then, the operating system swaps or pages the application to and from the temporary swap file as needed. The operating system determines the optimum setting for this swap file; however, the swap file size can be changed.

The rest of the chapter is devoted to questions and exercises to help with all hard drive concepts. Good luck on them!

 Name _____

HARD DRIVE REVIEW QUESTIONS

1. What is the difference between a floppy drive and a hard drive?

2. How many surfaces are on a hard drive platter?

3. How many read/write heads are normally used with each hard drive platter?

4. What is the difference between a track and a cylinder?

Use Hard Exercise Figure #1 for Questions 5–9:

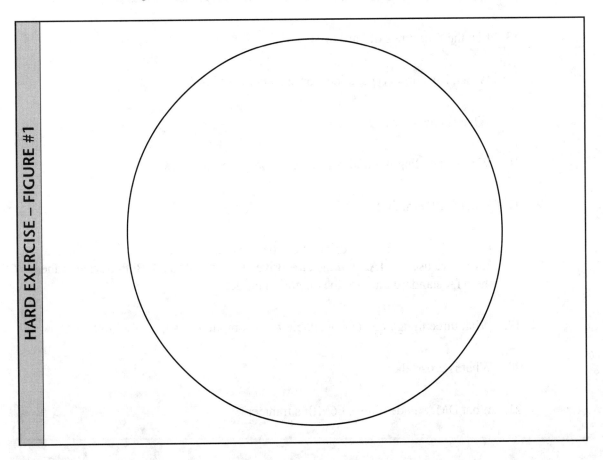

HARD EXERCISE – FIGURE #1

5. Draw and label Track 0.

6. Draw and label a Track 90.

7. Draw and label a Track 600.

8. Draw at least 9 sectors.

9. Shade in Track 90, Sector 3.

10. What is another name for zone bit recording?

11. Whavois interleaving?

12. What interleave ratio is most common with today's hard drives?

13. List the four types of hard drives.

14. Which hard drive type is the slowest and the oldest?

15. What is encoding?

16. Which encoding method is used with today's hard drives?

17. What is PIO mode 5?

18. [T / F] An IDE hard drive and tape drive are connected to an IDE cable. The hard drive uses DMA2 and the tape drive uses PIO Mode 3. Both devices adhere to the ATA standard and use the operation modes.

19. What three things must be available for a computer to support Ultra DMA?

20. What is crosstalk?

21. What DMA mode allows 66MBps transfers?

22. How is the Ultra ATA/66 cable different from older IDE cables?

23. What is the minimum UDMA mode that requires the 80-conductor IDE cable?

24. Describe how to determine if an operating system supports DMA transfers.

25. How many IDE connectors are standard on motherboards?

26. Which hard drive type has the ability to daisy chain multiple devices using the same controller?

27. What SCSI standard has a maximum data transfer rate of 80MBps?

28. What SCSI standard is associated with the term *Ultra*?

29. What are the three steps to configuring an ST506 or an ESDI hard drive?

30. How many cables connect to an ST506 drive? List them.

31. [T / F]   The connector closest to the twist on the ST506 34-pin cable connects directly to the controller.

32. [T / F]   When two IDE devices connect to the same cable, only one device transmits at a time.

33. Describe the difference between primary master and secondary master.

34. [T / F]   IDE hard drives are normally the fastest type of IDE device.

35. [T / F]   When only one device connects to an IDE cable, configure that device as master and attach the device to the center connector for optimum performance.

36. Explain why it is best not to mix IDE devices that use different operation modes.

37. Describe how to configure two IDE devices using cable select.

38. List the three criteria for using cable select.

39. Explain what happens if two devices are set to cable select and connected to a 40-conductor IDE cable.

40. [T / F]   IDE hard drives are used in laptops.

41. Explain how to add a second hard drive in a portable computer.

42. List three things to consider when adding a SCSI hard drive.

43. What is a SCSI chain?

44. Why must external SCSI devices be powered on before the computer is turned on?

45. List at least two reasons why you should be careful in choosing the SCSI ID for a SCSI device.

46. What is the highest priority SCSI ID?

47. What SCSI ID is normally assigned to the SCSI adapter?

48. What SCSI ID is normally assigned to a bootable hard drive?

49. One SCSI device has ID 4 and another device on the same bus has SCSI ID 14. Which device has the highest priority?

50. List one reason why installing or removing terminators on a SCSI hard drive is important.

51. [T / F]   A SCSI chain uses termination for proper operation.

52. List the three categories of terminators.

53. What types of devices require active terminators?

54. [T / F]   Passive and active terminators can be used on the same SCSI chain.

55. [T / F]   An HVD device can use a LVD/HVD terminator otherwise known as a differential terminator.

56. Which type of terminator is backward compatible with SE signaling?
     [HVD / LVD / Differential / PSST]

57. What SCSI standard defined LVD?

58. What are the two types of terminators used with LVD devices?

59. Explain when to use a SCSI segment.

60. A host adapter supports two SCSI segments. On one segment are LVD devices configured as SCSI IDs 14, 2, and 8. On the second SCSI segment are SE devices configured for SCSI IDs 6, 5, and 2. Are these configurations valid? Why or why not?

61. Describe how host adapters that support multiple SCSI channels are helpful to technicians.

62. Draw the SCSI symbol for SE.

63. If a SCSI adapter attaches to two internal hard drives, where do you install the terminators?

64. If a SCSI adapter attaches to an internal hard drive and an external tape drive, where do you install the terminators?

65. What is the significance, if any, of an external SCSI device with only one connector on the back of the device?
     A. No significance
     B. A pass through terminator must be used.
     C. The device should be taken out of the external casing and installed internally.
     D. The device should be the first device on the chain because it is internally terminated (permanently).

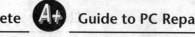

66. What is a *hard drive type* that must be entered into a computer's CMOS Setup program and why is it important this number is accurate?

67. What is the most common BIOS setting for IDE hard drives?

68. What is the purpose of the Block mode IDE BIOS setting?

69. What does a low-level format do to a hard drive?

70. What DOS program is used to low-level format some ST506 hard drives?

71. What does partitioning the hard drive mean?

72. What program is used with NT/2000 to partition the drive once the operating system is installed?

73. List three file systems.

74. [T / F]   FAT32 supports disk compression.

75. List two differences between NTFS and NTFS5.

76. What is the maximum partition size for NTFS/NTFS5?

77. [T / F]   All pre-existing NTFS partitions are automatically upgraded to NTFS5 when Windows 2000 is installed.

78. Why should you partition a 16.2GB hard drive?

79. How many logical drives can an extended partition have?

80. In Windows 98, a single hard drive has one primary partition and two logical drives in the extended partition. What drive letter is assigned to the second logical drive?

81. In NT, a system has two installed hard drives. The first drive has a primary partition and one logical drive in the extended partition. The second hard drive has a primary partition. What drive letter is assigned to the second drive's primary partition?

82. When using Windows 95, a system has two installed hard drives. The first drive has a primary partition and two logical drives in the extended partition. The second drive has a primary partition and one logical drive in the extended partition. What drive letter is assigned to the logical drive on the second hard drive?

83. A Windows 98 system has two installed hard drives. The first drive has a primary partition and one logical drive in the extended partition. The second hard drive has an extended partition and one logical drive. What is the drive letter assigned to the second hard drive's logical drive?

84. [T / F] Removable media can be partitioned under Windows 2000.

85. Explain the difference between spanned and striped volumes.

86. What command is used to high-level format a hard drive?

87. What web site allows creating a boot disk for various operating systems?

88. Describe the process used to create a Windows 95/98 boot disk.

89. What type of virus spreads to other computers via the Internet?

90. List three things to check if a hard drive has recently been installed and it does not work properly.

91. When powering on a computer, you notice the hard drive does not spin at all. What will you check?

92. Upon powering up a computer system, you receive a "Drive Not Ready" error message. What are you going to do?

93. A system with an IDE hard drive and a SCSI hard drive will not boot from the SCSI hard drive. What are you going to do?

94. List the boot process if Windows 95 is loaded on a bootable hard drive.

95. List the boot process if Windows NT is loaded on a bootable hard drive.

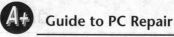
96. Lists three things to check when a working hard drive quits.

97. Upon powering on a computer, you receive a "Bad or Missing Command Interpreter" error message. What are you going to do?

98. What three things help with Windows 2000 boot problems?

Use Hard Exercise Figure #2 for Questions 99–101:

HARD EXERCISE – FIGURE #2

Advertisement for a computer:

Intel Pentium III 400MHz
256MB memory
18.0GB hard drive
8x8x32 CD-RW
Diamond Stealth 3D Graphic with 16MB
17" monitor
56K modem
MS mouse
Creative Lab SB64 sound card

99. If you were to buy a second hard drive just like the one listed in Figure #2, which of the three steps required to set up a hard drive would be done by the manufacturer?

100. If you were to buy a second hard drive just like the one shown in Figure #2, what two processes must you perform to set up the hard drive?

101. If you were to build a system like this and assuming the hard drive and CD-RW are IDE devices, how would you connect them to the hard drive (which connectors and what settings on each device)?

 Name _____

HARD DRIVE FILL-IN-THE-BLANK

1. The hard drive system consists of _____, _____, _____, and, as an option, _____.

2. One hard disk metal plate is called a _____.

3. The _____ are the part of the hard drive that actually transmit or receive the 1s and 0s to or from the hard drive.

4. The _____ is a part of the hard drive that holds the read/write heads.

5. One concentric circle on one surface of a hard drive platter is known as a _____.

6. One particular track on each and every platter collectively is known as a _____.

7. A _____ is the smallest division on a hard drive surface. Tracks are divided into these.

8. _____ allows more sectors on the drive by placing more sectors on the outer tracks than on the inner tracks.

9. An _____ hard drive is common in today's computers and cheaper than SCSI hard drives.

10. The ATA standard is associated with the _____ interface.

11. Two methods used to transfer data between IDE hard drives and RAM are _____ and _____.

12. Of the two methods listed in Question 11, the _____ mode is faster.

13. Another name for busmaster DMA is _____.

14. _____ is hard drive intelligence software used for error reporting.

15. The proposed _____ standard allows hard drives to expand to 144PB.

16. A _____ hard drive is used in network servers and whenever expandability (adding devices that do not necessarily have to be hard drives) is an issue.

17. Another name for a SCSI bus is a _____.

18. The three SCSI software standards are _____, _____, and _____.

19. Hard drives receive one or more drive letters from the operating system and they normally start with the drive letter _____.

20. IDE drives are set up using the _____ setting instead of drive select jumpers.

21. The four most common IDE jumper settings for hard drives are _____, _____, _____, and _____.

22. An internal IDE Zip drive normally comes preset to the _____ setting.

23. The primary IDE motherboard connection normally uses I/O address _____ and IRQ _____.

24. The IDE cable's maximum specified length is _____ inches.

25. The middle cable select connector (slave setting) is the color _____ according to the specification.

26. Another name for a SCSI controller is _____.

27. A number assigned to a SCSI device that determines the device's priority on the SCSI bus is the _____.

28. Standard SCSI devices can use SCSI IDs _____ through _____; 16-bit SCSI devices can use SCSI IDs _____ through _____.

29. The _____ terminator is the most common type.

30. The two types of SE terminators are _____ and _____.

31. An _____ terminator is not very popular, but is used on a few SCSI-2 devices.

32. A _____ divides the SCSI bus into two parts.

33. The [SCSI symbol] SCSI symbol designates a _____ device, terminator, or cable.

34. _____ is a term that means connecting SCSI devices together.

35. The two most common SCSI cables are _____ and _____.

36. The _____ interface is named after the BIOS interrupt that handles communication with the hard drive and causes drives to have a 504MB limitation.

37. A BIOS chip that supports hard drives larger than 504MB is known as a _____ BIOS.

38. The _____ BIOS setting allows two 16-bit IDE data transfers to occur simultaneously.

39. The step in preparing the hard drive that assigns drive letters to the hard drive is known as _____.

40. _____ is the command used to partition the hard drive.

41. Windows 2000 supports the _____, _____, and _____ file systems.

42. The _____ command changes a FAT partition to NTFS.

43. Windows 98 uses either the _____ or _____ file system

44. A _____ is the minimum amount of space a file occupies; the number of sectors for each one is determined by the size of the partition.

45. Only one _____ exists which is the first partition created on a hard drive.

46. When partitioning a hard drive, there can be only one primary partition and one _____, but within this section, multiple logical drives can be created.

47. An extended partition holds _____ drives.

48. The _____ is where the hard drive's partition information is kept.

49. The very first sector on a hard drive is called the _____.

50. The Windows 20000 partition that holds the majority of the operating system files is called the _____ partition.

51. The first detected hard drive is normally assigned the drive letter _____.

52. The two types of storage defined by 2000's Logical Disk Management tool are _____ and _____.

53. A _____ volume uses a minimum of three hard drives.

54. The _____ process sets up the file system.

55. The _____ is like the table of contents for a hard drive using DOS; at least two are on every hard drive.

56. A hard drive that contains system files and is used to load software when the computer is turned on is known as a _____ hard drive.

57. The _____ are COMMAND.COM, MSDOS.SYS, and IO.SYS on Microsoft DOS machines.

58. The _____ contains the system files.

59. To fix a partition table using DOS 6 or higher, type _____.

60. To transfer system files from a bootable floppy to the hard drive, type _____ from the A:\> prompt.

61. A _____ virus infects the MBR.

62. The NT/2000 _____ file is used to display multiple operating system boot options.

63. The _____ program detects and repairs lost clusters.

64. File _____ occurs when a file is located on non-consecutive clusters.

65. The _____ program places files in contiguous (adjacent) sectors.

66. A disk _____ speeds up hard drive data access.

Name _____

CONFIGURATION AND CABLING OF ST506 HARD DRIVES
PAPER EXERCISE

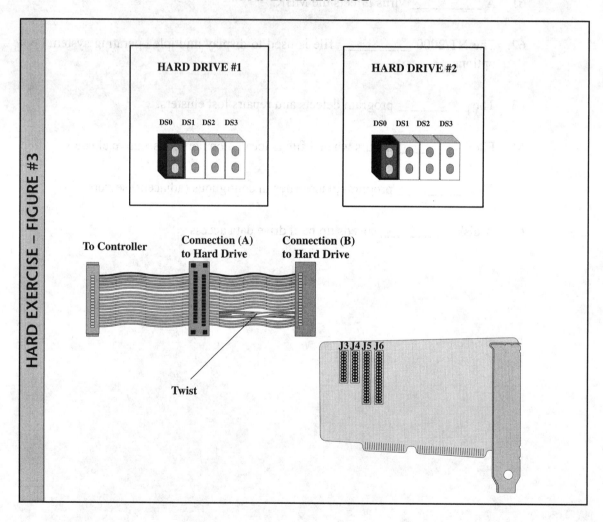

Look at Hard Exercise Figure #3 for Questions 1–9:

Question 1: Assume the hard drives shown in Hard Exercise Figure #3 will be installed in the same computer using a twisted cable like the one shown. Hard Drive #1 is to be the C: drive. Both drives have the drive select jumper set to the first position. Which drive select [DS0 / DS1 / DS2 / DS3] will be chosen for Hard Drive #1?

Question 2: Hard Drive #2 will become the D: drive. Which drive select [DS0 / DS1 / DS2 / DS3] will you choose for Hard Drive #2?

Question 3: To which cable connector will the C: drive be connected ?
[Connector A / Connector B]

Question 4: Hard Drives #1 and #2 come with a terminator installed. What will be done about the terminators?

    A. Leave both terminators installed.
    B. Remove both terminators.
    C. Install the terminator on the drive connected to the B connection and remove the terminator on the drive connected to the A connection.

Question 5: Assuming that a controller card and cable like the ones shown in Hard Drive Exercise Figure #3 are used, which connector [J3 / J4 / J5 / J6] connects to the end of the cable labeled "To controller"?

Question 6: What is the specific purpose of the 34-pin cable shown in Hard Drive Exercise Figure #3?

Question 7: The ST506 hard drive normally comes with two cables: one like that shown in Hard Exercise Figure #3 and a 20-pin cable. What is the purpose of the 20-pin cable that connects to the hard drive?

Question 8: To which connector [J3 / J4 / J5 / J6] will Hard Drive #1's (the C: drive) 20-pin cable connect?

Question 9: To which connector [J3 / J4 / J5 / J6] will Hard Drive #2's (the D: drive) 20-pin cable connect?

Question 10: Which hard drive type improved on ST-506 by allowing the heads to move directly to a cylinder instead of moving one cylinder at a time?

    A. ESDI
    B. IDE
    C. SCSI

Name _____

CONFIGURATION AND CABLING OF IDE HARD DRIVES
PAPER EXERCISE

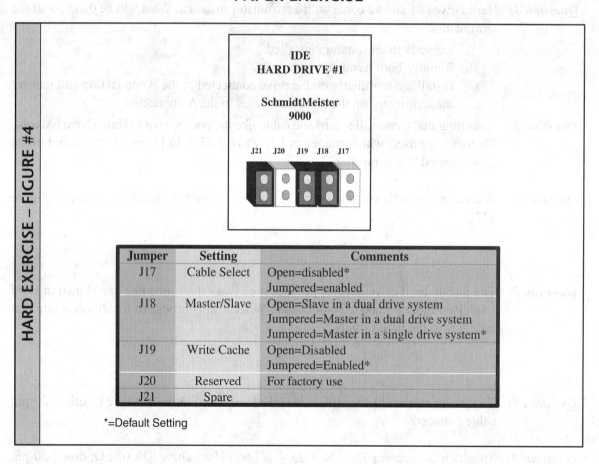

HARD EXERCISE – FIGURE #4

IDE HARD DRIVE #1

SchmidtMeister
9000

J21   J20   J19   J18   J17

Jumper	Setting	Comments
J17	Cable Select	Open=disabled* Jumpered=enabled
J18	Master/Slave	Open=Slave in a dual drive system Jumpered=Master in a dual drive system Jumpered=Master in a single drive system*
J19	Write Cache	Open=Disabled Jumpered=Enabled*
J20	Reserved	For factory use
J21	Spare	

*=Default Setting

See Hard Exercise Figure #4 for Question 1:

Question 1: Using the drawing below, circle the jumpers to be enabled (set) to configure IDE Hard Drive #1 as if it is the only drive connected to an IDE port.

J21   J20   J19   J18   J17

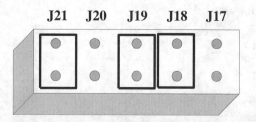

Look at Hard Exercise Figure #5 for Questions 2 and 3:

HARD EXERCISE – FIGURE #5

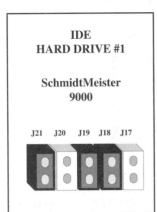

Jumper	Setting	Comments
J17	Cable Select	Open=disabled* Jumpered=enabled
J18	Master/Slave	Open=Slave in a dual drive system Jumpered=Master in a dual drive system Jumpered=Master in a single drive system*
J19	Write Cache	Open=Disabled Jumpered=Enabled*
J20	Reserved	For factory use
J21	Spare	

*=Default Setting

Question 2:   Using the drawing below, circle the jumpers to be enabled (set) to configure IDE Hard Drive #1 as the master drive connected to an IDE port. Keep in mind that IDE Hard Drive #2 shares the same cable with Hard Drive #1.

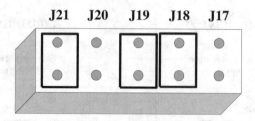

IDE Hard Drive #1

Question 3:   Using the drawing below, circle the jumpers to be enabled (set) to configure IDE Hard Drive #2 as the slave drive. Keep in mind that IDE Hard Drive #2 shares the same cable with Hard Drive #1.

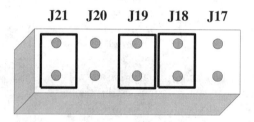

IDE Hard Drive #2

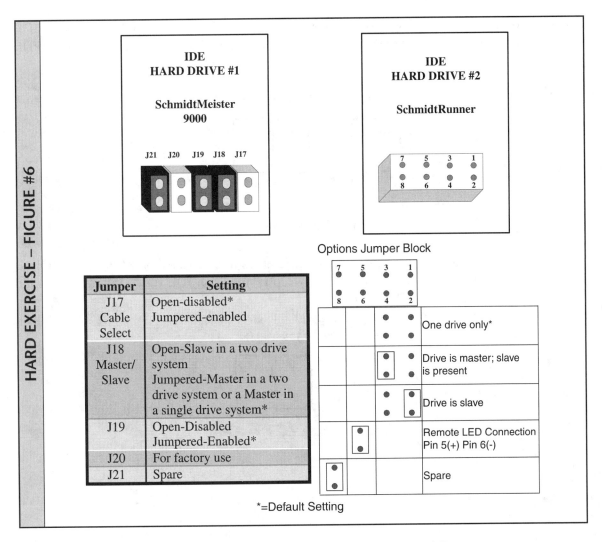

HARD EXERCISE – FIGURE #6

IDE
HARD DRIVE #1

SchmidtMeister
9000

J21 J20 J19 J18 J17

IDE
HARD DRIVE #2

SchmidtRunner

7 5 3 1
8 6 4 2

Options Jumper Block

7 5 3 1
8 6 4 2

Jumper	Setting
J17 Cable Select	Open-disabled* Jumpered-enabled
J18 Master/ Slave	Open-Slave in a two drive system Jumpered-Master in a two drive system or a Master in a single drive system*
J19	Open-Disabled Jumpered-Enabled*
J20	For factory use
J21	Spare

One drive only*

Drive is master; slave is present

Drive is slave

Remote LED Connection Pin 5(+) Pin 6(-)

Spare

*=Default Setting

Hard Exercise Figure #6 is needed when answering Questions 4 and 5:

Question 4:   Using the drawing below, circle the jumpers to be enabled (set) to configure IDE Hard Drive #1 as the master drive connected to an IDE port. Keep in mind that IDE Hard Drive #2 shares the same cable with Hard Drive #1.

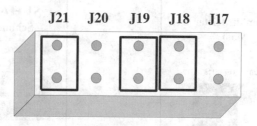

J21   J20   J19   J18   J17

IDE Hard Drive #1

Question 5:   Using the drawing below, circle the jumpers to be enabled or set to configure IDE Hard Drive #2 as the slave drive. Keep in mind that IDE Hard Drive #2 shares the same cable with Hard Drive #1.

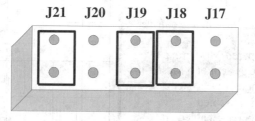

J21   J20   J19   J18   J17

IDE Hard Drive #2

Name _____

CONFIGURATION AND CABLING OF SCSI HARD DRIVES
PAPER EXERCISE

HARD EXERCISE – FIGURE #7

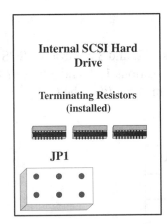

Internal SCSI Hard Drive

Terminating Resistors (installed)

JP1

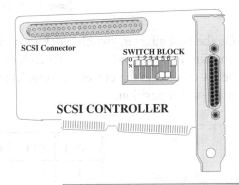

SCSI Connector

SWITCH BLOCK
0 1 2 3 4 5 6 7

SCSI CONTROLLER

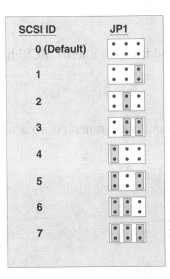

SCSI ID	JP1
0 (Default)	
1	
2	
3	
4	
5	
6	
7	

SCSI ID	Switch Block Positions		
	1	2	3
0	0	0	0
1	0	0	1
2	0	1	0
3	0	1	1
4	1	0	0
5	1	0	1
6	1	1	0
7 (Default)	1	1	1

Setting	Switch Block Position 7
Terminated	1 (Default)
Not terminated	0

1=ON
0=OFF

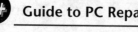
Look at Hard Exercise Figure #7 to answer Questions 1–4:

Question 1: Hard Exercise Figure #7 shows a SCSI controller that handles internal and external SCSI devices. In this configuration, install one internal hard drive that boots the computer. To what position(s) will JP1 be set on the internal hard drive? Circle the correct jumper setting(s) for JP1.

JP1

Question 2: On the host adapter, switch block positions 1, 2, and 3 control the SCSI ID. To what position will the controller's switch block positions 1, 2, and 3 be set? Use the chart below and fill in the correct setting. Mark an X in *either* the OFF or ON column for each switch position.

SW1	OFF	ON
1		
2		
3		

Question 3: Will the terminators be installed or removed from the internal SCSI hard drive?

Question 4: The host adapter's switch block position 7 controls termination. To what position (ON or OFF) will switch 1 position 7 be set?

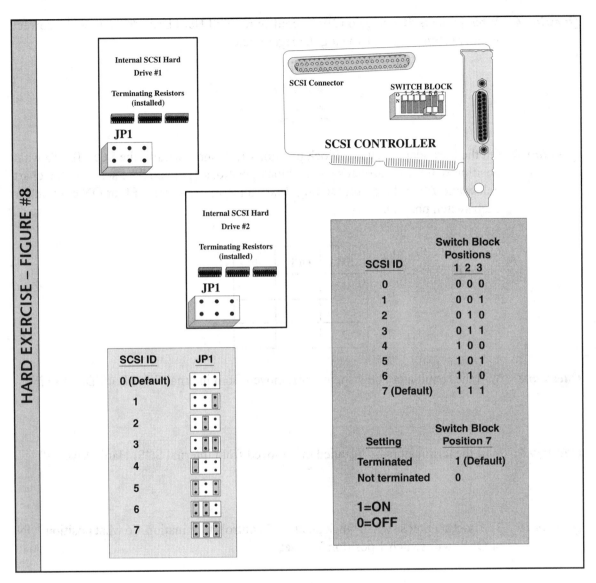

Look at Hard Exercise Figure #8 to answer Questions 5–10.

Question 5:   Hard Exercise Figure #8 shows the same SCSI controller used in Figure #7. In this configuration, however, two internal hard drives connect to the controller. Internal Hard Drive #1 boots the computer. What jumpers, if any, go on JP1 to configure Internal SCSI Hard Drive #1? Circle the correct jumper setting(s) for JP1 using the figure below.

JP1

Question 6: What jumpers, if any, go on JP1 to configure SCSI Hard Drive #2? Circle the correct jumper setting(s) for JP1 using the figure below.

JP1

Question 7: On the host adapter, switch block positions 1, 2, and 3 control the SCSI ID. To what position will the controller's switch block positions 1, 2, and 3 be set? Use the chart below and fill in the correct setting. Mark an X in *either* the OFF or ON column for each switch position.

SW1	OFF	ON
1		
2		
3		

Question 8: Will the terminators be installed or removed from internal SCSI Hard Drive #1?

Question 9: Will the terminators be installed or removed from internal SCSI Hard Drive #2?

Question 10: The host adapter's switch block position 7 controls termination. To what position (ON or OFF) will switch 1 position 7 be set?

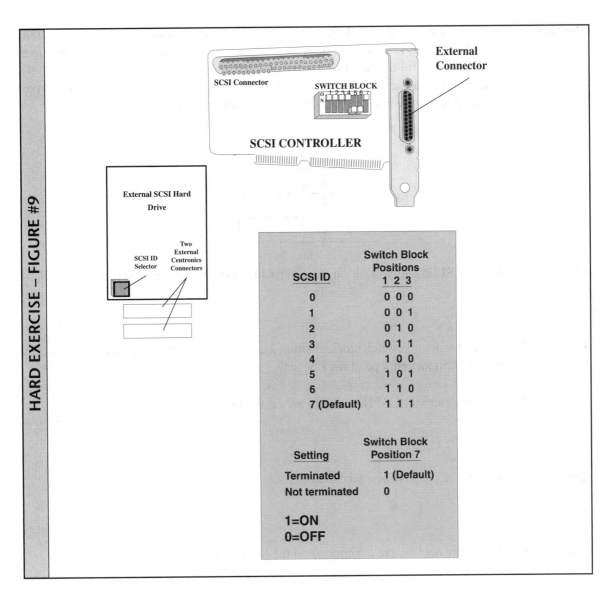

HARD EXERCISE – FIGURE #9

Hard Exercise Figure #9 is needed for Questions 11–14:

Question 11: In Hard Exercise Figure #9, the same SCSI controller is used, but with one external SCSI hard drive. The external hard drive boots the computer. Switch block positions 1, 2, and 3 control the SCSI ID for the adapter. To what position will the controller's switch block positions 1, 2, and 3 be set? Use the chart below and fill in the correct setting. Mark an X in *either* the OFF or ON column for each switch position.

SW1	OFF	ON
1		
2		
3		

Question 12: What SCSI ID will you set on the external hard drive's SCSI ID selector?

Question 13: The host adapter's switch block position 7 controls termination. To what position (ON or OFF) will switch 1 position 7 be set?

Question 14: Will the external SCSI Hard Drive be terminated? If so, how?

Question 15: What is the purpose of a terminator?

Question 16: How many devices are terminated on the SCSI chain?

Question 17: What is the purpose of the SCSI ID?

Question 18: [T / F] The lower the SCSI ID, the higher the priority on the SCSI bus.

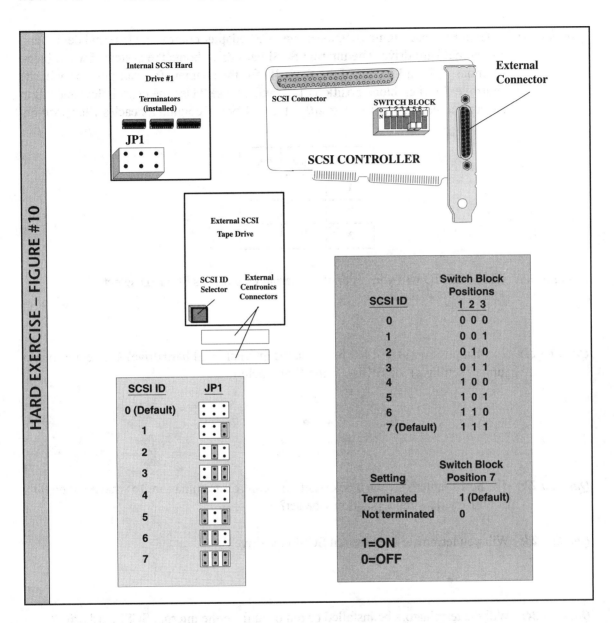

Look at Hard Exercise Figure #10 when answering Questions 19–24:

Question 19: In Hard Exercise Figure #10, the same SCSI adapter controls an external device and an internal hard drive. The internal SCSI hard drive boots the system. Switch block positions 1, 2, and 3 control the SCSI ID for the adapter. To what position will the controller's switch block positions 1, 2, and 3 be set? Use the chart below and fill in the correct setting. Mark an X in *either* the OFF or ON column for each switch position.

SW1	OFF	ON
1		
2		
3		

Question 20: What SCSI ID will you set on the external tape drive's SCSI ID selector?

Question 21: To what position(s) will JP1 be set on the internal SCSI hard drive? Circle the correct jumper setting(s) for JP1 using the figure below.

JP1

Question 22: The host adapter's switch block position 7 controls termination. To what position (ON or OFF) will switch 1 position 7 be set?

Question 23: Will you terminate the external SCSI tape drive?

Question 24: Will the terminators be installed or removed from the internal SCSI hard drive?

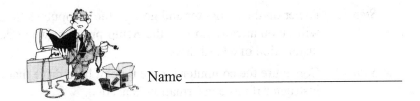

Name _____

SINGLE IDE HARD DRIVE INSTALLATION EXERCISE

Objective: To install an IDE hard drive correctly

Parts: IDE hard drive and documentation for the drive (if possible)
IDE cable
Tools
Anti-static materials

CAUTION: Observe proper grounding procedures when installing hard drives.

Step 1. Remove the cover from the computer. Use proper anti-static procedures.

Step 2. Configure the hard drive for master by referring to the documentation included with the hard drive or provided by the instructor. IDE hard drives are normally pre-configured to the master setting.

Step 3. Locate pin 1 on the hard drive's connector

Question 1: How was pin 1 identified on the hard drive connector?

Step 4. Locate an available drive bay in the computer system.

Step 5. Attach any mounting hardware needed to install the hard drive into the computer case and slide the hard drive into the computer case.

Step 6. Connect the power connector to the new drive.

Step 7. Connect the 40-pin signal cable to the hard drive verifying that the pin 1 connects to the hard drive connector's pin 1.

Step 8. Locate pin 1 on the motherboard or the adapter's IDE connector.

Question 2: How was pin 1 (in Step 8) identified?

Step 9. Connect the other end of the 40-pin cable to the motherboard or to the adapter ensuring the cable's pin 1 connects to the adapter or motherboard's pin 1.

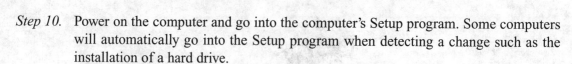
Step 10. Power on the computer and go into the computer's Setup program. Some computers will automatically go into the Setup program when detecting a change such as the installation of a hard drive.

Step 11. Configure the computer for the type of hard drive that is being installed. Contact the instructor if more information is needed.

Step 12. If the hard drive is not new, the system should boot from the hard drive. Otherwise, if the drive is new, the hard drive must be partitioned and high-level formatted. (Both are covered later in the chapter.)

Step 13. Power off the computer and re-install the computer's cover.

Question 3: If adding a CD-ROM to the same cable used for the hard drive, would the hard drive be left as master and the CD-ROM set to slave, or would the hard drive need to be re-configured as the slave and the CD-ROM drive set as the master device? Explain your answer.

_____ *Instructor's Initials*

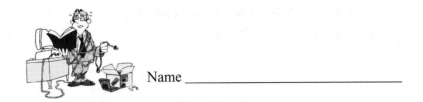

Name _____

SCSI ADAPTER AND DEVICE INSTALLATION EXERCISE

Objective: To install a SCSI device correctly

Parts: SCSI device, adapter (or motherboard with built-in SCSI), and documentation
SCSI cable(s)
Tools
Anti-static materials

CAUTION: Observe proper grounding procedures when installing hard drives.

Step 1. Remove the cover from the computer. Use proper anti-static procedures.

Step 2. Configure the SCSI adapter's SCSI ID by referring to the documentation included with the adapter or provided by the instructor. Most SCSI adapters come preset to SCSI ID 7 and should be left in this position for optimum operation. Refer to the adapter's documentation for more information.

Step 3. Install the SCSI adapter into an available slot in the computer.

Step 4. Configure the SCSI device for the proper SCSI ID and termination by referring to the device's documentation.

Question 1: What SCSI ID was chosen for the SCSI device?

Question 2: Did you terminate the SCSI device? Why or why not?

Question 3: Did you terminate the SCSI host adapter or motherboard? Why or why not?

Step 5. Locate pin 1 on the SCSI device's connector.

Step 6.   Locate pin 1 on the SCSI adapter.

Question 4:   How is pin 1 identified on the SCSI device's connector?

Question 5:   How is pin 1 identified on the SCSI adapter?

Step 7.   If the SCSI device is internal, locate an available drive bay in the computer system.

Step 8.   If the SCSI device is internal, attach any mounting hardware needed to install the device into the computer case. Slide the device into the computer case.

Step 9.   Connect the power connector to the SCSI device.

Step 10.   Connect the SCSI cable to the device, ensuring the cable's pin 1 attaches to the connector's pin 1.

Step 11.   Connect the other end of the SCSI cable to the SCSI adapter, ensuring pin 1 on the cable attaches to the adapter's pin 1.

Step 12.   Power on the computer and install any SCSI software necessary for the adapter and the SCSI device.

Step 13.   If the installation process did not call for a computer reboot, warm boot the computer after the software is installed to ensure all changes take effect.

Step 14.   If a scanner, tape backup unit, or other similar device is being installed, the device may require additional software installation for proper operation. Refer to the documentation that comes with the SCSI device for more information.

Question 6:   Does the SCSI device work? If not, refer to the chapter's section on troubleshooting.

_____ *Instructor's Initials*

Name _____

PARTITION THE HARD DRIVE INTO ONE PRIMARY PARTITION EXERCISE

Objective: To partition a hard drive into one primary partition

Parts: A bootable disk containing the same operating system version as the hard drive and the FDISK command

Step 1.   With the bootable DOS disk (that contains the FDISK command) inserted into drive A:, power on the computer.

Step 2.   Press **Enter** each time you are prompted for the date and time.

Step 3.   At the A:> prompt, type **FDISK** and press **Enter**. For DOS skills, refer to the DOS chapter.

Question 1:   What is the purpose of the FDISK command?

Step 4.   At the menu that appears choose

4 *Display partition information*, press **Enter**. A message appears stating that no partitions are defined. If a table appears with partition information, go to the exercise entitled Delete the Hard Drive's Partition(s) Exercise.

Step 5.   Press **ESC** to return to the FDISK Options screen.

Step 6.   At the main menu, choose

1 *Create DOS partition*, press **Enter.**

Step 7.   At the next menu that appears choose

1 *Create Primary DOS partition*, press **Enter**.

Step 8.   At the prompt "Do you wish to use the maximum available size for a primary DOS partition?" type **Y** (for Yes). A message appears stating that the system will restart. A prompt appears to insert a bootable DOS disk.

Question 2:   How many primary DOS partitions can be on a hard drive?

Question 3:   How many extended partitions can be on a hard drive?

Question 4:   How many logical drives can be on a hard drive?

Question 5:   List one reason why a new hard drive might need to be partitioned in today's computing environments.

Step 9.   Insert the bootable disk into Drive A: and press **Enter** to reboot the system. Error messages may appear about drive C: at this time. Press **F** for Fail as many times as necessary until the A:> prompt appears. This is okay because the hard drive must be high-level formatted before information can be written on it.

Step 10.   Press **Enter** each time you are prompted for the date and time.

Step 11.   At the A:> prompt, type **FDISK** and press **Enter**.

Step 12.   From the menu, choose:

> **4** *Display Partition size*

You should see something like the example below:

Partition	MB	USAGE
C: 1	100	100%

Show this display to the instructor.

_____*Instructor's Initials*

Step 13.   Press **ESC** to return to the FDISK Options screen.

Step 14.   Press **ESC** to exit FDISK.

Step 15.   A prompt appears reminding you to ensure that a bootable system disk is inserted into the A: drive.

Step 16.   Each partition must be high-level formatted before data can be written to the drive. Reference the High-level Format Exercise found later in the chapter.

Name _____

PARTITION THE HARD DRIVE INTO ONE PRIMARY AND ONE EXTENDED PARTITION EXERCISE

Objective:　　To partition a hard drive into one primary and one extended partition

Parts:　　A bootable disk containing the same operating system version as the hard drive, and the FDISK command

Step 1.　　With the bootable DOS disk (that contains the FDISK command) inserted into drive A:, power on the computer.

Step 2.　　Press **Enter** each time you are prompted for the date and time.

Step 3.　　At the A:> prompt, type **FDISK** and press **Enter**. For DOS skills, refer to Appendix A.

Question 1:　　What is the difference between a primary partifion and an extended partition?

Step 4.　　At the menu that appears choose

　　　　4 *Display partition information*, press **Enter**. A message appears stating that no partitions are defined. If a table appears with partition information, go to the exercise entitled Delete the Hard Drive's Partition(s) Exercise.

Step 5.　　Press **ESC** to return to the FDISK Options screen.

Step 6.　　At the menu that appears choose

　　　　1 *Create DOS partition*, press **Enter**.

Step 7.　　At the next menu that appears choose

　　　　1 *Create Primary DOS Partition*, press **Enter**.

Step 8.　　At the prompt "Do you wish to use the maximum available size for a primary DOS partition?" type **N** (for No).

Step 9.　　At the prompt "Enter Partition size:" type a number that is 60 percent of your total hard drive size. For example, if the hard drive is a 30MB hard drive, then choose 18. Press **Enter** after typing the number. A message appears at the bottom of the screen indicating the Primary DOS partition was created.

Question 2:　　What size (in MB) is chosen for the primary DOS partition?

Step 10.   Press **ESC** to continue. You will be back at the FDISK Options screen and will receive a message at the bottom of the screen, something similar to "Warning! No Partitions are set active." Disk 1 cannot be started unless a partition is set to active.

Step 11.   At the menu, choose:

> **2**   *Set Active Partition*, press **Enter**. Enter the number of the partition you want to make active: **1**, press **Enter**. You will receive a message that Partition 1 was made active.

Step 12.   At the menu, choose:

> **1**   *Create DOS partition*, press **Enter.**

Step 13.   At the next menu, choose:

> **2**   *Create Extended DOS partition*, press **Enter.**

Step 14.   At the prompt "Enter Partition Size:" enter a number that is your total amount of hard drive space less the number you chose in Question 2. For example, if you have a 30MB hard drive and you entered **18** (MB) for Question 2, then you would choose **12** (MB) for this prompt (30MB-18MB=12MB). After you type your number for the extended partition, press **Enter**. You will receive a message at the bottom of the screen indicating the extended partition was created.

Question 3:   What partition size (in megaytes) did you choose for Step 14?

Step 15.   Press **ESC** to continue. You will receive a message that states that no logical drives are defined.

Step 16.   When prompted for the Logical Drive Size, enter the same number that you chose for Step 12 and press **Enter**. You will receive a message that all available space in the extended DOS partition is assigned to the logical drives.

Step 17.   Press **ESC** to continue.

Question 4:   [T / F]   All data is lost when a hard drive is repartitioned using the DOS FDISK command.

Question 5:   [T / F]   Partitioning is a step required on all new hard drives installed into a computer system.

Question 6:   [T / F]   A logical drive is the same thing as an extended partition.

Step 18. From the menu, choose:

4 *Display Partition size.*

You should see something like the example below:

Partition	MB	USAGE
C: 1	18	60%
2	12	40%

Show this display to the instructor.

_____*Instructor's Initials*

Step 19. When prompted "Do you want to display logical drive info? Y/N," enter **Y** (for Yes) and press **Enter**. You should see something like the following:

LOGICAL DRIVE	MB	USAGE
D: 1	12	100%

Question 7: Why does the first screen that you saw in Step 16 show the second partition as 40 percent (or whatever your number is), but the logical drive of that partition shows usage as 100 percent?

Step 20. Press **ESC** to return to the Display Partition Information screen.

Step 21. Press **ESC** to return to the FDISK Options screen.

Step 22. Press **ESC** to exit FDISK.

Step 23. A prompt appears stating to ensure that a bootable system disk is inserted into the A: drive.

Question 8: If you are adding a second hard drive to a computer system and the new hard drive is partitioned into just one partition, what drive letter is assigned to the logical drive in the extended partition on the first hard drive?

Step 24. Each partition must be high-level formatted before data can be written to the drive. Reference the High-level Format Exercise found later in the chapter.

_____ *Instructor's Initials*

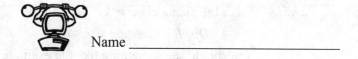

Name _____

DELETE THE PARTITION(S) ON THE HARD DRIVE

Objective: To delete a hard drive partition

Parts: A bootable DOS disk (with the same version of DOS as the hard drive) as well as the FDISK command

Step 1.   With the bootable DOS disk (that contains the FDISK command) inserted into drive A:, power on the computer.

Step 2.   Press **Enter** each time you are prompted for the date and time.

Step 3.   At the A:> prompt, type **FDISK** and press **Enter**. For DOS skills, refer to Appendix A.

Step 4.   At the menu that appears choose

        4 *Display partition information*, press **Enter**.

Question 1:   Does the screen displayed in Step 4 show that an extended partition exists?

Question 2:   If an extended partition exists on the hard drive, what logical drive letter(s) are assigned? *HINT:* If an extended partition with logical drives does exist, then a message appears on the bottom of the screen in Step 4 prompting "Do you want to display the logical drive information (Y/N)?"

Step 5.   Press **ESC** until the FDISK Options screen appears.

Step 6.   At the FDISK options menu, choose

        3 *Delete DOS Partition or Logical DOS Drive*, press **Enter**.

Step 7.   If the answer to Question 1 "Does the screen shown in Step 4 show that an extended partition exists?" is NO, move ahead to Step 18. If the answer is YES, continue to Step 8.

Step 8.   At the Delete DOS Partition or Logical DOS Drive menu, choose

        3 *Delete Logical DOS Drive (s) in the Extended DOS partition*, press **Enter**. A warning message appears at the bottom of the screen stating that all information in the logical drive will be deleted if the logical drive is deleted.

Step 9. At the prompt "What drive do you want to delete?" type in the drive letter of the logical drive shown on the screen. The normal choice is **D**. Press **Enter**.

Step 10. At the "Enter Volume Label" prompt, enter the volume label listed in the table at the top of the screen followed by **Enter**. If there is no volume label listed, simply press **Enter**.

Step 11. At the "Are you sure (Y/N)?" prompt, press **Y** and press **Enter**.

Step 12. Repeat Steps 9–11 as necessary for any remaining logical drives.

Step 13. Press **ESC** until the **FDISK Options** menu appears again.

Step 14. At the FDISK options menu, choose

      3 *Delete DOS Partition or Logical DOS Drive*, press **Enter**.

Step 15. At the Delete DOS Partition or Logical DOS Drive menu, choose

      2 *Delete Extended DOS Partition*, press **Enter**. A warning message appears at the bottom of the screen stating that all of the information in the extended partition will be deleted if the extended partition is deleted.

Step 16. At the "Do you wish to continue (Y/N)?" prompt, type **Y** and press **Enter**. A message at the bottom of the screen appears stating that the Extended DOS Partition was deleted.

Step 17. Press **ESC** to return to the FDISK Options menu.

Step 18. At the FDISK options menu, choose

      3 *Delete DOS Partition or Logical DOS Drive*, press **Enter**.

Step 19. At the Delete DOS Partition or Logical DOS Drive menu, choose

      1 *Delete Primary DOS Partition*, press **Enter**. A warning message appears at the bottom of the screen stating that all information in the primary partition will be deleted if the partition is deleted.

Step 20. At the prompt "What primary partition do you want to delete?" press the number corresponding to the primary partition as shown on the top of the screen. The normal response is **1** (and press **Enter**).

Step 21. At the prompt "Are you sure (Y/N)?" press **Y** and press **Enter**.

Step 22. The computer must restart after deleting the partition. Follow the directions on the screen and remember to insert the bootable disk into drive A: when rebooting the system. In order to create a new partition or multiple partitions, use the exercises found earlier in the chapter.

_____*Instructor's Initials*

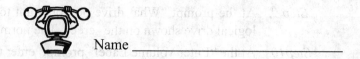

Name _____

HIGH-LEVEL FORMAT EXERCISE

Objective: To high-level format a hard drive correctly

Parts: A bootable disk containing the same operating system version that you want the hard drive to boot from, as well the FORMAT command

Step 1. With the bootable disk that contains the FORMAT command in drive A:, power on the computer.

Step 2. Press **Enter** each time you are prompted for the date and time.

Step 3. From the A:> prompt, type **FORMAT C:/S** and press **Enter**. For DOS skills, refer to the DOS chapter.

Step 4. When asked "Proceed with format Y/N?", type **Y** (for Yes) and press **Enter**. At the end of the FORMAT, you will be prompted to insert a system disk into the A: drive. Insert the bootable disk into the A: drive *before* pressing **Enter**.

Question 1: Why is the FORMAT command considered to be a high-level format? Exactly what is being done at this stage?

Question 2: For what is the /S switch used when combined with the FORMAT command?

Step 5. After the formatting of the logical drive C: is complete, remove the bootable disk from drive A:.

Question 3: Do you have to perform a high-level format on all logical drives? Explain.

Step 6. Reboot the computer by pressing **CTRL+ALT+DEL**.

Question 4: Does the computer boot to the C: drive? If not, perform the exercise again.

_____ *Instructor's Initials*

Optional instructions for formatting other logical drives:

Step 7. For each logical drive that you have created, a high-level format must be performed. Type the following command at the C:> prompt: **FORMAT D:** and press **Enter**.

Step 8. When asked "Proceed with format Y/N?" type **Y** (for Yes) and press **Enter**.

Question 5: Why would you NOT put a /S after the command used in Step 7?

Step 9. Perform Steps 7 and 8 for each logical drive. However, instead of typing FORMAT D:, type **FORMAT E:** or **FORMAT F:**, depending on the logical drive being formatted.

_____*Instructor's Initials*

If you just installed DOS version 6 onto the hard drive, you have a similar computer, and you would like to copy all the files from one drive to another, go to the next exercise.

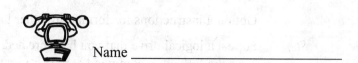
Name _____

COPYING FILES FROM ONE COMPUTER TO ANOTHER USING A SPECIAL CABLE

Objective: To use the Interlink program that comes with DOS

Parts: A bootable DOS disk containing the INTERLNK.EXE and INTERSVR.EXE files
The Interlink program from DOS 6 and higher machines works on lower DOS version machines
A special 3-wire serial cable, a 7-wire null-modem cable, or a bi-directional parallel cable (sometimes called a LapLink, Interlink, or Brooklyn Bridge cable)

When using the DOS Interlink program, the computer from which you want to copy files is the Server; the computer to which you want to copy files is the Client.

Step 1.   Insert the bootable disk into the Client computer. Power on the computer.

Step 2.   Press **Enter** when prompted for the date and the time.

Step 3.   From the A:> prompt, type **DIR** and press **Enter**. For DOS skills, refer to the DOS chapter.

Step 4.   Look at the directory listing for a file called **CONFIG.SYS**. If there is a file called CONFIG.SYS, type **REN CONFIG.SYS CONFIG.BAK** and press **Enter**.

Step 5.   Type the following command at the DOS prompt:

COPY CON:CONFIG.SYS and press **Enter**. *You will receive a blank screen.*

The blank screen is normal! Nothing is going to happen, no messages, nothing.

Step 6.   At the blank screen type:

Files=20 and press **Enter.**

Buffers=40 and press **Enter.**

Device=C:\INTERLNK.EXE and press **Enter.**

Step 7.   Press **F6**, then press **Enter**. The screen displays a message that one file copied.

Step 8.   Connect the special cable between the two serial or parallel ports (depending on which cable you use).

Step 9.   With the bootable disk still in drive A:, reboot the computer you were just typing on by pressing **CTRL+ALT+DEL**. You see a message that Interlink is installed. If you do not see this, perform Steps 5 through 9 again.

Step 10.   Press **Enter** each time you are prompted for the date and time.

Step 11.   Go to the Server computer from which you want to copy files.

Step 12.   At the DOS prompt, type **VER** and press **Enter**.

Question 1: What DOS version is this machine?

Optional Step 12a. If the computer you are at is *not* DOS 6 or higher, you must complete this step. Get the disk from the Client computer with the Interlink files. Insert the disk into the computer. Type the following command:

COPY A:\INTRSVR.* **C:\DOS** and press **Enter**. Put the disk back in the Client computer. You receive a message that one file was copied.

Step 13. Type the following commands on the Server machine (the one on which you are currently working):

C: and press **Enter**.

CD\DOS and press **Enter**.

INTERSVR and press **Enter**.

Step 14. On the Client machine, be sure that the bootable floppy is inserted into the A: drive and type the following command:

INTERLNK and press **Enter**. Notice that you are connected to the other computer and that each of the other computer's floppy and hard drive(s) are assigned a drive letter, one drive letter per device. For example, you should see something on the screen as shown below. If nothing on your screen is similar to the example below, contact your instructor.

Example of Interlink screen:
Port=LPT1

This Computer (Client)	Other Computer (Server)
E: equals	A:
F: equals	C:
G: equals	D:

Question 2: What does your screen show? Write your drive letters and what they equal below:

_____ *Instructor's Initials*

Step 15. Type the drive letter followed by a colon that equals the other computer's C: drive and press **Enter**. For example, in the example shown in Step 14, the drive letter would be F:. You are now connected to the other computer's drives. This exercise is especially useful if you need to install software from a 3.5-inch disk and the computer you are working on does not have this type of disk drive or has a disk drive that is the wrong capacity.

Question 3: What drive letter did you choose?

Question 4: Did you remember to put a colon after the drive letter and press **Enter**?

Step 16. Copy any files that you want from the Server computer. If you want to copy all the files from the Server, you would simply have to type **CD\DOS** and press **Enter**; **XCOPY F:*.* C:\ /E** and press **Enter**. If you happen to be on a DOS version lower than DOS 5, you would have to type **CD\DOS** and press **Enter**; **XCOPY F:*.* C:\ /E /S** and press **Enter**. If asked "Overwrite C:\COMMAND.COM (Y/N/All)?" (or something similar), press **N** for No and then press **Enter**.

Step 17. When you are finished, press **ALT+F4** on the Server computer to disconnect the link.

Question 5: List other ways in which you think this program could be useful to you as a technician.

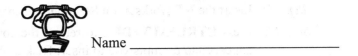

Name _____

PARTITION AND HIGH-LEVEL FORMAT NT WORKSTATION WITH FAT16 AND NTFS

Objective: To partition NT Workstation into two partitions—one with FAT and one with NTFS

Parts: DOS/WINDOWS 95 boot disk with FDISK and FORMAT commands
NT Workstation boot disks and CD
Drivers for any network cards or SCSI hard drives as needed

Step 1.   Boot the computer with a DOS or Windows 95 boot disk that has the FDISK command on it.

Step 2.   From the prompt, type **FDISK**.

Step 3.   Use menu option 3 to delete any partitions already on the drive. See the exercise on deleting partitions for more information.

Step 4:   Press **1** to create a partition. Press **Enter**.

Step 5.   Press **1** to create a primary partition. Press **Enter**.

Step 6.   When asked if you want to use the maximum available size for the partition, type **N** for No and press **Enter**.

Step 7.   Contact your instructor for the amount to type into the "Enter partition size" brackets. 300MB is recommended.

_____ *Instructor's Initials*

Type in the number from your instructor and press **Enter** to go to the next screen.

Question 1:   How many megabytes were used in Step 7?

Step 8.   Press the **ESC** key to continue.

Step 9.   Press **2** to set the partition you just created as an active partition.

Step 10.   At the "Enter the number of partition you want to make active" prompt, enter the number of the partition you just created. (Normally this is 1). Press **Enter**.

Step 11.   Press the **ESC** key to continue.

Step 12.   Press the **ESC** key to exit the FDISK program.

Step 13.   You will be prompted to restart the computer. Leave the boot disk in drive A:.

Step 14.   At the A:> prompt, type **FORMAT C: /S**. Press **Enter**.

Step 15.   Insert the NT Workstation Setup Disk 1 into drive A:.

Step 16.   Press **CTRL+ALT+DEL** to reboot the computer. The Windows setup blue screen appears and prompts you to insert Disk 2. Press **Enter** once the disk is inserted.

Step 17.   When the Welcome to Setup screen appears, press **Enter.**

Step 18.   Press **Enter** for mass storage device detection.

Step 19.   Insert Setup Disk 3 when prompted and press **Enter**.

Step 20.   Once NT detects any storage devices, they are displayed on the screen. Contact your instructor to see if you need to specify any additional devices and insert the manufacturer's disk.

_____ *Instructor's Initials*

Press **Enter** if no additional devices are needed. Press **S** if told to do so by the instructor.

Step 21.   Insert the CD when prompted and press **Enter**.

Step 22.   When the license agreement appears, press **Page Down** until the last window appears, then press **F8**.

Step 23.   NT displays the basic hardware found. If this matches your computer, press **Enter**. Contact your instructor if the list is incorrect.

Step 24.   To select what space on the hard drive is used to hold NT, use the arrow key to select **unpartitioned space** located below the C: FAT partition. Once highlighted, press **C** to create a partition.

Step 25.   The partition size is entered already. Press **Enter** to create the partition. You return to the partition screen when finished.

Step 26.   Use the arrow keys to highlight the **D:partition** and press **Enter**. A message appears that the partition is unformatted.

Step 27.   Use the arrow keys to highlight the **Format the partition using the NTFS file system** option and press **Enter**. The drive formats.

Step 28.   A window appears with the default directory of WINNT displayed. Press **Enter**.

Step 29.   Press the **ESC** key to skip the exhaustive drive search.

Step 30.   When prompted, remove all floppy disks and CDs and press **Enter** to restart the computer.

Step 31.   When prompted, insert the NT Workstation CD and click on the **OK** button.

Step 32.   In the Windows NT Setup window, click the **Next** button.

Step 33.   On the Setup options, the typical computer option is enabled. Click the **Next** button.

Step 34.   Contact your instructor for what to type in the Name and Organization boxes.

_____ *Instructor's Initials*

Step 35. When prompted for a CD key, contact your instructor for the correct number.

_____ *Instructor's Initials*

Step 36. After typing the correct number, click on the **Next** button.

Step 37. When prompted for a computer name, contact the instructor for a name.

_____ *Instructor's Initials*

Question 2: What name did you assign your computer?

Step 38. After entering the computer name, click on the **Next** button.

Step 39. When prompted for a password, contact the instructor.

_____ *Instructor's Initials*

Question 3: Is a password going to be used? If so, write the password here.

Step 40. If the instructor gave you a password, type it in the Password and Confirm Password boxes. If no password is required, leave the boxes blank. Click on the **Next** button to continue.

Step 41. Click in the **Do not create an emergency repair disk** option and click on the **Next** button.

Step 42. Click on the **Next** button to install the most common components.

Step 43. Click on the **Next** button to install NT networking.

Step 44. Contact your instructor to see whether networking is to be set up on the computer.

_____ *Instructor's Initials*

Step 45. Click **Next** after selecting the option preferred by the instructor.

Optional Step 46. If networking was selected, you have to install the appropriate drivers. Contact the instructor for the appropriate disks and follow the prompts to install the network drivers.

Optional Step 47. Contact the instructor about whether to use DHCP and whether to make the computer a member of a domain or a workgroup.

Step 48. Click on the **Finish** button to complete the installation.

Step 49. Select the correct time zone for your area by clicking on the time zone. Click on the **Close** button.

Step 50. Click the **OK** button when NT detects your display.

Step 51. Click on the **OK** button.

Step 52. Remove any floppy disks and CDs and press the **Restart Computer** button.

_____ *Instructor's Initials*

Name _____

CREATING NT SETUP DISKS (INCLUDING BOOT DISK)

Objective: To create a set of NT Setup disks

Parts: A computer that has a CD-ROM installed
                NT Installation CD
                Three blank formatted disks

Step 1.   Go to a command prompt. If on Windows 95, Windows 98, or Windows NT, click on the **Start** button, select **Programs**, and click on the **MS-DOS Prompt**.

Step 2.   From the prompt, type **CD X:** where *X* is the drive letter of the CD-ROM.

Step 3.   Insert the NT Installation CD into the CD-ROM.

Step 4.   Type **CD I386**.

Step 5.   If the computer is running DOS, Windows 3.x, Windows 95, or Windows 98:

            type **START WINNT /OX** and press **Enter**.

            If the computer is running Windows NT:

            type **START WINNT32 /OX** and press **Enter**.

Step 6.   Click on the **Continue** button.

Step 7.   Follow the instructions on the screen to insert each of the three blank disks. Click on the **OK** button between the dialogues for each disk.

_____ *Instructor's Initials*

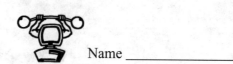

Name _____

CREATING WINDOWS 2000 SETUP DISKS (INCLUDING BOOT DISK)

Objective: To create a set of Windows 2000 Setup disks

Parts: A computer that has a CD-ROM installed
2000 Installation CD
4 blank formatted disks

Note: The Windows 2000 Setup disks can be created while working in any operating system.

Step 1.   Boot the computer and log on if necessary. Contact the instructor or lab assistant for userid and password.

Step 2.   Insert the Windows 2000 installation CD into the CD-ROM.

Step 3.   Click on the **Start** button, click on the **Run** option.

Step 4.   In the Open dialog box, type *x:***\bootdisk\makeboot.exe a:** where *x:* is the drive letter associated with the CD-ROM. Click on the **OK** button.

Step 5.   Follow the directions on the screen inserting disks when prompted. When all four disks have been created, a message appears that the Setup boot disks were made successfully.

_____ *Instructor's Initials*

Step 6.   Remove the last disk. Close the window.

Step 7.   Follow the instructions on the screen to insert each of the three blank disks. Click on the **OK** button between the dialogues for each disk.

Name _____

DOS CHKDSK EXERCISE

Objective: To use the CHKDSK program to claim lost clusters

Parts: A computer with DOS loaded

Note: If you have the MS-DOS SCANDISK program, you should use it instead of CHKDSK.

Question 1: Why should you use MSDOS SCANDISK instead of CHKDSK?

Step 1. Turn the computer on and boot from the hard disk.

Step 2. From the DOS prompt, type

CD\DOS and press **Enter.**

CHKDSK and press **Enter.**

For DOS skills, refer to the DOS chapter. CHKDSK alerts you with a message if a file needs to be fixed, but does not fix the error. If CHKDSK reports only lost clusters, then it is safe, (and usually a good idea), to rerun CHKDSK on the same drive with the /F option. When CHKDSK finishes, the system returns to the DOS prompt.

Question 2: Did CHKDSK report any lost clusters? If so, go to Step 3. If CHKDSK did not report any problems, you may just answer the questions below, skip Step 3. If CHKDSK found problems other than lost chains of clusters, then you need to use disk utility software. Contact your instructor for more information.

Optional Step 3. From the DOS prompt, type

CHKDSK /F. When asked if you want to convert the lost chains to files, answer **Y** (for yes). After CHKDSK is through, you will find one or more files in the root directory with names like FILE000.CHK, FILE001.CHK, or similar. You may view these files and then delete them if no critical information is within them. Contact your instructor if you cannot decide whether or not to delete the files.

Question 3:   What does the CHKDSK program do?

Question 4:   What would be an indication on the hard drive that CHKDSK needs to be run?

Question 5:   Why does the DEFRAG program require CHKDSK or SCANDISK be performed before it is executed?

Question 6:   What does the */F* switch do when used with the CHKDSK command?

Name _____

DOS SCANDISK EXERCISE

Objective: To use the DOS SCANDISK program

Parts: A computer with MS DOS 6.X or greater loaded

Note: SCANDISK should be performed before any defragmentation utility. If you run SCANDISK on a compressed drive, you are offered the choice of checking the physical (host) hard drive before you check the compressed drive. This is the best option when using a compressed drive.

Step 1.   Power on the computer.

Step 2.   From the DOS prompt, type **SCANDISK** and press **Enter**.

For DOS skills, refer to the DOS chapter. The SCANDISK utility immediately begins testing the file structure of your disk. A message box appears stating that the file structure testing was completed. You are asked if you want to perform a surface scan.

Question 1:   What does a surface scan do?

Step 3.   Press **Enter** to accept the **YES** default when the scan is complete. If SCANDISK finds a problem with the hard drive, a message box appears with three options: *Fix It, Don't Fix It,* or *More Info.* Choose **More Info** to get additional information and/or recommendations. Choose **Fix It** to allow SCANDISK the opportunity to repair the problem. At the end of the SCANDISK check, a final report appears on the screen. Sometimes recommendations are provided. This information is also in the SCANDISK.LOG file that can be brought into a word processor and printed if desired. If a hard drive has repeated problems, keep the SCANDISK.LOG files for documentation on the problems.

Step 4.   At the end of the scan, you can either view the log of any problems that SCANDISK found by pressing **Enter** or you may press the **right arrow** once to get to the EXIT prompt and press **Enter** to exit SCANDISK.

Question 2:   [T / F]   SCANDISK can repair any and all problems with hard drives.

Question 3:   [T / F]   SCANDISK is a better utility than CHKDSK.

Question 4:   [T / F]   SCANDISK is only available with Microsoft DOS.

Question 5:   [T / F]   The SCANDISK.LOG is *not* to be used as a diagnostic tool.

_____ *Instructor's Initials*

Name _____

WINDOWS 9X SCANDISK EXERCISE

Objective: To use the Windows 95 or Windows 98 SCANDISK program

Parts: A computer with Windows 95 or Windows 98 loaded

   Note: SCANDISK should be performed before any defragmentation utility is used.

Step 1.   Power on the computer.

Step 2.   Click on the **Start** button.

Step 3.   Click on the **C:** drive in the Select the drive(s) you want to check for errors box.

Step 4.   In the Type of Test area, click on the **Standard** radio button.

Step 5.   Click on the **Start** button.

Question 1:   What does the SCANDISK program do?

Question 2:   SCANDISK can repair any and all problems with hard drives.

Question 3:   [T / F]   SCANDISK is a better utility than CHKDSK.

Question 4:   [T / F]   SCANDISK is only available with Windows 95 or Windows 98.

_____ *Instructor's Initials*

Name _____

NT HARD DRIVE CHECK EXERCISE

Objective: To check the disk for bad sectors and attempt to recover the data

Parts: A computer with Windows NT loaded

Step 1.   Double-click on the **My Computer** icon.

Step 2.   Right-click on the drive letter of the drive to be scanned such as C:.

Step 3.   On the displayed menu, click on **Properties**.

Step 4.   Click on the **Tools** tab.

Step 5.   In the Error Checking section, click on the **Check Now** button.

Step 6.   In the dialog box, click in the **Scan for and attempt recovery of bad sectors** option.

Step 7.   Click the **Start** button.

Step 8.   Click the **OK** button when the check is complete.

Step 9.   Click the **OK** button to close the Properties window.

Step 10.   Click the **Close** box to close the My Computer window.

_____ *Instructor's Initials*

Name _____

WINDOWS NT CHKDSK EXERCISE

Objective: To use the Windows NT CHKDSK program

Parts: A computer with NT Workstation or NT Server loaded.

Step 1.   Power on and logon to the computer. Contact the instructor or lab assistant for the userid and password if needed.

Step 2.   Click on the **Start** button.

Step 3.   Point to the **Programs** menu option.

Step 4.   Click on the **Command Prompt** menu option.

Step 5.   Type **CHKDSK /R** and press **Enter.**

    The Windows NT CHKDSK program combines the functionality of the DOS CHKDSK and SCANDISK programs. It can be used to check FAT and NTFS volumes.

Question 1:   What does a surface scan do?

Question 2:   [T / F]   SCANDISK can repair any and all problems with hard drives.

Question 3:   [T / F]   SCANDISK is a better utility than CHKDSK.

Question 4:   [T / F]   SCANDISK is only available with Windows 95 or Windows 98.

_____ *Instructor's Initials*

Name _____

WINDOWS 2000 CHECK DISK EXERCISE

Objective: To use the Windows 2000 Check Disk utility

Parts: A computer with Windows 2000 loaded

Step 1.   Power on and logon to the computer. Contact the instructor or lab assistant for the userid and password if needed.

Step 2.   Close any running programs.

Step 3.   Double-click on the **My Computer** desktop icon.

Step 4.   Right-click on a hard drive icon (the drive being checked). Select the **Properties** menu item.

Step 5.   Click on the **Tools** tab and click on the **Check Now** button. The Check Disk dialog box appears.

Step 6.   The Automatically fix file system errors option allows error detection and attempts repair. The Scan for and attempt recovery of bad sectors option does error detection, attempts repairs, and tries to recover unreadable information. Click once in **each box** to enable these options; then click on the **Start** button.

Question 1:   What is your indication that the test is being conducted?

Question 2:   Were any errors found?

_____ *Instructor's Initials*

Step 7.   When the scan completes, click the **OK** button in the dialog box.

Name _____

HARD DRIVE DEFRAGMENTATION EXERCISE (DOS)

Objective: To defragment the hard drive

Parts: A computer with IBM PC DOS 6.X or MS DOS 6.X or greater loaded

The Defragmentation Utility comes with IBM's PC DOS 6.X and MS DOS 6.X. This program should not be used until after running CHKDSK /F or SCANDISK. See the Running CHKDSK or Running SCANDISK exercises for more details.

Step 1.   Power on the computer.

Step 2.   From the DOS prompt, type **VER** and press **Enter**.

Question 1:   Do you have DOS version 6 or greater? If not, please go to a computer that has DOS version 6.

Step 3.   Type at the DOS prompt **CD\DOS** and press **Enter**.

Step 4.   Type at the DOS prompt **DEFRAG** and press **Enter**.

Step 5.   At the prompt "Choose the Drive You Want to Optimize," choose the default of **C:**.

Step 6.   Click on **OK** or press **TAB** to get to the OK button and press **Enter**.

Step 7.   When you see the message "Recommended Optimization Method" choose **Configure** by pressing the **right arrow** once to highlight the word Configure and then pressing **Enter**. The program goes to the menu at the top of the screen.

Step 8.   Choose **Optimization Method** by pressing the **down arrow** twice, press **Enter**.

Step 9.   Choose the default of **Full-Optimization** by pressing **Enter**. You return to the menu.

Step 10.   At the menu, choose **Begin Optimization** by pressing the **up arrow** twice and then pressing **Enter**. You see the layout of the files on your hard drive and the file shuffling that occurs during defragmentation. The length of time this exercise takes varies from computer to computer. While the program is executing, go to the end of this exercise and answer the questions starting with Question 2.

Step 11.   After the defragmentation is complete, a message box appears that says "Finished Condensing?" press **Enter**.

Step 12.   Another message box appears stating that the optimization is complete. Press the **right arrow** twice to highlight **Exit Defrag**, then press **Enter**. You return to the DOS prompt.

Questions 2–5 (Use Help or the Map Legend for additional assistance.):

Question 2:   What does [•] mean while DEFRAG is running?

Question 3:   What does an **X** in a block mean <OR RECREATE THE SYMBOL (AN X IN A BLOCK).> while DEFRAG is running?

Question 4:   What does [ ] mean while DEFRAG is running?

Question 5:   What is the difference between the Full Optimization option and the Unfragment Files Only option?

Name _____

HARD DRIVE DEFRAGMENTATION EXERCISE (WINDOWS 9X)

Objective: To defragment the hard drive correctly while using Windows 95/98

Parts: A computer with Windows 95 or Windows 98 loaded

Step 1.   Power on the computer.

Step 2.   From the desktop, double-click on **My Computer**.

Step 3.   With the right mouse button, click once on the icon for the hard drive that is to be defragmented.

Step 4.   Using the left mouse button, click once on the **Properties** menu item. (The Properties window appears.)

Step 5.   Click once on the **Tools** tab at the top of the Properties window.

Step 6.   Click on the **Start** button to begin defragmenting the hard drive. If more control is needed over the defragmentation process, click on the Advanced Options button instead of the Start button. For more details on the Advanced Options, refer to the chapter text.

Step 7.   When the defragmentation is finished, a dialog box appears stating that the program is complete. Click on the **Yes** button to exit the disk defragmentation program.

Step 8.   Click once in the **Close** box of the Properties window.

Step 9.   Click once in the **Close** box of the Control Panel window.

_____ *Instructor's Initials*

Name _____

HARD DRIVE DEFRAGMENTATION EXERCISE (WINDOWS 2000)

Objective: To defragment the hard drive correctly while using Windows 2000

Parts: A computer with Windows 2000 installed

Note: The process can take more than 60 minutes on larger hard drives. You may want to defragment a floppy disk instead. This will let you save time but still see what this utility can do.

Step 1.   Power on the computer. Logon using the userid and password provided by the instructor or lab assistant if necessary.

Step 2.   Close any running programs.

Step 3.   Double-click on the **My Computer** desktop icon.

Step 4.   Right-click on a hard drive icon (the drive being checked). Select the **Properties** menu item.

Step 5.   Click on the **Tools** tab and click on the **Defragment Now** button. The Disk Defragmenter window appears.

Step 6.   In the Disk Defragmenter window, click on the desired drive.

Step 7.   Click on the **Analyze** button. A bar is displayed showing the disk's fragmentation in graphical format. Blue bars represent contiguous files; red bars are fragmented files; and green bars are system files. White areas represent free hard drive space.

Question 1:   Does the hard drive have ample free space?

Step 8.   Click on the **Defragment** button. The Pause button can be used to temporarily halt the utility. The Stop button can be used to halt the utility.

Question 2:   Is the drive fragmented?

_____ *Instructor's Initials*

Step 9. When the hard drive has been defragmented, a dialog box appears. Click on the **OK** button.

Step 10. Click on the **View Report** button. A dialog box shows details about what was done, and the type of file system being used.

Step 11. Close the Disk Defragmenter window.

_____ ***Instructor's Initials***

Name _____

INTERNET DISCOVERY

Objective: To obtain specific information on the Internet regarding a computer or its associated parts

Parts: Access to the Internet

Scenario used for Questions 1–3: You have just purchased a Maxtor DiamondMax Plus 60 UDMA 100 hard drive.

Question 1:   What IDE setting is the default for this drive? Write the answer and the URL where you found this information in the space below.

Question 2:   What BIOS setting does Maxtor recommend trying first when installing this drive?

Question 3:   What cable is required with this drive?

Question 4:   Find an Internet site that shows the drive parameters for older hard drives. Find how many heads, cylinders, and sectors per track a Seagate ST138N hard drive has. You cannot use Seagate's web site. Write the URL and hard drive information in the space below.

Question 5:   The IBM 7210 external DVD-RAM drive uses the SCSI interface. What signaling method does this drive use? [SE \ HVD \ LVD] Circle the correct answer and write the URL in the space below.

Question 6:   A customer has an Epson Expression 1680 SCSI scanner. What SCSI IDs are available for this scanner and what is its default SCSI ID setting? What kind of SCSI connector does it have? Write the answers and the URL in the space below.

Question 7:   A customer has an HP CD-Writer Plus internal 8100i IDE drive. What is the default IDE setting for this drive? Does this drive support cable select? Write the answers and the web site where you found this information in the space below.

NOTES

10

Chapter 10:
Multimedia Devices

OBJECTIVES

After completing this chapter you will
- Understand various CD and DVD technologies.
- Understand the meaning of a CD or DVD's *x* factor.
- Understand how a CD drive works.
- Know the different interfaces used with CD and DVD drives and be able to configure the drive.
- Understand the basic operation of a sound card.
- Understand the software associated with CD and DVD drive installation.
- Be able to install a sound card.
- Be able to use various operating system tools to verify drive and sound card installation.
- Troubleshoot CD drive, DVD drive, and sound card problems.

KEY TERMS

A3D	EAX
AAC	flats
average access time	FML/C
average seek time	frequency response range
caddy	frequency response time
caddy loaded	hardware decoder
CD	laser lens
CD-R	magneto-optical
CD-ROM	MIDI
CD-RW	MP3
CDFS	MSCDEX.EXE
DDCD	MultiRead
decoder	PD
device driver	pits
device name	power rating
DirectX	region code
DS3D	shielding
DVD-R	slot loaded
DVD-RAM	software decoder
DVD-ROM	tray loaded
DVD-RW	UDF
DVD+RW	WORM
dye polymer	

MULTIMEDIA OVERVIEW

The term *multimedia* has different meanings for people because there are many types of multimedia devices. This chapter focuses on the most popular areas—CD technologies, DVD, sound cards, and speakers. Once these concepts are understood, other devices are similar to install and troubleshoot. The chapter is not intended as a buyer's guide or an electronics "how it works" book, but it is a guide for technicians with emphasis on installation and troubleshooting. Multimedia devices can be a lot of fun once they are installed. They can also cause headaches during installation.

CD-ROM OVERVIEW

A **CD-ROM (Compact Disk-Read Only Memory)** is a drive that uses disks that store large amounts of information (628MB and higher). The disk for the CD-ROM drive is known as a **CD**, CD-ROM disk, or just disk. The data contained on these disks are audio files, software applications, and graphics. CD-ROMs are very important in today's business and home computers because software applications are so large. Rather than occupy valuable hard drive space with applications and graphics, CD-ROMs provide a means of running an application or storing large graphics or audio files on a compact disk. Using one CD rather than 40 3.5" disks saves time and makes software installation or software application loading easier. Most computers today have a CD-ROM drive, but it is being replaced by DVDs (covered later in this chapter). Technicians must definitely understand CD technologies.

CD-ROM drives have a variety of controls on their front panel. The most common are listed as follows:

- Headphone jack—used to connect a set of headphones to the CD-ROM and listen to audio output.
- Volume control button—used to control headset volume.
- Start/stop buttons—used to start or stop CD playing.
- Eject button—used to manually eject a CD or CD tray.

CD-ROM DRIVE SPEEDS

CD-ROMs come in a variety of types classified by the X factor: 1X (single speed), 2X (double speed), 3X (triple speed), 4X (quad speed), 6X, 8X, 10X, 12X, 16X, 32x, and higher. Multimedia Table #1 shows the transfer rates for several CD-ROM drive types.

MULTIMEDIA – TABLE #1

CD–ROM Transfer Speeds

Type of CD-ROM Drive	Typical Transfer Rate (in Kilobytes per second)
1 X	150
2 X	300
4 X	600
8 X	1200
10 X	1500
12 X	1800
16 X	2400
24 X	3600
32X	4800
36X	5400
40X	6000
48X	7200

There are drives being advertised as 100X. These drives use hard drive space to cache the CD contents and provide faster speeds (1.5MBps). See the CD-ROM Buffers/Cache section later in the chapter on how this works.

The particular CD drive depends on several factors—the microprocessor installed, how much RAM is in the system, what video card is used (PCI, AGP, ISA, VL-bus), and how much video memory is on the video card. Note that DVD drives have the same dependency factors and also use *x* factors.

Take, for example, an 8X CD-ROM drive installed in two different computers. One computer has a 133MHz Pentium, 8MB of RAM, and an ISA video adapter with 1MB of video memory. Another 133MHz Pentium computer has 16MB of RAM and a PCI video adapter with 2MB of video memory. The CD-ROM drive in the second example can put graphics on the screen or play audio files much faster than the first drive. The increased amount of system RAM, increased amount of video adapter RAM, and the use of a video card that is PCI or AGP, not ISA, all contribute to the performance increase. Buying a faster CD-ROM drive does not necessarily mean the drive performs to expectations. As with all computer devices, components in the computer must work together to provide the fastest data transfer. Many people do not realize buying the latest and greatest X factor CD-ROM drive does not provide faster access. The drawback to CD-ROM drives is they operate much slower than hard drives.

Two confusing specifications of CD-ROMs are average seek time and average access time. The **average seek time** is the amount of time the drive requires to move randomly around the disk. The **average access time** is the amount of time the drive requires to find the appropriate place on the disk and retrieve information. Multimedia Table #2 lists average access times for different CD-ROM drives. Keep in mind that the lower the access time number, the better the performance.

CD–ROM Access Times

Type of CD-ROM Drive	Typical Access Speed (in milliseconds—ms)
1X	400
2X	300
4X	150
8X	120
10-12X	100
16-24X	90
32X and higher	85 or less

MULTIMEDIA – TABLE #2

CD-ROM drive access times are much slower than hard drives and CD-ROM drive manufacturers usually quote access times using only optimum test conditions. When buying or recommending a CD-ROM drive to a computer user or customer, check magazines or online data for the latest test performance results.

CD-ROM DRIVE BUFFERS/CACHE

One way to increase CD-ROM data transfer is through buffer memory located on the CD-ROM drive. When requesting data, the drive looks ahead on the CD for more data than requested and places the data in the buffers. The buffer memory ensures data is constantly sent to the microprocessor instead of the microprocessor waiting for the drive's slow access time. Buffer sizes typically range from 64KB to 2MB and higher. A drive should not be installed or purchased unless it has a minimum of 500KB buffer.

Starting with the Windows 95 operating system, Microsoft includes a CD-ROM cache as part of the operating system. The cache is adjustable, although it is normally set to the correct position. Right-click on the *My Computer* desktop icon. Select the *Properties* item from the drop-down menu. Click on the *Performance* tab and click on the *File System* button. Click on the *CD-ROM* tab and check the Supplemental cache size slide bar as well as the Optimize access pattern for setting.

One way to improve a computer's disk caching ability is to change the computer role. This can be done through the System control panel or by right-clicking on the *My Computer* desktop icon as described in the previous paragraph. Click on the *Performance* tab, click on the *File System* button, click on the *Hard Disk* tab, and change the Typical role of this computer to Network server.

THEORY OF CD-ROM DRIVE OPERATION

A CD-ROM disk is created from a master copy. The plastic disk is coated with a reflective, metallic aluminum alloy. The aluminum alloy layer is covered by a thin layer of lacquer for protection. The aluminum alloy is the layer of the CD where data is stored. CD-ROM disks are usually single-sided. A label is normally on the *opposite side* of the data.

A CD has thousands of circular tracks in a continuous spiral from the innermost area of the disk to the outside rim. The spiral tracks are similar to the grooves in an LP record. Instead of grooves, the CD has **pits**—indentations along the track. **Flats** or lands separate the pits. The pits and lands vary in length and represent stored data on the disk.

Reading information from a CD involves using a laser diode or another laser beam producing device within the CD-ROM drive. The laser beam shines through the protective coating to the aluminum alloy layer where data is stored. To reach the aluminum alloy layer, the laser beam passes through an optical system, which is a series or combination of lenses, prisms and mirrors. A servo motor inside the drive positions the beam on the right track through the use of the optical system. The laser beam reflects back through the optics to a photodiode detector that converts the reflected beam of light into 1s and 0s.

The light beam reflected to the photodiode detector changes in intensity when passing over the lands and the pits. The light reflected by a pit area is not as bright as the light reflected from a land area. While the disk rotates, the light beam creates a series of on and off flashes received by the photodiode. Once detected, the flashes of light convert to 1s and 0s. The transition between the lands and the pits create the variation of light intensity. Multimedia Figure #1 shows an inside view of a CD-ROM drive.

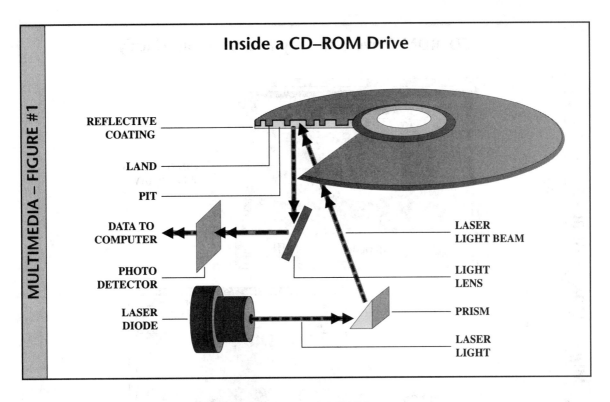

INTERNAL AND EXTERNAL CD-ROM DRIVES

A CD-ROM can be internally mounted in an available bay or it can be an external unit that sits beside the computer. If a CD-ROM uses the IDE interface, it must be an internal device because the interface does not support external devices. However, external SCSI CD-ROM drives can be purchased. A drawback to internal CD-ROM drives is that the drive requires a drive bay, but internal CD-ROM drives are cheaper than external drives.

CD-ROM DISK LOADING

Three methods exist for inserting a compact disk (CD) into a CD-ROM drive: tray loaded, caddy loaded, and slot loaded. A **tray loaded** CD-ROM drive has a tray that slides out from the CD-ROM drive. A CD is placed in the tray and the tray retracts into the drive. A **caddy loaded** CD-ROM drive uses a disk **caddy** that holds the CD. After inserting the disk, close the caddy lid and insert the entire caddy into the CD-ROM drive. A **slot loaded** CD inserts into a slot in the front of the CD-ROM. Some car CD-ROMs have this type of mechanism. See Multimedia Figure #2 for an example of a tray loaded CD-ROM drive and a CD-ROM disk caddy.

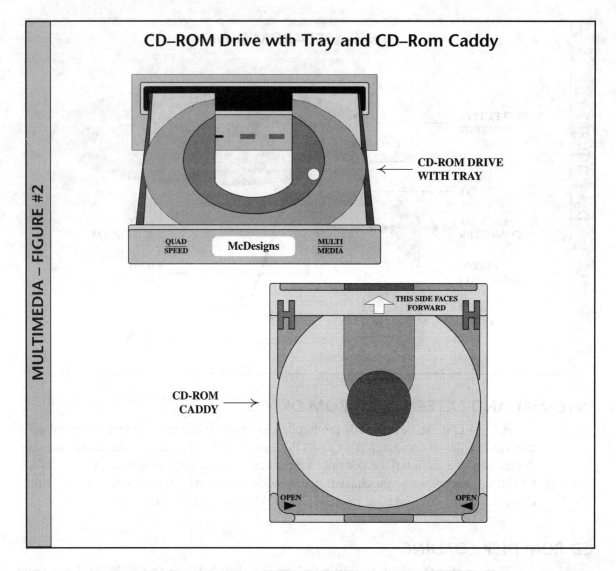

CD-ROM drives that use a caddy usually have only one caddy. Finding the one caddy when it's needed can be a hassle for some people. Using a caddy takes more time to install disks, but it provides a more secure and cleaner environment for the CD disks. Tray-loaded CD-ROM drives are less expensive than caddies, but more likely to have a worse MTBF—Mean Time Between Failure. MTBF is the average number of hours before a device is likely to fail. Another point to consider is some CD-ROM drives that use the caddy system can be vertically mounted on their side instead of the normal horizontal position. Most tray loading CD-ROM drives cannot be vertically mounted. Check the CD-ROM drive's documentation if this is an issue.

The third method, slot loaded CD-ROMs, have the disadvantage of disk jams. If a CD jams in the drive, the drive may have to be removed from the computer and disassembled to retrieve the disk. Most CD-ROMs use tray loaded mechanisms.

CD-R (COMPACT DISK RECORDABLE)

Being able to create CDs is important in today's home and business environments. Two CD technologies, CD-R (Compact Disk Recordable) and CD-RW (CD Rewritable) allow this to become a reality. The two technologies have many similarities and CD-RW is the most popular. Technicians should understand the differences between the two.

CD-R (Compact Disk Recordable) drives have the ability to create CDs but they can only write once to a particular disk. These disks cannot be erased. CD-R technology is sometimes called **WORM (Write Once-Read Many)** technology. CD-R drives are used to make backups or distribute software on CDs. Disks written by CD-R drives have a temperature sensitive dye coating. To write data, the laser beam strikes the disk, changing the disk's color. This alters the disk's reflective property providing a way to distinguish between 1s and 0s. A disk written by a CD-R drive can be read by a standard CD-ROM drive. CD-R drives are no longer as expensive as in years past.

CD-R drives come in IDE, SCSI, and USB models. The models are based on their X factor speed for reading and writing. For example, one model might be a 2x6, which is a drive that can write data at 2X speed (300 KBps) and read data at 6X (900 KBps) CD-ROM speed. Another model is a 4x4 that reads and writes at 4X CD-ROM speed (600KBps).

One problem with CD-R drives occurs when data is written to the CD-R disk. If the CD-R drive does not receive data in a steady stream, a buffer underrun error occurs and the CD-R disk is ruined. To avoid this problem, use a high-end computer with at least 64MB RAM and a fast hard drive.

An important feature to look for in a CD-R or CD-RW drive is supporting multiple sessions. This is known as a multisession CD-R or CD-RW. A multisession drive has the ability to store data on a CD and then add to it later. The earliest CD-R drives could not read a multisession CD. Some CD-R drive manufacturers use a standard known as **UDF (Universal Disk Format)**; however, Windows 95 does not support UDF, but Windows 98 and Windows 2000 both support UDF.

Adaptec Corporation has a driver for Windows 95 called DirectCD that overcomes the Windows 95/UDF problem. However, the CD created in the CD-R drive cannot be read by DOS, Windows 3.x, or Macintosh computers. Another problem is that some CD-ROM drives cannot read the disks created by a CD-R drive. On the problem CD-ROM drives, the laser is not calibrated to read recordable disks that have a surface different than that on regular CDs. An indication of this problem is if a disk created by a CD-R drive is readable by some CD-ROM drives, but not others. There is no solution to this problem except to replace the drive.

Most CD-R blank disks hold 650MB (sometimes labeled as 74min). However, some manufacturers distribute 700MB disks. Not all CD-Rs can write or read CDs of this capacity. There are software packages that allow writing to 700MB disks such as Roxio Inc.'s (a newly formed subsidiary of Adaptec) Easy CD Creator. Another type of disk used in CD-Rs is the mini-disk. Many CD drives can accept both the common 5-inch and the mini 3-inch CDs. Look at the CD drive tray to see if there is a 3-inch diameter depression in the center of the tray. If so, the depression is for the 3-inch CDs. Place the mini CD in the depression, close the tray, and most CD drives will be able to read the disk.

Sony and Phillips worked together to create a new CD format that extends the CD capacity to 1.3GB. The drives that can use this specification can also read regular CDs, CD-R disks, and CD-RW disks. The drives that support this standard cannot currently read or write DVD media, but are compatible with Windows 9x, ME, NT, and 2000. The disks that use this format are known as **DDCD (Double Density CD)**.

The keys to creating CDs (as well as DVDs) are as follows:
- Interface type
- Size of drive buffers
- Amount of free hard drive space
- Amount of operating system multitasking

SCSI CD-Rs provide the fastest transfer rate followed by USB. When creating a CD, the computer must transmit a steady stream of data that is written in a continuous format on the CD. The memory buffers included with the CD-R drive help with this task, but a computer that does not have enough free hard drive space or RAM can still slow down or abort the recording process. Creating a CD takes time and you should not be performing other tasks such as playing a game or working in another application when recording a CD. This takes away from CPU time, available RAM, and available hard drive space.

Most CD creation software packages allow you to select the hard drive partition where the data is cached before it is written to the CD. Make sure you select a partition that has twice the amount of free space as the data being written. For example, if 100MB of data is going on to a CD, make sure 200MB of hard drive space is available. If the computer continuously displays errors when writing a CD, most CD recording software allows you to reduce the recording speed. This will take longer, but increases chances of success. Turn off power management and screen savers when creating a CD (or DVD).

Some people like creating an emergency boot CD that allows the computer to start in case of hard drive failure. This is only a benefit if your BIOS supports booting from a CD. If the drive is IDE, it must connect to IDE motherboard connectors to boot the computer. If connected to a SCSI interface, the host adapter must support booting from a CD. Many computer manufacturers supply a CD for restoring a system back to factory defaults. However, all applications and operating system environment settings are lost.

There are software programs that help create a bootable CD such as Roxio Inc.'s Easy CD Creator. Normally when creating the boot CD, the computer is started from a bootable floppy (so the operating system files on the hard drive are not in use). The software used to create the bootable CD is loaded and the CD is created. Always test a bootable CD *before* a hard drive failure occurs.

CD-RW (CD REWRITABLE)

CD-RW (Compact Disk ReWritable) (sometimes called CD-E for Compact Disk Erasable) can write multiple times to a disk. These disks are good for data backup, data archiving, or data distribution on CDs. The disks normally hold 650MB of data. CD-RWs can be connected to a SCSI chain, IDE cable, USB port, or FireWire port.

Originally, this technology known as **Phase-change Dual (PD)** technology used a laser to change the reflective properties of the disk. Now to read a PD disk, a PD/CD drive with a high-powered, more expensive laser is used. CD-RW or CD-E drives create disks that can be read on any standard CD-ROM drive with **dye-polymer** technology which uses a laser to heat the CD. This creates a bump on the disk that reflects light differently than the flat areas on the CD.

The good thing about CD-RW drives is that most of them are backward compatible. The reflective properties of a CD-RW disk are different (lower) than regular CD-ROM disks. Many drives that support CD-RW disks are labeled as MultiRead.

MultiRead or MultiRead2 is an OSTA (Optical Storage Technology Association) specification that states the CD-RW drive is backward compatible with CD-ROM and CD-R disks. Look for these words when purchasing a CD-RW drive.

Check with the individual CD-ROM drive manufacturer to determine if a particular model can read CD-RW disks. The drawback to CD-RW disk is the disks wear out after multiple writes.

CD STANDARDS

CDs are classified according to their standard (data format). Manufacturers of CD-ROM drives occasionally use the CD standards to state what type of disks their CD-ROM drive reads. The standards can be grouped generically into "colored books." Multimedia Table #3 summarizes the standards for each.

CD Standards

Standard	Purpose
Red Book	Audio CD
Yellow Book	Data CD
Green Book	CD-i format
Orange Book	Recordable CD format (Part I is for magneto-optical. Part II is for write -once disks. The standard also includes the specification for a PhotoCD.)
White Book	Video CD format
Blue Book	CD Extra format to include data and audio
Scarlet Book	SACD (Super Audio CD) format that allows six channel sound
Purple Book	DDCD (Double Density CD) format
ISA 9660	File naming format
Joliet	Extension to ISO 9660 that allows CDs to use long filenames
Rock Ridge	Filename and symlink extensions (to be used with Unix)
CD-RFS	Sony's incremental packet writing file system
CD-UDF	Incremental packet -writing file system
CD-Text	Phillips audio CD standard

MULTIMEDIA – TABLE #3

MAGNETO-OPTICAL DRIVES

A similar technology used for reading and writing compact disks is **magneto-optical** (**MO**). These disks do not have the drawbacks of the dye-polymer or phase-change technologies. However, magneto-optical disks cannot be used in regular CD-ROM drives but require a magneto-optical drive. For data backups or archiving, magneto-optical drives are great. They also use a laser beam to heat the surface of the disk, then a magnet applies a charge to the surface. They can be erased by reheating the disk and using the magnet to erase the data. Magneto-optical disks are read using the laser similar to CD-ROM technology.

DVD-ROM

A technology known as the DVD-ROM drive makes the CD-ROM drive obsolete. **DVD-ROM** (also called DVD) originally stood for Digital Video Disk, then Digital Versatile Disk. Some people confuse DVD-Video with DVD-ROM. DVD-Video holds a video DVD and the DVD-Video player connects to a TV. DVD-ROM is the technology used in computers (although most DVD-ROM drives now support DVD-Video and allow playing DVD movies). DVD-ROMs will usually read DVDs, audio CDs, and application CDs.

DVD disks provide more storage capacity than a CD-ROM disk, but can still play CDs used in regular CD-ROM drives. The disks used with DVD drives are the same diameter and thickness as traditional CDs and like CDs, the DVD disks tolerate dust, dirt, and fingerprints. The data on the DVD disk has pits that are smaller and more closely spaced than CD-ROM disks. Because of this, DVDs cannot be read by CD drives. DVD disks provide high video resolution and high quality sound unmatched in the computer industry and can transfer data at 1.3MBps. DVD disks should satisfy the industry demand for increased storage.

DVDs are used for audio and video entertainment such as movies, video games, and interactive TV, as well as Internet access and software applications that currently require more than one CD. The DVD-ROM drives currently come in two different configurations, 4.7GB and 8.5GB. The 4.7GB format (sometimes known as DVD-5) has a single layer of data on one side of the disk. The 8.5GB capacity (known as DVD-9) uses two layers on the same side to increase storage capacity.

Two other capacities are 9.4GB and 17.1GB. The 9.4GB disk (also referred to as DVD-10) uses a single layer on both sides of the disk. The 17.1GB disk (DVD-18 is another name) has two layers on both sides of the disk. This capacity disk is difficult to manufacture.

A great deal of industry forethought went into making the DVD drive standards. From the start, DVD-ROM drives could read single-layer, dual-layer, dual-sided, and dual-sided/dual-layer disks as well as the existing audio and application CDs. The DVD-ROM drives originally were not able to read CD-R disks. However, the new CD-R2 disks are supposed to be compatible with CD-R drives, regular CD-ROM drives, and DVD-ROM drives.

If DVD-ROM technology is to be used, the computer needs several items. Refer to the list below.

- A 133MHz Pentium microprocessor as a bare minimum—a Pentium II or higher is better
- A DVD-ROM drive and possibly an interface card—the DVD-ROM drives use SCSI, ATAPI (IDE), or the USB interface
- A PCI/AGP audio/video adapter that handles MPEG-2 video and AC-3 audio
- Windows 98/Me/NT/2000 operating system

- An optional **decoder**—if DVD movies are to be played and if the computer is not 300MHz Pentium II or higher. The decoder can be hardware or software-based. A hardware decoder (sometimes called a MPEG-2 decoder) provides the best performance (especially in older computers). A software decoder puts the burden on the CPU to decode and uncompress the video data from the DVD. Video card manufacturers have added MPEG-2 video decoding support to decrease the CPU's load.

When a technician looks at a DVD drive's specifications or technical manual, several items can be a bit confusing when first learning about DVDs. A sample specification lists below:

Interface: ATAPI Ultra-DMA Mode 2 (33.3MBps)/MW-DMA Mode-2 (16.6MBps)

Disk format: DVD-ROM, DVD-R, DVD-RW, DVD-Video, CD-DA, CD-ROM, CD-R, CD-RW, CD-I, Video CD, Photo-CD

Disk storage capacity: DVD-ROM 4.7GB & 8.5GB; CD-ROM 656MB & 748MB

Data buffer size: 512KB

Speed: 16X DVD-ROM/40X CD

Mount position: Horizontal and vertical

The *interface* parameter determines the connector and rules for how the drive is configured before installation. This sample drive uses IDE (ATAPI). The drive follows the same rules as an IDE hard drive or CD drive in that you must configure it for master or slave and use a 40-pin (80-conductor is best) cable to connect to an IDE connector on an adapter or the motherboard. The other choices you might see are SCSI and USB. The specification also shows the modes supported UDMA 2 and MW-DMA 2. UDMA stands for Ultra DMA and this concept was covered in the Hard Drives chapter. UDMA allows the PCI bus to take control of the system bus and transfer directly to RAM without having to go through the CPU. MW-DMA uses standard DMA where the CPU was asked permission for the IDE interface to control the bus and transfer directly to RAM. MW stands for multi-word meaning that two 16-bit transfers could occur simultaneously. A technician needs to pay attention to the interface parameter because (1) the correct configuration, cabling, and type of connector/adapter is defined by the interface parameter; (2) the operating system and BIOS should be able to support the technologies offered (for example, UDMA transfers are important to a DVD device); and (3) different interfaces offer different speed performances.

The *disk format* specification defines what type of disks the DVD-ROM accepts. This is especially important for computer users who press their own CDs, and technicians who use pressed CDs in their support functions. The *data storage capacity* specification is similar in that it determines what type of disk capacities are supported.

DVD-ROM *speed* normally shows two different numbers—the speed at which DVDs operate and the speed at which CDs operate. The CD speed is always the larger of the two numbers. This is a performance issue. *Data buffer size* is important for DVD playback performance. This is the amount of memory included on the drive. The CD-ROM section on buffers and cache apply to DVDs as well. The last parameter, *mount position* is important to the technician doing the DVD-ROM installation. Some cases might only have a vertical drive slot available, or an external DVD-ROM attaches to a computer where there is only space available if the DVD-ROM is installed on its side.

A software development that helps with DVD technology is Microsoft's DirectX. **DirectX** allows people who write software such as games or web design to not have to write code to directly access specific hardware. DirectX translates generic hardware commands into special commands for the hardware. This speeds up development time for hardware manufacturers and software developers. DirectX takes the operating system and the audio and video functions into a new computer dimension. It incorporates support for the Universal Serial bus, 1394 bus, Accelerated Graphics Port, MPEG-1, MPEG-2, MMX extensions, and Microsoft's Talisman graphics architecture. DirectX has a direct impact on the new DVD market because of the lack of audio and video standards needed with the new PCI audio/video adapter. DirectX has pieces of software code that software providers use so their software works with PCI adapters. DirectX is available in Windows 9x, NT, and Windows 2000 and updated versions are available on Microsoft's web site.

To protect DVD software, movies, and audio, a DVD drive has a **region code**. The world is divided into six regions and the DVD drive must be set for the correct region code or else the DVDs made for that area do not work. When a DVD is inserted, the decoder checks what region it is configured for (or in the case of software decoding, what region the drive is configured for) and then checks the DVD region code and if the two match, the movie plays. Multimedia Table #4 shows the region codes.

DVD Region Codes

DVD Region Code	Geographic Area
1	USA and Canada
2	Europe, Near East, Japan, and South Africa
3	Southeast Asia
4	Australia, Middle America, and South America
5	Africa, Asia, and Eastern Europe
6	China

MULTIMEDIA – TABLE #4

Some DVD drives do not require this setting (region free). The current standards allow five region changes before the drive is locked. If you have a hardware decoder, make sure that you configure it for the appropriate region. If using software decoding, the program must be configured for the correct region and it too normally allows five changes. There are freeware programs on the Internet to check the drive for its region requirements without incrementing the number of times the region code has been changed.

DECODERS

MPEG (Moving Picture Experts Group) created a compression technique called MPEG2 used by DVDs. The computer must decompress the video and audio from the DVD, and this is called decoding. There are two methods for decoding: hardware and software. A **hardware decoder** requires a PCI adapter and less work is put on the computer's CPU because the adapter does the decoding. The adapter decodes both video and audio. This solution is good for slower computers. Hardware decoder adapters can have an output jack to connect to a TV or the video adapter may have a TV output, but the quality is not as good as a TV that uses a DVD-video player.

With **software decoding**, no PCI adapter is needed, but CPU power is. A 400MHz processor is the minimum to use. Software decoders provide varying playback quality. The installed video adapter must support DirectX's overlay mixers in order to do software decoding. Most video cards now include this feature but not all do. Some software decoders require an AGP video card or their performance is weak unless an AGP video card is installed. Software decoding also requires a PCI sound card. The sound card needs to support 48KHz decoding for DVDs.

For faster operations with a software decoder, enable DMA transfer for the DVD-ROM. Go into Device Manager and expand the CD-ROM section. Right-click on the *DVD* and select the *Properties* option. Click on the *Settings* tab and click on the *DMA* checkbox if it is currently unchecked. If the video and sound adapters support Windows acceleration, adjust the acceleration setting. For video, use the Display control panel, click on the *Settings* tab, click on the *Advanced* button, click on the *Performance* tab and slide the bar tab all the way to the right to the *Full* setting. For audio, use the Multimedia control panel. Click on the *Audio* tab, click on the *Advanced Properties* button in the Playback section. Click on the *Performance tab* and slide the *Hardware Acceleration* bar tab all the way to the right to the *Full* setting. Finally, you can lower the video resolution, which does not affect DVD quality.

Decoder adapters are prone to hardware conflicts because of the number of devices installed in the system. Use Device Manager to check for conflicts or the System Information utility in Windows 2000. Windows 2000 does not include any software decoders so one will have to be purchased.

OTHER DVD TECHNOLOGIES

The different types of DVD technologies currently in the market place are DVD-ROM, DVD-RAM, DVD-R, DVD-RW, and DVD+RW. DVD-ROM is the most common but that is changing. Compatibility with the various CDs and DVDs are issues to be aware of today.

DVD-RAM uses phase-change technology like CD-RW where a laser heats the disk to magnetically charge it. This technology allows data to be rewritten on a DVD-RAM disk. These disks are incompatible with older DVD-ROM drives, but look for the MultiRead2 capability discussed in the CD section of this chapter. There are two capacities of DVD-RAM disks, 2.6GB and 5.2GB. The 2.6GB disk uses only one side, but the 5.2GB model uses two sides. The single-sided disks can usually be read by DVD-ROM drives.

The DVD-RAM disk has grooves and lands. The lands are the areas between the grooves. Data is written on both the grooves and the lands. DVD-RAM is more a removable storage and backup medium than a video recording option. DVD-RAM disks can usually write to a DVD-RW disk (covered a few paragraphs later) and can read them.

DVD-R uses WORM technology and is similar to CD-R drives. DVD-R disks can use one or two sides and are available in 3.95GB, 4.7GB, and 9.4GB. When articles or advertisements mention DVD-R disks they sometimes show two different types, DVD-R(A) and DVD-R(G). The DVD-R(A) targets the "authoring" business for professional development of DVDs. DVD-R(G) is more for home users and lay people. Both can be read by most DVD players and drives, but DVD-R(G) drives usually cannot write to DVD-R(A) media. Advertisements usually distinguish between the media by referring to the DVD-R(G) disks as general purpose and the DVD-R(A) disks as authoring. The disks are written to once and can be used in DVD-ROM drives. The disks have grooves and lands like DVD-RAM, but the grooves are closer together and data is written only on the grooves.

DVD-RW (DVD-ReWritable) is similar to DVD-R except that you can erase and rewrite information on the disk. DVD-RW uses 4.7GB disks and most DVD-ROM drives and DVD-Video players support this format. The drives use a phase-change technology similar to CD-RW. The DVD-RW disks can be written to multiple times. This technology is sometimes known or seen as DVD-R/W or DVD-ER.

DVD+RW is also rewritable but is not endorsed by the DVD forum. Phillips, Sony, HP, Mitsubishi, Yamaha, and Ricoh are part of the DVD+RW consortium to push this technology. The target market is video recording (not data storage) and DVD+RW is backward compatible with DVD-ROM drives and DVD video players. The disks hold 2.8GB per side.

DVD STANDARDS

The DVD formats are organized according to "Book" specifications. Multimedia Table #5 summarizes these standards.

MULTIMEDIA – TABLE #5

DVD Specifications

DVD Specification	Purpose
Book A	Defines read-only specifications (DVD-ROM)
Book B	The second read-only specification defining DVD-Video
Book C	The third read-only specification defining DVD-Audio
Book D	Defines DVD-R and the writable format
Book E	The second writable format defining DVD-RAM
Book F	The third writable format defining DVD-RW

DRIVE INTERFACES AND CONNECTIONS

CD and DVD drives can use IDE, SCSI, USB, FireWire, or a proprietary (non-standard) interface. The IDE interface is the most common. The differences between these are great. You should reference the Hard Drive, Motherboard, and Serial chapters for more information on each of these technologies. Many users want technicians to add a CD or DVD drive or a kit to their computer system or upgrade their existing drive. A kit includes the CD-ROM drive, a sound card, a cable that connects the audio signals to the sound card, software drivers for the drive and sound card, a set of external speakers, and sometimes extra software bundles such as entertainment or encyclopedias. The particular interface the technician recommends to the customer depends on several factors. The following questions will help customers decide what interface to use.

- Is the drive going to be an external device? If so, SCSI, USB, and FireWire are the best choices.
- Is the drive going to be an internal device? If so, is price an issue? Internal CD-ROM drives can be IDE or SCSI. IDE is less expensive than SCSI, but the SCSI interface has much more expandability than IDE.
- Does the customer plan to add more devices such as a scanner or tape backup unit in the near future? If so, SCSI, USB and FireWire have more expandability than IDE.

When connecting a drive to an IDE connector with a hard drive connected, verify that the device is configured as the slave. If the drive connects to the IDE connector and is the sole device connected, verify that the drive is configured as the master. Some older CD-ROMs do not work unless connected as the slave; check the drive documentation. Refer to the chapter on hard drives for more information on setting the master/slave setting.

For the best performance, connect the drive as secondary master by putting it on a separate IDE interface from any installed hard drive(s). Make sure the BIOS has the motherboard's secondary connector enabled. For CD-R, CD-RW, DVD-R, or DVD-RW drives, look for DMA or UDMA transfer mode support. See the hard drive IDE section for more information on these transfer modes.

The expansion capabilities of the SCSI interface make it a good choice for these drives. However, SCSI drives are traditionally more expensive than IDE, but the gap has recently narrowed. Microsoft's Windows 9x, NT, and 2000 provide drivers for SCSI devices.

When installing a SCSI CD-R, CD-RW, DVD-R, or DVD-RW, look to see if the device allows bus mastering. This speeds up SCSI transfers. See the SCSI section in the hard drive chapter for more information on SCSI bus mastering.

SCSI CD-ROM drives require software compatibility with the SCSI adapter such as ASPI, CAM, or LADDR. Most SCSI CD-ROM drives today use the SCSI-2 standard.

A SCSI drive must usually have the SCSI ID set to a SCSI ID *other than* 0, 1, or 7. The terminator on the drive is installed or removed based on where the device connects along the SCSI chain. If the drive is at either end of the SCSI chain, terminate the drive. Refer to the hard drive chapter's SCSI configuration section for more information on setting the SCSI ID and termination.

Proprietary drives come as a kit with their own adapter. Even though they may be cheaper than SCSI or IDE CD-ROM kits, they are best *to be avoided*. Proprietary drives are not usually compatible with other devices such as sound cards. When replacement or upgrading is necessary, compatible drives may be hard to find.

DRIVE UPGRADES

If the customer wants to upgrade a drive, find out why. Many times, slow access is due to the computer's other components, not the drive. Use the same questions listed previously for a new drive, but only after finding out from the customer why they want to upgrade the device. If it is a 1X or a 2X CD-ROM drive, upgrade the drive, but be sure the other parts of the computer complement the CD-ROM drive's performance. The following questions help when upgrading drives.

- Does the customer want sound (speakers)? If so, a kit might be necessary or if the customer is an audiophile, then special speakers may be needed.
- What microprocessor does the customer have? CD-ROMs currently available now do not perform well on a system such as a 386SX. The customer should

have a Pentium or higher CPU. For DVDs, the minimum CPU depends on which decoding method is being used.

- Is there an available slot in the computer for a sound card? Also, check if there are sound connections built into the motherboard. If so, a sound card may not be needed. DVD users sometimes require a hardware decoder, which means an adapter (plus available slot). They also want sound (sound card or built-in motherboard sound port). The sound card should use PCI and support 48KHz decoding if software decoding is being used.

- Is the customer going to be using CDs that are video-intensive? If so, what type of interface is the video adapter? AGP provides the best throughput and performance for video. How much memory is on the video adapter? 2MB is the minimum amount of memory that should be on the video adapter. 8MB of memory should be on the video card if DVDs are being used. DVDs require that the video adapter support DirectX's overlay mixers if software decoding is being used.

- Does the customer have enough RAM on the motherboard? 64MB is the bare minimum for Windows 9x if the drive does writing. For Windows 2000, 128MB is recommended.

- In order to achieve the best DVD effects, connect a sound system that accepts digital audio input and supports Dolby Digital surround sound.

PREVENTIVE MAINTENANCE FOR CD AND DVD DRIVES

When LP records were used, handling of the records was quite a problem. Fingerprints, dust, and dirt greatly affected the performance of the record. CDs and DVDs are less prone to these problems because they have a protective coating over the aluminum alloy-based data layer. When reading information, the laser beam ignores the protective coating and shines through to the data layer. Even if the disk has dirt on the protective coating, the laser beam can still operate because the beam is directed at the data layer rather than the disk surface. An exception to this is surface material with reflective properties. The reflection could reflect and distort the laser beam thus causing distortion or data corruption. Another exception is if the dust or dirt completely blocks the laser beam. A heavy accumulation of dust and dirt can reduce the quality of the data retrieved from the disk.

Special cleaning disks, cloths, and kits are available. When using the cleaning cloth, wipe the disk from the inside (near the center hole) to the outside of the disk (*not* in a circular motion) on the side of the disk that has data. (If you cannot tell, just wipe both sides.) Proper handling of the disk aids in good performance. As with audio CDs used in stereos, handle the disk on the outside edge of the disk. Never touch the surface of the disk. Fingerprints, oil from hands, dust, and dirt on the CD disk can also cause performance problems. Store the disk in a cool location.

If a disk is scratched, mild abrasives or special disk repair kits are available. Examples of mild abrasives include plastic, furniture, or brass polish. When applying the abrasive, do not rub in circles. Instead, use the same technique as cleaning: start from the innermost portion of the disk and rub outward. The abrasive can remove the scratch if it is not too deep. A wax such as furniture or car wax can be used to fill the scratch if it is not removed by the abrasive.

A special component of the CD-ROM drive, the **laser lens** (also known as the objective lens), is responsible for reading information from the CD disk. The laser lens is susceptible to dust and dirt accumulation. If the laser lens gets dust, dirt, or moisture on it, the drive may report data or read errors. Some CD-ROM drives have the lens encased in an airtight enclosure and others have a self-cleaning laser lens. If the drive does not have this feature, laser lens cleaning kits are available at computer and music stores. Also, the laser lens can be cleaned with an air blower like ones used on a camera lens. Cleaning the laser lens should be a preventive maintenance routine just like cleaning the heads on a floppy disk drive. Some drive manufacturers include a special plate to keep dust away from the internal components. In any case, keep the disk compartment closed to prevent dust and dirt from accumulating on the laser lens and other CD parts.

NEW TECHNOLOGIES

There are two major trends for increasing data storage capacities—hybrid magneto-optical drives and FML/C. **Magneto optical drives** and hard drives have been around for years, but a push to combine the two technologies is here. One company calls it NFR (Near Field Recording) and their product has a laser that mounts in an optical flying read/write head to increase the amount of data stored on a disk.

FML/C (Fluorescent MultiLayer Disk/Card) uses a fluorescent dye that is embedded in pits and grooves on each layer of the disk or card. When a laser is used, fluorescent light reflects back from the disk that is a different wavelength of the laser's light beam. Current technology uses something similar to this in the dual-layer DVDs, but more layers cannot be added because the laser beam causes interference and scatter. Coating each layer with a fluorescent material removes this barrier and allows multiple layers to be created. A 20-layer DVD would be able to hold about 100GB. The technology would require deeper grooves and data pits.

To further increase capacity, a blue laser can be used. Current drives use red lasers. Blue laser technology has a shorter wavelength, which means that smaller data pit sizes can be used to create higher disk capacities. Blue laser technology is much more expensive than red lasers, but the potential is there.

CD AND DVD DRIVE INSTALLATION

The steps for installing an internal drive are similar to installing any drive. The steps that follow are for an internal drive installation.

1. Install any necessary mounting brackets onto the drive.
2. Check what interface (IDE or SCSI) the drive uses. Set the appropriate master/slave, SCSI ID, or termination according to the drive interface type. Refer to the documentation included with the drive for the proper configuration of these settings.

Most IDE drives are pre-configured as the slave device. Some drives will work even if it is the only device connected to the IDE connector (even though single IDE are normally set to master). Always refer to the drive's documentation for configuration issues. Manufacturers are trying to limit frustration and technical support calls by making the devices easier to install. Technicians should set the device properly because they know better! For best performance, connect the drive as secondary master without any other devices attached to the interface.

3. (optional) Turn off computer power and install the appropriate adapter into the system if necessary. Set any interrupt, I/O address, or DMA channel as needed. Refer to the documentation included with the adapter.
4. Install the drive into the computer.
5. Attach the power cable to the drive.
6. Attach the interface cable to the drive and the adapter or motherboard.

Be careful when attaching the interface cable from the drive to the adapter or motherboard. Verify the cable's pin 1 attaches to the drive's pin 1. Pin 1 on the drive is sometimes hard to detect because the connector on the drive is frequently black in color. Look very carefully for an etched arrow on the connector on the drive. Some drive manufacturers place a drawing on top of the drive illustrating the proper orientation. Most cables and drives are keyed so the cable only inserts one way.

7. (optional) Attach the audio cable from the drive to the sound card. If sound is provided through the USB or IEEE 1394 (FireWire) bus, this step is unnecessary.

The drive is now installed but is not operational until software drivers are installed properly.

If the drive is an IDE drive installed into a computer with an auto-detect BIOS, successful installation is indicated if the BIOS detects the drive when the computer reboots. If not, check the BIOS to ensure the interface is enabled.

CD-ROM AND DVD DRIVER INSTALLATION

Hardware will not function unless the operating system detects it. A **device driver** is a small piece of software that stays in RAM to allow communication with a piece of hardware. The driver is included with the drive and, through the installation process, adds to the registry. The general steps for installing a device driver are outlined below but always use the manufacturer's installation steps.

1. Power on the computer.
2. The Windows 9x or 2000 operating system normally detects that a device has been installed. If it does not, use the Add New Hardware control panel. The operating system contains drivers for many devices, but it is always best to use the driver provided by the manufacturer or the latest driver from the Internet. You can change device drivers using various control panels or Device Manager. When the system prompts and asks you if you want Windows to search for a driver, select the option where you can install the driver from the manufacturer. With NT, the vendor normally supplies an installation program that is executed using the RUN utility. Use NT Diagnostics and the Multimedia control panel to determine if the drive is detected.

In older operating systems, a line was added to the CONFIG.SYS file. A drive letter is assigned to the drive (such as D:, E:, etc.) by the operating system. After a drive letter is assigned, the drive is accessible to the system. **MSCDEX.EXE** is a program provided with DOS and Windows 3.x that assigns a drive letter to the CD-ROM drive. This is still important for DOS-based applications and games. More MSCDEX.EXE information is available in a later section.

The software device driver for the CD-ROM drive usually goes in the CONFIG.SYS file in a statement such as the following:

DEVICE=C:\CPQIDECD.SYS /D:IDECD001

or

DEVICE=C:\SB14\SB14CD.SYS /D:IDECD001

or

DEVICE=C:\CDROMDRV.SYS /D:MSCD000

The *D:* switch is the device name used by the CD-ROM device driver. The **device name** is an eight-character name unique for each CD-ROM drive. The device name is very important in later steps.

When installing a read or read/write drive that supports DMA transfers, you may need to enable DMA bus mastering. To verify if the operating system support DMA transfers, use Device Manager. Click on the *Disk Drives* option to expand the selections. Click on the specific hard drive you want to check. Click on the *Properties* button and select the *Settings* tab. Look for a DMA checkbox. If the checkbox has a check inside it, the DMA transfer mode is enabled. If unchecked, click inside the box, click on the *OK* button and restart the computer. Go into Device Manager again. If the box is unchecked, your BIOS does not support DMA transfers. If the computer locks because you enabled DMA transfers through the operating system and then does not allow you to disable it, disable DMA in CMOS Setup. Once disabled, start the operating system and disable DMA in the operating system. For NT, you must edit the registry directly to enable DMA bus mastering. Go to the Microsoft web site for instructions.

TROUBLESHOOTING THE DEVICE DRIVER

Before any additional steps are taken, a technician should be sure the device driver loads correctly and no problems occur. No other software procedures work if the device driver does not detect the drive. After installing the driver for the first time, the installation software sometimes displays a message that states the computer must be restarted for the changes to take effect. Use Device Manager in Windows 9x and 2000 to verify driver installation. Check that no conflicts exist with the drive. In NT, use NT Diagnostics and the Multimedia control panel.

In a DOS or Windows 3.x computer, if the driver loads without a problem, usually the driver prompts with a message such as "1 drive detected." Others might have quite lengthy messages, but look for an indication that a CD-ROM drive is found such as "Number of drives installed: 1." These messages are a technician's first clue that the driver is installed properly!

If the device driver message reads something like "No drive found" or "Number of installed drives: 0," then an interrupt, I/O address, or DMA conflict is very likely. Also, check the path for the correct device driver. For example, DEVICE=C:\CDROM\CDROMDRV.SYS /D:MSCD000 in the CONFIG.SYS file, indicates that the file, CDROMDRV.SYS, is in the CDROM directory on the hard drive. Verify that the directory exists and that the software driver (such as CDROMDRV.SYS) exists in the mentioned directory. Sometimes errors occur during the install process and the driver is not in the directory specified by the CONFIG.SYS statement, or the driver was not placed in the directory (or anywhere) by the installation process. If the directory or file is missing, delete all directories and files created during the install process and re-install the software driver again.

Do not proceed until the device driver loads properly and the system detects the drive. No other software installation steps work properly until the system sees the drive when the device driver loads correctly. Another problem could be with incorrect configuration and cabling of the drive. Recheck all master/slave, SCSI ID, termination settings and the correct cabling between the drive and the interface connector. Other things to check include the adapter seating, BIOS setting for secondary IDE interface, and power cable.

THE MSCDEX.EXE PROGRAM

When a computer does not work, a technician must work from a DOS prompt. In order to access a CD or DVD drive, DOS drivers must be loaded. The MSCDEX.EXE program provides access and assigns a drive letter to the CD-ROM drive in the DOS environment and Windows MS-DOS mode. The MSCDEX.EXE program has some switches that provide flexibility and enhancement to the program. Multimedia Table #6 summarizes the switches available with MSCDEX.EXE.

MULTIMEDIA – TABLE #6

MSCDEX.EXE Switches

Switch	Purpose
/D:*driver1*	Used to specify the specific device name
/E	Used to use expanded memory for sector buffers if expanded memory is available
/K	Used to recognize CD-ROM drive volumes encoded in Kanji
/L:*letter*	Assigns a specific drive letter to a CD-ROM drive
/M:*number*	Specifies the number of sector buffers
/S	Allows sharing of CD-ROM drives in networked environments
/V	Verbose switch used to provide more details when MSCDEX is loaded

The /D:*driver1* switch must include the exact device name given when the CD-ROM device driver loads in CONFIG.SYS.

For example, if the CONFIG.SYS line is DEVICE=C:\CPQIDECD.SYS */D:IDECD001*, the corresponding MSCDEX.EXE statement in the AUTOEXEC.BAT file would be C:\WINDOWS\MSCDEX.EXE */D:IDECD001*. The two device names must match in both statements to provide a drive letter to the CD-ROM drive. The MSCDEX.EXE requires the */D:driver1* to load properly.

Multiple CD-ROM drives can be controlled by the same MSCDEX.EXE line in the AUTOEXEC.BAT file. For example, if the CONFIG.SYS file contains two lines where each line controls a separate CD-ROM drive, then the two drives are assigned drive letters by the MSCDEX.EXE program. The CONFIG.SYS lines are below:

DEVICE=C:\CPQIDECD.SYS */D:IDECD001*
DEVICE=C:\CDROM\CDROMDRV.SYS */D:MSCD000*

The corresponding MSCDEX.EXE line in the AUTOEXEC.BAT file is below:
C:\WINDOWS\MSCDEX */D:IDECD001* */D:MSCD000*

The drive that uses the IDECD001 device name obtains the first available drive letter. The drive that uses MSCD000 as a device name gets the next drive letter because it is the second line.

MSCDEX.EXE's */E* switch is for using expanded memory for sector buffering. If at all possible, do not use this option due to the slow nature of expanded memory. The */L:letter* option assigns a specific drive letter to the CD-ROM drive instead of letting the system assign the next available drive letter. For example, C:\WINDOWS\MSCDEX.EXE /D:MSCD000 /L:J assigns the drive the letter J:. The number of drive letters available is determined by the LASTDRIVE statement in the CONFIG.SYS file. For example, if the CONFIG.SYS file contains the statement LASTDRIVE=F and the MSCDEX.EXE line in AUTOEXEC.BAT is C:\WINDOWS\MSCDEX /D:MSCD000 /L:G, then the CD-ROM drive would *not* get a drive letter because the assignment of the drive letter G: is not allowed by the system due to the LASTDRIVE statement. If the last drive statement is a problem, one indication is when MSCDEX.EXE loads and the message "Not enough drive letters available" appears.

Whenever the message "Not enough drive letters available" appears, check the LASTDRIVE statement in the CONFIG.SYS file. Modify the statement to include enough drive letters for the parameter specified in MSCDEX.EXE's */L:letter* switch.

The */M:number* switch specifies the number of memory buffers set aside for speedier access to the CD-ROM drive's data. Eight is the normal setting for one CD-ROM drive (with an increase of four for each additional CD-ROM installed). Increasing the number of sector buffers decreases the amount of conventional memory available because some memory is used by the MSCDEX.EXE buffers. An alternative to the */M:number* switch used with MSCDEX.EXE is to use the SmartDrive disk caching program.

TROUBLESHOOTING THE MSCDEX.EXE INSTALLATION

The technician must first determine by restarting the computer if the CD-ROM drive is assigned a drive letter. When the message "Starting MS-DOS" or "Starting PC DOS" appears on the screen, press the *F8* key to single step through the CONFIG.SYS and AUTOEXEC.BAT files. Pay particular attention when the MSCDEX.EXE program loads. A message similar to the following appears:

MSCDEX Version 2.23

Copyright (C) Microsoft Corp. 1986-1993. All rights reserved.

    Drive D: = Driver IDECD001 Unit 0

If no drive letter is assigned to the CD-ROM drive, then verify the CD-ROM device driver in the CONFIG.SYS file loads correctly and detects a CD-ROM drive. Also, be sure the correct device name is in the MSCDEX.EXE command found in the AUTOEXEC.BAT file. The device name used in the CD-ROM driver /D switch (CONFIG.SYS file) *must* match the device name in MSCDEX.EXE's /D switch (AUTOEXEC.BAT file). Finally, verify the path is correct and the directory listed in the AUTOEXEC.BAT line contains the MSCDEX.EXE program.

CD-ROM DRIVES (WINDOWS 95/98/NT/2000)

Windows 9x and 2000 support IDE and SCSI drives by default. **CDFS (CD-ROM File System)** is the Windows 95/98/NT/2000 32-bit protected mode CD-ROM file system driver. CDFS is an improvement over the older MSCDEX caching program used in the DOS/Windows environment because (1) conventional memory is not used, (2) CDFS is larger and smarter than MSCDEX, (3) multitasking is improved for CD-ROM access, and (4) CDFS provides a more intelligent and balanced use of memory, both for applications and for caching the CD-ROM drive. The CDFS cache is different than the one used for files from disks or networks because the CD-ROM cache can be paged to the hard disk when CD-ROM activity pauses. Applications have more room in memory to operate, and this keeps the hard disk's file cache from being flushed when a large multimedia stream is retrieved from the CD-ROM drive. Retrieving data from cache to a hard disk drive is still faster than accessing the information from the CD-ROM drive.

The CDFS cache is dynamic and grows or shrinks as needed. It requires no configuration or specific allocation of memory set by the user. However, an optional supplemental cache setting is available. This holds directory, file, and path table information for the CD-ROM drive. The supplemental CD-ROM cache improves CD streaming and reduces the drive's seek latency time.

 An indication that the supplemental CD-ROM cache needs to be adjusted might be if the CD-ROM drive does not play files as fast as it should.

An exercise at the end of the chapter illustrates how to configure the Windows 9x and 2000 CD-ROM supplemental cache size.

Some CDs designed for Windows have an Autorun feature, which starts an application when the CD is inserted into the drive. Some people find the Autorun feature annoying. If so, use the following steps to disable the Autorun feature:

1. Double-click on the *My Computer* icon and double-click on the *Control Panel* folder icon.
2. Double-click on the *System control panel* icon and click on the *Device Manager* tab.
3. Click on the *CD-ROM* icon. A new icon with the model of CD-ROM installed should be treed below the CD-ROM icon.
4. Click once on the icon for the *CD-ROM* installed in the system and click on the *Properties* button. Click on the *Settings* tab and click once to uncheck the *Auto-insert notification* option.
5. Close the Properties window and close the control panel window.

If the Auto-insert notification is enabled, and an audio CD is inserted into the CD-ROM drive, the Windows CD Player automatically launches. Windows takes control of the CD and disables the front panel controls on the CD Player program. Even after CD Player closes, the front panel controls of the CD-ROM drive remain disabled. To fix this problem, eject the disk. Then, hold down the *Shift* key and reinsert the audio CD. Another fix is to press the *Play* button twice on the drive's front panel (if available).

An advantage to assigning a specific drive letter to a CD or DVD drive is for future hard drive upgrades or new hard drive installations. For example, if a computer has one hard drive (C:) and one CD-ROM drive (D:) and you install a second hard drive, it is assigned drive letter D: and the CD-ROM drive changes to drive letter E: (depending on the operating system).

The problem with changing a drive letter is that some applications place the drive letter of the drive as the path to the location of certain software components. When the drive letter changes and the software application runs, application errors occur. The software must be reloaded.

Assign the CD or DVD drive a drive letter such as F: or G: from the very beginning, and more hard drives can be installed or the existing hard drive(s) can be re-partitioned into more logical drives without reassigning the drive letter. An exercise at the end of this chapter outlines the steps for reassigning the CD-ROM drive letter using Windows 9x, NT, and 2000.

SOUND CARDS

Since CD and DVD technology emphasize video and sound, no chapter on multimedia is complete without talking about sound. CD and DVD drives have the capability of producing sound, usually through a front headphone jack. Audio CDs can be played on these drives, but the CDs do not sound as good through headphone jacks as they do through a stereo system or speakers. A better alternative is to connect the drive to a sound card. A cable connects from the back of the CD or DVD drive to the sound card. Look at Multimedia Figure #3 for an illustration of an audio cable used to connect a CD-ROM drive to a sound adapter.

MULTIMEDIA – FIGURE #3

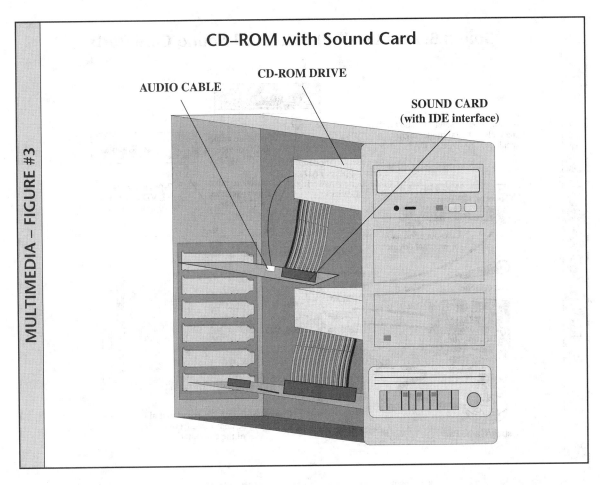

CD–ROM with Sound Card

CD-ROM DRIVE

AUDIO CABLE

SOUND CARD
(with IDE interface)

Notice in Multimedia Figure #3 how an audio cable goes from the back of the drive to the adapter. This cable carries the audio signals from the drive to the adapter and then out to the speakers.

Some sound adapters will not support every CD-ROM drive. Also, many drives have proprietary connectors for the audio cable. For this reason, most people prefer CD-ROM drive kits.

A few CD drives sold separately from the adapter include the interface cable, audio cable, mounting brackets, and screws. If you have an old CD-ROM, keep the old screws. A CD-ROM kit takes some of the hassle out of the purchase.

Many sound cards have the IDE or SCSI interface and a MIDI (Musical Instrument Digital Interface) built into the adapter, and a jack for microphone input. **MIDI (Musical Instrument Digital Interface)** is used to create synthesized music. A 15-pin female connector on the back of the sound adapter connects a joystick or a MIDI device such as a MIDI keyboard. Multimedia Figure #4 shows a typical sound board and ports.

MULTIMEDIA – FIGURE #4

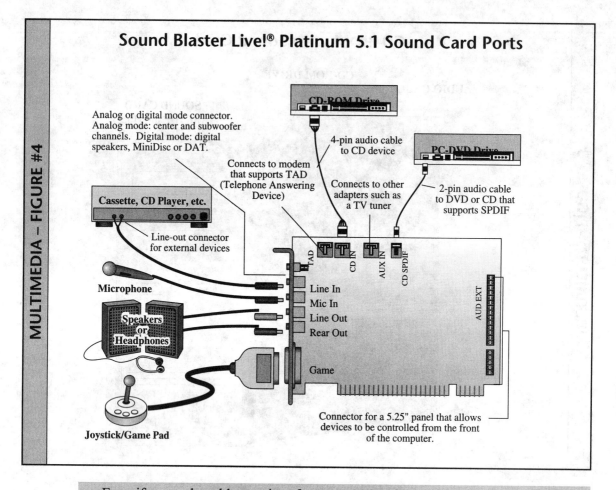

Sound Blaster Live!® Platinum 5.1 Sound Card Ports

Analog or digital mode connector.
Analog mode: center and subwoofer
channels. Digital mode: digital
speakers, MiniDisc or DAT.

Connects to modem
that supports TAD
(Telephone Answering
Device)

Connects to other
adapters such as
a TV tuner

4-pin audio cable
to CD device

2-pin audio cable
to DVD or CD that
supports SPDIF

CD-ROM Drive

PC-DVD Drive

Cassette, CD Player, etc.

Line-out connector
for external devices

Microphone

Speakers
or
Headphones

TAD   CD IN   AUX IN   CD SPDIF

Line In
Mic In
Line Out
Rear Out

AUD EXT

Game

Joystick/Game Pad

Connector for a 5.25" panel that allows
devices to be controlled from the front
of the computer.

Even if a sound card has an interface connection for the drive, the CD or DVD drive does not have to connect to the sound card. Instead, the CD-ROM drive can connect to an IDE motherboard connector or still yet to another IDE adapter installed in the system. Just remember to connect an audio cable from the drive to the sound card for CD or DVD-based audio to be heard.

An initiative between Microsoft and Intel resulted in the PC Design Guides. These are available on the Internet at www.pcdesguide.org. Connector colors and connector icons (labeling) are defined. For example, the audio Line In port's color is light blue whereas the audio Line Out port's color is lime. With sound cards having so many connectors on the card, understanding the common labeling is imperative. The documentation may not always be handy or easy to get. Multimedia Table #7 illustrates the recommended port icons relating to sound cards.

PC Design Symbols

Port	Icon
SCSI	
Gameport/Joystick	
Audio In*	
Audio Out*	
Microphone	
Serial Port 1	
Serial Port 2	
Headphone	

*Alternate designs by Hewlett-Packard

Also in the PC Design document are basic audio requirements. This section defines the basic hardware requirements for audio-based applications. For example, if a device supports DOS applications, the operating system or a emulator must be used so that device does not try to communicate directly with ISA resources (IRQ, DMA, I/O address). The audio subsystem needs to make the digital audio stream available to the operating system kernel. This allows USB and FireWire devices to accept the audio digital signal and convert it in the external device. This keeps noise inside the computer from interfering with this digital signal.

Two major types of sound files are MIDI (.MID) and Wave (.WAV) files. Most multimedia disks use Wave files for sound, but most game CDs use MIDI files. Getting a sound adapter that can process both files is important. An alternative format is **MP3** (MPEG-1 Audio Layer-3) that compresses a file into about one-twelfth its original size. Windows

98 and 2000 have a player built into the operating system and others are available on the Internet. MP3 files have a file extension of *mp3*. MP3 is slowly being replaced by **AAC** (Advanced Audio Compression), which does better compression. Some software applications require a sound card to be Sound Blaster-compatible. Creative Labs' audio cards are called Sound Blasters.

SOUND CARD THEORY OF OPERATION

Sound cards have a variety of options that can include an input from a microphone, an output to a speaker, a MIDI interface, and the ability to generate music. Take the example of bringing sound into the computer through a microphone connected to a sound card. Sound waves are shown as an analog waveform as in Multimedia Figure #5.

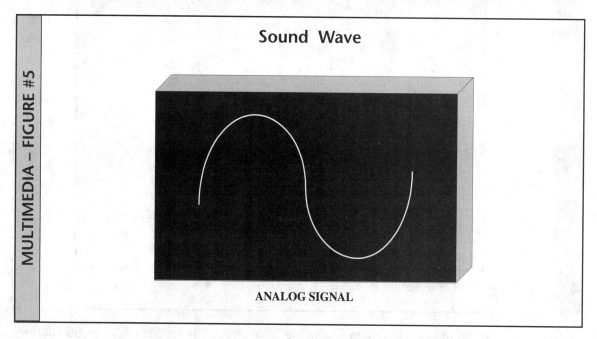

MULTIMEDIA – FIGURE #5

Sound Wave

ANALOG SIGNAL

Computers work with digital signals (1s and 0s) so the sound card must take the analog signal and convert it to a digital format to send the sound into the computer. Sound cards can also take the digital data from a CD and output the sound to the speakers. To convert an analog waveform to 1s and 0s, samples of the data are taken. The more samples taken, the truer the reproduction of the original signal.

The first sound cards made for the computer sampled the data using 8 bits. Eight 1s and 0s can give a total of 256 (2^8=256) different values. The analog waveform goes above and below a center value of 0. Because one of the eight bits denotes negative or positive value, only 7 bits can represent sampled values. 2^7=128. The values can be 0 through +127 or 0 through −127 (total value range is between −127 and +127). Multimedia Figure #6 shows an example of sampling.

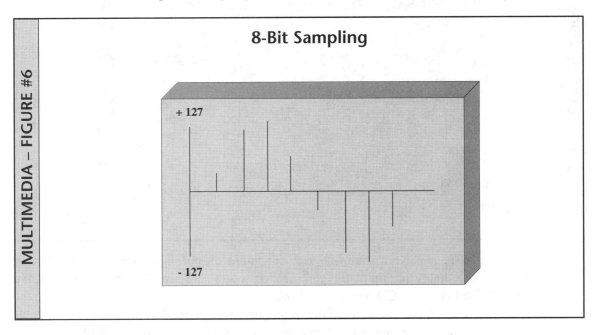

MULTIMEDIA – FIGURE #6

8-Bit Sampling

+ 127

- 127

The more samples taken by the sound card, the closer the reproduction is to the original sound signal. The sound card's **frequency response** is the number of samples taken. For a good reproduction of sound, the sound wave is sampled at twice the range desired. For example, a person's hearing is in the 20Hz to 20KHz range. Twice that range is approximately 40,000 samples per second. The frequency response for a musical CD is 44,100 samples per second, a good quality sound reproduction for human ears. The first sound cards for computers used eight bits to sample the sound wave and had a frequency response of approximately 22,000 samples per second (22KHz). The sound produced from the original sound cards was better than the beeps and chirps previously heard from the computer. The sound was still grainy, better than an AM radio station but not as good as a FM radio station or a musical CD.

16-bit sound cards arrived next for computers. The number of possible levels sampled with 16 bits is 65,536 (2^{16}=65,536). When positive and negative levels are sampled, the range is −37,768 to +37,768. The frequency response with 16-bit sound cards is 44KHz, the same resolution as stereo audio CDs. The increase in the number of sampling levels and the frequency response allows sound cards to produce quality sound equal to audio

CDs. Look at Multimedia Figure #7 for an example of 16-bit sampling. Keep in mind that when more samples are taken, the sound card provides a better frequency response.

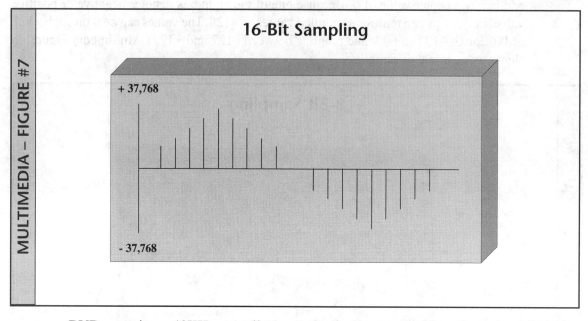

16-Bit Sampling

+ 37,768

- 37,768

MULTIMEDIA – FIGURE #7

DVDs require a 48KHz sampling rate for audio output. Therefore, the PC design specification states that the two recommended sound card sampling rates are 44.1KHz and 48KHz to support CD and DVD needs.

Many users do not understand that 8-bit and 16-bit sound board descriptions are the number of possible sample levels. Many people believe that the *x*-bit number describes the board for an ISA slot, which is not the case!

When buying or recommending a sound adapter, be sure it is a PCI adapter which uses a minimum of 16 bits for sampling. For DVDs, make sure the sound card supports 48KHz especially when using DVD software decoding.

INSTALLING SOUND CARDS

Because sound cards can include an IDE interface, a MIDI interface, audio output (and possibly a host of other ports), they frequently require multiple resource settings. The CD-ROM drive interface port requires an interrupt, I/O address, and DMA setting separate from the audio portion, as well as the MIDI portion of the sound card. This can be quite time-consuming and frustrating to a technician when installing a CD-ROM drive and sound card into a system that contains other adapters and devices. Having a PCI audio card makes resource management a lot easier.

The steps to installing a sound card are similar to any other adapter. Always refer to the manufacturer's instructions when installing devices and adapters. Power off the computer, remove the computer case and locate an empty expansion slot (make sure it is the appropriate type of slot). Attach appropriate cables such as the audio cable from the CD or DVD to the adapter. Attach external devices such as speakers. Power on the computer. Windows 9x and 2000 should detect that new hardware has been installed. Load the appropriate device drivers for the sound card. For NT, the procedure may be the same, but sometimes an installation program is used to install the sound card driver.

If you install a sound card into a computer that has sound built into the motherboard, you must disable the onboard sound before installing the new adapter.

Once a sound card is installed, there are normally other programs and utilities from the sound card manufacturer that you can install as you would any other application.

SOUND CARDS USING WINDOWS 9X/NT/2000

Most sound adapters are plug and play capable and compatible with Windows 9x and 2000. When installing a PnP sound card, Windows automatically determines the existing device and adapter resources, then allocates unused resources to the new PnP sound card. If the sound card is a legacy (non-PnP) card, the Add New Hardware wizard must be used.

Windows 9x does not need a configuration utility (such as was needed in DOS/Windows 3.x days). However, a configuration utility can be used to enter legacy card settings, even though Windows 9x is loaded and configured. Sometimes in Windows 9x, the CD-ROM drive and sound card must be set up differently for the Windows 9x operating system and the Windows 9x MS-DOS mode. This is necessary if the CD-ROM drive and the sound card functions will be used in both modes. Reference the manuals included with the CD-ROM and the sound card or contact the manufacturers when setting up the devices in both modes. Also, refer to the DOS or Windows MS-DOS mode section for more information on troubleshooting CD-ROM drives and sound cards with problems only in the MS-DOS mode. Just remember a configuration utility can cause a conflict with any operating system.

Windows 9x multimedia accessories are used to test the CD-ROM drive, sound card, microphone, etc. To test the audio section of the sound card, the CD audio MCI driver must be installed. To verify if the driver is enabled, perform the following steps:

1. Access the Control Panel by double-clicking on the *My Computer* icon, then double-click on the *Control Panel* folder icon.
2. Double-click on the *Multimedia* icon and click on the *Advanced* tab.
3. Click the *plus sign* next to Media Control Devices in the Multimedia Devices list. If CD Audio Device (Media Control) does not appear in the list, the driver is not installed. Go to the next section on how to install the driver. If *CD Audio Device* (Media Control) is in the list, click on it and go to the fifth step.
4. Click the *Properties* button and click on the *Use This Media Control Device* checkbox in the Properties dialog box. Close the *Control Panel* window.

If the CD audio MCI driver is not installed, the Windows 9x Media Player cannot play audio CDs. Many technicians forget this step and begin troubleshooting the installation of the sound card or the CD-ROM drive when the problem is a software driver. To install the MCI audio driver so the Windows 9x CD player will play audio CDs, perform the following steps:

1. Access the control panel by double-clicking on the *My Computer* icon, then double-click on the *Control Panel* folder icon.
2. Double-click on the *Add New Hardware* option and click on the *Next* button.
3. Click on the *No* button when asked if you want to have Windows 9x search for your hardware. Then click on the *Next* button.
4. Click on the *Sound, Video, and Game Controllers* option from the Hardware Types list and click on the *Next* button.
5. From the Manufacturers list, click on *Microsoft MCI*.
6. From the Models list, click on the *CD Audio Device (Media Control)* option, click the *Next* button, and click on the *Finish* button. Close the *Control Panel* window.

An exercise at the end of this chapter explains how to test an audio CD using the Windows 9x's CD player.

In NT Workstation, the Multimedia control panel is used to configure and view multimedia devices. Access the control panel by double-clicking on the *My Computer* desktop icon, double-clicking on the *Control Panel* folder, and double-clicking on the *Multimedia* control panel icon. The Multimedia control panel has five tabs—Audio, Video, Midi, CD Music, and Devices. Multimedia Table #8 outlines each tab's function.

NT's Multimedia Control Panel Tabs

Multimedia Tab	Function
Audio	Allows audio option configuration such as output volume, recording volume, and whether to display the volume control icon on the taskbar.
Video	Allows video playback configuration
MIDI	Allows selection of a MIDI instrument and customizing MIDI options
CD Music	Allows CD audio option configuration such as which CD-ROM and the headphone volume
Devices	Displays a list of NT drivers. You can add, remove, and configure drivers from this tab.

MULTIMEDIA – TABLE #8

With Windows 2000, the Sounds and Multimedia control panel is used to change sounds and adjust multimedia settings. The control panel has only three tabs, Sounds, Audio, and Hardware. Multimedia Table #9 summarizes the functions of each tab.

MULTIMEDIA – TABLE #9

2000's Sounds and Multimedia Control Panel Tabs

Sounds and Multimedia Tab	Function
Sounds	Allows sound scheme selection, creation of a custom sound scheme, and adjustment of sound volume
Audio	Allows specifying default audio devices for recording and playback and configuring advanced settings of these devices.
Hardware	Lists connected multimedia devices. Allows viewing and changing configuration settings such as volume and drivers. A troubleshooting wizard is also available through this tab.

All Windows operating systems allow controlling volume through a taskbar volume icon located in the lower right portion of the screen. When you double-click on this icon, a Play Control window opens.

If sound is not coming from the computer, one of the first things to check is the *Mute* checkboxes located in the Play Control window.

Audio drivers are vastly improved in Windows 98 and 2000. Microsoft has **WDM (Windows Driver Model)** that accommodates multiple streams of real-time audio and allows a kernel-mode process to handle audio management. This means that the operating system can control all aspects and improve audio performance. Digital audio can be redirected to any available output including USB and IEEE1394 (FireWire).

Windows also includes a set of APIs (Application Programming Interface) which are commands that developers use to communicate with the sound card. DirectX is a specific API that has commands relating to audio. In DirectX3, Microsoft added **DS3D (DirectSound3D)** that has more 3D audio effect commands. Two improvements for DS3D are A3D and EAX. **A3D** was developed by Aureal Semiconductor. It supports hardware acceleration and allows simulation of audio sounds in certain environments, such as a tunnel or underwater. **EAX (Environmental Audio Extensions)** was developed by Creative Labs. It allows software and game developers to create realistic audio environments such as muffling effects and audio directional effects (which direction a sound comes from).

SPEAKERS

Most people connect speakers to the sound card. Sound cards usually have built-in amplification to drive the speakers. Amplification is measured in watts. Most sound cards provide up to 4 watts of amplification, which is not enough for a full-bodied sound. Many computer speakers have built-in amplifiers to boost the audio signal for a much better and fuller sound quality. Amplification is a good feature to look for in speakers. The speaker's **power rating** is how loud the volume can go without distorting the sound and is expressed in watts-per-channel. Look for the RMS (root-mean-square) power rating. 10-15 watts-per-channel is an adequate rating for most computer users.

Another important measurement for speakers is the **frequency response range,** which is the frequency range of sounds the speaker can reproduce. People are able to hear from 20Hz to 20KHz and the range varies for each person. Therefore, whether or not a computer speaker is appropriate depends on the person listening to it.

> The best advice to give someone regarding speakers is to listen to them without headphones, using an audio (non-software) CD.

Speakers usually have a magnet inside them that can cause distortion to a device such as a monitor. These magnets can also cause damage to disks and other storage media. Because speakers have magnets, they should be shielded. **Shielding** cancels out the magnetic interference and keeps the interference away from other devices. The best and fastest CD drive and sound card combination can be downgraded by using inexpensive, poorly shielded speakers.

Most computers come with speakers. Sometimes these speakers are very inexpensive; often they are powered only by batteries. Speakers with an external power source are best. Computer speakers normally connect one speaker to the sound card port and the other speaker is daisy-chained to the first speaker. Some speakers have an external volume control. Be careful of this. It is just another thing to check for when sound does not occur.

USB and IEEE1394 (FireWire) can be used to provide speakers. This is a good solution because digital audio is sent over the bus and the external speaker converts the signal into sound. When audio is converted inside the computer, interference from internal electronic components, as well as from external sources (especially if an expansion slot does not have an adapter installed and the case has an opening), can cause audio interference. The drawback to USB is that it puts more work on the CPU. However, with today's processor power, this may not be an issue. Below is a list of extras to look for in speakers:

- An external volume control when your significant other is talking to you from another room.
- Headphone jacks
- Headphone and microphone pass-through connectors (So you do not have to dislodge the computer to reach the jacks.)
- AC adapter
- The proper connectors for the speakers to connect to the sound card (If the connectors are wrong, Radio Shack or music stores carry converters.)

- If the sound card is capable of 3D sound, you might want to consider obtaining a four or six speaker system.

When speakers power on, there may be a popping sound emit from them. This is normal, but if the sound continues after the speakers are powered on, the speaker is probably picking up interference from the computer or another device. Move the speakers further from the computer to see if it solves the problem.

TROUBLESHOOTING WINDOWS CD/DVD DRIVE PROBLEMS

Some of the troubleshooting steps found in the Troubleshooting the Device Driver, The MSCDEX.EXE program, and Troubleshooting the MSCDEX.EXE Installation sections, such as checking the cables, SCSI ID, master/slave jumper, etc., also apply to Windows 9x. By using the latest drivers and correcting interrupt, DMA channel, and I/O address conflicts, most installation problems are resolved.

Always check the easy stuff first such as verifying that a CD or DVD is installed in the drive. Ensure the disk is inserted correctly (label-side up). Verify that the drive has a drive letter assigned by using the My Computer desktop icon. If no drive letter is present for the device, check power and cabling and configuration settings such as master/slave, SCSI ID, and SCSI termination. If a drive letter is available, use Device Manager to see if any resource conflicts exist. This is the most common problem if the operating system sees the drive, gives it a drive letter, and the device does not operate.

Windows 95/98 also has the Troubleshooter wizard in Help. The following steps enable the Windows 9x Troubleshooter wizard.

1. Click on the *Start* button and select the *Help* option.
2. Click on the *Contents* tab. The Help Topics box appears.
3. Double-click on the *Troubleshooting* option.

The Windows 9x and 2000 Setup program checks for the existence of at least four device classes, of which the CD-ROM is one. If the initialization fails during hardware detection, Windows 9x creates the DETCRASH.LOG file, which has information about the module that was running and the I/O port or memory resources that was accessed when the failure occurred. Sometimes a CD-ROM drive quits working because of the Setup program's detection process. When Setup is attempted again through another power-up, the Safe Recovery part of Setup skips the CD-ROM device and continues through Setup.

If Windows locks when booting and appears to be locking up on the CD-ROM drive detection, Windows 9x or 2000 might not be able to find the CD-ROM drive because a hardware conflict occurred. Turn off the computer and power on again. When Windows loads, run the Add New Hardware control panel to allow Windows to search for, find, and configure the drive again.

The following is a list of problems with possible solutions or troubleshooting recommendations:

1. The system locks when the CD-ROM drive is found because the driver for the CD-ROM drive is a real-mode software driver and not a Windows 9x driver. If this happens, turn off the computer and try powering on again. When Windows loads, use the Add New Hardware control panel to load the proper CD-ROM driver.

2. Every time the computer restarts with Windows 9x, a message appears stating that "Your system configuration has changed" and Windows 9x goes into the hardware configuration program. This is usually because the proper Windows 9x driver is not loaded. To get rid of the message, use the Add New Hardware control panel. Do *not* allow Windows 9x to detect the hardware, but instead, choose *No* and load the proper drivers from disk.

3. If a drive's disk tray cannot be opened, make sure there is power attached to the drive. Some drives have an emergency eject button or instructions provided with the drive.

4. If a CD or DVD drive is not recognized by the operating system, check cables, power cords, and configuration (master/slave, SCSI ID, termination).

5. If a CD or DVD drive's busy indicator light flashes slowly (more slowly than normal), the disk may be dirty or the laser lens is dirty. Refer to the manufacturer's web site for their recommendations on cleaning the laser lens. See the Preventive Maintenance section for details on how to clean a disk.

6. If a CD or DVD drive cannot read all types of disks, refer to the drive manual to see what disks are supported. Not all disk formats are supported by all drives. You may need to install a software application for the particular disk being used.

7. If upgrading from Windows 9x to 2000 and the CD or DVD drive does not work or performs inadequately, upgrade the driver.

8. If a CD or DVD does not operate properly, try the disk in another machine or try a different disk.

9. If a DVD sound track works, but the video is missing or distorted, check cabling between video adapter and DVD decoder. Verify video drivers and that the video adapter supports DVD playback. Set the display resolution to 800x600 16-bit colors using the Display control panel.

10. If a DVD movie suddenly stops playing, the DVD may be double-sided and needs to be flipped over. Also make sure you have not paused the movie and check the video resolution settings.

11. If you receive an illegal DVD region error or region code error, change the region using the methods described earlier.

12. If a SCSI drive is installed and Windows sees extra drives, your SCSI IDs are conflicting.

13. If a DVD drive only reads CD, then the most likely problem is with bus

mastering or the DVD drivers. Go to the manufacturer's web site for the latest drivers. To reinstall the Windows bus mastering drivers, use Device Manager and go to the *Hard disk controllers* section. Expand the category and locate the item for *Bus Master Controller*. Click on the entry and click on the *Remove* button. Restart Windows and the operating system should reinstall the driver. A service pack for the operating system may contain updated drivers available on the Microsoft web site.

14. Many DVD problems are solved by (1) reinstalling DirectX or obtaining the latest version of DirectX, (2) installing the latest drivers for the DVD drive, video adapter, and sound card, or (3) screen resolution is too high (set is to 800x600 with 16-bit color for DVDs). A computer should have approximately 80% free system resources when playing DVDs. For optimum performance, do not multitask (have other applications loaded).

15. If you add DVD to a system, be careful that the video adapter can handle DVD playback. Sometimes a DVD player error occurs stating that you have low video memory. Make sure the latest video card drivers are loaded. If playback is still a problem, adjust the video card's refresh rate to a lower value by right-clicking on the *desktop*, click on the *Properties* item, and click on the *Settings* tab. The steps from here on may vary because of video adapter manufacturers. You are searching for the refresh rate settings. Click on the *Advanced* button and click on the *Adapter* tab. Use the drop-down tool box to set a lower refresh rate.

16. When troubleshooting Windows 2000 multimedia applications and devices, two tools are handy—Sounds & Multimedia control panel and the DirectX Diagnostic tool. To access the Sounds and Multimedia control panel, click on the *Start* button, point to the *Settings* option, and click on *Control Panel*. Double-click on the Sounds & Multimedia control panel icon. Click on the *Hardware* tab. Under the device section, click (right or double) on the device you want to check. The Properties button shows the version of driver being used. The Troubleshoot button is new to Windows operating systems and helps when diagnosing a specific multimedia device.

The DirectX Diagnostic Tool is used in troubleshooting multimedia devices and DirectX drivers. You can view the driver, view system information, and test multimedia devices with this tool. To access the DirectX Diagnostic Tool, click on the *Start* button. Click on the *Run* menu option. Type *DXDIA* and click on the *OK* button. The *DirectX Drivers* tab shows the name, version, and size of all DirectX drivers installed on the computer. The Sound tab shows sound card settings and allows you to test DirectSound. The Music tab shows MIDI settings and allows testing DirectMusic. The Input tab displays all installed input devices and drivers. The More Help tab allows you access to the Windows 2000 System Information tool by clicking on the *MSINFO* button.

TROUBLESHOOTING WINDOWS SOUND PROBLEMS

Check the easy stuff first. (1) Are speakers plugged into the correct port on sound card? (2) Is the volume control muted? (If so, take it off mute.) (3) Is the volume control on the speakers turned up? (4) If from within Windows, the device appears to be playing the disk, but no sound can be heard, then the problem is definitely in the sound system. (5) Do the speakers have power? (6) Is the cable from the drive to the sound card attached securely to the correct port?

The following is a list of common problems and solutions:

1. If the speaker is picking up unwanted sounds, make sure there are no empty adapter slots in the computer that leave an opening in the case. Next check the speaker wires for cuts, move the sound card to another PCI or ISA slot, and move the speakers further away from the computer. Finally, move the computer away from the offending device or the offending device away from the computer.

2. If sound is a problem, verify installation of the correct sound drivers. Go into the System Control Panel. Click on the *Device Manager* tab. Double-click on the *Sound, Video, and Game Controllers* option. Look for the specific sound driver for the sound card installed in the computer. Many sound drivers can be disabled due to a hardware conflict. Check the *General* tab in the sound driver section to determine if the driver is enabled or disabled. The exercises at the end of this chapter help with Windows 9x CD-ROM drive and sound card installation.

3. If any problem requires you to update the sound card driver, download your driver upgrade and use Device Manager. Click on the + *(plus sign)* by the Sound, Video, and Game Controllers option and the installed devices appear. Click on the *line* that represents the sound card and click on the *Properties* button. Click on the *Driver* tab and click on the *Update Driver* button. Follow the directions on the screen.

4. If the sound card is not working, check Device Manager or NT Diagnostics to see if the sound card is listed twice. If there are two entries for the same sound card, remove both of them by clicking on *each entry* and clicking on the *Remove* button. Restart Windows and the operating system should detect the adapter and either install a device driver or prompt for one. For best results, use the latest device driver from the sound card manufacturer.

5. If a sound card is not working, use Device Manager to see if there are any resource conflicts. Windows 2000 has a System Information tool to check for conflicts.

6. If a WAV sound playback error occurs, use Device Manager to locate the sound card and then click on *sound card* line. Click on the *Properties* button. On either the General or Settings tab, make sure the *Disable in this hardware profile* checkbox is clear (unchecked). If it is enabled, click once in the *checkbox*

to remove the checkmark. Then, use the Multimedia control panel and click on the *Advanced* or *Devices* tab. Double-click on the *Audio Devices*. Click on the sound card and click on the *Properties* button. Verify that the *Use audio features on this device* is selected. If disabled, click to select it. Click on the *OK* button multiple times until you exit the Multimedia control panel. Go back into the Multimedia control panel. Click on the *Audio* tab. Ensure the installed sound adapter is listed in the Preferred Device section. If not, select it and click on the *OK* button multiple times until you exit the Multimedia control panel. Restart windows and try playing a WAV file again.

7. If you do not see a sound icon in the bottom right corner of the screen, use the Multimedia (Sounds and Multimedia for Windows 2000) control panel to ensure the sound card is listed and use the Device Manager (NT Diagnostics in NT) to check for a resource conflict.

8. If audio is low no matter what disk or system sound is played, the speakers may not be amplified speakers or they may not be connected to the correct sound card port. Also, do not forget to check the computer's sound settings.

9. If one disk does not output sound, but other disks work fine, the disk may use a later version of DirectX than the one installed. Check the recommended DirectX version for the disk.

TROUBLESHOOTING SOUND PROBLEMS
(DOS OR WINDOWS MS-DOS MODE)

The only reason to continue to learn about sound in DOS mode is when users have DOS applications or DOS games. If sound does not come out of the CD-ROM drive after the drivers and software load, the following troubleshooting tips will help.

1. Be sure an audio CD or a CD containing audio files is inserted into the CD-ROM drive.

2. Try playing an audio CD from a DOS CD-ROM control program. Some manufacturers include both a Windows and a DOS program for controlling the CD-ROM drive. To start the program, change into the directory that contains the software and type the command that starts the CD-ROM control program. If the CD plays from the DOS program and not from the Windows program, Windows is most likely missing the audio driver for the sound card.

3. If sound no longer comes out of the speakers, check the speaker cables. Also, a corrupted SYSTEM.INI file can cause this problem. Copy your backup of SYSTEM.INI and replace the file. If no backup exists, check for any file that starts with SYSTEM in the Windows 3.x directory. Some programs such as Norton Utilities make a backup of the SYSTEM.INI file when installed.

4. Check for an interrupt, I/O address, or DMA conflict on the audio portion of the sound card.

5. Check the proper installation of the audio cable.
6. Check that the speakers or headphones connect to the CD-ROM drive or to the sound card.
7. If using speakers, check the insertion of the cable jack on the back of the sound card. Verify the speakers have batteries installed or an AC adapter connected.
8. If using headphones, verify that the headphones work on another device before using to test the drive.
9. Get updated drivers from the sound card manufacturer's web site.
10. When using a configuration utility such as Creative Lab's CTCU or Intel's ICU, the settings for the PnP sound card may need to be changed several times before finding a non-conflicting combination.
11. If the computer halts when the configuration manager loads, check for a memory conflict or remove the HIGHSCAN switch from the EMM386 statement in CONFIG.SYS.
12. If the monitor's image quality decreases after installing a sound card with speakers, move the speakers away from the monitor.
13. If the speakers produce a humming noise and are AC powered, move the speaker power cord to a different wall outlet. Plugging the speakers into the same circuit as the computer is best.

For more in-depth, product-specific troubleshooting, refer to the documentation or the web site of the sound card or CD-ROM drive manufacturer. Many sound card manufacturers no longer provide documentation for the DOS Windows environment or the Windows MS-DOS mode.

 Name _____

MULTIMEDIA DEVICES REVIEW QUESTIONS

1. What are some other names for disks that operate in CD-ROMs?

2. Why are CD-ROMs so important for today's computer users?

3. What is a CD-ROM's x-factor?

4. What factors influence what x-factor CD-ROM to install in a system?

5. [T / F]   A CD-ROM that has a 400ms access speed is faster than one with a 250ms access speed.

6. [T / F]   CD-ROM drives are slower than hard drives.

7. For what are CD-ROM buffers used?

8. [T / F]   CD-ROM data is normally on the same side as the disk label.

9. Describe how a CD-ROM reads data.

10. [T / F]   CD-ROMs can be external devices.

11. What are the three ways to load a CD into a drive? Which method do you prefer, and why?

12. A CD-R lists as a 4x12. What does this mean?

13. What is a buffer underrun?

14. [T / F]   Windows 2000 supports UDF.

15. What is a mini-disk?

16. List three factors that influence CD creation.

17. Is the USB interface faster than the SCSI interface in reference to CD creation?

18. A drive is labeled MultiRead. What does this mean?

19. What CD standard defines the DDCD format?

20. What is the difference between DVD-Video and DVD-ROM?

21. What is DVD-9?

22. What is UDMA and how is it beneficial to a DVD drive?

23. What is the DVD region code for the U.S.?

24. What are the two types of DVD decoders?

25. What DVD technology writes data on both the grooves and the lands?
     [DVD-ROM / DVD-RAM / DVD-R / DVD-GL]

26. [T / F] DVD-R drives can use both sides of the disk.

27. What is the endorsed DVD type that can read, write, and erase disks?

28. What DVD specification defines DVD-RW?

29. What type of interface is most common for CD-ROM drives in today's computers?

30. What interfaces are available for CD and DVD drives?

31. What are some considerations when choosing a CD or DVD drive interface?

32. A customer has a Pentium II computer with 64MB of RAM running Windows 98. The video adapter is an AGP adapter with 4MB of video memory on the adapter. The user has an IDE hard drive installed in the computer that plugs directly into the motherboard. The customer wants to upgrade the computer by adding a CD drive and sound card. What CD interface and drive setting would you recommend?

33. What are some considerations when upgrading a CD-ROM?

34. [T / F] CDs have a protective coating to shield the disk and even with a small amount of dirt on it, the disk functions.

35. Describe how to use a CD cleaning cloth.

36. [T / F] All CD-ROM drives have a self-cleaning laser lens.

37. What type of laser is currently used in DVD and CD drives?
    [Green / Purple / Blue / Red]

38. What interface type does not require an audio cable connection between an adapter and a CD or DVD drive?

39. How can you tell if a CD or DVD drive's device driver loads in Windows 2000?

40. List two things that could cause an IDE CD or DVD drive to not load a device driver.

41. A user has a DOS application that uses a CD. When the system boots, the error "Not enough drive letters available" appears. What MSCDEX switch needs to be added?

42. [T / F] The Windows 9x CD-ROM cache must initially be set by the user or the technician for optimum performance.

43. What is one indication that the CD-ROM supplemental cache might need to be adjusted?

44. What is Autorun?

45.   Why should a CD or DVD drive letter be set to a higher one on a new machine?

46.   [T / F]   CDs played through a drive's headphone jack is as good as a stereo.

47.   [T / F]   Some CD-ROM drives have proprietary audio cables.

48.   [T / F]   A CD-ROM connected to an IDE motherboard connector can play sound through a sound card.

49.   What is the PC Design recommended port color for Line In?

50.   Draw the PC Design symbol for a serial port.

51.   What is MP3?

52.   What does Sound Blaster-compatible mean?

53.   Why is 40,000 samples per second a good sampling rate for a sound card?

54.   What does having a 16-bit sound card mean?

55.   What sampling rate is required for DVD?

56.   [T / F]   Sound cards require a device driver.

57.   A motherboard has integrated sound ports. You install a sound card, but the drivers will not load. What will you do?

58.   What Windows 98 control panel is used to verify the sound card device driver loaded?

59.   What NT Multimedia control panel tab is used to list installed drivers?

60.   What Windows 2000 control panel is used to view the sound card drivers?

61. What Windows 2000 control panel tab contains a troubleshooting wizard for multimedia devices?

62. Sound does not emit from the speakers. What is the first thing to check?

63. What is shielding as it relates to speakers?

64. What is a drawback to using USB speakers?

65. What should you do if the CD or DVD's light constantly flashes slowly?

66. Before a SCSI CD is installed, the system shows A:, C:, and D: drives. Once installed, the system shows A:, C:, D:, E:, F:, G:, H:, I:, and J:. What is the problem?

67. List three easy checks for sound problems.

68. What Device Manager option is used to check for sound card resource conflicts?

69. A sound icon does not appear on the desktop. What will you check?

 Name _____

MULTIMEDIA DEVICES FILL-IN-THE-BLANK

1. A CD-ROM's _____ specification is the time it takes to find specific data.

2. On a CD, a _____ is an indentation along the spiral track.

3. On a CD, the area that separates the pits is a _____.

4. The CD-ROM's _____ reads data from the CD.

5. If a CD drive uses the _____ interface, the drive must be an internal unit.

6. A CD drive that can write data one time is known as a _____.

7. A _____ CD drive can write data to a disk and then add more data at a later date.

8. _____ drives can write multiple times to a CD.

9. _____ drives use a laser beam to read the CD and then it writes data to the disk.

10. _____ drives combine audio and video entertainment with backward compatibility with CDs.

11. Microsoft's _____ contains multimedia software to speed up video and audio applications.

12. The _____ decoder requires a PCI adapter.

13. A DVD technology that can read, write, and erase disks, but is not endorsed by the DVD Forum is _____.

14. _____ is an optical technology that places a fluorescent dye on each disk layer.

15. Most IDE CD and DVD drives come preconfigured to the _____ setting.

16. A piece of software that allows the operating system to communicate with the CD or DVD drive is a _____.

17. The _____ DOS program assigns a drive letter to the CD-ROM.

18. Windows 2000's CD-ROM support that uses extended memory is _____.

19. An _____ connects a CD-ROM to a sound card.

20. The _____ interface is used to create synthesized music.

21. Multimedia disks normally use sound files with the _____ file extension.

22. Most game CDs used sound files that end with the _____ file extension.

23. _____ is Windows 2000's audio driver built into the operating system.

24. Creative Lab's audio enhancements are known as _____.

25. A rating for how loud the volume can be without distorting sound is a speaker's _____.

26. The _____ is the range of sounds a speaker or sound card can reproduce.

27. A CD drive's tray will not eject. Check the _____ cable to the drive.

28. Two tools used with Windows 2000 to troubleshoot DVD drives are _____ and _____.

29. _____ is selected from the System control panel to update sound drivers.

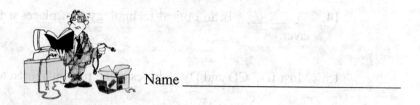

Name _____

INTERNAL CD-ROM DRIVE INSTALLATION EXERCISE

Objective: To install a CD-ROM drive

Parts: CD-ROM drive and documentation for the drive (if possible
Adapter (if needed)
Device driver
Interface cable
Tools
Anti-static materials
Available drive bay

CAUTION: Observe proper grounding procedures when installing a CD-ROM drive.

Step 1.   Remove the cover from the computer. Use proper anti-static procedures.

Step 2.   (optional) Install any mounting brackets necessary to install the CD-ROM drive inside the computer.

Step 3.   Check what interface the CD-ROM drive uses (IDE, EIDE, SCSI, or proprietary). Set the appropriate master/slave, SCSI ID, or termination settings depending on the drive interface type. Refer to the documentation included with the CD-ROM for the proper configuration.

Question 1:   What type of interface does the CD-ROM drive use?

Question 2:   What is an advantage of this type of interface?

Step 4. (optional) Install any interface adapter into the system. If using a sound card, an exercise later in the chapter explains how to install it. Set any interrupt, I/O address, or DMA channel as necessary ensuring these settings do not conflict with any other device or adapter installed in the system. Refer to the documentation included with the adapter. Before installing an adapter of any type inside a computer, you should know what interrupts and I/O addresses are being used by the devices and adapters already installed. If you do not know this information, go to Using Microsoft Diagnostics (MSD), Examining System Resources Using Windows 95/98, Examining System Resources Using NT Workstation, or Examining System Resources Using Windows 2000 Professional exercises found in Chapter 3. Make any notes regarding installed devices and the interrupts and I/O addresses already used.

Question 3: What would be one indication of an interrupt conflict between the CD-ROM drive and any other device in the system?

Step 5. Install the CD-ROM drive in the computer. Keep in mind the IDE interface cable connection may be short in length.

Step 6. Attach the power cable to the CD-ROM drive.

Step 7. Attach one end of the interface cable to the CD-ROM drive. Verify that the cable's pin 1 attaches to the drive's pin 1. The drive's pin 1 is sometimes hard to detect because the connector is black. Look very carefully for an etched arrow on the connector on the drive. Some drive manufacturers place a drawing on top of the drive that illustrates the proper orientation for the cable.

Step 8. Attach the other end of the interface cable to the motherboard or adapter interface connector. Verify the cable's pin 1 connects to the CD-ROM drive's pin 1.

Step 9. Power on the computer, verifying that no POST error codes appear.

_____ *Instructor's Initials*

Once the CD-ROM drive is installed, software drivers are required in the DOS/Windows environment. Go to the CD-ROM Software Installation (DOS/Windows 3.x) exercise. If using Windows 9x or 2000), the operating system detects the installation of a new hardware component and configures the device or prompts for a driver disk supplied by the CD-ROM drive manufacturer. If NT is being used, an NT installation program is available with the drive. Always refer to the manufacturer's instructions when installing any device.

Name _____

CD-ROM DRIVE SOFTWARE INSTALLATION
(DOS/WINDOWS 3.X) EXERCISE

Objective: To install software necessary for proper CD-ROM operation

Parts: CD-ROM driver and documentation for the drive
Microsoft Windows installation disks or a disk that contains the MCI CD Audio
software
A CD-based software application or files
(Optional) An audio CD

Step 1.   Install the software driver for the CD-ROM drive. Refer to the documentation included
with the drive for the command that starts the installation process. For DOS skills,
refer to the DOS chapter. Most software driver installation procedures prompt the
technician to reboot the computer for the changes to take effect. If the installation
procedures do not prompt for this, restart the computer with a warm boot.

Step 2.   When the computer restarts and the message "Starting MS-DOS" or "Starting PC
DOS" appears on the screen, press the **F8** key and step through the CONFIG.SYS
drivers one by one. Reply **Y** for Yes to the prompt to load each driver. Look specifically
for the driver for the CD-ROM drive and determine if the driver detects the installation
of a CD-ROM drive.

Question 1:   Did the software driver for the CD-ROM drive load okay and detect a CD-ROM
drive? If a CD-ROM drive is detected, write the message that indicates this in the
space below. If the CD-ROM drive is not detected by the software driver, troubleshoot
the CD-ROM and driver by referring to this chapter's section on troubleshooting.

Step 3.   Using a text editor, such as Microsoft's EDIT, verify that the MSCDEX.EXE program
is in the AUTOEXEC.BAT file. Most CD-ROM software driver installation programs
either put this line in the AUTOEXEC.BAT file or prompt the technician to add this
line manually. In either case, make sure you use the proper switches depending on the
system and if other caching programs such as SmartDrive are used.

Question 2: Is the MSCDEX.EXE line in the AUTOEXEC.BAT file? If not, add the line using the proper switches and correct device name with the program.

Question 3: What switches are used with the MSCDEX.EXE command and what is the function of each switch?

Step 4. Restart the computer. When the message "Starting MS-DOS" appears on the screen, press **F8** to single step through the CONFIG.SYS and AUTOEXEC.BAT files. Pay particular attention when the MSCDEX.EXE program loads. A message similar to the following should appear:

MSCDEX Version 2.23

Copyright (C) Microsoft Corp. 1986-1993. All rights reserved.

Drive D: = Driver IDECD001 Unit 0

Question 4: Did the MSCDEX.EXE program detect the CD-ROM drive? If not, perform troubleshooting techniques as described in the CD-ROM chapter.

Question 5: What drive letter did the operating system assign to the CD-ROM drive?

Step 5. Install any additional software included with the CD-ROM drive and test as necessary.

Question 6: Does the CD-ROM drive work?

Step 6. If the CD-ROM drive is to be checked for sound through a front panel headphone connection, perform Steps 10 through 20 in the SOUND CARD INSTALLATION EXERCISE.

_____ *Instructor's Initials*

Optional

Step 7. If performing no other work inside the computer, reinstall the computer's cover.

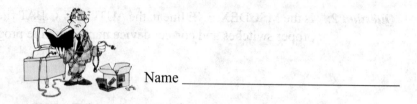

Name _____

SOUND CARD INSTALLATION EXERCISE
(DOS/WINDOWS ENVIRONMENT)

Objective: To install a sound card correctly in the DOS/Windows environment

Parts: Sound Card and documentation
          Sound Card software and drivers
          Audio cable
          Audio CD
          Tools
          Anti-static materials
          Available expansion slot

CAUTION: Observe proper grounding procedures when installing a sound card.

Step 1. Unless the sound card is a plug and play (PnP) adapter, use the sound card documentation to set any jumpers or switches for the DMA channel, interrupt, and I/O address for each part of the sound card (MIDI, audio output, etc.). If the card is a PnP adapter, proceed to Step 2. Before installing an adapter of any type, you should know what interrupts and I/O addresses are used by the devices and adapters already installed in the computer. If you do not know this information, go to the RUNNING MICROSOFT DIAGNOSTICS exercise or use software you have available to obtain this information. Make any notes regarding installed devices and the interrupts and I/O addresses already used. For DOS skills, refer to the DOS chapter.

Step 2. Remove the computer's cover.

Step 3. Insert and secure the sound card in an available slot.

Step 4. If the sound card has an external volume control, turn the volume to the maximum position.

Optional

Step 5. If the CD-ROM drive is to use the sound card as an interface connection, attach the interface cable from the CD-ROM drive to the sound card. Verify that the cable's pin 1 attaches to the adapter connector's pin 1.

Step 6. Attach an audio cable from the CD-ROM drive to the sound card. Verify that the cable's pin 1 attaches to the adapter connector's pin 1.

Step 7. Power on the computer.

Question 1:   Is the sound card a plug and play sound card? If yes, proceed to Step 8. If the sound card is not a plug and play card, go to Step 9.

Step 8.   If the computer has a plug and play BIOS, the BIOS configures the plug and play card. The settings configured by the BIOS may conflict with legacy (non-PnP) cards. A configuration manager and configuration utility may be necessary to configure the plug and play sound card even though the computer has a PnP BIOS. If the computer does *not* have a plug and play BIOS, use the Intel Configuration Manager (ICM) and ISA Configuration Utility (ICU) or one provided by the sound card's manufacturer and configure the PnP sound card.

Step 9.   Load any software drivers and any applications required for sound card operation. Refer to the sound card manual for any specific loading instructions.

Step 10.   Verify the installation of Windows 3.x's MCI CD Audio software driver by double-clicking on Window's **Main** program group.

Step 11.   Double-click on the **Control Panel** icon.

Step 12.   Double-click on the **Drivers** icon.

Step 13.   If the Windows 3.x's [MCI] CD Audio driver is not loaded, click on the **ADD** button. Choose [MCI] CD Audio driver from the list shown and insert the appropriate Windows disk as prompted on the screen.

Step 14.   Once the driver loads, close all open windows.

Step 15.   Double-click on the **Accessories** program group.

Step 16.   Open the **Media Player** program by double-clicking on the icon.

Step 17.   Insert an audio CD into the CD-ROM drive.

Step 18.   Verify that speakers connect to the sound adapter (if installed), motherboard, or verify that headphones attach to the CD-ROM drive.

Step 19.   Click on the **Device** option from the Media Player menu bar.

Step 20.   Click once on the **CD Audio** option from the drop-down menu. After a few seconds the CD player-like buttons on the Media Player screen darken. Once the buttons darken, click once on the **left-most right arrow icon.** The CD begins to play if the software is properly installed.

Question 2: Does the CD-ROM drive/sound card produce sound? If not, refer to the troubleshooting section of the CD-ROM chapter and troubleshoot the CD-ROM drive and sound card software programs and the CD-ROM drive/sound card installation. Keep in mind the sound card may need to be re-configured multiple times for successful operation of all. Remember that interrupt, DMA channel, and I/O conflicts are the source of 95 percent of sound card problems.

_____ *Instructor's Initials*

Step 21. Turn off the computer

Step 22. Reinstall the computer's cover.

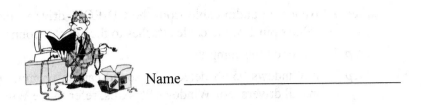

Name _____

SOUND CARD INSTALLATION EXERCISE (WINDOWS 9X)

Objective: To install a sound card correctly in the Windows 95/98 environment

Parts: Sound Card and documentation
Sound Card software and Windows 95/98 drivers
Audio cable
Audio CD
Tools
Anti-static materials
Available expansion slot

CAUTION: Observe proper grounding procedures when installing a sound card.

Step 1.   Unless the sound card is a plug and play (PnP) adapter, use the sound card's documentation to set any jumpers or switches for the DMA channel, interrupt, and I/O address for each part of the sound card (MIDI, audio output, etc.). If the card is a PnP adapter, proceed to Step 2. Before installing an adapter of any type inside a computer, you should know what interrupts and I/O addresses are used by the devices and adapters already installed in the computer. If you do not know this information, go to the Chapter 3 EXAMINING SYSTEM RESOURCES USING WINDOWS 95/ 98 exercise or use the software available to obtain this information. Make any notes regarding installed devices and the interrupts and I/O addresses used.

Step 2.   Remove the computer's cover.

Step 3.   Insert and secure the sound card in an available slot.

Step 4.   If the sound card has an external volume control, turn the volume to the maximum position.

Optional

Step 5.   If the CD-ROM drive is to use the sound card as an interface connection, attach the interface cable from the CD-ROM drive to the sound card. Verify that the cable's pin 1 of the cable attaches to the adapter connector's pin 1.

Question 1:   Which is better, using the sound card's connector, a separate adapter, or the motherboard connection for the CD-ROM interface? Explain your answer.

Step 6. Attach an audio cable from the CD-ROM drive to the sound card. Verify that the cable's pin 1 of the cable attaches to the adapter connector's pin 1.

Step 7. Power on the computer.

Step 8. If Windows 95/98 detects the sound card, a prompt appears asking if you want to install drivers. For Windows 95 skills, refer to the Windows 95 chapter. Click on the **Yes** button. Then another prompt asks for the Windows 95/98 installation disk, CD, or a manufacturer-provided disk. Do not use Windows 3.x drivers. Get Windows 95/98 drivers from the sound card manufacturer. After installing the software, the computer reboots. Proceed to Step 18. If Windows 95/98 does not automatically detect the sound card, Windows 95/98 must be forced to look for the hardware. Proceed to Step 9.

Steps 9 through 17 handle the situation that Windows 95/98 does not automatically detect the sound card.

Step 9. Click on the **Start** button.

Step 10. From the Start menu, select the **Settings** option.

Step 11. From the Settings menu, select the **Control Panel** option. The Control Panel window appears.

Step 12. Double-click on the **Add New Hardware** icon.

Step 13. Click on the **Next** button. A prompt asks if you want Windows 95/98 to search for new hardware.

Step 14. Click on the **No** button.

Step 15. Click on the **Next** button. A prompt tells you to pick from a list of hardware categories.

Step 16. Click on the **Sound, Video, and Game Controllers** option followed by a click on the **Next** button.

Step 17. Enter any IRQ, I/O address, DMA channel, etc. information requested (depending on the sound card installed).

Question 2: [T / F] Windows 95 is a plug and play operating system.

Question 3:   [T / F]   Windows 95 requires a plug and play BIOS to operate.

Step 18.   After the system reboots, if the adapter does not work, check the cabling, use the USING WINDOWS 95/98's DEVICE MANAGER TO MODIFY HARDWARE RESOURCES exercise, or use this chapter's troubleshooting section. Keep in mind the sound card may need to be re-configured multiple times for successful operation of all components such as the audio output and MIDI. Remember that interrupt, DMA channel, and I/O conflicts are the source of 95 percent of sound card problems.

_____ *Instructor's Initials*

Step 19.   Turn off the computer.

Step 20.   Reinstall the computer's cover.

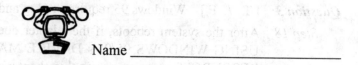

Name _____

SETTING THE CD-ROM SUPPLEMENTAL CACHE SIZE (WINDOWS 9X)

Objective: To optimize the Windows 95/98 CD-ROM cache

Parts: A computer with Windows 95/98 loaded and a CD-ROM drive installed

Step 1.   Power on the computer and boot to Windows 95/98. Refer to the Windows 95 chapter for Windows 95 skills.

Step 2.   Double-click on the **My Computer** icon.

Step 3.   Double-click on the **Control Panel** folder icon.

Step 4.   Double-click on the **System** icon.

Step 5.   Click once on the **Performance** tab.

Step 6.   Click once on the **File System** button located at the bottom of the screen in the Advanced Settings section.

Step 7.   Click on the **CD-ROM** tab.

Step 8.   Click on the **down arrow** in the **Optimize access pattern for:** window.

Step 9.   Select the proper speed of the CD-ROM drive installed in the system. Note that selecting a faster speed CD-ROM drive than what is installed does *not* increase performance.

Step 10. Drag the slidebar in the **Supplemental cache size** option to the far right setting. The setting of the slidebar changes the amount of memory allocated for the cache in the statement, "Windows will use ?? kilobytes of physical memory to perform these optimizations while data is being accessed." at the bottom of the window.

Step 11. Click once on the **OK** button to accept the settings.

Step 12. Close the System Properties window. A dialog box appears on the screen stating that the computer must be restarted for the changes to take effect.

Step 13. Click once on the **Yes** button to restart the computer.

_____ *Instructor's Initials*

Name _____

CHANGING THE CD-ROM DRIVE LETTER EXERCISE (WINDOWS 9X)

Objective: To change the CD-ROM drive letter assignment in the Windows 95/98 environment

Parts: A computer with Windows 95/98 loaded and a CD-ROM drive

Step 1.   Power on the computer and boot to Windows 95/98. Refer to theWindows 95 chapter for Windows 95 skills.

Step 2.   Double-click on the **My Computer** icon.

Step 3.   Double-click on the **Control Panel** folder icon.

Step 4.   Double-click on the **System** icon.

Step 5.   Click on the **Device Manager** tab.

Step 6.   Double-click the **CD-ROM** subbranch.

Step 7.   Double-click on the **CD-ROM drive**. If the CD-ROM drive is not in the tree, a DOS device driver controls the drive. To change the drive letter for a DOS-based device driver, edit the MSCDEX.EXE line in the AUTOEXEC.BAT file. See the chapter section on MSCDEX.EXE.

Step 8.   Click on the **Settings** tab.

Step 9.   Two Reserve Drive Letter fields (Start and End) are at the bottom of the dialog box. Set the drive Start range and End range to the same drive letter of your choice.

Question 1:   What drive letter did you choose for the CD-ROM drive?

Step 10.   Click on the **OK** button.

Step 11.   Close the System Properties window.

Step 12.   Close the Control Panel window.

Step 13.   Reboot Windows 95/98 using the **Start** button.

Step 14.   Verify the drive letter change using Explorer or going through the My Computer icon on the desktop.

Question 2:   How was the drive letter verified?

_____ *Instructor's Initials*

Name _____

CHANGING THE CD-ROM DRIVE LETTER USING WINDOWS NT WORKSTATION

Objective: To use the Disk Administrator tool effectively in changing the CD-ROM drive letter

Parts: Computer with Windows NT Workstation installed

Step 1. Power on the computer and verify that the Windows NT Workstation loads.

Step 2. Logon to Windows NT using the userid and password provided by the instructor or lab assistant.

Step 3. Double-click on the **My Computer** icon.

Question 1: What drive letter is assigned to the CD-ROM?

Step 4. Close the **My Computer** window by clicking on the **Close** box (the one with the X) in the upperright corner of the window.

Step 5. Click on the **Start** button.

Step 6. Point to the **Programs** option.

Step 7. Point to the **Administrative Tools (Common)** option.

Step 8. Click on the **Disk Administrator** option.

Step 9. If Disk Administrator has never been run, select the **Yes** option when asked to write a disk signature to disk 0. Otherwise, proceed to Question 2.

Question 2: List all of the drive letters assigned to the fixed-disk drives and CD-ROM.

Step 10. Click on the **white block** with the CD-ROM drive letter inside.

Step 11. Click on the **Tools** menu.

Step 12. Click on the **Assign Drive Letter** option.

Step 13. In the Assign Drive Letter dialog box, click the **radio** button beside the Assign Drive Letter.

Step 14. Click on the **arrow** button to select a drive letter that is not assigned to another drive. (Refer to Question 2 for drive letters already assigned.)

Question 3:   List below the drive letter that you selected.

Step 15.   Click on the **OK** button.

Step 16.   Select **Yes** when asked to confirm drive letter change.

Question 4:   Did the drive letter for the CD-ROM change?

Step 17.   Close the **Disk Administrator** windows.

Step 18.   Click on the **Start** button.

Step 19.   Click on **Shut Down.**

Step 20.   Click on the radio button next to **Restart the computer.**

Step 21.   Click on the **Yes** button.

Step 22.   When the computer restarts, logon to Windows NT using the userid and password provided by the instructor or lab assistant

Step 23.   Double-click on the **My Computer** icon.

Question 5:   What drive letter is assigned to the CD-ROM?

Question 6:   Is the assigned drive letter the same as the one that you assigned in Step 14? If not, redo the exercise.

_____ *Instructor's Initials*

Step 24.   Close the **My Computer** window.

Name _____

CHANGING THE CD-ROM DRIVE LETTER IN WINDOWS 2000 PROFESSIONAL

Objective: To change the CD-ROM's logical drive letter assignment on a Windows 2000 Professional computer

Parts: Computer with Windows 2000 Professional and a CD-ROM installed.

At times, it may become necessary to change the logical drive letter assignment for a CD-ROM.

Step 1. Power on the computer and verify that Windows 2000 Professional loads.

Step 2. Logon to Windows 2000 Professional using the userid and password provided by the instructor or lab assistant.

Step 3. From the Start menu, choose **Settings, Control Panel**, and then double-click on the **Administrative Tools** option.

Step 4. Double-click **Computer Management**. The Computer Management MMC (Microsoft Management Console) opens.

Step 5. Expand the **Storage** icon and select the **Disk Management** option. The Disk Management window opens.

Question 1: How many drives are listed in the Disk Management window?

Step 6. From the Disk Management window, right-click the **CD-ROM icon** and select **Change Drive Letter and Path**.

Question 2: What drive letter is currently assigned to the CD-ROM?

Step 7. Select **Edit**. The Edit Drive Letter or Path window opens.

Step 8. From the Assign a Drive Letter or Path drop-down menu, select an available **drive letter** and click on the **OK** button.

Question 3:   Are previously assigned drive letters listed as available?

Step 9.   Confirm the drive letter change by selecting **Yes** at the confirmation window.

Step 10.   The new drive letter assignment will appear in the Disk Management window.

_____ *Instructor's Initials*

Name _____

PLAYING AN AUDIO CD USING WINDOWS' CD PLAYER

Objective: To understand how to use Windows 95/98's CD Player program

Parts: A computer with Windows 95/98 loaded, a CD-ROM drive installed, and the MCI audio driver loaded. Refer to the chapter steps on how to verify (and install) the MCI audio driver.

An audio CD

Step 1. Power on the computer and boot to Windows 95/98. Refer to Windows 95 chapter for Windows 95 skills.

Step 2. Insert an audio CD into the CD-ROM drive.

Step 3. Click on the **Start** button.

Step 4. From the Start menu, choose the **Program** option.

Step 5. From the Program's submenu, choose the **Accessories** option.

Step 6. From the Accessories menu, choose the **Multimedia** option.

Step 7. From the Multimedia submenu, click on the **CD Player** option.

Step 8. Click on the **Play** button (the right arrow) on the CD graphic.

Question 1: Does the audio CD play? If not, verify the installation of the MCI audio driver. If the driver is installed, refer to the Windows 95/98 sound troubleshooting section of this chapter.

Step 9. Click on the **Stop** button on the CD graphic.

Step 10. Close and exit and **CD Player** program.

_____ *Instructor's Initials*

Name _____

PLAYING AN AUDIO CD USING WINDOWS NT WORKSTATION

Objective: To understand how to play an audio CD on a Windows NT Workstation

Parts: Windows NT Workstation with CD-ROM and sound card installed and configured
Audio CD
A Windows NT Workstation that has a CD-ROM and sound card installed and
configured has the ability to play both data and audio CDs. There are two methods
to access and play audio CDs, Autorun and manually. To play an audio CD on
Windows NT Workstation, follow these steps:

Playing an audio CD using the Autorun feature:

Step 1.   Insert an audio CD into the CD-ROM drive.

Step 2.   The Windows NT Workstation CD Player utility starts automatically and begins playing
the audio CD on track 1.

Playing an audio CD manually:

Step 1.   Insert an audio CD into the CD-ROM drive.

Step 2.   From the Start menu, choose **Programs, Accessories, Multimedia**, and then select
CD Player. The CD Player utility starts.

Step 3.   From the CD Player utility, select the **Play** button (>). The CD Player utility begins
playing track 1 of the audio CD.

Step 4.   To pause the CD Player, select the **Pause** button (||)

Step 5.   To change song tracks, select the **Previous Track** (|<<) or the **Next Track** (>>|)
buttons, or select the desired track from the **Track drop-down menu**.

Question 1:   How many tracks does your audio CD have?

To stop the CD Player utility:

Step 1.   Select the **Stop** button.

Step 2.   When finished playing the audio CD, close the CD Player utility.

_____ *Instructor's Initials*

Name _____

PLAYING AN AUDIO CD USING WINDOWS 2000 PROFESSIONAL

Objective: To understand how to play an audio CD on Windows 2000 Professional

Parts: Windows 2000 Professional computer with CD-ROM and sound card installed and configured
Audio CD
A Windows 2000 Professional computer that has a CD-ROM and sound card installed and configured has the ability to play both data and audio CDs. There are two methods to access and play audio CDs, auto-run and manually. To play an audio CD on Windows 2000 Professional, follow these steps:

Playing an Audio CD using the Autorun feature:

Step 1. Insert an audio CD into the CD-ROM drive.

Step 2. The Windows 2000 Professional CD Player utility starts automatically and begins playing the audio CD on track 1.

Playing anx Audio CD manually:

Step 1. Insert an audio CD into the CD-ROM drive.

Step 2. From the Start menu, choose **Programs, Accessories, Entertainment**, and then select **CD Player**. The CD Player utility starts.

Step 3. From the CD Player utility, select the **Play** button (>). The CD Player utility begins playing track 1 of the audio CD.

Step 4. To pause the CD Player, select the **Pause** button (||)

Step 5. To change song tracks, select the **Previous Track** (|<<) or the **Next Track** (>>|) buttons, or select the desired track from the **Track drop-down menu**. If your Windows 2000 Professional computer has multiple installed CD-ROM drives, you can select other audio disks in other drives from the **Disk drop-down menu.**

Question 1: How many tracks does your audio CD have?

To stop the CD Player utility:

Step 1.   Select the **Stop** button.

Step 2.   When finished playing the audio CD, close the CD Player utility.

_____ *Instructor's Initials*

Name _____

INTERNET DISCOVERY

Objective: To obtain specific information on the Internet regarding a computer or its associated parts

Parts: Access to the Internet

Question 1:   Find an Internet site that sells DVD drives. List the cost and the web site.

Question 2:   What is the cost of a disk that works in a DVD+RW drive? List the cost and web site.

Question 3:   Find an Internet site that tells you whether or not a DVD+RW drive is backwards compatible with CD-R and CD-RW drives. List the URL for the site in the space below.

Question 4:   An NT computer has a Pinnacle Micro optical SCSI drive installed. When the system boots, the SCSI controller detects the drive, but NT does not. Find the solution on the Internet. Write the solution and the Internet address.

Question 5:   A Windows 95 computer has a HP CD-Writer Plus model 7200I CD-RW drive. After installing the drive, you cannot reboot the computer. Find the solution on the Internet. Write the solution and the Internet address.

Question 6:   A Windows 95 computer has a Creative Labs PC-DVD Encore 6X DVD drive. Whenever you access the DVD software, the message "no drive detected" appears. Find the solution on the Internet. Write the solution and the Internet address.

Question 7:   You just installed a Philips CM206 model of CD-ROM into a computer and you notice that the green light on the front of the drive stays on all the time. Find the solution on the Internet. Write the solution and the Internet address.

Question 8:   You just installed a Maxoptix magneto-optical drive (model TMT3-1300) into a computer running Windows NT 4.0. What program must be downloaded from the Internet to dismount the media on this computer? Also, list the site where you found the answer.

Question 9:   On a TEAC CD-RW drive, you get buffer underruns very frequently. Find the possible solutions on the Internet. List the site and three solutions.

NOTES

Chapter 11:

Serial Devices, Mice, and Keyboards

OBJECTIVES

After completing this chapter you will

- Understand the difference between serial and parallel data transfers.
- Understand how a UART controls the serial port and how to determine which UART is installed.
- Configure a serial port and all its associated system resources and individual settings.
- Understand basic handshaking between a DTE and DCE.
- Use basic tools to determine which system resources can be assigned to new serial devices.
- Understand basic modem concepts and analog modem limitations.
- Be able to distinguish between analog modems, cable modems, and digital modems.
- Perform basic modem troubleshooting.
- Know the different types of mice and how to perform preventive maintenance on them.
- Know the different types of keyboards and how to perform preventive maintenance on them.

KEY TERMS

ADSL	error correction	phone line isolator
asynchronous	fax modem	PS/2 mouse
baud	FIFO setting	RS232C
bps	flow control	RTS
breakout box	full duplex	RTS/CTS
bus mouse	half duplex	serial mouse
cable modem	handshaking	start bit
capacitive keyboard	ICS	stop bit
combinational mouse	ISDN	straight-through cable
CTS	LAPM	synchronous
data bits	loopback plug	UART
data compression	mechanical keyboard	upstream
DCE	mechanical mouse	voice/fax modem
digital modem	MNP	xDSL
dongle	modem	XON/XOFF
downstream	null modem cable	
DTE	optical mouse	
echo mode setting	parity	

SERIAL DEVICES OVERVIEW

Serial devices can be challenging to install. Some technicians dread installing or troubleshooting serial devices, but if they are understood, technicians can conquer them easily. Serial devices can be difficult because (1) the serial ports may share an interrupt with another serial device, (2) serial devices may have proprietary cables, and (3) software is not always compatible with the serial device. Many serial devices support uncommon configurations. Maintaining the standards covered in Chapter 3, System Configuration, avoids these types of conflicts. Reviewing the sections on interrupts and I/O addresses is a good idea before trying to understand serial devices.

Common serial devices include mice, modems, digitizers, and plotters. Serial Figure #1 shows common serial devices.

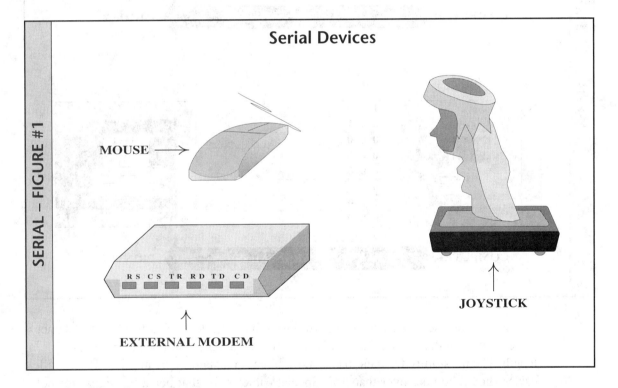

Serial devices transmit or receive information one bit at a time. In contrast, parallel devices transmit data eight bits at a time. Serial transmissions are much slower than parallel transmissions because one bit is sent at a time instead of eight. Serial Figure #2 compares serial and parallel transmissions.

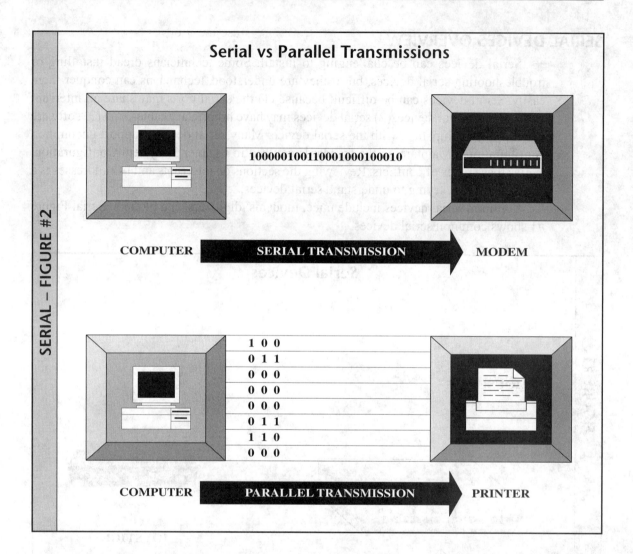

Serial vs Parallel Transmissions

100000100110001000100010

COMPUTER   **SERIAL TRANSMISSION**   MODEM

| 1 0 0 |
| 0 1 1 |
| 0 0 0 |
| 0 0 0 |
| 0 0 0 |
| 0 1 1 |
| 1 1 0 |
| 0 0 0 |

COMPUTER   **PARALLEL TRANSMISSION**   PRINTER

SERIAL – FIGURE #2

Even though serial transmissions are slower than parallel, they travel longer distances more accurately than parallel transmissions. Serial cables should be no more than 50' in length. The possibility for data loss is more likely in distances greater than 50'. Parallel cables should be no longer than 15'. Special cables exist that boost the signal for both serial and parallel devices to extend the maximum cable length. Contact any computer cabling vendor for the specifics.

Serial devices are frequently external and connect to a serial port. A device such as an internal modem may be on an adapter. Serial ports are also known as asynchronous ports, COM ports, or RS232 ports. **Asynchronous** transmissions add extra bits to the data to track when each byte starts and ends. The extra bit sent first is the **start bit** and the extra bit sent last is the **stop bit**. **Synchronous** transmissions rely on an external clock to time the data reception or transmission.

RS232C is a standard serial interface approved by the EIA (Electrical Industries

Association). Because serial devices on computers use the 9 or 25-pin male connector (normally 9-pin) specified by the RS232C standard, the devices are sometimes known as RS232 serial devices. Serial Figure #3 illustrates the two serial ports found on a motherboard or on an adapter.

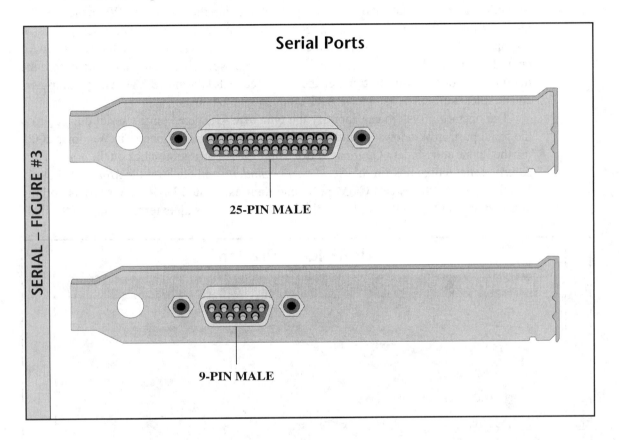

Serial Ports

25-PIN MALE

9-PIN MALE

SERIAL – FIGURE #3

The transmission speed of serial devices is calculated in **bits per second** or **bps**. Bits per second (bps) is the number of bits the serial device receives or transmits in one second. The speed settings for serial devices include 110, 300, 1200, 2400, 4800, 9600, 19200, 38400, 57600, and 115200. Some devices can be set to different speeds. The application software must match the serial device's bits per second rate.

Some people use the term *baud* to designate a modem's speed, but this is not common anymore. **Baud** is the number of times an analog signal changes in one second. If a signal was sent between two modems and the signal changed 600 times in one second, the device was communicating at 600 baud. However, with today's signaling methods (modulation techniques to be technically accurate), modems can send several bits in one cycle, so it is more accurate to communicate using the terms bits per second.

The chip that controls the serial device is a **UART (Universal Asynchronous Receiver/ Transmitter)**. For motherboards with built-in serial ports, the UART chip is on the motherboard. Internal modems have a UART chip built into the adapter. Serial ports built into an adapter have a UART chip on the adapter. The UART chip converts a data byte into a serial data stream of single 1s and 0s for transmission. It also receives the single bit stream and stores the data in its own buffer. UARTs have buffers to allow the microprocessor to handle other tasks instead of constantly checking with the serial port. When the UART's buffer is full, the chip initiates an interrupt to the microprocessor. The microprocessor responds and transfers the data from the UART buffer into RAM. Before the 16550 UART chip, the older UARTs lost data. Received data was overwritten with new data before the microprocessor had time to transfer the first received data into RAM. Many computers and adapters still have the older UART chips to save on costs.

The operating system can identify the type of UART used on the serial device or on the serial port. In Windows 9x and NT, use the Modems control panel; in Windows 2000, use the Phone and Modem Options control panel. Once you double-click on the *appropriate control panel* icon, click on the *COM port* or *modem*, and click on the *More info* button. Serial Figure #4 shows two COM ports and their associated UART. COM1 has nothing attached to it and is built into the motherboard. COM5 has an external modem attached.

UART Identification

More Info...

Port Information

Port:	COM1
Interrupt:	4
Address:	3F8
UART:	NS 16550AN

More Info...

Port Information

Port:	COM5
Interrupt:	3
Address:	DFE0
UART:	NS 16550AN
Highest Speed:	115K Baud

SERIAL – FIGURE #4

UPGRADING THE UART CHIP

A socketed UART is one that is *not* soldered, but plugged into a chip socket. To upgrade a socketed 8250 or 16450, buy a newer UART for approximately $15–20 to replace the existing one. If a soldered UART chip is on a serial adapter, replace the adapter with one that has a more current UART. If the motherboard contains a soldered UART chip, see if a jumper can disable the serial port, switch, or through the system's Setup program. If the serial port can be disabled, disable it and buy a separate serial adapter that contains an upgraded UART. Look at Serial Figure #5 for a socketed UART.

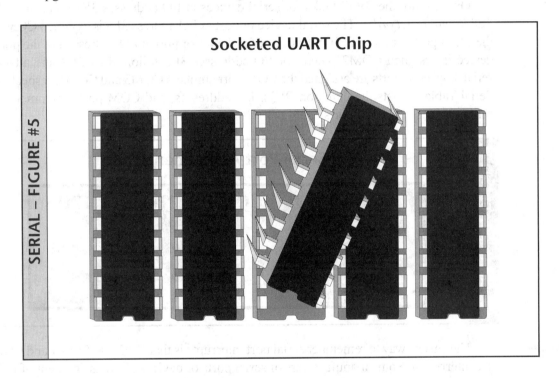

Socketed UART Chip

SERIAL – FIGURE #5

HOW TO CONFIGURE SERIAL DEVICES

Three major issues exist when configuring serial ports or serial devices: (1) assigning an interrupt, (2) assigning an I/O address, and (3) assigning a COM port number. Serial ports can share interrupt.

No two serial devices that operate simultaneously can share the same interrupt! For example, putting a mouse and a modem on the same interrupt is unadvisable because most modem applications use a mouse. While using the modem, if the mouse is moved, the modem will quit working.

Serial devices are normally assigned IRQ3 or IRQ4 although some manufacturers allow other IRQ (Interrupt Request) number assignments. An IRQ allows each device to request the microprocessor's attention.

Each serial port or device *must* be assigned a different I/O (Input/Output) address! An I/O address is a device's mailbox number so that the microprocessor can differentiate between devices. No single I/O address may be shared by two devices. The assigned I/O address determines the serial port's COM port number.

Every serial device or port must have a different COM port number! External serial devices inherit the COM port name assigned to the motherboard or adapter serial port to which the serial device connects. The operating system assigns the serial port a COM port number such as COM1, COM2, COM3, or COM4.

On boot up, the BIOS looks for serial devices at I/O addresses 3F8, 2F8, 3E8, then 2E8 *in that exact order*. The serial device or port at I/O address 3F8 is assigned COM1 as the COM port number. If BIOS finds a serial device or port at I/O address 2F8, the port or device is assigned COM2. Then, for I/O addresses 3E8 followed by 2E8, the attached serial devices or ports are assigned the COM port numbers COM3 and COM4, respectively. Serial Table #1 lists the common IRQs, I/O addresses, and COM port assignments for serial devices and serial ports.

SERIAL – TABLE #1

Serial Port Assignments

I/O Address	COM Port Name	IRQ
3F8	COM1	4
2F8	COM2	3
3E8	COM3	4
2E8	COM4	3

The easiest way to remember serial port interrupts is that $1 + 3 = 4$; COM1 and COM3 use Interrupt 4. Some manufacturers of serial ports or devices allow assignment of IRQs, COM names, and I/O addresses other than the ones listed in Serial Table #1. Use the assignments as they are listed in Serial Table #1 and stay out of trouble! For example, for the first serial device in the computer, assign it IRQ4 and I/O address 3F8h. The serial device becomes COM1.

Windows 9x, NT, and 2000 automatically assign COM names just as DOS does. If a serial device has a non-standard I/O address, Windows can assign the device a COM name higher than COM4, such as COM5, COM6, etc. Windows supports a total of 128 serial ports. However, even if the operating system sees the serial device and assigns it a higher COM port number, 16-bit Windows 3.x software or DOS software applications may not be able to communicate with the serial device.

Avoid settings other than those listed in Serial Table #1 if at all possible. Adhering to the standards set in the table prevents conflicts! Serial ports should be configured in I/O address and COM port order. Otherwise, the BIOS and the operating system reassign the COM port name. The BIOS COM port assignment, the serial port's COM port assignment, *and* the software's setup of the COM port must all agree if the serial device is to operate. The same is true for the IRQ and I/O address settings.

If the only serial adapter in a system is set to COM2 at I/O address 2F8, the computer's BIOS detects that no serial port exists at I/O address 3F8. Then, the BIOS checks at I/O address 2F8 and detects the adapter's serial port. The operating system assigns the serial adapter to port number COM1, even though the adapter jumpers are configured to COM2. This can create a conflict. Remember, the BIOS looks for the I/O address first at 3F8, then 2F8, 3E8, and 2E8. The operating system assigns COM names to the serial ports in COM1, COM2, COM3, and COM4 based on the sequence of the I/O addresses detected no matter how the board is configured.

If a computer has two serial ports at I/O addresses 3F8 and 2F8, the operating system assigns the serial port at I/O address 3F8 to COM1 and assigns the serial port at I/O address 2F8 to COM2. Assume an internal modem is then installed. The modem is set to I/O address 2E8 and to COM4. When installing the modem, the operating system assigns the modem to COM3 (even though 2E8 is normally for COM4). Because this is so confusing, the same steps are listed below.

1. BIOS detects I/O address 3F8.
2. The operating system assigns the port at I/O address 3F8 the COM port name of COM1.
3. BIOS detects I/O address 2F8.
4. The operating system assigns the port at I/O address 2F8 the COM port name of COM2.
5. BIOS scans for I/O address 3E8. Because no adapter or port is at this I/O address, the operating system does not assign a COM port.
6. BIOS detects I/O address 2E8.
7. The operating system assigns the port at I/O address 2E8 the *next* COM port name, COM3, not COM4.

Even with the internal modem jumpered for I/O address 2E8 and COM4, the BIOS reassigns the setting to COM3. Now, if the software has been configured to COM4, the modem will not work. This is why serial devices are so bothersome to install.

The order in which the I/O addresses are found is the order the serial devices and ports are assigned COM names!

Rather than use a software utility to determine serial port addresses, use the DEBUG command to see the serial port I/O addresses detected by the BIOS. An exercise at the end of the chapter details the steps. After documenting all currently used resources, set the new serial device settings to the next COM port name, an unused IRQ, and an unused I/O address. Never install a serial device without knowing the resources already in use.

Most software applications used with serial devices require configuration. For example, if using a communication software package with a modem, the communications software must be configured for the specific interrupt and I/O address that the modem uses. The application settings *must* match the serial device settings or the software will not operate with the serial device.

The DOS MODE command configures serial ports for the DOS environment. Windows 9x and 2000 use the System control panel. NT uses the Ports control panel. Exercises at the end of the chapter show how to view serial device resources. Whether using DOS/Windows, Windows 9x, NT, or 2000, a technician must be aware of the hardware resources used and what resources are available for serial devices.

MORE SERIAL PORT SETTINGS

A good understanding of how serial devices operate is essential to a technician's knowledge base. Before installing a serial device and configuring its associated software, a technician must be familiar with the terminology associated with serial device installation.

Data bits is a setting for how many bits make up a data word. The data bits setting is normally 8 bits per data word on a serial device, but can be seven or lower. **Parity** is a simple method of checking data accuracy. Most think of parity as even parity or odd parity. Take the example of a computer that uses even parity. If the data sent is 10101010, a total of four 1s are sent, plus a 0 for the parity bit. Four is an even number therefore the parity bit is set to a 0 because the total number of 1s must be an even number when even parity is used. If the data sent is 10101011, a total of five 1s are sent, plus an extra 1 for the parity bit. Because five is an odd number and the system uses even parity, then the extra parity bit is set to a 1 to make the total number of 1s an even number. When parity is used, both computers must be set to the same setting. The parity system is very basic for data error checking. The choices for parity include none, odd, even, space, and mark. With a space parity setting, both computers always set the parity bit to 0. With the mark parity setting, both computers always set the parity bit to 1.

 If communicating with an online service through a modem, the parity setting of the modem must match the parity setting of the online service modem. The normal setting in this case is none.

Stop bits in serial data communications are the number of bits sent to indicate the end of the data word. The number of stop bits can be 1, 1.5, or 2. One stop bit is the common choice. The **FIFO settings** option is used to enable or disable the UART chip's FIFO buffer. This setting gives the microprocessor time to handle other tasks without the serial device losing data. If data is lost, it will have to be retransmitted later when the microprocessor turns its attention back to the serial device.

The **flow control** setting in serial communications determines how two serial devices communicate. Flow control can be set using software or physical pins on the serial port (hardware). Another name for flow control is handshaking. This setting allows a serial device to tell the sending serial device, "Wait, I need a second before you send any more data." For communication to occur using hardware handshaking, things must happen in an exact sequence. **Handshaking** is the order in which things happen in order for two serial devices to communicate. Knowing this order helps with troubleshooting. Serial Table #2 delineates the hardware flow control.

Hardware Handshaking

SERIAL – TABLE #2

Order of Execution	Explanation
Both devices (the DTE and the DCE) power on and are functional.	
The DTE sends a signal over the DTR (Data Terminal Ready) line.	The DTE says, "I'm ready."
The DCE sends a signal over the DSR (Data Set Ready) line.	The DCE says, "I'm ready, too."
The DTE sends a signal over the RTS (Request to Send) connector pin.	The DTE (such as the computer) says, "I would like some data."
The DCE sends a signal on the CTS (Clear to Send) connector pin.	The DCE (such as the modem) says, "OK, here comes some data."
Data transmits one bit at a time over a single line.	

The two common methods for flow control are XON/XOFF (software method) and RTS/CTS (hardware method). The **XON/XOFF** handshaking sends special control characters when a serial device needs more time to process data or is ready to receive more data. If one modem needs the remote modem to wait a minute, it will send a certain character (usually CTRL S). Then, when the modem is ready to accept more data, a different control character (usually CTRL Q) is sent.

RTS/CTS (hardware handshaking) uses specific wires on the serial connector to send a signal to the other device to stop or start sending data. The **CTS (Clear to Send)** and the **RTS (Request to Send)** signals indicate when it is okay to send data.

The RS232 serial communication standard was developed during a time when mainframes were the norm. A mainframe terminal known as a DTE connected to a modem known as a DCE. In today's world, **DTE (Data Terminal Equipment)** includes computers and printers. On a DTE serial connector, certain pins initiate communication with a DCE device, such as a modem. Serial Table #3 shows the common signal names as well as the common abbreviations for the signals used with DTE devices.

SERIAL – TABLE #3

DTE Signal Connections

Signal Abbreviation	Signal Name
TD	Transmit Data
DTR	Data Terminal Ready
RTS	Request to Send

DCE (Data Circuit-terminating Equipment) includes devices such as modems, mice, and digitizers. On the DCE side, the signal names relate more to receiving data. Serial Table #4 lists the common signal names used with DCE devices.

SERIAL – TABLE #4

DCE Signal Connections

Signal Abbreviation	Signal Name
RD	Receive Data
DSR	Data Set Ready
CTS	Clear to Send
CD	Carrier Detect
RI	Ring Indicator

SERIAL CABLES

Anyone who has been a technician for any length of time will admit that serial devices have always been difficult to configure. In addition to the problems with interrupts, I/O address, and COM ports, serial cables are also a problem. All serial cables are not the same. Some serial device manufacturers require proprietary serial cables. Watch out for serial printers, plotters, and digitizers. Actually, beware of all serial devices and their cables. Be certain to use the correct cable.

Because a computer serial port is either a 9 or 25-pin male connector, a 9-to-25 or 25-to-9-pin converter may be necessary when connecting a serial device. If a computer has a 9-pin serial port and the serial device has a 25-pin connector, the cable for the device may have a 25-pin connector on each end of the cable. If this is true, a simple solution is to buy a 9-to-25-pin converter as shown in Serial Figure #6.

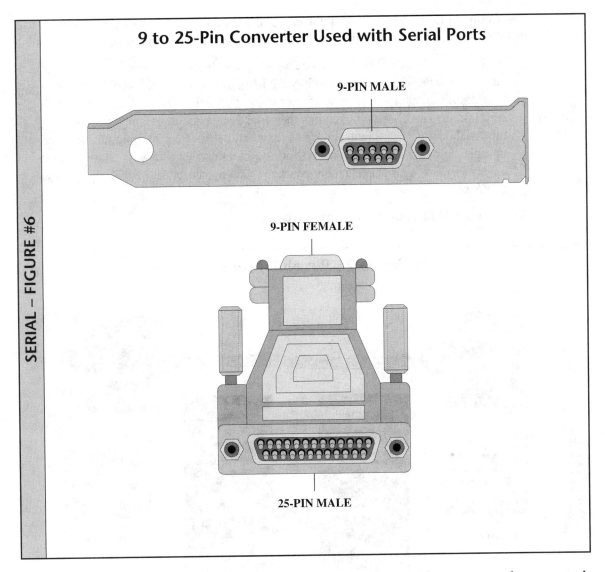

9 to 25-Pin Converter Used with Serial Ports

9-PIN MALE

9-PIN FEMALE

25-PIN MALE

If an external serial modem has a 25-pin connector and it connects to the computer's 25-pin serial connector, a **straight-through serial cable** is used for the device. A **null modem cable** connects two computers without the use of a modem. Some people are confused that null modem serial cables are *not* used by modems. That is because they do not understand the null modem cable's use. A null modem connection allows (1) file transfer between computers, (2) remote control of another computer, and (3) game playing between two players on separate computers. Take for example an older computer with only a 5.25" floppy drive that needs an application loaded, but you only have 3.5" disks. You can connect the two computers with a null-modem cable and load the application from the newer computer's 3.5" floppy drive to the older computer's hard drive. DOS has a program called INTERLINK that allows this connection. The Windows program is called the Direct Cable

Connection or DCC. An exercise at the end of the Hard Drive chapter explains how to use INTERLINK. Null modem cables also connect a computer to some serial peripherals.

Be very careful with 9-to-25-pin or 25-to-9-pin null modem cables. Many pinout variations exist. The best bet is to buy a 25-to-25-pin null modem cable and use a 9-to-25-pin adapter (converter) if necessary. The only way to determine which serial cable to purchase is by reading the serial device documentation or contacting the serial device's manufacturer. However, many cables frequently come packaged in a plastic bag with no documentation. Be careful what you buy! Mark all null modem cables with a permanent marker or with colored electrical tape so the cable is distinguishable from other serial cables.

Serial Figure #7 illustrates a null modem cable.

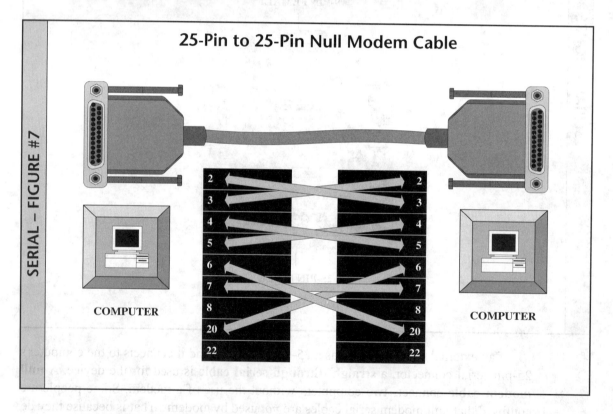

SERIAL – FIGURE #7

25-Pin to 25-Pin Null Modem Cable

COMPUTER

COMPUTER

Serial Figure # 8 shows a straight-through serial cable. Notice in Serial Figures #7 through #9 you cannot tell the difference between the cables except if you had the pinouts such as the ones shown. Serial Figure #9 shows a modem connected to a computer's 25-pin port, the same cable can be used to connect a 9-pin serial device to a 25-pin computer port.

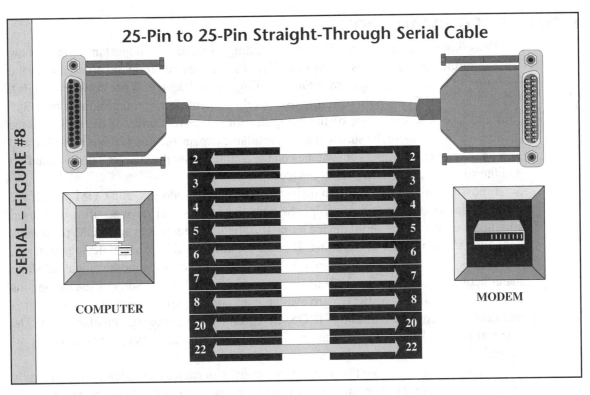

SERIAL – FIGURE #8

25-Pin to 25-Pin Straight-Through Serial Cable

COMPUTER

MODEM

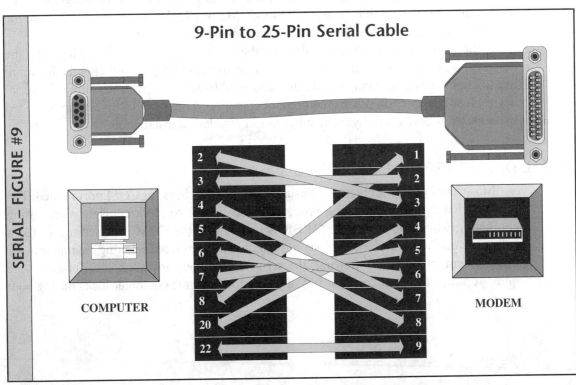

SERIAL– FIGURE #9

9-Pin to 25-Pin Serial Cable

COMPUTER

MODEM

SERIAL DEVICE INSTALLATION

Installing serial devices can be very frustrating. If there is an important time to know what is in the computer, it is when installing a serial device. To avoid frustration, take inventory of what is in the system *before* installing a serial device. Write down every IRQ, I/O address, and COM port currently used in the system. Place your findings on a 3x5 card and tape it to the inside of the computer for future reference. If the serial device requires its own adapter, be sure there is an available expansion slot. If it is a non-plug and play adapter, set the jumpers or switches on the adapter using the adapter's documentation and the rules for configuring serial devices.

If possible, give every device a different interrupt, I/O address, and COM port. If the serial device must share an interrupt, be sure the other serial device will *not* be used simultaneously with the serial device being installed. I/O addresses and COM ports *must* be unique to each device and adapter. If possible, keep within the serial device interrupt, I/O address, and COM port standards. Refer to Serial Table #1 for those standards. Many manufacturers allow non-standard configurations of serial devices. Sometimes, the options of IRQ2, IRQ5, IRQ9, or IRQ15 are available (as well as other interrupts). Sound cards and network cards sometimes use IRQ5. Be careful when choosing non-standard IRQs. The software package used with the serial device must be able to recognize the serial port as well.

To install a serial device that uses an expansion slot such as a modem, you frequently have to disable any built-in motherboard serial ports through the Setup program. Even though modems can often be configured as COM3 or COM4, it is best to configure the internal modem as COM2 especially if a serial mouse takes COM1.

If the serial device is plug and play and the system supports plug and play, plug the device in and let the system configure it. Refer to the Configuration chapter for more information on plug and play installation and troubleshooting. After installing the serial device, load any software drivers required for operation. Also, install any software included with the serial device. Always remember to test any device installation.

SERIAL DEVICE TROUBLESHOOTING

Most serial device problems are usually IRQ, I/O address, or COM port related. The serial device that is not working properly could be due to (1) a configuration setting conflicting with another device, (2) BIOS reassigning the COM port setting, or (3) a software's configuration setting does not match the serial device setting. Symptoms for this problem include the following: the serial device does not work, a different device quits working, the serial device works and then locks, or the computer locks during boot up. To solve this problem, go back to the discovery stage. Find out what is already installed in the computer. Try disabling serial ports not being used. Do not trust utilities to be completely accurate. Verify every setting through documentation. Use DEBUG to see which COM ports the BIOS detects.

Other problems with serial devices are below.

1. Always check the simplest solution first. Check the cable attachment. Check for bent pins on the connector and cable. This is more common than you would think.

2. If the device is external, check to see if it needs an external power source and, if so, that the external power source is working. Be sure you plugged the external device into the correct COM port and that the cable fits securely to the connector. The PC Design recommends the color teal be used to color-code serial ports. The PC Design port markings are as follows:

   First serial port |O|O|

   Second serial port |O|O|

3. Check if the UART is outdated. Upgrade the UART if possible. If the UART is soldered into the motherboard, consider buying an expansion card with a newer UART installed.

4. The wrong serial cable can cause many problems. The serial device may work intermittently or not at all. If possible, swap with a known good cable. Make sure you have not used a null modem cable by mistake. Contact the device manufacturer to see if the device needs a proprietary serial cable. If the serial device manufacturer is out of business and the correct serial connections are critical, use a **breakout box**. This allows a technician to determine the required wiring between two devices such as a computer and a serial printer. Breakout boxes are most useful when a manufacturer uses a proprietary serial cabling scheme and the cable pinouts are unknown. The breakout box allows you to connect a cable on one side of the box and a cable on the other side of the box. It is then used to tie a pin from one connector to the same or different numbered pin on the connector on the other side of the box.

5. Some software packages do not support the same IRQ, I/O address, or COM port as the serial device. Change the serial device settings to match the software or upgrade the software.

6. Some software packages simply do not support the serial device attached to the computer. Check with the software manufacturer, upgrade the software, replace the software, or replace the serial device.

7. Serial cables should not be longer than 50'; however, different grades of cable exist. Even a short, poorly made cable can be susceptible to outside interference. Cable interference is not normally a problem. If a cable is at fault or it works intermittently, do not keep the cable; throw it away! You may forget that it is bad and attempt to reuse it.

8. If the serial port is suspect, install a loopback plug and run a diagnostic that checks the port. A **loopback plug** is a 9 or 25-pin connector that plugs into the serial port. Once diagnostics execute, signals are sent out the serial port and looped back into the port. The loopback plug tests both the receive and transmit pins. Some diagnostic programs come packaged with the loopback plug. Remember that ports do not normally go bad, but lightning storms can damage an external modem's serial port.

9. Never forget that serial device drivers and other drivers or TSRs can conflict. Refer to the memory chapter for more help in this area.

10. Check the system's BIOS settings and verify the COM port used by an external serial device is not disabled in Setup, or does not conflict with an internal serial device.

MODEMS OVERVIEW

A very common serial device is a modem. A **modem (modulator/demodulator)** connects the computer with the outside world through a phone line. A modem converts a signal transmitted over the phone line to digital 1s and 0s read by the computer. A modem also converts the digital 1s and 0s from the computer and modulates them onto the phone line's carrier signal for transmission. Modems normally connect to a remote modem through the phone line. Modem communication normally uses hardware flow control (RTS/CTS) instead of software. Even though modems can be internal or external peripheral devices, Serial Figure #10 shows two modems connecting two computers.

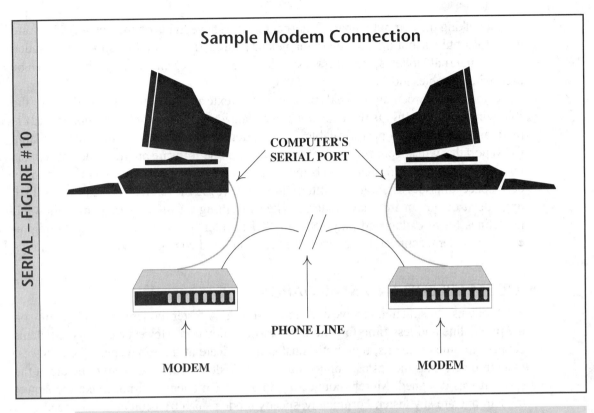

SERIAL – FIGURE #10

Sample Modem Connection

COMPUTER'S
SERIAL PORT

PHONE LINE

MODEM   MODEM

When connecting a modem to a phone line, be very careful with the cable. Some modems have two jacks on the back of the modem. The modem jack labeling varies, but one is usually labeled PHONE and the other labeled LINE. The LINE jack is for the cable that goes from the modem to the phone wall jack. The modem's PHONE jack is an optional jack to connect a telephone to the modem. Some people do not want to give up the wall jack for only the computer modem.

At a medium or large organization, it may be worthwhile to standardize modem settings such as COM2, IRQ3, I/O address 2F8. This will simplify setup, troubleshooting, and helpdesk calls, eliminating the need to spend time determining how an individual computer is set and checking for conflicts. All company technicians will know where to begin resolving the most time-consuming problems, those that are *not* conflict-related.

PROS AND CONS OF INTERNAL AND EXTERNAL MODEMS

The pros and cons of external modems are numerous. Internal modems require less space than an external modem, but they do require an expansion slot, generate more heat, and place a larger load on the computer's power supply. External modems connect to an existing serial port. Internal modems are cheaper than external modems. Internal modems come with their own UART so a technician does not have to wonder if the UART can keep up with the speed of the modem. External modems can easily connect to a different computer without taking the computer apart. External modems have lights on the outside. These are great for troubleshooting. However, many shareware exist, as well as software included with the internal modems, that allow a simulation of the external modem lights that can be used when troubleshooting.

Choosing between an internal modem and an external modem narrows down to the following questions: (1) Is there an existing expansion slot for an internal modem? (2) Is there an existing serial port available for an external modem? (3) Is there an available COM port that will not conflict with other devices? Some software programs do not support non-standard IRQ assignments. (4) Is money an issue? If so, get an internal modem. (5) Is desk space an issue? If so, get an internal modem. (6) Is the UART chip an issue? If so, upgrade it or get an internal modem. When installing an internal modem, follow all guidelines for any plug and play, ISA, or PCI adapter installation. When installing an external modem, connect it to an existing serial port and configure the port accordingly.

MODEM SPEEDS AND STANDARDS

Modems transmit and receive at different speeds. A faster modem means less time on the phone line and less time for microprocessor interaction. However, because modems connect to other modems, they both must communicate at the same speed. The slowest modem determines the fastest connection speed. A slow modem can only operate at the speed it was designed. Merely connecting to a faster modem will not make the slower modem operate any faster. Fortunately, speedy modems can transmit at lower speeds.

Communication mode standards developed by CCITT help with modem compatibility. For two modems to communicate with one another, they must adhere to the same protocol or set of rules. The CCITT (Comité Consultantif Internationale de Téléphonie et de Télégraphie) V standards regulate modem speeds and compatibility. CCITT standards are now listed in articles or textbooks as ITU (International Telecommunications Union) standards. For all communication standards check the TIA (Telecommunications Industry Association) and ITU web sites. ITU V.10 through V.34 are standards for interfaces and voice-band modems. ITU V.35 through V.37 standards deal with wideband modems. ITU standards V.40 through V.42 deal with error control.

Modem **error correction** ensures the data is correct at the modem level rather than have the computer's microprocessor handle or oversee it. A modem with error correction capabilities provides for overall faster computer performance. Microcom, Inc. has its own standards for error correction as well as CCITT. The **MNP (Microcom Network Protocol)** Levels 1 through 4 determine standards for error correction. Some of the CCITT standards include the MNP data compression standard levels as well.

Like error correction, data compression is also a part of some of the modem standards. **Data compression** converts data into smaller sizes before transmitting it. Compressing the data allows faster transmissions (less data to be transmitted). A drawback to modems using some types of data compression occurs with files such as .ZIP, .GIF, or .JPG. These files have already been compressed. The modem tries to uncompress the files, then recompress them for transmission. This process may actually slow down the computer's overall performance. Some of the ITU standards concern data compression. MNP Level 5 is the data compression standard from Microcom. Serial Table #5 lists some of the modem standards and their features.

SERIAL – TABLE #5

Communications Standards

Standard	Comments
V.17	14.4 Kbps and lower fax ITU standard
V.22	1200 bps modem ITU standard
V.22bis	2400 bps modem ITU standard
V.29	9600 bps and lower fax ITU standard
V.32	9600 bps and lower modem ITU standard
V.32bis	14.4Kbps and lower modem ITU standard
V.32turbo	Non-CCITT (ITU) standard for 12Kbps data transfer
V.FAST	Non-CCITT (ITU) standard for 28.8 Kbps data transfer. The *working name* for the V.34 standard until the standard became a reality.
V.FC	(Also known as V.Fast Class) Rockwell 28.8 Kbps standard with data compression and error correction. Does not support speeds less than 14.4Kbps.
V.34	28.8 Kbps modem ITU standard. In October of 1996, the standard changed to allow 33.6 Kbps transfers. Automatically adjusts to lower speeds if line problems occur.
V.34bis	ITU data compression standard
V.42	ITU error correction standard. Covers Microcomís Levels 1 through 4 for error correction. Also known as **LAPM (Link Access Procedure for Modems)**.
MNP-4	Microcom error correction standard
V.42bi s	ITU data compression standard
MNP-5	Microcom data compression standard
V.90	56K modem ITU standard. In February, 1998, the standard resolved the battle between the two 56Kbps standards: X.2 and K56flex.
MNP-10	Microcom standard for monitoring line conditions. Can adjust modem speed up or down depending on the state of the line.

Some new proposed standards are V.92, V.44, and V.59. V.92 will increase data rates and support something known as Quick Connect and Modem on Hold. Quick Connect allows faster initial connections (handshaking) and Modem On Hold allows modems to stay connected while you talk on the phone. V.44 improves data compression and V.59 is a standard for performing diagnostics.

When recommending a modem, nothing less than a V.34 modem is satisfactory in today's computing environments. Be sure the modem supports V.42 error correction as well as MNP Level 4 error correction. If the modem is an external unit, verify that it connects to an adapter or motherboard port with a 16550 or higher UART chip. If V.42bis is not available on a modem and Microcom's MNP Level 5 data compression standard is available, disable the MNP-5 data compression when transferring pre-compressed (.ZIP, .JPG, .GIF, etc.) files. MNP-5 does not detect if the file is already compressed. MNP-5 tries to uncompress the file and then recompress it thereby taking longer. V.42bis recognizes a compressed file and does not try to uncompress it.

As a general rule of thumb, the modem's speed setting should be set to its maximum throughput. If the modem supports data compression, higher speeds are possible. Serial Table #6 lists the maximum modem speeds based on the type of modem and the type of data compression used. Check the modem's documentation for the maximum speed setting.

General Guidelines for Maximum Modem Speeds

Modem Type	Type of Data Compression	Speed Setting (in bps)
V.22bis	MNP-5	4800
V.22bis	V.42bis	9600
V.32	MNP-5	19200
V.32	V.42bis	38400
V.32bis	V.42bis	38400 or 57,600

SERIAL – TABLE #6

56KBPS MODEMS

The phone line limit was once thought to be 28.8Kbps, then 33.6Kbps. Now modem manufacturers push even that limit. However, always keep in mind many areas of the country cannot go above 28.8Kbps because some phone companies will not guarantee their phone lines above a certain speed. Check with the phone company for this figure.

Nevertheless, the 56Kbps data transfer rate is only possible if the transmitted (analog) signal converts to digital one time during the data transmission. Digital phone lines are *quieter* than their analog counterparts, have less noise on the line, and allow faster data transmissions. Take the example of a person dialing into their office network from their home. Serial Figure #11 illustrates this example.

SERIAL – FIGURE #11

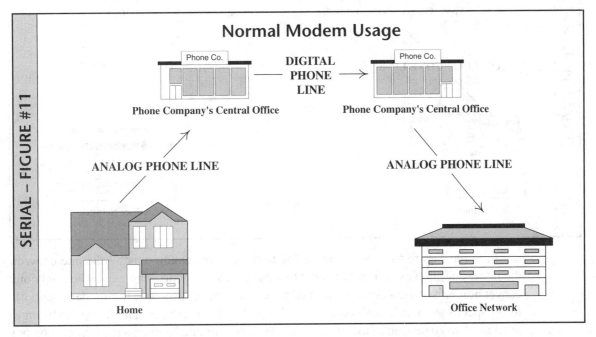

Normal Modem Usage

Notice in Serial Figure #11 how the signal converts twice. The first time the signal is converted is when the analog signal enters the phone company's central office. Between central offices, the signal stays digital. Then, when the signal leaves the central office to travel to the work building, the signal converts from a digital signal to an analog signal. 56Kbps transmission speeds do not support two conversions.

If the workplace has a digital line from the phone company or if a person dials into an Internet provider that has a digital phone connection, a 56Kbps modem is practical. Serial Figure #12 shows the difference.

SERIAL – FIGURE #12

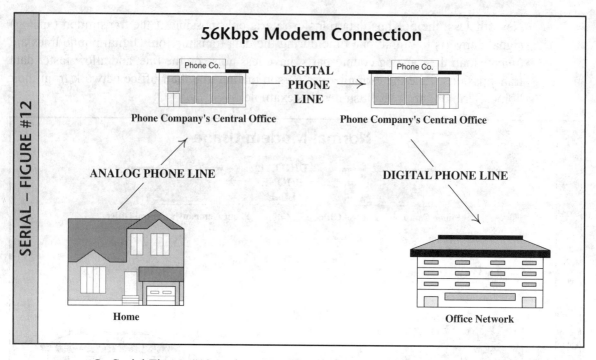

In Serial Figure #12, only one analog to digital conversion exists—the one between the home and the first central office. 56Kbps speeds, in theory, can exist when only one conversion exists. However, if the modem cannot run at 56Kbps, the modem supports lower speeds such as 33.6Kbps and 28.8Kbps. Studies estimate that 56Kbps will run at 56Kbps 10 to 20 percent of the time, about the same estimated percentage of time 33.6Kbps and 28.8bps modems run at their top speed. The problem is lack of standards. As with all new technologies, standards allow individual devices to communicate with other devices inside the computer and outside.

The V.90 standard resolved the battle between the two *proposed* Kbps modem standards, K56flex and x2. The K56flex proposal came from Lucent Technologies and Rockwell, International. 3Com supported the x2 proposal.

FAX MODEMS AND VOICE/FAX MODEMS

A **fax modem** allows a modem to use the computer and printer as a fax machine. The modem portion brings the data to the computer. The facsimile (fax) software allows viewing, printing, replying to, or sending a fax. The way that a regular modem sends data is different from the way a fax machine sends data, so a modem can do faxes only if it is a fax modem. Not all computer-based fax machines can handle modem data transfers, but a fax modem does both modem and fax transfers.

Fax standards handled by CCITT (ITU now) are in groups. Group I through Group IV concern fax machines. Group I and Group II are slow. The Group III standard is used by most computers today and has two subclasses, Class 1 and Class 2. Class 1 Group III fax machines can send and receive faxes. Class 2 fax machines handle more of the low-level communication details, (the protocol work), and the software manages the communication session as well as the fax image. The Class 2 standard took a long time to be approved. Some Class 2 modems adhered to the specification *draft* version rather than the approved version. An industry practice is that a fax machine that adheres to the final Class 2 standard is marked as a Class 2.0 standard instead of being listed as a Class 2. A Group III bis fax modem transfers data up to 14,400bps. Group IV fax modems transmit over a digital ISDN line at speeds up to 64Kbps. ISDN technology is discussed later in the chapter.

A **voice/fax modem** combines features from a voice mailbox system in the modem. The software handles messages for multiple people similar to multiple answering machines or a business voice system. A drawback to a voice/fax modem in a computer is that the computer stays on all the time. This is not a preferable situation unless the computer and modem are properly protected. Another drawback is some people have automated virus software dialing random numbers looking for a system with a voice/fax modem system. Once connected to the system, a virus will download to the system.

Some computer users want to connect their computer-based fax machine to their phone line and have the computer distinguish between an incoming fax and a phone call. A fax switch is available from computer and phone stores that distinguish between a voice call and a fax machine call. Another option is a service available from some telephone service providers that provides two phone numbers associated with the same phone line—one for the fax machine and one for voice. The service is known by different names such as Distinctive Ring, Ident-a-Ring, or SmartRing.

CABLE MODEMS

One of the hottest items in the modem industry is **cable modems** which connect a computer to a cable TV's network. Cable modems can be internal or external devices. If the cable modem is external, a NIC (Network Interface Card) is installed in the computer. The NIC connects to the cable modem and the cable modem connects to the cable TV network. If the cable modem is internal, there are two possible connections depending on the cable TV company. (1) The internal cable modem has a 56K analog modem built into it that is used to upload information to the Internet. The cable modem itself is used to bring information down from the Internet. (2) The internal cable modem uses a separate 56K analog modem to upload information.

The cable modem operation is not hard to understand. Internet data comes in through the cable TV coax cable. The coax cable plugs into the cable modem. The cable modem then sends the information out its built-in Ethernet port. A network cable connects from the cable modem's Ethernet port into an Ethernet port on the computer. To send data to the Internet, the reverse happens. The computer sends the data out its Ethernet port into the cable modem. The cable modem sends the data out the coax cable onto the cable TV company's network.

Two terms that are often associated with cable modems are upstream and downstream. **Upstream** refers to data that is sent from your home to the Internet. **Downstream** refers to the data pulled from the Internet into your computer, as when you download a file or view a web page. With cable modems, downstream transfer rates are faster than upstream transfers. Downstream speeds can be as high as 35Mbps, but are normally in the 1.4Mbps range. Upstream speeds vary, but with an external cable modem tend to be between 128Kbps and 500Kbps. Even though upstream speeds are slower, cable modems are a huge improvement over analog modems.

The speed of a cable modem connection depends on two things: (1) your cable company and (2) how many people in your neighborhood share the same cable TV channel. In a cable TV configuration, each cable channel uses 6MHz of the cable's bandwidth. The cable company designates one of the 6MHz channels as Internet access. Several homes can use the same channel, which reduces the amount of bandwidth each house has available. If you have three neighbors who all use the same cable vendor and they all are Internet warriors, you will have slower access than if you were the only person in the neighborhood connected.

The minimum amount of hardware needed to have a cable modem depends on the cable company's specifications. Normally, the minimum CPU needed is Pentium or higher, 64MB or RAM, and 100 to 150MB of free hard drive space. Whether or not you need an internal modem, Ethernet card, etc., depends on the company from which you receive the cable modem. Some companies include them as part of their rate. Serial Figure #13 illustrates cable modem connections with an internal cable modem.

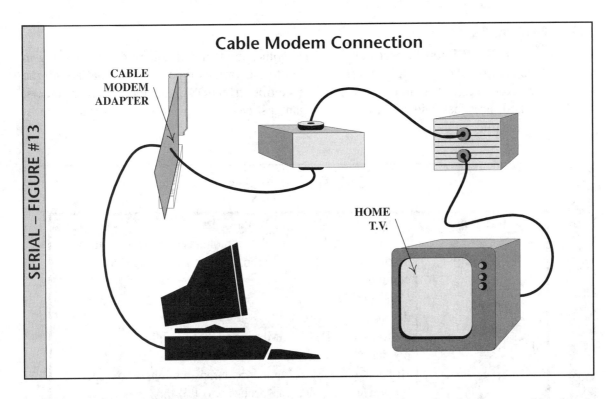

Cable Modem Connection

Some cable companies install the cable modem and associated software and hardware as part of their package. If required to install the modem, always follow the manufacturer's installation instructions. The modem installs similar to any other adapter. The Network chapter has tips on configuring network adapters.

DIGITAL MODEMS AND ISDN

Digital modems connect the computer directly to a digital phone line rather than a traditional analog phone line. One type of digital phone line available from the phone company is an ISDN line. An **ISDN (Integrated Services Digital Network)** line has three separate channels: two B channels and a D channel. The B channels handle data at 64Kbps transmission speeds. The D channel is for network routing information and transmits at a lower 16Kbps. The two B channels can combine into a single channel for video conferencing, thus allowing speeds up to 128Kbps. They are available in large metropolitan areas for reasonable rates, making it an affordable option for home office use, but due to recent technologies such as cable modems and xDSL modems (covered in the next section), ISDN is not a popular option today.

xDSL MODEMS

xDSL (Digital Subscriber Line) is another modem technology that is growing in popularity. The x in the term xDSL refers to the various types of DSL that are on the market. The most common one is **ADSL (Asymmetrical DSL),** but there are many others. ADSL uses faster downstream speeds than upstream. This performance is fine for most home Internet users.

SERIAL – TABLE #7

DSL Technologies

DSL Type	Comments
ADSL	Asymmetrical DSL—most common, faster downloads than uploads, speeds up to 8.4Mbps although 1.5M is most common
CDSL	Consumer DSL—slower than ADSL (1Mbps downloads), developed by Rockwell
DSL Lite or G.Lite	Slower than ADSL (1.5Mbps to 6Mbps), gaining in popularity
HDSL	High bit-rate DSL—symmetrical transmissions (equal speed for downloads/uploads), speeds up to 1.5Mbps
RADSL	Rate-Adaptive DSL—developed by Westell and allows modem to adapter to phone line condition, speeds up to 2.2Mbps
SDSL	Symmetric DSL—same speeds (up to 1.5Mbps) in both directions
VDSL	Very high data rate DSL—emerging technology with speeds up to 53Mbps
x2/DSL	3Com technology with a 56K modem that is upgradeable to DSL when it is available in a consumer's area

With DSL modems, bandwidth is not shared between people in the same geographical area. The bandwidth paid for is exclusive to the user. DSL is not available in all areas. A web site called DSL Reports (www.dslreports.com) has a listing of major DSL vendors and geographical areas plus a rating on the service. Serial Table #7 shows the most common DSL types.

With DSL, an internal or external DSL modem can be used and connected to the regular phone line. The phone line can be used for calls, faxes, etc., at the same time as the modem. If external, the modem can connect to a USB port or Ethernet network card. If the

DSL implementation uses an internal modem, it occupies an expansion slot (usually PCI) and configures the same way an internal modem does. Always follow the manufacturer's installation instructions. Some vendors install the DSL modem and configure the computer as part of their package.

Because the A+ exam and most computer support classes do not cover networking very deeply, this chapter does not go into firewalls and network security. However, it is very important when installing cable modems and DSL modems to look at information on proxy servers, firewalls, disabling file sharing, etc. When using these technologies, the computer is more prone to attacks, viruses, and taking/looking at the computer files or taking over the computer. Also be aware that Windows 98 Second Edition (Windows 98SE) and 2000 provide the ability to share a single Internet connection between multiple computers. The feature is called **ICS (Internet Connection Sharing)**.

LAPTOP MODEMS

Portable computers commonly have a modem PC Card installed in them. Modem PC Cards are Type II cards that fit into a Type II or a Type III slot. Many modem cards are combo cards—they are both a modem and a NIC. Modem PC Cards have a special connector that attaches to them called a **dongle** that allows an RJ-11 cable to be plugged into the card. Some vendors' dongles are proprietary. A spare dongle is recommended in the laptop case.

MODEM PREVENTIVE MAINTENANCE

The old adage "an ounce of prevention is worth a pound of cure" is never more true than it is in the case of modems. A power surge can come across a phone line just as it can travel through an electrical outlet. Most people think and worry about the computer problems that could be a result of power surges, but they do not stop to think about surges through the phone line. To provide protection for the modem and the computer, purchase a special protection device called a **phone line isolator** or a modem isolator at any computer or phone store. A power surge through the phone line can take out many components inside the computer, including the motherboard.

Some surge protectors also have modem protection. A phone cable from the computer plugs into the surge protector. A separate phone cable connects to another jack on the surge protector and the other end plugs into the phone wall jack. The surge protector must, of course, be plugged into a grounded outlet.

TROUBLESHOOTING MODEMS

All the previously mentioned troubleshooting tips for serial ports also apply to modems. However, some additional tips listed below apply to modems.

1. If the modem is an external unit, turn the modem's power off and back on, then try the modem again. If the modem is internal, reboot the computer and try the steps again.

2. If the modem does not dial the number, does not output a dial tone, or a message appears stating that the modem is not responding, check that the phone cord connects to the correct jack on the modem and to the wall phone jack. Also, be sure the correct serial cable is used, the cable secures properly to the modem and the computer, and the COM port setting is correct. Check the flow control setting or check if the phone line requires a special number such as a 9 to dial an outside line. Remove the cable from the phone outlet to the modem and plug it into a phone. The phone outlet should have a dial tone and work correctly.

3. If the modem starts to dial, but then hangs up, check if the phone cable from the wall jack to the modem inserts into the correct modem jack. This symptom also occurs if the "No dial tone" message appears.

4. If the modem hangs up after some time, other equipment (such as fax machines, answering machines, and portable phones) can cause the problem. Also, other people picking up the phone line and disconnecting the modem's connection is a common occurrence. To verify if other equipment causes the problem, disconnect the other devices on the phone line and see if the problem goes away. Also, check the UART chip to see if it is fast enough. Another problem can be the call waiting feature. Is call waiting enabled on the same phone line the modem uses? If so, disable call waiting or place a *70, (or whatever number disables call waiting for your phone) before the phone number to be dialed. Check with the modem at the other end to see if it is having problems. Lower the speed of the modem and try to connect. Turn off data compression or error checking to see if one of these settings is causing the problem.

5. Phone line problems can cause a modem to transmit at a lower speed. Some modems try to correct or compensate for phone line noise. This is a very common occurrence. Have the phone company check the line. Special modem lines provide a cleaner line and are available for home users. Check with the local phone company for details.

6. If the modem is an external unit and constantly transmits and receives at a lower speed, check the UART chip to see if it is fast enough for the modem.

7. If garbage (random characters) appears on the screen, check the handshaking, parity, stop bit, and baud rate settings. Most dial-up services require some type of emulation settings, such as VT-100 or ANSI. Check with the system provider or operator for the proper settings (or try each setting until one works).

8. Verify that the modem works by using the Windows HyperTerminal program. After setting the modem's parameters, type *ATE1M1V1* (using all caps). Some modems are case sensitive when using modem commands. Press *Enter.* The modem should reply with an OK on the screen. If not, the modem may not be a Hayes-compatible modem. The ATE1M1V1 is from the U.S. Robotics and

Hayes modem command set. *AT* in ATE1M1V1 means Attention and must precede all other commands. *E1* tells the modem to echo whatever is sent out. *M1* turns on the modem's speaker. *V1* places the modem in verbal mode. Check the modem's documentation to be sure it understands the ATE1M1V1 command. If that is not the problem, the modem may be set up on the wrong COM port in the Terminal settings. Go back and reconfigure the settings for a different COM port. The Hayes modem command ATZ resets the modem. Each modem normally comes with a manual that lists each command it understands.

9. Another HyperTerminal check is as follows: after setting the modem's parameters, type *ATDT* and press *Enter.* The *DT* in this command tells the modem to use touch-tone dialing. A dial tone should emit from the modem speaker. If not, the modem may not be a Hayes-compatible modem and it may not understand the command ATDT. Check the modem documentation to be sure it understands the command. Then, check the modem's connection to the wall jack and the modem's speaker volume level. Refer to the modem manual. If the phone line requires a special number to connect to an outside phone line, place that number immediately after the ATDT command.

10. If a modem is having trouble connecting, disable the error control feature.

11. Check with the other modem site to determine if the other modem and modem settings are operational.

12. If a letter appears twice on the screen for every letter typed, check the echo mode setting in the communications software package. The *echo* mode setting is sometimes called the local echo setting and when enabled, sends typed commands through the modem to the screen. The setting needs to have the local echo turned *off*. If nothing appears on the screen when you type, turn the local echo setting *on*. Some software settings refer to turning the local echo off as the full duplex mode and turning the local echo on as the half duplex mode. **Full duplex** means that two devices can send each other data simultaneously. **Half duplex** means that two devices can send each other data, but only one device can transmit at a time.

13. If the modem dials, but the high pitched, screeching noise that indicates connection to another modem or fax does not sound, check the phone number. The phone number dialed may be incorrect or the prefix such as a 1 for long distance may be inadvertently omitted. Another possibility is the modem is dialing too fast for the phone line. Consult the modem's manual for slowing down the dialing.

14. Use an external modem's lights to troubleshoot the problem. Manufacturers label the external lights differently, but the concept is the same. Most modems use hardware handshaking, so watching the lights and listening for the dial tone and the high pitched noises are good troubleshooting hints. Look back at Serial Table #2 for the order in which handshaking occurs. Internal modems

frequently have software to show a pictorial status of the internal modem as if the modem was external. Serial Table #8 shows the common external modem status lights.

SERIAL – TABLE #8

Common External Modem Lights

Abbreviation	Purpose
CD	Carrier Detect
MR	Modem Ready
RD	Receive Data
SD	Send Data
TR	Terminal Ready

15. If the modem is Hayes-compatible, type *AT&F* to restore the factory settings and often solve obscure problems. Serial Table #9 lists common modem commands. These commands are important to know for the A+ Certification.

SERIAL – TABLE #9

Common Modem Commands

Command	Purpose
AT	Precedes modem commands
ATDT	Dials a number using touch-tone. Put a space after this command and follow it with the phone number.
AT&F	Reset to factory default settings
ATZ	Reset to power on settings
*70	Disables call waiting

WINDOWS MODEM INSTALLATION AND TROUBLESHOOTING

Follow the same basic serial port rules when using Windows as when in the DOS/ Windows environment. However, Windows supports plug and play and many modems are plug and play. In theory, the installation should go much smoother, but that is not always the case. Modems, more than any other device, cause the most trouble.

Windows has an Install New Modem wizard that automates the modem installation process. Often conflicts arise and other devices stop working or the modem does not work after using this wizard. Many technicians avoid using the wizard to automatically detect the modem. Instead, manually select from a list of manufacturers and models or use the disk from the modem manufacturer. This is the best choice. If the wizard selects the modem type, it might only pick a compatible model. This frequently causes the conflict and the modem does not work, or does not have all of its capabilities. Some plug and play modems require specific settings on power up. The settings can be manually input through the Device Manager.

In Windows, if the modem is not dialing at all, check the port setting by using the Modem control panel. On the *General* tab, select the correct modem. Then, click on the *Properties* button to see the port listing. Check the port settings by clicking on the *Connection* tab. Windows has a Modem Diagnostic Tool available through the Diagnostic tab in the Modem control panel. Also, try disabling the error control, or changing the flow control setting by using *Device Manager*. Click on the *plus* symbol by the Modem icon. Click on the modem installed in the computer. Click on the *Properties* tab and then the *Connection* tab. Select the *Advanced* button. Adjust the error control and flow control by clicking in the checkboxes beside each option.

Sometimes Windows disables a modem. To verify the modem is enabled, use the System control panel. Select the *Device Manager* tab. Click once on the *plus sign* (+) beside the modem category. Select the modem from the sublist. Then, click on the *Properties* button. Verify the Device Usage checkbox next to the modem configuration. Click on the *Resources* tab to determine if Windows detects a resource conflict with any other installed device. Resolve resource conflicts the same way you would resolve any other I/O address, IRQ, or memory address conflict. Refer to the Configuration chapter for more resource conflict information.

If the modem keeps losing connection, use the prior troubleshooting tips and try placing the modem at a lower speed. Use the Modem control panel to set the lower speed. If the modem works using the Windows HyperTerminal program, but will not work with a different 32-bit communication application, try reinstalling the communication program.

THE MOUSE

A common serial input device is a mouse. A **serial mouse** connects to a 9 or 25-pin male port on the computer. All rules for setting serial port configurations apply to a serial mouse as well. Some motherboard manufacturers place a mouse connector on the motherboard. A mouse that connects to this port is known as a **PS/2 mouse**. A PS/2 mouse does not have to be purchased from IBM, but because IBM PS/2 computers first used this port, the name stuck with this type of mouse. The PC Design document recommends that the mouse port be color-coded green. Serial Figure #14 shows a PS/2 connector on the motherboard.

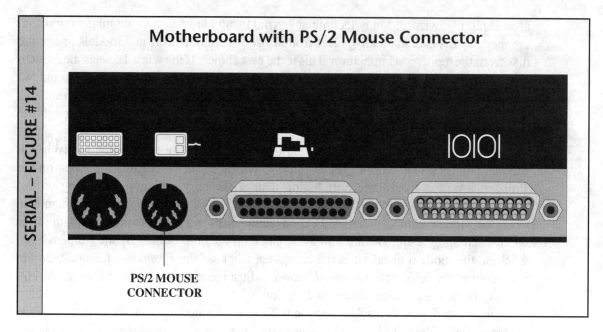

Motherboard with PS/2 Mouse Connector

PS/2 MOUSE
CONNECTOR

Buying a motherboard with a built-in mouse port saves on a COM port. The built-in mouse port normally uses IRQ12, not IRQ3 or IRQ4 like a serial mouse. Note that a mouse can also connect to a USB port. The recommended PC Design icon is as follows:

A popular model of mouse is a combinational mouse. The **combinational mouse** plugs into a motherboard PS/2 mouse port or into a serial port. The mouse has a mini-DIN connector like the PS/2 mouse connector and a cable that adapts the mini-DIN connector to a 9 or 25-pin serial port connector. This adapter cable will not work on a mouse that does not have the capability to plug into both port types. A regular serial mouse can only plug into serial ports. A regular PS/2 mouse only plugs into a motherboard mouse port. Only a combinational mouse plugs into both.

A **bus mouse** connects to its own adapter and is normally used when no serial ports are available. A bus mouse is not that common and should be used only when necessary. Taking up an expansion slot for a mouse is not necessary unless too many other serial devices are in the computer. Look at Serial Figure #15 for a bus mouse adapter.

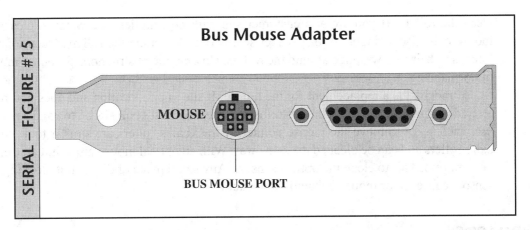

A mouse normally requires a software driver for Windows. If a mouse software driver is suspect, download a new driver from the manufacturer's web site, reload the driver, or use a generic mouse driver. Most mouse problems, however, are resource conflict related or dirt related. Conflicts also occur when installing a system for the first time or adding a new piece of hardware such as a modem that conflicts with the mouse's interrupt or I/O address.

Using a mouse frequently causes its internal parts to become dirty. Before explaining how to clean a mouse, understanding the basic internal mouse workings is important because the two topics interrelate. There are two basic types of a mouse—a mechanical mouse and an optical mouse. A **mechanical mouse** uses a rubber ball inserted into the bottom of the mouse. The rubber ball turns small metal, rubber, or plastic rollers mounted on the side. The rollers relay the mouse movement to the computer. An **optical mouse,** on the other hand, has optical sensors to detect the direction the mouse ball moves. It does not have a rubber ball at all, but uses reflections from LEDs using a grid pattern mouse pad to detect mouse location. A mechanical mouse is more common than an optical mouse.

MOUSE PREVENTIVE MAINTENANCE

Mouse cleaning kits are available in computer stores, but normal household supplies also suffice. For the mouse with a rubber ball, the ball gets dirty and clogged with lint and dirt. Turn the mouse over and rotate the ball's retainer ring or access cover counter clockwise. Remove the mouse ball's retainer ring or access cover. A mouse sometimes has screws that secure the ball's access cover.

After removing the cover, turn the mouse over, cupping your hand over the mouse ball. Catch the mouse ball as it falls into your hand. To clean the mouse ball, use a mild detergent, soapy water, contact cleaner, or alcohol. Rinse the mouse ball and dry completely with a lint-free cloth. With compressed air or your breath, blow out where the rubber ball sits in the mouse.

With a mechanical mouse, the rollers inside the mouse ball also get dirt on them that cause erratic mouse behavior. Use a cotton swab or lint-free cloth with rubbing alcohol to clean the rollers. If you are at a customer site with no supplies, use water to clean the mouse ball. Use a fingernail or tweaker screwdriver to scrape the rollers. Occasionally, threads or hair gets wrapped around the rollers. Unwrap the obstructions for better mouse performance.

A trackball is a replacement for the mouse. It sits in one location and does not move around on a mouse pad or on the desk. Instead, the trackball's ball sits on top and a person uses their palm to move the mouse pointer. A trackball's rollers are similar to a mouse ball's rollers and can be cleaned the same way. With an optical mouse, use a lint-free cloth or compressed air to clean the optical sensors. Any small piece of dirt or lint blocking the sensors causes poor mouse behavior and reaction.

KEYBOARDS

Keyboards are input devices that connect to the keyboard port. The recommended PC Design color code for the keyboard port is purple and the icon is

There are two main types of keyboards, capacitive and mechanical. **Mechanical keyboards** use a switch for each key. When the switch gets dirty, it sticks. Mechanical keyboards require more cleaning and are more error-prone than their capacitive counterparts. A **capacitive keyboard** is more reliable than a mechanical keyboard and more expensive because of the electronics involved in the design. IBM computers use capacitive keyboards. Keyboards have two main types of connectors, a larger 5-pin DIN and a 6-pin mini-DIN, also known as a PS/2 connector similar to the mouse PS/2 connector. See Serial Figure #16 for the 5 and 6-pin keyboard DIN connectors.

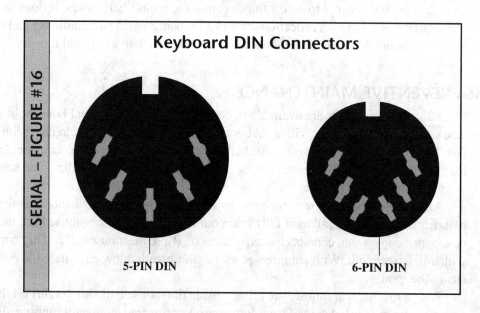

Keyboard DIN Connectors

SERIAL – FIGURE #16

5-PIN DIN

6-PIN DIN

KEYBOARD PREVENTIVE MAINTENANCE

Keyboards also need periodic cleaning, especially because most are some type of mechanical keyboard. Keyboard cleaning kits and wipes are available at computer stores. Simply turn the keyboard upside down and shake it to get out the paper bits and paper clips. Compressed air also helps with keyboard cleaning. If the keys are dirty from finger oils, turn the computer off before cleaning the keys. Then, using keyboard cleaning wipes or an all-purpose cleaner and an old cloth, wipe the keyboard keys. A cotton swab can get between the keys and a lint-free swab is best. Make sure the keyboard is completely dry before re-energizing.

KEYBOARD TROUBLESHOOTING

If a particular key is not working properly, remove the key cap. The chip removal tool included with PC tool kits is great for this. They are not great for removing chips, but they are good for removing key caps. A tweaker (small, flat-tipped) screwdriver also does a good job. After removing the key cap, use compressed air around the sticky or malfunctioning key.

Keyboards and mice are normally considered throw-away technology. The customer's cost to pay a technician to keep cleaning a keyboard over and over again would pay for many new capacitive keyboards. Keep this in mind when troubleshooting the cheaper devices. If coffee or a soft drink spills into the keyboard, all is not lost. Many people have soaked a keyboard in a bathtub, a flat pan of water, or the dishwasher's top rack. If you use a dishwasher, do not use detergent and run it through only one rinse cycle. Distilled or boiled water cooled down to room temperature is best. The keyboard can later be disassembled and/or scrubbed with lint-free swabs or cloths. Remember, though, keyboards are inexpensive and easily replaced!

Name _____

SERIAL DEVICES, MICE, AND KEYBOARDS REVIEW QUESTIONS

1. List two serial devices.

2. Why are serial devices sometimes difficulct to install?

3. Which device transmissions travel farther, serial or parallel?

4. Which device transmissions travel faster, serial or parallel?

5. [T / F] Serial devices transmit seven bits at a time.

6. Explain the difference between serial and parallel transmissions.

7. Which of the following are names for a computer's serial port? (Pick all that apply)
   [COM port / Asynchronous port / Synchronous port / LPT port
   / RS-232 port]

8. Describe the most common type of serial port found on the back of a computer.

9. Which of the following controls the computer's serial port?
   [UART / ROM BIOS / CMOS / CPU]

10. Where can a UART chip be located? (Pick all that apply)
    A. On the motherboard
    B. On a serial adapter
    C. In an external modem
    D. On an internal modem

11. What are the UART buffers for?

12. How can you determine what UART is being used in Windows 2000?

13. What is the difference between a socketed and a soldered UART?

14. List three major issues for configuring serial ports.

15. [T / F] Serial devices can share an interrupt as long as they operate simultaneously.

16. Which of the following must be unique for each serial port? (Pick all that apply)
    [COM port number / Interrupt / I/O address / DMA channel
    / Bus mastering address]

17. Which of the following is the correct order for I/O addresses which BIOS assigns COM port numbers?
    A. 2E8, 2F8, 3E8, 3F8
    B. 2E8, 3E8, 2F8, 3F8
    C. 3F8, 2F8, 3E8, 2E8
    D. 3F8, 3E8, 2F8, 2E8

18. [T / F] Serial ports always receive COM port numbers in I/O address order.

19. Which COM ports are normally assigned to IRQ4? (Pick all that apply)
    [COM1 / COM2 / COM3 / COM4]

20. Which COM ports are normally assigned to IRQ3? (Pick all that apply)
    [COM1 / COM2 / COM3 / COM4]

21. Explain why assigning a COM port out of order can give the COM port a different number.

22. The Windows 9x [Serial Device / Ports / System / Multimedia] is used to configure serial devices.

23. List five common modem speed settings.

24. Why do modems not normally use parity checking?

25. What setting determines how two serial devices establish communication?
    [Data bits / Stop bits / Parity / Flow control]

26. What are two common flow control methods?

27. What does CTS stand for?

28. What does RTS stand for?

29. Explain the difference between a DCE and a DTE.

30. Define handshaking.

31. Explain what happens when hardware handshaking is used.

32. [T / F] All serial cables are either 9-to-25-pin or 25-to-25-pin.

33. Scenario: An external modem has a 25-to-25-pin cable. The computer to which the modem attaches has two 9-pin serial ports. What is the most inexpensive way to connect the modem to the computer?
    A. Buy a 9-to 25-pin null modem cable
    B. Buy a 9-to-25-pin straight through cable
    C. Buy a 9-to-25-pin converter
    D. Buy a new modem

34. Why should a technician be careful when buying a 9-to-25-pin null-modem cable?

35. List three recommendations to remember when installing a serial device.

36. List five troubleshooting tips for serial ports.

37. What are the majority of serial problems and why is this an issue?

38. If a modem has only one RJ-11 port, what plugs into the port?
    A. A cable that connects to another modem
    B. A cable that plugs into a phone
    C. A cable that plugs into a phone outlet
    D. A cable that connects to another computer

39. Describe two advantages to external modems.

40. Describe two advantages to internal modems.

41. Describe how modem software can be an issue.

42. What ITU standards deal with modem data compression?

43. What ITU standards deal with fax modems?

44. What modem feature does the V.44 standard target?

45. What is a drawback to modem data compression?

46. [T / F]   A modem should be set to its maximum speed.

47. What is the biggest limitation to a 56Kbps modem transmitting at 56Kbps?

48. [T / F]   A 56Kbps modem is a good investment for a home modem. Explain your answer.

49. What two competing 56Kbps standards were used to create the V.90 modem standard?

50. Which ITU Fax Group standard is used by most computers?

51. If a customer wants to be able to receive and send faxes through their modem, what Group III, ITU class is necessary?
    [Class 1 / Class 2 / Class 3 / Class 4]

52. [T / F]   A cable modem is a good investment for a home modem. Explain your answer.

53. Explain when a NIC would be used with a cable modem.

54. List one drawback to a cable modem.

55. [T / F]   Digital modems require a digital phone line.

56. What does *asymmetrical* mean in relation to an ADSL modem?

57. What is x2/DSL?

58. Can a phone be used at the same time as a DSL modem?

59. What interface does a DSL internal modem use?

60. What type of PC Card does a laptop modem use?

61. What is a phone line isolator?

62. List five different troubleshooting tips for modems.

63. What happens if call waiting is enabled on a phone line with a modem attached?

64. List at least two things that can cause a modem to transmit at a lower than maximum speed.

65. If a modem does not sound a dial tone, what is the most likely conflict if the modem worked before?

66. What does a TR modem light indicate?
    [Terminal Ready / Transmit/Receive / Transmit Ready / Transmit Reset]

67. Explain whether plug and play technology makes serial device configuration harder, easier, or neither.

68. Where do you go to start the Windows 9x modem diagnostic utility?

69. How can you verify that Windows has *not* disabled a modem?

70. Describe the difference between how a mechanical and an optical mouse works?

71. [T / F] An optical mouse is more common than a mechanical mouse.

72. Which type of keyboard is more reliable?

73. How often should a keyboard and mouse be cleaned? Explain your answer.

74. What does the term throw-away technology mean?

75. [T / F] Keyboards are considered to be throw-away technology.

Name _____

SERIAL DEVICES, MICE, AND KEYBOARDS FILL-IN-THE-BLANK

1. _____ transmissions require a clock to send or receive data.

2. The _____ bit is used with asynchronous transmissions and signals the beginning of transmission.

3. The _____ bit is used with asynchronous transmissions and signals the end of transmission.

4. A serial device transmission speed is measured in _____.

5. A(n) _____ converts a data byte into single transmission bits.

6. Serial devices are normally assigned the interrupts _____ or _____.

7. The normal data bits per data word is _____ bits per word on a serial device.

8. The normal parity setting for a modem is _____.

9. The _____ modem setting enables the UART's buffer.

10. The _____ flow control method uses specific wires to signal data transmission.

11. The _____ flow control method uses control characters to signal data transmission.

12. Modems use a _____ cable.

13. To connect two computers and transfer data between them without a modem, a _____ cable is used.

14. A device used to help with serial pinouts is a _____.

15. A device that allows a computer to connect to a phone line is a _____.

16. _____ takes a signal from the phone line and converts it to digital format for input into the computer.

17. A modem that has _____ keeps the microprocessor from having to verify the accuracy of the data.

18. A modem that has _____ must transmit less data than one that does not have this ability.

19. Two features in the V.92 standard are _____ and _____.

20. A _____ handles voice messaging and allows documents to be sent over phone lines.

21. A _____ modem connects a computer to a TV network using coaxial cable.

22. When using a cable modem, the term _____ refers to data pulled from the Internet.

23. Computer modems are normally _____. [analog, digital]

24. A type of digital phone line that has three channels is _____.

25. An ISDN line consists of two _____ channels and one _____ channel.

26. The ISDN B channel transfers data at _____bps.

27. The ISDN D channel transfers data at _____bps.

28. _____ is an emerging type of DSL that allows speeds up to 53Mbps.

29. _____ is a Windows 2000 feature that allows multiple computers to use one Internet connection.

30. A _____ is used with a laptop to connect a modem to a phone line.

31. The Hayes modem command _____ causes a Hayes-compatible modem to perform as if picking up a phone—it issues a dial tone.

32. The Hayes modem command _____ resets a Hayes-compatible modem.

33. The Windows 9x _____ wizard handles a modem installation.

34. A _____ mouse connects to a serial computer port.

35. A _____ mouse connects to a 9-pin DIN connector.

36. A _____ is an input device that works like a mouse except that it does not move on a mouse pad or desk, it stays stationary and a ball moves the tracking object.

Name _____

MSD UART IDENTIFICATION EXERCISE

Objective: To use MSD to identify the UART

Parts: Working computer with Microsoft Diagnostics (MSD) loaded

Step 1.   Power on the computer and go to the command prompt.

Step 2.   Change into the directory (DOS or WINDOWS) that contains the Microsoft Diagnostics (MSD.EXE) program. Refer to the DOS chapter for DOS skills.

Step 3.   Start the Microsoft Diagnostics program by typing **MSD** at the prompt.

Step 4.   Press **C** on the keyboard to access the COM Ports option.

Step 5.   Look at the COM Ports information window. The headings across the top are COM1, COM2, COM3, and COM4. For each COM port, different criteria are listed below. Look for the last piece of information in the column. That is the UART chip used criteria.

Question 1:   What UART does COM1 use?

Question 2:   Does the system being tested have a COM2 port?

Question 3:   If the system has a COM2 port, what UART does COM2 use?

Step 6.   Press **Enter** to return to the first screen of the MSD program.

Step 7.   Press **F3** to quit MSD.

Name _____

DETERMINING THE UART USING WINDOWS 9X

Objective: To use Windows 95/98 to identify the UART

Parts: Working computer with Windows 95/98 loaded

Step 1.   Power on the computer and verify that Windows loads.

Step 2.   Double-click on the **My Computer** icon.

Step 3.   Double-click on the **Control Panel** folder icon.

Step 4.   Use the scroll bars to locate the **System** icon.

Step 5.   Double-click on the **System** icon.

Step 6.   Click once on the **Device Manager** tab.

Step 7.   In the displayed list, click once on the **plus** (+) symbol beside the Ports option.

Step 8.   Double-click on the **Communications Port** subitem under Ports.

Step 9.   Click once on the **Port Settings** tab.

Step 10. Click on the **Advanced** button.

Step 11. If the **Use FIFO buffers (requires 16550 compatible UART)** checkbox is checked, then the computer has a 16550 or higher UART. To determine the exact UART, remove the cover from the computer, find the UART, and look at the number on the chip.

Question 1: Does Windows 95/98 detect a 16550 or higher UART in the computer?

Step 12. Click on the **Cancel** button.

Step 13. Click on the **Cancel** button in the Communications Properties window.

Step 14. Click on the **Cancel** button in the System Properties window.

Optional alternate method is in Steps 15 through 19:

Step 15. From the Control Panel window, double-click on the **Modems** icon. (Use the scroll bars to locate the icon if necessary.)

Step 16. Click on the **Diagnostics** tab.

Step 17. Click once on **COM1** to select the port.

Step 18. Click on the **More Info** button. The port information is at the top of the window.

Question 2:   What UART does the port use?

Step 19.   Click on the **OK** button.

Step 20.   Close all windows on the desktop.

_____ *Instructor's Initials*

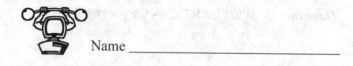

Name _____

DETECTING I/O ADDRESSES WITH THE DEBUG PROGRAM

Objective: To use DEBUG to identify I/O addresses

Parts: Working computer with the DEBUG command available

Step 1. Power on the computer and go to the command prompt.

Step 2. At the command prompt, type **DEBUG**. A dash appears on the line following the DEBUG command.

Step 3. At the dash on the screen, type **D40:0** and press **Enter**. Hexadecimal values display on the screen.

The D in the D40:0 command is the dump command meaning that the system is dumping the contents of a range of memory addresses. The 40:0 is the memory address where the I/O address information begins. The hexadecimal values of the active serial ports display first, followed by the parallel ports. Deciphering the hexadecimal numbers is tricky, but Serial Exercise Figure #1 helps explain the values. *The first line of the output is all that matters!*

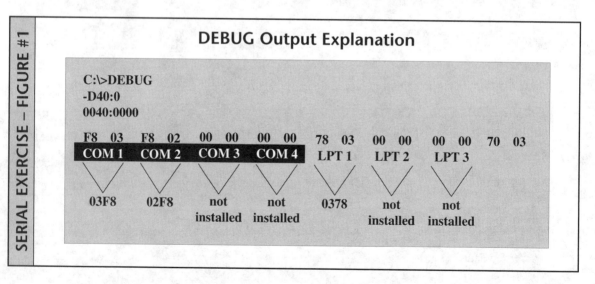

DEBUG Output Explanation

```
C:\>DEBUG
-D40:0
0040:0000
```

F8 03	F8 02	00 00	00 00	78 03	00 00	00 00	70 03
COM 1	COM 2	COM 3	COM 4	LPT 1	LPT 2	LPT 3	
03F8	02F8	not installed	not installed	0378	not installed	not installed	

SERIAL EXERCISE – FIGURE #1

Notice in Serial Exercise Figure #1 how four different values are associated with COM1, COM2, COM3, and COM4. The four values represent the I/O address for the associated COM port. However, the address displays backward and this confuses most people. For example, COM1 lists as F8 03, but in reality, the values represent I/O address of 03F8. A port address of 00 00 is an unused (or undetected) port.

Question 1: Using Serial Exercise Table #1, write the COM port assignments and associated I/O addresses found in the computer. Once finished, have a classmate verify the COM port assignments.

	COM Port Name	I/O Address
EXERCISE – TABLE #1	COM1:	
	COM2:	
	COM3:	
	COM4:	

Classmate's printed name: _____

Classmate's initials: _____

Step 4. To exit the DEBUG program, type **Q** and press **Enter**.

Question 2: Determine if a serial device connects to the serial ports detected by the BIOS or if the serial device is a separate adapter. For the serial ports being used, use Serial Exercise Table #2 to log this information. For example, if an internal modem is using COM1, then write modem in the first space available in the Device column.

	Port	Device
EXERCISE – TABLE #2	COM1:	
	COM2:	
	COM3:	
	COM4:	

Name _____

WINDOWS 9X COMMUNICATION PORT SETTINGS EXERCISE

Objective: To use Windows 95/98 to identify serial port settings

Parts: Working computer with Windows 95/98 loaded

Step 1.   Power on the computer and verify that Windows loads.

Step 2.   Double-click on the **My Computer** icon.

Step 3.   Double-click on the **Control Panel** folder icon.

Step 4.   Use the scroll bars to locate the **System** icon.

Step 5.   Double-click on the **System** icon.

Step 6.   Click once on the **Device Manager** tab.

Step 7.   In the displayed list, click once on the **plus** (+) symbol beside the Ports option.

Step 8.   Double-click on the **Communications Port** subitem under Ports.

Step 9.   Click once on the **Port Settings** tab.

Question 1:   What is the bits per second rate for COM1:?

Question 2:   What is the number of data bits for COM1:?

Question 3:   What is the flow control method used?

Question 4:   What is the current parity setting?

Step 10.   Click once on the **down arrow** in the Parity section.

Question 5:   What parity options are available?

Step 11.   Verify that the parity setting is set to the original setting. Refer to the answer given for Question 4.

Step 12.   Click on the **Resources** tab.

Question 6:   What I/O address does COM1: have?

Question 7:   What IRQ does COM1: have?

Question 8:   Do the I/O address and IRQ assignments adhere to the standard for configuring serial devices?

Question 9:   To what setting is the Settings based on: selection set?

Step 13.   Click once in the **Use automatic settings** checkbox to deselect it.

Step 14.   To change the setting, click on the **down arrow** in the **Setting based on:** section. A list of configurations appears.

Step 15.   Click once on a **configuration selection** different than the one specified in Question 9.

Question 10:   What happened to the I/O range and the IRQ settings? What are they set to now?

Question 11:   Does the chosen setting adhere to the standard for configuring serial devices? Refer to the chapter's Serial Table #2.

Step 16.   Set the **Setting based on:** selection back to the original configuration. Look back to the answer given for Question 9.

Step 17.   Click on the **Cancel** button.

Step 18.   Click on the **Cancel** button from within the System Properties window.

Step 19.   Close all open windows on the desktop.

_____ *Instructor's Initials*

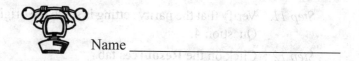

Name _____

EXTERNAL SERIAL DEVICE INSTALLATION (DOS/WINDOWS 3.X)

Objective: To connect an external serial device to a computer that uses DOS and/or Windows 3.x and configure the serial port for proper operation

Parts: Computer with DOS or Windows installed and an available serial port
Serial device
Appropriate serial cable
Tools

CAUTION: Observe proper grounding procedures when installing an external serial device.

Step 1.   Power on the computer.

Step 2.   Examine the back of the computer for serial ports.

Question 1:   How many total serial ports does the computer have?

Question 2:   Is there a serial port available (not being used by another serial device)? If not, install a serial adapter before continuing with this exercise.

Step 3.   Using the computer's Setup program, MSD (Microsoft Diagnostics), DEBUG, or any other similar program, determine the COM ports, IRQs, and I/O address assignment for the computer's serial ports and any internal serial device, such as a modem. Also, list any serial devices connected to the serial ports or any internal serial devices. Use Serial Exercise Table #3 to document the results. Leave any spaces blank if no device is found or if the COM port is not available.

EXERCISE – TABLE #3

COM Port	IRQ	I/O Address	Device Connected
COM1			
COM2			
COM3			
COM4			
COM__			
COM__			

Step 4. Use software such as MSD or a visual inspection around the port to determine the type of UART installed.

Question 3: What UART is installed?

Question 4: Is the UART fast enough for the device being installed? If not, contact the instructor.

Step 5. Locate the serial port to which the external serial device will attach.

Question 5: Based on the findings in Step 3, what interrupt, I/O address, and COM port assignments will be used by the external serial device being installed?

Step 6. Power off the computer.

Step 7. Attach the serial cable to the serial device.

Step 8. Attach the serial cable to the computer's serial port.

Step 9. Power on the external serial device.

Step 10. Power on the computer.

Step 11. Load any software drivers necessary for the external device. Refer to the serial device manual.

Step 12. If the external device is a modem, use Windows 3.x's Terminal program to test the modem. See the chapter exercise on using Windows Terminal program if unfamiliar with it.

Step 13. Install any software applications that come with the external serial device. If the application requires configuration parameters, refer to Question 5 for that information.

Question 6: Does the external serial device work? If not, refer to the chapter's troubleshooting sections and repair the problem.

Question 7: Do all other serial devices in the computer still operate? Verify this to be sure. If not, refer to the chapter's troubleshooting sections and repair the problem.

_____ ***Instructor's Initials***

Name _____

EXTERNAL SERIAL DEVICE INSTALLATION EXERCISE (WINDOWS 9X)

Objective: To connect an external serial device to a computer that uses Windows 95/98 and configure the serial port for proper operation

Parts: Computer with Windows 95/98 installed and an available serial port
Serial device
Appropriate serial cable
Tools

CAUTION: Observe proper grounding procedures when installing an external serial device.

Step 1.   Power on the computer and verify that the operating system loads.

Step 2.   Examine the back of the computer for serial ports.

Question 1:   How many total serial ports does the computer have?

Question 2:   Is there a serial port available (not being used by another serial device)? If not, install a serial adapter before continuing with this exercise.

Step 3.   Double-click on the **My Computer** icon.

Step 4.   Double-click on the **Control Panel** folder icon.

Step 5.   Use the scroll bars to locate the **System** icon.

Step 6.   Double-click on the **System** icon.

Step 7.   Click once on the **Device Manager** tab.

Step 8.   In the displayed list, click once on the **plus** (+) symbol beside the **Ports** option.

Step 9.   Double-click on the **Communications Port** subitem under Ports.

Step 10.   Click once on the **Port Settings** tab.

Step 11.   Click on the **Resources** tab.

Step 12.   Using the information displayed on the screen, complete Serial Exercise Table #4. Leave any applicable spaces blank if no device is found or if the COM port is not available.

COM Port	IRQ	I/O Address	Device Connected
COM1			
COM2			
COM3			
COM4			
COM__			
COM__			

EXERCISE – TABLE #4

Step 13. Click on the **Cancel** button.

Step 14. Click on the **Cancel** button from within the System Properties window.

Step 15. Close all open windows on the desktop.

Step 16. Use software or a visual inspection of the port (the one to which the serial device will attach) to determine the type of UART installed.

Question 3: What UART is installed in the computer?

Question 4: Is the UART fast enough for the device being installed? If not, contact the instructor.

Step 17. Locate the serial port to which the external serial device will attach.

Question 5: Based on the findings in Step 12, what interrupt, I/O address, and COM port assignments will be used by the external serial device being installed?

Step 18. Power off the computer.

Step 19. Attach the serial cable to the serial device.

Step 20.   Attach the serial cable to the computer's serial port.

Step 21.   Power on the external serial device.

Step 22.   Power on the computer.

Step 23.   Load any software drivers necessary for the external device. Refer to the serial device manual.

Step 24.   If the external device is a modem, use Windows HyperTerminal program to test the modem. (See the chapter exercise on using the Windows HyperTerminal program if you are unfamiliar with it.)

Step 25.   Install any software applications included with the external serial device. If the application requires configuration parameters, refer to Question 5 for that information.

Question 6:   Does the external serial device work? If not, refer to the chapter's troubleshooting sections and repair the problem.

Question 7:   Do all other serial devices in the computer still operate? Verify this to be sure. If not, refer to the chapter's troubleshooting sections and repair the problem.

_____ *Instructor's Initials*

Name _____

INSTALLING A SERIAL MOUSE USING WINDOWS NT WORKSTATION

Objective: To install a serial mouse on a Windows NT Workstation computer

Parts: Computer with Windows NT Workstation installed
Serial mouse
Available serial (COM) port

Windows NT Workstation has support for both PS2 style mice and serial mice. This exercise demonstrates how to install a serial mouse.

Step 1.   With the Windows NT Workstation computer turned off, connect a serial mouse to an appropriate COM port.

Question 1:   How many pins does a standard serial mouse connector have?

Step 2.   Power on the computer and verify that Windows NT Workstation loads.

Step 3.   Logon to Windows NT Workstation using the userid and password provided by the instructor or lab assistant.

Step 4.   After login, Windows NT Workstation detects the new serial mouse and installs a driver for it.

Question 2:   Which COM port is your serial mouse installed on?

_____ *Instructor's Initials*

Name _____

INSTALLING A SERIAL MOUSE USING WINDOWS 2000 PROFESSIONAL

Objective: To install a serial mouse on a Windows 2000 Professional computer.

Parts: Computer with Windows 2000 Professional installed
Serial mouse and an available serial (COM) port

Windows 2000 Professional will normally be installed on computers that support PS2 style mice. It may become necessary to install a serial mouse on a Windows 2000 Professional computer in the event the PS2 mouse port or mouse becomes disabled.

Step 1.   With the Windows 2000 Professional computer turned off, connect a serial mouse to an appropriate COM port.

Question 1:   How many pins does a standard serial mouse connector have?

Step 2.   Turn the computer on and verify that Windows 2000 Professional loads.

Step 3.   Logon to Windows 2000 Professional using the userid and password provided by the instructor or lab assistant.

Step 4.   After login, Windows 2000 Professional detects the new serial mouse and installs a driver for it.

Question 2:   Which COM port is your serial mouse installed on?

_____ *Instructor's Initials*

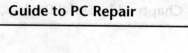

Name _____

INSTALLING AN INTERNAL MODEM USING WINDOWS NT WORKSTATION

Objective: To install and configure an internal modem in Windows NT Workstation

Parts: Computer with Windows NT Workstation installed
Internal modem with drivers for NT Workstation

Windows NT Workstation does not support plug and play. Because of this, you may have to do more modem configuration to prevent it from conflicting with other system resources.

Step 1.   Manually configure the modem with a COM port and IRQ that does not conflict with any of your computer's existing system settings.

Question 1:   What IRQ and COM port settings did you use?

Step 2.   Remove the computer case, and using proper ESD precautions, install the internal modem in an appropriate slot. Secure the modem with a retaining screw.

Step 3.   Plug an analog phone line into the proper modem port.

Step 4.   Turn on the computer and verify that Windows NT Workstation loads.

Step 5.   Logon to NT Workstation using the userid and password provided by the instructor or lab assistant.

Step 6.   From the Start menu, point to the **Settings** option, click on the **Control Panel** option, and then double-click on the **Modems** control panel icon. Click **Next** to allow Windows NT to attempt to detect the modem.

Question 2:   How many COM ports did Windows NT query?

Step 7.   When Windows NT detects the modem, check what type of modem was detected. If the detected type is not right, click **Change** and select the proper modem type from the list or click **Have Disk** and enter a path to the driver location.

Step 8.   When the proper modem is listed, click on the **Next** button.

Question 3:   What modem type did you select to install?

    Step 9.   After Windows NT installs the modem driver, click the **Finish** button to complete the installation.

_____ *Instructor's Initials*

Name _____

INSTALLING AN INTERNAL MODEM USING WINDOWS 2000 PROFESSIONAL

Objective: To install and configure an internal modem in a Windows 2000 Professional computer

Parts: Computer with Windows 2000 Professional installed
Internal modem

Windows 2000 Professional supports both plug and play and non-plug and play modems.

To install a plug and play modem, follow these steps:

Step 1. Remove the computer case and using proper ESD precautions, install the internal modem in an appropriate slot. Secure the internal modem with a retaining screw.

Question 1: Into what type of bus slot did you install the internal modem?

Step 2. Plug a phone cable into the proper port on the modem and ensure the other end is attached to a phone jack that works.

Step 3. Power on the computer and verify that Windows 2000 Professional loads.

Step 4. Logon to 2000 Professional using the userid and password provided by the instructor or lab assistant.

Step 5. After login, Windows 2000 Professional automatically detects the new internal modem and installs and configures a driver for it.

To install a non-plug and play modem, follow these steps:

Step 1. Manually configure the modem with a COM port and IRQ that does not conflict with any of the computer's existing system settings.

Step 2. Remove the computer case and using proper ESD precautions, install the internal modem in an appropriate slot. Secure the internal modem with a retaining screw.

Step 3. Power on the computer and verify that Windows 2000 Professional loads.

Step 4. Logon to 2000 Professional using the userid and password provided by the instructor or lab assistant.

Step 5. From the Start menu, choose **Settings**, click on the **Control Panel** option, and then double-click on the **Add/Remove Hardware** icon. Click on the **Next** button.

Step 6. Select **Add/Troubleshoot a device** and click on the **Next** button. Windows searches for plug and play devices. When Windows finds no new plug and play devices, the Choose a Hardware device window opens.

Step 7. Select **Add a New Device** and click on the **Next** button.

Step 8. Select **No, I want to select the hardware from a list**, and click on the **Next** button.

Step 9. From the Hardware Type window, scroll down and select **Ports [COM and LPT]**, and then click on the **Next** button.

Step 10. Choose **(Standard Port Types)**, select **Communications Port**, and then click on the **Next** button.

Step 11. From the Add New Wizard Properties window, select the resource settings that match the new modem and click **OK**.

Question 2: Which IRQ and I/O address settings did you assign your modem?

Step 12. Restart the computer for the new port settings to take effect.

Step 13. When the computer restarts, from the Start menu choose **Settings, Control Panel**, and then double-click **Phone and Modem Options**.

Step 14. Select the **Modems** tab, and then click **Add**.

Step 15. From the Install new modem window click **Next**. Windows queries installed COM ports attempting to detect a modem to install.

Question 3: How many COM ports did windows query?

Step 16. When the new modem is detected click **Next**. Windows will install the driver for the new modem. Click **Finish** to complete the modem installation.

_____ *Instructor's Initials*

Name _____

INSTALLING AN EXTERNAL MODEM ON WINDOWS NT WORKSTATION

Objective: To understand how to install an external modem on Windows NT Workstation

Parts: Windows NT Workstation
External modem with power cable
Serial cable

You can install both internal and external modems on a Windows NT Workstation. In this exercise, you will install an external modem.

Step 1.   Using an appropriate RS-232 serial cable (9 or 25-pin), connect the external modem to a COM port on the Windows NT Workstation computer, and connect the modem's power supply. Turn on the external modem.

Step 2.   Power on the computer and verify that NT Workstation loads.

Step 3.   Logon to Windows NT Workstation using the userid and password provided by the instructor or lab assistant.

Step 4.   From the Start menu, choose **Settings**, and then select **Control Panel**. The Control Panel opens.

Question 1:   What other method can be used to open the Control Panel?

Step 5.   Double-click the **Modems** control panel icon and click the **Next** button. Windows queries the available COM ports to detect the modem.

Step 6.   When Windows detects the new modem, the **Install New Modem** window opens.

Step 7.   If the modem type listed is incorrect, click **Change**. Select the proper modem type from the list, or if your modem is not listed, click **Have Disk** and enter a path to the modem driver files.

Step 8.   When the proper modem type is selected, click **OK**.

Step 9.   Click **Next** and the Location Information window opens.

Step 10.   From the Location Information window, enter your **Area Code**, **Outside line access numbers** (if any), and your **dialing type** (tone or pulse). Click **Next**.

Step 11.   Click **Finish** to complete your modem installation. The Modems Properties window opens.

Step 12. From the Modems Properties window, highlight the newly installed modem and select **Properties**. From the General tab, you can adjust the modem's speaker volume and the maximum Port Speed. From the Connection tab, you can configure your connection preferences, call preferences, and advanced connection preferences.

Question 2: Which COM port is your modem installed on? (Hint: Check the Modems Properties-General page)

Step 13. Close the Modems Properties window.

_____ *Instructor's Initials*

Name _____

INSTALLING AN EXTERNAL MODEM ON WINDOWS 2000 PROFESSIONAL

Objective: To understand how to install an external modem on a Windows 2000 Professional computer.

Parts: Windows 2000 Professional computer
External modem and power cable
9 or 25-pin serial modem cable

You can install both internal and external modems on a Windows 2000 Professional computer. In this exercise, you will install an external modem.

Step 1.   Using the appropriate RS-232 serial cable (9 or 25-pin), connect the external modem to a COM (serial) port on the Windows 2000 Professional computer, and connect the modem's power supply. Turn on the external modem.

Step 2.   Power on the computer and verify that Windows 2000 Professional loads.

Step 3.   Logon to Windows 2000 Professional using the userid and password provided by the instructor or lab assistant.

Step 4.   From the desktop, right-click on the **My Computer** icon, select **Properties**, and then choose the **Hardware** option. The **System Properties/Hardware** window opens.

Step 5.   Select **Device Manager**, and then expand the **Ports** icon. The configured COM and LPT ports display.

Question 1:   How many COM ports are listed?

Question 2:   Which COM port is your modem attached to?

Step 6.   Close Device Manager and select the **Hardware Wizard** button. The Add/Remove Hardware Wizard starts. Click on the **Next** button.

Question 3:   What other method can be used to start the Add/Remove Hardware wizard?

Step 7. Select **Add/Troubleshoot a device**, and click on the **Next** button. Windows searches for new hardware.

Step 8. When Windows finds the new modem, the Found New Hardware Wizard executes. Click on the **Next** button.

Step 9. Select **Search for a suitable driver for my device**, and click on the **Next** button.

Step 10. Insert the modem manufacturer's driver disk into the appropriate drive (usually the floppy drive or CD-ROM), select the drive to search, and click on the **Next** button.

Step 11. Sometimes when the driver is found, multiple modems are listed. Select the appropriate driver for the modem attached and click on the **Finish** button. Windows installs the modem driver.

_____ *Instructor's Initials*

Step 12. Select **Finish** to close the Found New Hardware wizard and click **Next** at the New Hardware Detection window.

Step 13. Select **Finish** to complete the modem installation and then click on the **OK** button to close the System Properties window.

_____ *Instructor's Initials*

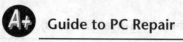
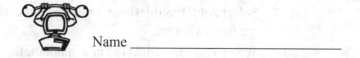

Name _____

USING HYPERTERMINAL ON WINDOWS 9X

Objective: To use the Windows 95/98/NT HyperTerminal program to test a modem

Parts: A computer with a modem, Windows 95/98/NT loaded, and the HyperTerminal program loaded

Question 1: Before beginning this exercise, gather information about the modem's serial port. Use Serial Exercise Table #5 to record the information.

EXERCISE – TABLE #5		
Modem (internal or external)?		
IRQ		
I/O address		
COM Port		
Maximum bps (speed)		

Step 1. Power on the computer and verify the operating system loads.

Step 2. Click on the **Start** button in the desktop's bottom left corner.

Step 3. Select **Programs** from the Start menu.

Step 4. Select **Accessories** from the menu.

Step 5. Click once on **HyperTerminal** from the next menu. The HyperTerminal window appears.

Step 6. Double-click on the **Hypertm.exe** icon. The Connection Description window appears.

Step 7. In the Connection Description window, type **COMPUSERVE TEST** in the Name: field.

Step 8. Using the slide bar, click once on the icon of your choice.

Step 9. Click on the **OK** button. The phone number window appears. The cursor blinks in the phone number field.

Step 10. Type **346-3247** in the Phone number: field.

Step 11. Verify the **Connect using** field. Verify the correct modem is selected or the modem's correct COM port setting is selected. Click on the **down arrow** to change if necessary.

Step 12.   Click on the **OK** button.

Step 13.   Click on the **Dialing Properties** button.

Question 2:   Check with the instructor to see if the phone line requires a special number to access an outside line. If so, what is that number?

Step 14.   If a special number is needed to connect to an outside telephone line (reference Question 2), click once in the **To access an outside line, first dial:** text box. Type in the special number needed to access an outside phone line.

Step 15.   If call waiting is available on the phone line, verify that the **This location has call waiting** checkbox is checked. Then, click on the **down arrow** to select the numbers to disable it. If you are unsure of the numbers to disable call waiting, contact the instructor.

Step 16.   Click on the **OK** button.

Step 17.   In the Connect window, click on the **Modify** button.

Step 18.   In the Area Code: text field, click once after the last number shown.

Step 19.   Press the **backspace** key **three** times until the area code numbers disappear.

Step 20.   Type **800** in the Area Code: field.

Step 21.   Click on the **Configure** button.

Step 22.   Verify the COM port name is correct, the speaker volume is turned up, and the maximum modem speed settings are correct. Refer to Serial Exercise Table #6 at the beginning of this exercise for the correct COM port name. Modify the settings as necessary.

Step 23.   Click on the **Connection** tab.

Step 24.   Verify that the **Data bits** setting is **8**. Verify that the **Parity** setting is **None**. Verify that the **Stop bits** setting is **1**.

Question 3:   Were all settings for Step 24 set correctly? If not, what settings had to be changed?

Step 25.   Click on the **Advanced** button.

Step 26.   Verify the **Use error control** checkbox is checked.

Question 4:   Was the Use error control checkbox checked?

Step 27.   Verify the **Use flow control** checkbox is checked.

Question 5:   Was the Use flow control checkbox checked?

Step 28.   Verify the **Hardware (RTS/CTS)** radio button is selected.

Step 29.   Click on the **OK** button.

Step 30.   Click the **OK** button in the Properties window.

Step 31.   Click the **OK** button in the CompuServe Test Properties window. The Connect window is on the desktop.

Step 32.   Verify the telephone number shown is 1 800 346-3247. If the phone number is incorrect, redo Steps 17 through 31.

Step 33.   Click **Dial** in the Connect window. The dial tone sounds as the modem dialing outputs screeching noises to the speaker. After that, the modem connects to the dialed service, the Connect window disappears, and a blinking cursor is on the Terminal screen. If this works, the modem is working fine. If other software applications do not access the modem properly, troubleshoot the software application's specific settings. If the modem does not connect to the other modem, recheck the modems IRQ, I/O address, COM port, speed setting, parity setting, stop bits setting, data bits setting, etc.

Question 6:   Does the modem work? If not, troubleshoot the modem. Refer to the chapter troubleshooting sections for more assistance.

_____ ***Instructor's Initials***

Step 34.   Press **Enter** after the modem connects to CompuServe. The Host Name: prompt appears.

Step 35.   At the Host Name: prompt, type **PHONES** and press **Enter**.

Step 36.   After reading the screen, press **Enter**.

Step 37.   Press **1** and **Enter** to find U.S. access numbers.

Step 38.   After reading the screen, press **Enter**.

Step 39.   Select the correct number for the speed of the modem being used and press **Enter**.

Step 40.   Enter the **school's phone number** or **your home phone number** as shown in the example on the screen. Then, press **Enter**. The local CompuServe phone numbers display on the screen.

Step 41.   Click on the Close box in the upper right corner of the window. A dialog box appears stating that you connected.

Step 42.   Click on the **Yes** button to close the session.

Step 43.   At the Do you want to save session CompuServe Test dialog box, click on the **No** button.

Step 44.   Close all windows on the desktop.

Name _____

USING HYPERTERMINAL ON WINDOWS NT WORKSTATION

Objective: To understand how to use the HyperTerminal application on NT Workstation

Parts: Windows NT Workstation with modem installed and configured

The HyperTerminal application allows a user to establish a connection with remote servers through a modem. In this exercise, you will configure a HyperTerminal connection

Step 1.   Power on the computer and verify that Windows NT Workstation loads.

Step 2.   Logon to Windows NT Workstation using the userid and password provided by the instructor or lab assistant.

Step 3.   From the Start menu, choose **Programs, Accessories,** and then select **HyperTerminal**. The Hyper Terminal utility starts and the Connection Description window opens.

Question 1:   Can you start the HyperTerminal utility if you do NOT have a modem installed and configured?

Step 4.   From the Connection Description window, enter a name for the connection, choose an icon for the connection, and click **OK**. The Connect To window opens.

Step 5.   From the Connect To window, select the **Country/Region** to dial, enter the **Area Code and Phone Number** to dial, choose the modem to use for the connection, and click **OK**. Contact the instructor or lab assistant for this information if necessary. The Connect window opens.

Step 6.   From the Connect window, insure the dial-up information is correct and click **Dial**. HyperTerminal places the call.

Step 7.   If prompted, enter any required information such as username and password to establish the connection.

Question 2:   Will you have to go through this entire connection process every time you make a HyperTerminal connection?

Step 8.   When you end the HyperTerminal session, you will be prompted to save the connection information for future use. Choose **Yes** to save the connection information. The connection appears in the Start menu, Programs, Accessories, HyperTerminal folder.

_____ *Instructor's Initials*

Name _____

USING HYPERTERMINAL ON WINDOWS 2000 PROFESSIONAL

Objective: To understand how to use the HyperTerminal application on a Windows 2000 Professional computer

Parts: Windows 2000 Professional computer with modem installed and configured

The HyperTerminal application allows a user of a Windows 2000 Professional computer to establish a connection with remote servers through a modem. In this exercise, you will configure a HyperTerminal connection.

Step 1.   Power on the computer and verify that Windows 2000 Professional loads.

Step 2.   Logon to Windows 2000 Professional using the userid and password provided by the instructor or lab assistant.

Step 3.   From the Start menu, point to **Programs**, **Accessories**, **Communications**, and then click on the **HyperTerminal option**. The HyperTerminal utility opens.

Question 1:   Can you start the HyperTerminal utility if you do NOT have a modem installed and configured?

Step 4.   If this is the first time HyperTerminal has run, enter the appropriate dialing information in the Location Information window and click on the **OK** button. Select the location you are dialing from and click **OK**. The Connection Description window opens.

Step 5.   From the Connection Description window, enter a name for the connection, select an icon for the connection, and click **OK**. The Connect To window opens.

Step 6.   From the Connect To window, select the **Country/Region** you are dialing, enter the **Area Code and Phone Number** to dial, choose the correct installed modem to use for the connection, and click **OK**. Contact the instructor or lab assistant for this information if necessary. The Connect window opens.

Step 7.   From the Connect window, ensure the dial-up information is correct and click **Dial**. HyperTerminal places the dial-up call.

Step 8.   If prompted, enter any required information such as username and password to establish the connection.

Question 2:   Will you have to go through this entire connection process every time you make a HyperTerminal connection?

Step 9.   When the HyperTerminal session has ended, you will be prompted to save the connection information for future use. Choose **Yes** to save the connection information. The connection appears in the Start menu, Programs, Accessories, Communications, HyperTerminal folder.

_____*Instructor's Initials*

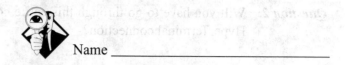

Name _____

INTERNET DISCOVERY

Objective: To obtain specific information regarding a computer or its associated parts on the Internet

Parts: Access to the Internet

Question 1:   You just updated an NT Workstation computer to Windows 2000. Now two modems display in the configuration. What is the problem and at what URL did you find information about this problem?

Question 2:   Where are the dip switches located on the US Robotics Courier Internal V.Everthing modem.

Question 3:   Find one vendor of VDSL and write their URL in the space below.

Question 4:   What is the difference between 3Com's VSP and VSP Plus?

Question 5:   You have a customer who has a Boca Research M144AI 14.4 Internal Express Fax/Modem. What COM ports is it capable of using? Which IRQs? What is the default I/O address? Write the answers and the web address in the space below.

Question 6:   You are working on a Maxtech XPV56P Net Pacer V.90 internal 56K voice modem. You go to the Internet to find out what you check first if the modem connects, but no data appears on the screen. Write the answer and the web address in the space below.

Question 7: You are working on a Windows 95 computer that has a Digicom Systems ModemBlaster Flash 56K modem installed. The modem worked when using one of the older applications, but has a problem when executed under a new application. Use the Internet to see the first thing you should do. Write the answer and the web address in the space below.

Question 8: Locate a cable modem web site that explains how to increase speed on a cable modem. Write the URL in the space below as well as the recommendation.

NOTES

12

Chapter 12:
Video

OBJECTIVES

After completing this chapter you will
- Describe the components of the video subsystem.
- Differentiate among monitor types.
- Understand basic monitor theory and terminology.
- Recommend a resolution for a particular monitor size.
- Describe different types of video memory.
- Be able to install a video adapter and associated software.
- Perform basic video troubleshooting techniques.

KEY TERMS

ACPI	monochrome monitor
active matrix	multi-scan monitor
AGP	passive matrix
analog monitor	picture cell
aperture grille	pixel
APM	raster
color monitor	RDRAM
CRT	refresh rate
degausser	resolution
digital monitor	screen saver
dot pitch	SGRAM
dot triad	shadow mask
DPMS	single-ported memory
dual-ported memory	SVGA
flat panel	UVGA
flyback transformer	vertical scan rate
grayscale monitor	VGA
horizontal scanning frequency	video processor
interlacing	VIS
LCD	VRAM
MDRAM	WRAM

VIDEO OVERVIEW

Video quality is very important to computer users. The monitor displays the data and is one of the most expensive components. Users usually derive the most gratification from their monitor, though sound quality is now becoming as important. Technicians must look at video as a subsystem that consists of the monitor, the electronic circuits that send the monitor instructions, and a cable that connects them. The electronic video circuits are on a separate video adapter or built into the motherboard. Video Figure #1 illustrates a computer's video subsystem.

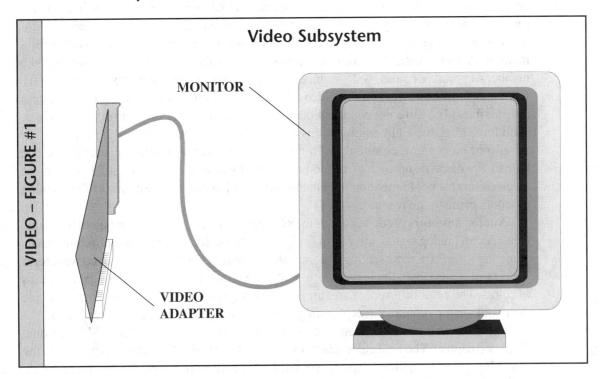

Video Subsystem

VIDEO – FIGURE #1

MONITOR

VIDEO ADAPTER

TYPES OF MONITORS

Monitors can be classified several ways—color or non-color, analog or digital signals used to produce colors, and the type of video adapter used. Understanding all three classifications gives you a good perspective about monitors.

The first computer monitors manufactured were monochrome. **Monochrome monitors** project a single color (white, amber, or green) on a black background. Computer systems that run an air conditioning system, a telephone exchange, or print servers (computers that handle a printer in a network environment) all use a monochrome monitor because the output is text only—no graphics. **Color monitors** display many colors for text and graphics.

Grayscale monitors display various shades of black and white. Grayscale monitors are used by artists who do not work in colors as well as by design engineers who work in the CAD (computer-aided design) environment.

The first monochrome monitors and the first two types of color monitors were **digital monitors** that accepted digital signals from the video adapter. The drawback to these digital monitors was that they could not display many colors.

Digital electronics use voltage levels to represent the binary data where the 1s and 0s turn something on or off. There are no varying levels. Color monitors project different colors using red, green, and blue guns (sometimes called electron guns) inside the monitor (one gun per color). A digital 1 or 0 goes from the video adapter to turn the specific color gun on or off. The number of bits used determines the number of colors visible on a monitor. A mathematical relationship exists between the number of bits used and the number of possible colors — 2^x=number of colors (where x is the number of color bits). For example, if three pins on the video adapter control color, then eight different colors are possible. (The different combinations of the 1s and 0s determine the different colors. With three pins, the eight combinations are 000, 001, 010, 011, 100, 101, 110, and 111. So, if four bits control colors, then 16 different colors are available because 2^4=16. The human eye discerns up to 16.7 million colors that would require at least 24 pins on the video connector not to mention the other pins needed to control the monitor. Then analog monitors came to the rescue.

Analog monitors produce numerous colors more easily than the older digital monitors. Consider an analog signal waveform for the color red. Imagine different places along the waveform representing different shades of red. Now combine the red waveform with a similar green and blue waveform and you can see how monitors produce millions of colors. The color differences are limitless! Analog monitors have digital circuits inside them, but analog monitors accept analog signals, not digital signals, to display colors.

The first type of video adapter used with computers was the MDA (Monochrome Display Adapter). The first color adapter was the CGA (Color Graphics Adapter) then the EGA (Enhanced Graphics Adapter) arrived. All the earlier monitors, monochrome, CGA, or EGA, were digital monitors and connected to a 9-pin female D-shell connector. IBM then produced the **VGA (Video Graphics Array)** monitors. They were the first analog monitors used in mass quantities and IBM established the VGA standard. Other types of monitors advertised include **SVGA (Super VGA)** and **UVGA (Ultra VGA)**. VESA (Video Electronics Standards Association) came up with a standard for SVGA and is called VBE (VESA BIOS extension) and it covers resolutions up to 1280x1024 with 16 million colors. UVGA is not a video standard, but usually refers to the 1024x768 resolution. The VGA, SVGA, and UVGA monitors all connect to a 15-pin, three-row, D-shell connector. Look back to Chapter 1's Introduction Figure #9, for a refresher on the video connectors.

One of the most important things to remember about video is the video adapter must match the type of monitor.

MONITOR TERMINOLOGY AND THEORY

Monitors are manufactured in different sizes. The most common sizes are 15-inch, 17-inch, and 21-inch. The video industry has traditionally defined the monitor size as the diagonal length of the picture tube, but there is no industry standard that defines a specific monitor size measurement. The monitor case encloses the **CRT (Cathode Ray Tube),** the main part of a monitor, and covers part of it. The size of the CRT, also called the picture tube, may not be what the computer user sees. Many manufacturers now list the viewable area or the **VIS (Viewable Image Size)** of the CRT to clarify the monitor size. Because Windows 9x, NT, and 2000 allow so many windows to be open on the screen, a 17-inch or larger monitor is recommended to allow more working room. Windows 98 and 2000 support multiple monitors connected to the same computer and the desktop image is split across the monitors.

Monitors have three electron guns, one each for the colors red, green, and blue, while other monitors have only one electron gun that directs the three color beams. The guns shoot a beam of electrons aimed at a phosphorous dot on the back of the monitor tube. When the electron beam hits the phosphor, the dot glows and appears on the front of the screen. All figures, icons, and letters on the screen are nothing more than closely spaced dots glowing at different intensities.

A monitor has three phosphorous dots called a **dot triad** (or dot trio) grouped together at each location on the screen. The dot triad consists of a dot for red, green, and blue. When the beam of electrons hit a phosphor dot, the dot begins to glow. The beam intensity varies to create different color intensities. Because the electron beam guns hit the phosphorous dots from different angles, a **shadow mask,** which is a metal plate with holes, keeps the beam directed at the proper dot. See Video Figure #2 for an illustration of how the three guns direct electron beams through the shadow mask to cause the phosphorous dots to glow.

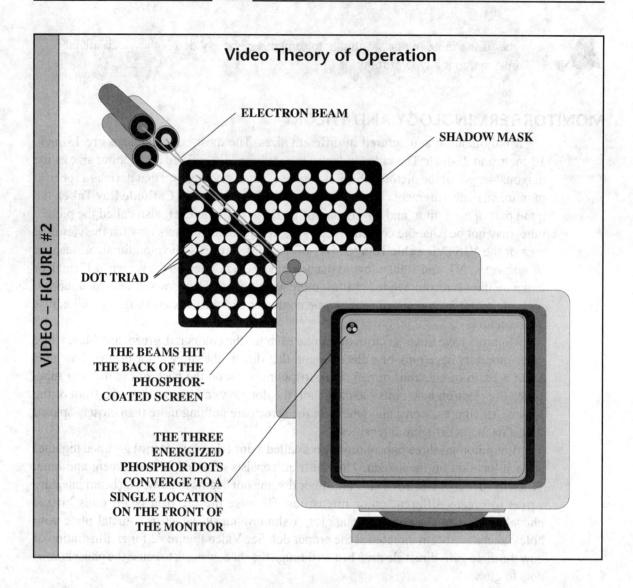

VIDEO – FIGURE #2

Video Theory of Operation

ELECTRON BEAM

SHADOW MASK

DOT TRIAD

THE BEAMS HIT THE BACK OF THE PHOSPHOR-COATED SCREEN

THE THREE ENERGIZED PHOSPHOR DOTS CONVERGE TO A SINGLE LOCATION ON THE FRONT OF THE MONITOR

Keep in mind that Video Figure #2 shows the shadow mask holes quite large, but in reality, they are the size of pin holes.

A variation of the shadow mask is a Phillips Magnavox creation, the Invar shadow mask. This reduces the heat problem of the traditional shadow mask. Another shadow mask used in NEC's Chromaclear monitors has elliptical slots instead of holes.

The phosphorous dot triad converges to make one dot on the screen called a **pixel**, short for picture element. Some view a pixel as one dot on the screen, but it takes the three different colored phosphorous dots to create the single image called a **picture cell**. Perhaps a better definition for a pixel is the smallest displayable unit on the screen.

The monitor's **dot pitch** is the distance between like-colored phosphorous dots on adjacent dot triads. Video Figure #3 illustrates dot pitch.

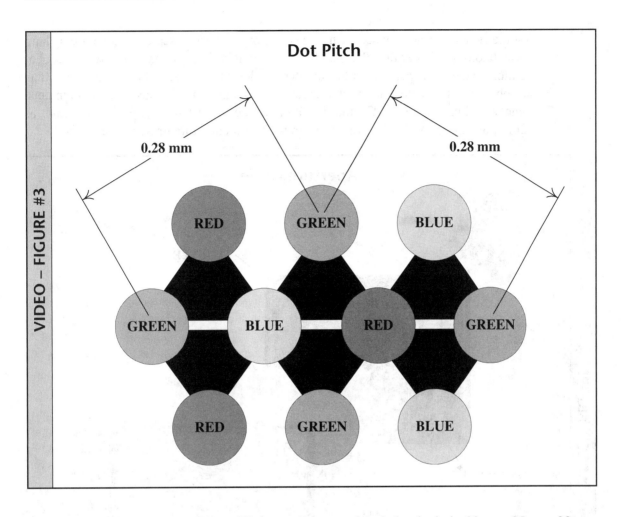

VIDEO – FIGURE #3

Dot Pitch

0.28 mm   0.28 mm

Dot pitch is measured in millimeters. Common dot pitches include .39mm, .35mm, .28mm, .26mm, .25mm, etc.

The lower the monitor's dot pitch, the smaller the distance between the dot triads. The lower the dot pitch number, the better the picture quality. For example, a monitor with a .28mm dot pitch is better than one with a .35mm dot pitch.

For any monitor that uses a shadow mask (including those with an Invar shadow mask), the dot pitch should be .28mm or smaller for a quality image. On any type of shadow mask, the closer the holes are to one another, the better the dot pitch.

An alternative to the shadow mask is an **aperture grille**, used in Sony Trinitron monitors that have very fine vertical wires instead of holes like the shadow mask. The vertical wires allow more electrons to reach the screen thereby producing deeper color intensities. The aperture grille wires are not as susceptible to heat and distortion as the shadow mask. However, to keep the fine vertical wires from moving or vibrating, horizontal wires are needed. These extra stabilizing wires can be seen on bright images (which is not acceptable in some fields of exact science such as medical or scientific research). Some users claim this technology is better than the shadow mask, but it is simply a matter of preference. For monitors that use an aperture grille, dot pitch is relevant in a horizontal direction only. The phosphor used to create a dot on the screen is coated in vertical strips rather than in dots. Some very high quality CRTs that use an aperture grille have dot pitches as small as .22mm, or smaller. Video Figure #4 illustrates how an aperture grille creates a pixel.

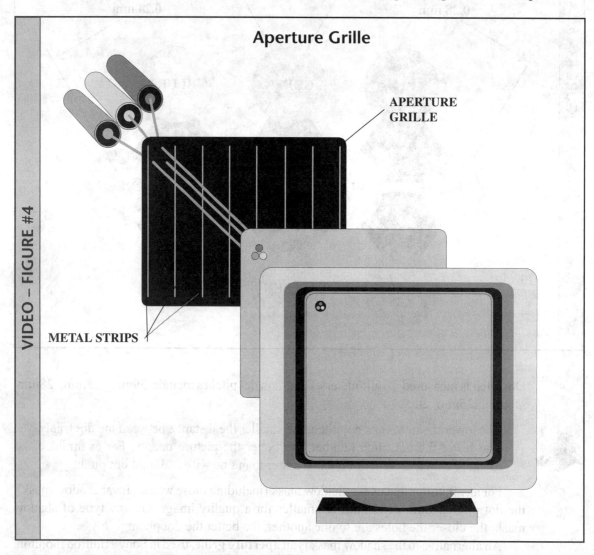

Aperture Grille

APERTURE GRILLE

METAL STRIPS

VIDEO – FIGURE #4

The minimum acceptable dot pitch for a monitor using an aperture grill is .25mm. However, manufacturers use different terminology to describe dot pitch when the monitor uses the aperture grille technology. Possible dot pitch descriptions include *grill pitch*, *horizontal mask pitch*, and *mask pitch*. Some Sony monitors use a variable aperture grille technology. On these monitors, two dot pitches are given, one for the center and one for the edges. Proper dot pitch is a user preference. The user must stare at the monitor all day long and needs a dot pitch suitable for his or her eyes.

Dot pitch is an important feature in choosing a monitor's **resolution,** which is the maximum number of pixels on the monitor. Two numbers separated by an *x* meaning *by* describe a monitor's resolution, such as 640x480. The first number, 640, is the number of pixels that fit horizontally across the screen. The second number, 480, describes the number of pixels that fit vertically on the screen. The possible monitor resolutions depend on the monitor and the video adapter.

Some describe SVGA as a monitor that displays an 800x600 resolution and a UVGA monitor as one that displays a 1024x768 resolution. Again, this is just what the industry accepts.

The higher the monitor's resolution, the smaller the pixel appears on the screen. Picking a higher resolution will make the icons in Windows appear smaller. Many users do not know or understand this concept and set their resolution too high relative to their monitor size.

Video Table #1 lists common monitor sizes with some recommended resolutions.

VIDEO – TABLE #1

Recommended Resolutions

Monitor Size	Resolution
14"	640x480
15"	640x480
17"	800x600 or 1024 x 768
19"	1024x768 or 1280x1024
20" or 21"	1024x768, 1280x1024, or 1600x1200

Another monitor feature that determines how sharp an image appears on the screen is its **refresh rate**. This is the maximum times a screen is scanned in one second, measured in Hz. The pixels on the screen do not stay excited very long and must be refreshed occasionally to stay lit. The electron beams start at the top left corner of the screen and cross to the right. Once the beam reaches the right side, it turns off momentarily as it returns to the left. Then, the electron beam refreshes the pixels in the row beneath the first horizontal row. The electron beam continuously sweeps left to right, scanning every row of pixels. The video card directs the electron beam and tells the beam which pixels need to be energized. The speed that the beam traverses the screen is the **horizontal scanning frequency** (also known as HRR or Horizontal Refresh Rate). This frequency is calculated by taking the inverse of the amount of time to go from the beginning of one line to the beginning of the next line. Horizontal scanning frequencies are measured in kilohertz (kHz) determined by the video adapter. Video adapters have horizontal scanning frequencies ranging from 35 to 90kHz. The **vertical scan rate** (also known as VRR or Vertical Refresh Rate) is the number of times the electron beam draws from the top left corner, to the bottom right corner, and back again to the top left. The horizontal scanning frequency is the rate for one line to be drawn whereas the vertical scan rate deals with drawing the entire screen. A slow vertical scan rate can cause a monitor to appear to flicker because the phosphors lose their intensity unless they are refreshed frequently.

A refresh rate greater than 60Hz is the bare minimum for a 14-inch or 15-inch monitor. A 72Hz, 75Hz, or 85Hz refresh rate is better especially if purchasing a 17-inch or 20-inch monitor. The VESA standard defines 85Hz as the minimum refresh rate.

With a 72Hz refresh rate, the entire video screen redraws 72 times per second. The refresh rate includes the time it takes the electron beam to return from the bottom right corner to the top left corner of the screen. The monitor's refresh rate is for a specific resolution. If the electron beam has to handle more pixels, it will naturally take longer. Therefore, before purchasing or recommending a monitor to customers, be sure you know the resolution they need. Then, look at the refresh rate for that particular resolution. For the video card to control the electron beam, the video adapter's specifications *must* match the monitor's refresh specifications. Video card capabilities are the main factor in determining what refresh rate the monitor uses, provided the monitor can perform it.

A monitor that can lock onto different vertical and horizontal scanning frequencies is a **multi-scan monitor** (also called multi-synch or multiple-frequency). Many users like these monitors due to their flexibility in connecting to a variety of adapters giving the user an upgrade path. Multi-scan monitors are common today.

To set the refresh rate for the monitor, use the Display control panel. Select the *Settings* tab and click on the *Advanced* button. The Properties window appears for the display adapter installed. Select the *Adapter* tab and click on the *Refresh rate down arrow*. A listing of possible settings is displayed. The Optimal setting is the default. If you select another setting, click on the *Apply* button and a warning message normally appears. Click on the *OK* button and the monitor changes. A dialog box asks if you want to keep this setting. Selecting *No* will reset back to the default. If the mouse does not work or the mouse pointer does not appear on this screen, just press *Enter* and the *No* selection will be accepted.

A monitor that uses **interlacing** scans only the odd numbered pixel rows. Then, the electron beam returns and scans the even numbered pixel rows. Interlacing causes a flickering on the screen but is cheaper than scanning every horizontal pixel row. Some manufacturers use non-interlacing techniques up to a specific resolution. At higher resolutions, the monitor reverts to interlaced mode. Check the monitor's refresh rate specifications for the resolution at which the monitor will be operated most often. Be sure the monitor uses the non-interlaced mode of operation for that resolution.

LCD (LIQUID CRYSTAL DISPLAY)

LCD (Liquid Crystal Display) is a video technology used with laptops and flat screen monitors. There are two basic types of LCD: passive matrix and active matrix. The difference between the two lies in how the screen image is created.

The cheaper of the two, **passive matrix** is made up of rows and columns of conductors. Each pixel is located at the intersection of a row and a column. (This is a similar concept to a cell in a spreadsheet.) Current on the grid determines whether a pixel is turned on or off. Each pixel has three cells in a color monitor, one for red, one for green, and the other for blue. Another name for passive matrix is STN (SuperTwist Nematic), which is a technology that twists light rays to improve the display's contrast. Passive matrix displays are not as bright as active matrix displays.

Active matrix displays have a transistor for each pixel. The number of transistors depends on the maximum resolution. An 800x600 resolution requires 480,000 transistors (800 times 600). This technology provides a brighter display (more luminance). Active matrix monitors take more power than passive matrix, but both of them require less power than CRT-based displays. Another name for active matrix monitors is TFT (Thin Film Transistor). TFT displays use three transistors per pixel (one for each color).

LCDs do not have multiple frequency settings like CRTs do, nor do they flicker (no beam tracing across and down the screen). The number of pixels on a screen is a fixed amount. Manufacturers use image scalers to change LCD resolution. LCDs have now come into the desktop and tower computer realm. The monitors that use this technology are called flat panel displays. With **flat panel** displays, the viewing area is the same as the LCD measurements (so no trick advertisements). Popular sizes include 14-inch, 15-inch, 17-inch, and 18-inch. LCDs take a lot less power, do not have tubes like CRTs, and take less desktop space.

Flat panel monitors are digital, but some can work off an analog adapter (like the one most likely installed in your computer now). These new digital monitors are more expensive, but offer better quality. The issue of colors with the old digital monitors is no longer relevant since the monitors use transistors to control colors. With the better flat panel monitors, you need an AGP adapter that has a DVI (Digital Video/Visual Interface). Video Figure #5 shows a video adapter with VGA, DVI, and TV out ports. The DVI port is a 24-pin connector.

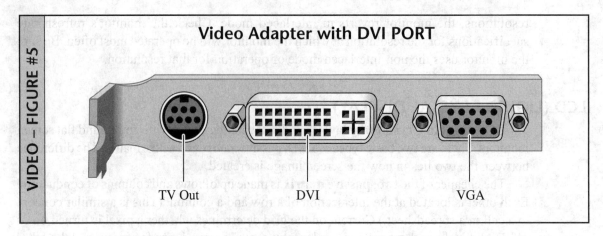

VIDEO – FIGURE #5

Video Adapter with DVI PORT

TV Out   DVI   VGA

Using an analog adapter is not recommended for connecting a flat panel display. The computer uses digital signals. The digital gets converted to analog at the video adapter; it is sent to the monitor as analog; and then the monitor has to convert it back to digital for the display output.

MONITOR PREVENTIVE MAINTENANCE

It is simple to perform preventive maintenance on a monitor. Static builds up on the face of the monitor and the screen attracts dust and dirt like any television. Anti-static cleaning wipes are available at computer and office supply stores. A monitor can also be cleaned with a soft dampened cloth and mild household detergent, glass cleaner, or isopropyl alcohol. Do not allow any liquid to get near the edge of the CRT. The liquid can seep inside the monitor case and cause damage. If using a CRT cleaning spray or glass cleaner, spray the cleaner on the cloth, not on the monitor. If the monitor has a non-glare screen or any type of special coating, see the manufacturer's instructions for cleaning it.

Unless specifically trained for monitor repair, never remove the monitor case. The monitor holds 20,000 or more volts (depending on the monitor size and components). Voltage can still be present after turning off the power. Most technicians who work on monitors have special training working on high voltage equipment. If you must remove the monitor case to work inside a monitor, a few safety rules include: (1) do not wear the anti-static grounding strap, (2) unplug the AC cord from the monitor or wall outlet, (3) do not work alone, (4) discharge the capacitors located inside the monitor, and (5) do not use regular test equipment to measure the monitor's high voltages.

MONITOR ENERGY EFFICIENCY

A monitor's life span is normally 20,000 to 60,000 hours. The heat generated inside a monitor can reduce the life span of the monitor's components. Some monitors called green monitors have energy conservation capabilities. These monitors have software that reduces the power leaving only enough to allow the monitor to be quickly reactivated to a useable state. The Environmental Protection Agency produced Energy Star guidelines to which many monitor manufacturers adhere. Many BIOS chips now support and have settings in the CMOS for energy efficient monitors.

VESA produced a **DPMS (Display Power Management Signaling)** standard that defines the signals used to tell the monitor to reduce power. If a video adapter is not DPMS-compatible, some adapters use a software program as an alternative. Microsoft and Intel developed the **APM (Advanced Power Management)** standard that allows the BIOS to control hardware power modes. With the Windows 98 operating system (and 2000), Microsoft presented **ACPI (Advanced Configuration and Power Interface)** that expanded the standard to also control power modes for CD-ROMs, network cards, printers, and other attached devices. The Power chapter has more information on ACPI.

In Windows 9x and 2000, this option is disabled by default. To enable the feature, use the Display control panel. Click on the *Screen Saver* tab and click on the *Settings* button to display the Power Management Properties window. Video Figure #6 shows this window.

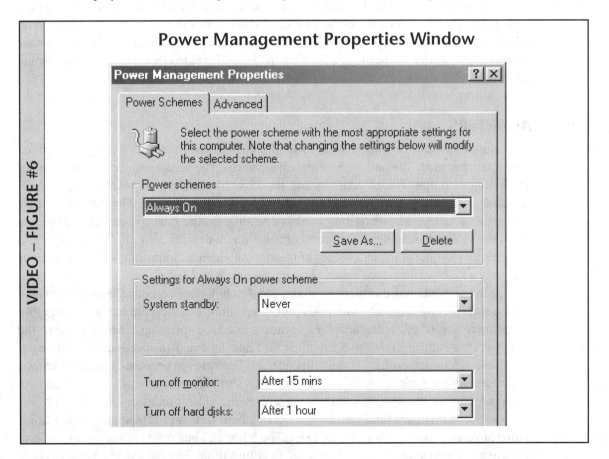

VIDEO – FIGURE #6

Power Management Properties Window

Only use the energy efficiency CMOS settings, energy efficiency software, or Windows' energy efficiency settings if the monitor supports it. A non-green monitor can be damaged if you enable these settings when the monitor does not support energy efficiency modes of operation. Check the monitor's documentation to determine if it supports energy efficiency modes.

SCREEN SAVERS

In the olden days when monitors did not have fast refresh rates, screen savers were very important. A **screen saver** changes the image on the monitor constantly to keep any particular image from *burning* into the screen. With old monitors, if an image stayed on the screen for an extended period of time, an imprint of the image was left on the screen permanently. Today's monitors have high enough refresh rates so screen savers are not necessary, but are now an entertainment art form. Screen savers can provide password protection that may be important to some users and are important for flat panel monitors.

In Windows, to enable the screen saver, use the Display control panel. Click on the *Screen Saver* tab and click on the *Screen Saver down arrow* to display an options list. The Blank Screen option takes the least amount of memory and does not use CPU time. Another resource saver is to remove the display's wallpaper option (also found through the Display control panel).

VIDEO ADAPTERS

Using millions of colors, motion, sound and video combined, the computer's video subsystem has made dramatic technological advances. The video adapter controls most of the monitor's output. Video adapters use the ISA, EISA, VL-bus, MCA, PCI, or AGP interface. The bus connects the video card to the microprocessor. The microprocessor accepts data in 16-, 32-, or 64-bit chunks depending on the microprocessor and the bus interface. (Refer to Chapter 2 for more information on the different microprocessors and bus interfaces.) One of the challenges of interfacing video is finding a good video adapter that uses a high-performance system architecture such as AGP.

On the motherboard, the microprocessor and the chipset are responsible for how quickly data travels to and from the video adapter. Such things as upgrading the chipset, the microprocessor, or the video adapter to a faster interface speed up video transfer to the monitor. However, special features on the video adapter can also speed up video transfer.

Some video adapters have their own processor. The **video processor** (sometimes known as a video coprocessor or video accelerator) assists in video communication between the video adapter and the system's microprocessor. Some video processors are 64 or 128-bit processors. Many users (and technicians) have a hard time understanding how a 128-bit video processor works in a 32-bit PCI slot. The 64 or 128 bits refers to the number of bits the video adapter's accelerator chip accepts at one time. The 64 bits (or higher) video processor controls many video functions on the video adapter otherwise handled by the microprocessor. Anytime information is processed on the adapter rather than the microprocessor, performance is faster. When signals pass to the microprocessor through an expansion slot, performance slows. Most video cards today contain a video processor because video is one of the biggest bottlenecks in a computer system.

One way of speeding up a video adapter's performance is to *shadow* the video adapter's ROM chip through the computer system's Setup program. Shadowing the video ROM chip means the software inside the ROM chip is copied into the RAM chips. Accessing instructions from RAM is faster than from a ROM chip, especially a ROM chip on an adapter.

VIDEO MEMORY

One of the most important functions of the video processor is to transfer data to and from the video adapter's memory. Memory chips on the video adapter can be regular DRAM chips (including FPM and EDO — see the Memory chapter for more information on chip technologies), VRAM, or WRAM memory chips. **VRAM (Video RAM)** and **WRAM (Windows Accelerator Card RAM,** or sometimes just called Window RAM) chips are **dual-ported**; they have separate read and write data paths and can be written to and read from simultaneously. DRAM chips are **single-ported**; they are read from or written to, but not simultaneously. The single-ported memory chips have a single data path in and out of the chips. Video adapters that use dual-ported memory have greater performance at resolutions greater than 800x600 and at higher color levels. The difference between the two is WRAM is cheaper than VRAM. The type of video memory can make a big difference in video performance. Refer to the video adapter documentation on the type of video memory chips to use.

Other advances in single-port memory chips include RDRAM, SGRAM, and MDRAM. **RDRAM (Rambus DRAM** or sometimes called Direct Rambus DRAM) is proprietary technology developed by Rambus, Inc. **SGRAM (Synchronous Graphics RAM)** chips allow the video data to clock up to four times quicker than traditional DRAM technologies. **MDRAM (Multi-bank Dynamic RAM)** chips act like multiple independent memory chips with a 32-bit path. MDRAM refreshes the monitor more efficiently than VRAM or WRAM.

The objective is to get the data in and out of the video card's memory chips as fast as possible for a reasonable cost. The adapter must handle a large amount of data due to the increasing number of pixels and colors displayed. Ample, fast memory on the video card allows higher resolutions and more colors to appear on the screen without the screen appearing to flicker. Dual-ported memory allows for faster data flow in and out of the memory chips, and advances in single-ported memory chips allow faster throughput while keeping the cost low.

All parts of the video subsystem must work together to get a clear picture on the screen. A very expensive video adapter with 16 trillion megabytes of memory connected to a monitor with a poor dot pitch will display a distorted picture on the screen. An expensive monitor connected to an ISA video adapter with only 256KB of memory will not provide the fastest refresh rates. The monitor appears to flicker as a result. The video adapter needs to be an AGP card. Furthermore, the adapter needs to contain enough memory to sustain the number of colors at the specific resolution the user must work. A technician cannot perform magic on poorly matched video components. The only solution is to upgrade the weak link.

Memory on the video card stores screen information as a snapshot of what appears on the screen. Common memory chip capacities include 256KB, 512KB, 1MB, 2MB, 4MB, 8MB, 16MB, 32MB, and 64MB. The video adapter manufacturer determines the maximum amount of video memory. Some manufacturers make video adapters that are not upgradeable. Check the adapter's documentation before making a purchase or recommendation. The ability to upgrade video card memory is important to computer users.

The amount of video adapter memory will determine the number of colors available at a specific resolution.

To determine the amount of video memory an adapter needs, multiply the total number of pixels (the resolution) by the number of bits needed to produce a specific number of colors. Different combinations of 16 1s and 0s create 65,536 (64K) possible combinations as $2^{16}=65,536$. For example, take a system that needs 65,536 colors at the resolution of 1024x768. To determine the minimum video memory necessary, multiply 16 (number of bits needed for 64K of colors) times 1024 times 768 (the resolution). The 12,582,912 result is the number of bits needed to handle the combination of 65K colors at 1024x768. Divide the bits by eight for the number of *bytes* needed. This is the minimum amount of memory needed on the video card: 12,582,912 divided by 8 = 1,572,864 or 1.5MB. The user needs more video memory if more colors, a higher resolution, or video motion is desired.

What if a user wanted 256K colors at an 800x600 resolution? What is the minimum amount of video memory needed for the system? Different combinations of 18 1s and 0s produce 256K colors ($2^{18}=262,144$). 18 times 800 times 600 equals 8,640,000 bits. 8,640,000 divided by 8 equals 1,080,000 bytes. The user would need at least 1MB of video RAM.

Video Table #2 lists the number of bits required for different color options.

Bits Required for Colors

No. of Bits	No. of Colors
4	16
8	256
16	65,536 (65K)
24	16,777,216 (16M)

There are also video cards that offer 32-bit color. The extra bits are used for color control and special effects such as animation and game effects. If determining the amount of video memory seems confusing, an exercise is at the end of the chapter to help you practice configuring different scenarios. Video Table #3 contains a chart that helps with the minimum amount of video memory needed for specific configurations.

Video Memory Requirement Examples

Amt of Memory	Color Depth	Resolution
1MB	16-bit (65,536 colors)	640x480
2MB	24-bit (16 million colors)	800x600
2MB	16-bit (65,536 colors)	1024x768
4MB	24-bit (16 million colors)	1024x768

If 2-D or 3-D graphics are being used, the above calculations can be used, but more memory is needed. For 2-D graphics, multiply the answer by 16 more bits. For 3-D graphics, multiply the final number by 48 bits. (One byte is used to process the front dimension, one byte to process the back dimension, and one byte for the third dimension). Then divide by eight to find out how many bytes.

INSTALLING A VIDEO ADAPTER

The first step in installing a video adapter is to do your homework: (1) Make sure that you have the correct interface type and an available motherboard slot. PCI and AGP are the most common, but keep in mind that monitors can attach to a USB or IEEE 1394 (FireWire) port. (2) Gather tools. The most common tool needed is a Phillips head screwdriver to remove the slot-retaining bracket and to reinsert the screw that holds the adapter. (3) Download the latest drivers for the video adapter including any video BIOS updates. (4) Make sure the adapter has a driver for the operating system you are using.

Before installing the adapter, power the computer off and unplug it. For best results and to prevent component damage, use an anti-static wrist strap. Access the motherboard by removing a side panel or removing the computer's cover. Remove any previously installed video adapters (if performing an upgrade) by removing the screw. Use both hands and lift the board upward; you may need to rock the board slightly from side to side to remove it. If no video adapters are installed, remove the slot retaining screw and remove the expansion slot cover. Place the retaining screw to the side.

Sometimes with tower computers, it is best to lay the computer on its side to insert the video adapter properly. Line the video adapter's metal connectors up with the interface slot. Push the adapter into the expansion slot. Make sure the adapter is flush with the expansion slot. Make sure sections of the adapter's gold connectors are not showing because the card is skewed. Reinstall the retaining screw. Connect the monitor to the external video connector. Power on the monitor and computer.

Note that Windows 98 and 2000 support multiple monitors connected to the same computer (using multiple video adapters). If this configuration is required, do only one monitor at a time. The steps outlined here are for a single video adapter installation.

A video adapter usually has a set of drivers or software to enable the adapter to work to its full potential. Any adapter that connects to a SVGA or higher monitor usually needs a driver for optimum performance. Individual software drivers from the manufacturer provide system compatibility and performance boosts. The Internet provides a wonderful way for technicians to obtain current video drivers from adapter manufacturers. Be sure to use the proper video driver for the operating system. Always follow the adapter manufacturer's instructions for installing their drivers. The next two paragraphs are generic steps.

On Windows 98 or 2000, the system usually prompts with the Found New Hardware dialog box. Click on the *Next* button. Continue through the next two screens until the point where you can select the *Have Disk* button. This is so you can install the drivers downloaded from the Internet. Use the *Browse* button to select the driver location (normally the CD drive or floppy drive) and follow the prompts on the screen until finished.

For NT Workstation, many manufacturers request that the machine be booted using the VGA Mode option. Once loaded, the Display control panel is used to install the new driver. Select the *Settings* tab and click on the *Display Type* button. Click on the *Change* button followed by the *Have Disk* button. Use the *Browse* button to select the driver location (normally the CD drive or floppy drive) and follow the prompts on the screen until finished.

Windows prompts you to restart the computer. After restarting the computer, you can adjust the various settings such as refresh rate, resolution, number of colors, screen saver, and power saver.

TROUBLESHOOTING VIDEO

When troubleshooting a video problem, check the simple solutions first. Verify the monitor's power light is on. If not, check the power cable connectors and the wall outlet. Verify that no one changed the brightness and contrast settings. Do not assume anything! Double check the monitor cable connected to the video port. Ask the user if any new software or hardware has been recently installed or upgraded.

In the video subsystem, if a piece of hardware is defective, then it is the monitor, adapter, or cable. If replacement is necessary, always do the easiest solution first. Replace the monitor with one that is working . If monitor replacement is not practical, then check for a conflict with non-energy efficient monitors. Disconnect the monitor from the adapter then power on the monitor and turn the brightness control to its highest position. Is there a raster? A **raster** is the monitor's brightness pattern—a bright white screen. If the raster appears, the problem is likely the video adapter. When disconnecting energy efficient monitors from the video adapter, the monitors go into their low power mode. This check does not work on monitors in the low power mode.

Most video problems are *not* hardware-related; most are software-related. There are many symptoms of a software driver problem. Anything wrong on the display can be a result of a bad driver, an incompatible driver, or an incorrect driver. The best way to be sure is to download the exact driver for the monitor or the display adapter from the Internet, or obtain it from the manufacturer and load it. Some troubleshooting tips relating to video are listed below. Remember, these are only suggestions. Contact the monitor manufacturer or the video adapter manufacturer for specific instructions on troubleshooting their equipment.

1. If the monitor screen is completely black, check the monitor power light. If it is off, check the power connection at the monitor, wall outlet, and surge protector. Try a different outlet or surge protector. Verify that the wall outlet has power. If the monitor power light is on, check the brightness and contrast settings. Try disconnecting the monitor from the adapter to determine if there is a raster. If a blank screen saver is enabled, press a key or move the mouse. If pranksters are around, watch out for black letters on a black background setting. Boot to Safe Mode and change the settings.

2. Carefully examine the monitor's cable ends. The pins can easily bend and not fit properly into the connector, yet the cable appears to plug correctly into the connector. If you find one or more bent pins, carefully use needlenose pliers to gently straighten the pins.

3. If the CRT goes bad, it is probably more cost effective to replace the entire monitor. Most monitors cost more to repair than to replace. One monitor

component that frequently goes bad is the **flyback transformer** that boosts the voltage to the high levels the CRT requires. The cost of flyback transformers varies from model to model. Get a price quote before replacing.

4. If you suspect a video driver problem, change the video driver to a standard (generic) driver to see if the problem goes away and to prove that it is a software driver problem.

5. If the screen appears distorted around the edges of the monitor or the color appears distorted, check for any other equipment such as other monitors, speakers, magnets, and fluorescent lighting that might cause interference with the monitor. Move the monitor from its current location to see if the situation improves or move the computer to another location to see if the problem goes away.

6. Another possible problem with color distortion is CRT magnetization from an outside source. Degaussing circuits neutralize a magnetic field. Some monitors have degaussing controls built into them, so try letting the monitor's internal degaussing circuits fix the problem. Turn the monitor and computer on for one minute. Then, turn off the monitor. Leave the monitor off for 30 minutes. Then, turn the monitor on again for one minute followed by turning it off and leaving it off for 30 minutes. Continue to do this for several cycles. If this does not solve the problem, try manually degaussing the CRT. A **degausser** or degaussing coil is available from electronic stores and can be used to remove the CRT magnetization. Also, a local television repair shop might perform this procedure inexpensively.

Before turning on the degausser, remove all magnetic media such as floppy disks, from the immediate area. Remove your wrist watch. Do not turn on the degausser near the rear of the monitor. Power on the monitor. This procedure sometimes causes anxiety as the colors on the screen go through all sorts of geometric distortions. Do not panic! This is only temporary. Turn on the degausser and bring the coil within a couple of inches to the center of the screen. Take the coil VERY slowly toward the monitor's top corner edge. VERY slowly, trace around the outside edges of the monitor screen, returning to the original starting position in the center of the screen. Hold the degausser pointed toward the center of the screen and back SLOWLY away from the monitor. Turn the degausser off when you are approximately four or five feet away from the monitor.

7. If the output appears distorted check video cables and refresh settings. On LCD monitors, use the vendor-provided software to make adjustments.

8. If the screen has intermittent problems, check the video adapter's documentation to see how to lower the refresh rate. The monitor and the adapter's refresh rates must match. Check the monitor's documentation for its refresh settings.

9. If a cursor appears momentarily before the computer boots, then nothing is displayed or a distorted display appears. Check for a video driver problem.

10. A color monitor displaying in monochrome (black and white) most likely has a video driver problem, a memory conflict, or a software utility problem.

11. Over time, a monitor may need a focus or brightness adjustment. Even though some monitors have external adjustments for this, some monitors place the adjustments inside the monitor case. Even monitors with external adjustment knobs can be adjusted further by adjustments located inside the monitor case. When performing the internal adjustments, follow all previously mentioned safety procedures when working inside the monitor. Other adjustments can also be made through the monitor's front panel button or through vendor-supplied software.

12. If the computer emits one long beep and three short beeps, check that the video card is properly seated in the expansion slot. You may have to push very hard on the adapter for a new expansion slot.

13. If you change the resolution or number of colors and the output is distorted, reboot to Safe Mode and reduce the resolution or number of colors.

WINDOWS VIDEO PROBLEMS

Windows 9x and higher require a VGA or higher monitor. The operating system automatically detects the monitor type during the initial installation. If an exact monitor type is not available, Windows 95/98 configures the setting for a generic type.

To change the monitor type, use the Display control panel *Settings* tab. Then, click on the *Change* button from the *Change Display Type* window. Click on the *Have Disk* option to use the disk provided by a monitor manufacturer.

To install the standard VGA driver in Windows click on the *Start* button, point to *Settings*, and click on the *Control Panel* option. Double-click on the *Display* icon. Click on the *Settings* tab and then click on the *Advanced* button. Click on the *Adapter* tab and click on the *Change* button. Click on the *Next* button followed by clicking on the *Display a list of all the drivers in a specific location so you can select the driver you want* option. Click on the *Next* button. Click on the *Show all devices* option. Click the *Standard Display Types* in the Manufacturers window. Click the *Standard Display Adapter (VGA)* option in the Models window. Click on *OK* and click the *Next* button three consecutive times. Click on the *Finish* button followed by the *Close* button twice.

On initial Setup, the operating system configures the video adapter based on the type of adapter detected. If Windows cannot detect the type of video adapter, it uses a generic video driver (Standard Display Adapter VGA), which does not use all the capabilities of the installed video adapter. However, the video driver can be changed later after Setup finishes.

Windows is not supposed to hang during the boot process because of video driver incompatibility. Instead, the operating system loads a default video driver. If video is a problem while working in Windows, boot to Safe Mode and then load the correct driver.

The following are more troubleshooting tips for Windows video problems. Again, the best source of information is the video adapter or monitor's manufacturer. Most problems do involve the video driver or compatibility issues with the chipset, video card, and operating system.

1. Always check the monitor settings to verify the monitor detection is accurate. In Windows 9x, use the Display control panel's *Settings* tab. To change the display type listed, click once on the *Change Display Type* button. If the monitor manufacturer does not appear in the manufacturer's box list, click on the *Standard Monitor Types* option. In the Models box, click on the appropriate monitor type that matches the type of monitor connected to the computer. For Windows 98, Click on the *Start* button, point to the *Settings* option, and click on *Control Panel*. Double-click on the *Display* icon. Click on the *Settings* tab and then click *Advanced*. Click on the *Change* button from the Monitor tab. In the Manufacturers window, click the monitor manufacturer that you desire. If your monitor manufacturer is not in the list, click on the *Standard Monitor Types* option. In the Models window, click on the correct monitor and click on the *OK* button three times.

2. During the GUI mode portion of Windows 2000 Setup, the screen goes black and finally a stop message appears. There are two solutions to this problem: (1) update the system BIOS or (2) move the video adapter to the first PCI slot on the motherboard.

3. Check to be certain the video adapter does not cause a memory conflict with another adapter. To check for an upper memory area conflict, start the operating system from the command prompt by typing *WIN /D:X*. This startup option tells Windows 9x to *not* use the Upper Memory Blocks for any of its programs. If Windows 95/98 boots properly after using the switch, a memory conflict exists.

4. To check for resource conflicts, use the Device Manager's *Display Adapter* option. For NT, use NT Diagnostics.

5. A screen saver password has been forgotten. In Windows 9x, search the C: drive for files that have the *pwl* extension. Delete these files and reboot the computer. In NT or 2000, there are programs on the Internet that can help with this task.

6. If video performance appears to be slow, adjust the monitor to a lower resolution or a lower number of colors (or both). See the exercise at the end of this chapter for step-by-step instructions. Check the video adapter driver to determine if it matches the installed adapter or if it is generic. Obtain the specific adapter's latest driver from the Internet.

7. If Windows 9x continues to show general protection (GP) faults in various applications, check if the video driver is a Windows 3.x driver. If so, get an updated driver from the manufacturer or use a standard Windows 95/98 driver.

8. Anytime an operating system will not load because of video, use the generic VGA driver until Windows is installed and then install the proper video driver.

9. While installing Windows 2000 and selecting a video mode, a dialog box keeps reappearing to select a video adapter. Select the standard VGA driver, continue loading the operating system and once loaded, install the proper video driver.

Name _____

VIDEO REVIEW QUESTIONS

1. What parts make up a computer's video subsystem?

2. What is the difference between a grayscale monitor and a monochrome monitor?

3. What is the difference between an analog and a digital monitor?

4. [T / F] XEGA monitors are the most popular monitor type for computers today.

5. How can you tell by looking at a video adapter's port if it accepts an analog or an older digital monitor?

6. [T / F] The monitor type must match the video adapter.

7. Why is a monitor's size an issue?

8. What is VIS?

9. What is the purpose of a monitor's electron gun?

10. What component directs the electron beam to the proper location on the front of the monitor screen?

11. Which is better, a .25mm or .28mm dot pitch?

12. What is the difference between a shadow mask and an aperture grille?

13. What is dot pitch and how does it relate to resolution?

14. [T / F] For monitors using an aperture grille, dot pitch is only relevant in a horizontal direction.

15. What resolution is good for a 17-inch monitor?

16. What determines the monitor's refresh rate?
    A. The monitor specifications
    B. The video adapter specifications
    C. The video adapter and the monitor specifications
    D. The motherboard
    E. The ROM BIOS
    F. The microprocessor

17. Why is the vertical scan rate important?

18. What is a good refresh rate for a monitor?

19. [T / F] Today's monitors normally support only one refresh rate.

20. What term best describes when a monitor's electron beam scans the odd pixel
     rows and then scans the even pixel rows?
     [Refreshing / Interlacing / Beaming / Video Skipping]

21. What type of video technology is used with laptop displays?

22. Describe the difference between active and passive matrix displays.

23. If an active matrix display uses TFT technology, how many transistors are required
     for an 800x600 resolution?

24. How do technicians usually change resolution on an LCD?

25. [T / F] Flat panel displays consume less power than CRTs.

26. Explain why having an analog adapter is not the preferred method for connecting a
     flat screen monitor.

27. How do you keep a monitor static-free?

28. [T / F] Monitors are frequently disassembled by technicians because the parts are so inexpensive.

29. Should a monitor be left on 24 hours a day? Explain your answer.

30. What is a green monitor?

31. [T / F] Windows 2000 supports ACPI.

32. What control panel is used to enable a monitor's energy saving features?

33. [T / F] A non-green monitor can be damaged if energy efficiency software is enabled.

34. [T / F] Today's analog monitors require a screen saver or an image could permanently burn into the display.

35. A computer user has a flat screen monitor. What do you recommend in regard to a screen saver?

36. What adapter interface would you recommend for video?
    [ISA / EISA / MCA / VL-bus / PCI / AGP] Explain your answer.

37. What is a video accelerator?

38. [T / F] Shadowing the video ROM chip provides faster video performance.

39. List three ways to increase video performance on a computer.

40. Which type of video memory chips is single-ported?

41. Why is having memory on the video adapter so important?

42. How much video memory is needed for 32K of colors at 1024x768?
    [1MB / 2MB / 4MB / 512KB]

43. How many colors can a 24-bit video adapter display?
    [16 / 256 / 64K / 256K / 1M / 16M]

44. What steps should be performed *before* installing a video adapter?

45. [T / F] Monitors can use USB and FireWire to attach to a system.

46. [T / F] When installing a new video adapter, NT normally displays the Found New Hardware dialog box.

47. When troubleshooting a non-green monitor, you disconnect the monitor cable and the monitor has a raster. Is the problem most likely in the monitor or video adapter?

48. Why are software problems more prevalent than hardware problems in the video subsystem?

49. How do you prove the video driver is causing the problem?

50. How do you remove a screen saver password when using Windows 9x?

51. During Windows 2000 installation, the screen goes blank. The installation process stops. What is one thing you can do?

Name _____

VIDEO FILL-IN-THE-BLANK

1.   _____ monitors display only one color.

2.   SVGA monitors connect to a _____-pin port.

3.   The main part of the monitor is the _____.

4.   The combination of a red dot, green dot, and blue dot is a _____.

5.   The smallest unit visible on a monitor is a _____.

6.   The distance between two dots is a monitor's _____.

7.   The total number of pixels on a monitor is the monitor's _____.

8.   The speed the horizontal beam crosses the monitor is the _____.

9.   The vertical scan rate is more commonly called a monitor's _____.

10. A monitor that has the ability use various vertical and horizontal scan rates is a _____.

11. The _____ type of passive matrix LCD improves brightness by twisting light rays.

12. An active matrix display with a resolution of 1024x768 has _____ transistors.

13. _____ displays are LCDs used on tower computers.

14. A 24-pin port on a video adapter is commonly called a _____.

15. _____ is the standard produced by VESA used for power saving monitors.

16. A _____ offers password protection and entertainment for today's computer users, but on an older computer, it is used to prevent an image from burning into the screen.

17. The _____ does processing on the video adapter normally performed by the microprocessor on the motherboard.

18. Memory chips with separate read and write data paths are said to be _____.

19. _____ video memory helps with the efficiency of refreshing the screen.

20. The monitor's brightness pattern is its _____.

21. A _____ is used to neutralize a magnetic field around the CRT that causes color distortions.

22. Windows 9x's _____ control panel is used to change the type of monitor.

23. A computer beeps once then three times. Check the _____.

24. To check for resource conflicts in NT, use _____.

Name _____

CHANGING THE RESOLUTION AND NUMBER OF COLORS USING WINDOWS 9X EXERCISE

Objective: To change the video resolution and number of colors using Windows 95/98

Parts: A computer with a color monitor and Windows 95 or 98 loaded

Step 1. Power on the computer and verify that the operating system has loaded.

Step 2. Click on the **Start** button.

Step 3. Select **Settings** from the Start menu.

Step 4. Click on the **Control Panel** option.

Step 5. Double-click the **Display** control panel.

Step 6. Click once on the **Settings** tab.

Notice how the Color Palette's down arrow sets the number of possible colors.

Question 1: What part or component determines the number of Color Palette settings available?

Question 2: What is the Color Palette's setting now?

Step 7. Click once on the Color Palette's **down arrow**.

Question 3: How many different color choices are available?

Question 4: What is the difference between a 16-bit and a 24-bit color palette?

Step 8. Use the Color Palette's **down arrow** to select the *lowest* color setting (usually 16 colors).

Step 9. Locate, but do *not* change, the Desktop Area's slidebar that controls the monitor resolution.

Question 5:   Looking at the Desktop Area's slidebar, what is the current resolution setting?

Step 10.   While holding the mouse button down, move the Desktop Area's slidebar back and forth to determine the possible resolutions.

Question 6:   How many different resolutions are available?

Question 7:   What determines the number of resolutions possible?

Step 11.   While holding the mouse button down, move the Desktop Area slidebar to the left to the *lowest* resolution setting. Notice in the open window, the size of the icons showing on the monitor.

Step 12.   While holding the mouse button down, move the Desktop Area slidebar to the right to the *highest* resolution setting. Notice how the icons on the monitor screen get smaller in the open window.

Windows 95 does not require restarting the computer every time you choose a different resolution!

Question 8:   Why do icons get smaller at a higher resolution?

Step 13.   Using the Color Palette's **down arrow** select the *highest* color setting.

Step 14.   While holding the mouse button down, move the Desktop Area's slidebar back and forth to determine the different number of resolutions possible.

Question 9:   How many different resolutions are available?

Question 10: What is the relationship (if any) between the number of colors and the possible resolution settings?

Step 15. Set the Color Palette back to its original setting. Refer back to the Question 2 answer.

Step 16. Set the Desktop Area slidebar back to the original setting. Refer back to the Question 5 answer.

Step 17. Have a classmate verify that the settings are in their original state.

Classmate's printed name: _____

Classmate's initials: _____

Step 18. Click on the **Change Display Type** button. The Change Display Type window is where the video adapter and the monitor type can be changed if necessary. On initial Setup, Windows 95/98 configures the video adapter based on the type of controller on the adapter.

Question 11: What adapter type shows in the Change Display Type window?

Question 12: What monitor type shows in the Change Display Type window?

Step 19. Click on the **Cancel** button.

Step 20. In the Display Properties window, click on the **Cancel** button.

Step 21. Close **all windows** on the desktop.

Name _____

CHANGING RESOLUTION AND COLORS ON WINDOWS NT WORKSTATION

Objective: To change the desktop settings in Windows NT Workstation

Parts: Windows NT Workstation

At times, it is necessary to adjust the desktop settings to match individual preferences or application requirements.

Step 1.   Turn the computer on and verify that Windows NT Workstation loads.

Step 2.   Logon to Windows NT Workstation using the userid and password provided by the instructor or lab assistant.

Step 3.   Right-click the **desktop** and choose **Properties**. The Display Properties window opens.

Step 4.   Choose the **Settings** tab.

Step 5.   From the Color Palette drop-down menu, select an appropriate colors setting.

Question 1:   How many color settings are available?

Step 6.   From the Desktop Area box, choose a resolution setting either higher or lower than your current setting.

Question 2:   How many resolution settings are available?

Step 7.   Select the **Test** button to test your new desktop configuration settings. When the Testing Mode window opens, click **OK**.

Step 8.   The new desktop settings will be applied and displayed for 5 seconds. If the new settings are acceptable, click **Yes**.

Step 9.   Click **OK** to accept the new settings and close the Display Properties window.

_____ *Instructor's Initials*

Name _____

CHANGING RESOLUTION AND COLORS ON WINDOWS 2000 PROFESSIONAL

Objective: Understand how to change the desktop settings in Windows 2000 Professional

Parts: Windows 2000 Professional computer

At times, you may find it necessary to adjust the desktop settings to match individual preferences or application requirements.

Step 1.   Turn the computer on and verify that Windows 2000 Professional loads.

Step 2.   Log on to Windows 2000 Professional using the userid and password provided by the instructor or lab assistant.

Step 3.   Right-click the **desktop** and choose **Properties**. The Display Properties window opens.

Step 4.   Choose the **Settings** tab.

Question 1:   What configuration options are available from the Settings tab?

Step 5.   From the Colors drop-down menu, select an appropriate colors setting.

Question 2:   How many colors settings are available?

Step 6.   From the Screen Area box, select a resolution setting either higher or lower than the existing setting.

Question 3:   What is the highest resolution setting available on your computer?

Step 7.   Select **OK**. A warning screen appears stating that Windows will apply the new settings. Click **OK**.

Step 8.   When the new settings have been applied, you have 15 seconds to confirm them. If you do not confirm within 15 seconds, the old settings will be reapplied automatically.

Step 9.   Click **Yes** within 15 seconds to confirm and apply the new desktop settings.

_____ *Instructor's Initials*

Name _____

CHANGING REFRESH RATE USING WINDOWS 9X

Objective: Understand how to change the monitor's refresh rate in Windows 95/98.

Parts: Windows 95/98 computer

At times, you may find it necessary to adjust the monitor's refresh rate to match individual preferences or match the monitor with the video adapter.

Step 1.   Turn the computer on and verify that Windows 9x loads.

Step 2.   Double-click on the **My Computer** desktop icon and double-click on the **Control Panel** folder icon.

Step 3.   Double-click on the **Display** control panel icon. The Display Properties window opens.

Step 4.   Click on the **Settings** tab.

Question 1:   What do the words *"800x600 pixels"* (or whatever number of pixels is listed in the Screen area section) mean to you?

Question 2:   What type of monitor is listed under the Display section?

Step 5.   Click on the **Advanced** button and select the **Adapter** tab.

Step 6.   Locate the **Refresh Rate** section and click on the **down arrow**.

Question 3:   List a couple of refresh rates available with this monitor.

_____ *Instructor's Initials*

Step 7.   Click on the **Cancel** button and then click on the **Cancel** button again.

Step 8.   Close the **Control Panel** window.

Name _____

CHANGING REFRESH RATE USING WINDOWS 2000

Objective: Understand how to change the monitor's refresh rate in Windows 2000.

Parts: Windows 2000 Professional computer

At times, you may find it necessary to adjust the monitor's refresh rate to match individual preferences or match the monitor with the video adapter.

Step 1.   Turn the computer on and verify that Windows 2000 has loaded. Login using the userid and password provided by the instructor or lab assistant.

Step 2.   Double-click on the **My Computer** desktop icon and double-click on the **Control Panel** folder icon.

Step 3.   Double-click on the **Display** control panel icon. The Display Properties window opens.

Step 4.   Click on the **Settings** tab.

Question 1:   What do the words *800x600 pixels* (or whatever number of pixels is listed in the Screen area section) mean to you?

Question 2:   How many bits are being used for colors?

Step 5.   Click on the **Advanced** button and select the **Adapter** tab.

Step 6.   Click on the **List All Modes** button. (Note that the Monitor tab may also contain a list of refresh rates in Windows 2000.)

Step 7.   Locate the Refresh Rate section and view the different refresh rates.

Question 3:   List a couple of refresh rates available with this monitor.

_____ *Instructor's Initials*

Step 8.   Click on the **Cancel** button and then click on the **Cancel** button again.

Step 9.   Close the **Control Panel** window.

Name _____

DETERMINING THE AMOUNT OF VIDEO MEMORY PAPER EXERCISE

Question 1:   What is the minimum memory (512KB, 1MB, 2MB, 4MB, or 8MB) a video adapter needs if a user wants a 1024x768 resolution with 16 million colors available?

Question 2:   What is the minimum memory (512KB, 1MB, 2MB, 4MB, or 8MB) a video adapter needs if a user wants an 800x600 resolution with 65,536 colors available?

Question 3:   A video card has 1MB of memory and is a 24-bit color adapter. The user wants to display 16 million colors at a resolution of 800x600. Is the amount of installed memory on the video adapter adequate? Justify your answer.

Question 4:   A video card has 4MB of memory. The user wants a resolution of 1024x768 and 16 million colors. Is the amount of installed memory on the video adapter adequate? Justify your answer.

Question 5:   What is the minimum recommended memory for a video card purchased for a brand new system? Explain your answer.

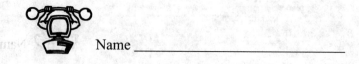
Name _____

DETERMINING THE MINIMUM VIDEO MEMORY INSTALLED

Objective: To understand how to calculate the amount of video memory based on the number of color bits and resolution settings

Parts: Windows computer

Step 1.   Turn the computer on and verify that the operating system loads. Login using the userid and password provided by the instructor or lab assistant.

Step 2.   Double-click on the **My Computer** desktop icon and double-click on the **Control Panel** folder icon.

Step 3.   Double-click on the **Display** control panel icon. The Display Properties window opens.

Step 4.   Click on the **Settings** tab.

Question 1:   In the Colors section, what is the number of bits used for color?

Bonus: How many colors can be displayed using the number found in Question 1?

Question 2:   In the Screen area section, what is the current resolution setting? (This number is listed as *x* by *x* pixels.)

Question 3:   Calculate the amount of memory required by multiplying the two numbers together that make up the resolution. This is the number listed as your answer to Question 2. (For example, if the resolution is listed as 800x600, the calculation would be 800 times 600 equals 480,000.)

_____ X _____ = _____

horizontal bits   vertical bits   TOTAL1

Question 4:   Take the result of Question 3 (TOTAL1) and multiply by the number of color bits (listed as the answer to Question 1). The result is the minimum amount of video memory installed *in bits*.

$$\underline{\hspace{3cm}} \text{X} \underline{\hspace{3cm}} = \underline{\hspace{3cm}}$$

   TOTAL1   color bits   TOTAL2

Question 5:   Take the result of Question 4 (TOTAL2) and divide by eight to determine the minimum amount of video memory installed *in bytes*.

$$\underline{\hspace{3cm}} \div \underline{\hspace{3cm}} = \underline{\hspace{3cm}}$$

   TOTAL2   8   video memory in bytes

Name _____

INTERNET DISCOVERY

Objective: To access obtain specific information on the Internet regarding a computer or its associated parts

Parts: Access to the Internet

Question 1: A customer calls in stating that they are using the WizardWorks software produced by the WizardWorks Group. When the user tries to run the game, all they get is a blank screen. Write down two possible solutions and the URL for where you found the answer.

Question 2: The following statement is found on the Internet, "When a monitor goes bad you are usually stuck with replacing it." List the URL where you found this quote.

Question 3: What does the term *pincushion distortion* mean as it relates to monitors? Find a web site that puts it in plain English and write down the URL.

Question 4: You just upgraded from NT Workstation to 2000 Professional. Now the display does not work properly. You have a clone monitor with an Accel Graphics Eclipse video adapter installed. What is the most likely problem and where did you find this answer on the Internet?

Question 5: Locate a web site that explains the different types of video memory and displays a chart of the differences. Write the URL in the space below.

13

Chapter 13:
Printers

OBJECTIVES

After completing this chapter you will

- Understand basic printing concepts.
- Know how each type of printer operates.
- Understand how printers require and use software.
- Perform a printer installation.
- Perform preventive maintenance on printers.
- Be able to control printers in the Windows operating system and make appropriate printer adjustments.
- Recognize and troubleshoot printing problems in the Windows environment.
- Be able to solve common printer problems and solutions.

KEY TERMS

Add Printer wizard	fuser cleaning pad	print spooler
bi-directional printing	fusing roller	printhead
conditioning roller	HPPCL	printwire
cpi	IEEE 1284	raster font
cps	ink jet printer	ream
default printer	internal font	RET
density control blade	laser printer	scaleable font
developing cylinder	marking subsystem	soft font
dot matrix printer	outline font	SPP
dpi	ozone filter	switch box
ECP	paper transport	toner puddling
EMF	PDL	transfer corona
EPP	pin firing	transfer roller
erase lamp	PostScript	TrueType font
felt side	primary corona	vector font
font	print cartridge	wax side
font cartridge	print driver	wire side
font size	print engine	write-black laser printer
font style	print server	write-white laser printer

PRINTERS OVERVIEW

Printers are a difficult subject to cover because so many different models exist. (Of course, that can be said about any peripheral.) But the principles are the same for different categories of printers. The best way to begin is to look at what printers have in common. All printers have three subsystems: (1) the paper transport subsystem, (2) the marking subsystem, and (3) the print engine subsystem.

The **paper transport** subsystem pulls, pushes, or rolls, etc. the paper through the printer. Printers use various methods such as belts, tractor feeds, and rollers to pass the paper through the printer. The **marking subsystem**, or marking engine, is the part of the printer responsible for placing the image on the paper. This subsystem includes ribbons, ink cartridges, toner cartridges, any part moving each of these, and anything else necessary to print the image. The **print engine** is the brains of the operation. It accepts data and commands from the computer and translates the commands into motion. The print engine subsystem also redirects feedback to the computer when necessary. Keep the three printer subsystems in mind when setting up a printer and troubleshooting it. Knowing how a specific type of printer places an image on the paper also helps when troubleshooting the printer.

PARALLEL AND USB PORTS

Printers connect to the parallel, serial, or USB ports. When connected to the parallel port data transmits eight bits at a time with possible speeds up to 2Mbps (depending on your printer, port, BIOS, and operating system). The parallel cable should be no longer than 15 feet, although 25 feet can work. Look back to Serial Figure #2 for the transmission differences between serial and parallel ports and to the Serial chapter for more information on serial devices. They will not be covered here since a serial printer configuration has the same issues as any other serial device. Even though USB transmits one bit at a time, it supports speeds up to 12Mbps. One device is allowed to request up to 6Mbps.

Most printers attach to a PC using either the parallel or USB port. The print speed is usually equitable between the two ports. The parallel port is a 25-pin female connector built into the motherboard or integrated on an adapter (sometimes, with other ports as well). Look back to Introduction Figure #10 for a picture of a parallel port. The USB port can also be integrated into the motherboard or on a separate adapter. Introduction Figure #13 shows a USB port.

The operating system assigns names to the parallel ports. The motherboard BIOS detects any parallel ports based on their I/O addresses just as with serial ports. The parallel port names are assigned in the I/O address order found—378, 278, and 3BC (normally). This is not as big a conflict as serial ports because computer users do not normally want to add as many printers as they do serial devices. The parallel port names are LPT1:, LPT2:, and LPT3:. The assignment of port names uses the same concept as assigning COM port names. Just as with serial ports, the DEBUG command shows the parallel ports that the BIOS chip detects. Device Manager (in Windows 9x and 2000) or NT Diagnostics (in NT Workstation) can be used to show the port I/O address. Because this is a confusing concept, the steps are listed below.

1. BIOS detects I/O address 378.
2. The operating system assigns the port at I/O address 378 the LPT port name of LPT1.
3. BIOS detects I/O address 278.
4. The operating system assigns the port at I/O address 278 the LPT port name of LPT2.

Printer Figure #1 lists the output of the DEBUG command when two printer ports are installed in the system. An exercise at the end of the chapter outlines this process.

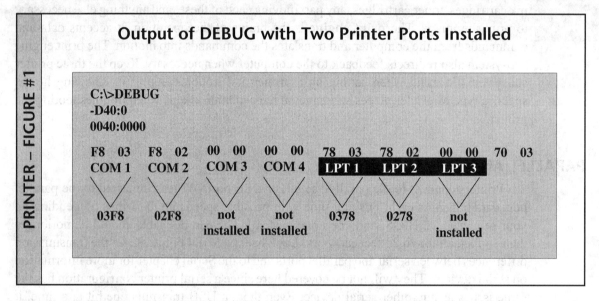

PRINTER – FIGURE #1

Output of DEBUG with Two Printer Ports Installed

```
C:\>DEBUG
-D40:0
0040:0000
```

| F8 03 | F8 02 | 00 00 | 00 00 | 78 03 | 78 02 | 00 00 | 70 03 |
| COM 1 | COM 2 | COM 3 | COM 4 | LPT 1 | LPT 2 | LPT 3 | |

| 03F8 | 02F8 | not installed | not installed | 0378 | 0278 | not installed |

The printer does not need to use an interrupt if printing through DOS or Windows. However, other devices that connect to the parallel port may require an interrupt or work faster than a printer.

With USB printers, the USB host controller (built into the motherboard or on an adapter) powers up and queries all USB devices as to what type of data transfer they want to perform. Printers use bulk transfer on the USB, which means that data is sent in 64 byte sections. The USB host controller also assigned each USB a device so that the host controller can track them. Even though USB can provide power to smaller devices, a USB printer normally has its own power source.

USB is a good alternative because it frees up the parallel port for other devices. Most computers ship with a single parallel port installed. By using a USB printer, the parallel port can be used for tape backup, hard drive, scanner, or another parallel device. USB uses only one interrupt for the devices connected to the bus.

IEEE 1284 STANDARD & SPP, EPP, ECP

The parallel port on the computer has sustained very few changes over the years. The IEEE committee established a standard in 1984 called **IEEE 1284**. Before there were any established standards, the parallel device received data from the computer through the **Standard Parallel Port (SPP).** The data traveled in one direction only—from the computer to the printer.

To allow status data to travel from the printer back to the computer, Intel Corp., Xircom, Inc., and Zenith Data Systems Corp., designed a standard known as **EPP (Enhanced Parallel Port).** The IEEE 1284 standard incorporates the EPP standard as one mode of parallel communication. EPP allows bi-directional communication. With **bi-directional printing**, the printer can notify the computer that the cover is open, the printer is off-line, or the paper is out, etc. Even though bi-directional printing allows two-way communication between the printer and the computer, it is only one direction at a time. Either the computer is sending information to the printer or the printer is sending information to the computer. In addition to allowing bi-directional transmissions, EPP transmits data at 500 KBps to 2 MBps, which is faster than SPP's 50 Bps to 150 Bps transfer rate.

Microsoft and Hewlett-Packard improved the EPP standard by creating the **Enhanced Capabilities Port (ECP)** standard. IEEE 1284 also includes ECP as a parallel communication mode that allows bi-directional communication. However with ECP, simultaneous bi-directional communication can occur over the parallel port. ECP mode allows the printer to communicate with the computer at the same time the computer is sending data to the printer. The ECP also supports data compression and DMA transfers that allow faster data exchange.

Four criteria determine whether a parallel device such as a printer and a computer can communicate using ECP.

1. The computer's parallel port must support ECP. If the port is built into the motherboard, check Setup to determine if the port allows ECP configuration. If the parallel port is built into a separate adapter, check the adapter's documentation.
2. The printer must support ECP. Check the printer's documentation.
3. A parallel port driver that handles the ECP communication between the port and the device is needed. The operating system can contain this software. For example, Windows 95, 98, and NT support ECP transfers; the DOS/Windows environment does not.
4. One also needs an ECP cable to connect the computer and the parallel device. Any cable that is IEEE 1284 compliant works in the ECP mode (if the other three criteria are in place). An IEEE 1284-compliant cable that connects the printer to the computer is not the same as a Laplink or Interlink cable (which are also bi-directional).

 A parallel cable should be no longer than 15 feet.

The IEEE 1284 standard supports three different connectors used with the parallel port. Type A in the IEEE standard is the 25-pin female port normally found on the back of the computer. Type B in the IEEE standard is the 36-pin Centronics connector found on the printer. Type C in the IEEE standard is a connector like the Centronics connector on the printer except smaller. The new connector is not widely used in the industry.

NOTICE: All the troubleshooting tips given in this chapter assume the printer connects to a parallel and USB ports. If the printer connects to a serial port, troubleshoot the serial problems as you would any other serial device. Refer to the Serial Devices chapter for more information on troubleshooting serial port problems.

PRINTER SWITCH BOXES

Instead of using two ports to connect two printers to the same computer, some people prefer a **switch box** that connects two printers to one computer or connects one printer to two computers. An inexpensive switch box allows sharing a resource such as a color laser printer. Switch boxes reduce the cost per computer when a resource is shared between multiple workstations.

An automatic switch box automatically detects which computer is sending the data to the printer. A manual switch box, sometimes called an A/B switch box, requires a person to pick which printer (if multiple printers connect to a computer) or which computer (if multiple computers connect to the same printer) by turning a dial. Printer Figure #2 shows a common automatic switch box configuration.

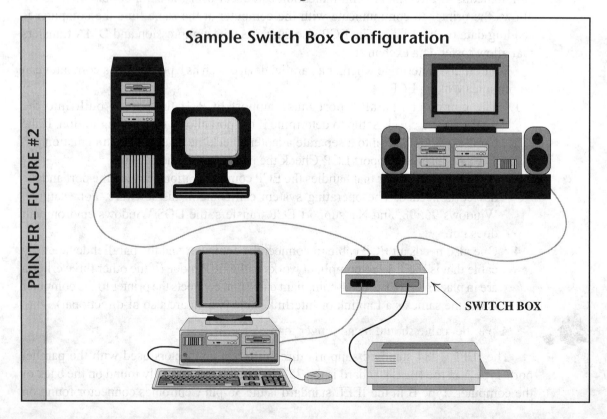

Sample Switch Box Configuration

PRINTER – FIGURE #2

SWITCH BOX

Always use an automatic switch box if using a laser printer. A manual switch box causes problems because the voltage levels created when taking laser printers on or off line appear as noise spikes through the cables. The noise spikes or a bad switch connection can damage the parallel port or the laser printer. Be aware that some laser printers will not function connected to a switch box. They require a direct connection to the computer. A USB printer is a viable alternative to a switch box.

NETWORKED PRINTERS

Many home users and almost all businesses use networked printers (printers that can be used by more than one computer). Printers can be networked using several different methods:

- A printer that is connected to a computer can be *shared* or made available to other computers through the Windows operating system. The other computers must be networked in some way.
- A printer can have a network card integrated into it or installed that allows it to participate as a network device.
- A printer can attach to a network device called an external **print server** (similar to attaching a printer to a computer) and the print server attaches to the network.

A networked printer can reduce costs. Laser printers can be expensive especially ones that produce high speed, high volume output, high quality, and color output. Buying one printer and allowing other users to access it from their own desktop can be cost effective. It also reduces the amount of office or home space needed. Network printing is a viable alternative to using a computer's parallel or USB port.

CATEGORIES OF PRINTERS

Printers can be categorized according to how they put an image on paper. The printer categories are dot matrix, ink jet, and laser. There are more, but these make up the majority of printers used in the workplace and home. Computer users normally choose a printer based on the type of printing done. **Dot matrix printers** are good for text printing, although they can produce limited graphics. They use ribbons that keep the overall printing costs down. The cost per page for a dot matrix printer is usually less than a penny. A dot matrix printer is the only printer of the three categories that prints multipart forms and the 132 column wide paper needed by some industries. If not for these two features, dot matrix printers would be extinct.

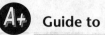

Most home computer users prefer **ink jet printers**. They are much quieter, weigh less, and produce higher quality graphics than dot matrix printers. The ink jet printer uses a **print cartridge** that holds the ink instead of a ribbon. A slight disadvantage to an ink jet printer is the ink is not completely waterproof like the laser printer output. Ink jet cartridges are usually $25 to $35 apiece for black ink and more for the color cartridges. The cost of the ink cartridges plus paper makes the cost of an ink jet printer as high as 12 cents per page. Color ribbons are available for dot matrix printers, but ink jet printers are the masters of color printing. Color output is most affordable through ink jet technology.

Laser printers, however, produce the highest quality output at the fastest rate. With such a claim, the cost of the technology rises. Laser printers are common in the corporate network environment where users share peripherals and are used for graphic design and computer-generated art where high quality printing is a necessity. Some laser printers can produce color output like ink jet printers but at a much higher cost. The cost for a color laser printer is prohibitive for most home computer users.

Each of the three basic printer types is discussed in greater detail in the next sections. The theory of operation for each printer type mainly concerns the marking subsystem.

DOT MATRIX PRINTERS

Dot matrix printers are called impact printers because of the way they create an image on the paper. They have a **printhead** that holds tiny wires called **printwires**. The wires individually strike a ribbon hard enough to create a dot on the paper. The dots collectively form letters or images. The speed that the printhead can place characters on the page is its **characters per second (cps)** specification rating. The number of printwires in the printhead determines the quality of print. The more printwires, the better the print quality. The most common printwires are 9, 18, and 24. The 24-pin printers can print Near Letter Quality (NLQ) output.

Each printwire connects to a solenoid coil. When current flows to the printwire, a magnetic field causes the wire to move away from the printhead and out a tiny hole. The print wire impacts a ribbon to create a dot on the paper. Printer Figure #3 shows a dot matrix printhead. To show the individual printwires, the casing that covers the printwires has been removed from the illustration.

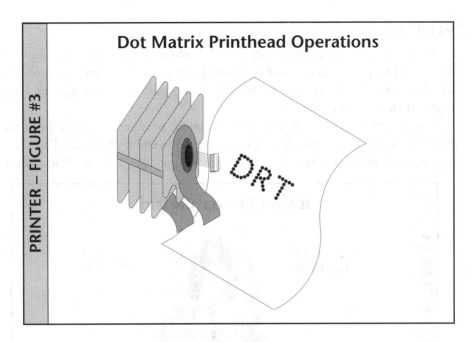

Dot Matrix Printhead Operations

PRINTER – FIGURE #3

Each wire connects to a spring that pulls the printwire back inside the printhead. The images created are nothing more than a series of dots on the page. Dot matrix printers are impact printers because the printwire springs out of the printhead. The act of the printwire coming out of the printhead is called **pin firing**. The impact of the printer physically striking the ribbon, which in turn touches the paper, causes dot matrix printers to be noisy.

Because the printwire impacts the ribbon, one of the most common points of failure with dot matrix printers is the printhead. It can be expensive to frequently replace one in a high-usage situation. However, refurbished printheads are available at a reduced price and they work fine. The companies who refurbish them usually replace the faulty wires and test the printhead thoroughly.

Dot matrix printers are the workhorses of printers. One advantage to a dot matrix printer is that it will print multiple part forms such as invoices, purchase orders, shipping documents, or wide forms. Laser and ink jet printers cannot produce multiple part forms. They can only make multiple copies of the same document. Multiple part forms print easily on dot matrix because the printer impacts the paper so hard. The maximum number of multiple copies each dot matrix printer handles depends on the printer model.

Do not stack things on top of any printer, especially a dot matrix printer. The printhead gets hot and you should not add to the heat by stacking things on top of the printer. Keep the printer in a cool environment to avoid overheating. Most dot matrix printers print bi-directionally. When the printhead gets too hot, the printer stops printing bi-directionally and prints only in the left-to-right direction. This is a normal condition and not a problem situation as some users might think. If the printer is used continuously, thus keeping the printhead hot, consider purchasing a second printer to handle the workload.

INK JET PRINTERS

Ink jet printers are much quieter than dot matrix printers. They also have a printhead, but the ink jet's printhead does not have metal pins that fire out from the printhead. Instead, the ink jet's printhead has many tiny nozzles that squirt ink onto the paper. Each nozzle is smaller than a strand of human hair.

One great thing about ink jet printers is that the printhead includes the nozzles *and* the reservoir for ink. When the ink runs out, replace the entire printhead. The ink jet printer's printhead is known as the print cartridge. Printer Figure #4 shows an ink jet printer cartridge.

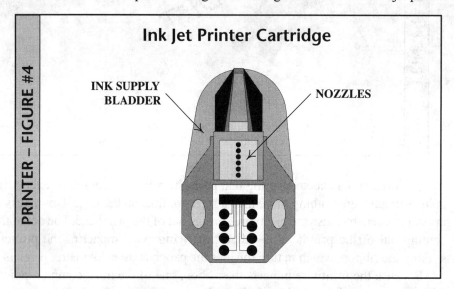

Ink Jet Printer Cartridge

PRINTER – FIGURE #4

INK SUPPLY BLADDER

NOZZLES

An ink jet cartridge has 50 or more nozzles instead of the 9, 18, or 24 metal pin configuration the dot matrix has. That is one reason why the ink jet quality is so much better than a dot matrix. Furthermore, every time the print cartridge is replaced, the printer gets a new printhead. Replacing the printhead, one of the most frequently used parts, keeps repair costs low.

Ink jet printers, also called bubble jet printers, use thermal (heat) technology to place the ink onto the paper. Each print nozzle attaches to a small ink chamber that attaches to a larger ink reservoir. A small amount of ink inside the chamber heats to boiling temperatures. Once the ink boils, a vapor bubble forms. As the bubble gets hotter, it expands and goes out through the print cartridge's nozzle onto the paper. The size of the ink droplet is approximately two ten-thousandths (.0002) of an inch, smaller than a human hair. As the small ink chamber cools down, suction occurs. The suction pulls more ink into the ink chamber for the production of the next ink droplet.

An alternative for producing the ink dots is to use piezo-electric technology, which uses pressure, not heat, to eject the ink onto the paper. The Seiko Epson Corporation uses this technology to obtain 1440x720 dpi and higher resolutions. **DPI** is the number of **dots per inch** a printer outputs. The higher the DPI, the better the quality of ink jet or laser printer output.

Most ink jet printers have different modes of printing. The draft mode uses the least amount of ink and the near letter quality (NLQ) mode uses the most ink. The quality produced by the ink jet printer is close to a laser printer, but in most high-end ink jet printers, the output is actually a higher dots per inch (DPI).

Some ink jet printers can produce color output. The color produced by an ink jet printer does not last as long as photographs. Color ink jet printers usually have a black cartridge for normal printing and a separate color cartridge for the colored ink or even separate cartridges for each color. Buying an ink jet printer that uses a single cartridge for colors is cheaper on the initial printer purchase but more expensive in the long run. The black ink usually runs out much quicker than the colored ink. Users should buy an ink jet model with separate cartridges for black ink and colored ink.

Ink jet printers are perfect for small businesses, home computer users, and individual computer office work. For higher output, the laser printer is more appropriate. A drawback to using ink is the ink sometimes smears. Different ink manufacturers vary greatly in how they respond to this problem. If the paper gets wet, some ink jet output becomes a mess. The ink also smears when touching the printed page before the ink dries. The ink can also soak into the paper and bleed down the paper. Using good quality paper helps with this particular problem. Some manufacturers have a printer operation mode that slows down the printing to give the ink time to dry. See this chapter's section on printer supplies for more information on choosing the correct paper for different printers.

LASER PRINTERS

The term *laser* stands for light amplification by stimulated emission of radiation. A laser printer operates similar to a copy machine's electro-photographic process. Before describing how a laser printer works, identifying the major parts inside the laser helps understand how it works. Printer Figure #5 shows a side view of a laser printer with a toner cartridge installed.

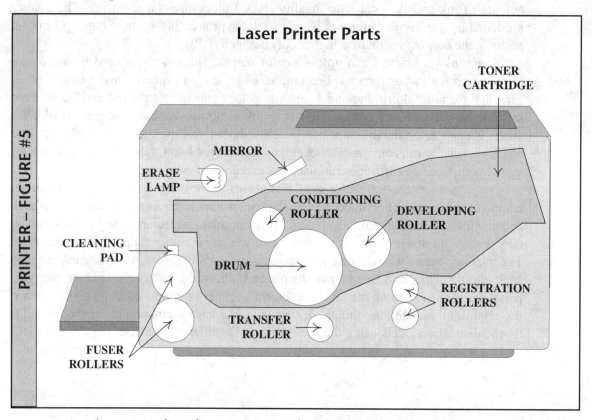

Laser Printer Parts

PRINTER – FIGURE #5

As an overview, the computer sends 1s and 0s out the parallel port and down the parallel cable to the printer. The data transmits either through an array of LEDs or through a laser beam. The light beam strikes the photosensitive drum located inside the toner cartridge. Laser toner particles are attracted to the drum. The paper feeds through and the toner transfers to the paper. The toner is then fused or melted into the paper.

Hewlett-Packard developed steps for the laser printing process. The six steps outlined below describe what happens when a laser printer prints a page. A computer technician must be very familiar with the laser printing process for certification and for troubleshooting laser printers.

- **Conditioning:** Get the drum ready for use. Before any information goes onto the drum, the entire drum must have the same voltage level. The **primary corona**, also known as the main corona, is a thin wire located inside the toner cartridge. The primary corona has up to –6000vdc applied to it. A primary control grid is located between the primary corona and the drum and it controls the amount of voltage applied to the drum's surface (approximately –600 to –1000 volts). Some printer manufacturers use a **conditioning roller** instead of a primary corona. No matter what method the manufacturer uses, the drum receives a uniform electrical charge.

- **Writing:** Put the 1s and 0s on the drum's surface. Whether the printer uses a laser beam or an LED array, the light reflects to the drum surface in the form of 1s and 0s. Every place the beam touches, the drum's surface voltage reduces to approximately –100 volts. Wherever the beam hits, the area no longer has a huge negative charge, but instead, has a reduced negative voltage. The image on the drum is nothing more than dots of electrical charges and is invisible at this point in the process.

- **Developing:** Get the toner on the drum (develop the image). A **developing cylinder** (also called a developing roller) located inside the toner cartridge (right next to the drum) has a magnet that runs the length of the cylinder. When the cylinder rotates, toner is attracted to the cylinder because the toner has iron particles in it. The toner receives a negative electrostatic charge. The magnetic charge is a voltage level between –200 and –500 volts. The magnetized toner particles are attracted to the places on the drum where the light beam strikes. A **density control blade** controls the amount of toner allowed through to the drum. The blade usually connects to a toner control knob located inside the printer. The computer user can adjust the toner control knob to vary the print density. The image is no longer transparent on the drum. During this step, the image is black on the drum surface.

- **Transferring:** The image transfers to the paper. A **transfer corona** or a **transfer roller** (depending on the manufacturer) is located at the bottom of the printer. The transfer corona or roller places a positive charge on the back of the paper. The positive charge is strong enough to attract the negatively charged toner particles from the drum. The toner particles leave the drum and go onto the paper. At this point, the image is on the paper; however, the particles are held only by their magnetic charge.

- **Fusing:** Melt the toner into the paper. Heat and pressure make the image permanent on the paper. The paper, with the toner particles clinging to it, immediately passes through **fusing rollers** that apply pressure to the toner. The top roller applies intense heat (350º F) to the toner and paper that literally squeezes and melts the toner into the paper fibers.

 Always remember to allow a laser printer to cool down completely before working in the fusing roller area.

A cleaning pad located above the top fusing roller lightly coats the roller with silicon oil to prevent the paper sticking to the roller, which is often coated with Teflon. The cleaning pad also removes any residual toner from the roller.

A laser printer frequently makes an unusual noise. The noise heard is the fusing rollers turning when the printer is not in use. Otherwise, the fusing rollers would have an indentation on one side. Users not familiar with laser printers sometimes complain about this noise but it is a normal function of the laser printer.

- **Cleaning:** Wipe off any toner left on the drum. Some books list this as the first step, but the order does not matter because the process is a continuous cycle. During the cleaning stage a wiper blade or brush clears the photosensitive drum of any excess toner. Then an **erase lamp** neutralizes any charges left on the drum so the next printed page begins with a clean drum.

Some books, manuals, and reference materials use the six phases of the electrophotographic process instead of Hewlett-Packard's (HP) terms. The six phases are listed in Printer Table #1 with the equivalent HP terms. Keep in mind the same thing happens in each phase, only different terms are given to each phase.

PRINTER – TABLE #1

Laser Printer Process Terms

Electrophotographic Phase and Term	Electrophotographic Process	HP Term
Phase 1 Charge	Charge the photoconductive drum	Conditioning
Phase 2 Expose	Expose the photoconductor	Writing
Phase 3 Develop	Develop the image	Developing
Phase 4 Transfer	Transfer the image onto the paper	Transferring
Phase 5 Fuse	Fuse the image to the paper	Fusing
Phase 6 Clean	Clean the photoconductor	Cleaning

Every laser printer that uses the six-phase process is known as a **write-black laser printer**. These laser printers produce a black dot every place the beam touches the drum. Most laser printers use the write-black technology. **Write-white laser printers** reverse the process and the toner attracts everywhere the light beam does *not* touch the drum surface. Write-black printers print finer details, but write-white laser printers can produce darker shades of black areas.

To help with the inundation of data, Printer Table #2 lists the major parts of a printer with a short description of the purpose of each part.

PRINTER – TABLE #2

Laser Printer Parts

Part	Purpose
AC power supply	The main power supply for the printer
Cleaning blade	Wipes away excess toner from the drum before printing the next page
Cleaning pad	Applies oil to the fusing roller to prevent sticking. It also removes excess toner during the fusing stage.
Conditioning roller	Used instead of a primary corona wire to apply a uniform negative charge to the drum's surface
Control panel assembly	The user interface on the printer
Density control blade	Controls the amount of toner allowed on the drum (usually user adjustable)
Developing cylinder	Rotates to magnetize the toner particles before they go on the drum. Also called the developing roller.
Drum (photosensitive)	Accepts the light beams (data) from LEDs or a laser. Can be permanently damaged if exposed to light.
ECP (Electronic Control Package)	The main board for the printer. Usually holds most of the electronic circuitry, the CPU, and RAM.
Erase lamp	Neutralizes any residual charges on the drum before printing the next page
Fusing assembly	Holds the fusing roller, conditioning pad, pressure roller, and heating unit
Fusing rollers	Applies pressure and heat to fuse the toner into the paper
High voltage power supply	Provides a charge to the primary corona or conditioning roller, which in turn puts a charge on the drum
Main motor	Provides the power to drive several smaller motors that drive the gears, rollers, and drum
Primary corona (main corona)	Applies a uniform negative charge to the drum's surface
Scanner unit	The scanner unit includes a laser or an LED array that is used to write the 1s and 0s onto the drum surface.
Toner	Powder made of plastic resin particles and organic compounds bonded to iron oxide
Toner cartridge (EP cartridge)	Holds the conditioning roller, cleaning blade, drum, developing cylinder, and toner. Always remove before shipping a laser printer.
Transfer corona wire (transfer roller)	Applies a positive charge on the back of the paper to pull the toner from the drum onto the paper

PAPER

The type of paper used in a printer can affect its performance and cause problems. Dot matrix printers are the most forgiving because a mechanism physically impacts the paper. Ink jet printers, on the other hand, spray ink onto the paper, so the quality of paper determines how well the ink adheres to the paper. If the paper absorbs too much of the ink, the printout appears faded. If it does not absorb enough ink, it will run down the paper. For the laser printer, how well the paper heats and absorbs the toner also affects the printed output.

A **ream** of paper contains 500 sheets. At the end of most reams is an arrow that points to the side on which to print. If the paper manufacturer does not have an arrow, then the printable side is usually rougher than the other side. The printable side is the **wire side**. The other side of the paper is the **felt side** or **wax side**. Paper is rated according to pounds with 20 lb. paper as the most common. An ink jet printer works best with 24–28 lb. paper. Any paper 16 lbs. or less will probably not pass through any printer easily and cause paper jams. Always refer to the printer documentation for the recommended paper poundage.

Some expensive paper has a watermark visible if you hold the paper up to a light. The paper feels rough on the watermark. Sometimes ink jet printers and laser printers do not print properly on the watermark. Erasable bond paper also does not work well in laser printers because the paper does not allow the toner to fuse properly. Every type of paper imaginable is available for ink jet and laser printers: transparency paper for overhead projectors, high gloss, water resistant ink jet paper, fabric paper, greeting cards, labels, recycled, etc. Recycled paper may cause printer jams and produce lower print quality.

The highest quality paper available does not work well if the surrounding area has too much humidity. Humidity is paper's worst enemy. It causes the paper to stick together as well as reduce the paper's strength causing feed problems. Paper affected by humidity is sometimes noticeable because of the lumpy look it gives the paper. If any damaged paper is detected, discard it immediately. For best printing results, keep paper stored in a non-humid storage area.

Another simple and useful task to do is fan the paper before you insert it into the printer's bin. Also, do not overfill a printer's paper bin. For best results, only fill a printer's paper bin three-quarters full.

REFILLING CARTRIDGES AND REINKING RIBBONS

Much controversy exists when it comes to reinking dot matrix printer ribbons, refilling ink jet cartridges, or buying remanufactured laser cartridges. Many people concerned about the environment recycle their cartridges. Even if a company or an individual user decides not to purchase remanufactured products, some send their old empty cartridges to companies that do the remanufacturing. Refilling ink cartridges significantly lowers the printing costs.

If you refill the ink cartridges, add new ink before the old cartridge runs completely dry. This seems to give better results. If refilling ink cartridges, be sure the refill ink emulates the manufacturer's ink. Some ink refill companies use inferior ink that, over time, has a corrosive effect on the cartridge housing. A leaky cartridge or one that bursts causing ink to get into the printer is nothing but trouble.

Some ink refill companies have an exchange system. The old ink cartridges are placed into a plastic sealed bag and returned to the company where they are remanufactured. In return, the company ships a remanufactured cartridge filled with ink. If the empty ink cartridge sent to the company does not fit their standards criteria, the cartridge is thrown away.

When it comes to laser cartridge remanufacturing, the most important components are the drum and wiper blade that cleans the drum. Many laser cartridge remanufacturers use the same parts over and over again. A quality refill company will disassemble the cartridge and inspect each part. When the drum and wiper blade are worn, they are replaced with new parts.

Reinking a dot matrix printer ribbon is not a good idea. It can cause a mess and the ink is sometimes an inferior quality that causes deterioration of the printhead over time. Because dot matrix printer ribbons are so inexpensive, just replace them.

PRINT DRIVERS

How an application outputs to a printer is determined by the operating system used. In the DOS environment, every application includes print drivers. A **print driver** is a small piece of software specifically written for a particular printer. The print driver enables the printer's specific features and allows an application to communicate with the printer. The number of print drivers included with a DOS application depends on the software manufacturer.

Every printer model needs a print driver for each DOS application. Windows applications use a single print driver—one written for the specific printer.

Windows ships with various print drivers, all of which allow basic communication and access to the printer. For best results and performance, use the driver provided by the manufacturer or better yet, one downloaded from the Internet. Use the driver designed for the operating system installed.

Printers must accept as much data as possible from the computer, process that data, output it, communicate to the computer the need for more data, accept more data, and continue the process all over again. With Windows, a print spooler is used. A **print spooler**, or Print Manager, is a software program that intercepts the printer's request to print. Instead of going directly to the printer, the data goes to the hard drive. The spooler then controls the data from the hard drive going to the printer. Some printers come with their own Print Manager that replaces the one included with Windows.

The print spooler's transmission retry option is the number of seconds the Print Manager waits before giving up on trying to send the printer more data. If the document contains multiple fonts, font sizes, or graphics, the transmission retry settings may need to be changed. For Windows, use the Printers control panel. Right-click on the *specific printer.* Select *Properties* from the drop-down menu and click on the *Details* tab to change the transmission retry setting.

FONTS

A **font** is a group of printable characters from a particular style such as Times New Roman, Script, Arial, and Courier. The **font style** refers to the appearance of the type such as bold or italic. The **font size** is in points such as 10pt. or 12pt. The larger the point size, the larger the type appears on the paper. Point size is different from **characters per inch (cpi)**. The larger the cpi, the smaller the font size.

The most basic font is the raster font. **Raster Fonts** are nothing more than dots creating an image. Dot matrix printers frequently use raster fonts. **Vector fonts** are a little more complicated and are created from a mathematical formula. All characters created using vector fonts are simply a series of lines between two points. Vector fonts are also known as **outline fonts**. The outline of each character is used to produce the printed output. The outline defines the shape of the character, but not the size. Outline fonts are **scaleable,** meaning the character can be created at any size. The most advanced type of outline font is the **TrueType font** with characters that can be scaled (enlarged or shrunk) and rotated (turned on its side or upside down).

A printer can load fonts or use fonts three ways: (1) internally, (2) from a font cartridge, or (3) from the hard drive. A printer's **internal fonts** are stored inside the printer on a ROM chip. Internal fonts speed up printer performance. **Font cartridges** are add-on features for printers that allow different fonts to be loaded into the printer's memory. Fonts that load from the hard drive, known as **soft fonts**, are the slowest type of fonts. The fonts come from the hard drive and transmit to the printer instead of all the processing done in the printer. Nevertheless, storing fonts on the hard drive keeps down printer costs.

Each printer has its own **page description language (PDL)** that is a translator between the computer and the printer. The page description language handles the overall page look and has commands that treat the entire document as a single graphic. The two most popular page description languages are Adobe Systems Inc.'s **PostScript** and Hewlett-Packard's **Printer Control Language (HPPCL).**

If a document is created in a computer that has a PostScript printer driver loaded, and the document is taken to another computer without a PostScript printer driver, there is a good chance the document will not print properly.

PRINTER INSTALLATION

A printer is one of the easiest devices to install. Always refer to the printer documentation for exact installation and configuration specifics. The steps to install a printer that attaches to a parallel port are listed below:

1. Take the printer out of its box and remove any shipping materials. The number one problem with new printers not working properly is all the shipping safeguards are not removed properly.
2. Connect the printer cable from the printer to the computer. Using a cable that complies with the IEEE 1284 standard is important for today's computers.

3. Connect the power cord from the printer to the wall outlet, surge protector, or UPS outlet.
4. Load paper and ribbon/ink/cartridge into the printer according to manufacturer's instructions.
5. Turn on the printer and verify the power light is on.
6. If the printer has a self-test routine, execute it by referring to the printer documentation. The self-test ensures a printer is operational.
7. Turn on the computer.
8. Install the print drivers by following the manufacturer's instructions for the operating system.
9. Perform a test print that verifies communication between the computer and printer.

For USB devices, the installation process is a little bit different. The same basic steps are done except some devices have you install the driver before the USB printer is connected to the USB port! Always refer to the manufacturer's installation instructions for connecting USB printers. The overall steps are to unpack the printer, install paper and ribbon/ink/cartridge, connect power cord, connect cable to printer and computer, load driver, and test. The only difference is whether you install the driver before or after connecting the device.

The key to a successful printer installation is to read the printer documentation, use a good cable, load the latest printer drivers (from the manufacturer), and test. Many hours of frustration for the computer user and the technician can be avoided by doing the research during the install, not after a problem occurs.

PRINTER PREVENTIVE MAINTENANCE

People sometimes forget to plug their printer into a surge protector or UPS. The printer can be damaged by electrical storms and power fluctuations just as a computer can. The laser printers' AC power module and fuser assembly are especially susceptible to power problems. Protect any printer as well as the computer, but always make sure that the UPS has the ability to handle the higher power laser printer.

If the printer has trouble feeding the paper, always be sure you are using the correct type of paper and that printing occurs on the correct side. Refer to the chapter section on paper. One vendor quotes that 80 percent of all paper jams are due to inferior paper quality, poor paper condition such as humidity, or an operator-related problem such as the wrong paper size selected in the software program.

Dot matrix printers are very hardy and require little maintenance except for cleaning. However, dot matrix printers that use tractor-fed paper periodically require vacuuming. The chaff produced by the tractor-fed paper accumulates on the bottom of the printer and spreads throughout the printer.

Rubber rollers are normally found in the paper transport system. Over time, the rollers become slick from use. Special cleaners such as Rubber Rejuvenator are available for rubber printer rollers that have a hard time picking up the paper and sending it through the printer. Some printers have a special cleaning page for cleaning the rollers. Through software or pushing front panel buttons, print the cleaning page and run it back through the printer. Refer to the printer's manual for exact procedures. If a cleaner is unavailable, scrub the rollers with a wire brush or sandpaper to roughen them up a bit to enable them to better pick up the paper. If you do not have sandpaper or a wire brush, use the sharp edge of a paper clip to roughen up the rubber part of the roller so it can grip the paper.

Laser printers, on the other hand, do require some periodic maintenance. If any toner appears inside the printer, do *not* use a normal vacuum cleaner! The toner particles seep through the vacuum cleaner bag into the vacuum's motor (where the particles melt). Special vacuum bags are available for some vacuum cleaners.

If the laser printer has a transfer corona instead of a transfer roller, clean it when you replace the toner cartridge. Many laser printers include a small cleaning brush (usually green) to clean the corona wire. Some new toner cartridges come with a cotton swab just for the purpose of cleaning the transfer corona. The transfer corona wire is normally in the bottom of the printer protected by monofilament wires. Be extremely careful not to break the wires or the transfer corona. Insert the swab between the monofilament wires and rub the wire with the swab.

Sometimes the primary corona wire inside the toner cartridge becomes dirty. If the wire is accessible, it can be cleaned using a cotton swab. Sometimes, if either corona wire has particles clinging to it, you can use a small amount of alcohol to dampen the swab and remove the dirt.

Ozone is a gas produced by the laser printer. The printer's **ozone filter** removes the gas as well as any toner and paper dust particles. The ozone filter needs replacing after a specific number of usage hours. Check the printer's documentation for the filter's replacement schedule. Simply vacuuming the ozone filter does not clean it. The ozone molecules are trapped and absorbed by the ozone filter. If you forget to replace the ozone filter, people in the immediate vicinity may develop headaches, nausea, irritability, and depression. Some laser printers do not have an ozone filter. With these printers, the surrounding area must be well ventilated.

The **fuser cleaning pad** (sometimes known as the fuser wand) sits above the top fusing roller and is normally replaced at the same time as the toner cartridge. However, the cleaning pad sometimes becomes dirty before it is time to replace the cartridge. If so, remove the cleaning pad. Hold the pad over a trash can. Take a small flat-tipped screwdriver and use the shaft to rub along the felt pad. Replace the cleaning pad and wipe the screwdriver with a cloth.

The fusing roller sometimes has particles that cling to it. Once the assembly cools, *gently* scrape the particles from the roller. A small amount of alcohol on a soft, lint-free cloth can help with stubborn spots.

If the laser printer uses a laser beam to write data to the photosensitive drum, the laser beam does not directly touch the drum. Instead, at least one mirror, if not more, is used to redirect the laser beam onto the drum's surface. The mirror(s) need to be cleaned periodically with a lint-free cloth.

After performing preventive maintenance on a printer, the pages may appear smudged or slightly dirty. Run a couple of print jobs through the printer to allow the dust to settle (so to speak). Never do any kind of maintenance on any computer part or peripheral without testing the results of the maintenance or the repair!

Quality printer replacement parts and preventive maintenance kits are important to the technician. If a printer must be sent away for repair, warranty work, etc., make sure to remove the toner cartridge, platen knobs, and power cords before boxing the printer. Call the receiving company to see if you should send the toner cartridge in a separate box.

PRINTERS IN THE WINDOWS ENVIRONMENT

The operating system plays a big part in controlling the printer. When working in a Windows environment, three areas are essential for a technician to know (besides knowing how to print): (1) configuration utilities, (2) resource allocation and viewing, and (3) printer settings. Sometimes these areas overlap, but a technician must be able to configure and maintain a printer in Windows.

To print in Windows, use one of the following methods:

- Open the file in the appropriate application. Click on the *File* menu item and click on the *Print* option.
- Drag the file to print to the printer's icon in the Printers folder.
- Create a shortcut icon on the desktop for a specific printer and drag the file to this icon.
- Right-click on the filename and select the *Print* option.
- From within the application, press the *CTRL+P* keys down and the print window appears.
- From within an application, click on the printer icon located under the menu bar.

The Windows Printers control panel is used frequently to add a printer, remove a printer, temporarily halt a print job (pause the printer) and define or change printer settings such as resolution, paper type, paper orientation, etc. The Windows Add Printer wizard steps you through the installation process. This utility starts automatically when Windows detects a newly installed printer. Once the wizard starts you must select whether the printer is a local printer (used by only one computer) or a network printer. If the local printer option is selected, you will have to install a print driver. For best performance, use the latest printer manufacturer's driver for the operating system installed. You must also select the port to which the printer attaches (COM or LPT). The wizard also asks if this printer is to be the default printer.

A **default printer** is the one that applications use without any configuration changes. Even if you reply *No* to this prompt, a printer can be changed to the default printer at a later date.

To configure a printer as a default printer, access the Printers control panel. Right-click on the *appropriate printer* icon (the one that you want to set as the default). Click on the *Set As Default* item. The default printer has a checkmark above the printer icon in the Printers control panel window.

Right-clicking on a *printer* icon also gives you access to the *Properties* option. Through this selection, several tabs are available (depending on the printer model). Common tabs include General, Details, Sharing, Paper, Graphics, Fonts, and Device Options. Printer Figure #6 shows a printer's Properties window.

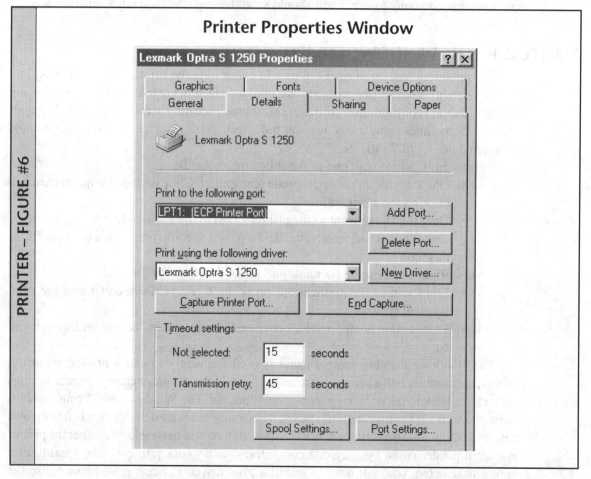

Use Device Manager in Windows 9x and 2000 to examine system resources. With NT, use NT Diagnostics and the Ports control panel to see the interrupts and I/O addresses. Windows 98 and Windows 2000 have a great utility called MSINFO (System Information)

that shows conflicts without having to expand each Device Manager category. To access MSINFO in Windows 98, click on the *Start* button, point to *Programs*, *Accessories*, and *System Tools*. Click on the *System Information* item. Double-click on the *Hardware Resources* option. Click on the *Conflicts/Sharing* selection and after a couple of seconds, the right side shows the IRQ number along with the name of the device and frequently the manufacturer.

To access System Information in 2000 Professional or 2000 Server, click on the *Start* button and point to the *Settings* selection. Point to the *Control Panel* option and double-click on the *Administrative Tools* control panel icon. Double-click on the *System Information* icon. Click on the + *(plus sign)* next to the *Components* folder. Click on the *Problem Devices* folder. Any devices with hardware conflicts are listed in the right window. The tabs could be different on each printer, but many of them are the same. Printers Table #3 lists the most common printer Properties window tabs and general purpose.

PRINTER – TABLE #3

Printer Properties' Tabs Overview

Tab	Comments
General	Displays the printer name and has a button for printing a test page
Details	Used to specify the port, install or display driver, configure Windows printer communication parameters including timeout, pool, and port configuration
Sharing	Used to share the printer over a network
Paper	Used to set paper orientation, size, and tray number
Graphics	Allows setting resolution, graphics intensity (darkness), and graphics mode
Fonts	Used to display and install printer fonts
Device Options	Used to adjust print density and quality, display amount of RAM installed in printer, and adjust printer memory tracking

The General tab's Print Test Page button is important for a technician to determine if the operating system can perform basic communication with the printer. The Detail tab is very important because a new driver can be loaded from here.

Look back to Printer Figure #6 and locate the Capture Printer Port, End Capture, Spool Settings, and Port Settings buttons as well as the Timeout settings section. The Capture Printer Port and End Capture buttons are used in a networking environment to map the printer port to a network drive. This is handy when printing from older DOS applications in a network environment. NT and Windows 2000 do not have this option in the Properties window. Instead, you must issue a command from a command prompt (NET USE command).

The Spool Settings option details how the print spool operates. Printers Figure #7 shows this screen.

Spool Settings Button

Spool Settings [?] [X]

- ● Spool print jobs so program finishes printing faster
    - ○ Start printing after last page is spooled
    - ● Start printing after first page is spooled
- ○ Print directly to the printer

Spool data format: EMF ▼

EMF
RAW

- ○ Enable bi-directio
- ○ Disable bi-directional support for this printer

[OK]   [Cancel]   [Restore Defaults]

The first section has the place to enable Windows 9x print spooling through the Spool print jobs as program finishes printing faster radio button. In NT and 2000, this option is on the Advanced tab and it is called Spool the document (for enabling spooling) or Print directly to a printer (for no print spooling). If spooling is turned on (enabled), then data is sent to be temporarily stored on the hard drive. Whenever the printer is ready to accept data, it is retrieved from the hard drive. This frees up the application so your printer can do other tasks.

Spooling should be disabled if the computer does not have at least 300MB of free hard drive space. Note that if a printer is shared (other computers can print to the printer through a network), spooling must be enabled and as much free hard drive space available as possible. Some people use older computers to connect printers to a network. These computers are not used for anything but print spooling. They are designated as print servers.

Some devices such as tape drives, which run off the parallel port, require or function better when spooling is disabled. The SPOOL32.EXE program controls the spooling function. Also, when troubleshooting printer problems, the spooler can be disabled to eliminate it as the problem source.

Once spooling is enabled, there are two more choices: Start printing after the last page is spooled or Start printing after the first page is spooled. These two selections determine when data is sent from the spooler (hard drive) to the printer: after the entire document has been written to the hard drive or as soon as the first page has been written to the drive.

The next section is also important—Spool data format. This setting determines how the data is stored on the hard drive. The EMF (Enhanced MetaFile) is the default setting and it is a 32-bit non-printer dependent format that performs faster than RAW. If you are having printing problems, and the documentation or your research directs you to change the spooling data format, this is the setting referenced. The RAW data format is printer-specific and it requires extra time to convert the printing data before it is saved to the hard drive. In NT and Windows 2000, this setting is normally found under PrintProcessor (General tab in NT and Advanced tab in Windows 2000) and it is called Always Spool RAW Datatype.

The Port Settings button is used to enable print spooler for DOS printing and whether or not to check the port before sending data. The Timeout settings section is used to define the amount of time (1) Windows waits for the printer to come online (the Not Selected option) or (2) how long Windows waits for the printer to be ready before reporting an error (the Transmission retry setting). If you have a laser printer that takes a long time to warm up, you send documents before a printer has time to come online and it frequently displays an error, or you have problems when large documents print, adjust these settings.

WINDOWS PRINTER TROUBLESHOOTING

Windows uses a single print driver for all applications. Windows has a Troubleshooter tool. To access the tool in Windows 95, click on the *Start* button and click on *Help*. Click on the *Contents* tab and double-click on the *Troubleshooting* topic. Enter the Troubleshooter by double-clicking on the *If you Have Trouble Printing* option. Follow the screens to troubleshoot the printer.

To access the Troubleshooter tool in Windows 98, click on the *Start* button. Click on the *Help* option and then click on the *Troubleshooting* option. Click on the *Windows 98 Troubleshooters* selection and then click on *Print*. Follow the screens to troubleshoot the printer.

In NT Workstation, access the Troubleshooter tool by clicking on the *Start* button and clicking on the *Help* option. Select the *Index* tab and type in *printers* in the text box. Double-click on the *Troubleshooting* selection and the troubleshooter displays in the right window.

Windows 2000's Troubleshooter tool is accessed by clicking on *Start* and clicking on the *Contents* tab. Click on the first topic, *Start Here*. Click on the *Troubleshooting and Maintenance* option. A list of troubleshooters appears in the right window. Click on the *Print* option for printer checks.

If the Troubleshooter tool does not help, run a self-test on your printer. Refer to the printer's documentation for how to perform this test. Many printers require you to hold down a specific button while powering on the printer. If the self-test works, the printer is usually fine and the problem lies in the cable, port, IRQ, I/O address, software driver, or printer settings.

If the self-test worked, try printing from Notepad. Restart the computer and click on the *Start* button. Point to *Programs* and then point to *Accessories*. Click on the *Notepad* option. Type a few characters in the blank window. Click on the *File* menu option and click on *Print*. If the file prints, then your problem may involve printing from only one application. Troubleshoot the problem application by reloading it or contacting the company who produces the application.

If Notepad printing does not work, try printing from a command prompt. In Windows 95, restart the computer and press *F8* when the message "Starting Windows 95" appears. For Windows 98, hold the *CTRL* key down while the computer boots. If this does not work, use the *F8* key as Windows starts. Windows 2000 also used the F8 key to bring up the Advanced Startup Menu options. NT does not have this option of booting from a command prompt. You could insert a boot disk and boot from it and do the steps. For Windows 9x and 2000, select the *Safe Mode Command Prompt Only* option.

Note that the following commands work for a printer attached to a LPT port (parallel port). Some USB printers do not use standard LPT or PRN port settings. For a dot matrix or ink jet printer, type the following command:

COPY C:\WINDOWS\MOUSE.TXT LPT1

For a laser printer, type the following command:

COPY C:\WINDOWS\MOUSE.TXT LPT1 /B

For a postscript laser printer, type the following command:

COPY C:\WINDOWS\SYSTEM\TESTPS.TXT LPT1

For Windows NT and 2000, click on the *Start* button and select the *Command Prompt* option. At the prompt, type the following command:

DIR > LPT1

For a postscript printer connected to an NT or 2000 computer, type the following command:

COPY C:\WINNT\SYSTEM\TESTPS.TXT LPT1

Note: The commands listed above assume the printer connects to LPT1 and the operating system is loaded in the default directories on the hard drive. Also, when you copy a file, you may have to press form feed or resume on the printer to get the paper to eject.

When copying test files directly to the printer from the command prompt, the operating system and the print driver are out of the loop. If this test does *not* work, remove any print-sharing devices such as a switch box. Connect the printer directly to the port and try the test again. If no print sharing devices are installed, perform a printer self-test and check the printer's power cables and connections. The problem is in the printer, port, cable, IRQ, or I/O address settings.

If you print from a prompt, but not with Windows, the print spool setting or bi-directional printing setting may need adjustment. Restart the computer. To remove the print spooling, use the Start menu's *Settings*, *Printers* option. Right-click on the problem printer icon. Select the *Properties* option. Refer to the chapter section on these settings for specific operating systems.

To disable bi-directional printing, in the same window click on the *Disable bi-directional support for this printer* radio button. Try printing from Notepad. If the printing works, try different combinations of spool settings and bi-directional support settings for optimum performance.

Free hard drive space is important for print spooling. Insufficient free space can cause print jobs to have problems. Another problem may be the printer driver conflicts with the installed video driver. To determine if the video driver is the problem, change the video driver to a generic one such as the VGA driver. If the problem goes away, there is a definite conflict.

If the printer works, then the printer, port, and printer cable are all operational and the problem is in the operating system. To see if the printer driver is the problem, use the Add Printer wizard to install the Generic/Text Only printer driver. See the exercise for more information.

While using an ECP port, if there are problems printing or the output is garbled, the ECP option can usually be changed to the SPP through Setup. To configure for non-ECP printing, double-click the *System* control panel. Click on the *Device Manager* tab. Click on the *Ports* branch. Double-click on the *ECP* port. On the Driver tab, click on the *Change Driver* button. Click on the *Show all devices* button. Click on *Standard Port Types* in the Manufacturers window. In the Models window, click *Printer Port*. Click on the *OK* button. Continue clicking on the *OK* button until you return to the System Properties window. Then, click on the *Close* button. In NT, use the NT Diagnostics tool.

If there are problems printing to any bi-directional printer, Device Manager does not allow changing an ECP port to run in SPP mode, or unusual characters appear on the printout, etc., try using the alternate LPT.VXD file. The operating system CD-ROM has the alternate LPT.VXD file located in the DRIVERS\PRINTER\LPT folder. The file is also available on the Internet from Microsoft. Rename the old LPT.VXD file located in SYSTEM subdirectory. Then copy the alternate LPT.VXD file into the SYSTEM subdirectory. Restart the computer when you finish copying the file.

If you reload the printer driver, the old printer driver must be removed first. Some manufacturers have very specific instructions for removing their driver. Always follow their directions. Most of them do something similar to the following: click on the *Start* button and select the *Settings* option followed by the *Printers* option. Right-click on the *printer* icon for the printer driver to be deleted. Click on the *Delete* option. Click on the *Yes* button when prompted if all the associated printer files are to be deleted. To reinstall the printer, use the Add Printer wizard. Refer to the steps at the end of the chapter if necessary.

GENERAL PRINTER TROUBLESHOOTING

The printing hardware subsystem consists of the printer, cable, and communications port. If something is wrong with the hardware, it is normally one of these three areas. Always check the connections and the power between each area. The printer has the highest failure rate of the three because it is a mechanical device with motors, plastic gears, and moving parts. Printers normally have a self-test routine. Refer to the printer's documentation to determine how to run the test. On some printers, you hold down a specific front-panel button or two while applying power. Others require changing a dip switch. If a printer's self-test operates properly, the printer is operational. If the printer checks out, the problem is the port, the cable, or software. Another problem could be that the printer is not configured for the correct parallel, serial, or network port. Check that the printer is configured for the proper port. Refer to the printer's documentation for specifics on how to configure the printer for a specific port.

If the printer is having trouble feeding paper, the first clue is to see how far the paper has gone along the paper path before it jammed or could not go any farther. Many paper feeding problems are due to poor paper quality or the rubber rollers that move the paper along the paper path. Refer back to this chapter's preventive maintenance section on rubber rollers.

The second highest failing part is the port. A loopback plug and diagnostics can be used to troubleshoot the parallel port to see if it fails. A loopback plug is a special connector that attaches to the parallel port. Diagnostic routines send signals out a pin that is tied to a different pin. The test checks to see if the signal returns back into the computer. Some diagnostics include the parallel port loopback plug as part of its package. Connect a working printer to the port and print from a command prompt.

If the printer uses the USB, the following is a checklist for troubleshooting:

- If the computer stops responding and the USB device is suspect, power the computer off and then back on again.
- The BIOS settings may have to be enabled for USB devices. Different BIOS manufacturers list the USB settings differently. Check for an Enabling on-board USB setting or under the PCI section. If you install a USB host adapter and the motherboard also supports USB ports, you may have to disable the motherboard ports through BIOS.
- Use Device Manager to check and see if USB is listed. Look at the Universal Serial Bus controllers section. If it is not, check BIOS settings or update BIOS. If the USB device is listed, ensure no resource conflicts exist.
- If there is a USB hub connected to the USB port, disconnect the hub and connect the USB printer directly into the USB port to see if the problem is the hub.
- With the computer's power on, disconnect the USB printer and reconnect it. Go into Device Manager and ensure that there is only one listing for the USB printer.
- Some USB devices have device drivers. Check on the Internet for updated drivers.
- Disconnect the USB printer while the computer is powered on. Power down the computer. Power back on the computer. Insert the USB printer cable into the USB port. The system should automatically detect and install the printer.

- Verify the USB device works by plugging it into another USB port or another computer's USB port.
- Check that the proper USB cable is being used.

The last part to check is the printer cable. Remember cables are not normally faulty. Just watch out for enabling the ECP mode without having a cable that handles ECP operations. A USB cable can be rated as high-speed or low-speed. The high-speed cables have more shielding and can support the higher 12Mbps (40Mbps for USB 2.0-rated cables). If a high-speed USB device attaches to a low-speed cable, data loss can occur. Make sure you have the proper USB cable for a printer that attaches to a USB port.

On the software side, troubleshooting involves narrowing the problem down to the print driver. Because Windows uses one print driver for all applications, check the printing from within several software packages. Use a simple text program such as Notepad to see if simple text will print. Printers need memory to print multiple pages of complex graphics. If the printer prints a couple pages and then stops, or prints half a page, ejects the paper, and then prints the other half of the page and ejects the paper, then the printer's memory needs upgrading. If printing does not occur in all of the software packages tested, the problem is most likely the software driver. See the earlier section for specific Windows tips.

DOT MATRIX PRINTER TROUBLESHOOTING

When technicians state that a printhead is not firing, one or more of the printwires are not coming out of the printhead to impact the ribbon. A printhead that is not firing is evidenced by one or more white lines that appear where the printed dots should be. On a printed page, the white line appears horizontally in the middle of a line. The most likely problem is the printhead. However be aware that the problem could be a bad driver transistor on the main circuit board or a loose cable that attaches to the printhead. But, because the printhead is a mechanical part, it is the most suspect.

If the printed page appears to have light print, adjust the printhead gap to place the printhead closer to the ribbon or replace the ribbon. If the print is light, then dark, the printer ribbon may not be advancing properly. One of the shafts that insert into each end of the ribbon may not be turning properly. Under the shaft is a set of gears that do not always mesh properly. Also, there is a motor that handles ribbon movement; the motor may need replacement. A faulty ribbon can also cause the carriage to seize up. Remove the ribbon and power up the printer. If the carriage moves when the ribbon is removed, but it will not move when the ribbon is installed, replace the ribbon. Some printers have belts that move the printhead across the page. If a belt is worn, loose, or slipping, erratic printing occurs.

If the printer prints continuously on the same line, be sure the setting for tractor-fed paper or friction-fed paper is correct. After that, the motor that controls paper movement may need replacement. If the printer moves the paper up a small bit after printing, the model may have the Auto Tear Off feature enabled. The Auto Tear Off feature is used with perforated forms used in many businesses. See the printer's documentation to disable this feature.

INK JET PRINTER TROUBLESHOOTING

Ink jet printers frequently have a built-in printhead cleaning routine. Access the routine through the printer's buttons or through software. Most manufacturers recommend cleaning the ink jet cartridge only when there is a problem such as lines or dots missing from the printed output. Otherwise, cleaning the ink jet cartridge with this method wastes ink and shortens the print cartridge's life span.

Usually ink jet manufacturers include an alignment program to align the dots more precisely. Use the alignment program when vertical lines or characters do not align properly. Always refer to the printer's documentation for troubleshooting programs such as the printhead cleaning and alignment routines.

LASER PRINTER TROUBLESHOOTING

Lasers have more mechanical and electronic circuitry than the other printer types, which means there are more things that can go wrong. The following list contains some common symptoms and possible solutions.

- Black streaks appear on the paper or the print is not sharp—check fuser cleaning pad for toner particles and use a small screwdriver to scrape off the excess particles before reinstalling.
- Output appears darker in some spots than others—remove the toner cartridge. Gently rock the toner cartridge back and forth to redistribute the toner. If this does not fix the problem, turn down the toner's density by adjusting a dial setting. Refer to the printer's documentation for this adjustment. The dial adjustment may be necessary if the printer is using a technology known as **RET (Resolution Enhancement Technology).** A drawback to RET is a phenomenon known as **toner puddling** where more toner dots are in some locations than in others.
- Print appears light—adjust the darkness setting on the printer or through the printer's operating system settings. Damp paper could also cause this symptom. Use fresh paper of the proper weight and finish. If the print appears consistently dark, adjust the darkness setting. Clean the mirrors inside the printer if necessary.
- A horizontal line appears periodically throughout the printout—the problem is one of the rollers. Check all rollers to see if they are dirty or gouged and need replacing. The rollers in the laser printer are not all the same size, so the distance between the lines is the circumference of the roller. That is an easy way to tell which rollers are definitely not the problem or which ones are likely candidates. A printing error that occurs every 3.75 inches indicates the drum is defective.

- White vertical line(s) appear—the corona wires may have paper bits or something else stuck on them. This can also be caused by something being caught in the developer unit (located in the cartridge). Replace the cartridge to see if this is the problem.

Many laser problems involve the toner cartridge. That is good because the cartridge is one part people normally have on hand. Various symptoms can occur because of the toner cartridge: smearing, horizontal streaking, vertical streaking, faded print, one vertical black line, a single horizontal black line, a white streak on one side, etc. One of the easiest things to do is to remove the toner cartridge, hold the cartridge in front of you with both hands, and rock the cartridge away from you and then back toward you. Reinsert the cartridge back into the printer and test.

Sometimes, the primary corona wire or the conditioning roller inside the toner cartridge needs to be cleaned. Clean the corona wires using the provided brush or with a cotton swab. Dampen the cotton swab with alcohol, if necessary. Clean the conditioning roller with a lint-free cloth. Dampen the cloth with alcohol, if necessary.

To prove if a problem is in the toner cartridge or elsewhere in the printer, send any output to the printer. Wait until the printer is through with the writing stage and before the toner fuses to the paper, open the laser printer cover and remove the paper. (Determining exactly when to open the cover may take several attempts.) If the paper is error-free, the problem is most likely in the transfer corona (or transfer roller) or fusing assembly.

Another common problem occurs when the laser printer does not have enough memory. One symptom is that when printing, the printer blinks as if it is accepting data. Then, the printer quits blinking and nothing appears or the printer prints only half the page. This could also be caused by insufficient hard drive space when spooling is enabled. Some printers give an error code if there is not enough memory. For example, in a Hewlett-Packard laser printer, the error code 20 indicates insufficient memory. If the printer needs more memory, upgrade it, send the print job fewer pages at a time, reduce the printer resolution such as from 1200 dpi to 600 dpi, reduce the size of the graphics, or standardize the fonts. Font standardization can be accomplished by not using as many font types, styles, or font sizes. When print spooling is enabled, make sure there is ample hard drive free space. Delete old files/applications and run SCANDISK to make more space available.

Experience is the best teacher when it comes to printers. Work on a couple of dot matrix models, a couple of ink jet printers, and a couple of laser printer models, and you will see the majority of problems. Each type of printer has very few circuit boards to replace. Normally the problems are in the moving parts. Many printer problems are software-related. The following exercises help set up printers for the Windows environments. The exercises for the chapter follow the review questions.

Name _____

PRINTER REVIEW QUESTIONS

1. What subsystems do all printers have in common?

2. What major printer subsystem handles dot matrix printer ribbon movement?

3. What major printer subsystem handles moving the paper from the fuser rollers to a laser printer's output bin?

4. What major printer subsystem tells the printer how to print a particular font size?

5. What major printer subsystem sends an error message that the ink jet printer is out of paper?

6. [T / F]   Most printers connect to the parallel or serial port.

7. If a customer asks for a printer recommendation, which type of printer would you recommend and why?

8. A computer user has one printer installed on the parallel port. Which of the following ports can be used to connect a second printer that has both parallel and USB capabilities? (Pick all that apply)
   [LPT1 / LPT2 / LPT3 / LPT378 / COM1 / COM2 / USB]

9. Of the possible answers shown in Question 8, which port would be the normal choice?

10. How does the first parallel port get the port name of LPT1?

11. What is the first I/O address scanned by the BIOS for parallel ports?

12. What is the second I/O address scanned by the BIOS for parallel ports?

13. If a system has only one parallel printer attached and it is assigned I/O address 278, what LPT port number is the printer assigned and why?

14. What type of connector does an ECP parallel port have on the back of the computer?
    [25-pin male / 25-pin female / Centronics / Mini-Centronics]

15. Explain the difference between SPP, EPP, and ECP printer ports.

16. How can you tell if a computer has an ECP port?

17. Describe the three connectors supported by the IEEE 1284 standard.

18. Which switch box [automatic or manual] is best for a laser printer and why?

19. List two ways to share a printer with another computer.

20. What type of printer is best for multipart forms?

21. What are some common dot matrix printhead pin configurations?

22. What does a dot matrix printhead *not firing* mean?

23. A dot matrix printer that normally prints bi-directionally starts printing only left to right. How do you fix this problem?

24. Why is an ink jet cartridge better than a dot matrix printhead?

25. What is the major difference between ink jet printers and dot matrix printers?

26. [T / F]   Most ink jet printers use heat to make the ink squirt onto the paper.

27. What can a user do who is having problems with ink smearing on an ink jet printer's output ?

28. What stage of the laser printing process prepares the photosensitive drum for use?

29. Explain how data is written to the laser printer drum.

30. [T / F] The laser printer's conditioning phase precedes the writing phase.

31. How does the toner inside a laser printer's toner cartridge get magnetically charged?

32. [T / F] The amount of toner allowed onto the laser printer's drum is normally adjustable.

33. Explain how the toner permanently adheres to the paper from a laser printer.

34. A customer calls to explain that their new laser printer makes this funny sound like it is printing something every 30 minutes, but nothing comes out of the printer. What is the solution to this problem?

35. [T / F] In the laser printing process, another name for the Conditioning phase is the Expose stage.

36. Do reinked dot matrix printer ribbons produce the same output as a new ribbon? Explain your answer.

37. Do refilled ink jet cartridges produce the same output as a new ink jet cartridge? Explain your answer.

38. Explain criteria to expect when purchasing remanufactured laser toner cartridges.

39. A Windows 2000 computer has Visio 2000, Office 2000, Adobe Illustrator, and Cisco Network Designer loaded. How many print drivers are needed for this computer?

40. [T / F] NT Workstation works best with an NT print driver.

41. [T / F] A Windows 9x printer driver works in Windows 3.x.

42. Explain what a hard drive has to do with a print spooler.

43. Give an example of a font.

44. [T / F] PostScript is a page description language every laser printer supports.

45. What printer check proves that the printer is operational (not checking for communication between the operating system and the printer)?

46. What is different about installing a USB printer?

47. What is the best preventive maintenance routine for a dot matrix printer?

48. How do you handle printer rollers that slip and cause the paper to not feed properly through the printer?

49. Why should you *not* use compressed air to remove toner from a laser printer?

50. Why should you *not* use a regular vacuum cleaner to remove toner from a laser printer?

51. List two ways to print from Windows.

52. What Windows utility helps with printer installations?

53. What is the difference between a network printer and a local printer?

54. What port is commonly chosen during a new printer installation assuming the printer connects to a parallel port?

55. List an instance when a printer *would not* be chosen as a default printer during the installation process.

56. What control panel is used to set a printer as the one used by applications?

57. What tool do you use in Windows 2000 to check for resource conflicts?

58. For what is the Device options printer tab used?

59. What printer properties tab contains the Print test page button?

60. What Windows 2000 tab allows print spool configuration?

61. What is a print server?

62. What is the default spool data format?

63. Describe the steps to access the Troubleshooter tool in Windows 98.

64. Describe the steps to access the Troubleshooter tool in Windows 2000.

65. If the Troubleshooter tool does not solve a printing problem, what is your next step?

66. If you can print from a command prompt, but not when Windows loads, what might be the problem?

67. If you copy a file to the printer, how do you eject the paper from the printer?

68. List two USB troubleshooting tips.

69. If a white line appears across one row of dot matrix print, what are the possible suspect components?

70. What is the most likely laser printer suspect component if a horizontal white line appears periodically throughout a printed page?

71. List one symptom of insufficient memory on a laser printer.

 Name _____

PRINTER FILL-IN-THE-BLANK

1. The _____ program can be used to see the serial and parallel ports detected by the BIOS.

2. The first printer detected in the system is assigned the name _____.

3. The IEEE _____ standard covers parallel devices.

4. _____ printing allows the printer to send messages that display on the computer.

5. The _____ standard improves on the Enhanced Parallel Port (EPP) standard.

6. Any _____-compatible cable works in the ECP mode.

7. A device that allows two printers to connect to the same parallel port is a _____.

8. A _____ switch box has a knob on the front to switch between printers.

9. A print _____ can be a computer that connects to a printer and a network, but is not used for production.

10. An _____ printer produces color output at a moderate price.

11. The _____ printer produces the highest quality output at the fastest rate.

12. The _____ printer is also called an impact printer.

13. Dot matrix _____ houses the printwires that strike the ribbon to produce a dot on the paper.

14. A dot matrix printer speed is measured in _____.

15. The _____ on a dot matrix printer needs replacing at times because the pins strike a ribbon.

16. _____ printers have tiny nozzles from which ink squirts onto the paper.

17. The _____ holds an ink jet printer's ink and functions as the printhead.

18. Ink jet and laser printer output is commonly measured in _____. The higher this number, the better the quality of the output.

19. _____ printers operate on the same principle as a copy machine.

20. The way in which 1s and 0s write to the laser printer's surface is by using a _____ or a _____.

21. The _____ or the _____ applies an uniform negative voltage to the laser drum.

22. _____ is powder made of plastic resin particles and organic compounds bound to iron oxide.

23. The _____ controls the amount of toner allowed onto the drum.

24. The _____ or the _____ applies a positive voltage on the back of the paper in a laser printer.

25. The _____ sits on top of the fusing roller and lubricates it.

26. A _____ laser printer produces a black image every place light touches the drum.

27. The laser printer's _____ removes gas, toner, and dust produced by the printer.

28. Printing should always occur on the _____ side of the paper.

29. A _____ is a piece of software needed for printer operation.

30. Storing data on the hard drive until the printer needs it is called _____.

31. _____ fonts are the most basic type.

32. _____ fonts are created from a mathematical model.

33. _____ fonts can be rotated.

34. _____ fonts are loaded from the hard drive.

35. _____ and _____ are the two most common page description languages for laser printers.

36. The _____ needs to be replaced when the laser printer's toner cartridge is replaced.

37. The default Windows printer has a _____ above the printer icon in the Printers window.

38. The _____ printer Properties tab is used to set printing resolution.

39. The Windows 98 _____ program control spooling.

40. An alternative to the EMF spool data format is _____.

41. Windows has a _____ tool to help with printing problems.

42. Ink jet printers frequently have a built-in _____ cleaning routing to clean the ink jet cartridge.

43. A drawback to laser printing Resolution Enhancement Technology is _____.

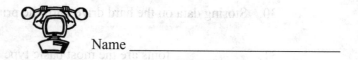
Name _____

ADDING WINDOWS 95/98'S GENERIC/TEXT ONLY PRINTER DRIVER EXERCISE

Objective: To add or change a Windows 95/98 printer driver

Parts: A computer with Windows 95/98 installed
Windows 95/98 CD-ROM

Step 1.   Power on the computer and verify the operating system loads.

Step 2.   To determine if a printer driver is already selected as the default, click on the **Start** button.

Step 3.   Select **Programs**, then **Accessories**, then click on the **Notepad** option.

Step 4.   Click on the **File** menu option.

Step 5.   Click on the **Page Setup** option.

Step 6.   Click on the **Printer** button at the bottom of the window.

Question 1:   Is any printer listed in the Name box? If so, write the printer name in the space below.

_____

Step 7.   Click on the **Cancel** button.

Step 8.   Click on the Page Setup window's **Cancel** button.

Step 9.   Click once in the Notepad **Close** box.

Step 10.   To install a printer driver click on the **Start** button.

Step 11.   Select the **Settings** option, then click on the **Printers** option.

Step 12.   Double-click on the **Add Printer** icon. The Add Printer wizard starts.

Step 13.   Click on the **Next** button.

Step 14.   Use the slide bar in the Manufacturers window to locate the **Generic** option.

Step 15.   Click once on the **Generic** option. The Generic/Text Only option appears in the Printers window.

Step 16.   Click on the **Next** button. The port window appears and LPT1 is highlighted.

Step 17.   Click on the **Next** button.

Step 18.   When prompted if Windows 95 is to use the Generic/Text Only printer as the default printer, click on the **Yes** radio button.

Step 19.   Click on the **Next** button.

Step 20.   When asked whether or not to print a test page, be sure the **Yes** radio button is selected.

Step 21.   Click on the **Finish** button. When prompted for the installation disk or CD, install it into the appropriate drive.

Step 22.   If the test page prints correctly, click on the **Yes** button. If the test page does not print correctly, click on the **No** button and the Windows 95 printer troubleshooting wizard starts.

Question 2:   Did the printer print the test page correctly? If not, troubleshoot the printer using the tips presented in the chapter or using Windows 95's Help.

_____ *Instructor's Initials*

Step 23.   To remove the Generic/Text Only printer driver, right-click on the **Generic/Text Only** icon.

Step 24.   Click on the **Delete** option from the drop down menu.

Step 25.   Click the **Yes** button to confirm the driver deletion.

Step 26.   Click the **Yes** button to the prompt stating that some unnecessary files will be deleted. A prompt appears if a printer driver was present before installing the Generic/Text Only driver. Click on the **OK** button, if necessary.

Question 3:   Why would a technician need to install the Generic/Text Only driver?

_____ *Instructor's Initials*

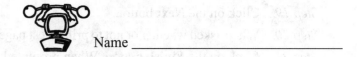
Name _____

DETECTING PARALLEL PORT I/O ADDRESSES WITH THE DEBUG PROGRAM EXERCISE

Objective: To use DEBUG to determine the parallel port I/O addresses

Parts: A working computer with the DEBUG command available

Step 1.   Power on the computer and go to the command prompt. Refer to the DOS chapter for DOS skills.

Step 2.   At the command prompt type **DEBUG**. A dash appears on the line following the DEBUG command.

Step 3.   At the dash on the screen, type **D40:0** and press **Enter**. Hexadecimal values display on the screen.

 The hexadecimal values of the active serial ports are displayed first, followed by the parallel ports. Deciphering the hexadecimal numbers is tricky, but Printer Exercise Figure #1 helps explain the values. The first line of the output is all that matters!

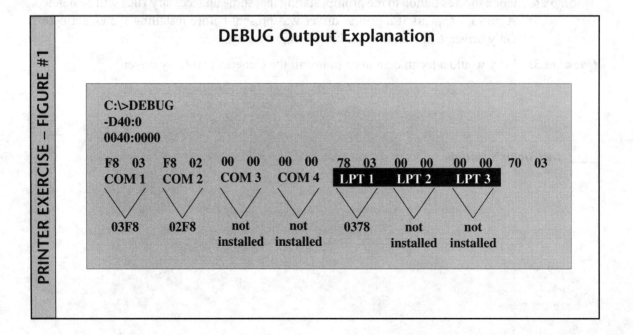

PRINTER EXERCISE – FIGURE #1

DEBUG Output Explanation

```
C:\>DEBUG
-D40:0
0040:0000
```

F8 03	F8 02	00 00	00 00	78 03	00 00	00 00	70 03
COM 1	COM 2	COM 3	COM 4	LPT 1	LPT 2	LPT 3	

| 03F8 | 02F8 | not installed | not installed | 0378 | not installed | not installed |

Notice in Printer Exercise Figure #1 how three different values are associated with LPT1, LPT2, LPT3. The three values represent the I/O address for the associated LPT port (if installed). However, the addresses display backward and this confuses people. For example, LPT1 is listed as 78 03, but in reality, the values represent I/O address of 0378h. A port address of 00 00 is an unused (or undetected) port.

Question 1:   How many parallel ports does BIOS detect?

Question 2:   What I/O addresses does each parallel port take? Use Printer Exercise Table #1 to place this information.

PRINTER EXERCISE – TABLE #1

Port Name	I/O Address
LPT1:	
LPT2:	
LPT3:	

_____ *Instructor's Initials*

Step 4.   To exit the DEBUG program, type **Q** and press **Enter.**

Name _____

USING MSD FOR LPT PORT IDENTIFICATION EXERCISE

Objective: To use Microsoft Diagnostics to determine LPT ports

Parts: A working computer with Microsoft Diagnostics (MSD) loaded

Step 1. Power on the computer and go to the command prompt. Refer to the DOS chapter for DOS skills.

Step 2. Change into the directory (DOS or WINDOWS) which contains the Microsoft Diagnostics (MSD.EXE) program.

Step 3. Start the Microsoft Diagnostics program by typing **MSD** at the prompt.

Step 4. Press **L** to access the LPT Ports... option.

Step 5. Look at the LPT Ports information window. The headings down the left side are LPT1, LPT2, and LPT3. For each LPT port, different criteria are listed to the right. The second column labeled Port Address contains the I/O addresses for each parallel port.

Question 1: What I/O address does LPT1 use?

Question 2: Does the system being tested have a device assigned to the LPT2 port?

Step 6. Press **Enter** to return to the first screen of the MSD program.

Step 7. Press **F3** to quit MSD.

Name _____

INSTALLING A LOCAL PRINTER ON A WINDOWS 95/98 COMPUTER

Objective: To install a local printer on a Windows 95/98 computer

Parts: Windows N95/98 computer with NIC installed and configured, and a printer physically attached to a printer port

Before a Windows 95/98 computer can send a print job to a local printer, the driver for that printer must be installed and configured.

Step 1.   Turn on the computer and verify that Windows 95/98 loads.

Step 2.   If necessary, logon to Windows 95/98 using the userid and password provided by the instructor or lab assistant.

Step 3.   Double-click on the **My Computer** desktop icon and then double-click on the **Printers** icon. The Printers folder opens.

Question 1:   What is another way to access the Printers folder?

Step 4.   Double-click on the **Add Printer** icon and the Add Printer wizard starts.

Step 5.   Click on the **Next** button, select the **Local printer** option, and then click on the **Next** button.

Step 6.   Select the appropriate printer **Manufacturer** and then select the appropriate printer **Model.** If the appropriate printer is not listed, click on the **Have Disk** button, enter a path to the driver files (such as A: or the drive letter of the CD-ROM), and click on the **OK** button.

Step 7.   After selecting the printer, click on the **Next** button.

Step 8.   From the Available Ports window, select the   to which the printer is attached and click on the **Next** button.

Question 2:   How many LPT ports are listed as available?

Step 9.   Enter a name for your printer in the **Printer Name** field, select **Yes** for Windows to use this printer as the Default Printer, and then click on the **Next** button.

Question 3:   Where will this printer name be displayed?

_____

_____

Step 10.   Select **Yes** to print a test page and click on the **Finish** button.

Step 11.   If prompted, insert the Windows 95/98 installation CD-ROM, or enter a path to the installation files.

Step 12.   The local printer will be installed. If the installation is successful, a printer test page prints.

_____ *Instructor's Initials*

Name _____

INSTALLING A LOCAL PRINTER ON A
WINDOWS NT WORKSTATION COMPUTER

Objective: To install a local printer on a Windows NT Workstation

Parts: Computer with NT Workstation loaded and a printer physically attached to a printer port

Optionally, the appropriate print driver for the printer attached or the NT Workstation CD

Before an NT Workstation can send a print job to a local printer, the driver for that printer must be installed and configured.

Step 1.   Turn the computer on and verify that NT Workstation has loaded.

Step 2.   Log on to NT Workstation using the userid and password provided by the instructor or lab assistant.

Step 3.   Double-click on the **My Computer** desktop icon and then double-click on the **Printers** folder. The Printers folder opens.

Question 1:   What is another way to access the Printers folder?

Step 4.   Double-click the **Add Printer** icon, and the Add Printer Wizard starts.

Step 5.   Select **My Computer** and then click on the **Next** button and the Ports window opens.

Question 2:   How many LPT and COM ports are listed in the Ports window?

Step 6.   Choose the printer **Manufacturer** of your printer and then select the printer **Model**. If the attached printer is not listed, click on the **Have Disk** button, insert the print driver disk or CD, enter a path to the driver files (such as A: or the drive letter for the CD-ROM), and click on the **OK** button.

Step 7.   Select the appropriate printer mode and click on the **Next** button.

Step 8.   Enter a **Name** for the printer in the **Printer Name** field and click on the **Next** button. The Sharing and Additional Drivers window opens.

Question 3:   What name did you assign to the printer?

Step 9.   Select the **Not Shared** option, leave the Share Name field blank, and click on the **Next** button.

Step 10.   Select the **Yes** option to print a test page and click on the **Finish** button.

Step 11.   If prompted, insert the Windows NT Workstation CD-ROM or enter a path to the installation files.

Step 12.   The printer installation process finishes and returns to the Printers Folder. If the installation is successful, a printer test page prints.

Question 4:   Did a test page print successfully? If not, redo the exercise. Take special precautions when selecting the appropriate print driver.

_____ *Instructor's Initials*

Name _____

INSTALLING A LOCAL PRINTER ON A
WINDOWS 2000 PROFESSIONAL COMPUTER

Objective: To install a local printer on a Windows 2000 Professional computer

Parts: Computer with Windows 2000 Professional loaded and a printer physically attached to a printer port

Optionally, the appropriate print driver for the printer attached or the 2000 Professional CD

Before a Windows 2000 Professional workstation can send a print job to a local printer, the proper print driver must be installed and configured.

Step 1.   Turn the computer on and verify that Windows 2000 Professional loads.

Step 2.   Log on to Windows 2000 Professional using the userid and password provided by the instructor or lab assistant.

Step 3.   From the Start menu, point to **Settings**, and then click on the **Printers** option. The Printers folder opens.

Step 4.   Double-click the **Add Printer** icon, and the Add Printer Wizard starts.

Step 5.   Select **Next**, and the Local or Network Printer window opens.

Step 6.   Select the **Local Printer** option, deselect the **Automatically detect my Plug and Play printer** option, and then select **Next**. The Select Printer Port window opens.

Question 1:   How many LPT and COM ports appear as available?

Step 7.   Choose **Use the following port**, highlight the port the printer attaches to, and then click **Next**.

Step 8.   Select the appropriate printer manufacturer, select the appropriate printer model, and then click **Next**. If your printer is not listed, click on the **Have Disk** button, insert the disk that contains the print driver such as the CD-ROM or the floppy, and enter a path to the driver files. Click on the **Next** button. Contact the instructor or lab assistant if you are unsure about which printer to select or if you have trouble installing the driver.

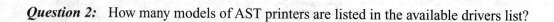

Question 2: How many models of AST printers are listed in the available drivers list?

Step 9. From the Name Your Printer window, enter a name for the printer, choose the **Yes** option to use this printer as the default printer, and then click on the **Next** button.

Step 10. From the Printer Sharing window, choose the **Do Not Share This Printer** option, and click on the **Next** button.

Step 11. From the Print Test Page window, choose **Yes** to print a test page and click on the **Next** button.

Step 12. From the Completing the Add Printer Wizard window, review the settings you have chosen and click on the **Finish** button.

Step 13. If prompted, insert the Windows 2000 CD-ROM installation disk or enter a path to the installation files (such as A: or the drive letter for the CD-ROM).

Step 14. The printer installation process will finish and return you to the Printers folder. If the installation process is successful, a printer test page prints.

Question 3: What signifies the printer you just installed is the default printer?

_____ *Instructor's Initials*

Name _____

USING A FREEWARE UTILITY TO EXAMINE PRINTER RESOURCES

Objective: To view the current system settings relating to a printer.

Parts: Computer with operating system loaded and access to a local or networked printer
Internet access
Software program that can uncompress files

Skills: Before starting this exercise, you should be able to download a zipped file and install a freeware utility onto the local hard drive.

Before and after a printer is installed, a technician needs to check on printer settings and system resources. This exercise uses a utility from Sisoftware called Sandra Standard.

Step 1.   Turn the computer on and verify the operating system loads. If necessary, logon using the userid and password provided by the instructor or lab assistant.

Step 2.   Access the Internet and go to www.sisoftware.demon.co.uk/sandra. Download the **Sandra Standard** utility.

Step 3.   Unzip the Sandra Standard program and install it by double-clicking on the **Setup** icon.

Step 4.   Once installed, click on the **Start** button, point to **Programs**, point to **SiSoft Utilities**, and click on **SiSoft Sandra 2001te Standard**. The Sandra utility appears on the screen.

Step 5.   Click on the **OK** button to clear the tip.

Step 6.   Double-click on the **I/O Settings** icon. The I/O Settings–SiSoft Sandra window appears.

Step 7.   Scroll down until you find the I/O address range for the LPT1 port.

Question 1:   What I/O address does the LPT1 port use?

Step 8.   Look on the back of the computer and see if the computer has USB ports. Then, scroll through the list and see if you find the USB Universal Host Controller.

Question 2:   Does the computer have USB ports? If so, what I/O address does the USB host controller use?

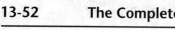

Step 9.   Click on the **OK** button.

Step 10.   Double-click on the **Printer and Fax Information** icon. The Printer and Fax Information–SiSoft Sandra window appears.

Step 11.   In the top Printer area, click on the **down area** to view all printing options installed. The number of options depends on the software and hardware installed on this machine.

Question 3:   How many options are available?

Step 12.   Select a physical printer from the drop down list.

Step 13.   Locate the General Information field for this printer.

Question 4:   What is the Printer Type, local or networked?

Question 5:   To what type of port does the printer connect [USB, serial, or parallel]?

Step 14.   Locate the Printer Settings field for this printer.

Question 6:   What is this printer's Data type?

Question 7:   Is the printer shared?

Question 8:   Is spooling enabled for this printer?

Question 9:   Is this printer the default printer?

Question 10: Is the printer online?

Question 11: Is this printer the default printer?

Question 12: Is bi-directional support enabled?

　　Step 15.   Scroll down until you see the Printer Driver section.

Question 13: What is the Printer Driver ID for this printer?

Question 14: What printer driver version is installed?

　　Step 16.   Locate the *Printer Driver Settings* section.

Question 15: What type of print technology is used?

Question 16: What printer mode is being used?

Question 17: What is the print quality setting?

Step 17. Find the Supported Paper Types section.

Question 18: How many paper types are supported by this printer?

Step 18. Scroll down until you see Supported Printer Modes.

Question 19: How many modes does this printer support?

Step 19. Locate the Printer Device Mode Characteristics area.

Question 20: How many device fonts are installed?

Step 20. Find the Printer Driver Raster Capabilities heading.

Question 21: Does the printer support bitmaps larger than 64K?

Step 21. Scroll down until you find Printer Driver Text Capabilities.

Question 22: Can the printer draw raster fonts?

_____ *Instructor's Initials*

Question 23: Locate the Performance Tips section if possible. Does the software list any performance tips? If so, write one of them in the space below.

Step 22. Click on **OK** button.

Step 23. Close the **SiSoft Sandra** window.

 Name _____

INTERNET DISCOVERY

Objective: To obtain specific information on the Internet regarding a computer or its associated parts

Parts: Access to the Internet

Question 1:   Using the Internet, determine what type of ports an Epson Stylus Photo 875DC printer supports? Write the ports and the URL where you found this information in the space below.

Question 2:   You just installed an Okidata OkiJet 2020 inkjet printer. When you turn the printer on, the red alarm light is illuminated along with all the rest of the colored lights. What is wrong? Find the solution on the Internet and write the URL as well as the solution in the space below.

Question 3:   A customer has a Xante Laserpress 1800 laser printer. While working on the printer, you power the printer up. The printer starts to warm up and before it comes on line, you shut the printer off. The user goes a little nuts and says to you, "You should not do that." "Do what?" you say. The customer replies, "Turn the printer off and on like that when it is warming up. You can permanently destroy a part inside the printer." You laugh. Using the Internet, determine whether this is true or not. Write the URL where you found this information in the space below and write whether it is or is not true.

Question 4:   A customer has a Minolta-QMS magicolor 6100 DeskLaser printer. Does this printer have Windows 2000 drivers? Write the answer and URL in the space below.

NOTES

Chapter 14:

Introduction to DOS

OBJECTIVES

After completing this chapter you will
- Execute and understand basic DOS commands.
- Understand and be able to use the DOS file structure and its limitations.
- Understand the purpose of the AUTOEXEC.BAT and CONFIG.SYS files.
- Be able to create a file using a text editor.
- Be able to copy and delete commands.
- Be able to set and unset attributes on files and directories.

KEY TERMS

archive attribute
ATTRIB
AUTOEXEC.BAT
batch file
boot
CD
command interpreter
command prompt
COMMAND.COM
CONFIG.SYS
COPY
COPY CON
device driver
DIR
directory
DOSKEY
ECHO OFF
EDIT
executable files
extension
external command

filename
FORMAT
hidden attribute
internal command
IO.SYS
MS-DOS
MSDOS.SYS
operating system
PATH
pipe symbol
PROMPT
read-only attribute
root directory
subdirectory
switch
SYS
system attribute
TYPE
wildcard
XCOPY

DOS OVERVIEW

Microcomputers require software to operate. An **operating system** is software that coordinates the interaction between hardware and any software applications running, as well as the interaction between a user and the computer. An operating system contains commands that both the user and the computer understand. For example, if you typed the word *hop* into a computer, hop is not a command. Therefore, the computer does not know what to do. If you type the letters *DIR*, the computer recognizes the command and displays a directory or a listing of files. Operating systems also handle file and disk management. Examples of operating systems for today's microcomputers are OS/2, UNIX, Windows 9x, NT Workstation, Windows 2000, and Windows XP.

Quite a few computer problems are software-related and many hardware installations have software programs that allow the hardware to work. Running diagnostic software is something a technician also performs from time to time. Even with the advent of newer and more powerful operating systems, a technician still must enter basic commands into the computer while troubleshooting. DOS skills are still very important for a technician. When an operating system does not work, the technician must be able to input commands from a prompt.

DOS COMMANDS

In the past, many manufacturers created their own DOS version, but Microsoft controls the operating system market today. Microsoft's DOS is known as **MS-DOS**. Three DOS files enable a machine to **boot** or come up to a usable point. Two of the files are hidden. Microsoft DOS hidden system files are **MSDOS.SYS** and **IO.SYS**. The third file is **COMMAND.COM**, also known as the **command interpreter**, which is responsible for processing every command typed into the computer. These three files load from a disk, or reside and load from the hard drive. Most commands with a particular manufacturer's DOS version will not work on other machines unless the other computer has the same version of DOS. These commands are still used with today's operating systems, but they have a different purpose.

DOS has two types of commands, internal and external. **Internal commands** are not visible when viewing files on a disk or hard drive, but after you enter the commands, they will execute. Internal commands are built into the COMMAND.COM file and execute much faster than external commands. An example of an internal command is DIR. **External commands** can be seen when viewing files on a disk or a hard drive. External commands execute slower than internal commands because the external commands must retrieve data from the disk or hard drive. One example of an external command is XCOPY.

Drive letters are assigned to hardware devices when a computer boots. For example, the first floppy drive gets the drive letter A:. The colon is part of the device's drive letter. The first hard drive in a system gets the drive letter C:. The devices detected by the operating system can use drive letters A: through Z:.

All communication with DOS begins at the **command prompt**, or simply a prompt. A command prompt might look like A:\> or C:\> or C:\DOS>. It can be changed to provide different information such as the drive letter, the date, or the time. The exercise that follows this section demonstrates how to change the command prompt. Commands are typed using a keyboard. Capitalization does not matter when using DOS, but DOS commands MUST be typed in a specific format and in a specific order. Practicing DOS commands is the best way to become proficient.

DOS FILE STRUCTURE

DOS files can be organized like chapters in a book. However, DOS files are grouped into **directories**. The starting point for all directories is the **root directory**. From the root directory, other directories can be made. The root directory is limited as to how many files it can hold.

The floppy drive's root directory can hold a maximum of 128 files or directories. The hard drive's root directories can hold up to 512 files or directories. A hard drive will send an "out of space" error message if there are more than 512 files in the root directory. The hard drive may have many gigabytes of available space and still give the error just because the root directory is filled. Creating directories is a good way for organizing files and keeping the root directory uncluttered.

The DOS file structure is called a tree because of how the directories are structured with limbs (directories) extending outward. Reference DOS Figure #1 for an example of how a hard disk's file structure might be organized.

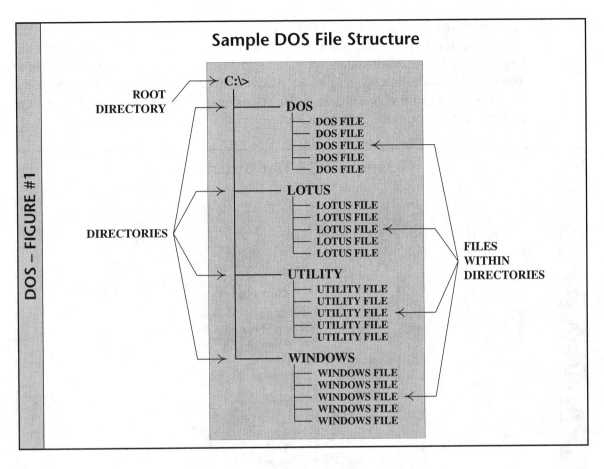

DOS – FIGURE #1

Sample DOS File Structure

Notice in DOS Figure #1 how each directory has a unique name. An infinite number of files can exist under each directory. Each **filename** within a directory must be unique, but other directories can contain the same file. For example, let us assume that the CHERYL.TXT file exists in the DOS directory. A different CHERYL.TXT file (or the same one) can exist in the WINDOWS, LOTUS, or UTILITY directory (or all three directories for that matter). However, a second CHERYL.TXT file cannot exist in the DOS directory.

Files are kept in directories or in the root directory. A **subdirectory** can be created beneath another directory. For example, if a DOS directory has the name BOOK, below the directory can be subdirectories titled CHAP1 and CHAP2, CHAP3, etc. In DOS, a filename *cannot* contain the following characters:

. (period)	; (semicolon)	/ (forward slash)
, (comma)	" (quotation marks)	\ (backslash)
| (vertical bar)	? (question mark)	[(left bracket)
: (colon)	= (equal sign)	] (right bracket)
* (asterisk)	(space)	

In addition to naming a file, in DOS you frequently have to add an extension to the name. An **extension** is an addition to the filename and it can be up to three characters in length. The filename and the extension are separated by a period. An example of a filename with an extension is BOOK.DOC where BOOK is the name of the file and DOC is the extension. In today's operating systems, extensions are automatically added by the application that creates the document. Reference DOS Figure #2 for this structure.

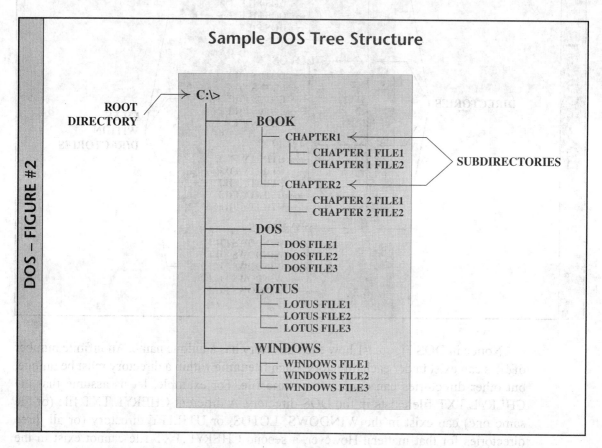

Sample DOS Tree Structure

DOS – FIGURE #2

Notice in DOS Figure #2 that the BOOK directory has more than one subdirectory. Many more subdirectories can be added to the BOOK directory as well. Each subdirectory's name must be unique; however, the same subdirectory name can be used under other directories. For example, the LOTUS directory could contain a CHAPTER1 and a CHAPTER2 subdirectory just like the book directory does.

The best way to become proficient with DOS is to use it. The following exercise illustrates basic commands.

Name _____

BASIC DOS COMMANDS

Objective:　To execute basic DOS commands

Parts:　A computer with a Windows operating system loaded
A disk with DOS files
A blank disk

For each step requiring a typed command the Enter key must be pressed to execute the DOS command. This instruction will *not* be given with each step.

Step 1.　Power the computer on and boot from the hard disk. If a logon password is needed, contact the instructor or lab assistant. When Windows loads, exit to a DOS prompt. The steps to get to a prompt are listed below for various Windows operating systems.

Windows 98: (1) Click on the **Start** button, point to **Programs**, and click on the **MS-DOS Prompt** option, (2) click on the **Start** button, click on the **Run** option, and type in **COMMAND** at the dialog box and press **Enter**, (3) boot from a bootable disk, (4) during startup, hold down either the **CTRL** key or press the **F8** key to access the Command-Prompt-Only mode.

NT Workstation: (1) Click on the **Start** button, point to **Programs**, and click on the **Command Prompt** option, (2) click on the **Start** button, click on the **Run** option, type in either **CMD** or **COMMAND** (both work), and click on the **OK** button.

Windows 2000: (1) Click on the **Start** button, click on the **Run** option, type in **CMD** or **COMMAND** (both work) in the dialog box, and click on the **OK** button.

Question 1:　Does a prompt display? If not, and you followed every step correctly, contact your instructor.

Question 2:　Write down the prompt displayed on the computer screen.

Step 2.　From the command prompt, type **CD**

The prompt changes to C:\>. If a message appears stating invalid command or invalid directory, you made a typing error. If you suspect an error, verify the backslash is after CD and there are no extra spaces. The backslash starts from the left side and goes to the right: \. Other commands use a forward slash, which would be in the

opposite direction (/). CD is the command for Change Directory, which tells the operating system to go to a different directory in the tree structure. The \ after the CD command tells the operating system to go to the root directory. An alternative way of typing this command is CD \. Notice the space between the CD command and the backslash. There are usually different ways to do every command from a prompt. Note that the CD\ command allows you to return to the root directory at any time.

Step 3. At the command prompt, type **DIR**

A list of files and directories appears. Files are the items that show an extension (up to three characters) out to the right of the filename, file size, and file creation date. Directories have a <DIR> entry to the right of the name.

DOS files can have names up to eight characters long. DOS files normally have file extensions and a name. File extensions frequently give clues as to which application created the file. An extension is an addition to the filename and can be no more than three characters. An extension usually identifies the software package that created the file. A period (.) separates the name from the extension. The file CHERYL.DOC has a name of CHERYL and DOC is the extension. The complete filename includes the eight-character name as well as the period and the extension. In the prior example, CHERYL.DOC is the filename.

Question 3: List one file and one directory shown on the screen.

Step 4. When the number of files exceeds what can be shown on the screen, the files quickly scroll off the screen until all files finish displaying. The DIR command has a switch that controls this scrolling. A **switch** begins with a forward slash and enhances or changes the way a DOS command performs. At the DOS prompt, type **DIR /P**

After looking at the data on the screen, press **Enter** again. Continue pressing **Enter** until the DOS prompt reappears. The DIR command's /P switch tells DOS to display the files one page at a time.

Step 5. At the prompt, type **DIR /W**

Question 4: What is the function of the /W switch?

Multiple switches can be used with a DOS command.

Step 6. At the prompt, type **DIR /W/P**

Using the DIR command /W and /P switches cause files to display in a wide format, one page at a time.

Step 7. Different versions of DOS have documentation with online help. To find out the DOS version loaded on the computer, at the DOS prompt, type **VER**

Question 5: Who is the operating system manufacturer and what version is being used on the computer?

Step 8. At the prompt, type **DIR /? |more**

A short explanation of the command appears followed by the command's syntax (instructions or rules for how the command is to be typed). A technician needs to be able to understand command syntax to function when a computer is broken. The | symbol is called the **pipe symbol** and it is discussed later in this chapter. The |more command tells the operating system to display the output one page at a time. Answer the following two questions and then press any key to continue until you return to a prompt.

Question 6: Write the DIR syntax in the space below.

Question 7: Write down one switch that can be used with the DIR command along with a short explanation of its purpose.

Step 9. Type **CD\XXXXX** where the *XXXXX* is replaced by the name of the directory you wrote down as an answer to Question 3. For example, in Question 3, if I wrote the directory name, CASINO, I would type CD\CASINO at the prompt.

Step 10. Type **DIR A*.***

The *A*.** is not a switch. This part of the command is directing the operating system to list all files or subdirectories that start with the letter A. The **.** part means all files. The directory you chose may not have any files or subdirectories that start with the letter A and the operating system displays the message "File not found", if this occurs. The * is known as a wildcard for DOS. A **wildcard** substitutes for one or more characters. The first asterisk (*) is the wildcard for any name of a file. The second asterisk (*) is the wildcard for any extension.

Question 8: Are any files or subdirectories that start with the letter A listed? If so, write one of them in the space below. If not, did the operating system let you know this? If so, write the message displayed.

Step 11. Type **CD..**

The **..** tells the operating system to move back (up) one directory in the tree structure. Since you are one level down (because of typing the CD*XXXXX* command), this command brings you back to the root directory.

Question 9: If you wanted to display a list of all commands in the root directory that start with the letter C, what command would you type? Try this command on the computer to see if it works.

Question 10: Does the COMMAND.COM file appear in the list of commands that start with the letter C?

Question 11: What is the purpose of the COMMAND.COM file?

ON YOUR OWN

Step A. Change to the directory that contains Windows. The directory's name is normally WINDOWS or WINNT. If you cannot determine what directory contains Windows, contact your instructor or lab assistant. Write the command you used to do this.

Step B. List three Windows files that begin with the letter D.

Step C. Look for the DRWATSON.EXE file. Is the file there?

Step D. Return to the root directory. Write the command you used.

Step 12. Insert a disk then type **DIR A:**

Watch for the light to appear on the floppy drive.

Question 12: What drive letter does the first bootable hard drive normally get?

Question 13: See if the disk has any files on it. List one filename from the disk if it has files. Do not forget to include the extension.

The following steps wipe (format) a diskette:

Step 13. From the prompt, type

FORMAT A:

A message similar to the following appears on your screen

C:\>FORMAT A:

Insert new diskette for drive A:

and press **Enter** when ready...

Step 14. Insert a disk into the floppy drive (the A: drive) then press **Enter**.

The FORMAT command erases all files on a floppy disk.

Step 15. At the prompt for volume label, simply press **Enter**.

Step 16. At the prompt to format another, type **N** (for no and press **Enter**).

Step 17. At the prompt, type **A:**

Question 14: How does the prompt change?

_____ *Instructor's Initials*

Step 18. Remove the floppy disk from the A: drive.

Step 19. From the prompt, type **PROMPT PT**

Question 15: What happened to the command prompt on the screen?

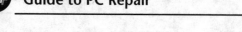
Step 20. From the prompt, type **PROMPT Technicians rule the world $g**

Question 16: Write down what the command prompt looks like now.

Step 21. From the prompt, type **PROMPT $P $D $T $G**

Step 22. From the prompt, type **PROMPT $P $G**

The command prompt is in its normal format.

_____*Instructor's Initials*

ON YOUR OWN

Step E. Using the ?, find at least one possible value (such as $P) for the PROMPT command that has *not* been used. Write the value as well as a short explanation of the value's purpose.

Step F. Type the command to return to the hard drive. Write the command used.

MORE DOS COMMANDS

In the previous exercise, the **CD** command changes the prompt to a different directory. The CHDIR command could have been used instead. CHDIR is the full command name for change directory and the CD command is a shortcut. Be aware there are many shortcuts and methods that can be used to issue the same command. This chapter is designed as an overview of DOS and does not cover all possible ways of doing the same task. Besides, most technicians have reference books on the operating systems they support.

In the exercise, the **FORMAT** command is used for the first time. The FORMAT command prepares a disk for use. Most disks come preformatted; however, there are vendors who still sell unformatted disks. You may want to completely wipe all information from the disk by using the FORMAT command. In Windows 9x, you can use the FORMAT command with the */S* switch to create a boot disk. The disk contains the system files (the two hidden files and COMMAND.COM). A similar result can be achieved using the **SYS** command. For example, if you type *SYS A:* from the command prompt, the two hidden files and COMMAND.COM copy over to a floppy disk (making the disk bootable). The SYS command is a valuable program for technicians especially when working with hard drives and system problems. For NT Workstation and Windows 2000, the installation disks are used as a boot disk.

Be aware that older DOS versions' SYS command does not work the same as today's versions. The format is the same, but with older versions of DOS, only the two hidden files copy to the disk. Also, with older versions, the COMMAND.COM file must be copied separately to make a disk or hard drive bootable.

THE AUTOEXEC.BAT FILE

In the exercise, the **PROMPT** command changed the appearance of the command prompt. However, when the computer boots for the first time, the command prompt is already there. This is because of a special file called the **AUTOEXEC.BAT** file that executes every time the computer starts if it exists in the root directory. The AUTOEXEC.BAT file can execute multiple commands, one right after another. Today's operating systems set the prompt through the IO.SYS file, but it can be changed by adding the PROMPT command to the AUTOEXEC.BAT file. An example of an AUTOEXEC.BAT file is in DOS Figure #3.

DOS – FIGURE #3

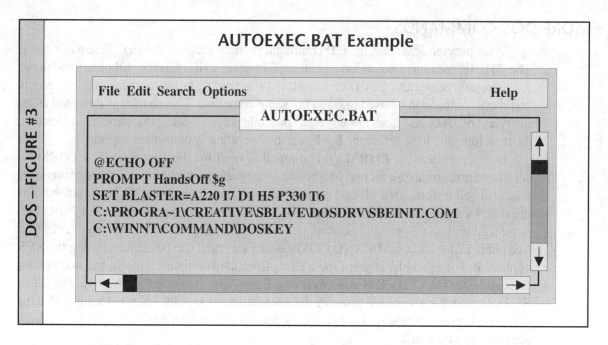

AUTOEXEC.BAT Example

File Edit Search Options   Help

AUTOEXEC.BAT

```
@ECHO OFF
PROMPT HandsOff $g
SET BLASTER=A220 I7 D1 H5 P330 T6
C:\PROGRA~1\CREATIVE\SBLIVE\DOSDRV\SBEINIT.COM
C:\WINNT\COMMAND\DOSKEY
```

The first line of the AUTOEXEC.BAT is @ECHO OFF. The **ECHO OFF** command prevents other AUTOEXEC.BAT commands from showing on the screen while the computer boots. The @ symbol in front of ECHO OFF keeps the words *ECHO OFF* from also showing. The second line of the AUTOEXEC.BAT file is PROMPT HandsOff $G, which is a similar command to the one used in the exercise. It sets the command prompt's appearance.

The third line, SET BLASTER sets configuration parameters for a Creative Labs SoundBlaster card. The fourth line, C:\PROGRA~1\CREATIVE\SBLIVE\ DOSDRV\SBEINIT.COM directs the operating system to execute the SBEINIT.COM file when the computer starts. The rest of the command tells the operating system where to find the file. (In a subdirectory called DOSDRV, which is a subdirectory of SBLIVE, which is a subdirectory of CREATIVE, which is a subdirectory called PROGRA~1, which is located on the hard drive.)

A common command is PATH. This command was always placed in the AUTOEXEC.BAT file during DOS days. The **PATH** command instructs the operating system where to look for commands. An example of a path statement for today's operating system is as follows:

PATH=C:\;C:\WINNT;C:\WINNT\COMMAND;C:\PROGRA~1\DELL\RESOLU~1\COMMON\BIN

When a command is typed at the prompt, the operating system first looks in the current directory for the file. If the file is not there, the PATH statement takes effect. The operating system looks in the root directory. If the file is not in the root directory, it looks in the WINNT directory. If the file is not in the WINNT directory, it looks in the COMMAND subdirectory (which is located under the WINNT directory). The COMMAND subdirectory holds DOS commands for the Windows operating systems. If the file is not there, the operating system looks in the BIN file, which is a subdirectory of the COMMON directory (which is a subdirectory of the RESOLU~1 directory, which is a subdirectory of the DELL directory, which is a subdirectory of the PROGRA~1 directory, which is located on the hard drive). After all that, you can now understand why operating systems today are much easier to use.

Today's operating systems load the PATH statement through the IO.SYS file. The PATH statement can be replaced or added to by statements placed in the AUTOEXEC.BAT file or by typing a new PATH statement at the prompt.

The PATH statement should always include (1) the root directory, (2) the directory that contains the operating system files, and (3) any frequently used directory.

When working from a prompt, you do not have to type a file's name and extension, only the filename. The operating system simply looks for files that have file extensions of COM, EXE, or BAT. These files are **executable files**. For ease of troubleshooting, all lines in the AUTOEXEC.BAT file should contain the file's full path (even though the file may be in one of the directories listed in the PATH statement).

The fifth line involves the DOSKEY program. **DOSKEY** allows the use of the arrow keys to bring up previously entered commands. DOSKEY is a favorite of many technicians and is used to save time while typing commands. DOS Table #1 lists the keys used with DOSKEY.

Keys Used with DOSKEY

Key	Function
Up arrow	Recalls the last typed command
Down arrow	Recalls commands
ESC	Clears current command
F7	Command history
F8	Searches command history
F9	Selects a command by number
ALT+F7	Clears command history

DOS – TABLE #1

Even if the DOSKEY program is not used, the function keys on the keyboard allow a small amount of command control. For example, the F1 function key displays the last command one character at a time. The F3 function key displays all the previous DOS command characters.

The AUTOEXEC.BAT file is a potential source of problems with computers. Because the commands do not show on the screen, one cannot easily tell if all programs and commands in the AUTOEXEC.BAT file execute. Today's Windows operating systems provide an easy way to troubleshoot AUTOEXEC.BAT file problems through the use of the F8 key or through a startup menu.

Much more information about troubleshooting specific problems with the AUTOEXEC.BAT file is included in the Memory, Hard Drive, and Multimedia chapters.

THE TYPE COMMAND

Another useful command is the **TYPE** command used to display text (.TXT) or batch (.BAT) files on the screen. Many times README.TXT or READ.ME files are included with software applications and utilities. The TYPE command allows viewing these files; however, most of the time, these files occupy more than one screen. So, using the |more parameter after the TYPE command permits viewing the file one screen at a time. For example, TYPE README.TXT|MORE allows viewing the text file one page at a time. Sometimes a technician needs a printout of a text file. In this case, use the redirect symbol, (the greater than sign >). For example, if the name of the file to be printed is README.TXT, then typing TYPE README.TXT >LPT1 sends the text file to the parallel port printer instead of the screen.

THE CONFIG.SYS FILE

The two files that execute automatically (if present) are AUTOEXEC.BAT and CONFIG.SYS. The **CONFIG.SYS** file customizes and configures the computer's environment. It contains parameters such as how many files a program uses or how many file buffers are allocated. Pieces of software called **device drivers** allow hardware devices to operate. Device drivers load through the CONFIG.SYS file.

Restart the computer for the changes made to the CONFIG.SYS or AUTOEXEC.BAT files to take effect.

An example CONFIG.SYS file is in DOS Figure #4.

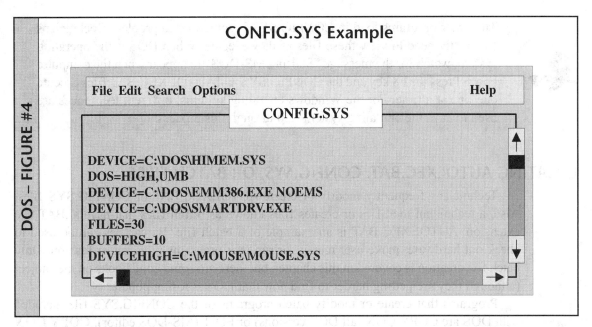

DOS – FIGURE #4

CONFIG.SYS Example

File Edit Search Options   Help

CONFIG.SYS

DEVICE=C:\DOS\HIMEM.SYS
DOS=HIGH,UMB
DEVICE=C:\DOS\EMM386.EXE NOEMS
DEVICE=C:\DOS\SMARTDRV.EXE
FILES=30
BUFFERS=10
DEVICEHIGH=C:\MOUSE\MOUSE.SYS

DOS Figure #4 shows a CONFIG.SYS file from a DOS machine. Today's computers frequently have no CONFIG.SYS statements or even a CONFIG.SYS file because these same parameters are replaced by (1) commands executed through the IO.SYS file or (2) the installed hardware uses 32-bit drivers loaded from the registry instead of the CONFIG.SYS file. If a Windows-based computer has a CONFIG.SYS file it is because an older driver is being used or a default parameter such as files and buffers is being changed. Because the concept of CONFIG.SYS is important because it may be used and contain commands that cause the computer problems, the lines in Figure #4 need to be covered.

The first three lines shown in DOS Figure #4 are for memory management. More details on these individual commands are in the Memory chapter. The fourth line of the CONFIG.SYS file, DEVICE=C:\DOS\SMARTDRV.EXE is a disk caching manager. The DEVICE= statement at the beginning of the line shows that the SMARTDRV.EXE file loads as a device driver. Another device driver shown in DOS Figure #4 is on line 7, DEVICEHIGH=C:\MOUSE\MOUSE.SYS. The MOUSE.SYS is the device driver that allows the mouse to operate. When using DOS, device drivers always load via the CONFIG.SYS file. Device driver files normally have the file extension of .SYS or .EXE.

Lines 5 and 6 of the CONFIG.SYS file in DOS Figure #4 set various parameters for DOS programs. The FILES= statement sets how many files can be open at one time. The BUFFERS= statement sets aside a certain amount of RAM for DOS to use when transferring information to and from a disk. This number is normally lower when using a caching program such as SMARTDRV.EXE.

The order programs load in CONFIG.SYS is sometimes a problem. Technicians frequently need to view these files as they execute. When DOS is the operating system, watch for the message "Starting MS-DOS" to appear when the computer boots. Press the F8 key and the CONFIG.SYS and AUTOEXEC.BAT files execute one line at a time. For the Windows operating systems, different techniques are used to have the operating system step through this process.

CREATING AUTOEXEC.BAT, CONFIG.SYS, OR BATCH FILES

Technicians frequently modify or create AUTOEXEC.BAT or CONFIG.SYS files. Also, a technician modifies or creates files known as **batch files** that have a .BAT file extension. AUTOEXEC.BAT is an example of a batch file. Batch files can be used to check out hardware, make user menus, or run user programs in an easier fashion. Only batch file creation is covered in this chapter, but there are some good books on the subject (although they are getting harder to find now that DOS is losing popularity).

Programs that create or modify batch programs or the CONFIG.SYS file included with DOS are COPY CON (all DOS versions) or EDIT (MS-DOS editor). **COPY CON** (COPY CONSOLE) is the hardest to work with because once you enter a line and press Enter, the line cannot be modified except through an editor or by creating the entire file again. The **EDIT** editor that comes with DOS and Windows is much easier to handle.

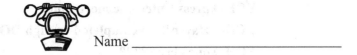

Name _____

COPY CON AND AUTOEXEC.BAT EXERCISE

Objective: To use the COPY CON to create a file

Parts: Windows 9x computer and floppy disk OR a bootable disk (to be used with NT or Windows 2000)

For each step requiring a typed command the Enter key must be pressed to execute the DOS command. This instruction will *not* be given with each step.

Step 1.   Power the computer on and boot from the hard disk. If a logon password is needed, contact the instructor or lab assistant. When Windows loads, exit to a DOS prompt. If you forgot how, reference the previous exercise.

Step 2.   If you are on a Windows 9x computer (check with the instructor or lab assistant if unsure or use the VER command from the prompt), insert a disk into the A: drive and type **FORMAT A: /S**

A message appears stating Insert new disk for drive A: and press **Enter** when ready. If the message does not appear, perform Step 2 again. Follow the directions on the screen. At the "Volume label (11 characters, Enter for none)?" prompt, press **Enter**. Disk space and serial number information appear. At the "Quick Format another (Y/N)?" prompt, press **N** for No then press **Enter**.

If you are on an NT Workstation or Windows 2000 computer, insert a bootable disk.

Step 3.   To verify that the disk is bootable, reboot the computer with the disk inserted into the floppy drive. The A:\> prompt appears. If the prompt does not appear, redo Step 2 or obtain another bootable disk.

Question 1:   What does making a disk or a drive *bootable* mean?

Step 4.   Note that when Enter is pressed after each line, no messages appear!
From the C:\ command prompt, type
COPY CON: A:\AUTOEXEC.BAT
@ECHO OFF
ECHO This is a fine mess you've gotten me into Ollie.
ECHO This computer is about to EXPLODE if you
PAUSE.

ECHO press Enter one more time.

ECHO Haven't we completed enough DOS exercises for

ECHO one class?????

ECHO LATER GATOR.

Press **F6**. A caret (^) and a Z appear on the screen. Press **Enter**. A message appears stating that one file copied.

Step 5.   Reboot the computer and watch for the messages created in Step 4 to appear on the screen as the AUTOEXEC.BAT file automatically executes.

Question 2:   Did the AUTOEXEC.BAT file run okay? If the AUTOEXEC.BAT file does not run correctly, perform Steps 4 and 5 again.

Step 6.   Have a classmate verify the AUTOEXEC.BAT file executes properly.

Classmate's printed name: _____

Classmate's initials: _____

Step 7.   Remove the disk from the floppy drive.

Step 8.   Reboot the computer.

Name _____

EDIT COMMAND EXERCISE

Objective: To use the EDIT editor to create a file

Parts: A computer with the EDIT editor loaded
A bootable disk

For each step requiring a typed command the Enter key must be pressed to execute the DOS command. This instruction will *not* be given with each step.

Step 1.   Power the computer on and boot from the hard disk. If a logon password is needed, contact the instructor or lab assistant. When Windows loads, exit to a DOS prompt. If you forgot how, reference the first exercise.

Step 2.   If a printer is attached to the computer, type **TYPE C:\AUTOEXEC.BAT>LPT1**

If a printer is not attached, type **TYPE C:\AUTOEXEC.BAT**

Question 1:   Does the AUTOEXEC.BAT file appear on the screen? If not, is there an AUTOEXEC.BAT file loaded on the hard drive's root directory? If there is a file on the hard drive, you made a mistake in your typing. Write one line from the AUTOEXEC.BAT file and explain its purpose.

Step 3.   Insert a bootable disk into the A: drive.

Question 2:   What three files make a disk *bootable* in a DOS environment?

Step 4.   From the prompt type **EDIT A:\AUTOEXEC.BAT**

The EDIT editor screen appears. The filename, AUTOEXEC.BAT is across the top center of the screen. The cursor blinks in the upper left corner.

Step 5.   Type the following using the backspace or arrow keys to correct any mistakes. Press **Enter** to move the cursor to the next line.

@echo off

Echo Sure as Schmidt we are about to get this editing down.

Echo This Schmidt woman is working our fingers to the bone.

Pause

> **Echo No one told me that we would have to type so much.**
>
> **Echo Folks from Tennessee are cool! Go VOLS!**

Step 6.   Press **ALT**. The word *File* on the menu bar highlights.

Step 7.   Press **F**. The File drop-down menu appears.

Step 8.   Press **X**. A message box appears stating "Loaded file is not saved. Save it now?"

Step 9.   Press **Y** for YES. The command prompt appears.

Step 10.   Reboot the computer and watch for the messages created in Step 5 to appear on the screen as the AUTOEXEC.BAT file automatically executes.

Question 3:   Did the AUTOEXEC.BAT file run correctly? If not, perform Steps 3 through 10 again. Also, the disk may not be bootable.

Step 11.   Have a classmate verify the AUTOEXEC.BAT file executes properly.

Classmate's printed name: _____

Classmate's initials: _____

Step 12.   Remove the disk from the floppy drive.

Step 13.   Reboot the computer from the hard drive.

Name _____

DOSKEY COMMAND EXERCISE

Objective: To use the DOSKEY program efficiently

Parts: A computer with a Windows operating system loaded
A formatted disk

For each step requiring a typed command the Enter key must be pressed to execute the DOS command. This instruction will *not* be given with each step.

Step 1.   Power the computer on and boot from the hard disk. If a logon password is needed, contact the instructor or lab assistant. When Windows loads, exit to a DOS prompt. If you forgot how, refer to the first exercise.

Step 2.   To install the DOSKEY program from the prompt, type **DOSKEY**

Step 3.   Insert the floppy disk into the floppy drive.

Step 4.   From the command prompt, type

A:

MD\SPECIAL

Step 5.   Verify the creation of the directory by typing **CD\SPECIAL**

Question 1:   Did the command prompt change to the A:\SPECIAL> directory? If not, redo Steps 2 through 5.

Step 6.   The DOSKEY program allows use of the arrow keys and function keys (the F1 through F12 keys on the keyboard). Press the **up arrow** once. The last typed command appears at the prompt. If the last command does not appear, then DOSKEY is not loaded properly. Perform Steps 1 through 6 again.

Step 7.   Press the **up arrow** until the MD\SPECIAL command appears at the command prompt. *Do not* press Enter when the command appears.

Step 8.   Press the **left arrow** key 3 times until the blinking cursor is under the *I* in SPECIAL. *Do not* press Enter. The arrow keys, when used with DOSKEY, allow movement through the command line.

Step 9.   While the cursor is blinking under the letter I, type the letter **T**. *Do not* press Enter. The command should now read MD\SPECTAL. DOSKEY is automatically in the typeover mode.

Step 10. Press **INS** (Insert), but *do not* press Enter. The cursor changes to a blinking box.

Step 11. While the cursor is a blinking box over the letter *A*, type the letter **R**. The command changes to SPECTRAL, because pressing the INS key causes DOSKEY to go into the insert mode.

Step 12. Press **Enter** to create a directory named SPECTRAL.

Step 13. Press the **up arrow** key once. The last command typed appears on the screen.

Step 14. Press **ESC** (Escape) once. ESC erases the current command from the command prompt.

Step 15. Press **F7** once. A list of all typed commands appears on the screen.

Step 16. Press **F9** once. The Line Number prompt appears. While in DOSKEY, F9 allows you to Enter a specific command based on a line number (that showed when you pressed F7).

Step 17. Type the number corresponding to the **A:** command, then press **Enter**. The A: command appears at the command prompt.

Step 18. Press **ESC** to clear the command.

Step 19. Press and *hold down* **ALT**. While holding ALT down, press **F7** once, then release both keys. DOSKEY uses ALT+F7 to clear the list of commands DOSKEY tracks. Sometimes, pressing the F7 key is cumbersome to use because the command list is so long. Clearing the command list allows DOSKEY to start over tracking commands.

Step 20. Press **F7** to verify the command list is clear.

_____ *Instructor's Initials*

COPYING FILES

Two commands used most frequently to copy files are COPY and XCOPY. The difference between the two commands is that **COPY** is an internal command and **XCOPY** is an external command residing on a disk or a hard drive. Either command is able to copy a file to a different disk, copy a file from one directory to another, copy a group of files using wildcards, or rename a file as it is being copied. XCOPY can copy multiple files and directories under other directories, but the COPY command cannot. With older versions of DOS, the COPY command replaces a file with the same name as the file being copied, without any warning or prompting. However, with newer versions of operating systems, a warning message appears asking if the file is to be replaced. The COPY and XCOPY commands have three parts with each part separated by a space:

1. The command itself (COPY or XCOPY)
2. The source (the file being copied)
3. The destination (where the file is being copied)

The destination is optional if the file copies into the current directory. For example, if working from the A:\> command prompt and copying the DOCUMENT file from the hard drive's root directory, then the command could be COPY C:\DOCUMENT. The destination is omitted because the file will automatically copy to the current drive and directory (which is A:\)

The command requires all three parts if the destination is *not* the current drive and directory. For example, take the situation of being at the C:\> command prompt. To copy the FORMAT.COM command from the hard drive to a disk located in the A: drive, type the following command:

COPY C:\WINDOWS\COMMAND\FORMAT.COM A:

Note that the COPY command is first. Then the source, the location and name of the file being copied—C:\WINDOWS\COMMAND\FORMAT.COM is next. Last is the destination, A:\, where the file is to be placed. If the current directory is the C:\WINDOWS\COMMAND hard drive directory, then the source path does not have to be typed. Instead, the command would look like the following:

C:\WINDOWS\COMMAND> COPY FORMAT.COM A:

The backslash (\) after the A: is not necessary if the floppy drive does not have directories. The COPY command does not need the entire path in front of the command because COPY is an internal command. Internal commands are part of COMMAND.COM and the operating system can always find internal commands no matter where in the tree structure the command executes.

New technicians commonly make mistakes in specifying a command's correct path. If you are a beginner, the safest way is to type the complete path of both the source and destination locations. Before using any command, consider these questions:

1.   What command do you want to issue?
2.   Where is the command located in the tree structure?
3.   Where in the tree structure are you currently working?
4.   If you are copying a file or moving a file, in what directory does the file need to be placed?

THE XCOPY COMMAND

The XCOPY command is more powerful and faster than the COPY command. The XCOPY command allows the copying of directories, subdirectories, and files. The syntax or typing format for the XCOPY command includes the command, a source, and a destination just like the COPY command. If the destination is omitted, the XCOPY command copies the source files to the current directory. If you have a disk containing files in subdirectories to be copied to a different capacity disk, the XCOPY is a great command to use.

THE ATTRIB COMMAND

The **ATTRIB** command sets, removes, or shows the attribute of a file or a directory. Attributes change how a file or directory is displayed on the screen or what can be done with the file or directory. Possible attributes include read-only, archive, system, and hidden. The **read-only attribute** protects files so they cannot be accidentally changed or deleted. For example, the AUTOEXEC.BAT and CONFIG.SYS files start and configure a computer. Make these two files read-only so they are not accidentally changed or deleted by a user. The **archive attribute** marks files that have changed since they were last backed up by a backup program. The RESTORE, XCOPY, and MSBACKUP commands use the archive attribute as well as any other backup software program. The **system attribute** designates a file as a system file. Files with this attribute do not show in directory listings. The **hidden attribute** allows file hiding and even directory hiding. Technicians frequently use the hidden attribute. If another person has hidden some files and the technician wants to see the files without having to change the attributes of all the files, then the DIR command displays all the files no matter which attributes the files possess.

Set each attribute using the +x switch where the +R switch adds the read-only attribute, the +S switch adds the system attribute, the +H adds the hidden attribute, and the +A adds the archive attribute. Remove each attribute using the –R, –S, –H, or –A switch with the ATTRIB command. One command can set more than one attribute on files or directories. For example, to make the CHERYL.TXT file hidden and read-only, type *ATTRIB +R +H CHERYL.TXT.*

An excellent use of the archive attribute is to copy multiple files onto a disk. Normally, if copying too many files, there is no warning that the disk cannot hold all the files until it is too late and the disk runs out of room. Traditionally, people used the BACKUP and RESTORE commands to get around this problem. However, the ATTRIB command (with the +*A* switch) and the XCOPY command (with the /*M* switch) together can copy files across multiple disks. For example, all the DOS files require more than one disk. If copying all the files to a disk, the operating system copies as many files as possible, then produces an error saying the destination disk is full. To prevent this problem, use the ATTRIB command and assign all the files the archive attribute. Type *ATTRIB +A C:\TESTDIR*.** then insert a disk into the A: drive and type *XCOPY C:\TESTDIR*.* A: /M*. When the XCOPY command stops and displays the error message that the destination disk is full, insert a new floppy into the A: drive and repeat the command. The /*M* switch tells XCOPY not to copy the same files over. The /*M* switch only copies files that have the archive attribute set. Once the file copies, the files no longer have the archive attribute.

Most technicians have a bootable disk with their favorite utilities and commands on it. Different DOS versions come with different utilities. Even the two hidden files and COMMAND.COM are different between vendors and between versions of DOS.

You never know what DOS version you will encounter. Therefore, the DOS version on the bootable disk is the same version of ATTRIB that needs to be on the disk. Be careful executing DOS commands from a floppy disk if the machine did not boot from that floppy.

MOVING AROUND IN DOS

The most frequently used command for moving around in the cumbersome tree structure is CD (Change Directory). Take, for example, a disk with a TEST1 directory has subdirectories called SUB1, SUB2, and SUB3 as shown in DOS Figure #5.

DOS – FIGURE #5

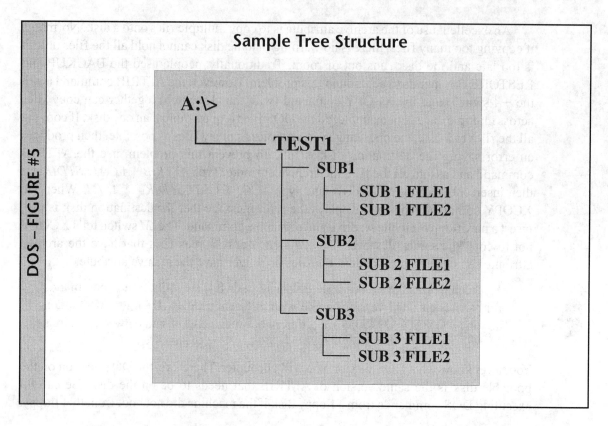

Sample Tree Structure

```
A:\>
   |
   |_____ TEST1
                     |___ SUB1
                     |      |___ SUB 1 FILE1
                     |      |___ SUB 1 FILE2
                     |
                     |___ SUB2
                     |      |___ SUB 2 FILE1
                     |      |___ SUB 2 FILE2
                     |
                     |___ SUB3
                            |___ SUB 3 FILE1
                            |___ SUB 3 FILE2
```

Assume the prompt is at A:\>. To move to the SUB2 subdirectory, type the command *CD TEST1\SUB2*. The command prompt changes to A:\TEST1\SUB2 >. Another command that will work is CD A:\TEST1\SUB2. To move to a subdirectory that is on the same level as the SUB2 directory (such as SUB1 or SUB3), several commands are possible. The easiest and fewest keystrokes are CD SUB1. Notice there is not a backslash (\) between the CD and the SUB1. Omit the backslash only when moving along the same level in the tree structure shown in DOS Figure #5. The commands CD\SUB1, or CD A:\TEST1\SUB1, or CD TEST1\SUB1 will each take you to subdirectory SUB1. However, if the prompt is currently located at the root directory, (A:\>), either A:\TEST1\SUB1 or CD TEST1\SUB1 must be used. The other commands given do not operate properly because of the current location within the tree structure. Practice is the only way to master moving around from a prompt. The following exercises should help with these concepts.

Name _____

COPY COMMAND EXERCISE

Objective: To use the COPY command correctly

Parts: A computer with a Windows operating system loaded
A formatted disk

For each step requiring a typed command the Enter key must be pressed to execute the DOS command. This instruction will *not* be given with each step.

Step 1.   Power the computer on and boot from the hard disk. If a logon password is needed, contact the instructor or lab assistant. When Windows loads, exit to a DOS prompt. If you forgot how, refer to the previous exercise.

Step 2.   In this next step, the command you type depends on the operating system installed. Make sure you know which operating system you are using before you type the command. If the command does not work, contact the instructor or lab assistant. The commands below assume standard operating system installation.

In Windows 9x: type **CD\WINDOWS\COMMAND**

In NT or Windows 2000: type **CD\WINNT\SYSTEM32**

Question 1:   What is the purpose of the CD command?

Step 3.   Type **COPY FORMAT.COM A:**

A message appears stating that one file copied. If the message does not appear, redo Steps 2 and 3. Since the prompt is currently at the COMMAND directory, the full source path does not have to be typed. The destination is the A: drive's root directory.

Step 4.   Type **COPY XCOPY.EXE A:**

A message appears stating that one file copied. If the message does not appear, perform Step 4 again.

Question 2:   Do a directory of the floppy disk to verify the two files copied properly. List the command used to perform this step. If the files are not on the disk, redo the steps again.

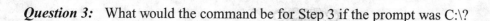

Question 3: What would the command be for Step 3 if the prompt was C:\?

Question 4: Could the backslash (\) be omitted in the command's destination (A:\)? Why or why not?

Step 5. From the prompt, type the following commands:

A:

CD

MD\TEST

The first command, A:, makes the floppy drive the default. The CD\ command instructs the operating system to change the directory to the root directory. The MD command is used to make a directory. The MD\TEST command creates a directory called TEST.

Step 6. Type **COPY A:*.* A:\TEST**

A message appears stating that two files copied. If a message does not appear, redo this step.

Question 5: What does the command in Step 6 do?

Step 7. To verify Step 6, type the following commands:

CD\TEST

DIR

The command prompt should be A:\TEST>. Both the FORMAT and the XCOPY commands should appear on the screen. If not, redo the exercise.

Step 8. From the prompt, type **CD..**

The system returns to the root directory.

Step 9. From the prompt, type **DIR A:\TEST**

Question 6: What is the difference between Step 7 and Step 9?

Step 10. Multiple files can be copied using wildcards. To start, we must create another directory. Type **MD FUN**

Notice how this command is different from Step 5. It does not include a backslash between MD and the directory name. The backslash is not required. The backslash is required if the default prompt is not in the directory if the subdirectory is being created. For example, I have a directory called CHERYL. The prompt is at the root directory. If I wanted to create a subdirectory under CHERYL called CLASSES, from the prompt, I would type MD CHERYL\CLASSES. If the prompt was A:\CHERYL>, I would simply type MD CLASSES.

Step 11. Type **COPY A:\TEST*.* A:\FUN**

When the copying is complete, a message appears stating how many files copied. If the message does not appear, perform the step again. COPY is the command. In the part A:\TEST*.*, the A: tells what drive (the floppy drive). The \TEST portion tells the operating system that the files to copy are in the TEST directory that is off the root directory (the backslash before TEST designates the root). The *.* tells the operating system what files to copy. The backslash separates the directory name from the filename. Since we want all of the files in the TEST directory top be copied to FUN, wildcards are used. Otherwise we would have to type a command for every file to be copied. The A:\FUN is the destination. This tells the operating system to place the copied files on the floppy drive in a directory called FUN.

Question 7: Why are two asterisks used in Step 11?

Question 8: Is the A:\TEST a necessary part of Step 8's command? Why or why not?

Step 12. The COPY command can also copy a file and rename it at the same time. For example, to copy the AUTOEXEC.BAT file to a disk and rename the file to AUTOEXEC.BAK, type the following command: **COPY C:\AUTOEXEC.BAT A:\AUTOEXEC.BAK**

A message appears stating that one file copied. If the message does not appear, perform the step again.

Question 9: Verify the AUTOEXEC.BAK file is placed in the floppy disk's root directory. Write the command used to verify the copying.

_____ *Instructor's Initials*

Step 13. In today's operating system, the PATH command is automatically loaded through the IO.SYS command. To view the current PATH statement, type **PATH** from the C:\> prompt.

Question 10: Write the computer's path.

_____

ON YOUR OWN

Step A. Create a backup copy of the CONFIG.SYS file located in the hard drive's root directory to the floppy disk's root directory. Name the file CONFIG.BAK. Complete everything using *one* command. Write the command in the space below:

Step B. Verify that the CONFIG.BAK file is in the floppy drive's root directory. Write *each* command used to verify the file in the space below:

Step C. Look on the hard drive to see what directories are available. Use the PATH command to set the path used by the operating system to search for executable files and include at least two hard drive directories. Write the command used to complete this task.

_____

_____ *Instructor's Initials*

Step 14. Remove the floppy disk and reboot the computer.

Name _____

XCOPY, RD, AND DELETE COMMANDS EXERCISE

Objective: To use the XCOPY and DELETE commands correctly

Parts: A computer with a Windows operating system loaded
                 A formatted disk

For each step requiring a typed command the Enter key must be pressed to execute the DOS command. This instruction will *not* be given with each step.

Step 1. Power the computer on and boot from the hard disk. If a logon password is needed, contact the instructor or lab assistant. When Windows loads, exit to a DOS prompt. If you forgot how, refer to the previous exercise.

Step 2. Insert a disk into the A: drive and create two files, one called FRIEND.TXT and another called FOE.TXT, and place the files in the A: drive's root directory. Use an editor to create the two files. Type two lines of text in each file.

Question 1: Have a classmate verify the creation of each file using the TYPE command. Write the commands they use to do this in the space below.

Classmate's printed name: _____

Classmate's initials: _____

Step 3. From the C:\> prompt, type **XCOPY A:\F*.* A:\TEST1**

A message might appear asking if TEST1 is a file or a directory. If so, press **D** for directory. A message appears stating the number of files copied. If the message does not appear, redo Steps 2 and 3.

Question 2: What does the command in Step 3 do?

There are several ways to delete files in DOS, but today's operating systems only include the DEL (DELETE) command for deleting files.

Step 4. Verify that the files copied.

Question 3: Have a classmate verify the creation of the directory and that the files copied. Write the commands they use to do this in the space below.

Classmate's printed name: _____

Classmate's initials: _____

    Step 5. From the C:\> prompt, type **DEL A:\TEST1*.***

Question 4: Verify that the files are deleted from the TEST1 directory. Write the commands to verify this operation in the space below.

_____***Instructor's Initials***

    The RD or RMDIR (Remove Directory) command removes the directory name only if all the directory's files are deleted prior to issuing the RD command.

    Step 6. From the C:\> prompt, type **RD A:\TEST1**

        This command removes the TEST1 directory.

    Step 7. Verify that the directory is gone by typing **DIR A:\TEST1**

ON YOUR OWN

    Step A. Verify the disk is in the first floppy drive and type the following commands:

        A:

        MD\TEST2

        CD\TEST2

        MD SUB1

        MD SUB2

        MD SUB3

Question 5: What would have happened if the command typed was MD\SUB1, MD\SUB2, and MD\SUB3?

Step B. Using an editor, create three files called FILE1, FILE2, FILE3 and place the files in the SUB1 subdirectory. Verify that the files are created and in the current directory before proceeding.

Step C. Using the XCOPY command, copy all of the files located in SUB1 subdirectory to the SUB2 and SUB3 subdirectories on the floppy disk.

Question 6: Verify the files copy to each subdirectory. Write the commands you used to perform this step in the space below.

Question 7: Draw a tree of the floppy disk's file structure in the area below.

_____ *Instructor's Initials*

Step 8. Removing subdirectories is a chore from the command prompt. Directories and subdirectories must be empty before the RD command can be used. From the A:\> prompt, type
DEL A:\TEST2\SUB1*.*
This command deletes all files in the SUB1 subdirectory.

Step 9. To remove the SUB1 subdirectory, type **RD A:\TEST2\SUB1**
Only the SUB1 subdirectory is deleted.

Question 8: Verify the SUB1 subdirectory has been deleted. Write the command you use in the space below.

ON YOUR OWN

Step D. Delete the files in the SUB2 and SUB3 subdirectories.

Step E. Remove the SUB2 and the SUB3 subdirectories.

_____*Instructor's Initials*

Name _____

ATTRIB COMMAND AND MOVING AROUND
IN THE TREE STRUCTURE EXERCISE

Objective: To use the ATTRIB command and to work correctly from a prompt when dealing with directories and subdirectories

Parts: A computer with a Windows operating system loaded
A formatted disk

For each step requiring a typed command the Enter key must be pressed to execute the DOS command. This instruction will *not* be given with each step.

Step 1.   Power the computer on and boot from the hard disk. If a logon password is needed, contact the instructor or lab assistant. When Windows loads, exit to a DOS prompt. If you forgot how, refer to the previous exercise.

Step 2.   Insert the disk into the floppy drive. On the disk, make a directory called JUNK. Type

A:

MD JUNK

Step 3.   Under the JUNK directory, make subdirectories called SUB1, SUB2, and SUB3. Type

CD JUNK

MD SUB1

MD SUB2

MD SUB3

Step 4.   Return to the floppy drive's root directory. Be sure the root directory is the default directory by looking at the command prompt after returning to the root directory.

Question 1:   What command makes the floppy drive's root directory the default directory? What does the command prompt look like?

Step 5.   Make a new directory called TRASH from the root directory of the floppy drive. Within the TRASH directory, make subdirectories called SUB1, SUB2, and SUB3. Type

MD TRASH

CD TRASH

MD SUB1

MD SUB2

MD SUB3

Step 6. Return to the floppy drive's root directory.

ON YOUR OWN

Step A. Make a new directory called GARBAGE from the floppy drive's root directory. Within the GARBAGE directory, make subdirectories called SUB1, SUB2, and SUB3. Write each command you use.

Step B. Create three files called SPECIAL1.TXT, SPECIAL2.TXT, and TICKLE.TXT. Place them in the GARBAGE\SUB1 subdirectory on the floppy drive. Write each command you use.

Step C. Copy all files that begin with the letter *S* from the GARBAGE\SUB1 subdirectory and place them in the TRASH\SUB3 subdirectory on the floppy drive. Write each command you use.

Step D. Copy the file that begins with *T* from the GARBAGE\SUB1 directory of the hard drive and place them in the SUB2 subdirectory of the JUNK directory. Write each command that you use.

_____ *Instructor's Initials*

Step 7. The TREE command is useful for viewing the file structure of a disk or a drive. Type **TREE**

An image of the disk tree structure is displayed on the screen. If it does not appear, perform the step again.

Step 8. The TREE command also verifies files within the tree structure using the /F switch. Type the following:

A:

TREE /F

A listing of the three directories, TRASH, GARBAGE, and JUNK is displayed as well as the SUB1, SUB2, and SUB3 subdirectories. The /F switch causes the files within each subdirectory to appear. The SUB2 subdirectory of JUNK holds the TICKLE file. The SUB1 subdirectory of GARBAGE holds the SPECIAL1, SPECIAL2, and TICKLE files. The SUB3 subdirectory of TRASH holds the SPECIAL1 and SPECIAL2 files. Repeat the On Your Own steps if these files do not appear on the screen.

Step 9. To make the SPECIAL1 and SPECIAL2 files read-only, use the ATTRIB command with the +R switch. Type

ATTRIB +R A:\TRASH\SUB3*.*

Step 10. To verify the read-only attribute is set, type

DIR A:\TRASH\SUB3*.*

The SUB3 subdirectory should list two files. Both have an *R* beside them indicating that the read-only attribute is set. If the two files do *not* have the read-only attribute set, perform Steps 9 and 10 again.

Step 11. The best way to prove that the files are read-only is to try and delete them. Type

DEL A:\TRASH\SUB3*.*

A message appears on the screen stating "All files in directory will be deleted. Are you sure (Y/N)?"

Step 12. From the prompt, type **Y** for Yes. A message appears on the screen stating, "Access denied." Then, the command prompt appears. If the access denied message does not appear, the files were deleted which means the read-only attribute was not set. If this is the case, perform On Your Own Step B, followed by Steps 9, 10, 11, and 12 of this exercise.

Step 13. Hiding a directory is always useful to a technician. Users who constantly delete directories or files by mistake can sometimes be controlled using the ATTRIB command's +H switch. Type

ATTRIB +H A:\JUNK\SUB2

No message appears on the screen. The command prompt appears again.

Step 14. To verify that the directory is hidden, type **DIR A:\JUNK*.***

The file should not appear.

Step 15. Use the ATTRIB command to verify that the directory is hidden by typing the following:

ATTRIB A:\JUNK\SUB2

The directory listing appears with an *H* beside the name.

Step 16. The two hidden files that make a disk or a drive bootable are automatically marked as system files. Type

ATTRIB C:*.*

The two system files appear, similar to the example below:

     A   SHR   C:\IO.SYS

     A   SHR   C:\MSDOS.SYS

The SHR indicates that the two hidden files have the system, hidden, and read-only attributes set. If a similar display does not appear, type the command in Step 15 again. If there are more files than will fit on one screen, type

ATTRIB C:*.* |more

The symbol before the word *more* is called the pipe symbol. For most keyboards, create the pipe symbol by holding down the Shift key and pressing the backslash key. The symbol looks like two vertical dashes on the keyboard key. The pipe symbol and the word *more* are used with many DOS commands that do not have a switch such as /P to display one screen at a time.

ON YOUR OWN

Step E. Hide the SPECIAL1.TXT file located in the SUB1 subdirectory of the GARBAGE directory. Write the command you used.

Step F. Verify that the SPECIAL1.TXT file is hidden, by using the DIR and ATTRIB commands. Write the command you used.

_____ *Instructor's Initials*

Step G. Remove the hidden attribute from the SPECIAL1.TXT file in the SUB1 subdirectory of the GARBAGE directory. Use Help, if necessary to find the switch to remove an attribute. Write the command used in the space below.

Step 17. Have a classmate verify that the SPECIAL1.TXT file is no longer hidden.

Classmate's printed name: _____

Classmate's initials: _____

Step 18. Make the current drive the floppy drive's root directory. If the command prompt is not A:\>, try this step again and refer to prior notes and exercises.

Step 19. Moving around within subdirectories can be a challenge, when you first use a prompt. Move to the SUB3 subdirectory of the TRASH directory by typing

CD TRASH\SUB3

The command prompt changes to A:\TRASH\SUB3>.

Step 20. Moving to the SUB2 or the SUB1 directory is much simpler because the SUB1 and SUB2 directories are on the same level as SUB3. Type

CD SUB1

The command prompt changes to A:\TRASH\SUB1>.

Step 21. A shortcut to move up one directory is to type CD.. from within the SUB1 subdirectory and the prompt immediately changes to one level up (the TRASH directory). Type

CD..

The command prompt changes to A:\TRASH.

Step 22. Using the CD.. command again returns one level back in the directory structure to the root directory of the floppy drive. Type

CD..

The command prompt changes to A:\.

ON YOUR OWN

Step H. From the root directory of the floppy drive change to the SUB2 subdirectory of the GARBAGE directory. Write the command used in the space below.

Step I. How can one verify that the current directory is A:\GARBAGE\SUB2?

Step J. From the A:\GARBAGE\SUB2 subdirectory, change the current directory to the SUB3 subdirectory of the TRASH directory. Write the command you use.

Step 23. Have a classmate verify that the current directory is A:\TRASH\SUB3.

Classmate's printed name: _____

Classmate's initials: _____

Step 24. Using the CD.. command, move from A:\TRASH\SUB3 to A:\TRASH.

Step 25. Using the CD.. command, move from A:\TRASH to A:\.

ON YOUR OWN

Step K. Using the ATTRIB, DEL, and RD commands delete the TRASH and GARBAGE directories including all subdirectories underneath them. Write the commands used in the space below.

Step L. Using the ATTRIB, DEL, and the RD command, delete the JUNK directory and all subdirectories underneath. Write the commands used in the space below.

_____ *Instructor's Initials*

Name _____

DOS REVIEW QUESTIONS

1. What does an operating system do for a microcomputer?

2. List at least two operating systems.

3. What file is known as the command interpreter?

4. [T / F] All system files are the same between DOS versions.

5. [T / F] Internal commands are part of the command interpreter.

6. What is the difference between internal and external commands?

7. Give an example of what the command prompt looks like.

8. [T / F] The root directory is limited in how many files can exist there.

9. Why should directories be created on a hard disk instead of placing every file in the root directory?

10. What is the difference between a directory and subdirectory?

11. What command always allows you to move to the root directory?

12. Which of the following DOS filenames are valid? (Pick all that apply)
     [RAINA.TXT / KARLTEXT2 / KARA.EXE / TROUBLE.SYS / THOMAS.BAT]

13. What is the purpose of the FORMAT command's /S switch?

14. Which of the following commands controls how the command prompt appears?
     [SHOW / TREE / VIEW / PROMPT]

15. What do the PG parameters do when used with the PROMPT command?
    A. Displays the path and > sign
    B. Displays the drive letter and the > sign
    C. Keeps the prompt from showing on the screen
    D. Tells DOS where to find commands

16. What does the SYS command do?

17. What is the purpose of the path statement in the AUTOEXEC.BAT file?

18. [T / F] Every computer requires the AUTOEXEC.BAT file.

19. What file extensions does DOS look for to execute? (Pick all that apply)
    [.BAT / .TXT / .WIN / .COM / .HLP / .EXT / .EXE]

20. What program allows the use of arrow keys to bring up previously entered DOS commands?

21. Which of the following keystrokes allows you to view the last executed DOS command by single characters?
    [F1 / F3 / F5 / F7 / F8]

22. Which of the following keystrokes brings up the last executed DOS command?
    [F1 / F3 / F5 / F7 / F8]

23. Which of the following commands is for viewing text files on the screen?
    [VIEW / SCREEN / OUTPUT / TYPE / EDIT]

24. What is the purpose of the CONFIG.SYS file?

25. [T / F] Every computer requires the CONFIG.SYS file.

26. [T / F] The COPY CON command is easier to use than Microsoft's EDIT editor when editing or creating a file.

27. What are some common mistakes technicians make when using the COPY or XCOPY commands?

28. [T / F] The COPY command does not always require a destination.

29. Which of the following commands can be used to delete a file? (Pick all that apply)
    [DELTREE / DEL / ERADICATE / RD]

30. [T / F] The ATTRIB command cannot hide directories.

31. List two file attributes.

Name _____

DOS FILL-IN-THE-BLANK

1. A computer needs an _____ to operate.

2. All viewable DOS commands are known as _____ commands.

3. The first floppy drive is assigned the drive letter _____.

4. The first hard drive partition is assigned the drive letter _____.

5. All DOS work is done from the _____.

6. DOS files are grouped into _____.

7. The _____ directory is the starting place for all files and directories.

8. DOS filenames can be up to _____ characters and have _____ letter extensions.

9. The _____ command is used to move around in the tree structure.

10. The _____ command is used to erase floppy disks.

11. The _____ command is used to transfer system files to a disk.

12. The _____ file, if found, is a batch file that executes when the computer boots.

13. _____ is the DOS command that keeps batch file commands from showing on the screen.

14. The _____ statement tells the operating system where to search for files.

15. The _____ program allows easy access to previously typed commands.

16. The _____ file customizes the computer's environment.

17. _____ are pieces of software that allow hardware to operate.

18. _____ is the text editor shipped with Microsoft DOS.

19. The _____ DOS command is an external command used for copying files, directories, and subdirectories.

20. ATTRIB +R A:\TEST\TEST1.DOC sets the _____ attribute on the _____ file.

21. The _____ command shows the DOS file structure.

22. The _____ symbol used with the word more is frequently used to show one screen of data at a time.

 Name _____

INTERNET DISCOVERY

Objective: To obtain specific information on the Internet regarding a computer or associated parts

Parts: Access to the Internet

Question 1:   Locate an Internet site that lists DOS commands and shows different examples of the commands. Write the URL in the space below.

Question 2:   Use the Internet to find the DOS commands that Windows 2000 supports when working from a prompt.

Question 3:   Find a web site that explains the use of the DISKCOPY command. The site cannot be one used for Questions 1 or 2.

Question 4:   Find the steps to create a Windows 98 boot disk on the Internet. Write down the site(s) you found.

Question 5:   Using the Internet, locate a site that details how to write a BATCH file.

Question 6:   Describe the steps to change the drive letter for an Iomega Zip drive when using 2000 Professional. Also write the URL of the Internet location where you found this information in the space below.

NOTES

15

Chapter 15:

Windows 98

OBJECTIVES

After completing this chapter you will

- Understand the major differences between Windows 98 and other operating systems.
- Be able to identify, explain, and use common desktop icons.
- Be able to manage files and folders.
- Understand the purpose of the registry, how it is organized into subtrees, and understand the function of each subtree.
- Be able to edit, backup, and restore the registry.
- Be able to install and troubleshoot Windows 98.
- Be able to install hardware and software on a Windows 98 computer.
- Understand the boot process and be able to troubleshoot boot problems including using Safe Mode.
- Be able to create and use an Emergency Repair Disk.
- Understand Windows 98 power and resource management capabilities.
- Know when to access and how to use Dr. Watson, System Monitor, and Resource Meter.

KEY TERMS

Apply button	GUI	shortcut
ASD.EXE	Help button	Show Desktop
boot sector virus	icon	Start button
Cancel button	Internet Explorer	Startup menu
checkbox	macro virus	stealth virus
clean install	MSINFO	System Configuration
Close button	multi-boot	System File Checker (SFC.EXE)
cooperative multitasking	My Computer	system files
desktop	My Documents	System Monitor
dialog box	OK button	taskbar
Dr. Watson	OnNow	textbox
drop-down menu	path	Trojan horse virus
dual-boot	polymorphic virus	user profile
ESCD	preemptive multitasking	Version Conflict Manager
extension	Quick Launch bar	virtual machine
file	radio button	virus
file virus	Recycle Bin	window
folder	registry	Windows Explorer
GPF	Resource Meter	worm virus

WINDOWS 98 OVERVIEW

Microsoft's Windows 98 is a popular operating system normally used by home users and small businesses. It is a 32-bit operating system that supports plug and play, DVD drives, TV tuner adapters, FireWire, USB, multitasking, 16-bit applications, and 32-bit applications. Windows 98 is more stable than Windows 95; Microsoft states that over 3,000 Windows 95 bugs were fixed in 98. Windows 98 also has better system maintenance and monitoring utilities, and it supports more hardware than Windows 95. Windows 98 supports older (16-bit) applications better and takes less hard drive space and memory than NT Workstation and 2000 Professional, but it does not have the built-in security capabilities that NT and 2000 offer. Microsoft's Windows 98 home page is at http://www.microsoft.com/windows98/.

Internet Explorer, a web browser for connecting to the Internet, is integrated into Windows 98. Windows 98 also supports Internet conferencing and Internet connection sharing. DOS, Windows 3.x and Windows 95 can be upgraded to Windows 98. There are two versions of Windows 98. The file systems that Windows 98 supports for hard drive partitions are FAT16 and FAT32. A FAT16 partition can be converted to a FAT32 partition using the CVT1.EXE command from a command prompt. Once a partition is converted to FAT32, it cannot be reconverted to FAT16. For CDs, Windows 98 uses the CDFS file system (Compact Disk File System) and UDF (Universal Disk Format). CDFS for CDs and UDF for CDs and DVDs. See the Multimedia chapter for more discussion on these file systems. When a computer's drive has already been formatted with a HPFS or NTFS partition, a FAT16 partition must be created before installing Windows 98.

WINDOWS 98 BASICS

After booting Windows 98 and possibly logging on to a network (this is optional), the desktop appears. The login screen can be bypassed as in Windows 95. If the computer is networked, a user can login to a network server or login to a network workgroup (peer-to-peer network). The **desktop** is the area where all work in 98 begins. It is the interface between the user and the computer files, applications, and hardware. The desktop is part of the operating system's **GUI (Graphical User Interface)** environment. The desktop consists of icons and shortcuts. An **icon** is a graphical representation of an application, file, folder, or utility. A **shortcut** is a special type of icon created by the user to quickly access a file or application.

When you double-click on an icon or shortcut, you open an application, file, or window that allows you to interface with various devices installed or connected to the computer. A **window** is a part of the screen that belongs to a specific application or utility. Windows are a normal part of the working environment through the desktop. A shortcut icon looks like any other desktop icon except that it has a bent arrow in the lower left corner. A shortcut represents a path (location on the drive) to a file, folder, or program. It is a link (a pointer) to where the file or application resides on a disk. When you double-click on a shortcut

icon, the shortcut icon tells Windows where to find the specific file that the icon represents. If the shortcut represents an application, the application opens. If the shortcut represents a document, the application used to create the document appears along with the document. A shortcut offers faster access to an application or file than going through the Start button or through the My Computer icon. Users and technicians frequently place shortcuts on the desktop and you must know how to create one. Users create shortcuts to their favorite applications or to documents used frequently.

Sometimes the desktop is cluttered with things the user puts on it. An exercise at the end of the chapter demonstrates how to clean up the desktop. One of the 98 features you can set for the desktop is Auto Arrange. When the Auto Arrange option is enabled, the desktop icons cannot be moved.

One way to modify the desktop is by changing the wallpaper scheme. A wallpaper scheme is a background picture, pattern, or color. Other changes to the desktop are altering the color scheme (which is used in displaying folders), and enabling a screen saver (which is the picture, color, or pattern that displays when the computer is inactive). An exercise at the end of the chapter describes how to change each of these. WIN98 Figure #1 shows an illustration of the Windows 98 desktop.

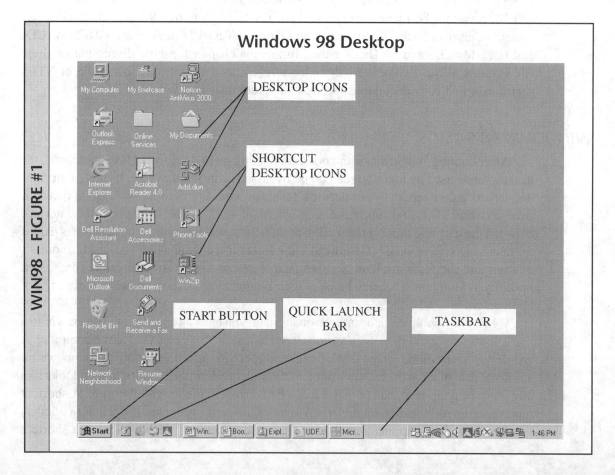

As mentioned before, icons are an important part of the Windows 98 desktop. The desktop consists of various icons such as My Documents, My Computer, Recycle Bin, and Internet Explorer. These can be seen in WIN98 Figure #1. The **My Documents** icon is used to quickly access the My Documents folder (directory) on the hard drive. The My Documents folder is the default location for files the user saves. The **My Computer** icon is used to access the hardware, software, and files located on the computer. The **Recycle Bin** is used to hold files and folders that the user deletes. When a file or folder is deleted, it is not really gone. Instead, it goes into the Recycle Bin. The deleted file or folder can be removed forever from the Recycle Bin, just as a piece of trash can be removed from a real trash can. The deleted files and folders in the Recycle Bin take up hard drive space. A technician must remember that some users cannot (or do not remember) to empty the Recycle Bin. The **Internet Explorer** icon is used to start the Internet Explorer application, which is used when communicating across the Internet. Internet Explorer is Microsoft's Internet communications package.

Other common desktop items include the Start button, Quick Launch bar, and the taskbar. The **Start button** is located in the lower left corner of the desktop and is used to launch applications and utilities, find files and other computers, get help, and add/remove hardware and software. If the Start button does not appear on the desktop, hold the *CTRL* key down and press the *ESC* key. Another way to bring up the Start menu is by pressing the *Windows key* on the keyboard. This is the key that has the Windows graphic on it.

The Shut Down Start button option is used to shutdown the computer, restart the computer, restart the computer in MS-DOS mode, and possibly put the computer in standby. The Restart the computer in MS-DOS mode option restarts the computer and boots to a command prompt. From there, you can shut off the computer, type commands at the prompt, or type WIN to start the GUI Windows 98 environment. The Standby option is available on computers that support power saving features. Standby is helpful on laptop computers to save on battery life.

The Log Off Start button option stops the current environment and brings up a dialog box for a user name and password. This is so others can log into a network or onto the computer with a user name and password and display their own customized desktop. Press the *ESC* key to bypass the dialog box. The Run Start button option starts an application or brings up a command prompt window. The Help option is for Windows 98 general usage and troubleshooting assistance. The Find Start button option helps to locate files and remote network devices.

The Settings option is used to access various suboptions that allow computer configuration. This is one of the most commonly used Start menu options for technicians. Look in WIN98 Figure #2 at the Settings menu. The Control Panel option is used to access various utilities that customize the Windows 98 environment such as the display, mouse, CD-ROM, etc. The Printers selection is used to install, configure, or monitor a printer. The Taskbar and Start Menu item is used to customize the taskbar or Start button menu. Folder Options brings up a dialog box that allows you to change how files and folders appear on the screen. The Active Desktop option allows enabling, disabling, or customizing the Active

Desktop environment. The Windows Update submenu item is used to connect to the Microsoft Web site to access the most recent drivers and operating system updates.

The Documents selection contains the 15 most recently used files (provided the application supports this option). The Favorites Start menu item is a list of preferred web sites. The Programs choice allows access to applications installed in the computer. WIN98 Figure #2 shows the Start button.

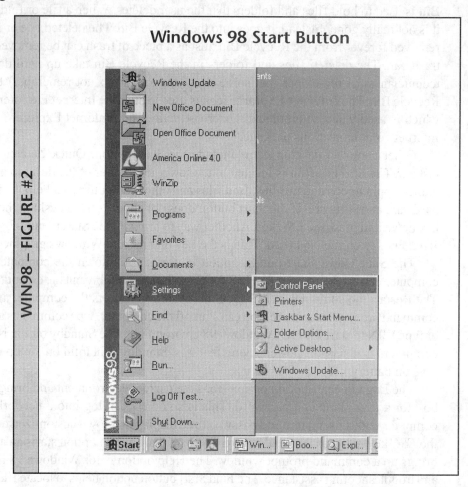

The **Quick Launch bar** is a set of icons to the right of the Start button and allows you to launch applications with one click on a Quick Launch icon. The Quick Launch bar is a great addition to the GUI operating system for those people who have many windows open at one time. An important icon on the Quick Launch bar is the **Show Desktop** icon. This icon looks like a desk with a pencil touching a piece of paper. A click on the Show Desktop icon reduces all windows and displays the desktop. Another Quick Launch icon is the Internet Explorer. Click once on this icon and the Internet Explorer application opens. If a user does not prefer the Quick Launch bar, right-click on an *empty taskbar space,* point to the *Toolbars* option, and click on *Quick Launch*.

An important desktop item is the taskbar. The **taskbar** is the bar that runs across the bottom of the screen. The taskbar holds buttons that represent applications or files currently loaded into memory. The taskbar also holds icons that allow access to system utilities. These utilities can include a clock icon for the date and time, an icon of a speaker for volume control, and an icon for a virus utility. Look back to WIN98 Figure #1 to identify the taskbar. An exercise at the end of the chapter helps you to become familiar with desktop components.

Technicians frequently interact with the Windows 98 operating system through a dialog box. A **dialog box** is used by the operating system and with Windows applications and allows you to configure application or operating system preferences. The most common features found in a dialog box are a checkbox, textbox, tabs, a drop-drown menu, a Help button, a Close button, an OK button, and a Cancel button. A **textbox** is an area where you can type a specific parameter. When you click inside a textbox, a vertical line appears, which is the insertion point. Any typed text is placed to the right of the insertion point. Notice in WIN98 Figure #3 how the Top, Bottom, Inside, Outside, etc., options are textboxes. Textboxes sometimes have up or down arrows that can be used to select a preset option or you can simply type your own parameter.

Tabs normally appear across the top of a dialog box. Each tab normally holds a group of related options. Click once on the tab to bring that particular major section to the window forefront. The tabs in WIN98 Figure #3 are Margins, Paper Size, Paper Source, and Layout.

The **Help button** is used to provide context sensitive assistance and is the question mark located in the upper right corner of the dialog box. When you click on the Help button (the question mark), the cursor turns into an arrow with a question mark attached. Click on any item you want basic information on: a pop-up window appears on the screen. To close the pop-up window, click anywhere on the screen. The **Close button**, which is an X located to the right of the Help button, is used to close the dialog box. When the Close button is used, changes that have been made in the dialog box are not applied.

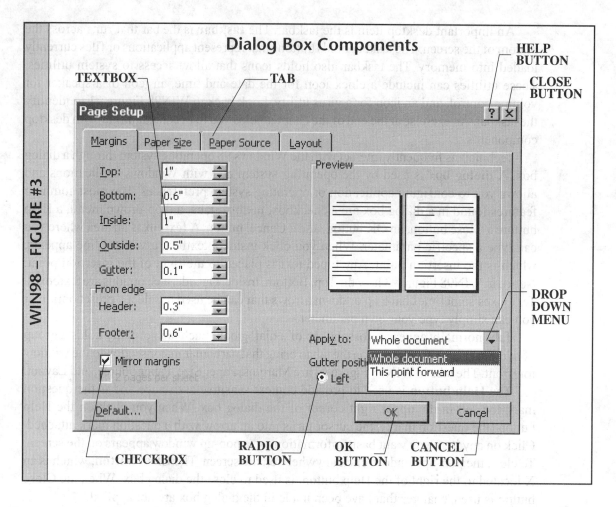

Dialog Box Components

WIN98 – FIGURE #3

When checked, a **checkbox** option is enabled or turned on. As shown in WIN98 Figure #3, clicking inside the checkbox enables the Mirror margins option. When an option is enabled, a checkmark appears in the checkbox. A **radio button** is a round circle, which behaves in the same way. A radio button is enabled when a solid dot appears in the radio button. Click once on a blank radio button and a solid dot appears in the radio button center. Click once on a radio button with a dot in it, and the dot disappears and the option is disabled.

Drop-down menus are presented when you click on a down arrow. The example in WIN98 Figure #3, shows a drop-down menu that appears when you click on the *down arrow* in the section marked *Apply to*. Clicking on the *preferred option* in the drop-down menu causes that option to appear in the drop-down window.

The **OK button** and the **Cancel button** are standard in a dialog box. When you click on the OK button, all options selected or changed within the dialog box are applied. When you click on the Cancel button, all changed options in the dialog box are not applied; the options are left in their original state. Another related button that can be found in a dialog box, but is not shown in WIN98 Figure #3, is the Apply button. The **Apply button** is used to make changes immediately (before clicking on the OK button). One example is when changes are made to the desktop's background.

 New technicians often make the mistake of clicking on the Close button (the button with an X). When a dialog box is closed with the Close button, no changes in the dialog box window are saved or applied.

MANAGING FILES AND FOLDERS

Technicians are always creating, deleting, and moving files and folders. It is important that you are able to do these tasks quickly and without error. The important thing to remember is to think about what file and folder you want to work with, where the files and folders are located now, and where you want the files or folders to be eventually.

A drive letter followed by a colon represents every drive in a computer. For example, the floppy drive is represented by A: and the first hard drive partition is represented by C:. The CD-ROM drive, DVD, or Zip drive are all represented by a drive letter followed by a colon. Disks or drives hold files. A **file** is an electronic container that holds computer code or data. Another way of looking at it is thinking of a file as a box of bits. A file is kept on some type of media, such as a floppy disk, Zip disk, hard drive, tape, or CD. Each file is given a name called a filename. An example of a filename is 98CHAP.DOC.

Files are kept in folders. A **folder** holds files and can also contain other folders. In older operating systems, a folder was called a directory. Every file and folder is given a name. It is easier to understand file and folder names if we look at how older operating systems named files and folders and then look at how Windows 98 names differ. In older operating systems (DOS), a filename could *not* contain the following characters:

. (period)	; (semicolon)	/ (forward slash)
, (comma)	" (quotation marks)	\ (backslash)
| (vertical bar)	? (question mark)	[(left bracket)
: (colon)	= (equal sign)	] (right bracket)
* (asterisk)	(space)	

In DOS, you would frequently have to add an extension to the name. An **extension** is an addition to the filename and it can be up to three characters in length. The filename and the extension are separated by a period. An example of a filename with an extension is BOOK.DOC where BOOK is the name of the file and DOC is the extension.

With Windows 95/98/NT/2000, the application normally adds an extension to the end of the filename. In most windows, Windows 98 does not automatically show the extensions. To view the extensions in Windows Explorer, click on the *View* menu option. Click on the *View* tab and on the *Hide file extensions for known file types* check box, which will remove the check from the box. Click on the *OK* button.

When Windows recognizes an extension, it associates that extension with a particular application. WIN98 Figure #4 illustrates common icons that Windows 98 uses when it recognizes an extension. An exercise at the end of this chapter will demonstrate how to get Windows to recognize a new file extension.

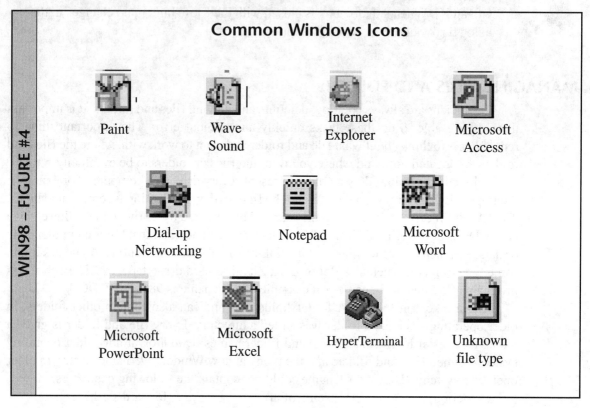

Common Windows Icons

WIN98 – FIGURE #4

Paint   Wave Sound   Internet Explorer   Microsoft Access

Dial-up Networking   Notepad   Microsoft Word

Microsoft PowerPoint   Microsoft Excel   HyperTerminal   Unknown file type

Filename extensions can tell you a lot about a file, such as which application created the file or what purpose the file has. WIN98 Table #1 lists the most common file extensions, their purposes, and which application typically creates the extension.

WIN98 – TABLE #1

Common File Extensions

Extension	Purpose or Application
386	Used by Windows 3.x for device drivers
AI	Adobe Illustrator
BAT	Used in DOS environments for batch files. Combines executable commands into one file and uses one command to start the batch file.
BMP	Bitmap file
CAB	Cabinet file—a compressed file that holds operating system or application files
COM	Command file—an executable file that opens an application or tool
DLL	Dynamic Link Library file —contains executable code that can be used by more than one application and is called upon from other code already running
DOC	Microsoft Word
DRV	Device driver —a piece of software that enables an operating system to recognize a hardware device
EPS	Encapsulated postscript file
EXE	Executable file—a file that opens an application
GIF	Graphics interchange file
HLP	Windows-based help file
INF	Information or setup file
INI	Initialization file—Used in Windows 3.x environment to control applications and the operating environment. Used in 95, 98, NT, and 2000 to be backward compatible with Windows 3.x
JPG or JPEG	Joint Photographic Experts Group file format— graphics file
MPG or MPEG	Movie clip file
PCX	Microsoft Paintbrush
PDF	Adobe Acrobat—portable document format
PPT	Microsoft PowerPoint
RTF	Rich text format
TIF or TIFF	Tag image file format
TXT	Text file
VXD	Virtual device driver
WKS	Lotus worksheet
WPS	Microsoft Works text file format
WRI	Microsoft WordPad
XLS	Microsoft Excel
ZIP	Compressed file

Filenames in Windows 98 can be up to 255 characters in length. These extended filenames are commonly called long filenames. Folders and filenames can contain all characters, numbers, letters and spaces *except* the following:

/ (forward slash)	" (quotation marks)	\ (backslash)
| (vertical bar)	? (question mark)	: (colon)
* (asterisk)		

As you can see, the list is much shorter (which means more characters are allowed) in Windows 98.

An example of a long filename is WINDOWS 98 CHAPTER.DOC. Any time a document has been saved with one of these long filenames and is taken to an older computer with an operating system that does not support long filenames, the filename is shortened to a maximum of eight characters. Windows does this by using the first six characters of the filename, deleting any spaces, and using two special characters—a tilde (~) and a number. For example, WINDOWS 98 CHAPTER.DOC would be shortened to WINDOW~1.DOC. If there were two files named WINDOWS 98 CHAPTER.DOC and WINDOWS 98 INDEX.DOC, the two files would be saved as WINDOW~1.DOC and WINDOW~2.DOC, respectively.

When saving a file in a Windows application, the application automatically saves the file to a specific folder. This is known as the default folder. With Windows 98, this folder is the My Documents folder. In documentation, installation instructions, and when writing down the exact location of a file, the full path is used.

A file's **path** is like a road map to the file and includes the drive letter plus all folders and subfolders, as well as the filename and extension. For example, if the CHAP1.DOC file is in the MY DOCUMENTS folder on the first hard drive partition, the full path is C:\MY DOCUMENTS\CHAP1.DOC. The first part is the drive letter where the document is stored, C:. The *C:* represents the first hard drive partition. The name of the document is always at the very end of the path. In the example given, CHAP1.DOC is the name of the file. Everything in between the drive letter and the filename is the name of one or more folders where the CHAP1.DOC file is located. The folder in this example is the MY DOCUMENTS folder.

If the CHAP1.DOC file is located in a subfolder called COMPUTER BOOK, which is located in the folder called MY DOCUMENTS, then the full path is C:\MY DOCUMENTS\COMPUTER BOOK\CHAP1.DOC. Notice how the backslashes in the path are always used to separate the folder names as well as separate the drive letter from the first folder name.

Windows Explorer is the most common application used to create, copy, or move files or folders; however, the My Computer window can also be used in a similar fashion. When you are copying a file or folder, use the Copy/Paste functions. When you are moving a file or folder, use the Cut/Paste functions.

When you delete a file or folder from a floppy or Zip disk, the file or folder is permanently deleted. When you delete a file or folder from a hard drive, the file or folder is automatically sent to the Recycle Bin. The contents of the Recycle Bin take up hard drive space and many users do *not* realize that they are not really deleting the file, but simply moving it to the Recycle Bin. To delete a file permanently from the hard drive, hold down the *SHIFT* key while pressing the *DELETE* key on the keyboard. Otherwise, you will have to remember to empty the Recycle Bin periodically. An exercise at the end of the chapter illustrates how to copy, move, and delete files and folders. WIN98 Figure #5 shows how the A+ COMPLETE BOOK.DOC long filename looks in graphical form using the Windows Explorer application.

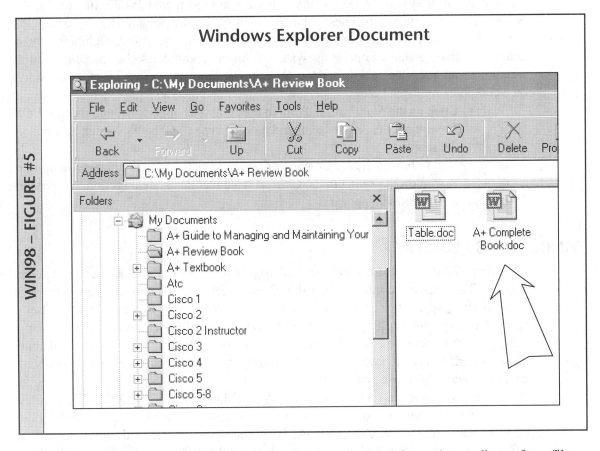

WIN98 – FIGURE #5

My Computer and Windows Explorer can be used for setting attributes for a file or folder. The file and folder attributes are read-only, hidden, archive, and system. The read-only attribute marks a file or folder so that it cannot be changed. The hidden attribute marks a file or folder so that it is not visible through My Computer or Windows Explorer unless someone changes the default view for the window. Some applications use the archive attribute to control which files or folders are backed up. The system attribute is placed on certain files used to boot Windows 98.

To change a file or folder's attributes, use My Computer or Windows Explorer to locate the file or folder. Right-click on the file or folder name. Click on the *Properties* option and the Properties window opens. Toward the bottom of the window is an *Attributes* section. Click inside one or more of the attribute checkboxes to enable or disable an attribute. A checkmark in a checkbox means an attribute is enabled. An empty checkbox means an attribute is disabled. If the file is not a system file, the system attribute is unavailable. Click on the *Apply* button when finished setting the attributes.

DETERMINING THE WINDOWS 98 VERSION

The operating system version is very important to a technician. With Windows 95, 98, NT, and 2000, upgrades or patches to the operating system are provided by way of service packs. A service pack fixes problems with the operating system. A technician must determine what version of operating system is on the computer so he/she can research whether or not a service pack is needed. Ways to determine what version of 98 is loaded on a computer are listed below.

- Click on the *Start* button. Point to the *Programs* option. Point to the *MS-DOS Prompt* option. At the command prompt, type *ver*. The 98 version appears on the screen.
- Right-click on the *My Computer* desktop icon. Click on the *Properties* option. A window appears. On the General tab under the System section, the version of Windows 98 appears.

WINDOWS 98 REGISTRY

Every 32-bit software and hardware configuration is stored in a database called the registry. The **registry** contains such things as folder and file property settings, port configuration, application preferences, and user profiles. A **user profile** contains a user's specific configuration settings, such as what applications the user has access to, desktop settings, user preferences, and the user's network configuration. The registry loads into memory during the boot process. Once in memory, the registry is updated continuously by changes made to software and hardware.

The registry is made up of two files—SYSTEM.DAT and USER.DAT. The registry files are stored in the folder where the Windows 98 files are located, which is normally the C:\WINDOWS folder. The SYSTEM.DAT holds computer-specific hardware settings, plug and play configurations, and application settings. USER.DAT holds user-specific files (the user profile settings) such as logon names, desktop settings, and Start button settings. Both files have the hidden attribute set by default. If the system is configured for multiple users (user profiles), a USER.DAT file is built for each user and is normally kept in the C:\WINDOWS\PROFILES*USER*\USER.DAT (where *USER* is the user name. If the system is configured for multiple users (user profiles).

In the Windows 3.x environment, .INI files were used instead of the registry. Each .INI file contained application-specific data, hardware configuration information, the computer environment configuration, and so forth. Windows 98 still has the SYSTEM.INI, PROTOCOL.INI, and WIN.INI files located in the default Windows 98 folder (normally

C:\WINDOWS) as well as the C:\COMMAND.COM, C:\AUTOEXEC.BAT and C:\CONFIG.SYS files so that older 16-bit applications can operate under Windows 98. To see the contents of these files, click on the *Start* button, click on the *Run* option, and type *SYSEDIT* in the dialog box. The System Configuration Editor opens with the SYSTEM.INI, WIN.INI, PROTOCOL.INI, AUTOEXEC.BAT, and CONFIG.SYS files open in separate windows.

The registry is divided into five subtrees. Subtrees are also sometimes called branches or hives. The five standard subtrees are as follows: HKEY_LOCAL_MACHINE, HKEY_USERS, HKEY_CURRENT_USER, HKEY_CURRENT_CONFIG, and HKEY_CLASSES_ROOT. Each of these subtrees has keys and subkeys that contain values related to hardware and software settings. WIN98 Table #2 lists the five subtrees and the function of each.

WIN98 – TABLE #2

Windows 98 Registry Subtrees

Registry Subtree	Subtree Function
HKEY_LOCAL_MACHINE	Holds global hardware configuration. Included in the branch is a list of hardware components installed in the computer, the software drivers that handle each component, and the settings for each device. This information is not user-specific.
HKEY_USERS	Keeps track of individual users and their preferences.
HKEY_CURRENT_USER	Holds a specific user's configuration such as software settings, how the desktop appears, and what folders the user has created.
HKEY_CURRENT_CONFIG	Holds information about the hardware profile that is used when the computer first boots.
HKEY_CLASSES_ROOT	Holds file associations and file links. The information held here is what allows the correct application to start when you double-click on a filename in Explorer or My Computer (provided the file extension is registered).

HYKEY_DYN_DATA is another subtree, but it is a dynamic subtree. This subtree contains current information about the status of hardware devices and software loaded during the current Windows session. The registry can contain other subtrees that are user-defined or system-defined depending on what hardware and software is installed in the computer.

In Windows 95, each registry key had a size limit of 64KB. This restriction was removed in Windows 98. In Windows 98, each registry key size is unlimited, but individual values within each subkey are limited to 16KB.

EDITING THE WINDOWS 98 REGISTRY

Most changes to Windows 98 are made through various control panels, but sometimes the only way to make a change is to edit the registry directly.

> Before making changes to the registry, be sure to make a backup of the registry. An exercise at the end of the chapter illustrates this procedure.

Windows 98 ships with a registry editor called REGEDIT. Some technical problems can only be corrected by editing the registry. The registry editor is not a tool for average users, but for technicians; thus it is not available through the Start menu or through System Tools. The REGEDIT program is accessed through the *Start* button. Click on the *Run* option, type *REGEDIT* in the dialog box, and click on the *OK* button.

With the REGEDIT program, subtrees are listed in the left window. Notice in WIN98 Figure #6 how the Registry Editor subtrees appear in the left window. Clicking on the + (plus) symbol beside each subtree, brings up more subkeys. When you click on a folder in the left window, values appear in the right window. These values are the ones you must change sometimes to fix a problem. In WIN98 Figure #6, you can see that the subtree HKEY_LOCAL_MACHINE\Hardware\Description\System\CentralProcessor\0 has an Identifier value of x86 Family 6 Model 8 Stepping 3. An exercise at the end of this chapter demonstrates how to work with the REGEDIT program.

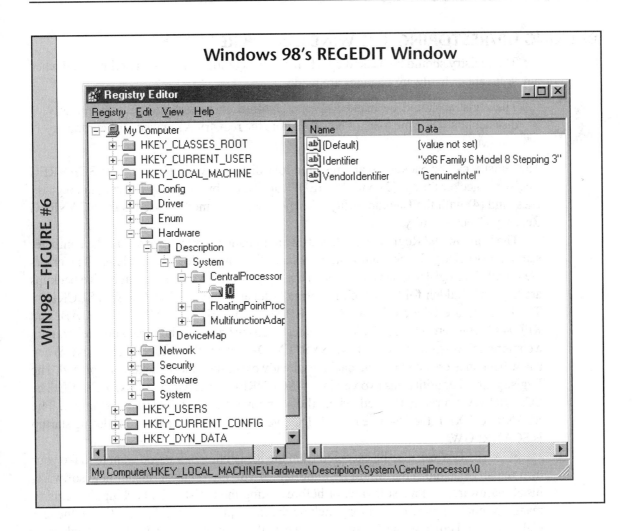

WIN98 – FIGURE #6

Windows 98's REGEDIT Window

BACKING UP/RESTORING THE WINDOWS 98 REGISTRY

The registry should be backed up whenever the computer is fully functional and when any software or hardware changes are made.

> The registry should be backed up and restored on a working computer *before* disaster hits. The time to learn how to restore the registry is *not* when the computer is down.

The registry can be backed up and restored four different ways: (1) using the SCANREG Registry Checker utility, (2) with REGEDIT utility, (3) by manually copying the registry files, and (4) with the Backup utility. The most common method used is the SCANREG Registry Checker utility.

The Windows 98 Registry Checker utility automatically starts every time the computer starts. The Registry Checker automatically scans the registry for any problems. If no errors are found, the Registry Checker backs up the registry once a day. By default, five backups are kept in a hidden folder, which is normally located in C:\WINDOWS\SYSBCKUP). The backups are labeled RB000.CAB, RB001.CAB, RB002.CAB, RB003.CAB, and RB004.CAB where RB000.CAB is the oldest registry backup. These backup files contain a compressed version of USER.DAT, SYSTEM.DAT, WIN.INI, and SYSTEM.INI. When a new backup is created and five backups already exist, the oldest backup is replaced. The Registry Checker utility has two versions—SCANREGW.EXE and SCANREG.EXE. The SCANREGW version is used when the Windows 98 GUI interface is active. The SCANREG.EXE is the 16-bit real-mode DOS version. The version that runs during startup is SCANREGW.

SCANREGW can also be executed from the Run dialog box if you want to make your own registry backup. This would be important if you are going to install new software, install hardware, remove software, or before editing the registry. To back up the registry manually, click on the *Start* button, click on the *Run* option, type *SCANREGW* in the text dialog box, and click on the *OK* button. You can also start Registry Checker through Start button ➔ Programs ➔ Accessories ➔ System Tools ➔ System Information. When the Microsoft System Information window opens, click on the *Tools* menu option and select *Registry Checker*. The SCANREGW program executes.

The Registry Checker runs and verifies that the registry does not have any errors, displays a message that the registry has already been backed up that current day, and prompts with the question, "Would you like to back it up again?" Click on the *Yes* button to make a backup of the registry. A prompt on the screen appears when the backup has completed successfully.

You can customize the Registry Checker utility by editing the SCANREG.INI file. The SCANREG.INI file is normally located in the C:\WINDOWS folder and you can edit it by opening the SCANREG.INI file in any text editor program such as Notepad or WordPad. WIN98 Table #3 lists the SCANREG.INI file entries and possible values.

WIN98 – TABLE #3

Windows 98 SCANREG.INI Entries

Entry	Explanation and Values
Backup=	0—disables registry backup 1—registry is backed up the first time the computer is started on a specific day
BackupDirectory=	Default is blank, which means that backups are saved to the WINDOWS\SYSBCKUP hidden folder. *x:\destination_path* where *x:\destination\path* is the drive letter and path for where the registry backups are to be stored
Files=	By default, this value does not exist, but is used to add files to the registry CAB backup file. *x:\path\filename* where *x:\path\filename* where *filename* is the name of the file to be backed up and *x:\path* is the drive letter and folder where the file is located
MaxBackupCopies=	Default is 5 Valid values are 0 to 99
Optimize=	Default value is 1, which means that the Registry Checker utility automatically optimizes the registry if it contains 500KB of unused space. Value of 0 means that the Registry Checker utility does not automatically optimize unused space in the registry.

The SCANREG program is normally used when the system does not boot properly, but it can be executed from the command prompt or from the *Run* dialog box. When the system does not boot properly, power on the computer, press and hold the *CTRL* key down, and then choose the *Safe Mode Command Prompt Only* from the Windows Startup menu. If the Startup menu does not appear, start the computer and press the *F8* key. This process is for computers that use the EZDrive tool. Once a command prompt appears, type *scanreg /restore*. If an error message appears, type *cd\default_folder\command* where *default_folder* is the folder where 98 is loaded (normally the WINDOWS folder). The Microsoft Registry Checker window appears. In the window, the backup file date, the words "started" or "not started," and the name of the file are listed. The first criterion for selecting a file is to select one that is started. Then, select the file with the most current date. Use the arrow keys to select the appropriate file and press *Enter* or press the *C* key to cancel.

The SCANREG.EXE program has several options that can be used to customize the way it works. WIN98 Table #4 lists the switches that can be used with the SCANREG command.

Windows 98 SCANREG Switches

WIN98 – TABLE #4

Switch	Explanation
/"comment=*text*"	*text* is a descriptive comment that is added to the registry backup
/autoscan	The registry is automatically scanned and backed up without displaying any prompts (if there is no backup for that specific day already)
/backup	Backs up the registry
/fix	This switch is used to repair the registry and optimize it by removing unused space
/opt	Optimizes the registry by removing unused space
/restore	Brings up the Registry Checker window and allows a specific registry backup file to be selected for repairing a system that will not boot or operate correctly
/scanonly	Checks the registry for errors and displays a message if problems are found

The REGEDIT program allows you to export the registry to a file that has an extension of .REG. The backed up file can be edited with a text editor, if necessary. The file can also be imported back into the computer. Access the REGEDIT program by clicking on the *Start* button, clicking on the *Run* option, and typing *REGEDIT* in the dialog textbox. Click on the *OK* button. Click on the *Registry* menu item and select *Export Registry File*. In the Filename textbox, type the name of the registry backup file. Make note of the full path where the file is located. Ensure that the *All* radio button in the Export Range section is selected and click on the *Save* button. Do not double-click on this file unless you want the information currently in the registry to be overwritten by the information contained in the file. This is a good method to use when doing manual registry changes. If the changes are not working properly, double-click on the registry backup icon (the file you just saved) and the original registry information will be imported back into the active registry files.

To edit the file, use My Computer or Windows Explorer to locate the file. Right-click on the file's icon and select the *Edit* option. If the registry is large, you will be asked if it is okay to open the file with WordPad rather than Notepad.

To import the registry file, you can start the REGEDIT program the same way previously described, click on the *Registry* menu item, and select the *Import Registry File* option.

Most of the time, the GUI interface will not be working when you need to do this. A file exported from REGEDIT can be imported using a command prompt. Start the computer in MS-DOS mode. Type *REGEDIT /L:system_file_path /R:user_file_path filename_path* where *system_file_path* is the location of the SYSTEM.DAT file, *user_file_path* is the location of the USER.DAT file, and *filename_path* is the complete path and filename of the saved (exported) registry. REGEDIT can be used from a command prompt for the export as well as other things. The most commonly used command-prompt commands are listed below.

- REGEDIT /L:*system_file_path* /R:*user_file_path filename_path*
- REGEDIT /L:*system_file_path* /R:*user_file_path* /C *filename_path2*
- REGEDIT /L:*system_file_path* /R:*user_file_path* /E *filename_path3* [*reg_path*]
- REGEDIT /L:*system_file_path* /R:*user_file_path* /D *reg_path2*

system_file_path is the full path of the SYSTEM.DAT file. *user_file_path* is the location of the USER.DAT file. *filename_path* is the complete path and filename of the saved (exported) registry. /C is used to create a file. *filename_path2* is the file from which to create the registry. /E is used to export the registry. *filename_path3* is the file to which to export the registry. *reg_path* is the starting registry key from which to export the registry and the default is to export the entire registry. /D is used to delete the registry or a specific key. *reg_path2* is the registry key to delete.

The registry can be backed up manually using the COPY command. A command prompt is accessed through Start button ➲ Programs ➲ MS-DOS Prompt. Type *CD\WINDOWS* and press *Enter*. Type *ATTRIB –R –H –S SYSTEM.DAT* and press *Enter*. Type *ATTRIB –R –H –S USER.DAT* and press *Enter*. Type *COPY SYSTEM.DAT path* where *path* is the drive letter, folder, and possible subfolder where you want the copy to reside. Type *COPY USER.DAT path* where *path* is the drive letter, folder, and possible subfolder where you want the copy to reside. See the DOS chapter for instructions for working from the DOS prompt if necessary. Type *ATTRIB +R +H +S SYSTEM.DAT* and press *Enter*. Type *ATTRIB +R +H +S USER.DAT* and press *Enter*. Close the DOS prompt window.

The Backup utility is accessed through Start button ➲ Programs ➲ Accessories ➲ System Tools ➲ Backup. With the Backup utility, you can either back up the entire computer, or just back up the registry. To restore one or more files that were backed up with the Backup utility, either use the Backup utility and select the *Restore backed up files* radio button or if the computer does not boot to the GUI interface, the System Recovery tool can be used to restore the file. To use the System Recovery tool, boot the computer from the Windows 98 Startup disk and insert the Windows 98 CD into the CD-ROM. At the command prompt type *drive_letter:* and press *Enter* where *drive_letter* is the drive letter of the CD-ROM followed by a colon. Type *CD\TOOLS\SYSREC* and press *Enter*. Type *PCRESTOR* at the command prompt. The System Recovery wizard will begin and allow you to back up the system or specific files.

If an error message appears that Windows has detected a registry/configuration error, boot the computer into Safe Mode. The Registry Problem dialog box appears. Click on the

Restore from Backup and Restart option. Windows 98 will use one of its automatic backups to restore the registry.

PRE-INSTALLATION OF WINDOWS 98

Windows 98 can be installed from a central location or locally. Because this book focuses on the A+ Certification exam, only local installation is covered. The pre-installation of any operating system is more important than the installation process. Technicians who grab a disk or CD and load a new operating system without going through a logical process are asking for trouble. The steps to take before installing Windows 98 are outlined below:

1. Decide whether the installation will be an upgrade or a clean install.
2. Decide whether the computer will have more than one operating system installed.
3. Scan the computer for viruses.
4. Determine if the hardware is compatible.
5. Delete unwanted files and uninstall any applications no longer needed.
6. Obtain any drivers, upgrades, or hardware replacements.
7. Back up any data files necessary.
8. Disable any unnecessary TSRs before upgrading to Windows 98.

The first decision to make when planning to install Windows 98 is whether you are upgrading from another operating system or performing a clean install. A **clean install** is when you install an operating system on a computer that does not have one or the existing operating system is removed (the hard drive is formatted).

If the decision is to do an upgrade, then determine what operating system is already installed. Windows 98 supports upgrading from DOS 5 and higher, Windows 3.x, and Windows 95. When Windows 98 is installed as an upgrade from Windows 3.x or Windows 95, the user's applications and data are preserved if the operating system is installed in the same folder (directory) as the original operating system. If Windows 98 is installed in a different folder, then all applications must be reloaded.

A related issue, if upgrading to 98, is whether or not to convert the hard drive partition to FAT32. Once a partition is converted to FAT32, the partition cannot be changed. If you are unsure whether or not to convert the partition, leave it unchanged and later use the Drive Converter wizard to upgrade. Most people want to convert the partition to FAT32 for the following reasons:

- Use of cluster space is more efficient (4KB per cluster on drives up to 8GB).
- FAT32 supports larger hard drive partition sizes.
- Supports larger hard drives (up to 2TB).
- FAT32 is more robust than FAT16 because the root folder can be relocated and a backup copy of the FAT can be used.
- FAT32 is more flexible than FAT16 because the root folder is an ordinary cluster that can be located anywhere on the drive instead of the outer hard

drive track. This also means that the previous root folder entries limitation is no longer an issue.

- FAT32 allows FAT mirroring to be disabled, which allows a copy of the FAT (rather than the first one) to be active.

Sometimes a clean install is the best choice, especially if the current operating system is DOS or Windows 3.x. Because a clean install involves formatting the hard drive, the user's data must be backed up and all applications reinstalled once the Windows 98 installation is complete. In addition, all user-defined settings are lost if Windows 98 is installed into a different folder.

The second decision that must be made is whether or not Windows 98 will be installed along with one or more other operating systems. This is often called a dual-boot or multi-boot scenario. **Dual-boot** means that the computer can boot from two different operating systems. **Multi-boot** means the computer can boot from two or more operating systems. Windows 98 can be dual-booted with DOS 5 and higher, Windows 3.x, NT, and 2000. If this is desired, a separate hard disk partition should be created and used for each operating system. Multi-booting is beyond the scope of this chapter. See the Microsoft web site for more details.

The third pre-installation step is to scan the drive for viruses. The next section covers viruses in detail.

The fourth step when installing Windows 98 is to determine what computer hardware is installed and whether it is compatible with Windows 98. WIN98 Table #5 lists the minimum and preferred hardware requirements for installing Windows 98.

Windows 98 Minimum Requirements

WIN98 – TABLE #5

Component	Minimum
CPU	Intel 486DX (or compatible) 66MHz or higher
RAM	16MB
Free hard drive space	120MB
Input Device	Keyboard, mouse, or other pointing device
Multimedia Drive	CD-ROM
Floppy Drive	3.5" 1.44MB
Video	VGA or higher

An upgrade from Windows 95 or Windows 3.x takes a minimum of 120MB. If you are doing a new installation to a FAT16 file system, 165MB is the minimum and to a FAT32 file system is 140MB minimum. If you are installing Windows 98 to a partition or drive other than the C:, the C: drive still needs a minimum of 25MB for Windows 98 system and log files.

On the Windows 98 CD is a document called HCL (Hardware Compatibility List). Use this list to see compatible hardware. The most current list is on Microsoft's web site. Once you have verified all hardware, you may have to get Windows 98 device drivers (step 5) from the hardware device manufacturer or their web site. There are also notes about hardware in the Windows 98 README and SETUP.TXT files contained on the 98 Setup disks.

The sixth and seventh decisions are whether or not to delete unnecessary files and whether or not current backups are needed. As with any upgrade, hardware change, or software change, data should be backed up. A user's data is very valuable to him or her. Whether you are doing a clean install or an upgrade, if the user has data on the computer, it must be backed up before starting the installation process. Also, before backing up data, remove any unwanted files and/or applications to free up hard drive space.

The final step is to disable old TSRs no longer needed. If Windows 98 is being upgraded, disable any unnecessary TSR (Terminate and Stay Resident) programs and device drivers loaded through CONFIG.SYS, AUTOEXEC.BAT, or the STARTUP folder. Windows 98's SETUP.TXT file on the CD-ROM contains information about TSRs that are incompatible with the upgrade.

VIRUSES

When installing a new operating system on a computer that already has an operating system loaded, it is a good time to run a virus scan. A **virus** is a computer program that is designed to do something to your computer that changes the way the computer operates. The virus could infect the computer so it does not boot, infect a particular application so it operates differently, or erase files. Some viruses are written to cause mischief rather than harm. An example of this could be a program that puts a picture on the screen. Some people think that they can eliminate viruses by high-level formatting their hard drive. This is a mistake. Do not take a chance; take a few moments and scan the hard drive for viruses! Common types of viruses include the boot sector virus, the file virus, the macro virus, and the Trojan horse virus.

A **boot sector virus** is a program placed in the computer's boot sector. Because the computer loads boot sector code into memory, the virus loads into RAM at the same time. Once in memory, the virus can take control of computer operations and spread to other drives, such as floppy drives, hard drives, and drives located on a network.

A **file virus** replaces or attaches itself to a file that has a COM or EXE extension. COM or EXE files are commonly known as executable files. Executable files are used to start applications. By attaching itself to this type of file, a virus can cause the program to not start or operate properly as well as load into RAM and affect other COM or EXE files.

A **macro virus** is written for a specific application such as Microsoft's Excel or Word. A macro virus is written in a specific language and attaches itself to a document that was created in the application. Once the document is opened and loaded into memory (along with the virus), the virus can attach itself to other documents.

A **Trojan horse virus** pretends to be a normal application. When the virus executes, the computer does something that the user does not expect such as put a message or a picture on the screen or put a new screen saver up. A Trojan horse virus does not replicate (copy itself somewhere else). The virus can be used to gather information such as userids and passwords that can be later used to hack into your computer.

Three other types of viruses that infect computers are the stealth virus, polymorphic virus, and a worm virus. A **stealth virus** is a program written to avoid being detected by anti-virus software. When an anti-virus program executes, the stealth virus provides the anti-virus program with a fake image that makes the anti-virus program believe that no virus is present. A **polymorphic virus** is a virus that constantly changes its own program to avoid detection by an anti-virus program. A **worm virus** makes a copy of itself from one drive to another and can use a network to replicate itself. The most common types of worm viruses today are in the form of an e-mail message. Once the e-mail is opened, the worm virus is sent to every other user that is in an address book.

Common symptoms of a virus are listed below:

- Computer does not boot.
- Computer hard drive space is reduced.
- Applications will not load.
- An application takes longer to load than necessary or longer than normal.
- Hard drive activity increases, especially when nothing is being done on the computer.
- An anti-virus software message appears.
- The number of hard drive sectors marked as bad steadily increases.
- Unusual graphics or messages appear on the screen.
- Files are missing (deleted).
- A message appears that the hard drive cannot be detected or recognized.
- Strange sounds come from the computer.

If a virus is detected or even suspected, run an anti-virus program. Follow the program's directions for installing and executing. The time to get an anti-virus program is *before* a virus infects the computer, because the damage may be irreversible, especially if backups are not performed. Back up data often! Always back up data files before upgrading to a new operating system. Backups are an important part of any computer support plan. Maintaining the anti-virus program and keeping it up-to-date with the latest virus signatures is also very important. New viruses are constantly created, so the virus software must be kept current as well.

Some anti-virus software can be set to load into memory when the computer boots and runs continuously. Make sure you disable this feature when installing an operating system patch (service pack) or upgrade. The anti-virus software can prevent the upgrade or patch (service pack) from installing. Other types of software that can prevent an operating system from being upgraded are power management and disk management software/tools. Disable these utilities and applications before attempting an operating system installation or upgrade.

INSTALLATION/UPGRADE OF WINDOWS 98

Once all of the pre-installation checklist steps are complete, you are ready to install Windows 98. The installation process is easy if you performed the pre-installation steps. An exercise at the end of the chapter shows you the steps for both a clean install (one where no other operating system is on the machine) and an upgrade to Windows 98. The number one thing to remember when installing any operating system is do your homework first and the number of possible problems will be greatly reduced.

When installing Windows 98, the technician completes five major steps:

1. Prepare the computer to run SETUP.
2. Gather information about the computer.
3. Copy the Windows 98 files.
4. Restart the computer.
5. Set up the hardware and operating system.

The Setup program can be run from a Windows 95 GUI environment, from a Windows 3.1x GUI environment, or from a command prompt. If you are upgrading from Windows 95 and keeping the current configuration, run the Setup program from the Windows 95 interface by closing all programs including any anti-virus programs. Insert the Windows 98 CD into the CD-ROM drive. Normally, the Setup program automatically starts. If the Setup program does not automatically start, click on the *Start* button, click on the *Run* option, and type the drive letter for the CD-ROM followed by a colon and *\setup* in the text dialog box and press *Enter*. An example of the command is D:\setup. The Windows 98 Setup wizard starts.

If upgrading from Windows 95, but putting Windows 98 into a different directory than where the Windows 95 files are, insert the Windows 98 CD, insert the Windows 98 Setup Disk 1 into the floppy drive (or any bootable disk that contains CD-ROM drivers), and restart the computer. At the command prompt, type the CD-ROM drive letter followed by a colon, \setup and press *Enter.* An example of the command is D:\setup. The Windows 98 Setup wizard begins.

If upgrading from Windows 3.1x or higher, close all active programs including any anti-virus programs. Insert the Windows 98 CD into the CD-ROM. Open the Program Manager utility. Click on the *File* menu and click on the *Run* option. In the Open dialog box, type the CD-ROM drive letter followed by a colon, \setup and press *Enter.* An example of the command is D:\setup. The Windows 98 Setup wizard starts.

If you are installing Windows 98 on a new computer, one that has a reformatted hard drive, or on a computer that has NT loaded, insert the Windows 98 CD into the CD-ROM, insert the computer using the Windows 98 Startup Disk, and power on the computer. The Windows 98 Startup menu appears. Press *1* on the keyboard and press *Enter.* When the command prompt appears, type *setup* and press *Enter.* The ScanDisk program checks the hard drive for errors. When finished, press the *X* key and the Windows Setup program begins.

During the installation process, you are asked to enter a Product Key. The Product Key is located either on the certificate found on the back of the Windows 98 book (that shipped with the computer) or on the back of the 98 CD. In addition, during the setup process, you are prompted for the type of setup (typical, portable, compact, and custom) installation. The Typical option installs the most common components for Windows 98. This is the most frequently chosen option. The Portable option is used for laptop computers and installs Windows 98 components used on portable computers. The Compact option is the smallest possible number of 98 files that can be loaded and Windows 98 still work. The Custom option allows you to select the components to install.

The SETUP.EXE file can be used with various switches that control the setup process. WIN98 Table #6 lists the switches that can be used.

Windows 98 SETUP.EXE Switches

Switch or Option	Purpose
/?	Displays switches available with the SETUP command
/c	Bypasses SmartDrive
/d	Bypasses using the existing Windows configuration
/ie	Skips the Startup Disk screen
/ig	Used when Setup fails on an older Gateway or Micron computer
/ih	Runs ScanDisk in the foreground
/im	Ignores conventional memory checking
/iq	The /iq switch prevents checking for cross-linked files. (If the /is switch is used to bypass ScanDisk or if ScanDisk does not complete the disk check successfully, the drive is checked for cross-linked files.)
/is	Skips the disk check (ScanDisk)
/it	Bypasses checking for TSRs
/iv	Does not display billboards during the installation process
/l	Enables Logitech mouse support during Setup
/n	Disables mouse during Setup
/nh	Bypasses running the HWINFO.EXE program
/nr	Skips the registry check
/nx	Bypasses checking what version of Setup is running
/t:*temp_dir*	Defines where Setup is to copy the temporary files used during the installation process. The folder (directory) must already exist and any existing files in the directory are deleted.

If networking is installed, an Identification window appears prompting for the computer name, workgroup name, and a description of the computer. The computer name prompt is used to uniquely identify the computer across a network. The name can be up to 15 characters long and should not contain blank characters. The workgroup name can also be up to 15 characters and must be the same for all computers networked together. Contact the network administrator for what to type in this dialog box. The computer description box can contain up to 48 characters and contain spaces to describe the computer or the computer's location.

TROUBLESHOOTING THE WINDOWS 98 INSTALLATION

The key to troubleshooting the Windows 98 installation is to get the operating system installed as best you can and troubleshoot the problem with the tools provided with Windows 98. Windows 98 ships with a feature called Safe Recovery that allows the installation to continue after a failure. Installation problems can be caused by a number of factors. The bulleted list shows the most common causes and their associated solutions during the installation process.

- Legacy hardware—Finish the installation and troubleshoot the hardware problems after the install.
- Incompatible drivers—Obtain Windows 98 drivers from the hardware manufacturer.
- Existing drivers are incompatible or halt the installation/upgrade process— Obtain Windows 98 drivers from the hardware manufacturer. If upgrading from a previous operating system, edit the AUTOEXEC.BAT and CONFIG.SYS and put the REM command before each line so the drivers do not load.
- Incompatible TSRs—Remove TSRs or obtain updated ones from the software manufacturer. Make sure to remove power management and anti-virus programs.
- Minimum hardware requirements have not been met—Upgrade the hardware. The top items to check are the CPU (486DX 66MHz minimum), RAM (16MB minimum), and hard drive space (120MB minimum).
- A virus is on the hard drive—Run a virus-checking program and remove the virus.
- Pre-installation steps have not been completed—Go back through the list!
- The Windows 98 boot disk or CD is corrupted (not as likely as the other causes)—Try the disk in another machine and see if you can see the contents. For the CD, check to see if any scratches or dirt is on the surface. Clean the CD as necessary.
- The wrong Windows 98 product has been purchased—If upgrading from another operating system, buy a Windows 98 upgrade. If installing the operating system onto a computer that does not have one or you are dual-booting, purchase the Windows 98 full version.
- Incorrect Product Key—Type in the correct CD key to complete the Windows 98 installation. The Product Key is located either on the certificate found on the back of the Windows 98 book (that shipped with the computer) or on the back of the 98 CD.
- SmartDrive is enabled and needs to be bypassed—Refer to the previous table for a listing of Setup switches.

Several text files can be helpful in determining the installation problem. WIN98 Table #7 lists the text files and a description of each.

Windows 98 Startup Log Files

WIN98 – TABLE #7

Log File	Description
BOOTLOG.TXT	Hidden text file in the root directory that is created when Windows 98 boots for the first time. Contains a list of 98 components and drivers that load during the boot process. A line that states "Loading device" or "Loading Vxd" shows the driver or component attempt at loading. The line following this shows whether the attempt was successful. "Load Success =" is an indication of a successful load. Also used if the Logged Startup Menu option is chosen.
DETCRASH.LOG	Hidden file in the root directory that is used when Setup fails during the installation process. When Setup resumes, this file is used to determine where to restart the installation and to skip the troublesome device.
DETLOG.TXT	Hidden text file stored in the root directory that contains a chronological list of hardware devices found during the hardware detection phase. See DETCRASH.LOG entry.
NETLOG.TXT	Text file stored in the root directory that chronologically lists network components (client, protocol, adapter, and service) found during the network detection phase. If everything is fine, an "OK" message is at the end of the line. If an error such as "Couldn't determine…" or "File not found" appears, the entry could cause Setup to hang or not complete the installation properly.
SETUPLOG.TXT	Hidden text file stored in the root directory that chronologically lists what happens during the installation process. Used to determine where Setup fails.

Once Windows 98 loads, a tool called **Version Conflict Manager** can be used to help with driver conflicts. If Windows 98 loads a driver from the CD that replaces a driver that is already on the system, then 98 tracks that driver through the Version Conflict Manager. Access the Version Conflict Manger through Start button ➲ Programs ➲ Accessories ➲ System Tools ➲ System Information. Click on the *Tools* menu option and select *Version Conflict Manager*. Files that have been replaced are listed in the window. To return to a previous file version, click on the file and click on the *Restore Selected Files* button. The version of the file currently loaded is backed up to the VCM folder, which is located in the folder that Windows 98 is loaded (normally WINDOWS). The command that starts Version Conflict Manager is VCMUI.EXE.

If Windows 98 hangs during the ScanDisk, insert the Windows 98 boot disk, boot the computer, and at the command prompt type *setup /d* so that the installation procedure completes. If Windows 98 hangs (a) during the Setup program, (b) when attempting to load, or (c) at the End User License Agreement screen, you probably have anti-virus software enabled, either as a TSR or through CMOS. If the images on the screen become distorted, or if the Setup Wizard screen appears as a black square, anti-virus software may also be to blame. Stop the installation, disable the anti-virus software, and start the Setup program again. If you get an error message that Windows 98 could not decode a Setup (.CAB) file, several things could be wrong. They are listed below:

- CD-ROM vibrates too much—Remove the CD from the drive and rotate it one quarter of a turn, reinsert the CD and click OK.
- Computer is over-clocked—Try slowing the computer down by configuring the appropriate settings recommended by the computer manufacturer or the motherboard manufacturer.
- Computer has mismatched RAM—Check the memory chips and make sure that they are the same type, for example EDO, and that they are the same speed. If they appear fine, copy the contents of the WIN98 folder from the CD to an empty folder on the hard drive and run the Setup program from the hard drive.
- The computer has bus mastering or Ultra DMA enabled in the BIOS and in the Device Manager.
- Virus is on the computer—Run a virus check before restarting the Setup program. Make sure the anti-virus program is disabled before running Setup.
- Norton Autoprotect is enabled—Disable the Autoprotect from the entry in the Startup group.

If Windows 98 gets an error message that states "Invalid System Disk" after the system reboots the first time, a virus may be present; an anti-virus program is running and has not been disabled either through AUTOEXEC.BAT, STARTUP folder, or CMOS; or disk management software is enabled.

DUAL-BOOTING WINDOWS 98 AND NT

Sometimes users would like to try a new operating system, but keep their old operating system loaded as well. If this is the case, two operating systems can reside in one system and it is called dual-booting. Windows 98 can be dual-booted with DOS, Windows 3.x, Windows 95, NT, and 2000 Professional, but care must be taken. NT supports and uses either NTFS4 or FAT16 and Windows 98 supports and uses either FAT16 or FAT32. NT cannot read FAT32 partitions and Windows 98 cannot read NTFS4 partitions. If 98 is to access the files stored when using NT, both operating systems need to use FAT16 (but the FAT32 and NTFS features are lost). It is best if the two operating systems are placed on different hard drive partitions and Windows 98 loaded before NT is installed. If the computer currently dual-boots with NT from another operating system or environment such as DOS, Windows 3.x, or Windows 95, the Windows 98 Setup program can be executed from the other operating system.

Even though Microsoft does not support installing Windows 98 after NT has already been installed, it can be done. If this is what you want to do, make sure the Windows NT Workstation Emergency Repair Disk is up to date and handy before starting the installation process. Boot from a DOS disk or the Windows 98 Setup disk and install Windows 98 to a different partition. Use the NT Emergency Repair Disk to restore the NT startup files once 98 is installed. See the NT chapter for instructions. You may have to edit NT's BOOT.INI file to add the Windows 98 boot option. See Microsoft's web site for instructions on editing the BOOT.INI file.

Installing NT after Windows 98 is already installed is not a problem. Make sure you select a partition that does not contain Windows 98 or create a new one for the NT installation. A prompt appears during the installation process that allows you to select *Leave Current File System Intact*.

DUAL-BOOTING WINDOWS 98 AND 2000 PROFESSIONAL

Whenever more than one operating system is on a computer, it is best to put each operating system on a separate partition or a separate hard drive. If there is only one hard drive with one partition, you can use a disk partitioning utility, such as PowerQuest's Partition Magic or V Communication's Partition Commander, to repartition the hard drive without losing data. Never start a dual-boot situation or repartition the hard drive without having a full backup of the current system.

Windows 98 supports FAT16 and FAT32, Windows 2000 Professional supports FAT16, FAT32, and NTFS5. If Windows 98 and Windows 2000 Professional are to share files, then both the Windows 98 and the 2000 Professional partitions need to be FAT16 or FAT32, with FAT32 being the preferred choice. Windows 2000 Professional does not support the DriveSpace or DoubleSpace programs that are available with Windows 98. The dual-boot is easier to configure if Windows 98 is installed before Windows 2000 Professional.

If Windows 98 is already installed, insert the Windows 2000 CD. Once the Windows 2000 Setup Wizard screen appears, select the *Install a new copy of Windows 2000 (Clean Install)* radio button and click on the *Next* button.

After you agree to the license and enter the product key, the Select Special Options screen appears. Click on the *Advanced Options* button, select the *I want to choose the installation partition during Setup* checkbox and click on the *OK* button.

Continue through the rest of the Setup screens. The system reboots and enters the text mode portion of Setup. You will be prompted to choose a partition on which to install Windows 2000.

When prompted for a partition to install Windows 2000, make sure you select the partition that does not have Windows 98 already installed.

Files are copied and a boot screen allows you to select either Windows 98 or Windows 2000.

If Windows 2000 is already installed and you want to install Windows 98, make sure that a new partition has already been created for Windows 98 and create a Windows 2000 Emergency Repair Disk by clicking on the Start button ➲ Programs ➲ Accessories ➲ System Tools ➲ Backup. On the Welcome tab, click on *Emergency Repair Disk* button. Insert a disk into the floppy drive, follow the directions on the screen, and store in a safe location once the files are copied. Boot the system from the Windows 98 Startup disk or the Windows 98 CD. Start the Setup program (if it does not start automatically). Install Windows 98 into the partition that has already been created.

Once Windows 98 has been installed and checked, boot the system with the Windows 2000 CD and go into the Windows 2000 Setup program. Continue until you reach the screen that queries whether to install Windows 2000, repair the current installation, or quit. Select the *Repair the current Windows 2000 installation* option. You will be prompted to either use the recovery console or the Emergency Repair Disk. Select the *Emergency Repair Disk* option. The next screen offers a selection of a manual repair or a fast repair; select the *manual repair* options. Three options are pre-selected. Click in the *Verify Windows 2000 files* checkbox to deselect it. Follow the instructions on the screen to use the ERD to repair the boot sector and add the dual boot entry into the startup screen. If the boot menu is incorrect once the ERD has repaired the boot files, edit the BOOT.INI file to correct the boot screen.

CONFIGURING WINDOWS 98 OVERVIEW

One of the most common windows used by technicians is the Control Panel window. A control panel is a method for configuring various Windows 98 components. The Add New Hardware, Add/Remove Programs, and Printing control panels are used when installing or removing hardware and software. Each control panel icon represents a Windows utility that allows you to customize a particular part of the Windows 98 environment. The number of control panels displayed depends on the type of computer and the components contained within the computer. WIN98 Figure #7 shows some of the more common Windows 98 control panels.

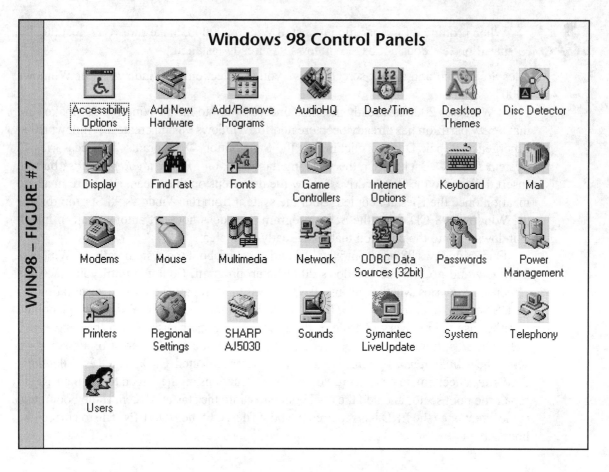

Technicians must know which control panel to use for changing a computer's configuration. WIN98 Table #8 shows the common Windows 98 control panels and the function of each.

WIN98 – TABLE #8

Windows 98 Control Panel Functions

Control Panel	Function
Accessibility Options	Controls keyboard, sounds, display, and mouse behavior for people with disabilities
Add New Hardware	Used when installing new hardware devices
Add/Remove Programs	Used to install or uninstall software applications
Date/Time	Used to set the date and time
Display	Used to change screen color, background color/pattern, object size, screen resolution, and screen saver
Fonts	Used to install, remove, or view system fonts
Game Controllers	Used to configure or test devices such as a joystick
Internet Options	Used to configure Internet connection settings
Keyboard	Used to install a keyboard driver and configure keyboard settings
Modem	Used to install or modify modem settings
Mouse	Used configure mouse settings
Multimedia	Used to install multimedia device drivers, configure properties for audio, video, and MIDI devices, and configure settings for playing audio CDs
Network	Used to add, remove, and configure network settings
Passwords	Used to configure user preferences and passwords
Power Management	Used to reduce electrical power use in devices such as a monitor or hard drive
Printers	User to add, remove, and modify printer settings
Regional Settings	Used to set the time zone, set the format for numbers and currency
Sounds	Used to change sounds used by Windows
System	Allows viewing system information, changing parameters related to system performance such as virtual memory and access Device Manager
Telephony	Used to install drivers and configure telephone devices (such as a fax or answering machine)
Users	Used to configure the computer for more than one person

Technicians must frequently add new hardware and software using the operating system. Windows 98 has specific tools for these functions. Using the correct procedure is essential for success. The following sections handle many of the tasks a technician must perform:

- Adding plug and play devices
- Adding non-plug and play devices
- Removing hardware components
- Adding a printer
- Installing/removing software

Hardware devices are physical components that connect to the computer. Hardware devices can be either plug and play, or non-plug and play. A device driver is a piece of software that allows hardware to work with a specific operating system. Some device drivers are automatically included with Windows 98. A technician must be aware of what hardware is installed into a system so that the latest Windows 98-compatible drivers can be downloaded and installed.

ADDING PLUG AND PLAY DEVICES

Plug and play devices are hardware and software designed to be automatically recognized by the operating system. The key to a successful plug and play device installation includes

- Possessing the most up-to-date device driver
- Following the directions provided by the device manufacturer

Always make sure that the computer is turned off when installing any new hardware component. Some plug and play devices can be inserted into the computer without restarting. These include a PC Card, a laptop into a docking station, and an USB device. However, devices such as internal modems or network cards require the computer to be turned off during installation.

Install the device according to the device manufacturer's instructions. Once installed, power on the computer. The Windows 98 Found New Hardware wizard appears. Windows 98 attempts to find a driver for the new device. If Windows 98 detect the plug and play device, the device gives Windows 98 a device ID. Windows 98 uses this device ID to look for the appropriate .INF file. A .INF file contains information used to install and configure the device. If a driver cannot be found, a dialog box appears. The best policy with any operating system is to use the latest driver even if the operating system detects the device. An exercise at the end of the chapter outlines how to install a new hardware driver.

ADDING NON-PLUG AND PLAY DEVICES

Legacy devices are also called non-plug and play devices. For devices that are not plug and play, use the Add New Hardware control panel. The Add New Hardware wizard allows hardware configuration and is used for hardware that is not automatically recognized by Windows 98. It is also used for plug and play devices that do not install properly with

Windows 98's automatic detection. Windows 98 prompts with the question asking if you want Windows 98 to search for non-plug and play devices. Select the *Yes* option. If Windows 98 finds the device, follow the rest of the prompts to install a driver for the device. If Windows 98 does not find the device, you must select the type of device that is being installed. Then, you must select the device manufacturer and device model from a list. A generic device or "other" option is available for most device categories. Have the Windows 98-compatible device driver ready, click on the *Have Disk* button and specify the drive and path to the driver. An exercise at the end of the chapter explains how to do this.

ADDING A PRINTER

Printers can be connected to a computer through the printer's parallel or USB port through a local area network. Only local printers (printers directly connected to a computer port) will be covered in this chapter. Networked printers will be explained in the Network chapter. Windows 98 can automatically detect printers. If Windows 98 detects the printer, the operating system installs the drivers, updates the registry, and allocates system resources to the printer. Printers that are normally detected automatically by Windows 98 are USB, FireWire, or infrared printers.

To install a printer, connect the printer to the appropriate computer port with the appropriate cable. Power on the computer, and the Windows 98 wizard normally detects and leads you through the installation process. However, if it does not, have the Windows 98-compatible printer driver ready, click on the *Start* button, point to the *Settings* selection, and click on the *Printers* option. When the Printers window opens, click on the *Add Printer* icon. Click on the *Next* button and select the *Local Printer* selection. When prompted for the printer driver, insert the CD or disk that contains the printer driver, and use the Browse button to locate the driver. Continue through the Add Printer wizard until the printer is installed.

To configure a printer as a default printer (the printer that applications normally use), locate the printer in the Printers folder. Access the Printers folder, by clicking on the *Start* button, point to the *Settings* option, and click on the *Printers* selection. Once you locate the appropriate printer icon, right-click on the icon. Click on the *Set as Default Printer* option. In the Printers folder, the default printer has a checkmark next to (above) the icon.

REMOVING HARDWARE DEVICES

When a plug and play hardware device is removed, Windows 98 automatically detects this and removes the resources and registry entries assigned to the device. When removing most non-plug and play hardware devices (all but printers), use Device Manager. Right-click on the *My Computer* desktop icon to access Device Manager. Click on the *Properties* option. Click on the *Device Manager* tab. Through Device Manager, a device can either be removed or disabled. When a non-plug and play device is removed, the driver does not load and any resources assigned to the device are now free. When a non-plug and play device is disabled, the resources assigned to the device are kept, but the device's driver does not load when the computer restarts.

To remove a device, click on the plus sign located beside the appropriate device category. Click on the name of the device being removed. Click on the *Remove* button. To disable a device, click on the plus sign located beside the appropriate device category. Click on the device name. Click on the *Properties* button. On the *General* tab in the Device Usage section is a checkbox that allows you to disable the device for a specific hardware profile. Click once in this checkbox to disable the device.

If you are removing a printer from the system, use the *Printers* control panel. Access this control panel by clicking on the *Start* button. Point to the *Settings* option and click on the *Printers* option. Right-click on the printer you want to delete and choose the *Delete* option.

INSTALLING/REMOVING SOFTWARE

No computer is fully functional without software and Windows 98 supports 16-bit and 32-bit applications. Most software today is 32 bit and comes on CD and includes an autorun feature. If the CD has the autorun feature, an installation wizard steps you through installing the software when the CD is inserted into the drive. If there is not an autorun feature on the CD or if the software is on a disk, then the Add/Remove Programs control panel is normally used to install or remove the software. Remember always to consult the application documentation for installation procedures.

To access the Add/Remove Programs control panel, click on the *Start* button and point to the *Settings* option. Click on the *Control Panel* option and then double-click on the *Add/Remove Programs* control panel icon. To install an application, click on the *Install/Uninstall* tab, click on the *Install* button, insert the application disk or CD, and click on the *Next* button. Windows 98 searches the floppy drive and CD for a Setup program. If one is found, continue the installation process. If one is not found, type the drive letter and path for the application's Setup program. Use the Browse button if necessary. Click on the *Finish* button to complete the process.

Close all active applications before starting the installation process. This will eliminate some complications.

The computer must frequently be rebooted after an application or Windows component has been installed.

To remove a software application, use the same Add/Remove Programs control panel; however, instead of clicking on the *Install* button, select the application to be removed and click on the *Add/Remove* button. Do not forget to check the application's documentation for specific removal procedures.

The Add/Remove Programs control panel can also be used to add operating system components, add programs across your network, and add or remove Windows components. The Windows Setup tab is used to add or remove operating system components. The Startup Disk tab is used to create a Windows 98 disk that can be used when Windows 98 does not boot properly.

Once an application is installed, launch the application by clicking on the *Start* button and pointing to the *Programs* option. Locate the *application name* and click on it. The application starts.

OVERVIEW OF THE BOOT PROCESS

Every operating system needs specific files that allow the computer to boot. These files are known as system files or startup files. The **system files** and their specific location on the hard drive are listed in WIN98 Table #9. The locations listed in WIN98 Table #9 assume that Windows 98 is loaded in the default folder (WINDOWS). If Windows 98 is loaded in a different folder, substitute the location WINDOWS for the name of the folder in which Windows 98 was initially loaded.

Windows 98 Startup Files

Startup File	Location and Purpose
AUTOEXEC.BAT	Root directory—used to load TSRs not designed to run under Windows 98
BOOT.INI	Root directory—used when multiple operating systems are present
CONFIG.SYS	Root directory—used to load 16-bit drivers not designed to run under Windows 98
DRVSPACE.BIN	WINDOWS\COMMAND—supports compressed drives
GDI.EXE	WINDOWS\SYSTEM—provides support for the graphical environment; one of Windows 98 core files
GDI32.DLL	WINDOWS\SYSTEM—provides support for the graphical environment
HIMEM.SYS	WINDOWS—driver for extended memory
IFSHLP.SYS	WINDOWS—driver for the 32-bit Installable File System Manager
IO.SYS	Root directory—boot file for real mode that loads drivers and TSRs listed in CONFIG.SYS and AUTOEXEC.BAT
KERNEL32.DLL	WINDOWS\SYSTEM—loads the main Windows components
KRNL386.EXE	WINDOWS\SYSTEM—loads Windows device drivers
LOGO.SYS	Root directory—contains a bitmap image
MSDOS.SYS	Root directory—contains boot parameters and provides backward compatibility for some applications
SYSTEM.DAT	WINDOWS—part of the registry database
SYSTEM.INI	WINDOWS—only exists to be backward compatible with older applications in the Windows 3.x environment
USER.EXE	WINDOWS\SYSTEM—provides user interface code; a Windows core file
USER32.DLL	WINDOWS\SYSTEM—provides user interface code
VMM32.VXD	WINDOWS\SYSTEM—contains real-mode load, executable virtual machine manager, and common static drivers (VxDs)
WIN.COM	WINDOWS—executable file that starts the Windows environment
WIN.INI	WINDOWS—only exists to be backward compatible with older applications in the Windows 3.x environment

The boot process is actually quite involved, but the major steps are as follows:

1. The computer powers on.
2. POST executes.
3. If the computer has a plug and play BIOS, plug and play adapters and devices are configured. If the computer does not have a plug and play BIOS, all ISA bus devices are enabled.
4. BIOS searches for an active partition on the hard drive.
5. BIOS reads the Master Boot Record, then locates and loads the information into sector 0 of the system partition. The contents of sector 0 define the type of file system and the location of the boot files, then start loading the file system.
6. Real-mode starts.
7. MSDOS.SYS boot configuration loads.
8. DRVSPACE.BIN loads if it is needed for compressed drives.
9. Prompts for a hardware profile if multiple profiles exist.
10. Bitmap image stored in LOGO.SYS loads.
11. SYSTEM.DAT loads.
12. DOS drivers and TSRs needed for backward compatibility load as specified by the CONFIG.SYS and AUTOEXEC.BAT files.
13. Initializes static VxDs in real mode specified by VMM32.VXD and the registry.
14. Starts protected-mode and loads WIN.COM.
15. Loads protected-mode VxDs as specified by VMM32.VXD, the registry, and the settings in the SYSTEM.INI file.
16. Loads KRNL386.EXE, GDI files, user libraries, Explorer shell, and network support (if needed).
17. Executes any programs located in the Startup folder and those referred to in the registry.

The only reason the AUTOEXEC.BAT, CONFIG.SYS, WIN.INI, and SYSTEM.INI files load is to make Windows 98 backward compatible with older operating systems, 16-bit TSRs, and 16-bit drivers.

IO.SYS SETTINGS

Windows 98's IO.SYS file is responsible for loading key files that were previously loaded through the CONFIG.SYS file. WIN98 Table #10 lists the files that are automatically loaded through IO.SYS and the default setting. If the computer needs a setting change, modify the setting by adding the line in the CONFIG.SYS file.

WIN98 – TABLE #10

Windows 98 Default IO.SYS Settings

Setting	Default Parameter and Purpose
buffers=	30—sets the number of file buffers to create for 16-bit programs
dos=high	No default setting—loads part of the operating system into the high memory area
fcbs=	4—sets the file control blocks that can be open for compatibility with very old software
files=	60—sets the file handle buffers to create
himem.sys	No default setting—enables access to extended memory
ifshlp.sys	No default setting—used to load device drivers
lastdrive=	Z—specifies the last drive letter available to be assigned by the operating system
setver.exe	No default setting—included for DOS compatibility
shell=command.com	No default setting—sets the default command interpreter
stacks=	9,256—specifies the number and size of data stacks to handle hardware interrupts

MSDOS.SYS SETTINGS

Windows 98 has a hidden, read-only system file called MSDOS.SYS that is located in the root directory. MSDOS.SYS enables backward compatibility with older DOS applications. The file holds multiple operating system boot options as well as the paths to important Windows 98 files such as the registry. There are lines of Xs in the MSDOS.SYS file. Do not remove the Xs. WIN98 Table #11 lists some of the more common options found in the MSDOS.SYS file.

Windows 98 MSDOS.SYS Settings

WIN98 – TABLE #11

Section	Setting	Default Setting and Purpose
[Options]	AutoScan=	1—enables a prompt to run ScanDisk; a value of 0 disables it; a value of 2 runs ScanDisk without prompting
[Options]	BootDelay=	2—seconds delayed after the "Starting Windows" message appears; a value of 0 disables the delay
[Options]	BootGUI=	1—enables the GUI interface; a value of 0 boots to a prompt
[Options]	BootKeys=	1—enables startup function keys; a value of 0 prevents startup keys from functioning and overrides the BootDelay= setting
[Options]	BootMenu=	0—enables/disables Startup menu automatically appearing; a value of 1 displays the Startup menu
[Options]	BootMenuDefault=	3 or 4—the number of the menu item to automatically start; a value of 3 is the default for a computer without networking installed; a value of 4 is the default for a computer with networking installed
[Options]	BootMenuDelay=	30—number of seconds before executing the default menu item
[Options]	BootMulti=	0—enables dual-booting; a value of 1 enables the F4 key (for DOS) or the F8 key (for the Windows 98 Startup menu)
[Options]	BootWin=	1—enables Windows 98 as the default operating system; a value of 0 makes another operating system the default; this setting is only useful with DOS-dual booted with Windows 98
[Options]	DoubleBuffer=	0—enables/disables double-buffering; a value of 0 disables it; a value of 1 enables it for SCSI controllers that require double-buffering
[Options]	LoadTop=	1—enables loading COMMAND.COM or DRVSPAC.BIN at the top of the conventional memory space; a value of 0 disables this feature
[Paths]	HostWinBootDrv=	C—drive letter for the boot drive root directory
[Paths]	WinBootDir=	Varies—defines the location of the startup files
[Paths]	WinDir=	Varies—specifies the folder where many of the Windows 98 files are located

TROUBLESHOOTING THE BOOT PROCESS

Windows 98 has a wealth of tools to help you when troubleshooting the boot process. One of the more common startup problem solving tools is the **Startup menu**. Access the Windows Startup menu by pressing the *CTRL* key when you boot the computer. If this does not work, press the *F8* key during the boot process. Each item in the Startup menu is used in different situations. The Startup menu options are as follows: Normal mode, Logged mode, Safe mode, Step-by-Step Confirmation mode, Command-Prompt-Only mode, Safe Mode Command-Prompt-Only mode, and Previous Version of MS-DOS. WIN98 Table #12 lists the purpose of each mode.

Windows 98 Startup Menu Options

Mode	Purpose
Normal	Used to boot Windows 98 in the normal fashion
Logged	Used to track the boot process and log each event in a file located in the root directory called BOOTLOG.TXT; used to determine where the boot failure occurs
Safe	Prevents the CONFIG.SYS and AUTOEXEC.BAT files from loading, prevents the [Boot] and [386enh] sections of the SYSTEM.INI file from loading, prevents the Load= and Run= parameters of the WIN.INI file from loading, prevents the items found in the Startup folder from loading, prevents portions of the registry from loading, prevents all device drivers except for the keyboard and mouse from loading, and loads a standard VGA driver
Step-by-Step Confirmation	Allows performing the boot process one step at a time to see where the problem occurs
Command-Prompt-Only	Used to troubleshoot DOS applications (only CONFIG.SYS, AUTOEXEC.BAT, COMMAND.COM, and the registry are loaded; the GUI does not load)
Safe Mode Command-Prompt-Only	Used if the computer does not boot to Safe Mode; does not load the HIMEM.SYS or IFSHLP.SYS files and does not execute WIN.COM to start the GUI. Various switches can be used at the command prompt with the WIN.COM file to troubleshoot the problem.
Previous Version of MS-DOS	Used to perform a DOS function that does not operate correctly under Windows 98

WIN98 – TABLE #12

Other tools that can be used for startup problems include the System Configuration utility, Microsoft System Information tool, Automatic Skip Driver, System File Checker, Startup and Shutdown Troubleshooter, and Registry Checker. Determining which tool to use and how to access the tool is the challenge.

The **System Configuration** utility is used when you suspect a problem with old device drivers or TSRs especially on a computer that has been upgraded to Windows 98. The System Configuration utility allows you to enable or disable entries in the AUTOEXEC.BAT, CONFIG.SYS, SYSTEM.INI, and WIN.INI files. The order in which the file entries load can also be controlled. These files are available in Windows 98 to be compatible with older operating systems and older applications. Access the System Configuration utility by clicking on the Start button ➲ Programs ➲ Accessories ➲ System Tools ➲ System Information. Click on the *Tools* menu option and select the *System Configuration Utility* from the drop-down menu. The easiest way to determine if one of the four files is causing the problem is to click on the *Diagnostic startup* radio button and click on the *OK* button. When the Windows 98 Startup menu appears, press the number corresponding to the *Step-by-Step Confirmation* setting. The command that starts the System Configuration utility is MSCONFIG.EXE located in the WINDOWS\SYSTEM subfolder. WIN98 Figure #8 shows the System Configuration Utility.

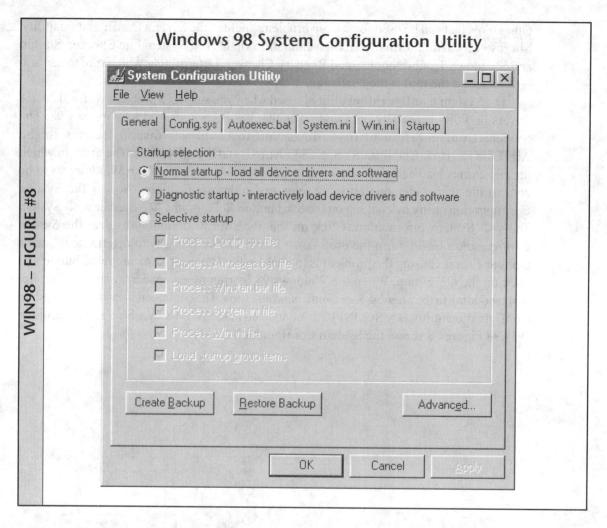

Windows 98 System Configuration Utility

WIN98 – FIGURE #8

The **MSINFO (Microsoft System Information)** tool is used to display information about system resources and can be used to detect conflicts between devices. Access the MSINFO tool by clicking on the Start button ➲ Programs ➲ Accessories ➲ System Tools ➲ System Information. Click on the *plus sign* beside the Hardware Resources option in the left window. Click on the *Conflicts/Sharing* setting to see resource conflicts between ISA devices and resources that are shared between PCI devices. Another popular option is the Forced Hardware view that lists devices that have been assigned resources manually. The Problem Devices selection allows you to view any devices that have problems and the History option shows seven days of driver history. The command to execute MSINFO tool is MSINFO32.EXE. WIN98 Figure #9 shows the Microsoft System Information tool.

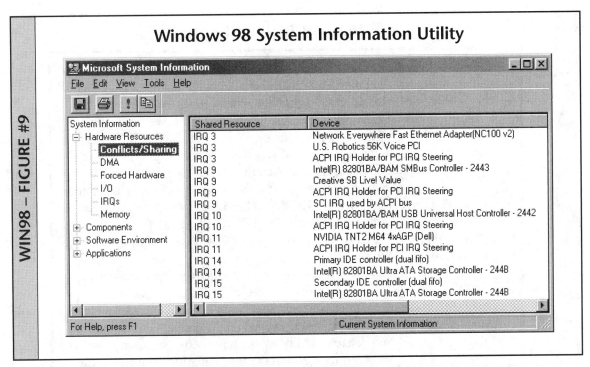

WIN98 – FIGURE #9

The MSINFO and the Windows Report tools update a file called HWINFO.DAT every time these tools execute. The HWINFO.DAT file is created during the installation process and holds a record of the computer's current hardware configuration, device drivers, and system resources. The MSINFO tool can be used to open the HWINFO.DAT file at any time.

The **ASD.EXE (Automatic Skip Driver Agent)** program is found in the same folder as where Windows 98 is installed. The Automatic Skip Driver tool determines which drivers fail to load during startup. After two failed attempts, ASD marks the device as defective and turns off the device driver. Access the Automatic Skip Driver Agent by clicking on the Start button ➲ Programs ➲ Accessories ➲ System Tools ➲ System Information. Click on the *Tools* menu option and select the *Automatic Skip Driver Agent* drop-down menu selection. If no problems are found, a dialog box appears on the screen.

Sometimes applications overwrite system files or files become corrupt. The **System File Checker (SFC.EXE)** is located in the WINDOWS\SYSTEM subfolder and protects your system files by checking them and repairing them if necessary. A prompt appears before the original files are restored.

Many error messages can appear in Windows 98. The technician's best source for information is the Internet. However, some common problems are listed in WIN98 Table #13.

WIN98 – TABLE #13

Windows 98 Troubleshooting

Message	Solution
A device referenced in SYSTEM.INI, WIN.INI, or registry could not be found	(1) Edit SYSTEM.INI and WIN.INI and look for all references to the device. Put a semicolon before the line. For Windows 9x, see if there is a 9x driver for the device. If so, leave the semicolon before the SYSTEM.INI line and reload the 9x driver if necessary. After rebooting the computer, if an application displays a message that it cannot find this file, the file needs to be recopied (usually to the WINDOWS \SYSTEM folder) and the semicolon removed from the SYSTEM.INI line. (2) To see which file caused the error, use MSCONFIG to choose Selective Startup and step through the startup process. (3) If a registry error occurs, back up the registry, use a registry editor to locate the driver in the HKLM System\ Current\ControlSet\Services\Vxd key. If you know the driver is no longer needed, highlight the Open subkey and delete it. If any application needs the missing file, a message appears that the file is missing. Reload the file from the application disk or CD.
Bad or missing COMMAND.COM	The COMMAND.COM file is missing. Replace from boot disk or CD.
Error in CONFIG.SYS line xx	Edit CONFIG.SYS and look at the line referenced in message. Check if the referenced file is in the listed folder. Check for typing errors on the line. Replace file in appropriate folder if necessary.
Error loading kernel. You must reinstall Windows.	Extract the KERNEL32.DLL file from Windows disk or CD and copy it to the WINDOWS\SYSTEM folder.
HIMEM.SYS not loaded or missing or corrupt HIMEM.SYS	Check the WINDOWS folder for the HIMEM.SYS file. Reload file from original disk, boot disk, or CD if the file is missing or corrupt.
Incorrect DOS version	The command or utility is from a different system version than the command interpreter loading during startup. Replace the command or COMMAND.COM and system files with the appropriate version or use the SETVER command to fool the application into using the command interpreter installed.
No operating system found	Boot from the appropriate boot disk and replace the operating system files by typing *SYS C:*.

Another error resulting from different causes is the Windows Protection Error. A Windows Protection Error is usually caused by a virtual device driver being loaded or unloaded. Sometimes the specific device driver (VxD) is mentioned in the error message. The following list cites the most common causes of a Windows Protection Error.

- Real mode driver conflicting with a protected mode driver
- Corrupt registry
- A virus has infected WIN.COM or COMMAND.COM or one of the files is corrupt
- Driver referenced in the registry has initialized and a conflicting SYSTEM.INI driver loads
- I/O or DMA address conflict (use Device Manager or MSINFO)
- Incorrect CMOS settings, such as CPU clock speed, cache, hard disk time out
- Serial mouse connected to a standard port replicator
- Motherboard chipset drivers are missing
- Motherboard has been replaced. (Sometimes Windows 98 must be reinstalled to recognize the new motherboard capabilities.)

Windows 98 comes with many troubleshooting wizards. One that relates to the boot process is the Startup and Shutdown troubleshooter. Access this troubleshooting wizard by clicking on the *Start* button and clicking on the *Help* button. Click on the *Index* tab and type *startup* in the textbox. Click on the *troubleshooting* option located beneath the word *startup*. In the right window, click on the *Click here* option to start the wizard.

Windows 98 has a Windows-based and a DOS-based program used to check the registry for errors and is commonly known as the Registry Checker. To start the Windows-based version, click on the *Start* button, click on *Run,* and type *scanregw.exe* in the textbox. If the computer will not boot into GUI mode, use the DOS-based program by typing *c:\windows\command\scanreg.exe* at the prompt. The Registry Checker automatically runs every time the computer starts.

Sometimes, when the computer will not boot, a startup disk (boot disk) is needed. Another time to use a startup disk is when the computer has a virus. Create a Windows 98 startup disk by clicking on the *Start* button, pointing to the *Settings* option, clicking on the *Control Panel* submenu option, and double-clicking on the *Add/Remove Programs* control panel. Click on the *Startup Disk* tab and click on the *Create Disk* button. One disk is needed for this procedure.

COMMAND PROMPT

Another useful tool used when Windows 98 crashes or does not boot properly is the command prompt. When the GUI mode does not work, a technician must be able to work from the command prompt. See the DOS chapter for more details on how to enter commands and move around in the directory structure. Access the command prompt by one of the following methods:

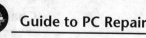
- During startup, hold down either the *CTRL* key or press the *F8* key to access the Startup menu. Select either the *Command-Prompt-Only* mode or the *Safe Mode Command-Prompt-Only* mode.
- Boot from a boot disk.
- Click on the *Start* button, point to *Programs*, and click on the *MS-DOS Prompt* option.
- Click on the *Start* button, click on the *Run* option, and type in *command* at the dialog box and press *Enter.*

The drive letters available at the command prompt might not be the same ones you used in the GUI environment. Some of the most frequently used Windows 98 commands are outlined below. The items enclosed by brackets [ ] are optional. Items in italics are command specific values you must enter. When the items are separated by a | (bar), one of the items must be typed.

ATTRIB   This command is used to control the attribute for a file or folder.

Syntax: attrib [+|-h] [+|-a] [+|-r] [+|-s] [*drive:*] [*path*] *filename* [/S]

Explanation: + Adds an attribute.
– Takes an attribute away.
h is the hidden attribute.
a is the archive attribute.
r is the read-only attribute.
s is the system attribute.
[*drive:*] is the drive there the file is located.
[*path*] is the directory/subdirectory where the file is located.
filename is the name of the file.
[*/S*] processes all files in all subdirectories specified by the *path.*

Example: **attrib +h c:\cheryl.bat** sets the attribute to hidden for a file called CHERYL.BAT located on the hard drive.

Notes: The DIR command (typed without any switches) is used to see which attributes are currently set. You may set more than one attribute at a time.

CD   This command is used to navigate through the directory structure.

Syntax: cd [*drive:*] [*path*] [..]

Explanation: [*drive:*] specifies the drive (if a different one than the current drive) to which you want to change.

[*path*] is the directory/subdirectory to reach the folder.
[..] is used to change to the parent directory (moves you back one directory).

Examples: C:\WINNT>**cd..**
C:\
This command moves you from the WINNT directory (folder) to the parent directory, which is the root directory (C:\).

C:\>**cd \WINDOWS**

This command moves you from the root directory to the WINDOWS directory on the C: drive.

CHKDSK   This command checks a disk for physical problems, lost clusters, cross-linked files, and directory errors. If necessary, the chkdsk command repairs the disk, marks bad sectors, recovers information, and displays the status of the disk.

Syntax: chkdsk [*drive:*] [*[path] filename*] [*/f*] [*/v*]

Explanation: [*drive:*] specifies the drive to check.
[*[path] filename*] specifies the directory and possibly the specific file to check.
[*/f*] fixes drive errors.
[*/v*] shows the full path for every file.

Example: **chkdsk d:** This command checks the disk structure on the D: drive.

Notes: This command can be used without switches.

CLS   The *cls* command clears the screen of any previously typed commands.

Example: C:\WINNT>**cls**

COPY   The *copy* command is used to copy a single file to the destination that you specify.

Syntax: copy [*/a*] [*/b*] source [*/a|/b*] [*target*] [*/a|/b*] [*/v*] [*/y*] [*/-y*]

Explanation: source is the file that you want to copy and it includes the drive letter and the path if it is different from your current location.
[*/a*] indicates an ASCII text file.
[*/b*] indicates a binary file.
[*target*] is the location you want to put the file and it includes the drive letter and path if it is different from your current location.
[*/v*] verifies that the copied files are written correctly.
[*/y*] suppresses prompting when overwriting an existing file.
[*/-y*] prompts when overwriting an existing file.

Example: **copy c:\cheryl.bat a:** This command takes a file called CHERYL.BAT that is located in the root directory of the hard drive and copies it to the floppy drive.

Notes: You can use wildcard characters such as * and ? with this command. You do not have to put a target if the file is going to the current location specified by the command prompt. By default, if a file already exists, you will be prompted whether or not to overwrite the file.

DEFRAG   The *defrag* command is used to defragment files on a drive.

Syntax: defrag

DEL   The *del* command is used to delete a file.

Syntax: del *name* [*/p*]

Explanation: *name* is the file or directory (folder) that you want to delete and it includes the drive letter and the path if it is different from your current location.
[*/p*] is used to prompt for confirmation before deleting.

Example: C:\WINDOWS>**del c:\cheryl.bat** This command deletes a file called CHERYL.BAT that is located in the WINDOWS directory of the hard drive.

Notes: You can use wildcard characters such as * and ? with this command.

DELTREE   The *deltree* command deletes a directory and all subdirectories and files located in the directory specified.

Syntax: deltree *path* [*/y*]

Explanation: *path* is the complete path to the directory to be deleted.
[*/y*] suppresses the prompt to confirm subdirectory deleting.

Example: **deltree c:\Cheryl\junk** This command deletes the JUNK directory and any files or subdirectories located in the JUNK directory.

Notes: Be very careful with this command.

DIR   The *dir* command is used to list files and folders and their attributes.

Syntax: dir [*drive:*] [*path*] [*filename*] [*/a*[[*:*]*attributes*]][*/b*] [*/l*] [*/o*[[*:*]*sortorder*]] [*/p*] [*/s*] [*/v*] [*/w*] [*/4*]

Explanation: [*drive:*] is the drive letter where the files are located.
[*path*] is the directory/subdirectory to reach the folder.
[*filename*] is the name of a specific file.
[*/a*[[*:*]*attributes*]] is used to display files that have specific attributes where the attributes are D, R, H, A, and S. D is for directories; R is for read-only; H is for hidden; A is for archive; and S is for system files. A + (plus sign) before the attribute means to select it and a – (minus sign) before the attribute means to not select it.
[*/b*] is for barebones format (it doesn't show heading or summary information).
[*/l*] displays the listing in lowercase.
[*/o*[[*:*]*sortorder*]] displays the listing in sorted order. Options you can use after the "o" are E, D, G, N, and S. E is by alphabetic file extension; D is by date and time with the oldest listing shown first; G shows the directories listed first; N displays by alphabetic name; and S displays by size from smallest to largest.
[*/p*] displays the information one page at a time.
[*/s*] includes subdirectories in the listing.
[*/v*] displays more information than normal (verbose mode).
[*/w*] shows the listing in wide format.
[*/4*] displays four digit years instead of two digit years.

Example: **dir c:\windows** This command shows all of the files and folders (and their associated attributes) for the WINDOWS folder that is located on the C: drive.

Notes: You can use wildcard characters such as * and ? with this command.

DISKCOPY   This command is used to copy the contents of one floppy to another floppy.

Syntax: diskcopy [*source*] [*destination*] [*/1*] [*/m*] [*/v*]

Explanation: [*source*] is the drive letter of the floppy that contains the file to copy.
[*destination*] is drive letter of the floppy that contains the disk receiving the copy.
[*/1*] copies one side of the floppy disk.
[*/m*] forces multiple pass copying using only memory.
[*/v*] verifies the copied information.

Example: **diskcopy a: a:** This command copies the information on one floppy (located in drive A:) to another floppy. The system prompts you to swap the floppy disks.

Notes: The *source* and *destination* drive letters can be the same. The system prompts you to change disks. The floppy disks must be the same capacity to use this command.

EDIT   The *edit* command brings up a text file editor.

Syntax: edit *name* [*/b*] [*/h*] [*/r*] [*/s*]

Explanation: *name* is the filename that you want to modify, view, or create and it includes the drive letter and the path if it is different from your current location.
[*/b*] forces the editor into monochrome mode.
[*/h*] displays the maximum number of lines per page.
[*/r*] brings up the file in read-only mode.
[*/s*] requires that short filenames be used.

Example: **edit c:\test\98final.txt** This command either brings a file called 98FINAL.TXT located in the TEST directory or it brings up the editor with a blank document that has the name 98FINAL.TXT.

Notes: You can use wildcard characters such as * and ? and multiple file specifications with this command.

EXIT   When using the command prompt from within the GUI environment, the *exit* command exits the command prompt.

Example: C:\WINNT>**exit**

EXTRACT   The *extract* command is used to uncompress a file from the Windows 98 CD or a CAB file. A CAB file is a shortened named for a cabinet file. A CAB file holds multiple files or drivers that are compressed into a single file. For Windows 98, the cabinet files are located in the WIN98 folder on the CD. Technicians frequently copy the CAB files onto the local hard drive (C:\WINDOWS\OPTIONS\CABS), so that when hardware and/or software is installed, removed, or reinstalled, the Windows 98 CD does not have to be inserted.

Syntax: extract *source* [*destination*] [*/a*] [*/c*] [*/d*] [*/e*] [*/y*]

Explanation: *source* is the name of the file including the path that you want to uncompress.

[*destination*] is the path to where you want to place the uncompressed file.

[*/a*] processes all CAB files.

[*/c*] copies source file to destination (used with DMF disks).

[*/d*] displays the CAB directory.

[*/e*] extracts all files.

[*/y*] is the parameter used if you do not want to be prompted before overwriting an existing file.

Example: C:\temp>**extract e:\win98\base6.cab** This command extracts (uncompresses) the cabinet file BASE6.CAB and puts it into the C:\TEMP directory (the default directory).

Notes: You may use wildcard characters with this command. When using the /d parameter, use with filename to avoid the CAB being extracted. The /e parameter is used in place of using wildcards.

FDISK   This command is used to view and change the hard drive partition(s).

Syntax: fdisk [*/status*] [*/mbr*] [*/x*]

Explanation: [*status*] displays partition information.

[*/mbr*] an undocumented switch used to repair the Master Boot Record.

[*/x*] ignores extended disk-access support.

Example: **fdisk** This command starts the FDISK partitioning program, which is used to create a DOS partition.

Notes: Use the /x switch if a disk access or stack overflow error appears.

FORMAT   The *format* command is used to format a disk and can be used to format it for a particular file system.

Syntax: format [*driveletter:*] [*/b*] [*/c*] [*/f:size*] [*/n:sectors*] [*/q*] [*/t:tracks*] [*/v:label*] [*/1*] [*/4*] [*/8*]

Explanation: [*driveletter:*] is drive letter for the disk or hard drive volume that you want to format.

[*/b*] allocates space for system files (boot sector).

[*/c*] tests clusters currently marked as bad.

[*/f:size*] The /f: must be part of the command followed by the size for floppy disk to format. The different sizes supported are as follows: 160, 180, 320, 360, 720, 1.2, 1.44, or 2.88.

[*/n:sectors*] The /n: must be part of the command followed by the number of sectors per track.

[*/q*] is the parameter used if you want to perform a quick format.

[*/t:tracks*] The */t:* must be part of the command followed by the number of tracks per disk side.

[*/v:label*] the */v:* must be part of the command followed by the name of the volume assigned.

[*/1*] is used to format a single side of a floppy disk.

[*/4*] is used to format a 5.25" 360K floppy disk in a 1.2M drive.

[*/8*] is used to format eight sectors per track.

Example: **format a: /f:720** This command formats the floppy for 720K.

IEXTRACT   This command is used to start the Internet Explorer Backup Information Extraction tool.

Syntax: iextract [*backup_name*] [*filename*] [*/l dir*] [*/w*]

Explanation: [*backup_name*] is the full path for the backup information file. The file must end in the .DAT extension.

[*filename*] is the name of the file to extract from the backup information file.

[*/l dir*] is the directory in which to save the extracted files.

[*/w*] provides an overwrite warning.

Notes: When using the *filename* parameter, multiple filenames can be used. The filenames are entered and separated by a space. The default is all files. When using the */l dir* parameter, the default is the current directory. When using the */w* parameter, the default is to automatically overwrite existing files.

MD   This command is used to create a directory (folder).

Syntax: md [*driveletter:*] [*dirname*]

Explanation: [*driveletter:*] is the drive letter for the disk or volume on which you want to create a directory (folder). It can also include the path.

[*dirname*] is the parameter used to name the directory (folder).

Example: **md c:\TEST**

Notes: You may not use wildcard characters with this command.

MEM   The *mem* command displays memory usage.

Syntax: mem [*/classify*] [*/debug*] [*/free*] [*/module module_name*] [*/page*]

Explanation: [*/classify*] displays programs according to memory usage, size of program, etc.

[*/debug*] displays memory module status and internal drivers.

[*/free*] displays the amount of available conventional and upper memory.

[*/module module_name*] displays a detailed listing of a specific module and where it is loaded in memory.

[*/page*] displays only one screen of information at a time.

Example: **mem /c** This command shows how memory is used by individual applications.

Notes: Each switch can be shortened to the first letter of the switch, for example, */classify* can be shortened to */c*.

MORE   The *more* command is used to display one screen at a time.

Syntax: more *filename* or *command*

Explanation: *filename* is the path and name of the file you want to display on the screen
command is a specific command to execute including the drive letter and full path for where the command is located

Example: **more c:\boot.ini**

Notes: The spacebar allows you to view the next page of a text file. The Enter key allows you to scroll through the text file one line at a time. The ESC key allows you to quit viewing the text file.

MOVE   The *move* command is used to change the location of one or more files

Syntax: move *source destination* [*/y|/-y*]

Explanation: *source* is the complete path for one or more files you want to move
destination is the complete path for the final place the files will reside.
[*/y*] Suppresses the prompt to confirm directory creation or overwriting existing files.
[*/-y*] prompts for directory creation or overwriting existing files.

Example: **move c:\test\98final.txt c:\mydocs\98class\98final.txt** This command moves the 98FINAL.TXT file from the TEST directory to the MYDOCS\98CLASS directory.

Notes: Directories can be relocated using this command.

MSCDEX   The *mscdex* command provides access to CD-ROM drives.

Syntax: mscdex [*/e/k/s/v*] [*/d:driver*] [*/l:drive_letter*] [*/m:buffers*]

Explanation: */e* uses expanded memory for storing sector buffers.
/k is used to recognize CDs encoded in Kanji.
/s allows CD-ROM sharing across a network.
/v displays memory statistics.
[*/d:driver*] specifies the CD-ROM driver.
[*/l:drive_letter*] specifies the drive letter assigned to the CD-ROM drive.
[*/m:buffers*] specifies the number of sector buffers.

PROMPT   This command is used to change how the command prompt displays.

Syntax: prompt [*text*] [*$$*][*$_*] [*$b*] [*$d*] [*$e*] [*$g*] [*$h*] [*$l*] [*$n*] [*$p*] [*$q*] [*$t*] [*$v*]

Explanation: [*text*] is any typed characters.
[*$$*] displays a dollar sign.

[*$_*] provides a carriage return and line feed after each time the Enter key is pressed.

[*$b*] displays the pipe symbol.

[*$d*] displays the current date.

[*$e*] displays the ASCII escape code 27, which is a left arrow symbol.

[*$g*] displays the greater than sign.

[*$h*] is for a backspace, which erases the previous character.

[*$l*] displays the less than sign.

[*$n*] displays the current drive.

[*$p*] displays the current drive and path.

[*$q*] displays the equal sign.

[*$t*] displays the current time.

[*$v*] displays the Windows version.

Example: **prompt pg** sets the prompt to look like C:\WINDOWS>.

Notes: Typing just the word *prompt* resets the prompt to the default setting.

RD   This command is used to remove a directory (folder).

Syntax: rd [*driveletter:*] [*path*]

Explanation: [*driveletter:*] is drive letter for the disk or hard drive volume that you want to remove a directory (folder).

[*path*] is the optional path and name of the directory (folder) you want to remove.

Example: **rd c:\TEST\JUNKDATA** removes a directory (folder) called JUNKDATA that is a subdirectory under a directory (folder) called TEST. This directory is located on the hard drive (C:).

Notes: You do not have to use the *driveletter:* parameter if the default drive letter is the same as the one that contains the directory to be deleted.

REN   The *ren* command is used to rename a file or directory (folder).

Syntax: ren [*driveletter:*] [*path*] *name1 name2*

Explanation: [*driveletter:*] is drive letter for the disk or hard drive volume that you want to rename a file or a directory (folder).

[*path*] is the optional path telling the operating system where to find the file or directory (folder) you want to rename.

name1 is the old name of the file or directory (folder) that you want to rename.

name2 is the new name of the file or directory (folder).

Example: **ren c:\cheryl.bat c:\newcheryl.bat**

Notes: The renamed file cannot be placed in a new location with this command. Move or copy the file after you rename it if that is what you want to do. The * and *?* wildcard characters are not supported.

SCANDISK   The *scandisk* command is used to check a drive for errors.

Syntax: scandisk [*driveletter:*] [*/a*] [*/n*] [*/p*]

Explanation: [*driveletter:*] is drive letter for the disk or hard drive volume that you want to check

[*/a*] checks all local hard disks

[*/n*] starts and exits ScanDisk automatically

[*/p*] runs ScanDisk without automatically correcting errors

Example: **scandisk c:** This command checks the C: drive for errors.

Notes: Use the Help function to find out more information about ScanDisk.

SCANREG   The *scanreg* command is used to check, repair, back up, and restore the registry.

Syntax: scanreg [*/backup*] [*/fix*] [*/restore*]

Explanation: [*/backup*] is used to back up the registry and system configuration files.

[*/fix*] is used to repair the registry.

[*/restore*] is used to select a backup copy of the registry to restore.

Example: **scanreg /fix** This command checks the C: drive for errors.

Notes: This command cannot be executed from within the GUI environment. You must boot to a command prompt.

SETVER   Command used to set or delete the DOS version number the Windows reports to an application.

Syntax to add an entry: setver [*path*] *filename x.xx*

Syntax to delete an entry: setver [*path*] *filename* /delete [*/quiet*]

Explanation: [*path*] is the drive letter and path where the SETVER command is located.

filename is the name of the application's executable file.

x.xx is the DOS version reported to the application by Windows.

/delete is the command to delete a version table entry for a specific program (specified by the *filename* parameter).

[*/quiet*] suppresses the message that normally displays when an entry is deleted.

SMARTDRV   The *smartdrv* command is used to install and configure disk caching for hard drives and CD-ROM drives running DOS mode drivers or MS-DOS-compatibility mode.

Syntax: smartdrv [*drive*[+|-]] [*/b:buffersize*] [*/c*] [*/e:elementsize*][*/f*][*initcachesize* [*wincachesize*]] [*/l*] [*/n*] [*/q*] [*/s*] [*/u*] [*/v*] [*/x*]

Explanation: [*drive*[+|-]] is the drives to set caching options on and has write-caching disabled unless the + (plus sign) is added. The + enables write-behind caching for the drive specified. The – disables all caching for the drive specified.

[*/b:buffersize*] specifies the size of the read-ahead buffer.

[*/c*] writes the information held in cache to hard drive.

[*/e:elementsize*] defines the number of bytes to transfer at a time.

[*/f*] writes any cached data to hard disk before command prompt returns.

[*initcachesize* [*wincachesize*]] *initcachesize* defines the amount of XMS memory (in KB) for the cache; *wincachesize* defines the amount of XMS memory (in KB) for the cache when using Windows.

[*/l*] keeps SmartDrive from loading into UMB.

[*/n*] does not write any cached data to hard disk before command prompt returns; the default is */f.*

[*/q*] suppresses status information.

[*/s*] displays additional status information.

[*/u*] does not load CD-ROM caching.

[*/v*] displays status information.

[*/x*] disables write-behind caching for all drives.

START	The *start* command runs an application from the command prompt.
Syntax:	start *name* [*/min*] [*/max*] [*/r*] [*/w*]
Explanation:	*name* is the filename of the application to execute.
	[*/min*] starts the program minimized.
	[*/max*] starts the program maximized.
	[*/r*] starts the program restored (in the foreground).
	[*/w*] does not wait until another program exits.
Example:	**start c:\windows\winmine.exe** This command starts the Mine Sweeper game that is located in the WINDOWS directory.
Notes:	The */r* parameter is the default.

SYS	The *sys* command is used to transfer the system files and command interpreter to a disk.
Syntax:	sys *source destination*
Explanation:	*source* is the path (drive letter and possibly directory if it is not the root directory) for where the system files are currently located.
	destination is the drive to which the system files are to be copied.
Example:	**sys a: c:** This command copies the system files that are on the A: drive to the C: drive.
Notes:	Do not use this command unless you know exactly what you are doing.

TYPE	The *type* command is used to display a text file.
Syntax:	type *filename*
Explanation:	*filename* is the path and name of the text file you want to display on the screen.
Example:	**type c:\boot.ini**

Notes: The spacebar allows you to view the next page of a text file. The Enter key allows you to scroll through the text file one line at a time. The ESC key allows you to quit viewing the text file.

VER   Displays the operating system version.

Syntax: ver

WSCRIPT   The *wscript.exe* is the command used to bring up a Windows-based script property sheet. This property sheet is used to set script properties. The command line version is CSCRIPT.EXE

XCOPY   The *xcopy* command is used to copy files and directories.

Syntax: xcopy *source* [*destination*] [/a] [/c] [/d[:date]] [/e] [/f] [/h] [/i] [/k] [/l] [/m] [/n] [/p] [/q] [/r] [/s] [/t] [/u] [w]

Explanation: *source* is the path (drive letter, directory, and subdirectory(ies)) where the files or folder being copied is currently located.

destination is the path (drive letter, directory, and subdirectory(ies)) where the files or folder being copied is currently located.

[/a] copies only the files that have the archive attribute set and does not change the archive attribute.

[/c] keeps on copying even if errors occur.

[/d[:*date*]] copies files changed on or after the date specified. If no date is specified, only the files that have a source time newer than the destination time are copied.

[/e] copies directories, subdirectories, and empty directories.

[/f] displays source and destination names when copying.

[/h] copies hidden and system files.

[/i] if the destination does not exist and more than one file is being copied, this assumes the destination is a directory.

[/k] copies the original file attributes.

[/l] lists files that would be copied.

[/m] copies only the files with the archive attribute set and removes the archive attribute.

[/n] destination file receives a computer generated short filename.

[/p] prompts before creating each destination file.

[/q] squelches the displaying of filenames as they copy.

[/r] overwrites read-only files.

[/s] copies directories and subdirectories, but not empty ones.

[/t] creates the directory structure, but does not copy files; does not include empty directories or subdirectories.

[/u] updates the files that already exist in the destination.

[/w] prompts before copying.

[/y] overwrites existing files automatically.

[/-y] provides a prompt before overwriting existing files.

Example: **xcopy c:\tests c:\backup\class\tests** This command copies the files located in the TESTS directory to the BACKUP\CLASS\TESTS subdirectory.

Notes: The default behavior of the XCOPY command is to reset the read-only attribute. Use the /k switch to override this XCOPY default. To create a directory structure including empty directories and subdirectories (and not copy files), use the /t /e switches together.

TROUBLESHOOTING APPLICATION PROBLEMS

Most computer problems occur when installing an operating system or a new hardware component, but applications can cause problems too. Application problems can occur when a new application is installed, a new operating system is installed, an operating system service pack or upgrade is installed, and during normal computer operation. The way in which an application problem is tackled depends on whether the application is 16-bit or 32-bit. This is because Windows 98 uses two types of multitasking—preemptive and cooperative. **Preemptive multitasking** is the operating system determining which application gets the microprocessor's attention and for how long. Preemptive multitasking is used with 32-bit applications. **Cooperative multitasking** relies on the application to relinquish control of the CPU and is the type of multitasking that 16-bit applications use.

An important concept when dealing with applications is the virtual machine. A **virtual machine** is a way for the operating system to appear as a separate computer to each application. Each 32-bit application runs in its own virtual machine. Each 16-bit DOS application runs in its own virtual machine. However, every 16-bit Windows application (an application designed for Windows 3.x) runs in one virtual machine. When a 16-bit Windows application crashes, all 16-bit applications that are loaded into memory crash as well.

Another important concept to remember is that 16-bit applications were not designed to interact with the registry. DOS applications are designed to interact and update the AUTOEXEC.BAT and CONFIG.SYS files. 16-bit Windows applications are designed to interact and update the AUTOEXEC.BAT, CONFIG.SYS, and various .INI files such as SYSTEM.INI and WIN.INI. Windows 98 still contains and supports these files in order to be backward compatible with older applications.

When an application error occurs, a **GPF (General Protection Fault)** error message appears. When a Windows 16-bit application GPF occurs, all other 16-bit Windows applications are halted until you exit the application that caused the error. In most cases, the other 16-bit applications must be closed as well. When a 32-bit application GPF occurs, no other application is affected. Sometimes when the GPF occurs, you are allowed to terminate the application from the GPF error window, but sometimes you must use a different method to quit the application. Press *CTRL+ALT+DEL* keys and the Close

Program window appears. Click on the *offending application* and then click on the *End Task* button.

Another useful utility to help with application problems is Dr. Watson. **Dr. Watson** has the ability to take a snapshot of the computer system when a fault occurs. For software applications, Dr. Watson can provide information about the problem cause. The Dr. Watson utility does not load by default in Windows 98. To start Dr. Watson in Windows 98, click on the *Start* button, point to the *Programs*, *Accessories*, and *System Tools* options, and then click on the *System Information* selection. From the Microsoft System Information window, click on the *Tools* menu option and choose the *Dr. Watson* menu item. A Dr. Watson icon appears in the taskbar system tray in the bottom right corner.

Dr. Watson takes a snapshot of the system and then the Dr. Watson window appears. On the Diagnosis tab is information relating to the system snapshot. WIN98 Figure #10 illustrates the Dr. Watson window.

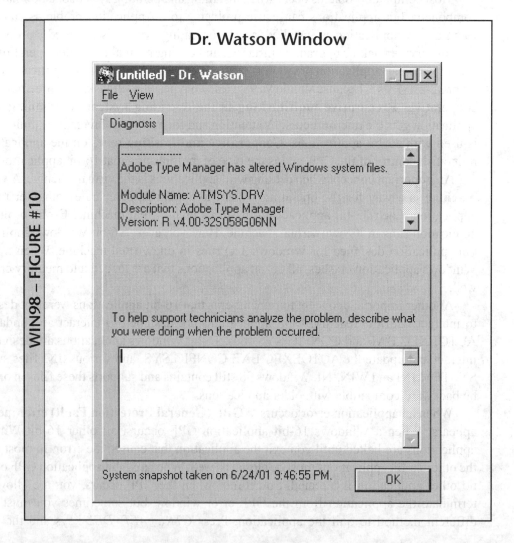

WIN98 – FIGURE #10

The Dr. Watson window also has blank space at the bottom so that the technician can insert notes.

Dr. Watson also includes an Advanced view that provides detailed information about the computer system. Click on the *View* menu option and select *Advanced view*. The Advanced view has many tabs across the top. To view more tabs, click on the right or left arrows located to the right of the tabs. Several important tabs include the Kernel drivers, User Drivers, MS-DOS drivers, and 16-bit Modules. These tabs separate the various drivers that can be used on Windows 98. WIN98 Figure #11 illustrates the Dr. Watson Advanced view.

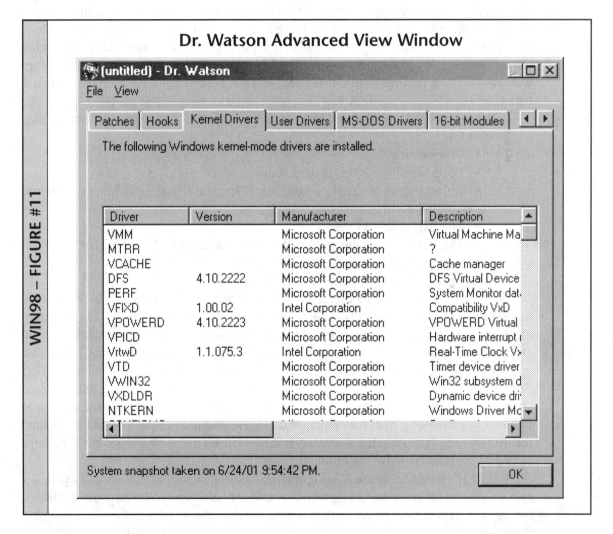

WIN98 – FIGURE #11

When Dr. Watson is running and an application error occurs, Dr. Watson logs the information into a file called WATSONxx.WLG file. The *xx* in the filename is a number that is automatically incremented by Dr. Watson. To view a saved file, click on the *File* menu option and select the *Open Log File* menu item. Any system snapshot can also be saved using the *Save* or *Save as* File menu options. To have Dr. Watson start every time the computer boots, create a shortcut to the WINDOWS\DRWATSON.EXE file, and place the shortcut in the WINDOWS\START MENU\PROGRAMS\STARTUP folder.

SHUTDOWN PROBLEMS

Before Windows 98 can shutdown, the operating system sends a message to all devices and applications. Each running device sends a message back saying it is okay to shutdown now. Any active application saves data that has not been previously saved and sends a message back to the operating system. If the system has trouble shutting down, it can be due to one of these two things. The most common problem is an application that is not responding back. When this happens, press *CTRL+ALT+DEL* to access the Close Program window. Click on the application that is causing the problem and click on the *End Task* button.

In Windows 98 Second Edition, other factors can cause a shutdown problem and they are listed below.

- IRQ steering
- BIOS/Windows 98 communication
- An anti-virus program is configured to scan the floppy disk drive before shutting down.
- The Exit Windows sound file is damaged.
- The Resume on Ring and LAN option is enabled in the BIOS.
- An incompatible device driver is loaded.
- Hardware is configured incorrectly.

IRQ steering is a feature that allows PCI devices to share the same IRQ. Some motherboard BIOSes do not fully support this option. To disable PCI but not IRQ steering, click on the *Start* button, point to the *Settings* option, and click on the *Control Panel* item. Double-click on the *System* control panel. Click on the *Device Manager* tab. Click on the + (*plus sign*) beside *System Devices*. Double-click on the *PCI Bus* item. Click on the *IRQ Steering* tab. Click on the *Use IRQ Steering* checkbox to remove the check and clear the setting. Click on the *OK* button and click on the *OK* button that allows the system to restart. After rebooting, shut the computer down. If the shutdown problem is not evident, the IRQ steering is causing the shutdown problem. Check the motherboard BIOS settings or update the BIOS to solve the problem.

ESCD (Extended System Configuration Data) provides the BIOS and operating system a means for communicating with plug and play devices. When the computer boots, the motherboard BIOS records legacy device configuration information. Plug and play devices use this information to configuring themselves without conflicting with legacy devices. To see if the communication between the BIOS and Windows 98 is a problem, click on the *Start* button, point to the *Settings* option, and click on the *Control Panel* item. Double-click on the *System* control panel. Click on the *Device Manager* tab. Click on the

+ (*plus sign*) beside *System Devices*. Double-click on the *Plug and Play BIOS* item. Click on the *Settings* tab. Click on the *Disable NVRAM/ESCD updates* checkbox. Click on the *OK* button and click on the *OK* button that allows the system to restart. After rebooting, shut the computer down, if the shutdown problem is not evident, the BIOS/Windows 98 communication is the problem. Update the BIOS or view the computer/motherboard manufacturer's web site for possible solutions.

Another method can be used to determine if the motherboard BIOS is causing a problem. Start the computer and hold the *CTRL* key down to bring up the Startup menu. If the Startup menu does not appear, restart the computer again and press the *F8* key during the startup process. From the Startup menu, select the *Command Prompt Only* option. At the command prompt, type *CD\WINDOWS\SYSTEM* and press *Enter*. At the command prompt, type *REN BIOS.VXD BIOS.OLD* and restart the computer. Once the computer boots, shutdown the computer. If the shutdown problem disappears, the BIOS is probably causing the problem. Update the BIOS or go to the computer manufacturer's web site for possible solutions.

If the anti-virus program is configured to scan the floppy disk drive before shutting down, disable this feature in the anti-virus program. Refer to the anti-virus application manual or on-line help for instructions. If the Exit Windows sound file is damaged, replace the file from the original Windows 98 CD. If the Resume on Ring and LAN option is enabled in the BIOS, disable it to see if it is causing Windows 98 to not shutdown properly. If you suspect device drivers, update all device drivers to their latest Windows 98-compatible versions. Use the Hardware Troubleshooter to determine if there are any conflicts in the system. To start the troubleshooting wizard, click on the *Start* button, click on *Help*, click on the *Index* tab, type *hardware* in the textbox, and click on the *troubleshooting* submenu item. Click on the *Click here* link in the right window and follow the directions on the screen.

PROBLEMS WITH MS-DOS MODE

Windows 9x executes a batch file called DOSSTART.BAT every time the Restart the Computer in MS-DOS mode, Restart in MD-DOS mode, or Exit to DOS option is selected. The commands included in the batch file are normally for mouse and CD-ROM support. Commands can be added to the DOSSTART.BAT by using the Notepad accessory. Click on the *Start* button, point to *Accessories*, and click on the *Notepad* option. Click on the *File* menu option and select *Open*. Click on the *Files of Type* down arrow and select *All files*. Locate the DOSSTART.BAT file and click on it. The file is normally located in the WINDOWS folder. Click on the *Open* button. Type the desired commands, click on the *File* menu option, and click on *Save*.

If the CD-ROM is not available from the command prompt, then the problem is probably that the DOSSTART.BAT file does not contain the MSCDEX line. See the CD-ROM chapter for information about creating this line. If the computer hangs when restarting in DOS mode, the problem is again most likely in the DOSSTART.BAT file. Use Notepad as previously described to edit and REM out one line at a time. Try restarting in DOS mode after each edit. Correct the line that causes the problem.

POWER AND RESOURCE MANAGEMENT

Windows 98 includes power management features through ACPI (Advanced Configuration and Power Interface) and the OnNow design. The motherboard, BIOS, and operating system must all support ACPI in order to use the power management features. ACPI supports the following:

- Specify a specific time the monitor turns off or on.
- Specify lower power when a laptop battery is low so that important applications are allowed to continue operating.
- Allow the operating system to lower the clock speed when applications do not need this capability.
- Allow the operating system to reduce power by not activating devices until they are needed.
- Put the computer in standby mode when it is inactive.
- Allow a fax/modem to continue receiving faxes even if the computer is in standby mode.

OnNow is a feature that allows a computer to be available to the user instantly when it is needed and to use the least amount of power possible when it is not needed.

In prior years, laptops were the first type of computers to have power management features. Power management was controlled through the motherboard BIOS. With these older systems, once the laptop received a signal to come out of sleep mode, it would take a considerable amount of time for the hard drive to spin up or the display to reappear. OnNow allows the operating system to control the power management features through ACPI. With OnNow-capable hardware and applications, the following features are possible:

- The moment the computer is brought out of sleep mode, it is instantly ready for use.
- Applications do not bring the computer out of sleep mode with background tasks.
- An application can be configured to bring the system out of sleep mode in order to connect automatically to the Internet for a download, receive a fax, or perform maintenance tasks.

To configure Windows 98 power management features, access the Power Management control panel by clicking on the *Start* button, pointing to the *Settings* option, and clicking on *Control Panel*. Double-click on the *Power Management* control panel icon. WIN98 Figure #12 shows the Power Management Properties window.

WIN98 – FIGURE #12

Power Management Control Panel

Mode	Purpose
Normal	Used to boot Windows 98 in the normal fashion
Logged	Used to track the boot process and log each event in a file located in the root directory called BOOTLOG.TXT; used to determine where the boot failure occurs
Safe	Prevents the CONFIG.SYS and AUTOEXEC.BAT files from loading, prevents the [Boot] and [386enh] sections of the SYSTEM.INI file from loading, prevents the Load= and Run= parameters of the WIN.INI file from loading, prevents the items found in the Startup folder from loading, prevents portions of the registry from loading, prevents all device drivers except for the keyboard and mouse from loading, and loads a standard VGA driver
Step-by-Step Confirmation	Allows performing the boot process one step at a time to see where the problem occurs
Command-Prompt-Only	Used to troubleshoot DOS applications (only CONFIG.SYS, AUTOEXEC.BAT, COMMAND.COM, and the registry are loaded; the GUI does not load)
Safe Mode Command-Prompt-Only	Used if the computer does not boot to Safe Mode; does not load the HIMEM.SYS or IFSHLP.SYS files and does not execute WIN.COM to start the GUI. Various switches can be used at the command prompt with the WIN.COM file to troubleshoot the problem.
Previous Version of MS-DOS	Used to perform a DOS function that does not operate correctly under Windows 98

Through the Power Management control panel, you can configure when the monitor and hard drive power are removed, how many minutes of inactivity puts the system into standby mode, a specific type of power scheme, and how the computer's sleep button and power button are used. The three types of power schemes supported by Windows 98 are Home/office, Portable/laptop, and Always on. The Home/office is for desktop computers used at work or home. The Portable/laptop scheme is designed to work with laptop batteries. The Always on scheme is for servers or any computer that must stay in operation at all times.

Many tools have already been covered that help with resource management, but two new ones are System Monitor and Resource Meter. **System Monitor** is a utility that tracks performance of individual system components, such as disk cache, file system, operating system kernel, and memory manager. Under each category are numerous individual selections. System Monitor helps identify where performance bottlenecks are located. To access System Monitor, click on the *Start* button, point to *Accessories* and *System Tools*, and click on the *System Monitor* option. The System Monitor utility may have to be installed to the System Tools program group.

System monitor has three views—line chart, bar chart, and numeric chart. WIN98 Figure #13 shows System Monitor using a bar chart.

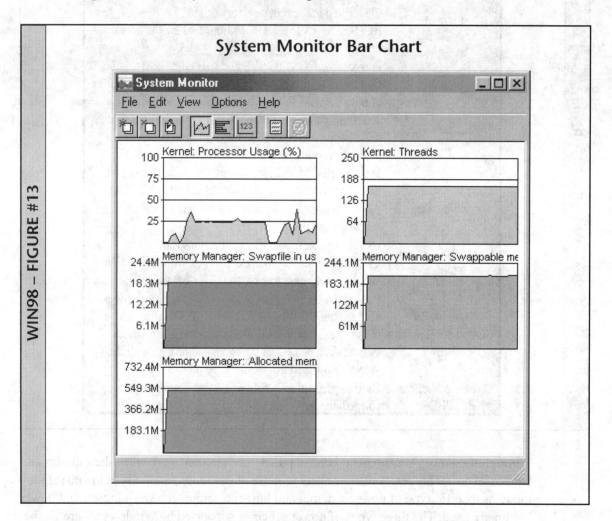

System Monitor Bar Chart

WIN98 – FIGURE #13

An exercise at the end of this chapter demonstrates System Monitor usage.

Resource Meter is a very simple graphical display of how Windows 98 is using memory. To access Resource Meter, click on the *Start* button, point to *Programs*, *Accessories*, and *System Tools* options, and click on the *Resource Meter* selection. A window with a Resource Meter description appears on the screen and then the Resource Meter becomes an icon on the taskbar system tray. Double-click on the icon that looks like a set of stairs with a colored bar across the bottom to display Resource Meter. Keep in mind that

Resource Meter consumes system resources just like any utility. After viewing Resource Meter, right click on the Resource Meter icon in the tzaskbar system tray and click on the *Exit* option.

The three Windows 98 core components, Kernel (system), User, and GDI, are shown with individual lines. The System line represents the Windows 98 kernel, which is the part of the operating system that supports input/output, task scheduling, and virtual memory management. The User line represents how much memory is being used to manage user input such as mouse usage, window sizing, etc. The GDI (Graphics Device Interface) core component line represents the amount of memory being used for screen and printer graphics. WIN98 Figure #14 shows the Resource Meter window.

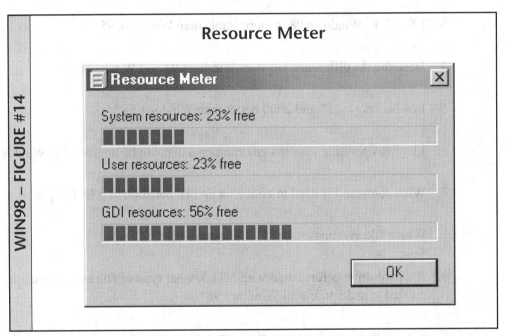

Resource Meter

WIN98 – FIGURE #14

Sometimes a technician must adjust the paging file size for optimum computer performance. The *System* control panel is used to set the virtual memory size. Once in the System control panel, click on the *Performance* tab. Click on the *Virtual Memory* button and two options are available—Let Windows manage my virtual memory settings (the default setting) and Let me specify my own virtual memory settings. Click on the *Let me specify my own virtual memory settings* radio button, select the hard drive partition and minimum/maximum amount of hard drive space. Click on the *OK* button when finished.

The minimum/maximum settings should contain the same value for maximum computer performance.

Name _____

WINDOWS 98 REVIEW QUESTIONS

1. What type of users are more prone to using Windows 98?

2. List three Windows 98 support features.

3. [T / F] Windows 98 is more stable than Windows 95.

4. Describe the difference between Windows 95 and Windows 98.

5. In what way is NT and 2000 better than Windows 98?

6. List two operating systems/environments that can be upgraded to Windows 98.

7. What command is used to convert a FAT16 partition to a FAT32 partition?

8. Which file systems are used by Windows 98 for CDs?

9. If a hard drive is formatted with NTFS, what type of file system partition must be created in order to install Windows 98?

10. What is the name for a graphical representation of an application, file, directory, or utility?

11. Describe an easy way to tell if an icon is a shortcut.

12. What happens when you double-click on a document shortcut icon?

13. List three common Windows 98 desktop icons.

14. What desktop icon is used to access the floppy drive?
    [My Documents / Internet Explorer / My Drives / My Computer]

15. [T / F]   Deleted files can be recovered from the Recycle Bin.

16. What keystroke combination brings up the Start menu?

17. You click on the *Start* button, click on *Shut Down*, and select the *Restart in MS-DOS* mode option. What command do you type to start the GUI environment?

18. What Start menu option is used to access various control panels?

19. What Quick Launch icon allows access to the desktop?

20. Describe the steps to close the Quick Launch bar.

21. What is the insertion point as it relates to a textbox?

22. What dialog box button is represented by an X?
    [Help / Close / Performance / Lock out]

23. What button is used to apply changes to a dialog box?
    [OK / Enable / Set / Change]

24. Describe the most common mistake made when working with dialog boxes.

25. What is another name for a folder?

26. Describe the process to view file extensions.

27. Describe the default icon used when Windows 98 does not recognize an extension.

28. What extension is used for a postscript file that has been encapsulated?

29. What file extension is found on Windows 98 files that are used to be backward compatible with Windows 3.x?

30. What file extensions do (or extension does) compressed files normally use?
    [COM / ZIP / WKS / INF]

31. What is the maximum length of a Windows 98 long filename?

32. [T / F]   The question mark can be used in a Windows 98 filename.

33. Give an example of a Windows 98 long filename.

34. A file is located in the TEST folder, which is a subfolder of WIN98 CLASS. The WIN98 CLASS folder is located in the MY DOCUMENTS folder on the first hard drive partition. Write the complete path to the QUIZ1 file located in the TEST folder.

35. List three file attributes and the purposes of each.

36. Describe the steps to set or remove a file attribute.

37. [T / F]   Folders can have attributes.

38. Give one method of determining the Windows 98 version.

39. Describe what is contained in a user profile.

40. What are the two files that make up the registry?

41. Which registry file holds user profiles?

42. What attribute is applied to the registry files by default?

43. When user profiles are implemented, where are the individual USER.DAT registry files stored?

44. Why is the CONFIG.SYS file still used in Windows 98?

45. What registry subtree tracks user preferences?

46. What is the size limitation for a Windows 98 subkey?
    [16K / 64K / 128K / Unlimited]

47. Before making chages to the registry, make a _____.
    [boot disk / backup tape / boot CD / registry backup]

48. Describe the steps to access REGEDIT.

49. When should a technician back up the registry?

50. List two methods for backing up the registry.

51. How often does the Registry Checker utility automatically back up the registry?

52. By default, how many backups are automatically retained by Windows 98?

53. List the two executable files that are used to start the Register Checker utility.

54. What Registry Checker executable file is used in the GUI environment?

55. Windows 98 is operational. You want to manually back up the registry using the Registry Checker utility. What command will you enter in the Run dialog box to start this process?

56. When is the SCANREG file used?

57. What SCANREG switch is used to repair the registry?

58. What SCANREG switch is used to select a backup registry file and install it on the computer?

59. What utility can be used to back up the operating system, registry, applications, and data?

60. List three pre-installation tasks.

61. What is the difference between a clean install and an upgrade?

62. [T / F] Once a partition is converted from FAT16 to FAT32, the process can be reversed.

63. List three reasons for using FAT32.

64. [T / F] When dual-booting, a separate hard drive partition should be used for each operating system.

65. How does a boot sector virus get loaded into RAM?

66. A Microsoft Excel spreadsheet has a virus. What type of virus normally affects these file types?

67. What type of virus is normally spread through e-mail?

68. List three symptoms of a virus.

69. When should an anti-virus program be installed?

70. What is the minimum microprocessor required to install Windows 98?

71. What is the minimum amount of RAM required to install Windows 98?

72. [T / F] The Windows 98 Setup program can be executed from a DOS prompt.

73. Describe the steps to upgrade from Windows 95 to Windows 98 and *not* have to reinstall applications.

74. What is the purpose of ScanDisk during a Windows 98 installation?

75. Where is the Windows 98 Product Key located?

76. What is the most commonly used Setup type for Windows 98?
     [Typical / Custom / Portable / Compact]

77. What Windows 98 SETUP.EXE switch is used on a Gateway computer that fails during Setup?

78. Windows 98 is being installed on a networked computer. What is the maximum number of characters for the computer name?

79. List three problems that cause the installation process to halt.

80. What startup log file is used by the computer when Setup fails?

81. If Setup cannot decode a CAB file, what could be the problem?

82. Which of the following can be dual-booted with Windows 98? (Pick all that apply) [DOS / Windows 3.x / Windows 95 / NT / 2000 Professional]

83. What file systems do NT and Windows 98 have in common?

84. [T / F]   Windows 98 can read, but not write, a file to an NTFS partition.

85. What three control panels are most often used to install hardware and software?

86. What control panel is used with CD-ROMs?

87. What control panel is used to access Device Manager?

88. What are two requirements for a successful plug and play device installation?

89. What is another name for a non-plug and play device?

90. How do you configure a printer as the default printer?

91. 16-bit TSRs load through what Windows 98 startup file?

92. What is the name of the Windows 98 extended memory manager file?

93. What is the purpose of the USER.EXE Windows 98 startup file?

94. What happens on a plug and play computer after POST executes?

95. What is the default number of buffers loaded by the IO.SYS file?

96. What MSDOS.SYS setting controls the number of seconds delayed after the "Starting Windows" message appears?

97. What MSDOS.SYS setting specifies where the Windows 98 files are located?

98. If the CTRL key does not bring up the Startup menu, what other key does?

99. What Startup menu option allows you to go through the boot process one line at a time?

100. In what instance is the System Configuration utility used?

101. Which program determines the drivers that do not load during startup?

102. What do you do if an error message appears stating that a device referenced in SYSTEM.INI could not be found?

103. What do you do if the computer displays a message that HIMEM.SYS is corrupt?

104. List three things that can cause a Windows Protection Error to appear.

105. Describe the steps to create a Windows 98 boot disk.

106. What command can be used from the command prompt to bring up a simple text editor?

107. What command is used to uncompress a Windows 98 CAB file?
[ZIP / UNZIP / EXPAND / EXTRACT]

108. What command is used to partition a hard drive?

109. What command can be used to provide CD-ROM drive access?

110. What command is used to repair the registry and is executed from a command prompt?

111. What command is used to bring up a Windows-based script property sheet?

112. What type of multitasking is used with 32-bit applications?

113. Describe the difference between preemptive and cooperative multitasking.

114. List the steps taken when an application crashes.

115. Describe the steps used to access the Dr. Watson utility.

116. List three problems that can cause Windows 98 to not shutdown properly.

117. What is the purpose of the DOSSTART.BAT file?

118. List three things ACPI can provide.

119. What control panel is used to control how long the system is idle before the Always on power scheme is activated?

120. What three components are displayed in the Resource Meter window?

Name _____

WINDOWS 98 FILL-IN-THE-BLANK

1. Windows 98 is a _____-bit operating system.

2. _____ is the web browser integrated into Windows 98.

3. The hard drive file systems supported by Windows 98 are _____ and _____.

4. The _____ file system is used for Windows 98 DVDs.

5. The name given to the area where all Windows 98 work is performed is _____.

6. A _____ is a special icon used for quick file or application access.

7. Shortcuts are normally placed on the _____.

8. The _____ desktop option keeps desktop icons from being moved.

9. A _____ is a picture, pattern, or color used for the desktop background.

10. A _____ is the picture, color, or pattern that appears when the computer is idle.

11. The _____ folder is the default location for file storage.

12. Deleted files go into the _____.

13. The _____ button is located in the lower left desktop corner.

14. The _____ Start menu option is used to restart the computer.

15. To access the troubleshooting wizards, select the _____ Start menu option.

16. The _____ Start menu option allows access to the fifteen most recently used files.

17. The _____ Quick Launch icon has an icon that looks like a desk with a pencil touching a piece of paper.

18. The _____ holds buttons that represent applications.

19. The dialog box's _____ button is represented by a question mark.

20. A _____ dialog box option contains a check when the option is enabled and blank when an option is not enabled.

21. With a _____ button, the circle is darkened when enabled.

22. A _____ holds data.

23. A _____ holds files.

24. .DOC is an example of an _____.

25. The _____ application uses the .PDF extension.

26. The _____ and _____ file extensions are used with executable files.

27. The _____ file extension is used with Windows 98 virtual device drivers.

28. _____, _____, and _____ are characters that can be used in long filenames.

29. The short filename for QUIZ1 FALL 2002.DOC is _____.

30. The _____ folder is the default folder for saving files in Windows 98.

31. The _____ and _____ desktop icons can be used to set file attributes.

32. To permanently delete a file, hold down the _____ key while pressing the DELETE key.

33. The Windows 98 database that stores hardware and software configuration information is called the _____.

34. The default location for the registry is _____.

35. The _____ registry file holds hardware settings.

36. In Windows 3.x, _____ files are used instead of the registry.

37. By default, Windows 98 stores the SYSTEM.INI file in the _____ folder.

38. A non-user-specific registry subtree that contains hardware components and drivers is _____.

39. The _____ registry subtree holds file links.

40. The default size limitation for a registry key in Windows 98 is _____.

41. The most common way to edit the registry is through _____.

42. The Windows 98 registry editor is called _____.

43. The _____ utility is the most common way to back up the registry.

44. The default path for automatic registry backups is _____.

45. The name of the latest automatic registry backup is _____.

46. The _____ SCANREG switch is used to back up the registry.

47. The _____ file extension is assigned to a registry backup when using REGEDIT.

48. A Windows 98 _____ preserves applications and data.

49. A computer acts strangely. One possible problem is a _____ may be present.

50. The _____ virus infects a .COM or .EXE file.

51. A virus that does not replicate itself, but can put a message on the screen is a _____ virus.

52. Windows 98 installation requires a minimum of _____ free hard drive space.

53. The _____ document on the Windows 98 CD contains a list of compatible hardware devices.

54. The _____ SETUP.EXE switch bypasses SmartDrive.

55. The _____ SETUP.EXE switch bypasses ScanDisk.

56. The workgroup name can contain up to _____ characters on Windows 98.

57. The _____ Windows 98 feature allows Setup to continue after a failure.

58. The Windows 98 _____ product must be purchased when going from Windows 95 to Windows 98.

59. The _____ file contains a list of components and drivers that load during the installation process.

60. A chronological listing of what happens during the installation process that is used to determine where Setup fails is the _____ startup log file.

61. The _____ tool is used with driver conflicts.

62. The _____ and _____ file systems are supported by both Windows 98 and 2000 Professional.

63. The _____ control panel is used to install a screen saver.

64. The control panel used to configure the computer for multiple operators is _____.

65. The _____ control panel is used to install a non-plug and play device.

66. The _____ button is clicked to allow you to specify the path to the latest device driver for a non-plug and play device.

67. _____ is used to remove most non-plug and play devices from the registry.

68. The _____ control panel is used to remove a printer.

69. Most software today is _____-bit.

70. The _____ control panel is used to install or delete applications.

71. Another name for startup files is _____.

72. _____ is the default folder for the GDI.EXE Windows 98 core file.

73. The _____ boot file loads TSRs and drivers found in CONFIG.SYS and AUTOEXEC.BAT.

74. The _____ Windows 98 executable startup file loads 32-bit device drivers.

75. The _____ executable startup file starts the Windows 98 GUI environment.

76. The _____ IO.SYS parameter loads part of the operating system into the HMA.

77. _____ is the last drive letter available to Windows 98 by default.

78. The _____ MSDOS.SYS setting configures to computer to automatically display the Startup menu.

79. The normal key pressed to access the Windows 98 Startup menu is _____.

80. The _____ Startup menu option is used when troubleshooting Windows 98 boot problems by not loading SYSTEM.INI, WIN.INI. CONFIG.SYS, AUTOEXEC.BAT, and Startup group items. However, the GUI environment does load.

81. The _____ Startup menu option is used for DOS application troubleshooting.

82. The _____ tool displays detected resource conflicts.

83. The _____ protects and repairs system files.

84. If the error message, "Error loading Kernel. You must reinstall Windows." appears, extract the _____ file.

85. The _____ command can be used from a prompt to remove the hidden attribute from a file.

86. The _____ command can be used from a command prompt to put hard drive files in contiguous order.

87. The _____ command can be used to prepare a disk for use from a command prompt.

88. The _____ command checks drives for errors.

89. The _____ command brings up a script property sheet from a command prompt.

90. _____ multitasking is when an application has control of the CPU.

91. A _____ occurs when an application crashes.

92. _____ is a utility used when application problems occur.

93. _____ allows PCI devices to share an IRQ.

94. _____ allows the BIOS and operating system to communicate with plug and play devices.

95. Windows 98 power management features are made available through _____ and _____.

96. _____ is a Windows 98 feature that allows a computer to be instantly available after being in standby mode.

97. _____ is a utility for tracking system component performance.

98. _____ shows memory resource usage.

99. Resource Meter is accessed through the _____ accessory.

100. The _____ control panel is used to adjust virtual memory size.

Name _____

WINDOWS 98 DESKTOP OPTIONS EXERCISE

Objective: To interact with and customize the Windows 98 desktop

Parts: Computer with Windows 98 installed

Step 1:   Turn on the computer and verify that the operating system loads.

Step 2:   If necessary, logon to Windows 98 using the userid and password provided by the instructor or lab assistant.

My Computer

Step 3:   Double-click on the **My Computer** desktop icon. A window appears.

Question 1:   Write down the drive letters that are available on your computer that show in the My Computer window.

Step 4:   Locate the three icons in the upper right corner of the window, a line, a window, and an X. The icon that looks like a straight line is used to minimize the screen, which means the application is still loaded in memory, but it does not show on the desktop. Instead, it shows up as an item on the Ttaskbar. The icon in the center can be of two varieties—a Maximize button, which looks like one window, or a Restore button, which looks like a window within a window. When a window is maximized it fills the entire screen. If you size the screen differently, you can click on the restore button and the window goes back the way it was. Click on the **X** icon.

Question 2:   What happened to the window when you clicked on the X button?

My Documents

Step 5:   Double-click on the **My Documents** icon. Click on the **View** menu option and ensure that there is not a checkmark beside the as Web page option. If a checkmark is present, click on the **as Web page** option to deselect it. The window shows files and possibly subfolders contained in the My Documents folder.

Step 6:   Click on the **View** menu option again. From the drop-down menu, click on the **Folder options**. A window opens with three tabs across the top. The General tab is used to select how the options look within the My Documents window. Click on the **Classic view** radio button. The View tab is used to select what files are shown by default. Technicians normally want to see all files, so under the Hidden Files folder option, select the **Show all files** option. To see extensions, make sure the checkbox beside Hide file extensions for known file types option is unchecked. To make hidden files available for all folders, click on the **Like Current Folder** button. The File Types tab is used to register a particular file type in Windows 98. The file types listed are the file types that Windows 98 knows about. Click on a file type listed in the **Registered file types** window. The normal file extension and program that opens the file lists in the File type details window section. This is where you would register your own file extensions so that Windows 98 automatically opens the document when you click on it.

Question 3:   List three file registered file types that Windows 98 has on your computer.

Step 7:   Click on the **Cancel** button.

Recycle Bin

Step 8:   Click on the **Start** button.

Step 9:   Point to the **Programs** option.

Step 10:   Point to the **Accessories** option.

Step 11:   Click on the **Notepad** option. The Notepad application opens with a blank document.

Step 12:   Type the following words: **Science and technology multiply around us. To an increasing extent, they dictate the languages in which we think and speak. Either we use these languages, or we remain mute. –J. G. Ballard**

Step 13:   Click on the **File** menu option.

Step 14:   Click on the **Save** menu option. The system defaults to the My Documents folder.

Step 15:   Type in the word **Technology** in the File name box.

Step 16:   Click on the **Save** button.

Step 17:   Click on the **X** (Close) button in the upper right corner to close the Notepad window.

Step 18:   Double-click on the **My Documents** icon on the desktop.

Step 19:   Locate the **Technology** document in the My Documents window. You may need to use the scroll bar to locate it.

Step 20:   Click once on the **Technology** document to select it.

Step 21:   Press the **Delete** key on the keyboard. A message appears on the screen asking if you are sure that you want to send the Technology document to the Recycle Bin.

Step 22.   Click on the **Yes** button.

Step 23.   In the My Documents window, click on the **X** (Close) button in the upper right corner.

Step 24.   Double-click on the **Recycle Bin** icon on the desktop.

Step 25.   Locate the **Technology** document. If it is not in the Recycle Bin, perform steps 8 through 24 again.

Step 26.   There are several ways to delete items from the Recycle Bin and they are listed below:

   A.   Click on the **File** menu option and select the **Empty Recycle Bin** option. This deletes all files from the Recycle Bin.

   B.   Click on the document you want removed from the disk entirely. Click on the **File** menu option. Click on the **Delete** option.

   C.   Click on the document you want to remove. Press the **Delete** key on the keyboard.

   D.   From the desktop, right-click on the **Recycle Bin** icon. Click on the **Empty Recycle Bin** option. This option deletes all files from the Recycle Bin.

   Use one of the methods listed above to delete the **Technology** document from the Recycle Bin and click on the **Yes** button to confirm the delete.

Desktop Icons

Step 27.   Sometimes users clutter the desktop with icons. One thing that helps with this clutter is to have the system arrange the desktop icons. The icons can be arranged by name, type, size, date, or allow the system automatically arrange them. To illustrate this function, go to the desktop area.

Step 28.   Right-click on a **blank desktop space.** Once a menu appears, point to the **Arrange Icons** option. If the Auto Arrange option has a checkmark beside it, click on the **Auto Arrange** option to remove the checkmark. If the Auto Arrange option does not have a checkmark beside it, click on an **empty portion of the desktop** to cancel.

Step 29.   Click on the **My Documents** icon and while continuing to hold the mouse button down, drag the icon to the center of the screen.

Step 30.   Click on the **Recycle Bin** icon and while continuing to hold the mouse button down, drag the icon to the top right portion of the screen.

Step 31.   Right-click on a **blank desktop space.** A menu appears.

Step 32.   Point to the **Arrange icons** menu option.

Step 33.   Click on the **By Date** menu option.

Question 4:   What changed on the screen?

Step 34. Right-click on a **blank desktop space** again. A menu appears.

Step 35. Point to the **Arrange icons** menu option.

Step 36. Click on the **Auto Arrange** option. If you look very carefully before the window closes, you can see a checkmark go beside the option. (You can also right-click on an **empty desktop space,** point to the **Arrange icons** option and see the checkmark.)

Step 37. Click on the **My Documents** icon and while continuing to hold the mouse button down, drag the icon to the center of the screen.

Question 5: What happened when you tried to move the My Documents icon?

Desktop Appearance

Step 38. Right-click on an **empty desktop area.** A menu appears.

Step 39. Click on the **Properties** option. The Display Properties window appears. (*Note:* this screen can also be accessed by clicking on the **Start** button, point to the **Settings** option, click on the **Control Panel** option, and double-click on the **Display** control panel icon.)

Step 40. Click on the **Background** tab. This tab controls how the background color and pattern appears.

Step 41. Click on the **Black Thatch** option and click on the **Apply** button.

Step 42. In the Display area, click on the **down arrow** and select the **Center** option. Click on the **Apply** button. You may have to click on the top of the Display Properties window and move the window to another area of the screen to see the effects of this step.

Question 6: What happened to the screen?

Step 43. In the Display area, click on the **down arrow** and select the **Stretch** option.

Step 44. Click on the **Apply** button.

Question 7: What happened to the screen?

Step 45. Click on the **Screen Saver** tab. This tab controls what screen saver, if any, loads and is used to control monitor power settings. A screen saver password can also be applied.

Step 46. Click on Screen Saver **down arrow.**

Question 8:   List one available screen saver.

Step 47.   Click on the **Appearance** tab at the top of the window. This tab controls the color scheme and size of letters displayed on the screen when various windows are open. This tab is good to use when people with vision problems need adjustments.

Question 9:   What color scheme is currently loaded?

Step 48.   Click on the Scheme **down arrow**.

Question 10:   List one theme available.

Step 49.   Click on the **Web** tab. The Web tab window allows you to define whether web content is allowed on the desktop. A common web content option would be stock quotes.

Step 50.   Click on the **Effects** tab.

Question 11:   For what is the Effects tab used?

Step 51.   Click on the **Settings** tab. The Settings tab allows you to define the number of colors available and the screen resolution (shown as Screen Area and is based on the video card's RAM).

Question 12:   How many colors are currently available?

Question 13:   What is the current screen resolution?

Step 52.   Click on the **Cancel** button.

Creating a Shortcut

Note: There are various ways to create a shortcut and only one way is demonstrated here.

Step 53.   Click on the **Start** button.

Step 54.   Point to the **Programs** option.

Step 55.   Click on the **Windows Explorer** option. You should make sure that the Windows Explorer window does not cover the entire screen. If it does, click on the **Restore** button, which is the middle button in the top right corner of the window (the one that looks like two windows stacked on top of one another).

Step 56.   Right-click (and continue to hold the right mouse button down) on **any file** or one designated by the instructor. Drag the file to an empty space on the desktop. Release the right mouse button and a menu pops up.

Step 57.   Click on the **Create Shortcut(s) here** option. The shortcut appears on the desktop as a shortcut icon.

Question 14:   What file did you choose to create a shortcut icon?

Step 58.   Close Windows Explorer by clicking on the **Close** button in the upper right corner. It is the one with an X in it.

Step 59.   Right-click on the shortcut icon you just created. Refer back to Question 14 if you forgot the name of it.

Step 60.   Click on the **Properties** option. A dialog box appears.

Question 15:   Write the path found in the Target textbox and describe what the path means.

Step 61.   Click on the **Find Target** button.

Question 16:   What happened when you clicked on the Find Target button?

Question 17:   Is the file that was used to create the shortcut icon visible?

Step 62.   Close the Explorer window by clicking on the **Close** button, which is the button in the upper right corner that has an X in it.

Question 18:   Find a way to create a shortcut using the mouse options rather than right-clicking. Write your steps in the space below.

_____ ***Instructor's Initials***

Step 63.   Using one of the methods learned previously, permanently delete the shortcut icon created during this exercise.

_____ ***Instructor's Initials***

Name _____

WINDOWS 98 TASKBAR OPTIONS

Objective: To interact with and customize the Windows 98 taskbar

Parts: Computer with Windows 98 installed

Step 1.   Turn on the computer and verify that the operating system loads.

Step 2.   If necessary, logon to Windows 98 using the userid and password provided by the instructor or lab assistant.

Step 3.   Locate the taskbar on the bottom of the screen. If it is not showing, move the mouse to the bottom of the screen and the taskbar pops up.

Step 4.   To modify or view the taskbar settings, right-click on a **blank area** of the taskbar. A menu appears. *Note:* You can also use the **Start** button, point to the **Settings** option, and click on the **Taskbar & Start Menu** option.

Step 5.   Click on the **Properties** option. The Taskbar Properties window appears.

Step 6.   Click on the **Taskbar Options** tab.

Step 7.   The four options available on this screen relate to how things are shown on the taskbar. The items with a check in the left checkbox are active. The Always on top option puts the taskbar visible on the screen at all times (even if a window is full size or maximized). The Auto hide option hides the taskbar during normal operation. Press **CTRL+ESC** or the **Start** button key on the keyboard (the one with the Windows emblem on it) to make the taskbar reappear. If both the Always on top and Auto hide options are checked, then the taskbar appears when you are in a window that is full size (maximized). The Show small icons in Start menu option reduces the size of the Start menu words. The Show clock option displays the clock icon in the right corner of the taskbar. Make sure the **Always on top** and **Show clock** options are the only ones with checkmarks in the checkboxes. To remove a checkmark, click in the checkbox that already contains a check in it. To put a checkmark in a box, click once in an empty box.

Step 8.   Click on the **Apply** button.

Step 9.   Click on the **OK** button.

Step 10.   Right-click on an **empty space** on the taskbar.

Step 11.   Point to the **Toolbars** option. A submenu appears.

Step 12.   Ensure that there is a checkmark beside the Quick Launch option. This setting allows the Quick Launch icons to appear on the desktop by the Start button. If a checkmark is missing, click once on the **Quick Launch** option.

Step 13. Using the skills you just learned, access the Taskbar Settings window.

Question 1: List the steps you performed to do Step 13.

Step 14. Click on the **Properties** option. Click on the **Question mark** icon in the upper right corner of the window. The question mark is an interactive help system. The pointer on the screen changes to an arrow with a question mark attached. Click on the **Always on top** option. A description of the option appears with the on-line help active.

Question 2: What text does the help balloon display?

Step 15. Click on the **Start Menu Programs** tab. The Start Menu Programs tab is used to customize the Start button and to delete files listed under the Start button's Documents option or previously accessed web sites.

_____ *Instructor Initials*

Step 16. Click on the **Cancel** button.

Name _____

WINDOWS 98 FILE EXTENSION EXERCISE

Objective: To associate a file extension with a file type

Parts: Computer with Windows 98 installed
Formatted 3.5" disk

Step 1. Turn on the computer and verify that the operating system loads.

Step 2. If necessary, logon to Windows 98 using the userid and password provided by the instructor or lab assistant.

Step 3. Click on the **Start** button and point to the **Programs** selection.

Step 4. Point to the **Accessories** option.

Step 5. Click on the **Notepad** menu selection.

Step 6. Type in the following:

However far modern science and techniques have fallen short of their inherent possibilities, they have taught mankind at least one lesson: Nothing is impossible. –Lewis Mumford

Step 7. Click on the **File** menu option.

Step 8. Click on the **Save** option from the drop-down menu.

Step 9. Insert a formatted disk into the floppy (A:) drive.

Step 10. Click on the **down arrow** in the **Save in** textbox.

Step 11. Click on the **3_ Floppy (A:)** option.

Step 12. In the File name textbox, type **Junk**.

Step 13. Click on the **Save** button.

Step 14. Close the Notepad application by clicking on the **Close** button (which is a button in the upper right corner with an X).

Step 15. Right-click on the **Start** button.

Step 16. Click on the **Explore** option.

Step 17. Click on the **View** menu option.

Step 18. Click on the **Folder Options** drop-down menu option.

Step 19. Click on the **View** tab in the Folder Options dialog box.

Step 20. If the **Hide file extensions for known file types** checkbox contains a checkmark, click inside the checkbox to remove the checkmark. If the checkbox is empty, ignore this step.

Step 21.   Click on the **OK** button.

Step 22.   In the left Explorer window, use the vertical scroll bar to locate the A: drive. Click on the **3_ Floppy (A:)** drive option.

Step 23.   Locate the **Junk.txt** file in the right window and double-click on the icon.

Question 1:   What happened? Did the Notepad application open with the Junk file open?

Step 24.   Close the Notepad application by clicking on the **Close** button (which is a button in the upper right corner with an X).

Step 25.   In the right Explorer window, right-click on the **Junk** filename.

Step 26.   Click on the **Rename** option. The name of the file, Junk.txt, is highlighted.

Step 27.   Type in **junk.abc** and press the **Enter** key. Junk.txt is renamed to junk.abc. A Rename warning box appears stating that if you change a filename extension, the file may become unusable. It also asks, "Are you sure you want to change it?" Click on the **Yes** button.

Question 2:   What does the junk.abc file icon look like now?

Step 28.   Double-click on the **junk.abc** file icon.

Question 3:   What happened when you double-clicked on the junk.abc file icon?

Step 29.   In the Choose the program you want to use section, scroll down until you reach the Notepad icon. Click on the **Notepad** icon and then click on the **OK** button.

Question 4:   What happened when you clicked on the OK button?

Step 30.   In the Notepad application, click on the **File** menu option. Then click on **New** from the drop-down menu.

Step 31.   Type in the following:

Technology is dominated by two types of people: Those who understand what they do not manage, and those who manage what they do not understand. –Source Unknown

Click on the **File** menu option.

Step 32.   Click on the **Save** option from the drop-down menu.

Step 33.   Click on the **down arrow** in the **Save in** textbox.

Step 34.   Click on the **3_ Floppy (A:)** option.

Step 35.   In the File name textbox, type **Junk2**.

Step 36.   Click on the **Save** button.

Step 37.   Close the Notepad application by clicking on the **Close** button (which is a button in the upper right corner with an X).

Step 38.   Using Explorer, rename the **Junk2.txt** file to **Junk2.abc**. Notice the file icon after the change.

Question 5:   How is the JUNK2.ABC icon different from before?

Step 39.   Double-click on the **Junk2.abc** icon.

Question 6:   What happened when you double-clicked on the Junk2.abc icon?

_____ *Instructor's Initials*

Name _____

WINDOWS 98 FILE AND FOLDER MANAGEMENT

Objective: To create folders, move files, and copy files to new locations

Parts: Computer with Windows 98 installed
Formatted 3.5" disk

Note: There are multiple ways to do some of the steps in this exercise. The steps that have an alternate method have the letters **ALT:** before the step. With these steps, you may pick either method of performing the step.

Step 1.   Turn on the computer and verify that the operating system loads.

Step 2.   If necessary, logon to Windows 98 using the userid and password provided by the instructor or lab assistant.

Step 3.   Click on the **Start** button and point to the **Programs** selection.

Step 4.   Point to the **Accessories** option.

Step 5.   Click on the **Notepad** option.

Step 6.   Type in the following:

No letters after your name are ever going to be a total guarantee of competency any more than they are a guarantee against fraud. Improving competence involves continuing professional development...That is the really crucial thing, not just passing an examination. –Colette Bowe

Step 7.   Click on the **File** menu option.

Step 8.   Click on the **Save** option from the drop-down menu.

Step 9.   Insert a formatted disk into the floppy (A:) drive.

Step 10.   Click on the **down arrow** in the **Save in** textbox.

Step 11.   Click on the **3_ Floppy (A:)** option.

Step 12.   In the File name textbox, type **Quote 1** and click on the **Save** button.

Step 13.   Click on the **File** menu option.

Step 14.   Click on the **New** menu option.

Step 15.   Type in the following:

People differ not only in their ability to do but also in their 'will to do.' –Paul Hersey

Step 16.   Click on the **File** menu option.

Step 17.   Click on the **Save** option from the drop-down menu.

Step 18. Click on the **down arrow** in the **Save in** textbox.

Step 19. Click on the **3_ Floppy (A:)** option.

Step 20. In the File name textbox, type **Quote 2** and click on the **Save** button.

Step 21. Click on the **File** menu option.

Step 22. Click on the **New** menu option.

Step 23. Type in the following:

I want to be scared again...I want to feel unsure again. That's the only way I learn, the only way I feel challenged. –Connie Chung

Step 24. Click on the **File** menu option.

Step 25. Click on the **Save** option from the drop-down menu.

Step 26. Click on the **down arrow** in the **Save in** textbox.

Step 27. Click on the **3_ Floppy (A:)** option.

Step 28. In the File name textbox, type **Quote 3** and click on the **Save** button.

Step 29. Click on the **File** menu option.

Step 30. Click on the **New** menu option.

Step 31. Type in the following:

Dreams can often become challenging, but challenges are what we live for. –Travis White

Step 32. Click on the **File** menu option.

Step 33. Click on the **Save** option from the drop-down menu.

Step 34. Click on the **down arrow** in the **Save in** textbox.

Step 35. Click on the **3_ Floppy (A:)** option.

Step 36. In the File name textbox, type **Quote 4** and click on the **Save** button.

Step 37. Click on the **File** menu option.

Step 38. Click on the **New** menu option.

Step 39. Type in the following:

Watch out for emergencies. They are your big chance. –Fritz Reiner

Step 40. Click on the **File** menu option.

Step 41. Click on the **Save** option from the drop-down menu.

Step 42. Click on the **down arrow** in the **Save in** textbox.

Step 43. Click on the **3_ Floppy (A:)** option.

Step 44. In the File name textbox, type **Quote 5** and click on the **Save** button.

Step 45. Close the Notepad application by clicking on the **Close** button (which is a button in the upper right corner with an X).

Step 46. Right-click on the **Start** button.

Step 47. Click on the **Explore** option.

Step 48. In the left window, use the vertical scroll bar to locate the A: drive. Click on the **3_ Floppy (A:)** drive option.

Step 49. In the right window, locate the five files you just created called Quote 1, Quote 2, Quote 3, Quote 4, and Quote 5. If the files are not there, redo steps 4 through 49.

_____ *Instructor's Initials*

Create a Folder

Step 50. In the right Explorer window, right-click on an **empty space.** Point to the **New** option and click on the **Folder** option. A folder appears in the right window with the words *New Folder* highlighted. Type **Learning Quotes** and press *Enter.*

Note: The method shown below that is preceded by the letters **ALT:** is an alternate way to perform the same steps shown in Step 50. You may use either method.

ALT: Click on the **File** menu option. Point to the **New** option and click on the **Folder** option. A folder appears in the right window with the words *New Folder* highlighted. Type **Learning Quotes** and press **Enter.**

Step 51. Create another new folder called **General Quotes** using the steps outlined in Step 50.

_____ *Instructor's Initials*

Copy a File

Step 52. In the right window, right-click on the file named **Quote 1**. A submenu appears. Click on the **Copy** option from the submenu.

ALT: In the right window, click on the file named **Quote 1**. Click on the **Edit** menu option. Click on the **Copy** option from the drop-down menu.

Step 53. In the right window, double-click on the **Learning Quotes** folder. Notice how the Windows Explorer Address line textbox changes to A:\Learning Quotes and the right window is empty because the folder does not have any files or subfolders in it yet.

Step 54. In the right window, right-click and a submenu appears. Click on the **Paste** option. The file named Quote 1 appears in the right window.

ALT: Click on the **Edit** menu option. Click on the **Paste** option from the drop-down menu. The file named Quote 1 appears in the right window.

Step 55. In the left window, click on the **3_ Floppy (A:)** drive option. Notice how the Window Explorer Address line textbox changes A:\.

Step 56. Copy the files named **Quote 2** and **Quote 3** into the **Learning Quotes** folder using the methods outlined in steps 52 through 54.

Copy Multiple Files

Step 57. In the left window, click on the **3_ Floppy (A:)** drive option.

Step 58. Locate the files called **Quote 4** and **Quote 5** in the right window.

Step 59. In the right window, click once on the **Quote 4** filename. The name highlights.

Step 60. Hold the **CTRL** key down and click once on the **Quote 5** filename. Both the Quote 4 and Quote 5 filenames highlight. *Note:* The CTRL key is used to select files that are not consecutive in a list (one right after the other). If you wanted to select files that are consecutive, use the SHIFT key to select the files.

Step 61. Right-click on the files named **Quote 4** and **Quote 5**. A submenu appears. Click on the **Copy** option from the submenu.

ALT: Click on the **Edit** menu option. Click on the **Copy** option from the drop-down menu.

Step 62. In the right window, double-click on the **General Quotes** folder. Notice how the Windows Explorer Address line textbox changes to A:\General Quotes and the right window is empty because the folder does not have any files or subfolders in it yet.

Step 63. In the right window, right-click on an **empty space** and a submenu appears. Click on the **Paste** option. The files named Quote 4 and Quote 5 appear in the right window.

ALT: Click on the **Edit** menu option. Click on the **Paste** option from the drop-down menu. The files named Quote 4 and Quote 5 appear in the right window.

_____ *Instructor's Initials*

Question 1: How many files are located in the A: root directory (A:\)?

Question 2: How many files are located in the A:\Learning Quotes folder?

Question 3: How many files are located in the A:\General Quotes folder?

Copying a File from One Folder to Another

Step 64. In the left window, click on the **3_ Floppy (A:)** drive option.

Step 65. In the left window, click on the **Learning Quotes** folder located under the Floppy (A:) option. The files Quote 1, Quote 2, and Quote 3 appear in the right window.

Step 66. In the right window, right-click on the file named **Quote 3.** From the submenu that appears, click on the **Copy** option.

ALT: In the right window, click on the file named **Quote 3.** Click on the **Edit** menu option. Click on the **Copy** option from the drop-down menu.

Step 67. In the left window, click on the folder called **General Quotes** located under the Floppy (A:) option. The files Quote 4 and Quote 5 appear in the right window and the Address textbox shows General Quotes.

Step 68. In the right window, right-click on an **empty space** and a submenu appears. Click on the **Paste** option. The file named Quote 3 appears in the right window along with the files named Quote 4 and Quote 5.

ALT: Click on the **Edit** menu option. Click on the **Paste** option from the drop-down menu. The file named Quote 3 appears in the right window along with the files named Quote 4 and Quote 5.

Step 69. Using the same procedures outlined in steps 64 through 68, copy the files named **Quote 1** and **Quote 2** from the **Learning Quotes** folder into the **General Quotes** folder. At the end of this step you should have three files (Quote 1, Quote 2, and Quote 3) in the Learning Quotes folder and five files (Quote 1, Quote 2, Quote 3, Quote 4, and Quote 5) in the General Quotes folder.

Moving a File

Step 70. Create a folder on the A: drive called **My Stuff**. Refer back to the steps earlier in the exercise if you need assistance.

Step 71. In the left window, click on the folder called **General Quotes**. In the right window, all five files appear.

Step 72. In the right window, click once on the file called **Quote 1** to highlight it.

Step 73. Hold the **CTRL** key down and click on the file called **Quote 3**. Both the Quote 1 and Quote 3 filenames are highlighted. *Note:* The CTRL key is used to select non-consecutive files, whereas the SHIFT key is used to select files that are listed consecutively (one right after another).

Step 74. Right-click on either **Quote 1** or **Quote 3** filename. Select the **Cut** option from the menu that appears. The Cut option is used to move a file from one folder to another folder.

ALT: Click on the **Edit** menu option. Click on the **Cut** option from the drop-down menu. The Cut option is used to move a file from one folder to another folder.

Step 75. In the left window, click on the **My Stuff** folder. The right window is empty because no files have been copied or moved into the My Stuff folder yet.

Step 76. In the right window, right-click and a menu appears on the screen. Select the **Paste** option from the menu. The Quote 1 and Quote 3 files appear in the right window.

ALT: Click on the **Edit** menu option. Click on the **Paste** option from the drop-down menu. The Quote 1 and Quote 3 files appear in the right window.

Step 77.   Using the procedures just learned, move the **Quote 1** file from the **Learning Quotes** folder into the **General Quotes** folder.

Question 4:   How many files are located in the A:\Learning Quotes folder?

Question 5:   How many files are located in the A:\General Quotes folder?

Question 6:   How many files are located in the A:\My Stuff folder?

_____ *Instructor's Initials*

Deleting Files and Folders

Step 78.   In the left Explore window, click on the **My Stuff** folder. The Quote 1 and Quote 3 files appear in the right window.

Step 79.   In the right window, click on the **Quote 1** filename. Hold the **SHIFT** key down and click on the **Quote 3** file name. Both the Quote 1 and Quote 3 filenames are highlighted.

Step 80.   Press the **Delete** key on the keyboard. A Confirm Multiple File Delete message appears on the screen asking, "Are you sure you want to delete these 2 items?"

Note: When deleting files from a floppy disk, the files do not get placed in the Recycle Bin. They are deleted. When deleting files from a hard drive, the files get placed in the Recycle Bin when you press the **Delete** key or select the Delete option from the File menu option. If you want to permanently delete a file from a hard drive (the file will not get placed in the Recycle Bin), hold the **SHIFT** key down while pressing the **Delete** key.

ALT: Click on the **File** menu option. Click on the **Delete** option from the drop-down menu. A Confirm Multiple File Delete message appears on the screen asking, "Are you sure you want to delete these 2 items?"

Step 81.   Click on the **Yes** button.

Step 82.   In the left window, click once on the **My Stuff** folder. The My Stuff folder highlights.

Step 83.   Press the **Delete** key on the keyboard. A Confirm Folder Delete message appears on the screen asking, "Are you sure you want to remove the folder "My Stuff" and all its contents?" Click on the **Yes** button.

ALT: Click on the **File** menu option. Click on the **Delete** option from the drop-down menu. A Confirm Multiple File Delete message appears on the screen asking, "Are you sure you want to remove the folder "My Stuff" and all its contents?" Click on the **Yes** button.

_____ *Instructor's Initials*

Step 84.   Using the procedures outlined in steps 78 through 83, delete the **Learning Quotes** folder and the **General Quotes** folders and all files contained within each folder.

Step 85.   Close the **Explore** window.

Challenge

Step 86.   Using Notepad, create three text files and save them to the floppy disk in a folder called My Files.

Step 87.   On the hard drive, create a folder called **Computer Text**.

Step 88.   Copy the two text files from the **My Files** folder on the floppy disk into the folder called **Computer Text** on the hard drive.

Step 89.   Move the third text file from the **My Files** folder on the floppy disk into the folder called **Computer Text** on the hard drive.

_____ *Instructor's Initials*

Step 90.   Permanently delete the folder called **Computer Text** from the hard drive and all files within this folder.

_____ *Instructor's Initials*

Step 91.   Delete the folder called **My Files** from the floppy disk and all files within this folder.

_____ *Instructor's Initials*

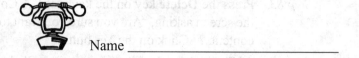

Name _____

USING REGEDIT IN WINDOWS 98

Objective: To familiarize yourself with the REGEDIT registry editing utility

Parts: Computer with Windows 98 installed

REGEDIT is a utility used for editing the Windows registry. With REGEDIT, you can view existing registry settings, modify registry settings values, or create new registry entries to change or enhance the way Windows operates.

In this lab, you will use REGEDIT to view the System BIOS and Video BIOS information on your computer.

CAUTION: Editing the registry can cause your computer to run erratically, or not run at all! When performing any registry editing, follow ALL directions carefully, including spelling, syntax use, etc. Failure to do so may cause your computer to fail!

Step 1.   From the Start menu, choose **Run**, type **REGEDIT**, and click **OK**. The REGEDIT utility opens.

Step 2.   In the left window, expand **HKEY_LOCAL_MACHINE**, **Hardware**, and **Description**, **System**, **CentralProcessor**, and then select the **0** folder.

Step 3.   In the right window, the Identifier and VendorIdentifier information display.

Question 1:   What is the CPU identifier for the computer?

Step 4.   In the left window, expand **HKEY_LOCAL_MACHINE**, **Software**, and **Microsoft**.

Question 2:   List three Microsoft applications loaded under the Microsoft folder.

Step 5.   In the left window, expand **HKEY_USERS**, **.DEFAULT**, **Control Panel**, **Appearance**, and then select the **Schemes** folder.

Question 3:   Name three schemes available to be chosen from the Display control panel as listed in the right window.

_____ *Instructor's Initials*

Step 6.   When finished viewing the information, close the **REGEDIT** utility.

Name _____

USING THE WINDOWS 98 REGISTRY CHECKER UTILITY
TO BACK UP THE REGISTRY

Objective: To use the Windows 98 Registry Checker utility to back up the registry

Parts: Computer with Windows 98 installed

Step 1.   Turn on the computer and verify that Windows 98 loads.

Step 2.   If necessary, logon to Windows 98 using the userid and password provided by the instructor or lab assistant.

Step 3.   Click on the **Start** button.

Step 4.   Point to the **Programs** option.

Step 5.   Point to the **Accessories** option.

Step 6.   Point to the **System Tools** option.

Step 7.   Click on the **System Information** option. The Microsoft System Information window opens.

Step 8.   Click on the **Tools** menu option and select **Registry Checker**. The following window appears. Click on the **Yes** button. A window appears with a message that the backup was successful. Click on the **OK** button.

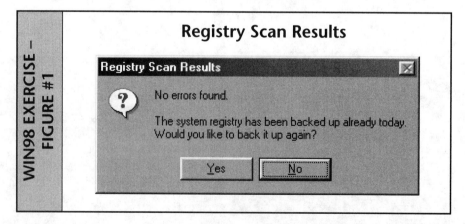

Step 9.   Notice the system data and time by double-clicking on the time display on the taskbar.

Question 1:   Write the system date and time in the space below.

Step 10.   Using Windows Explorer, locate the WINDOWS\SYSBCKUP folder. In the left Explorer window, click on the **WINDOWS\SYSBCKUP** folder.

Step 11.   In the right window, locate the RB000.CAB, RB001.CAB, RB002.CAB, RB003.CAB, and RB004.CAB files.

Step 12.   Right-click on each of these file icons and determine when the backup file was created.

Question 2:   Which backup filename was used to manually back up the registry in Step 8.

_____ ***Instructor's Initials***

Step 13.   Close the **System Information** window.

Name _____

USING THE REGEDIT TO EXPORT/IMPORT THE REGISTRY

Objective: To use REGEDIT to export the registry

Parts: Computer with Windows 98 installed

The REGEDIT program can be used to export a specific subtree or the entire registry as well as import the saved file when the computer does not operate properly.

Export the Registry or Subtree

Step 1. Turn on the computer and verify that Windows 98 loads.

Step 2. If necessary, logon to Windows 98 using the userid and password provided by the instructor or lab assistant.

Step 3. Click on the **Start** button and click on the **Run** option.

Step 4. Type **REGEDIT** and press **Enter.**

Step 5. Select the specific subtree to back up or click on the My Computer icon to back up the entire registry.

Step 6. Click on the **Registry** menu option.

Step 7. Select the **Export Registry File** selection from the drop-down menu. The Export Registry File dialog box appears.

Step 8. Select a location to save the file by clicking on the **down arrow** in the **Save in** box. Type a file name in the File name text box and click on the **Save** button.

_____ *Instructor's Initials*

Import the Registry or Subtree

Step 9. Turn on the computer and verify that the Windows 98 loads.

Step 10. If necessary, logon to Windows 98 using the userid and password provided by the instructor or lab assistant.

Step 11. Click on the **Start** button and click on the **Run** option.

Step 12. Type **REGEDIT** and press **Enter.**

Step 13. Click on the **Registry** menu option.

Step 14. Select the **Import Registry File** selection from the drop-down menu. The Import Registry File dialog box appears.

Step 15.   Select the file to be retrieved by clicking on the **down arrow** in the **Look in** box and clicking the filename. Click on the **Open** button. A dialog box appears when the file successfully imports. Click on the **OK** button.

_____ ***Instructor's Initials***

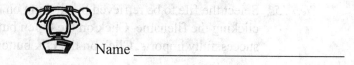

Name _____

UPGRADING FROM WINDOWS 95 TO WINDOWS 98

Objective: To upgrade Windows 95 to Windows 98

Parts: Computer with Windows 95 installed
Windows 98 Upgrade CD
1 blank floppy disk

Note: The installation process outlined below may differ due to computer differences. If the process is different, follow the directions on the screen. Contact your instructor or a lab assistant if you are unsure of the step.

Step 1.   Turn the computer on and verify that the operating system loads.

Step 2.   Insert the Windows 98 Upgrade CD into the CD-ROM or DVD drive.

Step 3.   The CD may automatically start. If it does, a message appears asking if you want to upgrade the existing operating system. Click on the **Yes** button. If the CD does not automatically start, click on the **Start** button. Click on the **Run** option. In the Open textbox, type **x:setup** where **x:** is the drive letter of the device containing the Windows 98 CD.

Step 4.   The Windows 98 Setup screen appears. Click on the **Continue** button.

Step 5.   You are asked if you would like to save the existing system files. Select **Yes**.

Step 6.   The license agreement appears on the screen. Read the agreement and click on the **I accept the agreement** radio button and then click on the **Next** button if you agree with the terms.

Step 7.   The Product Key screen appears. Enter the product key provided by the instructor, lab assistant, on the registration certificate, or located on the CD case. Click the **Next** button to continue. ScanDisk is performed (even though it is not seen on the screen) and Setup checks the registry.

Step 8.   The Select Directory screen appears. The default is C:\Windows. If this is the current folder where Windows 95 is installed, click on the **Next** button. If Windows 95 is installed in a different directory, click on the **Other directory** radio button and select the appropriate folder. The computer is checked for free hard drive space.

Step 9.   The Save System Files window appears. The system allows you to save the system files in case you want to uninstall Windows 98 and return to Windows 95. Click on the **Yes** radio button.

Step 10.   Establishing Your Location dialog box appears. Select the appropriate regional options and click on the **Next** button.

Step 11.   A prompt appears to create a Startup disk. Follow the directions on the screen and click on the **Next** button.

Step 12.   Click on the **Next** button to begin copying Windows 98 files. After copying files, you are prompted to restart the computer.

Step 13.   Click on the **Restart Now** button. Hardware detection begins and then the computer must restart again. After the restart, the Welcome to Windows 98 dialog box appears. If there is any problems during the installation process, troubleshoot the problem and being the installation again.

_____ *Instructor's Initials*

Name _____

CLEAN INSTALLATION OF WINDOWS 98

Objective: To install Windows 98 on a computer that does not have an operating system or one that the old operating system will be replaced (removed)

Parts: Windows 98 CD
1 blank floppy disk
Computer with formatted hard drive

Note: The installation process outlined below may differ due to computer differences. If the process is different, follow the directions on the screen. Contact your instructor or a lab assistant if you are unsure of the step.

Step 1. Insert the Windows 98 setup disk into the floppy drive and boot the computer. The Startup menu appears.

Step 2. Insert the Windows 98 CD into the CD-ROM and type **1** and press the **Enter** key.

Step 3. At the prompt, type **x:setup**, where **x:** is the drive letter of the device containing the Windows 98 CD, and press **Enter.**

Step 4. A message appears that ScanDisk is going to be performed. After the ScanDisk check, press the **X** key.

Step 5. The Welcome to Windows 98 Setup screen appears. Click on the **Continue** button.

Step 6. The licensing agreement appears on the screen. Read the agreement and click on the **I accept the Agreement** radio button and click the **Next** button. The Product Key window appears.

Step 7. Enter the product key provided by the instructor, lab assistant, on the registration certificate, or located on the CD case. Click the **Next** button to continue. The Select Directory window appears.

Step 8. The default Windows 98 folder is C:\WINDOWS. Contact the instructor or lab assistant to see if the default or a different drive/folder is to be used. If a different drive/folder is to be used, click on the **Other directory** radio button and click **next.** If the default directory is to be used, simply click on the **Next** button. The Preparing Directory screen appears.

Question 1:   What is the path for where Windows 98 is to be installed?

_____ *Instructor's Initials*

Step 9.   Setup checks the computers hardware and then displays the Setup Options screen. The default is Typical. Ensure the **Typical** radio button is selected and click on the **Next** button.

Step 10.   The User Information window appears. Type a name and a company in the textboxes and click on the **Next** button.

Step 11.   The Windows Components window appears. Ensure the **Install the most common components** radio button is selected and click on the **Next** button.

Step 12.   When the Identification screen appears, contact an instructor or lab assistant for the Name and Workgroup. The computer name must be unique and can be up to 15 characters. Spaces are not allowed. The workgroup name must be the same for all computers on the same network (if the computer is networked) and can be up to 15 characters; spaces are not allowed.

Question 2:   What computer name and workgroup name is to be used on this computer? Fill in the information below:

        Computer name _____

        Workgroup name _____

_____ *Instructor's Initials*

Step 13.   The Establishing Your Location window appears. Select the appropriate country and click on the **Next** button.

Step 14.   The Startup Disk screen appears. Click on the **Next** button. A prompt appears; insert the blank floppy disk into the A: drive and click on the **OK** button.

Step 15.   The Start Copying Files window appears. Click on the **Next** button and the Windows 98 files are copied to the computer hard drive. After copying, you are prompted to restart the computer.

Step 16.   Click on the **Restart Now** button. After the computer reboots, Windows 98 configures hardware and restarts again. The Welcome to Windows 98 screen appears.

_____ *Instructor's Initials*

Name _____

UPGRADING A HARDWARE DRIVER USING WINDOWS 98

Objective: To install an updated driver under the Windows 98 operating system

Parts: Computer with Windows 98 installed
Latest Windows 98 driver for the hardware device

Note: The installation process outlined below may differ due to computer differences. If the process is different, follow the directions on the screen. Contact your instructor or a lab assistant if you are unsure of the step.

Step 1.   Turn the computer on and verify that the operating system loads. If necessary, login to Windows 98 using the userid and password provided by the instructor or lab assistant.

Step 2.   Click on **Start** button, point to **Settings**, and click on the **Control Panel** menu option.

Step 3.   When the Control Panel window opens, scroll down to the **System** icon and double-click on it.

Step 4.   Click on the **Device Manager** button.

Step 5.   Click on the + **(plus sign)** beside the class of device you want to upgrade.

_____ *Instructor's Initials*

Step 6.   Right-click on the specific device you want to upgrade.

Step 7.   Click on the **Properties** option.

Step 8.   Click on the **Driver** tab.

Step 9.   Click on the **Update Driver** button. The Upgrade Device Driver wizard appears.

Step 10.   Click on the **Next** button.

Step 11.   Click on the **Display a list of the drivers in a specific location, so you can select the driver you want** radio button. Click on the **Next** button.

Step 12.   Click on the **Have Disk** button.

Step 13.   Insert the media that contains your updated driver into the floppy drive, Zip drive, CD-ROM, or DVD drive.

Step 14.   In the **Copy manufacturer's files from** box, type in the drive letter for the device that contains the updated driver followed by a colon and click on the **OK** button. An example of a driver device is A:. The Browse button can be used to locate a device driver as well.

Step 15. Click on the **Next** button and follow the instructions on the screen to complete the upgrade.

_____ *Instructor's Initials*

Name _____

INSTALLING A NON-PLUG AND PLAY DEVICE INTO A WINDOWS 98 COMPUTER

Objective: To install a non-plug and play device into a computer running Windows 98 and load the proper driver for it

Parts: Computer with Windows 98 installed
Non-plug and play device
Latest Windows 98 driver for the hardware device

Note: The installation process outlined below may differ due to computer differences. If the process is different, follow the directions on the screen. Contact your instructor or a lab assistant if you are unsure of the step.

Step 1.   Turn the computer off and install the piece of hardware according to the manufacturer's directions.

Step 2.   Turn the computer on and verify that the operating system loads. If necessary, login to Windows 98 using the userid and password provided by the instructor or lab assistant. The Found New Hardware window should *not* appear if the device is truly non-plug and play.

Step 3.   Start the Add New Hardware wizard by clicking on the **Start** button.

Step 4.   Point to the **Settings** option and then click on the **Control Panel** menu option.

Step 5.   When the Control Panel window appears, double-click on the **Add New Hardware** icon. The Add New Hardware wizard initializes. Click on the **Next** button to continue.

Step 6.   Click on the **Next** button so Windows 98 will search for plug and play devices. When 98 does not find a plug and play device, you have two options, let Windows search for new hardware or you manually select the hardware.

Step 7.   Click on the **No, I want to select the hardware from a list** radio button and click on the **Next** button.

Step 8.   Select the type of hardware you want to install and then click on the **Next** button.

Step 9.   Insert your device driver into the floppy drive, Zip drive, CD-ROM, or DVD drive.

Step 10.   Click on the **Have disk** button. In the **Copy manufacturer's files from** box, type in the drive letter for the device that contains the updated driver followed by a colon. An example of this would be A:. Click on the **Browse** button if you don't know where the file is located. Click on the **OK** button. You may be required to select your specific device or model from a list on the screen. If so, select the device and click the **Next** button. Contact an instructor or lab assistant if you don't know what to select.

Step 11.   Click on the **Finish** button.

_____ *Instructor's Initials*

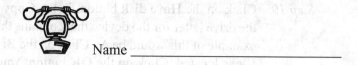
Name _____

INSTALLING A LOCAL PRINTER ON WINDOWS 98 COMPUTER

Objective: To understand how to install a local printer on a Windows 98 computer

Parts: Windows 98 computer and a printer physically attached to a printer port.

Before a Windows 98 computer can send a print job to a local printer, the driver for that printer must be installed and configured.

Step 1.   Turn on the computer and verify that Windows 98 loads.

Step 2.   If necessary, logon to Windows 98 using the userid and password provided by the instructor or lab assistant.

Step 3.   Double-click on the **My Computer** desktop icon and then double-click on the **Printers** icon. The Printers folder opens.

Question 1:   What is another way to access the Printers folder?

Step 4.   Double-click on the **Add Printer** icon and the Add Printer wizard starts.

Step 5.   Click on the **Next** button, select the **Local printer** option, and then click on the **Next** button.

Step 6.   Select the appropriate printer **Manufacturer** and then select the appropriate printer **Model.** If the appropriate printer is not listed, click on the **Have Disk** button, enter a path to the driver files (such as A: or the drive letter of the CD-ROM), and click on the **OK** button.

Step 7.   After selecting the printer, click on the **Next** button.

Step 8.   From the Available Ports window, select the port to which the printer is attached and click on the **Next** button.

Question 2:   How many LPT ports are listed as available?

Step 9.   Enter a name for your printer in the **Printer Name** field, select **Yes** for Windows to use this printer as the Default Printer, and then click on the **Next** button.

Question 3:   Where will this printer name be displayed?

Step 10.   Select **Yes** to print a test page and click on the **Finish** button.

Step 11.   If prompted, insert the Windows 98 installation CD-ROM, or enter a path to the installation files.

Step 12.   The local printer will be installed. If the installation is successful, a printer test page prints.

_____ *Instructor's Initials*

Name _____

USING THE WINDOWS 98 SYSTEM INFORMATION TOOL

Objective: To use the Windows 98 System Information tool to troubleshoot device conflicts

Parts: Computer with Windows 98 and the System Information tool installed

Step 1.   Turn on the computer and verify that Windows 98 loads.

Step 2.   If necessary, logon to Windows 98 using the userid and password provided by the instructor or lab assistant.

Step 3.   Click on the **Start** button and point to the **Accessories** and **System Tools** selections.

Step 4.   Click on the **System Information** option. If the System Information item is not highlighted, click on it.

Question 1:   What percentage of system resources is free?

Step 6.   Click on the + (**plus sign**) next to the **Hardware Resources** item.

Step 7.   Click on the **Conflicts/Sharing** item.

Question 2:   Are any devices sharing an IRQ? If so, list two devices in the space below.

Step 8.   Click on the **IRQs** item located under the Hardware Resources folder in the left window.

Question 3:   List any IRQ that is available for use by a new device.

Step 9.   Click on the **Memory** item located under the Hardware Resources folder in the left window.

Question 4:   List one memory address range used by the video adapter.

Step 10.   In the left window, click on the + (**plus sign**) next to the **Components** item.

Step 11. In the left window, click on the **Problem Devices** item. Any devices with hardware conflicts are listed in the right window. Keep in mind that you use the Device Manager program to correct any problems with resource allocation.

Question 5:   Do any devices have conflicts listed in the Problem Devices window? If so, write them in the space below.

_____ *Instructor's Initials*

Step 12. Close the System Information window by clicking on the **Close** button (the one with the X) in the upper-right corner of the window.

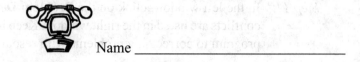

Name _____

HALTING AN APPLICATION IN WINDOWS 98

Objective: To use the Close Program window to halt an application

Parts: Computer with Windows 98 installed

At times, it may become necessary to halt a hung or stalled application. Windows 98 provides a method to accomplish this through the Close Program window.

Step 1. Turn the computer on and verify that Windows 98 loads.

Step 2. If necessary, logon to Windows 98 using the userid and password provided by the instructor or lab assistant.

Step 3. From the Start menu, choose **Programs, Accessories,** and then select **Notepad**. The Notepad utility opens.

Question 1: What other method can be used to start the Notepad utility?

Step 4. To access the Close Program window, simultaneously press **CTRL+ALT+DEL**. The Close Program window opens.

Question 2: Besides closing an application that is not responding to the operating system, what else can you do through the Close Program window?

Question 3: What applications are listed as open? List at least two of them.

_____ *Instructor's Initials*

Step 5. Click on the **Notepad.exe** application and select **End Task**. The Notepad application closes.

Name _____

CREATING A BOOT DISK USING WINDOWS 98

Objective: To create a boot disk that can be used when the computer does not boot properly

Parts: Computer with Windows 98
            Blank floppy disk

Step 1. Turn on the computer and verify that Windows 98 loads.

Step 2. If necessary, logon to Windows 98 using the userid and password provided by the instructor or lab assistant.

Step 3. Click on the **Start** button.

Step 4. Point to the **Settings** option.

Step 5. Click on the **Control Panel** option.

Step 6. Double-click on the **Add/Remove Programs** control panel.

Step 7. Click on the **Startup disk** tab.

Step 8. Click on the **Create disk** button. The Insert Disk window opens. Insert a floppy disk into the A: drive. Click on the **OK** button.

Question 1: Give one situation where a startup disk is useful.

_____ *Instructor's Initials*

Step 10. When the boot disk is created, use Explorer to examine the contents of the disk, the items in the AUTOEXEC.BAT file, and the items in the CONFIG.SYS file.

Question 2: Does the CONFIG.SYS include commands for CD-ROM support? How do you know?

Name _____

USING SYSTEM MONITOR IN WINDOWS 98

Objective: To use Windows 98's System Monitor tool

Parts: Computer with Windows 98 and the System Monitor tool installed

Step 1.   Turn on the computer and verify that Windows 98 loads.

Step 2.   If necessary, logon to Windows 98 using the userid and password provided by the instructor or lab assistant.

Step 3.   Click on the **Start** button, point to the **Accessories** and **System Tools** option, and click on the **System Monitor** selection.

Step 4.   Click on the **Edit** menu item and select the **Add item** function.

Step 5.   In the left window under Category, select **Kernel**. In the right window under Item, select the **Processor Usage (%)** item. Click on the **OK** button.

Step 6.   Use the same procedure for selecting a category and an item for the following components:

Category Item

Kernel	**Threads**
Memory Manager	**Swap file in use**
Memory Manager	**Swappable memory**
Memory Manager	**Allocated memory**

Step 7.   Select the **File System** category and just click once on the **Dirty data** item. Click on the **Explain** button.

Question 1:   What is the purpose of the Dirty data counter?

Step 8.   Click on the **Cancel** button.

Step 9.   The screen shows individual graphs for the components selected. If no graphs appear, click on the fourth button from the left for line charts.

_____ *Instructor's Initials*

Step 10.   Start several applications while keeping the graphics going. If connected to the Internet, download some files. When finished, click on the **Close** button.

Name _____

DR. WATSON AND SYSTEM FILE CHECKER

Objective: To use Windows 98 tools effectively when problems occur

Parts: Computer with Windows 98 loaded
Dr. Watson, System File Checker, and Registry Checker installed

Step 1.   Turn on the computer and verify that Windows 98 loads.

Step 2.   If necessary, logon to Windows 98 using the userid and password provided by the instructor or lab assistant.

Step 3.   Click on the **Start** button, point to the **Accessories** and **System Tools** option, and click on the **System Information** selection.

Step 4.   Click on the **Tools** menu item and select the **Dr. Watson**. A new icon appears on the right end of the taskbar next to the clock icon.

Step 5.   Double-click on the **Dr. Watson** taskbar icon. Dr. Watson records a snapshot of the system. The Diagnosis tab displays any problems found during the analysis.

Step 6.   Click on the **View** menu item and select **Advanced view**. 10 tabs appear across the top.

Step 7.   Click on the **System** tab. The System tab shows an overall view of the computer including what operating system version, amount of RAM installed, amount of resources available, amount of free space for the swap file, etc.

Question 1:   How much RAM does the computer have?

Step 8.   Click on the *Startup* tab. The Startup tab shows the applications that run every time the computer boots.

Question 2:   List three applications that load when the computer boots as found on the Startup tab.

Step 9.   Click on the **MS-DOS Drivers** tab. The MS-DOS Drivers screen displays a list of 16-bit drivers that load when the computer boots.

Question 3:   List three MS-DOS drivers.

_____ *Instructor's Initials*

Step 10.   Close the Dr. Watson tool by clicking on the **OK** button. Notice that the Dr. Watson utility is still active because the icon is still located on the taskbar. Right-click on the **Dr. Watson** icon located on the taskbar. Select the **Exit Dr. Watson** item. Dr. Watson closes.

Step 11.   Click on the **Microsoft System Information** button located on the taskbar. The Microsoft System Information window reappears on the screen.

Step 12.   Click on the **Tools** menu item and select the **System File Checker** option. The System File Checker window opens.

Step 13.   Ensure the **Scan for altered files** radio button is selected and click on the **Start** button. The system takes about a minute to scan the system files. When the scan is finished, a message displays. Click on the **OK** button. Click on the **Close** button to exit from the System File Checker window.

Step 14.   Click on the **Tools** menu item and select the **System File Checker** option again.

Step 15.   Click on the **Settings** button. The Settings window allows you to customize how the System File Checker tool works by allowing you to add/remove files to be checked, prompt before restoring system files, determine the default location for the good system files are stored, etc.

Step 16.   Click on the **View Log** button on the Settings tab. You may be prompted that the file is too big for Notepad and asked if it is okay to open the document in WordPad. If so, click on the **Yes** button. The default name of the log file is SFCLOG.TXT and it is stored in the WINDOWS folder by default. Close the **SFCLOG.TXT** file window.

Step 17.   Click on the **Search Criteria** tab. The Search Criteria tab lists files and folders that are checked through the System File Checker tool.

Question 4:   Locate the folder that contains the Windows 98 operating system (normally C:\WINDOWS). Are subfolders located in the WINDOWS folder checked by the System File Checker tool?

Step 18.   Click on the **Advanced** tab. The Advanced tab is where you can define the verification data file's default location.

Question 5:   What is the default location for the verification data file?

_____ *Instructor's Initials*

Step 19.   Click on the **Cancel** button to leave the System File Checker Settings window. Click on the *Close* button to exit the System File Checker utility.

Step 20.   Click on the **Close** button to exit the Microsoft System Information window.

Name _____

INTERNET DISCOVERY

Objective: To obtain specific information on the Internet regarding Windows 98

Parts: Access to the Internet

Question 1:   What is the URL for the Microsoft Windows 98 on-line help?

Question 2:   Locate a magazine article on the Internet that describes how to automatically log a user into a Windows 98 computer.

Question 3:   Locate a description of IRQ steering on the Internet and write the URL and basic description in the space below.

Question 4:   Find three different locations on the Internet that have the *Microsoft Windows 98 Resource Kit* book for sale. Find the lowest price on these three sites. Write the cost and the site in the space below.

Question 5:   Locate a site on the Internet that has Windows 98 troubleshooting tips that is not the Microsoft web site. Write the URL of this location in the space below.

Question 6:   At the Frank Condron's World O'Windows web site, he has Easter eggs listed for Windows 98. What panel is used to discover the Windows 98 Easter egg?

Chapter 16:

Windows NT Workstation

OBJECTIVES

After completing this chapter you will

- Understand the major differences between Windows NT Workstation and other operating systems.
- Be able to identify, explain, and use common desktop icons.
- Be able to manage files and folders.
- Understand the purpose of the registry, how it is organized into subtrees, and the function of each subtree.
- Be able to edit, back up, and restore the registry.
- Be able to install and troubleshoot Windows NT Workstation.
- Be able to install hardware and software on an NT Workstation computer.
- Understand the boot process and be able to troubleshoot boot problems including using Safe Mode.
- Be able to create and use an Emergency Repair Disk.
- Be able to access and use a command prompt.
- Be able to access tools that allow system monitoring.

KEY TERMS

Apply button	GUI	REGEDIT
baseline	HAL	REGEDT32
boot partition	Help button	registry
boot sector virus	icon	service
Cancel button	Internet Explorer	service pack
checkbox	macro virus	Start button
clean install	My Computer	stealth virus
Close button	Network Neighborhood	system files
desktop	NT Backup	system partition
dialog box	NT Diagnostics	tab
directory	NTVDM	Task Manager
drop-down menu	OK button	taskbar
dual-boot	path	textbox
ERD	Performance Monitor	Trojan horse
Event Viewer	PIF	virus upgrade
extension	polymorphic virus	user profile
file	radio butto	virus
file virus	RDISK	Windows NT Explorer
folder	Recycle Bin	worm virus

WINDOWS NT WORKSTATION OVERVIEW

Microsoft created NT Workstation for business computers operating in a networked environment. There are actually two major versions of NT—NT Server and NT Workstation. This chapter covers NT Workstation because it is on the A+ exam.

NT Workstation 4 can only be upgraded from a previous version of NT Workstation such as 3.5.1. It is possible to upgrade from Windows 3.x, but it is most likely that the computer will not have the appropriate hardware if it has Windows 3.x on it. NT Workstation 4 offers many enhancements to prior operating systems such as Window NT Workstation 3.5.1, Windows 3.x, Windows 95, and Windows 98. The NT Workstation enhancements are listed below:

- More efficient use of memory than NT Workstation 3.5.1.
- Improved graphics performance.
- True 32-bit operating system.
- Supports SMP (Symmetric Multiprocessing), which is the ability to run multiple processes on multiple CPUs.
- Better network security.
- Easier to use interface than Windows 3.x and NT Workstation 3.5.1.
- Support of long filenames.
- More reliable than Windows 3.x and Windows 95.
- Better application reliability.
- NT can be installed on RISC (Reduced Instruction Set) computers such as MIPS, Alpha, and PowerPC, as well as CISC (Complex Instruction Set) computers such as PCs and compatibles.

The file systems NT Workstation 4 supports are FAT16 and NTFS. For CD media, NT Workstation supports CDFS (Compact Disk File System). NT Workstation 4 does not support DVD media. See the multimedia chapter for more information on CDFS.

NT WORKSTATION BASICS

When NT Workstation boots, a login screen appears. The login screen cannot be bypassed as it can in Windows 95/98. A user can login to a network server, login to a network workgroup (peer-to-peer network), or login locally (as a stand-alone computer not participating in a network).

After logging in, the desktop appears. The **desktop** is the area where all work is performed. The desktop is the interface between you and the applications, files, and computer hardware. The desktop is part of a **GUI (Graphical User Interface)** environment. WINNT Figure #1 shows the NT Workstation desktop.

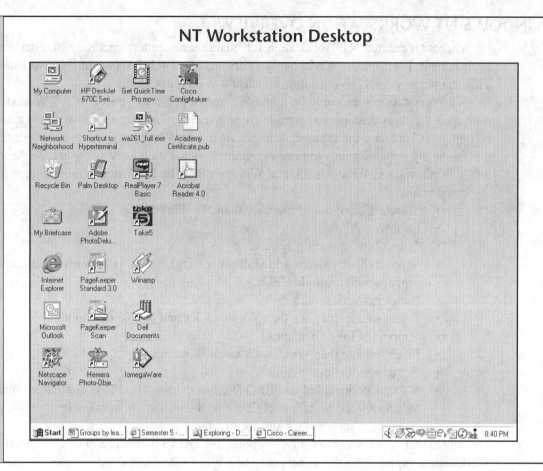

On the desktop are icons. **Icons** are graphics that can represent applications, files, the computer and its hardware devices, and shared network resources. In WINNT Figure #1, examples of icons include the My Computer icon, the Network Neighborhood icon, and the Recycle Bin icon.

The desktop can be modified to have a background or desktop pattern. This can include a graphic or a specific color. An exercise at the end of this chapter describes how to change the look of the desktop.

Notice in WINNT Figure #1 how part of the desktop includes the Start button and the taskbar. The **Start button,** located in the lower left corner of the desktop, is the most commonly used desktop item. The Start button is used to access applications, files, help, and utilities. WINNT Figure #2 shows how the Start button menu looks. The Start button can be customized by clicking on the *Start* button, pointing to the *Settings* option, and then clicking on the *Taskbar* option.

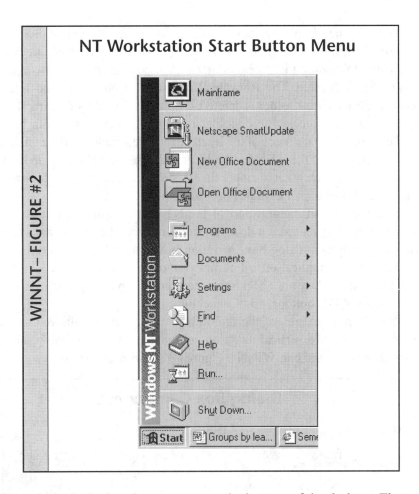

The **taskbar** is the bar that runs across the bottom of the desktop. The taskbar holds buttons that represent applications or files currently loaded into memory. The taskbar also holds icons that allow access to system tools. These tools can include an icon for changing or viewing the date and time, a speaker icon for adjusting speaker volume control, and an icon for a virus utility. In WINNT Figure #1, the files currently loaded into memory and displayed on the taskbar as a button are (1) a Word document called Groups by lea…, (2) an Internet Explorer session opened to Semester5…, (3) the Explorer application as shown by the Exploring-D… button, and another Internet Explorer session opened to Cisco-Career…. On the right portion of the taskbar in WINNT Figure #1, is the speaker icon, which is used to adjust speaker volume.

Other common desktop icons include My Computer, Internet Explorer, Network Neighborhood, and Recycle Bin. The **My Computer** desktop icon is used to access hardware, software, applications, and files located on or in the computer. To use the My Computer icon, simply move the mouse pointer to the icon and double-click on it. The same is true for all desktop icons.

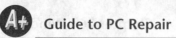

The **Internet Explorer** icon is used to start the Internet Explorer application. The **Network Neighborhood** icon only appears if the computer has a network card installed and is used to display and access all networked computers and networked devices in your workgroup or domain. The **Recycle Bin** is used to hold files and folders that the user deletes. When a file or folder is deleted, it is not immediately discarded; instead, it goes to the Recycle Bin. Once a file or folder is in the Recycle Bin, it can be removed. This is similar to the fact that a piece of trash can be retrieved from an office trash can. A technician must remember that these files and folders in the Recycle Bin take up hard drive space and that users frequently forget to empty the files and folders from the Recycle Bin. An exercise at the end of the chapter explains how to empty the Recycle Bin.

Windows are an integral part of the NT Workstation environment. Every time you double-click on an icon, a window appears. One type of window that a technician interacts with frequently is a dialog box. A **dialog box** is used by the operating system and with various software applications; it allows you to set various preferences. Common features found in a dialog box are checkboxes, textboxes, tabs, drop-down menus, Help buttons, Close buttons, OK buttons, and Cancel buttons.

A **textbox** is an area of the dialog box where you are allowed to type. Click in the blank text area and a vertical insertion point bar appears. All typing shows up to the right of the insertion point bar. WINNT Figure #3 shows a dialog box.

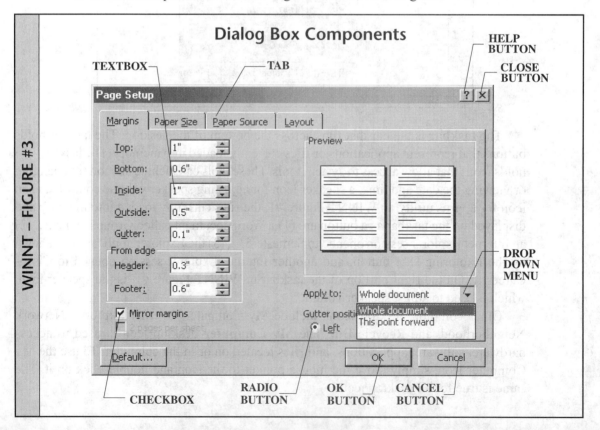

In WINNT Figure #3, the text boxes are the ones labeled *Top, Bottom, Inside,* and *Outside.* By clicking inside one of these boxes, you can manually type the margin setting or you can use the up and down arrows to select a number. Also in WINNT Figure #3 are the *Margins, Paper Size, Paper Source,* and *Layout* tabs. **Tabs** are frequently found across the top of a dialog box. Click once on a particular tab and a group of related options come to the forefront of the dialog box.

In the upper right corner of the dialog box shown in WINNT Figure #3 are the Help button and the Close button. The **Help button** has a question mark on it. When you click on the Help button, the cursor turns to an arrow with a question mark attached. Click on any item that you have a question about, and a popup window appears with basic information displayed. With older applications, a Help button may not be available for the dialog box. As an alternative, try pressing the *F1* key or *Shift + F1* keys to obtain help in the dialog box.

The **Close button** has an X on it and is used to close the dialog box window.

One of the most frequent mistakes new technicians make is clicking on the Close button. When a dialog box is closed with the Close button, no changes in the dialog box window are saved or applied.

If changes are made in a dialog box and you want to save these changes, click on the **OK button** located at the bottom of the dialog box to apply the changes and close the window. Another technique is to click on an optional button called the **Apply button** (which is not shown in WINNT Figure #3). Then, click on the OK button or the Close button to close the dialog box window.

Another common button shown in WINNT Figure #3 is the Cancel button. By clicking on the **Cancel button,** all changes made to the dialog box are ignored. The options are left in the state they were in before the dialog box was opened.

Other common items shown in WINNT Figure #3 are the checkbox, radio button, and drop-down menu. The **checkbox** appears beside an option that can either be enabled or disabled. When a check appears inside a checkbox, the option is enabled. When the checkbox is empty, the option is disabled. One click in a checkbox changes the option from its current state.

A **radio button** is similar to a checkbox, except it is a round circle. When a radio button has a solid dot in the middle, the option is enabled. When a radio button is a clear circle, the option is disabled. Click once inside the circle to change the option to its opposite state.

Drop-down menus are easy to spot because of the down arrow that appears to the right of the option. Notice in WINNT Figure #3 how the *Apply to:* option is a drop-down menu. Clicking on the down arrow causes a list of options to appear. In WINNT Figure #3 the two options are *Whole document* and *This point forward.* Click once on any option to place the selection in the drop-down menu window.

MANAGING FILES AND FOLDERS

Managing files and folders is an important part of NT Workstation. A technician must be able to create, delete, and move files and folders regularly. The easiest way to learn about files and folders is to start with the drive letter. A drive letter followed by a colon represents every drive in the computer. The first floppy drive in a system receives the drive letter A:. The first hard drive partition gets the drive letter C:. Other partitions receive consecutive drive letters (D:, E:, F:, etc.), usually before other devices. The CD-ROM, Zip® drive, or DVD is usually represented by a higher drive letter such as D:, E:, or F:.

Computer drives hold files and folders. A **file** is an electronic container that holds data or computer code. An example of a file is NT CHAPTER.DOC. A **folder** holds files and can also contain other folders. This is similar to an office folder that has memos and paper documents as well as other folders. A folder was called a **directory** in older DOS operating systems.

Every file and folder is given a name. It is easier to understand file and folder names if we look at how the older operating systems named files and folders and then look at how NT Workstation's names differ. In older operating systems (such as DOS), a file or folder name could contain all letters, numbers, and characters except for the following:

. (period)	; (semicolon)	/ (forward slash)
, (comma)	" (quotation marks)	\ (backslash)
| (vertical bar)	? (question mark)	[(left bracket)
: (colon)	= (equal sign)	] (right bracket)
* (asterisk)	(space)	

In DOS, in addition to naming a file or a folder, you frequently would have to add an extension to a filename. An **extension** is part of the filename and it can be up to three characters in length. The extension is separated from the first part of the filename by a period (.). Most people consider the extension to be part of the filename. An example of a filename (with an extension) is NTCHAP.DOC where *.DOC* is the extension. The good part about extensions today is that the applications normally add an extension automatically to the end of a filename. In most windows, NT Workstation does not automatically show the extensions. To view the extensions in Windows NT Explorer, click on the *View* menu option. Click on the *Folder Options* menu option. Click on the *View* tab and click on the *Hide file extensions for known file types* check box (which will remove the check from the box). Click on the *Apply* button.

When NT Workstation recognizes an extension, it associates that extension with a particular application. This means that NT Workstation assigns a known graphical icon to that file. An exercise at the end of the chapter teaches how to get NT Workstation to recognize a new file extension. WINNT Figure #4 illustrates common icons that NT uses when it recognizes an extension.

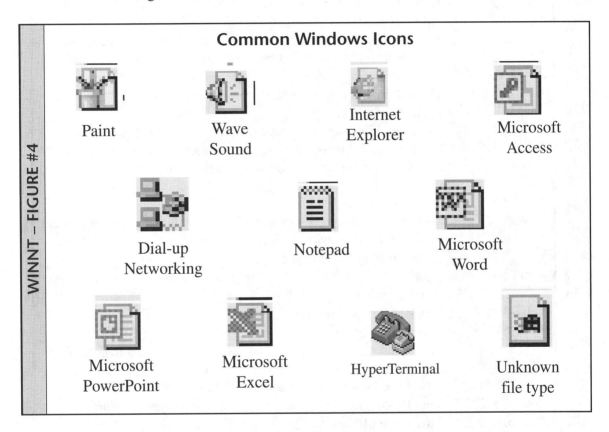

Common Windows Icons

Paint

Wave Sound

Internet Explorer

Microsoft Access

Dial-up Networking

Notepad

Microsoft Word

Microsoft PowerPoint

Microsoft Excel

HyperTerminal

Unknown file type

WINNT – FIGURE #4

Filename extensions can tell you a lot about a file, such as what application created the file or what purpose the file has. WINNT Table #1 lists the most common extensions, their purposes, and what application typically creates the extension.

WINNT – TABLE #1

Common File Extensions

Extension	Purpose or Application
386	Used by Windows 3.x for device drivers
AI	Adobe Illustrator
BAT	Used in DOS environments for batch files. Combines executable commands into one file and uses one command to start the batch file.
BMP	Bitmap file
CAB	Cabinet file—a compressed file that holds operating system or application files
COM	Command file—an executable file that opens an application or tool
DLL	Dynamic Link Library file —contains executable code that can be used by more than one application and is called upon from other code already running
DOC	Microsoft Word
DRV	Device driver—a piece of software that enables an operating system to recognize a hardware device
EPS	Encapsulated postscript file
EXE	Executable file—a file that opens an application
GIF	Graphics interchange file
HLP	Windows-based help file
INF	Information or Setup file
INI	Initialization file—Used in Windows 3.x environment to control applications and the operating environment. Used in 95, 98, NT, and 2000 to be backward compatible with Windows 3.x
JPG or JPEG	Joint Photographic Experts Group file format—graphics file
MPG or MPEG	Movie clip file
PCX	Microsoft Paintbrush
PDF	Adobe Acrobat—portable document format
PPT	Microsoft PowerPoint
RTF	Rich text format
TIF or TIFF	Tag image file format
TXT	Text file
VXD	Virtual device driver
WKS	Lotus worksheet
WPS	Microsoft Works text file format
WRI	Microsoft WordPad
XLS	Microsoft Excel
ZIP	Compressed file

Filenames in NT Workstation can be up to 255 characters. These extended filenames are commonly called long filenames. Folder names and filenames can have all characters, numbers, letters, and spaces except for the following

/ (forward slash)	" (quotation marks)	\ (backslash)
| (vertical bar)	? (question mark)	: (colon)
* (asterisk)		

An example of an NT Workstation long filename is NT WORKSTATION CHAPTER.DOC. Anytime a document has been saved with one of these long filenames and is taken to an older computer with an operating system that does not support long filenames, the filename is shortened to a maximum of eight characters. Windows does this by using the first six characters of the filename, deleting any spaces, and using two special characters—a tilde (~) and a number. For example, NT WORKSTATION CHAPTER.DOC would be shortened to NTWORK~1.DOC. If there were two files named NT WORKSTATION CHAPTER.DOC and NT WORKSTATION INDEX.DOC, the two files would be saved as NTWORK~1.DOC and NTWORK~2.DOC, respectively.

Anytime a file is saved on a disk, the reference for what drive and folder the file is saved to is known as the file's **path.** A path is like a roadmap of how to get to the file. An example of an NT path is as follows:

C:\MY Documents\A+ Book\NT WORKSTATION CHAPTER.DOC

To understand a path statement, look at the items in small chunks. In the previous example, C: is the drive letter where the document is stored. The C: represents the first hard drive partition. The name of the document is always at the very end of the path. In the example given, the name of the document is NT WORKSTATION CHAPTER.DOC. Everything in the middle of these two items is the name of the folders one must go through to find the NT WORKSTATION CHAPTER.DOC file. For example, the first folder listed in the example is *My Documents*. The My Documents folder is on the C: drive and is separated from the drive letter by a backslash (\). The next folder (which is a subfolder within the My Documents folder) is called *A+ Book*. The A+ Book folder is separated from the parent folder (My Documents) by another backslash (\). The A+ Book folder is also separated from the name of the document by a backslash (\).

NT Workstation ships with an application called Windows NT Explorer. **Windows NT Explorer** is the most common application used to copy or move files and folders. WINNT Figure #5 shows how the A+ BOOK HARDWARE FROM PAGEMAKER.DOC path looks in graphical form under the Windows NT Explorer utility.

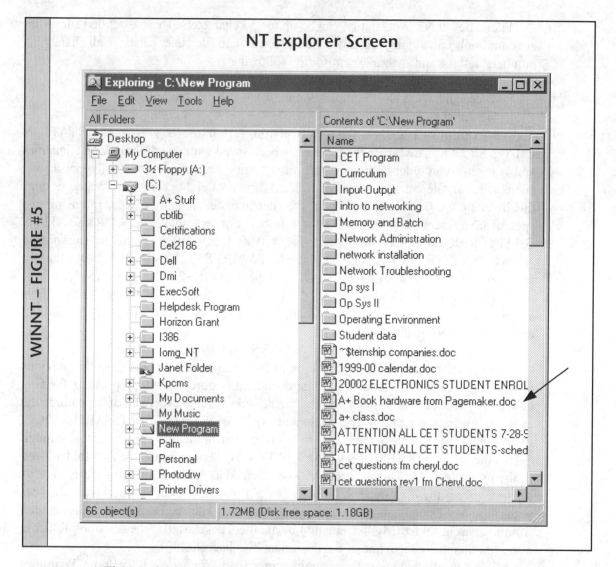

WINNT – FIGURE #5

NT Explorer Screen

The My Computer desktop icon can be used in a similar fashion to copy or move files and folders. Even though the graphical form is nice, technicians must thoroughly understand a file's path written in long format. Frequently, technical directions, advisories, support documents, etc., have the path written in long format, such as the example given earlier. An exercise at the end of the chapter illustrates creating a file, copying a file into a folder, moving the file to a different folder, deleting the file, and emptying the Recycle Bin to permanently delete the file.

My Computer and NT Explorer can be used for setting attributes for a file or folder. The file and folder attributes are read-only, hidden, archive, and system. The read-only attribute marks a file or folder so that it cannot be changed. The hidden attribute marks a file or folder so that it is not visible through My Computer or NT Explorer, unless someone changes the default view for the window. Some applications use the archive attribute to control which files or folders are backed up. The system attribute is placed on certain files used to boot NT Workstation.

To change a file or folder's attributes, use My Computer or NT Explorer to locate the file or folder. Right-click on the file or folder name. Click on the *Properties* option and the Properties window opens. Toward the bottom of the window is an *Attributes* section. Click inside one or more of the attribute checkboxes to enable or disable an attribute. A checkmark in a checkbox means an attribute is enabled. An empty checkbox means an attribute is disabled. If the file is not a system file, the system attribute is unavailable. Click on the *Apply* button when finished setting the attributes.

NTFS COMPRESSION

NT Workstation can use the NTFS and FAT file systems. In the NTFS file system, file and folder compression are supported. In NT Workstation, when you click on an NTFS compressed file, the file automatically uncompresses. After all work on the file is complete, the file recompresses when it is saved or the document is closed. Even though a compressed file or folder takes less space on the hard drive, the file or folder takes longer to access when it is compressed. Each file and folder in NTFS has a compression state of either compressed or uncompressed. Just because a folder is in a compressed state, does not mean that all files in the folder are compressed.

To set compression on a folder, open the Windows NT Explorer application by clicking on the *Start* button, pointing to the *Programs* option, and clicking on the *Windows NT Explorer* option. Select the folder that is to be compressed by clicking once on the folder name listed in the left Explorer window. Click on the *File* menu option and click on the *Properties* option. Click once in the *Compressed* checkbox and click on the *OK* button.

To enable file compression, follow a similar procedure. Start the Windows NT Explorer program by clicking on the *Start* button. Point to the *Programs* option and click on the *Windows NT Explorer* item in the submenu. In the left Explorer window, double-click on the name of the folder that contains the file. The files in the folder appear in the right NT Explorer window. Click once on the filename in the right NT Explorer window. Click on the *File* menu option. Click on the *Properties* menu option. Click once in the *Compressed* checkbox.

 The compression that comes with NT Workstation can only be accomplished if the partition has been formatted as NTFS (not FAT).

DETERMINING THE NT WORKSTATION VERSION

The operating system version is important to a technician when troubleshooting a computer. With NT Workstation, upgrades or patches to the operating system are provided with **service packs**. A service pack contains fixes for known operating system problems. Some application installation requirements list the minimum service pack that has to be installed before the software will install and/or operate properly. There are several ways to determine what version and service pack are installed with NT Workstation and they are listed below.

- When NT Workstation boots and the blue screen appears, the version and service pack level display.
- Click on the *Start* button. Click on the *Run* option. In the *Open* textbox, type *WINVER* and press *Enter.*
- Open Windows NT Explorer. Click on the *Help* menu item. Click on the *About* option. The version appears.

WINDOWS NT REGISTRY

With NT Workstation, every hardware and software configuration is stored in a database called the **registry.** The registry contains such things as folder and file property settings, application preferences and settings, driver files, environment settings, and user profiles. A **user profile** is all settings associated with a specific user including what application the user has access to, desktop settings, and the user's network configuration. The registry loads into RAM during the boot process. As changes are made to the computer's hardware and software settings, the registry updates continuously.

The registry consists of five subtrees. Subtrees are also called branches or hives. The five standard subtrees are HKEY_LOCAL_MACHINE, HKEY_USERS, HKEY_CURRENT_USER, HKEY_CURRENT_CONFIG, and HKEY_CLASSES_ROOT. Each of the subtrees has keys and subkeys containing values related to the settings that subtree tracks.

The registry can contain other subtrees depending on what software (applications, device drivers, or services) is added to the computer. A **service** is a process running on NT that provides a specific function to the computer. Examples of services include: DHCP client, computer browser, event log, net logon, and remote access connection manager. The registry is located in the %SYSTEMROOT%\SYSTEM32\CONFIG folder (where %SYSTEMROOT% is the boot partition and the name of the folder under the folder where NT Workstation is installed (normally C:\WINNT). WINNT Table #2 lists the five major subtrees and the function of each.

WINNT – TABLE #2

Windows NT Workstation Registry Subtrees

Registry Subtree	Subtree Function
HKEY_LOCAL_MACHINE	Holds global hardware configuration. Included in the branch is a list of hardware components installed in the computer, the software drivers that handle each component, and the settings for each device. This information is not user-specific.
HKEY_USERS	Keeps track of individual users and their preferences.
HKEY_CURRENT_USER	Holds a specific user's configuration such as software settings, how the desktop appears, and what folders the user has created.
HKEY_CURRENT_CONFIG	Holds information about the hardware profile that is used when the computer first boots.
HKEY_CLASSES_ROOT	Holds file associations and file links. The information held here is what allows the correct application to start when you double-click on a filename in Explorer or My Computer (provided the file extension is registered).

EDITING THE NT WORKSTATION REGISTRY

Most changes to the registry are accomplished through the various control panels, but some changes can only be done through the registry editor.

By default, only members of the Administrators and Power Users groups can edit the registry, but all users can view the registry.

Before making changes to the registry, make sure you make a backup of the registry. An exercise at the end of the chapter illustrates this procedure.

NT Workstation ships with two registry editors—**REGEDIT** and **REGEDT32.** Either editor can be used to change the registry. For most technicians, it is simply a matter of which view he/she prefers. However, there are some differences between the two. WINNT Table #3 shows some of the more important differences.

WINNT – TABLE #3

REGEDIT and REGEDT32 Differences

REGEDIT	REGEDT32
Provides more powerful search capabilities	Can display and edit values larger than 256 characters
All of the subtrees are shown in one window	The subtrees are shown in individual windows
Allows exporting the registry to a text file	Can look at and apply access permissions to the subtrees, keys, and subkeys.
Allows importing the registry from the command line	Can work with multiple registry files simultaneously

Exercises at the end of the chapter illustrate how to use the registry editors.

BACKING UP/RESTORING THE NT WORKSTATION REGISTRY

The registry should be backed up once a computer is initially configured and operating properly. The registry should also be backed up when any software or hardware changes are made.

The registry should be backed up and restored on a working computer *before* disaster hits. The time to learn how to restore the registry is *not* when the computer is down.

There are several ways to backup the registry and they are listed below.
- Use the NT Backup program*.
- Use the RDISK (Repair Disk) utility.
- Use the REGEDIT registry editor.

*Microsoft states that this option is the only supported option for backing up the registry.

The **NT Backup** program is accessed by first clicking on the *Start* button. Point to *Programs,* point to *Administrative Tools,* and click on the *Backup* option. The Backup dialog box appears. Select the *Windows* menu option and then click on the *Drives* option. Double-click on the drive letter that represents the boot drive (normally C:). In the bottom window, click on a checkbox to enable at least one file on this drive. At least one file must be chosen in order to backup the registry. Click on the *Backup* button. In the Backup Information dialog box, click once in the *Backup local registry* checkbox to enable the option. Click on the *OK* button.

The **RDISK (Repair Disk)** utility is used to create an **ERD (Emergency Repair Disk)** after NT is installed. When using the RDISK utility, two options are available—Update Repair Info and Create Repair Disk. The *Update Repair Info* button updates the emergency repair directory, which is a folder called Repair. The system then prompts you to create an ERD (Emergency Repair Disk). After NT is installed for the first time, the emergency repair folder is updated only using this *Update Repair Info* option. It is especially important to use the *Update Repair Info* option when making an updated ERD.

The *Create Repair Disk* button is used to create an ERD and use the information stored in the Repair folder. This option does not back up the current options to the Repair folder. Since the *Update Repair Info* option creates an ERD anyway, it is best to use the *Update Repair Info* option. An exercise at the end of the chapter details how to create an ERD.

One limitation of the RDISK program is that it does not update the default, security, or SAM files in the Repair folder. This means none of the user account information or changes are backed up. To do a complete update, use the RDISK / S command from the command prompt. This takes a bit of time. That is why most people prefer using some type of backup program to back up the registry. The BACKUP utility that ships with NT Workstation is a better method once the Repair folder has been updated using the RDISK program.

The REGEDIT program can also be used to back up or export the registry to backup media. To start the REGEDIT utility, click on the *Start* button. Click on the *Run* option and in the textbox type in *REGEDIT* and press *Enter.* In the REGEDIT window, click on the *Registry* menu item. Click on the *Export Registry File* option from the drop-down menu. Select the drive location where the registry will be saved. In the *File name* textbox, type in the name for the registry file backup. Click on the *Save* button. WINNT Figure #6 illustrates the REGEDIT utility.

WINNT – FIGURE #6

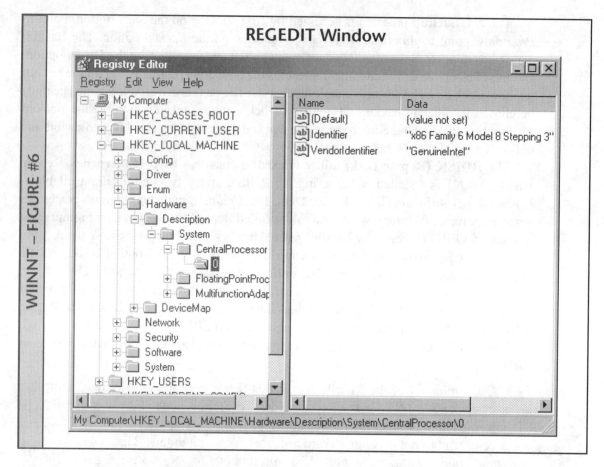

REGEDIT Window

The subtrees in WINNT Figure #6 are in the left window. Click on the plus sign (+) beside each subtree and more subkeys appear. Click on a folder and the folder values appear in the right window. For example, in WINNT Figure #6, the Hardware folder has a subfolder called Description. The Description folder has a subfolder called System. The System folder has a subfolder called CentralProcessor. The CentralProcessor folder has a subfolder called 0. Once the 0 subfolder is double-clicked, the values appear in the right window. The value names for the 0 subfolder are (Default), Identifier, and VendorIdentifier. The value data for the 0 subfolder is on the far right side of the right window. These values must be changed sometimes to repair technical problems.

PRE-INSTALLATION OF NT WORKSTATION

Skipping the installation planning is a bad habit for any technician, especially when installing an operating system. The planning stages save time (and time is money to any business). Technicians who skip the pre-installation steps find themselves troubleshooting the installation process unnecessarily. The following steps outline the various stages of NT Workstation pre-installation:

1. Decide whether the installation will be an upgrade or clean install.
2. Decide whether the computer will have more than one operating system installed.
3. Decide how you want to partition the hard drive.
4. Determine which type of file system NT Workstation will use.
5. Determine if the hardware is compatible.
6. Obtain any drivers, upgrades, or hardware replacements.
7. Determine if the software applications are compatible.
8. Obtain any patches, upgrades, or software replacements.
9. Scan the computer for viruses.
10. Remove any power management or disk management tools.
11. Delete any unwanted files and uninstall any unwanted applications.
12. Back up any data files necessary.
13. Determine the local administrator password.

A **clean install** places an operating system on a computer that does not already have an operating system installed. An operating system **upgrade** is when an operating system already exists on the computer and NT Workstation 4 will be installed on top of this operating system. Windows 3.x and a previous version of NT Workstation (such as 3.5.1) can be upgraded to NT Workstation 4; however, a computer that already has Windows 3.x will probably not have enough hardware to load NT Workstation 4.

When NT Workstation 4 is installed to a different folder than the existing operating system, the computer will automatically be configured to be a dual-boot system. **Dual-boot** means that the computer has two operating systems installed and you can boot from either one. If Windows 95/98 or OS/2 is already installed, remove the operating system or install NT to a different folder. The default installation folder for NT is WINNT.

If you decide that you are going to install NT on a machine that already has Windows 95/98, first check to see that all applications are supported by NT Workstation 4. Then, install NT into a separate directory on the hard drive. The system now has two operating systems and can boot from either of them. Reinstall all Windows 9x applications through NT. If Windows 95/98 is no longer desired, manually delete the folder that contains the Windows 95 or 98 operating system files.

A hard drive is usually more efficient when it is split into two or more partitions. (See the hard drive chapter for more information on partitions.) There are two types of NT Workstation partitions: system partition and boot partition. The **system partition** is the active hard drive partition that contains hardware-specific files used to load the operating system. The system partition is normally located on the C: hard drive partition. The **boot partition** is the hard drive partition that holds the majority of the NT Workstation operating system files. What is confusing is that the two types of NT partitions can be located on the same hard drive partition, or they can be on different partitions.

For example, take a hard drive that has one partition, C:. The files needed to boot the system are on C:, and the NT files, located in the WINNT folder, are also on the C: partition.

Therefore, in this example, both the system partition and the boot partition are on the same hard drive partition (C:).

Another example is a computer that has two partitions, C: and D:. The active partition that the computer boots from is C:. An extended partition with one logical drive is D:. The C: partition already has Windows 95 installed. This computer will be able to dual-boot from either Windows 95 or NT Workstation. When NT Workstation is installed, the files needed to load and boot NT are put on the C: partition (the NT system partition). The NT files are loaded to the WINNT folder on the D: partition (the NT boot partition).

NT Workstation can use either the FAT16 or the NTFS file system. The FAT file system should only be used if NT is to be dual-booted with an older operating system and there is only one hard drive partition formatted as FAT16. With the FAT16 file system, there is no file or folder compression. Nor are there as many permissions for individual files and folders. Also, the partition does not support large hard drive volumes greater than 2GB. The NTFS file system supports security options and long filenames.

The FAT partition can be converted to NTFS after the installation by using the CONVERT program. CONVERT *partition letter*: /FS:NTFS will convert a FAT partition to NTFS with no data loss. Take the example of the C: hard drive partition that is currently FAT16. The command used to convert the partition to NTFS is CONVERT C: /FS:NTFS. This command would be executed from a command prompt or by using the Run option from the Start menu.

The hardware requirements for NT Workstation are very important in the pre-installation checklist. Technicians who omit this step find themselves troubleshooting when actually there is nothing wrong except that the hardware requirements are not met. WINNT Table #4 lists the minimum requirements for NT Workstation.

NT Workstation Minimum Hardware Requirements

Component	Minimum
CPU	Intel 486 (or compatible) 33MHz or higher
RAM	12MB
Free hard drive space	120MB or more
Input Device	Keyboard, mouse, or other pointing device
Multimedia Drive	CD-ROM
Video	VGA or higher

WIINNT – TABLE #4

On the NT Workstation CD in the Support folder, there is a file called HCL.HLP. This is the hardware compatibility list that contains hardware devices compatible with NT Workstation. If a computer device is not listed here, check Microsoft's website at www.microsoft.com for the latest listing. Also check the device manufacturer's web site to see if it offers an NT driver for the device or if the driver is compatible with NT.

Microsoft provides a utility called NTHQ (NT Hardware Qualifier) that identifies what hardware is installed in the system. The NTHQ program is executed from a special floppy disk that you must make. Insert a blank floppy disk into the computer. Run the *MAKEDISK.BAT* file, (which is located on the NT Workstation CD in the SUPPORT\HQTOOL folder). After this program executes, reboot the computer from this special disk. If your computer will not boot from the disk, check BIOS settings to make sure the A: drive is the first boot device. The NTHQ program automatically executes. Once hardware has been verified, obtain the appropriate NT driver for the device. If the device is incompatible with NT, replace the hardware device with a compatible one *before* installing NT.

DOS applications, 16-bit, and 32-bit Windows-based applications can all operate under NT. However, any older application that tries to access hardware directly will not operate properly in the NT environment. One way you can know whether an application is compatible with NT is to try it. Some application manufacturers provide software upgrades (for a fee) so that the application can be run on NT. Contact the software manufacturer for any software compatibility issues. Microsoft also has some application compatibility notes on their web site.

When upgrading an operating system to NT Workstation, it is wise to free up hard drive space and clean off unwanted files and applications. Hard drive space is an important commodity to an operating system. As applications and operating systems increase in size, it is very important to have enough free hard drive space and enough RAM installed.

The last preparation steps before installing or upgrading NT Workstation are to determine what the name of the computer will be and what the local administrator passwords will be. NT Workstation was designed for a corporate networked environment. In a network, every computer must have a unique name. The company may have a standard for naming computers. Gather this information before starting an NT upgrade or installation.

A local administrator has full power over the NT Workstation computer. When someone logs in as the local administrator, he/she can create and delete user accounts, create and delete hard drive partitions, and use all of the administration tools that ship with NT Workstation. Some companies have standards for the local administrator account password. Check with the network administrator or desktop support supervisor to see if this is the case. Otherwise, determine what password will be set during the installation process. The password can be blank (not advised), or it can be up to 14 characters in length. Also, the password is case sensitive (unlike the username, such as Administrator).

VIRUSES

When installing a new operating system on a computer that already has an operating system loaded, it is wise to run a virus scan. A **virus** is a computer program designed to change the way the computer operates. The virus could infect the computer so it does not boot, or infect a particular application so it does not operate or performs differently, or erase files. Some viruses are written not to cause harm, but simply to cause mischief. An example of this could be a program that puts a picture on the screen. Common types of viruses include: the boot sector virus, the file virus, the macro virus, and the Trojan horse virus.

A **boot sector virus** is a program that is placed in the computer's boot sector. Because the computer loads boot sector code into memory, the virus loads into RAM at the same time. Once in memory, the virus can take control of computer operations and spread to other drives such as floppy drives, hard drives, and drives located on a network.

A **file virus** replaces or attaches itself to a file that has a COM or EXE extension. COM or EXE files are commonly known as executable files. Executable files are used to start applications. By attaching itself to this type of file, a virus can can prevent the program starting or operating properly. It can also load into RAM and affect other COM or EXE files.

A **macro virus** is written for a specific application such as Microsoft's Excel or Word. Macro viruses are written in a specific language and attach themselves to a document created in the application. Once the document (along with the virus) is opened and loaded into memory the virus can attach itself to other documents.

A **Trojan horse virus** pretends to be a normal application. When the virus executes, the computer does something the user does not expect, such as putting a message or a picture on the screen or launching a new screen saver. A Trojan horse virus does not replicate (copy itself somewhere else). The virus can be used to gather information such as userids and passwords that can later be used to hack into your computer.

Three other types of viruses that infect computers are the stealth virus, the polymorphic virus, and the worm virus. A **stealth virus** is a program written to avoid being detected by anti-virus software. When an anti-virus program executes, the stealth virus provides the anti-virus program with a fake image that makes the anti-virus program believe no virus is present. A **polymorphic virus** is a virus that constantly changes its own program to avoid detection by an anti-virus program. A **worm virus** makes a copy of itself from one drive to another and can use a network to replicate itself. The most common types of worm viruses today are in the form of an e-mail message. Once the e-mail is opened, the worm virus is sent to every other user in an address book.

Common symptoms of a virus are listed below:
- Computer does not boot.
- Computer hard drive space is reduced.
- Applications will not load.
- An application takes longer to load than normal.

- Hard drive activity increases (especially when nothing is being done on the computer).
- An anti-virus software message appears.
- The number of hard drive sectors marked as *bad* steadily increases.
- Unusual graphics or messages appear on the screen.
- Files are missing (deleted).
- A message appears that the hard drive cannot be detected or recognized.
- Strange sounds come from the computer.

If a virus is detected or even suspected, run an anti-virus program. Follow the program's directions for installing and executing. The time to get an anti-virus program is *before* a virus infects the computer because the damage may be irreversible, especially if backups are not performed. Back up data often! Always back up data files before upgrading to a new operating systems. Backups are an important part of any computer support plan.

Some anti-virus software can be set to load into memory when the computer boots and runs continuously. Make sure you disable this feature when installing an operating system patch (service pack) or upgrade. The anti-virus software can prevent the upgrade or patch (service pack) from installing. Other types of software that prevent an operating system from being upgraded are power management and disk management software/tools. Disable these utilities and applications before attempting an operating system installation or upgrade.

INSTALLATION/UPGRADE OF NT WORKSTATION

After all pre-installation steps are completed, you can start the installation process. NT Workstation uses the Setup program to install the operating system files. There are three ways to start the Setup program: (1) from an NT Workstation CD, (2) by launching the installation program from a local hard drive partition, and (3) across a network. When installing NT across a network, one of two files is used to start the Setup program—WINNT.EXE or WINNT32.EXE. WINNT.EXE is used to install NT Workstation to a computer that currently has DOS, Windows 3.x, Windows 95, or Windows 98 installed. The WINNT32.EXE file is used to upgrade from a previous version of NT Workstation.

There are two major parts of the installation process—the text mode (otherwise known as DOS mode) and the GUI mode (also known as Windows mode). In text mode, characters are shown on a plain blue background. During text mode, the hard drive is partitioned and formatted for either FAT or NTFS, the location of where to install the NT files is chosen, hardware is checked for minimum requirements, hard drives are detected, and some of the installation files are copied. During the GUI mode, the setup logs are created, the computer is named, the administrator password is entered, and the rest of the operating system files are copied. You may also create an Emergency Repair Disk, as well as install networking components. An exercise at the end of the chapter demonstrates how to install NT Workstation.

TROUBLESHOOTING THE NT WORKSTATION INSTALLATION

Various problems can cause the NT Workstation installation process to halt. If the system halts during text mode, go into the computer's BIOS and disable shadow RAM, virus utility, and power management utilities and try the installation process again.

If the computer halts during text mode and displays a STOP message, there is probably an incompatible piece of hardware or software installed in the computer, or a virus is present. If no error messages appear, but the computer halts during text mode, check the BIOS settings, especially on older ISA devices. If an error message appears during text mode that indicates the HAL.DLL is missing or corrupt or a similar HAL.DLL message, then the incorrect **HAL (Hardware Abstraction Layer)** is being loaded. This is a layer between the operating system and hardware devices. The HAL allows NT to run with different hardware configurations and components without affecting (or crashing) the operating system. To correct this, restart the Setup program. When the message appears that NT is examining your hardware configuration, press the *F5* key. Select the correct computer type from the list that appears. If the computer type is not listed there, obtain a HAL from the computer manufacturer. Then, select *Other* from the list and load the HAL provided by the computer manufacturer. Another indication that the HAL is incorrect is if Setup hangs while copying files to the hard drive.

If the computer halts during the GUI portion of Setup, restart the computer. The installation process attempts to continue from the place it left off. Incompatible hardware devices normally cause this. You can troubleshoot the device once Windows is installed. Also, if the system hangs at random intervals, an IRQ conflict, I/O address conflict, video setting, or SCSI setting is probably the culprit. Incompatible hardware devices are the most common problem during the installation process because they can cause both the text and GUI modes to halt. If the system hangs after the final reboot, the problem is most likely caused by incorrect information in the BOOT.INI file or an incorrect hardware configuration.

Installation problems can be caused by a number of factors. The bulleted list shows the most common causes and their associated solution during the installation process.

- Incompatible BIOS—Obtain compatible BIOS, upgrade to a compatible BIOS, replace motherboard with one that has a compatible BIOS, or do not upgrade/install NT Workstation.
- BIOS needs to be upgraded—Upgrade the BIOS.
- Incompatible hardware—Replace the hardware or do not upgrade/install NT Workstation.
- Incompatible drivers—Obtain NT drivers from the hardware manufacturer.
- Existing drivers are incompatible or halt the installation/upgrade process— Obtain NT drivers from the hardware manufacturer.
- Incompatible TSRs—Remove TSRs or obtain updated ones from the software manufacturer; otherwise, disable the TSR until after NT has been installed and then try re-enabling the TSR.

- Incompatible applications—Obtain upgrades from software manufacturer.
- Minimum hardware requirements have not been met—Upgrade the hardware. The number one thing to check is the CPU (486 33MHz minimum) and RAM (12MB minimum).
- A virus is on the hard drive—Run a virus-checking program to remove the virus.
- Pre-installation steps have not been completed—Go back through the list!
- The installation floppy disks or CD is corrupted (not as likely as the other causes)—Try the disk in another machine and see if you can see the contents. For the CD, check to see if any scratches or dirt is on the surface. Clean the CD as necessary.
- Incorrect CD key—Type in the correct CD key to complete the NT Workstation installation. The key is located on the CD case.
- Hard drives are not configured correctly—If a message appears that Setup did not find any hard drives on your computer and this is a new computer, check that the cable(s) are properly connected and that power connects to the drive. If the hard drive is EIDE, make sure it connects to the first controller on the motherboard. If the hard drive is IDE or EIDE, make sure the master/slave/single drive setting is correctly configured.
- Existing FAT32 partition—If a message appears that there is no valid partition on the hard drive and a previous operating system has been (or is) on the hard drive, there is a good possibility that the drive has been partition to FAT32. NT Workstation does not support FAT32. Back up the data and create a new partition (FAT or NTFS) if NT Workstation is to be installed.
- If Setup hangs while files are copying to the hard drive, the wrong HAL is installed (see previous section that describes the HAL file) or some BIOS settings are interrupting the copy process. Go into the computer's BIOS and disable video shadow RAM and the 32-bit enhanced file throughput settings.

CONFIGURING WINDOWS NT WORKSTATION OVERVIEW

Technicians must frequently add new hardware and software using the operating system. NT Workstation has specific tools for these functions. Using the correct procedure is essential for success. The following sections handle many of the tasks a technician must perform:

- Adding/removing hardware components
- Installing/removing software
- Adding a printer

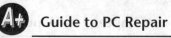

ADDING/REMOVING HARDWARE COMPONENTS

All hardware devices must have NT drivers in order to operate with NT Workstation. An important thing to remember is that the only type of user who can install hardware components by default is the Administrator. The Administrator uses various control panels to add hardware components in NT Workstation. WINNT Figure #7 illustrates control panels found in Windows NT Workstation.

WINNT – FIGURE #7

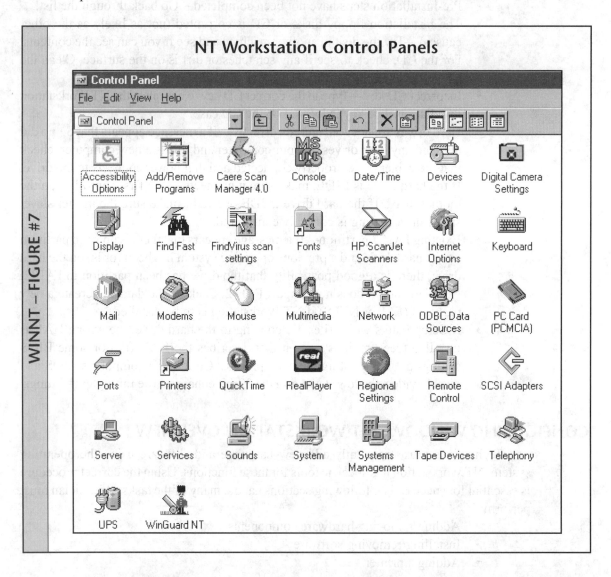

To access the control panels, click on the *Start* button. Point to the *Settings* option and then click on the *Control Panel* menu option. The number of control panels is determined by what hardware is installed in the computer. WINNT Table #5 lists common control panels and their functions.

NT Control Panel Functions

Control Panel	Function
Accessibility Options	Controls keyboard, sounds, display, and mouse behavior for people with disabilities
Add/Remove Programs	Used to install software applications
Console	Configures the command prompt window
Date/Time	Used to set the date and time
Devices	Used to start and stop device drivers; used to control how the device driver loads
Display	Used to install a monitor driver and configure monitor settings
Internet	Controls Internet connection settings
Keyboard	Used to install a keyboard driver and configure keyboard settings
Modems	Used to install a modem driver and configure modem settings
Multimedia	Used to install multimedia device drivers, configure properties for audio, video, and MIDI devices, and configure settings for playing audio CDs
Network	Used to install NIC drivers, add network software, and configure network connections
Ports	Used to configure serial ports
Printers	Used to add, remove, and configure printer settings
SCSI Adapters	Used to add and configure SCSI device drivers
Services	Stops, pauses, restarts, and configures various services including the event log service
Sounds	Used to change sounds used by Windows
System	Allows viewing system information and changing parameters related to system performance such as virtual memory
Tape Devices	Used to add tape device driver and configure tape device parameters
UPS	Configures UPS settings

WIINNT – TABLE #5

Knowing what control panel to use and what specific control panel tab to use to install a hardware device driver is sometimes confusing in NT. The following procedures are to help with the most common NT hardware installations.
- To load a monitor device driver, use the *Display* control panel, click on the *Settings* tab, and click on the *Change* button.

- To load a keyboard driver, use the *Keyboard* control panel, click on the *General* tab, and click on the *Change* button. To load a modem driver, use the *Modem* control panel, click on the *Add* button.
- To load a multimedia device driver such as a CD-ROM, joystick, or MIDI driver, use the *Multimedia* control panel, click on the *Devices* tab, and click on the *Add* button.
- To install a NIC driver, use the *Network* control panel, click on the *Adapters* tab, and click on the *Add* button.
- To install a SCSI adapter device driver, use the *SCSI Adapter* control panel, click on the *Drivers* tab, and click on the *Add* button.
- To install a tape drive device driver, use the *Tape Devices* control panel, click on the *Detect* button.

Two important things to remember about NT Workstation: (1) you must have administrator rights to install a hardware driver and (2) the driver needs to be compatible with NT.

INSTALLING/REMOVING SOFTWARE

No computer is complete without software. Various types of applications can be used with NT including DOS applications, 16-bit Windows applications, and 32-bit Windows applications. Not all older applications are compatible with NT, but the only way you can know is to load the application and try it. 16-bit applications are installed using the directions from the software manufacturer. 32-bit applications are installed using the Add/Remove Programs control panel. To access this control panel, click on the *Start* button. Point to the *Settings* option and click on the *Control Panel* menu option. When the control panel window appears, click on the *Add/Remove Programs* control panel. Follow the directions on the screen or the directions from the software manufacturer.

DOS applications run in a special environment called **NTVDM** (NT Virtual DOS Machine). NTVDM simulates a DOS environment inside NT Workstation. Each DOS application loaded into RAM (started), loads into one NTVDM. The environment the DOS application runs in can be customized through NT Workstation. Using My Computer or Explorer, right-click on the EXE file or shortcut that starts the DOS application. Select the *Properties* option from the drop-down menu. A Properties screen appears with tabs across the top. All of the settings made through this window are collectively known as the DOS application's **PIF** (**Program Information File**).

The two most common tabs used with DOS applications are Memory and Screen. The Memory tab allows setting memory parameters for the NTVDM that the DOS application is using. With this tab, you can specify a specific amount of expanded and extended memory. WINNT Figure #8 shows the Memory tab for the DOS application executable file called SHERLOCK.EXE.

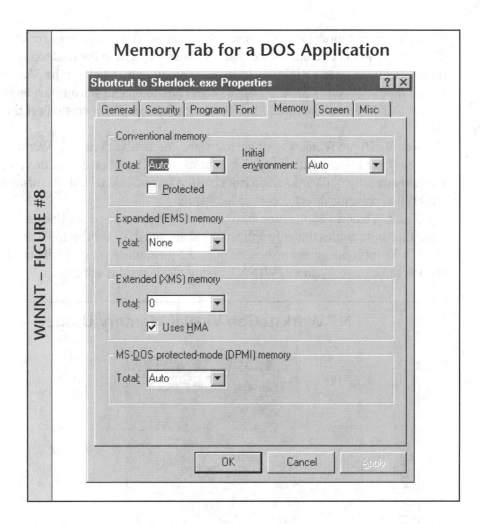

The other commonly used tab for a DOS application is the Screen tab. The Screen tab allows the DOS application to run in full-screen mode (the application takes up the entire screen and has no common Windows buttons) or in a window mode (the application runs inside a window that has common Windows buttons to control the window).

Not all DOS applications are compatible with NT Workstation. The only way to know is to install the software and attempt to execute it. If it doesn't work, try adjusting the memory settings described above for the specific amount and type of memory the DOS application requires. DOS applications frequently try to directly access hardware and NT has a built-in feature called HAL (Hardware Abstraction Layer) that prevents direct access to hardware.

16-bit Windows applications use WOW (Win16 on WIN32) which is a WIN16 environment simulator running inside a NTVDM. All 16-bit Windows applications run in a single NTVDM, which means that when one 16-bit Windows application fails, they all fail. You can configure each 16-bit Windows application to operate in its own NTVDM.

Create a shortcut for the icon that starts the program. (Use Explorer to create the shortcut. Click and drag the executable file that starts the program to the desktop and a shortcut is automatically created.) Right-click on the shortcut icon. Click on the *Shortcut* tab. Click on the *Run in Separate Memory Space* checkbox to enable starting the application in its own NTVDM and preventing other 16-bit applications from crashing if this application fails.

Not all 16-bit Windows applications are compatible with NT Workstation. This is because some 16-bit Windows applications use a VxD (virtual device driver) that accesses hardware directly. NT Workstation has a built-in feature called HAL (Hardware Abstraction Layer) that prevents direct access to hardware.

32-bit Windows application have their own memory space allocated—2GB for the operating system files that all applications share and 2GB for the application. This means that if a 32-bit application crashes, no other 32-bit application will fail because it does not use the same memory space. WINNT Figure #9 shows this concept.

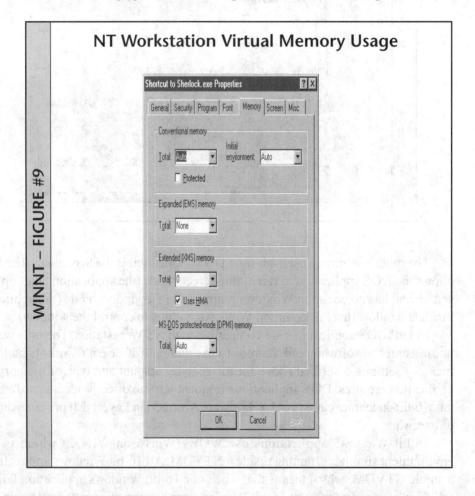

ADDING A PRINTER

Printers normally connect to a computer through the parallel port, a USB port, or through a local area network. Only local printers (printers directly connected to the computer) will be covered in this chapter. To install a printer under NT, use the Add Printer wizard. To access the Add Printer wizard, click on the *Start* button. Point to the *Settings* option and then click on the *Printers* option. Double-click on the *Add Printer* icon. WINNT Figure #10 shows this concept.

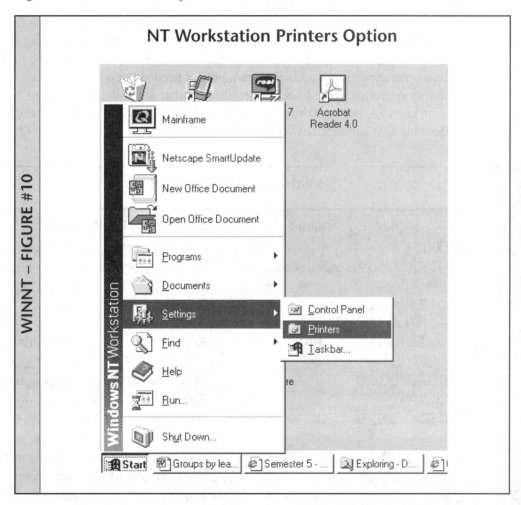

If you are installing a local printer, you must install an NT print driver that is specific for the printer model attached to the computer. An exercise in the Printers chapter demonstrates how to install a printer attached to an NT Workstation computer.

If multiple printers are available to an NT Workstation computer, one printer is marked as the default printer. A default printer is the one to which a computer prints unless a different one is chosen. To set the default printer, click on the *Start* button, point to the *Settings* option, and click on the *Printers* drop-down menu option. The Printers folder opens. Right-click on the printer that will be the default printer. From the drop down menu, click on the *Set As Default* option.

OVERVIEW OF THE BOOT PROCESS

With NT Workstation and Windows 2000, two types of partitions are important during the boot process—the system partition and the boot partition. The **system partition** is the active drive partition that has the files needed to load the operating system. The system partition is normally the C: drive (the active partition). The **boot partition** is the partition or logical drive where the NT operating system files are located. One thing that people sometimes forget is that the system partition and the boot partition can be on the same partition. These partitions are where certain files needed to boot are located.

Every operating system needs specific files that allow the computer to boot. These files are known as **system files** or startup files. The system files and their specific location on the hard drive are listed in WINNT Table #6.

Windows NT Boot Files

Startup Filename	File Location
BOOT.INI	Root directory of system partition
BOOTSECT.DOS (needed if dual or multi-boot system)	Root directory of system partition
HAL.DLL	%systemroot%\SYSTEM32*
NTBOOTDD.SYS (used with SCSI drives that have the SCSI BIOS disabled)	Root directory of system partition
NTDETECT.COM	Root directory of system partition
NTLDR	Root directory of system partition
NTOSKRNL.EXE	%systemroot%\SYSTEM32*
	*%systemroot% is the boot partition and the name of the folder where Windows NT is installed (normally C:\WINNT)

WINNT – TABLE #6

Information from Microsoft can be confusing at times because of the %systemroot% and %systemdrive% entries. This is because computers can be partitioned differently. If you install Windows NT Workstation onto a drive letter (a partition or logical drive) other than the active partition (normally C:), the startup files can be on two different drive letters. Also, you do not have to take the default folder name of WINNT to install NT. To account for these different scenarios, Microsoft uses the %systemroot% to represent the boot partition—the partition and folder that contains the majority of the NT Workstation files. On a computer with a single operating system, this would be C:\WINNT. The %systemdrive% represents the root directory of the same drive letter. On a computer with a single operating system, this would be C:\.

The boot process is actually quite involved, but the major steps are as follows:

1. The computer is powered on.
2. POST executes.
3. BIOS searches for an active partition on the hard drive.
4. BIOS reads the Master Boot Record, then locates and loads the information into sector 0 of the system partition. The contents of sector 0 define the type of file system and the location of the bootstrap loader file, then start the bootstrap loader. With NT Workstation, this file is NTLDR.
5. NTLDR starts the file system.
6. NTLDR reads the BOOT.INI file and displays the various operating system choices. If something other than NT Workstation is chosen, the BOOTSECT.DOS file takes over. If NT Workstation is chosen, the NTDETECT.COM file executes.
7. NTDETECT.COM detects the computer's hardware. A message appears on the screen saying "NTDETECT V4.0 Checking Hardware…"
8. NTLDR passes the hardware information to the NTOSKRNL.EXE file and displays the Startup screen. The message on the screen is "OS Loader V4.0." Press *Spacebar* now to invoke Hardware Profile/Last Known Good menu. This menu stays on the screen three to five seconds.
9. The operating system kernel, NTOSKRNL.EXE, executes and the HAL.DLL file loads. The message on the screen displays "Microsoft® Windows NT™ Version 4.0 (Build 1381) 1 System Processor (64 MB Memory)."
10. The registry key HKEY_LOCAL_MACHINE\SYSTEM loads. This registry key is located in the %SYSTEMROOT%\SYSTEM32\CONFIG\SYSTEM folder. This key has information found during the hardware detection process.
11. The WINLOGON.EXE file executes and the logon screen appears.

TROUBLESHOOTING THE BOOT PROCESS

Various problems exist that cause NT Workstation to not boot, but boot problems can usually be narrowed down to two main areas: (1) missing or corrupted boot files, or (2) configuration problems. When boot files are missing or corrupted, different error messages can appear. WINNT Table #7 shows some of the most common error messages seen with missing or corrupt boot files.

Windows NT Workstation Boot Problems

WINNT – TABLE #7

Symptom	Cause
Message Boot: Couldn't find NTLDR. Please insert another disk.	NTLDR file is missing or corrupt.
Message Error opening NTDETECT. Press any key to continue.	Timeout option for the boot loader located in the BOOT.INI file is set to 0 or the path of the operating system in the boot loader section of the BOOT.INI file is not the same as a path listed in the [operating systems] section of BOOT.INI.
Message The system did not load because of a computer disk hardware configuration problem. Could n ot read from the selected boot disk. Check the boot path and disk hardware. Please check the Windows NT documentation about hardware disk configuration and your hardware reference manuals for additional information. Boot failed.	The device or partition information regarding a path in the [operating systems] section of BOOT.INI is wrong.
Message multi(0)disk(0)rdisk(0) partition(1)\winnt\system\ntoskrnl.exe The system did not load because it cannot find the following file: C:\WINNT\SYSTEM32\NTOSKRNL.EXE. Please reinstall a copy of the above file.	The path information in the BOOT.INI file's [operating systems] section is wrong or NTLDR and/or BOOT.INI files are not in the root directory of the system partition.
Message I/O error accessing boot sector file multi(0)disk(0)rdisk(0)partition(1) \bootsect.dos	The BOOTSECT.DOS file is missing or corrupted. Restore the file from a backup copy.
When you select an operating system from the operating system selection screen, the selected operating system does not load.	Corrupted BOOT.INI file. The path information in the [operating systems] section of BOOT.INI is wrong.
Message "Invalid Partition Table"	A virus is on the hard drive or there is an error in the BOOT.INI file.
Blue screen appears after a power failure	The boot files are missing or corrupt.

When any of these error messages appear, the most common tool used is the ERD (Emergency Repair Disk). The ERD is a disk that can be made during the installation process and after NT Workstation is installed. An entire section is devoted to the ERD immediately following this section.

Other problems that can occur during the boot process are POST errors, STOP errors, and blue screens. POST errors are normally caused by an invalid/incorrect hardware configuration or a faulty piece of hardware. If NT Workstation has booted correctly prior to this POST error, press the *spacebar* on the keyboard when the message, "OS Loader V4.0. Press spacebar NOW to invoke Hardware Profile/Last Known Good menu" appears on the screen. By default, this message stays on the screen for approximately five seconds. Once you press the spacebar, a menu appears. Press the letter *L* to access the Last Known Good Configuration option. This allows you to change the configuration of the new device or disable it until you can determine the exact problem or get an NT driver for the device.

The same process of accessing the Last Known Good Configuration is used if you get a blue screen after a configuration change. If a blue screen appears after a power failure, there is a good chance that the boot files are missing or corrupt. Use the ERD or copy over the boot files to the correct location on the hard drive. If a STOP message appears, the registry may be corrupt. The registry can be reinstalled using a current ERD for the computer or reinstall the registry from a backup.

In older operating systems, a startup disk was used to begin the troubleshooting process. With NT Workstation, the startup disk is actually the set of three installation disks that came with the NT Workstation CD. If you cannot find these, you can go to any computer that has the same version of Windows NT Workstation loaded and make a set. Insert the NT Workstation CD, click on the *Start* button, and click on the *Run* option. In the dialog box, type *x:\i386\winnt32.exe /ox* where *x* is the drive letter that represents the CD-ROM. Click on the *OK* button and follow the prompts on the screen. You will need three floppy disks to complete this procedure. The installation disks are used when repairing a system using the ERD.

CREATING AN EMERGENCY REPAIR DISK

The ERD (Emergency Repair Disk) is used to fix system file problems, the partition boot sector, and startup environment settings, all of which can cause a computer to not boot properly. The ERD is unique to a specific computer. The ERD should be recreated anytime changes are made to the computer's configuration. An ERD can also be created during the installation process but it still needs to be recreated whenever changes are made.

To create an ERD, click on the *Start* button and click on the *Run* menu option. In the dialog box, type *RDISK /S*. If an error occurs, type the correct path for the RDISK program. By default, RDISK is located in the SYSTEM32 subfolder under WINNT. The RDISK program creates a disk that can be used for emergency repairs. The /S switch causes a backup of the Security Accounts Manager (SAM) database as well as the entire registry in a subfolder under WINNT called Repair. When prompted to create the ERD, click on the *Yes* button if you are simply updating the existing ERD.

If the computer system will not work and you want to use the ERD, you must actually start the NT Workstation installation process and get to the Welcome to Setup screen. Use the NT Workstation setup disks (you must get through Disk 3 before you see the Welcome to Setup screen). Once presented with the Welcome to Setup screen, press the *R* option, which is the To repair a damaged Windows NT version 4.0 installation, press R option that allows you to use the ERD to fix the computer. Once you press *R*, a menu appears. The menu has four selections that are all enabled. Press *Enter* to start the process. A prompt appears telling you to insert the ERD. The CHKDSK program runs and verifies the hard disk clusters. Each operating system file is checked and reinstalled if the file is missing or corrupt. The system and security portion of the registry is replaced (if you confirm that you want them replaced), and the boot sector and boot files are replaced. An exercise at the end of the chapter illustrates how to create an ERD.

NT COMMAND PROMPT

Understanding how to work from a command prompt is very important to a technician. One of my favorite sayings is that when an operating system does not work, you are looking at nothing but a command prompt. From the command prompt, you can start programs, manipulate files and folders, start and stop services, repair the master boot record, repair the boot sectors, or format the hard drive.

To work from the command prompt, three common methods exist to access the prompt:

- Click on the *Start* button, point to *Programs*, and click on the *Command Prompt* option.
- Click on the *Start* button, click on the *Run* option, type *cmd* in the dialog box and click on the *OK* button.
- Click on the *Start* button, click on the *Run* option, type *command* in the dialog box and click on the *OK* button.

More than one command prompt window can be opened at a time and each window can be customized in terms of what colors are used, the size of font, etc. To modify how the window looks, click on the *Control* menu button (upper left corner) and click on the *Properties* option. The size of the font used inside the window is controlled on the Font tab. The type of memory used for any commands typed in the command prompt window is controlled by the Memory tab. Whether the command prompt is placed inside a window or whether it is full-screen is controlled with the Screen tab. The Misc tab is used to control what Windows keystrokes are active and whether or not a screen saver is permitted. WINNT Figure #11 shows the command prompt Properties tabs.

WINNT – FIGURE #11

NT Command Prompt Window Properties

MS-DOS Prompt Properties   [?] [X]

Program | Font | Memory | Screen | Misc

MS
DOS
[MS-DOS Prompt]

Cmd line: [C:\WINDOWS\command.com]

Working: [   ]

Batch file: [   ]

Shortcut key: [None   ]

Run: [Normal window   ▼]

☑ Close on exit

[Advanced...]   [Change Icon...]

[OK]   [Cancel]   [Apply]

Some of the most frequently used commands from the command prompt are outlined below. The items enclosed by [] (brackets) are optional. Items in italics are command-specific values that you must enter. When the items are separated by a | (bar), one of the items must be typed.

ATTRIB   This command is used to control the attribute for a file or folder.

Syntax: attrib [+|-c] [+|-h] [+|-r] [+|-s] [*drive:*] [*path*] *filename*

Explanation: + adds an attribute

– takes an attribute away.

c is the compressed attribute.

h is the hidden attribute.

r is the read-only attribute.

s is the system attribute.

[*drive:*] is the drive where the file is located.

[*path*] is the directory/subdirectory where the file is located.

filename is the name of the file.

Example: **attrib +h c:\cheryl.bat** sets the attribute to hidden for a file called CHERYL.BAT located on the hard drive.

Notes: The DIR command (typed without any switches) is used to see what attributes are currently set. You may set more than one attribute at a time.

CD This command is used to navigate through the directory structure.

Syntax: cd [*drive:*] [*path*] [..]

Explanation: [*drive:*] specifies the drive (if a different one than the current drive) to which you want to change.

[*path*] is the directory/subdirectory to reach the folder.

[..] is used to change to the parent directory (moves you back one directory).

Examples: C:\WINNT>**cd..**

C:\

This command moves you from the WINNT directory (folder) to the parent directory, which is the root directory (C:\).

C:\>**cd \WINNT**

This command moves you from the root directory to the WINNT directory on the C: drive.

CHKDSK This command checks a disk for physical problems, lost clusters, cross-linked files, and directory errors. If necessary, the chkdsk command repairs the disk, marks bad sectors, recovers information, and displays the status of the disk.

Syntax: chkdsk [*drive:*] [/p] [/r] [/c] [/f] [/i] [/l:size] [/v] [/x]

Explanation: [*drive:*] specifies the drive to check.

[/p] forces the chkdsk check even if the volume is not identified as being bad.

[/r] locates bad sectors and attempts recovery on the sector's information.

[/c] skips cycle checking of NTFS volume folders.

[/f] fixes drive errors.

[/i] checks only index entries on NTFS volumes.

[/l:size] the /l: must be part of the command followed by the size (in kilobytes) of the log file for NTFS volumes.

[/v] With a FAT volume, the /v switch shows the full path for every file. With a NTFS volume, cleanup messages are displayed.

[/x] With NTFS, the switch forces the volume to dismount before checking the volume.

Example: **chkdsk d:** This command checks the disk structure on the D: drive.

Notes: This command can be used without switches. In order for this command to work, the AUTOCHK.EXE must be loaded in the SYSTEM32 folder or used with the correct path and run from the NT Workstation CD.

CLS   The *cls* command clears the screen of any previously typed commands.

Example: C:\WINNT>**cls**

CMD   The *cmd* command is executed from the Run dialog box. (Click on *Start* button, click on *Run* option, and type *CMD.EXE* in the dialog box.) A DOS window appears. Type *EXIT* from the prompt to close the window.

Syntax: cmd [/c *string*]

Explanation: [/c *string*] specifies that the command interpreter is to perform the command specified by the *string* option and then stop.

Example: **cmd /c chkdsk d:** This command runs the chkdsk program on the D: hard drive volume using the command line.

CONVERT   The *convert* command is used to convert a FAT partition to NTFS.

Syntax: convert [*drive:*] /FS:NTFS [/v] [*nametable: filename*]

Explanation: [*drive:*] specifies the drive to check.
[/v] is for verbose which means the output will contain more details.
[nametable: *filename*] creates a translation table with the name of the file wing that is typed with the *filename* parameter. The table is placed in the root directory of the converted drive.

Example: **convert C: /FS:NTFS /v** This command converts the C: partition from FAT to NTFS and displays more details on the output.

COPY   The *copy* command is used to copy a single file to the destination that you specify.

Syntax: copy *source* [*target*]

Explanation: *source* is the file that you want to copy and it includes the drive letter and the path, if it is different from your current location.
[*target*] is the location you want to put the file and it includes the drive letter and path if it is different from your current location.

Example: **copy c:\cheryl.bat a:**

This command takes a file called CHERYL.BAT that is located in the root directory of the hard drive and copies it to the floppy drive.

Notes: You do not have to put a target if the file is going to the current location specified by the command prompt. If a file already exists, you will be prompted whether or not to overwrite the file.

DATE   The *date* command is used to display the current date or allows you to change the date.

Syntax: date [*mm-dd-yy*]

Explanation: [*mm-dd-yy*] is the date you specify where *mm* stands for the month, *dd* stands for day and *yy* stands for year.

Example: **date**

Notes: If you do not want to change the date, simply press *Enter*.

DEL   The *del* command is used to delete a file.

Syntax: del *name* [*/p*] [*/f*] [*/s*] [*/q*] [*/a*]

Explanation: *name* is the file or directory (folder) that you want to delete and it includes the drive letter and the path if it is different from your current location.
[*/p*] is used to prompt for confirmation before deleting.
[*/f*] is used to force read-only files to be deleted.
[*/s*] is used to delete files from all subdirectories.
[*/q*] means quiet mode which does not prompt for confirmation.
[*/a*] is used to select files based on their attribute where the attributes are R, H, S, and A. A + (plus sign) before the attribute means "select it" and a – (minus sign) before the attribute means "do not select it."

Example: C:\WINNT>**del c:\cheryl.bat**

This command deletes a file called CHERYL.BAT that is located in the root directory of the hard drive.

Notes: You cannot use wildcard characters such as * and ? with this command while in the Recovery Console.

DIR   The *dir* command is used to list files and folders and their attributes.

Syntax: dir [*drive:*] [*path*] [*filename*] [*/a*] [*/b*] [*/c*] [*/d*] [*/l*] [*/n*] [*/o*] [*/p*] [*/q*] [*/s*] [*/t*] [*/w*] [*/x*] [*/4*]

Explanation: [*drive:*] is the drive letter where the files are located.
[*path*] is the directory/subdirectory to reach the folder.
[*filename*] is the name of a specific file.
[*/a*] is used to display files that have specific attributes where the attributes are D, R, H, A, and S. D is for directories; R is for read-only; H is for hidden; A is for archive; and S is for system files. A + (plus sign) before the attribute means "select it" and a – (minus sign) before the attribute means "do not select it."
[*/b*] is for barebones format (it doesn't show heading or summary information).
[*/c*] shows the file sizes with the thousands separator.
[*/d*] displays the file listing in a wide format sorted by column.
[*/l*] displays the listing in lowercase.
[*/n*] displays the listing in long list format.
[*/o*] displays the listing in sorted order. Options you can use after the "o" are E, D, G, N, and S. E is by alphabetic file extension; D is by date and time with the oldest

listing shown first; G shows the directories listed first; N displays by alphabetic name; and S displays by size from smallest to largest.

[/p] displays the information one page at a time.

[/q] displays the owner of the file(s).

[/s] includes subdirectories in the listing.

[/t] controls which specific time field is shown where the types of time fields are A, C, and W. A is for the last access date/time with the earliest shown first; C is for the creation date/time; and W is for the last written date/time.

[/w] shows the listing in wide format.

[/x] shows the 8.3 filename listing for long filenames.

[/4] displays four digit years instead of two digit years.

Example: **dir c:\winnt**

This command shows all of the files and folders (and their associated attributes) for the WINNT folder that is located on the C: drive.

Notes: You can use wildcard characters such as * and ? with this command in the Recovery Console. The attributes you can see are (1) *a* for archive, (2) *c* for compressed, (3) *d* for directory, (4) *e* for encrypted, (5) *h* for hidden, (6) *p* for reparse point, (7) *r* for read-only, and (8) *s* for system file.

DISKCOPY The *diskcopy* command is used to make an exact copy of one disk and put it on another.

Syntax: diskcopy [*drive1:*] [*drive2:*]

Explanation: [*drive1:*] is the source drive letter followed by a *:* (colon).

[*drive2:*] is the destination drive letter followed by a *:* (colon).

Example: C:\WINNT>**diskcopy a: a:**

Notes: The drive letters are only needed if the command prompt is a different drive and location.

DOSKEY The *doskey* command is used to start the DOSKEY program that allows commands to be recalled easily.

Syntax: doskey

Explanation: *sourcedrive:* is the drive letter that contains the original disk.

targetdrive: is the drive letter that will contain the copied disk.

Example: **diskcopy a: a:**

This command makes a copy of the disk that is currently in the A: drive, (the source drive), and prompts you to insert another disk, (the target drive), into the A: drive in order to make a copy of the original disk.

Notes: Since most computers contain only one floppy disk, you can copy a disk using the same drive letter for the *sourcedrive:* and the *targetdrive:*.

EXIT   The *exit* command exits the command prompt by closing the command prompt window.

Example: C:\WINNT>**exit**

EXPAND   The *expand* command is used to uncompress a file from the NT Workstation CD or a CAB file.

Syntax: expand *source* [*/f:filespec*] [*destination*] [*/y*] [*/d*]

Explanation: *source* is the name of the file including the path that you want to uncompress.
[*/f:filespec*] is the parameter used if a source contains more than one file.
[*destination*] is the path to where you want to place the uncompressed file.
[*/y*] is the parameter used if you don't want to be prompted before overwriting an existing file.
[*/d*] is the parameter used when you do not want to expand the folder that is contained in the source parameter.

Example: **expand.exe system._ system**

Notes: You may not use wildcard characters with the *source* parameter. You may use wildcard characters with the */f:filespec* parameter.

FDISK   The *fdisk* command is used to partition a FAT partition, repair the hard drive's Master Boot Record, and remove a virus from the Mmaster Boot Record.

Syntax: fdisk [*/mbr*]

Explanation: [*mbr*] is used to repair the hard drive's Master Boot Record and/or remove a virus from the Master Boot Record.

Example: **fdisk /mbr**

FORMAT   The *format* command is used to format a disk and can be used to format it for a particular file system.

Syntax: format [*driveletter:*] [*/q*] [*/fs:filesystem*] [*/a:size*] [*/c*] [*/f:size*] [*/n:sectors*] [*/t:tracks*]
[*/v:label*] [*/x*] [*/1*] [*/4*] [*/8*]

Explanation: [*driveletter:*] is drive letter for the disk or hard drive volume that you want to format.
[*/q*] is the parameter used if you want to perform a quick format.
[*/fs:filesystem*] is the parameter used if you want to specify a file system. Valid values are as follows:

    FAT
    FAT32
    NTFS

[*/a:size*] The /a: must be part of the command followed by the default allocation unit size. The different units supported by the three file systems are as follows:
    NTFS: 512, 1024, 2048, 4096, 8192, 16K, 32K, and 64K

FAT: 512, 1024, 2048, 4096, 8192, 16K, 32K, 64K, and (128K, 256K for sector size that is larger than 512 bytes)

FAT32: 512, 1024, 2048, 4096, 8192, 16K, 32K, 64K, and (128K, 256K for sector size that is larger than 512 bytes)

[*/c*] is used to compress the files on the volume by default.

[*/f:size*] The */f:* must be part of the command followed by the size for floppy disk to format. The different sizes supported are as follows: 160, 180, 320, 360, 640, 720, 1.2, 1.44, 2.88, or 20.8.

[*/n:sectors*] The */n:* must be part of the command followed by the number of sectors per track.

[*/t:tracks*] The */t:* must be part of the command followed by the number of tracks per disk side.

[*/v:label*] The */v:* must be part of the command followed by the name of the volume assigned

[*/x*] is used to dismount the volume first, if necessary.

[*/1*] is used to format a single side of a floppy disk.

[*/4*] is used to format a 5.25" 360K floppy disk in a 1.2M drive.

[*/8*] is used to format eight sectors per track.

Example: **format c: /fs:ntfs**

Notes: If no */fs:filesystem* parameter is specified, the NTFS file system is used. FAT is FAT16. FAT16 hard drive volumes cannot be more than 4GB in size, but should be formatted to 2GB to be compatible with DOS, Windows 3.x, and Windows 9x.

HELP This command displays information about specific commands.

Syntax: help [*command*]

Explanation: [*command*] is the name of the command for which you want help.

Example: **help expand**

Notes: If you do not specify the *command* parameter when using the Help command, all commands are listed.

LABEL This command is used to create, change, or delete the volume label of a disk.

Syntax: label [*driveletter:*] [*label*]

Explanation: [*driveletter:*] is the drive letter for the disk or hard drive volume on which you want to look at or control the name.

[*label*] is the new volume label (the name of the drive volume).

Example: **label a: labdisk** puts the name *labdisk* on the disk in the A: drive.

MD This command is used to create a directory (folder).

Syntax: md [*driveletter:*] [*dirname*]

Explanation: [*driveletter:*] is the drive letter for the disk or volume on which you want to create a directory (folder). It can also include the path.

[*dirname*] is the parameter used to name the directory (folder).

Example: **md c:\TEST**

Notes: You may not use wildcard characters with this command.

MEM This command is used to display the amount of available memory for a NTVDM session.

Syntax: mem [*/p*] [*/d*] [*/c*]

Explanation: [*/p*] stands for program and is used to display the programs currently loaded into memory.

[*/d*] stands for debug and it displays the status of programs loaded into memory as well as drivers.

[*/c*] stands for classify and it displays the status of programs loaded into conventional memory as well as the UMA.

MORE The *more* command is used to display a text file.

Syntax: more *filename* [*/c*] [*/e*] [*/p*] [*/s*] [*/t#*]

Explanation: *filename* is the path and name of the text file you want to display on the screen.

[*/c*] clears the screen before displaying a page of information.

[*/e*] enables extended features.

[*/p*] expands form feed characters.

[*/s*] takes multiple blank lines and condenses them into one blank line.

[*/t#*] The */t* must be part of the command followed by the number of spaces used to expand tabs. The normal setting is eight spaces.

Example: **more c:\boot.ini**

Notes: The spacebar allows you to view the next page of a text file. The *Enter* key allows you to scroll through the text file one line at a time. The *ESC* key allows you to quit viewing the text file.

PATH This command is used to display or set the search path used in locating executable files.

Syntax: path [*driveletter:*] [*path1*][*;path2*][*;path3...*]

Explanation: [*driveletter:*] specifies the drive letter for the drive to search.

[*path1*] is the name of the directory/subdirectory you want to have in the search path.

[*;path2*] is another directory/subdirectory to include in the search path.

Example: **path c:\winnt;c:\winnt\system32;c:\winnt\command**

Notes: Paths must be separated by a semicolon between each directory/subdirectory path.

PROMPT   The *prompt* command is used to change the default setting for how the command prompt looks.

Syntax: prompt [*option*]

Explanation: [*option*] is any text to appear as the prompt or one of the following options: $a (ampersand), $b (pipe symbol), $c (open parentheses), $d (current date), $e (ASCCI escape code 27), $f (close parentheses), $g (greater than sign), $h (backspace to delete a character that has been written to the prompt command line), $l (less than sign), $n (current drive), $p (current drive and path), $q (equal sign), $s (space), $t (current time), $v (DOS version number), $_ (ENTER-LINEFEED), $$ (dollar sign)

Examples: C:\WINNT>**prompt Cheryl's Computer$g** changes the prompt to look like Cheryl's Computer>.

C:\WINNT>**prompt cpgf** changes the prompt to look like (C:\WINNT>).

RD   This command is used to remove a directory (folder).

Syntax: rd [*driveletter:*] [*path*].

Explanation: [*driveletter:*] is the drive letter for the disk or hard drive volume that you want to remove a directory (folder).

[*path*] is the optional path and name of the directory (folder) you want to remove.

Example: **rd c:\TEST\JUNKDATA** removes a directory (folder) called JUNKDATA that is a subdirectory under a directory (folder) called TEST. This directory is located on the hard drive (C:).

Notes: You do not have to use the *driveletter:* parameter if the default drive letter is the same as the one that contains the directory to be deleted.

REN   The *ren* command is used to rename a file or directory (folder).

Syntax: ren [*driveletter:*] [*path*] *name1 name2*

Explanation: [*driveletter:*] is the drive letter for the disk or hard drive volume that you want to rename a file or a directory (folder).

[*path*] is the optional path telling the operating system where to find the file or directory (folder) you want to rename.

name1 is the old name of the file or directory (folder) that you want to rename.

name2 is the new name of the file or directory (folder).

Example: **ren c:\cheryl.bat c:\newcheryl.bat**

Notes: The renamed file cannot be placed in a new location with this command. Move or copy the file after you rename it if that is what you want to do. The * and ? wildcard characters are not supported.

SCANREG   The *scanreg* utility is used to scan a registry for strings.

Syntax: scanreg [*-s searchstring*] [*-k*] [*-v*] [*-d*] [*-r rootkey*] [*-c*] [*-e*] [*-n*]

Explanation: [*-s searchstring*] is used when searching for a specific string of letters (*searchstring*).

[*-k*] specifies to search keynames.

[*-v*] specifies to search value names.

[*-d*] specifies to search data.

[*-r rootkey*] specifies from which subtree to start searching; parameters are HKEY_LOCAL_MACHINE (or abbreviate as *lm*), HKEY_CURRENT_USER (or abbreviate as *cu*, HKEY_CLASSES_ROOT (or abbreviate as *cr*), and HKEY_USERS (or abbreviate as *us*).

[*-c*] specifies that the search is case sensitive.

[*-e*] returns only exact matches.

[*-n*] disables color output.

Example: **scanreg -s Windows -k -v -d**

Notes: The *scanreg* command is available on the NT Resource CD.

You must use the -k, -v, -d, or any combination of the three options.

The default subtree to start searching is HKEY_CURRENT_USER.

SCANREG searches are not case sensitive by default.

By default, SCANREG returns all matches.

START   The *start* command is used to run a program

Syntax: start [*path*] [*/min*] [*/max*] [*/separate*] [*/low*] [*/normal*] [*/high*] [*/realtime*]

Explanation: [*path*] is the drive letter, a colon, and the path to get to the program.

[*/min*] runs the program in a minimized window.

[*/max*] runs the program in a maximized window.

[*/separate*] runs 16-bit Windows programs in a separate NTVDM.

[*/low*] starts the application with a low idle priority class.

[*/normal*] starts the application with a normal priority class.

[*/high*] starts the application with a high priority class.

[*/realtime*] starts the program with a realtime priority class.

Example: **start c:\games\space.exe /separate** starts the SPACE program in its own NTVDM.

SYSEDIT   *Sysedit* is used to automatically open the AUTOEXEC.BAT, CONFIG.SYS, WIN.INI, and SYSTEM.INI files. Each of these files can be used by older applications and allows older 16-bit applications to run under NT.

Syntax: sysedit

TIME   The *time* command is used to display or change the computer's internal clock.

Syntax: time [*hh:mm:ss.ss*]

Explanation: [*hh:mm:ss.ss*] is the format used to change the time where *hh* is hours for a 24-hour clock, *mm* is minutes (0 to 59), and *ss.ss* is seconds (0 to 99) and hundredths of seconds. The hundredths of seconds is optional.

Example: **time 18:00:00** sets the clock to 6:00 p.m.

Notes: To view the system clock, just type the *time* command without any other parameters.

TREE   The *tree* command is used to graphically display a directory structure of a drive or a specific path.

Syntax: tree [*driveletter:*] [*path*]

Explanation: [*driveletter:*] is the drive that contains the directory you want to display.
[*path*] is the exact location of the directory for which you want to display the directory structure.

Example: **tree c:\winnt**

Notes: The *driveletter:* parameter is not needed if you are on the drive that contains the directory.

TYPE   The *type* command is used to display a text file.

Syntax: type *filename*

Explanation: *filename* is the path and name of the text file you want to display on the screen.

Example: **type c:\boot.ini**

Notes: The spacebar allows you to view the next page of a text file. The *Enter* key allows you to scroll through the text file one line at a time. The *ESC* key allows you to quit viewing the text file.

VER   The *ver* command is used to display the name and current version of NT.

Syntax: ver

Notes: The *ver* command does not show service pack information.

XCOPY   The *xcopy* command is used to copy files to the destination that you specify.

Syntax: copy *source* [*target*] [/w] [/p] [/c] [/q] [/f] [/i] [/l] [/u] [/s] [/e] [/t] [/k] [/r] [/h] [/a] [/m] [/n] [/z]

Explanation: *source* is the file(s) that you want to copy and it includes the drive letter and the path if it is different from your current location.

[*target*] is the location you want to put the file(s) and it includes the drive letter and path if it is different from your current location.

[/w] displays the message, "Press any key to begin copying file(s)."

[/p] prompts the confirmation of each destination file.

[/f] displays the source and destination names during copying.

[/l] creates a new destination directory if it doesn't exist.

[/u] copies only files that already exist in the destination.

[/s] copies all subdirectories from the source unless the subdirectory is empty.

[/e] copies all subdirectories from the source.

[/t] copies the subdirectory tree structure of the source without copying files.

[/k] copies and retains the read-only attribute of the source files.

[/r] copies read-only files.

[/h] copies hidden files and files with the system attribute.

[/a] copies source files that have the archive attribute set.

[/m] copies source files that have the archive attribute set and resets the attribute in the destination directory.

[/n] copies the source files using short filenames (8.3 format).

[/z] permits copying over a network in restartable mode.

Example: **xcopy c:\Cheryl*.* a:** This command takes a directory called CHERYL and copies all of the files held within that directory to the floppy drive.

Notes: You do not have to put a target if the file is going to the current location specified by the command prompt. If a file already exists, you will be asked whether or not you want to overwrite the file.

WINDOWS SCRIPTING

In a DOS environment, a batch file can provide how the operating system loads, how a particular application loads, a menu-driven environment, and other environment settings. With Windows 98, NT, and Windows 2000, Microsoft provides a Windows-based scripting tool called WSCRIPT.EXE. When the WSCRIPT tool is executed, a Windows-based dialog box appears and allows you to configure script properties.

For technicians, scripts can automate desktop shortcuts for users; and set or restrict access for the desktop, Start menu, network share mapping, network printer mapping, setting default printer, and launching applications. In Windows, scripts can be executed three different ways: (1) by double-clicking on an icon associated with a particular file, (2) by running a script from the Run dialog box, or (3) by typing WSCRIPT.EXE *script_name* (where *script_name* is the path and name of the previously created script) from the Run dialog box. The Windows scripting host is sometimes known as WSH. The scripting host is integrated into 2000 and the NT option pack and can be downloaded from Microsoft's web site. Microsoft also provides sample scripts and a tutorial.

TASK MANAGER, EVENT VIEWER, AND NT DIAGNOSTICS

Task Manager is a Windows-based utility that displays applications currently loaded into memory, processes that are currently running, microprocessor usage information, and memory usage data. To activate the Task Manager utility, press the *CTRL+ALT+DEL* keys. From the window options that appear, click on the *Task Manager* button. Two other ways toaccess Task Manager are (1) press *CTRL+ALT+ESC* and (2) right-click on the *taskbar* and then click on the *Task Manager* option.

One of the common uses of Task Manager is to exit from an application that is "hung up" or not responding. Task Manager can help with exiting the program. To exit from a 32-bit application, access the Task Manager window and click on the *Applications* tab. Locate the name of the troublesome application and click on it. Normally, the status shows the application as "not responding." Click on the *End Task* button. Close the Task Manager window.

To exit from a DOS or 16-bit Windows applications, access the Task Manager window and click on the *Processes* tab. Locate the appropriate NTVDM.EXE file that contains the program. Note that there may be more than one application running within the NTVDM if they are 16-bit Windows programs that have not been configured to run in separate NTVDMs. Click on the *End Process* button. Close the Task Manager window.

Event Viewer is a Windows tool used to monitor various events in your computer, such as when a driver or service does not start properly. One of the most common reasons a technician uses the Event Viewer is when she encounters the message "One or more services failed to start. Please see the Event Viewer for details." (As a side note, the individual administrative tool that controls the service or the Services control panel is used to manage the event. The Event Viewer is used to determine which service had the problem.)

The EventLog service starts automatically every time a computer boots. This service is what allows events to be logged. Event Viewer is then used to see the log. Event Viewer is a great troubleshooting tool because, even when a user cannot remember exactly what happens when a problem occurs, Event Viewer tracks the problems.

Event Viewer tracks three different categories of events: system events, security events, and application events. System events log events regarding system components. An example would be a driver that does not load during startup. Security events are only accessible to system administrators and contain information such as valid and invalid logon attempts and whether someone tried to access a protected file. An administrator can set what security events are logged and tracked by Event Viewer. Application events are associated with a specific program. The programmers that design the software decide which events to display in the Event Viewer's application log. All users can view the system log and the application log, but only a member of Administrators can view or enable security log information. The most commonly used log is the system log.

Access the Event Viewer by clicking on the *Start* button, pointing to the *Programs* option, pointing to the *Administrative Tools* option, and clicking on *Event Viewer*. The system events appear by default in the Event Viewer window. Double-click on any event that is shown in Event Viewer to see more information. Click the *Close* button to return to the full Event Viewer screen. To access the security events, click on the *Log* menu option. Select the *Security* option. To access application events, click on the *Log* menu option. Select the *Applications* option. To exit Event Viewer, click on the *Close* box in the upper-right corner or click on the *Log* menu option and select the *Exit* option.

Each system event is logged as one event per line. The following list describes each of the Event Viewer headings and what can be found below each heading:

- *Date* is the date the event occurred.
- *Time* is the time the event occurred.
- *Source* is the application, driver, system program, system component such as *the serial port, etc. that logged the event.*
- *Category* is the type of event such as logon, logoff, or policy change. This heading is mainly used with security events. Event is a number assigned by NT to a given event.
- *User* is the user logged on at the time the event occurred.
- *Computer* is the name of the computer on which the event occurred.

The Event Viewer can display five different types of events. The events are shown in WINNT Table #8.

NT Event Viewer Symbols

Symbol	Type of Event	Explanation
Blue circle with lower case "i"	Information	Normal system operations such as the system being initialized or shut down.
Yellow circle with exclamation mark inside	Warning	An event that is not critical, but one that you might want to take a look at. The system can still function, but some feature(s) may not be available.
Red hexagon with the words STOP inside	Error	An event failed. A specific event failed such as a service or device that failed to initialize properly.
Padlock symbol	Success Audit	You can audit a specific event. If successful, this symbol appears.
Key symbol	Failure Audit	When you specify a specific event to audit and the event fails, the yellow lock appears. An example is auditing a system login and someone tries to login that does not have a valid username or password.

WIINNT – TABLE #8

No new events are shown when the Event Viewer is accessed. To update the Event Viewer, press the *F5* key when the Event Viewer is active.

Sometimes a technician may need to clear all previous events in order to see what is currently happening with a particular problem. To restart event logging, click on the *Log* menu option. Click on the *Clear All Events* menu option. Click on the *No* button when asked if you want to save the log. Click on the *Yes* button when asked if you are sure that you want to clear the log. This process clears all prior logged events and only displays events that occur from this point forward. Press the *F5* key to refresh the Event Viewer screen. Also note that once events are cleared from the log, they cannot be retrieved. Save the events when prompted, if you want to keep the events that are currently logged before clearing the log.

If an error message appears stating that the Event Viewer log is full, start the *Event Viewer.* Click on the *Log* menu option and then click on the *Log Settings* selection. The Event Log Settings dialog box appears. Locate the *Change Settings For* option. Click on the *down arrow* and select the *log* to modify. This will normally be the system log or security log. To change the maximum amount of hard disk space allocated to the specific log, use the arrow in the *Maximum Log Size* text box to select up to a maximum size of 512K. You can also change how long events are kept. Locate the *Event Log* Wrapping section. Click on one of the following: *Overwrite events as needed, Overwrite events older than 0 days,* or *Do not overwrite events*. WINNT Figure #12 shows what the settings screen looks like.

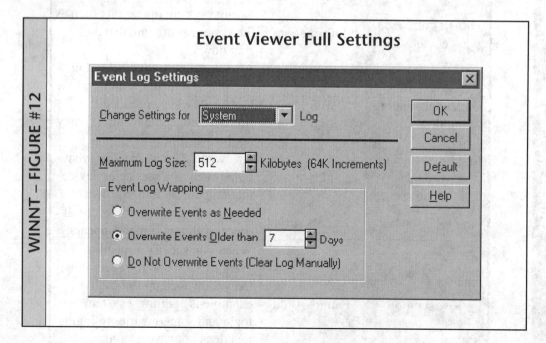

WINNT – FIGURE #12

NT Diagnostics is a utility that allows viewing configuration information about the computer's hardware, installed device drivers, and installed services. NT Diagnostics can help when troubleshooting configuration problems. The utility does not really perform any diagnostics; it simply displays information. To access NT Diagnostics, click on the *Start* button, point to *Programs*, point to *Administrative Tools (Common)*, and click on the *Windows NT Diagnostics* option. The tabs across the top of the window include Version, System, Display, Drives, Memory, Services, Resources, Environment, and Network.

The Version NT Diagnostics tab displays the version, service pack version, and NT serial number. A Print button on this screen allows a comprehensive listing of all NT Diagnostic information (from all of the various tabs). The System NT Diagnostics tab displays the installed HAL type, BIOS manufacturer and date, and the type of processor(s) installed in the computer. The Display tab lists video adapter information including chip type, BIOS date, driver, driver version, and amount of video memory. The Drives NT Diagnostics tab displays information about any drives connected to the computer, including hard drive partitions. The window also displays network connected drives (shares). Double-click on any drive and the amount of used space, number of bytes per sector, number of sectors per cluster, and available space is shown. The Memory NT Diagnostics tab displays physical memory and information about the paging file. This tab is useful in determining if the computer has enough physical memory or if the paging file needs to be adjusted.

The back row of NT Diagnostic tabs includes Services, Resources, Environment, and Network. The Services tab displays the current status of all services and device services. Double-click on any service to see detailed information such as the pathname to the service or device and any dependencies. There are two types of dependencies, service and group. Service dependencies are the services or drivers that must run before the particular service can start. Group dependencies are groups of services that must be running before the particular service can start.

The Resources tab is probably the most common tab used by technicians. On this display, IRQs, I/O port addresses, DMA channels, memory addresses, and devices can be shown by clicking on the appropriate button at the bottom of the tab. WINNT Figure #13 illustrates the Resources tab.

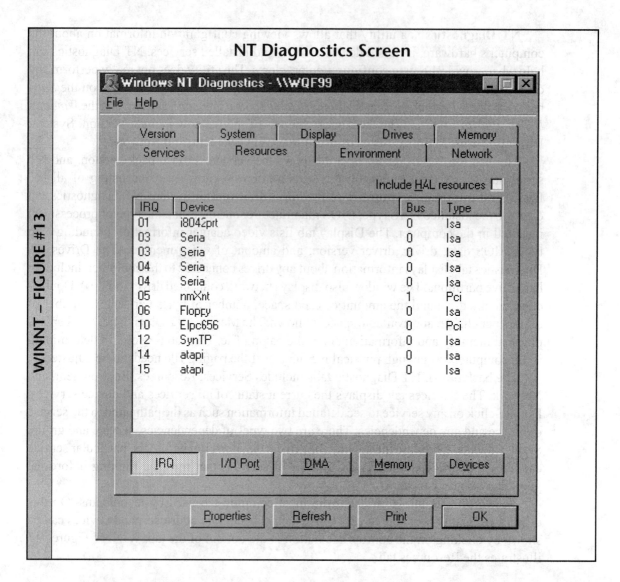

WINNT – FIGURE #13

The Environment tab lists the path to the command interpreter, how many processors are installed, and the directory where the majority of NT files are located. The Network tab shows the domain or workgroup name and what user is currently logged onto NT. Other buttons located on the bottom of the tab are Transports, Settings, and Statistics. The Statistics button is helpful when troubleshooting network problems because you can see the number of bytes transmitted, bytes received, network errors, failed sessions, server disconnects, hung sessions, etc.

TROUBLESHOOTING A SERVICE THAT DOES NOT START

Some NT services start automatically each time the computer boots. If one of these services has a problem, an error message normally appears during the boot sequence. You can use Event Viewer to see what particular service did not start. To control the service, use the individual administrative tool or the Services control panel. To access the Services control panel, click on the *Start* button. Point to the *Settings* menu option. Click on the *Control Panel* option. A window appears with all the control panels displayed. Double-click on the *Services* icon. To start or stop a service manually, click on its name. Click on the *Start* or *Stop* button as appropriate.

SHUT DOWN PROBLEMS

To shut down Windows NT Workstation properly, click on the *Start* button, click on the *Shut Down* option, click on the *Shut down the computer* radio button, and click on the *Yes* button. A shortcut is to press the *ALT+F4* keys after all applications are closed. If applications are open when you try to shut down NT, the operating system will attempt to close the applications and, if successful, it will shut down. If any documents have not been saved, you are prompted to save changes.

Before NT Workstation can shut down, the operating system sends a message to all devices, services, and applications. Each device that is running sends a message back saying it is okay to shut down. Any active application saves data that has not been previously saved and sends a message back to the operating system. Active system services also respond that it is okay to shut down. If the system has trouble shutting down, it is due to one of these three things. The most common problem is an application that is not responding. When this happens, press *CTRL+ALT+DEL* to access Task Manager. Click on the *Task Manager* button. Click on the *Applications* tab. Click on the application that has the words "not responding" in the Status column. Click on the *End Task* button. If a single application continually prevents NT Workstation from shutting down, contact the software manufacturer to see if there is a fix.

For services problems, boot the computer into Safe Mode and then shut down the computer. Take note as to whether or not the computer had any problems shutting down. If the process works, access the BOOTLOG.TXT file that is located in the root directory of the drive containing NT Workstation. Inside the file, take note of each service that is disabled because of booting into Safe Mode. Boot the computer normally. Stop each service one at a time to see which service is causing the problem.

Before troubleshooting non-responding devices, eliminate services and applications. A device usually does not cause a shut-down problem. While working on the computer, take notice of which devices you are using. Common ones are video, hard drive, CD-ROM, keyboard, and mouse. Verify that all of your devices have the most up-to-date drive loaded and that the driver is compatible with NT.

MONITORING SYSTEM PERFORMANCE

Another utility used to monitor the computer is the Performance Monitor tool. **Performance Monitor** allows creation of graphs, bar charts, and text reports. Specific resources such as memory and CPU usage can be tracked through Performance Monitor. An exercise at the end of the chapter shows how to use the Performance Monitor utility.

To access the Performance Monitor utility, click on the *Start* button, point to *Programs*, point to *Administrative Tools (Common)*, and click on the *Performance Monitor* option. The utility can be customized to show different counters. The button with a + (plus sign) is used to add various counters on the display. Some of the most important memory counters are Available Bytes and Pages/sec. The Available Bytes counter shows the amount of RAM available for running program processes. The Pages/sec counter shows the number of times per second that the information requested could not be found in RAM, and the data had to be retrieved from the hard drive. Since memory is a potential bottleneck for many computers, a technician should familiarize himself/herself with this technique.

Sometimes a technician must adjust the paging file size for optimum computer performance. Note that the paging file is known by various terms including swap file, paging file, or virtual memory. The *System* control panel is used to set the virtual memory size. Once in the System control panel, click on the *Performance* tab. Click on the *Change* button and the Virtual Memory window appears. Two values are selectable—Initial size and Maximum size. Both of these values should be the same for maximum computer performance. Once you change the values, click on the *Set* button. The Virtual Memory window may also be used to change the amount of space reserved for the registry.

Another potential bottleneck is the hard drive. The hard drive and memory work together because NT makes use of the paging file. The Performance Monitor charts you should watch are the Page Writes/sec and Pages Output/sec for memory and the Disk Writes/sec, Disk Write Bytes/sec, and Avg. Disk Write Queue Length for the logical disk option. A technician should practice working with the Performance Monitor utility before a problem occurs or the computer slows down.

The Task Manager utility may also be used to monitor your current system's performance. Sometimes a computer starts slowing down. A baseline is needed before the slowdown occurs. A **baseline** is a snapshot of your computer's performance during normal operations (before it has problems).

Start the Task Manager utility and click on the *Performance* tab to see the CPU usage and memory usage statistics. The first window on the left shows the CPU usage percentage. It is actually a percentage of time the processor is running a thread. A thread is a type of Windows object that runs application instructions. This percentage relates directly to the System Monitor's (Processor) %Processor Time counter. The first window on the right displays the CPU usage history, which is a graph of how busy the microprocessor has been over a period of time.

The second window on the left shows the amount of virtual memory being used. The amount shown is in kilobytes as evidenced by the K after the number. The number displayed directly relates to the System Monitor's (Memory) Committed Bytes counter. The second window on the right is a graph of the virtual memory used over time. Memory is a frequent bottleneck for computer performance issues. Task Manager can also be used to see the total amount of RAM installed and how much RAM is available. Task Manager is an invaluable tool for technicians when a computer is slowing down.

Name _____

WINDOWS NT WORKSTATION REVIEW QUESTIONS

1. [T / F] NT Workstation was developed for home computers.

2. List three NT Workstation enhancements.

3. [T / F] NT Workstation supports long filenames.

4. List two file systems that NT Workstation supports.

5. List the three login options for NT Workstation.

6. Describe what is meant by a GUI environment.

7. What button is located in the lower left corner of the desktop and is used to access applications?

8. What is the name of the bar that holds buttons that represent open applications?

9. List two things located on the taskbar.

10. What desktop icon is used to access files location on various drives?
    [My Computer / Internet Explorer / Network Neighborhood / Recycle Bin]

11. What desktop icon is used to access a remote computer?

12. Describe why items placed in the Recycle Bin take up hard drive space.

13. List three items commonly found in a dialog box.

14. What dialog box button is represented by a question mark?

15. What dialog box button is represented by an X?

16. What is the most common mistake made when using a dialog box?

17. What dialog box item allows a setting to be enabled or disabled by clicking inside a box?

18. What dialog box item allows a setting to be enabled or disabled by clicking inside a circle?

19. What drive letter is assigned to the first floppy drive?

20. A hard drive has been divided into two partitions. What drive letter is normally assigned to the second partition?

21. [T / F] A CD-ROM receives a drive letter in NT Workstation.

22. What is the name of the object that holds files in the NT operating system? [dialog box / CD case / folder / Task button]

23. In NT Workstation, what is the maximum number of extension characters?

24. In the filename NT QUIZ 4.DOC, which letters represent the extension?

25. [T / F] Windows NT Explorer automatically displays file extensions.

26. List three characters that cannot be used in an NT Workstation filename.

27. A user is working in Microsoft Word. He saves the document called LTR1 to a folder (directory) called WORDDOCS. The WORDDOCS folder is a subfolder (subdirectory) of the MY DOCUMENTS folder. Both folders are located on the D: hard drive volume. Write the complete path for the LTR1 document.

28. What device contains the file A:\REVIEW1?

29. What is the parent folder for the path C:\MY DOCUMENTS\GAME1?

30. What application is commonly used for copying files in NT Workstation?

31. [T / F] Compression is not supported under NTFS.

32. Describe the steps to compress a folder using NT Workstation.

33. Describe one method for determining the NT Workstation version.

34. During the boot process, the registry loads into what type of memory?
    [ROM / EEPROM / RAM / FLASH]

35. What are the five branches of the registry?

36. What registry hive has a list of hardware components and software drivers?

37. What registry hive tracks user preferences?

38. What registry branch holds the currently installed hardware profile?

39. You double-click on a document called TEST GRAPHICS.VSD and the Visio application opens with the TEST GRAPHICS.VSD file active in a window. What registry subtree tracked the file extension and associated it with the Visio application?

40. [T / F] The registry can contain only five subtrees.

41. Assuming that NT is loaded onto the first hard drive partition in the standard folder, write the path where the registry is located.

42. How are most changes made to the registry?

43. [T / F] Some changes to the operating system can only be done by editing the registry.

44. What default groups are allowed to edit the registry?

45. Which registry editor can edit values larger than 256 characters?

46. Which registry editor allows the registry to be exported to a text file?

47. Which registry editor allows simultaneous registry file editing?

48. What utility allows creation of an ERD?

49. What is the purpose of the *Update Repair Info* button when using RDISK?

50. [T / F] The Create Repair Disk button does not back up information to the REPAIR folder.

51. List three steps to take when planning for an NT Workstation installation.

52. What is the term given for the situation of an older operating system being replaced with a newer one?

53. What is the default folder for installing NT?

54. What is the name of the partition that contains hardware-specific files used to load the operating system?

55. What is the name of the partition that contains the NT operating system files?

56. [T / F] The system partition and the boot partition can reside on the same hard drive partition if NT Workstation is loaded and the partition is NTFS.

57. Describe one situation when the FAT16 file system should be used.

58. NT is loaded onto a drive partitioned for FAT16. It is the first hard drive partition. Write the complete command syntax used to convert the partition to NTFS.

59. [T / F] When using the CONVERT utility, all data files are lost, but the operating system files remain intact.

60. What is the minimum amount of RAM needed to load NT Workstation?

61. [T / F] NT Workstation requires a CD-ROM.

62. What is the minimum video requirement to install NT?

63. You have a sound card that is not listed in the HCL.HLP file. What will you do to verify it is compatible with NT?

64. What file is used to create the NTHQ program?

65. You have just created a disk and attempt to run the NTHQ utility to see if the hardware is compatible with NT. The computer will not boot from this disk. What is the first thing you will check?

66. [T / F] All DOS applications operate under NT Workstation.

67. What type of virus loads when the computer first starts?

68. What is the name of the virus that attaches to a specific application?

69. What are the types of viruses written to avoid detection?

70. List three symptoms of a virus.

71. Describe what to do with an anti-virus program when installing an operating system service pack.

72. [T / F] In a network environment, every computer must have a unique name.

73. [T / F] The NT local administrator password cannot be blank.

74. [T / F] The NT local administrator password is not case sensitive.

75. List two ways to start the NT installation process.

76. What is the name of the file used to install NT Workstation 4 onto a computer that currently has NT Workstation 3.5?

77. What are the two parts of the NT Workstation installation process?

78. During what installation mode is the hard drive partitioned?

79. During what installation mode is the computer named?

80. Describe two things to try if the system halts during the text mode portion of the installation.

81. During NT Workstation installation's text mode, a STOP message displays. What are two things that cause this?

82. What will you do if NT Workstation stops during the GUI portion of Setup?

83. What are the most likely causes of the system randomly hanging during installation?

84. What do you do if the BIOS is incompatible with NT?

85. A crucial device is incompatible with NT. What do you do?

86. What do you do if a software application is incompatible with NT?

87. During the installation process, Setup displays a message that no hard drives were found. What are two things to check?

88. What are the most likely problems if Setup hangs when copying files during the installation process?

89. Describe the steps to access the Display control panel

90. When using the Mouse control panel, what tab allows access to loading a mouse driver?

91. What is the name of the environment for DOS applications?
    [FAT16 / NTFS / PIF / NTVDM]

92. Describe the procedures for accessing a PIF.

93. What PIF tab is used to configure how a DOS application appears on the monitor?

94. What is WOW as it relates to 16-bit applications running on NT Workstation?

95. Two 16-bit applications are running. How many NTVDMs are active?

96. [T / F] When one 16-bit application locks, all 16-bit applications that are currently running are inaccessible.

97. [T / F] 16-bit applications cannot be configured to run in their own NTVDM.

98. Describe the steps to allow a 16-bit application to operate in its own NTVDM.

99. [T / F] All 16-bit applications are compatible with NT.

100. [T / F] If a 32-bit application fails, no other 32-bit application is affected in NT.

101. Describe the steps used to access the Add Printer wizard.

102. Where is the BOOT.INI file located?

103. NT Workstation is loaded on the C: drive. Write the complete path for the NTOSKRNL.EXE file.

104. Once the computer has power, what is the first step in the boot process?

105. What is the name of the operating system kernel in NT Workstation?

106. What are the two main areas of boot problems?

107. What file will you examine if the message, "The system did not load because of a computer disk hardware configuration problem" appears?

108. What could cause the error message "Invalid partition table"?

109. When would you use the Last Known Good profile?

110. Describe two methods used to access a command prompt when using NT Workstation.

111. Describe the steps used to access Task Manager.

112. List the steps necessary to halt a 32-bit application using Task Manager.

113. What are the three types of events that Event Viewer tracks?

114. What default user can define what security events are tracked?

115. [T / F] All users can view security log information.

116. Describe how to access Event Viewer on NT Workstation.

117. What do you do if the message, "Event Viewer log is full" appears?

118. What is the most commonly used NT Diagnostics tab?

119. List the steps to properly shut down NT Workstation.

120. What is the most common problem that causes NT Workstation to not shut down properly?

121. Describe the steps for adjusting the paging file size.

122. Describe the purpose of a baseline report.

123. List two tools commonly used to monitor a NT Workstation computer's performance.

124. What Task Manager tab is used to display a graph of CPU and memory usage?

 Name _____

WINDOWS NT WORKSTATION FILL-IN-THE-BLANK

1. NT Workstation can be upgraded from _____ or _____.

2. NT Workstation is a _____-bit operating system.

3. NT uses the _____ file system for CD media.

4. The interface between the user and the operating system starts with the _____, which is the area that appears after logging onto NT.

5. Graphical representations of files and applications are known as _____.

6. To access help, the _____ button is used.

7. A Microsoft Word document and a Visio document are loaded into memory. The Word document is currently displayed on the screen. To quickly switch to the Visio document, click the Visio document button located on the _____.

8. The _____ desktop icon is frequently used to access the web.

9. David Brown, a user on the local network, has shared a folder on his computer so others can access the documents in the folder. Lance Wallace wants to access David's folder, so he uses the _____ desktop icon.

10. Deleted files are placed in the _____.

11. A _____ is the part of a dialog box that allows typed entries.

12. Click on a dialog box's _____ to access a screen of related options.

13. To save dialog box changes, click on the _____ or the _____ button.

14. A down arrow represents a _____ in a dialog box.

15. The drive letter _____ represents the first hard drive partition.

16. NTTEST1.DOC is an example of a _____.

17. In older operating systems, a folder is known as a _____.

18. HOMEWORK ASSIGNMENT 1.DOC is an example of a _____ filename.

19. C:\MY DOCUMENTS\NT CLASS\HOMEWORK ASSIGNMENT1.DOC is an example of a _____.

20. When working with a path, folders and filenames are always separated by the _____ character.

21. Compression is not supported on a/an _____ partition.

22. The command used to view the NT Workstation version is _____.

23. Another name for the NT Workstation database is _____.

24. User specific settings are kept in a _____.

25. The _____ registry subtree holds global hardware configuration information.

26. The _____ registry branch holds settings for a specific user.

27. The _____ registry subtree holds file associations.

28. The two NT registry editors are _____ and _____.

29. Before editing the registry, do a _____.

30. The _____ registry editor has better search capabilities.

31. Registry subtrees are shown in individual windows when using the _____ registry editor.

32. The _____ program is the preferred method for backing up the registry in NT Workstation.

33. The NT Backup program is located under the _____ Programs option.

34. A disk used when NT Workstation fails is called a/an _____.

35. An installation where no other operating systems are installed is called a/an _____.

36. A computer has Windows 98 and NT Workstation installed. This is known as a _____ computer.

37. The two types of NT hard drive partitions are the _____ partition and the _____ partition.

38. NT can use the _____ or the _____ file systems on the hard drive.

39. The _____ program changes a FAT partition to NTFS.

40. NT requires a minimum of a _____ CPU.

41. NT requires a minimum of _____ hard drive space to install.

42. HCL.HLP is located in the _____ folder on the NT Workstation CD.

43. The _____ utility identifies NT-compatible hardware.

44. The MAKEDISK.BAT file is located in the _____ folder on the NT Workstation CD.

45. A _____ is a computer program designed to change the way the computer operates.

46. The _____ virus attaches to a .COM or .EXE file.

47. A _____ virus does not replicate, but is used to gather private information.

48. The most common types of _____ viruses are sent via an e-mail.

49. The maximum number of characters for a local administrator password is _____.

50. The _____ file is used to install NT onto a computer that currently has Windows 3.1.

51. During the NT Workstation installation process, the _____ mode displays characters on a blue background.

52. During the _____ installation mode, the administrator password prompt appears.

53. If NT hangs during the installation process after the final reboot, the problem is likely in the _____ file or an incorrect hardware configuration.

54. To obtain NT-compatible hardware drivers, contact the _____.

55. The CD key is located on the _____.

56. The only default user allowed to install hardware is the _____.

57. Various _____ are used to install hardware components.

58. The _____ control panel is used for CD-ROMs.

59. 32-bit applications are loaded using the _____ control panel.

60. Every DOS application loads into a single _____.

61. The _____ PIF tab allows extended and expanded memory configuration.

62. Each 32-bit application is allocated _____ of memory that is shared by operating system files and _____ for the application.

63. To install a printer, use the _____ wizard.

64. Another name for startup files is _____.

65. The NTLDR file is located in the _____ directory of the system partition.

66. The _____ boot file starts or loads the file system.

67. The _____ file displays the logon screen.

68. The _____ Run dialog box command brings up a DOS window and a prompt.

69. The _____ command is used to uncompress an NT file.

70. The _____ command is used to partition a FAT partition.

71. _____ displays applications and processes that are currently loaded in memory.

72. _____ is used to monitor drivers and services on NT Workstation.

73. The _____ control panel is used to stop a service.

74. The _____ mode is used for troubleshooting services problems that cause NT to not shut down properly.

75. _____ allows you to create graphs representing the computer's performance.

76. The default setting for virtual memory is _____ times the amount of installed RAM.

Name _____

WINDOWS NT WORKSTATION DESKTOP OPTIONS EXERCISE

Objective: To interact with and customize the Windows NT Workstation desktop

Parts: Computer with Windows 2000 installed

Step 1.   Turn on the computer and verify that the operating system loads.

Step 2.   Logon to NT Workstation using the userid and password provided by the instructor or lab assistant.

My Computer

Step 3.   Double-click on the **My Computer** desktop icon. A window appears.

Question 1:   Write down the drive letters that are available on your computer and that show in the My Computer windoW.

Step 4.   Locate the three icons in the My Computer's window upper right corner. The icons are a line, a window, and an X. Click on the **line** icon. The icon that looks like a straight line is used to minimize the screen, which means the window is still loaded in memory, but it does not show on the desktop. Instead, it shows up as an item on the taskbar. Click on the button labeled **My Computer** on the taskbar. The My Computer icon reappears on the screen. The icon in the center can be of two varieties—a maximize button, which looks like one window, or a Restore button, which looks like a window within a window. When a window is maximized it fills the entire screen. If you size the screen differently, you can click on the **Restore** button and the window goes back the way it was. Click on the **X** button.

Question 2:   What happened to the window when you clicked on the X button?

Recycle Bin

Step 5.   Click on the **Start** button.

Step 6.   Point to the **Programs** option.

Step 7.   Point to the **Accessories** option.

Step 8.   Click on the **Notepad** option. The Notepad application opens with a blank document.

Step 9.   Type the following words: **Education is what survives when what has been learnt has been forgotten. –B.F. Skinner**

Step 10.   Click on the **File** menu option.

Question 3:   What drive (and possibly folder) is listed in the Save in: dialog box?

Step 11.   Click on the **Save** menu option.

Step 12.   In the File name: textbox, type **Education**. The letters **.txt* are replaced.

Step 13.   Click on the **Save** button.

Step 14.   Click on the **X** (**Close**) button in the upper right corner to close the Notepad window.

Step 15.   Double-click on the **My Computer** desktop icon.

Step 16.   Locate the **Education** document in the proper location. Refer back to Question 3 if you forgot. You may need to use the scroll bar or double-click on a drive icon and possibly a folder icon to find your document. After trying to locate the file and you still cannot find it, contact a lab assistant or instructor.

Step 17.   Click once on the **Education** document to select it.

Step 18.   Press the **Delete** key on the keyboard. A message appears on the screen asking if you are sure that you want to send the education document to the Recycle Bin.

Step 19.   Click on the **Yes** button.

Step 20.   Click on the **X** (**Close**) button in the upper right corner.

Step 21.   Double-click on the **Recycle Bin** icon on the desktop.

Step 22.   Locate the **Education** document. If it is not in the Recycle Bin, perform steps 5 through 21 again.

There are several ways to delete items from the Recycle Bin and they list below:

A. Click on the **File** menu option and select the **Empty Recycle Bin** option. This deletes all files from the Recycle Bin.

B. Click on the document you want removed from the disk entirely. Click on the **File** menu option. Click on the **Delete** option.

C. Click on the document you want removed from the disk entirely. Press the **Delete** key on the keyboard.

D. From the desktop, right-click on the **Recycle Bin** icon. Click on the **Empty Recycle Bin** option. This option deletes *all* files from the Recycle Bin.

Use one of the methods listed above to delete the **Education** document from the Recycle Bin.

Desktop Icons

Step 23. Sometimes users clutter their desktop with icons. One thing that helps with this clutter is to have the system arrange the desktop icons. The icons can be arranged by name, type, size, date, or let the system automatically arrange them. To illustrate this function, go to the desktop area.

Step 24. Right-click on a blank desktop space. Once a menu appears, point to the **Arrange Icons** option. If the **Auto Arrange** option has a checkmark beside it, click on the **Auto Arrange** option to remove the checkmark.

Step 25. Click and hold the mouse button down while pointing to the **My Computer** icon and drag the icon to the center of the screen.

Step 26. Click and hold the mouse button down while pointing to the **Recycle Bin** icon and drag the icon to the top right portion of the screen.

Step 27. Right-click on a blank desktop space. A menu appears.

Step 28. Point to the **Arrange icons** menu option.

Step 29. Click on the **By Date** menu option.

Question 4: What changed on the screen?

Step 30. Right-click on a blank desktop space again. A menu appears.

Step 31. Point to the **Arrange icons** menu option.

Step 32. Click on the **Auto Arrange** option. If you look very carefully before the window closes, you can see a checkmark go beside the option. (You can also right-click on an empty desktop space again, point to the Arrange icons option and see the checkmark.)

Step 33. Click and hold the mouse button down while pointing to the **My Computer** icon and drag the icon to the center of the screen.

Question 5: What happened when you tried to move the My Documents icon?

Desktop Appearance

Step 34. Right-click on a desktop area. A menu appears.

Step 35. Click on the **Properties** option. The Display Properties window appears. (*Note:* This screen can also be accessed by clicking on the Start button, point to the Settings option, click on the Control Panel option, and double-click on the Display icon.)

Step 36. Click on the **Background** tab. This tab controls how the background color and pattern appears.

Question 6:   What are the default Wallpaper and Display settings?

Step 37.   Click on the **WINNT** option and click on the **Apply** button.

Question 7:   What happened to the screen?

Step 38.   In the Display: dialog box, click on the down arrow and select the **Tile** option. Click on the **Apply** button.

Question 8:   What happened to the screen?

Step 39.   Click on the **Appearance** tab at the top of the window. This tab controls the color scheme and size of letters displayed on the screen when various windows are open. This tab is good to use when people with vision problems need adjustments.

Step 40.   Click on the **Background** tab. Configure the wallpaper and display settings back to their original settings. Refer to Question 6 if you forgot what the settings were.

Step 41.   Click on the **OK** button. The Display Properties window closes.

Creating a Shortcut

Note: There are various ways to create a shortcut and only one way is demonstrated here.

Step 42.   Click on the **Start** button, point to the **Programs** option, and click on the **Windows NT Explorer** option. You should make sure that the Exploring window does not cover the entire screen. If it does, click on the Restore button, which is the middle button in the top right corner of the window (the one that looks like two windows stacked on top of one another).

Step 43.   Right-click (and continue to hold the right mouse button down) on any file or one designated by the instructor. Drag the file to an empty space on the desktop. Release the right mouse button and a menu pops up.

Step 44.   Click on the **Create Shortcut(s) here** option. The shortcut appears on the desktop as a shortcut icon.

Question 9:   What file did you choose to create a shortcut icon?

Step 45. Close the Exploring window by clicking on the **Close** button in the upper right corner. It is the one with an X in it.

Step 46. Right-click on the **shortcut** icon you just created. Refer back to Question 9 if you forgot the name of it.

Step 47. Click on the **Properties** option. A dialog box appears.

Question 10: Write the path found in the Target textbox and describe what the path means.

Step 48. Click on the **Find Target** button.

Question 11: What happened when you clicked on the Find Target button?

Question 12: Is the file that was used to create the shortcut icon visible?

Question 13: Can you locate the file that was used to create the shortcut icon? If not, contact a lab assistant or your instructor.

Step 49. Close the window you are working in by clicking on the **Close** button, which is the button in the upper right corner that has an X in it.

Step 50. In the Shortcut Properties window, click on the **OK** button to close the window.

Step 51. Click once on the shortcut desktop icon that you created to select it.

Step 52. Hold the **Shift** key down and press the **Delete** key. A message box appears asking if you are sure you want to delete the shortcut. Make sure the name of the shortcut file is the name of the shortcut you created. Refer to Question 9 if you forgot. If the name is not the same as the desktop shortcut icon you created, click on **No.** Otherwise, to delete the shortcut, click on the **Yes** button.

Step 53. Double-click on the **Recycle Bin** desktop icon.

Question 14: Is the desktop shortcut icon you created in the Recycle Bin? Why or why not? (Hint: In Step 52, what was done differently to delete the file?)

Question 15: Find a way to create a shortcut using the mouse options rather than right-clicking. Write your steps in the space below.

_____ *Instructor's Initials*

   Step 54.   Delete the shortcut icon you created for Question 15.

_____ *Instructor's Initials*

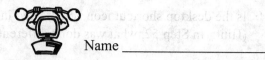

Name _____

CHANGING THE WALLPAPER AND DESKTOP PATTERN IN WINDOWS NT WORKSTATION

Objective: To understand how to change the appearance of the desktop in Windows NT Workstation

Parts: Computer with Windows NT Workstation installed and configured

At times it may be desirable to adjust the wallpaper and desktop patterns in Windows NT to provide a more pleasing or personalized look.

To change the Wallpaper and/or Desktop patterns, follow these steps:

Step 1.   Turn the computer on and verify that Windows NT Workstation loads.

Step 2.   Logon to Windows NT Workstation using the userid and password provided by the instructor or lab assistant.

Step 3.   Right-click on an empty part of the **desktop** and select the **Properties** option. The Display Properties window opens.

Question 1:   Which wallpaper and desktop pattern settings are currently selected?

Step 4.   From the **Pattern** window, scroll to and select the **Thatches** pattern. The Thatches pattern appears in the Preview window.

Step 5.   From the **Wallpaper** window, select **WINNT**. The WINNT wallpaper appears in the preview window.

Step 6.   To apply the new desktop settings, click on the **Apply** button and then click on the **OK** button.

_____ *Instructor's Initials*

Name _____

WINDOWS NT WORKSTATION TASKBAR OPTIONS

Objective: To interact with and customize the NT Workstation taskbar

Parts: Computer with Windows NT Workstation installed

Step 1.   Turn on the computer and verify that the operating system loads.

Step 2.   Logon to NT Workstation using the userid and password provided by the instructor or lab assistant.

Step 3.   Locate the taskbar on the bottom of the screen. If it is not showing, move the mouse to the bottom of the screen and the taskbar pops up.

Step 4.   To modify or view the taskbar settings, right-click on a blank area of the taskbar. A menu appears.

Step 5.   Click on the **Properties** option. The Taskbar Properties window appears.

Step 6.   Click on the **Taskbar Options** tab. The four options available on this screen relate to how things are shown on the taskbar. The items with a check in the checkbox to the left are active. The Always on top option puts the taskbar visible on the screen at all times (even if a window is full size or maximized). The Auto hide option hides the taskbar during normal operation. Press **CTRL+ESC** or the **Start** button key on the keyboard (the one with the Windows emblem on it) to make the taskbar reappear. If both the Always on top and Auto hide options are checked, then the taskbar appears when you are in a window that is full size (maximized). The Show small icons in Start menu option reduces the size of the Start menu words. The Show clock option displays the clock icon in the right corner of the taskbar. Make sure the **Always on top** and **Show clock** options are the only ones with checkmarks in the checkboxes. To remove a checkmark, click in the checkbox that already contains a check in it. To put a checkmark in a box, click once in an empty box.

Step 7.   Click on the **Apply** and then the **OK** buttons. If the apply button is grayed out, simply click on the OK button.

Step 8.   Right-click on an empty space on the **taskbar.**

Step 9.   Point to the **Toolbars** option. A submenu appears.

Step 10. Ensure that there is a checkmark beside the **Quick Launch** option. This setting allows the Quick Launch icons to appear on the taskbar by the Start button.

Step 11. Using the skills you just learned, access the Taskbar Settings window.

Question 1: List the steps you performed to do Step 11.

Step 12. Click on the **Properties** option. Click on the **Question mark** icon in the upper right corner of the window. The question mark is an interactive help system. The pointer on the screen changes to an arrow with a question mark attached. Click on the **Always on top** option. A description of the option appears with the on-line help active.

Step 13. Click on the **Start Menu Programs** tab. The Start Menu Programs tab is used to add or remove items from the Start menu or to clear the Documents list. The Documents list is a list of up to 15 recently used documents.

Step 14. Click on the **Clear** button in the Documents menu section of the window. The Clear button turns gray.

Step 15. Click on the **OK** button.

Question 2: What other options are available through the taskbar option list?

_____ ***Instructor's Initials***

Name _____

CONFIGURING WINDOWS NT WORKSTATION TO RECOGNIZE A NEW FILE EXTENSION

Objective: To understand how to configure Windows NT Workstation to recognize new file extensions

Parts: Computer with Windows NT Workstation installed and configured

Windows NT uses file extension associations to automatically start the associated application when a file is accessed. Usually these associations are configured when the applications are installed, however at times, you may find it necessary to manually configure these file extension associations.

To configure Windows NT Workstation to recognize a new file extension association, follow these steps:

Step 1.   Turn on the computer and verify that the operating system loads.

Step 2.   Logon to NT Workstation using the userid and password provided by the instructor or lab assistant.

Step 3.   Double-click on the **My Computer** desktop icon.

Step 4.   From the View menu item, choose **Options**, and then select **File Types**.

Question 1:   How many Registered File Types are listed?

Step 5.   To create a new file type, select **New Type**.

Step 6.   In the **Description** field, enter **Test Extension**.

Step 7.   In the **Associated Extensions** field, enter **DDC**.

Step 8.   From the **Actions** field, click **New**.

Step 9.   In the **Actions** field, type **Open**.

Step 10. In the **Application Used To Perform Action** field, browse to **C:\Program Files\Windows NT\Accessories\Wordpad**, and click on the **Open** button.

Step 11. Click **OK**. The Open action appears in the Actions field.

Step 12. Click on the **Close** button. The new DDC file type appears in the Registered File Types window.

Question 2:   What will happen if you double-click a file with the .DDC extension?

Step 13.   To test the new file type extension, create a text File with the **Notepad** or **WordPad** application.

Step 14.   Name the file **TESTFILE** and change the file extension to **DDC**.

Step 15.   Using My Computer or Explorer, double-click on the renamed **file** icon. WordPad or Notepad starts automatically and opens the text file.

_____ *Instructor's Initials*

Name _____

NT WORKSTATION FILE AND FOLDER MANAGEMENT

Objective: To create folders, move files, and copy files to new locations

Parts: Computer with Windows NT Workstation installed
Formatted 3.5" disk

Note: There are multiple ways to do some of the steps in this exercise. The steps that have an alternate method have the letters ALT: before the step. With these steps, you may pick either method of performing the step.

Step 1. Turn on the computer and verify that the operating system loads.

Step 2. Logon to NT Workstation using the userid and password provided by the instructor or lab assistant.

Step 3. Click on the **Start** button, point to the **Accessories** option, and click on the **Notepad** option.

Step 4. Type in the following:

Develop a passion for learning. If you do, you will never cease to grow. –Anthony J. D'Angelo

Step 5. Click on the **File** menu option and click on the **Save** option from the drop-down menu.

Step 6. Insert a formatted disk into the floppy (A:) drive.

Step 7. Click on the **down arrow** in the **Save in** box.

Step 8. Click on the **3_ Floppy (A:)** option.

Step 9. In the File name textbox, type **Quote 1**.

Step 10. Click on the **Save** button.

Step 11. Click on the **File** menu option and click on the **New** option.

Step 12. Type in the following:

The harder you try, the harder it is to fail. –Vince Lombardi

Step 13. Click on the **File** menu option and click on the **Save** option from the drop-down menu.

Step 14. Click on the **down arrow** in the **Save in** textbox.

Step 15. The 3_ Floppy (A:) option should already be selected, but if it is not, select this option. In the File name textbox type **Quote 2** and click on the **Save** button.

Step 16. Click on the **File** menu option and click on the **New** menu option.

Step 17. Type in the following:

My mother said to me, "If you are a soldier, you will become a general. If you are a monk, you will become the Pope." Instead, I was a painter and became Picasso. – Pablo Picasso

Step 18. Click on the **File** menu option and click on the **Save** option from the drop-down menu.

Step 19. Click on the **down arrow** in the **Save in** textbox.

Step 20. The 3_ Floppy (A:) option should already be selected, but if it is not, select this option. In the File name textbox type **Quote 3** and click on the **Save** button.

Step 21. Click on the **File** menu option and click on the **New** menu option.

Step 22. Type in the following:

Education has really only one basic factor: one must want it –G.E. Woodbury

Step 23. Click on the **File** menu option and click on the **Save** option from the drop-down menu.

Step 24. The 3_ Floppy (A:) option should already be selected, but if it is not, select this option. In the File name textbox type **Quote 4** and click on the **Save** button.

Step 25. Click on the **File** menu option and click on the **New** menu option.

Step 26. Type in the following:

A committee is a group that keeps minutes and loses hours. –Milton Berle

Step 27. Click on the **File** menu option and click on the **Save** option from the drop-down menu.

Step 28. The 3_ Floppy (A:) option should already be selected, but if it is not, select this option. In the File name textbox type **Quote 5** and click on the **Save** button.

Step 29. Close the Notepad application by clicking on the **Close** button (which is a button in the upper right corner with an X).

Step 30. Right-click on the **Start** button.

Step 31. Click on the **Explore** option.

Step 32. In the left window, use the vertical scroll bar to locate the A: drive. Click on the **3_ Floppy (A:)** drive option.

Step 33. In the right window, locate the five files you just created called **Quote 1, Quote 2, Quote 3, Quote 4,** and **Quote 5.** If the files are not there, redo steps 3 through 33.

_____ *Instructor's Initials*

Create a Folder

Step 34. In the right Exploring window, right-click on an **empty space.** Point to the **New** option and click on the **Folder** option. A folder appears in the right window with the words *New Folder* highlighted. Type **Class Quotes** and press **Enter**.

Note: The method shown below, that is preceded by the letters ALT:, is an alternate way to perform the same steps shown in Step 34. You may use either method.

ALT: Click on the **File** menu option. Point to the **New** option and click on the **Folder** option. A folder appears in the right window with the words *New Folder* highlighted. Type **Class Quotes** and press **Enter**.

Step 35. Create another new folder called **General Quotes** using either step outlined in Step 3

_____ *Instructor's Initials*

Question 1: List the files and folder contained on the A: drive.

Copy a File

Step 36. In the right window, right-click on the file named **Quote 1**. A submenu appears. Click on the **Copy** option from the submenu.

ALT: In the right window, click on the file named **Quote 1**. Click on the **Edit** menu option. Click on the **Copy** option from the drop-down menu.

Step 37. In the right window, double-click on the **Class Quotes** folder. Notice how the Address box changes to A:\Class Quotes (the path) and the right window is empty because the folder does not have any files or subfolders in it yet.

Step 38. In the right window, right-click and a submenu appears. Click on the **Paste** option. The file named Quote 1 appears in the right window.

ALT: Click on the **Edit** menu option. Click on the **Paste** option from the drop-down menu. The file named Quote 1 appears in the right window.

Step 39. In the left window, click on the **3_ Floppy (A:)** drive option. Notice how the Address box changes to A:\.

Step 40. Copy the files named **Quote 2** and **Quote 3** into the **Class Quotes** folder using the methods outlined in steps 36 through 39.

Copy Multiple Files

Step 41. In the left Exploring window, click on the **3_ Floppy (A:)** drive option.

Step 42. Locate the files called **Quote 4** and **Quote 5** in the right window.

Step 43. In the right window, click once on the **Quote 4** filename. The name highlights.

Step 44. Hold the **Shift** key down and click once on the **Quote 5** filename. Both the Quote 4 and Quote 5 filenames highlight.

Note: The Shift key is used to select files that are consecutive in a list (one right after the other). If you wanted to select files that are not consecutive (such as Quote 1 and Quote 5), use the Ctrl key to select the files.

Step 45. Right-click on the files named **Quote 4** and **Quote 5.** A submenu appears. Click on the **Copy** option from the submenu.

ALT: Click on the **Edit** menu option. Click on the **Copy** option from the drop-down menu.

Step 46. In the right window, double-click on the **General Quotes** folder. Notice how the Address line changes to A:\General Quotes and the right window is empty because the folder does not have any files or subfolders in it yet.

Step 47. In the right window, right-click on an **empty space** and a submenu appears. Click on the **Paste** option. The files named Quote 4 and Quote 5 appear in the right window.

ALT: Click on the **Edit** menu option. Click on the **Paste** option from the drop-down menu. The files named Quote 4 and Quote 5 appear in the right window.

Question 2: Write the full path statement for the Quote 4 document that resides in the General Quotes folder on the A: drive.

_____ *Instructor's Initials*

Copying a File from One Folder to Another

Step 48. In the left Exploring window, click on the **3_ Floppy (A:)** drive option.

Step 49. In the left Exploring window, click on the **Class Quotes** folder located under the Floppy (A:) option. The files Quote 1, Quote 2, and Quote 3 appear in the right window.

Step 50. In the right window, right-click on the file named **Quote 3.** From the submenu that appears, click on the **Copy** option.

ALT: In the right window, click on the file named **Quote 3.** Click on the **Edit** menu option. Click on the **Copy** option from the drop-down menu.

Step 51. In the left Exploring window, click on the folder called **General Quotes** located under the Floppy (A:) option. The files Quote 4 and Quote 5 appear in the right window and the Address textbox shows A:\General Quotes.

Step 52. In the right window, right-click on an **empty space** and a submenu appears. Click on the **Paste** option. The file named Quote 3 appears in the right window along with the files named Quote 4 and Quote 5.

ALT: Click on the **Edit** menu option. Click on the **Paste** option from the drop-down menu. The file named Quote 3 appears in the right window along with the files named Quote 4 and Quote 5.

Step 53.   Using the same procedures outlined in steps 48 through 53, copy the **Quote 1** and **Quote 2** files from the **Class Quotes** folder into the **General Quotes** folder. At the end of this step, you should have three files (Quote 1, Quote 2, and Quote 3) in the Class Quotes folder and five files (Quote 1, Quote 2, Quote 3, Quotre 4, and Quote 5) in the General Quotes folder.

Moving a File

Step 54.   Create a folder on the A: drive called **My Stuff**. Refer back to the steps earlier in the exercise if you need assistance.

Step 55.   In the left Exploring window, click on the folder called **General Quotes**. In the right window, all five files appear.

Step 56.   In the right window, click on the file called **Quote 1**.

Step 57.   Hold the **CTRL** key down and click on the file called **Quote 3**. Both the Quote 1 and Quote 3 file names are highlighted. *Note:* The CTRL key is used to select non-consecutive files, whereas the Shift key is used to select files that are listed consecutively (one right after another).

Step 58.   Right-click on either **Quote 1** or **Quote 3** filename. Select the **Cut** option from the menu that appears.

ALT: Click on the **Edit** menu option. Click on the **Cut** option from the drop-down menu.

Step 59.   In the left Exploring window, click on the **My Stuff** folder. The right window is empty because no file have been copied or moved into the My Stuff folder yet.

Step 60.   In the right window, right-click and a menu appears on the screen. Select the **Paste** option from the menu. The Quote 1 and Quote 3 files appear in the right window.

ALT: Click on the **Edit** menu option. Click on the **Paste** option from the drop-down menu. The Quote 1 and Quote 3 files appear in the right window.

Step 61.   Using the procedures just learned, move the **Quote 1** file from the **Class Quotes** folder into the **General Quotes** folder.

_____ *Instructor's Initials*

Question 3:   What files now exist in the General Quotes folder?

Deleting Files and Folders

Step 62.   In the left Exploring window, click on the **My Stuff** folder. The Quote 1 and Quote 3 files appear in the right window.

Step 63.   In the right window, click on the **Quote 1** filename. Hold the **Shift** key down and click on the **Quote 3** filename. Both the Quote 1 and Quote 3 filenames highlight.

Step 64.   Press the **Delete** key on the keyboard. A Confirm Multiple File Delete message appears on the screen asking, "Are you sure you want to delete these 2 items?"

Note: When deleting files from a floppy disk, the files are not placed in the Recycle Bin. They are deleted. When deleting files from a hard drive, the files get placed in the Recycle Bin when you press the Delete key or select the Delete option from the File menu option. If you want to permanently delete a file from a hard drive (the file will not get placed in the Recycle Bin), hold the **Shift** key down while pressing the **Delete** key.

ALT: Click on the **File** menu option. Click on the **Delete** option from the drop-down menu. A Confirm Multiple File Delete message appears on the screen asking, "Are you sure you want to delete these 2 items?"

Step 65.   Click on the **Yes** button.

Question 4:   Why do you think deleted files from a floppy drive are not placed in the Recycle Bin?

Step 66.   In the left Exploring window, click once on the **My Stuff** folder. The My Stuff folder highlights.

Step 67.   Press the **Delete** key. A Confirm Folder Delete message appears on the screen asking, "Are you sure you want to remove the folder My Stuff and all its contents?" Click on the **Yes** button.

ALT: Click on the **File** menu option. Click on the **Delete** option from the drop-down menu. A Confirm Multiple File Delete message appears on the screen asking, "Are you sure you want to remove the folder My Stuff and all its contents? " Click on the **Yes** button.

Question 5:   What folders are left on the floppy disk?

_____ ***Instructor's Initials***

Step 68.   Using the procedures outlined in steps 62 through 67, delete the **Class Quotes** folder and the **General Quotes** folders and all files contained within each folder.

Challenge Steps

Step 69.   Using Notepad, create **three text files** and save them to the floppy disk in a folder called **My Files**.

Step 70.   On the hard drive, create a folder called **Computer Text**.

Step 71.   Copy the two text files from the **My Files** folder on the floppy disk into the folder called **Computer Text** on the hard drive.

Step 72.   Move the third text file from the **My Files** folder on the floppy disk into the folder called **Computer Text** on the hard drive.

_____ *Instructor's Initials*

Step 72.   Permanently delete the folder called **Computer Text** from the hard drive and all files within this folder.

_____ *Instructor's Initials*

Step 73.   Delete the folder called **My Files** from the floppy disk and all files within this folder.

_____ *Instructor's Initials*

Name _____

EMPTYING THE WINDOWS NT RECYCLE BIN

Objective: To understand how to use the Windows NT Recycle Bin

Parts: Computer with Windows NT Workstation installed and configured

The Windows NT Recycle Bin is a handy fail-safe mechanism to protect from losing accidentally deleted files. Deleted files automatically are placed in the Recycle Bin from where they can be restored, or permanently deleted.

To use the Recycle Bin, follow these steps:

Step 1. Turn the computer on and verify that Windows NT Workstation loads.

Step 2. Logon to Windows NT Workstation using the userid and password provided by the instructor or lab assistant.

Step 3. Double-click the **My Computer** desktop icon and then double-click the **C: Drive**. The C: Drive directory structure displays in the My Computer window.

Step 4. Right-click on an **empty space** in the window, choose **New,** and then select **Text Document**. A new text document file appears in the window with the name highlighted.

Step 5. Type **TESTDOC** and press **Enter.** You have now created a blank text file on the C: drive.

Question 1: What file extension does TESTDOC have?

Step 6. Right-click the **TESTDOC** file and choose **Delete**. Confirm the file deletion by clicking **Yes**. The TESTDOC file has now been sent to the Recycle Bin.

Step 7. Double-click the **Recycle Bin** desktop icon. The Recycle Bin window opens with the TESTDOC file appearing in the window.

Step 8. Highlight the **TESTDOC** file and select the **File** menu option.

Question 2: Which option would you select to return the TESTDOC file to its previous location?

Step 9. Choose the **Empty Recycle Bin** option, and then click **Yes** to confirm the deletion. The TESTDOC file has been permanently deleted.

_____ *Instructor's Initials*

Name _____

USING REGEDIT IN WINDOWS NT WORKSTATION

Objective: To become familiar with the REGEDIT registry editing utility

Parts: Computer with Windows NT Workstation installed

REGEDIT is a utility used for editing the Windows registry. With REGEDIT you can find and view existing registry settings, modify registry settings values, or create new registry entries to change or enhance the way Windows operates.

In this lab, you will use REGEDIT to modify how your Windows NT Workstation participates in the Browser process.

CAUTION: Editing the registry can cause your computer to run erratically, or not run at all! When performing any registry editing, follow ALL directions carefully including spelling, syntax use, etc. Failure to do so may cause your computer to fail!

Step 1.   Turn on the computer and verify that the NT Workstation loads.

Step 2.   Logon to NT Workstation using the userid and password provided by the instructor or lab assistant.

Step 3.   Click on the **Start** button. Click on the **Run** option.

Step 4.   In the textbox, type in **REGEDIT** and press **Enter.** The REGEDIT utility appears.

Step 5.   In the left window, click on the + **(plus sign)** by the **HKEY_LOCAL_MACHINE** folder.

Step 6.   In the left window, click on the + **(plus sign)** by the **System** folder.

Step 7.   In the left window, click on the + **(plus sign)** by the **CurrentControlSet** folder.

Step 8.   In the left window, click on the + **(plus sign)** by the **Services** folder.

Step 9.   In the left window, click on the + **(plus sign)** by the **Browser** folder.

Step 10.   In the left window, click on the **Parameters** folder. The values contained in the Parameters folder list in the window on the right side.

Step 11.   In the right window, locate the MaintainServerList value.

Note: The MaintainServerList value controls how the local computer participates in Browser elections. It has three possible DATA values:

    A.   Yes: Will always participate as a Browser

    B.   No: Will not participate as a Browser

    C.   Auto: Can be a Browser if necessary

Question 1: What is the DATA value for your computer's **MaintainServerList** value?

Step 12. Double-click the **MaintainServerList** value. The **Edit String** window opens.

Step 13. If the current DATA value is **Auto**, change the value to **Yes**. If the current DATA value is **Yes**, change the value to **Auto**. If the current DATA value is **No**, change the value to **Auto**.

Question 2: What affect will the change made have on the computer's Browser status?

Step 14. Click on the **OK** button to close the **Edit String** window. The new DATA value appears in the REGEDIT window.

Question 3: When will the new registry setting take affect?

Step 15. Close the **REGEDIT** utility and reboot the computer.

_____ *Instructor's Initials*

Name _____

USING REGEDT32 IN WINDOWS NT WORKSTATION

Objective: To become familiar with the REGEDT32 registry editing utility

Parts: Computer with Windows NT Workstation installed

REGEDT32 is a utility used for editing the Windows registry. With REGEDT32 you can find and view existing registry settings, modify registry settings values, or create new registry entries to change or enhance the way Windows operates. In this lab, you will use REGEDT32 to create and configure a new registry setting to resize the desktop icons from the default of 32 pixels to 20 pixels.

CAUTION: Editing the registry can cause your computer to run erratically, or not run at all! When performing any registry editing, follow ALL directions carefully including spelling, syntax use, etc. Failure to do so may cause your computer to fail!

Step 1.   Turn on the computer and verify that the NT Workstation loads.

Step 2.   Logon to NT Workstation using the userid and password provided by the instructor or lab assistant.

Step 3.   Click on the **Start** button. Click on the **Run** option.

Step 4.   In the textbox, type in **REGEDT32** and press **Enter.** The REGEDT32 utility appears.

Step 5.   Click on the **HKEY_CURRENT_USER** window.

Step 6.   Expand the **Control Panel** folder by clicking on the **+ (plus sign)** beside it.

Step 7.   Expand the **Desktop** folder.

Step 8.   Select the **WindowMetrics** option.

Step 9.   Form the **Edit** menu item, click on the **Add Value** option. The Add Value window opens.

Step 10. In the Value Name field, type **Shell Icon Size**.

Step 11. In the Data Type field, choose **REG_SZ** and then click on the **OK** button. The String Editor opens.

Step 12. From the String Editor window, enter the value of **20**, (the default number of pixels in a desktop icon is 32) and click on the **OK** button. The new value displays.

Question 1:   How is the new value displayed in REGEDT32?

    Step 13.   Close the **REGEDT32** utility and reboot the computer for the new registry setting to take effect.

Question 2:   After the computer reboots, are your desktop icons smaller or larger than before? If not, perform the exercise again.

_____***Instructor's Initials***

Name _____

USING THE WINDOWS NT BACKUP UTILITY

Objective: To understand the proper use of the Windows NT Backup utility to backup and restore files

Parts: Computer with Windows NT Workstation and a backup tape drive installed and configured

Windows NT provides a backup utility that can be used to backup files to a tape drive and to restore the files in an emergency.

To backup files using the Windows NT Backup utility, follow these steps:

Step 1. Turn the computer on and verify that Windows NT Workstation loads.

Step 2. Logon to Windows NT Workstation using the userid and password provided by the instructor or lab assistant.

Step 3. From the **Start** menu, point to the **Programs** selection, then the **Administrative Tools** option, and double-click on the **Backup** menu selection. The Windows NT Backup utility starts.

Step 4. From the **Drives** window, select the **C: drive checkbox** to enable it. This action selects all files and folders on the C: drive for backup.

Note: To select specific files only, double-click the drive, then browse to and select specific files and/or folders.

Question 1: How many drives list in the Drives window?

Step 5. After choosing the files to be backed up, click on the **Backup** button to begin the backup process. The Backup Information window opens.

Step 6. From the Backup Information window, type **TESTTAPE** in the Tape Name field, choose **Verify After Backup**, select **Normal** for the backup type, and click on the **OK** button.

Question 2: What types of backups are available?

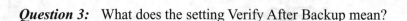

Question 3: What does the setting Verify After Backup mean?

Step 7. Windows NT Backup begins backing up the selected files and folders. The status of the backup can be monitored from the Backup Status window. When Windows NT Backup completes the backup process, a summary report displays. Click on the **OK** button to close the Backup Status window.

_____ ***Instructor's Initials***

To restore files and/or folders from a backup tape, follow these steps:

Step 8. Verify that the tape with the needed files is inserted into the tape drive.

Step 9. From within the Windows NT Backup utility, open the **Tapes** window. Browse to and select the files to be restored, and then click on the **Restore** button. The Restore Information window opens.

Step 10. Click on the **OK** button to begin the restore process.

Question 4: Can the files be restored to an alternate location?

Step 11. Confirm any file replacement messages by selecting **Yes to all**.

Step 12. When the restore process is completed, a summary report displays in the Restore Status window.

Step 13. Click on the **OK** button to close the Restore Status window and then exit the Windows NT Backup utility.

_____ ***Instructor's Initials***

Name _____

INSTALLING WINDOWS NT WORKSTATION

Objective: To understand how to install the Windows NT Workstation operating system on a computer

Parts: Computer without an operating system installed
Windows NT Workstation installation CD-ROM and setup disks

The method used to start the Windows NT Workstation installation process depends on whether or not your system supports booting from a CD-ROM.

If your computer supports booting from a CD-ROM, follow these steps:

Step 1.   Insert the Windows NT Workstation CD-ROM into the CD-ROM drive and start the computer. The computer boots from the CD and begins the installation process.

Step 2.   At the Welcome to Setup screen, press **Enter** to begin Windows NT Setup.

Step 3.   Setup detects the mass storage devices installed on your computer and displays a list of the detected devices. Press **Enter** to continue. Continue with Step 5.

If your computer does NOT support booting from a CD-ROM, follow these steps:

Step 1.   Insert the Windows NT Setup Disk 1 into the floppy drive and start the computer.

Note: If you do not have the Windows NT Setup floppy disks, you can create them from the installation CD. Insert the installation CD in a computer that has been booted with CD-ROM support. From a command prompt, change to the **I386** directory on the CD. Type **WINNT /OX** and press **Enter** when upgrading from DOS, WIN 3.x, or WIN9x, or type **WINNT32 /OX** and press **Enter** to upgrade an older version of NT or install a new version of NT. You are prompted to label and insert three floppy disks.

Step 2.   When prompted, change the floppy disks.

Step 3.   At the Welcome to Setup screen, press **Enter.** Windows prompts to detect the mass storage devices. Press **Enter** to continue.

Step 4.   Setup detects the mass storage devices installed and displays a list of the detected devices. Press **Enter** to continue.

From this point on, setup for both types of installations is identical

Step 5.   Page down through the Licensing Agreement and press **F8** to agree.

Step 6.   At the Hardware Components page, verify that the listed components match what is installed in the computer and press **Enter.**

Question 1:   Can these settings be changed later?

Step 7.   Highlight the **un-partitioned disk space** where you want to install Windows NT and press **Enter**.

Step 8.   Choose to format the partition as **NTFS** and press **Enter**.

Question 2:   What is one advantage of using the NTFS file system?

Step 9.   Press **Enter** to install Windows NT into the default **WINNT** directory.

Step 10.   Press **Enter** to have Windows Setup examine the hard disks. After the examination is complete, Setup begins copying files to the hard drive.

Step 11.   When prompted, remove all floppy disks and CDs from the drives and press **Enter** to restart the computer.

Question 3:   Why is it important to remove all disks before restarting?

Step 12.   The computer restarts and Setup enters the graphical (GUI) Setup mode. If you chose to use the NTFS file system format, Setup converts the partition to NTFS and restarts the computer a second time.

Step 13.   When prompted, re-insert the **Windows NT Installation CD-ROM** and click **OK**.

Step 14.   At the Gathering Information about your Computer window, click on the **Next** button.

Step 15.   Choose **Typical** installation and click **Next**.

Step 16.   Enter the **Name** and **Organization** information provided by the instructor or lab assistant, and click **Next**.

Step 17.   Enter the **CD-key** (found on the back of the CD case or provided by the instructor or lab assistant) and click **Next**.

Step 18.   Enter the **computer name** (provided by the instructor or lab assistant) and click **Next**.

Step 19.   Enter and confirm the **Password** (provided by the instructor or lab assistant) and click **Next**.

Step 20.   Select **No, Do not create an Emergency Repair Disk** and click on the **Next** button.

Question 4:   Can you create an Emergency Repair Disk later?

Step 21.   Select **Install the most common components**, and click on the **Next** button.

Step 22.   Click on the **Next** button to begin installing Windows NT Networking.

Step 23.   Choose **This computer will participate on a network**, select **Wired to the Network**, and click **Next**.

Step 24.   Select **Start Search**, and Setup searches for network adapters. When the network adapter is detected, click on the **Next** button.

Step 25.   Select the **TCP/IP Protocol**, click on the **Next** button, and click on the following **Next** button.

Step 26.   If directed by the instructor or lab assistant to use DHCP, choose **Yes** at the TCP/IP Setup window. If not using DHCP, choose **No**. Setup installs the selected networking components.

Question 5:   What does DHCP do?

Step 27.   If you are NOT using DHCP, enter an IP address and subnet mask provided by the instructor or lab assistant and click **OK**.

Step 28.   Click on the **Next** button to start the network.

Step 29.   At the Make this computer a member of window, enter the workgroup or domain information (provided by the instructor or lab assistant) and click on the **Next** button.

Step 30.   Click on the **Finish** button to complete Windows NT setup.

Step 31.   Select the appropriate **Time Zone** information and click on the **Close** button.

Step 32.   Test the selected video settings by selecting the **Test** button. If the settings are correct, click **Yes**, and then click **OK** twice.

Step 33.   When prompted, remove all floppy disks and CDs from the drives and select **Restart Computer**. The computer restarts using the newly installed Windows NT Workstation operating system.

_____ *Instructor's Initials*

Name _____

INSTALLING A DEVICE USING WINDOWS NT WORKSTATION

Objective: To understand the proper installation of devices using Windows NT Workstation

Parts: Computer with Windows NT Workstation installed and configured.
Internal or external peripheral device

Most devices installed on a Windows NT Workstation are installed using the device icons within Control Panel. Each device type has it's own specific installation steps, and you must follow the device-specific on-screen prompts and instructions for proper installation.

To install a device on a Windows NT Workstation, follow these general steps:

Step 1.   With the computer turned off, and following proper ESD precautions, install the device into the appropriate BUS slot or external port.

Step 2.   Turn the computer on and verify that Windows NT Workstation loads.

Step 3.   Logon to Windows NT Workstation using the userid and password provided by the instructor or lab assistant.

Step 4.   From the **Start** menu, point to the **Settings** option, and then select **Control Panel**.

Question 1:   How else can you open the Control Panel?

Step 5.   From the Control Panel window, double-click on the **Control Panel** icon that represents the device you are installing. Follow the appropriate device-specific instructions and steps to install the device.

Modems

Step 1.   Double-click the **Modems** control panel icon.

Step 2.   Click on the **Next** button to allow NT to detect the modem.

Step 3.   When the modem is detected, click on the **Next** button and follow the on-screen prompts to complete the installation.

Sound Cards

Step 1. Double-click the **Multimedia** control panel icon.

Step 2. Select the **Devices** tab.

Step 3. Click on and highlight **Audio Devices**, click on the **Add** button, and then follow the on-screen prompts to complete the device installation.

Network Adapters

Step 1. Double-click the **Network** control panel icon and select **Adapters**.

Step 2. Click **Add** and then follow the on-screen prompts to complete the device installation.

Ports

Step 1. Double-click the **Ports** control panel icon.

Step 2. Click on the **Add** button and follow the on-screen prompts to complete the device installation.

Printers

Step 1. Double-click the **Printers** control panel icon.

Step 2. Double-click **Add Printer** icon and follow the on-screen prompts to complete the device installation.

SCSI Adapters

Step 1. Double-click the **SCSI Adapters** control panel icon and select **Drivers**.

Step 2. Click on the **Add** button and follow the on-screen prompts to complete the device installation.

Tape Devices

Step 1. Double-click the **Tape Devices** control panel icon and select **Drivers**.

Step 2. Click on the **Add** button and follow the on-screen prompts to complete the device installation.

Note: If the device cannot be installed through a control panel, follow the device manufacturer's specific installation instructions.

_____ *Instructor's Initials*

Name _____

VIEWING MEMORY AREAS USING TASK MANAGER
AND NT DIAGNOSTICS

Objective: To understand how to view memory usage statistics in Windows NT Workstation

Parts: Computer with Windows NT Workstation installed and configured

At times, it is beneficial to view memory usage statistics to troubleshoot resource conflicts. NT provides two utilities that can be used for this, Task Manager and NT Diagnostics. Task Manager allows you to view the memory usage for individual processes whereas NT Diagnostics allows you to view overall memory usage statistics.

To use Task Manager, follow these steps:

Step 1.   Turn the computer on and verify that Windows NT Workstation loads.

Step 2.   Logon to Windows NT Workstation using the userid and password provided by the instructor or lab assistant.

Step 3.   Press **CTRL, ALT, and Delete** simultaneously. The Windows Security window opens.

Step 4.   Choose **Task Manager** and then select the **Processes** tab.

Step 5.   The currently running processes display along with each processes' CPU and Memory usage statistics.

Question 1:   How much memory are the Winlogon.exe and the Taskmgr.exe processes using?

To use the Windows NT Diagnostics utility, follow these steps:

Step 6.   Click on the **Start** button, point to **Programs, Administration Tools**, and then click on the **Windows NT Diagnostics** option.

Question 2:   What other method can be used to start Windows NT Diagnostics?

Step 7.   When the Windows NT Diagnostics window opens, select the **Memory** tab. The memory statistics display.

Question 3:   How much memory is set aside for file caching?

_____ *Instructor's Initials*

Name _____

USING NT DIAGNOSTICS

Objective: To understand the proper use of the NT Diagnostics utility

Parts: Computer with Windows NT Workstation installed and configured

Windows NT provides a diagnostic utility that can be used to view system information. This is especially useful for diagnosing and troubleshooting system errors and conflicts.

Step 1. Turn on the computer and verify that the Windows NT Workstation loads.

Step 2. Logon to NT Workstation using the userid and password provided by the instructor or lab assistant.

Step 3. From the **Start** menu, choose **Programs, Administrative Tools**, and then select **Windows NT Diagnostics**. The Windows NT Diagnostics utility starts.

Question 1: How else can you start Windows NT Diagnostics?

Step 4. Click on the **Version** tab. From the Version tab, you can view the version, service pack, registration key, and registration information for the computer.

Step 5. Select the **System** tab. From the System window, you can view system, HAL, BIOS, and CPU information.

Question 2: What type of processor is installed in the computer?

Step 6. Select the **Display** tab. From the Display window, you can view video adapter and display information.

Question 3: What type of video adapter is installed in the computer?

Step 7. Select the **Drives** tab. From the Drives window, you can view the hard drives and CD-ROM drives.

Step 8. Select the **Memory** tab. From the Memory window, you can view memory statistics for the system.

Question 4:   How much total physical memory is installed in the system?

Step 9.   Select the **Services** tab. From the Services window, you can view installed services and their status, as well as installed devices and their operational state.

Step 10.   Select the **Resources** tab. From the Resources window, you can view IRQ, I/O port, DMA, memory, and device statistics for your system.

Question 5:   Are any devices using DMA channels? If so, which devices?

Step 11.   Select the **Environment** tab. From the Environment window, you can view the system and local user environment variables.

Step 12.   Select the **Network** tab. From the Network window, you can view the network environment settings and statistics.

Question 6:   Is your workstation a member of a domain, or a workgroup?

_____ *Instructor's Initials*

Step 13.   Close the **Windows NT Diagnostics** utility.

Name _____

USING NT DIAGNOSTICS #2

Objective: To use the Windows NT Diagnostics tool to troubleshoot device conflicts

Parts: Computer with Windows NT Workstation installed

Step 1.   Turn on the computer and verify that the Windows NT Workstation loads.

Step 2.   Logon to NT Workstation using the userid and password provided by the instructor or lab assistant.

Step 3.   Click on the **Start** button.

Step 4.   Point to the **Programs** option.

Step 5.   Point to the **Administrative Tools (Common)** option.

Step 6.   Click on the **Windows NT Diagnostics** option. The Windows NT Diagnostics window opens. The tab that opens by default is the Version tab.

Question 1:   What version of NT Workstation is running and what, if any, service pack is installed?

Step 7.   Click on the **Resources** tab.

Question 2:   What IRQs are not used?

Step 8.   Click on the **I/O Port** button.

Question 3:   What device uses 03F7 I/O address space?

Step 9.   Click on the **DMA** button.

Question 4:   What device uses DMA channel 2?

Step 10.   Click on the **Memory** button.

Question 5:   What device uses the memory range 000A0000 – 000AFFFF?

Step 11.   Close the **NT Diagnostics** window.

_____ *Instructor's Initials*

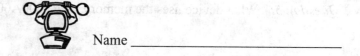

Name _____

INSTALLING A LOCAL PRINTER ON
WINDOWS NT WORKSTATION COMPUTER

Objective: To understand the installation of a local printer on a Windows NT Workstation

Parts: Computer with NT Workstation loaded and a printer physically attached to a printer port
(Option) The appropriate print driver for the printer attached or the NT Workstation CD

Before an NT Workstation can send a print job to a local printer, the driver for that printer must be installed and configured.

Step 1.   Turn the computer on and verify that NT Workstation loads.

Step 2.   Logon to NT Workstation using the userid and password provided by the instructor or lab assistant.

Step 3.   Double-click on the **My Computer** desktop icon and then double-click on the **Printers** folder. The Printers folder opens.

Question 1:   What is another way to access the Printers folder?

Step 4.   Double-click the **Add Printer** icon, and the Add Printer wizard starts.

Step 5.   Select **My Computer** and then click on the **Next** button and the Ports window opens.

Question 2:   How many LPT and COM ports are listed in the Ports window?

Step 6.   Choose the printer **Manufacturer** of your printer and then select the printer **Model**. If the attached printer is not listed, click on the **Have Disk** button, insert the print driver disk or CD, enter a path to the driver files (such as A: or the drive letter for the CD-ROM), and click on the **OK** button.

Step 7.   Select the appropriate printer mode and click on the **Next** button.

Step 8.   Enter a **name** for the printer in the **Printer Name** field and click on the **Next** button. The Sharing and Additional Drivers window opens.

Question 3:   What name did you assign to the printer?

Step 9.   Select the **Not Shared** option, leave the Share Name field blank, and click on the **Next** button.

Step 10.   Select the **Yes** option to print a test page and click on the **Finish** button.

Step 11.   If prompted, insert the Windows NT Workstation CD-ROM or enter a path to the installation files.

Step 12.   The printer installation process finishes and returns to the Printers Folder. If the installation is successful, a printer test page prints.

Question 4:   Did a test page print successfully? If not, redo the exercise. Take special precautions when selecting the appropriate print driver.

_____ *Instructor's Initials*

Name _____

CREATING AN ERD (EMERGENCY REPAIR DISK) USING NT WORKSTATION

Objective: To create an ERD on an NT Workstation computer

Parts: Computer with NT Workstation installed

Step 1.   Turn on the computer and verify that the NT Workstation loads.

Step 2.   Logon to NT Workstation using the userid and password provided by the instructor or lab assistant.

Step 3.   Click on the **Start** button.

Step 4.   Click on the **Run** option.

Step 5.   In the Open: textbox, type, **RDISK** and press **Enter.** The Repair Disk Utility appears on the screen.

Step 6.   Click on the **Update Repair Info** button. A prompt may appear that states that the repair information that was previously saved will be deleted. If this prompt appears, click on the **Yes** button.

Question 1:   What is the difference between using the Update Repair Info button and the Create Repair Disk options?

Step 7.   A prompt appears asking if you want to create an Emergency Repair Disk. Click on the **Yes** button to create an Emergency Repair Disk.

Step 8.   Insert a floppy disk into the A: drive and click on the **OK** button.

Step 9.   When finished, remove the disk, label it with the current date and store in a safe location.

Step 10.   Click on the **Exit** button to close the Repair Disk program.

_____ *Instructor's Initials*

Name _____

USING PERFORMANCE MONITOR IN WINDOWS NT WORKSTATION

Objective: To understand the proper use of the Performance Monitor utility in monitoring system performance in Windows NT Workstation

Parts: Computer with Windows NT Workstation installed and configured

Windows NT provides the Performance Monitor utility that can be used to monitor system performance

To monitor system performance using Performance Monitor, follow these steps:

Step 1.   Turn the computer on and verify that Windows NT Workstation loads.

Step 2.   Logon to Windows NT Workstation using the userid and password provided by the instructor or lab assistant.

Step 3.   From the **Start** menu, point to **Programs, Administrative Tools**, and then select **Performance Monitor**. The Performance Monitor utility starts.

Step 4.   Before Performance Monitor can be used to monitor system performance, you must configure the system counters to monitor. To add counters to Performance Monitor, click the + **(plus)** button on the Performance Monitor toolbar. The Add To Chart window opens.

Step 5.   From the Object drop-down menu, select **Processor**.

Question 1:   How many objects are available for adding system counters?

Step 6.   From the Counter window, hold the **CTRL** key down while selecting the following: **%Processor Time, %User Time, %Interrupt Time**, and **%Privileged Time**. Click on the **Add** button, and then click on the **Done** button to return to the Performance Monitor window.

Step 7.   Each of the selected counters will be represented on the Performance Monitor chart by different color. Minimize the **Performance Monitor utility** window by clicking on the icon with the line symbol in the top right corner of the window.

Step 8.   From the **Start** menu, choose **Programs, Accessories,** and then select **Notepad**.

Step 9.   Maximize the **Performance Monitor utility** window by clicking on the Performance Monitor icon located on the taskbar.

Question 2: Did starting the Notepad application cause any activity with the selected counters in Performance Monitor?

Step 10. Move the mouse cursor across the Performance Monitor screen.

Question 3: Did moving the mouse cursor cause any counter activity?

Question 4: If moving the mouse cursor caused counter activity, which of the selected counters show the most activity?

_____ ***Instructor's Initials***

Step 11. When finished with monitoring the selected counters, close the **Performance Monitor** utility.

Name _____

EVENT VIEWER USING NT WORKSTATION

Objective: To create a computer baseline report that can be used when the computer does not function properly

Parts: Computer with NT Workstation installed

Step 1.   Turn on the computer and verify that the Windows NT Workstation loads.

Step 2.   Logon to NT Workstation using the userid and password provided by the instructor or lab assistant.

Step 3.   Click on the **Start** button.

Step 4.   Point to the **Programs** option.

Step 5.   Point to the **Administrative Tools (Common)** option.

Step 6.   Click on the **Event Viewer** option.

Question 1:   What log is opened by default?

Question 2:   If any events list on the screen, write the two most recent events in the space below.

Step 7.   Scroll down through the events and note the different symbols that precede events.

Question 3:   How many different event symbols show in the Event Viewer system log? What does each symbol mean?

Step 8.   Double-click on an **event** in the system log.

Question 4:   What information does the Event Detail window give you that was not available on the original screen?

Step 9.   Click on the Event Detail **Help** button.

Question 5:   What happens to event data if you archive the event log in a TXT file?

Step 10.   Click on the **Close** button in the Event Viewer Help window.

Step 11.   Click on the **Close** button in the Event Detail window.

Step 12.   Click on the **Log** menu item and select the **Security** option.

Question 6:   What types of events are kept in the security log?

Step 13.   Click on the **View** menu option.

Question 7:   What is an alternative to viewing the newest information first?

Step 14.   Click on the **Log** menu item and select the **Log Settings** option.

Question 8:   What is the current setting for the Maximum Log Size option?

Step 15.   Click on the **Change Settings for Security** down arrow. The Maximum Log Size option is applicable to each type of event log.

Question 9:   How many types of logs are available in the drop-down menu and what are the names of the logs?

Step 16.   Click on the **Cancel** button.

Step 17.   Click on the **Log** menu item and select the **System** option.

Step 18.   Click on the **View** menu item and select the **Filter Events** option. The Filter Events option is a dialog box that allows you to define the event time period, event type, and event category. When filtering is enabled, the word Filtered appears in the title bar.

Question 10: What types of events are filtered by default?

Step 19. Click on the **Cancel** button in the Filter window.

_____ *Instructor's Initials*

Step 20. Click on the **Close** button in the Event Viewer window.

Name _____

HALTING AN APPLICATION USING TASK MANAGER
IN WINDOWS NT WORKSTATION

Objective: To use Task Manager to halt an application

Parts: Computer with Windows NT Workstation installed

At times, it may become necessary to halt a hung or stalled application. Windows NT Workstation provides a method to accomplish this through the Task Manager utility.

Step 1.   Turn on the computer and verify that Windows NT Workstation loads.

Step 2.   Logon to Windows NT Workstation using the userid and password provided by the instructor or lab assistant.

Step 3.   From the **Start** menu, point to **Programs, Accessories,** and then click on the **Notepad** option. The Notepad utility runs.

Question 1:   What other method can be used to start the Notepad utility?

Step 4.   To access Task Manager, simultaneously press the **CTRL, ALT**, and **DEL** keys and then select **Task Manager**.

Question 2:   What things can you view from Task Manager?

Step 5.   Select the **Applications** tab.

Question 3:   What applications are listed as open?

Step 6.   Highlight the **Notepad.exe** application and select **End Task**. The Notepad.exe application closes.

Step 7.   Close the **Task Manager** utility.

_____ *Instructor's Initials*

Name _____

INTERNET DISCOVERY

Objective: To access the Internet to obtain specific information regarding a computer or its associated parts

Parts: Access to the Internet

Question 1:   List two web sites that have information about troubleshooting the NT Workstation installation.

Question 2:   You have just loaded Norton AntiVirus and now NT Workstation does not boot. Find a web site that details what to do.

Question 3:   How do you create boot floppies for NT Workstation? Find a web site that describes how and write the URL in the space below.

Question 4:   What is Paged Pool Memory as it relates to NT Workstation? Find a definition for this term on the Internet and write the URL and the definition in the space below.

Question 5:   On the Microsoft Internet site, find a description of how to install NT Workstation unattended. Write the URL in the space below.

Question 6:   An internal 100MB Iomega Zip Drive is installed in an NT Workstation computer. The computer displays the error, "ASPI for Win32 not initialized." Find a URL that details the resolution process. Write the URL in the space below.

NOTES

17

Chapter 17:

Windows 2000 Professional

OBJECTIVES

After completing this chapter you will
- Understand the major differences between Windows 2000 Professional and other operating systems.
- Be able to identify, explain, and use common desktop icons.
- Be able to manage files and folders.
- Understand the purpose of the registry, how it is organized into subtrees, and the function of each subtree.
- Be able to edit, back up, and restore the registry, and back up/restore the System State.
- Be able to install and troubleshoot Windows 2000 Professional.
- Be able to install hardware and software on a Windows 2000 computer.
- Understand the boot process and be able to troubleshoot boot problems, including using Safe Mode.
- Be able to create and use an Emergency Repair Disk.
- Be able to use the Recovery Console and work from a command prompt to repair a computer using Windows 2000.
- Know when to access and how to use Computer Management console, Task Manager, Dr. Watson, and Event Viewer.

KEY TERMS

ACPI	dual-boot	My Documents	SMP
Apply button	EFS	My Network Places	Start button
archive attribute	encryption	OK button	stealth virus
baseline	ERD	path	system attribute
boot partition	Event Viewer	Performance Logs	system files
boot sector virus	Explorer	and Alerts	system key
Cancel button	extension	polymorphic virus	system partition
checkbox	file	Quick Launch bar	System State
clean install	file virus	radio button	tab
Close button	folder	read-only attribute	Task Manager
compression	GUI	Readiness Analyzer	taskbar
Computer	HAL	Recovery Console	textbox
Management	Help button	Recycle Bin	Trojan horse virus
Connect to the	hidden attribute	REGEDIT	user profile
Internet	icon	REGEDT32	virus
desktop	Internet Explorer	registry	WFP
dialog box	macro virus	service pack	window
Dr. Watson	multi-boot	shortcut	worm virus
drop-down menu	My Computer	Show Desktop	

WINDOWS 2000 PROFESSIONAL OVERVIEW

There are several versions of Windows 2000—Windows 2000 Professional, Windows 2000 Server, Windows 2000 Advanced Server and Windows 2000 Data Center Server. Windows 2000 Professional is an operating system designed for a computer workstation. Windows 2000 Professional is covered in this chapter because it is on the A+ Certification exam.

Windows 2000 Professional is an operating system designed for business workstations—computers in the workplace that are connected to a network. Windows 2000 is easy to install and you can upgrade from Windows 95, Windows 98, or NT Workstation. The installation can also be done across a network. In addition, Windows 2000 is more robust and more stable than previous workstation operating systems. Windows 2000 supports plug and play. The operating system supports many new hardware devices including DVD, WDM video capture devices, speakers, USB, AGP, multiple monitor support, FireWire, removable storage drives, infrared devices, and digital cameras. One important change is that with Windows 2000, the computer does not have to be restarted after every change, as it did with Windows 95/98. This feature is only available if the drivers being installed are Windows 2000 certified. See Microsoft's web site at http://www.microsoft.com for a complete listing of devices supported by Windows 2000.

Windows 2000 Professional is based on a 32-bit architecture. This operating system provides better performance than NT Workstation and Windows 95/98. Every 32-bit application under Windows 2000 and NT runs in its own memory space. When an application freezes or crashes, other 32-bit applications loaded into memory are not affected. Like NT Workstation, all 16-bit applications run in a single process called NTVDM (NT Virtual DOS Machine). If one 16-bit application crashes, any other 16-bit applications loaded into memory crash too. However, Windows 2000 Professional offers the option of running a 16-bit application in its own memory space to prevent this from happening. To allow a 16-bit application to run in its own memory space, go to a command prompt and type *Start /separate process_name*, where *process_name* is the name of the 16-bit application process.

Windows 2000 Professional can use up to 4GB of RAM and support **SMP (Symmetric Multiprocessing)**. SMP is the ability to support two processors that operate simultaneously. Each process being run by an application or the operating system is distributed equally across two microprocessors and makes sure that one processor does not become a bottleneck for the system.

A new Windows 2000 Professional feature is **WFP (Windows File Protection)**, which is a program that protects system files. WFP is a program that runs in the background. It detects whether a system file has been altered or deleted. In previous operating systems, applications or users changed the system files and thus made the operating system unstable. WFP detects when a system file has been altered, deleted, or overwritten. A copy of the original file is obtained from the DLLCACHE folder or the media from which Windows 2000 was installed. If the media is unavailable, a message appears on the screen prompting for the media. The copied file is put into the proper folder.

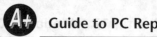
The file systems that Windows 2000 Professional supports include FAT16, FAT32, and NTFS. The NTFS version that Windows 2000 Professional supports is known as NTFS 5 (as opposed to NT Workstation's NTFS 4). See the Hard Drive chapter for more details on file systems. For CD and DVD media, Windows 2000 Professional supports CDFS (Compact Disk File System) and UDF (Universal Disk Format). See the Multimedia chapter for more discussion about these file systems.

WINDOWS 2000 BASICS

After a user logs on to Windows 2000, the desktop appears. The login screen cannot be bypassed as it can in Windows 95/98. A user can login to a network server, login to a network workgroup (peer-to-peer network), or login locally (as a stand-alone computer not participating in a network). The **desktop** is the area where all work is performed. It is the interface between the user and the computer files, applications, and hardware. The desktop is part of the operating system's **GUI (Graphical User Interface)** environment. WIN2000 Figure #1 shows an illustration of the Windows 2000 desktop.

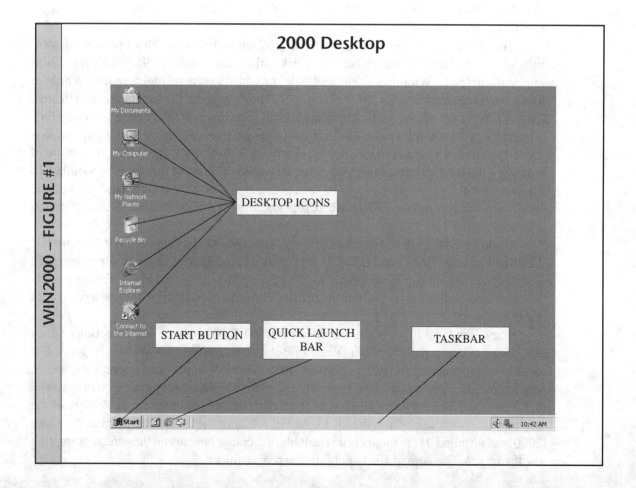

WIN2000 – FIGURE #1

The desktop consists of many icons. **Icons** are pictures on the desktop. When you double-click on them, you interface with various devices, files, and applications on your computer.

The desktop sometimes is cluttered with things the user puts on it. An exercise at the end of the chapter shows you how to clean up the desktop. Note that when you have the Auto Arrange option enabled, the icons on the desktop cannot be moved. The desktop can also be modified to have a wallpaper scheme (which is a background picture, pattern, or color), a color scheme (which is the color scheme used in displaying folders), and a screen saver (which is the picture, color, or pattern that displays when the computer is inactive). An exercise at the end of the chapter describes how to change each of these.

Whenever you open an application or utility, a **window** appears. Windows are a normal part of the desktop. The desktop consists of icons, the Start button, the Quick Launch bar, and the taskbar. Common icons include: My Documents, My Computer, My Network Places, and Recycle Bin.

The **My Documents** icon is used to quickly access the My Documents folder (directory) on the hard drive. The My Documents folder is the default location for files the user saves. The **My Computer** icon is used to access the hardware, software, and files located on the computer. The **My Network Places** icon is used to access network resources such as computers, printers, scanners, fax machines, and files. The **Recycle Bin** is used to hold files and folders the user deletes. When a file is deleted from a folder, it is not immediately discarded; instead, it goes into the Recycle Bin. Once a file or folder is in the Recycle Bin, it can be removed. This is similar to a piece of trash being retrieved from an office trash can. A technician must remember that these files and folders in the Recycle Bin take up hard drive space and that users frequently forget to empty the files and folders from the Recycle Bin. An exercise at the end of the chapter explains how to empty the Recycle Bin.

The **Internet Explorer** icon is used to start the Internet Explorer application. This application allows Internet connectivity. The **Connect to the Internet** icon is a Windows 2000 wizard that steps you through setting up an Internet connection. The Connect to the Internet is actually a common type of desktop icon called a shortcut. A **shortcut** is an icon that looks like any other icon except that it has a bent arrow in the lower left corner. A shortcut represents a path (location on the drive) to a file, folder, or program. It is a link (a pointer) to where the file or application resides on a disk. When you double-click on a shortcut icon, the shortcut icon tells Windows where to find the specific file that the icon represents. If the shortcut represents an application, the application opens. If the shortcut represents a document, the application used to create the document appears along with the document. A shortcut offers faster access to an application or file than going through the Start button or through the My Computer icon. Users and technicians frequently place shortcuts on the desktop and it is important that you know how to create one. Users create shortcuts to their favorite applications or to documents used frequently.

The **Start button** is located in the lower left corner of the desktop and is used to launch applications and utilities, search for files and other computers, get help, and add/remove hardware and software. WIN2000 Figure #2 shows the Start button.

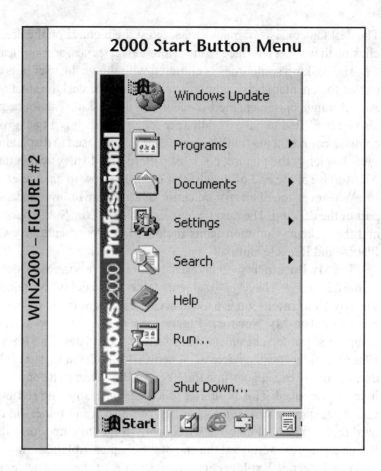

WIN2000 – FIGURE #2

The Shut Down Start button option is used to shut down the computer, logoff from the network, restart the computer, and possibly put the computer in standby or hibernate. The standby and hibernate options are available on computers that support power saving features. Standby is helpful on laptop computers to save on battery life. Hibernate is available on computers that support Windows 2000 power options and is similar to the shut down option except that it can be scheduled. At a specific time, the computer is shut down and when the computer restarts, the active components on the desktop at the time of hibernation are still there.

The Run Start button option is used for starting an application or bringing up a command prompt window. The Help option is used for Windows 2000 general usage and troubleshooting assistance. The Search Start button option is used to locate files, remote network devices, web sites on the Internet, and people in the Windows address book. The Settings option is used to access various suboptions that allow computer configuration. The Documents selection contains the 15 most recently used files (provided the application supports this option). The Programs choice allows access to applications installed in the computer. The Windows Update option is used to connect to the Microsoft Web site to access the most recent drivers and operating system updates.

The **Quick Launch bar** is a set of icons to the right of the Start button and allows you to launch applications with one click on a Quick Launch icon. An important icon on the Quick Launch bar is the **Show Desktop** icon. This icon looks like a desk with a pencil touching a piece of paper. Single-click on the Show Desktop icon to reduce all windows on the screen and display the desktop. If you click on the icon a second time, the original document (that was on the screen when you clicked the Show Desktop icon) reappears. Another Quick Launch icon is the Internet Explorer. Click once on this icon and the Internet Explorer application opens.

The **taskbar** is the bar that runs across the bottom of the screen. The taskbar holds buttons that represent applications or files currently loaded into memory. The taskbar also holds icons that allow access to system utilities. These utilities can include a clock icon for the date and time, an icon of a speaker for volume control, and an icon for a virus utility. Look back to WIN2000 Figure #1 to identify the taskbar. An exercise at the end of the chapter helps you get familiar with working with desktop components.

One type of window used with Windows operating systems is a dialog box. A **dialog box** allows you to set application or operating system preferences. The most common features found in a dialog box are a checkbox, a textbox, tabs, a drop-drown menu, a Help button, a Close button, an OK button, and a Cancel button. A **textbox** is an area where you can type a specific parameter. When you click inside a textbox, a vertical line appears which is the insertion point. Any typed text is placed to the right of the insertion point. Notice in WIN2000 Figure #3 how the Top, Bottom, Inside, Outside, etc. options are textboxes. Textboxes sometimes have up or down arrows that can be used to select a preset option, or you can simply type your own parameter.

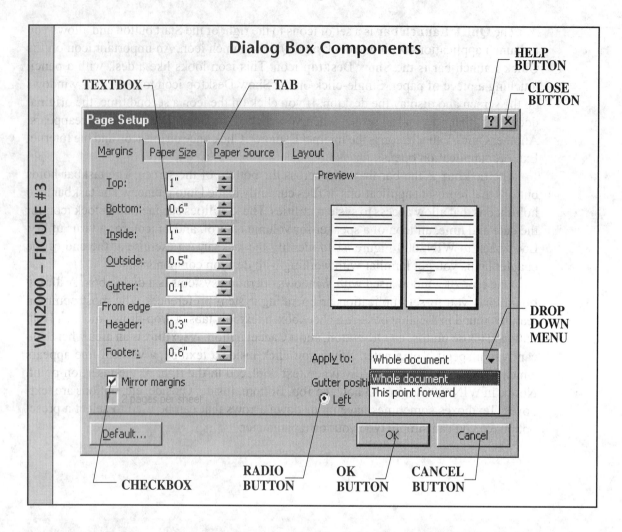

Dialog Box Components

WIN2000 – FIGURE #3

Tabs normally appear across the top of a dialog box. Each tab normally holds a group of related options. Click once on the tab to bring that particular major section to the window forefront. The tabs in WIN2000 Figure #3 are Margins, Paper Size, Paper Source, and Layout.

The **Help button** is used to provide context sensitive assistance and is the question mark located in the upper right corner of the dialog box. When you click on the Help button (the question mark), the cursor turns into an arrow with a question mark attached. Click on any item you want basic information on and a pop-up window appears on the screen. To close the pop-up window, click anywhere on the screen. The **Close button**, which is located to the right of the Help button and is an "X," is used to close the dialog box. When the Close button is used, no changes that have been made in the dialog box are applied.

A **checkbox** is an option that, when checked, is enabled or turned on. In WIN2000 Figure #3, clicking inside the checkbox enables the Mirror Margins option. When an option is enabled, a checkmark appears in the checkbox. A **radio button** is a round circle, but it operates the same way a checkbox does. A radio button is enabled when a solid dot appears inside it. Click once on a blank radio button and a solid dot appears. Click once on a radio button that has a dot in it, and the dot disappears. The option is disabled when no dot appears.

Drop-down menus are presented when you click on a down arrow. In WIN2000 Figure #3, the drop-down menu appears when you click on the down arrow in the section marked Apply to. Once presented with the drop-down menu, click on the preferred option and that option appears in the drop-down window.

The **OK button** and the **Cancel button** are standard buttons in a dialog box. When you click on the OK button, all options selected or changed within the dialog box are applied. When you click on the Cancel button, all changed options in the dialog box are not applied; the options are left in their current state. Another related button that can be found in a dialog box, but is not shown in WIN2000 Figure #2, is the Apply button. The **Apply button** is used to make changes immediately (before clicking on the OK button). This is useful when you want to see the results of your selection, such as when you are making changes to the desktop's background.

One of the most frequent mistakes new technicians make is clicking on the Close button without first applying or clicking OK for changes. When a dialog box is closed with the Close button, no changes in the dialog box window are saved or applied.

MANAGING FILES AND FOLDERS

Technicians are always creating, deleting, and moving files and folders. It is important that you are able to do these tasks quickly and without error. The important thing to remember is to think about what file and folder you want to work with, where the files and folders are located now, and where you want the files or folders to be eventually.

A drive letter followed by a colon represents every drive in a computer. For example, the floppy drive is represented by A: and the first hard drive partition is represented by C:. The CD-ROM drive, DVD, or Zip® drive are all represented by a letter followed by a colon. Disks or drives hold files. A **file** is an electronic container that holds computer code or data. Another way of looking at it is thinking of a file as a box of bits. A file is kept on some type of media such as a floppy disk, Zip disk, hard drive, tape, or CD. Each file is given a name called a filename. An example of a filename is 2000CHAP.DOC.

Files are kept in folders. A **folder** holds files and can also contain other folders. In older operating systems, a folder was called a directory. Every file and folder is given a name. It is easier to understand file and folder names if we look at how older operating systems named files and folders and then look at how 2000 names differ. In older operating systems (DOS), a filename could *not* contain the following characters:

. (period)	; (semicolon)	/ (forward slash)
, (comma)	" (quotation marks)	\ (backslash)
	(vertical bar)	? (question mark)	[(left bracket)
: (colon)	= (equal sign)	] (right bracket)
* (asterisk)	(space)	

In addition to naming a file in DOS, you would frequently have to add an extension to the name. An **extension** is an addition to the filename and it can be up to three characters in length. The filename and the extension are separated by a period. An example of a filename with an extension is BOOK.DOC where BOOK is the name of the file and DOC is the extension.

Normally with Windows 95/98/NT/2000, the application automatically adds an extension to the end of the filename. In most windows, Windows 2000 does not automatically show the extensions. To view the extensions in Windows Explorer, click on the *Tools* menu option. Click on the *Folder Options* menu option. Click on the *View* tab and click on the *Hide file extensions for known file types* checkbox (which will remove the check from the box). Click on the *OK* button.

When Windows recognizes an extension, it associates the extension with a particular application. WIN2000 Figure #4 illustrates common icons that Windows uses when it recognizes an extension and WIN2000 Table #1 lists the most common file extensions.

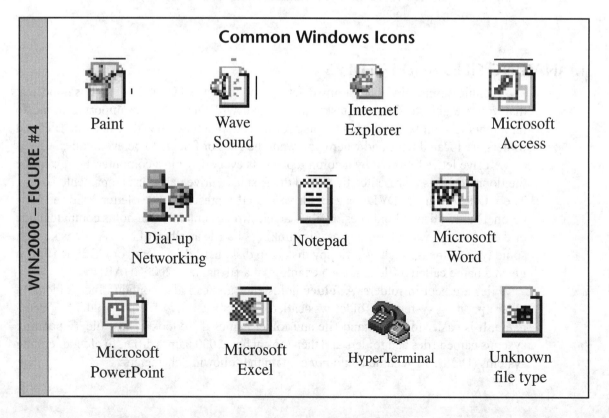

WIN2000 – FIGURE #4

Common Windows Icons

Paint

Wave Sound

Internet Explorer

Microsoft Access

Dial-up Networking

Notepad

Microsoft Word

Microsoft PowerPoint

Microsoft Excel

HyperTerminal

Unknown file type

WIN2000 – TABLE #1

Common File Extensions

Extension	Purpose or Application
386	Used by Windows 3.x for device drivers
AI	Adobe Illustrator
BAT	Used in DOS environments for batch files. Combines executable commands into one file and uses one command to start the batch file.
BMP	Bitmap file
CAB	Cabinet file—a compressed file that holds operating system or application files
COM	Command file—an executable file that opens an application or tool
DLL	Dynamic Link Library file —contains executable code that can be used by more than one application and is called upon from other code already running
DOC	Microsoft Word
DRV	Device driver—a piece of software that enables an operating system to recognize a hardware device
EPS	Encapsulated postscript file
EXE	Executable file—a file that opens an application
GIF	Graphics interchange file
HLP	Windows-based help file
INF	Information or Setup file
INI	Initialization file—Used in Windows 3.x environment to control applications and the operating environment. Used in 95, 98, NT, and 2000 to be backward compatible with Windows 3.x
JPG or JPEG	Joint Photographic Experts Group file format—graphics file
MPG or MPEG	Movie clip file
PCX	Microsoft Paintbrush
PDF	Adobe Acrobat —portable document format
PPT	Microsoft PowerPoint
RTF	Rich text format
TIF or TIFF	Tag image file format
TXT	Text file
VXD	Virtual device driver
WKS	Lotus worksheet
WPS	Microsoft Works text file format
WRI	Microsoft WordPad
XLS	Microsoft Excel
ZIP	Compressed file

Filenames in Windows 2000 Professional can be up to 255 characters. These extended filenames are commonly called long filenames. Folders and filenames can have all characters, numbers, letters, and spaces *except* the following:

/ (forward slash)	" (quotation marks)	\ (backslash)
| (vertical bar)	? (question mark)	: (colon)
* (asterisk)		

As you can see, the list is much shorter than the DOS list (which means more characters are allowed) with Windows 2000 Professional.

An example of a long filename is WINDOWS 2000 CHAPTER.DOC. Any time a document has been saved with one of these long filenames and is taken to a computer with an older operating system that does not support long filenames, the filename is shortened to a maximum of eight characters. Windows does this by using the first six characters of the filename, deleting any spaces, and using two special characters—a tilde (~) and a number. For example, 2000 PROFESSIONAL CHAPTER.DOC would be shortened to 2000PR~1.DOC. If there were two files named 2000 PROFESSIONAL CHAPTER.DOC and 2000 PROFESSIONAL INDEX.DOC, the two files would be saved as 2000PR~1.DOC and 2000PR~2.DOC, respectively.

When a file is saved in a Windows application, it automatically goes to a specific folder. This is known as the default folder. With Windows NT and 2000, this folder is the My Documents folder. In documentation, installation instructions, and when writing down the exact location of a file, the full path should be used. A file's **path** is like a road map to the file and includes the drive letter plus all folders and subfolders as well as the filename and extension. For example, if the CHAP1.DOC file is in the MY DOCUMENTS folder on the first hard drive partition, the full path is C:\MY DOCUMENTS\CHAP1.DOC. The first part is the drive letter where the document is stored, C:. The C: represents the first hard drive partition. The name of the document is always at the very end of the path. In the example given, CHAP1.DOC is the name of the file. Everything in between the drive letter and the filename is the name of one or more folders where the CHAP1.DOC file is located. The folder in this example is the MY DOCUMENTS folder.

If the CHAP1.DOC file is located in a subfolder called COMPUTER BOOK, which is located in the folder called MY DOCUMENTS, then the full path is C:\MY DOCUMENTS\COMPUTER BOOK\CHAP1.DOC. Notice how the backslashes in the path are always used to separate the folder names as well as separate the drive letter from the first folder name.

Explorer is the most common application used to create, copy or move files or folders; however, the My Computer window can be used in a similar fashion. When you are copying a file or folder, use the Copy/Paste functions. When you are moving a file or folder, use the Cut/Paste functions.

When you delete a file or folder from a floppy or Zip disk, the file or folder is permanently deleted. When deleting a file or folder from a hard drive, the file or folder is automatically sent to the Recycle Bin. The contents of the Recycle Bin take up hard drive space. Many users do not realize that they are not really deleting the file, but simply moving it to the Recycle Bin. To delete a file permanently from the hard drive, hold down the *Shift* key while pressing the *Delete* key on the keyboard and the file is permanently removed. Otherwise, you will have to remember to empty the Recycle Bin periodically. An exercise at the end of the chapter illustrates how to copy, move, and delete files and folders. WIN2000 Figure #5 shows how the A+ COMPLETE BOOK.DOC long filename looks in graphical form using the Explorer application.

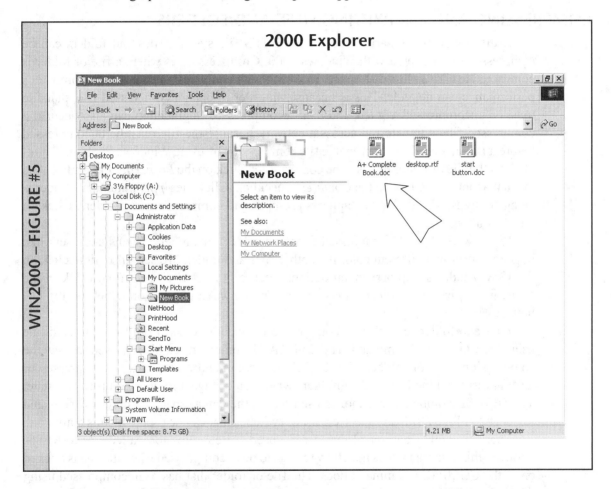

My Computer and Explorer can be used for setting attributes for a file or folder. The file and folder attributes are read-only, hidden, archive, and system. The **read-only attribute** marks a file or folder so that it cannot be changed. The **hidden attribute** marks a file or folder so that it is not visible through My Computer or Explorer unless someone changes the default view for the window. Some applications use the **archive attribute** to control which files or folders are backed up. The **system attribute** is placed on certain files used to boot 2000 Professional.

To change a file or folder's attributes, use My Computer or Explorer to locate the file or folder. Right-click on the file or folder name. Click on the *Properties* option and the

Properties window opens. Toward the bottom of the window is an *Attributes* section. Click inside one or more of the attribute checkboxes to enable or disable an attribute. A checkmark in a checkbox means an attribute is enabled. An empty checkbox means an attribute is disabled. If the file is not a system file, the system attribute is unavailable. Click on the *Apply* button when you are finished setting the attributes.

COMPRESSING AND ENCRYPTING FILES AND FOLDERS

If the hard drive is partitioned for the NTFS file system, files and folders can be compressed or encrypted with Windows 2000. **Compression** is where a file or folder is compacted to take up less disk space. However, with compression enabled, the computer's performance can degrade. This is because, in order to open a compressed file, that file must be uncompressed, copied, and then recompressed. Degradation can also occur if a compressed file is transferred across a network because the file must be uncompressed before it is transferred. You can enable file compression by using Windows Explorer. Right-click on the file or folder that is to be compressed. Click on the *Properties* option from the menu that appears. Click on the *Compress* checkbox. Click the *Apply* button. If a folder is being compressed, a dialog box appears prompting to compress any subfolders. Click on the *OK* button.

When working with compressed files and folders, many technicians and users like them to appear in a different color than other files and folders. To set this option, click on the *View* Windows Explorer menu option. Click on the *Options* selection. Click in the *Display compress files and folders with alternate color* radio button. Click on the *OK* button.

Files and folders can also be compressed or uncompressed from the command line using the COMPACT command. The COMPACT command can also be used to view the compression state of folders. The COMPACT command automatically compresses or uncompresses all the files and subfolders when you change a folder's compression state. The DIRUSE command line tool is used to see the actual space compressed files and folders take. Type *DIRUSE /?* to see a list of switches that can be used with this command.

There is another command that can be used for compression called COMPRESS; however, this command does not allow the file to be uncompressed when the file is clicked on as the COMPACT command does. The file or folder that has been compressed using the COMPRESS command must be uncompressed with the EXPAND command.

Encryption is a method of securing data from unauthorized users. Windows 2000 has a new encryption feature called **EFS (Encrypting File System)**. When a file or folder is encrypted with EFS, only the authorized user can view or change the file. Recovery Administrators have the ability to recover encrypted files if necessary. EFS is not compatible with any prior versions of Windows.

To encrypt a file in Windows 2000, use Windows Explorer. The hard drive volume must be partitioned as NTFS to enable encryption. Right-click on the file or folder to be encrypted. Click on the *Properties* option. Click on the *General* tab. Click on the *Advanced* button. Click in the *Encrypt Contents to Secure Data* option. Click the *OK* button. Click on the *Apply* button and then click on the *OK* button.

The CIPHER command line utility can be used to encrypt and decrypt files. The command can also be used to encrypt and decrypt files. If you type *CIPHER* from the command prompt without any switches, current file/folder encryption states are displayed on the screen. Type *CIPHER /?* to view the various switch options available with this command.

Another helpful command line tool with EFS is EFSINFO. The EFSINFO command displays information such as authorized users, recovery agents, etc. Type *EFSINFO /?* from the command prompt to view the switches available with this command.

DETERMINING THE WINDOWS 2000 VERSION

The operating system version is very important to a technician. With Windows 95, 98, NT, and 2000, upgrades or patches to the operating system are provided through **service packs** which fix problems within the operating system. A technician must determine what operating system version is on the computer so that he/she can research whether or not a service pack is needed. Several ways to determine what version of 2000 is loaded on a computer are listed below.

- Right-click on the *Start* button. Click on the *Explore* option. Windows Explorer opens. Click on the *Help* menu option. Click on the *About Windows* option from the drop-down menu.
- Click on the *Start* button. Click on the *Run* option. In the Open textbox, type *winver* and press *Enter*. A window appears with the version.
- Click on the *Start* button. Point to the *Programs* option. Point to the *Administrative Tools* option. Click on the *Computer Management* option. Right-click on the *Computer Management (Local)* option and then click on the *Properties* option.
- Click on the *Start* button. Click on the *Run* option. In the Open textbox, type *winmsd* and then press *Enter*.

WINDOWS 2000 REGISTRY

Every software and hardware configuration is stored in a database called the **registry**. The registry contains such things as folder and file property settings, port configuration, application preferences, and user profiles. A **user profile** contains a user's specific configuration settings such as what applications the user has access to, desktop settings, and the user's network configuration. The registry loads into memory during the boot process. Once in memory, the registry is updated continuously through changes made to software and hardware. The registry is divided into five subtrees. Subtrees are also sometimes called branches or hives. The five standard subtrees are as follows: HKEY_LOCAL_MACHINE, HKEY_USERS, HKEY_CURRENT_USER,

HKEY_CURRENT_CONFIG, and HKEY_CLASSES_ROOT. Each of these subtrees has keys and subkeys that contain values related to hardware and software settings. WIN2000 Table #2 lists the five subtrees and each function.

Windows 2000 Registry Subtrees

Registry Subtree	Subtree Function
HKEY_LOCAL_MACHINE	Holds global hardware configuration. Included in the branch is a list of hardware components installed in the computer, the software drivers that handle each component, and the settings for each device. This information is not user-specific.
HKEY_USERS	Keeps track of individual users and their preferences.
HKEY_CURRENT_USER	Holds a specific user's configuration such as software settings, how the desktop appears, and what folders the user has created.
HKEY_CURRENT_CONFIG	Holds information about the hardware profile that is used when the computer first boots.
HKEY_CLASSES_ROOT	Holds file associations and file links. The information held here is what allows the correct application to start when you double-click on a filename in Explorer or My Computer (provided the file extension is registered).

The registry can contain other subtrees that are user-defined or system-defined depending on what hardware and software is installed in the computer.

EDITING THE WINDOWS 2000 REGISTRY

Most changes to Windows 2000 are made through the various control panels, but sometimes the only way to make a change is to edit the registry directly.

> Before changing the registry, make sure you back up the registry. An exercise at the end of the chapter illustrates this procedure.

Windows 2000 has two registry editors called **REGEDIT** and **REGEDT32**. Both registry editors can be used to change the registry; however, there are some differences between the two. WIN2000 Table #3 shows some of the more important differences.

<table>
<tr><td colspan="2" align="center">**REGEDIT and REGEDT32 Differences**</td></tr>
<tr><td align="center">**REGEDIT**</td><td align="center">**REGEDT32**</td></tr>
<tr><td>Provides more powerful search capabilities</td><td>Can display and edit values larger than 256 characters</td></tr>
<tr><td>All of the subtrees are shown in one window</td><td>The subtrees are shown in individual windows</td></tr>
<tr><td>Allows exporting the registry to a text file</td><td>Can look at and apply access permissions to the subtrees, keys, and subkeys.</td></tr>
<tr><td>Allows importing the registry from the command line</td><td>Can work with multiple registry files simultaneously</td></tr>
</table>

WIN2000 – TABLE #3

With the REGEDIT program, subtrees are listed in the left window. WIN2000 Figure #6 shows the REGEDIT utility.

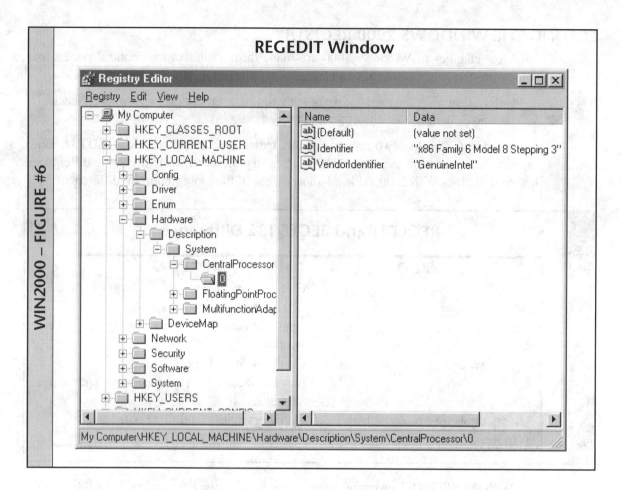

WIN2000 – FIGURE #6

Notice in WIN2000 Figure #6 how the subtrees show up in the left window. When you click on the + (plus) symbol beside each subtree, more subkeys appear. After several layers, when you click on a folder in the left window, values appear in the right window. These values are the ones you must sometimes change to fix a problem.

In REGEDT32, each registry hive appears in a separate window inside the Registry Editor window. Each subtree has individual folders with a + (plus) symbol beside them. Click on the plus symbol to view subkeys. Values appear in the right window as they do in the REGEDIT program. Each hive, or even part of a subtree, can be backed up individually.

BACKING UP/RESTORING THE WINDOWS 2000 REGISTRY

The registry should be backed up whenever the computer is fully functional and when any software or hardware changes are made.

The registry should be backed up and restored on a working computer *before* disaster hits. The time to learn how to restore the registry is *not* when the computer is down.

The registry can be backed up and restored several different ways. The two most common methods used are the REGEDIT and the Backup utilities. The REGEDIT program allows you to export the registry to a file that has the .REG extension. The backed up file can be modified with a text editor if necessary. The file can also be imported back into the computer.

The Backup utility is accessed through Start button ➲ Programs ➲Accessories ➲ System Tools ➲ Backup. The Backup utility is the preferred method for backing up the Windows 2000 registry. The Backup option to look for is the System State, which is discussed in the next section.

BACKING UP THE SYSTEM STATE

Another way to back up the registry is to use the Windows 2000 Backup utility. One option available in the Backup utility is the System State. The **System State** is a group of important Windows 2000 files including the registry, the system files, the boot files, and the COM+ Class Registration database. With the backup utility, you cannot back up or restore these items individually. They are all needed because they depend on one another to operate properly. The Backup utility is accessed through Start button ➲ Programs ➲ Accessories ➲ System Tools ➲ Backup. Click on the *Backup* tab. Click in the box next to *System State*. Select the destination and click on the *Start Backup* button. Once you click on the Start Backup button, the Backup Job Information dialog box appears. The *Advanced* option has a setting, *Automatically backup system protected files with the System State*. This option, when selected, backs up all system files in the %systemroot% folder (which is normally C:\WINNT). Click on the *OK* button to start the backup.

The registry files are located in a folder normally labeled %systemroot% \Repair\Regbackup (which is normally C:\WINNT\REPAIR\REGBACKUP). The registry can be restored without having to restore the other System State files.

 In order to use the Backup program, you must be an administrator or a member of the Backup Operators group.

An exercise at the end of the chapter illustrates this procedure.

RESTORING THE SYSTEM STATE AFTER A FAILURE

In order to correct a problem with the system files, registry, or Windows 2000 boot failure, you must restore the registry. You may also have to restore the System State files (which include the registry) to make the system operational again. To start the restoration process, install a copy of Windows 2000 to the same folder in which it was installed originally. When you are prompted to format the hard drive volume or leave it, select the *Leave the current file system intact* option. Use the Backup utility to restore the System State and/or the registry, (Programs ➲ Accessories ➲ System Tools ➲ Backup). Click on the *Restore* tab and select the device that holds the backed up files.

PRE-INSTALLATION OF WINDOWS 2000 PROFESSIONAL

Windows 2000 Professional can be installed from a central location or locally. Because this book focuses on the A+ Certification exam, only local installation is covered. The pre-installation of any operating system is more important than the installation process. Technicians that grab a disk or CD and load a new operating system without going through a logical process are just asking for trouble. The steps to be taken before installing Windows 2000 Professional are outlined below:

1. Decide whether the installation will be an upgrade or clean install.
2. Determine the file system(s) to be used.
3. Decide whether the computer will have more than one operating system installed.
4. Scan for viruses.
5. Determine if the hardware is compatible.
6. Obtain any drivers, upgrades, or hardware replacements.
7. Decide if the software applications are compatible.
8. Obtain any patches, upgrades, or software replacements.
9. Delete any unwanted files and uninstall any unwanted applications.
10. Back up any data files necessary.
11. Remove any power management or disk management tools.

The first decision to make when planning to install Windows 2000 Professional is whether to upgrade from another operating system or perform a clean install. A **clean install** puts an operating system on a computer without an operating system, or reformats the hard drive so that the computer's existing operating system is removed.

If the decision is to do an upgrade, then determine which operating system is already installed. Windows 2000 Professional supports upgrading from Windows 95, Windows 98, NT Workstation 3.51, and NT Workstation 4. When Windows 2000 Professional is installed as an upgrade, the user's applications and data are preserved if the operating system is installed in the same folder (directory) as the original operating system. If Windows 2000 Professional is installed in a different folder, then all applications must be reloaded.

Another decision you must make if upgrading to Windows 2000 Professional is whether or not to convert the hard drive partition to NTFS. Once a partition is converted to NTFS, the partition cannot be changed back. If you are unsure whether or not to convert the partition, leave it unchanged and later use the CONVERT.EXE program to upgrade. Most people want to convert the partition to NTFS for the following reasons:

- Security (individual files can be protected with NTFS).
- More efficient use of cluster space (the cluster size can be defined based on the user's needs with NTFS).
- NTFS supports file compression.
- NTFS supports larger hard drive partition sizes.

With Windows 2000, a new version of NTFS called NTFS 5 is used. In NTFS 5, a new type of encryption called EFS is supported and disk quotas can be set to monitor and limit user disk space. If upgrading from a prior version of NTFS, the drive is automatically configured for NTFS 5. If any NTFS 4 volumes are not powered during the installation process, the volume is automatically upgraded when the drive is mounted. If you want to dual-boot between Windows NT 4 and Windows 2000 Professional (have both operating systems loaded), make sure that NT Workstation service pack 4 or higher is installed because some of the features in NTFS 5 change the data structure on disks.

In order to take advantage of Windows 2000 Professional's reliability, enhancements, and security features, sometimes a clean installation is the best choice, especially if the current operating system is Windows 95 or Windows 98. Because a clean installation involves formatting the hard drive, the user's data must be backed up and all applications reinstalled once the Windows 2000 Professional installation is complete. Also, all user-defined settings are lost. Another important point to remember is that not all Windows 3.x, 95, and 98 applications are compatible with Windows 2000 Professional. Microsoft has a web site that addresses application compatibility and you should check at this site before making this decision—http://windows.microsoft.com/windows2000/reskit/webresources. You can also contact the company that developed your application and see the application is compatible with Windows 2000.

If the computer already has NT Workstation 3.5 or 4, then a Windows 2000 Professional upgrade is recommended. However, if there are hardware drivers for such devices as a DVD player, power management software, or network utilities loaded on the computer, a clean installation may be a better choice. Whichever is the case, the user's data and applications should be backed up and restored once the Windows 2000 Professional installation is complete.

The third decision that must be made is whether or not Windows 2000 Professional will be installed with one or more other operating systems. This situation is often called a dual-boot or multi-boot scenario. **Dual-boot** means that the computer can boot from two operating systems. **Multi-boot** means the computer can boot from two or more operating systems. Windows 2000 Professional can be dual-booted with DOS, Windows 3.1 or higher, Windows 95, Windows 98, NT Workstation, and OS/2. If this is desired, a separate hard disk partition should be created and used for each operating system. When doing a dual or multi-boot configuration, make sure that Windows 2000 Professional is installed *after* the other operating systems. Multi-booting is beyond the scope of this chapter. See the Microsoft web site for more details. The fourth step is to scan the system for viruses. Viruses are covered in the next section.

The fifth thing to do when installing Windows 2000 Professional is to determine what computer hardware is installed. WIN2000 Table #4 lists the minimum and preferred hardware requirements for installing Windows 2000 Professional.

WIN2000 – TABLE #4

Windows 2000 Professional Hardware Requirements

Component	Minimum	Preferred
CPU	Intel Pentium (or compatible) 133MHz or higher	Intel Pentium II (or compatible) 300MHz or higher
RAM	32MB	64MB
Free Hard Drive Space	650MB	2GB
Input Device	Keyboard, mouse, or other pointing device	Keyboard, mouse, or other pointing device
Multimedia Drive	CD-ROM or DVD	CD-ROM or DVD 12x or faster

Microsoft has a tool called **Readiness Analyzer** that checks your system for hardware and software compatibility issues. This tool can be downloaded from Microsoft's web site at http://www.microsoft.com/windows2000/upgrade/compat/default.asp. Be aware that the Readiness Analyzer might not be able to detect all hardware devices or software applications.

Another hardware check that you need to do is the BIOS on the motherboard. Windows 2000 operates best if the BIOS supports **ACPI (Advanced Configuration and Power Interface)**. Among other things, the ACPI BIOS allows Windows 2000 Professional to control plug and play features. If the BIOS is not an ACPI BIOS, plug and play features can only be handled by the BIOS, not the operating system. In a non-ACPI BIOS, resource settings configured manually cannot be reallocated by the operating system.

Look in the motherboard or computer documentation to see what BIOS is installed. Check the BIOS or computer manufacturer's web site to see whether the BIOS supports ACPI. The Microsoft web site also has a list of compatible BIOSes as well as links to other web sites. Some computers display the manufacturer and BIOS version when the computer first boots. During POST (when the memory count is displaying on the screen), press the *Pause* or *Break* key to be able to read the screen and jot down the BIOS information. Check your BIOS or computer manufacturer's web site to see if the BIOS supports ACPI. You can install Windows 2000 Professional without the BIOS supporting ACPI, but you will not have some of the Windows 2000 features.

Do *not* download a BIOS update unless you are sure it is compatible with your computer. Installing an invalid update can damage your computer system and cause it to cease operating.

Windows 95 and NT Workstation do not support ACPI, but if you are running Windows 98, click on the *Start* button. Point to the *Settings* option and click on the *Control Panel* option. Double-click on the *System* icon. Next, click on the *Device Manager* tab. Then, click on the + (plus symbol) beside the *System Devices* option. If the BIOS supports ACPI, it will be among those listed under System Devices.

Once you have verified all of your hardware, you may have to get Windows 2000 device drivers from the hardware device manufacturer or their web site. You may also need to upgrade the hardware device, which usually means replacing it. This is sometimes the cost of going to a bigger and better operating system. You may also decide at this point not to upgrade, but to buy a computer with Windows 2000 already installed.

The seventh determination you must make before installing Windows 2000 Professional is whether or not any existing software applications are compatible. The preparation for installing a new operating system is usually more work than the actual installation process, but any omitted step will cost you more time in the long run. Use the Readiness Analyzer or contact the developer of each software application to determine if it is compatible. You may also go to the software developer's web site. The information may be posted there. A list of compatible software is also listed on Microsoft's web site.

Once you have determined whether the software is compatible with Windows 2000, you may have to obtain software patches, upgrades, or buy a new version. This is best done before you install Windows 2000. Be proactive, not reactive—solve any problems you can *before* upgrading or installing any operating system.

As with any upgrade, hardware change, or software change, data must be backed up. It is almost funny that the worst people in the world for backing up data are technicians—the very ones who are entrusted with the clients' data and computer. Since Windows 2000 is really designed for the corporate/small business environment, backing up data is an essential step. Whether you do a clean install or an upgrade, if the user has data on the computer, it must be backed up before starting the installation process. Also, before backing up data, remove any unwanted files and/or applications that are no longer needed in order to free up hard drive space.

The last step in the pre-installation checklist is to remove any power or disk management tools loaded on your computer. Computer manufacturers for older operating systems frequently provide these types of tools. Power or disk management tools can interfere with the new tools provided with Windows 2000. Disable these utilities and applications before attempting an operating system installation or upgrade. One important note about disk drives is that you cannot install Windows 2000 on a compressed hard drive partition. Uncompress the partition before starting the Windows 2000 installation process.

VIRUSES

When installing a new operating system on a computer that already has an operating system loaded, it is wise to run a virus scan with the latest version of virus scanning software. A **virus** is a computer program designed to change the way the computer operates. The virus could infect the computer so it does not boot, or infect a particular application so it does not operate or performs differently, or erase files. Some viruses are written not to cause harm, but simply to cause mischief. An example of this could be a program that puts a picture on the screen.

Viruses can cause many unusual and frustrating problems during an operating system installation. Some people think that by high-level formatting their hard drives, they have killed all viruses. This is a mistake. Do not take a chance; take a few moments and scan the hard drive for viruses with the latest virus checker version! Common types of viruses include the boot sector virus, file virus, macro virus, and the Trojan horse virus.

A **boot sector virus** is a program that is placed in the computer's boot sector. Because the computer loads boot sector code into memory, the virus loads into RAM at the same time. Once in memory, the virus can take control of computer operations and spread to other drives such as floppy drives, hard drives, and drives located on a network.

A **file virus** replaces or attaches itself to a file that has a COM or EXE extension. COM or EXE files are commonly known as executable files. Executable files are used to start applications. By attaching itself to this type of file, a virus can prevent the program starting or operating properly. It can also load into RAM and affect other COM or EXE files.

A **macro virus** is written for a specific application such as Microsoft's Excel or Word. Macro viruses are written in a specific language and attach themselves to a document created in the application. Once the document (along with the virus) is opened and loaded into memory, the virus can attach itself to other documents.

A **Trojan horse virus** pretends to be a normal application. When the virus executes, the computer does something the user does not expect, such as putting a message or a picture on the screen or putting a new screen saver up. A Trojan horse virus does not replicate (copy itself somewhere else). The virus can be used to gather information such as userids and passwords that can later be used to hack into your computer.

Three other types of viruses that infect computers are the stealth virus, the polymorphic virus, and the worm virus. A **stealth virus** is a program written to avoid being detected by anti-virus software. When an anti-virus program executes, the stealth virus provides the anti-virus program with a fake image that makes the anti-virus program believe no virus is present. A **polymorphic virus** is a virus that constantly changes its own program to avoid detection by an anti-virus program. A **worm virus** makes a copy of itself from one drive to another and can use a network to replicate itself. The most common types of worm viruses today are in e-mail messages. Once the e-mail is opened, the worm virus is sent to every other user in an address book.

Common symptoms of a virus are listed below:

- Computer does not boot.
- Computer hard drive space is reduced.
- Applications will not load.
- An application takes longer to load than normal.
- Hard drive activity increases (especially when nothing is being done on the computer).
- An anti-virus software message appears.

- The number of hard drive sectors marked as *bad* steadily increases.
- Unusual graphics or messages appear on the screen.
- Files are missing (deleted).
- A message appears that the hard drive cannot be detected or recognized.
- Strange sounds come from the computer.

If a virus is detected or even suspected, run an anti-virus program. Follow the program's directions for installing and executing. The time to get an anti-virus program is *before* a virus infects the computer because the damage may be irreversible, especially if backups are not performed. Back up data often! Always back up data files before upgrading to a new operating system. Backups are an important part of any computer support plan.

Some anti-virus software can be set to load into memory when the computer boots and runs continuously. Make sure you disable this feature when installing an operating system patch (service pack) or upgrade. The anti-virus software can prevent the upgrade or patch (service pack) from installing. Other types of software that prevent an operating system from being upgraded are power management and disk management software/tools. Disable these utilities and applications before attempting an operating system installation or upgrade.

INSTALLATION/UPGRADE OF WINDOWS 2000 PROFESSIONAL

After all the pre-installation checklist steps are completed, you are ready to install Windows 2000 Professional. The installation process is easy if you performed the pre-installation steps. An exercise at the end of the chapter guides you through both a clean installation (one where no other operating system is on the machine) and an upgrade to Windows 2000. The number one piece of advice you need to follow when installing any operating system is this: Do your homework first. The number of possible problems will be greatly reduced.

There are two major portions of the installation process— the text mode (otherwise known as the DOS mode) and the GUI mode (also known as the Windows mode). In text mode, the monitor only shows characters with a blue background. The text mode portion of Setup checks for the proper minimum hardware requirements; detects plug and play devices and adapters; locates hard drives; creates the registry; partitions and formats the hard drive for the file system you select; copies most of the Windows 2000 installation files to begin the installation process; and restarts the computer to begin the Windows mode. During the GUI mode portion of Setup, hardware devices are detected, installed, and configured; the Setup logs are created; the operating system starts; and you are allowed to create an Administrator password.

TROUBLESHOOTING THE 2000 INSTALLATION

Various problems can cause the Windows 2000 installation process to halt. There are two major places the installation stops—during the text mode portion of setup or during the GUI mode portion of Setup. If the computer halts during text mode and displays a text message, there is probably an incompatible piece of hardware installed in the computer. If no error messages appear, but the computer halts during text mode, check the BIOS settings especially on older ISA devices. Make sure the *Reserved for ISA* option is selected in BIOS for any ISA devices. If your computer is non-ACPI, disable the *Plug and Play Operating System* setting in BIOS. If everything looks fine and Setup still hangs at the "Setup is inspecting your computer" screen, press the *F5* key. Select the *Standard PC* option from the menu that appears. This selection forces Windows 2000 to ignore ACPI settings.

If the computer halts during the GUI portion of Setup, restart the computer. The installation process attempts to continue from the place it left off. Incompatible hardware devices normally cause this. You can troubleshoot the device once Windows is installed. An incompatible hardware device is the most common problem during the installation process because it can cause both the text and GUI modes to halt.

Installation problems can be caused by a number of factors. The bulleted list below shows the most common causes and their associated solution during the installation process.

- Incompatible BIOS—Obtain compatible BIOS, replace motherboard with one that has a compatible BIOS, or do not upgrade/install Windows 2000 Professional.
- BIOS needs to be upgraded—Upgrade the BIOS.
- Incompatible hardware—Replace the hardware or do not upgrade/install Windows 2000 Professional.
- Incompatible drivers—Obtain Windows 2000 drivers from the hardware manufacturer.
- Existing drivers are incompatible or halt the installation/upgrade process—Obtain Windows 2000 drivers from the hardware manufacturer.
- Incompatible TSRs—Remove TSRs or obtain updated ones from the software manufacturer.
- Incompatible applications—Obtain upgrades from software manufacturer.
- Minimum hardware requirements have not been met—Upgrade the hardware. The number one things to check are the CPU (133MHz minimum) and RAM (32MB minimum).
- A virus is on the hard drive—Run a virus-checking program and remove the virus. One of the tools that comes on the 2000 Professional CD is InoculateIT anti-virus program (sometimes called the AV boot disk). To make a bootable disk that has the anti-virus program on it, insert the 2000 Professional CD into the CD-ROM and a 1.4MB disk in the floppy drive. Click on the *Start* button and click on the *Run* option. Click on the *Browse* button; locate and double-click on the drive letter that represents the CD-ROM. Locate the

VALUEADD folder, the 3RDPARTY subfolder, and the CA_ANTIV subfolder. Double-click on the CA_ANTIV subfolder. In the right window, double-click on the *MAKEDISK.BAT* file. Click on the *OK* button. To use the disk and run the anti-virus program, make sure the BIOS is set to boot from the floppy drive. Insert the disk into the floppy drive and boot the computer. When the menu appears, press *1* and follow the directions on the screen.

- Pre-installation steps have not been completed—Go back through the list!
- The installation floppy disks or CD are corrupted (not as likely as the other causes)—Try the disk in another machine and see if you can see the contents. For the CD, check to see if any scratches or dirt is on the surface. Clean the CD as necessary.
- Incorrect CD key—Type in the correct CD key to complete the 2000 installation. The key is located on the CD case.

Several text files can be helpful in determining the installation problem. WINNT.LOG and WINNT32.LOG are created during the installation process. SETUPLOG.TXT logs information detected during the text mode portion of Setup and includes device drivers that are copied. SETUPERR.LOG lists errors logged during the installation. SETUPACT.LOG and SETUPAPI.LOG are located in the folder that contains most of the Windows 2000 files (normally C:\WINNT). SETUPACT.LOG displays information about the files copied during the installation and SETUPAPI.LOG contains information about device driver files copied during installation. The NBTLOG.TXT is used when the Enable Boot Logging boot option is chosen and lists the drivers loaded during the boot process. BOOTLOG.TXT is located in the root directory and lists boot logging messages when booting from Safe Mode.

Different function keys can also help when troubleshooting the Windows 2000 installation process as well as troubleshooting boot problems. WIN2000 Table #5 shows a list of keystrokes that can be used.

Windows 2000 Professional Startup Keystrokes

Keystroke	Purpose
F5	System hangs at "Setup is inspecting your computer" screen. Select *Standard PC* from the list.
F6	Use when you need to go back and load 3rd party drivers
F7	Loads the normal HAL instead of ACPI HAL
F8	Brings up the Advanced Options menu
Shift+F10	Displays a command prompt during the GUI mode portion of installation

WIN2000 – TABLE #5

DUAL-BOOTING WINDOWS 2000 PROFESSIONAL AND NT

Sometimes users would like to try a new operating system, but keep their old operating system loaded as well. If this is the case, two operating systems can reside in one system and it is called dual-booting. Because Windows 2000 supports and uses NTFS 5 and NT Workstation supports and uses NTFS 4, it is best if the two operating systems are placed on different hard drive partitions. As soon as Windows 2000 is installed onto a partition formatted as NTFS, Windows 2000 upgrades the partition to NTFS 5 without any prompting.

NT Workstation should be installed first. Service pack 4 or later should also be installed. Install Windows 2000 to a different hard drive partition by inserting the Windows 2000 Professional CD. The CD normally starts automatically. A dialog box appears, asking if you want to install Windows 2000 Professional. Another dialog box appears asking if you want to install a new operating system or upgrade your old one. For a dual-boot situation, make sure you select that you want to install a new copy.

After installing all files and rebooting, a menu appears with the Microsoft Professional option, NT Workstation option, and NT Workstation (VGA Mode) option. To select which option is the default operating system, right-click on the *My Computer* desktop icon and click on the *Properties* option from the drop-down menu. Click on the *Advanced* tab and select the *Startup and Recovery* button. Select the default boot option.

CONFIGURING WINDOWS 2000 PROFESSIONAL OVERVIEW

One of the most common windows used by technicians is the Control Panel window. A control panel is a method for configuring various Windows 2000 components. The Add/Remove Hardware, Add/Remove Programs, and Printing control panels are used when installing or removing hardware and software. Each control panel icon represents a Windows utility that allows you to customize a particular part of the Windows 2000 environment. The number of control panels displayed depends on the type of computer and the components contained within that computer. WIN2000 Figure #7 shows some of the more common Windows 2000 Professional control panels.

WIN2000 - FIGURE #7

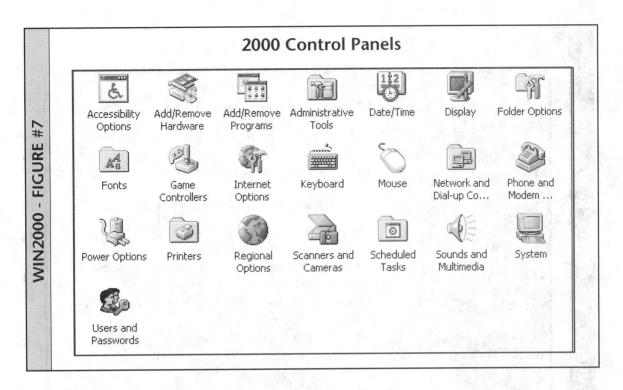

2000 Control Panels

Technicians must know which control panel to use for changing a computer's configuration. WIN2000 Table #6 shows the common Windows 2000 control panels and the function of each.

Windows 2000 Control Panels

Control Panel	Function
Accessibility Options	Used for people with a disability; it changes the way the keyboard, sounds, display, and mouse function within Windows
Add/Remove Hardware	Used to install and remove hardware devices
Add/Remove Programs	Used to install and remove software applications
Administrative Tools	Tools to monitor and configure Windows 2000
Date/Time	Used to change the date and time
Display	Controls monitor functions such as desktop appearance, screen saver, and size of objects
Folder Options	Used to change file associations and how folder contents are displayed
Fonts	Used to add or remove system fonts
Internet Options	Used to change settings related to an Internet connection
Keyboard	Used to change the keyboard driver, repeat rate, and cursor blink rate
Mouse	Used to change the mouse driver, click speed, and pointer shape
Network and Dial-up Connections	Used to add, remove and configure network connections
Phone and Modem Options	Used to install a modem and control modem and dialing properties
Power Options	Used to reduce electrical power use in devices such as a monitor or hard drive
Printers	Used to add, remove, and change the properties of a printer
Regional Options	Used to set the time zone, set the format for numbers and currency
Scheduled Tasks	Used to schedule things like backups and disk defragmentation utility
Sounds and Multimedia	Used to add/remove multimedia device drivers, set system event sounds, and change audio/video settings for multimedia devices
System	Allows viewing system configuration information, configuring the computer for multiple hardware configurations, and changing system settings
Users and Passwords	Used to add/remove user accounts, set passwords, and set/view various security settings

Technicians frequently must add new hardware and software using the operating system. Windows 2000 Professional has specific tools for these functions. Using the correct procedure is essential for success. The following sections handle many of the tasks a technician must perform:

- Adding plug and play devices
- Adding non-plug and play devices
- Removing hardware components
- Adding a printer
- Installing/removing software

Hardware devices are physical components that connect to the computer. Hardware devices can be either plug and play or non-plug and play. A device driver is a piece of software that allows hardware to work with a specific operating system. Some device drivers are automatically included with Windows 2000 Professional. A technician must be aware of what hardware is installed into a system so that the latest 2000-compatible drivers can be downloaded and installed.

ADDING PLUG AND PLAY DEVICES

Plug and play devices are hardware and software designed to automatically be recognized by the operating system. These include: USB devices; FireWire devices; SCSI devices; PC Card and CardBus devices; VL bus devices; PCI, ISA, and EISA devices; and printers. In order for Windows 2000 to fully support plug and play devices, the computer should have a BIOS that supports ACPI. Successful plug and play device installation involves the following:

- Possessing the most up-to-date device driver
- Following the directions provided by the device manufacturer

Always make sure that the computer is turned off when installing any new hardware component. Some plug and plug devices can be inserted into the computer without restarting. These include a PC card, a laptop into a docking station, and a USB device. However, devices such as internal modems or network cards require that the computer be turned off during installation.

Install the device according to the manufacturer's instructions. Once it is installed, power on the computer. The Windows 2000 Found New Hardware wizard appears. Windows 2000 attempts to find a driver for the new device. Plug and play devices make use of a special .CAB (cabinet) file called DRIVER.CAB which is located in %systemroot%\Driver Cache\i386 folder (where %systemroot% is normally C:\WINNT). This file is over 50MB and contains over 3,000 compressed files. If Windows 2000 detects new hardware, it will automatically search DRIVER.CAB for a driver. If a driver cannot be found, a dialog box appears. The best policy with any operating system is to use the latest driver, even if the operating system detects the device. An exercise at the end of this chapter outlines how to install a new hardware driver.

Remember that if the Windows 2000 Professional operating system cannot configure a plug and play device and prompts for a device driver, you must have administrator rights to install the driver.

ADDING NON-PLUG AND PLAY DEVICES

Devices, known as legacy devices, are also called non-plug and play devices. For devices that are not plug and play, Windows 2000 has a tool (wizard) called Add/Remove Hardware. The Add/Remove Hardware wizard allows hardware configuration and is used for hardware that is not automatically recognized by Windows 2000 Professional. It is also used for plug and play devices that don't install properly with Windows 2000's automatic detection. You must have administrator privileges in order to load device drivers for new hardware. An exercise at the end of the chapter explains how to do this.

ADDING A PRINTER

Printers can be connected to a computer through the printer's parallel port or through a local area network. Only local printers (printers connected to the computer's parallel port) will be covered in this chapter. Networked printers will be in the Network chapter. Windows 2000 can automatically detect printers. If Windows 2000 detects the printer, the operating system automatically installs the drivers, updates the registry, and allocates system resources to the printer. Automatically detected printers are normally USB, FireWire, or infrared printers.

To install a printer, connect the printer to the appropriate computer port with the appropriate cable. Power on the computer, and the Windows 2000 wizard normally detects and leads you through the installation process. However, if it does not, have the Windows 2000 printer driver ready, click on the *Start* button, point to the *Settings* selection, and double-click on the *Printers* option. When the Printers window opens, click on the *Add Printer* icon. Click on the *Next* button and select the *Local Printer* selection. When prompted for the printer driver, insert the CD or disk that contains the printer driver, and use the Browse button to locate the driver. Continue through the Add Printer wizard until the printer is installed.

To configure a printer as a default printer (the printer that applications normally use), locate the printer in the Printers folder. Access the Printers folder, by clicking on the *Start* button, point to the *Settings* option, and click on the *Printers* selection. Once you locate the appropriate printer icon, right-click on the icon. Click on the *Set as Default Printer* option. In the Printers folder, the default printer has a checkmark next to (above) the icon.

REMOVING HARDWARE DEVICES

When removing most hardware devices (all but printers), use the Add/Remove Hardware tool (wizard). To access this wizard, click on the *Start* button. Point to the *Settings* option and then click on the *Control Panel* option. Start the wizard by double-clicking on the *Add/Remove Hardware* icon located in the Control Panel window. Click on the *Uninstall/Unplug a device* radio button. Click on the *Next* button. Click on the *Uninstall a device* option and click on the *Next* button. Click the *Yes, I want to uninstall this device* option and click on the *Next* button. Click on the *Finish* button to complete the hardware removal.

If you are removing a printer from the system, use the Printers control panel. Access this control panel by clicking on the *Start* button. Point to the *Settings* option and click on the *Printers* option. Right-click on the *printer* you want to delete and choose the *Delete* option.

INSTALLING/REMOVING SOFTWARE

No computer is functional without software. One thing you should know about Windows 2000 is that it does not support some of the older 16-bit software. Most software today is 32-bit and comes on CD that includes an Autorun feature. If there is no Autorun feature, an installation wizard steps you through installing the software when the CD is inserted into the drive. If there is not an Autorun feature on the CD or if the software is on a disk, then the Add/Remove Programs control panel is used to install or remove the software.

To access the Add/Remove Programs control panel, click on the *Start* button and point to the *Settings* option. Click on the *Control Panel* option and then double-click on the *Add/Remove Programs* control panel icon. In the left panel in the window, click on the *Add New Programs* icon. Click on the appropriate *CD* or *Floppy* button depending on the type of media. Make sure the software disk or CD is inserted in the appropriate drive. If the Add New Programs cannot find a SETUP.EXE file on the designated disk, it prompts with a dialog box. Use the *Browse* button to locate the installation file. Click on the *Finish* button to complete the process.

To remove a software application, use the same Add/Remove Programs control panel; however, instead of clicking on Add New Programs, click on the *Change or Remove Programs* icon in the left panel. A list of installed applications appears in the right panel. Locate the software to be removed and click on its *name*. Click on the *Change/Remove* button. When asked if you are sure you want to remove this software, click on the *OK* button and close the Control Panel window.

The Add/Remove Programs control panel can also be used to add programs from Microsoft, add programs across your network, and add/remove Windows components. The Add Programs from Microsoft icon automatically opens a web browser to the Microsoft web site. There you can locate, download, and install software upgrades, patches, and service releases. The Add Programs from Your Network icon is used to install software from a network share on another computer. The Add/Remove Windows Components icon is used to add or remove standard Windows applets, games, accessibility options, and communication components.

Once an application is installed, launch the application by clicking on the *Start* button and pointing to the *Programs* option. Locate the application name and click on it. If the application does not appear on the list, do not panic. Windows 2000 has a feature that only shows the most commonly used programs in the Programs list. If the application name does not appear, point to the double down arrows at the bottom of the *Programs* submenu. The less frequently used program names appear on the screen.

COMPUTER MANAGEMENT CONSOLE

The **Computer Management** console is a large group of Windows 2000 tools displayed on one screen. The tools are called snap-ins and the 2000 Professional CD contains additional snap-ins that you can add to your system. To access the Computer Management console, click on the *Start* button, point to the *Settings* option, click on the *Control Panel* option, double-click on the *Administrative Tools* icon, and double-click on the *Computer Management* icon.

To add the Administrative tools to the Start button Programs option, right-click on an empty space on the taskbar. Click on the Properties option and click on the Advanced tab. Click in the Display Administrative Tools checkbox and click on the OK button.

WIN2000 Figure #8 shows a partial listing of a Computer Management console screen.

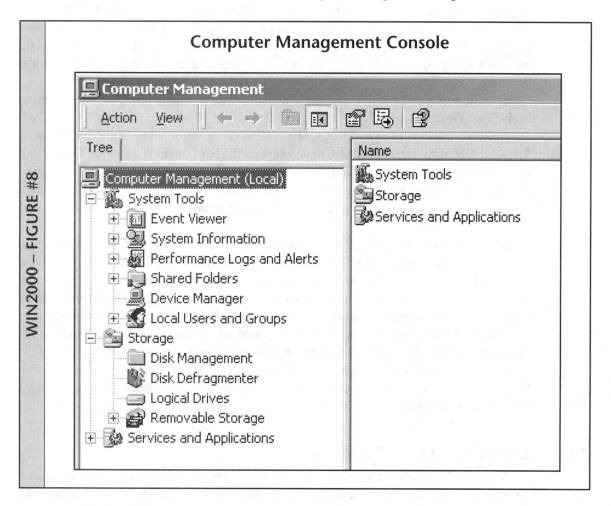

The Computer Management console allows a technician to manage shared folders, manage disk drives, start and stop services, look at performance logs and system alerts, and access Device Manager to troubleshoot hardware problems.

The three major tool categories found in the Computer Management console include: System Tools, Storage, and Services and Applications. The System Tools include: Event Viewer and Performance Logs and Alerts (both covered later in the chapter), System Information, Shared Folders, Device Manager, and Local Users and Groups. The System Information tool is used to provide information about the computer's hardware and software including IRQs, I/O addresses, conflicts, and memory addresses.

The Shared Folders tool is used to view shared folders, sessions, and files. Device Manager is used after installing a new hardware device and seeing if Windows 2000 could recognize the device. The Properties window's General tab can help diagnose hardware problems. This window also provides a Troubleshooter button that starts a specific troubleshooting wizard. The Local Users and Groups tool can be used to manage local user and group accounts.

The Storage Computer Management console category includes: Disk Management tool, Disk Defragmenter tool, Logical Drives, and Removable Storage. The Disk Management tool is used to enable RAID as well as create and manage hard drive volumes. The Disk Defragmenter tool is used to defragment the hard drive. The Logical Drives tool allows the management of local and mapped network drives. The Removable Storage option allows creation of media libraries that track where data is stored on removable disks such as Zip disks and CDs. Even if the removable media is removed, the library is still aware of what is on the media.

The Services and Applications section contains a multitude of options depending on the computer and what is loaded. Common options could include: Telephony, WMI Control, Services, DHCP, and DNS. One of the most frequently used options is Services. The Services section takes the place of the NT's Services control panel. A list of services installed on the computer are displayed in the right window when the Services option is clicked. Double-click on any service and a detailed window appears. The Recovery tab is a nice tool for technicians. The Recovery tab allows a technician to determine what happens when a service fails. For example, if the print service fails the first time, a restart occurs. Once the print service fails a second time, the print server can be restarted automatically. The third time the print service fails, a file can be executed that pages a technician.

OVERVIEW OF THE BOOT PROCESS

With NT Workstation and Windows 2000, two types of partitions are important during the boot process—the system partition and the boot partition. The **system partition** is the active drive partition that contains the files needed to load the operating system. The system partition is normally the C: drive (the active partition). The **boot partition** is the partition or logical drive where the Windows 2000 operating system files are located. People sometimes forget that the system and boot partitions can be on the same partition.

Every operating system needs specific files that allow the computer to boot. These files are known as **system files** or startup files. The system files and their specific location on the hard drive list in WIN2000 Table #7.

Windows 2000 Startup Files

Startup Filename	File Location
BOOT.INI	Root directory of system partition
BOOTSECT.DOS (needed if the computer is a dual or multi-boot system)	Root directory of system partition
CDLDR	Root directory of system partition
HAL.DLL	%systemroot%\SYSTEM32*
HYBERFIL.SYS	%systemdrive%**
NTBOOTDD.SYS (used with SCSI and some large IDE drives)	Root directory of system partition
NTDETECT.COM	Root directory of system partition
NTLDR	Root directory of system partition
NTOSKRNL.EXE	%systemroot%\SYSTEM32*
System key	%systemroot%\SYSTEM32\CONFIG*
	*%systemroot% is the boot partition and the name of the folder under the folder where Windows 2000 was installed (normally C:\WINNT).
	**%systemdrive% is the root directory on the drive where Windows 2000 boot files are located (normally C:\).

The table can be confusing because of all of the %systemroot% and %systemdrive% entries. This is because computers can be partitioned differently. If you install Windows 2000 onto a drive letter (a partition or logical drive) other than the active partition (normally C:), the startup files can be on two different drive letters. Also, you do not have to take the default folder name of WINNT to install Windows 2000. To account for these different scenarios, Microsoft uses the %systemroot% to represent the boot partition, the partition and folder that contains the majority of the Windows 2000 files. On a computer with a single operating system, this would be C:\WINNT. The %systemdrive% represents the root directory of the same drive letter. On a computer with a single operating system, this would be C:\.

If Windows 2000 is installed onto the C: drive and the C: drive is the active partition, then the BOOT.INI, BOOTSECT.DOS, HYBERFIL.SYS, NTBOOTDD.SYS, NTDETECT.COM, and NTLDR files would all be in the root directory of C:. The HAL.DLL and NTOSKRNL.EXE files would be located in the SYSTEM32 folder (that is located under the WINNT folder) on the C: drive. The system key would be in the CONFIG folder (that is located under the SYSTEM32 folder that is located under the WINNT folder) on the C: drive.

Another example: If you installed Windows 2000 onto the D: drive, but the C: drive is the active partition. The BOOT.INI, BOOTSECT.DOS, HYBERFIL.SYS, NTBOOTDD.SYS, NTDETECT.COM, and NTLDR files would all be in the root directory of C:. The HAL.DLL and NTOSKRNL.EXE files would be located in the SYSTEM32 folder (that is located under the WINNT folder) on the D: drive. The system key would be in the CONFIG folder (that is located under the SYSTEM32 folder that is located under the WINNT folder) on the D: drive.

The **system key** is a protection feature for Windows 2000 passwords. By default, the system key is stored on the local computer, but it can also be stored on a floppy disk used to boot Windows 2000. An algorithm secures the system key and it is stored in various locations through the registry.

The boot process is actually quite involved, but the major steps are as follows:

1. The computer is powered on.
2. POST executes.
3. BIOS searches for an active partition on the hard drive.
4. BIOS reads the Master Boot Record, then locates and loads the information into sector 0 of the system partition. The contents of sector 0 define the type of file system, the location of the bootstrap loader file, and start the bootstrap loader. With Windows 2000, this file is NTLDR.
5. NTLDR starts the file system.
6. NTLDR reads the BOOT.INI file and displays the various operating system choices contained within the BOOT.INI file. If something other than Windows 2000 is chosen, the BOOTSECT.DOS file takes over. If Windows 2000 is chosen, the NTDETECT.COM file executes.
7. NTDETECT.COM detects the computer's hardware.
8. NTLDR passes the hardware information to the NTOSKRNL.EXE file and displays the startup screen.
9. The operating system kernel, NTOSKRNL.EXE, executes and the HAL.DLL file loads. HAL stands for Hardware Abstraction Layer. This is a layer between the operating system and the hardware devices. The HAL allows Windows 2000 to run with different hardware configurations and components, without affecting (or crashing) the operating system.
10. The registry key HKEY_LOCAL_MACHINE\SYSTEM loads from the registry key located in %systemroot%\System32\Config\System. This key has information found during the hardware detection process.
11. The Windows 2000 Professional screen appears.
12. The Starting Up process bar displays.
13. The WINLOGON.EXE file executes and the logon screen appears.

TROUBLESHOOTING THE BOOT PROCESS

When Windows 2000 has startup problems, the Emergency Repair Disk, Recovery Console (both covered later in this chapter), and the Advanced Options menu are used. Many times startup problems are due to a virus. The AVBoot disk can be used to check the computer for a virus. The procedure for creating this is in the Troubleshooting the 2000 Installation section. Other utilities that can be used within Windows 2000 to help with MBR, boot sector, and system files are FIXBOOT, FIXMBR, System File Checker, and the Advanced Options menu.

To use FIXBOOT, type *FIXBOOT x:* command where *x:* is the drive letter of the volume that has the problem. To use FIXMBR, type *FIXMBR* from a command prompt. Both the FIXBOOT and FIXMBR commands are covered in the Recovery Console section later in the chapter. The System File Checker program can be run from the Run dialog box by typing *x:\WINNT\SYSTEM32\SFC.EXE /scannow* where *x:* is the drive letter where 2000 is installed. Indications that there is a problem with the Master Boot Record or the system files are as follows:

- Invalid partition table
- Error loading operating system
- Missing operating system
- A disk read error has occurred
- NTLDR is missing
- NTLDR is corrupt

When Windows 2000 has startup problems due to incompatible hardware or software, or a corrupted installation process, the Windows 2000 Advanced Options menu can help. This option can be selected by pressing the *F8* key when the *For troubleshooting and advanced startup options for Windows 2000, press F8* message appears on the screen during the boot process. Also, look back to WIN2000 Table #5 for a review of keystrokes that can be used to bring up different start options used in troubleshooting Windows 2000 Professional.

The most commonly used boot option is Safe Mode. In prior Windows operating systems, when the system had a problem it automatically booted into Safe Mode. This is not the case with Windows 2000. You must use the Advanced Startup Options to select Safe Mode.

Safe Mode is used when the computer stalls, slows down, does not work right, video is not working properly, intermittent errors appear or new hardware/software installation causes problems. When the computer boots in Safe Mode, the mouse, keyboard, CD-ROM, and VGA video device drivers are all that are loaded. After the computer boots to Safe Mode, you can disable or delete a system service; delete, reload or upgrade a device driver, and disable or delete a shortcut in the Startup folder, any of which can cause the computer to hang during startup. The bottom line is that Safe Mode puts the computer in a "bare bones" mode so you can troubleshoot problems.

Another menu item that is useful when troubleshooting device drivers is Boot Logging. This option creates a file called NTBTLOG.TXT that is placed in the %systemroot%

folder, (which is normally C:\WINNT). The NTBTLOG.TXT file contains a list of the drivers that load and the drivers that do not load. If you suspect a problem with a driver, use the *Enable Boot Logging* option from the Advanced Options menu to see if Windows 2000 loaded the driver. An exercise at the end of the chapter explains how to take advantage of this feature.

The other menu items are also used for troubleshooting and WIN2000 Table #8 shows the function of each menu option.

Windows 2000 Advanced Options Menu

Menu Option	Function
Safe Mode	Loads the bare minimum device drivers needed to boot the system.
Safe Mode with Networking	Loads the bare minimum device drivers needed to boot the system plus the network services and drivers needed for the computer to participate in a network.
Safe Mode with Command Prompt	Loads the bare minimum device drivers needed to boot the system, but does not load the GUI interface (EXPLORER.EXE). Instead, a command prompt displays.
Enable Boot Logging	Creates a log file called NTBT LOG.TXT in the %systemroot% folder (which is normally C:\WINNT). This file contains all drivers that load during startup and shows each driver's status.
Enable VGA Mode	This option is used when an incompatible or corrupted video driver has been loaded. It boots the system with a generic VGA driver so troubleshooting can be done.
Last Known Good Configuration	Whenever new hardware or software is installed that causes the system to crash or perform inadequately, use this option to load a previous system configuration that worked.
Debugging Mode	This option is used when debugging the operating system kernel.
Boot Normally	The Boot Normally option boots Windows 2000 with normal device drivers, registry, and startup folder files.

WIN2000 – TABLE #8

In older operating systems, a startup disk was used to begin the troubleshooting process. With Windows 2000, the startup disk is actually the set of four installation disks that came with the Windows 2000 Professional CD. If you cannot find these, you can go to any computer that has the same version of Windows 2000 Professional loaded and make a set. Insert the Windows 2000 Professional CD, click on the *Start* button, and click on the *Run* option. In the dialog box, type *x:\bootdisk\makeboot.exe a:* where *x* is the drive letter that represents the CD-ROM. Click on the *OK* button and follow the prompts on the screen. You will need four floppy disks to complete this procedure.

CREATING AN EMERGENCY REPAIR DISK

The **ERD (Emergency Repair Disk)** is used to fix system file problems, the partition boot sector, and startup environment settings, all of which can prevent a computer from booting properly. By default, the ERD does not contain a backup copy of the registry. Use the Backup utility to back up and restore the registry. You should make a new ERD whenever hardware or software changes are made to the computer. Store the disk in a safe place. The ERD contains the following files: AUTOEXEC.NT, CONFIG.NT, SETUP.LOG, NTLDR, NTDETECT.COM, BOOT.INI, NTBOOTDD.SYS, and HAL.DLL. The AUTOEXEC.NT and CONFIG.NT files are used to initialize the DOS environment. The SETUP.LOG lists the files installed by the Setup program. NTLDR is the file used to load Windows 2000; BOOT.INI is used to tell the computer which hard drive and which hard drive partition to use to boot Windows 2000. The NTBOOTDD.SYS is only used when the computer has a SCSI hard drive installed. The HAL.DLL file is used by Windows 2000 to keep hardware problems from crashing the operating system. An exercise at the end of the chapter illustrates how to make an ERD.

If the computer system will not work and you want to use the ERD, start the Windows 2000 installation process and get to the Welcome to Setup screen. Use the Windows 2000 Professional Setup disks (you must get through Disk 4 before you see the Welcome to Setup screen) or boot your computer from the Windows 2000 Professional CD. Once presented with the Welcome to Setup screen, press the *R* option, which is the *To repair a Windows 2000 installation by using the emergency repair process* option that allows you to use the ERD to fix the computer. Once you press *R*, you are asked if you want a manual repair or a fast repair. The manual repair allows you to select what portions of the operating system are repaired. The fast repair will check and try to repair system files, the partition boot sector, or the startup environment settings. Most people select the fast repair option. After making a selection, you are prompted to insert the ERD. Follow the instructions on the screen to complete the repair process. The computer must reboot after the repairs have been done.

RECOVERY CONSOLE

Another useful tool used when Windows 2000 crashes or does not boot properly is the Recovery Console. The **Recovery Console** boots the computer to a command prompt and allows access to the hard drive no matter what type of file system is being used (FAT, FAT32, or NTFS). From the command prompt, the administrator can manipulate files and folders, start and stop services, repair the Master Boot Record, repair the boot sectors, or format the hard drive. You must have the administrator password to access the full potential of this option.

The Recovery Console can be loaded to the hard drive and added to the Start menu, but it is not loaded by default. Normally, because the system is not working properly, the Recovery Console is started from the Windows 2000 CD or the Setup floppy disks. Start the computer from the Setup disks or CD. (If you do not have the Setup disks, go to a working 2000 computer and make some.) When the Setup program begins, press *Enter* at the *Setup Notification* screen. At the *Welcome to Setup* screen, press *R* (Repair a Windows 2000 installation). On the next screen, press *C* to access the Recovery Console. A screen appears that shows all of the Windows 2000 installations that are detected. Press the number corresponding to the Windows 2000 installation you want to work with. You are prompted for the local administrator password. Type the password to continue.

If the registry is corrupt or has been deleted, you are not prompted for an administrator password. Instead, the system boots to a prompt where you can use basic commands like CHKDSK, FIXBOOT, and FIXMBR to repair the system. However, you cannot access any folders on the hard drive.

The drive letters available at the Recovery Console command prompt might not be the same ones you used in the GUI environment. Use the MAP command to see the drive letters (and the volumes that do not have drive letters). The syntax for the MAP command is covered later in this chapter.

In order to work in the Recovery Console, you must be able to work from a command prompt. You may want to go through the DOS chapter in this book to understand the process and procedures needed when working from a command prompt. Some of the most frequently used commands at the Recovery Console command prompt are outlined below. The items enclosed by brackets are optional. Command specific values that you must enter are shown in italics. When the items are separated by a | (bar), one of the items must be typed.

ATTRIB   This command is used to control the attribute for a file or folder.

Syntax: attrib [+|-c] [+|-h] [+|-r] [+|-s] [*drive:*] [*path*] *filename*

Explanation: + adds an attribute.

– takes an attribute away.

c is the compressed attribute.

h is the hidden attribute.

r is the read-only attribute.

s is the system attribute.

[*drive:*] is the drive where the file is located.

[*path*] is the directory/subdirectory where the file is located.

filename is the name of the file.

Example: **attrib +h c:\cheryl.bat** sets the attribute to hidden for a file called CHERYL.BAT located on the hard drive.

Notes: The DIR command (typed without any switches) is used to see what attributes are currently set. You may set more than one attribute at a time.

CD   This command is used to navigate through the directory structure.

Syntax: cd [*drive:*] [*path*] [..]

Explanation: [*drive:*] specifies the drive (if a different one than the current drive) to which you want to change.

[*path*] is the directory/subdirectory to reach the folder.

[..] is used to change to the parent directory (moves you back one directory).

Examples: C:\WINNT>**cd..**

C:\

This command moves you from the WINNT directory (folder) to the parent directory, which is the root directory (C:\).

C:\>**cd \WINNT**

This command moves you from the root directory to the WINNT directory on the C: drive.

CHKDSK   This command checks a disk for physical problems, lost clusters, cross-linked files, and directory errors. If necessary, the chkdsk command repairs the disk, marks bad sectors, recovers information, and displays the status of the disk.

Syntax: chkdsk [*drive:*] [/p] [/r] [/c] [/f] [/i] [/l:size] [/v] [/x]

Explanation: [*drive:*] specifies the drive to check.

[/p] forces the chkdsk check even if the volume is not identified as being bad.

[/r] locates bad sectors and attempts recovery on the sector's information.

[/c] skips cycle checking of NTFS volume folders.

[/f] fixes drive errors.

[/i] checks only index entries on NTFS volumes.

[/l:size] the /l: must be part of the command followed by the size (in kilobytes) of the log file for NTFS volumes.

[/v] With a FAT volume, the /v switch shows the full path for every file. With a NTFS volume, cleanup messages are displayed.

[/x] With NTFS, the switch forces the volume to dismount before checking the volume.

Example: **chkdsk d:** This command checks the disk structure on the D: drive.

Notes: This command can be used without switches. In order for this command to work, the AUTOCHK.EXE must be loaded in the SYSTEM32 folder or used with the correct path and run from the Windows 2000 CD.

CLS The *cls* command clears the screen of any previously typed commands.
Example: C:\WINNT>**cls**

COPY The *copy* command is used to copy a single file to the destination that you specify.
Syntax: copy *source* [*target*]
Explanation: *source* is the file that you want to copy and it includes the drive letter and the path if it is different from your current location.
[*target*] is the location you want to put the file and it includes the drive letter and path if it is different from your current location.
Example: **copy c:\cheryl.bat a:**

This command takes a file called CHERYL.BAT that is located in the root directory of the hard drive and copies it to the floppy drive.

Notes: You cannot use wildcard characters such as * and ? with this command in the Recovery Console. You do not have to put a target if the file is going to the current location specified by the command prompt. If a file already exists, you will be prompted whether or not to overwrite the file. Compressed files that are copied from the 2000 CD are automatically uncompressed to the hard drive as they are copied.

DEL The *del* command is used to delete a file.
Syntax: del *name* [*/p*] [*/f*] [*/s*] [*/q*] [*/a*]
Explanation: *name* is the file or directory (folder) that you want to delete and it includes the drive letter and the path if it is different from your current location.
[*/p*] is used to prompt for confirmation before deleting.
[*/f*] is used to force read-only files to be deleted.
[*/s*] is used to delete files from all subdirectories.
[*/q*] means quiet mode which does not prompt for confirmation.
[*/a*] is used to select files based on their attribute where the attributes are R, H, S, and A. A + (plus sign) before the attribute means "select it" and a – (minus sign) before the attribute means "do not select it."
Example: C:\WINNT>**del c:\cheryl.bat**

This command deletes a file called CHERYL.BAT that is located in the WINNT directory on the hard drive.

Notes: You cannot use wildcard characters such as * and ? with this command while in the Recovery Console.

DIR   The *dir* command is used to list files and folders and their attributes.

Syntax: dir [*drive:*] [*path*] [*filename*] [/a] [/b] [/c] [/d] [/l] [/n] [/o] [/p] [/q] [/s] [/t] [/w] [/x] [/4]

Explanation: [*drive:*] is the drive letter where the files are located.

[*path*] is the directory/subdirectory to reach the folder.

[*filename*] is the name of a specific file.

[/a] is used to display files that have specific attributes where the attributes are D, R, H, A, and S. D is for directories; R is for read-only; H is for hidden; A is for archive; and S is for system files. A + (plus sign) before the attribute means "select it" and a – (minus sign) before the attribute means "do not select it."

[/b] is for barebones format (it doesn't show heading or summary information).

[/c] shows the file sizes with the thousands separator.

[/d] displays the file listing in a wide format sorted by column.

[/l] displays the listing in lowercase.

[/n] displays the listing in long list format.

[/o] displays the listing in sorted order. Options you can use after the "o" are E, D, G, N, and S. E is by alphabetic file extension; D is by date and time with the oldest listing shown first; G shows the directories listed first; N displays by alphabetic name; and S displays by size from smallest to largest.

[/p] displays the information one page at a time.

[/q] displays the owner of the file(s).

[/s] includes subdirectories in the listing.

[/t] controls which specific time field is shown where the types of time fields are A, C, and W. A is for the last access date/time with the earliest shown first; C is for the creation date/time; and W is for the last written date/time.

[/w] shows the listing in wide format.

[/x] shows the 8.3 filename listing for long filenames.

[/4] displays four digit years instead of two digit years.

Example: **dir c:\winnt**

This command shows all of the files and folders (and their associated attributes) for the WINNT folder that is located on the C: drive.

Notes: You can use wildcard characters such as * and ? with this command in the Recovery Console. The attributes you can see are (1) *a* for archive, (2) *c* for compressed, (3) *d* for directory, (4) *e* for encrypted, (5) *h* for hidden, (6) *p* for reparse point, (7) *r* for read-only, and (8) *s* for system file.

DISABLE   The *disable* command is used to disable a system service or hardware driver.

Syntax: disable *name*

Explanation: *name* is the name of the service or driver that you want to disable.

Notes: You can use the *listsvc* command to show all services and drivers that are available for you to disable. Make sure that you write down the previous START_TYPE before you disable the service in case you need to restart the service.

DISKPART   The *diskpart* command is used to manage and manipulate the hard drive partitions.

Syntax: diskpart [*/add*//*delete*] [*devicename*] [*drivename**partitionname*] [*size*].

Explanation: [*add/delete*] is used to create a new partition or delete an existing partition.
[*devicename*] is the name given to the device when creating a new partition such as \Device\HardDisk0.
[*drivename*] is drive letter used when deleting an existing partition such as E:.
[*partitionname*] is the name used when deleting an existing partition and can be used instead of the *drivename* option. An example of a *partitionname* is Device\HardDisk0\Partition2.
[*size*] is used when creating a new partition and is the size of the partition in megabytes

Notes: You can just type the *diskpart* command without any options and a user interface appears that helps when managing hard drive partitions.

ENABLE   This command is used to enable a system service or hardware driver.

Syntax: enable *name* [*start-type*]

Explanation: *name* is the name of the service or driver that you want to disable.
[*start-type*] is when you want the service or driver scheduled to begin. Valid start-types are as follows:
    SERVICE_BOOT_START
    SERVICE_SYSTEM_START
    SERVICE_AUTO_START
    SERVICE_DEMAND_START

Notes: You can use the *listsvc* command to show all services and drivers that are available for you to enable. Make sure that you write down the previous START_TYPE value before you enable the service in case you need to restart the old service or driver.

EXIT   The *exit* command exits the Recovery Console and restarts the computer.

Example: C:\WINNT>**exit**

EXPAND   The *expand* command is used to uncompress a file from the Windows 2000 CD or a CAB file. A CAB file is a shortened named for a cabinet file. A CAB file holds multiple files or drivers that are compressed into a single file. For Windows 2000, the cabinet files are located in the i386 folder on the CD. Technicians frequently copy the CAB files onto the local hard drive, so that when hardware and/or software is installed, removed, or reinstalled, the Windows 2000 CD does not have to be inserted.

Syntax: expand *source* [*/f:filespec*] [*destination*] [*/y*] [*/d*]

Explanation: *source* is the name of the file including the path that you want to uncompress.

[*/f:filespec*] is the parameter used if a source contains more than one file.

[*destination*] is the path to where you want to place the uncompressed file.

[*/y*] is the parameter used if you don't want to be prompted before overwriting an existing file.

[*/d*] is the parameter used when you do not want to expand the folder that is contained in the source parameter.

Example: **expand d:\i386\access.cp_ c:\winnt\system32\access.cpl** This command expands (uncompresses) the compressed file ACCESS.CP_ and puts it into the C:\WINNT\SYSTEM32 folder with the name ACCESS.CPL.

Notes: You may not use wildcard characters with the *source* parameter. You may use wildcard characters with the */f:filespec* parameter.

FIXBOOT   This command is used to rewrite the hard drive's boot sector.

Syntax: fixboot [*driveletter:*]

Explanation: [*driveletter:*] is the drive letter (and a colon) of the hard drive volume that you want to place in a new boot sector.

Example: **fixboot c:**

Notes: If you do not specify the *driveletter:* parameter, the boot sector that is repaired is the system boot volume's boot sector.

FIXMBR   This command rewrites the startup partition's Master Boot Record.

Syntax: fixmbr [*name*]

Explanation: [*name*] is the name of the device that you want to repair its Master Boot Record.

Example: **fixmbr \Device\HardDisk0**

Notes: If you do not type in the *name* parameter, Disk 0 is the default. Use the *map* command to see valid device names. Run a virus checker before using this command.

FORMAT   The *format* command is used to format a disk and can be used to format it for a particular file system.

Syntax: format [*driveletter:*] [*/q*] [*/fs:filesystem*] [*/a:size*] [*/c*] [*/f:size*] [*/n:sectors*] [*/t:tracks*] [*/v:label*] [*/x*] [*/1*] [*/4*] [*/8*]

Explanation: [*driveletter:*] is drive letter for the disk or hard drive volume that you want to format.

[*/q*] is the parameter used if you want to perform a quick format.

[*/fs:filesystem*] is the parameter used if you want to specify a file system. Valid values are as follows:

    FAT
    FAT32
    NTFS

[*/a:size*] The */a:* must be part of the command followed by the default allocation unit size. The different units supported by the three file systems are listed below.

   NTFS: 512, 1024, 2048, 4096, 8192, 16K, 32K, and 64K

   FAT: 512, 1024, 2048, 4096, 8192, 16K, 32K, 64K, and (128K, 256K for sector size that is larger than 512 bytes)

   FAT32: 512, 1024, 2048, 4096, 8192, 16K, 32K, 64K, and (128K, 256K for sector size that is larger than 512 bytes)

[*/c*] is used to compress the files on the volume by default.

[*/f:size*] The */f:* must be part of the command followed by the size for floppy disk to format. The different sizes supported are as follows: 160, 180, 320, 360, 640, 720, 1.2, 1.44, 2.88, or 20.8.

[*/n:sectors*] The */n:* must be part of the command followed by the number of sectors per track.

[*/t:tracks*] The */t:* must be part of the command followed by the number of tracks per disk side.

[*/v:label*] the */v:* must be part of the command followed by the name of the volume assigned.

[*/x*] is used to dismount the volume first, if necessary.

[*/1*] is used to format a single side of a floppy disk.

[*/4*] is used to format a 5.25" 360K floppy disk in a 1.2M drive.

[*/8*] is used to format eight sectors per track.

Example: **format c: /fs:ntfs**

Notes: If no */fs:filesystem* parameter is specified, the NTFS file system is used. FAT is FAT16. FAT16 hard drive volumes cannot be more than 4GB in size, but should be formatted to 2GB to be compatible with DOS, Windows 3.x, and Windows 9x.

HELP   This command displays information about specific Recovery Console commands.

Syntax: help [*command*]

Explanation: [*command*] is the name of the command for which you want help.

Example: **help expand**

Notes: If you do not specify the *command* parameter when using the Help command, all Recovery Console commands are listed.

LISTSVC   This command lists all of the services, hardware drivers, and their start-types. The *listsvc* command is useful to use before using the *disable* or *enable* command.

Syntax: listsvc

Example: C:\WINNT>**listsvc**

LOGON   The *logon* command is used to list all Windows 2000 and NT installations and prompts for the local administrator password.

MAP   This command is used to list the computer's drive letters, types of file systems, volume sizes, and physical device mappings.

Syntax: map [*arc*]

Explanation: [*arc*] is the Advanced RISC Computing path instead of the Windows device paths. This parameter is used when you are repairing or recreating the BOOT.INI file.

MD   This command is used to create a directory (folder).

Syntax: md [*driveletter:*] [*dirname*]

Explanation: [*driveletter:*] is the drive letter for the disk or volume on which you want to create a directory (folder). It can also include the path.

[*dirname*] is the parameter used to name the directory (folder).

Example: **md c:\TEST**

Notes: You may not use wildcard characters with this command.

MORE   The *more* command is used to display a text file.

Syntax: more *filename* [/*c*] [/*e*] [/*p*] [/*s*] [/*t#*]

Explanation: *filename* is the path and name of the text file you want to display on the screen.

[/*c*] clears the screen before displaying a page of information.

[/*e*] enables extended features.

[/*p*] expands form feed characters.

[/*s*] takes multiple blank lines and condenses them into one blank line.

[/*t#*] The /*t* must be part of the command followed by the number of spaces used to expand tabs. The normal setting is eight spaces.

Example: **more c:\boot.ini**

Notes: The spacebar allows you to view the next page of a text file. The Enter key allows you to scroll through the text file one line at a time. The ESC key allows you to quit viewing the text file.

RD   This command is used to remove a directory (folder).

Syntax: rd [*driveletter:*] [*path*]

Explanation: [*driveletter:*] is drive letter for the disk or hard drive volume that you want to remove a directory (folder).

[*path*] is the optional path and name of the directory (folder) you want to remove.

Example: **rd c:\TEST\JUNKDATA** removes a directory (folder) called JUNKDATA that is a subdirectory under a directory (folder) called TEST. This directory is located on the hard drive (C:).

Notes: You do not have to use the *driveletter:* parameter if the default drive letter is the same as the one that contains the directory to be deleted.

REN   The *ren* command is used to rename a file or directory (folder).

Syntax: ren [*driveletter:*] [*path*] *name1 name2*

Explanation: [*driveletter:*] is the drive letter for the disk or hard drive volume that you want to rename a file or a directory (folder).

[*path*] is the optional path telling the operating system where to find the file or directory (folder) you want to rename.

name1 is the old name of the file or directory (folder) that you want to rename.

name2 is the new name of the file or directory (folder).

Example: **ren c:\cheryl.bat c:\newcheryl.bat**

Notes: The renamed file cannot be placed in a new location with this command. Move or copy the file after you rename it if that is what you want to do. The * and ? wildcard characters are not supported.

SET   The *set* command is used to display and view different Recovery Console variables.

Syntax: set [*variable = value*]

Explanation: *variable* is one of the following:

AllowWildCards, which is the variable used to enable wildcard support for the commands that normally do not support wildcards.

AllowAllPaths, which is the variable that allows access to all of the computer's files and folders.

AllowRemovableMedia, which is the variable that allows files to be copied to removable media (floppy disk).

NoCopyPrompt, which is the variable that disables prompting when overwriting a file.

value is the setting associated with the specific variable.

Notes: To see all of the current settings, type *set* without a variable and the current settings display. The *set* command can only be used if it is enabled using the Group Policy snap-in. If the Windows 2000 Professional computer is contained in a Windows 2000 Server environment, you can use the Group Policy from the server to control this functionality. If you want to set the policy at the Windows 2000 Professional computer, click on the *Start* button, click on the *Run* option, and type *mmc* in the dialog box. Click on the *OK* button. Click on the *Console* menu option and select *Add/Remove Snap-in*. Click on the *Add* button. Click on the *Group Policy* option and then click on the *Add* button. Click on the *Local Computer* option from the Group Policy Object list. Click on the *Finish* button. Click on the *Close* button. Click on the *OK* button. Click on the + (*plus sign*) to expand the Local Computer Policy option. Click on the + (*plus sign*) to expand the Computer Configuration, Window Setting, Security Settings, and Local Policies folders. Click on the *Security Options* selection. Double-click on the *Recovery Console: Allow floppy copy and access to all volumes and folders* option. In the Local Security Policy Setting dialog box, select *Enabled*. Click on the *OK* button.

TYPE   The *type* command is used to display a text file.

Syntax: type *filename*

Explanation: *filename* is the path and name of the text file you want to display on the screen.

Example: **type c:\boot.ini**

Notes: The spacebar allows you to view the next page of a text file. The Enter key allows you to scroll through the text file one line at a time. The ESC key allows you to quit viewing the text file.

RESTORING THE REGISTRY THROUGH RECOVERY CONSOLE

If you have created an up-to-date Emergency Repair Disk (ERD) and you have chosen the option of backing up the registry to the Repair directory, you can use the Recovery Console command prompt to restore the registry. To perform this operation, start the recovery console. At the command prompt, type *cd repair\regback* and press *Enter*. Then, type *copy name drive:\system\system32\config* where *name* is the name of the registry file you want to restore, *drive* is the drive letter where the operating system is installed (normally C:), and *system* is the name of the folder where the operating system is installed (normally WINNT). Press *Enter*. Type *copy name drive:\system\system32\sam* and press *Enter*. Type *copy name drive:\system\system32\default* and press *Enter*. Type *copy name drive:\system\system32\security* and press *Enter*. Type *copy name drive:\system\system32 \Software* and press *Enter*. Type *copy name drive:\system\system32\system* and press *Enter*.

WORKING FROM THE COMMAND PROMPT

Technicians must sometimes work from the command prompt when the system is not working properly. That is what the Recovery Console tool is all about. There are other commands that technicians have used throughout the years, but in Windows 2000 the commands change a bit. There are several ways to access a command prompt when the computer is functional. These methods are listed below.

*   Click on *Start* button, click on the *Run* option, and type *command* in the dialog box.
*   Click on *Start* button, point to the *Programs* option, point to the *Accessories* option, and click on the *Command prompt* option.
*   Click on the *Start* button, click on the *Run* option, and type *cmd* in the dialog box.

The commands that were not covered in the Recovery Console section, but are still used are listed below with their associated switches.

CMD   The *cmd* command is executed from the Run dialog box. (Click on *Start* button, click on *Run* option, and type *CMD.EXE* in the dialog box.) A DOS window appears. Type *EXIT* from the DOS window to close the window.

Syntax: cmd [*/c string*]

Explanation: [*/c string*] specifies that the command interpreter is to perform the command specified by the *string* option and then stop.

Example: **cmd /c chkdsk d:** This command runs the chkdsk program on the D: hard drive volume using the command line.

DISKCOPY   The *diskcopy* command is used to make an exact copy of one disk and put it on another.

Syntax: diskcopy [*drive1:*] [*drive2:*]

Explanation: [*drive1:*] is the source drive letter followed by a *:* (colon).
[*drive2:*] is the destination drive letter followed by a *:* (colon).

Example: C:\WINNT>**diskcopy a: a:**

Notes: The drive letters are only needed if the command prompt is a different drive and location.

PROMPT   The *prompt* command is used to change the default setting for how the command prompt looks.

Syntax: prompt [*option*]

Explanation: [*option*] is any text to appear as the prompt or one of the following options:
$a (ampersand), $b (pipe symbol), $c (open parentheses), $d (current date), $e (ASCCI escape code 27), $f (close parentheses), $g (greater than sign), $h (backspace to delete a character that has been written to the prompt command line), $l (less than sign), $n (current drive), $p (current drive and path), $q (equal sign), $s (space), $t (current time), $v (DOS version number), $_ (ENTER-LINEFEED), $$ (dollar sign)

Examples: C:\WINNT>**prompt Cheryl's Computer$g** changes the prompt to look like Cheryl's Computer>
C:\WINNT>**prompt cpgf** changes the prompt to look like (C:\WINNT>)

WSCRIPT   The *wscript.exe* is the command used to bring up a windows-based script property sheet.

TASK MANAGER, DR. WATSON, AND EVENT VIEWER

Task Manager is a Windows-based utility that displays applications currently loaded into memory, processes that are currently running, microprocessor usage information, and memory usage data. To activate Task Manager press the *CTRL+ALT+DEL* keys and from the window options that appear, click on the *Task Manager* button. Two other ways of accessing this utility are (1) pressing *CTRL+ALT+ESC* and (2) right-clicking on the *taskbar* and then clicking on the *Task Manager* option.

One of the common uses of Task Manager is to exit from an application that is "hung up" or not responding. Task Manager can help with exiting the program. Once inside the Task Manager window, click on the *Applications* tab. Locate the name of the troublesome application and click on it. Normally, the status shows the application as "not responding." Click on the *End Task* button.

Dr. Watson is a utility that automatically loads when an application starts. Dr. Watson can detect and display troubleshooting information as well as create a text log file when a system or application error occurs. A technician might need this information when communicating with Microsoft or the application developer's technical support. Make notes of any messages that appear on the screen when any type of problem occurs.

To start Dr. Watson in Windows 2000, click on the *Start* button, click on the *Run* option, type *drwtsn32,* and press *Enter*. Click on the *application error* and click on the *View* button. The default location for the log file is C:\Documents and Settings\All Users\Documents\DrWatson. The name of the log file is drwtsn32.log. When an error occurs, Dr. Watson appends information to the end of this log file.

Event Viewer is a Windows tool used to monitor various events in your computer such as when a driver or service does not start properly. The EventLog service starts automatically every time a computer boots to Windows 2000. This service is what allows the events to be logged and then Event Viewer is used to see the log.

Access the Event Viewer by clicking on the *Start* button, pointing to the *Settings* option, double-clicking on the *Control Panel* option, and double-clicking on the *Administrative Tools* control panel icon. Then double-click on the *Event Viewer* icon. The left window contains the type of Event Viewer logs such as the system log, the security log and the application log. The system log displays events that deal with various system components, such as a driver or service that loads during startup. The type of system log events cannot be changed, added, or deleted. The security log can display events, such as when different users login to the computer (both valid and invalid logins). A technician can pick which events are displayed in the security log. The application log displays events associated with a specific program. The programmers that design the software decide which events to display in the Event Viewer's application log. All users can view the system log and the application log, but only a member of Administrators can view or enable security log information. The most commonly used log is the system log. Click on the *System log* option in the left panel. The system log events are displayed in the right window.

The event viewer can display five different types of events. The events are shown in WIN2000 Table #9.

WIN2000 – TABLE #9

Event Viewer Symbols

Symbol	Type of Event	Explanation
Lowercase "i"	Information	Normal system operations such as the system being initialized or shut down.
Exclamation mark	Warning	An event that is not critical, but one that you might want to take a look at. The system can still function, but some feature(s) may not be available.
X	Error	An event failed. A specific event failed such as a service or device that failed to initialize properly.
Yellow key	Success Audit	You can audit a specific event. If successful, this symbol appears.
Yellow lock	Failure Audit	When you specify a specific event to audit and the event fails, the yellow lock appears. An example is auditing a system login and someone tries to login that does not have a valid username or password.

If an error message appears stating that the Event Viewer log is full, start the Event Viewer. Note that you must be an administrator or a member of the Administrators group to perform this procedure. Click on the *Action* menu option and then click on the *Properties* selection. Click on the *General* tab. Click in the *Clear log* option. The Log Size option may need to be changed to one of the following: Overwrite events older than 0 days, Maximum log size, or Overwrite events as needed.

TROUBLESHOOTING A SERVICE THAT DOES NOT START

Some Windows 2000 services start automatically each time the computer boots. If one of these services has a problem, an error message normally appears during the boot sequence. You can use Event Viewer also as previously discussed or use the Services and Application tool available through the Computer Management administrative tool.

SHUT DOWN PROBLEMS

Before Windows 2000 can shut down, the operating system sends a message to all devices, services, and applications. Each device that is running sends a message back saying it is okay to shut down now. Any active application saves data that has not been previously saved and sends a message back to the operating system. Active system services also respond that it is okay to shut down. If the system has trouble shutting down, it is due to one of these three things. The most common problem is an application that is not responding. When this happens, press *CTRL+ALT+DEL* to access Task Manager. Manually stop any applications from running to see if that is causing the problem. If a single application continually prevents Windows 2000 from shutting down, contact the software manufacturer to see if there is a fix.

For services problems, boot the computer into Safe Mode and then shut the computer down. Take note as to whether or not the computer had any problems shutting down. If the process works, access the BOOTLOG.TXT file that is located in the root directory of the drive that contains Windows 2000. Once inside the file, take note of each service that is disabled because of booting into Safe Mode. Boot the computer normally. Stop each service one at a time to see which service is causing the problem.

To troubleshoot devices not responding, eliminate services and applications first. A device frequently does not cause a shut down problem. Then, while working on the computer, take notice of what devices you are using– common ones are video, hard drive, CD-ROM, keyboard, and mouse. Verify that all of your devices have the most up-to-date driver loaded and that the driver is compatible with Windows 2000.

MONITORING SYSTEM PERFORMANCE

Another utility used to monitor the computer is the Performance Logs and Alerts snap-in tool. **Performance Logs and Alerts** allows creation of graphs, bar charts, and text reports. An exercise at the end of the chapter shows how to use the Performance Logs and Alerts utility. This utility can also be customized to show different counters. The button with a + (plus sign) is used to add various counters to the display. Some of the most important memory counters are Available Bytes, Pages/sec, and Paging file\%Usage. The Available Bytes counter shows the amount of RAM available for running program processes. The Pages/sec counter shows the number of times per second the information requested could not be found in RAM, and the data had to be retrieved from the hard drive. The Paging file\%Usage counter shows what percentage of allocated space for the paging file is in use.

Sometimes a technician must adjust the paging file size for optimum computer performance. The System control panel is used to set the virtual memory size. Once in the System control panel, click on the *Advanced* tab. Click on the *Performance Options* button and two sections appear in the window—Application Response and Virtual Memory. Click on the *Change* button in the Virtual Memory section and the Virtual Memory window appears.

Two values are selectable—Initial size and Maximum size. Both of these values should be the same for maximum computer performance.

Once you change the values, click on the *Set* button. The default amount of virtual memory is 1.5 times the amount of RAM installed in the computer. The Virtual Memory window can also be used to change the amount of space reserved for the registry.

The Task Manager utility can be used to monitor your current system's performance. Sometimes a computer can start slowing down. A baseline report is needed before the slowdown occurs. A **baseline** report is a snapshot of your computer's performance during normal operations (when it does not have any problems).

Start the Task Manager utility by pressing *CTRL+ALT+DEL* and clicking on the *Task Manager* button (or right-clicking on an empty space on the taskbar and clicking on the *Task Manager* option). Click on the *Performance* tab to see the CPU usage and memory usage statistics. The first window on the left shows the CPU usage percentage. Actually, it is a percentage of time the processor is running a thread. A thread is a type of Windows object that runs application instructions. The first window on the right displays the CPU usage history, which is a graph of how busy the microprocessor has been over a period of time.

The second window on the left shows the amount of virtual memory being used. The amount shown is in kilobytes as evidenced by the K after the number. The second window on the right is a graph of the virtual memory used over time.

Memory is a frequent bottleneck for computer performance. Task Manager can also be used to see the total amount of RAM installed and how much RAM is available. Task Manager is an invaluable tool for technicians when a computer is slowing down.

Name _____

WINDOWS 2000 PROFESSIONAL REVIEW QUESTIONS

1. List two differences between Windows 2000 Professional and other operating systems.

2. [T / F]   Windows 2000 Professional does not support plug and play.

3. How many bits can Windows 2000 Professional handle at a time?
    [8 / 16 / 32 / 64]

4. What is the term given for supporting more than one CPU?

5. Windows 2000 is a _____ environment.
    [GUI / text-based / 16-bit / tailored]

6. What desktop icon is frequently used for quick access to a user's files?

7. What desktop icon is used to access deleted files?

8. What desktop icon is an installation wizard for Internet accessibility?
    [My Network Places / Network Neighborhood / Internet Explorer / Connect to the Internet]

9. Explain what a shortcut icon represents.

10. Give an example of what happens when the Show Desktop icon is clicked.

11. How can you tell when a radio button option is disabled?

12. What happens when a dialog box is closed using the Close button?

13. [T / F]   A disk drive is always represented by a drive letter and a colon.

14. List three characters that cannot be used in Windows 2000 Professional filenames.

15. A user is working in Microsoft Word. He saves the document called LTR1 to a folder (directory) called WORDDOCS. The WORDDOCS folder is a subfolder (subdirectory) of the MY DOCUMENTS folder. Both folders are located on the D: hard drive volume. Write the complete path for the LTR1 document.

16. Why is it so important to empty the Recycle Bin?

17. [T / F]   File and folder compression can degrade a computer's performance.

18. What command line utility is best to use to compress a file?
    [COMPACT / ENCRYPT / EFS / COMPRESS]

19. What command line utility shows authorized users and recovery agents?
    [ENCRYPT / COMPRESS / EFSINFO / CIPHER]

20. List one method of determining what Windows 2000 version is loaded on the computer.

21. Describe the purpose of a user profile.

22. What registry branch is *not* user-specific and contains global hardware configuration?

23. What registry branch holds information such as ".DOC extensions go with Microsoft Word".

24. [T / F]   A Windows 2000 Professional registry can only have five subtrees.

25. Which registry editor is best to use when performing a specific search?

26. Which registry editor allows exporting the registry to a text file?

27. When should a backup of the registry be performed?

28. Describe the steps to use the Backup utility to back up the registry and the system files.

29. List three things to do before installing Windows 2000.

30. What command is used to change a FAT partition into a NTFS partition?
     [FDISK / FORMAT / NTFS / CONVERT]

31. What type of virus loads when the computer first starts?

32. What is the name of the virus that attaches to a specific application?

33. What are the types of viruses written to avoid detection?

34. List three symptoms of a virus.

35. Describe what to do with an anti-virus program when installing an operating system service pack.

36. What is the minimum amount of hard drive space required to install Windows 2000 Professional?

37. [T / F] A CD-ROM or DVD is considered a Windows 2000 Professional minimum.

38. What BIOS feature is important for Windows 2000 to be able to control plug and play devices?

39. Which of the following operating systems support ACPI? (Select all that apply)
     [Windows 95 / Windows 98 / NT Workstation / NT Server / Windows 2000 Professional]

40. How can you tell if the BIOS supports ACPI on a Windows 98 computer?

41. Describe the difference between text mode and GUI mode (in regard to a Windows 2000 installation).

42. Which Windows 2000 Professional installation mode checks the computer to see if there is enough hard drive space?

43. Which Windows 2000 Professional installation mode creates the various startup logs?

44. What is the most common cause of a Windows 2000 installation stopping during the text mode portion of setup?

45. What do you do if your hardware drivers are incompatible with Windows 2000?

46. How can you tell if the Windows 2000 installation CD has corrupted files?

47. Where is the CD key located?

48. What text file is created when the computer boots to Safe Mode?

49. What keystroke is used so the Standard PC option can be selected?

50. What keystroke is used to select Safe Mode?

51. [T / F] USB devices can be plug and play.

52. What happens when you install a plug and play device and Windows 2000 cannot find a driver?

53. Who has the right to install a new device driver?

54. What control panel is used to install software in Windows 2000?

55. What is the name of the file Windows 2000 looks for when installing a new application?

56. What type of software can be installed with the Add/Remove Windows Components icon?

57. What console allows a technician access to Device Manager?

58. What type of partition contains the boot files?

59. [T / F] The boot partition and the system partition can be on the same hard drive volume.

60. Where is the NTLDR startup file located on the hard drive?

61. Explain the difference between %systemroot% and %systemdrive%.

62. Where is the default location of the system key?

63. What is the first step of the boot process?

64. What Windows 2000 startup file contains the operating system boot choices?

65. What Windows 2000 file is used to detect hardware devices?

66. What Windows 2000 file is used to display the logon screen?

67. List two messages that could indicate a MBR or system file problem.

68. Describe the process for getting into Safe Mode.

69. [T / F] When Windows 2000 has a driver problem, the operating system automatically boots into Safe Mode.

70. List one instance of when Safe Mode would be used.

71. Describe when the Enable VGA Mode would be used.

72. If a new Read/Write CD has just been installed in a computer and now the computer does not boot properly, what Advanced Options menu choice would be best to use?

73. [T / F]   With Windows 2000, the registry is automatically backed up when creating an ERD.

74. Which of the following files is *not* contained on an ERD?
[AUTOEXEC.NT / NTLDR / SETUP.LOG / CONFIG.SYS / NTDETECT.COM]

75. When working from a command prompt, what command shows the drive letters available under the Recovery Console?

76. What Recovery Console command is used to detect and repair disk problems?

77. In Recovery Console, what switch would be used with the DEL command so that no confirmation prompt appears?

78. What Recovery Console command is used to show all services and drivers available to disable?

79. Which of the following is the Recovery Console command used to uncompress a file from the Windows 2000 CD?
[CIPHER / UNLOCK / CHKDSK / EXPAND]

80. Which of the following is the Recovery Console command used to display a text file?
[MORE / DISPLAY / DIR / VIEW]

81. What Recovery Console command is used to change the name of a folder?

82. List the Recovery Console command that has the same basic function as the MORE command.

83. What command, when issued from the Run dialog box, brings up a command prompt?

84. What three keystrokes bring up Task Manager without clicking on any buttons?

85. What Task Manager tab shows an application that is "not responding"?

86. What utility is best to use when a service does not start properly?

87. What type of user can view the Event Viewer system log?

88. What type of Event Viewer symbol is used to show an error?

89. The Event Viewer is full. What procedure must be done?

90. Which of the following control panels display currently running services?
[Services / Administrative Tools / Networking / System]

91. [T / F] Currently running services can be stopped using the Services control panel.

92. What is the most common cause for the Windows 2000 computer not shutting down properly?

93. Which of the following control panels is used to change the paging file size?
[Memory / Hard Drive / System / Services]

94. [T / F] When setting the virtual memory paging size variables, both the Initial size setting and the Maximum size setting should be set to the same number.

Name _____

WINDOWS 2000 PROFESSIONAL FILL-IN-THE-BLANK

1. When a 16-bit application is running on Windows 2000 Professional, it runs in _____.

2. _____ is a Windows 2000 program that copies over system files if something happens to the original system files.

3. The three files systems supported by Windows 2000 are _____, _____, and _____.

4. _____ is the area where all work is done in the Windows 2000 environment.

5. The _____ desktop icon is used to access the floppy drive.

6. The _____ desktop icon is used to access a networked printer.

7. Another name for an icon with a bent arrow is _____.

8. The _____ button is the place to begin accessing programs, getting help, and finding files.

9. The _____ is the desktop icon that appears as a desk with a piece of paper on it.

10. The _____ is the desktop icon that holds buttons that represent applications loaded in RAM.

11. A _____ is the part of a dialog box that requires typing one or more parameters.

12. In a dialog box, the _____ button is represented by a question mark.

13. When you click on an empty checkbox, a _____ appears in the checkbox to show that the option is enabled.

14. A filename extension can be up to _____ characters in length.

15. In Windows 2000, a filename can be up to _____ characters.

16. In Windows 2000, _____ is the most commonly used application used to copy or move files and create folders.

17. In order for a folder to be compressed, the _____ file system must be used.

18. _____ folders take less space than folders that do not have this feature.

19. The _____ application is the application most commonly used to compress a folder.

20. _____ is the Windows 2000 encryption type.

21. _____ and _____ can view an encrypted file.

22. Another name for the Windows 2000 database is _____, which tracks all hardware and software.

23. The _____ registry branch holds Janet Patterson's desktop settings such as her dancing fish desktop.

24. A computer just booted. The registry branch that has the current hardware profile is _____.

25. The two registry editors for Windows 2000 are _____ and _____.

26. The _____ registry editor can display a value that is longer than 256 characters.

27. The _____ includes the registry, boot files, and the COM+ Registration database.

28. The _____ utility is used to restore the System State.

29. A user has a new hard drive that you install. It is the only hard drive in the system. You load Windows 2000 for the first time. This is known as a _____ install.

30. The _____ file system supports file compression.

31. A _____ is a computer program designed to change the way the computer operates.

32. The _____ virus attaches to a .COM or .EXE file.

33. A _____ virus does not replicate, but is used to gather private information.

34. The most common types of _____ viruses are sent via an e-mail.

35. The preferred CPU speed for a computer running Windows 2000 Professional is _____ or higher.

36. The _____ tool checks a computer's hardware and software to see if it is compatible with Windows 2000.

37. If a hard drive already has an operating system on it, before Windows 2000 is installed, the drive should be scanned for _____.

38. The anti-virus program that comes with the Windows 2000 Professional CD is _____.

39. The _____ text file holds information about device driver files and information about the text mode portion of setup.

40. The _____ keystroke allows you to bring up the Advanced Options menu.

41. The _____ control panel is used to remove a piece of hardware.

42. The _____ feature is when you insert a CD and an installation wizard appears.

43. The _____ Start button option is used to launch an application.

44. A group of common Windows 2000 tools displayed in one window is called the _____.

45. The two types of Windows 2000 partitions are _____ and _____.

46. The _____ partition contains the Windows 2000 Professional files.

47. The _____ startup file is needed if two operating systems are installed on the same computer.

48. The NTOSKRNL.EXE startup file is located in the _____ folder.

49. The normal path for the %systemroot% is _____.

50. The normal path for the %systemdrive% is _____.

51. The name of the Windows 2000 protection feature for passwords is _____.

52. The _____ Windows 2000 file starts the file system.

53. Four things that can help with boot problems are the _____ command, the _____ command, the _____ program, and the _____ menu.

54. The _____ Advanced Menu option loads device drivers and boots to a text-based screen.

55. The _____ command is used to make a set of four installation disks.

56. The _____ tool allows you to use commands from a prompt.

57. The _____ Recovery Console command is used to move around in the directory structure.

58. The _____ switch is used with the CHKDSK command to speed up the process by only checking NTFS index entries.

59. Use the _____ Recovery Console command to partition hard drives.

60. The _____ Recovery Console command is used to rewrite the master boot record.

61. The syntax for displaying the BOOT.INI file (which is located in the C: drive's root directory) is _____.

62. The _____ command is used to display and view different Recovery Console variables.

63. The _____ utility shows CPU usage.

64. The _____ utility displays a message when an application has an error.

65. The Event Viewer shows an _____ as an event that is not critical, but should be examined.

66. When the Event Viewer log is full, an _____ is the only type of user that can perform the procedure to repair the problem.

67. The _____ utility can be customized to display various system performance counters.

68. A _____ is a report of a computer's performance during normal operation and is used as a comparison when the computer slows down.

69. The Task Manager Performance tab can be used to view the _____ and _____ usage.

Name _____

WINDOWS 2000 DESKTOP OPTIONS EXERCISE

Objective: To interact with and customize the Windows 2000 desktop

Parts: Computer with Windows 2000 installed

Step 1.   Turn on the computer and verify that the operating system loads.

Step 2.   Logon to Windows 2000 using the userid and password provided by the instructor or lab assistant.

My Computer

Step 3.   Double-click on the **My Computer** desktop icon. A window appears.

Question 1:   Write down the drive letters that are available on your computer that show in the My Computer window.

Step 4.   Locate the three icons in the upper right corner of the window, a line, a window, and an X. The icon that looks like a straight line is used to minimize the screen, which means the application is still loaded in memory, but it does not show on the desktop. Instead, it shows up as an item on the taskbar. The icon in the center can be of two varieties—a maximize button, which looks like one window, or a Restore button, which looks like a window within a window. When a window is maximized it fills the entire screen. If you size the screen differently, you can click on the **Restore** button and the window goes back the way it was. Click on the **X** icon.

Question 2:   What happened to the window when you clicked on the X button?

My Documents

Step 5. Double-click on the **My Documents** window. On the left is the name of the folder, My Documents, and links to My Network Places and My Computer. On the right are the user files and folders.

Step 6. Click on the **Tools** menu option. From the drop-down menu, click on the **Folder options**. A window opens with four tabs across the top. The General tab is used to select how the options look within the My Documents window. The View tab is used to select what files are shown by default. Technicians normally want to see all files so select the **Show hidden files and folders** option, which is found under the Hidden files and folder selection. To make hidden files available for all folders, click on the **Like Current Folder** button. The File Types tab is used to register a particular file type in Windows 2000. The file types listed are the file types that Windows 2000 knows about. Click on a **file type** listed in the Registered file types window. The normal file extension and program that opens the file lists in the Details for 'x' extension section of the window. This is where you would register your own file extensions so that Windows 2000 can automatically open the document when you click on it. The Offline Files tab is used to allow the computer to store network files locally so the files are accessible when disconnected from the network.

Question 3: List three file registered file types that Windows 2000 has on your computer.

Step 7. Click on the **Cancel** button.

Recycle Bin

Step 8. Click on the **Start** button.

Step 9. Point to the **Programs** option.

Step 10. Point to the **Accessories** option.

Step 11. Click on the **Notepad** option. The Notepad application opens with a blank document.

Step 12. Type the following words: **Education is what survives when what has been learnt has been forgotten. —B.F. Skinner**

Step 13. Click on the **File** menu option.

Step 14. Click on the **Save** menu option. The system defaults to the My Documents folder.

Step 15. Type in the word **Education** in the File name box.

Step 16. Click on the **Save** button.

Step 17. Click on the **X** (Close) button in the upper right corner to close the Notepad window.

Step 18.   Double-click on the **My Documents** icon on the desktop.

Step 19.   Locate the Education document in the My Documents window. You may need to use the scroll bar to locate it.

Step 20.   Click once on the **Education** document to select it.

Step 21.   Press the **Delete** key on the keyboard. A message appears on the screen asking if you are sure that you want to send the Education document to the Recycle Bin.

Step 22.   Click on the **Yes** button.

Step 23.   In the My Documents window, click on the **X** (**Close**) button in the upper right corner.

Step 24.   Double-click on the **Recycle Bin** icon on the desktop.

Step 25.   Locate the **Education** document. If it is not in the Recycle Bin, perform steps 8 through 24 again.

Step 26.   There are several ways to delete items from the Recycle Bin. Use one of these methods to delete the **Education** document from the Recycle Bin and click on the **Yes** button to confirm the delete.

     A.   Click on the **File** menu option and select the **Empty Recycle Bin** option. This deletes all files from the Recycle Bin.

     B.   Click on the **document you want removed** from the disk entirely. Click on the **File** menu option. Click on the **Delete** option.

     C.   Click on the **document you want removed** from the disk entirely. Press the **Delete** key on the keyboard.

     D.   From the desktop, right-click on the **Recycle Bin** icon. Click on the **Empty Recycle Bin** option. This option deletes all files from the Recycle Bin.

Desktop Icons

Step 27.   Sometimes users clutter their desktop with icons. One thing that helps with this clutter is to have the system arrange the desktop icons. The icons can be arranged by name, type, size, date, or let the system automatically arrange them. To illustrate this function, go to the desktop area.

Step 28.   Right-click on a **blank desktop space.** Once a menu appears, point to the **Arrange Icons** option. If the **Auto Arrange** option has a checkmark beside it, click on the **Auto Arrange** option to remove the checkmark. If the **Auto Arrange** option does not have a checkmark beside it, click on an empty portion of the desktop to cancel.

Step 29.   Click on the **My Documents** icon and while continuing to hold the mouse button down, drag the icon to the center of the screen.

Step 30.   Click on the **My Network Places** icon and while continuing to hold the mouse button down, drag the icon to the top right portion of the screen.

Step 31.   Right-click on a **blank desktop space.** A menu appears.

Step 32.   Point to the **Arrange icons** menu option.

Step 33.   Click on the **By Date** menu option.

Question 4:   What changed on the screen?

Step 34.   Right-click on a **blank desktop space** again. A menu appears.

Step 35.   Point to the **Arrange icons** menu option.

Step 36.   Click on the **Auto Arrange** option. If you look very carefully before the window closes, you can see a checkmark go beside the option. (You can also right-click on an **empty desktop space,** point to the **Arrange icons** option and see the checkmark.)

Step 37.   Click on the **My Documents** icon and while continuing to hold the mouse button down, drag the icon to the center of the screen.

Question 5:   What happened when you tried to move the My Documents icon?

Desktop Appearance

Step 38.   Right-click on a **blank desktop area.** A menu appears.

Step 39.   Click on the **Properties** option. The Display Properties window appears. (*Note:* This screen can also be accessed by clicking on the **Start** button, point to the **Settings** option, click on the **Control Panel** option, and double-click on the **Display control panel** icon.)

Step 40.   Click on the **Background** tab. This tab controls how the background color and pattern appears.

Step 41.   Click on the **Blue Lace 16** option and click on the **Apply** button.

Step 42.   In the Picture Display area, click on the **down arrow** and select the **Center** option. Click on the **Apply** button. You may have to click on the top of the **Display Properties** window and move the window to another area of the screen to see the effects of this step.

Question 6:   What happened to the screen?

Step 43.   In the Picture Display area, click on the **down arrow** and select the **Stretch** option.

Step 44.   Click on the **Apply** button.

Question 7:   What happened to the screen?

Step 45.   Click on the **Screen Saver** tab. This tab controls what screen saver, if any, loads and is used to control monitor power settings. A screen saver password can also be applied.

Step 46.   Click on the **Screen Saver** down arrow.

Question 8:   List one available screen saver.

Step 47.   Click on the **Appearance** tab at the top of the window. This tab controls the color scheme and size of letters displayed on the screen when various windows are open. This tab is good to use when people with vision problems need adjustments.

Question 9:   What color scheme is currently loaded?

Step 48.   Click on the **Scheme** down arrow.

Question 10:   List one theme available.

Step 49.   Click on the **Web** tab. The Web tab window allows you to define whether web content is allowed on the desktop. A common web content option would be stock quotes.

Step 50.   Click on the **Effects** tab.

Question 11:   For what is the Effects tab used?

Step 51.   Click on the **Settings** tab. The Settings tab allows you to define the number of colors available and the screen resolution (based on the video card's RAM).

Question 12:   How many colors are currently available?

Question 13:   What is the current screen resolution?

Step 52.   Click on the **Cancel** button.

Creating a Shortcut

   Note: There are various ways to create a shortcut and only one way is demonstrated here.

Step 53.   Click on the **Start** button.

Step 54.   Point to the **Programs** option.

Step 55.   Point to the **Accessories** option.

Step 56.   Click on the **Windows Explorer** option. You should make sure that the Windows Explorer window does not cover the entire screen. If it does, click on the Restore button, which is the middle button in the top right corner of the window (the one that looks like two windows stacked on top of one another).

Step 57.   Right-click (and continue to hold the right mouse button down) on **any file** or one designated by the instructor. Drag the file to an empty space on the desktop. Release the right mouse button and a menu pops up.

Step 58.   Click on the **Create Shortcut(s) here** option. The shortcut appears on the desktop as a shortcut icon.

Question 14:   What file did you choose to create a shortcut icon?

Step 59.   Close Windows Explorer by clicking on the **Close** button in the upper right corner. It is the one with an X in it.

Step 60.   Right-click on the **shortcut** icon you just created. Refer back to Question 8 if you forgot the name of it.

Step 61.   Click on the **Properties** option. A dialog box appears.

Question 15:   Write the path found in the Target textbox and describe what the path means.

Step 62.   Click on the **Find Target** button.

Question 16:   What happened when you clicked on the Find Target button?

Question 17:   Is the file that was used to create the shortcut icon visible?

Step 63.   Click on the **Show Files** words that are underlined in the left part of the window.

Question 18:   Can you locate the file that was used to create the shortcut icon? If not, contact a lab assistant or your instructor.

Step 64.   Close the window you are working in by clicking on the **Close** button, which is the button in the upper right corner that has an X in it.

Question 19:   Find a way to create a shortcut using the mouse options rather than right-clicking. Write your steps in the space below.

Step 65.   Click on the **Cancel** button.

Step 66.   Using one of the methods learned previously, permanently delete the shortcut icon created during this exercise.

_____*Instructor's Initials*

Name _____

WINDOWS 2000 TASKBAR OPTIONS

Objective: To interact with and customize the Windows 2000 taskbar

Parts: Computer with Windows 2000 installed

Step 1.   Turn on the computer and verify that the operating system loads.

Step 2.   Logon to Windows 2000 using the userid and password provided by the instructor or lab assistant.

Step 3.   Locate the taskbar on the bottom of the screen. If it is not showing, move the mouse to the bottom of the screen and the taskbar pops up.

Step 4.   To modify or view the taskbar settings, right-click on a **blank area** of the taskbar. A menu appears. *Note:* You can also use the **Start** button, point to the **Settings** option, and click on the **Taskbar and Start Menu** option.

Step 5.   Click on the **Properties** option. The Taskbar and Start Menu Properties window appears.

Step 6.   Click on the **General** tab.

Step 7.   The five options available on this screen relate to how things are shown on the taskbar. The items with a check in the checkbox to the left are active. The Always on top option puts the taskbar visible on the screen at all times (even if a window is full size or maximized). The Auto hide option hides the taskbar during normal operation. Press **CTRL+ESC** or the **Start** button on the keyboard (the one with the Windows emblem on it) to make the taskbar reappear. If both the Always on top and Auto hide options are checked, then the taskbar appears when you are in a window that is full size (maximized). The Show small icons in Start menu option reduces the size of the Start menu words. The Show clock option displays the clock icon in the right corner of the taskbar. The Use Personalized Menus option allows you to hide menu items that you rarely use. Make sure the **Always on top** and **Show clock** options are the only ones with checkmarks in the checkboxes. To remove a checkmark, click in the **checkbox** that already contains a check in it. To put a checkmark in a box, click once in an **empty box.**

Step 8.   Click on the **Apply** button.

Step 9.   Click on the **OK** button.

Step 10. Right-click on an **empty space** on the taskbar.

Step 11. Point to the **Toolbars** option. A submenu appears.

Step 12.   Ensure that there is a checkmark beside the **Quick Launch** option. This setting allows the Quick Launch icons to appear on the desktop by the Start button.

Step 13.   Using the skills you just learned, access the **Taskbar Settings** window.

Question 1:   List the steps you performed to do Step 13.

Step 14.   Click on the **Properties** option. Click on the **Question mark** icon in the upper right corner of the window. The question mark is an interactive help system. The pointer on the screen changes to an arrow with a question mark attached. Click on the **Always on top** option. A description of the option appears with the on-line help active.

Question 2:   What text does the help balloon display?

Step 15.   Click on the **Advanced** tab. The Advanced tab is used to customize the Start button and to delete files that list under the Start button's Documents option or previously accessed web sites.

Step 16.   Click on the **Cancel** button.

_____*Instructor Initials*

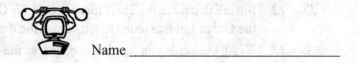

Name _____

WINDOWS 2000 FILE EXTENSION EXERCISE

Objective: To associate a file extension with a file type

Parts: Computer with Windows 2000 installed
Formatted 3.5" disk

Step 1.   Turn on the computer and verify that the operating system loads.

Step 2.   Logon to Windows 2000 using the userid and password provided by the instructor or lab assistant.

Step 3.   Click on the **Start** button and point to the **Programs** selection.

Step 4.   Point to the **Accessories** option.

Step 5.   Click on the **Notepad** menu selection.

Step 6.   Type in the following:

I hear and I forget. I see and I remember. I do and I understand. –Confucius

Step 7.   Click on the **File** menu option.

Step 8.   Click on the **Save** option from the drop-down menu.

Step 9.   Insert a formatted disk into the floppy (A:) drive.

Step 10.   Click on the **down arrow** in the Save in textbox.

Step 11.   Click on the **3_ Floppy (A:)** option.

Step 12.   In the File name textbox, type **Junk**.

Step 13.   Click on the **Save** button.

Step 14.   Close the Notepad application by clicking on the **Close** button (which is a button in the upper right corner with an X).

Step 15.   Right-click on the **Start** button.

Step 16.   Click on the **Explorer** option.

Step 17.   Click on the **Tools** menu option.

Step 18.   Click on the **Folder Options** drop-down menu option.

Step 19.   Click on the **View** tab in the Folder Options dialog box.

Step 20.   If the **Hide file extensions for known file types** checkbox contains a checkmark, click inside the **checkbox** to remove the checkmark. If the checkbox is empty, ignore this step.

Step 21.   Click on the **OK** button.

Step 22.   In the left window, use the vertical scroll bar to locate the A: drive. Double-click on the **3_ Floppy (A:)** drive option.

Step 23.   Locate the **Junk.txt** file in the right window and double-click on the icon.

Question 1:   What happened? Did the Notepad application open with the Junk file open?

Step 24.   Close the Notepad application by clicking on the **Close** button (which is a button in the upper right corner with an X).

Step 25.   In the Windows Explorer window on the right side, right-click on the **Junk** filename.

Step 26.   Click on the **Rename** option. The name of the file, Junk.txt, is highlighted.

Step 27.   Type in **junk.abc** and press the **Enter** key. Junk.txt is renamed to junk.abc. A Rename warning box appears stating that if you change a filename extension, the file may become unusable. It also asks, "Are you sure you want to change it?" Click on the **Yes** button.

Question 2:   What does the junk.abc file icon look like now?

Step 28.   Double-click on the **junk.abc** file icon.

Question 3:   What happened when you double-clicked on the junk.abc file icon?

Step 29.   Scroll down until you reach the **Notepad** icon. Click on the **Notepad** icon and then click on the **OK** button.

Question 4:   What happened when you clicked on the OK button?

Step 30.   In the Notepad application, click on the **File** menu option. Then click on **New** from the drop-down menu.

Step 31.   Type in the following: **The only real mistake is the one from which we learn nothing. —John Powell**

Step 32.   Click on the **File** menu option.

Step 33.   Click on the **Save** option from the drop-down menu.

Step 34.   Click on the down arrow in the **Save in** textbox.

Step 35.   Click on the **3_ Floppy (A:)** option.

Step 36. In the File name textbox, type **Junk2**.

Step 37. Click on the **Save** button.

Step 38. Close the Notepad application by clicking on the **Close** button (which is a button in the upper right corner with an X).

Step 39. Using Explorer, rename the **Junk2.txt** file to **Junk2.abc**. Notice the file icon after the change.

Question 5: How is the icon different from before?

Step 40. Double-click on the **Junk2.abc** icon.

Question 6: What happened when you double-clicked on the Junk2.abc icon?

_____*Instructor Initials*

Name _____

WINDOWS 2000 FILE AND FOLDER MANAGEMENT

Objective: To create folders, move files, and copy files to new locations

Parts: Computer with Windows 2000 installed
Formatted 3.5" disk

Note: There are multiple ways to do some of the steps in this exercise. Alternate methods are marked with the letters ALT:. You may pick either method of performing the step.

Step 1.   Turn on the computer and verify that the operating system loads.

Step 2.   Logon to Windows 2000 using the userid and password provided by the instructor or lab assistant.

Step 3.   Click on the **Start** button and point to the **Programs** selection.

Step 4.   Point to the **Accessories** option.

Step 5.   Click on the **Notepad** option.

Step 6.   Type in the following: **Develop a passion for learning. If you do, you will never cease to grow. —Anthony J. D'Angelo**

Step 7.   Click on the **File** menu option.

Step 8.   Click on the **Save** option from the drop-down menu.

Step 9.   Insert a formatted disk into the floppy (A:) drive.

Step 10.   Click on the **down arrow** in the Save in textbox.

Step 11.   Click on the **3.5-inch Floppy (A:)** option.

Step 12.   In the File name textbox, type **Quote 1** and click on the **Save** button.

Step 13.   Click on the **File** menu option.

Step 14.   Click on the **New** menu option.

Step 15.   Type in the following: **The man who graduates today and stops learning tomorrow is uneducated the day after. —Newton D. Baker**

Step 16.   Click on the **File** menu option.

Step 17.   Click on the **Save** option from the drop-down menu.

Step 18.   Click on the down arrow in the **Save in** textbox.

Step 19.   Click on the **3.5-inch Floppy (A:)** option.

Step 20.   In the File name textbox, type **Quote 2** and click on the **Save** button.

Step 21.   Click on the **File** menu option.

Step 22.   Click on the **New** menu option.

Step 23.   Type in the following: **Don't just learn the tricks of the trade. Learn the trade. — James Bennis**

Step 24.   Click on the **File** menu option.

Step 25.   Click on the **Save** option from the drop-down menu.

Step 26.   Click on the **down arrow** in the Save in textbox.

Step 27.   Click on the **3_ Floppy (A:)** option.

Step 28.   In the File name textbox, type **Quote 3** and click on the **Save** button.

Step 29.   Click on the **File** menu option.

Step 30.   Click on the **New** menu option.

Step 31.   Type in the following: **Nine-tenths of education is encouragement. —Anatole France**

Step 32.   Click on the **File** menu option.

Step 33.   Click on the **Save** option from the drop-down menu.

Step 34.   Click on the **down arrow** in the Save in textbox.

Step 35.   Click on the **3.5-inch Floppy (A:)** option.

Step 36.   In the File name textbox, type **Quote 4** and click on the **Save** button.

Step 37.   Click on the **File** menu option.

Step 38.   Click on the **New** menu option.

Step 39.   Type in the following: **Technology is dominated by two types of people: those who understand what they do not manage and those who manage what they do not understand. —Source unknown**

Step 40.   Click on the **File** menu option.

Step 41.   Click on the **Save** option from the drop-down menu.

Step 42.   Click on the **down arrow** in the Save in textbox.

Step 43.   Click on the **3.5 inch Floppy (A:)** option.

Step 44.   In the File name textbox, type **Quote 5** and click on the **Save** button.

Step 45.   Close the Notepad application by clicking on the **Close** button (which is a button in the upper right corner with an X).

Step 46.   Right-click on the **Start** button.

Step 47.   Click on the **Explore** option.

Step 48.   In the left window, use the vertical scroll bar to locate the **A: drive.** Click on the the **3.5 inch Floppy (A:)** drive option.

Step 49.   In the right window, locate the five files you just created called **Quote 1, Quote 2, Quote 3, Quote 4,** and **Quote 5.** If the files are not there, repeat steps 4 through 49.

____**Instructor's Initials**

Create a Folder

Step 50.   In the right Explorer window, right-click on an **empty space.** Point to the **New** option and click on the **Folder** option. A folder appears in the right window with the words New Folder highlighted. Type **Learning Quotes** and press **Enter**.

Note: The method shown below that is preceded by the letters ALT: is an alternate way to perform the same steps shown in Step 50. You may use either method.

ALT: Click on the **File** menu option. Point to the **New** option and click on the **Folder** option. A folder appears in the right window with the words New Folder highlighted. Type **Learning Quotes** and press **Enter.**

Step 51.   Create another new folder called **General Quotes** using the steps outlined in Step 50.

___*Instructor's Initials*

Copy a File

Step 52.   In the right window, right-click on the file named **Quote 1.** A submenu appears. Click on the **Copy** option from the submenu.

ALT: In the right window, click on the file named **Quote 1.** Click on the **Edit** menu option. Click on the **Copy** option from the drop-down menu.

Step 53.   In the right window, double-click on the **Learning Quotes** folder. Notice how the Windows Explorer Address line textbox changes to Learning Quotes and the right window is empty because the folder does not have any files or subfolders in it yet.

Step 54.   In the right window, right-click and a submenu appears. Click on the **Paste** option. The file named Quote 1 appears in the right window.

ALT: Click on the **Edit** menu option. Click on the **Paste** option from the drop-down menu. The file named Quote 1 appears in the right window.

Step 55.   In the left window, click on the **3_ Floppy (A:)** drive option. Notice how the Window Explorer Address line textbox changes to 3_ Floppy (A:).

Step 56.   Copy the files named **Quote 2** and **Quote 3** into the **Learning Quotes** folder using the methods outlined in steps 52 through 54.

Copy Multiple Files

Step 57.   In the left window, click on the **3_ Floppy (A:)** drive option.

Step 58.   Locate the files called **Quote 4** and **Quote 5** in the right window.

Step 59.   In the right window, click once on the **Quote 4** filename. The name highlights.

Step 60.   Hold the **Shift** key down and click once on the **Quote 5** filename. Both the Quote 4 and Quote 5 filenames highlight. *Note:* The Shift key is used to select files that are consecutive in a list (one right after the other). If you wanted to select files that are not consecutive, use the CTRL key to select the files.

Step 61. Right-click on the files named **Quote 4** and **Quote 5**. A submenu appears. Click on the **Copy** option from the submenu.

ALT: Click on the **Edit** menu option. Click on the **Copy** option from the drop-down menu.

Step 62. In the right window, double-click on the **General Quotes** folder. Notice how the Windows Explorer Address line textbox changes to A:\General Quotes and the right window is empty because the folder does not have any files or subfolders in it yet.

Step 63. In the right window, right-click on an **empty space** and a submenu appears. Click on the **Paste** option. The files named Quote 4 and Quote 5 appear in the right window.

ALT: Click on the **Edit** menu option. Click on the **Paste** option from the drop-down menu. The files named Quote 4 and Quote 5 appear in the right window.

_____*Instructor's Initials*

Question 1: How many files are located in the A: root directory (A:\)?

Question 2: How many files are located in the A:\Learning Quotes folder?

Question 3: How many files are located in the A:\General Quotes folder?

Copying a File from One Folder to Another

Step 64. In the left window, click on the **3_ Floppy (A:)** drive option.

Step 65. In the left window, click on the **Learning Quotes** folder located under the Floppy (A:) option. The files Quote 1, Quote 2, and Quote 3 appear in the right window.

Step 66. In the right window, right-click on the file named **Quote 3**. From the submenu that appears, click on the **Copy** option.

ALT: In the right window, click on the file named **Quote 3.** Click on the **Edit** menu option. Click on the **Copy** option from the drop-down menu.

Step 67. In the left window, click on the folder called **General Quotes** located under the Floppy (A:) option. The files Quote 4 and Quote 5 appear in the right window and the Address textbox shows A:\ General Quotes.

Step 68. In the right window, right-click on an **empty space** and a submenu appears. Click on the **Paste** option. The file named Quote 3 appears in the right window along with the files named Quote 4 and Quote 5.

ALT: Click on the **Edit** menu option. Click on the **Paste** option from the drop-down menu. The file named Quote 3 appears in the right window along with the files named Quote 4 and Quote 5.

Step 69.   Using the same procedures outlined in steps 72 through 76, copy the files named **Quote 1** and **Quote 2** from the **Learning Quotes** folder into the **General Quotes** folder. At the end of this step you should have three files (Quote 1, Quote 2, and Quote 3) in the Learning Quotes folder and five files (Quote 1, Quote 2, Quote 3, Quote 4, and Quote 5) in the General Quotes folder.

Moving a File

Step 70.   Create a folder on the A: drive called **My Stuff**. Refer back to the steps earlier in the exercise if you need assistance.

Step 71.   In the left window, click on the folder called **General Quotes**. In the right window, all five files appear.

Step 72.   In the right window, click once on the file called **Quote 1** to highlight it.

Step 73.   Hold the **CTRL** key down and click on the file called **Quote 3**. Both the Quote 1 and Quote 3 file names are highlighted. *Note:* The CTRL key is used to select non-consecutive files, whereas the Shift key is used to select files that are listed consecutively (one right after another).

Step 74.   Right-click on either **Quote 1** or **Quote 3** file name. Select the **Cut** option from the menu that appears. The Cut option is used to move a file from one folder to another folder.

ALT: Click on the **Edit** menu option. Click on the **Cut** option from the drop-down menu. The Cut option is used to move a file from one folder to another folder.

Step 75.   In the left window, click on the **My Stuff** folder. The right window is empty because no files have been copied or moved into the My Stuff folder yet.

Step 76.   In the right window, right-click and a menu appears on the screen. Select the **Paste** option from the menu. The Quote 1 and Quote 3 files appear in the right window.

ALT: Click on the **Edit** menu option. Click on the **Paste** option from the drop-down menu. The Quote 1 and Quote 3 files appear in the right window.

Step 77.   Using the procedures just learned, move the **Quote 1** file from the **Learning Quotes** folder into the **General Quotes** folder.

Question 4:   How many files are located in the A:\Learning Quotes folder?

Question 5:   How many files are located in the A:\General Quotes folder?

Question 6:   How many files are located in the A:\My Stuff folder?

Deleting Files and Folders

Step 78.   In the left Explorer window, click on the **My Stuff** folder. The Quote 1 and Quote 3 files appear in the right window.

Step 79.   In the right window, click on the **Quote 1** filename. Hold the **Shift** key down and click on the **Quote 3** filename. Both the Quote 1 and Quote 3 filenames are highlighted.

Step 80.   Press the **Delete** key on the keyboard. A Confirm Multiple File Delete message appears on the screen asking, "Are you sure you want to delete these 2 items?"

Note: When deleting files from a floppy disk, the files do not get placed in the Recycle Bin. They are deleted. When deleting files from a hard drive, the files get placed in the Recycle Bin when you press the Delete key, or select the Delete option from the File menu option. If you want to permanently delete a file from a hard drive (the file will not get placed in the Recycle Bin), hold the **Shift** key down while pressing the **Delete** key.

ALT: Click on the **File** menu option. Click on the **Delete** option from the drop-down menu. A Confirm Multiple File Delete message appears on the screen asking, "Are you sure you want to delete these 2 items?"

Step 81.   Click on the **Yes** button.

Step 82.   In the left window, click once on the **My Stuff** folder. The My Stuff folder highlights.

Step 83.   Press the **Delete** key on the keyboard. A Confirm Folder Delete message appears on the screen asking, "Are you sure you want to remove the folder "My Stuff" and all its contents?" Click on the **Yes** button.

ALT: Click on the **File** menu option. Click on the **Delete** option from the drop-down menu. A Confirm Multiple File Delete message appears on the screen asking, "Are you sure you want to remove the folder "My Stuff" and all its contents?" Click on the **Yes** button.

Step 84.   Using the procedures outlined in steps 86 through 91, delete the **Learning Quotes** folder and the **General Quotes** folders and all files contained within each folder.

Step 85.   Close the **Explorer** window.

Challenge

Step 86. Using Notepad, create **three text files** and save them to the floppy disk in a folder called **My Files.**

Step 87. On the hard drive, create a folder called **Computer Text.**

Step 88. Copy the two text files from the **My Files** folder on the floppy disk into the folder called **Computer Text** on the hard drive.

Step 89. Move the third text file from the **My Files** folder on the floppy disk into the folder called **Computer Text** on the hard drive.

_____*Instructor's Initials*

Step 90. Permanently delete the folder called **Computer Text** from the hard drive and all files within this folder.

_____*Instructor's Initials*

Step 91. Delete the folder called **My Files** from the floppy disk and all files within this folder.

_____ *Instructor's Initials*

Name _____

USING REGEDIT IN WINDOWS 2000 PROFESSIONAL

Objective: To become familiar with the REGEDIT registry editing utility

Parts: Computer with Windows 2000 Professional installed

REGEDIT is a utility used for editing the Windows registry. With REGEDIT, you can view existing registry settings, modify registry settings values, or create new registry entries to change or enhance the way Windows operates.

In this lab, you will use REGEDIT to view the System BIOS and Video BIOS information on your computer.

CAUTION: Editing the registry can cause your computer to run erratically, or not run at all! When performing any registry editing, follow ALL directions carefully, including spelling, syntax use, etc. Failure to do so may cause your computer to fail!

Step 1.   From the Start menu, choose **Run**, type **REGEDIT**, and click **OK**. The REGEDIT utility opens.

Step 2.   In the left window, expand **HKEY_LOCAL_MACHINE**, **HARDWARE**, and **DESCRIPTION**, and then select **System**.

Step 3.   In the right window, the System BIOS and Video BIOS information display.

Question 1:   What is the System BIOS date?

Question 2:   Who is the manufacturer of your System BIOS?

Question 3:   When was your Video BIOS manufactured?

_____*Instructor's Initials*

Step 4.   When finished viewing the System and Video BIOS information, close the **REGEDIT** utility.

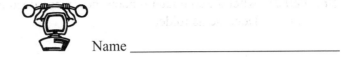

Name _____

USING REGEDT32 IN WINDOWS 2000 PROFESSIONAL

Objective: To become familiar with the REGEDT32 registry editing utility

Parts: Computer with Windows 2000 Professional installed

REGEDT32 is a utility used for editing the Windows registry. With it, you can find and view existing registry settings, modify registry settings values, or create new registry entries to change or enhance the way Windows operates.

In this lab, you will use REGEDT32 to create and configure a new registry setting to control how many document entries appear in Documents on the Start menu.

CAUTION: Editing the registry can cause your computer to run erratically, or not run at all! When performing any registry editing, follow ALL directions carefully, including spelling, syntax use, etc. Failure to do so may cause your computer to fail!

Step 1.   From the Start menu, click on the **Run** option, type **REGEDT32** in the textbox, and click **OK**. The REGEDT32 utility opens.

Step 2.   From HKEY_CURRENT_USER on Local Machine window, expand the following options: **Software**, **Microsoft, Windows, CurrentVersion,** and **Policies**, and then select the **Explorer** option.

Step 3.   From the Edit menu option, choose **Add Value**. The Add Value window opens. Editor opens.

Step 4.   The default number of documents that appear in the Start menu's Document folder is 15. From the **DWORD Editor** window, select the **Decimal** radio button, enter the value of **20** in the Data textbox, and click **OK**. The new DATA value displays in Hexadecimal format.

Question 1:   What is the Hexadecimal value of the new DATA value?

Step 5.   Close the **REGEDT32** utility and reboot the computer for the new registry setting to take effect.

Question 2:   After the computer reboots, how many documents can be displayed in the Start menu's Documents folder?

_____*Instructor's Initials*

Name _____

USING THE WINDOWS 2000 BACKUP UTILITY

Objective: To use the Windows 2000 Backup Utility to back up the registry

Parts: Computer with Windows 2000 installed

Step 1. Turn on the computer and verify that the Windows 2000 Professional loads.

Step 2. Logon to Windows 2000 using the userid and password provided by the instructor or lab assistant. Make sure that the userid is an Administrator userid or a userid that is a member of the Backup Operators group.

Step 3. Click on the **Start** button.

Step 4. Point to the **Programs** option.

Step 5. Point to the **Accessories** option.

Step 6. Point to the **System Tools** option.

Step 7. Click on the **Backup** option. The Backup Utility window opens.

Step 8. Click on the **Backup** tab.

Step 9. Click once in the **System State** checkbox to enable this option. A checkmark appears in the checkbox.

Step 10. At the bottom of the window, click on the **Browse** button to select a hard drive or any other type of media. Contact your instructor for the location to put the backed up files.

_____*Instructor's Initials*

Step 11. Type a **name** for the backup and click on the **Open** button.

Question 1: What name did you assign for the backup file?

Step 12. Click on the **Start Backup** button to begin the backup procedure. The Backup Job Information dialog box appears.

Step 13. Click on the **Advanced** option.

Step 14. Click on the **Automatically backup system protected files with the System State** option.

Step 15. Click on the **OK** button.

Step 16.   Click on the **Start Backup** button. A Backup Progress window appears.

Question 2:   How many estimated files will be backed up?

___

____*Instructor's Initials*

Step 17.   Click on the **Close** button.

Step 18.   Close the **Backup** window.

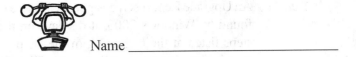

Name _____

UPGRADING FROM WINDOWS 95 OR 98
TO WINDOWS 2000 PROFESSIONAL

Objective: To upgrade an existing operating system to Windows 2000 Professional

Parts: Computer with Windows 95 or 98 installed
Windows 2000 Professional installation CD

Note: The installation process outlined below may differ due to computer differences. If the process is different, follow the directions on the screen. Contact your instructor or a lab assistant if you are unsure of the steps.

Step 1.   Turn the computer on and verify that the operating system loads.

Step 2.   Insert the Windows 2000 Professional CD into the CD-ROM or DVD drive.

Step 3.   The CD may automatically start. If it does, click on the **Setup** icon. If the CD does not automatically start, click on the **Start** button. Click on the **Run** option. Type in **x:setup** where *x:* is the drive letter of the device containing the Windows 2000 Professional CD.

Step 4.   A message appears on the screen that a newer operating system is being installed and asks if you want to continue. Click the **Yes** button.

Step 5.   The Welcome to Windows 2000 Setup wizard appears. Make sure the **Upgrade to Windows 2000** radio button is selected. Click on the **Next** button.

Step 6.   The licensing agreement appears on the screen. Read the agreement and click on the **I accept this agreement** radio button and then click on the **Next** button if you agree with the terms.

Step 7.   The Your Product Key screen appears. Enter the **product key** provided by the instructor or located on the CD case. Click the **Next** button to continue.

Step 8.   The Preparing to Upgrade to Windows 2000 screen appears. Click the **Next** button.

Step 9.   The Provide Upgrade Packs screen appears. Click on the **No, I don't have any upgrade packs** radio button. Click the **Next** button to continue.

Step 10.   If you have a file system other than NTFS, you will be prompted to upgrade to NTFS. Ask your instructor whether or not to upgrade to NTFS.

If an upgrade to NTFS is desired, click on the **Yes, upgrade my drive** radio button and then click on the **Next** button.

_____*Instructor's Initials*

Step 11. An Upgrade Report screen appears. If there was any incompatible hardware or software found by Windows 2000, it displays on the screen. Go back to the pre-installation steps listed at the beginning of the chapter for more assistance. Print the report or save it if the instructor tells you to. Click the **Next** button to continue.

Step 12. After some files are copied, the computer restarts several times.

Step 13. After the final restart, you must type in the **username and password** entered during the setup process.

_____*Instructor's Initials*

Name _____

CLEAN INSTALLATION OF WINDOWS 2000 PROFESSIONAL

Objective: To install Windows 2000 Professional on a computer without an operating system or on a computer on which the old operating system will be replaced (removed)

Parts: Computer appropriate hardware
Four Windows 2000 Professional installation disks
Windows 2000 Professional installation CD

Note: The installation process outlined below may differ due to computer differences. If the process is different, follow the directions on the screen. Contact your instructor or a lab assistant if you are unsure of the steps.

Step 1.   Turn the computer on and verify that the BIOS is set to boot from the floppy drive first and the hard drive second (A,C sequence). Contact an instructor or lab assistant for assistance on entering the BIOS SETUP program.

Step 2.   Insert the Windows 2000 Professional Disk 1 into the floppy drive.

Step 3.   Restart the computer. If the computer does not boot from the floppy disk, go back to Step 1.

Step 4.   Hardware detection starts and then you are prompted to insert Disk 2. Insert the Windows 2000 Profession floppy Disk 2 into the drive and press **Enter**. You will later be prompted for disks 3 and 4. Follow the directions on the screen.

Step 5.   After all files from the floppies have been copied, the Welcome to Windows 2000 Professional Setup screen appears. Press **Enter** to continue with the installation process.

Step 6.   The licensing agreement appears on the screen. Read the agreement and press the **F8** key if you agree to the terms.

Step 7.   The partitioning options appear next. Contact an instructor or lab assistant to find out if you are to create a partition, use an existing partition, or delete a partition.

Step 8.   Follow the directions on the screen and partition the hard drive.

Question 1:   What type of partitioning will you be doing on this computer? Write the instructions in the space below:

Step 9.   After the hard drive partition is created, more files are copied and the computer restarts.

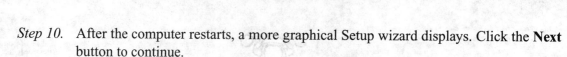
Step 10. After the computer restarts, a more graphical Setup wizard displays. Click the **Next** button to continue.

Step 11. The regional options such as language and time zone appear. Select the **appropriate option** for your area of the world. Click on either **Customize** button that appears on the screen to change the regional settings. Click on the **Next** button to continue.

Step 12. When the Personalize Your Software screen appears, contact an instructor or lab assistant for the Name and Organization to type.

Name _____

Organization _____

___*Instructor's Initials*

Step 13. The Product Key screen appears. Type in the **product key** that is located on the CD case or type in a **key** provided by your instructor. Click the **Next** button to continue.

Step 14. The Computer Name and Password screen appears. Contact an instructor or lab assistant for the Name and Administrator password.

Name _____

Password _____

___*Instructor's Initials*

Step 15. The Date and Time screen appears. Enter the **correct date and time** and click on the **Next** button.

Step 16. The Network Settings screen appears. Since networking is covered in the Networking chapter, click on the **Typical Settings** button. See the Networking chapter for complete network installation instructions.

Step 17. The Workgroup or Computer Domain screen appears. Click on the **No, this computer is not on a network or is on a network without a domain** radio button. Click on the **Next** button to continue.

Step 18. Setup continues to copy more files. When instructed to, remove the installation CD and click on the **Finish** button.

___*Instructor's Initials*

Name _____

UPGRADING A HARDWARE DRIVER USING WINDOWS 2000

Objective: To install an updated driver under the Windows 2000 operating system

Parts: Computer with Windows 2000 installed
                  Latest Windows 2000 driver for the hardware device

Note: The installation process outlined below may differ due to computer differences. If the process is different, follow the directions on the screen. Contact your instructor or a lab assistant if you are unsure of the steps.

Step 1.   Turn the computer on and verify that the operating system loads. Login to Windows 2000 using the userid and password provided by the instructor or lab assistant.

Step 2.   Click on **Start** button, point to **Settings**, and click on the **Control Panel** menu option.

Step 3.   When the Control Panel window opens, scroll down to the **System** icon and double-click on it.

Step 4.   Click on the **Hardware** tab.

Step 5.   Click on the **Device Manager** button.

Step 6.   Click on the + **(plus sign)** beside the class of device you want to upgrade.

_____*Instructor's Initials*

Step 7.   Right-click on the **specific device** you want to upgrade.

Step 8.   Click on the **Properties** tab.

Step 9.   Click on the **Driver** tab.

Step 10.   Click on the **Update Driver** button. The Upgrade Device Driver wizard appears.

Step 11.   Click on the **Next** button.

Step 12.   Click on the **Display a list of known drivers for this device so that I can choose a specific driver** radio button. Click on the **Next** button.

Step 13.   Click on the **Have Disk** button.

Step 14.   Insert the media that contains your updated driver into the floppy drive, Zip drive, CD-ROM, or DVD drive.

Step 15.   In the Copy manufacturer's files from box, type in the drive letter for the device that contains the updated driver followed by a colon and click on the **OK** button. An example of a driver device is A:. The Browse button can be used to locate a device driver as well.

Step 16.   Click on the **Next** button and follow the instructions on the screen to complete the upgrade.

_____ *Instructor's Initials*

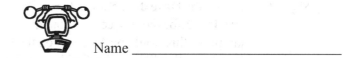

Name _____

INSTALLING A NON-PLUG AND PLAY DEVICE
INTO A WINDOWS 2000 COMPUTER

Objective: To install a non-plug and play device into a computer running Windows 2000 and load the proper driver for it

Parts: Computer with Windows 2000 installed
Non-plug and play device
Latest Windows 2000 driver for the hardware device

Note: The installation process outlined below may differ due to computer differences. If the process is different, follow the directions on the screen. Contact your instructor or a lab assistant if you are unsure of the steps.

Step 1.   Turn the computer off and install the piece of hardware according to the manufacturer's directions.

Step 2.   Turn the computer on and verify that the operating system loads. Login to Windows 2000 using the userid and password provided by the instructor or lab assistant. The Found New Hardware window should *not* appear if the device is truly non-plug and play.

Step 3.   Start the Add/Remove Hardware wizard by clicking on the **Start** button.

Step 4.   Point to the **Settings** option and then click on the **Control Panel** menu option.

Step 5.   When the Control Panel window appears, double-click on the **Add/Remove Hardware** icon. The Add/Remove Hardware wizard initializes. Click on the **Next** button to continue.

Step 6.   Ensure the Add/Troubleshoot a device radio button is selected, and then click on the **Next** button. A list of installed devices appears.

Step 7.   Click on the **Add a new device** option from the window and click on the **Next** button.

Step 8.   Click on the **No, I want to select the hardware from a list** option and then click on the **Next** button.

Step 9.   Select the type of hardware you want to install and then click on the **Next** button.

Step 10.   Insert your device driver into the floppy drive, Zip drive, CD-ROM, or DVD drive.

Step 11. Click on the **Have disk** button. In the Copy manufacturer's files from box, type in the **drive letter** for the device that contains the updated driver followed by a colon. An example of this would be A:. Click on the **Browse** button if you don't know where the file is located. Click on the **OK** button. You may be required to select your specific device or model from a list on the screen. If so, select the device and click the **Next** button. Contact an instructor or lab assistant if you don't know what to select.

Step 12. Click on the **Finish** button.

_____*Instructor's Initials*

Name _____

INSTALLING A PRINTER INTO A WINDOWS 2000 COMPUTER

Objective: To install a USB, IEEE 1394, or infrared printer as well as a printer attached to the parallel port on a computer running Windows 2000 and load the proper driver for it

Parts: Computer with Windows 2000 installed
Printer (with appropriate cabling if necessary)
Latest Windows 2000 driver for the printer

Note: The installation process outlined below may differ due to printer differences. If the process is different, follow the directions on the screen. Contact your instructor or a lab assistant if you are unsure of the steps.

Step 1.   Turn the computer off and install the piece of printer according to the manufacturer's directions.

Question 1:   Do you have a Windows 2000 driver for the printer being installed? If not, go on the printer manufacturer's web site and download the driver or obtain it from the instructor or lab assistant.

Step 2.   Turn the computer on and verify that the operating system loads. Logon to Windows 2000 using the userid and password provided by the instructor or lab assistant. The Found New Hardware wizard should appear. Follow the instructions on the screen to install the printer. When prompted for the printer driver, insert the CD or disk that contains the printer driver, and use the Browse button to locate the driver. Continue through the Add Printer wizard until the printer is installed.

Step 3.   If the Found New Hardware wizard does not appear, have the Windows 2000 printer driver ready, click on the **Start** button, point to the **Settings** selection, and double-click on the **Printers** option.

Step 4.   When the Printers window opens, click on the **Add Printer** icon.

Step 5.   Click on the **Next** button and select the **Local Printer** selection.

Step 6.   When prompted for the printer driver, insert the CD or disk that contains the printer driver, and use the Browse button to locate the driver. Continue through the Add Printer wizard until the printer is installed.

Step 7.   Print a test page to test the printer.

Question 2:   Did the printer print the test page? If not, troubleshoot the printer.

_____*Instructor's Initials*

 Name _____

CHECKING THE WINDOWS 2000 INSTALLATION

Objective: To verify any errors that occurred during the Windows 2000 installation

Parts: Computer with Windows 2000 installed

Step 1. Turn on the computer and login to Windows 2000 using the userid and password provided by the instructor or lab assistant.

Step 2. Right-click on the **Start** button. Click on the **Explore** option.

Step 3. In the left window, locate the drive letter on which Windows 2000 was loaded. (Normally this is the C: drive.) Contact the instructor or a student assistant if you are unsure. Click on the + **(plus sign)** beside the drive letter. If there is no plus signby the drive letter, but instead it is a minus sign, skip this step.

Step 4. In the left window, locate the folder in which Windows 2000 was loaded. (Normally this is WINNT.) Contact the instructor or a student assistant if you are unsure. Double-click on this folder.

Step 5. In the left window, locate the folder called WINDIR and click on the + **(plus sign)** beside this folder.

Step 6. Click on the **Tools** menu option.

Step 7. Click on the **Folder options** selection.

Step 8. Click on the **View** tab.

Step 9. Locate the Hidden files and folders option and ensure the radio button beside the Show hidden files and folders option is selected. If it is not, click in the **radio button** to enable it. Click on the **OK** button.

Step 10. In the right window, if files and folders do not appear, click on the **Show files** option. Locate the **SETUPACT.LOG** file and double-click on it. Notepad opens with this file. This file contains a listing of all installation actions performed.

Question 1: What was the first listing shown in the SETUPACT.LOG of what was done during the installation process?

Step 10. Close the SETUPACT.LOG file by clicking on the **Close** button (**X**) located in the upper right corner of the window.

Step 11.   In the right Explorer window, located the **SETUPERR.LOG** file and double-click on it. Notepad opens with this file. The SETUPERR.LOG file contains a listing of any errors that occurred during the Windows 2000 installation process.

Question 2:   Were any errors logged during the Windows 2000 installation? If so, write one of the errors in the space below.

Step 12.   Close the SETUPERR.LOG file by clicking on the **Close** button (**X**).

_____ *Instructor's Initials*

Name _____

USING THE BOOT LOGGING ADVANCED OPTIONS MENU

Objective: To use the Windows 2000 Boot Logging menu option to troubleshoot device drivers

Parts: Computer with Windows 2000 installed

Step 1.   Turn on the computer and press the **F8** key when the For troubleshooting and advanced startup options for Windows 2000, press F8 message appears.

Step 2.   Use the arrow keys on the keyboard and select the **Enable Boot Logging** menu option and press **Enter.**

Step 3.   After the system boots, login using the userid and password assigned by the instructor. Right-click on the **Start** button.

Step 4.   Click on the **Explore** option.

Step 5.   In the left window, locate and click on the **%systemroot%** folder (the folder that contains the majority of the 2000 files, which is normally C:\WINNT). Contact the instructor or a lab assistant if you are not certain of the drive letter or name of the folder.

Step 6.   In the right window, locate and double-click on the **NTBTLOG.TXT** file. Notepad opens with this file active on the screen. If the files and folders do not show on the screen, click on the **Show Files** option.

Step 7.   A driver that loads properly has the words *loaded driver* before the name of the driver.

Question 1:   List two drivers that loaded properly on your system.

Step 8.   A driver that does not load properly has the words *did not load driver* before the name of the driver.

Question 2:   Did any of the drivers on your system not load properly? If so, list at least one in the space below.

_____***Instructor's Initials***

Step 9.   Close the **NTBTLOG.TXT** document.

Step 10.   Close the **Explorer** window.

Step 11.   Shut down the computer.

Name _____

USING THE WINDOWS 2000 SYSTEM INFORMATION TOOL

Objective: To use the Windows 2000 System Information tool to troubleshoot device conflicts

Parts: Computer with Windows 2000 installed and the Computer Management tool installed

Step 1.   Turn on the computer and verify that the Windows 2000 Professional loads.

Step 2.   Logon to Windows 2000 using the userid and password provided by the instructor or lab assistant.

Step 3.   Click on the **Start** button and point to the **Settings** selection.

Step 4.   Point to the **Control Panel** option.

Step 5.   Double-click on the **Administrative Tools** control panel icon.

Step 6.   Double-click on the **System Information** icon.

Step 7.   Click on the + **(plus sign)** next to the **Components** folder.

Step 8.   Click on the **Problem Devices** folder. Any devices with hardware conflicts list in the right window. Keep in mind that you use the Device Manager program to correct any problems with resource allocation.

Question 1:   Do any devices have conflicts listed in the Problem Devices window? If so, write them in the space below.

Step 9.   Another good check for hardware conflicts is through the Hardware Resources option. Click on the + **(plus sign)** next to the Hardware Resources folder.

Step 10.   Double-click on the **Conflicts/Sharing** folder. Any device that lists under this folder has a resource conflict or is sharing a system resource. Do not forget that PCI devices can legitimately share system resources.

Question 2:   List two devices that are sharing system resources in the space below.

Step 11.   Click on the **IRQs** folder located under the Hardware Resources folder in the left window.

Question 3:   List any IRQ that is available for use by a new device.

Question 4:   Are any IRQs shared by two devices? If so, write them in the space below.

Step 12.   Click on the **Memory** folder located under the Hardware Resources folder in the left window.

Question 5:   List one memory address range used by the video adapter.

_____ *Instructor's Initials*

Step 13.   Close the System Information window by clicking on the **Close** box (the one with the **X**) in the upperright corner of the window.

 Name _____

HALTING AN APPLICATION USING TASK MANAGER IN WINDOWS 2000 PROFESSIONAL

Objective: To use Task Manager to halt an application

Parts: Computer with Windows 2000 Professional installed

At times, it may become necessary to halt a hung or stalled application. Windows 2000 Professional provides a method to accomplish this through the Task Manager utility.

Step 1.   Turn the computer on and verify that Windows 2000 Professional loads.

Step 2.   Logon to Windows 2000 Professional using the userid and password provided by the instructor or lab assistant.

Step 3.   From the Start menu, choose **Programs, Accessories,** and then select **Notepad**. The Notepad utility opens.

Question 1:   What other method can be used to start the Notepad utility?

Step 4.   To access the **Task Manager**, simultaneously press **CTRL, ALT,** and **Delete**, and then select **Task Manager.**

Question 2:   What things can you view from Task Manager?

Step 5.   Select the **Applications** tab.

Question 3:   What applications are listed as open?

Step 6.   Click on the **Notepad.exe** application and select **End Task**. The Notepad.exe application closes.

Step 7.   Close the Windows **Task Manager** window.

_____ *Instructor's Initials*

Name _____

CREATING AN ERD (EMERGENCY REPAIR DISK)

Objective: To create an ERD that can be used when the computer does not boot properly

Parts: Computer with Windows 2000 installed

Step 1.   Turn on the computer and verify that the Windows 2000 Professional loads.

Step 2.   Logon to Windows 2000 using the userid and password provided by the instructor or lab assistant.

Step 3.   Click on the **Start** button.

Step 4.   Point to the **Programs** option.

Step 5.   Point to the **Accessories** option.

Step 6.   Point to the **System Tools** option.

Step 7.   Click on the **Backup** option. The Backup window appears.

Step 8.   Click on the **Tools** menu option.

Step 9.   Click on the **Create an Emergency Repair Disk** option.

Question 1:   Give one situation where an Emergency Rescue Disk is useful.

Step 10. Insert a blank formatted floppy disk when prompted.

Step 11. Click on the **OK** button.

_____ *Instructor's Initials*

Step 12. When the ERD creation is complete, close the **Backup** window.

Question 2:   [T / F] The registry is backed up automatically when you create an ERD.

Name _____

USING THE PERFORMANCE UTILITY IN 2000 PROFESSIONAL

Objective: To use the Performance utility to track individual computer components

Parts: Computer with Windows 2000 installed and Administrative Tools loaded

Step 1.   Turn on the computer and verify that the Windows 2000 Professional loads.

Step 2.   Logon to Windows 2000 using the userid and password provided by the instructor or lab assistant.

Step 3.   Click on the **Start** button, point to the **Settings** option, and click on the **Control Panel** selection.

Step 4.   Double-click on the **Administrative Tools** control panel icon.

Step 5.   Double-click on the **Performance** icon. The Performance utility allows you to track individual computer component's performance. This is done through individual counters.

Step 6.   In the left window, click on the **System Monitor** item.

Step 7.   Click on the **Add button** (the button that has a plus sign on it) or right-click in the right window and click on the **Add Counters** option. The Add Counters dialog box opens.

Step 8.   Click on the **Performance object** down arrow. A list of system components appears such as Processor, physical disk, paging file memory, etc. Select the **Memory** performance object.

Step 9.   Once a system component has been selected, individual counters for that component can be selected and monitored. In the Select counters from list window, click on the **Available Bytes** counter. Click on the **Add** button.

Step 10.   Click on the **Performance** object down arrow. Select the **Paging File** performance object.

Step 11.   In the Select counters from list window, click on the **%Usage** counter. Click on the **Add** button.

Question 1:   Using the Explain button, find out for what the %Usage counter is used. Write the explanation in the space below.

Step 12.   Using the method outlined in steps 7 through 9, select two more counters to be monitored.

Question 2: What two counters did you add?

Step 13.   Click on the **Close** button. The right window in the Performance window displays a graph of the various counters. You may need to start some applications, do some cutting and pasting, or surf the Internet to see some of the counter activity. When finished, close the **Performance** window.

_____ *Instructor's Initials*

Name _____

INTERNET DISCOVERY

Objective: To access the Internet to obtain specific information regarding a computer or its associated parts

Parts: Access to the Internet

Question 1.   What is the URL for the Microsoft Windows 2000 Professional on-line help?

Question 2.   When Windows 2000 Professional is in Standby mode, a stop 0x9F error appears. What should you do? Write the URL and the answer in the space below.

Question 3.   Frank Condron has a web site for Windows 2000. On this web site, Frank describes what to do if you get a blue screen of death with the stop error of DATA_BUS_ERROR. What is Frank's solution and what is the URL where you found the solution?

Question 4.   ZD, Inc. has a web site for Windows 2000. Write the URL for this site.

Question 5.   Locate one book on the Internet that deals with troubleshooting Windows 2000 Professional. Write the name of the book, the author, and the URL in the space below.

Question 6.   How many service packs are currently available for Windows 2000 Professional? Write the number and URL where you found the answer in the space below.

NOTES

Chapter 18:

Introduction to Networking

OBJECTIVES

After completing this chapter you will

- Be able to differentiate between peer-to-peer and server-based networks.
- Be able to identify a network topology.
- Understand the different types of network cabling.
- Be able to explain the differences between various network access methods.
- Understand Ethernet issues.
- Identify OSI model layers.
- Be able to explain when a specific network protocol is used.
- Understand the difference between a MAC address and an IP address.
- Be able to correctly apply IP addressing concepts.
- Understand the purpose of DHCP, WINS, and DNS.
- Be able to properly configure a NIC for network connectivity.
- Be able to use common network troubleshooting tools.
- Be able to access a network printer.
- Understand dial-up networking concepts and define commonly used network terms.

KEY TERMS

application layer	frame	network number	subnet mask
backbone	FTP	network protocol	switch
bandwidth	full-duplex	network topology	TCP
baseband	half-duplex	NOS	TCP/IP
broadband	host number	NSLOOKUP	telnet
broadcast address	HTML	OSI model	token
browser	HTTP	packet	token passing
bus topology	hub	peer-to-peer network	tracert
coaxial cable	infrared	physical layer	transport layer
crosstalk	IP address	ping	twisted-pair cable
CSMA/CA	IPCONFIG	PPP	UDP
CSMA/CD	IPX/SPX	presentation layer	UNC
data link layer	ISP	ring topology	URL
default gateway	LAN	router	UTP
DHCP	loopback address	server-based network	VPN
DNS server	MAC address	session layer	WAN
DUN	mesh topology	single-mode	WINIPCFG
e-mail	multi-mode	SMTP	WINS server
Fast Ethernet	NetBEUI	SNMP	
FDDI	network	star topology	
fiber-optic cable	network layer	STP	

NETWORKING OVERVIEW

A **network** is two or more devices that can communicate with one another and share resources between the devices. A network allows computer users to share files; communicate via e-mail; browse the Internet; share a printer, modem, or scanner; and access applications and files. Networks can be divided into two major categories—LANs and WANs. A **LAN** (**Local Area Network**) is a group of devices that can share resources in a single area such as a room or a building. A **WAN** (**Wide Area Network**) is communication between LANs. The Internet is an example of a WAN as are two networks located in two different cities.

Networks are vital to businesses today. They can even be found in many homes. Many students come in to class saying that they want to learn networks. A technician must have a basic understanding of the devices that make up networks (computers, printers, modems, etc.) and then learn network devices. You cannot bypass computer repair and go straight into networking.

TYPES OF LOCAL AREA NETWORKS

There are two basic types of LANs, a server-based network and a peer-to-peer network. With a **server-based network**, computer users login to a main computer called a server where they are authenticated (authorized to use the network). The server is a more powerful computer than a normal workstation. The server contains information about who is allowed to connect to the network, and to what network resources (files, printer, and applications) the network user is allowed access. A **peer-to-peer network** does not have a central server. Instead, each computer is its own server. The computer user sets up passwords to allow others access to the resources. A user uses the network to access the remote files, printer, applications, etc., from their own workstation. Server-based networks are more common in businesses, whereas peer-to-peer networks are more common in homes and very small businesses. A server-based network can consist of 10 or more computers, in contrast to a peer-to-peer network which usually has fewer than 10 computers.

A server-based network is more secure than a peer-to-peer network. This is because the server is normally located in a locked network room or wiring closet. Also, the network users and what they are allowed to do (their network rights and permissions) are configured and stored on the network server. Servers have a special operating system loaded on them called a **NOS** (**Network Operating System**). Examples of network operating systems are Novell, Microsoft's NT Server, and Microsoft's 2000 Server. A network operating system has utilities that allow computer user management (who is allowed onto the network), resource management (what network applications, files, printers, etc. a user can use), and security management (what a user is allowed to do with a resource such as read, write, read and write, etc.). One userid and password is all a remote user needs to access many network resources located throughout the business organization. A network user can sit down at any computer in the organization, logon to the server, and start working with the network resources.

Network Figure #1 shows how a server-based network can be configured. The network has one server in the center, four workstations labeled Workstation 1, 2, 3, and 4, and two laser printers labeled LP1 and LP2. The server has a database of users, CSchmidt, RDevoid, and MElkins, and their associated passwords. The server also has three applications loaded—Microsoft Excel, Microsoft Project, and Microsoft Word. These applications and associated documents are stored on the server. Whether or not the users can access these applications and documents and what they can do within each document is also stored on the server. In the Permission column of the table located in Network Figure #1 is either R for Read or R/W for Read/Write. This is an indication of what the user can do in a particular application. For example, user CSchmidt has read and write access to Excel, Project, and Word. User MElkins can only read Excel and Word documents, but she can read and write Microsoft Project documents. User CSchmidt can print to either of the laser printers, but user RDevoid prints only to the LP1 laser printer.

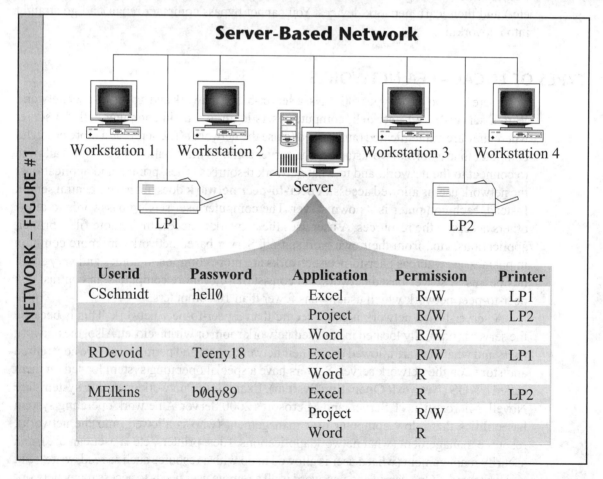

Server-Based Network

NETWORK – FIGURE #1

Workstation 1   Workstation 2   Server   Workstation 3   Workstation 4

LP1   LP2

Userid	Password	Application	Permission	Printer
CSchmidt	hell0	Excel	R/W	LP1
		Project	R/W	LP2
		Word	R/W	
RDevoid	Teeny18	Excel	R/W	LP1
		Word	R	
MElkins	b0dy89	Excel	R	LP2
		Project	R/W	
		Word	R	

Another benefit of server-based networks is that a user can sit down at any workstation, login to the server with their userid and password, and have access to all of their network resources. For example in Network Figure #1, computer user RDevoid can sit down at any workstation and have access to her Excel and Word documents and print to laser printer LP1.

A peer-to-peer network is not as expensive, nor as secure as a server-based network. A server is more expensive than a regular workstation plus it requires a network operating system. Since peer-to-peer networks do not use a dedicated server, costs are reduced. Instead of a network operating system, each workstation uses a regular operating system such as Windows 95, Windows 98, NT Workstation, or 2000 Professional. A peer-to-peer network is not as secure as a server-based network because each computer must be configured with individual userids and passwords. Network Figure #2 shows how a peer-to-peer network is configured.

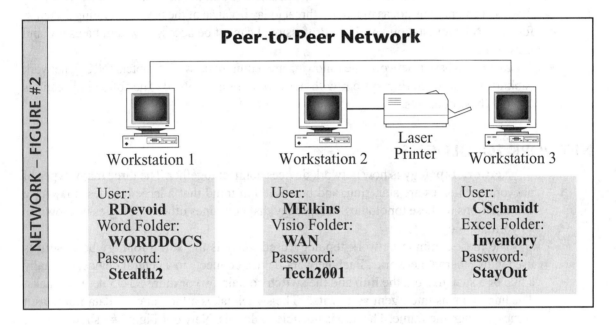

Peer-to-Peer Network

NETWORK – FIGURE #2

Workstation 1

User:
RDevoid
Word Folder:
WORDDOCS
Password:
Stealth2

Workstation 2

User:
MElkins
Visio Folder:
WAN
Password:
Tech2001

Laser Printer

Workstation 3

User:
CSchmidt
Excel Folder:
Inventory
Password:
StayOut

In Network Figure #2, there are three workstations labeled Workstation 1, 2, and 3. Workstation 2 has a shared printer. A shared printer is a printer connected to the computer that has been configured so that other network users can print to it. There are three people in this company, Raina Devoid, Cheryl Schmidt, and Melody Elkins. Raina Devoid normally works at Workstation 1 and Raina has shared a folder on the hard drive called WORDDOCS that has a password of Stealth2. Cheryl and Melody can access the documents located in the folder called WORDDOCS from their own workstations as long as they know the password is Stealth2. If Raina (who is sitting at Workstation 1) wants to access Melody's WAN folder, Raina must know and remember that the password is Tech2001. If Melody changes the password on the WAN folder, Melody must remember to tell the new password to anyone who needs access. The password is only used when accessing the WAN folder documents.

A peer-to-peer network password is only effective across the network. The password is not effective if someone sits down at the workstation. For example, if a summer intern, Ken Tinker, sits down at Workstation 3, Ken has full access to the Inventory folder and documents. Even though the folder is passworded for the peer-to-peer network, Ken is not using the network to access the folder so the password is useless.

Management of network resources is much harder to control on a peer-to-peer network than on a server-based network. Each user is required to manage the network resources on one computer and password management can become a nightmare. Remember with peer-to-peer networks, anyone who has the password can access the folder across the network. Server-based networks are normally more secure because (1) passwords are managed centrally at the server and (2) the server is normally locked in a wiring closet.

The problem of having access to a workstation and all its resources just by sitting down at a computer is not as much of a threat today because of the newer operating systems' features. NT Workstation and 2000 Professional cannot be accessed without a userid and password.

In order to have a network, the following are required: network adapters (NICs), network cabling, and an operating system with network options enabled. The following sections explore these concepts.

NETWORK TOPOLOGIES

Network topology is how network devices connect together. The three major types of network topologies are star, ring, and bus. Keep in mind that a large business may have combinations of these topologies. A topology that combines other topologies is known as a hybrid topology.

The most common network topology used today is the **star topology** because it is used with Ethernet networks. Each network device connects to a central device, normally a hub or a switch. Both the **hub** and the **switch** contain two or more RJ-45 network jacks. The hub is not as intelligent as a switch. The switch takes a look at each data frame as it comes through the frame. The hub is not able to do this. Network Figure #3 shows what a hub or switch looks like.

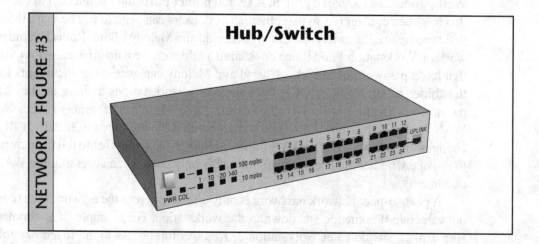

NETWORK – FIGURE #3

Hub/Switch

In a star topology, each network device has a cable that connects between the device and the hub or switch. If one computer or cable fails, all other devices continue to function. However, if the hub or switch fails, the network goes down. The hub or switch is normally located in a central location such as a network wiring closet. Network Figure #4 shows how a star topology is cabled. By looking at how each device connects to a central location, you can easily see why it is called a star.

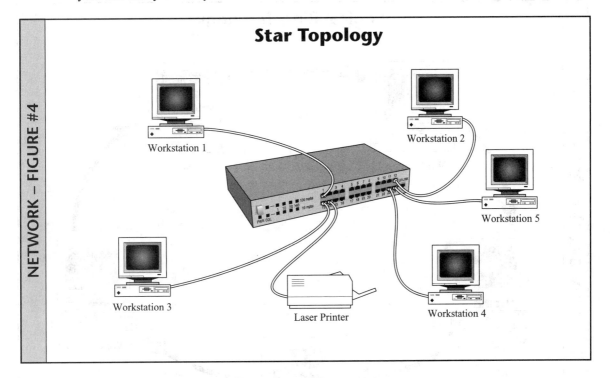

Star Topology

NETWORK – FIGURE #4

Workstation 1

Workstation 2

Workstation 5

Workstation 3

Laser Printer

Workstation 4

More cable is used in wiring a star topology than with the bus topology, but the type of cable used is cheap and this is not an issue for today's network managers. Star topologies are easy to troubleshoot. If one network device goes down, the problem is in the device, cable, or port on the hub/switch. If a group of network devices go down, the problem is most likely in the device that connects them together (hub or switch). Look back to Network Figure #4. If Workstation 1, Workstation 2, Workstation 3, Workstation 4 and Workstation 5 all cannot communicate with one another, the problem is the switch in the middle. If only Workstation 3 cannot communicate with the other network devices, the problem is in Workstation 3, the cable that connects Workstation 3, or in port 13 on the switch.

The **ring topology** is physically wired like a star, but operates differently. The ring topology is used in Token Ring networks. A token (a special network packet) passes from one network device to the next in a continuous fashion. Token Ring networks are wired like a star, but they operate like a logical ring. Network Figure #5 shows how the Token Ring network appears to be a ring.

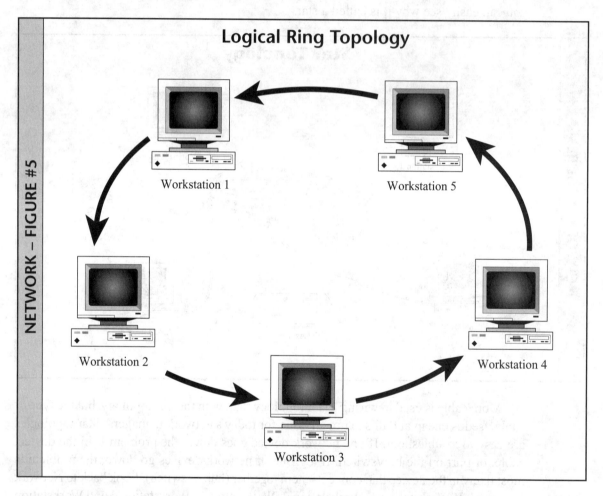

Logical Ring Topology

NETWORK – FIGURE #5

Workstation 1

Workstation 5

Workstation 2

Workstation 4

Workstation 3

The token passes from one workstation to another in a continuous loop. When the token does not contain data, it is known as a free token. As the free token is passed around the ring, any workstation wishing to transmit data takes the token and adds data. The data is sent around the ring until it reaches its destination. No other workstation can accept the data except for the destination network device. Once the data has been transmitted, a free token is placed on the ring again. No workstation can transmit until the free token comes back around the ring.

The **bus topology** is one of the oldest network topologies. All network devices connect to a single cable. If the cable has a break, the entire network is down. Bus topologies are also difficult to troubleshoot when there is a network problem. Network Figure #6 depicts a bus topology.

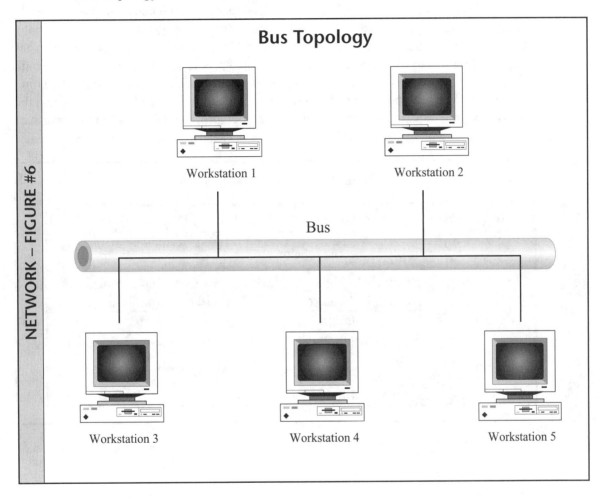

A mesh topology is not as common as other topologies, but a **mesh topology** is used when all network devices connect to each other. Mesh topology is more likely to be used in a WAN (Wide Area Network) rather than a LAN (Local Area Network). Mesh topologies take a lot of cabling, but if a cable breaks, the network still continues to function.

An example of a mesh topology is a college that has three main campuses—North, South, and West. Each campus has a connection to the other two campuses. For example, the North campus has a connection to the South and the West campuses. Each campus has important servers to which the other campuses need access. If the North campus to South campus connection breaks, the North campus can still reach the South campus by going through the West campus. Whenever a network can still function after a cable break, the network is said to be fault tolerant. A mesh topology provides the most fault tolerance of any network topology. Network Table #1 summarizes network topologies.

NETWORK – TABLE #1

Network Topologies

Topology	Advantages	Disadvantages
Bus	Takes less cable (cheaper)	Break in the bus, network is down
Mesh	Break in the cable, network still works (fault tolerant)	Expensive and complex (hard to reconfigure)
Ring	Easy to install	Expensive parts
Star	Easy to install, most common, break in workstation cable network still works (fault tolerant)	More expensive than bus

NETWORK CABLING

Networks require some type of medium to transmit data. This medium is normally some type of cable or air (when using wireless networking). The most common types of cable are twisted-pair and fiber-optic, although some very old networks have coax cable.

Twisted-pair cable comes in two types, shielded and unshielded. The acronyms used with this type of cable are STP for shielded twisted-pair and UTP for unshielded twisted-pair. The most common is UTP. With twisted-pair cable, all network devices connect to one central location such as a patch panel, hub, or switch. If one cable breaks, only the one device fails. Most people are familiar with twisted-pair cable because this type of cable is used in homes for telephone wiring. The type used with networking has eight copper wires. The wires are grouped in colored pairs. Each pair is twisted together to prevent crosstalk. **Crosstalk** occurs when a signal on one wire interferes with the signal on an adjacent wire. The wires are wrapped in a vinyl insulator. Network Figure #7 shows unshielded twisted-pair cable.

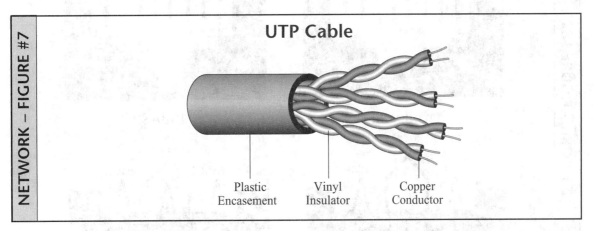

NETWORK – FIGURE #7

UTP Cable

Plastic Encasement   Vinyl Insulator   Copper Conductor

UTP cabling is measured in gauges. The most common measurements for UTP cabling are 22, 24, or 26 gauge unshielded twisted-pair cables. UTP cables come in different specifications called categories. The most common are categories 3, 4, and 5. People usually shorten the name Category 3 to CAT 3 or Category 5 to CAT 5. The categories determine, in part, how fast the network can run. Category 3 was mainly installed for telephone systems in many office buildings. Category 3 (CAT 3) is called a voice grade cable, but it has the ability to run up to 10Mbps Ethernet or 16Mbps Token Ring topologies. Networks that run 10Mbps are known as 10BaseT networks. 100Mbps Ethernet networks are known as Fast, 100BaseT4, and 100BaseT8. The 100BaseT4 networks use two pairs (four wires) of the UTP cable whereas the 100BaseT8 networks use all four pairs (8 wires). The most common type of UTP is CAT 5. Fairly new categories of UTP cable include CAT 5e, which is designed for 100Mbps on UTP and STP; CAT 6, which is designed for 1000Mbps on UTP and STP; and CAT 7, which is designed for 1000Mbps on UTP, STP, and fiber. UTP and STP cable are used in star and ring topologies.

In order to avoid extra troubleshooting time, most businesses install their network cabling according to the ANSI/TIA/EIA-568-A or 568-B standard. This standard specifies how far the cable can extend, how to label it, what type of jack to use, etc. Network Figure #8 illustrates the common cabling standards used in industry.

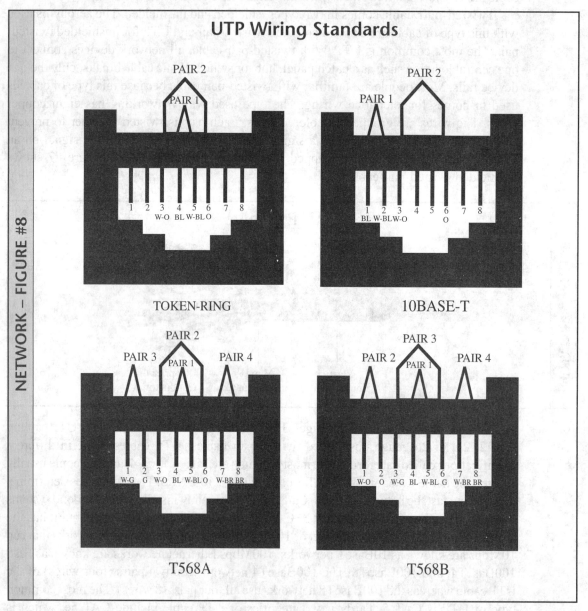

NETWORK – FIGURE #8

UTP Wiring Standards

STP (**Shielded Twisted-Pair**) cable has extra foil shielding that provides more shielding. Shielded twisted-pair cable is used in industrial settings where extra shielding is needed to prevent outside interference from interfering with the data on the cable.

When installing network cabling, it is important to insert the UTP cable fully into the

RJ-45 jack and to insert the colored wires in the standardized order. One of the most common mistakes that new technicians make when putting an RJ-45 connector on UTP cable is they put the cable into the RJ-45 connector backwards. Network Figure #9 shows the location of pin 1 on an RJ-45 connector.

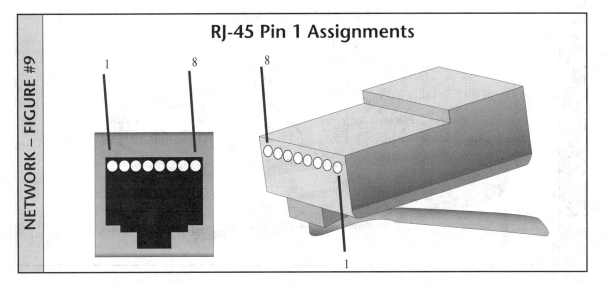

RJ-45 Pin 1 Assignments

NETWORK – FIGURE #9

Another common mistake is not pushing the wires to the end of the RJ-45 connector. Before crimping the wires into the connector, look at the end of the RJ-45 connector. You should see each wire jammed against the end of the RJ-45 connector.

Fiber-optic cable is made of glass or a type of plastic fiber and is used to carry light pulses. Fiber-optic cable can be used to connect a workstation to another device, but in industry, the most common use of fiber-optic cable is to connect networks together forming the network backbone. Copper cable is used to connect workstations together. Then fiber cable is used to interconnect the networks especially when the network is located on multiple floors or multiple buildings.

Fiber-optic cable is the most expensive cable type, but it also handles the most data with the least amount of data loss. The two major classifications of fiber are single-mode and multi-mode. **Single-mode** fiber-optic cable has only one light beam sent down the cable. **Multi-mode** fiber-optic cable allows multiple light signals to be sent along the same cable. Multi-mode fiber is cheaper than single-mode fiber and is good for shorter distance applications. But, single-mode fiber can transmit a signal farther than multi-mode.

Fiber-optic cabling has many advantages including security, long distance transmission, and bandwidth. Fiber-optic cabling is used by many government agencies because of the high security it offers. Light signals that travel down fiber are impossible to detect remotely, unlike signals from other cable media. Also, because light is used instead of electrical signals, fiber-optic cable is not susceptible to interference from EMI or RFI-producing devices.

Each fiber-optic cable can carry signals in one direction, so an installation normally has two strands of fiber-optic cable in separate jackets. Fiber is used in the ring and star topologies. Network Figure #10 shows a fiber-optic cable.

Fiber-Optic Cable

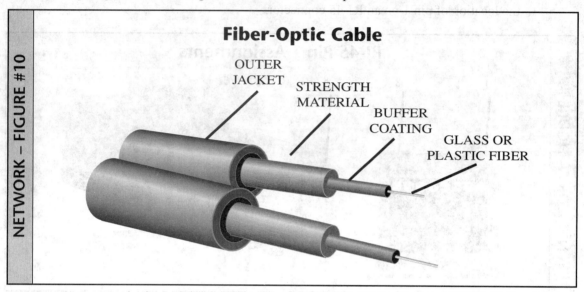

OUTER JACKET
STRENGTH MATERIAL
BUFFER COATING
GLASS OR PLASTIC FIBER

NETWORK – FIGURE #10

The last type of cable is **coaxial cable** (usually shortened to coax). Coax cable is used in older Ethernet 10Base2 and 10Base5 networks as well as mainframe and minicomputer connections. Most people have seen coax cable in their homes. The cable used for cable TV is coax cable, but is a different type than network cabling. Coax cable has a center copper conductor surrounded by insulation. Outside the insulation is a shield of copper braid, a metallic foil, or both, that protects the center conductor from EMI. Network Figure #11 shows a coax cable. Coax is used in star and bus topologies.

Coax Cable with Connector

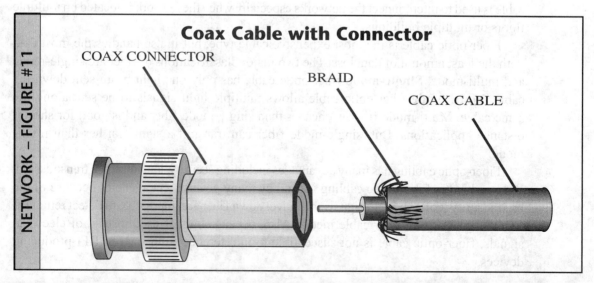

COAX CONNECTOR
BRAID
COAX CABLE

NETWORK – FIGURE #11

ACCESS METHODS

Before a computer can communicate on a network it must adhere to a set of communication rules to which all computers on the network comply. This set of communication rules is known as a common access method. Ethernet uses a common access method known as **CSMA/CD** (Carrier Sense Multiple Access/Collision Detect), whereas fiber networks and Token Ring use **token passing** as the common access method. Wireless networks and Apple networks use **CSMA/CA** (Carrier Sense Multiple Access/ Collision Avoidance). The purpose of the common access method is to ensure that each workstation has an opportunity to communicate with the other workstations.

With CSMA/CD, each workstation can place data onto the network cable at any time, but the network adapter checks the network cable to ensure that no other workstation is already transmitting. In the acronym CSMA/CD, the CS stands for "Carrier Sense" which means that it is checking the network cable for other traffic. "Multiple Access" means that multiple computers can access the network cable simultaneously. "Collision Detect" provides rules for what happens when two computers access the network at the same time. One point to remember is that collisions are common and normal on Ethernet networks.

Take an example of a busy highway. The highway represents the network cable and cars on the highway represent data traveling down the cable. Each intersection that crosses the highway is simply a computer wanting to connect onto the major highway. Using CSMA/CD, the workstation checks that no other traffic is traveling down the highway (cable). If the way is clear, data is allowed to go onto the highway. If two workstations happen to transmit at the same time, a collision occurs. Both workstations have to stop transmitting data for a specified amount of time and then try transmitting again.

A Token Ring adapter uses token passing as the common access method. This method differs from CSMA/CD because there are no collisions in the Token Ring environment. With token passing, a **token** (a small packet of data) is passed from one workstation to another. Only the workstation that possesses the token is allowed to transmit data. The token is passed around the ring from one workstation to another with each workstation receiving a turn. When a workstation wants to transmit, it changes one bit inside the token data frame, adds data, and then places the data frame onto the cable. If a workstation does not want to transmit any data, the token is passed to the next workstation.

CSMA/CA (Carrier Sense Multiple Access/Collision Avoidance) is used with wireless LANs (Local Area Networks) and Apple networks. Network devices listen on the cable for conflicting traffic just like CSMA/CD; however, with CSMA/CA, a workstation that wants to transmit data sends a jam signal onto the cable. The workstation then waits a small amount of time for all other workstations to hear the jam signal and then the workstation begins transmission. If a collision occurs, the workstation does the same thing as CSMA/ CD—the workstation stops transmitting, waits a designated amount of time, and then retransmits.

ETHERNET ISSUES AND CONCEPTS

Since Ethernet is the most common type of network, more time needs to be spent on some issues that deal directly with Ethernet. Some of these issues are full-duplex and half-duplex transmissions, network slowdowns, and increasing bandwidth.

Ethernet networks were originally designed to support either half-duplex or full-duplex data transmissions. **Half-duplex** transmission is data transmitted in both directions on a cable, but not at the same time. Only one network device can transmit at a time. One example of half-duplex transmission is using a walkie-talkie. **Full-duplex** transmission is data transmitted in both directions on a cable simultaneously. This is similar to a phone conversation. Both people can talk at the same time if they want to do so. Ethernet networks were originally designed for half-duplex transmission. Ethernet was also designed for a 10Mbps bus topology and still performs as if it is connected in a bus network. Due to CSMA/CD, each workstation has to listen to the cable to see if any other transmission is occurring. Then, if no other network device is transmitting, the workstation starts transmitting data. In a request for a web page, for example, data would travel back to the workstation from the web server. With half-duplex transmission, the workstation transmits and then later the web server transmits. The transmission could not occur simultaneously in both directions. The more workstations on the same network, the more collisions occur and the more the network slows down. In addition, with half-duplex Ethernet, less than 50 percent of the 10Mbps available bandwidth could be used because of collisions and the time it takes for a network frame to transmit across the wire.

Today's Ethernet networks support speeds of 10Mbps, 100Mbps, and 1000Mbps. Most Ethernet NIC cards are 10/100, which means they can run at either 10Mbps or 100Mbps. Ethernet networks are also known as 10Base2, 10BaseT, 100BaseT, and 1000BaseT. When considering the term 10Base2, the 10 means that the network runs at 10Mbps. Base means that the network uses baseband technology. The 2 in 10Base2 means that the maximum coax cable length is 185 meters (which is close to 200 meters). A 10Base2 network has terminators at the both ends of the coax cable bus network. The T at the end of 10BaseT means that the computer uses twisted-pair cable. The 100 in 100BaseT means that the network supports 100Mbps and the 1000 in 1000BaseT means that 1000Mbps is supported.

Ethernet networks now support full-duplex transmissions. With full-duplex implemented, collisions are not a problem. This is because full-duplex takes advantage of the two pairs of cables, one for receiving and one for transmitting. Full-duplex Ethernet creates a direct connection between the transmitting station at one end and the receiving circuits at the other end. Full-duplex allows 100 percent of the available bandwidth to be used in each direction. In order to implement full-duplex Ethernet, both network cards in the devices must have the ability and be configured for full-duplex.

Another way to speed up the network is to use a switch instead of a hub when connecting network devices together. Full-duplex Ethernet works great, but replacing hubs with switches also improves network performance. A switch has more intelligence than a hub. When a workstation sends data to a hub, the hub broadcasts the data out all ports except for the port the data came in on. This is inefficient. A switch, on the other hand, keeps a table of addresses. When a switch receives data, the switch forwards the data out the port for which it is destined. A switch looks very similar to a hub and it is sometimes hard to distinguish between the two. Switches are very common devices in today's business network environment.

NETWORK STANDARDS

The IEEE (Institute for Electrical and Electronics Engineers) committee created network standards called the 802 standards. Each standard is given an 802.x number and represents an area of networking. Standardization is good for the network industry so that different manufacturers' network components work with other manufactures' devices. Network Table #2 lists the various 802 standards.

NETWORK – TABLE #2

IEEE 802 Standards

802 Standard	Purpose
802.1	Bridging and Management
802.2	Logical Link Control
802.3	CSMA/CD Access Method
802.4	Token-Passing Bus Access Method
802.5	Token Ring Access Method
802.6	DQDB (Distributed Queue Dual Bus) Access Method
802.7	Broadband LAN
802.8	Fiber Optic
802.9	Isochronous LANs
802.10	Security
802.11	Wireless
802.12	Demand Priority Access
802.15	WPANs (Wireless Personal Area Networks)
802.16	Broadband Wireless Access
802.17	Resilient Packet Ring

For more information about the 802 standards, access the IEEE web site at http://standards.ieee.org/getieee802/index.html.

OSI MODEL

The International Standards Organization (ISO) has developed a model for network communications known as the OSI (Open Systems Interconnect) model. The **OSI model** is a standard for information transfer across the network. The model sets several guidelines including (1) how the different transmission media are arranged and interconnected, (2) how network devices that use different languages communicate with one another, (3) how a network device goes about contacting another network device, (4) how and when data gets transmitted across the network, (5) how data is sent to the correct device, and (6) how it is known if the network data was received properly. All of these tasks must be handled by a set of rules and the OSI model provides a structure into which these rules fit.

Can you imagine a generic model for building a car? This model would state that you need some means of steering, a type of fuel to power the car, a place for the driver to sit, safety standards, etc. The model would not say what type of steering wheel to put in the car, or what type of fuel the car must use, but is just a blueprint for making the car. In networking, there is such a model, and it is called the OSI model. The OSI model divides networking into different layers so that it is easier to understand (and teach). Dividing up the network into distinct layers also helps manufacturers. If a particular manufacturer wants to make a network device that works on layer 3, the manufacturer only has to be concerned with layer 3. This division makes networking technologies emerge much faster. Having a layered model also helps to teach network concepts. Each layer can be taught as a separate network function.

The layers of the OSI model (starting from the top and working down) are application, presentation, session, transport, network, data link, and physical.

OSI Model Layers

NETWORK – FIGURE #12

7	Application
6	Presentation
5	Session
4	Transport
3	Network
2	Data Link
1	Physical

Each layer of the OSI model uses the layer below it (except for the physical layer which is on the bottom). Each layer provides some function to the layer above it. For example, the data link layer cannot be accessed without first going through the physical layer. If communication needs to be performed at the third layer, (the network layer), then the physical and data link layers must be used first.

Certification exams contain questions about the OSI model and knowing the levels is a good place to start preparing for the exams. A mnemonic to help remember the OSI layers is: **A P**erson **S**eldom **T**akes **N**aps **D**uring **P**arties. Each first letter of the mnemonic phrase is supposed to remind you of the first letter of the OSI model layers. For example, *A* in the phrase is to remind you of the application layer. The *P* in Person is to remind you of the Presentation layer, and so on.

Each layer of the OSI model from the top down (except for the physical layer) adds information to the data being sent across the network. Sometimes this information is called a header. Network Figure #13 shows how a header is added as the packet travels down the OSI model. When the receiving computer receives the data, each layer removes the header information. Information at the physical layer is normally called bits. When referring to information at the data link layer, use the term *frame*. When referring to information at the network layer, use the term *packet*.

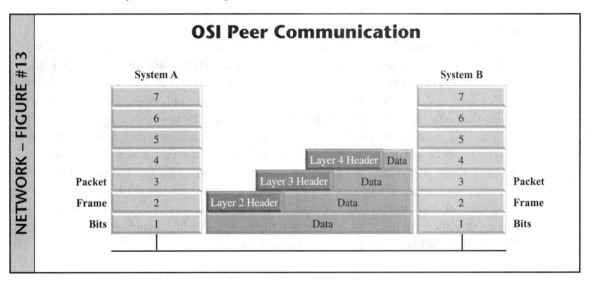

NETWORK – FIGURE #13

OSI Peer Communication

Each of the seven OSI layers performs a unique function and interacts with the layers surrounding it. The bottom three layers handle the physical delivery of data across the network. The **physical layer** (sometimes called layer 1) defines how bits are transferred and received across the network media without being concerned about the structure of the bits. The physical layer is where connectors, cable, and voltage levels are defined. The **data link layer** (sometimes called layer 2) provides the means for accurately transferring the bits across the network and it groups (encapsulates) the bits into usable sections called frames. The **network layer** (sometimes called layer 3) coordinates data movement between two devices. This layer provides path selection between two networks. Most companies and even some homes have a router that they use to connect to the Internet through their **ISP (Internet Service Provider)**.

The top four layers handle the ins and outs of providing accurate data delivery between computers and their individual processes, especially in a multi-tasking operating system environment. The **transport layer** (sometimes called layer 4) provides a service to the upper layers so they do not have to worry about the details of how data is sent. The transport layer provides such services as whether the data should be sent "reliably" or not. This is similar to getting a return receipt for a package at the post office.

The **session layer** manages the communication and synchronization between two network devices. The **presentation layer** provides a means of translating the data from the sender into data the receiver understands. This allows all types of computers to communicate with one another even though one computer may be using one language (such as EBCDIC), and another computer using a different language (such as ASCII). The **application layer** provides network services to any software applications running on the network. The application layer provides network services to a computer. This allows the computer to participate or enter the OSI model (the network). Some of the services the application layer provides include negotiating authentication (what type of authentication will be used in the communication), negotiating who has responsibility for error recovery, and negotiating quality of service across the network.

Certain network devices or components work at a specific OSI layer. For example, cables, connectors, repeaters, hubs, and patch panels all reside at layer 1 of the OSI model, the physical layer parts of the network card reside at layer 1 and part of the OSI model resides at layer 2. A switch also resides at layer 2, the data link layer. A **router**, a network device that determines the best path to send a packet, works at layer 3, the network layer.

The OSI model is very confusing when you are first learning about networking, but it is very important. Understanding the model helps every day when troubleshooting a network. Knowing where the problem is occurring narrows the field of what the solution may be. For example, if a computer has problems communicating with a computer on the same network, then the problem is most likely a layer 1 or a layer 2 problem because layer 3 takes care of communication between two networks. Check the cabling and NIC settings. Network Table #3 summarizes the OSI model for you.

NETWORK – TABLE #3

OSI Model

OSI Model Layer	Purpose
Application	Provides network services (file, print, and messaging services) to any software application running on the network
Presentation	Translates data from one character set to another
Session	Manages the communication and synchronization between network devices
Transport	Provides the mechanisms for how data is sent such as reliability and error correction
Network	Provides path selection between two networks. Routers reside at the network layer. Encapsulated data at this layer is called a packet.
Data Link	Encapsulates bits into frames. Can provide error control. MAC address is at this layer. Switches reside at data link layer.
Physical	Defines how bits are transferred and received. Defines the network media, connectors, and voltage levels. Data at this level is called bits.

NETWORK PROTOCOLS

A **network protocol** is a data communication language. There are three primary network protocols used: TCP/IP, NetBEUI, and IPX/SPX. **TCP/IP** is the most common network protocol and is used when accessing the Internet and most companies (and homes) use TCP/IP as their standard protocol. **IPX/SPX** is used when connecting to a Novell network, but Novell networks now use TCP/IP as their standard protocol. **NetBEUI** is a non-routable network protocol. This means that it can only be used on simple networks, not on multiple networks that are tied together. A common place for NetBEUI is on a peer-to-peer network.

NETWORK ADDRESSING

Network adapters normally have two types of addresses assigned to them—a MAC address and an IP address. The **MAC address** is used when two network devices on the same network communicate with one another. The MAC address is a 48-bit unique number that is burned into a ROM chip located on the NIC and is represented in hexadecimal. A MAC address is unique for every computer on the network. However, the MAC address has no scheme to it except that the first three bytes represent the manufacturer. The MAC address is known as a layer 2 address.

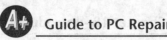

The **IP address** is a much more organized way of addressing a computer than a MAC address and it is sometimes known as a layer 3 address. The IP address is a 32-bit number that is entered into a NIC's configuration parameters. The IP address is used when multiple networks are connected together and when accessing the Internet. The IP address is shown using dotted decimal notation, such as 192.168.10.4. Each number is separated by periods and represents eight bits, and the numbers that can be represented by eight bits are 0 to 255.

IP addresses are grouped into classes. It is easy to tell which type of IP address is being issued by the first number shown in the dotted decimal notation. Class A addresses have any number from 0 to 127 as the first number. Class B addresses have any number from 128 to 191 as the first number and Class C addresses have numbers 192 through 223. For example, if a computer has an IP address of 12.150.172.39, the IP address is a Class A address because the first number is a 12. If a computer has an IP address of 176.10.100.2, it is a Class B IP address because the first number is 176.

An IP address is broken into two major parts—the network number and the host number. The **network number** is the portion of the IP address that represents which network the computer is on. All computers on the same network have the same network number. The **host number** is the portion of the IP address that represents the specific computer on the network. All computers on the same network have unique host numbers or they will not be able to communicate.

The number of bits that are used to represent the network number and the host number depends on which class of IP address is being used. With Class A IP addresses, the first eight bits (the first number) represent the network portion and the remaining 24 bits (the last three numbers) represent the host number. With Class B IP addresses, the first 16 bits (the first two numbers) represent the network portion and the remaining 16 bits (the last two numbers) represent the host number. With Class C IP addresses, the first 24 bits (the first three numbers) represent the network portion and the remaining eight bits (the last number) represent the host number. Network Figure #14 illustrates this point.

NETWORK – FIGURE #14

IP Addressing (Network Number and Host Number)

	Network	Host	Host	Host
Class A	000	0	0	0

	Network	Network	Host	Host
Class B	000	000	0	0

	Network	Network	Network	Host
Class C	000	000	000	0

In order to see how IP addressing works, it is best to use an example. A business has two networks connected together with a router. On each network, there are computer workstations and printers. Each of the networks must have a unique network number. For this example, one network has the network number of 193.14.150.0, and the other network has the network number of 193.14.151.0. Notice how these numbers represent a Class C IP address because the first number is 193.

With a Class C IP address, the first three numbers represent the network number. The first network has a network number of 193.14.150 and the second network has a network number of 193.14.151. Remember that each network has to have a different number than any other network in the organization. The last number of the IP address will be used to assign different network devices their IP address. On the first network, each device will have a number that starts with 193.14.150 because that is the network number and it stays the same for all devices on that network. Each device will then have a different number in the last portion of the IP address, for example, 193.14.150.3, 193.14.150.4, 193.14.150.5.

On the second network, each device will have a number that starts with 193.14.151 because that is the network number. The last number in the IP address changes for each network device, for example, 193.14.151.3, 193.14.151.4, 193.14.151.5, etc. No device can have a host number of 0 because that number represents the network and no device can have a host number of 255 because that represents something called the broadcast address. A **broadcast address** is the IP address used to communicate with all devices on a particular network. So, in the example given, no network device can be assigned the IP addresses 193.14.150.0 or 193.14.151.0 because these numbers represent the two networks. Furthermore, no network device can be assigned the IP addresses 193.14.150.255 or 193.14.151.255 because these numbers represent the broadcast address used with each network. An example of a Class B broadcast is 150.10.255.255. An example of a Class A broadcast is 11.255.255.255. Network Figure #15 shows this configuration.

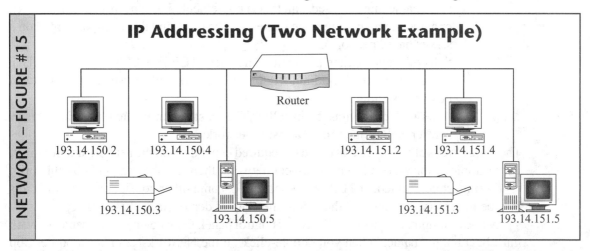

NETWORK – FIGURE #15

IP Addressing (Two Network Example)

Router

193.14.150.2   193.14.150.4   193.14.151.2   193.14.151.4

193.14.150.3   193.14.150.5   193.14.151.3   193.14.151.5

In addition to assigning a computer an IP address, you must also assign a subnet mask to the computer. The **subnet mask** is a number that the computer uses to determine which part of the IP address represents the network and which portion represents the host. The subnet mask for a Class A IP address is 255.0.0.0; the subnet mask for a Class B IP address is 255.255.0.0; the subnet mask for a Class C IP address is 255.255.255.0.0. Network Table #4 recaps this important information.

IP Address Information

Class	First Number	Network/Host Number	Standard Subnet Mask
A	0-127	N.H.H.H*	255.0.0.0
B	128-191	N.N.H.H*	255.255.0.0
C	192-222	N.N.N.H*	255.255.255.0

*N = Network number
& H = Host number

NETWORK – TABLE #4

The Complete A+ Guide to PC Repair has an appendix explaining how to subnet IP adresses.

CONFIGURING NETWORKING

When you install a NIC card in a computer, there are four things that must be configured before connecting to the network.

1. An appropriate driver for the NIC must be installed. The type of driver needed depends on which operating system is being used.
2. You must give the computer a unique name and either a workgroup name (the same name must be used, and this is implemented on a peer-to-peer network), or a domain name (the same name must be used, and this is implemented on a server-based network).
3. Select the appropriate protocol being used (TCP/IP, IPX/SPX, or NetBEUI). Conatct the network administrator for the protocol to use. The majority of businesses and homes use TCP/IP.
4. A network client must be installed. The most common client used in industry is Microsoft's client for Microsoft networks.

There are always other things that could be required depending on the network environment. For example, if the system is a peer-to-peer network, then file sharing (and possibly print sharing) must be enabled. If TCP/IP is configured, some other configuration parameters may be necessary. Exercises at the end of the chapter demonstrate these concepts.

Name a computer by using the Network control panel. Each device on the same network must be a unique name. When you double-click on the Network Neighborhood desktop icon, you can view the network device names. It can also be viewed by typing *nbtstat –n* from a command prompt. The command prompt can also be used to access network shares by using the **UNC (Universal Naming Convention).** For example, a computer called CSchmidt has a network share called TESTS. By typing *\\CSchmidt\TESTS* at the Run prompt, you can access the network share.

To share a folder, use My Computer or Explorer. Locate the folder to be shared. Right-click on the *folder.* Click on the *Sharing* option. Click on the *Sharing* tab and click in the *Shared As* radio button to enable sharing. In the Share Name text box, type a name for the network share. This name appears in other computers' Network Neighborhood or My Network Places when accessed across the network. In the Access Type section of the window, click on the *appropriate radio button* for the type of access remote users have to the folder. If a password is to be assigned, type it in the textbox. Click on the *OK* button and test from a remote computer.

In a network, it is common to map a drive letter to a frequently used network share. To map a drive letter to a network share, right-click on the *Network Neighborhood* or *My Network Places* (Windows 2000) desktop icon. Select the *Map Network Drive* option. Select a drive letter in the *Drive* box by clicking on the down arrow. In the *Folder* or *Path* box (depending on the operating system), type the *UNC* for the network share or use the *Browse* button or *Shared Directories* window (depending on the operating system) to select the network share. The Reconnect at Logon checkbox allows you to connect to the mapped drive every time you logon.

When configuring TCP/IP, an IP address and subnet mask must be assigned to the network device. The IP address is what makes the network device unique and what allows it to be reached by other network devices. There are two ways to get an IP address—(1) statically define the IP address and mask or (2) use DHCP.

When an IP address is statically defined, that means that someone manually enters an IP address into the computer. This is done through the Network control panel. The appropriate mask must also be entered. The correct IP address and mask can be obtained from the company's network administrator. Entering an IP address that is a duplicate of another network device renders the new network device inoperable on the network. Most support people do not statically define IP addresses unless the device is an important network device such as a web server, database server, network server, router, or switch. Instead, technicians use DHCP.

DHCP (Dynamic Host Configuration Protocol) is a method of automatically assigning IP addresses to network devices. A DHCP server (software configured on a network server or router) contains a pool of IP addresses. When a network device has been configured for DHCP and it boots, the device sends out a request for an IP address. A DHCP server responds to this request and issues an IP address to the network device. DHCP makes IP addressing easier and keeps network devices from being assigned duplicate IP addresses.

Another important concept that relates to IP addressing is a default gateway (or gateway of last resort). A **default gateway** is an IP address assigned to a network device that tells the device where to send a packet that is destined for a remote network. The default gateway address is the IP address of the router that is directly connected to that immediate network.

A router's job is to find the best path to another network. A router has various network numbers stored in memory. Consider Network Figure #16.

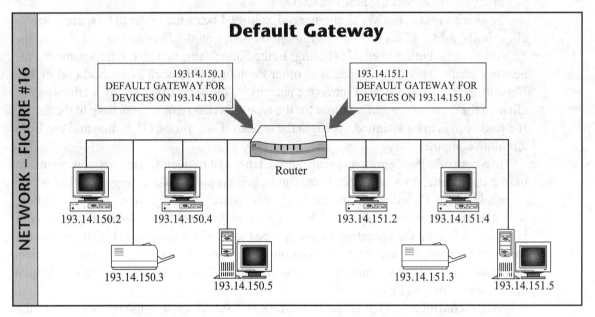

Default Gateway

193.14.150.1
DEFAULT GATEWAY FOR
DEVICES ON 193.14.150.0

193.14.151.1
DEFAULT GATEWAY FOR
DEVICES ON 193.14.151.0

Router

193.14.150.2   193.14.150.4

193.14.151.2   193.14.151.4

193.14.150.3

193.14.150.5

193.14.151.3

193.14.151.5

Network devices on the 193.14.150.0 network use the router IP address of 193.14.150.1 as a default gateway address. When a network device on the 193.14.150.0 network wants to send a packet to the 193.14.151.0 network, it sends the packet to the router's IP address that is on the same network (the gateway address). The router, in turn, looks up the destination address (193.14.151.x) in its routing table and sends it out the other interface (193.14.151.1) to the remote network device on the 193.14.151.0 network.

The default gateway address for all network devices on the 193.14.151.0 network is 193.14.151.1, the router's IP address on the same network. Any network device on 193.14.151.0 sending information to the 193.14.150.0 sends it to the default gateway address. For network devices on the 193.14.151.0 network, the gateway address is 193.14.151.1.

Network devices can receive their default gateway address from the DHCP server just like they can an IP address. The DHCP server must be configured for the appropriate default gateway address to give to network devices. An important note is that a DHCP server can give out IP addresses to network devices on remote networks as well as the network to which the DHCP server is directly connected. Default gateway addresses are important for network devices that need to communicate with network devices on other networks. The default gateway address is configured using the Network control panel under the TCP/IP section.

Other elements of TCP/IP information that may need to be configured are one or more DNS server IP addresses and one or more WINS server IP addresses. A **DNS (Domain Name System) server** is an application that runs on a network server that provides translation of Internet names into IP addresses. DNS is used on the Internet, so you do not have to remember the IP address of each site to which you connect. For example, DNS would be used to connect to Scott/Jones Publishing by translating the **URL** (**Universal Resource Locator**) www.scottjonespub.com into the IP address 167.160.239.173. A computer can receive the DNS server's IP address from DHCP if the DHCP server has been configured for this. A technician can also manually configure the system for one or more DNS server IP addresses through the Network control panel.

If a DNS server does not know a domain name (it does not have the name in its database), the DNS server can contact another DNS server to get the translation information. Common three letter codes used with DNS (three letters used at the end of a domain name) are com (commercial sites), edu (educational sites), gov (government sites), net (network related sites), and org (miscellaneous sites).

A **WINS** (**Windows Internet Naming Service**) **server** keeps track of IP addresses assigned to a specific computer name. When connecting to another computer, a user types a computer's name and not the computer's IP address. The WINS server translates the name to an IP address. The WINS server's IP address can be configured under the Network control panel. WINS is very important especially on computers that receive their IP address from DHCP. The IP address can change each time the computer boots because with DHCP, you can configure the DHCP server to issue an IP address for a specific amount of time. In addition, the DHCP server can send the WINS server's IP address to a network device just like the server sends the default gateway address and the DNS address. Another important fact about WINS is that newer DNS servers can now provide the computer name to IP address translation as well as the domain name to IP address translation.

NETWORK TROUBLESHOOTING

One way to troubleshoot a network is determine how many devices are affected. For example, if only one computer cannot communicate across a network, it will be handled differently than if several (or all) computers on a network cannot communicate. The easiest way to determine how many devices are having trouble is by using a simple test. Since most computers use TCP/IP, one tool that can be used for testing is the ping command. **Ping** sends a packet to an IP destination (that you determine) and a reply is sent back from the destination device (when everything is working fine). The ping command can be used to determine if the network path is available, if there are delays along the path, and whether the remote network device is reachable.

The ping utility can be used to test the NIC as well as the TCP/IP protocol running on the NIC with the command *ping 127.0.0.1*. The 127.0.0.1 IP address is what is known as a private IP address, which means it cannot be used by the outside world. The 127.0.0.1 is also known as a loopback address. A **loopback address** is not used to check connections to another computer, but is used to test a NIC card's own basic network setup.

If the ping is successful (a message that a reply was received from 127.0.0.1), then the TCP/IP protocol stack is working correctly on the NIC. If the ping responds with a no answer or 100% packet loss error, TCP/IP is not properly installed or functioning correctly on that one workstation.

The ping command can be used to check connectivity all around the network. Network Figure #17 shows a sample network that is used to explain how ping is used to check various network points.

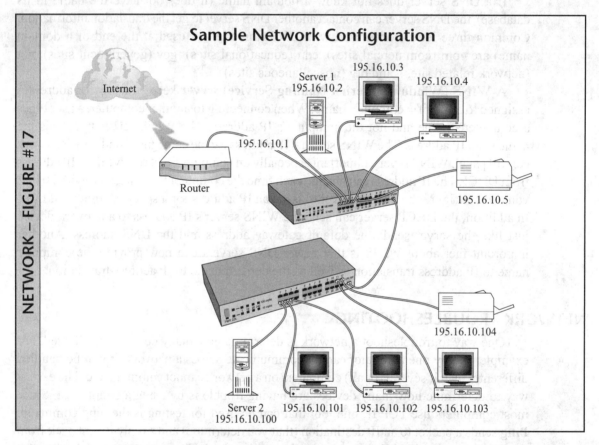

Sample Network Configuration

NETWORK – FIGURE #17

Internet

Router
195.16.10.1

Server 1
195.16.10.2

195.16.10.3

195.16.10.4

195.16.10.5

195.16.10.104

Server 2
195.16.10.100

195.16.10.101   195.16.10.102   195.16.10.103

The network consists of various network devices including two servers and two laser printers. The devices connect to one of two switches which are connected together using the uplink port. This port allows two similar devices to be connected together with a standard Ethernet cable or fiber cable. A router connects to the top switch and the router connects to the Internet.

The workstation that has the IP address 195.16.10.3 cannot access a file on Server2 (195.16.10.100). The first step in troubleshooting is to ping Server2. If this is successful (the destination reachable), the problem is in Server2 or the file located on the server. If the ping is unsuccessful, there is a problem elsewhere. Right now, the ping is unsuccessful, so ping another device that connects to the same switch. From workstation 195.16.10.3, ping Server1 (195.16.10.2) which connects to the same switch. This ping is successful and tells you the connection between the 195.16.10.3 workstation and the switch is good, the switch is working, the cable connecting to Server1 is fine, and Server1 is functioning. If the ping is unsuccessful, one of these things is faulty.

Now ping workstation 195.16.10.101 (a device other than the server on the remote switch), If the ping is successful, (1) the uplink cable is operational, (2) the second switch is operational, (3) the cable that connects workstation 195.16.10.101 to the switch is good, and (4) the 195.16.10.101 workstation has been successfully configured for TCP/IP. If the ping is unsuccessful, one of these four items is faulty. If the ping is successful, the problems could be (1) Server2's cable, (2) the switch port to which the server connects, (3) server NIC, (4) server configuration, or (5) the file on Server2.

To see the current IP configuration, use the WINIPCFG or IPCONFIG command from a DOS prompt. The **WINIPCFG** command is used with Windows 95 and Windows 98. The **IPCONFIG** command is used with Windows 98, NT Workstation, NT Server, 2000 Professional, and 2000 Server. To access the DOS prompt on Windows 95/98, click on the *Start* button. Point to the *Programs* option and click on the *MS-DOS Prompt* option, In NT Workstation or Server, click on the *Start* button, point to the *Programs* option, and click on the *Command Prompt* option. When using Windows 2000 Professional or Server, click on the *Start* button, point to *Programs*, point to the *Accessories* option, and click on the *Command Prompt* option. Network Figures #18 and #19 show you the switches and output of each command.

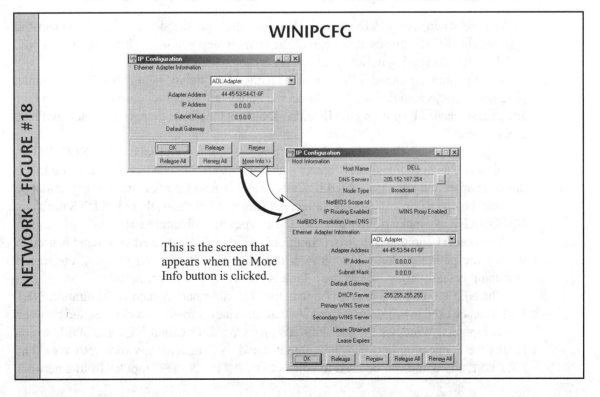

NETWORK – FIGURE #18

WINIPCFG

This is the screen that appears when the More Info button is clicked.

NETWORK – FIGURE #19

```
                        IPCONFIG

        C:\WINDOWS> ipconfig

        Windows 98 IP Configuration

        0 Ethernet adapter :

              IP Address . . . . . . . . . . : 0.0.0.0
              Subnet Mask. . . . . . . . . : 0.0.0.0
              Default Gateway. . . . . . . . :

        1 Ethernet adapter :

              IP Address . . . . . . . . . : 0.0.0.0
              Subnet Mask. . . . . . . . . : 0.0.0.0
              Default Gateway. . . . . . . . :

        2 Ethernet adapter :

              IP Address . . . . . . . . . : 192.168.10.10
              Subnet Mask. . . . . . . . . : 255.255.255.0
              Default Gateway. . . . . . . :

        C:\WINDOWS>ipconfig /?
        Command line options:
        /All - Display detailed information.
        /Batch [file] - Write to file or ./WINIPCFG.OUT
        /renew_all    - Renew   all adapters.
        /release_all  - Release all adapters.
        /renew  N    - Release adapter N.
        /release N    - Release adapter N.
```

Make sure when using WINIPCFG, that you click on the down arrow to select the appropriate NIC. Exercises at the end of the chapter step you through configuring a NIC and TCP/IP, and sharing network resources.

Use the ping command followed by the name of the device being tested, for example, ping *www.scottjonespub.com*. A DNS server translates the name to an IP address. If the site can be reached by pinging the IP address, but not the name, there is a problem with the DNS server.

A program that helps with DNS server troubleshooting is a tool called **NSLOOKUP**. NSLOOKUP is available on NT Server and 2000 Server. NSLOOKUP allows you to see domain names and their associated IP addresses. When an Internet site (server) cannot be contacted by its name, but can be contacted using its IP address, there is a DNS problem. NSLOOKUP can make troubleshooting these types of problems easier.

The **tracert** command is also a commonly used tool. The tracert command is used to display the path a packet takes through the network. The benefit of using the tracert command is that you can see where a fault is occurring in a larger network.

The NET command is also useful in network troubleshooting and configuration. NET DIAG can be used in Windows 98 and 2000 to run a hardware diagnostic program between two computers. Windows 98 and 2000 also have a utility called NET LOGOFF, which breaks the connection between the computer and its connected network resources. The NET USE command can be used to connect or disconnect the computer from a network resource and can be used to display information about network connections. For example, to view all the network connections currently in use, type *NET USE* and press *Enter*. In Windows 98 and 2000, the NET VER command displays the type and version of the network redirector. The NET VIEW command displays a list of computers in a workgroup or a specific computer's shared network resources. A good site for the NET command is www.computerhope.com/nethlp.htm.

CONFIGURING A NETWORKED PRINTER

There are three ways to network a printer.

- Connect a printer to a port on a computer that is connected to the network and share the printer.
- Setup a computer that is designated as a print server. Connect the print server to the network.
- A printer with a network connector installed is connected directly to the network.

Printers can also be password protected on the network. A networked printer is very common in today's home and business computing environment. Networking expensive printers such as laser printers and color printers is cost effective.

A printer that is connected to a workstation can be shared across the network by enabling File and Print Sharing. An exercise at the end of the chapter explains how to do this. Once File and Print Sharing is enabled, a printer is shared simply by clicking on the *Start* button, pointing to the *Settings* option, clicking on the *Printer* option, right-clicking on the printer to be shared, selecting *Properties*, and clicking on the *Sharing* option.

With Microsoft operating systems, networked printers are much easier to configure than they used to be. To connect and use a networked printer, use the Add Printer wizard. A prompt is available that asks whether the printer is local or networked. A local printer is one that is directly attached to the computer and a networked printer is one attached to another workstation, a print server, or directly connected to the network.

Even though print drivers normally automatically download, sometimes they cause printing problems. The best way to tackle this situation is to manually load the print driver for the networked printer.

DIAL-UP NETWORKING

DUN (Dial-up Networking) is a remote computer that dials into the Internet or a corporation using a modem. Another technology using dial-up networking is virtual private networking. **VPN (Virtual Private Networking)** is a remote computer connecting to a remote network by "tunneling" over an intermediate network such as the Internet or a LAN. Once connected, the remote user can make use of network devices as if they were directly connected to the network. Network Figure #20 illustrates these concepts.

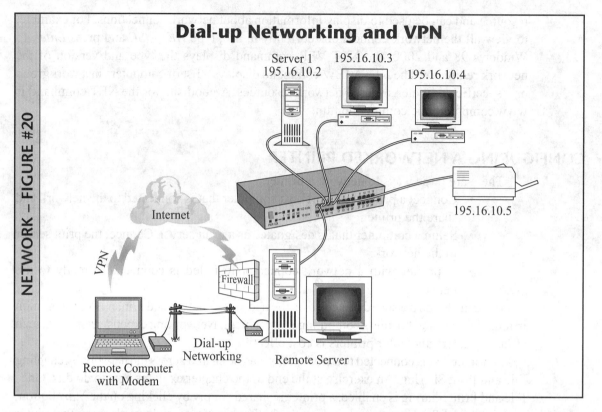

NETWORK – FIGURE #20

Dial-up Networking and VPN

The type of connection, protocol, and settings that you configure on the remote computer depends on the company to which you are connecting. The most commonly used protocol is TCP/IP, but Microsoft operating systems do support IPX/SPX and NetBEUI. A connection protocol used with dial-up networking is PPP. **PPP (Point-to-Point Protocol)** is a connection-oriented, layer 2 protocol that encapsulates data for transmission over phone lines. An older protocol that was used with dial-up networking and was the predecessor to PPP is SLIP (Serial Line Internet Protocol).

To make a dial-up networking connection, make sure a modem is properly installed. Then access the dial-up networking wizard by double-clicking on the *My Computer* desktop icon, double-clicking on the *Dial-up Networking* folder, and then double-clicking on the *Make New Connection* icon. If the Dial-up Networking folder is not there, you can install the required components using the Add/Remove Programs control panel.

In Windows 2000, click on the *Start* button, access the *Settings* option, and click on the *Network and Dial-up Connections* folder. The Make New Connection wizard is used to setup dial-up networking or configure a VPN connection.

Before creating a remote connection, you should always determine what parameters are to be entered *before* starting the configuration. Contact the network administrator for exact details on how to configure the remote connection. If the connection is to the Internet via an ISP, detailed instructions are available on the ISP's web site and/or with the materials that come with the Internet package from the ISP.

There are many types of network connections. Dial-up networking normally uses POTS (Plain Old Telephone System) or ISDN. Businesses use various types of network connections leased from the local phone company or a provider. Network Table #5 shows the types of network connections and speeds.

NETWORK – TABLE #5

Network Connections

Connection Type	Speed
POTS (Plain Old Telephone System)	2400bps to 115Kbps analog phone line
ISDN (Integrated Services Digital Network)	64Kbps to 1.544Mbps digital line
Frame Relay	56K to 1.544Mbps
56K point to point	56K guaranteed bandwidth between two points
T1	1.544Mbps guaranteed bandwidth between two points
T3	44Mbps guaranteed bandwidth between two points
DSL (Digital Subscriber Line)	256Kbps and higher; shares data line with voice line
ATM (Asynchronous Transfer Mode)	Up to 2Gbps

INTERNET SOFTWARE

Once a dial-up networking configuration or the LAN configuration tasks have been completed, you can connect to the Internet. Most people use a web browser when connecting to the Internet. A **browser** allows you to view web pages across the Internet. The two most common Internet browsers are Internet Explorer (also known as IE) and Netscape Navigator. Other web browsers include Opera Software's Opera and NeoPlanet, Inc.'s NeoPlanet. Internet Explorer comes with Microsoft operating systems. Netscape Navigator is available from Netscape Communications Corporation (http://home.netscape.com/) or free from some ISPs when you enroll with their service. If Internet Explorer is not loaded on the computer, add it using the Add/Remove Programs control panel or go to Microsoft's web site at www.microsoft.com to download the latest version.

Keeping the web browser current is important. Internet hackers frequently target Internet browsers and constant updates are provided that help with these attacks. Before upgrading, you should determine the web browser's current version. With any software application,

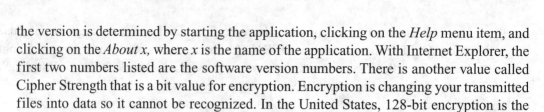
the version is determined by starting the application, clicking on the *Help* menu item, and clicking on the *About x,* where *x* is the name of the application. With Internet Explorer, the first two numbers listed are the software version numbers. There is another value called Cipher Strength that is a bit value for encryption. Encryption is changing your transmitted files into data so it cannot be recognized. In the United States, 128-bit encryption is the best.

Internet browsers frequently need plug-ins. A plug-in is an application designed to work with the browser. Common plug-ins are Macromedia Flash, Macromedia Shockwave, RealNetworks RealPlayer, Apple QuickTime, Adobe Acrobat Reader, and WinZip. Macromedia Flash allows web animations to be played. Macromedia Shockwave is for interactive multimedia graphics and audio applications. RealPlayer is for playing streaming audio and video, QuickTime is used for playing video clips. Acrobat Reader is for displaying PDF documents. WinZip is used for compressing and expanding ZIP files.

Another common tool for a web browser is an accelerator. An accelerator speeds up downloads and Internet browsing (surfing). Some accelerators are plug-ins for the web browser software and others are standalone applications. Various download and browsing accelerators are available on the Internet. One example is SpeedBit's Download Accelerator Plus; it's available at www.speedbit.com. Two other popular ones are Go!Zilla available from www.gozilla.com and NetSonic available from www.netsonic.com.

Another common Internet software application is an e-mail package. This software allows you to send messages across the Internet. Microsoft operating systems come with Windows Messaging (Inbox). Another popular freeware e-mail software program is Eudora Light. Many Internet providers also have their own e-mail package.

The e-mail service has to be configured. Many settings are configured through the Mail control panel. Two common settings are POP and SMTP server addresses. POP stands for Post Office Protocol and a POP3 server is a server used for retrieving e-mail. SMTP stands for Simple Mail Transport Protocol and a SMTP server is used for sending e-mail. These settings for the e-mail service are available from the network administrator or the ISP in their instructions for configuring dial-up networking.

A technician must be familiar with troubleshooting browser and e-mail applications. A good place to start is with the userid and password, POP3, and SMTP settings. In Internet Explorer, a technician needs to be familiar with the settings that can be configured under the Internet Options section of the Tools menu item. The Connections tab is a great place to start.

NETWORK TERMINOLOGY

In the networking field, there are tons of acronyms and terms with which you must be familiar. Below are a few terms that are the most common to help you get started in this area.

Backbone — The part of the network that connects multiple buildings, floors, networks, etc., together.

Bandwidth — The width of a communications channel that defines its capacity for data.

Baseband — A networking technology where the entire cable bandwidth is used to transmit a digital signal. Because LANs use baseband, there must be an access method used to determine when a network device is allowed to transmit (token passing or CSMA/CD).

Broadband — A networking technology where the cable bandwidth is divided into multiple channels. On these channels, simultaneous voice, video, and data can be sent.

E-mail — A shortened version of electronic mail. A method of communicating across the Internet by using communications software.

Fast Ethernet — An extension of the original Ethernet standard that permits data transmission of 100Mbps. Fast Ethernet uses CSMA/CD just like the original Ethernet standard. Different types of Fast Ethernet are 100BaseT4, 100BaseTX, and 100BaseFX.

FDDI (Fiber Distributed Data Interface) — A high-speed fiber network that uses the ring topology and the token passing access method.

Frame — A term used for the encapsulated data found at layer 2 of the OSI model.

FTP (File Transfer Protocol) — A protocol used when transferring files from one computer to another across a network.

HTML (Hypertext Markup Language) — The programming language used on the Internet for creating web pages.

HTTP (Hypertext Transfer Protocol) — A protocol used when communicating across the Internet.

Infrared — Many laptop computers have infrared ports on them that allow them to communicate with other devices (such as another computer or a printer) across a wireless network. The common term used with this is IrDA (Infrared Serial Data Link).

ISP (Internet Service Provider) — A vendor who provides access to the Internet.

Packet – A term used for the encapsulated data found at layer 3 of the OSI model.

SMTP (Simple Mail Transfer Protocol) — A protocol used for e-mail or transferring messages across a network from one device to another.

SNMP (Simple Network Management Protocol) — A protocol that supports network monitoring and management.

TCP (Transmission Control Protocol) — A layer 4 connection-oriented protocol that ensures reliable communication between two devices.

Telnet — An application that allows connection to a remote network device.

UDP (User Datagram Protocol) — A layer 4 connectionless protocol that applications use to communicate with a remote device.

Name _____

NETWORKING REVIEW QUESTIONS

1. A home user connects to the Internet. The ISP provides hard drive space for the user's web page. Is this a network? Why or why not?

2. What type of network is a large business most likely to have?

3. Which type of network is least secure and why?

4. What device is normally at the center of a star topology?

5. Which type of network topology takes the most cable and why?

6. Which type of topology does a Token Ring network use?

7. How are Token Ring networks cabled?

8. List three types of network media.

9. Match the following:
   A. CAT 3 UTP   _____ Most common type of cable
   B. CAT 5 UTP   _____ Used in 10Base2 networks
   C. Coax   _____ Voice-grade cable
   D. Fiber   _____ Backbone cable

10. What cabling standard is the most common for UTP cable?

11. What is the most common mistake technicians make when installing UTP?

12. What is the most expensive type of cable?
    [Coax / Fiber / UTP / STP]

13. What are the two types of fiber-optic cable and the difference between the two?

14. 10Base5 networks use what type of cabling ?

15. Ethernet networks use what type of access method?

16. Token Ring networks use what type of access method ?

17. What types of access methods are used when network devices "listen" to the cable before transmitting?

18. What does the *CD* mean in the term CSMA/CD and how does this affect Ethernet networks?

19. Explain token passing.

20. What type of access method is used when a workstation sends out a jam signal before transmitting data?

21. Explain the difference between half-duplex and full-duplex transmissions.

22. [T / F] Ethernet networks support half- and full-duplex transmissions.

23. List the speeds that Ethernet networks can operate.

24. What does the *10* mean in the term 10Base2?

25. What does the *2* mean in the term 10Base2?

26. Explain how full-duplex transmission helps with Ethernet collisions.

27. Which network device works at layer 1 and sends received data out all its ports?

28. List three guidelines provided by the OSI model.

29. Describe a benefit of using a layered model approach to networking.

30. Write down your own mnemonic phrase that describes the OSI model from bottom to top (layer 1 to layer 7).

31. What layer of the OSI model encapsulates data into frames?

32. What is an ISP?

33. The analogy of a post office return receipt is used to describe what OSI model layer?
    [Session / Network / Data link / Transport]

34. Sometimes, when logging into a network, you must provide a userid and password or authenticate yourself. What OSI layer handles authentication?
    [Session / Presentation / Application / Transport]

35. At what OSI model layer does a hub reside?

36. At what OSI model layer does a router reside?

37. Match the following:
    A. TCP/IP   _____ Used on Novell networks
    B. NetBEUI   _____ Used on the Internet
    C. IPX/SPX   _____ Used on peer-to-peer networks

38. What is the most common network protocol?

39. Which protocol is *not* routable?
    [TCP/IP | IPX/SPX | NetBEUI]

40. Which type of address is 48 bits in length?

41. Which type of address is *not* burned into a NIC ROM?

42. How many MAC address bits represent the NIC manufacturer?

43. Each number in an IP address represents how many bits?

44. Determine the class of IP address for each IP address shown below:

   _____ 156.122.10.59   _____ 201.56.199.45

   _____ 122.6.158.2   _____ 194.194.194.194

   _____ 172.10.148.253   _____ 58.22.12.10

45. Draw a line between the network number and the host number for each of the following IP addresses:

   141.2.195.177

   193.162.183.5

   100.50.70.80

46. Explain why no network device can have the number 255 as its host number.

47. List four network configuration tasks.

48. List one way to view network device names.

49. List two methods of assigning an IP address to a network device.

50. [T / F] Workstation IP addresses are normally statically defined.

51. Reference the following drawing:

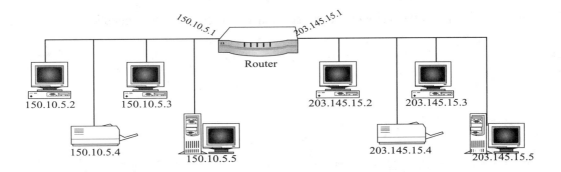

What IP address is the default gateway for host 150.10.5.2?

52. [T / F]   DHCP can provide IP addresses of the DNS and WINS servers to a host.

53. What command is used to determine if another network device is reachable?

54. What IP address is known as the NIC loopback address?

55. What are the two commands used on Microsoft networks to view the current IP configuration?

56. What NT and 2000 Server tool is used to troubleshoot DNS problems?

57. What tool is used to determine the path a packet takes through a network?

58. List three ways to network a printer.

59. What does DUN stand for and what does this term mean?

60. What is the term given for the part of the network that connects multiple buildings or floors.

61. What is the term given for layer 3 encapsulated data?

62. What is the name of the transport layer protocol that is connectionless?

Name _____

NETWORKING FILL-IN-THE-BLANK

1. A _____ is a group of devices connected together for the purpose of sharing resources.

2. The two basic types of networks are _____ and _____.

3. A home user has two computers connected together. Both computers have folders that are shared and accessible by the other computer. One computer has a printer attached that the other computer can also use. This is an example of a _____ network.

4. Of the two basic types of networks, the _____ network is more secure.

5. A _____ network should consist of no more than 10 computers.

6. The _____ network topology is the most common, used with Ethernet networks, and has a direct connection between a network device and a centrally located hub or switch.

7. With a _____ topology, all devices connect to a single cable.

8. Data from one cable interferes with another cable. This is known as _____.

9. _____ cable carries light pulses.

10. With a fiber-optic cable installation, _____ strands are normally used, one for each direction.

11. An _____ is the set of rules for how workstations transmit on a network.

12. Apple networks use _____ as an access method.

13. _____ transmission is when data is transmitted in both directions simultaneously.

14. A phone conversation is an example of _____ transmission.

15. The _____ in 100BaseT means that twisted-pair cable is used.

16. A _____ is better than a hub in Ethernet networks because this device is a layer 2 device and keeps a table of addresses for the network devices attached.

17. A UTP cable resides at the _____ layer of the OSI model.

18. The _____ layer provides best path selection through the network and the Internet.

19. The _____ layer provides reliable connectivity.

20. A mainframe terminal has data in one data format and a workstation has data in another format. Both devices are able to communicate across a network with the help of the _____ layer because this layer translates from one language to another.

21. A switch resides at the _____ layer of the OSI model.

22. Three network protocols are _____, _____, and _____.

23. The MAC address is considered a layer _____ address.

24. MAC addresses are represented in _____ format.

25. Each position in an IP address can be a number from _____ to _____.

26. 153.12.250.14 is a Class _____ IP address.

27. The term associated with sending a packet to all devices on a single network is _____.

28. The _____ is used to determine which part of an IP address is the network number.

29. The standard mask used with a Class C IP address is _____.

30. A technician configures a workstation to automatically receive an IP address. The IP address comes from a _____ server.

31. A _____ address is used when a network device wants to communicate with another network device located on a remote network.

32. _____ provides translation between a URL and an IP address.

33. _____ provides translation between a computer name and an IP address.

34. Newer _____ servers can provide computer name to IP address translation.

35. The command used to test the TCP/IP protocol on a NIC is _____.

36. The _____ command is used on Windows 2000 to view the IP configuration.

37. The _____ command is used to troubleshoot a remote network fault and to see the path a packet takes through several networks.

38. A _____ "tunnels" over an intermediate network to use remote network resources.

39. _____ is a layer 2 protocol used with dial-up networking.

40. The term given for encapsulated layer 2 data is _____.

41. A layer 4 connection-oriented protocol is _____.

Name _____

INSTALLING AND CONFIGURING A NIC USING WINDOWS 95/98

Objective: To be able to install and configure a NIC in a Windows 95/98 computer

Parts: Computer with Windows 95/98 installed, NIC card with driver

The method used to install a NIC in Windows 95/98 depends on whether the NIC is a plug and play device or a non-plug and play or legacy device.

Installing a Plug and Play NIC

Step 1.   With the computer turned off, remove the **computer cover**.

Step 2.   Using proper ESD precautions insert the **NIC** in a compatible bus slot and secure with a screw.

Step 3.   Turn the computer on and verify that Windows 95/98 loads.

Step 4.   Logon to Windows 95/98 using the userid and password provided by the instructor or lab assistant.

Step 5.   Windows 95/98 automatically detects and installs the NIC. If Windows 95/98 does not detect a driver for the NIC, you will be prompted for a driver location. If this is the case, insert the driver disk and enter the path to the driver. Proceed to the **Checking the Installation** section.

Installing a Non-Plug and Play or Legacy NIC

Step 1.   Using jumpers or a software configuration utility, configure the NIC so it will use system resources that do not conflict with any other device.

Step 2.   With the computer turned off, remove the **computer cover**.

Step 3.   Using proper ESD precautions, insert the **NIC** in a compatible bus slot and secure with a screw.

Step 4.   Turn the computer on and verify that Windows 95/98 loads.

Step 5.   Logon to Windows 95/98 using the userid and password provided by the instructor or lab assistant.

Step 6.   Click on the **Start** button, point to the **Settings** option, and double-click on the **Control Panel** option. The Control Panel window opens.

Step 7.   Double-click on the **Add/Remove Hardware** icon. The Add/Remove Hardware wizard opens. Select the **Next** button twice.

Step 8.   Windows searches for new plug and play devices. When Windows does not find any, you are given the option to allow Windows to search for non-plug and play devices or you can select the hardware from a list. Choose **No, I want to select the hardware from a list** and click on the **Next** button.

Step 9. Scroll down and select **Network Adapters** and then click on the **Next** button.

Step 10. Select the **NIC Manufacturer and Model** from the list. If the NIC is not listed, select **Have Disk**, enter a path to the driver files, and click **OK**.

Step 11. After selecting the proper NIC, click on the **Next** button.

Step 12. Select **Finish** to continue the installation. If prompted, enter the proper configuration information for the NIC and click **OK**.

Step 13. Restart the computer.

Checking the Installation

Step 1. From the **Start** menu, point to **Settings,** and then click on the **Control Panel** option.

Step 2. From the Control Panel window, double-click the **System** icon, and then select **Device Manager**.

Step 3. Expand **Network Adapters**, select the **network adapter** installed in the computer, and then click **Properties**.

Step 4. Click on the **General** tab.

Question 1: What is the device status of your NIC?

Step 5. Select the **Driver** tab.

Question 2: What is the driver version number of the NIC?

Step 6. Select the **Resources** tab.

Question 3: What resources are being used by the NIC?

Question 4: Are any devices conflicting with your NIC? If so, list them below.

Step 7. Click **OK** to close the Network Adapters Properties window.

_____ *Instructor's Initials*

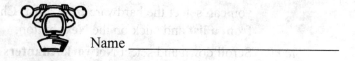

Name _____

INSTALLING AND CONFIGURING A NIC USING WINDOWS NT WORKSTATION

Objective: To be able to properly install and configure a NIC using Windows NT Workstation

Parts: Computer with Windows NT Workstation loaded
NIC card
Optional NIC driver disk

Installing a NIC using NT Workstation is different than using Windows 95, 98, or 2000 Professional because NT Workstation is not a plug and play operating system.

Step 1.   With the computer turned off, remove its cover.

Step 2.   Using proper ESD precautions, insert the **NIC** in a compatible bus slot and secure with a screw.

Step 3.   Turn the computer on and verify that Windows NT Workstation loads.

Step 4.   Logon to NT Workstation using the userid and password provided by the instructor or lab assistant.

Question 1:   What rights are required to be able to install a NIC in Windows NT Workstation?

Step 5.   Right-click on the **Network Neighborhood** desktop icon and select **Properties.** The Network window opens.

Question 2:   What alternate method can be used to open the Network window?

Step 6.   Select the **Adapters** tab, the Adapters Installation and Configuration window opens.

Step 7.   Click on the **Add** button and the Select Network Adapter window opens.

Step 8.   If the NIC that is installed in the computer is listed, click on it from the list. If the proper NIC is not listed, insert the NIC driver disk, click on the **Have Disk** button, and enter the path to the driver.

Step 9.   If prompted, insert the Windows NT Workstation CD-ROM, or enter the path to the installation files, and click on the **Continue** button.

Step 10.   If prompted, enter configuration information such as Ethernet ID, bus type, and slot number and click on the **OK** button.

Step 11.   Windows NT Workstation copies and installs the NIC driver files.

Step 12.   Click on the **Close** button to exit the Adapter Installation and Configuration window.

_____ *Instructor's Initials*

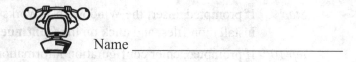

Name _____

INSTALLING AND CONFIGURING A NIC
USING WINDOWS 2000 PROFESSIONAL

Objective: To be able to properly install and configure a NIC using Windows 2000 Professional

Parts: Computer with Windows 2000 Professional installed
NIC card
Optional NIC driver disk

The method used to install a NIC in Windows 2000 Professional depends on whether the NIC is a plug and play device or a non-plug and play device (also known as a legacy device).

Question 1:   What type of NIC is to be installed into the computer, plug and play or non plug and play? Contact your instructor or lab assistant if unsure. Once the type of NIC is determined, follow the directions appropriate for the type of NIC: Installing a Plug and Play NIC or Installing a Non Plug and Play (legacy) NIC.

Installing a Plug and Play NIC

Step 1.   With the computer turned off, remove the **computer cover.**

Step 2.   Using proper ESD precautions, insert the **NIC** in a compatible bus slot and secure with a screw.

Step 3.   Turn on the computer and verify that Windows 2000 Professional loads.

Step 4.   Logon to Windows 2000 Professional using the userid and password provided by the instructor or lab assistant.

Step 5.   Windows 2000 Professional automatically loads the drivers and configures the NIC. If Windows 2000 Professional does not have a driver for the NIC, you will be prompted for a driver location. If this is the case, insert the driver disk into the floppy drive and enter the path to the driver (A:).

Step 6.   Go to the section labeled **Checking the Installation.**

Installing a Non-Plug and Play or Legacy NIC

Step 1.   With the computer turned off, remove the **computer cover.**

Step 2.   Using proper ESD precautions, insert the **NIC** in a compatible bus slot and secure with a screw.

Step 3.   Turn on the computer and verify that Windows 2000 Professional loads.

Step 4.   Logon to Windows 2000 Professional using the userid and password provided by the instructor or lab assistant.

Step 5.   Click on the **Start** button.

Step 6.   Point to the **Settings** option.

Step 7.   Click on the **Control Panel** option. The Control Panel window opens.

Step 8.   Double-click on the **Add/Remove Hardware** icon. The Add/Remove Hardware wizard opens.

Step 9.   Click on the **Next** button.

Step 10.   Choose the **Add/Troubleshoot a device** option, and select **Next**.

Step 11.   Windows searches for plug and play devices. When the search is over, select the **Add a new device** option from the **Choose a Hardware Device** window, and then click on the **Next** button.

Step 12.   Choose the **Yes, search for new hardware** option and click on the **Next** button.

Step 13.   Windows searches for non-plug and play hardware and displays devices found. Choose your NIC from the list and select **Next**.

Step 14.   In the **Found New Hardware** wizard window select the **Resources** button.

Step 15.   Ensure the resources assigned to the NIC are correct. Make any necessary changes and click on the **OK** button to return to the Found New Hardware Wizard window.

Step 16.   Select the **Finish** button twice to complete the installation.

Step 17.   Continue on to the **Checking the Installation** section.

Checking the Installation

Step 1.   Click on the **Start** button.

Step 2.   Point to the **Programs** option.

Step 3.   Point to the **Administrative Tools** option.

Step 4.   Click on the **Computer Management** option. The Computer Management window opens.

Step 5.   In the left window, select **Device Manager**.

Step 6.   In the right window, select the **+ (plus sign)** next to **Network adapters**.

Step 7.   Right-click on the NIC you just installed and select the **Properties** option from the menu. The Properties page opens.

Step 8.   Click on the **General** tab.

Question 1:   What is the device status of the NIC selected?

Step 9.   Select the **advanced** tab (if available).

Question 2:   Are any properties listed? If so, list one property and its value below.

Step 10.   Select the **Driver** tab.

Question 3:   What is the driver version number of your NIC's driver?

Step 11.   Select the **Resources** tab.

Question 4:   What resources are being used by your NIC?

Question 5:   Are any devices conflicting with your NIC? If so, list them below.

Step 12.   Click **OK** to close the Properties page.

_____ *Instructor's Initials*

Name _____

INSTALLING THE MICROSOFT CLIENT ON A WINDOWS 95/98 COMPUTER

Objective: Install the Microsoft Client on a Windows 95/98 computer

Parts: Windows 95/98 computer with NIC installed and configured

The Microsoft Client for Windows 95/98 enables a client computer to take advantage of the built-in Microsoft networking services in a Microsoft peer-to-peer network. It also allows a Windows 95/98 computer to access a Windows NT domain.

Step 1.   Turn on the computer and verify that Windows 95/98 loads.

Step 2.   If necessary, logon to Windows 95/98 using the userid and password provided by the instructor or lab assistant.

Step 3.   From the Start menu, point to the **Settings** option, click on the **Control Panel** option, and then double-click on the **Network** icon. The Network Properties window opens.

Question 1:   What is another way to access the Network Properties window?

Step 4.   Click on the **Add** button. The Select Network Component Type window opens.

Step 5.   From the Select Network Component Type window, choose **Client** and then select **Add**. The Select Network Client window opens.

Step 6.   Highlight the **Microsoft** option, select **Client for Microsoft Networks,** and then click on the **OK** button.

Question 2:   Which Microsoft network clients appear as available in the Select Network Client window?

Step 7.   From the Network Properties window, verify that **Client for Microsoft Networks** appears in the Installed Components window, and then click on the **OK** button.

Step 8.   If prompted, insert the Windows 95/98 CD-ROM in the drive or enter a path to the installation files.

Step 9.   When the Client for Microsoft Networks installation finishes, reboot the computer for the new client to take effect.

_____ *Instructor's Initials*

Name _____

INSTALLING NETWORKING ON A WINDOWS NT WORKSTATION COMPUTER

Objective: Install networking on a computer that uses NT Workstation

Parts: NT Workstation computer with NIC installed and configured

Note: The instructor or lab assistant must be prepared to answer questions such as these: Should the student select Workgroup or Domain network model? Is DHCP being used in the lab?

You must configure NT networking a bit differently than the other operating systems. The Network Setup wizard steps you through the installation process.

Step 1.   Turn on the computer and verify that NT Workstation loads.

Step 2.   Logon to Windows using the userid and password provided by the instructor or lab assistant.

Step 3.   From the **Start** menu, point to the **Settings** option, click on the **Control Panel** option, and then double-click on the **Network** icon. A dialog box appears stating that networking is not installed and asks if you want to install it. Click on the Yes button.

Question 1:   What is another way to access the Network Properties window?

Step 4.   The next prompt asks if you are wired to the network or if you are going to use a modem to connect. In a lab environment, you are probably wired to the network. Look at the back of the computer and see if a NIC is installed and a network cable connects to the NIC. If so, click on the **Wired to the network** checkbox and click on the **Next** button.

Step 5.   On the next screen, click on the **Start Search** button so the operating system looks for the installed NIC. This exercise assumes the NIC is installed, but if it hasn't been, you can click on the **Select from list** button and install the NIC drivers and then continue. The NIC appears in the window. Click on the **Next** button.

Step 6.   A list of protocols appears. Ensure the **TCP/IP Protocol** is selected and click on the **Next** button.

Step 7.   The Network Services screen appears. These default services are what allow your computer to participate in a peer-to-peer network or in a server-based network. Ensure that **RPC Configuration, NetBIOS Interface, Workstation,** and **Server** are all checked and click on the **Next** button.

Step 8.   A message appears that NT is going to install the components. Click on the **Next** button. Another screen appears that allows you to change your binding order. Simply click on the **Next** button. You may be asked to insert the NT installation CD or be prepared to type in the path to where the programs are stored. Contact your instructor or lab assistant if you are unsure what to do.

Step 9.   Since TCP/IP was selected, you will be asked if there is a DHCP server connected to the network. This is lab dependent. Most schools have a DHCP server, but contact the instructor or student assistant if unsure. If you select **No**, you must enter the IP address, mask, and default gateway information. If you select **Yes**, the computer will be assigned this information by the DHCP server.

Step 10.   Click on the **Next** button to start the NT networking services.

Step 11.   You are asked to give the computer a name and determine if the computer participates in a peer-to-peer network (Workgroup option) or a server-based network (Domain option); either way, you will have to enter either a workgroup name or a domain name. Contact the instructor or lab assistant for the correct names if you are unsure. Click on the **Next** button after all information has been entered.

Question 2:   What is the network name of your computer?

Question 3:   Is the computer participating in a peer-to-peer network or a server-based network?

Question 4:   Is DHCP being used?

Step 12.   Click on the **Finish** button to complete the installation.

Step 13.   The computer must reboot in order for the setting to take effect. Click on the **Yes** button to restart the computer.

Step 14.   After restarting and logging in, double-click on the **Network Neighborhood** desktop icon.

Question 5:   How many other computers do you see on the network?

_____ *Instructor's Initials*

Name _____

INSTALLING THE MICROSOFT CLIENT ON A
WINDOWS 2000 PROFESSIONAL COMPUTER

Objective: Correctly install Microsoft Client on a Windows 2000 Professional computer

Parts: Windows 2000 Professional Workstation with NIC installed and configured (Client for Microsoft Networks is not installed.)

Microsoft Client enables a computer to take advantage of the built-in Microsoft networking services in a Microsoft peer-to-peer network. It also allows a computer to access a Windows NT domain.

Step 1.   Turn on the computer and verify that Windows 2000 Professional loads.

Step 2.   Logon to Windows 2000 Professional using the userid and password provided by the instructor or lab assistant.

Step 3.   Right-click on the **My Network Places** desktop icon, and select the **Properties** option. The Network and Dial-up Connections window opens.

Step 4.   Right-click on the **Local Area Connection** icon and select the **Properties** option. The Local Area Connections window opens.

Question 1:   Which installed network components are being used by this connection?

Step 5.   Select the **Install** button. The Select Network Component Type window opens.

Step 6.   Choose the **Client** option, and then click on the **Add** button. The Select Network Client window opens.

Question 2:   What network clients are listed as available?

Step 7.   Select the **Client for Microsoft Networks** option, and click on the **OK** button.

Step 8.   If prompted, insert the Windows 2000 Professional installation CD-ROM or enter a path to the installation files.

Step 9.   When prompted, reboot the workstation for the new network settings to take effect.

_____ *Instructor's Initials*

Name _____

INSTALL AND CONFIGURE
THE TCP/IP PROTOCOL IN WINDOWS 95/98

Objective: Be able to install and configure the TCP/IP protocol on a Windows 95/98 computer

Parts: Windows 95/98 computer with a NIC installed and configured

The TCP/IP protocol is a routable protocol. It is the protocol that powers the Internet, so it is important that you understand how it is installed and configured.

Step 1.   Turn on the computer and verify that Windows 95/98 loads.

Step 2.   If necessary, logon to Windows 95/98 using the userid and password provided by the instructor or lab assistant.

Step 3.   Right-click on the **My Network Places** desktop icon, and then select **Properties.** The Network Properties window opens.

Question 1:   What other method can be used to access Network Properties?

Step 4.   Click on the **Add** button, and the Select Network Component Type window opens.

Question 2:   What network component types are listed as available?

Step 5.   Click on the **Protocol** item, and then click on the **Add** button. The Select Network Protocol window opens.

Step 6.   Click on the **Microsoft** option in the left window. In the right window, click on the **TCP/IP** option and then click on the **OK** button.

Step 7.   From Network Properties, scroll down and choose **TCP/IP** and then select **Properties**.

Step 8.   If you are using DHCP on your network, choose **Obtain an IP address automatically**. If you are *not* using DHCP on your network, choose **Specify an IP address**, and enter an **IP address** and **subnet mask**. Contact the instructor or a lab assistant if you are unsure which option to use.

Step 9. If needed, select **DNS configuration** and enter DNS information, select **Gateway** and enter gateway information, and select **WINS configuration** and enter WINS information. Again, contact the instructor or lab assistant if you are unsure which option to use.

_____*Instructor's Initials*

Question 3: Which of the following is responsible for host name to IP address resolution: DNS, gateway, or WINS?

Question 4: Which of the following is responsible for NetBIOS name to IP address resolution, DNS, gateway, or WINS?

Step 10. Click on the **OK** button and if prompted, insert the Windows 95/98 CD-ROM or enter the path to the installation files.

Step 11. Reboot the computer for the new settings to take effect.

_____*Instructor's Initials*

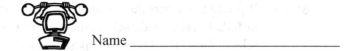 Name _____

INSTALL AND CONFIGURE THE TCP/IP PROTOCOL IN
WINDOWS NT WORKSTATION

Objective: Be able to install and configure the TCP/IP protocol on a Windows NT Workstation computer

Parts: Windows NT Workstation computer with a NIC installed and configured

The TCP/IP Protocol is a routable protocol. It is the protocol that powers the Internet, so it is important that you understand how it is installed and configured.

Step 1.   Turn on the computer and verify that NT Workstation loads.

Step 2.   Logon to NT Workstation using the userid and password provided by the instructor or lab assistant.

Step 3.   From the Start menu, point to the **Settings** option, click on the **Control Panel** option, and then double-click on the **Network** icon. The Network Installation and Configuration window opens.

Question 1:   What alternate method can be used to access the Network Installation and Configuration window?

Step 4.   Click on the **Protocols** tab. The Protocols window opens.

Question 2:   Which protocols are already installed on your computer?

Step 5.   Click on the **Add** button. The Select Network Protocol window opens.

Question 3:   List the protocols that are available for installation.

Step 6.   Select the **TCP/IP Protocol** option and click on the **OK** button.

Step 7.   If DHCP is used on the network, select **Yes** to use DHCP, otherwise select **No**. Contact the instructor or lab assistant if you are unsure which option to select.

Step 8. If prompted, insert the Windows NT Workstation CD-ROM or enter the path to the installation files and click on the **Continue** button. When TCP/IP finishes installing, select **Close**. The TCP/IP Properties page opens.

Step 9. If DHCP is used on the network, select **Obtain an IP address from a DHCP server.** If DHCP is not used, select **Specify an IP address** and enter the **IP address, subnet mask,** and **default gateway** information provided by the instructor or lab assistant.

Question 4: When DHCP is not used, which one of the following is optional: IP address, subnet mask, or default gateway?

Step 10. If directed by the instructor, click on the **DNS** tab and enter the provided DNS information. Click on the **WINS** tab and enter the provided WINS information.

Step 11. When all TCP/IP configuration information has been entered click on the **OK** button. NT Workstation goes through a bindings process, and you will be prompted to restart the computer. Restart the computer for the new settings to take effect.

_____*Instructor's Initials*

Name _____

INSTALL AND CONFIGURE THE TCP/IP PROTOCOL IN WINDOWS 2000 PROFESSIONAL

Objective: Be able to install and configure the TCP/IP protocol on a Windows 2000 computer

Parts: Windows 2000 Professional computer with a NIC installed and configured

The TCP/IP protocol is a routable protocol. It is the protocol that powers the Internet, so it is important that you understand how it is installed and configured.

Step 1.   Turn on the computer and verify that Windows 2000 Professional loads.

Step 2.   Logon to Windows 2000 Professional using the userid and password provided by the instructor or lab assistant.

Step 3.   Right-click on the **My Network Places** desktop icon, and then select **Properties**. The Network and Dial-up Connections window opens.

Step 4.   Right-click on the **Local Area Connection** icon, and then select **Properties**. The Local Area Connections page opens.

Step 5.   Choose **Install,** and the Select Network Component Type window opens.

Question 1:   What types of network components are available?

Step 6.   Choose **Protocol,** and then select **Add.** The Select Network Protocol window opens.

Question 2:   Which network protocols are available for installation?

Step 7.   Choose the **TCP/IP** protocol and then select **OK**.

Step 8.   If prompted, insert the Windows 2000 Professional CD-ROM into the drive, or enter the path to the installation files.

Step 9.   From the Local Area Connection window, highlight **TCP/IP,** and then select **Properties**. The TCP/IP Properties window opens.

Step 10. If you are using DHCP, select the **Obtain an IP Address Automatically** option. If you are *NOT* using **DHCP,** select the **Use the Following IP Address** option, and enter an **IP address,** a **subnet mask,** and the **default gateway** information provided by the instructor or lab assistant.

Question 3: Which of the following is optional: IP address, subnet mask, or default gateway?

Step 11. When you are finished entering TCP/IP configuration information, click on the **OK** button and close the Local Area Connections Properties window.

_____*Instructor's Initials*

Name _____

CREATING A STRAIGHT-THROUGH CAT 5 NETWORK CABLE

Objective: Create a functional CAT 5 UTP network cable

Parts: Category 5 UTP cable
RJ-45 connectors
CAT 5 stripper/crimper tool
UTP cable tester

Standard Ethernet networks are cabled with either CAT 5 UTP cable or RG-58 coaxial cable. In this exercise, you create a standard CAT 5 cable for use with either 10BaseT or 100BaseT networks connected through a central hub or switch.

Step 1.   Category 5 UTP cable consists of four twisted pairs of wires, color-coded for easy identification. The color-coded wires are colored as follows:

         Pair 1: White/Orange and Orange
         Pair 2: White/Blue and Blue
         Pair 3: White/Green and Green
         Pair 4: White/Brown and Brown

Step 2.   Using the **stripper/crimper tool**, strip approximately **1/2 inch** of the protective outer sheath to expose the four twisted pairs of wires. Most strippers have a strip gauge to ensure stripping the proper length. (See Network Exercise Figure 1.)

Note: In order to make it easier to sort the wire pairs, the sheathing can be stripped further than 1/2 inch, then the wires can be sorted properly and trimmed to the proper length.

Network Exercise Figure #1

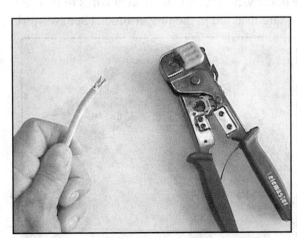

Step 3.   Untwist the exposed wire pairs. Be careful that you do not remove more twist than necessary. Sort the wires according to the following:

Wire 1: White/Orange   Wire 5: Blue

Wire 2: Orange   Wire 6: Green

Wire 3: White/Green   Wire 7: White/Brown

Wire 4: White/Blue   Wire 8: Brown

Ethernet cabling utilizes wires 1, 2, 3, and 6. Using the above wiring scheme means that the cable will use the White/Orange-Orange and White/Green-Green wire pairs. (See Network Exercise Figure 2.)

**Network
Exercise
Figure #2**

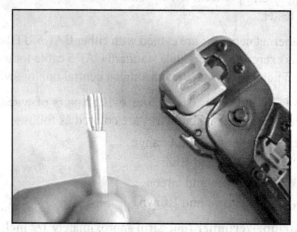

Question 1:   Will both ends of the cable need to follow the same wiring schematic?

Step 4.   Insert the sorted and trimmed **cable** into an **RJ-45 connector**. The RJ-45 connector's key should face downward. Verify that all eight wires fully insert into the RJ-45 connector and that they are inserted in the proper order. (See Network Exercise Figure 3.)

**Network
Exercise
Figure #3**

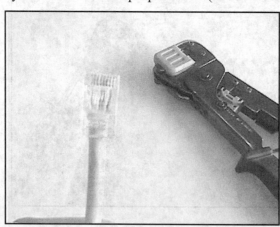

Step 5.   Insert the **cable-connector assembly** into the **stripper/crimper tool** and crimp the connector firmly. (See Network Exercise Figure 4.)

Network Exercise Figure #4

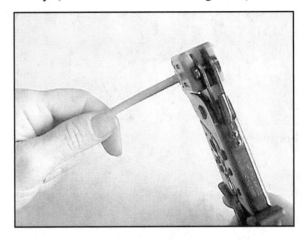

Step 6.   Remove the **cable/connector assembly** from the **stripper/crimper tool** and verify that the wires fully insert into the connector and that they are in the proper order. (See Network Exercise Figure 5.)

Network Exercise Figure #5

Step 7. Repeat steps 2 through 6 for the other end of the CAT 5 UTP cable. (See Network Exercise Figure 6.)

Network Exercise Figure #6

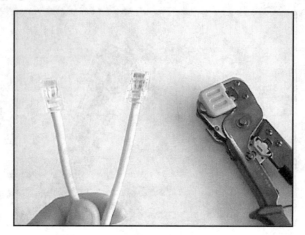

Question 2: Can the cable be used at this point?

Step 8. Before using the cable, it should be tested with a cable tester. This verifies that you have end-to-end continuity on individual wires and proper continuity between wire pairs. Insert the **RJ-45 connector** into the proper **cable tester receptacle** and verify that the cable is functional. (See Network Exercise Figure 7.)

Network Exercise Figure #7

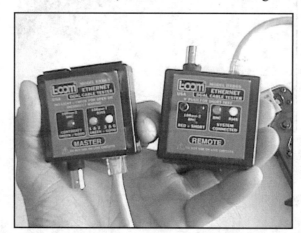

_____ *Instructor's Initials*

Name _____

CREATING A CAT 5 CROSSOVER NETWORK CABLE

Objective: Create a functional CAT 5 UTP crossover cable

Parts: Category 5 UTP cable
RJ-45 connectors
Stripper/crimper tool
UTP cable tester

In normal situations, straight-through CAT 5 UTP cabling is used to connect to a central hub or switch. In this exercise, you create a crossover CAT 5 cable for use when connecting two network devices—computers *without* using a central hub or switch.

Step 1.   Category 5 UTP cable consists of four twisted pairs of wires that are color-coded for easy identification. The color-coded wires are as follows:

Pair 1: White/Orange and Orange
Pair 2: White/Blue and Blue
Pair 3: White/Green and Green
Pair 4: White/Brown and Brown

Step 2.   Using the **CAT stripper/crimper tool**, strip approximately **1/2 inch** of the protective outer sheath to expose the four twisted pairs of wires. Most tools have a strip gauge to ensure stripping the proper length. (See Network Exercise Figure 8.)

Note: In order to make it easier to sort the wire pairs, the sheathing can be stripped further than 1/2 inch, the wires can then be sorted properly and trimmed to the proper length.

**Network
Exercise
Figure #8**

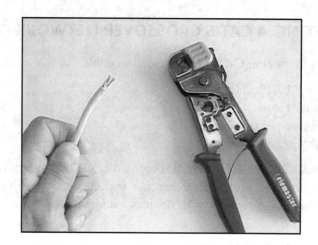

Step 3.   Untwist the exposed wire pairs. Be careful that you do not remove more twist than necessary. Sort the wires as follows:

Wire 1: White/Orange	Wire 5: Blue
Wire 2: Orange	Wire 6: Green
Wire 3: White/Green	Wire 7: White/Brown
Wire 4: White/Blue	Wire 8: Brown

Ethernet networks utilize wires 1, 2, 3, and 6. Using the above wiring scheme means the cable will use the White/Orange-Orange and White/Green-Green wire pairs. (See Network Exercise Figure 9.)

**Network
Exercise
Figure #9**

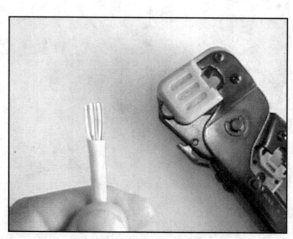

Question 1:   When making a crossover cable, will both ends of the cable need to follow the same wiring schematic?

Step 4.   Insert the sorted and trimmed **cable** into a **RJ-45 connector**. The RJ-45 connector's key should face downward. Verify that all eight wires fully insert into the RJ-45 connector, and that they are inserted in the proper order. (See Network Exercise Figure 10.)

Network Exercise Figure #10

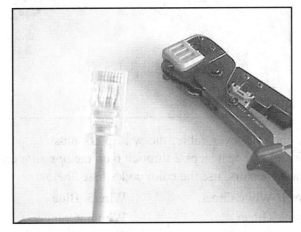

Step 5.   Insert the **cable-connector assembly** into the **CAT 5 stripper/crimper tool** and crimp the connector firmly. (See Network Exercise Figure 11.)

Network Exercise Figure #11

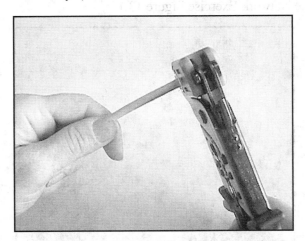

Step 6. Remove the **cable/connector assembly** from the **CAT 5 stripper/crimper** tool and verify that the wires are fully inserted into the connector and that they are in the proper order. (See Network Exercise Figure 12.)

Network Exercise Figure #12

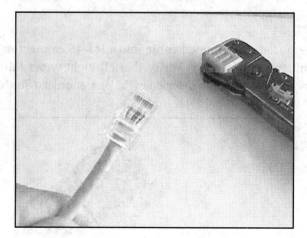

Step 7. To create the crossover cable, the wire pairs must be put in a different order. To accomplish this, repeat steps 2 through 6 on the *opposite* end of the cable, but when sorting the wire pairs, use the color codes listed below:

Wire 1: White/Green   Wire 5: Blue

Wire 2: Green   Wire 6: Orange

Wire 3: White/Orange   Wire 7: White/Brown

Wire 4: White/Blue   Wire 8: Brown

(See Network Exercise Figure 13.)

Network Exercise Figure #13

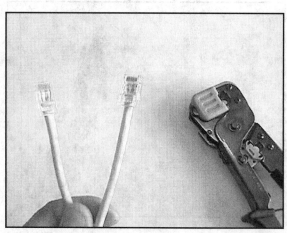

Question 2:   Can the crossover cable be used at this point?

Step 8.   Before using the crossover cable, it should be tested with a cable tester. This verifies that you have end-to-end continuity on individual wires and proper continuity between wire pairs. Insert the **RJ-45 connector** into the proper **cable tester receptacle** and verify that the cable is functional. *Note:* Your cable tester must have the capability to test crossover cables. (See Network Exercise Figure 14.)

**Network
Exercise
Figure #14**

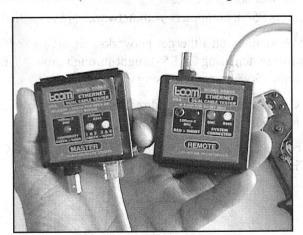

_____ *Instructor's Initials*

Name _____

CONNECTING TWO WINDOWS 95/98 COMPUTERS USING A CAT 5 CROSSOVER NETWORK CABLE

Objective: Connect two computers together using a CAT 5 crossover network cable

Parts: CAT 5 crossover network cable
Two Windows 95/98 computers with network cards installed and configured

In normal situations on Ethernet networks, all networked computers connect to a central hub or switch using CAT 5 straight-through cables. In this exercise, you connect two Windows 95/98 computers using a CAT 5 crossover cable.

Step 1.   Plug the **CAT 5 crossover cable** directly into the network cards' RJ-45 ports on the two Windows 95/98 computers.

Question 1:   Can you connect more than two computers together using a CAT 5 crossover network cable? Why or why not?

Step 2.   Turn the computers on and verify that Windows 95/98 loads.

Step 3.   Logon to both Windows 95/98 computers using the userid and password provided by the instructor or lab assistant.

Step 4.   Right-click on the **Network Neighborhood** desktop icon and select **Properties**. The Network Properties window opens.

Step 5.   From the General tab, select the **File and Print sharing** button. Verify that the **I want to be able to give others access to my files** checkbox is selected, and click **OK**.

Step 6.   Select the **Identification** tab. Verify that both computers are members of the same **workgroup**.

Step 7.   Click **OK** to close the Network Properties window.

Step 8.   If prompted, insert the Windows CD into the CD-ROM and restart the computers.

Step 9.   From the My Computer desktop icon, right-click on the **C:** drive, and select **Sharing**.

Step 10.   From the Sharing window, select **Shared as,** enter a share name, and click **OK**.

Question 2:   What is the significance of a share name?

Step 11.   After finishing sharing both C: drives, double-click on the **Network Neighborhood** desktop icon.

Step 12.   If the crossover cable connection is working, both computers should appear in the Network Neighborhood browser window. If it is not working, check the NIC configuration settings, the crossover cable, or redo the steps in this exercise. Show the instructor or lab assistant the two computer names in the Network Neighborhood browser window.

_____ *Instructor's Initials*

Name _____

SHARING A LOCAL PRINTER USING WINDOWS 95/98

Objective: Be able to share a local printer on a Windows 95/98 computer, so it will be available to other workstations

Parts: Windows 95 or 98 with a NIC installed and configured, and a printer physically attached and configured

A printer that is physically attached (local) to a networked workstation can accept and process print jobs from other workstations on the network. Before this can happen, the local printer must be shared on the network. Before a printer can be shared in Windows 95/98, Printer Sharing must be installed.

Installing Printer Sharing

Step 1.   Turn on the computer and verify that Windows 95/98 loads.

Step 2.   If necessary, logon to Windows 95/98 using the userid and password provided by the instructor or lab assistant.

Step 3.   Right-click on the **Network Neighborhood** desktop icon and select the **Properties** option. The Network Properties window opens.

Step 4.   Choose **File and Print Sharing,** select **I want to be able to allow others to print to my printers,** and then click on the **OK** button.

Question 1:   What will this setting allow you to share?

Step 5.   From the Network Properties window, click on the **OK** button.

Step 6.   If prompted, insert the Windows 95/98 installation CD-ROM or enter a path to the installation files.

Step 7.   Reboot the computer when prompted.

Sharing a Windows 95/98 Printer

Step 8.   From the **Start** menu, point to **Settings,** and then click on the **Printers** option. The Printers folder opens.

Step 9.   Right-click on a specific printer that is attached to the computer, and then select the **Sharing** option. The Printer Sharing window opens.

Step 10.   Select the **Shared As** radio button, and enter a share name of **TESTPRINT** in the Share Name field.

Step 11.   In the **Comment** field, enter a user-friendly description of this printer.

Step 12.   In the Password field, type the word **password.**

Qeestion 2:   What effect will setting a password have?

Step 13.   Click on the **Apply** button to save your sharing settings, re-enter the password **(password)** when prompted, and then click on the **OK** button.

Step 14.   Click on the **OK** button to exit the Printer Sharing window. Your printer is now shared and available on the network.

_____ *Instructor's Initials*

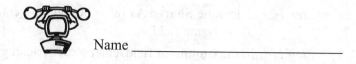

Name _____

SHARING A LOCAL PRINTER USING WINDOWS NT WORKSTATION

Objective: Be able to share a local printer on a Windows NT Workstation so it will be available to other workstations on the network

Parts: Windows NT Workstation with NIC installed and configured, and a printer physically attached and configured

A printer that is physically attached (local) to a networked workstation can accept and process print jobs from other workstations on the network. Before this can happen, the local printer must be shared on the network.

Step 1.   Turn on the computer and verify that NT Workstation loads.

Step 2.   Logon to NT Workstation using the userid and password provided by the instructor or lab assistant.

Step 3.   Click on the **Start** button, point to **Settings,** and then click on the **Printers** option. The Printers folder opens.

Question 1:   What other method can be used to access the Printers folder?

Step 4.   Right-click on the name of the printer that is attached to the workstation. Select the **Sharing** option. The Printer Sharing window opens.

Question 2:   What other method can be used to access the Printer Sharing window?

Step 5.   Click on the **Shared** radio button and enter a name in the Share Name field.

Question 3:   What name did you assign to the printer?

Step 6.   Click on the **OK** button to return to the Printers folder. The printer is now shared.

Question 4:   How can you verify that the printer has been shared?

_____ *Instructor's Initials*

Name _____

SHARING A LOCAL PRINTER USING WINDOWS 2000 PROFESSIONAL

Objective: Be able to share a local printer on a Windows 2000 Professional Workstation so it will be available to other workstations

Parts: Windows 2000 Professional Workstation with NIC installed and configured, and a printer physically attached and configured

A printer that is physically attached (local) to a networked workstation can accept and process print jobs from other workstations on the network. Before this can happen, the local printer must be shared on the network.

Step 1.   Turn on the computer and verify that Windows 2000 Professional loads.

Step 2.   Logon to Windows 2000 Professional using the userid and password provided by the instructor or lab assistant.

Step 3.   Click on the **Start** button, point to the **Settings** option, and then click on the **Printers** option. The Printers folder opens.

Step 4.   Right-click on the local printer attached to the workstation and select the **Properties** option. The printer's Properties window opens.

Step 5.   Click on the **Sharing** tab. From the Sharing window, you can share the printer, give it a share name, and install additional drivers for each type of Windows operating system connected to the network that will use the printer. You can also publish the printer in Active Directory if the workstation is part of a Windows 2000 domain.

Step 6.   Choose the **Shared as** option and type **TestShare** in the Share Name field.

Question 1:   If you have Windows NT 4.0 Workstations, Windows 98 client computers, and other Windows 2000 Professional Workstations on the network, and they all will be using this shared printer, which additional drivers should you install on this workstation?

Step 7.   Choose **Apply** and then click on the **OK** button. The printer's Properties window closes and then returns to the Printers folder. The local printer is now shared and is available to other workstations on the network.

Question 2:   How can you tell the printer has been shared?

_____ *Instructor's Initials*

Name _____

CONNECTING TO A NETWORKED PRINTER
IN WINDOWS 95/98

Objective: Understand how to connect to and use a networked printer on a Windows 95/98 computer

Parts: Windows 95/98 computer with NIC installed and configured and local printer installed and shared on the network

A printer that is physically attached (local) to a networked computer and shared on the network can accept and process print jobs from remote computers on the network. Before this can happen, the remote computers must connect to the shared printer and install the proper printer driver.

Step 1.   Turn the computers on and verify that Windows 95/98 loads.

Step 2.   Logon to Windows 95/98 using the userid and password provided by the instructor or lab assistant.

Step 3.   Click on the **Start** button, point to the **Settings** option, and then click on the **Printers** option. The Printers folder opens.

Step 4.   Double-click on the **Add Printer** icon and the Add Printer wizard runs.

Step 5.   Click on the **Next** button, select the **Network printer** option, and then click on the **Next** button.

Step 6.   Locate the shared printer, highlight the printer, and then click on the **OK** button. Contact the instructor or lab assistant if you cannot locate the shared printer. The printer's UNC name appears in the Network path or Queue Name field.

Question 1:   What does UNC stand for?

Step 7.   Choose **No** to the **Do you print from MS-DOS based programs** prompt, and click on the **Next** button.

Step 8.   Enter the name **LABTEST** for this printer in the Printer Name field.

Question 2:   Where does this printer name appear?

Step 9.   Select the **Yes** option in order to have Windows use this printer as the default printer, and then click on the **Next** button.

Step 10. Choose **Yes** to print a test page, and then select **Finish**.

Step 11. The printer driver downloads and installs on your local computer.

Step 12. To complete the connection, type **password** for the printer share password and then click on the **OK** button.

Question 3: Can the printer be used across the network without a network user supplying the password?

Step 13. If the printer connection and driver installation was successful, a printer test page prints.

_____ *Instructor's Initials*

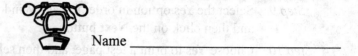

Name _____

CONNECTING TO A NETWORKED PRINTER IN
WINDOWS NT WORKSTATION

Objective: Be able to connect to and use a networked printer in Windows NT Workstation

Parts: Windows NT Workstation with NIC installed and configured and a local printer installed and shared on the network

A printer that is physically attached (local) to a networked computer and shared on the network can accept and process print jobs from remote computers on the network. Before this can happen, the remote computers must connect to the shared printer and install the proper printer driver.

Step 1.   Turn the computers on and verify that Windows NT Workstation loads.

Step 2.   Logon to Windows NT Workstation using the userid and password provided by the instructor or lab assistant.

Step 3.   Click on the **Start** button, point to the **Settings** option, and then click on the **Printers** option. The Printers folder opens.

Step 4.   Double-click on the **Add Printer** icon and the Add Printer wizard runs.

Step 5.   Choose **Network Printer Server** and then click on the **Next** button. The Connect to Printer window opens.

Step 6.   From the Connect to Printer window, browse through the available computers and shared printers until you locate the appropriate shared printer. After several minutes of browsing, contact the instructor or lab assistant if you cannot locate the shared printer.

Step 7.   Click on the **appropriate shared printer.** The Printer's UNC name appears in the Printer field. Click on the **Next** button.

Question 1:   The UNC name is made up of two parts. What do these two parts represent?

Step 8. Choose **Yes** for Windows applications to use this printer as the default printer, and then click on the **OK** button.

Step 9. The printer driver downloads and installs. Click on the **Finish** button to exit the Add Printer wizard. You have now connected to and installed the driver for a networked printer.

Question 2: How can you tell the printer has been connected to a shared printer?

_____ *Instructor's Initials*

Name _____

CONNECTING TO A NETWORKED PRINTER IN WINDOWS 2000 PROFESSIONAL

Objective: Connect to and use a networked printer in Windows 2000 Professional

Parts: Windows 2000 Professional with NIC installed and configured, and a local printer installed and shared on the network

A printer that is physically attached (local) to a networked workstation and shared on the network can accept and process print jobs from remote workstations on the network. Before this can happen, a remote workstation must connect to the shared printer and install the proper printer driver.

Step 1.   Turn the computer on and verify that Windows 2000 Professional loads.

Step 2.   Logon to Windows 2000 Professional using the userid and password provided by the instructor or lab assistant.

Step 3.   From the **Start** menu, point to **Settings**, and then click on the **Printers** option. The Printers folder opens.

Step 4.   Double-click on the **Add Printer** icon and the Add Printer wizard opens.

Step 5.   Click on the **Next** option, and the Local or Network Printer window opens.

Step 6.   Choose **Network Printer** and then select **Next.** The Locate Your Printer window opens.

Step 7.   If the workstation is part of an Active Directory domain, you could choose the **Find a printer in the directory** option or select the **Connect to a printer on the Internet or on your intranet** option and enter the URL for the printer. Contact the instructor or lab assistant if you are unsure about which option to choose.

Question 1:   What does the acronym URL stand for?

Step 8. Choose the **Type the printer name or click Next to browse for a printer** option and then click on the **Next** button. The Browse for Printer window opens.

Step 9. From the Browse for Printer window, browse through the available computers and shared printers until you find the appropriate shared printer. Contact the instructor or lab assistant if you are unsure about which printer to choose.

Step 10. Highlight the **shared printer.** The printer's UNC name displays in the Printer Name field. Click on the **Next** button.

Question 2: The UNC name is made up of two parts. What do these two parts represent?

Step 11. From the Default Printer window, choose **Yes** for Windows to use this printer as your default printer, and then select **Next**.

Step 12. From the Completing the Add Printer Wizard window, review the settings and click **Finish**.

Step 13. The printer driver automatically downloads from the host workstation and you return to the Printers folder after the driver downloads. You have now connected to and installed the driver for a networked printer.

Question 3: How can you tell the printer has been connected to a shared printer?

_____ *Instructor's Initials*

 Name _____

CREATING A DIAL-UP CONNECTION USING WINDOWS 95

Objective: Understand how to create a dial-up connection using the Windows 95 operating system

Parts: Windows 95 computer with a modem installed and Dial-up Networking installed and configured
Phone number of a dial-up server

The Windows Dial-up Networking (DUN) utility allows you to create and configure dial-up connections to dial-up access servers. In this exercise, you create a dial-up connection using Windows 95.

Step 1.   Turn the computer on and verify that Windows 95 loads.

Step 2.   Logon to Windows 95 using the userid and password provided by the instructor or lab assistant.

Step 3.   Double-click the **My Computer** desktop icon and then double-click the **Dial-up Networking** folder. The Dial-up Networking folder opens.

Question 1:   Can you create a new connection if a modem has not been installed?

Step 4.   Double-click the **Make New Connection** icon. The Make New Connection window opens.

Step 5.   Type **Test** in the Connection Name field and from the Select a device drop-down menu, select the **modem** to use for this connection. Click on the **Next** button.

Step 6.   Enter the **area code** and **phone number** of the Remote Dial-up Server you are dialing, select the **Country or Region code** from the drop-down menu, and click on the **Next** button. Contact the instructor or lab assistant for this information if you do not have it.

Step 7.   Click on the **Finish** button to create the **Test** connection.

Step 8.   Close the **Make New Connection** window. The Test Connection icon appears in the Dial-up Networking folder.

Question 2:   Can you modify the dialing properties of the Test connection after it has been created?

To use the Test connection, follow these steps:

Step 9.   Double-click on the **My Computer** desktop icon and then double-click the **Dial-up Networking** folder. The Dial-up Networking folder opens.

Step 10.   Double-click the **Test Connection** icon. The Connect to window opens.

Step 11.   Enter a **username** and **password** for the connection, verify the proper **phone number** is listed, and click on the **Connect** button. The Dial-up Networking utility will complete the connection to the remote dial-up server.

_____ *Instructor's Initials*

Name _____

CREATING A DIAL-UP CONNECTION USING WINDOWS 98

Objective: Understand how to create a dial-up connection using Windows 98

Parts: Windows 98 computer with a modem and Dial-up Networking installed and configured
Phone number of a dial-up server

The Windows Dial-up Networking (DUN) utility allows you to create and configure dial-up connections to dial-up access servers. In this exercise, you create a dial-up connection using Windows 98.

Step 1.   Turn the computer on and verify that Windows 98 loads.

Step 2.   Logon to Windows 98 using the userid and password provided by the instructor or lab assistant.

Step 3.   Double-click on the **My Computer** desktop icon and then double-click the **Dial-up Networking** folder. The Dial-up Networking folder opens.

Question 1:   Can you create a new connection if a modem has not been installed?

Step 4.   Double-click on the **Make New Connection** icon. The **Make New Connection** window opens.

Step 5.   Type **Test** in the Connection Name field and from the **Select a device** drop-down menu select the modem to use for this connection. Click on the **Next** button.

Step 6.   Enter the **area code** and **phone number** of the remote dial-up server to be dialed, select the **Country or Region code** from the drop-down menu, and click on the **Next** button. Contact the instructor or lab assistant for this number.

Step 7.   Click on the **Finish** button to create the Test connection.

Step 8.   Close the **Make New Connection** window. The Test Connection icon appears in the Dial-up Networking folder.

Question 2:   Can you modify the dialing properties of the Test connection after it has been created?

To use the Test connection, follow these steps:

Step 9.   Double-click on the **My Computer** desktop icon and then double-click the **Dial-up Networking** folder. The Dial-up Networking folder opens.

Step 10.   Double-click the **Test Connection** icon. The Connect to window opens.

Step 11.   Enter a **username** and **password** for the connection, verify the proper **phone number** is listed, and click on the **Connect** button. The Dial-up Networking utility will complete the connection to the remote dial-up server.

_____ *Instructor's Initials*

Name _____

CREATING A DIAL-UP CONNECTION USING WINDOWS NT WORKSTATION

Objective: Use the Dial-up Networking utility to create a dial-up connection in Windows NT Workstation

Parts: Computer with Windows NT Workstation and a modem and Dial-up Networking installed

Windows NT Workstation comes with Dial-up Networking to enable you to create a dial-up connection to a remote dial-up access server.

Step 1.   Turn the computer on and verify that Windows NT Workstation loads.

Step 2.   Logon to NT Workstation using the userid and password provided by the instructor or lab assistant.

Step 3.   Double-click on the **My Computer** desktop icon and then double-click the **Dial-up Networking** icon. The Dial-up Networking window opens.

Step 4.   To create a new dial-up connection, select **New**. The New Phonebook Entry wizard starts.

Step 5.   Type **Test** in the **Name the phonebook entry** field and click on the **Next** button.

Step 6.   From the Server window, select the type of dial-up connection you are configuring.

Question 1:   Which type of connection would you choose for browsing the web?

Step 7.   Choose **I am calling the Internet** and click **Next**.

Step 8.   Enter the **phone number** of the **Internet Service Provider (ISP)** you are calling and click **Next**.

Step 9.   Click **Finish** to complete the creation of the Test connection.

Question 2:   Where will the new connection appear?

Step 10. To use the Test connection, double-click the **My Computer** desktop icon and then double-click the **Dial-up Networking** icon.

Step 11. From the Phonebook Entry drop-down menu, select the **Test** connection.

Step 12. Select **Dial**, enter a **username, password**, and **domain** (if required), and click **OK**. Dial-up Networking dials the Internet Service Provider and completes the connection.

_____ *Instructor's Initials*

 Name _____

CREATING A DIAL-UP CONNECTION USING
WINDOWS 2000 PROFESSIONAL

Objective: Use the Dial-up Networking utility to create a dial-up connection in Windows 2000 Professional

Parts: Computer with Windows 2000 Professional and a modem installed
Phone number of a dial-up server

Windows 2000 Professional comes with Dial-up Networking to enable you to create a dial-up connection to a remote dial-up access server.

Step 1.   Turn the computer on and verify that Windows 2000 Professional loads.

Step 2.   Logon to Windows 2000 Professional using the userid and password provided by the instructor or lab assistant.

Step 3.   From the **Start** menu, choose **Settings,** and then select **Network and Dial-up Connections.**

Question 1:   What other method can be used to access Network and Dial-up Connections?

Step 4.   Double-click on the **Make New Connection** icon. The Network Connection wizard starts.

Step 5.   Click on the **Next** button.

Step 6.   From the Network Connection Type window, you can select the **type of connection** you are making.

Question 2:   Which connection type would you select to allow your computer to act as a Remote Dial-up Access Server?

Step 7.   Select **Dial-up to Private Network** and click on the **Next** button.

Step 8.   Enter the **Phone number** of the Remote Dial-up Access Server. Contact the instructor or lab assistant for the number. Click on the **Next** button.

Step 9.   Select **Create this connection for all users** and click on the **Next** button.

Step 10. Enter **Test** in the **Connection Name** field and click on the **Finish** button.

Step 11. New Dial-up connection appears in the Network and Dial-up Connection window.

Step 12. Double-click the **Test** connection icon, enter a **Username** and **Password** and click **Dial**. Dial-up Networking places the call and completes the connection to the remote dial-up access server.

_____ ***Instructor's Initials***

Name _____

INTERNET DISCOVERY

Objective: To access the Internet to obtain specific information regarding a computer or its associated parts

Parts: Access to the Internet

Question 1:   On an HP BRIO computer and after installing a 10/100 BT PCI Ethernet adapter, NT Workstation displays the error message, "At least one service failed to start." What is the problem, solution, and at what Internet address did you find the solution?

Question 2:   What does the term *Wake* on LAN mean and at what URL did you find the answer?

Question 3:   On a clone computer running Windows 95 and with a 3Com 3C359B adapter installed, the "Divide by zero error R6003" error appears. The computer is upgraded to Windows 98 and the problem does not change. What is the solution? List the URL where the answer was found.

Question 4:   How can you tell if an infrared device is within range on a Windows 2000 Professional computer? Write the answer and the URL in the space below.

Question 5:   Find an Internet site that explains the differences between CAT 5 and CAT 5E UTP cable. Write one difference and the URL in the space below.

Appendix A:

Subnetting

OBJECTIVES

After completing this chapter you will

- Understand the difference between major classes of IP addresses.
- When given an IP address, be able to identify its IP class.
- Determine the appropriate mask to use with each IP class.
- Understand and be able to subnet IP addresses.

KEY TERMS

broadcast
ISP
subnet
useable subnets
useable host numbers

SUBNETTING OVERVIEW

Any company that needs IP addresses can lease them from an **ISP** (Internet Service Provider. ISP's are organizations that provide individuals and businesses access to the Internet. If your company decides to connect to the Internet, a network administrator would contact an ISP and make arrangements for a connection to the Internet. Your connection to the Internet would be through the ISP's own network. You would have to provide the ISP with the number of IP address the company needs. ISP's have a limited number of IP addresses available to give out to their customers. The ISP will ask how many computers your company presently has and how many computers are planned for the near future.

Public IP addresses are in short supply due to the overwhelming popularity and success of the Internet. ISP's are reluctant to lease more IP addresses than a customer needs. The ISP may have 100 Class C IP addresses available to lease, but that does not mean the ISP will lease an entire Class C just because it was requested.

What if your company doesn't have enough computers to warrant a full Class C? For example, the Smiley Company has 30 computers and needs Internet access. The company predicts a growth of 20 additional computers over the next two years. If the Smiley Company contacts an ISP and asks for a full Class C block of addresses, the request would probably be denied. Remember that a full Class C contains 256 host addresses and the Smiley Company needs only 50 addresses. The ISP would probably lease a portion of the Class C to Smiley.

As another example, the WebBook Company has over 450 computers on its network with expected growth of 50 new computers this year. The ISP has 100 Class C's available for its customers and will have to dedicate at least two Class C's for the WebBook Company. The WebBook Company is not centralized in one building; it has several offices throughout the city. Each office has 30-60 computers that need Internet access. The ISP gives the company two full Class C's to organize as the network administrator sees fit. The network administrator can subdivide the Class C addresses to enable all external sites to have access to the Internet. The ISP does not care if the Class C is broken into smaller segments to fit a company's needs. When an IP addresses range is subdivided like this, it is called *subnetting*. Although the above examples are very simplified, it gives you a basic understanding of the process involved in acquiring and using IP addresses.

A **subnet** is a method used that divides the IP address into three parts rather than two. A normal IP address consists of two parts—a network number and a host number. Remember from the Network chapter that the number of bits used for the two parts depends on the class of IP address. Refer back to Network Figure #14 to refresh your memory. When subnetting is used, the IP address has three parts—a network number, a subnetwork number, and a host number.

Subnetting involves borrowing bits from the host portion of the IP address and creating the third part of the IP address—the subnetwork number, which is commonly called the subnet. Take a Class C IP address of 192.168.10.4. Because it is a Class C address, the first three octets are the network number—192.168.10. The last octet is the host or network

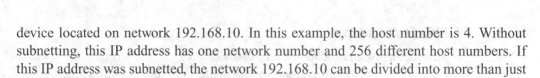

device located on network 192.168.10. In this example, the host number is 4. Without subnetting, this IP address has one network number and 256 different host numbers. If this IP address was subnetted, the network 192.168.10 can be divided into more than just one network. It can have a varying number of subnetworks.

Subnetting has three primary functions: (1) efficient use of one or more IP addresses, (2) reduces the money spent to lease IP addresses, and (3) divides the network into easier to manage portions. The effects of these three functions will be seen in the sections on how to subnet and why to subnet.

HOW TO SUBNET

When subnetting, bits are borrowed from the host portion of the IP address. Borrowing bits from the host creates a new number called a subnet.

 When subnetting, always borrow bits from the left-most host bits. Subnetting reduces the number of hosts, but allows more networks using a single IP address.

Take the example of a standard Class C IP address, 207.193.204.0. The numbers 207.193.204 is the network number and the last octet is used for host numbers. Subnet Figure #1 shows the bit positions for the last octet (Octet 4) for a standard Class C IP address.

Subnet Figure #1

bit positions

Class C Network No.			Hosts							
Octet1	Octet2	Octet3	Octet4							
			128	64	32	16	8	4	2	1
207.	193.	204.								

In order to subnet, bits are borrowed from the host bits to create a subnet field. The borrowed bits make up the subnet field. Subnet Figure #2 shows two bits borrowed from the *hosts* field for subnetting.

Subnet Figure #2

Class C Network No.			Subnet		Hosts					
Octet1	Octet2	Octet3	Octet4							
			128	64	32	16	8	4	2	1
207.	193.	204.								

Remember that bits are always borrowed from the left-most bits in the octet. Since two bits are being borrowed, bit positions 128 and 64 now represent subnet numbers. In Subnet Figure #2, you can see that the IP address still contains a network number and host numbers. The new addition to the IP address is called the subnet and is formed by taking left-most bits away from the host field. The standard Class C has eight bits that represent hosts, but now only six host bits remain because two bits were borrowed to create subnets.

SUBNETWORK NUMBERS

The subnet portion of an IP address can have varying combinations of 1s and 0s. For example, if two bits are borrowed for subnetting, the combinations of 1s and 0s are four different numbers—00, 01, 10, and 11. Subnet Figure #3 shows this concept.

Subnet Figure #3

Class C Network No.			Subnet		Hosts					
Octet1	Octet2	Octet3	Octet4							
			128	64	32	16	8	4	2	1
207.	193.	204.	0	0						
207.	193.	204.	0	1						
207.	193.	204.	1	0						
207.	193.	204.	1	1						

A mathematical formula can be used to determine how many subnets are formed when borrowing bits.

The number of subnets can be found by taking 2^x where x is the number of bits borrowed. For example, if two bits are borrowed $2^2 = 4$ or four subnetworks. If three bits are borrowed $2^3 = 8$ or eight subnetworks.

Look back at Subnet Figure #3. The *00* combination in the subnet field represents Subnetwork 0. The *01* combination in the subnetwork column designates it as Subnetwork 64. The 64 is obtained by a *1* being set in the *64* bit position. What subnetwork number is designated by a bit combination of *10* in the subnetwork column? The answer is 128 because there is a *1* set in the *128* bit position. Subnet Figure #4 shows how the various combinations of 1s and 0s create different subnetwork numbers.

Subnet Figure #4

Class C Network No.			Subnet		Hosts							Subnet No.
Octet1	Octet2	Octet3	Octet4									
			128	64	32	16	8	4	2	1		
207.	193.	204.	0	0								0
207.	193.	204.	0	1								64
207.	193.	204.	1	0								128
207.	193.	204.	1	1								192

Now that subnetwork numbers are understood, let's see how this applies to networks. Subnet Figure #5 shows two networks connected by a router. The networks are subnetted.

Subnet Figure #5

192.168.10.64 —— Router —— 192.168.10.128

In Subnet Figure #5, one network is 192.168.10.64 and the other network is 192.168.10.128. Even though a company purchased one Class C IP address, two networks can be created because of subnetting.

NUMBER OF HOSTS

An IP addressing rule is that every device on the network must have a unique IP address. How does this rule affect subnetting? Each subnet can have varying number of hosts. The number of hosts on each subnet depends on how many host bits have been borrowed to subnet. The more bits borrowed for subnetting, the fewer host bits remain for network devices. Subnet Figure #6 shows how this works in a Class C IP address with two bits borrowed for subnets.

Subnet Figure #6

Class C Network No.			Subnet		Hosts						Subnet No.
Octet1	Octet2	Octet3					Octet4				
			128	64	32	16	8	4	2	1	
207.	193.	204.	0	0	0	0	0	0	0	0	0
207.	193.	204.	0	0	0	0	0	0	0	1	
207.	193.	204.	0	0	0	0	0	0	1	0	
207.	193.	204.	0	0	0	0	0	0	1	1	
207.	193.	204.	0	0	0	0	0	1	0	0	
207.	193.	204.	0	0							
207.	193.	204.	0	0							
207.	193.	204.	0	0	1	1	1	1	1	1	
207.	193.	204.	0	1	0	0	0	0	0	0	64
207.	193.	204.	0	1	0	0	0	0	0	1	
207.	193.	204.	0	1	0	0	0	0	1	0	
207.	193.	204.	0	1							
207.	193.	204.	0	1							
207.	193.	204.	0	1	1	1	1	1	1	1	
207.	193.	204.	1	0	0	0	0	0	0	0	128
207.	193.	204.	1	0	0	0	0	0	0	1	
207.	193.	204.	1	0	0	0	0	0	1	0	
207.	193.	204.	1	0							
207.	193.	204.	1	0							
207.	193.	204.	1	0	1	1	1	1	1	1	
207.	193.	204.	1	1	0	0	0	0	0	0	192
207.	193.	204.	1	1	0	0	0	0	0	1	
207.	193.	204.	1	1	0	0	0	0	1	0	
207.	193.	204.	1	1							
207.	193.	204.	1	1							
207.	193.	204.	1	1	1	1	1	1	1	1	

The easiest way to determine the total number of hosts is to count the number of bits that are left for hosts. and raise the number 2 to that power. For example, in Subnet Figure #6, there are six hosts bits remaining. Take the number 2 and raise it to the number of host bits—$2^6 = 64$. This means that there are 64 different combinations of 1s and 0s in the host field for each subnetwork. One of the most important rules about subnetting concerns the first and last subnet and the first and last host addresses.

> When subnetting, the first and last subnetwork numbers and the first and last host numbers within each subnet cannot be used.

As previously discussed in the Network chapter, a network has an IP address that cannot be used by any network device. An example of a Class C network address is 192.107.10.0. A Class B network address is 152.124.0.0 and a Class A example is 11.0.0.0. When all of the host bits are 0s, that is considered the network or subnetwork number and that number cannot be assigned to a network device as a host number. Look back to Subnet Figure #7. The first subnetwork shown is 0. When all host bits are *0*, that is considered the subnetwork number. Some people call it the *wire*. Each combination of 1s and 0s after that point are host numbers on that subnetwork until the subnetwork number changes. The only exception to this is when all host bits are set to 1. When all of the host bits are a binary 1, this designates a **broadcast** for that network or subnetwork. Using the same network numbers given above as examples, the broadcast addresses would be 192.107.10.255 for the Class C network, 152.124.255.255 for the Class B network, and 11.255.255.255 for the Class A network. The broadcast address cannot be assigned to a network device. The broadcast address is used to communicate with all network devices simultaneously.

When borrowing two host bits from a Class C IP address, subnetworks 0, 64, 128, and 192 were created. Based on the rule stated above, subnetworks 0 and 192 cannot be used, so all that are left are subnetworks 64 and 128. These subnetworks that can be used are known as **useable subnets**. The first and the last subnet are considered unuseable because they contain all 0s and all 1s in the host bits. Subnet 0 contains all 0s in the host bits. Subnet 192 can contain all 1s in the host bits.

On subnetwork 64, the host numbers that are *possible* are 64 through 127. On subnetwork 64, the host numbers that are useable are 65 through 126. The host numbers that can be assigned to network devices are known as **useable host numbers**. For subnetwork 128, the possible host numbers are 128 through 191, but only 129 through 190 are used. This is found by using varying combinations of 1s and 0s through the host bits. Subnet Figure #7 illustrates this concept.

Subnet Figure #7

Class C Network No.			Subnet		Hosts						Subnet No.	Host No.
Octet1	Octet2	Octet3	Octet4								Subnet No.	Host No.
			128	64	32	16	8	4	2	1		
207.	193.	204.	0	1	0	0	0	0	0	0	64	
207.	193.	204.	0	1	0	0	0	0	0	1		65
207.	193.	204.	0	1	0	0	0	0	1	0		66
207.	193.	204.	0	1	0	0	0	0	1	1		67
207.	193.	204.	0	1	0	0	0	1	0	0		68
207.	193.	204.	0	1	0	0	0	1	0	1		69
207.	193.	204.	0	1	0	0	0	1	1	0		70
207.	193.	204.	0	1								
207.	193.	204.	0	1								
207.	193.	204.	0	1	1	1	1	1	1	0		126
207.	193.	204.	1	1	1	1	1	1	1	1		Broadcast
207.	193.	204.	1	0	0	0	0	0	0	0	128	
207.	193.	204.	1	0	0	0	0	0	0	1		129
207.	193.	204.	1	0	0	0	0	0	1	0		130
207.	193.	204.	1	0	0	0	0	0	1	1		131
207.	193.	204.	1	0	0	0	0	1	0	0		132
207.	193.	204.	1	0	0	0	0	1	0	1		133
207.	193.	204.	1	0								
207.	193.	204.	1	0								
207.	193.	204.	1	0	1	1	1	1	1	0		190
207.	193.	204.	1	0	1	1	1	1	1	1		191

One of the hardest concepts for students to grasp is that when determining what the decimal number is for an octet, you must use all eight octet bits in the number. Ignore the line drawn for the subnet bits. For example, in Subnet Figure #7, for subnetwork 64, the first useable host number is 65. Eight bits designate the number 65—01000001. Since there is a *1* in bit position 64 and a *1* in bit position 1, 64 + 1 = 65. The subnetwork number is 64 because the subnetwork columns have a *01* combination. The *1* is set in the 64 column. The host number is 67 because the decimal IP number represents all eight bits in an octet.

Subnet Figure #8 illustrates how a subnetted network has host numbers assigned to each network device. Notice that each device has numbers that relate to the range valid for each subnetwork.

Subnet Figure #8
Host Addresses on a Subnetted Network

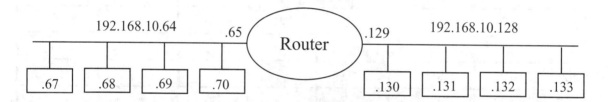

Notice in Subnet Figure #8 how the router received two host numbers. This is because inside the router, there are two Ethernet ports. Each of these ports receives a host number just as if it was a network card inside a computer. The host number assigned to the router's Ethernet port corresponds to a host number on the subnetwork the Ethernet port attaches to. Since the left side of the router is connected to Subnetwork 64, the router's port host address is .65, the first available host number on the subnetwork. The router's port does not have to receive the first host number in the subnetwork, but it is done this way in the figure to illustrate how a host number is assigned.

When subnetting, each device still has a unique IP address. The only difference that subnetting makes, is that each subnetwork has a range of valid host numbers for that individual subnetwork.

MASK REVIEW

In order to subnet, the subnet mask is used and is very important to understand. In the Network chapter you learned that a Class A IP address has a standard mask of 255.0.0.0. A Class B IP address has a standard mask of 255.255.0.0 and a Class C IP address has a mask of 255.255.255.0. For example, consider a computer that has an IP address of 150.150.150.150. The IP address is a Class B address. If the computer uses a standard mask, the mask entered would be 255.255.0.0.

Keep in mind that the mask distinguishes the network number from the host number. Using the same example used above of 150.150.150.150 and a mask of 255.255.0.0, yields the network number of 150.150.0.0 because of the mask used. An IP address of 193.206.52.4 with a mask of 255.255.255.0 has a network address of 193.206.52.

THE MASK WHEN SUBNETTING

The way that any network device knows that a subnet is being used is through the mask. This is why the mask is sometimes known as the subnet mask. The mask number stays the same up to the point that bits are borrowed. Then, in the octet where bits are borrowed, the new mask number is found by adding the bit positions together *that are borrowed* to create the subnet number. Look back to Subnet Figure #3. Since this is a Class C address, the normal mask is 255.255.255.0. However, since subnetting is implemented, the mask changes to 255.255.255.**192**. The 192 is found by adding the value of the bit positions being borrowed—bit position 128 and bit position 64 (the two bit positions borrowed to create the subnet number). 128 + 64 = 192. So, the new mask is 255.255.255.192. If three bits are borrowed in a C IP address, the last octet mask would be 224, (128 + 64 + 32). If four bits are borrowed in a Class C IP address, the last octet mask would be 240, (128 + 64 + 32 + 16). Examples of the new mask with each IP class are given later in the chapter.

SOLVING IP SUBNETTING PROBLEMS

When asked a subnetting problem, you can be presented with several pieces of information that describe the situation. Given that information, it will up to you to figure out the remaining pieces of information to solve the problem. The types of information that you must be able to identify are as follows:

Information
Class of IP address
Network Number
Mask
Total no. of networks/subnetworks
Total no. of hosts per network/subnetwork
Subnet numbers
Broadcast addresses
No. of bits borrowed
Useable hosts per network/subnetwork
Useable subnets

Class C Problem 1

Let's do one example without subnetting to make it simple and to explain how the chart works. Given the XYZ Company's Class C address of 201.15.6.0 and a mask of 255.255.255.0, you should be able to fill in the following information:

Information	Value
Class of IP address	C
Network Number	201.15.6.0
Mask	255.255.255.0
Total no. of networks/subnetworks	1
Total no. of hosts per network/subnetwork	256
Subnet numbers	N/A because there are no subnets
Broadcast addresses	201.15.6.255
No. of bits borrowed	N/A because there are no subnets
Useable hosts per network/subnetwork	254
Useable subnets	N/A because there are no subnets

Now that the purpose of the chart is clear, let's try an example with subnetting. Suppose the XYZ Company has four different networks throughout its factory, but only one full class C address. One option the company can do is to divide the class C address into four different subnetworks. The Class C IP address is 201.15.6.0. The network administrator decides the new subnet mask is 255.255.255.224. The following information is what we know so far:

Information	Value
Class of IP address	C
Network Number	201.15.6.0
Mask	255.255.255.224
Total no. of networks/subnetworks	??
Total no. of hosts per network/subnetwork	??
Subnet numbers	??
Broadcast addresses	??
No. of bits borrowed	??
Useable hosts per network/subnetwork	??
Useable subnets	??

If the mask is given, you can solve the rest of the unknowns and fill in the chart. The mask in this problem is 255.255.255.224. Since this is a Class C network and the default mask is 255.255.255.0, we know that some bits are being borrowed in the last octet because the number in the last octet has changed to 255.255.255.**224**. The first step is to break the last octet into binary to see how many bits are being borrowed for the subnetting. Subnet Figure #9 shows the last octet broken down into bits.

Subnet Figure #9

224 broken into bits ⟶

Class C Network No.			Subnet			Hosts				
Octet1	Octet2	Octet3	Octet4							
			128	64	32	16	8	4	2	1
255.	255.	255.	1	1	1	0	0	0	0	0 ⟵

Notice in Subnet Figure #9 how the first three bits are set to *1*. Since there is a *1* in the 128 column, a *1* in the 64 column, and a *1* in the 32 column, 128 + 64 + 32 = 224. This is just the process of converting decimal to binary as shown in earlier chapters.

The next step is to draw a vertical line between the 1s and the 0s. In the case of the 224 mask, a vertical line is drawn between the 32 and the 16 column. See Subnet Figure #10 to see where the vertical line is placed.

Subnet Figure #10

Class C Network No.			Subnet			Hosts				
Octet1	Octet2	Octet3	Octet4							
			128	64	32	16	8	4	2	1
255.	255.	255.	1	1	1	0	0	0	0	0

Once you have figured out where this line goes, you can answer many questions. Now you know the number of bits borrowed is three because there are three 1s set when you translate 224 into binary. Let's update the chart.

Information	Value
Class of IP address	C
Network Number	201.15.6.0
Mask	255.255.255.224
Total no. of networks/subnetworks	??
Total no. of hosts per network/subnetwork	??
Subnet numbers	??
Broadcast addresses	??
No. of bits borrowed	**3**
Useable hosts per network/subnetwork	??
Useable subnets	??

Once you know the number of bits borrowed, you can determine the number of subnetworks using the formula 2^x = number of subnetworks where x is the number of bits borrowed. So $2^3 = 8$ meaning that there are eight subnetworks. Again, update the chart with the new information.

Information	Value
Class of IP address	C
Network Number	201.15.6.0
Mask	255.255.255.224
Total no. of networks/subnetworks	**8**
Total no. of hosts per network/subwork	??
Subnet numbers	??
Broadcast Address	??
No. of bits borrowed	3
Useable hosts per network/subwork	??
Useable subnets	??

Also, since you know the number of bits borrowed, you can determine how many bits are left for hosts (network devices). Since three of the eight bits in the octet are borrowed for subnetworks, there are five bits left for hosts. The number of hosts per subnetwork can be found by using the formula 2^x = number of hosts where x is the number of host bits remaining after bits have been borrowed for subnetting. In our example, three bits were borrowed for subnetting. Five bits were left for hosts. $2^5 = 32$ hosts per subnetwork. Updating the chart shows the following:

Information	Value
Class of IP address	C
Network Number	201.12.6.0
Mask	255.255.255.224
Total no. of networks/subnetworks	8
Total no. of hosts per network/subnetwork	**32**
Subnet numbers	??
Broadcast addresses	??
No. of bits borrowed	3
Useable hosts per network/subnetwork	??
Useable subnets	??

Once you have determined the total number of subnets and the total number of hosts per subnet, you can determine the number of useable subnets and useable hosts per subnet. The number of useable subnets is the number of subnets minus two. Since there are 8 possible subnetworks, 8 – 2 = 6 useable networks. The number of useable hosts is the number of hosts per subnetwork minus 2. Since there are 32 possible hosts per subnetwork, 32 – 2 = 30.

Information	Value
Class of IP address	C
Network Number	201.15.6.0
Mask	255.255.255.224
Total no. of networks/subnetworks	8
Total no. of hosts per network/subnetwork	32
Subnet numbers	??
Broadcast addresses	??
No. of bits borrowed	3
Useable hosts per network/subnetwork	**30**
Useable subnets	**6**

We have determined that there are eight subnetworks available using the subnet mask of 255.255.255.224. Subnet Figure #11 shows the eight different subnetworks converted into decimal values.

Subnet Figure #11

Class C Network No.			Subnet	Hosts							Subnet No.
Octet1	Octet2	Octet3	Octet4								
			128	64	32	16	8	4	2	1	
201.	15.	6.	0	0	0	0	0	0	0	0	0
201.	15.	6.	0	0	1	0	0	0	0	0	32
201.	15.	6.	0	1	0	0	0	0	0	0	64
201.	15.	6.	0	1	1	0	0	0	0	0	96
201.	15.	6.	1	0	0	0	0	0	0	0	128
201.	15.	6.	1	0	1	0	0	0	0	0	160
201.	15.	6.	1	1	0	0	0	0	0	0	192
201.	15.	6.	1	1	1	0	0	0	0	0	224

Notice in Subnet Figure #11 that the subnetworks are grouped into multiples of 32. Also notice that the first column to the left of the line (the darker gray area) has a value of 32. The total subnetworks are as follows 0, 32, 64, 96, 128, 160, 192, and 224. These are all multiples of 32.

Now, we can update our list and put in the subnet numbers as shown below:

Information	Value
Class of IP address	C
Network Number	201.15.6.0
Mask	255.255.255.224
Total no. of networks/subnetworks	8
Total no. of hosts per network/subnetwork	32
Subnet numbers	**201.15.6.0, 201.15.6.32, 201.15.6.64, 201.15.6.96, 201.15.6.128, 201.15.6.160, 201.15.6.192, 201.15.6.224**
Broadcast addresses	??
No. of bits borrowed	3
Useable hosts per network/subnetwork	30
Useable subnets	6

Instead of running 1s and 0s in the subnet columns, you can determine that the subnetworks are in groups of 32, which is the value in the column left of the subnet line.

Now let's determine the broadcast addresses for each subnetwork. The broadcast address can be found by placing all 1s in the host bits for each subnetwork. Subnet Figure #12 shows the broadcast address calculation.

Subnet Figure #12
4th Octet in Binary

Subnet	IP Address Range	128	64	32	16	8	4	2	1
1	(201.15.6.0)	0	0	0	0	0	0	0	0
1	(201.15.6.31)	0	0	0	1	1	1	1	1
2	(201.15.6.32)	0	0	1	0	0	0	0	0
2	(201.15.6.63)	0	0	1	1	1	1	1	1
3	(201.15.6.64)	0	1	0	0	0	0	0	0
3	(201.15.6.95)	0	1	0	1	1	1	1	1
4	(201.15.6.96)	0	1	1	0	0	0	0	0
4	(201.15.6.127)	0	1	1	1	1	1	1	1
5	(201.15.6.128)	1	0	0	0	0	0	0	0
5	(201.15.6.159)	1	0	0	1	1	1	1	1
6	(201.15.6.160)	1	0	1	0	0	0	0	0
6	(201.15.6.191)	1	0	1	1	1	1	1	1
7	(201.15.6.192)	1	1	0	0	0	0	0	0
7	(201.15.6.223)	1	1	0	1	1	1	1	1
8	(201.15.6.224)	1	1	1	0	0	0	0	0
8	(201.15.6.255)	1	1	1	1	1	1	1	1

Notice in Subnet Figure #12 how each subnetwork is shown with the subnetwork number and the broadcast address for that subnetwork. Now for the final chart update.

Information	Value
Class of IP address	C
Network Number	201.15.6.0
Mask	255.255.255.224
Total no. of networks/subnetworks	8
Total no. of hosts per network/subnetwork	32
Subnet numbers	201.15.6.0, 201.15.6.32, 201.15.6.64, 201.15.6.96, 201.15.6.128, 201.15.6.160, 201.15.6.192, 201.15.6.224
Broadcast addresses	**201.15.6.31, 201.15.6.63, 201.15.6.95, 201.15.6.127, 201.15.6.159, 201.15.6.191, 201.15.6.223, 201.15.6.255**
No. of bits borrowed	3
Useable hosts per network/subnetwork	30
Useable subnets	6

Class C Problem 2

The Hi-IQ Company has leased one Class C address—200.200.200.0. The company has ten networks with 12 computers on each network. With this information the chart appears as follows:

Information	Value
Class of IP address	**C**
Network Number	**200.200.200.0**
Mask	??
Total no. of networks/subnetworks	**(10 needed)**
Total no. of hosts per network/subnetwork	**(12 needed)**
Subnet numbers	??
Broadcast addresses	??
No. of bits borrowed	??
Useable hosts per network/subnetwork	??
Useable subnets	??

To solve this problem, the first step is to determine the mask and from there, the rest is the same as the first example. To determine what mask is needed, you must discover how many bits to borrow. Remember to use the formula 2^x = total number of subnets – 2 = the number of useable subnets where x is the number of bits borrowed. If two host bits are borrowed (the minimum number for a Class C network), only two subnets are created (2^2=4–2=2). That number of subnets is not enough for the Hi-IQ Company. If three host bits are borrowed, six subnets are useable (2^3=8-2=6). Again, there are not enough subnets. If four host bits are borrowed, 14 subnets are useable (2^4=16–2=14). This is the correct number of bits to borrow for the Hi-IQ Company; however, the mask must still be determined.

When borrowing four host bits to create the subnets, the mask is found by adding the bit values for the highest most bits. See Subnet Figure #13.

Subnet Figure #13

Class C Network No.			Subnet				Hosts			
Octet1	Octet2	Octet3	Octet4							
			128	64	32	16	8	4	2	1
255.	255.	255.	1	1	1	1	0	0	0	0

The normal Class C mask is 255.255.255.0, but we are borrowing bits from the last octet, so we know the mask is going to be different. By adding the bit values for the bits being borrowed, the mask is found—128 + 64 + 32 + 16 = 240. The mask for this subnetted Class C address is 255.255.255.240. Updating the chart shows the following:

Information	Value
Class of IP address	C
Network Number	200.200.200.0
Mask	**255.255.255.240**
Total no. of networks/subnetworks	**16**
Total no. of hosts per network/subnetwork	(12 needed)
Subnet numbers	??
Broadcast addresses	??
No. of bits borrowed	**4**
Useable hosts per network/subnetwork	??
Useable subnets	**14**

Since the number of bits borrowed has been determined, it is easy to see how many host bits are left to determine the total number of hosts per subnetwork. Look back at Subnet Figure #13. At a quick glance, it is apparent that four bits remain for hosts. Using the formula 2^x = total number of hosts − 2 = the number of useable hosts where x is the number of host bits remaining. If four host bits are remaining, 14 host addresses are useable (2^4=16−2=14). This works well for the Hi-IQ Company since they have 12 computers on each network. Updating the chart with this information provides the following:

Information	Value
Class of IP address	C
Network Number	200.200.200.0
Mask	255.255.255.240
Total no. of networks/subnetworks	16
Total no. of hosts per network/subnetwork	16
Subnet numbers	??
Broadcast addresses	??
No. of bits borrowed	4
Useable hosts per network/subnetwork	14
Useable subnets	14

The only thing left to do is to figure out the subnetwork numbers and the broadcasts. Subnet Figure #14 shows only the subnetwork numbers by placing 0s in each of the host bits.

Subnet Figure #14

Class C Network No.			Subnet				Hosts				Subnet No.
Octet1	Octet2	Octet3	Octet4								
			128	64	32	16	8	4	2	1	
201.	15.	6.	0	0	0	0	0	0	0	0	0
201.	15.	6.	0	0	0	1	0	0	0	0	16
201.	15.	6.	0	0	1	0	0	0	0	0	32
201.	15.	6.	0	0	1	1	0	0	0	0	48
201.	15.	6.	0	1	0	0	0	0	0	0	64
201.	15.	6.	0	1	0	1	0	0	0	0	80
201.	15.	6.	0	1	1	0	0	0	0	0	96
201.	15.	6.	0	1	1	1	0	0	0	0	112
201.	15.	6.	1	0	0	0	0	0	0	0	128
201.	15.	6.	1	0	0	1	0	0	0	0	144
201.	15.	6.	1	0	1	0	0	0	0	0	160
201.	15.	6.	1	0	1	1	0	0	0	0	176
201.	15.	6.	1	1	0	0	0	0	0	0	192
201.	15.	6.	1	1	0	1	0	0	0	0	208
201.	15.	6.	1	1	1	0	0	0	0	0	224
201.	15.	6.	1	1	1	1	0	0	0	0	240

Notice that the first subnet has all 0s in the last octet. This is why the first subnets cannot be used as a useable subnet. Now let's get the broadcast numbers. Subnet Figure #15 shows only the broadcasts by placing 1s in each of the host bits.

Subnet Figure #15

Class C Network No.			Subnet				Hosts				Broadcast Address
Octet1	Octet2	Octet3	Octet4								
			128	64	32	16	8	4	2	1	
201.	15.	6.	0	0	0	0	1	1	1	1	15
201.	15.	6.	0	0	0	1	1	1	1	1	31
201.	15.	6.	0	0	1	0	1	1	1	1	47
201.	15.	6.	0	0	1	1	1	1	1	1	63
201.	15.	6.	0	1	0	0	1	1	1	1	79
201.	15.	6.	0	1	0	1	1	1	1	1	95
201.	15.	6.	0	1	1	0	1	1	1	1	111
201.	15.	6.	0	1	1	1	1	1	1	1	127
201.	15.	6.	1	0	0	0	1	1	1	1	143
201.	15.	6.	1	0	0	1	1	1	1	1	159
201.	15.	6.	1	0	1	0	1	1	1	1	175
201.	15.	6.	1	0	1	1	1	1	1	1	191
201.	15.	6.	1	1	0	0	1	1	1	1	207
201.	15.	6.	1	1	0	1	1	1	1	1	223
201.	15.	6.	1	1	1	0	1	1	1	1	239
201.	15.	6.	1	1	1	1	1	1	1	1	255

Notice how the last subnet has all 1s in the last octet. This is why the last subnet cannot be used as a useable subnet. Now let's update the chart with the subnetwork numbers and their associated broadcast addresses.

Information	Value
Class of IP address	C
Network Number	200.200.200.0
Mask	255.255.255.240
Total no. of networks/subnetworks	16
Total no. of hosts per network/subnetwork	16
Subnet numbers	**200.200.200.0, 200.200.200.16, 200.200.200.32, 200.200.200.48, 200.200.200.64, 200.200.200.80, 200.200.200.96, 200.200.200.112, 200.200.200.128, 200.200.200.144, 200.200.200.160, 200.200.200.176, 200.200.200.192, 200.200.200.208, 200.200.200.224, 200.200.200.240**
Broadcast addresses	**200.200.200.15, 200.200.200.31, 200.200.200.47, 200.200.200.63, 200.200.200.79, 200.200.200.95, 200.200.200.111, 200.200.200.127, 200.200.200.143, 200.200.200.159, 200.200.200.175, 200.200.200.191, 200.200.200.207, 200.200.200.223, 200.200.200.239, 200.200.200.255**
No. of bits borrowed	4
Useable hosts per network/subnetwork	14
Useable subnets	14

All important pieces of information needed to setup the network are now provided.

Class C Problem 3

A network administrator for the Total Cool Company is working on a computer. The computer's IP address is 204.210.179.142 with a mask of 255.255.255.192. The network administrator needs to know on which subnet the computer belongs. The information found by looking at the computer is the Class of IP address, the network portion of the IP address, and the mask. The following chart shows this information.

Information	Value
Class of IP address	C
Network Number	**204.210.179.0**
Mask	**255.255.255.192**
Total no. of networks/subnetworks	??
Total no. of hosts per network/subnetwork	??
Subnet numbers	??
Broadcast addresses	??
No. of bits borrowed	??
Useable hosts per network/subnetwork	??
Useable subnets	??

The first step in solving this problem is to discover how many bits are borrowed. A normal Class C mask is 255.255.255.0, but the one on this computer is 255.255.255.192. To find out how many bits are borrowed requires you to put 1s in Octet 4's bits until the bit positions add up to 192. Look at Subnet Figure #16 to see how this is done.

Subnet Figure #16

Class C Network No.			Subnet		Hosts					
Octet1	Octet2	Octet3	Octet4							
			128	64	32	16	8	4	2	1
255.	255.	255.	1	1						

Bit position 128 plus bit position 64 added together gives you 192. So, two bits are borrowed. Updating the chart with the number of bits borrowed shows the following:

Information	Value
Class of IP address	C
Network Number	204.210.179.0
Mask	255.255.255.192
Total no. of networks/subnetworks	??
Total no. of hosts per network/subnetwork	??
Subnet numbers	??
Broadcast addresses	??
No. of bits borrowed	**2**
Useable hosts per network/subnetwork	??
Useable subnets	??

Now that the number of bits borrowed is solved, you can determine the number of subnetworks using the formula 2^x = number of subnetworks where x is the number of bits borrowed and subtracting two because you cannot use the first or the last subnetworks. So $2^2 = 4$ minus 2 equals 2 meaning that there are two subnetworks. You can also determine the number of hosts on each network using the same method. 2^x = number of hosts where x is the number of host bits remaining after bits have been borrowed for subnetting. Then subtract two for the number of useable hosts. In our example, two bits were borrowed for subnetting. Six bits are left for hosts. $2^6 = 64$ hosts per subnetwork minus two for the subnetwork number and broadcast leaves 62 hosts per subnetwork. Updating the chart shows the following:

Information	Value
Class of IP address	C
Network Number	204.210.179.0
Mask	255.255.255.192
Total no. of networks/subnetworks	**4**
Total no. of hosts per network/subnetwork	**64**
Subnet numbers	??
Broadcast addresses	??
No. of bits borrowed	2
Useable hosts per network/subnetwork	**62**
Useable subnets	**2**

Now, the only thing left to do is to determine the subnet numbers. Look back to Subnet Figure #16. You can see that the line is drawn between the 32 and 64 bit positions. A shortcut is to look at the number to the *left* of the line and you can tell that the subnetwork numbers will be incremented in steps of 64, but filling in the chart with 0s in the host bits proves this shortcut. Subnet Figure #17 shows the subnetwork numbers.

Subnet Figure #17

Class C Network No.			Subnet		Hosts							
Octet1	Octet2	Octet3	Octet4									Subnet No.
			128	64	32	16	8	4	2	1	
204.	210.	179.	0	0	0	0	0	0	0	0	0
204.	210.	179.	0	1	0	0	0	0	0	0	64
204.	210.	179.	1	0	0	0	0	0	0	0	128
204.	210.	179.	1	1	0	0	0	0	0	0	192

A shortcut for finding the broadcast address is to subtract one from the subnetwork below the one you are working on because the broadcast address is always one less than the subnetwork number. Also remember that the last subnet will always have a broadcast address of 255. However, filling in the chart shows the full version. Subnet Figure #18 shows broadcasts for each of the subnetworks by putting 1s in the host positions.

Subnet Figure #18

Class C Network No.			Subnet		Hosts							
Octet1	Octet2	Octet3	Octet4									Broadcast Address
			128	64	32	16	8	4	2	1	
204.	210.	179.	0	0	1	1	1	1	1	1	63
204.	210.	179.	0	1	1	1	1	1	1	1	127
204.	210.	179.	1	0	1	1	1	1	1	1	191
204.	210.	179.	1	1	1	1	1	1	1	1	255

Now, update the chart to include the subnetwork numbers and broadcast addresses:

Information	Value
Class of IP address	C
Network Number	204.210.179.0
Mask	255.255.255.192
Total no. of networks/subnetworks	4
Total no. of hosts per network/subnetwork	64
Subnet numbers	**204.210.179.0, 204.210.179.64, 204.210.179.128, 204.210.179.192**
Broadcast addresses	**204.210.179.63, 204.210.179.127, 204.210.179.191, 204.210.179.255**
No. of bits borrowed	2
Useable hosts per network/subnetwork	62
Useable subnets	2

Now that the chart is complete, look at the sequence of network numbers or back at Subnet Figure #17 to determine what subnetwork IP address 204.210.179.142 falls. Subnetwork 0 is IP addresses 204.210.179.0 through 204.210.179.63. This does not include *.142*, so look at the next subnetwork. Subnetwork 1 is IP addresses 204.210.179.64 through 204.210.179.127. Again, *.142* is not in this range. Subnetwork 2 is IP addresses 204.210.179.128 through 204.210.179.191. This range of addresses does include *.142*, so IP address 204.210.179.142 is on subnetwork 204.210.179.128. Another way of solving for the subnetwork number is to *and* the IP address with the mask. Remember when anding two 1s together make a 1. All other combinations of 1s and 0s make a 0. Subnet Figure #19 shows the anding of the IP address 204.210.179.142 with the mask—255.255.255.192 with the result being the subnetwork number.

Subnet Figure #19

```
              1                 1                 1                 1
              2 6 3 1           2 6 3 1           2 6 3 1           2 6 3 1
              8 4 2 6 8 4 2 1   8 4 2 6 8 4 2 1   8 4 2 6 8 4 2 1   8 4 2 6 8 4 2 1
IP in
binary        1 1 0 0 1 1 0 0   1 1 0 1 0 0 1 0   1 0 1 1 0 0 1 1   1 0 0 0 1 1 1 0

Mask in
binary        1 1 1 1 1 1 1 1   1 1 1 1 1 1 1 1   1 1 1 1 1 1 1 1   1 1 0 0 0 0 0 0

Subnet in
binary        1 1 0 0 1 1 0 0   1 1 0 1 0 0 1 0   1 0 1 1 0 0 1 1   1 0 0 0 0 0 0 0
```

CLASS B SUBNETTING

Class B IP addresses are handled the same as Class C's with the exception of how many host bits can be borrowed for subnetting. With Class B IP addresses, the first two octets (16 bits) represent the network number and the last two octets (16 bits) represent host bits. Subnet Figure #20 shows this concept

Subnet Figure #20

Class B Network No.		Hosts	
Octet1	Octet2	Octet3	Octet4

When subnetting, host bits are borrowed to create subnets and they are always borrowed from the left-most host bits. Subnet Figure #21 shows a Class B IP address with three bits borrowed.

Subnet Figure #21

Class B Network No.		Subnets			Hosts												
Octet 1	Octet 2	Octet3								Octet4							
		128	64	32	16	8	4	2	1	128	64	32	16	8	4	2	1

The number of subnets is still found using the formula 2^x = total number of subnets where x is the number of bits borrowed. The useable subnets is found by subtracting two from the result just like it is done with Class C addresses. Look back to Subnet Figure 21. When three bits are borrowed, there are eight subnets and six useable subnets possible because $2^3 = 8$ and $8 - 2 = 6$.

To determine the total number of hosts, the same formula used when working with Class C addresses is applied: 2^x = number of hosts where x is the number of host bits remaining after bits have been borrowed for subnetting. Subtract the number two from this result to obtain the useable number of hosts per subnetwork. Look back to Subnet Figure #21. With three bits borrowed to perform subnetting, 13 bits remain. $2^{13} = 8,192$, which is the total number of hosts. To find the useable number of hosts per subnetwork, subtract two from 8,192. 8,192 − 2 = 8,190. So, 8,190 hosts are allowed on each subnet when borrowing three bits from a Class B address.

The normal subnet mask used with Class B IP addresses is 255.255.0.0. When implementing subnets, the third (and possible fourth) octet number changes. The mask is found by looking at the octet(s) where host bits are borrowed and adding the bit values together. Subnet Figure #22 shows how the mask is obtained when borrowing 3 bits from a Class B address.

Subnet Figure #22

Mask

Class B Network No.		Subnets			Hosts												
Octet 1	Octet 2	Octet3							Octet4								
		128	64	32	16	8	4	2	1	128	64	32	16	8	4	2	1
255	255	1	1	1													

When three bits are borrowed, the mask has 1s set in the first three bits of the third octet. These bit positions are 128, 64, and 32. Add these bit values together to get 224 (128 + 64 + 32 = 224). The mask for a Class B network with three bits borrowed is 255.255.224.0.

Now, for some more practice. The best way to learn Class B IP address subnetting is to practice, practice, practice.

Class B Problem 1

The PDQ, Inc. company has ten different networks located throughout the country, but has leased only one Class B address, 180.10.0.0. One option for the company is to divide the class B address into subnetworks. The network administrator must determine how many bits to borrow by looking at how many subnets the company needs. Since the company has ten networks, a minimum of four bits must be borrowed. $2^4 = 16$ and $16 - 2 = 14$ useable subnet numbers. (If three bits were borrowed, there would not be enough subnets because $2^3 = 8$ and $8 - 2 = 6$.) The network administrator has heard that a merger is imminent, so playing it safe, she decides to borrow five bits for subnetting. Borrowing five bits allows for 30 subnetworks because $2^5 = 32$ and $32 - 2 = 30$. Subnet Figure #23 shows how the mask is determined.

Mask

Subnet Figure #23

Class B Network No.		Subnets								Hosts							
Octet 1	Octet 2	Octet3								Octet4							
		128	64	32	16	8	4	2	1	128	64	32	16	8	4	2	1
255	255	1	1	1	1	1											

1s are placed in all subnetwork bit positions and those bit values are added together: 128 + 64 + 32 + 16 + 8 = 248. The mask used in the PDQ, Inc. network is 255.255.248.0. The chart below shows the information gathered thus far:

Information	Value
Class of IP address	B
Network Number	180.10.0.0
Mask	255.255.248.0
Total no. of subnetworks	**32**
Total no. of hosts per network/subnetwork	??
Subnet numbers	??
Broadcast addresses	??
No. of bits borrowed	5
Useable hosts per network/subnetwork	??
Useable subnets	**30**

The number of hosts can be determined by looking at how many host bits remain. Look back to Subnet Figure #13 and see that the number of remaining host bits is 11. 2^{11} = 2,048 total number of hosts for each subnet. Subtract two to obtain the number of useable hosts on each subnet: $2,048 - 2 = 2,046$ useable hosts on each subnet. The updated chart shows the following:

Information	Value
Class of IP address	B
Network Number	180.10.0.0
Mask	255.255.248.0
Total no. of subnetworks	32
Total no. of hosts per subnetwork	**2,048**
Subnet numbers	??
Broadcast addresses	??
No. of bits borrowed	5
Useable hosts per subnetwork	**2,046**
Useable subnets	30

Now for the real work—determining subnet numbers and broadcast addresses. Subnet Figure #24 shows the 1 and 0 patterns for determining subnetwork numbers. Due to the lack of space, not all subnetworks are shown, but enough subnets are shown to illustrate the pattern.

Subnet Figure #24

Class B Network No.		Subnets								Hosts								Subnet No.
Octet 1	Octet 2	Octet3								Octet4								Subnet No.
		128	64	32	16	8	4	2	1	128	64	32	16	8	4	2	1	
180	10	0	0	0	0	0	0	0	0	0	0	0	0	0	0	0	0	0.0
180	10	0	0	0	0	1	0	0	0	0	0	0	0	0	0	0	0	8.0
180	10	0	0	0	1	0	0	0	0	0	0	0	0	0	0	0	0	16.0
180	10	0	0	0	1	1	0	0	0	0	0	0	0	0	0	0	0	24.0
180	10	0	0	1	0	0	0	0	0	0	0	0	0	0	0	0	0	32.0
180	10	0	0	1	0	1	0	0	0	0	0	0	0	0	0	0	0	40.0
180	10	0	0	1	1	0	0	0	0	0	0	0	0	0	0	0	0	48.0
180	10	0	0	1	1	1	0	0	0	0	0	0	0	0	0	0	0	56.0
180	10	0	1	0	0	0	0	0	0	0	0	0	0	0	0	0	0	64.0
180	10	0	1	0	0	1	0	0	0	0	0	0	0	0	0	0	0	72.0
180	10	0	1	0	1	0	0	0	0	0	0	0	0	0	0	0	0	80.0
180	10	0	1	0	1	1	0	0	0	0	0	0	0	0	0	0	0	88.0
180	10	0	1	1	0	0	0	0	0	0	0	0	0	0	0	0	0	96.0
180	10	0	1	1	0	1	0	0	0	0	0	0	0	0	0	0	0	104.0
180	10	0	1	1	1	0	0	0	0	0	0	0	0	0	0	0	0	112.0
180	10	0	1	1	1	1	0	0	0	0	0	0	0	0	0	0	0	120.0
180	10	1	0	0	0	0	0	0	0	0	0	0	0	0	0	0	0	128.0
180	10			•														•
180	10			•														•
180	10	1	1	1	1	1	0	0	0	0	0	0	0	0	0	0	0	248.0

Notice how the subnetwork numbers are in increments of eight. When doing Class A and B subnetting, there is normally not enough time to write every combination of 1s and 0s. When first learning subnetting, you should definitely write out a few, but once you see the pattern emerge, you should do the first couple of subnets and the last subnet. Updating the chart with the subnetwork numbers yields the following:

Information	Value
Class of IP address	B
Network Number	180.10.0.0
Mask	255.255.248.0
Total no. of subnetworks	32
Total no. of hosts per subnetwork	2,048
Subnet numbers	**180.10.0.0, 180.10.8.0, 180.10.16.0, 180.10.24.0, 180.10.32.0, 180.10.40.0, 180.10.48.0, 180.10.56.0, 180.10.64,0, 180.10.72.0, 180.10.80.0, 180.10.88.0, 180.10.96.0, 180.10.104.0, 180.10.112.0, 180.10.120.0, 180.10.128.0, 180.10.136.0, 180.10.144.0, 180.10.152.0, 180.10.160.0, 180.10.168.0, 180.10.176.0, 180.10.184.0, 180.10.192.0, 180.10.200.0, 180.10.208.0, 180.10.216.0, 180.10.224.0, 180.10.232.0, 180.10.240.0, 180.10.248.0**
Broadcast addresses	??
No. of bits borrowed	5
Useable hosts per subnetwork	2,046
Useable subnets	30

All that is left in the chart is the broadcast address for each subnetwork. This is found by placing 1s in all of the host bits after the subnetworks are found. This too, will show an emerging pattern as Subnet Figure #25 illustrates:

Subnet Figure #25

Class B Network No.		Subnet								Hosts								Broadcast
Octet 1	Octet 2	Octet3								Octet4								Broadcast
		128	64	32	16	8	4	2	1	128	64	32	16	8	4	2	1	
180	10	0	0	0	0	0	1	1	1	1	1	1	1	1	1	1	1	7.255
180	10	0	0	0	0	1	1	1	1	1	1	1	1	1	1	1	1	15.255
180	10	0	0	0	1	0	1	1	1	1	1	1	1	1	1	1	1	23.255
180	10	0	0	0	1	1	1	1	1	1	1	1	1	1	1	1	1	31.255
180	10	0	0	1	0	0	1	1	1	1	1	1	1	1	1	1	1	39.255
180	10	0	0	1	0	1	1	1	1	1	1	1	1	1	1	1	1	47.255
180	10	0	0	1	1	0	1	1	1	1	1	1	1	1	1	1	1	55.255
180	10	0	0	1	1	1	1	1	1	1	1	1	1	1	1	1	1	63.255
180	10	0	1	0	0	0	1	1	1	1	1	1	1	1	1	1	1	71.255
180	10	0	1	0	0	1	1	1	1	1	1	1	1	1	1	1	1	79.255
180	10	0	1	0	1	0	1	1	1	1	1	1	1	1	1	1	1	87.255
180	10	0	1	0	1	1	1	1	1	1	1	1	1	1	1	1	1	95.255
180	10	0	1	1	0	0	1	1	1	1	1	1	1	1	1	1	1	103.255
180	10	0	1	1	0	1	1	1	1	1	1	1	1	1	1	1	1	111.255
180	10	0	1	1	1	0	1	1	1	1	1	1	1	1	1	1	1	119.255
180	10	0	1	1	1	1	1	1	1	1	1	1	1	1	1	1	1	127.255
180	10	1	0	0	0	0	1	1	1	1	1	1	1	1	1	1	1	135.255
180	10			•			1	1	1	1	1	1	1	1	1	1	1	•
180	10			•			1	1	1	1	1	1	1	1	1	1	1	•
180	10	1	1	1	1	1	1	1	1	1	1	1	1	1	1	1	1	255.255

 Do not forget to look at the entire octet when determining the decimal value for the octet.

The pattern that emerges is that the third octet increments by eight each time and the fourth octet is always 255. Also notice that the broadcast number is one less than the subnetwork number that follows. The completed chart lists below:

Information	Value
Class of IP address	B
Network Number	180.10.0.0
Mask	255.255.248.0
Total no. of subnetworks	32
Total no. of hosts per subnetwork	2,048
Subnet numbers	180.10.0.0, 180.10.8.0, 180.10.16.0, 180.10.24.0, 180.10.32.0, 180.10.40.0, 180.10.48.0, 180.10.56.0, 180.10.64,0, 180.10.72.0, 180.10.80.0, 180.10.88.0, 180.10.96.0, 180.10.104.0, 180.10.112.0, 180.10.120.0, 180.10.128.0, 180.10.136.0, 180.10.144.0, 180.10.152.0, 180.10.160.0, 180.10.168.0, 180.10.176.0, 180.10.184.0, 180.10.192.0, 180.10.200.0, 180.10.208.0, 180.10.216.0, 180.10.224.0, 180.10.232.0, 180.10.240.0, 180.10.248.0
Broadcast addresses	**180.10.7.255, 180.10.15.255, 180.10.31.255, 180.10.39.255, 180.10.47.255, 180.10.55.255, 180.10.63.255, 180.10.71.255, 180.10.79.255, 180.10.87.255, 180.10.95.255, 180.10.103.255, 180.10.111.255, 180.10.119.255, 180.10.127.255, 180.10.135.255, 180.10.143.255, 180.10.151.255, 180.10.167.255, 180.10.175.255, 180.10.183.255, 180.10.191.255, 180.10.199.255, 180.10.207.255, 180.10.215.255, 180.10.223.255, 180.10.231.255, 180.10.239.255, 180.10.255.255**
No. of bits borrowed	5
Useable hosts per subnetwork	2,046
Useable subnets	30

Class B Problem 2

One of the hardest concepts for students to grasp is when borrowed host bits are in more than one octet. In the next scenario, the Top Hats Co. has 2,000 locations located throughout the world. Each location has a network with approximately 20 computers. The Top Hats Co. has leased the Class B IP address of 189.208.0.0. The first step in solving this problem is determining how many bits to borrow. Subnet Table #1 helps with this decision:

Subnet Table #1

Borrowed Bits	No. of Host Bits	Total Subnets	Useable Subnets	Total Hosts	Useable Hosts
5	11	32	30	2048	2046
6	10	34	32	1024	1022
7	9	128	126	512	510
8	8	256	254	256	254
9	7	512	510	128	126
10	6	1024	1022	64	62
11	**5**	**2048**	**2046**	**32**	**30**
12	4	4096	4094	16	14
13	3	8192	8190	8	6

Looking at Subnet Table #1, you can see that borrowing 11 bits allows for the 2,000 Top Hat Co.'s locations throughout the world. By borrowing 11 bits, there are also enough remaining host bits to accommodate the computers at each site. The following chart summarizes the information gathered so far:

Information	Value
Class of IP address	B
Network Number	189.208.0.0
Mask	??
Total no. of subnetworks	**2,048**
Total no. of hosts per subnetwork	**32**
Subnet numbers	??
Broadcast addresses	??
No. of bits borrowed	**11**
Useable hosts per subnetwork	**30**
Useable subnets	**2,046**

To determine what mask is needed throughout the Top Hat Co.'s network, place 1s in the subnetwork field and add the bit value positions together for each octet. Subnet Figure #26 shows this concept:

Subnet Figure #26

Mask

Class B Network No.		Subnets											Hosts				
Octet 1	Octet 2	Octet3								Octet4							
		128	64	32	16	8	4	2	1	128	64	32	16	8	4	2	1
255	255	1	1	1	1	1	1	1	1	1	1	1					

The first two octets are the standard 255.255 numbers. The third octet is filled with 1's, so the third octet mask is 255—(128 + 64 + 32 + 16 + 8 + 4 + 2 +1 = 255). The fourth octet has three bits set, so the mask is 224—(128 + 64 + 32 = 224). The final mask for this problem is 255.255.255.244 and the information can be inserted into the chart:

Information	Value
Class of IP address	B
Network Number	189.208.0.0
Mask	**255.255.255.224**
Total no. of subnetworks	2,048
Total no. of hosts per subnetwork	32
Subnet numbers	??
Broadcast addresses	??
No. of bits borrowed	11
Useable hosts per subnetwork	30
Useable subnets	2,046

Now, the subnetworks must be determined. Subnet Figure #27 shows the breakdown of the subnets with 1s and 0s.

Keep in mind, when putting 1s and 0s in multiple subnetwork octets, treat them as one big group.

Subnet Figure #27

Class B Network No.		Subnets								Hosts								Subnets
Octet 1	Octet 2	Octet3								Octet4								Subnets
		128	64	32	16	8	4	2	1	128	64	32	16	8	4	2		
189	208	0	0	0	0	0	0	0	0	0	0	0	0	0	0	0		0.0
189	208	0	0	0	0	0	0	0	0	0	0	1	0	0	0	0		0.32
189	208	0	0	0	0	0	0	0	0	0	1	0	0	0	0	0		0.64
189	208	0	0	0	0	0	0	0	0	0	1	1	0	0	0	0		0.96
189	208	0	0	0	0	0	0	0	0	1	0	0	0	0	0	0		0.128
189	208	0	0	0	0	0	0	0	0	1	0	1	0	0	0	0		0.160
189	208	0	0	0	0	0	0	0	0	1	1	0	0	0	0	0		0.192
189	208	0	0	0	0	0	0	0	0	1	1	1	0	0	0	0		0.224
189	208	0	0	0	0	0	0	0	1	0	0	0	0	0	0	0		1.0
189	208	0	0	0	0	0	0	0	1	0	0	1	0	0	0	0		1.32
189	208	0	0	0	0	0	0	0	1	0	1	0	0	0	0	0		1.64
189	208	0	0	0	0	0	0	0	1	0	1	1	0	0	0	0		1.96
189	208	0	0	0	0	0	0	0	1	1	0	0	0	0	0	0		1.128
189	208	0	0	0	0	0	0	0	1	1	0	1	0	0	0	0		1.160
189	208	0	0	0	0	0	0	0	1	1	1	0	0	0	0	0		1.192
189	208	0	0	0	0	0	0	0	1	1	1	1	0	0	0	0		1.224
189	208	0	0	0	0	0	0	1	0	0	0	0	0	0	0	0		2.0
189	208	0	0	0	0	0	0	1	0	0	0	1	0	0	0	0		2.32
189	208					•												•
189	208					•												•
189	208	1	1	1	1	1	1	1	1	1	1	1	0	0	0	0		255.224

Updating the chart could take several pages with these subnetworks, but entering in a few of them shows the following:

Information	Value
Class of IP address	B
Network Number	189.208.0.0
Mask	255.255.255.224
Total no. of subnetworks	2,048
Total no. of hosts per subnetwork	32
Subnet numbers	**189.208.0.0, 189.208.0.32, 189.208.0.64, 189.208.0.96, 189.208.0.128, 189.208.0.160, 189.208.0.192, 189.208.0.224, 189.208.1.0, 189.208.1.32, ...189.208.1.224, 189.208.2.0, 189.208.2.32, 189.208.2.64, 189.208.2.96, 189.208.2.128, . . . 189.208.255.224**
Broadcast addresses	??
No. of bits borrowed	11
Useable hosts per subnetwork	30
Useable subnets	2,046

The last bit of information is the broadcast numbers. Simply put 1s in the host bits for each subnetwork. Subnet Figure #28 shows this process.

Subnet Figure #28

Class B Network No.		Subnets								Hosts								Subnets
Octet 1	Octet 2	Octet3								Octet4								Subnets
		128	64	32	16	8	4	2	1	128	64	32	16	8	4	2		
189	208	0	0	0	0	0	0	0	0	0	0	0	1	1	1	1		0.31
189	208	0	0	0	0	0	0	0	0	0	0	1	1	1	1	1		0.63
189	208	0	0	0	0	0	0	0	0	0	1	0	1	1	1	1		0.95
189	208	0	0	0	0	0	0	0	0	0	1	1	1	1	1	1		0.127
189	208								•									•
189	208								•									•
189	208	0	0	0	0	0	0	0	1	1	1	0	1	1	1	1		1.223
189	208	0	0	0	0	0	0	0	1	1	1	1	1	1	1	1		1.255
189	208	0	0	0	0	0	0	1	0	0	0	0	1	1	1	1		2.31
189	208	0	0	0	0	0	0	1	0	0	0	1	1	1	1	1		2.63
189	208								•									•
189	208	1	1	1	1	1	1	1	1	1	1	1	1	1	1	1		255.255

Of course updating the list with the broadcasts is quite lengthy too, but some have been inserted into the chart to illustrate the point.

Information	Value
Class of IP address	B
Network Number	189.208.0.0
Mask	255.255.255.224
Total no. of subnetworks	2,048
Total no. of hosts per subnetwork	32
Subnet numbers	189.208.0.0, 189.208.0.32, 189.208.0.64, 189.208.0.96, 189.208.0.128, 189.208.0.160, 189.208.0.192, 189.208.0.224, 189.208.1.0, 189.208.1.32, ...189.208.1.224, 189.208.2.0, 189.208.2.32, 189.208.2.64, 189.208.2.96, 189.208.2.128, . . . 189.208.255.224
Broadcast addresses	**189.208.0.31, 189.208.0.63, 189.208.0.95, 189.208.0.127, ...189.208.1.223, 189.208.1.255, 189.208.2.31, 189.208.2.63, 189.208.2.95, 189.208.2.127 ...189.208.254.63, 189.208.254.95, 189.208.254.127, 189.208.254.159, 189.208.254.191, 189.208. 254.255, 189.208.255.63, 189.208.255.95, 189.208.255.127, 189.208.255.159, 189.208.255.191, 189.208.255.255**
No. of bits borrowed	11
Useable hosts per subnetwork	30
Useable subnets	2,046

Of course, each of the broadcast addresses is in groups of 32 just like the subnetworks are. Do not forget to treat each octet as a group of eight bits when determining subnetwork numbers and broadcast addresses!

Class B Problem 3

The network administrator is working on a computer with the IP address of 157.208.190.144. The mask shows as 255.255.255.192. On what subnet is the computer attached? The information known so far is summarized in the following table:

Information	Value
Class of IP address	B
Network Number	157.208.0.0
Mask	255.255.255.192
Total no. of subnetworks	??
Total no. of hosts per network/subnetwork	??
Subnet numbers	??
Broadcast addresses	??
No. of bits borrowed	??
Useable hosts per network/subnetwork	??
Useable subnets	??

The first step is to determine how many host bits have been borrowed for subnetting. Subnet Figure #29 shows the mask (the borrowed bits).

Subnet Figure #29

Mask

Class B Network No.		Subnets										Hosts						
Octet 1	Octet 2	Octet3										Octet4						
		128	64	32	16	8	4	2	1	128	64	32	16	8	4	2	1
255	255	1	1	1	1	1	1	1	1	1	1						

As seen in Subnet Figure 29, there are ten borrowed host bits. Knowing this information, the total number of subnets, useable subnets, total number of hosts, and useable hosts can be determined by using the formula 2^x (where x is either the number of bits borrowed or the remaining bits) and then entered into the chart as shown below.

Information	Value
Class of IP address	B
Network Number	157.208.0.0
Mask	255.255.255.192
Total no. of subnetworks	**1,024**
Total no. of hosts per network/subnetwork	**64**
Subnet numbers	??
Broadcast addresses	??
No. of bits borrowed	**10**
Useable hosts per network/subnetwork	**62**
Useable subnets	**1,022**

The next thing is to determine the subnetwork numbers. Subnet Figure #30 shows a partial illustration of subnetwork numbers for this problem.

Subnet Figure #30

Class B Network No.		Subnets											Hosts				Subnets
Octet 1	Octet 2	Octet3								Octet4							Subnets
		128	64	32	16	8	4	2	1	128	64	32	16	8	4	2	
157	208	0	0	0	0	0	0	0	0	0	0	1	0	0	0	0	0.32
157	208	0	0	0	0	0	0	0	0	0	1	0	0	0	0	0	0.64
157	208	0	0	0	0	0	0	0	0	0	1	1	0	0	0	0	0.96
157	208	0	0	0	0	0	0	0	0	1	0	0	0	0	0	0	0.128
157	208	0	0	0	0	0	0	0	0	1	0	1	0	0	0	0	0.160
157	208	0	0	0	0	0	0	0	0	1	1	0	0	0	0	0	0.192
157	208	0	0	0	0	0	0	0	0	1	1	1	0	0	0	0	0.224
157	208					•											•
157	208					•											•
157	208	1	0	1	1	1	1	1	0	0	1	0	0	0	0	0	190.64
157	208	1	0	1	1	1	1	1	0	0	1	1	0	0	0	0	190.96
157	208	1	0	1	1	1	1	1	0	1	0	0	0	0	0	0	190.128
157	208	1	0	1	1	1	1	1	0	1	0	1	0	0	0	0	190.160
157	208	1	0	1	1	1	1	1	0	1	1	0	0	0	0	0	190.192
157	208	1	0	1	1	1	1	1	0	1	1	1	0	0	0	0	190.224
157	208	1	0	1	1	1	1	1	1	0	0	0	0	0	0	0	191.0
157	208	1	0	1	1	1	1	1	1	0	0	1	0	0	0	0	191.32
157	208					•											•
157	208					•											•
157	208	1	1	1	1	1	1	1	1	1	1	1	0	0	0	0	255.224

The answer to the problem is actually in Subnet Figure #30. The subnetwork numbers shown are the beginning address (the number for "the wire") for the subnet. For example, subnetwork 157.208.190.0 has addresses that extend from 157.208.190.0 through 157.208.190.31. Subnetwork 157.208.190.32 has addresses that extend from 157.208.190.32 through 157.208.190.63. The computer in this example has an IP address of 157.208.190.144. The solution is found by looking at a subnetwork number that is the smallest number below *190.144*. The answer is subnetwork 157.208.190.128. Since the solution is solved, there is no need to finish the chart or determine broadcast addresses. However, to determine the broadcast address for each subnetwork, the same method is used as shown before—put 1s in all of the host addresses and determine the decimal value for the octet.

> A shortcut for solving a problem that gives an IP address and a mask and asks for the subnetwork number is to put the IP address and mask in binary and *and* the two numbers together. Then convert the result to dotted decimal notation. Remember when *anding*, the only way to get a *1* is by anding two 1s together. Subnet Figure #31 shows this process.

Subnet Figure #31

	1 2 6 3 1 8 4 2 6 8 4 2 1	1 2 6 3 1 8 4 2 6 8 4 2 1	1 2 6 3 1 8 4 2 6 8 4 2 1	1 2 6 3 1 8 4 2 6 8 4 2 1
IP in binary	1 0 0 1 1 1 0 1	1 1 0 1 0 0 0 0	1 0 1 1 1 1 1 0	1 0 0 1 0 0 0 0
Mask in binary	1 1 1 1 1 1 1 1	1 1 1 1 1 1 1 1	1 1 1 1 1 1 1 1	1 1 0 0 0 0 0 0
Subnet in binary	1 0 0 1 1 1 0 1	1 1 0 1 0 0 1 0	1 0 1 1 1 1 1 0	1 0 0 0 0 0 0 0

Subnet in dotted decimal notation: 157.208.190.128

CLASS A SUBNETTING

Class A subnetting is handled the same as Class B's and C's with the exception of how many host bits can be borrowed for subnetting. With Class A IP addresses, the first octet (8 bits) represents the network number and the last three octets (24 bits) represent host bits. Subnet Figure #32 shows this concept.

Subnet Figure #32

Class A Network No.	Hosts		
Octet1	Octet2	Octet3	Octet4

When subnetting Class A IP addresses, bits are borrowed from the left-most host bits and can extend across octets 2, 3, and 4 because these are the Class A host bits. Subnet Figure #33 shows a Class A IP address with eleven bits borrowed from the first and second octets.

Subnet Figure #33

Class A Network No.	Hosts																							
Octet1	Octet2								Octet3								Octet4							
	128	64	32	16	8	4	2	1	128	64	32	16	8	4	2	1	128	64	32	16	8	4	2	1

With Class A subnets, the same formula, 2^x = total number of subnets (where x is the number of bits borrowed) is still used. The useable subnets is found by subtracting two from the result, just like it was done with Class B and Class C subnets. In Subnet Figure #33, 11 bits are borrowed from octets 2 and 3. 2^{11} = 2,048 total subnets and subtracting two yields the useable subnets—2,048 – 2 = 2,046.

The same formula is also used for determining total number of hosts. In Subnet Figure #33, 13 host bits remain. 2^{13} = 8,192 total host addresses. Subtracting two yields the useable host addresses—8,192 – 2 = 8,190. Keep consistent in how you solve IP subnetting problems and no exam can trip you up.

The normal subnet mask used with Class A IP addresses is 255.0.0.0. When implementing subnets, the second, third, and fourth octets can be used and therefore the mask changes for these octets. Subnet Figure #34 shows how the mask is obtained when borrowing 11 bits from a Class A address.

Subnet Figure #34

Mask

Class A Network No.	Hosts																							
Octet1	Octet2								Octet3								Octet4							
	128	64	32	16	8	4	2	1	128	64	32	16	8	4	2	1	128	64	32	16	8	4	2	1
255	1	1	1	1	1	1	1	1	1	1	1													

When borrowing 11 bits, the mask has 1s set in the second octet and the first three bits of the third octet. Octet 2 is all 1s, so the mask for octet 2 is 255. Octet 3 has 1s set in the first three bit positions. Add these bit values together to get 224. (128 + 64 + 32 = 224). The mask for a Class A network with 11 bits borrowed is 255.255.224.0.

The best way to learn Class A addresses (as it has been for the other classes) is to practice. They are done the exact same way as the other addresses except there are more host bits from which to borrow.

Class A Problem 1

The Super Duper Company has 5,000 locations world-wide. In each location, there are over 1000 computers. The super Duper Company has leased one Class A IP address, 19.0.0.0. One option for the company is to divide the class A address into subnetworks. The first task for the network administrator is to determine how many bits to borrow for subnetting. Subnet Table #2 summarizes some borrowed bits with corresponding number of subnets.

Subnet Table #2

Borrowed Bits	No. of Host Bits	Total Subnets	Useable Subnets	Total Hosts	Useable Hosts
5	19	32	30	524288	524286
6	18	64	62	262144	262142
7	17	128	126	131072	131070
8	16	256	254	65536	65534
9	15	512	510	32768	32766
10	14	1024	1022	16384	16382
11	13	2048	2046	8192	8190
12	12	4096	4094	4096	4094
13	**11**	**8192**	**8190**	**2048**	**2046**
14	10	16384	16382	1024	1022
15	9	32768	32766	512	510
16	8	65536	65534	256	254
17	7	131072	131070	128	126

Looking at Subnet Table #2, one can see that to assign subnetwork numbers to 5,000 locations, the Super Duper Co. must borrow 13 host bits. This also allows for 2,046 host addresses per location. Subnet Figure #35 shows how the subnet mask is determined using the 13 host bits for subnetworks.

Subnet Figure #35

Mask

Class A Network No.	Hosts																								
Octet1	Octet2								Octet3								Octet4							
	128	64	32	16	8	4	2	1	128	64	32	16	8	4	2	1	128	64	32	16	8	4	2	1
▶255	1	1	1	1	1	1	1	1	1	1	1	1	1											

With 13 bits borrowed, the mask has the standard 1s in the first octet (255), 1s in the second octet (255), and 1s in 5 bits of the third octet (248—128 + 64 + 32 + 16 + 8). So, the mask for the Super Duper Co. is 255.255.248.0. The chart below shows the information determined so far.

Information	Value
Class of IP address	A
Network Number	19.0.0.0
Mask	**255.255.248.0**
Total no. of subnetworks	8,192
Total no. of hosts per subnetwork	2,048
Subnet numbers	??
Broadcast addresses	??
No. of bits borrowed	11
Useable hosts per subnetwork	2,046
Useable subnets	8,190

Determining subnetwork numbers is done exactly the same way as Class B and Class C addresses are subnetted. Subnet Figure #36 shows a partial view of the Class A subnetworks. Octet 1 is not divided into bit positions because it is always 19. Octet 4 is not subdivided because it is always contains 0s for the subnetwork number. For presentation, Octet 4 is not shown, only Octets 2 and 3 where the subnetting occurs.

Subnet Figure #36

Mask

Class A Network No.	Hosts																Subnets
Octet1	Octet2								Octet3								Subnets
	128	64	32	16	8	4	2	1	128	64	32	16	8	4	2	1	
19	0	0	0	0	0	0	0	0	0	0	0	0	0	0	0	0	19.0.0.0
19	0	0	0	0	0	0	0	0	0	0	0	0	1	0	0	0	19.0.8.0
19	0	0	0	0	0	0	0	0	0	0	0	1	0	0	0	0	19.0.16.0
19	0	0	0	0	0	0	0	0	0	0	0	1	1	0	0	0	19.0.24.0
19							•							0	0	0	•
19							•							0	0	0	•
19	0	0	0	0	0	0	0	0	1	1	1	1	1	0	0	0	19.0.248.0
19	0	0	0	0	0	0	0	1	0	0	0	0	0	0	0	0	19.1.0.0
19	0	0	0	0	0	0	0	1	0	0	0	0	1	0	0	0	19.1.8.0
19	0	0	0	0	0	0	0	1	0	0	0	1	0	0	0	0	19.1.16.0
19							•							0	0	0	•
19	1	1	1	1	1	1	1	1	1	1	1	1	1	0	0	0	19.255.248.0

As you can see in Subnet Figure #36, there are 13 borrowed host bits. Subnetwork numbers increment in groups of eight (19.0.0.0, 19.0.8.0, 19.0.16.0, and so on up to 19.255.248.0). A few of the subnetwork numbers are filled into the chart so you can see the trend. To determine the broadcast address for each subnetwork, the same method used with Class C and Class B address is used—put all 1s in the host address and determine the decimal value (or take the shortcut and subtract one from the next subnetwork number). The final chart is as follows:

Information	Value
Class of IP address	A
Network Number	19.0.0.0
Mask	255.255.248.0
Total no. of subnetworks	8,192
Total no. of hosts per subnetwork	2,048
Subnet numbers	**19.0.8.0, 19.0.16.0, 19.0.24.0, 19.0.32.0 through 19.0.248.0, 19.1.0.0, 19.1.8.0, 19.1.16.0 through 19.1.248, 19.2.0.0 through 19.255.248.0**
Broadcast addresses	**19.0.15.255, 19.0.23.255, 19.0.31.255, 19.0.39.255 etc. through 19.0.255.255, 19.1.7.255, 19.1.15.255, 19.1.31.255 etc. through 19.1.255.255, 19.2.7.255 through 19.255.255.255**
No. of bits borrowed	11
Useable hosts per subnetwork	2,046
Useable subnets	8,190

Writing all of the subnet numbers and broadcast addresses would take up page after page of this text, so enough numbers are inserted for you to get the idea of the pattern. Once you do a couple of numbers and see the patterns, you can determine all of the subnet numbers.

 Name _____

SUBNETTING REVIEW QUESTIONS

1. A company has received a Class C IP address for their four networks. How many bits need to be borrowed?

2. A company uses a Class C mask of 255.255.255.224. What is the maximum number of hosts per subnetwork?

3. How many bits are borrowed in a Class C address if the mask is 255.255.255.240?

4. Given the IP address 199.14.180.4, what class IP address is this?

5. Given the IP address of 201.60.250.91 and a mask of 255.255.255.248, what is the subnetwork number?

6. Given the IP address 210.199.184.66 and the fact that a company borrows three bits to subnet, what mask is used?

7. What is the standard subnet mask for a Class C address?

8. What is the maximum number of bits that can be borrowed when using a Class C address?

9. What is the minimum number of bits that can be borrowed when using a Class C address?

10. Given the IP address 204.16.8.0 and a mask of 255.255.255.240. What is the first useable subnetwork number?

11. Given the IP address 197.56.2.141 and a mask of 255.255.255.192, what is the broadcast address for this subnetwork?

12. Given the broadcast address of 202.202.159.159 and a mask of 255.255.255.248, what is the subnetwork number?

13. A company has a policy of only 25 hosts per subnet. They have 20 networks. How many class C addresses does the company need?

14. How many bits are set in a standard Class C mask?

15. What is the maximum number of hosts on a Class C network?

16. Given the mask of 255.255.255.224 and an IP address of 200.200.200.200, on what subnetwork is the device?

17. Given an IP address of 193.15.10.105 and a mask of 255.255.255.252, what is the subnetwork number?

18. Given the mask of 255.255.255.248 and the fact that a Class C address is being used, how many host are on each subnet?

19. Given the IP address of 206.19.1.186 and a mask of 255.255.255.192, what are the two unusable subnets?

20. Given the IP address of 199.199.144.43 and a mask of 255.255.255.224, what is the last useable subnetwork number?

21. Given the IP address 130.14.207.39 and a mask of 255.255.240.0, how many total subnets are available?

22. Given the IP address 130.14.207.39 and a mask of 255.255.240.0, what is the subnetwork number associated with this IP address?

23. Given the IP address 188.188.188.188 and a mask of 255.255.255.128, what is the subnetwork number associated with this IP address?

24. Given the IP address 191.10.59.63 and six bits are borrowed, what is the mask?

25. A company has a Class B IP address, what is the maximum number of bits that can be borrowed and still have 100 hosts per subnetwork?

26. A company is leasing a Class A IP address and has 3000 networks. How many bits do they need to borrow?

27. Given the IP address 15.200.166.41 and a mask of 255.252.0.0, what is the subnetwork number?

28. What is the mask when 15 bits are borrowed and a Class A network address is being used?

29. Given the IP address 14.168.29.180 and a mask of 255.255.192.0, how many bits are borrowed for subnetting?

30. Given the IP address 14.168.29.180 and a mask of 255.255.192.0, what is the broadcast for this subnetwork?

31. How many bits are set with a Class A subnet mask of 255.255.240.0?

32. Given the IP address 120.150.150.150 and a mask of 255.255.240.0, what is the subnetwork number and broadcast address?

NOTES

B

Appendix B:

Certification Review Questions

Name _____

Question 1.   A 25-pin female port on the computer is a _____ port.

    A. Video
    B. Parallel
    C. Serial
    D. Network

Question 2.   Serial ports on the computer are _____. (Pick all that apply.)

    A. 9-pin male
    B. 9-pin female
    C. 25-pin male
    D. 25-pin female

Question 3.   The RJ-45 jack is most commonly found on _____.

    [Modems / Ethernet adapters / Video cards / Zip Drives]

Question 4.   A 9-pin female port on the computer can be _____. (Pick all that apply.)

    A. Monochrome video port
    B. Modem
    C. Serial port
    D. Token Ring port
    E. Parallel port

Question 5.   The RJ-11 port is for _____ .

    A. Monitors
    B. Networks
    C. Printers
    D. Modems

Question 6.   The speed rating shown on a microprocessor is for _____ operations.

    A. Internal
    B. External

Question 7.   A 15-pin female computer port is for _____ .

     A. Video
     B. Modems
     C. Printers
     D. Network adapters

Question 8.   Which of the following describes functions of the microprocessor? (Pick all that apply.)

     A. Distributes power to the adapters, devices, and motherboard
     B. Handles communications between computer components
     C. Stores user documents permanently
     D. Processes software instructions

Question 9.   A 100MHz 80486DX4 microprocessor runs at _____MHz externally.

     A. 25
     B. 33
     C. 50
     D. 75
     E. 100

Question 10.   Which of the following is *not* an Intel microprocessor?

     A. 80386DX
     B. 80486SX
     C. 80586DX
     D. 80487SX

Question 11.   A user wants to buy a computer for desktop publishing. What architecture or local bus would be best for video performance?

     A. PC Card
     B. ISA
     C. EISA
     D. AGP
     E. PCI
     F. VL-bus

Question 12.   Into which PC Card slot will a Type II card fit? (Pick all that apply.)

     [I / II / III]

Question 13.   What architecture or local bus can provide the best performance when transferring between the Pentium II microprocessor and an adapter?

    A. PC Card

    B. ISA

    C. EISA

    D. MCA

    E. PCI

    F. VL-bus

Question 14.   What architecture or local bus is primarily for laptop computers?

    A. PC Card

    B. ISA

    C. EISA

    D. MCA

    E. PCI

    F. VL-bus

Question15.   What math coprocessor goes with the 80486SX?

    A. 80487

    B. 80487SX

    C. 80486DX

    D. 80486SX

Question 16.   If a multimeter is used to check the power supply output that goes to the hard drive, to what setting will the multimeter be set?

    A. AC volts

    B. DC volts

    C. Ohms

    D. Farads

Question 17.   If a multimeter is used to check the input to the power supply, to what setting will the multimeter be set?

    A. AC volts

    B. DC volts

    C. Ohms

    D. Farads

Question 18. The ability to transfer information between devices without microprocessor intervention is _____.

    A. Bus mastering
    B. Direct memory access
    C. Plug and play
    D. High memory access

Question 19. Motors inside the computer normally use _____ volts and electronic components normally use _____ volts.

    A. -5 / -12
    B. +5 / +12
    C. +12 / +5
    D. -12 / -5

Question 20. When a computer is powered on, a cursor does *not* appear in the monitor's left corner. Which of the following is the LEAST suspect?

    A. Monitor
    B. Power supply
    C. Hard drive
    D. Motherboard

Question 21. [T / F] Maintaining polarity is important when measuring DC volts.

Question 22. Which of the following devices ensures that power is constantly provided to the computer?

    A. Surge protector
    B. Power Conditioner
    C. Power Supply
    D. UPS

Question 23. Which of the following items should you check when replacing a power supply? (Pick all that apply.)

    A. The correct wattage
    B. The power supply accepts AC input
    C. The size of the power supply as well as the position of the on/off switch
    D. The output voltages provided to the hard drive

Question 24. [T / F] A voltage spike can affect any component even if a surge suppressor is installed.

Question 25.   In the United States, a selectable power supply should be set to the _____ setting.

    A. 110
    B. 220
    C. 5
    D. 12

Question 26.   ACPI is a standard for _____.

    [Power management / PCI adapters / Laptops only / Printers]

Question 27.   Which of the following indicate the power supply is faulty? (Pick all that apply.)

    A. The fan on the power supply does not turn
    B. The power LED on the front of the computer does not come on
    C. The power light on the monitor does not come on
    D. There is no cursor in the upper left corner of the monitor

Question 28.   Which of the following are important to consider when adding an adapter? (Pick all that apply.)

    A. Unique interrupt
    B. Expansion slot location
    C. Unique I/O address
    D. Unique ROM address

Question 29.   What is the name of the routine that is performed when a computer is powered on?

    A. Startup test routine
    B. BIOS startup
    C. System check routine
    D. Power on self test

Question 30.   What power supply is used with a Pentium 4 motherboard?

    [SFX / LPX / ATX12V / NLX]

Question 31.   Which of the following helps determine if a problem is software or hardware? (Pick all that apply.)

    A. Did POST produce any audio errors or display any error codes?
    B. Single-stepping through the AUTOEXEC.BAT and CONFIG.SYS files
    C. Determining if the problem only occurs in one software application
    D. Running diagnostics on the hardware

Question 32.   Which of the following is NOT true about memory?

  A. An access time of 50ns is faster than 60ns
  B. A bank of memory contains chips of the same capacity
  C. All memory banks must contain chips
  D. Memory POST errors usually being with a 2

Question 33.   A user has two 8MB 72-pin SIMMs in a Pentium. The user wants to upgrade to 32MB. Two SIMM sockets are available on the motherboard. What will you recommend?

  A. Remove the two 8MB SIMMs and buy one 32MB SIMM
  B. Remove the two 8MB SIMMs and buy two 16MB SIMMs
  C. Add one 16MB SIMM
  D. Add two 8MB SIMMs

Question 34.   Which of the following commands allows use of the UMBs by TSRs?

  A. DEVICE=C:\WINDOWS\HIMEM.SYS
  B. DEVICE=C:\WINDOWS\EMM386.EXE
  C. DOS=HIGH
  D. DOS=UMB

Question 35.   [T / F]   Windows 95 needs the SmartDrive command in the AUTOEXEC.BAT file to acccess extended memory.

Question 36.   [T / F]   Virtual memory is faster than a RAM drive.

Question 37.   A user has a mouse configured for COM1, IRQ3. After installing an internal modem to COM2, IRQ4 I/O address 3F8, neither the mouse, nor the modem works. What is the most likely problem?

  A. The modem is incompatible with the operating system
  B. IRQ conflict
  C. I/O address conflict
  D. COM port conflict

Question 38.   Which of the following provides the fastest access?

  A. CD-ROM
  B. DRAM
  C. SRAM
  D. Hard drive
  E. Floppy drive

Question 39.   You have just installed a new CD-ROM drive and sound card, but no sound comes out of the speakers. What will be your first troubleshooting step?

A. Replace the CD-ROM
B. Check the CD-ROM drive for an IRQ conflict
C. Replace the sound card
D. Check that the CD-ROM's audio cable connects to the sound card

Question 40.   A 601 error code indicates a _____ problem.

A. RAM
B. Hard drive
C. Floppy drive
D. CMOS

Question 41.   If a SCSI device driver is causing the computer system to hang, what should be the next step?

A. Single-step through the CONFIG.SYS until the problem device driver is discovered
B. Bypass the AUTOEXEC.BAT file
C. Bypass the CONFIG.SYS file
D. Bypass both the AUTOEXEC.BAT and CONFIG.SYS files

Question 42.   What is the *first* step when installing a new hard drive in a computer today?

A. Copy the system files over
B. Partition the new hard drive
C. Low-level format the new hard drive
D. High-level format the new hard drive
E. Copy the COMMAND.COM file over from a bootable floppy

Question 43.   What is the *last* step when installing a new bootable hard drive in a computer today?

A. Copy the system files over
B. Partition the new hard drive
C. Low-level format the new hard drive
D. High-level format the new hard drive
E. Copy the COMMAND.COM file over from a bootable floppy

Question 44.   SCANDISK _____

A. places files in non-contiguous sectors into contiguous sectors.
B. partitions the hard drive.
C. partitions the floppy disk.
D. checks and fixes problems in the FAT and with lost or cross-linked files.

Question 45.   Scenario: A computer has an internal SCSI device and an external SCSI device connected to the same adapter. Which of the following is *false* concerning termination?

    A. The internal device must be terminated
    B. The external device must be terminated
    C. The adapter must be terminated

Question 46.   Which of the following commands performs disk caching?

    A. DEFRAG
    B. CACHE
    C. SMARTDRV
    D. HDCACHE

Question 47.   [T / F] All new hard drives must be high level formatted before data can be stored on it.

Question 48.   What command is used to assign a logical drive a drive letter for the first time?

    A. DEBUG
    B. FORMAT
    C. ASSIGN
    D. FDISK

Question 49.   A computer boots up with the message "Bad or Missing Command Interpreter." What should be done?

    A. Change the drive type in CMOS
    B. Copy over COMMAND.COM from a bootable floppy disk
    C. Re-partition the hard drive
    D. High-level format the hard drive
    E. Use DEBUG to recover from the error

Question 50.   What is the maximum FAT16 partition size that is compatible between all Microsoft operating systems?

    A. 32MB
    B. 2GB
    C. 4GB
    D. 8GB

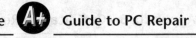

Question 51.   The two primary specifications for evaluating a CD-ROM drive are:

     A.   Access speed
     B.   Transfer rate
     C.   Compatibility with other devices
     D.   Acceleration speed
     F.   Mean time between failures

Question 52.   [T / F]   The SmartDrive program should not be used with Windows 95 in normal operations.

Question 53.   To install a CD-ROM drive as a second device on the IDE connector, the CD-ROM drive must:

     A.   be set to SCSI ID 1
     B.   be terminated
     C.   be set to SLAVE
     D.   be set to drive select 1

Question 54.   [T / F]   Adapters frequently have ROM chips installed on them.

Question 55.   Scenario: A newly installed CD-ROM drive will not operate. Which of the following would be checked *first*?

     A.   Check the hard drive's interface cabling
     B.   Check the audio cable
     C.   Check the configuration settings such as the SCSI ID, terminators, or the Master/Slave setting
     D.   Verify that the CD-ROM drive's device driver loads
     E.   Verify that the sound card's device driver loads
     F.   Verify that the SmartDrive program loads
     G.   Verify that the MSCDEX program loads

Question 56.   Scenario: The light on the CD-ROM lights up when the CD-ROM device driver loads in CONFIG.SYS, but the CD-ROM drive does not appear as a drive letter in Window's File Manager. Which of the following is checked *first*?

     A.   Check the interface cabling
     B.   Check the audio cable
     C.   Check the configuration settings such as the SCSI ID, terminators, or the Master/Slave setting
     D.   Verify that the CD-ROM drive's device driver loads
     E.   Verify that the sound card's device driver loads
     F.   Verify that the SmartDrive program loads
     G.   Verify that the MSCDEX program loads

Question 57.   Which of the following is the most common problem with sound card installations:

    A. Plug and Play configurations
    B. Resource conflicts such as interrupts, I/O addresses, DMA channels
    C. Audio output
    D. Compatibility with CD-ROM drives

Question 58.   A SCSI CD-ROM drive is to be installed in a computer. The CD-ROM must be set to:

    A. SCSI ID 0
    B. SCSI ID 1
    C. A SCSI ID not used by any other device or the SCSI adapter
    D. Master
    E. Slave

Question 59.   [T / F]   Hard drives are faster than RAM.

Question 60.   Which of the following COM ports are used with IRQ3? (Pick all that apply.)

    A. COM1
    B. COM2
    C. COM3
    D. COM4

Question 61.   Which of the following ports allow information to be transferred between two devices, two computers, or a device and a computer? (Pick all that apply.)

    A. Serial port
    B. IDE port
    C. Video port
    D. Parallel port
    E. Mouse port

Question 62.   Approximately how many bits per second does a 28.8 modem transmit?

    A. 270-290
    B. 2,700-2,900
    C. 28,000-29,000
    D. 280,000-290,000
    E. 2,800,000-2,900,000

Question 63. The smallest video element on a monitor is a _____.

    A. dot pitch
    B. pixel
    C. aperture grille
    D. dot triad

Question 64. What is the minimum amount of memory for a 1024x768 resolution with 256K colors?

    A. 512K
    B. 1MB
    C. 2MB
    D. 4MB

Question 65. After installing a new video adapter, Windows 95 locks, what should you do?

    A. Buy a new video adapter
    B. Reinstall the old video adapter
    C. Restart Windows 95 in the MS-DOS mode
    D. Restart Windows 95 in the Safe mode

Question 66. Which of the following devices is affected most by EMI?

    A. Printer
    B. Mouse
    C. Hard drive
    D. Monitor
    E. Floppy drive

Question 67. Which of the following devices should you avoid wearing an anti-static wrist strap when repairing?

    A. Monitor
    B. Ink jet printer
    C. Hard drive
    D. Laser printer

Question 68. Which of the following printers should you avoid connecting to a manual switch box?

    A. Dot matrix
    B. Ink jet
    C. Laser
    D. Thermal

Question 69. Which of the following are the most common pin configurations for dot matrix printers? (Pick all that apply.)

A. 9
B. 18
C. 24
D. 27
E. 32

Question 70. What is the *first* step when installing a printer?

A. Take the printer out of the box and inspect it for damage
B. Load the print driver
C. Connect the cable to the computer
D. Connect the cable to the printer

Question 71. What step of the laser printing process places the image on the drum?

A. Conditioning
B. Fusing
C. Transferring
D. Developing

Question 72. What step in the laser printing processes follows the transfer stage?

A. Charge
B. Fuse
C. Develop
D. Expose

Question 73. What laser printer part allows the proper amount of toner to the drum surface?

A. Toner roller
B. Toner regulator
C. Density control blade
D. Drum sensor

Question 74. Which of the following parts is least likely to cause a paper jam in a laser printer?

A. Fuser rollers
B. Erase lamp
C. Drum
D. Transfer rollers

Question 75.   The charge applied to the laser's drum during the conditioning stage applies a
                   _____ voltage.

      A.   Negative
      B.   Positive
      C.   Neutral

Question 76.   Paper should be printed on which side first? (Pick all that apply.)

      A.   Side with the arrow
      B.   Felt side
      C.   Wax side
      D.   Wire side

Question 77.   [T / F]   TrueType fonts are scalable.

Question 78.   [T / F]   Soft fonts are faster than internal fonts.

Question 79.   Which of the following extensions are executable in DOS? (Pick all that apply.)

      A.   .TXT
      B.   .BAT
      C.   .INI
      D.   .EXE
      E.   .COM
      F.   .SYS

Question 80.   Which of the following commands will keep users from accidentally erasing the
                   AUTOEXEC.BAT file?

      A.   REN +H C:\AUTOEXEC.BAT
      B.   NONERASE C:\AUTOEXEC.BAT
      C.   UNDELETE C:\AUTOEXEC.BAT
      D.   ATTRIB +R C:\AUTOEXEC.BAT

Question 81.   Which of the following files make a DOS disk bootable? (Pick all that apply.)

      A.   IO.SYS
      B.   AUTOEXEC.BAT
      C.   MSDOS.SYS
      D.   COMMAND.COM
      E.   CONFIG.SYS
      F.   WIN.COM

Question 82.   Which of the following files is a common device driver found in CONFIG.SYS?

     A. MOUSE.EXE

     B. PATH=C:\WINDOWS

     C. MOUSE.SYS

     D. DEVICE.SYS

Question 83.   Which of the following keystrokes bypasses the AUTOEXEC.BAT and CONFIG.SYS files in Windows 9x?

     A. F1 and pick the Bypass option

     B. F3 and pick the Bypass option

     C. F5 and pick the Safe Mode option

     D. F8 and pick the Safe Mode option

Question 84.   Which of the following is an example of when you would use the System Monitor tool?

     A. When the "Missing Operating System" message appears

     B. When Device Manager shows a resource conflict

     C. When a system that has 384MB of RAM shows a message that 90% of system resources are in use

     D. When you have ample hard drive space, ample RAM, but when you go to print, an error message appears that the printer needs servicing

Question 85.   Which of the following files are considered part of the Windows 9x registry? (Pick all that apply.)

     A. COMMAND.COM

     B. AUTOEXEC.BAT

     C. USER.DAT

     D. SYSTEM.INI

     E. CONFIG.SYS

     F. SYSTEM.DAT

Question 86.   Which of the following would be done when Windows 95 displays "Starting Windows 9x," but never boots?

     A. Boot the computer into MS-DOS mode and reload Windows 95

     B. Boot the computer into Safe Mode and check for a device conflict

     C. Boot the computer from a bootable disk and reload the registry

     D. Repartition the hard drive for a 32-bit File Allocation Table

NOTES

Appendix C:
Glossary

1.2MB disk A 5.25" floppy disk without a hub ring commonly known as double-sided, double-density disk that only works in a 1.2MB floppy drive.

1.44MB disk A high density 3.5" floppy disk having both write-protect and high density windows that cannot be used in 720KB floppy drives.

2.88MB disk A 3.5 inch data storage diskette known as extra-high density and labeled EHD or ED. These are relatively rare because they work only in 2.88MB floppy drives.

360KB disk A 5.25" floppy disk commonly known as double-sided, double-density. Normally has a reinforced center hub ring and works best in a 360KB floppy drive.

3DNow! A microprocessor CPU technology developed by Advanced Micro Devices for 3-D applications.

56Kbps modem A modem that produces higher transmission speeds and uses traditional phone lines. Actual modem speed is determine by the number of analog to digital conversions that occur through the phone system.

720KB disk A 3.5" floppy disk commonly known as double-sided, double-density, and works best in a 720KB floppy drive.

A

A3D An audio standard developed by Aureal Seminconductor that supports hardware acceleration and allows simulation of sounds in certain environments such as a tunnel or underwater.

a:drive The product name of a floptical drive developed using a patented laser servo technology. Also known as a LS-120 drive.

AAC (Advanced Audio Compression) a sound file format that provides file compression.

AC (Alternating Current) The type of electrical power from a wall outlet.

AC circuit tester A device used to check a wall outlet's wiring.

access time The amount of time it takes to retrieve data from memory or a device.

ACPI (Advanced Configuration and Power Interface) Allows motherboard and operating system to control the power needs and modes of operation of various devices.

active matrix A technology used in LCD monitors where displays have a transistor for each pixel. Contrast with passive matrix.

active terminator A type of end to a SCSI chain that allows for longer cable distance and provides correct voltage for SCSI signals.

actuator arm Holds the read/write heads over hard disk platters.

adapter Electronic circuit card that connects into an expansion slot. Also called a controller, card, controller card, circuit card, circuit board, and adapter board.

Add Printer wizard A Windows utility used to install a local or network printer.

ADSL (Asymmetrical DSL) Provides speeds up to 8.4Mbps, but 1.5M is the most common rate. Provides faster downloads than uploads.

AGP (Accelerated Graphics Port) An extension of the PCI bus (a port) that speeds up 3-D graphics in software applications. AGP is used for video adapters.

amp A measurement of current.

analog monitor A monitor that uses analog signals to obtain different color levels.

anti-static wrist strap A strap connecting the technician to the computer that equalizes the voltage potential between the two to prevent ESD.

aperture grille An alternative to the shadow mask used by Sony in their Trinitron monitors that uses wires instead of holes to direct the color beams to the front of the monitor.

application layer Layer 7 of the OSI model that defines how applications and the computer interact with a network, and negotiates services such as authentication, error recovery and quality of service.

apply button Located in bottom right corner of a dialog box; clicking on it saves any changes the user has applied to the window.

APM (Advanced Power Management) Allows the operating system to control the power needs of the computer's hard drive and monitor when computer is not in use. It cannot control external devices. The APM standard has since evolved into an ACPI standard.

architecture A set of rules governing the physical structure of the computer. It regulates bit transfer rate, adapter SETUP configuration, and so forth. Three types of architectures used in PCs are ISA, EISA, and MCA.

archive attribute A designation that can be attached to a file that marks whether the file has changed since it was last backed up by a software program. The RESTORE, XCOPY, and MSBACKUP commands use the archive attribute as well as third party backup software applications.

ARCnet   (Attached Resource Computer network) One of the early Local Area Networks but is now surpassed by Token Ring and Ethernet network adapters. An ARCnet adapter could have a BNC connector, a RJ-45 connector, or all three. It may also have DIP switches.

ASD.EXE   (Automatic Skip Driver) A command used in Windows 98 that determines which drivers fail to load during startup. After two failed attempts, ASD marks the device as defective and turns off the device driver. Access the Automatic Skip Driver Agent by clicking on the Start button ➲ Programs ➲ Accessories ➲ System Tools ➲ System Information. Click on the Tools menu option and select the Automatic Skip Driver Agent drop-down menu selection. If no problems are found, a dialog box appears on the screen.

ASPI   (Advanced SCSI Programming Interface) A type of software drive that supports SCSI devices.

asynchronous   Transmissions that do not require a clock signal, but instead use extra bits to track the beginning and end of the data.

ATA standard   The original IDE interface that supported two drives.

ATAPI   (AT Attachment Packet Interface) The hardware side of the IDE specification that supports devices like CD-ROM and tape drives.

ATTRIB   A command used to designate a file as hidden, archived, read-only, or as a system file.

AUTOEXEC.BAT   A file that contains multiple lines that executes every time the computer boots. Today's operating systems use a startup folder, but the AUTOEXEC.BAT file is still processed for older, 16-bit commands.

average access time   The time required to find and retrieve data on a disk or in memory.

average seek time   The time required for a drive to move randomly about the disk.

B

backbone   Network part that connects multiple buildings, floors, networks, etc., together.

bandwidth   The communications channel width that defines its capacity for carrying data.

bank   One or more memory chips that work together to transfer data to and from the CPU and a device.

baseband A networking technology where the entire cable bandwidth is used to transmit a digital signal.

baseline A snapshot of a computer's performance (memory, CPU usage, etc.) during normal operations (before a problem or slowdown is apparent).

basic disk A Windows 2000 term for a drive that has been partitioned and formatted.

basic storage A Windows 2000 term for a partition. Contrast with dynamic storage.

batch file A file that has the extension of BAT that executes multiple commands when a single command is entered at a prompt. The AUTOEXEC.BAT file is an example of a batch file.

baud The number of times an analog signal changes in one second. If a signal is sent that changes 600 times in one second, the device communicates at 600 baud. Today's signaling methods (modulation techniques to be technically accurate), modems can send several bits in one cycle, so it is more accurate to talk in bits per second.

BEDO (Burst Extended Data Out) A type of memory that speeds up sequential accesses to a memory chip.

Berg connector A type of power connector that extends from the computer's power supply to various devices.

BIOS See ROM BIOS.

bi-directional printing Printing that occurs from left to right and right to left to provide higher printing speeds.

bit An electrically charged 1 or 0.

blackout A total loss of AC power.

boot A term used to describe the process of a computer coming to a useable condition.

boot partition A type of partition found in Windows NT and 2000 that contains the operating system. The boot partition can be in the same partition as the system partition, which is the part of the hard drive that holds hardware-specific files.

boot sector Previous called DBR or DOS boot record, this section of a disk contains information about the system files (the files used to boot the operating system).

boot sector virus   A virus program placed in a computer's boot sector code, which can then load into memory. Once in RAM, the virus takes control of computer operations. The virus can spread to installed drives and drives located on a network.

boot volume   A Windows 2000 term that describes a storage unit that contains the 2000 operating system.

bps   (bits per second) The number of 1s and 0s transmitted per second.

breakout box   A device that allows serial connection pinouts.

broadband   A networking technology where the cable bandwidth is divided into multiple channels; thus, the cable can carry simultaneous voice, video and data.

broadcast   See broadcast address

broadcast address   IP address used to communicate with all devices on a particular network.

brownout   A loss of AC power due to electrical circuits being overloaded.

browser   A program that views web pages across the Internet. Common web browsers are Internet Explorer, Navigator, Opera, and NeoPlanet.

burst EDO   See BEDO

bus   Electronic lines that allow 1s and 0s to move from one place to another.

bus frequency multiple   A motherboard setting for the internal microprocessor speed.

bus mouse   A mouse connected to a 9-pin DIN connector normally used when the computer does not have a built-in mouse port.

bus topology   Network wherein all devices connect to a single cable. If the cable fails, the network is down.

bus-mastering   A feature allowing an adapter to take over the external data bus from the microprocessor to execute operations with another bus-mastering adapter.

busmaster DMA   Another name for UDMA. Allows the IDE interface to control the PCI bus for faster transfers.

byte   Eight bits grouped together as a basic unit.

C

C-RIMM (Continuity RIMM) A blank module used to fill empty memory slots on the motherboard when using RIMMs, because the memory banks must be tied together. RIMMs (a trademark of Rambus, Inc.) are packaged RDRAMs (Rambus DRAM).

cable modem A modem that connects to the cable TV network.

cable select A setting used on IDE devices when connected to a special cable. The cable connector determines which device is master and which one is slave.

cache memory A type of memory designed to increase microprocessor operations.

caddy A holder for a compact disk that inserts into the CD-ROM drive.

caddy loaded A term used to describe how a CD inserts into a CD drive. With caddy loaded, the CD inserts into a holder, which in turn, gets inserted into the drive.

CAM A type of software driver that supports SCSI devices.

cancel button Located in bottom right corner of the window, clicking on it ignores any changes the user has made and restores parameters to their original state.

capacitive keyboard A reliable, but more expensive, keyboard.

capacitor An electronic component that can hold a charge.

card services The second software layer that allows PC Cards to operate.

CardBay A PC card standard that allows laptop computers to be compatible with USB and IEEE 1394 serial interfaces. It is backward compatible and does not require a driver or support by the operating system.

CardBus An upgraded standard from the 16-bit local bus standard to the PCMCIA that allows 32-bit transfers at up to 33MHz speeds.

CAS (Column Address Strobe) In a memory module, CAS indicates how long (in clock cycles) for the processor to move on to the next memory address. Therefore, the smaller the number, the better (i.e., faster). Also knows as CAS latency, or CASL.

cascaded interrupt A bridged interrupt system using two interrupt controller chips in which priority requests travel from the second chip over the first chip and onto the microprocessor.

CD (Compact Disk) A disk that holds large amounts of data, such as audio, video, and software applications.

CD-E (Compact Disk-Erasable) A CD drive that can write data multiple times to a particular disk.

CD-R (Compact Disk-Recordable) A CD drive that can create a compact disk by writing once to the disk. See also WORM.

CD-ROM See CD-ROM drive

CD-ROM drive A device that holds CDs and is used for audio and data files.

CD-ROM kit An upgrade to a computer system which includes the CD-ROM drive, sound card, cable, speakers, and drivers.

CD-RW (Compact Disk ReWritable) A CD drive that can write data multiple times to a particular disk.

CDFS (CD-ROM File System) A Windows CD file system with a dynamic cache which does not require specific configuration or memory allocation by the user.

CGA (Color Graphics Adapter) An adapter used with old color digital monitors.

checkbox Provides the user the ability to enable an option or not. Clicking in the checkbox places a checkmark that enables the option. Clicking again removes the checkmark that disables the option.

chipset Motherboard chips that work in conjunction with the microprocessor to allow certain computer features, such as motherboard memory and capacity.

CHS addressing (Cylinders Heads Sectors addressing) The method the BIOS uses to talk to the hard drive based on the number of cylinders, heads, and sectors of the drive.

clamping speed The time elapsed from an overvoltage condition to when surge protection begins.

clamping voltage The voltage level at which the surge protector begins to protect the computer.

clean install Loading an operating system on a computer that does not already have one installed.

clone A term used to describe a computer that copied the original IBM PC.

close button Located in upper right corner of a dialog box with an X, it is used to close the dialog box window.

cluster The minimum amount of space that one saved file occupies.

CMOS (Complementary Metal Oxide Semiconductor) A special type of memory on the motherboard in which Setup configuration is saved.

COAST (Cache on a Stick) A type of cache memory module used on motherboards.

coaxial cable Type of network cabling used in older Ethernet networks as well as mainframe and minicomputer connections. Has copper core, surrounded by insulation and shielding from EMI.

cold boot Executes when the computer is turned on with the power switch. Executes POST.

color monitor A type of monitor that displays information using various number of colors. Contrast with monochrome monitor.

combinational mouse A mouse that allows connection to a PS/2 mouse port or a serial port.

command interpreter The part of the operating system that translates commands entered at a prompt into code that the computer understands. An example of a command interpreter is the COMMAND.COM file.

command prompt Otherwise known as a prompt. A text-based environment where commands are entered.

COMMAND.COM A file known as the command interpreter that loads when the computer boots.

compression Compacting a file or folder to take up less disk space

computer Unit that performs tasks using software applications. Also referred to as a microcomputer or PC.

Computer Management A Windows 2000 console that displays a large group on snap-in tools on one screen.

conditioning roller Used in a laser printer to generate a large uniform negative voltage to be applied to the drum.

CONFIG.SYS A file that contains multiple lines used to control or configure the computer environment such as memory, CD-ROM, screen display, etc. The file is no longer required in today's operating systems, but if needed for old device drivers, the operating system loads it.

Connect to the Internet A desktop icon representing a Windows 2000 wizard that steps you through setting up an Internet connection.

continuity A resistance measurement to see if a wire is good or broken.

conventional memory The memory map area from 0 to 640KB reserved for RAM chips in which DOS, DOS applications, and some of the Windows operating system are mapped.

cooperative multitasking A type of multitasking used by Windows 3.x and 16-bit applications under Windows 9x. This type of multitasking relies on the application to relinquish control of the CPU.

COPY A DOS command used to transfer one or more files from one place to another.

COPY CON: A command used to copy the characters entered from a keyboard (the console). An archaic way to create batch files.

cpi (characters per inch) A printing measurement that defines how many characters are printed within an inch. The larger the CPI, the smaller the font size.

cps (characters per second) The number of characters a printer prints in one second.

CPU See microprocessor

CPU bus frequency A motherboard setting for external microprocessor speed.

CRC (Cyclic Redundancy Check) An advanced method of data error checking.

crosstalk A type of EMI where signals from one wire interfere with the data on an adjacent wire.

CRT (Cathode Ray Tube) The main part of a monitor, the picture tube.

CSMA/CA (Carrier Sense Multiple Access/Collision Avoidance) A common access method (set of communication rules governing networked devices) used in wireless and Apple networks.

CSMA/CD (Carrier Sense Multiple Access/Collision Detect) A common access method (set of communication rules governing all network devices) used by Ethernet.

CTS (Clear to Send) Part of the RTS/CTS hardware handshaking communication method. Specific wires on the serial connector are used to send a signal to the other device to stop or start sending data. The CTS and RTS (Request to Send) signals indicate when it is okay to send data.

current A term that describes how many electrons are going through a circuit.

cylinder   On a stack of hard drive platters, the same numbered concentric tracks of all platters.

D

D-shell connector   A connector with more pins or holes on the top side than the bottom so that a cable inserts in only one direction. Examples include parallel, serial, and video ports.

daisy chaining   Connecting multiple devices together through cabling.

data bits   A serial device setting for how many bits make up a data word.

data compression   A method of converting data into smaller sizes before transmission.

data link layer   Layer 2 of the OSI model, it accurately transfers bits across the network by encapsulating (grouping) them into frames (usable sections).

DBR   (DOS Boot Record) Area of a disk that contains system files.

DC   (Direct current) The type of power the computer needs to operate.

DCE   (Data Circuit Terminating Equipment) A term that refers to serial devices such as modems, mice, and digitizers.

DDCD   (Double Density CD) A CD disk format developed by Sony and Phillips that extends capacity to 1.3GB. The drives that can use this specification can also read regular CDs, CD-R disks, and CD-RW disks.

DDR DIMM   A type of Dual In-Line Memory Module with 184 pins and one notch used in AMD Athlon computers and higher-end servers.

DDR RAM   (Double Data Rate RAM) A memory module that can send data on both the rising and falling sides of a clock signal, unlike SDRAM that sends data only on the rising clock cycle. Therefore, DDR RAM can send twice as much data as SDRAM.

decoder   In DVD drives, the MPEG-2 video must be converted and the decoder is the way to convert the data. The two types of decoders are hardware and software.

default printer   When a computer can use multiple printers, one of the printers is marked as the default. This is the printer that all applications use. A computer user must change the printer to a different one though the Print dialog window. To mark a printer as default, right-click on the printer icon and click on the Set as default option.

default gateway   The IP address of the Layer 3 device, such as a router, that is directly connected to its immediate network. It tells a device on its network where to send a packet destined for a remote network.

defragmentation   A process of reordering and placing files in contiguous sectors.

degausser   A device that demagnetizes monitors. Also called a degaussing coil.

density control blade   A part inside the laser printer's toner cartridge that controls the amount of toner released to the drum.

desktop   The area of the monitor where all work is performed. It is the interface between the user and the applications, files and hardware, and is part of the graphical user interface environment.

developing cylinder   A component inside the laser printer's toner cartridge that applies a static charge to the toner so it will be attracted to the drum. Sometimes called a developing roller.

device driver   Special software that allows an operating system to access a piece of hardware.

Device Manager   A Windows 9x/2000 program used to view and configure hardware.

device name   A part of the CONFIG.SYS line that is eight characters and unique for each CD-ROM drive.

DHCP   (Dynamic Host Configuration Protocol) A method to automatically assign IP addresses to network devices from a pool of IP addresses.

dialog box   A window used by the operating system that allows user interaction to set preferences on various software parameters.

DIB   (Dual Independent Bus) Using two buses (a backside and frontside bus) to relieve the bottleneck when the CPU communicates with RAM, L2 cache, chipset, PCI bus, etc.

differential terminator   A SCSI terminator used with HVD SCSI devices. It cannot be used with other SCSI types.

digital modem   A modem that transmits directly on digital phone lines.

digital monitor   A monitor that uses digital signals to determine the amount of colors displayed. Digital monitors were used with the older computers, but are becoming more prevalent today.

DIMM   (Dual In-line Memory Module) A style of 168-pin memory chip normally used for RAM chips on Pentium and higher motherboards.

DIN connector   A round connector with small holes, normally keyed with a metal piece or notch so that cable only inserts one way. Examples include keyboard and mouse connectors.

DIP   (Dual In-line Package) A style of memory chip that has a row of pins down each side and is normally used for ROM chips.

DIP switch   Physical switch located on older computers' motherboards to manually set configuration. It normally comes in slide-type or rocker-type switch.

DIR   A DOS command that is used to display the contents of a directory.

directory   In older operating systems, an electronic container that holds files and even other directories.

DirectX   A Microsoft DVD technology that integrates multimedia drivers, application code, and 3-D support for audio and video.

disk   Media used to store data.

disk cache   A portion of RAM set aside for hard drive data and speeds up hard drive operations. A cache on a hard drive controller is also known as a data buffer.

Disk Cleanup   A Windows 2000 utility that helps free up hard drive space by emptying the Recycle Bin, removing temporary files, removing temporary Internet files, removing offline files, etc.

DMA channel   (Direct Memory Access channel) A number assigned to an adapter which allows the adapter to bypass the microprocessor to communicate directly with the RAM chips.

DNS server   (Domain Name System server) Application on network server that translates Internet names into IP addresses.

dongle   A connector that attaches to a PC Card modem (on a laptop) that allows a phone cable to be attached to the modem. The other end of the phone cable connects to the phone outlet.

DOSKEY   A DOS program that can still be used with today's operating systems that makes working from a prompt easier. The program allows easy recall of previously typed commands.

dot matrix printer Sometimes called an impact printer because of the printer physically impacting a ribbon that places an image on the paper.

dot pitch The distance between like-colored phosphorous dots on adjacent dot triads.

dot triad A grouping of three phosphorous color dots combined to make a single image on the monitor.

downstream A term used to describe information pulled from the Internet such as when viewing web pages or downloading a file.

dpi (dots per inch) A printer measurement used with ink jet and laser printers that refers to how many dots are produced in an inch.

DPMS (Display Power Management Signaling) A standard that defines the signals used to inform the monitor to reduce it's power.

Dr. Watson A Windows utility that detects and displays troubleshooting information when a system or program error occurs.

DRAM (Dynamic Random Access Memory) One of two major RAM types that is less expensive, but slower than SRAM. DRAM requires periodic refreshing of the electrical charges holding the 1s and 0s.

drive select setting A number assigned to a drive that enables the controlling circuits to distinguish between two drives.

drive type A number that corresponds to a drive's geometry assigned during Setup configuration.

driver See device driver

drop-down menu Option box with down arrow; clicking on the arrow reveals additional choices for the option.

DS3D (DirectSound 3D) A Microsoft development included in DirectX3 that adds more 3D audio effect commands.

DTE (Data Terminating Equipment) A term that refers to computers and printers.

dual-boot Ability to boot from one of two installed operating systems.

dual-ported (memory) A type of video memory that allows data reads and writes simultaneously.

DUN (Dial-Up Networking) A remote computer that dials into the Internet or a corporation using a modem.

DVD-R WORM technology used with DVD drives that is similar to CD-R drives. DVD-R disks can use one or two sides and are available in 3.95GB, 4.7GB, and 9.4GB. DVD-R disks are sometimes shown as two different types, DVD-R(A) and DVD-R(G). DVD-R(A) targets the "authoring" business for professional development of DVDs. DVD-R(G) is more for home users and lay people. Both can be read by most DVD players and drives, but DVD-R(G) drives usually cannot write to DVD-R(A) media.

DVD-RAM See DVD Rewritable

DVD-ROM A technology that produces disks with superior audio and video performance and increased storage capacity.

DVD-RW (DVD-ReWritable) is similar to DVD-R except that you can erase and rewrite information on the disk. DVD-RW uses 4.7GB disks and most DVD-ROM drives and DVD-Video players support this format. This technology is sometimes known or seen as DVD-R/W or DVD-ER.

DVD+RW (DVD Read and Write) A drive that can be read from, written to, and holds 3GB.

dye polymer A technology for making CD-E or CD-RW disks by laser-heating the disk surface to produce light reflecting bumps.

dynamic disk A Windows 2000 term for volumes that can be resized and managed without rebooting.

dynamic storage A Windows 2000 disk that has been configured for the 2000 operating system. The unit can be resided and managed without rebooting and contains primary partitions, extended partitions, logical drives, and dynamic volumes.

E

EAX (Environmental Audio Extensions) Creative Labs' development that allows software and game developers to create realistic audio environment such as muffling effects and audio directional effects (which direction a sound comes from).

ECC (Error Correcting Code) An alternative method of checking data accuracy. ECC uses a mathematical algorithm to verify accuracy. ECC is more expensive than parity and the motherboard or memory controllers must also have additional circuitry to process ECC.

echo mode setting   Sometimes called the local echo setting. The setting that displays typed commands.

ECHO OFF   A DOS command that prevents characters from being displayed on the screen. Normally loaded when the computer first boots to prevent the AUTOEXEC.BAT and CONFIG.SYS files from showing.

ECHS   (Extended CHS) A method by which both the hard drive and the BIOS perform cylinders, heads, and sector translation.

ECP   (Enhanced Capabilities Port) A parallel communication standard that allows simultaneous bi-directional communication.

EDIT   A command used to bring up a text editor. A text editor allows file creation and modification.

EDO   (Extended Data Out) A technology to speed up DRAM access.

EFS   (Encryption File System) An encryption feature of Windows 2000 Professional; only the authorized user may view or change a file encrypted with EFS.

EIDE   (Enhanced Integrated Drive Electronics) A term that signifies two IDE connectors (four devices) and support of the ATAPI standard.

EISA   (Extended Industry Standard Architecture) Developed by a consortium of manufacturers in response to IBM's MCA standard. EISA utilizes a 32-bit 10MHz standard.

e-mail   Electronic message sent via the Internet.

EMF   (Enhanced MetaFile) A spooled print data format that defines how data is stored on the hard drive (spooled) before being sent to the printer. EMF is the default setting and it is a 32-bit non-printer dependent format that performs faster than RAW. If you are having printing problems, and the documentation or your research directs you to change the spooling data format, this is the setting referenced. The RAW data format is printer-specific and it requires extra time to convert the printing data before it is saved to the hard drive.

EMI   (ElectroMagnetic Interference) Electronic noise generated by electrical devices. Also called ElectroMagnetic Radiation (EMR).

EMS   (Expanded Memory Specification) See Expanded Memory.

encoding   The way in which binary 1s and 0s are placed on the hard drive.

encryption   Method of securing data from unauthorized users.

EPP (Enhanced Parallel Port) A parallel port communication standard that allows bidirectional communication.

erase lamp A component inside a laser printer that neutralizes any charges left on the drum so that the next printed page receives no residuals from the previous page.

ERD (Emergency Repair Disk) A copy of the REPAIR folder created when backing up the registry in Windows 2000 Professional and NT Workstation.

error correction Standard for the modem to check the data for errors rather than the microprocessor.

ESCD (Extended System Configuration Data) Started being used in Windows 98 and it provides the BIOS and operating system a means for communicating with plug and play devices. As the computer boots, the BIOS records legacy device configuration information. Plug and play devices use this information to configure themselves and avoid conflicts.

ESD (ElectroStatic Discharge) Occurs when stored up static electricity is discharged in an instantaneous surge of voltage. Cumulative effects of ESD weaken or destroy electronic components.

ESDI (Enhanced Small Devices Interface) The second generation of hard drive interfaces which increased hard drive capacities over the older ST506 drives.

Ethernet A network system that carries computer data along with audio and video information. Ethernet adapters are the most common network cards. They may have a BNC, a RJ-45, a 15-pin female D-shell connector, or a combination of these ports. The RJ-45 connector is the most common.

Event Viewer A Windows tool used to monitor various events in the computer.

exabyte (EB) One billion times one billion bytes or 2^{60} power. (1,152,921,504,606,800 bytes)

executable file A file with a BAT, EXE, or COM extension that starts an application, utility, or command. A file upon which the operating system can take action.

expanded memory A 64KB space in the memory map normally reserved for ROM chips (640KB to 1MB range) that allows paging up to 32MB of memory, 64KB at a time. Also known as LIM memory standard or Expanded Memory Specification (EMS).

expansion slot Motherboard socket into which adapters are connected.

Explorer A Windows-based application which details certain information for all folders and files on each drive. It is used most commonly to copy or move files and folders. Sometimes called Windows Explorer or NT Explorer.

extended memory The area of the microprocessor's memory map above 1MB. Also known as XMS.

extended partition A hard drive division.

extension In operating systems, the adding of three characters following the file name and a period (.). The extension associates the file with a particular application that executes the file.

external command A command located on a disk that the operating system must locate before the command can execute.

external data bus The electronic lines that allow the microprocessor to communicate with external devices. Also known as external data path. See also Bus.

F

Fast Ethernet An extension of original Ethernet standard that allows data transmission of 100Mbps.

FAT (File Allocation Table) A method of organizing a computer's file system.

FAT16 File system supported by DOS, Windows 9x, NT, and 2000. DOS and Windows 9x have a 2GB limit. Windows NT and 2000 have a 4GB limit.

FAT32 The file system used by Windows 95 Service Release 2, Windows 98, and 2000 that supports hard drives up to 2TB in size.

fax modem A device that functions as a modem and uses the printer and computer as a fax machine.

FDDI (Fiber Distributed Data Interface) High speed fiber network that uses ring topology and token passing access method.

FDISK A command used to partition a hard drive.

felt side The side of the paper which should not be printed on. Also known as the wax side.

female port   A type of connector on a motherboard or a separate adapter with recessed portions (or holes) that accept a male cable's pins.

fiber-optic cable   An expensive network cabling made of plastic or glass fibers that carry data in the form of light pulses. Handles the greatest amount of data with least amount of data loss. Comes in single-mode and multi-mode.

FIFO setting   A serial device setting that enables or disables the UART's buffer.

file   Electronic container holding data or computer code that serves as a basic unit of storage.

file system   Defines how data is stored on a drive. Examples of file systems include FAT16, FAT32, NTFS4, and NTFS5.

file virus   A program that replaces or attaches to executable files (those with .COM or .EXE extensions). The virus can cause the application to not start or operate properly. It can also load into RAM and affect other executable files.

filename   A term used to describe the name of a file. In older operating systems, the filename was limited to eight characters plus a three character extension. Today's operating systems allow filenames up to 255 characters in length.

FireWire   See IEEE 1394

firmware   Combines hardware and software attributes. An example is a ROM chip (tangible) which has instructions (software) written into it.

Flash BIOS   A type of motherboard memory that allows updates by disk or downloading Internet files.

flash memory   A type of non-volatile memory that holds data when the power is off.

flat panel   A type of LCD monitor used with desktop and tower computers that take less power than CRTs and less desktop space. The monitors can be digital, but some can work off an analog adapter. This issue of colors that was prevalent with old technology digital monitors is no longer relevant since flat panels use transistors to control colors.

floppy disk   A flexible disk (or diskette) made of oxide-coated mylar most popular today in 3-inch drive sizes. Disks have much less capacity compared to a hard drive, but were designed as portable, temporary and relatively low cost. Therefore, floppy disk data should be backed up at least once.

floppy drive   A device which allows data storage to floppy disks.

floptical drive   Floppy drives that use optical technology to move the read/write heads over the disk surface.

flow control   A serial device setting that determines the communication method.

flyback transformer   A component inside the monitor that boosts the voltage to very high levels.

FML/C   (Fluorescent MultiLayer Disk/Card) A new CD/DVD-type technology that uses a fluorescent dye embedded in pits and grooves on each layer of the disk or card. When a laser is used, fluorescent light reflects back from the disk that is a different wavelength of the laser's light beam. A 20-layer DVD would be able to hold about 100GB. The technology would require deeper grooves and data pits.

folder   In Windows-based operating systems, an electronic container that holds files as well as other folders. Folders were previously called directories in older operating systems.

font   A group of printable characters of a particular style such as Times New Roman, Script, Arial, and Courier.

font cartridge   A printer add-on feature that allows different fonts to be loaded into the printer's memory.

font size   The point size of a particular font and is abbreviated pt. such as 10pt. or 12pt.

font style   A particular feature of a font such as bold or italic.

form factor   The shape and size (height, width and depth) of motherboards, adapters, memory chips, power supplies, etc. Before building or upgrading, make sure the device's form factor fits in the computer case!

FORMAT   A command used to prepare a disk for use.

formatted (disk)   A disk that has been prepared to accept data.

FPM   (Fast Page Mode) A technology to speed up DRAM access speed.

FPT   (Forced Perfect Termination) A special type of active terminator that can be used with SE devices.

fragmentation   Occurs over time as files are saved on the hard drive in clusters not adjacent to each other which slows hard disk access time.

frame   The encapsulated data found at layer 2 of the OSI model.

frequency response   The number of samples taken by a sound card.

frequency response range   The range of sounds a speaker can reproduce.

FSB   (Front Side Bus) Part of the Dual Independent Bus that connects the CPU to the motherboard components.

FTP   (File Transfer Protocol) A standard used when transferring files from one computer to another across a network.

fullduplex   A serial device setting that allows the sending and receiving device to send data simultaneously. On a cable, the ability to transmit data in both directions simultaneously.

fuser cleaning pad   The pad located above the laser printer's fuser roller that lightly coats it with silicon to prevent the paper sticking to the roller.

fusing roller   A laser printer part responsible for heating the toner and melding it into the paper.

G

game port   An input port that connects a joystick to the computer.

generic enabler   One of three basic layers of software that allow a PC card to operate. Sometimes called a super driver, it allows assignment of interrupts and input/output addresses.

gigabyte   Approximately one billion bytes of information (exactly 1,073,741,824 bytes).

gigahertz   One billion cycles per second (1Ghz). Expresses the speed of a microprocessor.

GPF   (General Protection Fault) An application error that appears in the Windows environment.

grayscale monitor   A monitor that displays images in shades of gray instead of colors.

grounding   Occurs when the motherboard or adapter is not installed properly and has a trace touching the computer's frame.

GUI (Graphical User Interface) In newer operating systems, user selects files, programs, and commands by clicking on pictorial representations (icons), rather than typing commands at a command prompt.

H

HAL (Hardware Abstraction Layer) The layer between the operating system and hardware devices that allows Windows to run different hardware configurations and components without crashing the operating system.

halfduplex A serial device setting that allows either the sending or the receiving device to send data, one device at a time. On a cable, the ability to transmit in both directions but not at the same time.

handshaking The method two serial devices negotiate communications.

hard drive A sealed data storage medium on which information is stored. Also called a hard disk.

hardware A tangible item one can touch and feel like the keyboard or monitor.

hardware decoder Sometimes called a MPEG-2 decoder that provides the best performance (especially in older computer) when converting a MPEG DVD file into a format that can be displayed. A software decoder puts the burden on the CPU to decode and uncompress the video data from the DVD. Video card manufacturers have added MPEG-2 video decoding support to decrease the CPU's load.

head crash Occurs when a read/write head touches a platter, causing damage to the heads or the platter.

head parking utility Software in older computers that pulls the read/write heads away from the data storage platters to minimize damaging physical contact (hence, the phrase head crash). Today's hard drives park the heads automatically.

heaps Memory allocated to Windows core files that records every Windows action, such as each mouse click, each re-sizing of a window, etc. In Windows 3.x, the GDI.EXE memory heap is limited to 64KB and the USER.EXE memory heap is divided into two 64KB sections. For Windows, the heaps are unlimited.

help button Located in upper right corner of a dialog box as a question mark button, clicking on it allows access to information on various topics.

hertz A measurement of electrical frequency equal to one cycle per second. Abbreviated Hz.

hidden attribute A file designation that keeps a file from being seen in directory listings. However, with today's operating systems, this attribute does not help because the operating system makes it very easy to see hidden files.

high level format Process that sets up the file system for use by the computer. It is the third and last step in preparing a hard drive for use.

HMA (High Memory Area) The first 64KB above 1MB in the memory map that can be used as an extension of conventional memory.

horizontal scanning frequency The rate in which a monitor's beam moves across the screen.

host adapter Another name for a SCSI adapter.

host number Portion of an IP address that represents the specific network device.

hot Wire that brings AC current from the power supply to the PC's front panel or the term used to describe the smaller flat AC outlet connection.

HPPCL (Hewlett-Packard's Printer Control Language) A popular print software that translates between the printer and the computer.

HTML (Hypertext Markup Language) Programming language used to create Internet web pages.

HTTP (HyperText Transfer Protocol) A standard for Internet communication.

hub A device used with the Universal Serial Bus or in a star network topology that allows multiple device connections. A network hub cannot look at each data frame coming through its ports like a switch does.

hub ring A reinforcement ring found in the center of 360K disks.

HVD (High Voltage Differential) A SCSI-2 standard that allows longer SCSI bus lengths and required a differential terminator. HVD was removed from the SCSI-3 standards.

HyperTransport AMD's futuristic I/O architecture in which a serial-link design allows devices to communicate in daisy chain fashion without interfering with any other communication. Thus, I/O bottleneck is mitigated.

I

I/O address (Input/Output address) A port address that allows an external device to communicate with the microprocessor. It is analogous to a mailbox number.

icon Operating system graphic that represents a file, application, hardware, and shared network resources.

ICS   (Internet Connection Sharing) A feature provided by Windows 98 Second Edition and 2000 that allows a single Internet connection to be shared between multiple computers.

IDE   (Integrated Drive Electronics) An interface that supports internal hard drives, CD drives, DVD drives, Zip drives, and tape backup units.

IEEE 1284 A standard that defines what connections are used with printers and how data is transferred through the parallel port.

IEEE 1394 The standard for high-speed audio and video device data transfers known as FireWire. It supports connection of up to 63 devices.

IML (Initial Microcode Load) A special section on hard drives installed in IBM computers that holds BIOS information.

InfiniBand A futuristic input/output architecture wherein point-to-point device connections are made through a switching fabric. The I/O link is established only for the duration of the data transfer and then is torn down.

infrared A technology utilizing infrared light that allows devices to communicate across a wireless network. Examples are laptop computers, printers, and hand-held computing devices.

ink jet printer A type of printer that squirts ink through tiny nozzles to produce print. Ink jet printers produce high quality, high resolution, color output.

INT 13 interface Short for Interrupt 13, a standard that allows a system BIOS to locate data on the hard drive.

integrated motherboard A motherboard that contains ports such as the mouse, keyboard, serial, and parallel ports.

interface   A set of rules that govern how a device is configured or accessed. Examples of hard drive interfaces are ST506, ESDI, IDE, and SCSI.

interlacing   A scanning method used with monitors in which only the odd numbered pixel rows are scanned followed by the even numbered pixel rows.

interleaving   The method of numbering platter sectors for the most efficient transfer of data between the hard drive and the controller.

internal command   A command that is part of the command interpreter that the operating system does not have to locate in order to execute. An example of an internal command is DIR.

internal data bus   The electronic lines inside a microprocessor. See also Bus.

internal font   A font stored inside a printer in its memory.

Internet Explorer   A Windows-based application used to access the Internet through a network or dial-up access.

interrupt   See IRQ

IO.SYS   A system file used to boot an operating system. In today's operating systems, the IO.SYS file is used to configure the computer environment (things that used to be done through the CONFIG.SYS file).

IP address   A type of network adapter address used when multiple networks are linked. Known as a Layer 3 address and is a 32-bit binary number with groups of eight bits separated by a dot. This numbering scheme is also known as dotted-decimal notation. Each eight-bit group represents numbers from 0 to 255. An IP address example is 113.19.12.102.

IPCONFIG   A command used with Windows 98, NT, and 2000 to see the current IP settings.

IPX/SPX   (Internet Packet Exchange/Sequenced Packet Exchange) A network protocol used to connect to a Novell network.

IRQ   (Interrupt ReQuest) A microprocessor priority system which assigns a number to each expansion adapter or port to facilitate orderly communication.

IRQ steering   A PCI bus property that allows many PCI devices to share the limited and fixed number of IRQs, thus preventing competing devices to slow or stop CPU processing.

ISA   (Industry Standard Architecture) The oldest of the three types of computer architectures. Allows 16-bit data transfers.

ISDN   (Integrated Services Digital Network) A digital phone line that has three separate channels, two B channels and a D channel. The B channel allows 64Kbps transmission speeds. The D channel allows 16Kbps transmissions.

ISP   (Internet Service Provider) A vendor that provides connection to the Internet.

J

joule dissipation capacity   A measure of a surge protector ability to absorb overvoltage power surges. The higher the capacity, the better the protection.

jumper   A plastic cover for two metal pins on a jumper block.

K

keyboard   Allows users to communicate and input data to the computer.

keyboard port   DIN connector on the motherboard into which only the keyboard cable must connect.

keyed   A connector or cable that has an extra metal piece or not that allows correct connections.

kilobyte   Approximately 1,000 bytes of information (exactly 1,024 bytes).

L

L1 cache   Fast memory located inside the microprocessor.

L2 cache   Fast memory located inside the microprocessor on Pentium Pros and higher and located on the motherboard on lower microprocessor-based motherboards.

L3 cache   Any cache fast memory installed on the motherboard when both L1 and L2 cache is on the microprocessor.

LADDR   (Layered Device Driver Architecture) A type of software drive that supports SCSI devices.

LAN   (Local Area Network) A group of devices sharing resources in a single area such as a room or a building.

LAPM   (Link Access Procedure for Modems) Another name for Microcom's error correction levels.

laser lens   A component of the CD-ROM drive that reads the data from the compact disk. Also known as the objective lens and is susceptible to dust accumulation.

laser printer   A type of printer that produces output using a process similar to a copy machine. Laser printers are the most expensive type of printer.

layered block device driver   Windows software that manages hard drives by working with groups of bytes (blocks) instead of one byte at a time.

LBA   (Logical Block Addressing) A method for the system BIOS to talk to the hard drive using sector intelligence translation.

LCD   (Liquid Crystal Display) A video technology used with laptops and flat screen monitors. The two basic types of LCD are passive matrix and active matrix.

LIM   (Lotus Intel Microsoft) The LIM memory standard was developed by Lotus, Intel and Microsoft to solve the limitations of conventional memory. See also expanded memory.

line conditioner   Device to protect the computer from over and undervoltage conditions as well as adverse noise conditions. Also known as a power conditioner.

local bus   A data channel that attaches to the microprocessor with a different expansion slot than ISA, EISA, and MCA.

logical drive   Dividing the extended partition into separate units which appear as separate drive letters.

Logical Disk Management   A Windows 2000 snap-in tool that allows storage device management.

loopback address   A private IP address of 127.0.0.1 that is used to test a NIC card's basic network setup.

loopback plug   A device used in troubleshooting that allows port testing.

lost clusters   Sectors on a disk that the file allocation table cannot associate with any file or directory.

low-level format   Creates and numbers all sectors on the hard drive as well as erases all existing data. It is the first step in preparing a hard drive for use and is done at the factor for IDE and SCSI hard drives.

LS-120 drive   (laser serve 120MB) Using a patented laser servo technology to access data up to five times faster than the traditional drive. Also known as a:drive.

LVD   (Low Voltage Differential) A SCSI signaling type that is required on all SCSI devices that adhere to the Ultra SCSI standards. It uses a lower voltage than HVD (which means shorter cabling distances), but longer cable lengths than SE allows. LVD is backwards compatible with SE.

M

MAC address One of two types of addresses assigned to network adapters used when two devices on same network communicate. Known as a Layer 2 address.

macro virus Program that attaches to a document written by a specific application such as Microsoft PowerPoint. Once the document in opened into RAM, the virus attaches to other documents.

magneto-optical A technology for reading and writing multiple times to a compact disk.

male port A connector on a motherboard or adapter with protruding pins that accepts a cable with a female connector.

marking subsystem Also called the marking engine. The part of the printer that places the image on the paper.

master A jumper setting used to configure an IDE device. The master is the controlling device on the interface.

math coprocessor A separate chip added to the motherboard to perform number-crunching functions.

MBR (Master Boot Record) A program that reads the partition table to find the primary partition used to boot the system.

MCA (MicroChannel Architecture) A proprietary system developed by IBM, which is not compatible with ISA architecture.

MDRAM (Multi-bank Dynamic RAM) Memory used with video adapters that acts like multiple independent 32-bit memory chips.

mechanical keyboard A keyboard cheaper in design than capacitive keyboards and more prone to failure.

mechanical mouse A mouse that uses a rubber ball to move the pointer.

megabyte Approximately one million bytes of data (exactly 1,048,576 bytes).

megahertz The speed at which microprocessors and coprocessors are measured. Equal to one million cycles per second, abbreviated MHz. See also Hertz.

memory The part of the computer that temporarily stores applications, user documents, and system operating information.

memory address A unique address for memory chips.

memory map   A graphical representation the amount of a microprocessor's memory addresses.

mesh topology   Network where all devices connect to each other by cabling to provide link redundancy and the maximum fault tolerance.

microcomputer   See computer

microprocessor   The central electronic chip that determines the processing power of a computer.

MIDI   (Musical Instrument Digital Interface) An interface built into a sound card to create synthesized music.

MMX   Microprocessors that have 57 more multimedia instructions that speed up multimedia applications such as sound and video.

MNP   (Microcom Network Protocol) A set of error correction standards.

modem   (modulator/demodulator) A device which connects a microcomputer to a phone line.

modem isolator   See phone line isolator

Molex connector   A type of power connector that extends from the computer's power supply to various devices.

monitor   Displays information from the computer to the user.

monochrome monitor   A type of monitor that displays only one color such as amber, white, or green.

motherboard   The main circuit board of a microcomputer. Also known as the mainboard, planar, or systemboard.

mouse   A data input device that moves the cursor or select menus and options.

mouse port   A DIN connector on the motherboard which should only accept the mouse cable.

MOV   (Metal Oxide Varistor) An electronic component built into some surge protectors to absorb overvoltage spikes or surges.

MP3   (MPEG-1 Audio Layer-3) A sound format that compresses an audio file and has the extension of mp3.

MS-DOS Microsoft's version of DOS that is an old operating system.

MSCDEX.EXE A DOS-based program that assigns a drive letter to the CD-ROM drive.

MSD (Microsoft Diagnostics) A program that ships with DOS and Windows 3.x used to help in resource conflicts.

MSDOS.SYS A boot (system) file used in the MS-DOS environment. Today's operating systems use this file to hold multiple boot option settings as well as the paths to important Windows files such as the registry.

MSDS (Material Safety Data Sheet) A document that contains information about a product, its toxicity, storage, and disposal.

MSINFO (Microsoft System Information) A tool in the Windows 98 environment used to display information about system resources and detect device conflicts.

multiplier A motherboard setting used to determine CPU speed (multiplier times bus speed equals CPU speed).

multi-boot The computer can start up from two or more operating systems.

multi-mode A type of fiber-optic cabling that allows multiple light signals to be sent along the same cable.

multi-scan monitor Sometimes called multi-synch monitor and it supports multiple horizontal and vertical scanning frequencies.

MultiRead Sometimes called MultiRead2 is an OSTA (Optical Storage Technology Association) specification that states the CD-RW drive is backward compatible with CD-ROM and CD-R disks. Look for these words when purchasing a CD-RW drive.

My Computer The desktop icon that allows access to files, applications, software and hardware located in or on the computer.

My Documents The default folder (directory) location on the hard drive for files the user saves. Also, the icon that quickly accesses the default directory.

My Network Places The Windows 2000 Professional desktop icon used to access network resources.

N

nanosecond   A billionth of a second.

NetBEUI   A non-routable network protocol commonly found on peer-to peer networks. Can work only on simple networks, not on routed networks.

network   Two or more devices capable of communicating and sharing resources between them.

network layer   Layer 3 of the OSI model that coordinates data movement between two devices on separate networks.

Network Neighborhood   Windows icon on desktop that appears only if the computer has a network card installed. Is used to display and access networked computers and devices within its domain.

network number   Portion of an IP address that represents which network the computer is on.

network protocol   Specifications that define the network data communication procedures to follow when sending and receiving data. Most common protocols are TCP/IP, IPX/SPX and NetBEUI.

network topology   Maps how the physical or logical paths of network devices connect.

NIC   (Network Interface Card) An adapter used to connect a device to a network.

non-cascaded interrupt   An interrupt system in which two controller chips are not bridged together.

non-parity   A type of memory chip that is cheaper and does not do error checking.

non-volatile memory   Memory that remains even when the computer is powered off. ROM and flash memory are examples of non-volatile memory.

NOS   (Network Operating System) Special operating system on a server containing utilitiesfor managing users, resources, and security.

NSLOOKUP   A NT Server and 2000 Server troubleshooting tool that displays network domain names and their associated IP addresses.

NT Backup   Windows NT program to make a registry backup.

NT Diagnostics   Windows NT utility that shows configuration information about the computer's hardware, device drivers and installed services, such as IRQs, I/O addresses, DMA channels, and memory addresses of the system.

NT Explorer   See Explorer

NTFS   File system used with Windows NT and 2000. NT's version is called NTFS4 and 2000's version is NTFS5.

NTFS4   File system used by Windows NT.

NTFS5   File system used by Windows 2000; NT can be upgraded to NTFS5 with a service pack.

NTVDM   (NT Virtual DOS Machine) Simulates a DOS environment inside NT Workstation and Windows 2000 when a DOS application is being run.

null modem cable   A cable that connects two computers together without the use of a modem.

O

ohm   A measurement of resistance.

OK button   Located in bottom right hand of dialog box; clicking on it saves any changes applied and closes the window.

on-die cache   L2 cache when housed in the microprocessor packaging.

OnNow   A Windows power feature that allows a computer to be instantly available when needed, but use the least amount of power when not in use.

operating system   A piece of software used to load a computer and make it operational.

optical mouse   A mouse that has optical sensors used to move the pointer.

OSI model   (Open Systems Interconnect) A standard for information transfer across a network that was developed by the International Standards Organization. The model has seven layers – each layer uses the layer below it, and each layer provides some function to the one above it.

outline font   Fonts computed from a mathematical formula and also known as vector fonts.

overclocking   Manually changing the front side bus speed and/or multiplier to increase CPU and system speed.

overvoltage   A condition when the AC voltage is over the rated amount of voltage.

overdrive   A chip that upgrades the performance of the microprocessor.

ozone filter   A part of the laser printer that filters out the ozone produced by the printer.

P

packet   Encapsulated data found at layer 3 of the OSI model.

page   In Windows 9x/NT/2000 disk caching, memory space is divided into 4KB blocks called pages. The operating system swaps or pages the application to and from the temporary swap file as needed, if RAM is not large enough to handle the application.

paper transport   The part of a printer that moves paper through the printer.

parallel port   A 25-pin female D-shell connector used to connect a printer to a motherboard. Transfers eight bits of data at a time to parallel devices, such as printers, tape drives, Iomega's Zip drives and external hard drives.

parity   A method of checking data accuracy.

parity chip   A memory chip on a memory bank that checks for data accuracy.

partition table   Holds the information about the types and locations of partitions created. Occupies the outermost track on the platter (Cylinder 0, Head 0, Sector 1), and is part of the Master Boot Record.

partitioning   Dividing a hard drive so that the computer system sees more than one drive. Partitioning is the second step in preparing a hard drive for use.

pass through terminator   A type of terminator used with SCSI devices that has an extra connector on it and allows a device that does not have terminators to be terminated through the connector that attaches to the cable.

passive matrix   A type of LCD monitor used with laptops and now in flat screen displays. Contrast with active matrix.

passive terminator   One type of SCSI chain end that is susceptible to noise interference over long cable distances. Used with SCSI-1 devices.

patch   A piece of software that fixes a specific problem in an application or operating system.

path   Reference that tells where a file is located among drives and folders (directories).

PC   (Personal Computer) A common name for a microcomputer, taken from the IBM PC brand.

PC Card   A common local bus architecture used in laptops. Also known as PCMCIA.

PC100   SDRAM standard DIMM developed by Intel designed for the 100 MHz front side bus.

PC133   SDRAM standard DIMM developed by Intel designed for 133 MHz front side bus, but will also work with 100MHz motherboards (the speed will be 100 MHz).

PCI   (Peripheral Component Interconnect) A common 64-bit, 66MHz local bus standard found in today's computers.

PCMCIA   (Personal Computer Memory Card Industry Association) See PC Card

PD   (Phase-change Dual) A laser technology used to make CD-E or CD-RW disks.

PDL   (Page Description Language) Software inside the printer that translates between the printer and the computer. Two examples are HPPCL and PostScript.

peer-to-peer network   One of two basic types of LANs, wherein each computer user acts as a server. Passwords are created for resources others on the network are allowed to use (if they know the password). Usually found in homes or very small business, comprised of ten or fewer computers.

Performance Logs and Alerts   A Windows 2000 utility that allows creation of graphs, bar charts, and text reports.

Performance Monitor   Name of Windows NT that monitors resources such as memory and CPU usage, and allows creation of graphs, bar charts and text reports.

Performance utility   Name of Windows 2000 Profession utility that monitors memory usage aspects.

petabyte (PB)   One thousand terabytes (2^{50} power) (1,125,899,906,842,600 bytes).

phone line isolator   A surge protector for the modem protecting against power fluctuations in a phone line. Also known as a modem isolator.

physical layer Layer 1 of the OSI model, it defines how bits are sent and received across the network without regard to their structure.

picosecond A trillionth of a second.

picture cell The smallest image shown on the front of a monitor made up of three color phosphorous dots.

PIF (Program Information File) The customized property settings of a DOS application when run inside a NTVDM special environment. NTVDM simulates a DOS environment inside Windows NT and 2000.

pin 1 A designated pin on every cable and connector which must be mated when attaching the two. Usually designated by a stenciled or etched number, a color stripe, etc.

pin firing The act of a printwire coming out of a dot matrix printer's printhead and impacting the paper.

ping A network troubleshooting command used to test TCP/IP communications and determine if a network path is available, whether any delays exist along the path, and if a remote network device is reachable. Use ping with the private IP address 127.0.0.1 to test a NIC's basic network setup.

pipe symbol A character (|) used at the command prompt that allows control of where or how the output of the command is processed. For example a command can be "piped" to display only one screen at a time.

pipeline Separate internal data buses that operate simultaneously inside the microprocessor.

pipeline burst cache A type of cache memory that allows microprocessors and memory to process instructions faster.

pipelining Using L2 cache memory to speed up the process microprocessors and memory use to obtain software instructions.

pits Areas along the track of a compact disk.

pixel Short for picture element. The smallest displayable unit on a monitor.

platter A metal disk of a hard drive on which binary data is recorded.

plug and play (PnP) A bus specification that allows automatic configuration of an adapter.

point enabler Type of PC card software layer that allows assignment of system resources such as interrupts, I/O addresses, etc. In using a point enabler, the PC card does not need socket services or card services. Use it only if the PC card is the only PC card installed in the computer.

polymorphic virus A program that changes constantly to avoid detection by anti-virus scanning.

port A connector located on the motherboard or on a separate adapter.

POST (Power On Self Test) Startup software contained in the BIOS chip that tests individual hardware components.

PostScript A type of printer software that translates between the printer and the computer.

power A measurement expressed in watts that represents how much work is being done.

power good signal A signal sent to the motherboard from the power supply during POST that signifies that power is acceptable.

power rating A measurement expressed in watts-per-channel which represents how loud the speaker volume can go up without distorting the sound.

power supply A device that converts AC voltage into DC voltage that the computer can use.

PPP (Point-to-Point Protocol) A connection-oriented Layer 2 protocol that encapsulates data for transmission over remote networks. Supports TCP/IP and IPX/SPX.

preemptive multitasking A type of multitasking used of 32-bit applications in Windows. With preemptive multitasking, the operating system determines which application gets the microprocessor's attention and for how long.

presentation layer Layer 6 of the OSI model that defines how data is formatted, encoded, converted and presented from the sender to the receiver, even though different computer language is used.

preventive maintenance Something that is done to prolong the life of a device.

primary corona A wire in the laser printer responsible for generating a large negative voltage to be applied uniformly to the laser's drum.

primary partition The first detected drive on the hard drive.

print cartridge   Also known as an ink cartridge. The container that holds the ink and the nozzles for the ink jet printer.

print driver   A piece of software that coordinates between the operating system and the printer.

print engine   The part of a printer that translates commands from the computer and provides feedback when necessary. The print engine is the brains of the printer operation.

print server   A device (computer or separate device) that connects to a printer used by multiple people through a network.

print spooler   Also known as a print manager. A software program that intercepts the request to print and sends print information to the hard drive where it is sent to the printer whenever the microprocessor is not busy with other tasks. A print spooler allows multiple print jobs to be queued inside the computer so other work can be performed.

printer emulation   A printer configuration allowing the printer to be configured to be a different type. Printers emulating other ones do not usually perform to their maximum.

printhead   The part of the dot matrix printer that holds the printwires and impacts the ribbon.

printwire   A component of the dot matrix printer's printhead that is a single wire that connects to a spring and impacts a ribbon to make a single dot on the paper.

prompt   See command prompt

protected mode   A computer operating mode that allows applications to access memory above 1MB.

PS/2 mouse   A mouse that connects to a 6-pin DIN port.

Q

Quick Launch bar   In Windows 98 and 2000 it is located to the right of the Start button in the task bar; clicking on a quick launch icon opens the application.

R

radio button   Similar to a checkbox, it is a round space on a dialog box that allows the user to enable an option by clicking in it. A solid dot in the button means the option is enable; absence of the dot means a disabled option.

Raid 5 volume   A Windows 2000 term that describes putting data on three or more hard drives and one of the three drives is used for parity.

RAM   (Random Access Memory) A volatile type of memory that loses its data when power to the computer is shut off.

RAM drive   A virtual hard disk created from RAM.

RapidIO   A futuristic input/output architecture promoted by Motorola and Mercury Computers. This standard supports I/O interconnections for chip-to-chip, board-to-board, and device-to-device.

raster   A monitor's brightness pattern.

raster font   The most basic type of font normally used by dot matrix printers to create images.

RDISK   (Repair Disk) NT Workstation utility used to create an Emergency Repair Disk after NT is installed. Caution: RDISK does not update security, SAM or default files in the repair folder; use the RDISK /S command for a complete update.

RDRAM   Memory chip developed by Rambus, Inc. that transfers data at rates up to 600MHz.

Readiness Analyzer   A tool that checks for hardware and software compatibility conflicts

read-ahead caching   A type of disk caching that attempts to guess what the next data requested will be and loads that data into RAM.

read-only attribute   A designation that can be applied to a file so the file is not accidentally erased.

read/write head   The part of a floppy or hard drive that electronically writes binary data on disks.

real mode   A computer operating mode found in older computers (8088) in which applications could not access memory above 1MB.

ream   500 sheets of paper.

Recovery Console   A Windows 2000 tool that allows administrator to boot the computer to a command prompt and access the hard drive.

Recycle Bin   Location in Windows-based operating systems where user deleted files and folders are held. This data is not discarded from the computer. The user must then empty the Recycle Bin to complete erase the data.

reference disk   Disk for older IBM PS/2 computers containing its SETUP program, advanced diagnostics, and special utilities for the hard drive.

refresh   Rewriting the information inside memory chips.

refresh rate   The maximum time a monitor's screen is scanned in one second.

REGEDIT   A Windows utility used to modify and backup the registry.

REGEDT32   One of two Windows NT and 2000 registry editors. See also registry and REGEDIT.

region code   A setting on a DVD drive or disk that specifies a geographic region. There is a maximum number this setting can be changed and the drive must match the disk in order to play.

registered SDRAM   Used in network servers and higher end computers, it delays all data transfers by one clock cycle to ensure accuracy and also allows for larger capacity DIMMs. Also called buffered SDRAM.

registry   A central Windows database file which holds hardware and software configuration information.

reserved memory area   The area of a microprocessor from 640KB to 1MB of memory addresses. Used for ROM chips.

resistance   A measurement of how much opposition is applied to a circuit in ohms.

resolution   The number of pixels shown on a monitor or output on a printer.

Resource Meter   A Windows 9x utility used to show how Windows is using memory.

RET   (Resolution Enhancement Technology) A technology used with laser printers that allows higher resolutions by adjusting toner output.

return   Wires that return AC current from the PC's front panel to the power supply. Also, it is a term used to refer to the center (round) AC outlet plug. Other terms used are common or neutral.

RFI (Radio Frequency Interference). A specific type of EMI noise that occurs in the radio frequency range. Often results from operation of nearby electrical appliances or devices.

ring topology Network that is physically wired like a star network but, logically, passes control from one device to the next in a continuous fashion, using a Token Ring.

RIMM A trademark of Rambus, Inc. that is a type of memory module used on video adapters and motherboards.

riser board A board that connects to the motherboard that holds adapters.

ROM (Read-Only Memory) A non-volatile type of memory that keeps data in chips even when the computer is shut off.

ROM BIOS (ROM Basic Input/Output System) A read-only memory chip that contains computer start-up software, and important hardware configuration parameters.

root directory The starting place for all files on a disk. A floppy is limited to 127 entries and a hard drive to 512 entries. The designation for a floppy drive's root directory is A:\ and for the hard drive is C:\.

router A network device that determines the best path to send a packet. Works at OSI model Layer 3.

RS232C A serial interface standard.

RTS (Request to Send) Part of the RTS/CTS hardware handshaking communication method. Specific wires on the serial connector are used to send a signal to the other device to stop or start sending data. The CTS (Clear to Send) and RTS signals indicate when it is okay to send data.

RTS/CTS (Request to Send/Clear to Send) A method of serial device handshaking that uses signals on specific pins of the connector to signal the other device when to stop or send data.

S

sag A momentary undervoltage condition that occurs when the wall outlet AC voltage drops.

scaleable font Fonts that can be created at any size. Outline fonts are an example of a scaleable font.

SCAM (SCSI Configured AutoMatically) A SCSI feature that automatically assigns priority numbers to each attached device.

SCANDISK A software program used to detect and repair lost clusters.

screen saver A piece of software that constantly changes the image shown on the monitor to keep a particular image from burning into the screen.

SCSI (Small Computer System Interface) An interface standard that connects multiple small devices to the same adapter via a SCSI bus.

SCSI bus The bus shared by all devices that attach to one SCSI adapter.

SCSI chain All devices and cabling that attach to a SCSI adapter.

SCSI channel A SCSI bus. Some SCSI host adapters support more than one SCSI channel.

SCSI ID The priority number assigned to each device connected by a SCSI chain.

SCSI segment A SCSI bus that has been divided into two electrical units, but is still logically one bus.

SDRAM (Synchronous DRAM) Provides very fast burst memory access (approximately 100MHz) by placing new memory addresses on the address bus before prior memory address retrieval and execution completes.

SE (Single Ended) A type of SCSI electrical signal and terminator used with most SCSI devices. Both active and passive terminators can be used with this signaling method.

SEC cartridge (Single Edge Contact cartridge) Intel's cartridge design for its Pentium II that mounts onto the motherboard.

sector The smallest amount of storage space on a disk or platter which holds 512 bytes of data.

sector translation A way of translating the cylinder, head, sector, and head information from the BIOS into a single number that the hard drive understands.

self-parking heads When powering off the computer, hard drive automatically pulls the read/write heads away from the data storage platters to minimize damaging physical contact.

SEPP cartridge (Single Edge Processor Package cartridge) An Intel cartridge design for Celeron processors.

serial ATA Follow-on future standard to ATA/133 for IDE devices.

serial mouse   A mouse that connects to a 9 or 25-pin serial port.

serial port   Either a 9-pin male D-shell connector or a 25-pin male D-shell connector. Transmits one bit at a time and used for input devices such as mice, modems, digitizers, trackballs, etc.

server-based network   A basic type of LAN wherein users login to a controlling computer, called a server, that knows who is authorized to connect to the LAN and what resources the user is authorized to access. Usually found in business, comprised of ten or more computers.

service   Windows NT process that provides a specific function to the computer.

service pack   Upgrade or patch provided by a manufacturer for an operating system.

service release   Software available from a manufacturer to fix a known problem (bug) in their applications program.

session layer   Layer 5 of the OSI model that manages communication and administrative functions between two network devices.

setup   Software that tells the computer about itself and the hardware it supports such as how much RAM memory, type of hard drive installed, current date and time, etc.

SFC.EXE   See System File Checker

SGRAM   (Synchronous Graphics RAM) Memory chips used on video adapters and graphics accelerators to speed up graphics-intensive functions.

shadow mask   A screen used in monitors that direct the electron beams to the front of the monitor.

shielding   Cancels out and keeps magnetic interference from devices.

shortcut   Icon with a bent arrow in lower left corner. It is a link to file, folder or program on a disk. If the file is a document, it opens the application used to create the document.

Show Desktop   Clicking on this icon reduces all open windows on the screen and shows the desktop. Click it again and the original document reappears.

SIMM   (Single In-line Memory Module) A style of 30-pin or 72-pin memory chip used for RAM.

simple volume A Windows 2000 term for the storage unit that contains the files needed to load the 2000 operating system. The system volume and the boot volume can be the same unit.

sine wave Pattern for AC voltage in its correct form. UPS DC battery power is converted into AC voltage by an inverter. A good UPS produces sine wave AC voltage; a cheaper UPS produces a square wave, which is not as effective.

single An IDE setting used when only one device connects to the interface and cable.

single-mode A type of fiber-optic cabling that sends one light beam down the cable.

single-ported (memory) Memory that can be written to or read from, but not simultaneously.

SIPP (Single In-line Pin Package) An older type of DRAM chip used on 80286 and 80386 based motherboards.

slave An IDE setting for the second device added to the cable. The device should be a slower device than the master.

Slot A Cartridge or slot used with Athlon processors.

slot loaded A term used to describe how a CD loads into a CD drive. With a slot loaded drive, the CD simply inserts into a horizontal opening on the drive front. Some car CD players have this type of CD loading too.

S.M.A.R.T. (Self-Monitoring Analysis & Reporting Technology) Part of ATA-3 IDE standard for power management, drive analysis, and failure reporting.

SmartDrive A DOS and Windows 3.x software that creates a disk cache in extended memory for floppy, hard and CD-ROM drives.

SmartMedia A card, smaller than a credit card, used to hold audio and video files.

SMP (Symmetric MultiProcessing) The ability for an operating system to support two CPUs simultaneously.

SMTP (Simple Mail Transfer Protocol) A standard used for e-mail, or for transferring message across a network from one device to another.

SNMP (Simple Netowrk Management Protocol) A standard that supports network monitoring and management.

SO-DIMM (Small Outline-DIMM) Special, smaller DIMM used in laptop computers.

SO-RIMM   (Small Outline-RIMM) Special, smaller RIMM used in laptop computers.

Socket A   CPU holder on motherboards for AMD Duron and Athlon microprocessors.

socket services   The most basic software layer that allows PC Cards to operate.

soft font   Fonts loaded from the hard drive instead of being stored inside the printer. Soft fonts take longer to load than internal fonts.

software   An application consisting of a set of instructions that makes the hardware work.

software decoder   A type of DVD decoder that puts the burden on the CPU to decode and uncompress the MPEG-2 video data from the DVD. Video card manufacturers have added MPEG-2 video decoding support to decrease the CPU's load. Contrast with hardware decoder.

solder joints   Solder connections on the back of motherboards and adapters.

sound card   An adaptor card (also known as an audio card) with several ports that converts digital signals to audible sound, and also the reverse. Common devices that connect to the ports include microphone, speakers and joystick.

spanned volume   A Windows 2000 term used to describe hard drive space created from multiple hard drives.

SPD   (Serial Presence Detect) A feature of SDRAM DIMM PC100 and PC133 standard. The system BIOS can read an EEPROM, and adjust motherboard timings for best CPU to RAM performance.

spike   An overvoltage condition of short duration and intensity.

SPP   (Standard Parallel Port) A name given before parallel standards were created to signify unidirectional data transfers from the computer to the parallel device.

SPS   (Standby Power Supply) A device that provides power to the computer only after it first detects a AC voltage power out condition.

square wave   The AC voltage pattern described by a cheaper, and thus less effective, UPS.

SRAM   (Static Random Access Memory) SRAM is faster but more expensive than DRAM. SRAM is also known as cache memory, or L2 cache.

SSE   (Streaming SIMD Extension) Intel's microprocessor technology that speeds up 3-D applications.

ST506   The oldest hard drive interface standard that transmits data serially.

standoffs   Plastic connectors on the bottom side of motherboards.

star topology   Most common Ethernet network topology where each device connects to a central hub or switch. If an individual device or cable fails, the rest of network keeps working. But, if the hub or switch fails, the entire network goes down.

start bit   A bit used in asynchronous communications that signals the beginning of each data byte.

Start button   Located in the lower left hand corner of the Windows desktop; it is used to access and launch applications, files, utilities and help, and add/remove hardware and software.

Startup menu   A term used with today's operating systems that describes a menu that allows various operating system boot environments such as Safe Mode. The menu is used when an operating system problem occurs.

stealth virus   A virus program that presents a fake image to anti-virus scanning to make itself invisible to the scanning.

stop bit   A bit used in asynchronous communications that signals the end of each data byte.

STP   (Shielded Twisted-Pair) Network cable with extra foil to outside noise from interfering with data on the cable.

straight-through cable   A cable without physically crossed (twisted) wires.

striped volume   Windows 2000 term describing had data is written across two to thirty-two hard drives. It is different from a spanned volume in that each drive is used alternately instead of filling the first hard drive before going to the second hard drive. Other names include striping or Raid 0.

subdirectory   A directory contained in another directory. Today's subdirectories are called folders.

subnet   A portion of a network number that has been subdivided so that multiple networks can use separate parts of a single network number. Subnets allow more efficient use of IP addresses. Also called subnetwork or subnetwork number.

subnet mask   A number the computer uses to determined which part of an IP address represents the network and which portion represents the host.

Super 7 socket A CPU holder for AMD's K6-2 and K6-III processors.

surge An overvoltage condition like a spike but with a longer duration.

surge protector A device to help protect power supplies from overvoltage conditions. Also known as surge strip or surge suppressor.

SVGA (Super VGA) A type of monitor that displays at least a 800x600 resolution and connects to a 15-pin D-shell connector.

swap file A temporary file in hard disk space used by Windows that varies in size depending on the amount of RAM installed, available hard drive space, and the amount of memory needed to run the application.

switch In star networks, a Layer 2 central controlling device. Looks at each data frame as it comes through each port. Another definition of a switch is an option used when working from a command prompt that allows the command to be controlled or operated on differently.

switch bank A grouping of DIP switches that allow configuration setting.

switch box A device that allows connection of two or more computers to a single printer or multiple printers to a single computer.

synchronous Transmissions that require the use of a clock signal.

SYS A command that is used to transfer the system files from one disk to another.

system attribute A file designation to mark a file as a system file. By default, files with this attribute set, do not show in directory listings.

System Configuration A Windows 9x utility that allows boot files and settings to be enabled/disabled for troubleshooting purposes. Files affected are AUTOEXEC.BAT, CONFIG.SYS, WIN.INI, SYSTEM.INI, and the startup folder. The command that brings this utility up is SFC.EXE.

System File Checker A Windows 98 utility that scans, protects, and repairs the system files. A prompt appears before the original files are restored.

system files Startup files the operating system needs to boot up the computer.

system key A protection feature for Windows 2000 passwords stored on the local computer or a network computer.

System Monitor Name of Window utility that monitors specific computer components and allows creation of graphs, bar charts and text reports.

system partition   A type of active hard drive partition found in Windows NT and 2000 that contains the hardware-specific files needed to load the operating system.

system resources   The collective set of interrupt, I/O address, and DMA configuration parameters. Also, when used in Windows 3.x and Windows 9x, NT or Windows 2000 environments, this term is defined as the amount of memory being used by specific applications.

System State   In Windows 2000 the System State contains a group of interrelated files including the registry, system files, boot files and COM+ Class Registration database. One cannot backup or restore these files individually.

system volume   Windows 2000 term describe the storage space that holds Windows 2000 files.

T

tab   Often found along top of dialog boxes, clicking on a tab displays a group of related standard options which users may optionally change to their personal preferences.

Task Manager   Windows-based utility that displays memory and microprocessor usage data, and displays currently loaded applications as well as currently running processes.

taskbar   On a Windows program, the bar that runs across the bottom of the desktop. This bar holds buttons that represent files and applications currently loaded into the PC's memory. It also holds icons representing direct access to system tools.

TCP   (Transmission Control Protocol) A OSI model Layer 4 standard that ensures reliable communication between two devices.

TCP/IP   (Transmission Control Protocol/Internet Protocol) Most widely used network protocol by businesses and homes in connecting to the Internet. Developed by the Defense Advanced Research Projects Agency in the 1970's, it is the basis of the Internet.

Telnet   An application that allows connection to a remote network device.

terabyte   (TB) Approximately one trillion bytes of information (2^{40} power). (1,099,511,627,776 bytes).

terminator   Used to designate the end of a floppy drive cable. Also known as a terminating resistor.

textbox   An area with a dialog box where the user may type preferred parameters applied to the software in use.

thread A unit of programming code that receives a slice of time from Windows so it can run concurrently with other units of code or threads.

token Small data packet passed from one networked device to another in a ring topology. Only the device holding the token may communicate.

token passing The common access method (set of communication rules governing network devices) used by fiber and Token Ring networks.

Token Ring A type of adapter for networks. The ports on this type of adapter have a RJ-45 or a 9-pin female D-shell connector. Some adapters have a green sticker with 4/16 on it to indicate 4Mbps/16Mbps run speeds.

toner puddling A side effect sometimes experienced on laser printers that use Resolution Enhancement Technology. The toner dial must be adjusted to reduce the amount of toner released to the paper so that it does not appear to have too much toner in one area of the paper.

tracert A network troubleshooting command that displays the path a data packet takes through a network, thus allowing one to see where a fault occurs in larger networks.

track A concentric circle on a formatted floppy disk or a hard drive platter.

trackball An input device that replaces a mouse.

transfer corona A wire inside the laser printer that applies a positive charge on the back of the paper so the toner is attracted to the paper as it moves through the printer.

transfer roller A roller inside the laser printer that replaces the transfer corona. The roller applies a positive charge on the back of the paper so the toner is attracted to the paper as it moves through the printer.

translating BIOS A system BIOS that allows communication with hard drives larger than 504MB.

transport layer Layer 4 of the OSI model, it determines details on the how the data is sent, supervises the validity of the transmission, and defines protocol for structuring messages.

tray loaded A method to insert a CD or DVD into a drive. With the tray loaded method, one push of a button ejects a disk container. Insert the disk into the drive and press gently on the tray (or push the button again) and the tray pulls back inside the drive.

Trojan horse virus   A virus program that appears to be a normal application, but when executed, changes something. It does not replicate, but could gather information which can later be used to hack into one's computer.

TrueType font   A type of outline font that can be scaled and rotated.

TVS rating   (Transient Voltage Suppressor) Measure of the surge protector's ability to guard against overvoltage conditions. The lower the TVS rating, the better.

twisted cable   A type of floppy or hard drive cable having crossed wires which physically moves the drive selection jumper position from the second to the first position.

twisted-pair cable   Network cable of eight copper wires twisted into 4 pairs. Comes shielded and unshielded.

TYPE   A command used to display a file's contents on the screen.

Type A-B-C fire extinguisher   A type of extinguisher used on either Type A, Type B, or Type C fires.

Type C fire extinguisher   A type of extinguisher used only on electrical fires.

U

UART   (Universal Asynchronous Receiver/Transmitter) A chip that coordinates the serial port or device activity.

UDF   (Universal Disk Format) A CD-R drive standard used by some manufacturers.

UDMA   (Ultra DMA) Allows the IDE interface to control the PCI bus for faster transfers.

UDP   (User Datagram Protocol) A Layer 4 connectionless standard that applications use to communicate with a remote device.

UMA   (Upper Memory Area) An area of the memory map between 640K and 1MB that was traditionally reserved for ROM chips. Unused portions of the UMA can be made into UMBs.

UMB   (Upper Memory Block) Chunks of the memory map between 640KB and 1MB that are unused by ROM chips and can be used for software.

undervoltage   A condition when AC power drops below 100 volts which may cause the computer's power supply to draw too much current and overheat.

UNC (Universal Naming Convention) A method used from a command prompt to connect to a network share using the format *devicename* *sharename*.

upgrade Installing a newer or more powerful operating system where one already exists.

UPS (Uninterruptable Power Supply) A device that provides power for a limited time to a computer or device during a power outage.

upstream A term used to describe information that is sent to the Internet such as an e-mail transmission or uploading a file to a server.

URL (Universal Resource Locator) A method of accessing Internet resources.

USB (Universal Serial Bus) A bus that allows 127 devices to be connected to a single computer port.

USB port A port on the motherboard or an adapter that allows connection of up to 127 devices.

useable host numbers The number of host bits (and associated IP addresses) that can be used by network devices residing in a subnetwork.

useable subnets The number of subnetworks that can be used when an IP network number is subdivided to allow more efficient use of IP addresses.

user profile All settings associated with a specific user including desktop settings, network configurations and applications that user has access to. It is part of the registry.

UTP (Unshielded Twisted Pair) Most common network cable. Comes in different categories for different uses. See also twisted-pair cable.

UVGA (Ultra VGA) A type of monitor that displays at least a 1024x768 resolution or greater and connects to a 15-pin D-shell connector.

V

VCACHE A dynamic disk caching program by Windows 95 that uses read-ahead and write-behind caching.

VCM (Virtual Memory Channel) A memory chip alternative to SDRAM. Developed by NEC Electronics, Inc., it fits in DIMM slots, but the chipset must support it.

vector font A font derived from a mathematical formula. Plotters frequently use vector fonts.

vendor-specific enabler   A PC card software layer that allows assignment of interrupts and I/O addresses. It will operate only with the manufacturer's specific PC card, and requires socket services and card services software.

Version Conflict Manager   A Windows 98 utility that helps with driver conflicts.

vertical scan rate   The rate the monitor's electron beam draws the entire screen.

VFAT   (Virtual File Allocation Table) A file system used by Windows 95 to organize a computer's files.

VGA   (Video Graphics Array) A type of monitor that displays at least a 640x480 resolution or greater and connects to a 15-pin D-shell connector.

video port   A connector on a motherboard or separate adapter for hooking up the monitor. Two variations are the 9 pin and 15 pin female D-shell connectors.

video processor   Sometimes known as the video coprocessor or video accelerator. The processor on the video adapter that coordinates communication between the adapter and the main microprocessor.

virtual machine   A way for the operating system to appear as a separate computer to each application. In Windows 98, each 32-bit application runs in its own virtual machine and each 16-bit DOS application runs in its own virtual machine. However, every 16-bit Windows application (an application designed for Windows 3.x) runs in one virtual machine. When a 16-bit Windows application crashes, all 16-bit applications that are loaded into memory crash as well.

virtual memory   A method of simulating extra memory by using the hard disk space as if it were RAM.

virus   Program designed to change something in the way a computer originally operated.

VIS   (Viewable Image Size) The actual area of the monitor seen by a user.

VL-bus   (Video Electronics Association Video Local Bus) A type of local bus developed for transmitting large volume of video data. Also know as VESA.

voice/fax modem   A modem that combines the features of a voice mailbox system with a modem.

voltage   A term used to describe how much pressure is applied to push electrons through a circuit.

volatile memory   Memory that does not remain when power is removed.

volt The measurement for voltage.

VPN (Virtual Private Networking) A remote computer connecting to a remote network by "tunneling" over an intermediate network, such as the Internet or a LAN.

VRAM (Video RAM) Dual-ported memory found on video adapters.

VRM (Voltage Regulator Module) A component on the motherboard that adjusts the voltage sent to the microprocessor. Used with lower voltage microprocessors.

W

Wake on LAN A BIOS and adapter feature that allows a network administrator to remotely control power to a workstation, and allows a computer to come out of the sleep mode.

Wake on Ring A BIOS and adapter feature that allows a computer to come out of sleep mode when the telephone rings, so the computer can accept fax, e-mail, etc., when the user is absent.

WAN (Wide Area Network) Two or more LANs communicating, often across large distances. The most famous WAN is the Internet.

warm boot Restarting the computer by pressing CTRL-ALT-DEL. Puts less strain on the computer than a cold boot.

watt Electrical measure in which computer power supplies are rated.

wax side The side of the paper which should not be printed on. Also known as the felt side.

WFP (Windows File Protection) Windows 2000 Professional feature that protects system files. If WFP detects a file that is altered, deleted or overwritten, it obtains a copy of the original file and places the copied file in the proper folder.

wildcard A special character used at the command prompt when typing commands. The ? character is used to designate "any" for a single character place, whereas the * character denotes any characters from that place forward. For example, the command DIR CH?RT.COM shows all commands that starts with CH and ends with RT.COM with any character any the middle. So the screen could show CHART.COM, CHORT.COM, CHERT.COM, etc. The command DIR CH*.* shows all commands that start with CH and end with any extension. So the files that could appear are CHART.COM, CHERYL.DOC, CHANCE.EXE, CHUCKLE.TXT, etc.

window The work area created on the desktop when an application or utility is opened.

Windows Explorer   See Explorer

WINIPCFG   A command used with Windows 9x to see current IP configuration.

WINS server   (Windows Internet Naming Service server) Keeps track of IP addresses assigned to a specific computer name.

wire side   The side of the paper which should be printed on. The wire side is normally shown by an arrow on the end of a paper ream.

word size   The number of bits the CPU can process at one time.

WORM   (Write Once-Read Many) A technology that writes data once to a disk. Often used to make backups or to distribute software.

worm virus   A virus program that replicates from one drive to another. The most common worm virus today is e-mail message that, once opened, sends the virus to every address in the user's address book.

WRAM   (Window RAM) Dual-ported memory found on video adapters.

write-back cache   A technique whereby the microprocessor stores 1s and 0s for later writing to regular memory when the microprocessor is not busy.

write-behind caching   A type of disk caching that stores data on the RAM and later records it to the disk.

write-black laser printer   A type of laser printer that produces a black dot every where the beam touches the drum. Write-black printers produce finer details than write-white laser printers.

write-protect notch   Located on the right side of a 5.25" disk, if covered, it prevents new data from being written on the disk.

write-protect window   An opening on a 3.5" floppy disk with a sliding tab. When the tab is closed, no new data may be written on the disk.

write-through cache memory   A technique whereby the microprocessor writes 1s and 0s into cache memory at the same time it writes data to regular memory.

write-white laser printer   A type of laser printer that produces a dot everywhere the beam does not touch the drum. Write-white printers produce darker shades of black than write-black printers.

X

x2/DSL A DSL technology provided by 3COM that allows a 56K modem to be upgraded to DSL when made available in a geographic area.

XCOPY An external command used to transfer files from one place to another in the DOS environment.

XMS (Extended Memory Specification) See Extended Memory.

XON/XOFF A method of handshaking that uses special control characters to coordinate data transmissions.

Z

zone bit recording A method of putting more sectors on the outer tracks of a hard drive platter than on the inner tracks.

ZV port (Zoomed Video Port) A new PC Card that allows data transfer from a PC Card to a VGA video adapter.

Appendix D:

Index

C

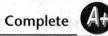

D

G

O

P

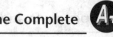

U

W

X

Y

Z